Modern Industrial Organization

Fourth Edition

The Addison-Wesley Series in Economics

Abel/Bernanke
Macroeconomics

Bade/Parkin
Foundations of Economics

Bierman/Fernandez
Game Theory with Economic Applications

Binger/Hoffman
Microeconomics with Calculus

Boyer
Principles of Transportation Economics

Branson
Macroeconomic Theory and Policy

Bruce
Public Finance and the American Economy

Byrns/Stone
Economics

Carlton/Perloff
Modern Industrial Organization

Caves/Frankel/Jones
World Trade and Payments: An Introduction

Chapman
Environmental Economics: Theory, Application, and Policy

Cooter/Ulen
Law and Economics

Downs
An Economic Theory of Democracy

Ehrenberg/Smith
Modern Labor Economics

Ekelund/Tollison
Economics

Fusfeld
The Age of the Economist

Gerber
International Economics

Ghiara
Learning Economics

Gordon
Macroeconomics

Gregory
Essentials of Economics

Gregory/Stuart
Russian and Soviet Economic Performance and Structure

Hartwick/Olewiler
The Economics of Natural Resource Use

Hoffman/Averett
Women and the Economy

Hubbard
Money, the Financial System, and the Economy

Hughes/Cain
American Economic History

Husted/Melvin
International Economics

Jehle/Reny
Advanced Microeconomic Theory

Klein
Mathematical Methods for Economics

Krugman/Obstfeld
International Economics

Laidler
The Demand for Money

Leeds/von Allmen
The Economics of Sports

Lipsey/Courant/Ragan
Economics

Melvin
International Money and Finance

Miller
Economics Today

Miller
Understanding Modern Economics

Miller/Benjamin/North
The Economics of Public Issues

Miller/Benjamin
The Economics of Macro Issues

Mills/Hamilton
Urban Economics

Mishkin
The Economics of Money, Banking, and Financial Markets

Parkin
Economics

Perloff
Microeconomics

Phelps
Health Economics

Riddell/Shackelford/Stamos/Schneider
Economics: A Tool for Critically Understanding Society

Ritter/Silber/Udell
Principles of Money, Banking, and Financial Markets

Rohlf
Introduction to Economic Reasoning

Ruffin/Gregory
Principles of Economics

Sargent
Rational Expectations and Inflation

Scherer
Industry Structure, Strategy, and Public Policy

Schotter
Microeconomics

Stock/Watson
Introduction to Econometrics

Studenmund
Using Econometrics

Tietenberg
Environmental and Natural Resource Economics

Tietenberg
Environmental Economics and Policy

Todaro/Smith
Economic Development

Waldman
Microeconomics

Waldman/Jensen
Industrial Organization: Theory and Practice

Weil
Economic Growth

Williamson
Macroeconomics

Modern Industrial Organization

Fourth Edition

Dennis W. Carlton
University of Chicago
Jeffrey M. Perloff
University of California, Berkeley

PEARSON
Addison Wesley

Boston San Francisco New York
London Toronto Sydney Tokyo Singapore Madrid
Mexico City Munich Paris Cape Town Hong Kong Montreal

To Janie and Jackie

Editor in Chief: Denise Clinton
Acquisitions Editor: Adrienne D'Ambrosio
Director of Development: Sylvia Mallory
Managing Editor: Jim Rigney
Senior Production Supervisor: Nancy Fenton
Senior Media Producer: Melissa Honig
Marketing Manager: Deborah Meredith
Design Supervisor: Regina Kolenda
Interior Designer: Leslie Haimes
Cover Designer: Leslie Haimes
Illustrator: Jim McLaughlin
Senior Prepress Supervisor: Caroline Fell
Senior Manufacturing Buyer: Hugh Crawford
Compositor: Nesbitt Graphics, Inc.
Cover Image: Stella, Frank (b. 1936) © Copyright ARS, NY. Agbatana II. 1968. Polymer and fluorescent polymer paint on canvas. 10' × 15'. © Copyright ARS, NY. Musee d'Art et d'Industrie, Saint-Etienne. Photo credit: Giraudon

PIE ISBN 0-321-22341-1

6 7 8 9 10—CRW—08

Brief Contents

Contents

PART 1 *Introduction and Theory* 1

PART 2 *Market Structures* 55

PART 6 Government Policies and Their Effects 595

Preface

There's no IO without U.—Sesame Street

Modern Industrial Organization, Fourth Edition, combines the latest theories with empirical evidence about the organization of firms and industries. It goes beyond the descriptive traditional structure-conduct-performance approach by using the latest advances in microeconomic theory, including transaction-cost analysis, game theory, contestability, and information theory. Practical examples illustrate the role of each theory in current policy debates, such as whether mergers promote economic efficiency (Chapter 2), whether predatory pricing is likely to be a serious problem (Chapter 11), whether preventing manufacturers from restricting distributors' prices benefits consumers (Chapter 12), whether providing consumers with more information about prices or products increases welfare (Chapter 13), whether advertising is harmful (Chapter 14), whether joint ventures are the best means of encouraging research (Chapter 16), whether current antitrust laws promote competition and increase welfare (Chapter 19), and whether government regulation does more harm than good (Chapter 20).

Modern Industrial Organization is designed for use by both undergraduate and graduate students. The theories presented in the chapters require only a microeconomics course as a prerequisite and do not involve calculus. Technical appendixes supplement selected chapters and provide a rigorous foundation for graduate students. Starred sections are relatively difficult and may be skipped.

We have used this book in both undergraduate and graduate courses. In our undergraduate courses, we rely on the chapters and skip the technical appendixes. In graduate courses, we use the chapters and technical appendixes along with supplementary readings based on selected articles that are discussed within chapters or recommended at the end of chapters.

Structure of the Book

The first half of the book covers the basics of competition, monopoly, oligopoly, and monopolistic competition. Chapter 1 discusses the basic approach used in the book. Chapter 2 discusses the reasons why firms exist, merger activity, and costs. Chapters 3 and 4 develop the basics of microeconomic theory—costs, competition, monopoly, barriers to entry, and externalities—that we use throughout the rest of the book. Variations on the standard models (such as a dominant firm facing a competitive fringe) are also presented.

Chapters 5 through 7 explain the recent developments in the theory of oligopoly and monopolistic competition. Chapter 5 covers cooperative oligopoly behavior (cartels), and Chapter 6 examines both cooperative and noncooperative behavior based on game theory. Chapter 7 focuses on monopolistic competition and product differentiation. Chapter 8 concludes the first part of the book with a thorough review and assessment of empirical work on market structure.

The remainder of the book covers the "new industrial organization"—material that is often missing from traditional texts. These topics, essential for applying the theories of industrial organization to everyday problems, are at the heart of many public policy debates and are the focus of considerable recent research. Chapters 9 and 10 cover common pricing strategies such as price discrimination through quantity discounts and tie-in sales. Chapter 11 examines strategic behavior where firms determine the best ways to do battle with their rivals. Chapter 12 discusses common business practices between manufacturers and distributors (vertical integration and vertical restrictions) and the dramatic changes in public policy toward these practices in recent years. The next two chapters, Chapters 13 and 14, address the problems that arise when consumers are not perfectly informed and when firms must advertise their products. The role of time is introduced in Chapters 15 and 16, which analyze how the durability of a product affects the market and how innovation can be encouraged. Chapter 17 considers evidence on the ways markets operate, and explores how modern microeconomic models of industrial organization may affect the macroeconomic economy. Chapter 18 examines the industrial organization issues that arise in international trade. The two concluding chapters, Chapters 19 and 20, analyze antitrust policy and government regulation.[1]

Although we believe that *Modern Industrial Organization* contains innovative ideas, we recognize that any textbook must borrow from existing research. We have tried to indicate when we have relied on the insights of others. However, we may have occasionally omitted a reference to an author whose ideas predated ours. We apologize for any such oversights.

Changes in the Fourth Edition

There are three major changes in the Fourth Edition. First, we have added many new applications, as well as discussions of important recent policies and new theories. Much of this new material is based on significant findings from more than 250 relevant articles and books published since our last edition. We have substantially updated material on cartels, particularly international cartels, and antitrust activities (Chapter 5); we have included a new section on estimation issues concerning differentiated

---

[1]Sometimes commonly used words have special meanings in the law that differ from the standard usage by economists and the general public. We try to use clear language to express economic rather than legal principles. For example, we might say that the "price of wheat in the market in Chicago affects the price of wheat in the market in Kansas City." Although such a statement uses the word *market* loosely, the point of the statement—that the prices of wheat in Chicago and Kansas City are related—is clear. In an antitrust trial, however, a specific legal definition of a market (see Chapter 19) is used and whether there are two separate markets or a single combined market is often of central interest. Our statement should not be interpreted to mean that there are necessarily two distinct wheat markets in Chicago and Kansas City for legal purposes.

goods oligopolies (Chapter 7); we have added a major new section on Sutton's modern approach to structure-conduct-performance analysis (Chapter 8); and we have substantially updated our discussion of patents and copyrights (Chapter 16) and regulation (Chapter 20).

Second, we have updated 18 examples and added 51 new examples. For instance, in one updated application, we conducted a new study of how the prices of Coke and Tropicana orange juice vary across grocery stores within a city. Our new examples spotlight a range of current events, among them the Enron scandal, the importation of low-price drugs from Canada, genetically modified organisms, the effect of 9/11 on flag sales, Blockbuster's innovative pricing polices, mergers in Europe, a monopsony in hiring priests, the change of China's tobacco monopoly to dominant firm status, the international vitamins cartel, the value of minivans, the certification of thoroughbreds, counterfeit Halal meat, Napster and piracy issues, and many others.

Third, we have significantly augmented our Web site, **www.aw-bc.com/carlton_perloff,** with extensive supporting material. Still-timely material that we removed from the Third Edition is available on the Web site. Further, we have written many new applications for the site.

Alternative Course Outlines

To cover the entire book takes two quarters or semesters. The book is designed, however, so that shorter courses can be constructed easily by choosing selected chapters, as shown in the following proposed reading lists.

Chapter 2 through 4 review and extend the basic material that is often covered in an intermediate microeconomics course: the theory of the firm, costs, the theory of competition, the theory of monopoly, and externalities. These chapters can be reviewed quickly for students with extensive preparation in microeconomics. Chapters 2 through 8 comprise the basic material for any course. Depending on the interests of the students and the instructor, a one-quarter or semester course could then sample a few of the chapters in the remainder of the book to obtain a flavor of the ways industrial organization can be used to study real-world problems.

All courses:
Carefully cover the core material in Chapters 2 and 5–8.

For courses that do not assume a strong background in microeconomic theory:
Cover Chapters 3 and 4.

Courses that assume a strong background in microeconomic theory:
Quickly review Chapters 3 and 4.

Courses that require calculus:
Include the technical appendixes and material on the Web.

Policy-oriented courses:
Cover international trade, antitrust, and regulation (Chapters 18 through 20). As time allows, include strategic behavior (Chapter 11), price discrimination (Chapters 9

and 10), vertical relationships (Chapter 12), limited information, advertising, and disclosure (Chapters 13 and 14), government policies toward innovation (Chapter 16), and macroeconomics (Chapter 17).

Regulation courses:
Regulations are dealt with throughout the book. Cover, in particular, externalities (Chapters 3 and 4), vertical relations (Chapter 12), limited information (Chapter 13), advertising and disclosure (Chapter 14), government policies toward innovation (Chapter 16), international trade (Chapter 18), and other government regulation (Chapter 20).

Business courses:
Include strategic behavior (Chapter 11), price discrimination (Chapter 9 and, optionally, nonlinear pricing, Chapter 10), vertical relations (Chapter 12), information and advertising (Chapters 13 and 14), and international trade (Chapter 18).

Courses that stress the latest theories:
Include strategic behavior (Chapter 11), vertical relations (Chapter 12), information and advertising (Chapters 13 and 14), government policies toward innovation (Chapter 16), market operation (Chapter 17), and international trade (Chapter 18).

Advanced courses:
Add chapters on nonlinear pricing (Chapter 10) and durability (Chapter 15).

Acknowledgments

We are especially grateful to George Stigler, our departed colleague, for his encouragement and insightful comments. His contributions to industrial organization influenced this and every other text in the field. We also thank the many people who helped us in the planning, writing, revising, and editing of this book:

Donald L. Alexander, *Western Michigan University*
Mark Bagnoli, *Michigan State University*
Kyle Bagwell, *Northwestern University*
Gustavo Bamberger, *Lexecon, Inc.*
Francis Bloch, *Brown University*
Giacomo Bonanno, *University of California, Davis*
Ralph Bradburd, *Williams College*
Reuven Brenner, *McGill University*
Timothy Bresnahan, *Stanford University*
Jeremy Bulow, *Stanford University*
David Butz, *University of California, Los Angeles*
Catherine Carey, *Western Kentucky University*
Kathleen Carroll, *University of Maryland, Baltimore County*
Phillip P. Caruso, *Western Michigan University*

Richard Clarke, *AT&T Bell Laboratories*
Charles Cole, *California State University, Long Beach*
John Connor, *Purdue University*
Ron Cotterill, *University of Connecticut*
Keith Crocker, *Pennsylvania State University*
Anna P. Della Valle, *New York University*
Craig A. Depken II, *University of Texas, Arlington*
Frank Easterbook, *University of Chicago,* and *Judge, Federal Court of Appeals*
Nicholas Economides, *New York University*
Gregory Ellis, *University of Washington*
Robert Feinberg, *American University*
Daniel Fischel, *University of Chicago*
Trey Fleisher, *Metropolitan State College of Denver*
Alan Frankel, *LECG*
Drew Fudenberg, *Harvard University*
Anita Garten, *A. Garten Consulting*
Robert Gertner, *University of Chicago*
Richard Gilbert, *University of California, Berkeley*
J. Mark Gidley, *White and Case*
Luis Guash, *University of California, San Diego*
Timothy Guimond, *Lexecon, Inc.*
Jonathan Hamilton, *University of Florida*
Mehdi Haririan, *Bloomsburg University*
Gloria Helfand, *University of Michigan*
James Holcolm, *University of Texas, El Paso*
Charles Holt, *University of Virginia*
Jorge Ibarra-Salazar, *ITESM*
Adam Jaffe, *Brandeis University*
Harvey James, *University of Missouri*
Larry Karp, *University of California, Berkeley*
Theodore Keeler, *University of California, Berkeley*
Alvin Klevorick, *Yale University*
William Kolasky, *Wilmer, Cutler and Pickering*
Dan Kovenock, *Purdue University*
John Kwoka, *George Washington University*
William Landes, *University of Chicago*
Richard Langlois, *University of Connecticut*
Jim Lee, *Fort Hays State University*
Bart Lipman, *Carnegie-Mellon University*

Nancy Lutz, *Yale University*
William Lynk, *Lexecon, Inc.*
Frank Mathewson, *University of Toronto*
Rachel McCulloch, *Brandeis University*
James Meehan, *Colby College*
John Menge, *Dartmouth College*
Robert Michaels, *California State University, Fullerton*
Richard A. Miller, *Wesleyan University, Connecticut*
David E. Mills, *University of Virginia*
Herbert Mohring, *University of Minnesota*
Janet Netz, *Purdue University*
Gregory Pelnar, *Lexecon, Inc.*
Marty Perry, *Rutgers University*
Nicola Persico, *University of Pennsylvania*
Russell Pittman, *Justice Department*
Richard Posner, *University of Chicago,* and *Judge, Federal Court of Appeals*
Stanley Reynolds, *University of Arizona*
Richard Rogers, *University of Massachusetts*
Andrew Rosenfield, *Lexecon, Inc.*
Thomas Ross, *University of British Columbia*
Charles K. Rowley, *George Mason University*
Stephen Salant, *University of Michigan*
Garth Saloner, *Stanford University*
Steven Salop, *Georgetown University*
Richard Schmalensee, *Massachusetts Institute of Technology*
Suzanne Scotchmer, *University of California, Berkeley*
Robert Sherwin, *Analysis Group*
Steven Sklivas, *Columbia University*
Edward Snyder, *University of Michigan*
Pablo Spiller, *University of California, Berkeley*
Mark Stegman, *University of North Carolina*
George Stigler, *University of Chicago*
Stephen Stigler, *University of Chicago*
Joseph Stiglitz, *Columbia University*
Dmitry Stolyarov, *University of Michigan*
Valerie Suslow, *University of Michigan*
Ming-Je Tang, *University of Illinois*
Mihkel M. Tombak, *Helsinki School of Economics*
Lien Tran, *Federal Trade Commission*

W. van Hulst, *Tilburg University*
Frank van Tongeren, *Erasmus University of Rotterdam*
Klaas van't Veld, *University of Michigan*
John Vernon, *Duke University*
Rickard Wall, *Linköping University*
Roger Ware, *Queen's University*
Avi Weiss, *Bar-Ilan University*
Leonard Weiss, *University of Wisconsin*
Gregory Werden, *Department of Justice*
Douglas West, *University of Alberta*
Lawrence White, *New York University*
Oliver Williamson, *University of California, Berkeley*
Robert Willig, *Princeton University*
Asher Wolinsky, *Northwestern University*
Brian Wright, *University of California, Berkeley*
Edwin Zimmerman, *Covington & Burling*

We are grateful to Keith Crocker, Stan Reynolds, and particularly Gregory Pelnar, who have made invaluable contributions to several editions. We thank David Buschena, Gary Casterline, Hayley Chouinard, Laona Fleischer, George Frisvold, Carolyn Harper, Colleen Loughlin, David Mitchell, Margaret Sheridan, and Deborah Zimmermann for excellent research assistance. We gratefully acknowledge the typing and other assistance of Julie Rodriguez and Hazel Young.

We thank our four excellent acquisitions editors: George Lobell (who provided extensive help on the First Edition), John Greenman (who arranged for much of the supplemental material for the Second Edition and the early stages of the Third Edition), Denise Clinton (who was very supportive on our Third Edition), and Adrienne D'Ambrosio (who helped to create the Fourth Edition). We are particularly grateful to Director of Development Sylvia Mallory, who has been extremely helpful as a development editor and in arranging for the supplements (with Diana Theriault) and creating a Web site (with Melissa Honig). Nancy Fenton and Julie DeSilva ably handled production and art coordination. Cynthia Benn and Robin MacFarlane provided careful copy editing and proofreading. Jim McLaughlin carefully drew all the two-color figures. Regina Kolenda directed the design of both the text and the cover, and Nesbitt Graphics executed the paging, resulting in the most attractive edition yet.

This book benefited extensively from the comments of our many students who cheerfully served as "guinea pigs," reading and using earlier editions and drafts of this version. Most importantly, we thank our families for their support.

Each author blames the other for any mistakes. Each takes credit for any good jokes.

Dennis W. Carlton
Jeffrey M. Perloff

PART ONE

Introduction and Theory

CHAPTER 1

Overview

Leave all hope, ye that enter. —*Dante Alighieri*

This text presents both traditional and new theories of **industrial organization**: the study of the structure of firms and markets and of their interactions. Introductory microeconomics analyzes idealized models of firms and markets; this text takes a closer, more realistic look at them, warts and all.[1] In introductory physics, one first disregards gravity and friction in studying the movement of bodies, and then adds these complications to the analysis. The study of industrial organization adds to the perfectly competitive model real-world frictions such as limited information, transaction costs, costs of adjusting prices, government actions, and barriers to entry by new firms into a market. It then considers how firms are organized and how they compete in such a world. This chapter describes some of the approaches that help to organize the study of industrial organization and gives an overview of the material in later chapters. Finally, it describes some of the analytic tools that are used.

Models

There are at least two major approaches to the study of industrial organization, and, because they are compatible as organizing principles, this text uses both of them. The first approach, *structure-conduct-performance,* is primarily descriptive and provides an overview of industrial organization. The second,

[1]We use the terms *market* and *industry* loosely and interchangeably. In antitrust cases, important distinctions are made between these terms, as is discussed in later chapters.

price theory, uses microeconomic models to explain firm behavior and market structure.

According to the structure-conduct-performance approach, an industry's **performance** (the success of an industry in producing benefits for consumers) depends on the **conduct** (behavior) of its firms, which, in turn, depends on the **structure** (factors that determine the competitiveness of the market).[2] The structure of an industry depends on basic conditions, such as technology and demand for a product. For example, in an industry with a technology such that the average cost of production falls as output increases, the industry tends to have only one firm, or possibly a small number of firms. If only one firm (a monopoly) sells output in an industry, it may be able to set a price that is well above its marginal costs of production. If the basic conditions make the demand for the monopoly's product relatively inelastic (people are relatively insensitive to price), then the price in that market is higher than if the demand is relatively elastic (people are price sensitive).

Figure 1.1 illustrates the relationships among structure, conduct, and performance and shows how basic conditions and government policy interact. The relationships among the five boxes are complex. For example, government regulations affect the number of sellers in an industry, and firms may influence government policy to achieve higher profits. Similarly, if entry barriers lead to monopoly and monopoly profits, new industries may develop new, substitute products that affect the demand for the original product. Empirical researchers who rely on this paradigm typically use data at the industry level. They ask, for example, if industries with certain structural features (for example, few firms) have high prices.

The structure-conduct-performance approach is a very general way to organize the study of industrial organization, and can be used to organize the material in the rest of this book. The second major approach, the price theory paradigm, can also be used to organize and interpret this material.

Price Theory

Price theory models analyze the economic incentives facing individuals and firms to explain market phenomena. George J. Stigler (1968), an early proponent of this analytical approach, believed that industrial organization researchers should use microeconomic theory to design empirical studies of markets and of the effects of public policy. Today, most industrial organization research and courses are well grounded in microeconomic theory. Two reasons for the shift to this approach are the recent availability of data at a more micro level and advances in price theory. In recent years, three specific theoretical applications of price theory have won substantial support—transaction cost analysis, game theory, and contestable market analysis—and help to explain structure, conduct, and performance.

---

[2]The structure-conduct-performance approach was developed at Harvard by Edward S. Mason (1939, 1949) and his colleagues and students, such as Joe S. Bain (1959).

FIGURE 1.1 Structure, Conduct, and Performance

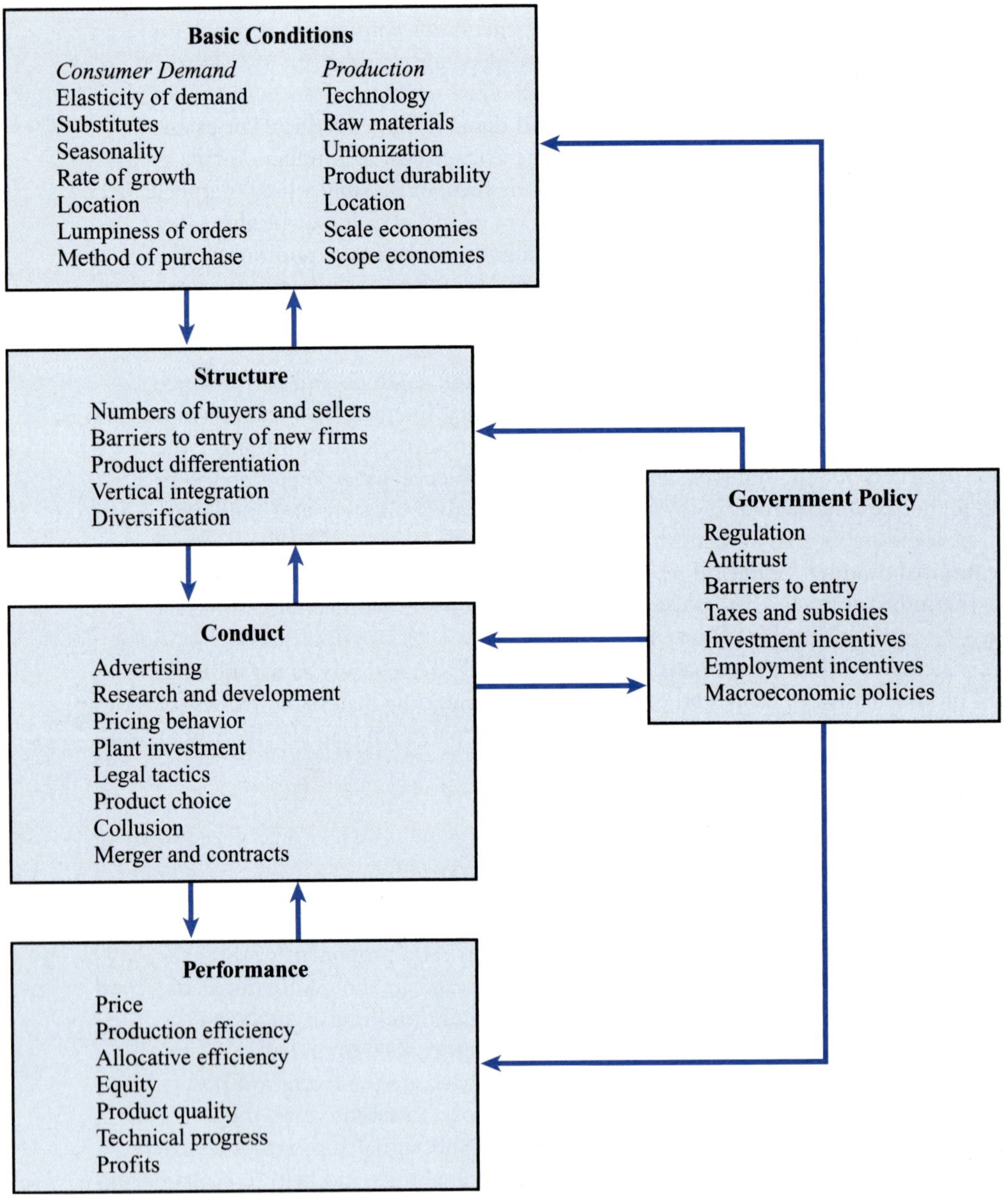

Transaction Costs

Transaction costs are the expenses of trading with others above and beyond the price, such as the cost of writing and enforcing contracts. Using formal price theory analysis, the transaction cost approach uses differences in transaction costs to explain why structure, conduct, and performance vary across industries.

Over 60 years ago, Ronald H. Coase (1937) explained that a firm and a market are alternative means of organizing economic activity. Coase emphasized that the use of the marketplace involves costs. These costs help to determine market structure. For example, where the cost of buying from other firms is relatively low, a firm is more likely to buy supplies from others than produce the supplies itself.

Oliver Williamson (1975, 8–10), one of the major proponents of the transaction cost approach, says that four basic concepts underlie this analysis:

1. Markets and firms are alternative means for completing related sets of transactions. For example, a firm can either buy a product or a service or produce it.
2. The relative cost of using markets or a firm's own resources should determine the choice.
3. The transaction costs of writing and executing complex contracts across a market "vary with the characteristics of the human decision makers who are involved with the transaction on the one hand, and the objective properties of the market on the other" (p. 8).
4. These human and environmental factors affect the transaction costs across markets and within firms.

This approach aims to identify a set of environmental and human factors that explain both the internal organization of firms and organization of industries. The key environmental factors are *uncertainty* and the *number of firms*; the key human factors are *bounded rationality* and *opportunism.* **Bounded rationality** is the limited human capacity to anticipate or solve complex problems. Problems arise when uncertainty is combined with bounded rationality, or where the managers of the few firms in an industry behave opportunistically (take advantage of a situation).

Thus, in a world of great uncertainty, it may be too difficult or costly to negotiate contracts that deal with all possible contingencies. As a result, firms may produce internally even though, otherwise, it would be cost-effective to rely on markets.

When the number of firms is small and individuals are opportunistic, firms may not want long-term contracts for fear of being victimized in the future. For example, a firm that relies on another to supply a factor that is essential to its production process may be exploited because it cannot operate if its supply is stopped. This problem is likely to be important if there are few alternative suppliers.

Thus, reliance on markets is more likely when (1) there is little uncertainty and (2) there are many firms (competition) and limited opportunities for opportunistic behavior. When these conditions are reversed, firms are more likely to produce for themselves than to rely on markets. The transaction cost approach has been very successful because of its broad explanatory power.

Game Theory

Another approach that is increasingly important to economic theorists is game theory (von Neumann and Morgenstern 1944), which uses formal models to analyze conflict and cooperation between firms and individuals. Competition among firms is viewed as a game of strategies, or battle plans of the actions of a firm, that describe the behavior of each firm. A firm's strategy determines, for example, its output, price, and advertising level. In the game, firms compete for profits. Game theory describes how firms form their strategies and how these strategies determine the profits.

Game theory provides insights in games in which there are relatively few firms. Much of this text concerns such markets, and many of the models it presents are examples of game theory.

Contestable Markets

The importance of entry to the competitive process has been recognized for a long time. Demsetz (1968) and Baumol, Panzar, and Willig (1982) emphasize that industries with only a few firms (or just one) can be very competitive if there is a threat of entry by other firms. Markets in which many firms can enter rapidly if prices exceed costs and can exit rapidly if prices drop below costs are called contestable. As Baumol, Panzar, and Willig explain, firms are reluctant to enter an industry if it is very costly to exit.

With few firms but easy entry and exit, the market is contestable and can have the properties of a competitive market: Price equals marginal cost and strategic behavior is irrelevant. There are few known examples of such markets. If there are few firms in an industry and entry or exit is difficult, the market is not contestable and the strategic behavior studied by game theorists is relevant.

Organization

Where I am not understood, it shall be concluded that something very useful and profound is couched underneath. —*Jonathan Swift*

The main objective of this text is to provide a systematic presentation of the basic theories—both traditional and new—of how firms and markets are organized and how they behave. Rather than treating structure and conduct as given, the text explains them as the outcome of individuals' maximizing behaviors. That is, it shows how the price theory models provide the underpinnings for the structure-conduct-performance paradigm. The paradigms complement each other, and both are useful for developing an understanding of industrial organization.

Basic Theory

Chapter 2 reviews basic microeconomic theories about costs and introduces the theory of the firm. The chapter starts by covering the internal organization and ownership of firms, pointing out that the division between firms and markets is not always clear and that the structure of an industry may change rapidly as costs shift. It examines the role of mergers and acquisitions in achieving efficiency in production.

The chapter then turns to costs. Special attention is paid to costs because they are crucial in explaining market structure. For example, costs (especially transaction costs) are crucial in determining whether it pays for a firm to produce an input or buy it in a market. The chapter reviews several cost concepts and discusses empirical evidence on costs.

Market Structures

The theory and empirical evidence on basic market structures are covered in Chapters 3 through 8. Table 1.1 shows the basic taxonomy used in this text to describe several structures. The number of firms in a market and the ease of entry and exit by new firms determine the type of structure.

When a market has many potential buyers and sellers and has no entry or exit barriers, the market structure is that of **competition**. When one firm sells to many buyers, and no new sellers can enter, the firm is a **monopoly**. Conversely, the only firm that buys from many sellers is a **monopsony**. If sellers can influence price even though they face competition from other firms, the market structure is either oligopolistic or monopolistic competition. An **oligopoly** is a small group of firms in a market with substantial barriers that prevent new sellers from entering the market. If there are no substantial barriers to entry and exit and each firm has some control over the price of its product, then the market is one of **monopolistic competition**: Firms can set price above the competitive level but earn zero profit.

The market structure often depends on the presence or absence of barriers to entry and exit, which are discussed in Chapter 3. For example, a new airline company cannot offer service between New York and Tokyo without permission from both the

TABLE 1.1 **Some Basic Market Structures**

	Sellers		Buyers	
Market Structure	Entry Barriers	Number	Entry Barriers	Number
Competition	no	many	no	many
Monopoly	yes	one	no	many
Monopsony	no	many	yes	one
Oligopoly	yes	few	no	many
Oligopsony	no	many	yes	few
Monopolistic competition	no	many	no	many

United States and Japan. Such permission is usually not granted unless a company currently flying ceases operation; thus, a government-created entry barrier exists in this market.

Chapters 3 and 4 review and extend the theory of competition and monopoly. Chapter 3 discusses the basic theory of competition. Competitive firms are too small to affect the market price, so they take that price as given (the firms are said to be **price takers**) and choose how many units of output to produce. The chapter shows that such behavior has desirable consequences for social welfare. It is the market structure to which all other structures are compared. Because there are no barriers to entry, firms enter competitive markets whenever positive profits can be made. This influx of sellers drives profits to zero for all firms in the market in the long run.

In contrast, as the only firm in the market, a monopoly (Chapter 4) is a **price setter**: It determines the price of its good, and typically sets it above the competitive level. The ability to price profitably above the competitive level is referred to as **market power**, and such conduct leads to welfare losses by society. Because of entry barriers, the monopoly can earn positive economic profits in the long run. Analogously, monopsony results in a lower price than a competitive market would set, which also has undesirable welfare implications.

Chapter 4 introduces another structure, which is not described in Table 1.1. It is a hybrid of the competitive and monopolistic structures, in which there is a *dominant firm* and a *competitive fringe*. The dominant firm has some market power so that it can set prices, and the other (fringe) firms are price takers. For example, such a structure is observed where a monopoly in one country competes in world markets with a higher-cost competitive industry located in another country.

Chapter 5 shows how monopoly-like conduct may occur in a market with more than one firm. The firms may form a **cartel**: an association of firms that explicitly agree to coordinate their activities, typically to maximize joint profits. That is, the separate firms imitate the behavior of a monopoly. If they all restrict output and raise the industry price above the competitive level, they can increase their profits. Government antitrust laws may be used to prevent explicit cartels from forming. The chapter considers why cartels form in only some industries and why they fall apart. Members of cartels are shown to have an incentive to cheat on one another. This chapter shows how cartel theory provides an explanation of oligopoly behavior in the absence of explicit agreements.

Chapter 6 continues our study of oligopolies. Unlike competitive and monopolistic firms, oligopolistic firms expect their rivals to react to their behavior or strategies. Using game theory, we consider when oligopolies compete vigorously and when they do not. The chapter presents some experimental evidence on oligopolistic behavior.

Chapter 7 studies monopolistic competition by modifying the oligopoly model of Chapter 6 in two ways. First it allows entry. In monopolistic competition, unlike in an oligopoly, entry by new firms drives economic profits to zero. Thus, other things being equal, removing entry barriers typically increases output.

Second, Chapter 7 considers the implications of product differentiation on social welfare and the effect of government interventions in these markets. For example, consumers presumably prefer low prices and many choices of differentiated products. Thus, government intervention that results in fewer firms and products but lower average prices may be a mixed blessing. Whether consumers prefer slightly higher prices with more variety becomes an empirical question for each market.

Chapter 8 surveys the available empirical evidence on performance and market structure in the United States and other economies. Tests of the market structure theories discussed in Chapters 3 through 7 are examined. Both traditional and modern empirical approaches to assessing performance are presented.

Business Practices: Strategies and Conduct

Chapters 9 through 12 cover general business practices using some of the latest research in game theory and transaction cost theory. In the basic market structures, covered in the earlier chapters, firms concentrate on only a few strategies: Firms vary only price, output levels, or the degree of differentiation of their products, usually on a once-only basis.

Chapters 9 and 10 concentrate on complex pricing behavior. Chapter 9 covers **price discrimination**: A firm charges different categories of customers different unit prices for the identical good. Firms with market power can increase their profits by charging some consumers who are less price sensitive a higher price than others for identical products. Chapter 10 deals with other pricing schemes that are related to price discrimination. For example, an electrical utility may charge one price to be connected to the system and another for each kilowatt consumed. Similarly, a firm may sell you one of its products only if you agree to buy another.

Chapter 11 considers sophisticated competitive strategies in dynamic game theory models. For example, a firm may set such a low price that it drives its competitors out of business and then raises its price. Similarly, a firm may engage in behavior designed to raise its rivals' costs, so they cannot compete as effectively. Other more complex strategies involve exchanging (or not exchanging) information with competitors.

Chapter 12 examines the reasons for vertical integration. When a firm produces an input itself, the firm is said to be *vertically integrated.* Costs help to determine whether the firm vertically integrates or not. The chapter discusses why some industries buy inputs and others produce them. It also examines the welfare implications of vertical integration.

Chapter 12 then discusses why some firms, instead of vertically integrating, use *vertical restraints.* For example, an automobile manufacturer may require that its dealers, which are independent firms, agree in contracts about the way they will conduct their business. Thus, the manufacturer uses contractual restrictions to approximate vertical integration. The recent change in public policy toward vertical restraints is discussed.

Information, Advertising, and Disclosure

Chapters 13 and 14 examine the effects of limited information on markets and how strategic behavior by firms can alter information. Chapter 13 discusses the effect of information on quality and prices in a market and shows that many typical properties of a competitive market disappear if information is limited. Limits on consumer information often give firms market power; thus, better information may reduce market power and increase competition.

Chapter 14 examines advertising and how it may either increase or decrease welfare. The chapter also explains how laws designed to limit lying or to require disclosure of important facts to consumers may have paradoxical effects.

Dynamic Models and Market Clearing

Except for Chapter 11's discussion of multiperiod strategies, the models discussed prior to Chapter 15 use a **static analysis**: models of markets that last for only one period. Like snapshots, static models tell us what happens at a point in time. Typically, static models are used for long-term analysis. In contrast, multiperiod or dynamic models describe the evolution of markets and firm behavior over time. Although such models are more difficult to use than static ones, they provide additional insights.

Chapters 15, 16, and 17 use models in which current actions affect future profits. Chapter 15 examines firms' decision making in markets for durable goods. For example, would a car that lasts 15 years produce higher or lower profits for the manufacturer than one that lasts 10 years? One surprising result of this investigation is that a durable goods monopoly may have more market power if it rents its product than if it sells it.

Chapter 16 considers how government behavior affects technological change. New discoveries that reduce production costs or create new products are obviously highly desirable. Unfortunately, a competitive industry produces too few inventions because inventors do not capture the full value of their discoveries. To encourage greater inventive activity, governments provide many incentives. For example, governments grant patents that allow inventors to be monopoly sellers of new products.

Chapter 17 is the only chapter to deal explicitly with macroeconomic issues. However, as in the other chapters, the focus is on price theory. This chapter examines how a market adjusts over time as a function of its structure. Other means of *clearing a market* (forcing quantity demanded to equal quantity supplied) besides price adjustments are also discussed.

Government Policies and Their Effects

Chapters 18, 19, and 20 analyze the effects of government actions that increase or decrease welfare. Chapter 18 examines how market structure and government actions affect international trade markets. Particular attention is paid to the effects of tariffs, subsidies, and quotas on the performance of markets.

Chapter 19 considers *antitrust* laws, which are intended to prevent conduct that adversely affects welfare, such as the formation of cartels or mergers that might lead to substantial market power. The chapter points out, however, that antitrust laws sometimes have been used to prevent rather than encourage competitive behavior.

Finally, Chapter 20 discusses how governments regulate business conduct and market structure. The chapter examines the effects of the recent trend toward deregulating markets. Unfortunately, regulation does not always benefit consumers or society. Government intervention in some markets leads to inefficiency, and many laws proposed with the noblest objectives benefit special interest groups at the expense of the general population.

CHAPTER 2

The Firm and Costs

Few have heard of Fra Luca Parioli, the inventor of double-entry bookkeeping; but he has probably had much more influence on human life than has Dante or Michelangelo. —*Herbert J. Muller*

A **firm** is an organization that transforms *inputs* (resources it purchases) into *outputs* (valued products that it sells). It earns the difference between what it receives as revenue and what it spends on inputs, which are used in manufacturing and selling. For example, a steel firm builds a plant, hires workers, purchases raw materials, and then produces and sells steel. The firm decides the quantity of resources to buy, how to combine the resources to make steel, and how and where to sell it. The firm makes a profit if it sells its steel for more than the cost of producing and selling the steel.

We start by discussing the objective, organization, and ownership of firms. Most firms try to maximize their profits. To maximize profit, a firm must produce its output at the least possible cost, given technology and the price of inputs.

Next we examine costs. Knowledge of costs is necessary to understand industrial organization for three reasons. First, many of the predictions of economic theory, such as those involving price and firms' size, revolve around concepts like marginal costs and profits. Without a knowledge of cost concepts, one cannot understand or empirically test these predictions. Second, theoretical work (Baumol, Panzar, and Willig 1982) emphasizes that oligopoly behavior depends crucially on certain types of fixed cost. Third, governments often regulate industries in which competitive entry leads to unusually high costs. Knowing how to regulate these industries requires an intimate familiarity with cost concepts (see Chapter 20).

This chapter introduces the concepts of marginal, average, and variable costs and then discusses some subtleties associated with economic costs. It analyzes the theory and evidence concerning economies of scale and concludes with a discussion of costs for a multiproduct firm.

The key issues we study in this chapter are:

1. Most firms maximize profits.
2. Acquisitions and other mergers may (but do not always) force firms to operate efficiently and profitably.
3. Economists use the concept of an opportunity cost that includes a normal profit.
4. The costs of a single-product firm depend on the prices of factors of production and the output level.
5. A multiproduct firm's cost of producing a single product depends on factor prices, the output level of that product, and the output level of its other products.
6. Production processes may have various properties such as economies of scale and economies of scope.

The Firm

Most goods and services produced in Western countries are produced by firms. In the United States, firms produce 84 percent of national production, the government produces 11 percent, nonprofit institutions (such as some universities and hospitals) produce 5 percent, and private households produce less than 0.1 percent.[1] In contrast, the government's share of total national production can be much higher in developing countries, reaching 43 percent in Ethiopia, 44 percent in Kyrgyzstan, 46 percent in Yemen, and 59 percent in Lesotho, though it is less than 5 percent in Guinea, Ireland, and Luxembourg (Heston et al., 2002). We now examine the objective, organization, and ownership of firms.

The Objective of a Firm

Most firms are *for-profit* firms: They exist to make money. Unless we state otherwise, when we refer to a firm we mean a for-profit firm and not a firm that exists for charitable or other nonprofit reasons.

The standard assumption in most economic models is that the primary objective of a manager of a firm is to maximize the firm's profits. The manager must sell the optimal amount of output, and the firm engages in **efficient production**: No more output could be produced with existing technology, given the quantity of inputs used.

[1]These are shares of the U.S. gross domestic product for 2002 from the U.S. Department of Commerce, Bureau of Economic Analysis, National Income and Products Accounts Table 1.7, Gross Domestic Product by Sector (**www.bea.doc.gov/bea/dn/nipaweb**). These figures exclude nonmarketed output of private households such as meal production.

Managers may have objectives other than profit maximization, however. For example, if managers want to control a large firm, they may maximize sales rather than profits. Similarly, managers may spend the firm's money on luxurious offices, company planes, and other amenities that reduce the profitability of the firm but benefit managers directly.

Various forces keep managers from deviating from profit-maximizing behavior. If a firm is run inefficiently and unprofitably, it may be driven out of business by rival firms that do maximize profits. Managers who lose their jobs when their firm is driven out of business or who are fired for inefficiency or laziness find it difficult to obtain new jobs. Incentives, such as stock ownership and other bonuses, also motivate managers to maximize profit. Thus, throughout most of this book, we assume that profit maximization is a reasonable approximation of a firm's objectives.

In Chapter 12, we examine how firms are organized to make them as efficient and profitable as possible, why failing to monitor causes problems, and what incentives firms provide employees to minimize these problems.[2]

Ownership and Control

Firms are owned and controlled in a variety of ways. A firm must raise money to finance itself, decide how its business is to be managed, and distribute its revenues to those who have contributed to its activity.

Forms of Ownership. The three basic business forms in the United States are sole proprietorships (single owner), partnerships (multiple owners), and corporations. Before the twentieth century, most firms were sole proprietorships or partnerships. Sole proprietors and partners are personally liable for the debts of their business. *All* the owners' assets, not just those invested in the business, are at risk. For example, a partner bears full personal liability for the debts of a failed business if the other partners have no assets, even if the business fails through no fault of the partner with the assets. Partnerships have a second problem as well. If one member of a partnership leaves, the entire partnership is automatically dissolved. To continue, the business must form a new partnership.

In the United States, 87 percent of business sales are made by corporations, even though only 20 percent of all firms are corporations. Nearly 72 percent of all firms are sole proprietorships. Sole proprietorships tend to be small, however, so they are responsible for only 5 percent of all sales. Partnerships are 8 percent of all firms and make 9 percent of sales.[3]

Corporations are companies whose capital is divided into shares that are held by individuals who have only limited responsibility for the debts of the company. That is, a shareholder has **limited liability**: If the corporation fails (is unable to pay its bills), the

---

[2]For classic works on these issues see March and Simon (1958), Cyert and March (1963), Marris (1964), and Williamson (1964). See **www.aw-bc.com/carlton_perloff** "How Firms Are Organized" for a discussion of these issues.

[3]Data for 1999 from the *Statistical Abstract of the United States,* Table 699, 2002:471.

stockholders need not pay for the debt using their personal assets. A shareholder's losses are limited to the price paid for the stock. With limited liability, individuals are more willing to buy shares than they would be if they could lose more than they paid to acquire the shares.

Today, most sales in the United States are made by corporations. Large corporations whose stock is publicly traded account for the bulk of economic activity and own a large percentage of all assets. According to the *1997 Census of Manufactures* (2001), out of 316,952 manufacturing firms, 246,189 (78 percent) are corporations. In manufacturing, corporations produce 95 percent of all the value added, account for 94 percent of all new capital expenditures, and hire 94 percent of all workers and 93 percent of all production workers. Individual proprietorships are 16 percent of all manufacturing firms but produce only 0.7 percent of the value added. Partnerships are about 4 percent of all manufacturing firms and produce 1.6 percent of the value added.

The importance of corporations has risen over time. In 1947, they comprised only 49 percent of all manufacturing firms (compared to 78 percent in 1997) and produced 92 percent of the value added (compared to 95 percent in 1997).

The rise of the corporation coincided with the need to increase the size of firms (see Example 2.1). The money needed to finance large enterprises could be efficiently raised only through the corporate form of organization. Otherwise, investors were not willing to accept the potential liabilities arising from the actions of managers whom they neither knew nor had the ability to monitor. The increase in the importance of the corporation and the coincident rise in stock trading is a relatively recent phenomenon of the last 100 years. In 1900, only 113 companies were listed on the New York Stock Exchange; in 1920, there were 391; today, over 1900 companies are listed.[4]

A corporation may raise money by selling shares of stock. Its shareholders elect a board of directors to run the corporation. In practice, the board of directors of a large corporation rarely becomes involved in day-to-day affairs; it delegates that responsibility to officers of the company. In large corporations, after the stock is issued, the stock is typically traded publicly (for example, IBM stock is traded on the New York Stock Exchange) and is not necessarily concentrated in the hands of a few key employees. Once stock is issued, the corporation receives nothing when individuals buy or sell the shares on a stock market.

Shareholders (also called *equity owners* because they own rights to the capital or equity of the firm) are entitled to receive dividend payments, which come out of the corporation's profits. Dividends are one way stockholders earn returns on their investments, but even if a corporation pays no dividends, shareholders can earn returns. If the price of the stock rises above what the shareholder paid, the shareholder can sell it for a profit.

Corporations also raise money by issuing debt. They promise to pay those who lend them money (*debt holders*) a stipulated amount of interest plus repayment of the loan. For example, General Electric might sell a *note* for $1 million in which it promises to pay 10

---

[4] *Wall Street Journal,* December 24, 1900, 1920, and telephone communications with the New York Stock Exchange. The number of companies is calculated as the number listed in the table entitled "New York Stock Exchange Composite Transactions," which appears daily in the *Wall Street Journal.* Some companies may not appear if their stock was not traded.

EXAMPLE 2.1 *Value of Limited Liability*

The rise of limited liability coincided with an increase in the size of firms. If it is efficient for firms to become large, and limited liability is the best structure for large firms to have, then a group of firms could limit competition if they could get a law passed that grants limited-liability protection to them alone. In Scotland until 1879, limited liability was granted to only three Edinburgh banks; all other competing banks had to accept unlimited liability.

We would expect that the limited-liability banks were larger and more successful than the others. In fact, even though over 50 banks with unlimited liability failed between 1845 and 1879, none of the three limited-liability banks failed. Furthermore, data from 1825 indicate that the three limited-liability banks averaged about 10 times the assets of the average bank with unlimited liability. After 1879, laws were changed, and all banks effectively became protected by limited liability.

Source: Carr and Mathewson (1988). See also Rasmusen (1988) for a discussion of ownership form and banks.

percent, or $100,000, per year for three years and repay the $1 million at the end of three years. Debt holders are paid first; stockholders are paid from what remains.

Table 2.1 illustrates this distinction between the claims of debt holders and shareholders. Suppose a corporation raises $1 million by borrowing $500,000 at 20 percent interest and selling 500,000 shares at $1 each. The corporation invests in Project 1, which has an equal chance of succeeding or failing. If the project succeeds, the corporation earns $2 million, of which $100,000 goes to interest payments and $500,000 to repay the loan. The remaining $1,400,000 goes to shareholders as dividends. If the project fails, the corporation goes out of business and sells its machines for $500,000, which goes to the debt holders.

On average, debt holders expect to receive a payoff of $550,000 (= 1/2 × $600,000 + 1/2 × $500,000), and equity owners expect to receive a payoff of $700,000 (= 1/2 × $1,400,000 + 1/2 × 0). The expected return on an investment is the expected payoff in excess of the initial investment divided by the initial investment, which the table shows is 10 percent for debt holders and 40 percent for equity owners.

The example shows that the expected return is higher for equity owners than for debt holders and that the payoff is not as variable for debt holders as for equity owners. In general, because debt holders get paid before equity owners, it is safer to hold debt. But, because debt is less risky, the expected return tends to be lower than for equity owners—if it were not, no one would hold equity. As the firm becomes more *highly leveraged*—increases its ratio of debt to equity—the expected returns to the equity holders rise. That is why stock prices fluctuate more for companies with high debt/equity ratios than for companies with low debt/equity ratios, all other things equal.

The amount of taxes firms pay depends on whether they are corporations, single proprietorships, or partnerships. For example, corporate income is taxed before it is

TABLE 2.1 Returns to Debt Holders and Equity Owners

Project 1			
Outcome of Project	Probability	Payoff Received by Debt Holders	Payoff Received by Equity Owners
Success	.5	$600,000	$1,400,000
Failure	.5	500,000	0
Expected payoff		$550,000	$700,000
Initial investment		500,000	500,000
Expected payoff minus initial investment		50,000	200,000
Expected return		10%	40%

Project 2			
Outcome of Project	Probability	Payoff Received by Debt Holders	Payoff Received by Equity Owners
Success	.5	$600,000	$1,300,000
Failure	.5	600,000	0
Expected payoff		$600,000	$650,000
Initial investment		500,000	500,000
Expected payoff minus initial investment		100,000	150,000
Expected return		20%	30%

distributed to a shareholder, who then pays personal income taxes. In contrast, income from proprietorships and partnerships is not directly taxed; it flows untaxed to the owners, who then pay personal income taxes.

Separation of Ownership and Control. The dramatic rise in the importance of the corporation caused a clamor in the 1930s about whether this organizational form was efficient. The debate was precipitated in part by *The Modern Corporation and Private Property*, by Berle and Means (1932), who argued that the corporate form separates ownership from control.[5] With separation of ownership and control, the owners of a

[5]Their book was and still is very influential. See Leibenstein (1966) and "The Symposium on Berle and Means" in the *Journal of Law and Economics*, June 26, 1983.

corporation, the shareholders, are typically not the managers, who are employees of the corporation. In contrast, single proprietorships and partnerships are run by the owners.

When control is separated from ownership, managers may not attempt to maximize profits and may pursue other objectives, like maximizing their own incomes, not working hard, and having plush offices (see Example 2.2).

In many corporations, there is often no single shareholder with the incentive to monitor managers' actions. Shareholders elect a board of directors to minimize the conflicts that arise because of the separation of ownership and control. The board's primary function is to act as an agent for the shareholders and oversee the efficient management of the company. But who monitors the board of directors? If they do a bad job, how will they be punished? One potential punishment is that they may not be re-elected and may acquire bad reputations that make it difficult for them to get other good jobs. For example, in 1992, when facing massive debts, the large retailer R. H. Macy & Co. brought in outside directors to take control and to ensure that, in the event of a filing for bankruptcy, a majority of the board members would not be company employees.[6]

This control over the board of directors and over the managers may be inadequate to ensure profit-maximizing behavior. Therefore, according to Berle and Means, the actions of corporations cannot be predicted by a traditional economic analysis based on profit maximization. They implied that the severity of the Great Depression was at least in part attributable to the rise of this new and inefficient form of business.

Aside from the conflict that Berle and Means pointed out between equity owners and managers, conflict can also arise between debt holders and equity owners. For example, suppose the firm in Table 2.1 has already raised its $500,000 from debt holders and $500,000 from equity holders and is deciding between Project 1, which we've already examined, and Project 2, which pays $600,000 if it fails and $1,900,000 if it succeeds. The total expected payoff to the latter project is $1,250,000, as before. Yet the division of the payoff between equity owners and debt holders is different: Debt holders now receive $600,000 for sure, whereas the equity owners can expect to receive $650,000. The payoffs of the new project are summarized in the table.

The debt holders prefer this new project, but the equity owners prefer the original one. Because debt holders recognize that their interests may diverge from those of equity owners, debt holders often insist on **bond covenants**, which are restrictions on the corporation's choices of investment projects or further financing.

One interpretation of Berle and Means is that they were focusing attention on the monitoring problems and conflicts that arise as a firm grows. There is nothing inefficient about incurring costs as long as they are offset by benefits. Large corporations are not inefficient just because they entail monitoring costs. These costs can be offset by the benefits of larger size and the ability to raise money cheaply.

[6]Laura Evenson, "Macy's Board Facing Major Shakeup," *San Francisco Chronicle,* April 25, 1992: B1–B2.

EXAMPLE 2.2

Conflicts of Interest Between Managers and Shareholders

The stock market decline beginning March 2000 was followed by a series of revelations that managers had perpetrated outrageous fraud. The managers had engaged in actions that directly benefited themselves at the expense of unsuspecting shareholders. Often the frauds involved misreporting earnings to mislead investors and to raise the price of the stock at least temporarily.

One of the most spectacular frauds involved Enron. Enron had been primarily a natural gas pipeline company until it transformed itself into an energy-trading company. With the deregulation of energy markets, there was great incentive for buyers and sellers of energy to trade with each other through a variety of sometimes complicated contracts. Enron became a hugely successful company whose stock price by 2000 was four times what it had been four years earlier, and whose annual revenue was $200 billion. Then in fall 2001, everything began to come apart. Enron executives had apparently set up partnerships for themselves that did business with Enron. The partners allegedly stood to earn significant profits. The investments performed poorly for Enron, and huge losses piled up—losses that were unknown to the public because they were not explicitly revealed in the accounting information released by Enron. In November 2001, Enron made the startling announcement that it was correcting its past accounting numbers and was writing off several hundred million dollars of earnings; the firm disavowed its past four years of audited financial statements. Enron declared bankruptcy, and litigation followed.

Several Enron executives pleaded guilty to felonies, and others, proclaiming innocence, were indicted. Enron's auditor, Arthur Andersen, one of the leading accounting firms in the world, was convicted of obstruction of justice in connection with the shredding of documents and subsequently fell apart.

This scandal was only one of many. Massive frauds were uncovered in other industries. One of the largest telecommunication firms, WorldCom (now called MCI), was thrown into bankruptcy as a result of poor investments that were allegedly not handled

Size of Firms. A firm may expand because it wants to produce more of its basic output or because it chooses to produce inputs as well or distribute its output. The market and the firm are alternative means of providing goods and services. The higher the costs of doing business with other firms, the more tasks a firm performs itself. For example, as the relative costs of dealing with others changed, General Motors went from purchasing car bodies from others, as it did before 1926, to producing the car bodies itself.[7]

Although a firm may want to grow so as to avoid the cost of doing business with other firms, a larger firm faces higher costs and greater difficulty monitoring its own

[7]See the April 2000 issue of the *Journal of Law and Economics* for four articles that examine and dispute this claim.

properly in its accounts nor revealed. In addition, WorldCom made a loan of about $400 million to its CEO. The Securities and Exchange Commission (SEC) began to look into tightening accounting standards to prevent firms from reporting income in ways that, while technically accurate, distort a company's overall financial picture. Congress passed the Sarbanes-Oxley Act, which increases firms' reporting requirements and attempts to limit possible conflicts of interest between managers and shareholders.

Finally, the use of stock options as a device to pay and motivate employees came under scrutiny. An option provides the owner with the right to buy a stock at a fixed price. So, for example, an option on Microsoft at a strike price of $10 allows the owner to purchase one share of Microsoft stock for $10 even if the stock price is $50. Firms, especially high-tech companies, give options to employees to motivate them. If an employee receives an option for $10 when the stock is trading at $5, the option is not worth much. But the option becomes valuable if the stock price rises substantially. The option creates a strong incentive for employees to act to raise the stock price. Some observers believe that options so cloud executives' thinking that they are encouraged to misreport earnings and to engage in actions that cause stock prices to rise for long enough that they can exercise their options. Maybe, but an executive should expect that a fraudulent short-run strategy will be discovered when the company's stock eventually plummets.

There is not yet a simple answer as to why fraud was so prevalent in the late 1990s (nor even whether the amount of fraud was unusually large historically, given the opportunities), but two facts are clear. First, the conflict between managers and shareholders is a real one. Second, the use of accounting gimmicks and even the use of options (which may be a reasonable method to pay employees in many industries) are likely to diminish. In 2003, Microsoft, one of the largest granters of options as a payment device, announced that it would use stock ownership rather than options to motivate employees.

Source: David Nicklaus, "WorldCom Scandal Shows Dark Side of Stock Option Plans," *St. Louis Post Dispatch*, July 3, 2002:C1; "Running Out of Options," *Newsweek*, July 21, 2003:40; "'24 Days' Behind Enron's Demise," *Wall Street Journal*, August 8, 2003:C1.

managers and employees so as to ensure that they operate efficiently and profitably. The optimal size of a firm depends on this trade-off between the advantages and disadvantages of expanding. For example, Bill Gates, head of the software firm Microsoft, contends that[8]

> [A]ll large organizations are in a certain sense less efficient than small organizations. But they can do things that are super important and need to be done. Believe me, when I wrote and reviewed every line that went into the code, the overall quality of the code—according to me—was higher. And I've had to compromise.

[8]"Gates: Our Only Advantage Is We Bet on Windows." *InfoWorld*. August 3, 1992:102.

In Chapter 12, we contend that a firm is more profitable if it performs only those actions that it is good at and relies on others (the market) for other essential actions.

Most U.S. firms are small, though larger firms account for most employment and sales. In 1999, 56 percent of all manufacturing firms had nine or fewer employees and accounted for 4 percent of all manufacturing employees (*Statistical Abstract of the United States,* 2002, Table 715). The U.S. economy had about 6 million companies, roughly 89 percent of which employed fewer than 20 people. Only 0.3 percent of firms had 500 or more employees, but they accounted for 50 percent of all employees. The top 200 U.S. manufacturing firms in terms of value added accounted for about 22 percent of manufacturing employment and 40 percent of value of shipments of manufacturers in 1997 (*Concentration Ratios in Manufacturing,* 1997, Table 1).

The share of employment and assets of the largest U.S. firms has fallen since 1970. Because machines have become more productive, manufacturing output is now produced with fewer employees. For example, the fraction of the nonagricultural labor force in manufacturing declined from about 34 percent in 1950 to about 13 percent by the end of 2001 (*Economic Report of the President,* 2003, Table B–46). As a result, employment has shifted to industries such as services in which firms tend to be relatively small.

Mergers and Acquisitions

A firm may increase its size by expanding through investment, such as by building new factories, or by means of a **merger**: a transaction in which the assets of one or more firms are combined in a new firm. We use the term *merger* to include acquisitions. There are three types of mergers:

- **Vertical merger:** A firm combines with its supplier.
- **Horizontal merger:** Firms that compete within the same market combine.
- **Conglomerate merger:** Firms in unrelated lines of businesses combine.

Reasons for Mergers and Acquisitions

There are many explanations for mergers. The main motive is usually to increase profitability. Unfortunately for firms, not all mergers result in greater profitability. Moreover, some mergers may be profitable for the firm yet harm society by reducing efficiency. We now contrast the motives for mergers that increase efficiency with those that do not.

Mergers That Increase Efficiency. Acquisitions and other mergers that increase efficiency are desirable for society. There are a number of reasons why takeovers of existing firms may promote efficiency, including increasing scale to an optimal level, creating synergies, and improving management.[9]

[9]Although takeovers are common in the United States and United Kingdom, they are virtually nonexistent in Japan. Takeovers were rare in Germany before unification. Privatized East German state companies are being acquired: "Bidding for Europe's Takeover Business." *The Economist,* September 12, 1992:81.

Combining firms may reduce duplication or produce other benefits from increased size. For example, the firms may be able to save management costs by using a single set of managers to run both firms.

As the costs of factors of production change, the optimal size of a firm (that is, the output at which average cost is minimized) may increase. In the late 1800s the cost of transportation fell because of the development of railroads, and the cost of communication fell because of the advent of the telegraph and telephone. Further, the development of financial markets (for example, bond and stock markets) lowered the cost of raising large sums of money. These developments probably caused the optimal size of a firm to increase and led to the importance of the large corporation as the major organizational form in the U.S. economy.

Reduced transaction costs could explain why two firms that engage in different activities might prefer to merge. Bittlingmayer (1985) contends that the Sherman Act of 1890 created uncertainty about the legality of contracts between direct competitors and thereby created an incentive for firms that had been cooperating with each other through contracts to merge.

Firms that engage in different but complementary activities may benefit from mergers because of synergies or **economies of scope**: It is less costly for one firm to perform two activities than for two specialized firms to perform them separately. If one firm excels at designing fast cars and another firm excels at designing attractive cars, the two firms may gain by merging.

Acquiring a badly run firm and installing better management produces gains. Suppose the current managers of a firm are doing a poor job. The firm generates a large amount of cash, but the managers keep investing the money in unprofitable projects and raising their salaries, so that stockholders see little, if any, of the cash as a dividend. Stockholders could urge the board of directors to control management, but that may be difficult, especially if some members of the board are managers.[10]

An alternative way to discipline managers is to allow shrewd investors to discover inefficiently run firms. Such investors could then "take over" (acquire or gain control of) the inefficient firm at a low price, improve it, and either resell it or pass along the increased dividends to shareholders.

Imagine that the stock of the firm is worth \$100 per share, based on the low dividends that current management is paying shareholders. You discover that this firm is badly run, acquire it, fire the current management, improve the firm's operations, and double dividends. As a result, the value of your stock in the company doubles to \$200 per share. The threat that someone like you could come along and buy enough shares to gain control of the company might so scare the managers of the firm that they perform efficiently to avoid losing their jobs.

To gain control of the firm, you could offer to buy a controlling number of shares of stock from the current shareholders. Shareholders, however, stand to gain if (a) they

---

[10]Groups of investors may pressure firms to perform well. A study by Lilli Gordon for the California Public Employees' Retirement System finds that "relationship investors" (those who gain a seat on the board and induce the firm to behave well) have higher returns than the market as a whole. "A Fund in Wolf's Clothing?" *The Economist,* January 30, 1993:68.

keep their stock while you take over the firm, improve its performance, and raise dividends; (b) they sell to you at a price above \$100; or (c) they hold on to their stock and you fail to gain control of the firm, but your attempt motivates current managers to improve their performance. Of course, the firm's managers may not care at all about the shareholders, and they may fight the attempted takeover in order to protect their comfortable jobs. If the managers are unsuccessful in preventing the firm from changing hands, a **hostile takeover** occurs. Battles to prevent hostile takeovers are intense, and managers often use clever tactics.[11]

It is also possible that the firm's managers believe that they could significantly improve profits if only the board of directors would allow them to fire employees, sell off parts of the business, and embark on new projects. Such radical changes in operation might not appeal to either shareholders or the board, so the managers themselves might decide to buy out the firm. A firm that is being taken over by its managers is said to be **going private**, because there are no longer any outside stockholders to whom management must answer. But how could a group of managers afford to buy out a corporation? One way is to use a **leveraged buyout (LBO)**, in which bonds based on the corporation's assets are sold in order to raise a tremendous amount of money. These bonds are sometimes called **junk bonds**, which are high-yield bonds backed by a corporation's assets and are considered riskier than typical corporate bonds. Junk bonds became popular in the 1980s as a way for investors to raise money to acquire control of a firm. It is safer to own a junk bond than a share of stock in the same firm because bondholders are paid before stockholders.

Mergers That Reduce Efficiency. Some mergers are disastrous: They reduce both efficiency and profitability.[12] Here, we focus on mergers where the new owners of a firm profit from the merger, yet production efficiency is reduced or other efficiency losses occur. Although the owners of the new firm may benefit, society loses. Such mergers may occur to take advantage of tax codes, for reasons of short-run exploitation, or to extend market or political power.

Because of the complexities of the U.S. tax code, firms may have a financial incentive to merge even if there is no gain from increased economic efficiency. Suppose Firm 1 has \$100 in profits and Firm 2 has \$100 in losses. If the corporate tax rate is 50 percent, Firm 1 must pay \$50 in taxes, and Firm 2 pays nothing. If Firms 1 and 2 combine, their profit is zero. The profits of Firm 1 are offset by the losses of Firm 2, so the combined firm owes no taxes. The government gets \$50 less, but the profit of the new firm is \$50 more than the combined profits of the two firms had they not merged. Thus, although no economic efficiencies are created (the same amount of inputs is used to produce the same amount of outputs), the merger is privately profitable. Tax

[11]See **www.aw-bc.com/carlton_perloff** "Hostile Takeovers" for a discussion of how managers avoid hostile takeovers.

[12]For example, managers may desire to control large firms because they enjoy power, and they may pursue a policy of acquisition not because it is profitable but because it appeals to their ego, which may bias their judgment about value (Roll 1986).

reasons alone, however, do not account for much merger activity (Auerbach and Reishus 1988).

People might acquire a firm to take advantage of short-run gains, even if there are long-run losses. Suppose a firm has implicitly agreed to employ loyal workers even during slack times. As a result of this arrangement, workers receive lower wages in return for steadier employment. If management reneged on its arrangement and fired workers during slack times, workers would never again trust management. If you buy an inefficient firm and get rid of surplus labor in slack times, you can make a short-run gain. Workers will soon demand higher wages to compensate them for less steady employment, but in the meantime, you can run the firm more profitably than the previous management. Your action may harm the firm in the long run as the wage payments rise. Still, the short-run gain to the acquiring firm could offset the long-run loss (Shleifer and Summers 1988).[13]

If a sufficient number of firms in one industry merge, the resulting firm would face less competition and acquire additional *market power*: the ability of a firm to set price profitably above competitive levels. As we explain in Chapter 3, if price is greater than the competitive level, too little output is produced (production is inefficient). Therefore, the elimination of competitors through merging could lead to higher prices for consumers. Antitrust laws in the United States and in most other industrialized countries forbid mergers that are likely to reduce competition and lead to higher prices.

Some observers point to the relaxation of antitrust scrutiny as one of the reasons for the U.S. merger wave of the 1980s and 1990s. However, there is little evidence of significant increases in market power overall or in market concentration (Pautler 2001, White 2002). Even if firms are in different industries, so that there are no concerns about a reduction in competition, their amalgamation may create a potent political force that could influence legislation to their benefit at the expense of the rest of society.

Merger Activity in the United States

Although newspaper articles often claim that the current period—starting with the Reagan era—is the period of greatest merger activity in history, even greater merger activity occurred in earlier times, when one adjusts for the size of the economy. Surprisingly, it is difficult to obtain consistent data on merger activity over time.[14] In early periods, data were kept on manufacturing and mining primarily. Over time these industries have declined in relative importance in the U.S. economy. The early data sources report only "large" transactions, ignoring mergers between small firms. As a result, measures of merger activity are biased downward, especially in earlier periods when firms tended to be smaller.

[13]Even if the firm's actions are inefficient, the firm's long-run losses from the higher wages could be offset by the firm's short-term gains.

[14]This section is based on Golbe and White (1988), and Andrade and Stafford (2001).

FIGURE 2.1 Annual Number of Mergers and Acquisitions

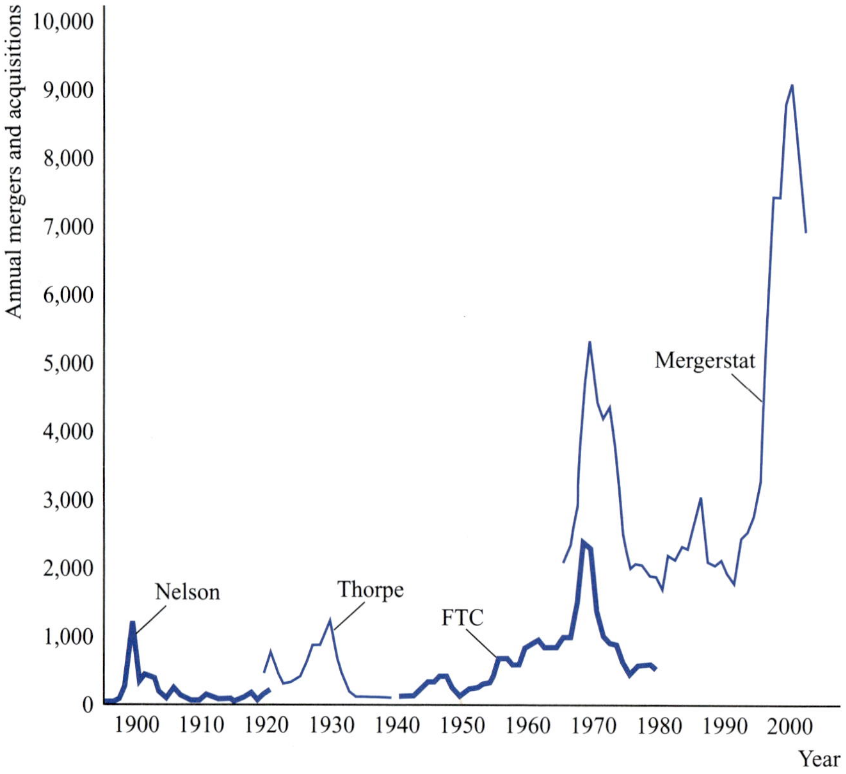

Notes: Nelson: Data derived by Nelson (1959) for manufacturing and mining. Thorpe: Data derived by W. Thorpe, reported in Nelson (1959, 166) for manufacturing and mining. FTC: Continuation of Thorpe series by Federal Trade Commission. Mergerstat: *Mergerstat Review* (2003).

Source: Adapted from Golbe and White (1988). Figure 9.6, in Alan J. Auerbach, ed., *Corporate Takeovers*. Copyright 1988 by the National Bureau of Economic Research. All rights reserved.

Bursts of merger activity appear to coincide with booms in the stock market for reasons that are not fully understood. Figure 2.1 shows the number of mergers since 1900 based on data from various sources. In the figure, there are five periods of extensive merger activity: one near the turn of the century, a second in the late 1920s, a third in the late 1960s, a fourth in the 1980s, and a fifth in the 1990s.

George Stigler (1950) called the first wave near the turn of the century the *merger to monopoly* movement. During this period, the U.S. economy was undergoing widespread changes in response to the development of railroads and communications. The stock market became a more important source of capital, and this period witnessed the creation of firms that, to this day, remain large and successful—among them, General Electric and U.S. Steel. The end of the first merger wave in the early 1900s coincided with a downturn in economic activity and with the Supreme Court's 1904 decision in the Northern Securities case, in which the Court found that certain (horizontal) mergers violated the antitrust law of the Sherman Act, which was passed in 1890.[15]

Stigler (1950) called the second wave in the 1920s the *merger to oligopoly* movement. The third wave in the 1960s is called the *conglomerate merger* movement because many of these mergers produced conglomerate firms or holding companies that own many firms that produce in different markets. There is no common name for the fourth wave. It was in this merger wave that hostile takeovers became more common, although they still remained a small share (less than 25 percent) of overall merger activity. The fifth wave could be labeled the *deregulation merger* wave because nearly half of the mergers took place in industries that had recently been deregulated, such as airlines, telecommunications, media, and banking.

News reports often proclaim that the 1980s and 1990s had unparalleled merger activity. Based on the pure number of mergers (Figure 2.1) or the nominal (not adjusted for inflation) value of the mergers, these statements are true. However, the economy is much larger today than near the turn of the century. If we compare mergers to the size of the economy, there was greater activity near the turn of the century. Figure 2.2 shows the ratio of the number of transactions per billion dollars of inflation-adjusted or "real" gross national product (GNP). Thus, the merger activity since the 1980s, though substantial, is not unprecedented.

Merger Activities in Other Countries

Traditionally, mergers were much less common in Europe than in the United States. Now, however, mergers, hostile takeovers, and "going public" transactions are becoming more common in Europe, though there are still fewer mergers than in the United States. For example, the number of European Community mergers rose from 575 in 1984 to 1,159 in 1988 (Schmittmann and Vonnemann 1992). The number of mergers involving at least one of the top 1,000 EC firms rose from 185 in 1984/85 to 492 in 1988/89 (Jacquemin 1990). From 1980 to 1992, 95 mergers or acquisitions occurred in the U.S. defense industry and 40 in the comparable European industry (Reppy 1994).

One of the most debated issues in transitional central and eastern European economies has been the restructuring of state-owned enterprises. Some countries—such as Czechoslovakia and Russia—have privatized existing enterprises, while others—including Hungary and Poland—have tried to transform their enterprises before selling them. Regardless of the strategy these transitional economies used, they experienced massive and spontaneous breakups of state-owned enterprises at the beginning of the reforms.

---

[15] *Northern Securities Co. vs. U.S.*, 193 U.S. 197 (1904).

FIGURE 2.2 Annual Number of Mergers and Acquisitions per Billion Dollars of Real GNP

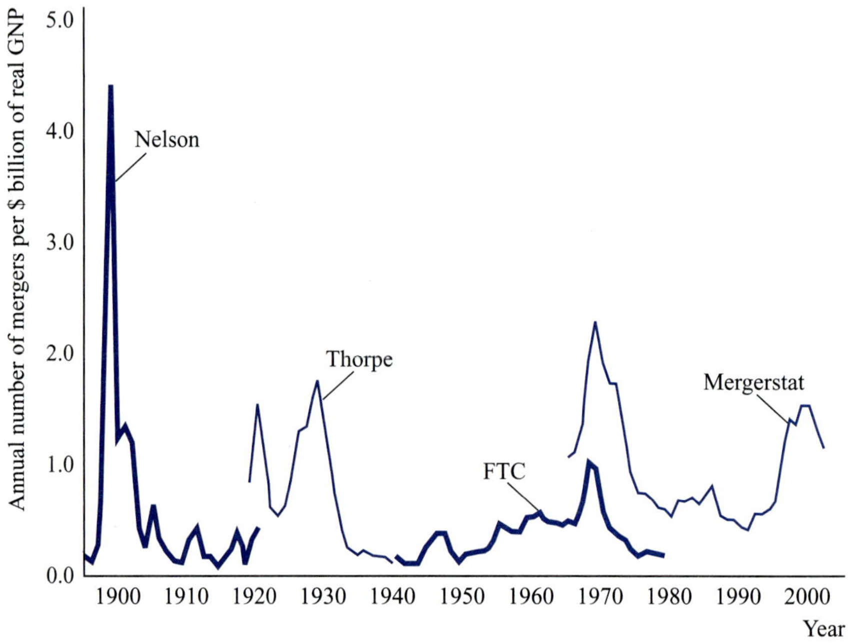

Note: Annual number of mergers and acquisitions per billion dollars of real GNP (in 1982 dollars); Nelson Series, FTC "Broad" series and Mergerstat.

Source: Adapted from Golbe and White (1988). Figure 9.7, in Alan J. Auerbach, ed., *Corporate Takeovers*.

For instance, the number of industrial enterprises employing more than 25 workers went from about 700 in 1990 to 2,000 by mid-1992 in Czechoslovakia. Most industries have become less concentrated: The largest firms' share of the industry has declined in terms of both value of output and employment. This shift in industrial activities from large to small or medium-sized enterprises in the first years of transition was brought about by a combination of breakups of large companies and rapid entry of new firms.

Empirical Evidence on the Efficiency and Profitability of Mergers

Much debate has arisen about whether the recent wave of mergers and acquisitions benefits the economy. Obviously acquisitions and mergers that lead to production efficiency are desirable. Some worry, however, that many mergers and acquisitions merely involve a reshuffling of ownership that produces short-run stock gains for financial manipulators who are not interested in the long-term health of firms. Others are concerned that mergers create greater market power that hurts consumers by raising prices. Andrade and Stafford (2001) and Mueller (1997) survey the recent studies of the evidence on mergers and acquisitions. Earlier studies include Bradley, Desai, and Kim (1988), Jarrell, Brickley, and Netter (1988), Jarrell and Poulsen (1987), Jensen (1988), Jensen and Ruback (1983), Romano (1985), Scherer (1988), and Shleifer and Vishny (1988). The following paragraphs summarize the findings of these studies.

Returns to Acquired Firm. Shareholders of an acquired firm receive a premium of about 16 to 25 percent above the stock price prevailing prior to the acquisition activity. Much of the increase in the share price of an acquired firm occurs just *before* public announcement of the transaction. The premium received by shareholders rose significantly as a result of the Williams Act, which required firms to reveal their takeover plans, and the gains to shareholders of acquired firms have increased over time.

Effects of Preventing Mergers. Management tactics to thwart takeovers reduce the probability of a takeover but raise the acquisition price, if the takeover is successful. When someone fails to gain control of a firm, the increase in its stock price caused by that person's bidding is completely eliminated, and price returns to its previous level.

The evidence is mixed on the effect of defensive provisions such as supermajority amendments, greenmail, and poison pills on stock prices. Managers (who often own some stock) may try to enact a shareholder agreement under which anyone who seeks to gain control of the firm must obtain the approval of a supermajority (more than 50 percent) of the firm's shareholders. Such a rule makes it easier for a group of current shareholders to prevent a takeover. Adoption of supermajority amendments lowers a firm's stock price, presumably because of the reduced likelihood of a takeover.

A firm may try to dissuade a particular individual from taking over the firm by using **greenmail**, in which the firm buys back the shares of the person who is trying to take over the firm (and only that person's shares) at a premium. Greenmail has a negative effect on a firm's stock price. A firm that changes its state of incorporation to take advantage of the new state's strong antitakeover laws enjoys a slight increase (though not a statistically significant one) in its share price.

In **poison-pill** arrangements, the corporation must make stock available at bargain prices to original shareholders—but not to someone who takes over the firm—if the firm is taken over, thereby diluting the value of the new owner's stock. These arrangements significantly lower the stock price of the firm. Poison pills decrease the value of taking over the firm, raising the costs of acquisition and thereby reducing a potential buyer's incentives to try to acquire the firm.

Returns to Acquiring Firm. The shareholders of an acquiring firm do not earn substantial, above-average rates of return as a result of the acquisition. They do slightly better in hostile takeovers than in friendly mergers. The return to stockholders of acquiring firms has declined over time from about 4 percent in the 1960s to −3 percent in the 1980s and 1990s. The return to acquirers depends on whether the target is purchased with stock or cash, with acquirers doing better when cash is used. The use of stock as a means of payment increased by about 50 percent from the 1980s, with about 60 percent of transactions in the 1990s financed entirely by stock.

When faced with a hostile takeover attempt, a firm's managers may seek a friendly firm or individual, known as a **white knight**, to come to their rescue, obtain control of the firm, and leave current management in place. White knights, on average, overpay for the firms they acquire.

Returns to Society. Overall, total shareholder value of the combined companies rises about 2 to 7.5 percent after the consolidation. The increased value of a consolidated firm is not typically due to the creation of market power.

If the new firm acquires market power, the price consumers face will rise. This increased market power, however, also benefits the rivals of the combined firm, and hence their stock prices should rise. If the transaction is motivated by greater efficiency in production, the combined firm will be a more efficient competitor, and the stock price of its rivals should decline in anticipation of the increased competition. Stillman (1983), Eckbo (1983), and Banerjee and Eckard (1998), investigating the merger wave at the turn of the nineteenth century, conclude that the second explanation is more consistent with the evidence.

Instead of using stock-price data, some researchers look directly at accounting data from the consolidated firm to see if the new firm is more efficient. Data problems are more severe with this approach than with looking at stock prices because accounting data are often difficult to interpret. Moreover, the estimated efficiency gains for the firm are likely to be smaller than those estimated from data on stock prices because those figures apply to the increase in the *equity* value (not total value, which includes debt) that results from acquisition. In Mueller's (1997) survey of 20 studies covering 10 countries, only a few studies find increased profitability from merger. Two particularly ambitious U.S. studies, Scherer (1988) and Ravenscraft and Scherer (1987), do not find increases in profits after acquisition based on their examination of profit data by line of business from the 1960s and 1970s. In contrast, Lichtenberg and Siegel (1987) examine the productivity of individual plants using more recent data and detect significant improvements in efficiency in plants whose ownership had changed. Moreover, they find that the plants most likely to undergo an ownership change were those that were performing poorly. Andrade and Stafford (2001) criticized Scherer's studies for failing to control for industry benchmarks. Controlling for such benchmarks reveals that mergers generally improve the efficiency of the firm and lead to increased profits. Finally, that mergers are often concentrated in the same industries in any one time period lends further support to an efficiency rationale for mergers (Jovanovic and Rousseau 2001).

Moreover, contrary to what some commentators allege, there is no evidence that consolidated firms are "myopic" and cut back on research and development (R&D). Hall (1988) finds that R&D spending is not influenced by the change in control.

In summary, stock market evidence supports the view that merger activity improves efficiency and creates value. Shareholders of target firms are the primary beneficiaries of this increased value. As legislation and new management tactics have made it more difficult to gain control of firms, the returns to shareholders of target firms have increased and those to shareholders of acquiring firms have decreased. Moreover, there appears to be no increase in market concentration and market power, so consumers do not lose. Nor is there a reduction in R&D.

Additional research on profits subsequent to consolidation, not on stock prices, is needed to confirm these efficiency gains. Without such research, some may argue that mergers and takeovers create illusory stock market value that represents either the unjustified transfer of wealth from those dependent on the acquired firm (for example, employees) to its shareholders, or valuation errors by the stock market. The work of Andrade and Stafford (2001) appears to confirm the stock market evidence regarding the efficiencies of mergers.

Cost Concepts

By running efficiently, a firm can produce output at the lowest possible cost. Every firm needs to know what it costs to produce its products if it is to make sensible business decisions. There are a variety of ways to measure costs, and some cost concepts are more appropriate for certain problems than others. This section explores these different cost concepts and some subtleties in understanding them.

Types of Costs

Firms typically incur costs that do not vary with output and costs that do. A fixed cost (F) is an expense that does not vary with the level of output. A fee a government charges for a firm to incorporate and conduct business is a fixed cost. Whether the firm produces a lot or a little, it must pay the fee. Another example is the monthly rent that a lawyer must pay for an office after signing a one-year lease. The monthly rent must be paid regardless of how much business the lawyer does.

If the firm and the lawyer decide to go out of business, they would not renew their incorporation or rental agreement for the next year. But what if they decide to go out of business just one month after they began? Must they still pay their fee or monthly rental? If they have paid in advance, can they get a refund? The answer depends on the law or contract. The firm probably prepaid the entire incorporation fee, which is not refundable. The lawyer, although obligated to pay a monthly rent, may be able to rent to someone else and recoup some, if not all, of the cost. The portion of fixed costs that is not recoverable is a **sunk cost**. A sunk cost is like spilled milk: Once it is sunk, there is no use worrying about it, and it should not affect any subsequent decisions. In contrast, a fixed cost that is not sunk *should* influence decisions. For example, whether or not the lawyer should go out of business depends in part on how costly it is to get out of the lease (the financial penalty for breaking the lease). Costs, including fixed costs, that are not incurred if operations cease are called **avoidable costs**.

Variable costs (VC) are costs that change with the level of output, q. Because variable costs vary with output, we normally write them as a function of output: $VC(q)$. Typically, as output increases, so does the need for labor, electricity, and materials, so variable costs depend on the wages and prices that a firm must pay for inputs.

Total costs (C) are the sum of all fixed and variable costs: $C = F + VC$. Associated with the concepts of total cost and variable cost is marginal cost (MC), which is the *increment,* or addition, to cost that results from producing one more unit of output.[16] Because fixed cost does not change as output increases, the increase in total cost when output increases is identical to the corresponding increase in variable cost.

It is important to distinguish between the concept of marginal cost and the various concepts of average cost. There are three common types of average cost: *average total cost* (sometimes simply called *average cost*), *average variable cost,* and *average fixed cost*:

- Average cost (AC) (sometimes called *average total cost* or ATC) is total cost divided by output: $AC = C(q)/q$.
- Average variable cost (AVC) is variable cost divided by output: $AVC = VC(q)/q$.
- Average fixed cost (AFC) is fixed cost divided by output: $AFC = F/q$.

Because AC is the sum of AVC and AFC, AVC and AFC cannot exceed AC:

$$AC(q) = \frac{C(q)}{q} = \frac{VC(q) + F}{q} = \frac{VC(q)}{q} + \frac{F}{q} = AVC(q) + AFC(q).$$

Even though marginal cost is independent of fixed costs and average cost is not, it is *not* necessarily true that, at any given output level, marginal cost is less than average cost. The reason that marginal cost may exceed average cost is that marginal cost refers to *changes* in cost, not to levels.

Imagine going into a supermarket to buy fruit. You carry a bag and put in some apples, which naturally differ in weight. The total weight of the apples in the bag and the associated average weight per apple are easily determined. Suppose you *add* a very small apple to your bag. Its weight is the increment to the weight of the apples in the bag (the marginal weight). But the weight of the small apple is less than the average weight of the apples already in the bag, so the average weight falls. If, instead, you add a very large apple, its marginal weight exceeds the average weight of the apples already in the bag, so the average weight rises. The marginal weight is totally determined by the *one* additional apple. The average weight (after the additional apple) is determined in large part by the apples that were already there. Analogously, marginal cost can be either above or below average cost.

To illustrate further the relationship of marginal cost, average cost, and average variable cost, Table 2.2 shows how the various cost measures vary as output increases. In this example, the fixed cost is \$100 regardless of whether production occurs or not (output = 0). This fixed cost is an obligation that cannot be avoided by going out of business, so the fixed cost is sunk or nonrecoverable.[17]

---

[16] If $C(q)$ is the total cost of producing q units, then the marginal cost is $MC = dC(q)/dq$.

[17] If part of the fixed cost were recoverable, as when a license fee is refundable, then the relevant cost for output of zero would be only the sunk cost. For example, a firm that goes out of business but obtains a \$60 refund on its \$100 state license fee has costs of \$40 for producing nothing.

TABLE 2.2 An Example of Cost Concepts

Output	Fixed Cost	Average Fixed Cost	Total Variable Cost	Average Variable Cost	Total Cost	Average Total Cost	Marginal Cost
0	100		0		100		
1	100	100	10	10	110	110	10
2	100	50	19	9.5	119	59.5	9
3	100	33.3	25	8.3	125	41.7	6
4	100	25	32	8.0	132	33	7
5	100	20	40	8.0	140	28	8
6	100	16.7	49	8.2	149	24.8	9
7	100	14.2	60	8.6	160	22.9	11
8	100	12.5	73	9.1	173	21.6	13
9	100	11.1	88	9.8	188	20.9	15
10	100	10	108	10.8	208	20.8	20

In the table, the variable cost rises from 0 to 108 as output expands from 0 to 10. Total cost—the sum of fixed plus variable costs—rises from 100 to 208 as output expands to 10. Marginal cost equals the increase in total costs that results from producing an additional unit of output. It initially falls, reaches a minimum of 6 at 3 units of output, and then rises.

Average variable cost equals total variable cost divided by output, and average total cost equals total cost divided by output. Average total cost always exceeds average variable cost, but as shown, marginal cost may be less than, equal to, or greater than average total or average variable cost.

There is a geometric relationship between *MC*, *AVC*, and *AC* as depicted in Figure 2.3. When *MC* is below *AVC*, the *AVC* curve is falling. When *MC* is above *AVC*, the *AVC* curve is rising. When *MC* equals *AVC*, the *AVC* is at its minimum. A similar relationship exists between *MC* and *AC*. Figure 2.3 also shows that, as output increases, average fixed cost (*AFC*) approaches zero and *AVC* and *AC* get closer together.

The apples example can be used to illustrate why *AC* rises if *MC* exceeds it or falls if *MC* is below it. If you add an apple that is heavier than the average apple, the average weight of the basket increases. Conversely, if you add a lighter-than-average apple, the average weight falls.

In general, total costs depend on the amount of output produced as well as the prices of the factors of production (for example, wages of workers and the price of raw materials). Figure 2.3 illustrates how a typical (short-run) average cost curve varies with output: Average cost eventually rises as output expands because it becomes more

FIGURE 2.3 Cost Curves

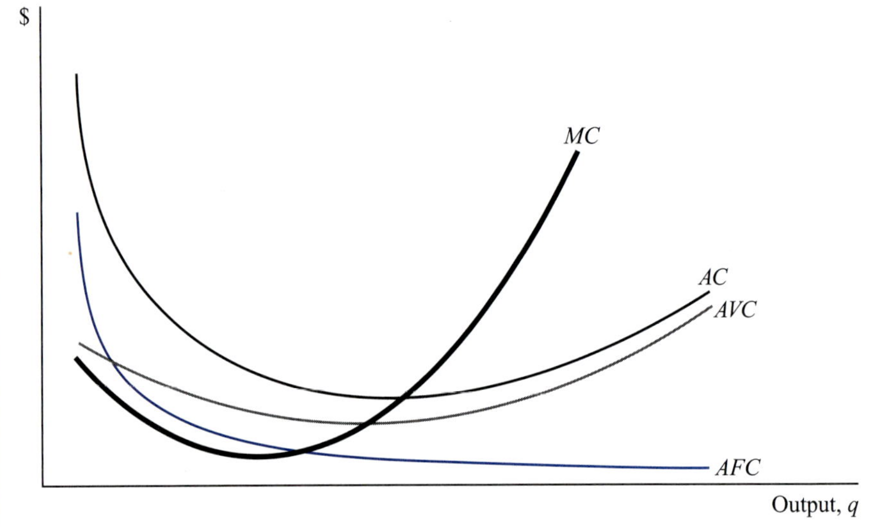

costly to produce as output increases within a given plant. The curves are based on the assumption that the prices of the factors of production (for example, wages of employees) are held constant. If, for example, wages were to rise, then the entire average cost curve would shift up. It is *not* necessarily true that the curve would shift straight upward because the minimum-cost output may well change. That is, the size of a firm that yields minimum average cost depends on the wages of labor and costs of all other factors of production.

A cost curve summarizes an enormous amount of information. For instance, knowing how the cost curve changes as wages or other factor prices change, one can infer a firm's **production technology**: the relationship between inputs and output reflecting the maximum possible output that can be produced from a given set of inputs. In other words, knowing the cost function of a firm and knowing its technology are equivalent.[18] For example, suppose the wage rate is \$10 per hour, and workers are the only input used to produce corn (seeds are free). To plant 1 bushel of corn costs \$10, to plant 2 bushels costs \$20, and so on. From this information on costs and

[18]Let $\mathbf{x}$ = an input or vector of inputs (for example, labor and raw materials), q = output, $\mathbf{w}$ = wage rate (and other unit prices for inputs), $F(\mathbf{x})$ = the production function (output as a function of inputs). The cost function $C(q, \mathbf{w})$ is derived by solving the following problem: Minimize the cost of producing q units subject to the constraint that q units are produced according to the engineering relationship between q and $\mathbf{x}$. Knowledge of $C(q, \mathbf{w})$ allows one to infer $F(\mathbf{x})$ under reasonable assumptions (using "duality theory," which is explained in Varian 1992, Ch. 6).

wages, we can infer that the production technology is that one worker can plant 1 bushel of corn per hour.

Cost Concepts

Although the definitions of the various cost concepts may seem straightforward, several complicated issues are associated with them. We now explore the most important ones.

Cost Factors in Addition to Output. A firm's costs depend on how much it produces for any given set of input prices. But factor prices are generally not the only influence on cost (Alchian 1959). The costs of production depend not only on how much is produced but also on *how fast*. Producing something quickly is more costly than producing it slowly. Moreover, variation in the rate of production over time matters. For example, steady production of 60 units/hour for 10 hours might involve lower costs than 100 units/hour for 2 hours plus 50 units/hour for 8 hours, even though total production is 600 units in either case.

It might be cost effective for a firm to spend money to make its plant highly adaptable to different levels of production. If a business is seasonal (for example, New Year's cards), the relevant cost is not the cost of producing a specific output but rather the cost of producing the range of outputs experienced during the year. If output fluctuates between 25 and 100 units per month, then a plant with a cost curve like AC_1 in Figure 2.4 might well be more efficient (that is, have lower total cost) than one with the curve AC_2, even though the minimum of the AC_2 curve is lower than that of the AC_1 curve.

The Short Run Versus the Long Run. The **short run** is a time period so brief that some factors of production cannot be costlessly varied. The **long run** is a period of time sufficiently long that all factors of production can be costlessly varied. For example, at the end of the year, the lawyer who rented an office is free to renew the lease or lease a new space. However, during the course of the year, the lease may not be broken without cost (there are sunk costs). In this example, the short run is less than one year, whereas the long run is one year or longer.

FIGURE 2.4 Cost Curves of Different Technologies

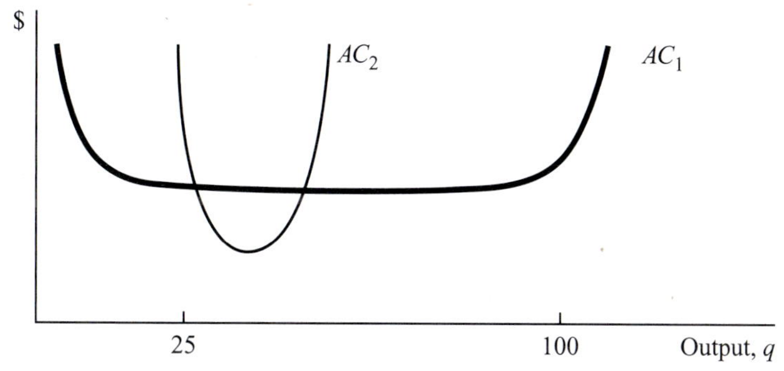

Another example illustrating the difference between short and long run has to do with installed machinery, which is costly to move and reinstall. If machines last for one year and must then be replaced, the number of machines can be regarded as predetermined in the short run of one year, though not in the long run. More generally, the short run is that time period during which the number of machines and physical space (the plant) are fixed and cannot be varied except at so substantial a cost that it is never profitable. In the short run, the firm must make do with its current plant and stock of machines. In the long run, the firm can alter its capital: It can buy new machines, discard old ones, and even move into a different plant designed to allow production of any given level of output at minimum cost.

The distinction between short and long run is not precise. Indeed, there is a continuum of runs, with increasingly more adjustment possible as the length of the run increases. The firm must incur greater costs, **adjustment costs**, as it increases the speed at which it adjusts its operations.[19]

A firm can configure itself in any way it wants in the long run, but in the short run its choices are constrained. Therefore the long-run average cost is always at least as low as the short-run average cost. This relationship between long-run and short-run costs implies that the long-run curve is the *envelope* of the short-run curves; that is, the long-run average cost curve (*LRAC*) is the relevant section of whichever short-run average cost curve (*SRAC*) is lowest at that particular quantity, as Figure 2.5 shows. In the short run, suppose that the firm can only have a single plant size. In the figure, there are three possible *SRAC* curves, AC_1, AC_2, and AC_3. Notice that the *LRAC* is not always the minimum point of a short-run average cost curve. In Figure 2.5, the least expensive way to produce 100 units is to use Plant 2, even though that is not the output that minimizes average cost in Plant 2 but *is* the output that minimizes average cost in Plant 3. In textbooks, one typically draws the long-run average cost curve so that it eventually rises as output expands, which means that the firm's efficient size (the largest output that minimizes average cost) is finite.

Opportunity Cost. As Adam Smith said, "The real price of everything is the toil and trouble of acquiring it." That is, an action's **opportunity cost** is the value of the best forgone alternative use of the resources employed in that action. For example, if a firm hires three workers at the going wage of $10 per hour, then its labor cost is $30 per hour. In this example, the opportunity cost and the actual out-of-pocket costs are the same. Suppose, instead, that one of the three workers is the firm's owner, who does not receive a wage. An economist still measures the opportunity cost of the three workers at $30 per hour: The labor used by the firm is worth $30 because another firm would value the labor at that amount.

We can use opportunity costs to determine whether it is profitable to continue an activity. To return to the example, suppose that each worker produces 1 unit of output per hour, which sells for $9. The owner calculates the profits earned in one hour as the revenue of $27 minus the cost (using opportunity cost as the measure) of $30 for a net

[19]See **www.aw-bc.com/carlton_perloff** "Adjustment Costs" for details.

FIGURE 2.5 Long-Run Cost Curve

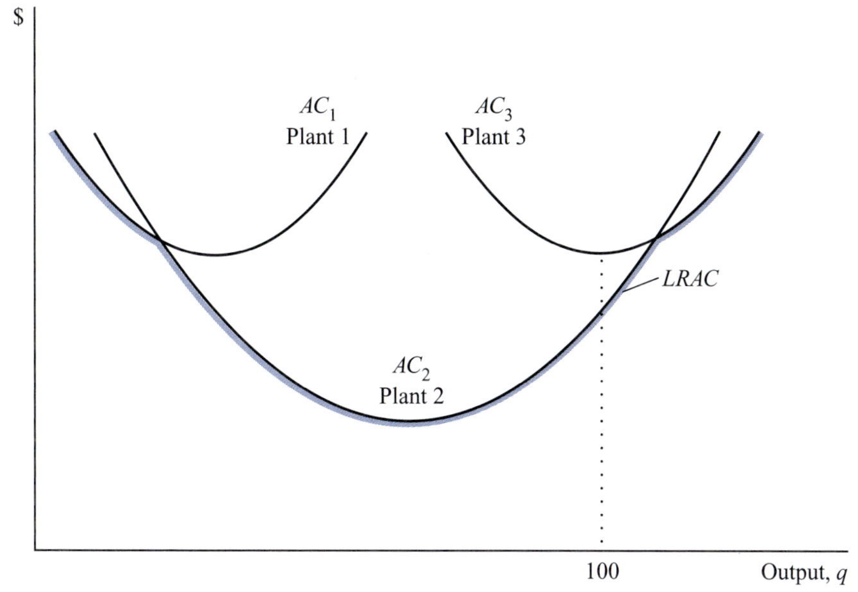

loss of \$3. The presence of a loss shows that the owner should cease production and work for someone else at \$10 per hour. Clearly, the owner is better off earning \$10 per hour than earning \$7 (= \$27 − \$20) in wages.

The opportunity cost concept is very useful in determining whether a firm should continue to use an asset that it owns when that asset could be rented readily. Consider a firm that owns the building it occupies. If the building could be rented to another tenant for \$1,000 per month, then the firm should count that amount as its cost of occupying the building. It is the forgone earnings of not renting out the building. If the firm cannot afford to pay itself rent (because doing so would result in a negative profit), then the firm should realize that its use of the building is not the most profitable—it would be better to go out of its current business and rent the building.

Surprisingly, if all costs are valued at their opportunity cost, then profit need only be *zero* to make remaining in business worthwhile. Opportunity cost values *all* resources used at the highest value they could receive elsewhere. If revenues just cover costs, then all resources (for example, the owner's time, the firm's building) are being used in an efficient manner and would not be worth more if used elsewhere. Because opportunity cost values each resource at its most profitable alternative use, economists sometimes say that opportunity cost attributes a **normal profit** (best possible profit from an alternative use of the resource) to all of the firm's resources.

Expensing Versus Amortizing. Suppose that a firm rents a machine by the month for \$100 and then decides to purchase the machine outright for its market price of \$10,000.

Should it count all $10,000 as a fixed cost incurred in its month of purchase, or should it spread the cost over the months the machine will be used? When costs are counted as they are incurred, they are said to be **expensed**; when they are spread out over the useful life of the machine, they are said to be **amortized**. If the firm amortizes the cost of the machine, how much should it charge itself? The answer clearly affects how the firm judges its performance.

The simple answer to any question about the appropriate cost to assign a durable asset is that the relevant cost is the *rent* that the owner could earn by renting the asset to someone else. This calculation is often easy—when a firm owns an office building and uses only some of the space for its own needs, it determines the appropriate market rent when it rents space. In other cases, the appropriate rent may not be available; for example, there is no rental market for blast furnaces. How should the cost of such assets be treated? One answer is to calculate the cost of owning an asset as the lost interest on its value (if it were sold for $100, that $100 could be earning interest) plus the depreciation on the asset. Economic **depreciation** is the decline in the value of an asset during the year (for example, using a machine causes it to wear out and fall in value). Even when installed assets cannot be resold, one can still use this method to calculate a rent.[20] The resulting profit calculation reveals whether the firm's decision to install the machine was a good one and whether further investment would be profitable.

Economies of Scale

A firm's average costs may remain constant, rise, or fall as its output expands. If average cost falls as output increases, the firm is said to have **economies of scale** (or **increasing returns to scale**); if average costs do not vary with output, it has **constant returns to scale**; and if average cost rises with output, the firm is said to have **diseconomies of scale** (or **decreasing returns to scale**). In Figure 2.3, the firm first enjoys economies of scale, then (at least for one output level) it has constant returns, and then it suffers from decreasing returns to scale. If a firm enjoys economies of scale at all output levels, then it is efficient for one firm to produce the entire market output (see the discussion of "natural monopoly" in Chapter 4).

Reasons for Economies of Scale

There are many reasons to expect a firm's average costs to decline, at least initially, as its output expands. One is that fixed setup costs do not vary with the level of output. For example, a publishing company typically incurs substantial costs to have a book written. Editors must be paid and the plates for printing made. If 100 rather than 50 books are produced, the cost does not rise by a factor of 2 because the additional books require few additional costs. Another example is an automobile stamping facility. Typically, special dies must be made to press the parts into their unique shapes. The more parts produced with each die, the lower the average total cost of production.

[20]See **www.aw-bc.com/carlton_perloff** "Depreciation."

Average costs tend to fall with increased output for a second reason. As output expands, a firm can use its labor in more specialized tasks. For example, at low levels of business, one lawyer may handle both divorce and bankruptcy cases. As the law firm expands, one lawyer may specialize in divorce, while another specializes in bankruptcy, and each one can develop expertise in one area. If a training cost is associated with developing expertise in each task, only a firm that requires frequent repetition of each task finds it worthwhile to train separate workers for each task (see Example 2.3).

If a firm manufactures several products in one plant, the length of the production run could increase as output expands. Consider a paper manufacturer that sells three

EXAMPLE 2.3 *Specialization of Labor*

Why doesn't everyone work individually and sell finished products to others as needed? One answer is that it can be more efficient to break down production processes into several small steps in which workers specialize. Two examples illustrate the advantages of breaking production into several tasks.

Writing at about the time of the American Revolution, Adam Smith (1937, 4–5) offered an example to show that the division of labor can have important advantages in the "very trifling manufacture" of pin-making:

> [A] workman not educated to this business . . . nor acquainted with the use of machinery employed in it . . . could scarce, perhaps, with his utmost industry, make one pin a day, and certainly could not make twenty. But in the way in which this business is now carried on, not only the whole work is a peculiar trade, but it is divided into a number of branches, of which the greater part are likewise peculiar trades. One man draws out the wire, another straightens it, a third cuts it, a fourth points it, a fifth grinds it to the top for receiving the head; to make the head requires two or three distinct operations; to put it on, is a peculiar business, to whiten the pins is another; it is even a trade by itself to put them into the paper; and the important business of making a pin is, in this manner, divided into about eighteen distinct operations, which, in some manufactories, are all performed by distinct hands, though in others the same man will sometimes perform two or three of them. I have seen a small manufactory of this kind where ten men only were employed, and where some of them consequently performed two or three distinct operations. . . . [T]hey could, when they exerted themselves, make among them about twelve pounds of pins in a day [or] upward of forty-eight thousand pins in a day.

Similarly, Henry Ford became the largest automobile manufacturer in the early 1900s, and probably the most profitable, by developing mass production. He adapted the conveyor belt and assembly line so that he could produce a standardized, inexpensive car in a series of tasks in which individual workers specialized. He achieved cost savings despite paying wages that were considerably above average.

grades of paper. To produce each grade requires a separate setup of the production line. If the firm is small and has only one production line, then two switchovers are needed to produce the three grades daily. But if the firm triples in size, it can have one production line for each grade and thus avoid switching costs.

Certain physical laws generate scale economies; the best known concerns the relationship between volume and surface area. Suppose a chemical firm plans to make a certain liquid in a spherical container. The volume of the sphere is $(4\pi r^3)/3$ where r is the sphere's radius. The cost of the sphere depends on how much steel it takes to make it. That cost is related, not to volume, but to the surface area of the sphere, which equals $4\pi r^2$. Doubling the radius raises volume (and output) by a factor of 8, but raises surface area by only a factor of 4.

Similarly, there is a natural economy of scale in the holding of inventories and replacement parts because of the law of large numbers. This statistical law holds that random events tend to cancel out if there are enough of them, so that a firm's inventory as a fraction of its sales shrinks as the firm grows.[21]

Total Costs Determine Scale Economies

Even if economies of scale characterize some functions of a firm, diseconomies of scale may characterize other functions. Whether the firm experiences economies of scale overall depends on the contribution of each function to overall cost. For example, just because an individual plant has economies of scale in production, one should not conclude that it is most efficient to have only one plant producing. Such a false conclusion ignores other types of costs, such as monitoring costs and transportation costs.

Suppose that a firm produces pasteurized milk and delivers it to grocery stores. The fewer the plants, the farther, on average, the milk has to be shipped, and the higher the transportation costs. Even if there are substantial economies of scale in production, it is not efficient to have one plant if transportation costs are very high. The relevant average cost curve is the sum of the cost of producing the milk and the cost of transporting it to customers.

Figure 2.6 shows the AC curve of production, AC_P. It slopes downward initially, indicating economies of scale in production. The average cost of transporting raw materials to the plant and transporting the milk to customers is AC_T. As more milk is produced in one location, it must be shipped farther, and so average transportation costs rise. The sum of these two curves is the overall average cost, AC, which is the relevant curve for determining the cost of operation. The output at the minimum of the AC curve would be smaller if the transportation costs increase so that AC_T becomes steeper. That means, all else equal, that the optimal size of the plant becomes smaller as transportation costs become more important. Many small-scale plants are common in industries characterized by high transportation costs.

The location of a plant is influenced by the relative costs of transporting raw materials to the plant compared to transporting the output from the plant to customers.

[21] See **www.aw-bc.com/carlton_perloff** "Scale and Inventories" for a detailed explanation.

FIGURE 2.6 Total Average Cost

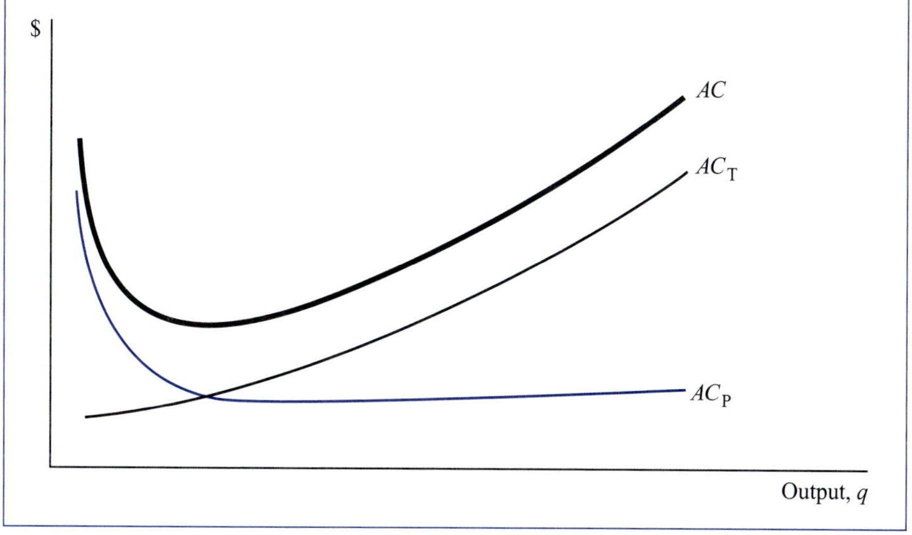

The higher the cost of transporting raw materials, the closer the plant will be to their source. For example, shipping bromine is expensive (and dangerous) compared to shipping bromide fluids (which are made from bromine). Therefore, bromide fluid plants tend to be located close to facilities that make bromine.

Conversely, if raw materials come from many different locations, or if they are readily available in many locations, the differences across locations in the transportation costs for obtaining raw materials may be insignificant, so the plant tends to locate close to its customers. For example, cement is costly to transport, and the main raw material, limestone, is widely available. Therefore, cement plants tend to locate close to their customers.

The decision of how many plants a firm should have depends on both the cost of transporting raw materials and finished products and the economies of scale in production.[22] The more important the economies of scale in production, the more likely that production is concentrated in only a few plants. The greater the transportation costs (and the greater the dispersion of customers), the more likely that production is decentralized in several plants.

A Measure of Scale Economies

Scale economies exist if average cost falls as output expands. As long as marginal cost is below average cost, economies of scale exist; if marginal cost exceeds average cost, there are diseconomies of scale. This relationship suggests that a natural measure of scale

[22]See Scherer et al. (1975) for an extended analysis.

economies is the ratio of average to marginal cost.[23] If $s = AC/MC$, then economies of scale exist if $s > 1$, constant returns to scale exist if $s = 1$, and diseconomies of scale exist if $s < 1$ (see Appendix 2A).[24]

Empirical Studies of Cost Curves

Economists often estimate firms' cost curves and economies of scale. Because economies of scale refer to cost savings that arise as output increases, it is important in any study of economies of scale to verify that output is the *only* variable accounting for cost differences among firms (or for the same firm over time). Large firms may differ from small firms in many ways; for example, they may produce more products or perform different functions, such as marketing.

Cost differences between firms are due to economies of scale only if the two firms studied produce the same products and perform the same functions. If one firm markets its product itself, whereas the other, smaller firm does not, an analysis that failed to account for this difference would find diseconomies of scale: Average costs would appear to rise as output expands, when in fact the opposite may be the case.

Some studies focus on whether economies of scale characterize certain specific functions, such as purchase of equipment and operating costs. Other studies ask the more general question of whether economies of scale characterize the entire operations of a firm or group of firms (see Example 2.4).

Economies of Scale in Total Manufacturing Costs

Some firms have U-shaped long-run average cost curves. At the lowest point of the curve, output q^*, the average cost curve is flat. Empirical studies of manufacturing firms often find that cost curves are L-shaped: As output rises, the average cost curve slopes down sharply, slopes down more slowly, and finally is flat. That is, for small output levels, there are large economies of scale, but for large outputs, those economies are exhausted and average costs are constant. On L-shaped cost curves, we can determine the lowest output level, q^*, such that the long-run average cost curve is essentially flat.

---

[23]This discussion of economies of scale is based on the cost function, which answers the question: What is the minimum cost of producing a given amount of output? A natural measure of scale economies is the ratio of average cost to marginal cost. Instead, one could base the definition of economies of scale on the production function, which answers the question: How much output is produced with given amounts of labor and raw materials? That is, economies of scale exist if an equal percentage increase in the use of all factors of production results in a proportionately greater expansion of output. So, for example, if a firm increases its use of its two inputs, labor and raw materials, by 10 percent, economies of scale exist if output rises by more than 10 percent. A natural measure of scale economies, therefore, is the percentage of output expansion generated by an increase of 1 percent in the use of all inputs. One can show that these two measures are equivalent in a competitive industry.

[24]If a firm makes zero profit, then s measures the ratio of costs to revenues.

EXAMPLE 2.4 *Indiana Libraries*

According to DeBoer (1992), Indiana libraries have U-shaped average cost curves when circulation is used as the measure of output. However, most libraries operate on the strictly declining portion of the *AC* curve. Average cost (including costs of labor, books, utilities, and equipment, but not capital costs such as rent and debt-service expenditures) is \$3.62 for a small library with a circulation of 2,000 per year, \$2.59 at a circulation of 10,000, and reaches its minimum of \$2.13 at a circulation of 350,000. As the circulation rises beyond 350,000 books, average cost rises slightly.

A government can use this information to determine how much more it costs to have several branch libraries rather than a single central library. For example, the average cost is 5.5 percent higher with four branch libraries with 50,000-book circulations rather than a central library with a 200,000-book circulation.

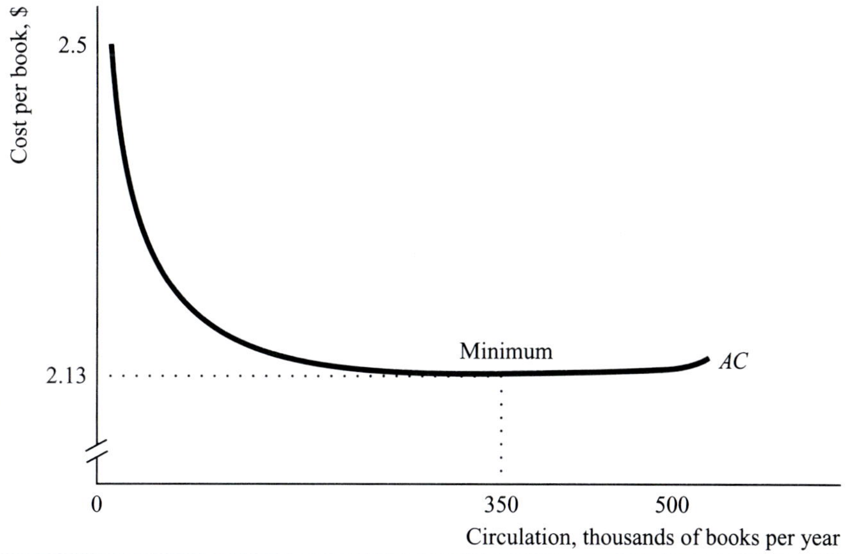

A plant's **minimum efficient scale** (*MES*) is the smallest output (q^*) it can produce such that its long-run average costs are minimized. The size of the *MES* plant, especially in relation to the overall market, is useful for judging how many firms could operate in a market.

A useful measure of the importance of scale economies is the measure of the cost disadvantage incurred by a plant that is smaller than the *MES*. If this disadvantage is small, then economies of scale are unimportant.

Table 2.3 lists some engineering estimates of *MES* for various industries in the United Kingdom together with the cost disadvantage that would be incurred if plants equal in size to 50 percent of the *MES* were built. Pratten (1971) found that in only about 25 percent of the cases examined was the cost disadvantage of producing in the

TABLE 2.3 **Estimates of Minimum Efficient Scale (MES)**

Product	*MES* (physical output per year)	*MES* as a Percent of U.K. Market	Percent Increase in Unit Cost Incurred by a Plant of 50% *MES*
Oil	10 million tons	10	5
Chemicals			
Ethylene	300,000 tons	9	25
Dye	large	100	22
Sulfuric acid	1 million tons	30	1
Beer (brewery)	at least 1 million barrels	3	9
Steel production	9 million tons	33	5–10

Source: Pratten (1971) as reported in Siberston (1972, 380).

suboptimal size plant more than 10 percent. Weiss (1976) used Pratten's results to show that, for most industries, the size of the *MES* plant is typically a small percentage of total U.S. output. This work implies that for most industries, plant economies of scale are not so significant as to preclude having many firms in an industry.

Survivorship Studies

Another approach to measuring economies of scale is due to Stigler (1968b), who made use of the following simple but powerful observation: If a particular plant size is efficient, eventually all plants in the industry should approach that size. Any plant or firm size that survives for a long time is efficient. Accordingly, Stigler classified the fraction of output from petroleum-refining plants of various sizes, as Table 2.4 shows. Stigler uses these data to conclude that the very smallest and the very largest plants are inefficient, because their share of industry output declined over time.

TABLE 2.4 **Distribution of Petroleum Refining**

Plant Size (percent of industry total)	Percent of Industry Capacity 1947	1950	1954
under .1	8.22	7.39	6.06
.1–.2	9.06	7.60	7.13
.2–.3	5.45	4.99	7.28
1.5–2.5	17.39	23.64	22.45
2.5–4.0	21.08	16.96	15.54

Source: Stigler (1968b, 69).

TABLE 2.5 **Number of Beer Plants**

Annual Capacity (thousands of barrels)	1959	1971	1979
0–25	11	2	2
26–100	57	19	8
101–250	51	19	6
251–2000	88	67	26
2001–3000	5	9	6
3001–4000	3	3	7
4001+	2	7	20

Source: Elzinga (1986, 215).

If all firms face similar cost conditions, a survivorship study reveals the efficient plant size as the industry replaces its obsolete plants. If firms face different costs or produce *different* products, their optimal scales will vary, and a survivorship study can only identify the *range* of efficient plant sizes. In other words, economies of scale measure how costs fall as output expands, *holding all else constant.* If other factors are not constant across plants, a survivorship study does not reveal the efficient plant size but merely describes the range of efficient plant sizes.

Since Stigler's initial study, there have been numerous applications of his survivorship method to other industries (see, for example, Rogers 1992). For example, there has been a dramatic decline in the number of beer plants since 1947. The number of plants fell from 465 in 1947, to 253 in 1958, 108 in 1974, 96 in 1978, and 80 in 1983. Table 2.5 illustrates the composition of beer plants by size (annual capacity). It shows that, from 1959 to 1979, the share of the smallest plants diminished and the share of the largest plants grew. The data suggest that, in the beer industry, economies of scale at the plant level have become increasingly important. In the 1980s and 1990s, however, many microbreweries opened, suggesting the development of a new technology.

Cost Concepts for Multiproduct Firms

Most firms do not produce a single product; it is typical for a firm to make several different, perhaps related, products. For example, a doughnut shop produces filled doughnuts and plain doughnuts, a doctor treats sore throats and skin rashes, and a plumber fixes sinks and bathtubs. A firm that produces many different products is called a *multiproduct firm.*[25] The multiproduct nature of firms does not materially affect the analyses in most of this text. However, it is important to remember that treating

[25] See Baumol, Panzar, and Willig (1982) and Panzar (1989) for detailed studies of multiproduct firms.

firms as multiproduct is more realistic than not and that, in some cases, ignoring the multiproduct characteristics of firms can lead to improper conclusions or regulations (see Chapter 20).

Adaptation of Traditional Cost Concepts for a Multiproduct Firm

If a firm produces two or more products, one cannot measure *the* average cost or *the* marginal cost because there is no one measure of output. One can, however, define cost concepts that are analogous to those in a single-product environment. For example, if q_1 units of Product 1 and q_2 units of Product 2 are produced, the marginal cost of producing Product 1 is the additional cost incurred by increasing q_1 to $q_1 + 1$, holding the output of Product 2 constant at q_2. In this definition, the marginal cost of Product 1 depends not only on the level of output for Product 1 but also on q_2. Marginal cost for Product 2 is defined analogously.

Unlike marginal cost, average costs are not as easy to define in a multiproduct context. The problem arises in trying to decide whether to divide total cost by the output of Product 1, q_1, or Product 2, q_2. Perhaps total cost should be divided by the sum, $q_1 + q_2$. There is no single right answer, but several relevant average cost concepts have been suggested (see Appendix 2A).

Aside from the extrapolation of the concepts of marginal and average cost to a multiproduct environment, there are some cost concepts that arise only in a multiproduct setting. The most important such cost concept is economies of scope (see Appendix 2A for some others).

Economies of Scope

When it is cheaper to produce two products together (joint production) rather than separately, there is an economy of scope (Baumol, Panzar, and Willig 1982; Panzar and Willig 1977a). For example, a steer produces beef and hide. Although it is possible to use some steers just for hide and others just for beef, it would be inefficient with current technology.

Economies of scope imply that it is efficient to produce two or more products together; they do not necessarily imply that these products should be produced by a single firm. For example, consider how steel is made. First, iron ore is melted down into pig iron in a blast furnace; the molten pig iron is then run into a steel-making furnace.

It is possible to conceive of two separate firms, side by side, one of which makes pig iron and the other steel, with a pipe carrying the molten pig iron between the two firms.[26] As we discuss in Chapter 12, when firms must rely heavily on each other, transaction costs are high and each firm is liable to be exploited. High transaction costs

[26]Pipes are used to connect two separate firms in some industries. For example, a lead additive used to be added to gasoline to prevent engine knock. In the early 1980s, an Exxon gasoline refinery in Louisiana was located beside a plant owned by the Ethyl Corporation that made the lead additive and delivered it by pipe to Exxon.

explain why only a single firm typically produces all the products for which economies of scope exist.

Many possible factors contribute to economies of scope, and one of the most important is the use of common inputs. In the example of producing beef and hide, it is easy to see why it might be best to produce both simultaneously rather than using one steer for beef and another for hide.

Knowledge is one of the most important common inputs for producing and selling related products. Information about one product is likely to be relevant for another closely related product. For example, knowing how to market steel bars efficiently (knowing among other things where customers are located) might help in marketing steel sheets. Or knowing how to manufacture steel bars efficiently (knowing where to obtain low-price iron ore) might contribute to the efficient manufacture of steel sheets. In such situations, it is efficient to produce and sell these products together. Otherwise, resources like information would have to be duplicated wastefully. Moreover, because it is difficult to buy and sell information, a single firm often produces related products.

A final example of using common input arises when a person's physical presence is required for certain services. Consider a plumber who handles a wide variety of plumbing problems and can fix sinks as well as bathtubs. It might be that a plumber who repairs only sinks could service them better than a more versatile plumber. For that matter, there might be gains from specializing further and having one plumber repair sink washers and another repair sink stoppers. But a homeowner would have to call several plumbers to diagnose the problem before finding the right specialist. In other words, because of the *indivisibility* involved in diagnosing a problem (you need one person physically present to do it), it would be inefficient if that person were unable to fix a wide range of plumbing problems. If the gains from specialization in plumbing were great, it might be worth having specialists—perhaps even a specialist at diagnosing problems. But as long as the gains are small, such specialization is unlikely.

Economies of Scale and Economies of Scope

Firms often produce many products to gain economies of scope in marketing and distribution. A salesperson who sells white bread to a store can also sell rolls. A store may prefer to deal with one person who can satisfy all its needs rather than with several different salespeople. A firm that produces and sells many products can specialize production by plant, thereby obtaining economies of scale in production while maintaining a full product line. The disadvantage of such specialization is that transportation costs may rise as individual products must be shipped farther. See Examples 2.5 and 2.6.

Specialization in Manufacturing

Firms often produce different products in the same plant. The U.S. Bureau of the Census publishes a measure of how specialized each plant's output is for each industry. The specialization ratio for an industry equals shipments of products in the particular industry divided by total shipments of all products for all plants listed as being in the industry. For example, suppose there is only one plant that makes steel bars and the

EXAMPLE 2.5

The Baking Industry

The baking industry provides an excellent example of multiplant specialization. Until recently, bakeries typically produced a wide range of products (breads, rolls, cakes) and served relatively small geographic areas. Because bakery products are perishable, shipping distances were limited in earlier times. The development of improved preservatives extended the shelf life of baked goods with the result that shipping distances could be increased. Bakeries began to acquire nearby bakeries and use *reciprocal baking* to produce their products. Reciprocal baking means that plants become specialized in particular products and then ship their products to each other, so that each geographic area is served by a full line. Reciprocal baking allows bakery firms to take advantage of scale economies and still preserve the economies of scope in marketing that come from having a full product line.

plant also makes steel wire. If the plant sells \$100 worth of steel bars and \$50 worth of steel wire, it is classified as producing in the steel bar industry. The specialization ratio for this industry is 2/3, or 66.7 percent. The specialization ratio for an industry is typically in excess of 80 percent. This high share indicates that individual manufacturing plants (not necessarily firms) are relatively specialized.

A tabulation of the number of different industries in which one firm operates indicates that 146 of the top 200 manufacturing firms (in terms of shipments) operated in 11 or more different industries in 1968 (Scherer 1980, 76). Dunne, Roberts, and Samuelson (1988) study all manufacturing firms (which numerically are dominated by very small firms) and find that in 1982, firms on average produced between one and two separate products. Multiplant firms on average produced between two and three separate products.

An Example of an Industry with Economies of Scope

Friedlaender, Winston, and Wang (1983) estimate a multiproduct cost function for each of the four U.S. auto makers. They postulate that costs depend on prices of various inputs (for example, wages, raw materials) and various outputs (for example, small cars, large cars, and trucks). Their statistical procedure also adjusts for the differing physical specifications of small and large cars and trucks.

They use a generalization of the scale economy measure s for a multiproduct firm (Equation 2A.1 in Appendix 2A). They find that $s = 1.23$ for General Motors at a typical point, suggesting that GM has economies of scale. That is, if GM expanded output of small cars, large cars, and trucks by 10 percent, costs would rise by about 8 percent (10/1.23).

They are also able to measure the degree of economies of scope (see Equation 2A.2 in Appendix 2A), which depends on the group of outputs being considered. For example, the economy of scope, SC, of producing large cars together with small cars and trucks is defined as

EXAMPLE 2.6 *Electricity Minimum Efficient Scale and Scope*

There are both scale and scope economies in electricity distribution. Yatchew (2000) estimates that the minimum efficient scale is achieved by utilities with about 20,000 customers in Ontario (and about 30,000 customers in New Zealand). He observed Canadian utilities with between 600 and 220,000 customers. Consequently, he concludes that the merger of utilities that increases their size is unlikely (in most cases) to produce savings in distributing electricity due to scale economies. He also finds that those Canadian utilities that deliver electricity and other municipal services (46 percent of utilities deliver other services such as water and sewage) had costs that were 7 to 10 percent lower than those that delivered only electricity, indicating economies of scope.

$$SC = \frac{C(\text{large cars alone}) + C(\text{small cars} + \text{trucks}) - C(\text{large cars} + \text{small cars} + \text{trucks})}{C(\text{small cars} + \text{trucks})},$$

where C stands for the total cost of producing the indicated outputs. SC indicates the percentage increase in costs that would occur if large cars were produced separately from small cars plus trucks. For GM, this number equals 25 percent, which indicates that there are substantial benefits from combining the production of large cars with small cars plus trucks. Surprisingly, no economies of scope arise from producing trucks together with small and large cars; it appears that truck production could occur in a separate firm with no loss of efficiency.

SUMMARY

In Western countries, most output is produced by firms and most of these firms are profit maximizers. Large firms in the United States and elsewhere are organized as corporations with limited liability. Corporations typically raise money by issuing debt and equity (stock). The corporation must make sure that its managers operate to maximize profits and do not pursue different goals that would adversely affect other concerned parties, such as debt holders and shareholders.

Large corporations are run by managers and not by the owners. If managers do not run firms efficiently or maximize profits, the firm may be driven out of business or taken over by others. Not all acquisitions and mergers of firms necessarily lead to greater efficiency and profitability, though. Since the 1980s, merger activity has reached a relatively high level (though not as high as at the turn of the century). Much, but not all, empirical analysis indicates that takeovers create economic value and that shareholders of the acquired companies capture the lion's share of the gains.

To maximize profit, a firm must minimize the cost of producing a given level of output. An economist's definition of cost is based on the concept of an opportunity cost, which includes a normal profit. A cost function shows how much it costs the firm to produce various amounts of output, or, in the case of a multiproduct firm, various combinations of different outputs. A cost function depends not only on the output produced, but also on the price of the factors of production such as the wages of workers and the price of raw materials.

There are many different types of costs: sunk costs, fixed costs, variable costs, avoidable costs, marginal costs, average variable costs, and average total cost. Some cost functions exhibit economies of scale, while others do not. A typical manufacturing process exhibits economies of scale at least initially. But the other functions of the typical firm, such as administration, monitoring, marketing, and delivery, may entail costs that exhaust all scale economies and lead to an optimal firm size.

When a firm produces several different products, an analysis of costs requires the development of cost concepts analogous to those used with a single-product firm, and the development of new cost concepts such as economies of scope. Cost concepts for a multiproduct firm explicitly recognize that the cost of producing one product depends on the amount of other products that are produced.

PROBLEMS

1. Are large firms more likely to have monitoring problems? If so, why do large firms exist?
2. Firms can raise money by issuing debt: pieces of paper that are IOUs. Why didn't firms issue debt in the 1920s and remain as either single proprietorships or partnerships?
3. For each situation below, discuss how two separate firms could carry out the activities. Identify those areas in which transaction costs are highest and you would expect to see only one firm.
   a. Oil pipelines, once built, cannot be moved. A pipeline ends at an electric power facility, which buys oil.
   b. A golf course locates beside a hotel.
   c. A postcard manufacturer wants a readily available supply of custom-made paper.
   d. A candy manufacturer needs to purchase sugar daily.
4. *(Difficult)* The managers of Firm A recommend that Firm A purchase Firm B because the purchase will diversify the business of Firm A. Diversification of risks is a desirable strategy for individual shareholders, but if shareholders can diversify their risks by holding stock in Firm B, is there any reason for Firm A to purchase Firm B? Suppose labor turnover is costly; could that provide an efficiency saving to support the proposed purchase? (*Hint:* If output is less variable, labor employment can be steadier.)
5. In the very short run, practically all costs are fixed. Does that mean that marginal cost is zero?
6. If there are economies of scope and if the price for each product equals marginal cost, is it possible for a firm to cover all its costs? If the firm's average cost of production declines the more it produces, can a price equal to marginal cost ever cover all its costs?
7. Suppose the cost of producing q_1 cars and q_2 trucks is $10{,}000 + 70q_1 + 80q_2$. Calculate the marginal cost of producing cars and the measure of scope economies when $q_1 = 100$ and $q_2 = 200$.
8. Why can the measure of economies of scope not exceed one as long as marginal costs are always positive?
9. Suppose there are a wide range of plant sizes in an industry. What do you conclude about the shape of the average cost curve if the plants are in the same area? Assume plants in the same area face similar costs. How does your answer change if the plants are located in different countries?

Answers to the odd-numbered problems are given at the back of the book.

SUGGESTED READINGS

Coase (1937) first asked why firms exist and gave a clear answer. Williamson (1975, 1985), Alchian and Demsetz (1972), and Klein, Crawford, and Alchian (1978) expand on this topic. See the interesting exchange between Coase and Klein and others in the April 2000 issue of the *Journal of Law and Economics*. Most of the discussions in these books and articles are relatively nontechnical. Calvo and Wellisz (1979) and Holmstrom (1979) explain the role of supervision and observability more formally. The articles in Auerbach (1988a) and Kaplan (2002) present the major theories and empirical evidence on mergers and acquisitions.

APPENDIX 2A

Cost Concepts for a Multiproduct Firm

When moving from a single-product to a multiproduct environment, one must adapt some of the definitions of cost and develop some new concepts to characterize cost.[1]

Total Costs

Suppose that $C(q_1, q_2)$ represents the cost of a firm that produces q_1 units of Product 1 and q_2 units of Product 2. The marginal cost of producing Product 1 at any given output level is defined, as in the single-product case, as the incremental cost of producing one more unit of Product 1—except now it is necessary to specify not only how much of Product 1 is being produced but also how much of Product 2. In mathematical terms, the marginal cost of Product 1 is just the (partial) derivative of $C(q_1, q_2)$ with respect to q_1.

Average Costs

What meaning can be given to the concept of average cost? The answer is that there is no unambiguous measure of average cost. Although total cost is well defined, there is no one unique output level to choose when two products are produced. One could define total output as $q_1 + q_2$, but that literally would be akin to adding apples and oranges. In fact, there is no reason why any linear combination of output, $a_1q_1 + a_2q_2$, is better than any other, where a_1 and a_2 are any two numbers.

If one specifies the proportions in which Products 1 and 2 are produced, it is possible to define an average cost concept, called *ray average cost* (*RAC*). Let λ_1 and λ_2 be the proportions in which Products 1 and 2 are produced, so $q_i = \lambda_i q$ implicitly defines q, a scale of output measure. Then, *RAC* is defined as total costs divided by q. That is,

$$RAC(q) = \frac{C(\lambda_1 q, \lambda_2 q)}{q}.$$

Using $RAC(q)$, one can define increasing ray average costs, constant ray average costs, and decreasing ray average costs. $RAC(q)$, of course, depends on the values of λ_1 and λ_2. If λ_1 and λ_2 are arbitrarily given, the multiproduct case reduces to the single-product case. For any given value of λ_1 and λ_2, we can calculate *RAC* and then find the scale, q, that minimizes *RAC*—just as in the single-product case. However, the scale at which *RAC* is minimized along different rays (different combinations of λ_1 and λ_2) generally differs.

[1]See Baumol, Panzar, and Willig (1982, Ch. 3, 4) and Panzar (1989) for a detailed treatment of these topics.

For example, consider an automobile company that makes small and large cars. If it is required to have a 50 percent mix, its average production cost may be minimized at 1 million units of each type of car. However, if the mix is 25:75 percent, its average production costs may be minimized at 1 million small cars and 3 million large cars.

It is possible to show that $RAC(q)$ falls, rises, or is constant as q increases, depending on whether s (a measure of scale economy) is above, below, or equal to 1, where[2]

$$s = \frac{C(q)}{q_1\frac{\partial C}{\partial q_1} + q_2\frac{\partial C}{\partial q_2}}. \tag{2A.1}$$

That is, s is the multiproduct analogue of the ratio of average to marginal cost. As in the single-product case, if firms are pricing at marginal cost, then s is the ratio of costs to revenues. In the single-product case, if s exceeds 1 so that AC exceeds MC, AC decreases with q, whereas if s is below 1 so that AC is less than MC, AC rises with q. Similarly, in the multiproduct case, if s exceeds 1, RAC falls with q, whereas if s is below 1, RAC rises with q. Thus, s can be viewed as measuring the proportionate increase in total costs from a percentage increase in the amount of *all* outputs. If s exceeds 1, costs increase by less than the percentage increase in output.

In addition to RAC, there are several cost concepts that do not have a clear analogy to the single-product case. Consider the cost of producing q_2 units of Product 2:

- The *incremental costs* of increasing Product 2 from 0 to q_2 holding Product 1 constant is $IC_2 = C(q_1, q_2) - C(q_1, 0)$.
- The *average incremental costs* of increasing Product 2 from 0 to q_2 holding Product 1 constant is $AIC_2 = [C(q_1, q_2) - C(q_1, 0)]/q_2$.

The incremental cost of producing q_2 units of Product 2 includes any fixed cost associated with the production of q_2 and depends on the assumed production of q_1.

Economies of Scale

The *product-specific economies of scale* (PS_i) of q_i, holding the other output, q_j, constant is defined using the AIC:

$$PS_i \equiv \frac{AIC_i}{MC_i}.$$

[2] *Proof:*

$$\frac{dRAC(q)}{dq} = \frac{1}{q}\left[\lambda_1\frac{\partial C}{\partial q_1} + \lambda_2\frac{\partial C}{\partial q_2}\right] - \frac{1}{q^2}C(q) = \frac{1}{q^2}\left[\lambda_1 q\frac{\partial C}{\partial q_1} + \lambda_2 q\frac{\partial C}{\partial q_2} - C(q)\right]$$
$$= \frac{1}{q^2}\left[q_1\frac{\partial C}{\partial q_1} + q_2\frac{\partial C}{\partial q_2} - C(q)\right].$$

Hence, $dRAC(q)/dq > 0$ if and only if $\Sigma q_i\, \partial C/\partial q_i > C(q)$, or $1 > C(q)/(\Sigma\, q_i\, \partial C/\partial q_i)$, or $1 > s$.

PS_i is the same as the scale measure *s* defined earlier for the particular case where all outputs except q_i are held fixed. The *AIC* cost function is like a typical single-product average cost function. The multiproduct cost function is converted into a single-product function by fixing the level of all outputs except one.

Economies of Scope

Most firms produce more than one product because it is cheaper to produce them together rather than separately. The term *economy of scope* refers to the savings that result from doing so. Consider the production of q_1 units of Product 1 and q_2 units of Product 2. The cost of producing each separately is $C(q_1, 0) + C(0, q_2)$; the cost of producing them together is $C(q_1, q_2)$. Economies of scope, *SC*, are measured as

$$SC = \frac{[C(q_1, 0) + C(0, q_2) - C(q_1, q_2)]}{C(q_1, q_2)}. \tag{2A.2}$$

SC measures the relative increase in cost that would result if the products were produced separately.[3] If *SC* is everywhere positive, it is cheaper to produce the products together. If marginal costs are positive, *SC* cannot exceed 1.[4]

When a firm increases its output of several products, it takes advantage of both economies of scope and economies of scale if they exist. It is possible for these two types of economies to have offsetting effects. A cost function is *trans-ray convex* at a given point if the cost of producing a linear combination of any two appropriately chosen output vectors is less than the weighted cost of producing the outputs separately.[5]

An Example

Suppose that it costs \$100 to rent a machine that can produce either red balloons or blue balloons. Let q_1 be the number of red balloons and q_2 the number of blue balloons. Suppose the cost function is $C(q_1, q_2) = 100 + q_1 + 2q_2$.

---

[3]If $\partial^2 C/\partial q_1 \partial q_2 < 0$, then Products 1 and 2 have *weak cost complementarity*. Increased production of one product lowers the marginal cost of the other. Here, economies of scope must necessarily exist (Panzar 1989).

[4]*Proof:* If $SC > 1$, $C(q_1, 0) + C(0, q_2) - C(q_1, q_2) > C(q_1, q_2)$ or $[C(q_1, 0) - C(q_1, q_2)] + [C(0, q_2) - C(q_1, q_2)] > 0$. But each term in the parentheses must be negative if the marginal cost is positive. Therefore, the inequality cannot hold, and *SC* cannot exceed 1.

[5]The formal definition of trans-ray convexity (Baumol, Panzar, and Willig 1982, Ch. 4, Def. 4D1) is: "A cost function $C(q)$ is trans-ray convex through some point $q^* = (q_1^*, \ldots, q_n^*)$ if there exists any vector of positive constants $w_1, \ldots, w_n$ such that for every two output vectors $q^a = (q_1^a, \ldots, q_n^a)$ and $q^b = (q_1^b, \ldots, q_n^b)$ that lie on the hyperplane $\Sigma\, w_1 q_i = w_0$ through point q^* (so that they satisfy $\Sigma\, w_i q_i^a = \Sigma\, w_i q_i^b = \Sigma\, w_1 q_1^*$), for any *k* such that $0 < k < 1$ we have

$$C(kq^a + [1 - k]q^b) \leq kC(q^a) + [1 - k]C(q^b)."$$

Trans-ray convexity can be related to conditions associated with natural monopoly (Panzar 1989).

The cost function shows that it costs \$1 to produce an additional red balloon but \$2 to produce an additional blue balloon, after the machine is purchased. Now several of the cost concepts that have been discussed can be illustrated.

The marginal cost of Product 1 is the derivative of $C(q_1, q_2)$ with respect to q_1. In this case, the marginal cost of Product 1 is constant and equals 1. The marginal cost of Product 2 is also constant and equals 2.

Next, we turn to the ray average cost. Suppose $\lambda_1 = .5$ and $\lambda_2 = .5$. Then

$$C(.5q, .5q) = 100 + .5q + 2 \times .5q = 100 + 1.5q.$$

Hence

$$RAC(q) = \frac{(100 + 1.5q)}{q} = \frac{100}{q} + 1.5.$$

In this example, *RAC* falls as q increases.

The measure of scale economies, s, is

$$s = \frac{C(q_1, q_2)}{\left(q_1\dfrac{\partial C}{\partial q_1} + q_2\dfrac{\partial C}{\partial q_2}\right)} = \frac{100 + q_1 + 2q_2}{q_1 + 2q_2} = \frac{100}{q_1 + 2q_2} + 1.$$

Thus, in this example, the measure of scale economies must exceed 1, so scale economies are always present.

If q_1 were produced separately, the cost would be $C(q_1, 0) = 100 + q_1$. Similarly, if q_2 were produced separately, the cost would be $C(0, q_2) = 100 + 2q_2$. The cost of producing q_1 and q_2 separately is

$$C(q_1, 0) + C(0, q_2) = 200 + q_1 + 2q_2.$$

This latter cost is clearly greater than the cost of producing them together, $C(q_1, q_2)$. Using equation (2A.2), we can calculate economies of scope as

$$\begin{aligned} SC &= \frac{[C(q_1, 0) + C(0, q_2) - C(q_1, q_2)]}{C(q_1, q_2)} \\ &= \frac{[(100 + q_1) + (100 + 2q_2) - (100 + q_1 + 2q_2)]}{[100 + q_1 + 2q_2]} \\ &= \frac{100}{100 + q_1 + 2q_2}. \end{aligned}$$

Because *SC* exceeds zero everywhere, it is cheaper to produce the two goods together rather than separately.

By fixing the level of output of one of the products, say q_2, we can calculate $AIC(q_1)$ as $[C(q_1, q_2) - C(0, q_2)]/q_1$ or

$$AIC(q_1) = \frac{[(100 + q_1 + 2q_2) - (100 + 2q_2)]}{q_1} = \frac{q_1}{q_1} = 1.$$

Thus, AIC is constant and equals 1. (Notice that the marginal cost of Product 1 is also constant and equals 1.) Because AIC is constant, there are no product-specific economies for q_1 (or for q_2), yet there are overall scale economies.

PART TWO

Market Structures

CHAPTER 3

Competition

Thou shalt not covet; but tradition approves all forms of competition.
—Arthur Hugh Clough

Perfect competition provides a benchmark against which the behavior of other markets is judged. The chapter starts by examining perfect competition, even though its strong assumptions apply to only a few markets. Next, two useful tools of analysis, elasticities and residual demand curves, are discussed. Then the chapter shows that competition has desirable efficiency and welfare properties. These properties, however, depend crucially on the assumptions of free entry and exit and on no externalities (firms bear the full costs of their actions). The chapter discusses the adverse effects if these conditions do not hold. The chapter concludes with examples of industries that most economists would characterize as reasonably competitive.

In this chapter, we stress five key points:

1. Perfect competition has many desirable properties.
2. Free entry and exit is a crucial factor in determining whether a market is perfectly competitive and efficient.
3. One important measure of welfare is maximized under perfect competition.
4. The desirability of perfect competition is reduced in the presence of externalities such as pollution.
5. Even if some of the necessary conditions for perfect competition do not hold, markets can come close to achieving the desirable properties of perfect competition.

Perfect Competition

Even though perfect competition is rarely, if ever, encountered in the real world, we study the perfect competition model because it provides an ideal against which to compare other models and markets. In later chapters, we examine how actual markets deviate from perfectly competitive ones, and determine which markets are likely to have the greatest deviations. The desirable properties of a perfectly competitive economy explain why economists generally favor competition. That a market deviates from the perfectly competitive model does not necessarily mean that the performance of a market can be improved, however, as is discussed at length throughout the book.

Assumptions

We define **perfect competition** as a market outcome in which all firms produce a homogeneous, perfectly divisible output; producers and consumers have full information, incur no transaction costs, and are price takers; and there are no externalities. That is, the main assumptions of perfect competition are:

- *Homogeneous Perfectly Divisible Output.* All firms sell an identical product. Consumers view the products of various firms as the same and hence are indifferent between them.
- *Perfect Information.* Buyers and sellers have all relevant information about the market, including the price and quality of the product. Firms can produce and consumers can buy a small fraction of a unit of output. As a result, the amount of output demanded or supplied varies continuously with price. This technical assumption avoids problems caused by large discrete changes in either supply or demand in response to small price changes.
- *No Transaction Costs.* Neither buyers nor sellers incur costs or fees to participate in the market.
- *Price Taking.* Buyers and sellers cannot individually influence the price at which the product can be purchased or sold. Price is determined by the market, so each buyer and seller takes the price as given.
- *No Externalities.* Each firm bears the full costs of its production process. That is, the firm does not impose externalities—uncompensated costs—on others. For example, pollution produced by a firm is an externality because the firm does not recompense the victims.

Some economists also assume that a perfectly competitive market has a large number of buyers and sellers. If there are many similar firms, no one firm can charge a price above the market price without losing all its customers, so the firm views the price at which it can sell as beyond its control. Similarly, consumers cannot find a firm willing to sell below the market price, so consumers must view the market price as beyond their control. Moreover, even if there are relatively few firms in a market, no firm can raise its price above the market price without losing all its customers if another firm can quickly enter the market and underprice it. Thus, because we assume firms and consumers are price takers, we do not also assume either that there are a large number of firms, or free entry and exit.[1] Competitive markets typically have a large number of firms and consumers, but industries can have all the properties of perfect competition even though there are few firms in those industries.

The Behavior of a Single Firm

Let us first examine the incentives of a typical firm. Suppose a firm has the short-run cost curves in Figure 3.1 and faces a market price of p_0. How much should it produce? Indeed, should it produce anything at all?

Profit Maximization. The objective of any firm, including a competitive firm, is to maximize its profits (or, equivalently, minimize its losses). The competitive firm's profits, π, are

$$\pi = pq - C(q),$$

where p is price, q is output, and $C(q)$ is total cost. As a result of the price-taking assumption above, the firm can sell all it wants at price p. (For example, the firm is too small a part of the market to influence the market price). That is, the firm faces a horizontal demand curve at price p.

It is profitable for the firm to expand output as long as the extra revenue from selling an additional unit exceeds the extra cost of producing that unit. The extra revenue from selling an additional unit is *price,* and the extra cost is the *marginal cost* (MC). That is, the optimal (profit-maximizing) production rule for a competitive firm is to expand its output until its marginal cost, MC, equals price, p.

Figure 3.1 illustrates the profit-maximizing decisions of a competitive firm facing a market price p_0. If the firm were producing a quantity greater than q_0, then p_0 would be less than MC, and the firm could increase its profits by reducing its output. If the firm were producing less than q_0, then p_0 would be greater than MC, and the firm could increase its profits by expanding its output. At output q_0, p equals MC, and profits are maximized.[2] In Figure 3.1, the shaded box represents profits.[3]

---

[1]We could derive the result that firms are price takers from these other assumptions. We make price taking an assumption for simplicity of presentation.

[2]The firm's objective is to

$$\max_q \pi = pq - C(q).$$

Its first-order condition is found by differentiating π with respect to q and setting that equal to zero: $p - C'(q) = 0$, where $C'(q) = dC(q)/dq$ is MC. This first-order condition—price equals marginal cost—is a necessary condition for profit maximization. The second-order condition is $C''(q) < 0$. That is, the second-order condition, which is a sufficient condition for profit maximization, is that the MC be upward sloping at the equilibrium.

[3]A firm's profits are total revenue minus total cost: $\pi = pq - C$, where pq (price times quantity) is total revenue. We can rewrite profits as average profits per unit (average revenue, p, minus average cost, $AC = C/q$) times the number of units sold (q), or $\pi = (p - AC)q$. Thus, profits can be shown graphically as a box with a height equal to average profits per unit, $p - AC$, and a length equal to the number of units, q, the firm sells.

FIGURE 3.1 Cost Curves and Profit Maximization

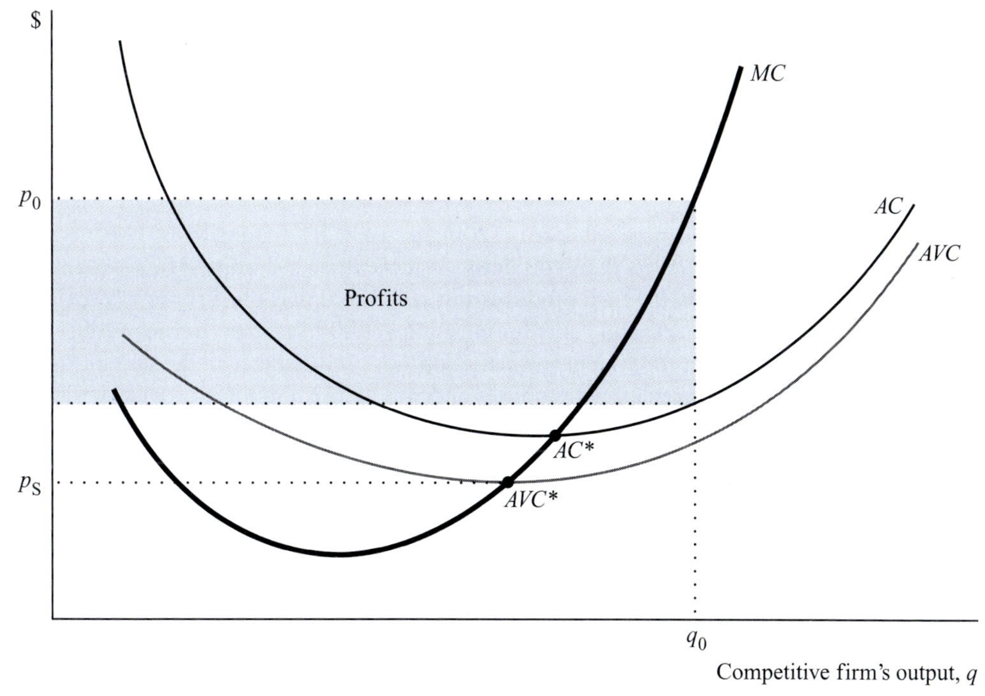

If the price, p, rises above p_0, the firm earns higher profits at its current output, but it earns even higher profits if it expands output until $p = MC$. If price falls below p_0, the firm earns lower profits at q_0, but it suffers less of a reduction if it reduces its output until $p = MC$. Thus, as the price rises, the firm moves up its marginal cost curve, and its profits rise; as the price falls, the firm moves down its marginal cost curve to minimize the reduction in its profits. Increases and decreases in profits signal a firm either to expand or contract output respectively.

Shutdown Decision. A firm produces only if doing so is more profitable than not producing. It produces only if the revenues from producing exceed **avoidable costs**: the costs that are not incurred if a firm ceases production. The revenues earned in excess of avoidable cost are called **quasi-rents**, which are the payments above the minimum amount necessary to keep a firm operating in the short run.

For simplicity, assume that all fixed costs are sunk. An example of a sunk cost given in Chapter 2 is that a firm is not refunded its incorporation fee if it ceases operating. In this case, avoidable costs are the same as variable costs. Thus, the rule for deciding whether to remain in business is: Produce and sell only if revenues are at least as great as total variable cost. Equivalently, the firm should produce and sell at price p only if p equals or exceeds average variable cost (AVC).

Minimum average cost (the lowest point on the *AC* curve), AC^*, is greater than minimum *AVC*, AVC^*, in the short run, because average costs are average variable costs plus average fixed costs. Thus, a firm finds it more profitable to produce than to shut down if price is below minimum average cost, $p < AC^*$, but above minimum average variable cost, $p > AVC^*$. It is more profitable to produce and earn some revenue in excess of variable cost than to shut down and earn no revenues (which can help offset the fixed costs). That is, the firm chooses to produce even though it is losing money when all costs are considered. Consider an example to clarify this apparent contradiction.

Suppose a firm's fixed cost is $200 and sunk. Its marginal cost (*MC*) is constant at $10 at quantities less than 100 units. At more than 100 units, *MC* is extremely high. If the price is $10, the firm produces and sells 100 units. The firm just covers its production cost and makes no contribution to the $200 fixed cost: It loses $200.

If the price is $9, the firm is better off not producing at all, because it loses an additional $1 for every unit it produces and would lose $300 if it produced 100 units. It is better to shut down and lose only $200 than to produce and suffer greater losses.

If the price is $11, by producing 100 units, the firm now more than covers variable cost: It earns $100 above variable cost. It still loses money overall ($-200 + 100 = -100$) because of the fixed cost of $200, but it is better to lose $100 than $200. The point of the example is that the decision to produce or not is *independent* of the fixed sunk cost. If fixed costs are sunk (incurred whether the firm produces or not), they should be ignored in deciding whether to produce.

If all fixed costs are sunk, a firm operates if p is greater than or equal to AVC^* but not if p is less than AVC^*. The price at which a firm ceases production is the **shutdown point**, which is p_s in Figure 3.1. That is, if price exceeds AVC^*, the firm operates along its *MC* curve. The firm's **supply curve** reflects the quantity that a firm is willing to supply at any given price. The competitive firm's supply curve, then, is the portion of the *MC* curve above AVC^*, the shutdown point.

If a firm suffers losses in the short run (the period in which costs are sunk), should it continue to operate and remain unprofitable in the future?[4] No. In the long run, a firm that is losing money will not reinvest—it will not continue to sink costs. Short-run losses are a signal that the firm should not invest further to replace plant and equipment. In the long run, a rational firm shuts down if it expects to have losses in each period forever. It prefers to cease production rather than invest in new facilities or maintenance and lose even more.

When a firm loses in the short run, its revenues are below the long-run opportunity cost of its resources. Because opportunity cost includes a normal profit, a firm that is making a loss may not literally be paying out more money than it receives; it is simply earning less than it could have earned had it invested its (already) sunk costs elsewhere.

[4]As described in Chapter 2, the short run and the long run are useful abstractions, but in reality adjustment costs determine how fast an industry can adjust to change. The time needed to adjust to any change depends on the current state of the industry and the size of the needed adjustment. See **www.aw-bc.com/carlton_perloff** "Adjustment Costs."

If fixed costs are not sunk, the shutdown decision depends on whether revenues exceed *avoidable* costs. An example (in Chapter 2) of an avoidable cost is the lawyer who can pay a penalty to break a lease. If some fixed costs are avoidable, a price equal to AVC^* is not high enough to prevent the firm from shutting down. Use the numbers from above and suppose that the fixed cost of $200 represents a yearly rental payment and that, for a $100 penalty fee, the landlord will release the lawyer from the obligation to pay $200. The firm compares losing $100 for sure (the penalty fee) with producing and earning revenues minus production costs minus the $200 rental payment. If price is $10, the firm earns $0 per sale and is stuck paying the $200 of fixed cost; therefore, it prefers to pay the $100 penalty and go out of business. Even if price were $10.50 so that the firm would make 50¢ on each of its 100 units sold, it would still be better to pay the $100 penalty and go out of business.

The price at which shutdown occurs is above average variable cost and closer to average cost the greater the proportion of fixed costs that are avoidable. In the extreme, when there are no sunk costs (all fixed costs are avoidable), the shutdown point coincides with the minimum point on the *AC* curve. Thus, if it has no sunk costs, a firm shuts down before it incurs economic losses.

The Competitive Market

Given the behavior of individual competitive firms, we can derive a market supply curve. The intersection of the market supply curve and the market demand curve determines the competitive equilibrium.

The Short-Run Equilibrium. We start by supposing that there are n identical firms and that all fixed costs are sunk in the short run. The short-run **market supply curve**, S in Figure 3.2b, is the horizontal sum of the supply curves of each firm, the *MC* curve above the minimum of the *AVC* curve in Figure 3.2a. The horizontal portion of the market supply curve reflects (1) that no output is forthcoming if price is below the shutdown point and (2) that at a price slightly above the shutdown point, all firms produce.

The intersection of the demand curve with the short-run market supply curve determines the *short-run equilibrium price,* p_0, and quantity, Q_0. The amount that firms want to supply at the equilibrium price exactly equals the amount that consumers demand at that price. There are no unsatisfied buyers and no unsatisfied sellers. All buyers pay and all sellers receive the same price.

In the short-run equilibrium in Figure 3.2, a typical firm may earn a profit, which provides an incentive for firms to enter the market. However, such entry cannot occur in the short run because firms cannot build new plants in the short run.

The Long-Run Equilibrium. In the long run, firms can adjust their levels of capital so that they can enter this market. Short-run profits or losses induce firms to enter or leave the market until price is driven to the minimum long-run average cost, AC^*, in the long run.

In Figure 3.2, firms are making a positive profit at the short-run equilibrium price p_0, which is determined by the intersection of the market demand curve and the original short-run market supply curve. In the long run, these profits induce new firms to

FIGURE 3.2 Short-Run Equilibrium

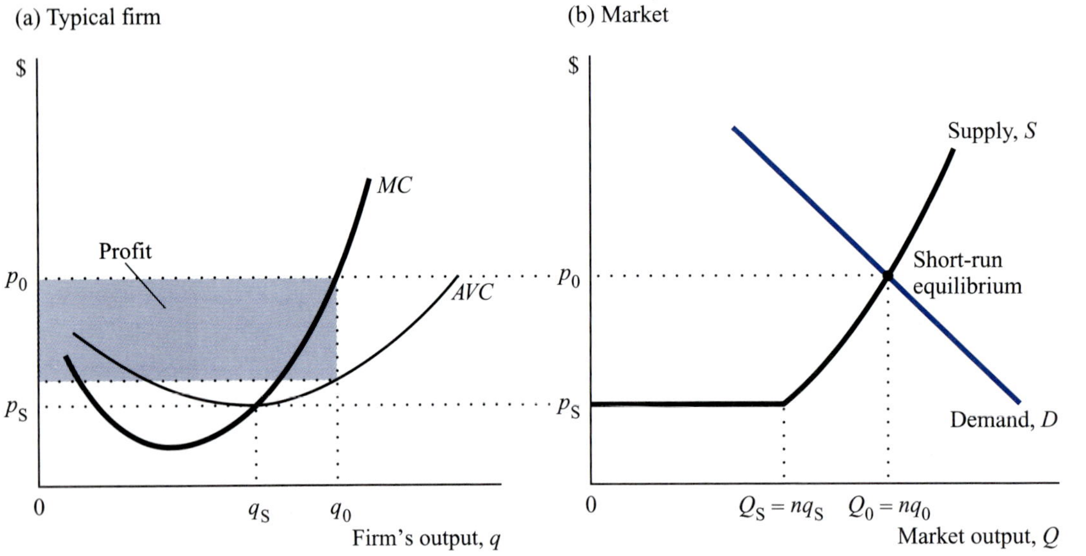

enter this market. If the number of firms that can potentially produce at the same cost is very large, the long-run supply curve is horizontal at the minimum of the average cost curve, AC^*, as Figure 3.3 shows. The long-run equilibrium is determined by the intersection of the demand curve and the long-run market supply curve. In Figure 3.3, the market is in a new short-run *and* long-run equilibrium because the demand curve, *D,* intersects both the long-run supply curve and the new short-run supply curve corresponding to the equilibrium number of firms, n^*. The equilibrium price is $p^* = AC^*$, and equilibrium output is $Q^* = n^*q^*$. In this long-run equilibrium, firms make zero profit.

Similarly, short-run losses induce firms to leave the market and reduce output until price rises again to yield normal (zero) profits. In long-run equilibrium, firms receive economic profits of zero, which is just enough to induce them to remain in the market.

The Slope of the Long-Run Supply Curve. In this last example, a very large number of firms could enter the market and produce at the same marginal and average costs as the existing firms. Consequently, the long-run perfectly competitive supply curve was perfectly flat at AC^*, which is the minimum average cost of production. However, the long-run supply curve need not be flat.

If an expansion of output causes the prices of some key inputs to rise, the long-run supply curve tends to be upward sloping. As the output of wheat produced increases, farmland becomes more valuable, and the land rents (or the opportunity cost of owning the land) increase. As rents increase, the average cost curve of each farmer rises so the minimum average cost, AC^*, increases. Thus, the long-run supply curve for the

FIGURE 3.3 Long-Run Equilibrium

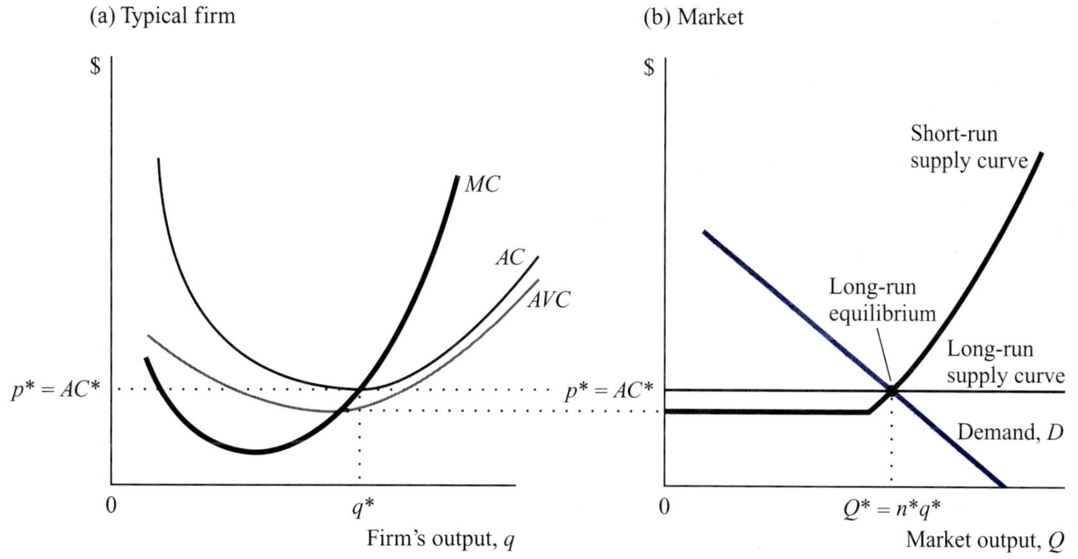

wheat market (whose height is traced out by the minimum average cost points) rises as output expands.

Whenever some factors of production (such as fertile land) are in fixed supply, their price gets bid up as market output expands. Prices of key inputs may fall as output expands if there are economies of scale. If input prices fall as output expands, the long-run market supply curve could slope down. The long-run supply curve of a market tends to be flat as long as the market accounts for only a small fraction of any one factor's total employment.

Another reason why the long-run supply curve may be upward sloping is that there are only a few firms that can produce at low costs. For market output to increase, less efficient firms have to enter the market. In Figure 3.4a, there are n_1 low-cost, efficient firms with marginal cost curve MC and average cost curve AC_1. The minimum point on AC_1 is AC^*_1, which is obtained if the firm produces q_1 units of output. For market output levels up to $Q_1 = n_1 q_1$, these low-cost firms can produce at the minimum average cost, AC^*_1, so the long-run supply curve is flat at AC^*_1 up to Q_1, as Figure 3.4b shows. If less than Q_1 is demanded, some of these n_1 firms exit the market.

If the market demand is slightly larger than Q_1, the average cost of production must rise. The market supply curve is the horizontal sum of the supply curves of the n_1 firms: Their marginal cost curves above AC^*_1. Thus, because there are no more low-cost firms, the market supply curve rises beyond Q_1.

Now suppose that there are n_2 other firms that can produce this product with the same marginal cost curve as the first n_1 firms but with an average cost curve, AC_2, with a higher minimum average cost, AC^*_2 ($> AC^*_1$). That is, these high-cost firms have larger fixed costs than do the low-cost firms.

FIGURE 3.4 Upward-Sloping Long-Run Supply Curve

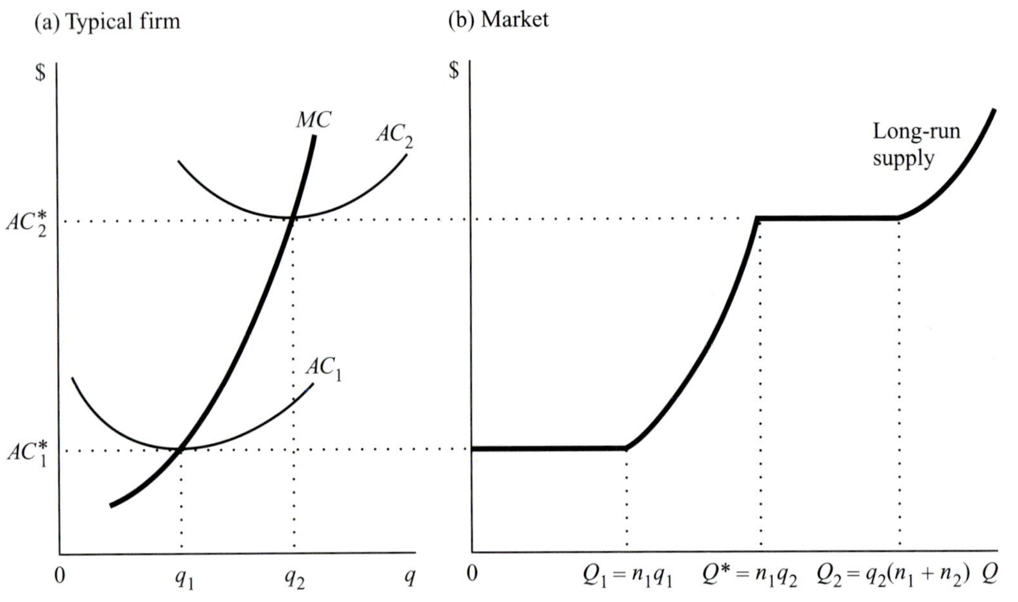

If the quantity demanded is slightly greater than $Q^* = n_1q_2$, the price is AC^*_2 and some high-cost firms enter the market. Increases in market demand beyond this point are met by additional high-cost firms entering the market and producing q_2 at an average cost of AC^*_2. When the quantity demanded can no longer be met by entry by additional high-cost firms, the long-run supply curve again rises, tracing out the sum of the marginal cost curves of all the firms in the market. That is, the long-run supply curve rises for output greater than $Q_2 = Q^* + n_2q_2 = q_2(n_1 + n_2)$.

If the quantity demanded exceeds n_1q_1 but is less than Q^* (that is, the second group of firms has not entered the market), the low-cost firms earn an unusual return (profit) to their scarce knowledge or other scarce resource that enables them to produce at relatively low costs. That is, they earn a **rent**: a payment to the owner of an input beyond the minimum necessary to cause it to be used. If the quantity demanded exceeds Q_2, both types of firms earn rents on their scarce know-how or other scarce input.[5]

[5]In some markets where firms must incur substantial sunk costs so that only a few firms can efficiently produce, a competitive equilibrium may be impossible. In such markets where no competitive equilibrium exists, the market exhibits instability, including price wars and bankruptcies. Here, firms may temporarily make above-normal profits; these profits attract other firms, the additional competition results in all the firms in the market making losses, some firms exit, the remaining firms make above-normal profits, and the process repeats. The study of when interactions between firms and consumers will lead to stability is called the theory of the core. See Clark (1923), Telser (1978), and **www.aw-bc.com/carlton_perloff** "Nonexistence of Competitive Equilibrium."

Elasticities and the Residual Demand Curve

Throughout the rest of this book, we make repeated use of two related concepts to analyze both competitive and noncompetitive industries: (1) the price elasticity of demand or supply, and (2) the demand curve facing a single firm, which is called the firm's *residual demand curve*. The price elasticity of supply or demand aids in understanding how a market responds to changes in either demand or supply. The residual demand facing a single firm allows an analyst to comprehend the behavior of a single firm. We now examine how the elasticity of the residual demand curve is related to the assumption that a competitive firm cannot affect price.

Elasticities of Demand and Supply

If either the demand or the supply curve shifts, the competitive equilibrium changes, and the shapes of the demand and supply curves influence how the new equilibrium compares to the old. For example, if the demand curve is perfectly flat, the competitive price remains unchanged, even if the supply curve shifts radically.

One concept used to characterize the shape of demand or supply curves is the price elasticity of demand or supply (often the word *price* is omitted). The **elasticity of demand** is the percentage change in quantity demanded in response to a given small percentage change in price.[6] Similarly, the **elasticity of supply** is the percentage change in quantity supplied in response to a given small percentage change in the price. The elasticity of demand is always a negative number, and the elasticity of supply is usually, but not always, positive.

If a 1 percent increase in price leads to a more than a 1 percent reduction in the quantity demanded (so that the total amount paid in the market falls), a demand curve is called **elastic**. That is, an elastic demand curve has an absolute value of the elasticity of demand greater than 1 (the absolute values of 1 and -1 are both 1). It is common to omit the phrase *the absolute value of* when discussing the price elasticity of demand. The statement, "The price elasticity of demand is 2," is interpreted to mean that the price elasticity is -2.

When the absolute value of the elasticity of demand is 1, the demand curve is said to have **unitary elasticity**. In that case, a 1 percent change in price causes a 1 percent change in the quantity demanded, and the total amount paid (total revenues) remains constant. If the absolute value of the elasticity of demand is less than 1, the demand curve is **inelastic**: A 1 percent increase in price causes less than a 1 percent decline in the quantity demanded, and the total amount paid rises.

[6]The price elasticity of demand at price p and quantity Q is the percentage change in quantity divided by the percentage change in price (if that change is small): $(\Delta Q/Q)/(\Delta p/p) = (p/Q)(\Delta Q/\Delta p)$. Because the elasticity is the ratio of two percentage terms, the elasticity is invariant to changes in scale of either price or quantity (it is a *pure* number—without scale itself). For example, if price is measured in cents rather than in dollars, the elasticity is unchanged even though the slope of the demand curve, $\Delta Q/\Delta p$, does change. The technical definition of the price elasticity is $(p/Q)(dQ/dp)$.

In general, the elasticities of demand and supply depend upon many economic factors, such as the level of output, the availability of substitute products, and the ease with which suppliers can alter production. For example, as more substitute products are available, consumers find it easier to substitute for a product if its price rises, which makes its demand curve more elastic. Similarly, the more flexible the production process of a firm, the more likely it is that the firm can greatly increase production in response to a price increase, which tends to increase the elasticity of supply.

The Residual Demand Curve of Price Takers

Competitive firms are often described as *price takers.* They believe that they cannot affect the market price and must accept, or take, it as given. There are three equivalent ways to describe a firm's inability to affect price, all of which are used in this chapter:

- A competitive firm is a price taker.
- The demand curve facing a competitive firm is horizontal at the market price.
- The elasticity of demand facing a competitive firm is infinite.

A firm is a price taker if it faces a horizontal demand curve, because a horizontal demand curve has an infinite price elasticity of demand. If a firm facing an infinite price elasticity raises its price even slightly, it loses all its sales. Equivalently, by lowering its quantity, the firm cannot cause the price to rise. In contrast, a firm facing a downward-sloping demand curve can raise its price by decreasing its output.

If the number of firms in a market is large, the demand curve facing any one firm is nearly horizontal (elasticity of demand is infinite) even though the demand curve facing the market is downward sloping with a low elasticity. Indeed, for most market demand curves, there do not have to be very many firms in a market for the elasticity of demand facing a particular firm to be large.

To show this result, it is necessary to determine the demand curve facing a particular firm: the **residual demand curve.** A firm sells to people whose demands are not met by the other firms in the market. For positive quantities of residual demand, the residual demand, $D_r(p)$, is the market demand, $D(p)$, minus the supply of other firms, $S_o(p)$:

$$D_r(p) = D(p) - S_o(p).$$

If $S_o(p)$ is greater than $D(p)$, $D_r(p)$ is zero.

Figure 3.5b shows the market demand curve and the supply curve of all the firms except one. Figure 3.5a shows the residual demand curve facing a particular firm, which is the horizontal difference between the quantity demanded by the market at a given price minus the supply of other firms at that price. For example, at a price of $5, market demand is 10,050 units and the supply of the other firms is 9,950 units in Figure 3.5b. Thus, market demand exceeds their supply by 100 units at $5, so the remaining firm faces a residual demand of 100 units at that price.

FIGURE 3.5 Derivation of Residual Demand Curve

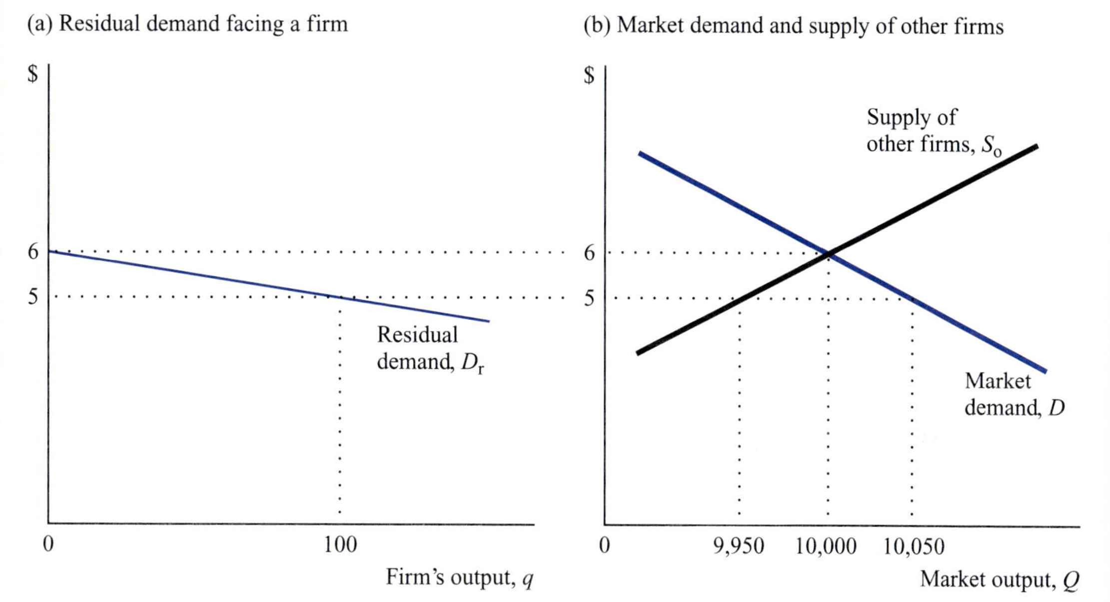

At \$6, the supply of other firms equals the market demand. The residual demand facing the firm in Figure 3.5a is zero. Were the price to rise even higher, other firms would be willing to supply even more than is demanded. Thus, at any price greater than or equal to \$6, the firm in panel a sells no units.

The residual demand curve facing the firm, Figure 3.5a, is much flatter than the market demand curve in Figure 3.5b. Similarly, the single firm's demand elasticity is much higher than the market elasticity. For example, the elasticity of demand for the individual firm is -11 at \$5.50, whereas the corresponding market elasticity of demand is approximately -0.027.[7] In other words, the firm's residual demand curve is over 400 times as elastic as the market demand curve at this price.

More generally, if there are n identical firms in the market, then the elasticity of demand facing Firm i is

$$\epsilon_i = \epsilon n - \eta_o(n - 1), \tag{3.1}$$

[7]For a linear demand curve, $Q = a - bp$, the elasticity of demand is the slope of the demand curve, $dQ/dp = -b$, times p/Q. Thus, the elasticity of demand of the residual demand curve is $-100(5.50/50) = -11$ and the elasticity of demand of the market demand curve is $-50(5.50/10{,}025) \approx -0.027$.

where ϵ is the market elasticity of demand (a negative number), η_o is the elasticity of supply of the other firms (a positive number), and $(n - 1)$ is the number of other firms.[8]

Thus, for a given market elasticity, as the number of firms in a market, n, increases, the elasticity facing a single Firm i, ϵ_i, grows large in absolute value (more negative). Similarly, the larger the elasticity of supply of the other firms, η_o, or the more other firms there are, the larger in absolute value (more negative) is the elasticity of demand facing Firm i.

Table 3.1 shows how the elasticity of demand facing a single firm varies with the number of firms and the market elasticities, given that the supply of other firms is completely inelastic ($\eta_o = 0$). For example, if the market elasticity is unitary ($\epsilon = -1$) and there are 50 firms, then $\epsilon_i = -50$. That is, if a firm were to increase its price by 1 percent, the quantity it sells would fall by about 50 percent. If the market demand elasticity is -0.5 and there are 1,000 firms, $\epsilon_i = -500$, so that if the firm were to raise its price by a tenth of a percent, the quantity it sells would fall by 50 percent. Thus, even if the supply of the other firms is completely inelastic, if there are a large number

TABLE 3.1 **Price Elasticity for a Single Firm**

	Market Elasticity		
Number of Firms n	Inelastic $\epsilon = -0.5$	Unitary $\epsilon = -1$	Elastic $\epsilon = -5$
10	−5	−10	−50
25	−12.5	−25	−125
50	−25	−50	−250
100	−50	−100	−500
500	−250	−500	−2,500
1,000	−500	−1,000	−5,000

Note: Because the supply of the other identical firms is assumed to be perfectly inelastic ($\eta_o = 0$), the elasticity of demand facing a particular firm is $\epsilon_i = n\epsilon$.

[8]The residual demand curve facing any one firm is $D_r(p) = D(p) - S_o(p)$. Differentiating $D_r(p)$ with respect to p, we obtain

$$\frac{dD_r}{dp} = \frac{dD}{dp} - \frac{dS_o}{dp}.$$

Let the quantity produced by one firm be $q = Q/n$ and the total quantity produced by all the other firms be $Q_o = (n - 1)q$. Multiplying both sides of the expression above by p/q and multiplying and dividing the first term on the right-hand side by Q/Q and the second term by Q_o/Q_o, this expression is

$$\frac{dD_r}{dp}\frac{p}{q} = \frac{dD}{dp}\frac{p}{Q}\frac{Q}{q} - \frac{dS_o}{dp}\frac{p}{Q_o}\frac{Q_o}{q},$$

where $q = D_r(p)$, $Q = D(p)$, and $Q_o = S_o(p)$. This expression is rewritten as $\epsilon_i = \epsilon n - \eta_o(n - 1)$ in Equation 3.1.

EXAMPLE 3.1 *Are Farmers Price Takers?*

In most U.S. agricultural markets there are a large number of farms, and no farm has as much as even 1 percent of total sales. As a result, the elasticity of demand facing each farm is extremely large. Farms are price takers.

We can roughly calculate the residual demand price elasticity facing an individual farm. For simplicity, we assume that other farms have an inelastic supply ($\eta_o = 0$), which may be a reasonable assumption in the short run. Less accurately, we assume that all farms are approximately the same size, so that each farm's share of the market is equal to 1 divided by the number of farms. The following table shows the approximate elasticity of demand facing each farm.

Crop	Estimated Market Demand Elasticity	Number of Farms	Each Farm's Residual Demand Elasticity
Fruits			
apples	−.20	28,160	−5,620
grapes	−1.03	19,961	−20,560
peaches	−.82	14,459	−11,856
Vegetables			
asparagus	−.65	2,672	−11,140
cucumbers	−.30	6,821	−2,046
dry onions	−.16	3,296	−527
sweet peppers	−.25	6,271	−1,568
tomatoes	−.38	14,366	−5,459

Sources: Number of Farms: U.S. Department of Commerce, Bureau of the Census, 1997 Census of Agriculture; Survey of Elasticities: You; Epperson, and Huang (1998).

Thus, each farm faces a gigantic price elasticity. For example, were a grape farm to increase its price by as little as 0.001 percent (one-thousandth of one percent), the quantity demanded from the farm would fall by 21 percent. Each farm is a price taker.

of firms in the market, the elasticity of demand facing a single firm is very large, as Example 3.1 illustrates.

Efficiency and Welfare

The welfare of the people is the chief law. —*Cicero*

The competitive equilibrium has desirable efficiency and welfare properties. Indeed, no one can be made better off without making someone else worse off in the competitive equilibrium.

Efficiency

The competitive equilibrium of price and quantity has two desirable efficiency properties. First, production is efficient in the sense that there is no possible rearrangement of resources (such as labor, machines, and raw materials) among firms that can increase the output of one product without reducing the output of at least one other product.

Second, consumption is efficient. The value that a buyer places on consuming the good is exactly equal to the marginal cost of producing that good (remember, the competitive price equals the marginal cost of production). Moreover, no rearrangement of goods among consumers can benefit a consumer without harming at least one other consumer.

Welfare

We now describe a common measure of welfare, show that competition maximizes this measure of welfare for any given distribution of income, and illustrate that departures from competition lower welfare. In particular, in the next section, we show that restrictions that prevent firms from entering a market lower welfare.

Consumer Surplus. Typically, consumers value the goods they purchase above the amount they actually pay for them. **Consumer surplus** is the amount above the price paid that a consumer would willingly spend, if necessary, to consume the units purchased.

A good's demand curve reflects the value that consumers place on consuming additional units of a good. For example, the demand curve in Figure 3.6 indicates that

FIGURE 3.6 Consumer Surplus and Producer Surplus

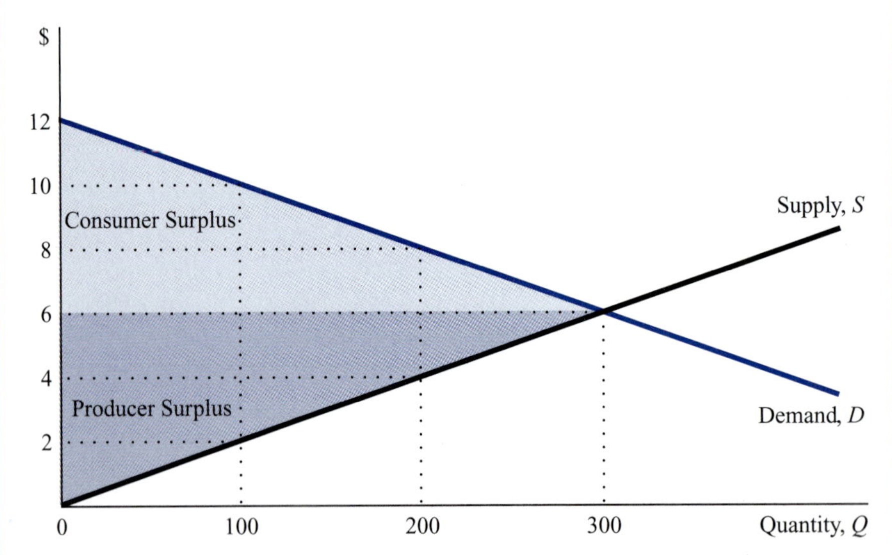

consumers would pay $10 for 100 units of the good, $8 for 200 units, and $6 for 300 units.

In the competitive equilibrium in Figure 3.6, consumers pay $6 for 300 units. They would have been willing to spend $4 more for the first 100 units, $2 more for the first 200 units, and no extra amount for 300 units. The total consumer surplus is the shaded area below the demand curve and above the equilibrium price of $6 up to the equilibrium quantity of 300 units.[9] This area equals $900 (= [$12 − $6] × 300/2).

In the competitive market, consumers paid $1,800 to buy the 300 units. In this example, consumer surplus is 50 percent of the amount they actually pay. If consumers could have had the choice of buying 300 units or none, they would have been willing to spend up to $2,700 (the $1,800 they spent, plus the extra $900 in consumer surplus) to purchase the 300 units.

Producer Surplus. Similarly, firms may receive more for the goods they sell than it costs them to produce those goods. **Producer surplus** is the largest amount that could be subtracted from a supplier's revenues and yet the supplier would still willingly produce the product.

We can use information from the supply curve to calculate firms' producer surplus. A supply curve represents the marginal cost of producing output. For example, in Figure 3.6, it costs firms $2 to produce 100 units, $4 to produce 200 units, and $6 to produce 300 units. The producer surplus is the area above the supply curve and below the market price up to the quantity sold. The producer surplus is the area equal to $900, which is above the supply curve and below the price of $6 up to 300 units. That is, firms would be willing to pay $900 for the right to sell 300 units of the good at $6 rather than selling none at all.

Welfare. One common measure of welfare from a market is the sum of consumer surplus and producer surplus. This measure of welfare is the value that consumers and producers would be willing to pay to purchase the equilibrium quantity of output at the equilibrium price.

Figure 3.6 illustrates that this measure of welfare is maximized at the competitive equilibrium. For example, if fewer units were produced, welfare would fall, as we now show.

Deadweight Loss. The cost to society of a market's not operating efficiently is called **deadweight loss** (*DWL*). It is the welfare loss—the sum of the consumer surplus and producer surplus lost—from a deviation from the competitive equilibrium.

For example, the competitive equilibrium is at price p_0 and quantity Q_0 in Figure 3.7. At Q_0, the value that a consumer places on additional consumption equals the marginal cost of producing the good. If the government taxes this good or restricts its

[9]Consumer surplus is an accurate measure of consumer well-being if there are no income effects (a change in a consumer's income leaves demand unchanged). Even when there are income effects, changes in consumer surplus can provide a close approximation to changes in welfare (Willig 1976).

FIGURE 3.7 Deadweight Loss from a Tax

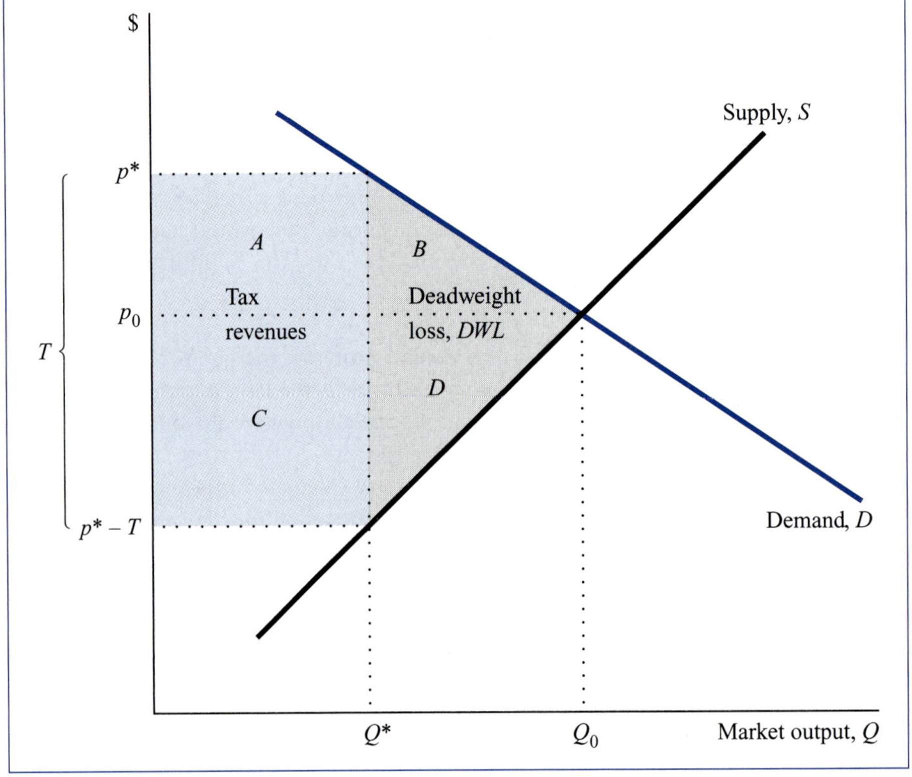

sale, this link between the value the consumer places on an additional unit and the cost of producing it is broken, which lowers welfare.

Suppose that the government collects a tax of T per unit of goods sold. If a customer pays p, the government takes T of that, and the firm receives $p - T$. Thus, the tax creates a wedge of T between the value that the marginal demander places on the good (as shown by the demand curve) and the cost that the marginal supplier is willing to incur to produce the good (as shown by the supply curve). The imposition of the tax reduces the quantity sold from Q_0 to Q^*. The price consumers pay rises to p^*, and the price firms receive falls to $p^* - T$.

In this after-tax equilibrium, the amount sold, Q^*, is less than in the competitive equilibrium, Q_0, and the value consumers place on consuming an additional unit, p^*, now exceeds the marginal cost of producing it by T. Consumers suffer a loss of consumer surplus equal to areas A and B (the area between p^* and p_0, to the left of the demand curve). Suppliers suffer a loss of producer surplus equal to areas C and D (the area between p_0 and $p^* - T$ to the left of the supply curve). The government receives tax revenues equal to TQ^*, boxes A and C. Thus, the transfer from consumers and producers to the government (the tax revenues = boxes *A* and *C*) is less than the combined loss of the consumers and producers. This extra cost to society due to reduced output is the deadweight loss, which equals the sum of the triangles *B* and *D* in Figure 3.7.[10]

The deadweight loss triangle is the total loss to society if the government makes good use of the tax revenues. The *DWL* triangle is an efficiency loss because the marginal cost of producing a good is less than the marginal willingness of consumers to pay for it.

As long as the government makes efficient use of this money, the tax revenues are not an efficiency loss. Rather, the tax revenues reflect a redistribution of income from buyers and sellers of this good to those who benefit from the government's use of these funds.

Entry and Exit

As we show throughout the rest of this book, ease of entry and exit plays a critical role in determining market structure and the subsequent performance of firms. If firms that are as efficient as those already in the market cannot easily enter, existing firms may be able to exercise market power by setting prices above marginal cost.

Restrictions on Entry

In many industries, governments or groups of firms collectively set licensing requirements that restrict entry (see Example 3.2). An example of an entry restriction is the limit on the number of taxicabs allowed in many cities throughout the world. Such entry restrictions elevate prices above competitive levels.

Figure 3.8 illustrates how a restriction on entry leads to a price above the long-run competitive equilibrium price. In this market, a large number of firms could produce with identical cost curves, as panel a shows.

Figure 3.8b shows two long-run supply curves for a market where all firms have identical costs. In the absence of a government restriction on entry, there are 150 firms in this market. The competitive equilibrium is determined by the intersection of the supply curve for 150 firms and the market demand curve. The equilibrium price is p_0, and each firm is producing at the minimum of its long-run average cost curve, AC^*.

---

[10]The deadweight loss triangle can be expressed in terms of the elasticities of demand and supply. For simplicity, assume that the supply curve is perfectly horizontal (infinitely elastic). Then the deadweight loss triangle = $-1/2\Delta p\Delta Q$, where $\Delta p = p^* - p_0$ and $\Delta Q = Q^* - Q_0$. The elasticity of demand, ϵ, is (approximately) equal to $(\Delta Q/Q_0)(p_0/\Delta p)$. Define t as $\Delta p/p_0$, which is the percentage change in the price due to the tax. The deadweight loss triangle equals

$$-\frac{1}{2}\Delta p\Delta Q \approx -\frac{1}{2}\frac{\Delta p}{p_0}p_0Q_0\left(\frac{\Delta Q}{Q_0}\frac{p_0}{\Delta p}\right)\frac{\Delta p}{p_0} \approx -\frac{1}{2}t^2R\epsilon,$$

where R is the revenue, p_0Q_0, and ≈ means *approximately equal*. Thus, the deadweight loss depends on the size of the market, R, in addition to t and ϵ.

EXAMPLE 3.2

Restrictions on Entry Across Countries

Most countries restrict new businesses from entering. Virtually every country requires that a potential new firm fill out certain forms and pay fees to become a legal business. Some countries prohibit entry in certain industries.

A World Bank survey of entry restrictions in 85 countries found that the ease of entry varied substantially across countries. It takes two business days to enter a typical business in Australia or Canada, but 152 days in Madagascar. The average for the 85 countries surveyed was 47 days.

To determine the cost of entry, the researchers calculated the ratio of fees plus the cost of time in applying as a percentage of per capita annual gross domestic product (GDP). Again, the range across countries was enormous: The lowest ratio was less than 0.5 percent for the United States, the highest was more than 4.6 times per capita GDP in the Dominican Republic, and the average was 47 percent of per capita GDP.

Are there any patterns to help explain which countries have the most onerous restrictions? Yes. In general, rich countries have fewer restrictions than poor countries. Countries with greater political freedoms, less corruption, and smaller illegal sectors tend to have fewer entry restrictions. Leaders of governments in poor, underdeveloped countries generally set rules that protect existing businesses from competition, perhaps benefiting their friends, their relatives, or themselves, all of whom may have business interests.

Source: Djankov et al. (2002).

FIGURE 3.8 Long-Run Equilibrium with an Entry Restriction

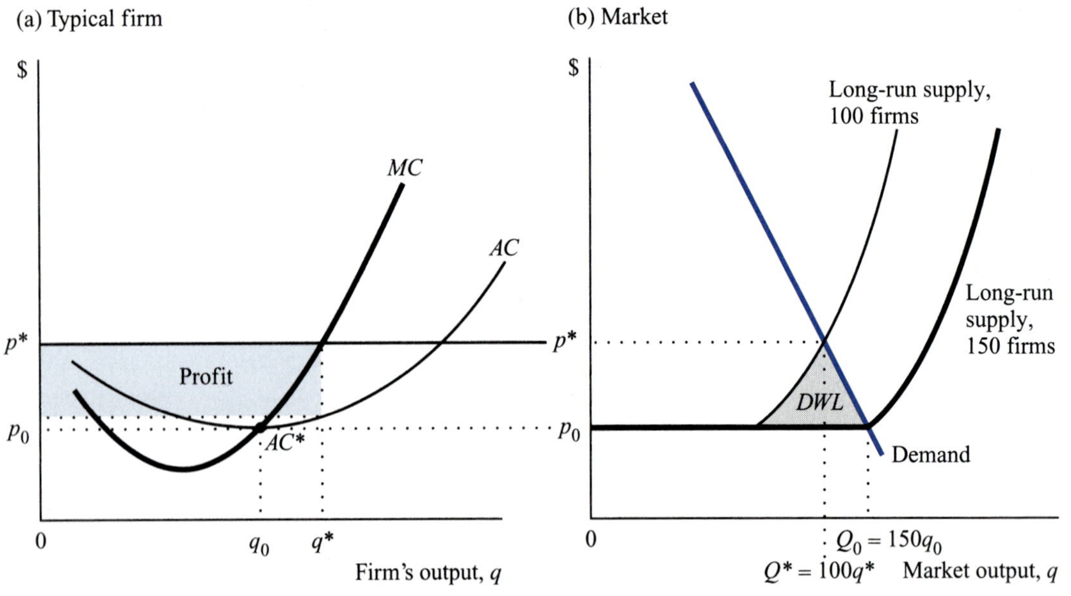

If the government restricts the number of firms in the market to 100, the long-run supply curve lies to the left of the original one. With this restriction on entry, the new equilibrium price is p^*. The entry restriction, therefore, results in consumers' paying a price, p^*, higher than the unrestricted competitive price, p_0, and consuming only Q^*, which is less than the unrestricted competitive quantity, Q_0.

The shaded area *DWL* in Figure 3.8b is the lost welfare from restricting entry. It reflects the loss of consumer surplus from paying p^* rather than p_0 that is not captured by the firms.

The entry restriction is inefficient for two reasons. First, there is a loss in efficiency due to restricting output from Q_0 to Q^*. Second, the average cost of production is greater with entry restrictions. With free entry, each firm produces q_0 and the average and marginal cost of production is p_0. With the restriction, firms produce q^* units at a marginal cost of p^* and an average cost above p_0 in Figure 3.8a. The area between the two supply curves to the left of Q^* in Figure 3.8b is a measure of this increased cost. The entire shaded area in Figure 3.8b is the deadweight loss caused by both sources of inefficiency from the entry restriction.

A firm that is among the 100 firms allowed into the market is better off than if there were no entry restrictions. The elevated price raises the profits of each of these 100 firms (the shaded area in Figure 3.8a) above the level that would have existed had the equilibrium number of firms, 150, been allowed to enter. With free entry, each firm produces at minimum average costs, and profits are zero. Thus, entry restrictions are like a tax on the consumption of a good. A tax, however, transfers money from consumers and producers to the government. In contrast, the entry restrictions transfer money from consumers to firms that were able to operate in this market. Consequently, the Federal Trade Commission (FTC) opposes many such barriers: see Example 3.3.

EXAMPLE 3.3

FTC Opposes Internet Bans That Harm Competition

Preventing Internet shopping may raise the price of some goods. In 2003, the Federal Trade Commission (FTC) issued a report concluding that removing bans on interstate wine sales over the Internet would save consumers as much as 21 percent on relatively expensive wines and increase consumer choice. In 26 states, including New York, Florida, Massachusetts, and Pennsylvania, laws (many dating from the Prohibition era) ban direct-to-consumer shipping from out of state, in part to prevent sales to minors. However, the FTC concluded that shipping wine directly to homes does not lead to more underage drinking. One reason is that many states require an adult to sign to accept wine deliveries.

The FTC has worked to reduce barriers to online trade in other markets. For example, they argued before Connecticut's Board of Examiners for Opticians against regulations making it difficult for online vendors to sell contact lenses to consumers. Similarly, they opposed barriers to online sales of caskets in Oklahoma.

Sources: Federal Trade Commission, **www.ftc.gov/os/2003/07/winereport2.pdf, www.ftc.gov/opa/2003/07/wine.htm**.

Competition with Few Firms—Contestability

In some markets, total output is small relative to the efficient size of a firm. In other words, the economies of scale in production and sales are important so that only one or a few firms can efficiently produce in the market. Even in such a setting, it is possible for competition to work (Demsetz 1968, Baumol, Panzar, and Willig 1982), although the process is different from the competitive markets we have been analyzing.

If many identical firms are capable of entering the market and producing, no firm is able to earn more than the normal level of profits in the long run. If there is free entry into and exit from a market instantaneously (no sunk costs), firms have an incentive to enter whenever price exceeds average cost. Markets with free instantaneous entry and exit are called perfectly *contestable* (Baumol, Panzar, and Willig 1982).

Residential garbage collection may be an example of a contestable market. There are economies of scale in providing residential garbage collection in a single town (see Example 20.4). It would be inefficient for more than one firm to traverse the same route to pick up garbage. A town can solicit bids from garbage collection firms and choose the lowest bidder. Competition among bidders ensures that the town is served at the lowest possible cost, even though only one firm actually provides the service.[11]

In contrast, in a market that is protected from entry, price remains above marginal cost because no firm can enter the market and drive down price. Thus, restrictions on entry are the reason that many markets are not perfectly competitive, so that prices are above marginal cost.

Definition of Barriers to Entry

Is entry difficult in most markets? To answer this question, we need to define what we mean by a *barrier to entry.* A common definition of a **barrier to entry** is anything that prevents an entrepreneur from instantaneously creating a new firm in a market. This definition may not be useful, however, as it implies that virtually every market has a barrier to entry. Under this definition, the cost of hiring labor or the cost of building a plant is an entry barrier. Moreover, it implies that any market in which entry takes time has a barrier to entry.

Unfortunately, the term *barrier to entry* is often used to refer to both the costs of entering and the time it takes for entry to occur. Because the term has several meanings, confusion has resulted sometimes, even though the proponents of the various definitions agree that higher costs of entry raise prices. See Carlton (2004).

---

[11]A complication arises with economies of scale. If the bidding competition drives profits to zero so that price equals average cost and if there are economies of scale, price *exceeds* marginal cost. If price does not equal marginal cost, the allocation of resources is inefficient. A more efficient way to finance garbage collection service is to charge a fee per pickup that reflects marginal cost, and to charge a separate fee for the right to have garbage picked up at all. Under this scheme, if residents want garbage picked up twice a week, they would pay the fixed fee plus twice the fee per pickup. Such two-part pricing schemes are studied in Chapter 10.

The economic theories discussed in this book predict the erosion of profits by entry only in the long run. Thus, one reasonable approach is to focus on long-run barriers to entry, which prevent new firms from entering a market even though an existing firm earns long-run profits.

If there are many firms that can enter with identical cost curves and face identical prices, then no one firm can succeed in the long run at earning profits that exceed costs without inducing additional entry. Only by having some advantage over new entrants can a firm earn persistently higher profits than other actual or potential firms. Because long-run profits can only persist if a firm has an advantage over potential entrants, a logical definition of a **long-run barrier to entry** is a cost that must be incurred by a new entrant that incumbents do not (or have not had to) bear.[12]

Entry Barriers. A good example of a long-run barrier to entry is a patent. Under most patent systems, the government grants an inventor the monopoly right to sell the invention for a fixed period of time. A patent creates a legal monopoly through a long-run barrier to entry. To compete against an incumbent firm with a patent, a potential entrant has to either invent around the patent or license it from the incumbent firm.[13] Because the incumbent firm has the right to exclude anyone from using the patent, it can prevent entry. The incumbent probably had to invest in research and development in order to acquire the patent. If the same avenue of research and development is not available once a patent has been granted, the potential entrant faces a cost that is greater than that of the incumbent.[14]

An incumbent may use a variety of strategies designed to raise the cost of entry, all of which require the incumbent to exploit some asymmetry between it and a potential entrant in order to raise the cost to a potential entrant above its own. When it is successful, the incumbent firm can create a long-run barrier to entry. These strategic responses are studied in detail in Chapter 11.

Exit Barriers. An important consideration in understanding a firm's incentive to enter a market is, paradoxically, the firm's ability to exit the market. If it is costly to exit a market, the incentives to enter are reduced. It is costly to exit a market if there are sunk costs that cannot be recovered. For example, suppose that a firm in a market must have very specialized equipment that is difficult to resell. A firm contemplating entry into that market realizes that if the unusual profit opportunities in the market are short lived, it may not pay to enter. In contrast, if there are no costs to enter or exit, then instantaneous entry and subsequent exit, sometimes called *hit-and-run entry*, by outside

---

[12]This definition is adapted from Stigler (1968a). See also von Weizsäcker (1980), who adds the condition that an entry barrier must lower consumer welfare. See McAfee, Mialon, and Williams (2004) for a discussion of various definitions of barriers to entry.

[13]As discussed in Chapter 16 on patents, the holder of a patent may allow other firms to use the invention in return for a license fee. That fee, however, is the barrier to entry, for it is the amount that an entrant must pay that the incumbent does not pay.

[14]As discussed in Chapter 16, patents have an offsetting benefit. Were it not for the unusually high profits a patent holder obtains from its monopoly, firms would not sink large amounts into the research and development that leads to discoveries. Thus, society probably would be worse off in the absence of this barrier to entry.

firms guarantees that prices will not exceed costs at each instance.[15] Therefore, costs of exit serve to *prevent entry*, just as do costs of entering a market.

General Evidence on Entry and Exit. Agriculture, construction, wholesale and retail trade, and services are generally thought to have easy entry and exit. In contrast, in some manufacturing industries, mining, and in certain regulated industries (public utilities and some insurance industries), entry and exit may be more difficult. According to the Economic Report of the President (2003, Table B 12), the composition of the U.S. gross domestic product in 2001 by sector is agriculture, 1 percent; construction, 5 percent; mining, 1 percent; manufacturing, 14 percent; transportation and public utilities, 8 percent; wholesale trade, 7 percent; retail trade, 9 percent; finance/insurance, and real estate, 2 percent; services, 22 percent; and government, 13 percent.

There are several interesting recent studies on entry and exit, including Berry (1992), Bresnahan and Reiss (1988, 1990, 1991), Dixit (1989), Geroski (1991), Lieberman (1990), Pakes and Ericson (1999), Mazzeo (2002), and Schary (1991). For example, Bresnahan and Reiss examine markets with only a few producers of professional services (such as rural markets for doctors) and ask how large a market must become before a single firm enters. They then ask how much more the market has to grow for two, three, and more firms to enter. They find that competition acts very quickly to reduce price and profits. Although initial entrants can charge a high price, the entry of two additional firms appears to produce competition. They also obtain a measure of sunk costs by comparing the size at which exit occurs to the size at which entry occurs. The larger a sunk cost, the smaller is the market size that triggers exit compared to the market size that induces entry.

The empirical literature suggests that there is much entry and exit and that entrants tend to be small. These high rates of entry and exit are roughly equal in stable industries (Caves 1998). Dunne, Roberts, and Samuelson (1988) find that entrants are much smaller than the average firm in a manufacturing industry. They produce 17 percent of the output level of existing firms and account for about 11 percent of industry output on average.[16] Similarly, exiting firms, which produce 11 percent of industry output, only produce one-fifth the output of the average firm. Despite entry, the four largest firms in an industry stay in that group on average for over 10 years (Caves 1998). Birch (1987), using Dun and Bradstreet data for all sectors (not just

[15]Baumol, Panzar, and Willig (1982) emphasize this point and are responsible for popularizing the concept of hit-and-run entry and relating it to contestability. See also Eaton and Lipsey (1980). Weitzman (1983) shows that hit-and-run entry is equivalent to a horizontal supply curve.

[16]There are not many economic models about how new firms enter and grow in an industry. Simple application of the competitive model suggests no difference between a new entrant and an existing firm. More realistic models based on differences in knowledge can generate specific growth processes for new firms and a distribution of firm sizes. See Jovanovic (1982), Jovanovic and MacDonald (1984), Hopenhayn (1992), and Ericson and Pakes (1995). See also Evans (1987a, b), Hall (1987) and Syverson (2003). Sutton (1997) and Caves (1998) report that the variability of a firm's growth rate first falls and then levels off with firm size, that a firm's average growth rate diminishes with size, and that a firm's probability of survival increases with age and size. See Sutton (1997) for a discussion of Gibrat's Law, which postulates a log-normal distribution for firm size.

manufacturing), finds that about half of all new entrants fail within five years and that despite their high rate of failure, entrants over a period of a few years are a significant source for the creation of (net) new jobs. However, employment by entrants accounts for a disproportionately small share of total employment and does not generate a disproportionately higher share of employment growth (Davis, Haltwanger, and Schuk 1996).

In many new industries, a massive entry of small firms is followed by a shakeout that eliminates the weakest firms. The surviving firms then grow both in size and in functions until the industry eventually goes into decline. This pattern is explained by the models of entry and exit discussed in this chapter in which firms learn whether they are efficient and, if not, exit.

The beer, auto, and tire industries followed this pattern. For example, in the beer industry, massive entry in the 1870s doubled the number of firms. Massive exit in the 1880s reduced the number of firms by 40 percent. Firms that entered just prior to the shakeout had higher survival probabilities than firms that entered after the shakeout had begun.

The spike in entry followed by a spike in exits can be pronounced. The number of tire manufacturers rose from about 170 in 1915 to about 270 in 1921, fell back down to about 150 around 1925, and dropped to approximately 50 by the beginning of the Depression in the early 1930s. Similarly, the number of auto firms increased from about 150 in 1905 to 250 in 1910, fell back to 150 by 1915, and dropped to below 30 by 1930.[17]

Identifying Barriers to Entry

Bain (1956) pioneered the modern approach to analyzing barriers to entry. He identified three such barriers:

- Absolute cost advantage
- Economies of large-scale production that require large capital expenditures
- **Product differentiation**: related products that have varying characteristics so that consumers do not view them as perfect substitutes (for example, Apple computers are not perfect substitutes for IBM computers)

An absolute cost advantage allows an incumbent firm to earn excess profits without fear of new firms entering the market. For example, suppose Firm A can produce at a constant cost of $2 per unit, whereas all other potential firms could produce at a cost of $5. Firm A can set its price at $4, which is above its per unit cost, earn an unusually high profit, and yet not fear entry. Because it is less clear that the other two barriers fit our definition of long-run entry barriers, let us examine them in more detail.

If both an incumbent and a new entrant can enjoy the same benefits of economies of scale, why should an incumbent be able to earn excess profits? Some argue that a new entrant would have difficulty raising money (or be unwilling to invest its own money) to finance a large expenditure. It is not necessarily true that it is more difficult

[17]Klepper (2000) and Hovarth, Schivardi, and Woywode (2001) [statistics read from their graphs].

to raise money for large than small projects.[18] If capital markets work properly (banks and others are willing to loan money for profitable activities), raising capital should be no more difficult for a profitable large-scale project than for a profitable small-scale project. There should be many investors for good projects.

But is it reasonable that the scale of a firm has no effect on the incentives to enter? If large *sunk* costs are associated with entry and if entry is unsuccessful, the entrant's losses are large. In such a setting, threats of strategic behavior (for example, vigorous price cutting) may prevent new entry. The greater the risk of encountering strategic behavior and the greater the potential loss, the more potent is the threat of strategic entry deterrence. In such a case, the need for large-scale investment that involves large sunk costs could well provide a disincentive for a potential entrant because it would have so much to lose (see Chapter 11).

Product differentiation (firms produce similar but not identical products) can create a long-run barrier to entry. For example, consumer goodwill toward established brand names may make it more difficult for a new brand to enter. Of course, an advantage may accrue to the first firm to introduce a new product. That firm may have a **first-mover advantage**: the first firm to enter incurs lower marketing costs because it faces no rivals (see Chapter 11). Later firms face higher marketing costs because they must compete against the first.[19] If the presence of the incumbent raises the marketing costs of the second firm to enter, then the first firm has a permanent advantage—a long-run barrier to entry—and can maintain high prices.[20] For example, because the product of the first firm in the market is familiar to customers, they may be reluctant to switch to a new brand (Schmalensee 1982).

The Size of Entry Barriers by Industry

A number of methods are used to assess long-run barriers to entry. Some economists use subjective judgments to predict how difficult it would be for a new firm to enter a market. These estimates can be based on how frequently entry has occurred in the past.

Other measures of barriers to entry are based on the answers to questions like the following: What would be the cost disadvantage if a new entrant's plant was half the size of the incumbent's? How much higher are the entrant's costs because of the incumbent's patents or acquired expertise? Tables 3.2 and 3.3 reproduce Bain's characterization of the extent of barriers to entry in certain industries.

Harris (1976) examined the rate of entry into those industries that Bain and later Mann (1966) considered difficult to enter, and found that several of these industries had significant entry. The entry barriers identified by Bain and Mann that did seem to

[18]Dunne, Roberts, and Samuelson (1988) find that existing firms that choose to enter a new business enter at a larger scale than do newly created firms. Possibly, capital market imperfections are more easily overcome by existing firms than by entrepreneurs without track records or existing firms are more confident of their likely success.

[19]Sometimes the second firm to enter has lower marketing costs than the first firm, which had to spend money educating consumers about the use and desirability of the new type of product.

[20]Caves and Porter (1977) stress the importance of *mobility barriers* that prevent firms in an industry from moving into different segments of that industry.

TABLE 3.2 Bain's Barriers to Entry

Industry	Scale Economy	Product Differentiation	Absolute Cost	Capital Requirement
Automobiles	3	3	1	3
Cigarettes	1	3	1	3
Liquor	1	3	1	2
Shoes	2	1–2	1	0
Soap	2	2	1	2
Steel	2	1	3	3
Tractors	3	3	1	3
Tires and tubes	1	2	1	2
Meat packing	2	2	2	0–1
Cement	2	1	1	2
Flour	1	1–2	1	0

Note: Higher scores indicate greater entry barriers.

Source: Bain (1956, 169)

TABLE 3.3 Bain's Overall Barriers to Entry

Industry	Overall Barriers
Automobiles	Very high
Cigarettes	Very high
Liquor	Very high
Soaps	Substantial
Steel	Substantial
Tractors	Very high
Flour	Moderate to low
Cement	Moderate to low
Meat packing	Moderate to low
Tires	Moderate to low
Rayon	Moderate to low

Note: Industries with very high barriers could elevate price 10 percent or more above competitive levels. Substantial and moderate-to-low entry barriers allow prices to be in excess of competitive levels by 7 percent and 4 percent respectively.

Source: Bain (1956, 170).

restrict entry were those having to do with product differentiation. Only long-run barriers to entry can prevent prices from eventually falling to equal marginal cost.

From a practical point of view, if the long run is very long, knowing that profits will eventually be driven to zero may not matter much to incumbent firms. Large short-run profits are still desirable. The time it takes for entry to expand output enough to eliminate unusually high profits may be more informative than the size of the long-run entry barrier.

The speed with which entry into various industries erodes profits may differ across competitive and noncompetitive industries. Most researchers find that profit erosion takes longer in concentrated industries (Stigler 1963) and in high-profit industries (Connolly and Schwartz 1985). Dunne, Roberts, and Samuelson (1988) find that differences in entry and exit rates across manufacturing industries persist over time. Moreover, there is considerable dispersion in entry and exit rates across industries. They find that the rates of entry and exit in a market are highly related. Industries with high rates of entry also have high rates of exit. In roughly half the manufacturing industries, entrants account for 7 to 25 percent of industry value, and exiting firms account for 8 to 25 percent of value.

Externalities

A competitive market may lack desirable welfare properties for reasons in addition to inefficient taxes and restrictions on entry. The competitive equilibrium is nonoptimal when a valuable good has no price or the wrong price. Unfortunately, many *goods* (such as information and fresh air) or *"bads"* (such as pollution and garbage) may not be priced in our economy. An **externality** occurs when consumers or firms do not bear the full cost (benefit) from the harm (good) their actions do to others.

Pollution is one of the most important examples of a **negative externality**, which is an uncompensated action that harms someone. Pollution is a bad that has no price. In the absence of government regulations, manufacturing firms do not pay for the pollution they create, so they ignore the cost to society of pollution in deciding how much output to produce. That is, their *private marginal cost* (their out-of-pocket production cost) of making one more unit is less than the *social marginal cost* (the private marginal cost plus the damage from the pollution). As a result, they produce more than is socially optimal. Such distortions, or inefficiencies in production due to improper pricing, are referred to as **market failures**.

An uncompensated action that benefits others is a **positive externality**. For example, when you plant a beautiful garden in view of your neighbor, your neighbor receives a free benefit. Two important examples of positive externalities involve the generation and dissemination of information, which can benefit many people at once. When Henry Ford developed the assembly line, other firms benefited from his innovation without compensating him. Many consumers who don't buy *Consumer Reports* learn of its ranking of automobiles and benefit from this in-formation. Whereas too much is typically produced in industries with negative externalities, too little is typically produced in industries with positive externalities.

Information is also described as a **public good**: a commodity or service whose consumption by one person does not preclude others from also consuming it. Another example of a public good is national defense. In addition to being an externality, pollution is a public bad (an undesirable public "good"). In contrast, a *private good*, such as a hot dog, is consumed by only one consumer—it cannot be consumed by another as well. An externality can be either a private or public good or bad. We now show that externalities arise when property rights are not clearly defined (Coase 1960).

You have **property rights** when you own or have exclusive rights to use some asset such as a good or service. Others must compensate you if they wish to use your property. For example, you may have property rights to a particular car, but no clearly defined area of a highway belongs to you alone. You share the highway with others. Each driver claims a temporary property right in a portion of the highway by occupying it (thereby preventing others from occupying the same space). Competition for space on the highway can lead to congestion (a negative externality), which slows up every driver on a highway. (See Example 3.4).

EXAMPLE 3.4

Increasing Congestion

According to the annual reports of the Texas Transportation Institution (TTI) at Texas A&M University, U.S. highway congestion and its costs have increased substantially over the last two decades. TTI estimates the cost from congestion in 75 areas around the United States at $67.5 billion in 2000, which reflects 3.6 billion hours of delay and 5.7 billion gallons of excess fuel consumed. In Los Angeles—the most congested city—the annual delay per peak-hour traveler was 136 person-hours, up from 47 hours in 1982. For all areas, the average annual delay increased from 16 hours to 46 hours from 1982 to 2000. The annual congestion cost per peak road traveler was $2,510 in Los Angeles and averaged $1,160 across the country. In addition, stalled traffic causes increased air pollution.

The only way to reduce this congestion is to decrease the number of simultaneous users of the highways or to increase the highways' capacity. According to the TTI, preventing congestion from growing between 1999 and 2000 would have required 1,780 new lane-miles of freeway and 2,590 new lane-miles of streets, or an average of 6.2 million additional new trips per day taken by either carpool or transit, or other operational improvements that allowed 3 percent more travel to be handled on the existing systems, or some combination of these actions.

One approach to controlling the congestion externality would be to impose a toll on users who travel during peak hours, where the toll equals the externality cost. Such a toll would force drivers to take into account the cost they impose on others when they travel.

Source: **mobility.tamu.edu/ums/study/short_report.stm, mobility.tamu.edu/ums/study/appendix_A/**

Where property rights are clearly defined so there are no externalities, competitive markets are efficient. For example, growing wheat does not affect a farmer's neighbors or anyone else usually, and farmers have the right to produce and sell the wheat as they choose. In contrast, if property rights are not well defined, markets may be inefficient. For example, if a software company cannot protect its property right to its computer programs and prevent other firms from selling them, these programs provide a positive externality (the company is not compensated for use of its programs). As a result, too few resources are devoted to producing software. Unfortunately, externalities are common. Specific examples include pollution and fisheries.[21]

Limitations of Perfect Competition

Some markets satisfy most of the assumptions of the perfect competition model. For example, on the New York Stock Exchange, many people buy and sell shares of stock of individual firms like IBM. Individuals who own the stock but want to sell it ask their brokers to sell, and those who want to buy ask their brokers to buy. There are many well-informed participants in the stock market, and the price of a particular stock is determined by the forces of supply and demand. Most individuals correctly believe that they have no effect on the price of the stock. Although this market comes close to satisfying the assumptions for perfect competition, most do not.

The model of perfect competition is directly relevant to only a few markets, and much of this book is devoted to analyzing the consequences of more realistic models of economic behavior. In these more realistic models, firms are able to influence price and their rivals' actions, engage in advertising and other marketing activities to inform and influence consumers, and undertake research and development to produce more efficiently.

Many people observe that, even in perfectly competitive markets, welfare is nonoptimal if the distribution of income is "unjust." Individual wealth depends on assets (for example, money, machines) and skills. Competition does not necessarily reward the deserving. It rewards those who are the most productive and those who own productive assets.

If the distribution of income is not just, why does anyone care about efficiency? After all, efficiency means only that one person cannot be made better off without another being made worse off. If there is only $10,000 to distribute and Debbie gets $9,999 and Rebecca gets $1, that is efficient because all $10,000 is distributed. But so is $1 for Debbie and $9,999 for Rebecca. There are many efficient points; in fact, *any* division of the $10,000 between Debbie and Rebecca is efficient. The particular efficiency point that the competitive equilibrium produces depends on the initial owner-

[21]See **www.aw-bc.com/carlton_perloff** "Pollution" for a more extensive discussion of pollution and externalities, and of how the assignment of property rights to either firms or consumers can lead to an efficient outcome.

ship of assets. Public policy may assert that it is unjust for either Debbie or Rebecca to receive only \$1 while the other receives \$9,999, and might prefer \$5,000 to Debbie and \$5,000 to Rebecca. It might even find \$4,999 to Debbie and \$4,999 to Rebecca preferable to the policy of \$9,999 for one and \$1 for the other. That means that an *inefficient* policy may be preferred to an efficient one! Why then do economists seem to stress efficiency?

One answer is that the morally just (however defined) distribution of income can be achieved by competition plus a system of appropriate income redistribution. That is, the government could assign wealth initially according to society's moral values, and then competition would lead society to an efficient outcome. One interpretation of this result is that it is up to the government to achieve the moral distribution of wealth through nondistorting taxation, and it is up to the competitive process to achieve efficiency.

Economists can objectively discuss whether economic efficiency is achieved, but they are no better equipped than others to discuss the best or most moral income distribution. They may analyze how the distribution of income changes as a result of certain policies, but they cannot scientifically determine whether one distribution is ethically superior to another.

The Many Meanings of Competition

We have been specific about the definition of perfect competition. Many non–economists and even many economists use the term *competition* loosely to apply to markets that we refer to as noncompetitive.

Some people use the term *competition* to refer to a market in which a few price-setting firms compete vigorously for sales. Each firm tries to obtain customers for itself at the expense of its rivals. In this interpretation, competition is used to describe rivalry between firms that can affect market price. This use of the term differs from our definition, where a perfectly competitive firm is a price taker that can sell all it wants at the market price.

Even though few industries fit the requirements of perfect competition, economists often speak of certain types of industries as being reasonably competitive if they have certain characteristics. Price-taking behavior, many firms, and free entry and exit are often used as criteria to judge the competitiveness of a market. Free entry and exit typically result in firms eventually earning zero profits. For example, in some states, it is very easy to become a barber, and there are often many independent barber shops in an area. Even though barbers are not identical in either quality or prices and all consumers are not aware of all barber shops, most economists would describe the provision of haircuts by barber shops as a reasonably competitive market.

Another example of a reasonably competitive market is steel scrap. Firms in that market collect used steel, process it, and sell it to steel firms. Entry into the steel-scrap market is easy and quick, the product sold is fairly homogeneous, and there are published quotations of prices. Even though transaction prices undoubtedly vary from firm to firm, the large number of sellers acting independently would cause most economists to label this market as reasonably competitive.

Some discussions involving public policy use the term *competitive* in a still different way: A competitive market is one that requires no intervention to improve its performance; a noncompetitive market is one that has some defect that should be corrected. This usage of the terms *competitive* and *noncompetitive* can be confusing. The confusion arises because intervention can sometimes improve the performance of industries that satisfy all the assumptions of perfect competition—as can occur, for example, when the government encourages inventive activity. Conversely, the failure of a market to satisfy all the assumptions of perfect competition does not necessarily mean that some intervention can improve market performance.

SUMMARY

In perfect competition, all firms produce homogeneous, perfectly divisible output; producers and consumers have full information, incur no transaction costs, and are price takers; and there are no externalities. If all these conditions hold, use of resources is efficient. Welfare defined as consumer surplus plus producer surplus is maximized.

Government interventions in competitive markets such as taxes and restrictions on entry and exit reduce the efficiency of these markets. Government intervention may be helpful, however, if some of the assumptions of perfect competition do not hold. For example, where property rights are not clearly defined or high transaction costs prevent negotiated solutions, polluting competitive firms do not pay for the damage they cause, and produce too much pollution. The optimal government policy reduces the pollution.

The assumptions of perfect competition do not hold in many industries. Subsequent chapters explore firms' behavior and the consequences of departures from perfect competition.

PROBLEMS

1. Will a tax of \$1 per unit of output change the optimal scale of a competitive firm if all firms are identical and any firm can enter the market?

2. The government imposes a fixed fee per year on each firm that operates in a competitive market. What happens to output, the optimal scale of a firm, and price if there is free entry into the market?

3. Suppose a competitive market consists of identical firms with a constant long-run marginal cost of \$10. (There are no fixed costs in the long run.) Suppose the demand curve at any price, p, is given by $Q = 1{,}000 - p$.

   a. What are the price and quantity consumed in the long-run competitive equilibrium?

   b. Suppose one new firm enters that is different from the existing firms. The new firm has a constant marginal cost of \$9 and no fixed costs but can only produce 10 units (or fewer). What are the price and the quantity consumed in long-run competitive equilibrium? Are these the same as in (a)? Explain.

   c. Are positive economic profits inconsistent with a long-run competitive equilibrium?

   d. Identify the marginal cost of the last unit sold in (b). Is it \$10 or \$9? That is, if demand fell by 1 unit, would the new entrant or the other firms reduce output?

   e. How much profit do the less efficient firms in (b) earn?

   f. In the long-run competitive equilibrium, must the profit of the marginal entrant (the next firm to enter the market if demand expands or, alternatively, the next firm to leave the market if demand contracts) be zero?

4. If the market demand curve is $Q = 100 - p$, what is the market price elasticity of demand? If the supply curve of individual firms is $q = p$ and there are 50 identical firms in the market, draw the residual demand facing any one firm. What is the residual demand elasticity facing one firm at the competitive equilibrium?

5. When is a firm's shutdown point equal to the minimum point on its average cost curve?

6. The U.K. produces and imports eggs. Suppose that the government imposed a quota on imports: Foreign suppliers could export no more than Q eggs (regardless of price). What effect does this quota have on the foreign supply curve of eggs, the total U.K. supply curve of eggs, the equilibrium price, British consumers, and British producers?

Answers to the odd-numbered problems are given at the back of the book.

CHAPTER 4

Monopolies, Monopsonies, and Dominant Firms

Aeroflot Airlines: You Have Made the Right Choice.
—Ad campaign for the only airline in the then Soviet Union

A firm is a **monopoly** if it is the only supplier of a product for which there is no close substitute. A monopoly sets its price without fear that it will be undercut by a rival firm. A monopoly faces a downward-sloping demand curve and sets a price above marginal cost. As a result, less is sold than if the market were competitive (where price equals marginal cost) and society suffers a deadweight loss.

This chapter analyzes a monopoly's behavior and the consequences of that behavior. It also discusses how a monopoly is maintained and asks whether monopoly is always bad. The effects of externalities in a monopolized market are discussed next. The chapter then turns to two related topics. It examines monopsony, which is a monopoly on the buying side of the market. Then it discusses what happens to a monopoly if higher-cost competitive firms enter its market.

The six key questions we answer in this chapter are:

1. How does monopoly compare to competition in terms of prices and welfare?
2. How are monopolies created and maintained?
3. Are there markets in which there are benefits to monopoly?
4. Are all firms that earn profits monopolies, do all monopolies earn profits, and can monopolies earn profits in the long run?
5. How does a monopsony exercise its market power?
6. What happens to a monopoly if smaller, price-taking firms enter its market?

Monopoly Behavior

Because a monopoly faces a downward-sloping market demand curve, it can raise its price above marginal cost. To maximize its profit, it has an incentive to produce its output efficiently. A firm's behavior and government regulations influence the firm's ability to become and remain a monopoly.

Profit Maximization

Price, n. Value, plus a reasonable sum for the wear and tear of conscience in demanding it. —*Ambrose Bierce*

Like a competitive firm, a monopoly sets its level of output to maximize its profits. Because the market demand curve is downward sloping, the more the monopoly sells, the lower the price it receives.

The market demand curve constrains the monopoly. In its quest to maximize profit, it can set only price or only quantity—not both. If the monopoly sets quantity, the market price is determined by the market demand curve. If it sets price, the quantity is determined by the market demand curve.

Given the demand curve in Figure 4.1, if the monopoly wants to sell Q_0 units of its product, it charges price p_0. If it wishes to sell one more unit, it has to lower its price to p_1.

If the monopoly lowers its price to p_1, its revenues may rise or fall. The monopoly gains revenue on the extra unit it sells at price p_1, Area B in Figure 4.1. To sell that extra unit, however, it must cut its price from p_0 to p_1 on the original Q_0 units, resulting in a loss of revenues of $(p_0 - p_1)Q_0$, Area A in Figure 4.1.

When discussing a competitive firm's behavior in Chapter 3, we did not have to consider this loss of revenue due to lower price. Because a competitive, price-taking firm faces a horizontal demand curve, the price it receives does not fall if it expands its quantity.

If Area B is larger than Area A in Figure 4.1, then selling the extra unit causes revenues to rise. The extra revenues, $p_1(Q_0 + 1) - p_0Q_0$, that a firm receives when it produces one more unit of the product is called the **marginal revenue**.[1] Hence, the marginal revenue equals area B minus Area A. If the monopoly did not have to lower its price to sell the additional unit, then the increment to revenues from selling an additional unit would simply be the initial price, p_0. But because the demand curve

[1]Marginal revenue, MR, is the change in revenue from selling an additional unit. Total revenue is $p(Q)Q$, where $p(Q)$ is the inverse demand curve (p is a decreasing function of Q). Marginal revenue is equal to $p + Q(\Delta p/\Delta Q)$, where $(\Delta p/\Delta Q)$ is the decline in price necessary to sell the additional unit. Using calculus,

$$MR = \frac{d(p(Q)Q)}{dQ} = p + \frac{dp}{dQ}Q.$$

FIGURE 4.1 Demand Curve Facing a Monopoly

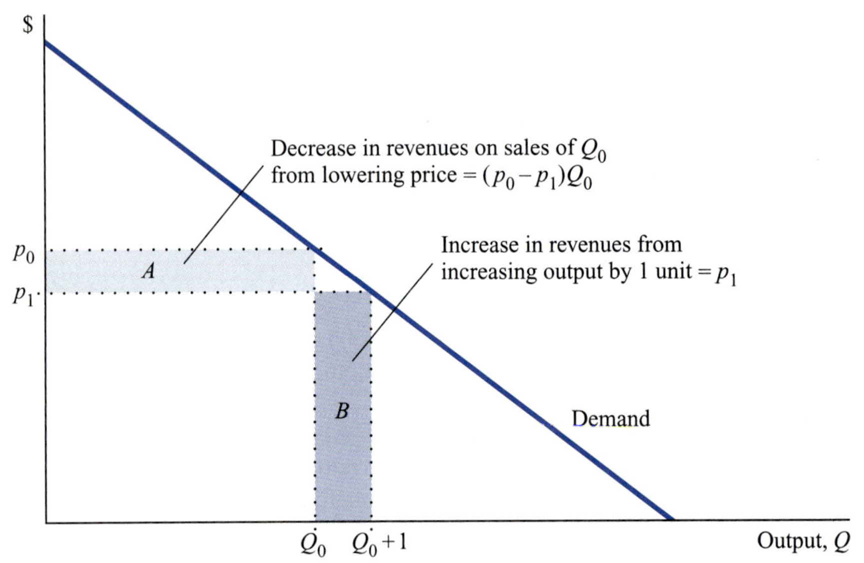

is downward sloping, the monopoly must lower its price to sell more units. Therefore, the marginal revenue is always less than the price for a monopoly, as Figure 4.2a illustrates.[2] For a firm in a perfectly competitive market, marginal revenue equals price.

Marginal revenue and total revenue are closely related. When marginal revenue is positive, total revenue increases as output expands, but when marginal revenue is negative, total revenue falls as output expands. As a result, total revenues are maximized (Figure 4.2b) when marginal revenue equals zero (Figure 4.2a).[3]

A monopoly maximizes its profit rather than its revenue (just as a competitive firm does). Profit is maximized at a smaller quantity than is revenue, as Figure 4.2b illustrates.

---

[2]If a straight-line demand curve, as in Figure 4.2a, hits a horizontal line at Q, the corresponding marginal revenue curve is also a straight line and hits the horizontal line at $Q/2$. To prove this result, let the straight-line demand curve be $p = a - bQ$. Total revenue is $R = pQ = aQ - bQ^2$. The marginal revenue curve is obtained by differentiating R with respect to Q: $MR = a - 2bQ$. The demand curve hits the horizontal axis ($p = 0$) at $Q = a/b$. The marginal revenue curve hits the horizontal axis ($MR = 0$) at $Q = a/(2b)$.

[3]If the monopoly wants to maximize revenues through its choice of Q,

$$\max_{Q} R = p(Q)Q,$$

it sets its marginal revenues equal to zero (first-order condition):

$$MR = p + \frac{dp}{dQ}Q = 0.$$

FIGURE 4.2 Monopoly Profit Maximization

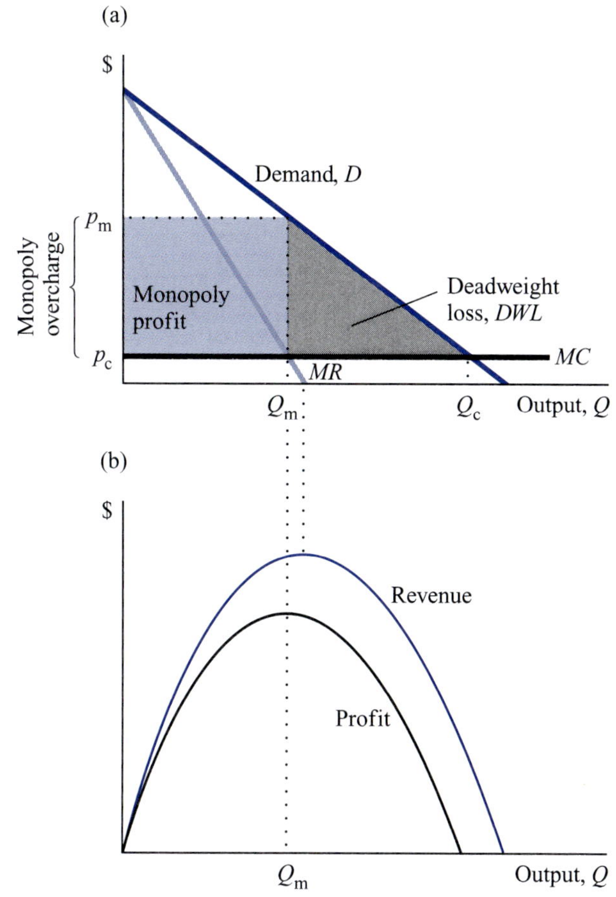

A monopoly maximizes its profit when the extra revenue from selling one more unit just equals the extra cost of producing that last unit of output. That is, profit is maximized where *marginal revenue equals marginal cost:*[4]

$$MR = MC. \tag{4.1}$$

[4]If the monopoly wants to maximize profits through its choice of Q

$$\max_{Q} \pi = p(Q)Q - C(Q),$$

it sets its marginal profits equal to zero (first-order condition):

$$\frac{d\pi}{dQ} = MR - MC = \left(p + \frac{dp}{dQ}Q\right) - \frac{dC}{dQ} = 0.$$

(continues)

Figure 4.2a illustrates this profit-maximizing relationship. The profit-maximizing monopoly output, Q_m, is smaller than the competitive output, Q_c, determined by the intersection of the demand curve with the marginal cost curve (which we assume would be the supply curve if the market were competitive) at price p_c. The monopoly does *not* have a supply curve that can be specified solely as a function of price because the monopoly's output depends on marginal revenue (which depends on the slope of the demand curve) and marginal cost.

The properties of the demand curve determine the monopoly *overcharge*: the amount by which the monopoly price, p_m, exceeds the marginal cost or competitive price, p_c, in Figure 4.2a. A relationship exists between the monopoly overcharge and the price elasticity of demand.

The elasticity of demand is a characteristic of the demand curve and is defined as the percentage change in quantity that results from a 1 percent change in price. If the elasticity of demand is very high (a large negative number), then the curve is said to be *elastic*. With a very elastic demand, a small price change induces a very large change in the quantity demanded. If the elasticity is low (a number between -1 and 0), the demand curve is *inelastic*, and a price change of 1 percent has relatively little effect on the quantity demanded.

Marginal revenue can be written as[5]

$$MR = p\left(1 + \frac{1}{\epsilon}\right), \tag{4.2}$$

where ϵ is the elasticity of demand. Thus, marginal revenue is positive if the demand curve is elastic ($\epsilon < -1$). It is negative if the demand curve is inelastic ($-1 < \epsilon < 0$). The elasticity of demand, in general, depends on not only the particular demand curve but also the point (the price and quantity pair) on the demand curve. For example, the elasticity of demand could decrease as price becomes lower.

By substituting Equation 4.2 for *MR* in Equation 4.1, we can write the profit-maximizing condition for the monopoly as:

$$\frac{p - MC}{p} = -\frac{1}{\epsilon}. \tag{4.3}$$

Thus, it sets $MR = MC$. Another condition for profit maximization is that the marginal revenue curve cut the marginal cost curve from above, as in Figure 4.2a. That is, the second-order condition must hold:

$$\frac{d^2\pi}{dQ^2} = \frac{dMR}{dQ} - \frac{dMC}{dQ} < 0.$$

A monopoly uses the same shut-down condition as does a competitive firm. In the short run, if price is below average variable cost, the monopoly stops producing.

[5]Differentiating revenue, $R = p(Q)Q$, with respect to Q, we find that the marginal revenue is

$$MR = p + \frac{dp}{dQ}Q = p\left(1 + \frac{dp}{dQ}\frac{Q}{p}\right) = p\left(1 + \frac{1}{\epsilon}\right),$$

where ϵ is defined as $(dQ/dp)(p/Q)$.

The left-hand side of Equation 4.3 is the **price-cost margin**: the difference between price and marginal cost as a fraction of price, $[p - MC]/p$. As the equation shows, the price-cost margin depends on only the elasticity of demand the monopoly faces. The price-cost margin is also called the **Lerner Index** of market power (Lerner 1934).

Equation 4.3 shows that the monopoly's price is close to MC when the demand is very elastic, and the price increasingly exceeds MC as the demand becomes less elastic. For example, if the elasticity of demand is -2, price is twice marginal cost. If the elasticity is -100 (very elastic), price equals $1.01MC$. The higher the elasticity of demand, the closer is the monopoly price to the competitive price. Therefore, the key element in an investigation of market power is the price elasticity of demand. Where the elasticity of demand is relatively inelastic, a monopoly markup may be substantial, as Example 4.1 illustrates.

Market and Monopoly Power

In contrast to a price-taking competitive firm, a monopoly knows that it can set its own price and that the price chosen affects the quantity it sells. A monopoly can set its price above its marginal cost but does not necessarily make a supracompetitive profit. For example, if a monopoly incurs a fixed cost, its profit may be zero (the competitive level) even if its price exceeds its marginal cost.

It is common practice to say that whenever a firm can profitably set its price above its marginal cost without making a loss, it has *monopoly power* or *market power*. One might usefully distinguish between the terms by using *monopoly power* to describe a firm that makes a profit if it sets its price optimally above its marginal cost, and *market power* to describe a firm that earns only the competitive profit when it sets its price optimally above its marginal cost. However, people do not always make this distinction, and generally use the two terms interchangeably, sometimes creating confusion.

EXAMPLE 4.1 *Monopoly Newspaper Ad Prices*

When the *Houston Post* shut down in April 1995, the managing editor of the sole surviving paper, the *Houston Chronicle*, received dozens of calls from concerned *Post* readers worried about one thing: Would the *Chronicle* pick up the *Post's* comics? Local advertisers also were very concerned: What would happen to newspaper advertising prices?

Ad rates skyrocketed by nearly 62 percent from January 1995 (before the *Post* folded) to December 1996. The rate for a one-column inch ad in a daily paper rose from \$252.64 to \$409.00 per day, and Sunday rates jumped from \$294.84 to \$477.28. These rates increased by much more than readership, which rose 32 percent on weekdays and 23 percent on Sunday. Thus, a loss of competition resulted in a substantial increase in price.

Source: Iver Peterson, "New Realities of Life in a One-Paper Town," *New York Times*, December 30, 1996:C5.

The Incentive for Efficient Operation

Organized crime in America takes in over forty billion dollars a year and spends very little on office supplies. —*Woody Allen*

The consequences of inefficient behavior are different for monopolies and competitive firms. An inefficient competitive firm may not be able to remain in business because it is unprofitable, but an inefficient monopoly can profitably remain in business. This observation has led some to conclude that the monopoly strives less hard to be efficient (called *x-inefficiency* by Leibenstein 1966) than does a competitive firm.

This argument is rejected by many economists who believe that monopolies, like other firms, prefer more to less. Monopolies want to maximize profits, and the only way a firm can do so is to minimize its costs at its chosen output level. Therefore, to postulate that monopolies want to maximize profits is to assume implicitly that they also minimize their costs. No firm—monopolistic or competitive—wants to throw money away. If improving the efficiency of operations increases profits, the firm should do it, whether it is a monopoly or a competitor.

A monopoly, however, may not have the same *ability* to produce as efficiently as a competitive firm. A firm in a market with many other firms can observe what other firms are doing. It can observe, for example, whether its own costs of production are above or below the market price. Because the market price reflects the efficiency of the other firms in the market, a competitive firm knows that it can improve its production efficiency if its costs of production are high relative to the market price. In contrast, a monopoly has no other firms to look at and may have no other standard by which to judge how efficiently it is operating. Therefore, a competitive firm may operate more efficiently than does a monopoly because it is more difficult for a monopoly to monitor internal efficiency than it is for a competitive firm.

Monopoly Behavior over Time

If demand is inelastic ($-1 < \epsilon < 0$), it is not possible to satisfy the profit-maximization condition of Equation 4.3. Thus, a monopoly never operates on the inelastic portion of its demand curve. If a monopoly were operating in the inelastic portion of its demand curve, it could increase its profits by raising its prices until it was operating in the elastic portion of its demand curve. In the inelastic portion of the demand curve, a 1 percent increase in the monopoly's price causes the quantity sold to fall by less than 1 percent, so that revenues increase. With reduced output, however, the monopoly's costs must fall, so that total profits must rise. Thus, if the monopoly is operating in the inelastic portion of the demand curve, it should keep increasing its price, obtaining ever more profits, until it is in the elastic portion of the demand curve.[6]

[6]What if there were no elastic portion of the demand curve? The monopoly would produce just a small amount of output, charge an infinite price, and make infinite profits. That this story is implausible underscores the empirical irrelevance of a monopoly's demand curve that is everywhere inelastic.

This observation, however, applies only in the context of a simple, timeless model. In actual markets, demand curves shift over time. As a result, a rational monopoly changes its price over time.

Consumers may have a more inelastic demand curve in the short run than in the long run. In the short run there are limitations on how fast consumers can substitute away from a product in the face of a price increase. Therefore, if a monopoly takes advantage of an inelastic portion of its short-run demand curve and raises its price, its consumers are more likely to substitute away from its product in subsequent periods. Thus, a monopoly may operate in the inelastic portion of its short-run demand curve to avoid long-run substitution.

The oil market provides an excellent example of the time it takes to substitute away from a product. When the Organization of Petroleum Exporting Countries (OPEC) raised the price of oil in the early 1970s, total consumption of energy changed very little in the first year. However, the quantity of oil demanded fell sharply over the next several years as consumers adjusted to the increased price and began to take energy-saving measures.

The Costs and Benefits of Monopoly

A monopoly is socially reprehensible in the hands of others.

If a monopoly restricts its output and raises its price above marginal cost, society suffers a deadweight loss. We first examine why such behavior leads to a deadweight loss. Then we use our understanding of how monopolies arise to show that, in certain circumstances, there are benefits associated with monopolies. Indeed, in certain situations, monopoly may be preferable to competition.

The Deadweight Loss of Monopoly

In order to maximize its profit, a monopoly sets its output where its marginal revenue curve intersects its marginal cost curve, as Figure 4.2a shows. The gap between the monopoly's price and marginal cost represents the difference between the value (price) that buyers place on the product and the marginal cost of producing it. This gap is similar to the one caused by a tax on a competitive market (Chapter 3). In both cases, price and output differ from their competitive levels, and there is a deviation between the demand price (as given by the demand curve) and the supply price (as given by the marginal cost curve).

If consumers must pay a monopoly price p_m that is above the competitive price p_c, they lose consumer surplus equal to the sum of the monopoly profits and the deadweight loss in Figure 4.2a. The monopoly profit is less than the consumer surplus loss. Thus, society suffers a deadweight loss (the *DWL* triangle in Figure 4.2a) that equals the consumers' loss less the monopoly's gain. This *DWL* triangle is the area below the demand curve, above the marginal cost curve, and to the right of the equilibrium monopoly quantity.

Thus, both monopoly and an inefficient tax cause a deadweight loss. However, who keeps the transfer from consumers differs: Tax revenues go to the government, whereas the monopoly keeps the monopoly profit. Even fairly small deadweight losses may be associated with a large redistribution of wealth, as the "monopoly profit" box in Figure 4.2a illustrates.

Many researchers have estimated the deadweight loss that monopoly imposes on the U.S. economy. In a pioneering paper, Harberger (1954) calculated that the deadweight loss is small: less than 0.1 percent of the gross national product (GNP: a measure of the value of all goods and services in our economy).[7] Later researchers repeated these calculations based on different assumptions. Worcester (1973), for example, also finds that the *DWL* is small: 0.4 to 0.7 percent. Kamerschen (1966) estimates the *DWL* at 6 percent and Cowling and Mueller (1978) estimate that it is between 4 and 13 percent.[8] Jenny and Weber (1983) find that the *DWL* in France is as high as 7.4 percent.

Rent-Seeking Behavior

The gods help those that help themselves. —*Aesop*

Some researchers contend that the efficiency loss to society is much larger than the *DWL* triangle. They argue that an amount equal to some or all of the monopoly profits is also an efficiency loss.

Monopoly profits can be regarded as a transfer from consumers to the monopoly, just as tax revenues are a transfer of income from consumers to the government. By itself, a transfer of income does not affect efficiency. Only if the monopoly restricts output below competitive levels is there an efficiency effect.

However, Posner (1975) argues that the monopoly profits may also represent a loss to society to the extent that it creates incentives for a firm to use real resources to become a monopoly. For example, suppose that a firm can become a monopoly by persuading the government to pass a law that restricts entry into the market. The use of a firm's resources to hire lobbyists, lawyers, and economists to argue its case before legislators is a cost to society, because these resources could have been productively employed elsewhere.

If there is a positive monopoly profit, as in Figure 4.2a, a firm would be willing to spend an amount up to these profits in order to become a monopoly. Of course, the firm would like to spend as little as possible, but the opportunity to earn monopoly profit could create the incentive to use valuable resources up to the amount of monopoly profits in order to secure the monopoly.[9] Because firms compete to earn the "rent"

[7]Stigler (1956) and Cowling and Mueller (1978) criticize Harberger's methodology on technical grounds.

[8]See, however, Masson and Shaanan (1984) for a critique of this last result.

[9]Whether the firm would dissipate the entire monopoly profit depends on the institutional details as to how the monopoly can be acquired (Fisher 1985).

(monopoly profits) from the monopoly, the expenditure of resources to attain government-created monopoly profits is called **rent seeking**.

If rent seeking occurs, the calculation of the deadweight loss from monopoly must include that part of the transfer that is dissipated by the firms seeking to become the monopoly. Thus, the cost of monopoly is greater than the *DWL* triangle that Harberger calculated: The loss equals the *DWL* triangle plus at least part of the monopoly profits.

Posner recalculates the deadweight loss from regulated and unregulated monopoly on the extreme assumption that the entire amount of monopoly profit is dissipated in rent-seeking activities. His estimates of deadweight loss as a percent of revenues exceed previous estimates. For example, Posner found deadweight losses of up to 30 percent of revenues for some of the industries he examined (such as motor carriers, physician services, and oil). His insight was that a great part of the loss to the economy from monopoly (or, more generally, noncompetitive pricing) is directly traceable to the existence of government institutions that insulate some firms from competition. If he's correct, the recent rescinding of many government regulations (see Chapter 20) will provide sizable benefits to society.

Monopoly Profits and Deadweight Loss Vary with the Elasticity of Demand

Monopoly profits and the *DWL* triangle depend on the shape of the demand curve. We illustrate how monopoly profits and deadweight loss vary with the elasticity of demand with a linear demand curve,

$$p = a - bQ.$$

The light demand curve in Figure 4.3 is for $a = \$60$ and $b = 0.5$. Given a constant marginal and average cost, $MC = AC = \$10$, the monopoly sells $Q_m = 50$ units at $p_m = \$35$, where the elasticity of demand is -1.4. The monopoly's profit is Area $A = \$1{,}250$, and the deadweight loss is area $D = \$625$.[10]

We now rotate the demand curve so as to vary the elasticity of demand. The demand curve is rotated around the point where it crosses the *MC* line, at 100 units. That is, for all the demand curves examined, if price were set efficiently at $MC = \$10$, consumers would buy 100 units. Because the demand curve is linear, the marginal revenue curve is also linear and crosses the horizontal *MC* line at half the distance that the demand curve does. Thus, the profit-maximizing monopoly equilibrium quantity of 50 units is unchanged as we rotate the demand curve.

---

[10]Let $t\ (= [p_m - p_c]/p_c)$ be the monopoly markup above the competitive price. For small t, the monopoly *DWL* triangle can be approximated as

$$-1/2t^2 R\epsilon,$$

where R would be the revenues if the product were sold at the competitive price ($p_c Q_c$) and ϵ is the elasticity of demand. *DWL* does not necessarily rise as the absolute value of ϵ increases because t is inversely related to ϵ, and as t changes, so does R. Holding R constant, *DWL* falls as the absolute value of ϵ increases.

FIGURE 4.3 Monopoly Profits and Deadweight Loss Vary with the Elasticity of Demand

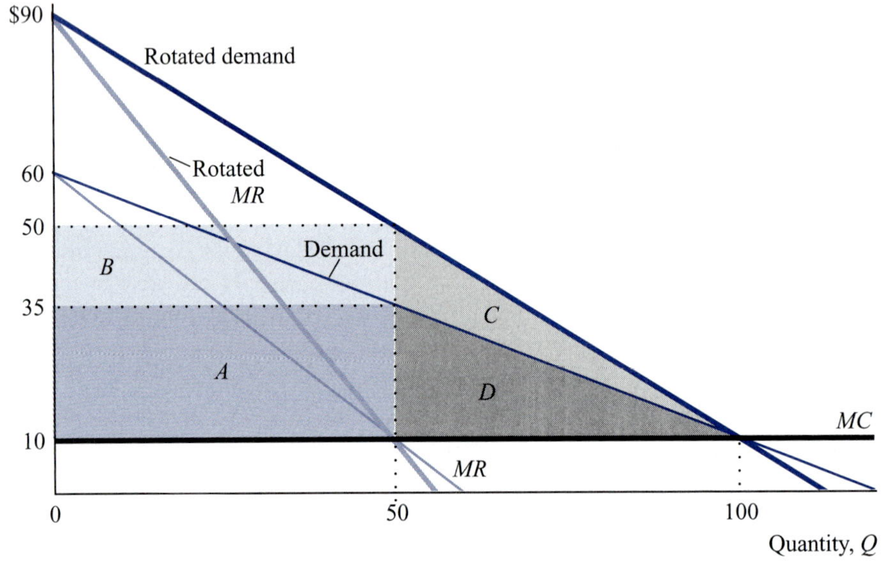

The thick blue demand curve in Figure 4.3 shows a demand curve that has been rotated so that its intercept with the price axis, a, is \$90, which is higher than the original \$60 intercept. The thick blue demand curve intercepts the price axis at \$90. The monopoly sells the same quantity as before, $Q_m = 50$, but at a higher price, $p_m =$ \$50, so that the demand elasticity falls (in absolute value) from -1.40 to -1.25 (becomes less elastic), as Table 4.1 illustrates. The monopoly profit rises to $A + B =$ \$2,000, and the deadweight loss increases to area $C + D =$ \$1,000.

TABLE 4.1 Monopoly Profits and Deadweight Loss Vary with the Price Elasticity of Demand

Intercept of Demand Curve with Price Axis	Elasticity of Demand at $Q = 50$	Monopoly Price	Deadweight Loss	Monopoly Profit
\$ 30	−2.00	\$20	\$ 250	\$ 500
60	−1.40	35	625	1,250
90	−1.25	50	1,000	2,000
120	−1.18	65	1,375	2,750
150	−1.14	80	1,750	3,500

As the demand curve becomes less elastic at the monopoly equilibrium, people are less willing to do without this good: An increase in price causes the quantity they purchase to fall by less than if demand were more elastic. The monopoly, realizing this opportunity exists, increases its equilibrium price and earns a larger monopoly profit. As the demand curve becomes steeper at a given quantity (demand is more inelastic), the deadweight loss increases.

The Benefits of Monopoly

The welfare harms from monopoly may be offset by several benefits. These benefits are ignored in the static analysis above where we calculated deadweight losses. For example, the prospect of receiving monopoly profits may motivate firms to develop new products, improve products, or find lower-cost methods of manufacturing. Were it not for the quest to obtain monopoly profits, firms might innovate less.

The benefit of monopoly is most clearly recognized in research and development (see Chapter 16). If a firm succeeds in developing a new product, it can obtain a patent that prohibits other firms from using the patented technology for a fixed number of years—currently 20 years in the United States. Were it not for the patent, the innovative firm might discover that, within a matter of weeks, other firms had copied the new product. The innovative firm would then receive no more than the competitive level of profits and would not recover its expenditures on research and development. The firms that copied the product would have no research and development expenditure to recover. The ability of other firms to copy a new product removes the innovating firm's incentive to invest in research and development. The patent system attempts to deal with this problem by granting the innovating firm the sole property right to commercially exploit its innovation.

Naturally, if monopoly had no offsetting benefits, competition would be preferable. For example, if all firms in a competitive market decide to merge, and if the merger does not lead to a more efficient market, then the only result is the creation of a monopoly. As long as new entry takes time, the firms could price above their marginal cost. Because there is no benefit from this action, such behavior should be discouraged. One responsibility of the Department of Justice and the Federal Trade Commission is to scrutinize each merger carefully to make sure that its effect is not simply to raise prices to consumers.

Creating and Maintaining a Monopoly

There are several ways in which a firm may become and remain a monopoly. One possibility is that all the firms *merge* (combine into a single firm) or act in concert as a monopoly would. We address these possibilities in detail in Chapter 5 and in Example 4.2. Another possibility is that the firm takes strategic actions that prevent entry by other firms, as we discuss in Chapter 11 and in Example 4.3. Here, we examine three other reasons why a firm is able to create and maintain a monopoly:

EXAMPLE 4.2

Monopolizing by Merging

United States

In 2001, the Federal Trade Commission (FTC) accused the Hearst Corporation of illegally acquiring a monopoly over medical drug databases that are used by pharmacies and hospitals. Hearst bought Medi-Span, which was the only major competitor for Hearst's database company, First DataBank, according to the FTC. The FTC went on to contend that Hearst withheld information necessary for its premerger antitrust review. After Hearst acquired Medi-Span, it raised prices, doubling some and tripling others, according to the FTC and Express Scripts, a pharmacy-benefit management company. In its settlement with the FTC, Hearst agreed to return $19 million to customers. Later, Hearst paid more than $26 million to Express Scripts and other class-action plaintiffs in a private antitrust suit in 2002.

South Africa

South African Breweries controls 98 percent of South Africa's beer sales, with its 14 brands, including Castle, Lion, Heineken, Guinness, Amstel, and Carling Black Label. It was formed by a merger of two major competitors in 1979 because South Africa had virtually no antitrust laws. A company spokesman claims that the firm has little market power because the market is "fully contestable" with no legal barriers to entry. The firm's control of distribution channels may be responsible for its ability to maintain its high market share.

Sources: "FTC Accuses Hearst of Creating Monopoly," *San Francisco Chronicle*, April 15, 2001:D2; "Hearst Settles Dispute with FTC," *Milwaukee Journal Sentinel*, December 15, 2001:D1; Peter Shinkle, "Express Scripts Drops Antitrust Suit vs. Hearst; Maryland Heights Company with Share in FTC Settlement," *St. Louis Post-Dispatch*, May 23, 2002:C11; Donald G. McNeil, Jr., "In South African Beer, Forget Market 'Share'," *New York Times*, August 27, 1997:C1, C4; Bernard Simon, "Private Sector; An Old School Brewer for Miller," *New York Times*, February 2, 2003:3.2.

The firm may have special knowledge, the government may protect it from entry, or the market may only be large enough for a single firm to produce profitably.

Knowledge Advantage

A firm may be a monopoly because only it knows how to produce a certain product or it can produce the product at lower cost than other firms. A firm may have special knowledge that enables it to produce a new or better product that others cannot imitate. The firm may try to keep secret its special knowledge so as to prevent rivals from imitating it (see Example 4.4). A firm with an important secret faces a downward-sloping demand curve for its product and does not fear the entry of rival firms or the introduction of products that are close substitutes.

EXAMPLE 4.3 *Controlling a Key Ingredient*

In 2000, the attorneys general of 33 states and the Federal Trade Commission settled a lawsuit with Mylan Labs (and its suppliers) for $100 million. The suit contended that Mylan Labs cornered the market on the active ingredients for two drugs used to treat Alzheimer patients and then raised the price of the drug Clorazepate more than 3,000 percent (from about 2¢ a tablet to over 75¢) and increased the price of the drug Lorazepam more than 2,000 percent (from about 1¢ a tablet to over 37¢).

Source: **www.state.ia.us/government/ag/mylan.htm**.

Similarly, a firm may have special knowledge about production techniques that enable it to produce the same product at lower cost than other firms, which may be unable to discover the production technique of the efficient firm. We illustrate this possibility in Figure 4.4. Initially all the firms in a competitive market have a constant marginal cost, m_1, so the equilibrium price, p_1, equals m_1 and the equilibrium quantity is Q_1. One firm discovers a new production technique that it can keep secret and that lowers its marginal costs from m_1 to m_0. It faces a *residual demand curve* (the unmet demand after all other firms sell as much as they want at a given price) that is horizontal at p_1 (equal to m_1) up to Q_1 because many firms can produce and sell at price m_1. Beyond Q_1 (prices less than p_1), the residual demand curve coincides with the market demand curve because below p_1 no other firm can profitably produce.

If m_0 is close to m_1, the firm may maximize its profit by selling at a price equal to p_1. However, in Figure 4.4, m_0 is enough less than m_1 that the profit-maximizing monopoly price is less than m_1 but above m_0. Because the residual demand curve has a kink in it at Q_1, the corresponding marginal revenue curve is discontinuous at the output, Q_1. The marginal revenue curve is horizontal where the residual demand curve is horizontal and slopes down where the residual demand curve is downward

EXAMPLE 4.4 *Preventing Imitation—Cat Got Your Tongue?*

Why are violin strings called *catgut* when they are really made of sheep intestines? An old Roman named Erasmo (c. 130 AD) started making strings for musical instruments out of sheep intestine. The demand grew. Because it was considered extremely bad luck to kill a cat, Erasmo identified his product as *catgut* so nobody would imitate it and ruin his monopoly.

Source: L. Boyd, "Grab Bag," *San Francisco Chronicle*, October 27, 1984:35.

FIGURE 4.4 Monopolization Through Efficiency

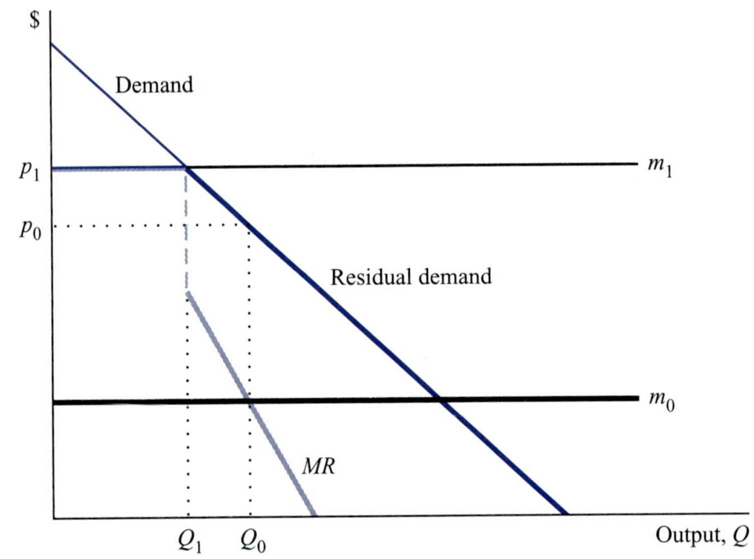

sloping. To maximize its profit, the firm with the secret process produces Q_0 units of output where its marginal revenue curve equals its marginal cost curve. The firm sets its price at p_0, which is less than $p_1 = m_1$, so no other firm remains in the market.

Government-Created Monopolies

A firm may be a monopoly because the government protects it from entry by other firms. For example, suppose a firm invents a new product and realizes that imitation *is* possible technically. In most countries, the original innovating firm can obtain legal protection to prevent entry for some period of time. The law on intellectual property, in particular the patent law, grants a legal monopoly to a firm that has discovered a new product or technique. A firm can obtain a patent (see Chapter 16) on a new product that prevents any other firm from copying its product and competing with it for a fixed period of years.

Aside from the patent laws, other types of government (or government sanctioned) restrictions on entry can serve to create and maintain monopolies. Generally, government restrictions on entry allow at least a few firms to produce, but they prevent the normal competitive forces from driving price and profits down to competitive levels (see Example 4.5).

For example, in many cities, one must purchase medallions, of which only a fixed number are sold by local authorities, to operate a taxicab. The United States, by granting exclusive (monopoly) rights to portions of the electromagnetic spectrum, gave broadcast television stations at least $40 billion in present-value terms for the first 30 years of television (Isé and Perloff 1997).

EXAMPLE 4.5 *Protecting a Monopoly*

An 1872 law established the U.S. Postal Service (USPS) monopoly on mail delivery. In 1971, the USPS started an express mail service. A 1979 amendment to the 1872 law broke the agency's monopoly on urgent mail, establishing as the definition of *urgent,* mail that must arrive by noon the next day or lose its value. However, the USPS has the right to decide what is urgent and what is not.

How serious was the Postal Service's competition on express mail? By 1994, the USPS's share of the express mail market had fallen to just under 15 percent. Worse, to the horror of postal officials, the federal government contracted with Federal Express for next-day delivery of government parcels at a price of $3.75, well below the Postal Service's overnight Express Mail rate of $9.95.

The USPS fought back. From 1990 through 1993, the Postal Service fined 21 companies for violating the USPS's legal monopoly on mail delivery, collecting more than $542,000 in fines from these companies that sent "nonurgent" mail by private couriers such as Federal Express, UPS, and DHL.

For example, an Atlanta-based credit-reporting company, Equifax Inc., was assessed a $30,000 penalty, making up the loss to the Postal Service for routine business mail it sent by express services. Postal officials say they recovered $4 in lost revenue for every $1 spent on enforcement.

In 1994, the USPS issued a postal inspectors' audit that found that five federal agencies—the General Services Administration (GSA) and the departments of Agriculture, Health and Human Services, Treasury, and Energy—routinely infringed on the USPS's monopoly on first-class mail by using Federal Express to ship materials that were not time sensitive.

The report warned that the agencies, which accounted for one-third of the 4.3 million government packages moved by Federal Express in the first two years of the contract, "are incurring a substantial liability for postage"—the revenue that would have otherwise gone to the Postal Service. The USPS did not demand any payments for the postage, but postal officials pressured the GSA to train federal mailroom personnel as to what kind of materials they can legally send by Federal Express.

Armed with news reports of USPS fines on private firms and pressure on federal agencies, outraged private companies went to Congress for legislation ending the Postal Service's practices. Smarting from bad publicity and congressional pressure, the USPS announced that it would cease its practice of raiding businesses to check up on their use of commercial overnight delivery services, and stopped complaining about federal agencies. Nice try, though.

Sources: Michael A. Goldstein, "Can the U.S. Postal Service Market Itself to Success?" *Los Angeles Times Magazine,* December 22, 1996:14; Bloomberg News, "UPS Aims to Curb Postal Service Monopoly," *The Dallas Morning News,* April 14, 1998:9D; Bill McAllister. "Must It Get There Overnight?: Agencies Improperly Bypassing Postal Service, Inspectors Report," *Washington Post,* January 12, 1994:A17; "Private Couriers and Postal Service Slug It Out," *New York Times,* February 14, 1994:D2.

Until recently, U.S. states required someone wishing to build an in-patient medical facility to obtain a certificate of need by demonstrating that a new facility was needed. Using these laws, an early entrant could make entry by potential competitors difficult. In part because of these laws, Community Psychiatric Centers, a chain of psychiatric hospitals in the United States and Britain, had annual earnings growth of 15 to 30 percent between 1969 when it went public and 1985.[11]

Similarly, trade barriers can be used to prevent entry. For example, in 1992, the Ontario government agency that monopolizes the sale of beer in that province, the Liquor Control Board of Ontario, announced a ban on American beer imports. Similarly, China places a 230 percent tariff (tax on foreign products) on foreign cigarettes to protect the China National Tobacco Corporation, which sells 1.75 trillion of the 5 trillion cigarettes sold throughout the world and accounts for 12 percent of the revenue of the Chinese government.[12]

Natural Monopoly

In some markets, it is efficient for only one firm to produce all of the output. When total production costs would rise if two or more firms produced instead of one, the single firm in a market is called a **natural monopoly**.

A firm is a natural monopoly if it can produce the market quantity, Q, at lower cost than can two or more firms. Let $q_1, \cdots, q_k$ be the output of the k (≥ 2) firms in a market that produce an identical product so that total market output equals the sum of the firms' output: $Q = q_1 + \cdots + q_k$. If each firm has a cost function $C(q_i)$ and one firm can produce Q at lower cost than the sum of the k firms,

$$C(Q) < C(q_1) + C(q_2) + \cdots + C(q_k),$$

then the least expensive (most efficient) way to produce is to have one firm produce all Q units. A cost function is said to be *subadditive* at Q if this inequality holds, so subadditivity is a necessary condition for the existence of a natural monopoly (Sharkey 1982; Baumol, Panzar, and Willig 1982).

A natural monopoly often has falling average costs and constant or falling marginal costs in the region in which it operates. A strictly decreasing average cost curve implies subadditivity (though the opposite does not necessarily follow).

Suppose that the average cost curve of a natural monopoly is downward sloping, and that the firm can produce 100 units at an average cost of $10 per unit. The firm's total cost of producing that many units is $1,000. Now suppose that a second firm with identical costs enters the market. If each of these two firms produces 50 units, their average cost of production is higher than before because the average cost curve is downward sloping. If their average cost is $15 per unit, for example, their combined

---

[11] See **www.aw-bc.com/carlton_perloff** "Model of Insanity."

[12] Glenn Collins, "U.S. Tobacco Industry Looks Longingly at Chinese Market, but in Vain," *New York Times*, November 20, 1998:A10.

total cost of producing 100 units is $1,500. Thus, a single firm can produce 100 units at lower cost than can two firms.

It is often argued (but may not be true) that electrical, gas, telephone, and cable television are natural monopolies. There is a relatively high fixed cost for running an electric power line or a phone line to a home or firm, but constant or falling marginal costs of supplying the service. As a result, marginal cost is constant or falls, and average cost falls as output increases.[13]

If production is characterized by economies of scale everywhere, then average cost declines as output increases, and it is always less costly for one firm to produce any given output than for several firms to produce that output. Therefore, when average cost falls with output, there is a natural monopoly. A natural monopoly can occur even if average cost is not declining everywhere with output. For example, if a U-shaped average cost curve reaches a minimum at an output of 100, it may be most efficient for only one firm to produce an output of 101 even though average cost is rising at that output. Therefore, economies of scale are a sufficient but not a necessary condition for natural monopoly.[14]

Profits and Monopoly

Many people associate high profits with monopoly or too little competition, normal profits with competition, and losses with excessive competition. Although each of these beliefs has some element of truth, none is correct. We now show why these beliefs do not hold in general by answering three questions: (1) Is anyone who earns positive profits a monopoly? (2) Does a monopoly always earn positive profits? (3) Should the government allow mergers that create monopoly in a market that was suffering short-run losses?

Is Any Firm That Earns a Positive Profit a Monopoly?

Although a monopoly may earn positive profits, it does not follow that any firm that earns a positive profit is a monopoly. The previous chapter discusses the possibility that certain scarce resources, such as land, can earn rents. For example, a wheat farmer who owns particularly productive land earns a large profit. This profit is attributable to the land that is owned and should properly be called a rent. The farmer behaves competitively, taking price as given and operating where price equals marginal cost. This

[13]The empirical literature, however, leaves some doubt as to whether many utilities exhibit increasing returns to scale, which implies downward-sloping marginal and average cost curves. Moreover, showing that there are scale economies in one range of output is not sufficient to demonstrate that a firm is a natural monopoly (that is, the cost function is subadditive). See, for example, Fuss and Waverman (1981) and Evans and Heckman (1982a, 1982b). Shin and Ying (1992) argue that local telephone exchange carriers were not natural monopolies prior to deregulation. Friedlaender (1992) finds evidence of substantial returns to scale for railroads.

[14]In Chapter 20, we examine how governments regulate natural monopolies and the conditions under which other firms will try to enter a market with a natural monopoly.

farm is a competitive firm; rents on factors of production do not indicate a monopoly. As long as output is not restricted so that price equals marginal cost, there is no market power. Scarce resources can command very high prices and those who own those resources benefit. For example, star athletes earn high salaries (rents) even though they are not monopolies that restrict output.

Does a Monopoly Always Earn a Positive Profit?

Although a monopoly earns a larger profit than a competitive firm would, it is not true that a monopoly always earns a positive profit. In the short run, a monopoly can make losses, just as a competitive firm can. A monopoly that faces a sudden decline in demand may continue to operate even though it makes a negative short-run profit (its price is less than its average cost) if its price is above its average variable cost. Losses in a market do not imply that it is competitive. In the long run, when there are no sunk costs, no firm continues to operate if there are only losses in the market.

As in competition, the length of time that losses will be earned by a monopoly depends on how long the short run lasts—how long it takes for the plant and equipment to wear out, forcing a decision on whether to replace them. In some markets, the short run may be very long. For example, railroad tracks can last for years or possibly decades. Therefore, one might expect that a monopoly railroad could earn a negative profit on its investments for a long time before deciding to exit the market.

Briefly, in the long run, a competitive firm makes zero economic profit, whereas a monopoly makes a zero or positive profit. In the short run, both competitive firms and monopolies may make losses or profits.

Are Monopoly Mergers to Eliminate Short-Run Losses Desirable?

A merger of firms into a monopoly can eliminate competition and allow the merged firm to exercise market power and raise price so that the losses are eliminated. Firms in a market where all firms are losing money often argue for a merger for this reason (see Example 4.6). This motivation for merger appears to have a certain logical appeal—if

EXAMPLE 4.6 *EU Allows Merger to Eliminate Losses*

In 2003, the European Union allowed Rupert Murdoch's News Corporation to merge Telepiu, which had two-thirds of all pay-TV subscribers in Italy, with its own Italian pay-TV firm, Stream, to create a new firm called Sky. EU Competition Commissioner Mario Monti conceded that his decision "will create a quasi-monopoly on the Italian market." He justified his actions by saying that a weak business environment allowed room for only one firm to survive in this market, as both Stream and Telepiu had been losing money.

Source: Raf Casert, "EU Commission Allows Murdoch's News Corp. to Forge 'Quasi-Monopoly' in Italian Pay TV," Associated Press, April 2, 2003.

the merger eliminates the losses, perhaps it is efficient for the merger to occur. However, such a merger harms society!

If a merger enables firms to set a price in the short run that is greater than the level at which they would have priced had they remained competitive, then the merger imposes a deadweight loss on society. The existence of sunk costs in the short run that cause short-run losses cannot be eliminated by merging firms. The merger only changes the amount of competition that firms face. Because the merger does not eliminate sunk costs, it is inefficient to allow firms to form a monopoly and thus allow the price to rise.

Monopsony

A single buyer in a market is called a **monopsony**. A monopsony's decision on how much to buy affects the price it must pay (just as a monopoly's choice of output affects the price it receives). The monopsony decides how much to purchase by choosing a price-quantity pair on the market supply curve. Monopsony is the flip side of monopoly. Both a monopoly and a monopsony recognize that their actions affect the market price.

A monopsony determines how much to buy in much the same way that a monopoly determines how much to produce. A monopsony buys more of the good as long as the value of the extra consumption as given by its demand curve equals or exceeds its marginal cost of consuming one more unit.

If there is a competitive labor market, each firm takes the wage rate as given, and the marginal cost of hiring one more worker is simply the wage rate. Now suppose there is only one local employer (buyer of labor services): a monopsony. In Figure 4.5,

FIGURE 4.5 Deadweight Loss from Monopsony

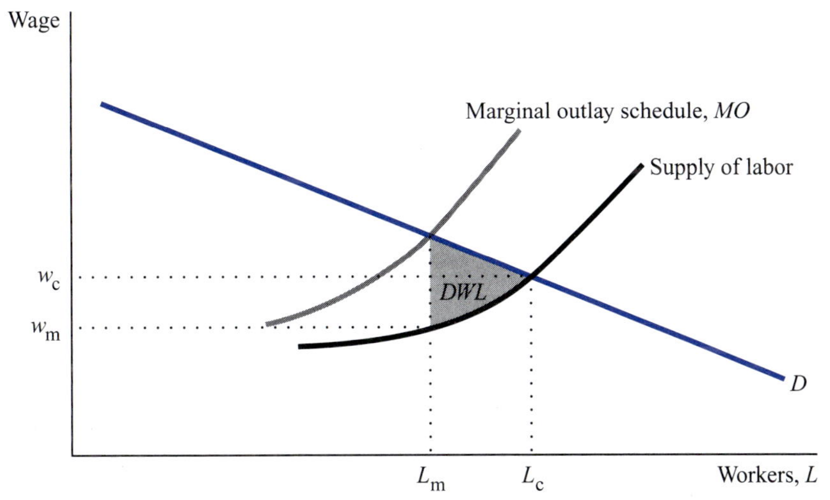

it faces an upward-sloping supply curve for labor. In order to hire an extra worker, the monopsony must not only pay that worker a slightly higher wage rate but also pay *all* its other workers a slightly higher wage rate, because only by raising the wage can extra labor be induced into the marketplace.

If the monopsony must raise its wage from, say, \$5 to \$6 to induce that last individual to work for the firm, the monopsony's extra cost of hiring the additional worker is not just \$6; it is \$6 plus the \$1 increase in wages that must be passed along to each of its original workers. If it originally had 100 workers, its total wage bill rises from \$500 to \$606: an increase of \$106. The monopsony recognizes that *its* marginal cost of hiring the additional worker is \$106 rather than \$6 and takes that into account in deciding whether to hire the additional worker. The monopsony hires an extra worker only if the marginal benefit as given by its labor demand curve exceeds its marginal cost of hiring an additional worker.

The marginal cost to a monopsony of buying additional units (hiring additional workers) is described by a **marginal outlay schedule**, which is analogous to a marginal revenue curve. As Figure 4.5 illustrates, the marginal outlay schedule lies above the upward-sloping supply curve because the monopsony must raise the wage for all its workers to hire an extra worker. A profit-maximizing monopsony hires L_m workers, where its marginal benefit, as given by its demand curve, equals its marginal outlay. Because the marginal outlay curve lies above the supply curve, the monopsony hires fewer workers, L_m, than would a competitive market, which hires L_c workers (determined by the intersection of the demand curve and the supply curve). In other words, a monopsony restricts output just as a monopoly does.

The monopsony wage rate, w_m, is below the competitive wage rate, w_c. Using a definition analogous to the one for market power, we can define monopsony power as the ability to profitably set wages (or other input prices) below competitive levels. At the monopsony solution (L_m, w_m) in Figure 4.5, there is a gap between the demand curve and the supply curve. A gap between the demand curve (which represents the marginal benefit to society of consumption) and the supply curve (which represents the marginal cost to society) reflects a loss in efficiency. The monopsony deadweight loss triangle (Figure 4.5) is analogous to the deadweight loss that results from monopoly (Figure 4.2a).

Most labor economists believe there are few monopsonized labor markets in the United States. Example 4.7 identifies one such market. The most frequent examples given of monopsony in the labor market concern single-company towns, local employment markets, and sports leagues. For example, a major league baseball player can work in the United States only if he plays for a team that belongs to either the American or National Leagues. Collectively, these teams are the sole buyer in the United States for the services of a major league baseball player. To the degree that the teams agree not to compete for players, they gain monopsony power. To offset such monopsony power, baseball players can form a union to obtain monopoly power in selling their labor services.

Monopsony is most likely in markets where resources are specialized to a few uses. Moreover, even if resources are initially specialized to one use, as with a piece of custom-designed machinery (or a plant in a specific location serving a single buyer),

EXAMPLE 4.7 *Priest Monopsony*

Newspapers repeatedly report a "shortage" of Catholic priests, citing sources both inside and outside the church hierarchy. Between 1960 and 2000, the number of priests declined 13 percent even as 55 percent more Catholics had joined their local parishes. Strikingly, other religious denominations are not suffering from a "shortage of clergy."

Why the difference between churches? Is it due to changing tastes among potential priests or some other factor? Daniel Condon (2002) attributes the difference to the fact that the Catholic Church exercises monopsony power, whereas other churches and synagogues permit an active, competitive labor market for clergy. Individual Catholic parishes do not compete for clergy, who are instead assigned by the central church authority (diocese). Wages vary little across parishes, although priests in wealthy parishes may receive larger fees for performing wedding and funeral services.*

Condon estimates that Catholic priests earn 41 percent less than non-Catholic officiants, controlling for education, experience, location, and whether they are provided rent-free housing. He concludes (p. 894) that the true differential is "more pronounced when one considers that Catholic clergy have a condition of employment (celibacy) that would require additional monetary compensation for most."

*Academics at a Catholic university may face an even greater problem. For them, it's publish or parish.

monopsony may not persist in the long run. The reason is that no one will make new custom-designed machinery (or new investments in a plant) for a specific buyer if they earn a depressed return compared to what they can earn from making other machines (or building a plant elsewhere). In other words, few resources are specialized in the long run, and therefore it is unlikely that monopsony can persist in the long run.

Another way to explain the preceding point is as follows. If resources are not specialized to a particular market in the long run, then the long-run supply curve tends to be flat (highly elastic). As Chapter 3 explained, a flat long-run supply curve is most likely to occur when the market in question uses only a relatively small fraction of the total consumption of its inputs. Long-run monopsony power is impossible if the long-run supply curve is flat because price cannot be lowered below the competitive price.

If the long-run supply curve is flat, there may not be any monopsony power even in the short run. Suppose that before a firm enters a market, it has many alternative uses for the resources it owns. After it enters the market, it specializes its machines so that it has very few alternative uses for its assets. Suppose that it will only enter a particular market if it receives \$10 per unit of output (which is the long-run average cost). The sole buyer, the monopsony, agrees to pay \$10. After the firm enters, it is committed, at least for some time, in the sense that its machines are specialized to this particular market. If the monopsony lowers its price to \$9, it may not pay for the firm to exit immediately. But the firm will not replace the specialized machines when they wear out, and the monopsony may eventually have no one willing to supply the product. Even if the buyer again promises \$10 per unit to induce a supplier to enter, no firm would believe the buyer in light of its previous behavior. So, for a buyer that is concerned about a long-run source of supply, it may not pay to exercise short-run monopsony power.

Dominant Firm with a Competitive Fringe

Where does the gorilla sleep?
Anywhere the gorilla wants to sleep.

What happens to a monopoly if other, higher-cost firms enter its market? Or, similarly, what happens if a lower-cost firm enters a market with many price-taking, higher-cost firms? After entry, the lower-cost firm has a relatively large share of the market. If one firm is a price setter and faces smaller, price-taking firms, it is called a **dominant firm**. It typically has a large market share. The smaller, price-taking firms, called **fringe firms**, each have a very small share of the market, though collectively they may have a substantial share of the market.

There are several industries in which one firm has a large share of the industry sales. For example, Kodak's share of the photographic film business has been estimated at 65 percent.[15] Hewlett-Packard is estimated to have 59 percent of laser printer sales.

We begin by discussing what makes a firm dominant. We then analyze how entry limits a dominant firm's market power. We examine two extreme cases. In the first, entry by other firms is impossible. In the second, entry by competing fringe firms can occur instantaneously. The analysis shows that a dominant firm's price-setting behavior depends on the ease of entry by fringe firms.

We draw two main conclusions. First, it is generally not in a profit-maximizing dominant firm's best interest to set its price so low that it drives all competitive-fringe firms out of the market. Second, the presence of competitive-fringe firms or the threat of entry by additional firms may force a dominant firm to set a price lower than the price a monopoly would set (see Example 4.8).

If a sufficiently large number of price-taking firms can enter the market, a dominant firm cannot continue to charge a price higher than the minimum average cost of these new firms. Indeed, if potential entrants' costs are as low as the dominant firm's, the dominant firm eventually has no more market power than any other firm.

[15] A firm's share of sales in an industry depends crucially on how the industry is defined, and hence is often controversial, especially in court proceedings.

EXAMPLE 4.8 *Price Umbrella*

It is often asserted that a dominant firm provides a *pricing umbrella* for smaller firms. As long as competing firms price at or below the level of the dominant firm, they will be able to find buyers. If their products are inferior (say because they are risky to use for legal reasons), the fringe firms have to set their prices substantially below the dominant firm's.

In many countries, phone monopolies charge rates that are more than twice those in the United States, where competition has kept rates relatively low. This price difference causes problems for the monopolies.

"Callback" services offer some customers a way to evade paying high monopoly prices. A callback service provides a "trigger" number connected to a computer in the United States. The customer calls that number using the monopoly service and hangs up before the phone is answered, paying nothing for the incomplete call. The computer calls the customers back and offers an American dial tone, which can be used to place a call anywhere in the world for rates well below the monopoly price. In some cases, the callback rates are less than the price of a local call. Hundreds of American companies provide these services, and the rate of use has grown exponentially over time. Ghana's monopoly is reported to lose $1 million each week to callback and Internet services.

To protect local monopolies, governments in many countries—including Argentina, Canada's Northwest Territories, China, Malaysia, Saudi Arabia, South Korea, and Uganda—try to stop these services. The U.S. operators believe they are beyond the reach of local laws. For example, when Uganda blocked all calls to the Seattle, Washington, area code where one service, Kallback, is based, the company routed the calls through a different area. When other countries tried to identify and block the services by picking up the touch-tone beeps used to complete calls, Kallback added a voice-recognition system. As a firm spokesman said, "It's a cat and mouse game. It's kind of fun."

Source: "Don't Call US," *The Economist,* 338(7947), January 6, 1996:55; **www.kallback.com**; "Telecom Loses $1m a Week, Communications Experts Say," *Ghanaian Chronicle,* February 7, 2003.

Why Some Firms Are Dominant

All animals are equal, but some animals are more equal than others.

—George Orwell

Why do some firms gain substantial market power, while others do not? At least three possible reasons are sufficient to create a dominant firm-competitive fringe market structure.

The first reason is that *dominant firms may have lower costs than fringe firms.* There are at least four major causes of lower costs:

- A firm may be more efficient than its rivals. For example, it may have better management or better technology that allows it to produce at lower costs. Such a technological advantage may be protected by a patent.
- An early entrant to a market may have lower costs from having learned by experience how to produce more efficiently.
- An early entrant may have had time to grow large optimally (in the presence of adjustment costs) so as to benefit from economies of scale. By spreading fixed costs over more units of output, it may have lower average costs of production than a new entrant could instantaneously achieve.
- The government may favor the original firm. The U.S. Postal Service does not pay taxes or highway user fees, which reduces its cost relative to that of competing package delivery services.

A second important reason is that *a dominant firm may have a superior product* in a market where each firm produces a differentiated product. This superiority may be due to a reputation achieved through advertising or through goodwill generated by its having been in the market longer.

A third reason is that *a group of firms may collectively act as a dominant firm.* As Chapter 5 shows, groups of firms in a market have an incentive to coordinate their activities to increase their profits. A group of firms that explicitly acts collectively to promote its best interests is called a *cartel.* If all the firms in a market coordinate their activities, then the cartel is effectively a monopoly; if only some of them do so, then the group acts as a dominant firm facing a competitive fringe of noncooperating firms.

One example of a dominant firm is the cartel consisting of Philippine coconut-oil-producing firms that act in concert but face a fringe of firms in other countries that act as price takers. With nearly four-fifths of the world's export market, the Philippine cartel has dominant-firm market power with a Lerner Index of 0.89 (Buschena and Perloff 1991).

Whether a dominant firm can exercise market power in the long run depends crucially on the number of firms that can enter the market, how their production costs compare to those of the dominant firm, and how fast they can enter. We now examine the dominant firm-competitive fringe model under two alternative extreme assumptions about the ease of entry.

The No-Entry Model

Consider a market with a dominant firm and a competitive fringe in which no additional fringe firms can enter. Two key results emerge from an analysis of this model: (1) It is more profitable to be the *gorilla* of a market than a mere fringe firm. (2) The existence of the fringe limits the dominant firm's market power—that is, it is more profitable to be the only firm in a market (a monopoly) than merely a dominant firm.

Assumptions. Five crucial assumptions underlie this no-entry model:

1. *There is one firm that is much larger than any other firm because of its lower production costs.* Although a market may be characterized by a small group of relatively large firms rather than a single dominant firm, we concentrate on the case of the single dominant firm for simplicity.
2. *All firms, except the dominant firm, are price takers,* determining their output levels by setting marginal cost equal to the market price (p).
3. *The number of firms (n) in the competitive fringe is fixed: No new entry can occur.* That is, the dominant firm knows that it can raise the market's price without causing new firms to enter the market or existing firms to build additional plants.
4. *The dominant firm knows the market's demand curve, $D(p)$.* Each firm produces a homogeneous product, so that there is a single price in this market.
5. *The dominant firm can predict how much output the competitive fringe will produce at any given price;* that is, it knows the competitive fringe's supply curve, $S(p)$.

The first three assumptions determine that this market has a dominant firm facing a competitive fringe with no more than n firms. The last two assumptions ensure that the dominant firm knows enough to be able to set its output level optimally.

The Dominant Firm's Reasoning. Suppose you ran the dominant firm. How would you choose your output level? Given your firm's large size, you could drive up the market's price by restricting your output. Unfortunately for you, as your dominant firm lowers its output and price rises, the competitive fringe output increases because the fringe supply curve, $S(p)$, is increasing in p. As a result, market output falls less than you would like, and the market price does not rise as high as it would if your firm had a monopoly.

Thus, your dominant firm's problem is much more complex than that of a monopoly, which merely needs to consider the market demand curve (with its corresponding marginal revenue curve) and its marginal cost curve to determine its profit-maximizing output. Your dominant firm, in contrast, must consider not only those factors, but also how the competitive fringe responds to your actions.

To maximize your profits, you must take the competitive fringe's actions into account when setting your policy. A convenient way to calculate your optimal price level is to do the following thought experiment. For lack of an ability to stop them, let the fringe firms sell as much as they want at the market price: the price you set. Except at the very highest prices, the competitive fringe does not produce enough to meet all of the market's demand. Your dominant firm, then, is in a monopoly position with respect to this residual demand. Thus, you can determine your optimal output by a two-step procedure. First, determine your firm's residual demand curve; then, act like a monopoly with respect to the residual demand. This two-step procedure can be illustrated with the use of graphs.

A Graphic Analysis of Dominant-Firm Behavior. The first step is to determine the long-run residual demand curve facing the dominant firm. Figure 4.6 shows two graphs: (a) one for a representative competitive-fringe firm and for the entire competitive fringe, and (b) one for the dominant firm.

FIGURE 4.6 The Dominant Firm and the Competitive Fringe

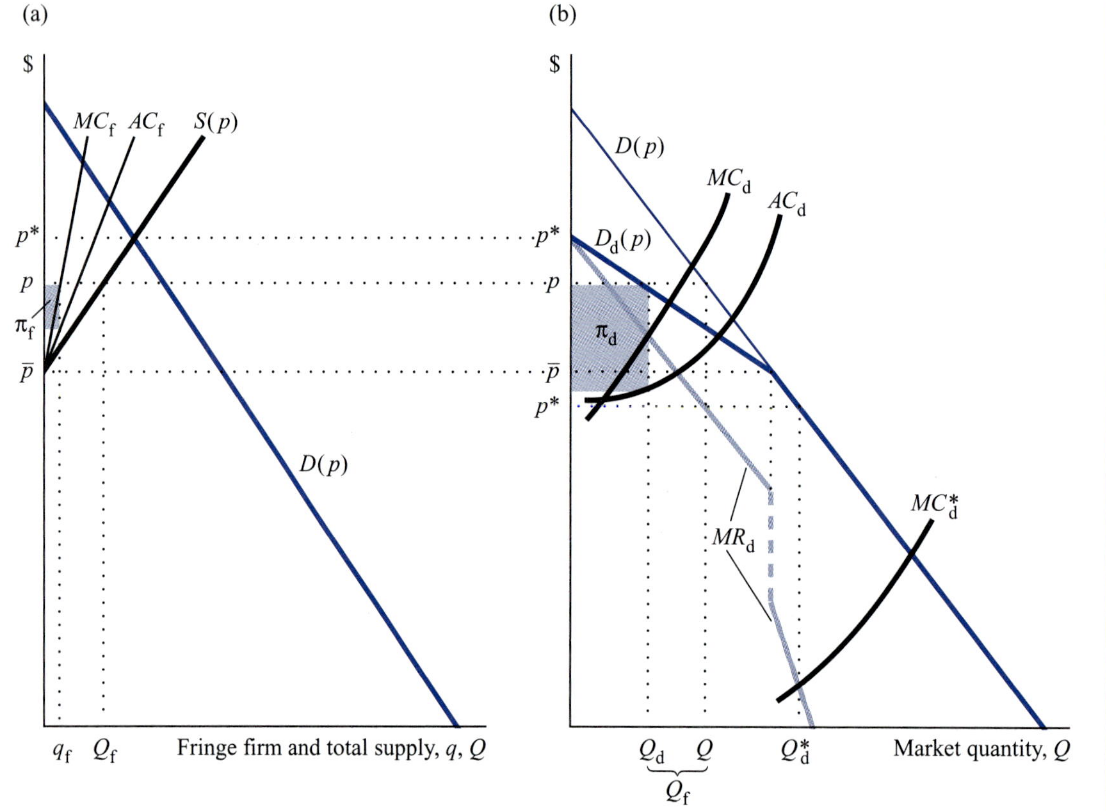

The graph on the left, Figure 4.6a, shows the market demand curve, $D(p)$, and the supply curve of a typical, price-taking, competitive-fringe firm. The fringe firm's supply curve is its marginal cost curve above the minimum of its average cost curve $\bar{p}$. That is, the fringe firm's shutdown price is $\bar{p}$. Above $\bar{p}$, each fringe firm makes positive economic profits. At $\bar{p}$, each fringe firm makes zero profits and is indifferent between operating and shutting down.[16] Below $\bar{p}$, each firm shuts down, and the dominant firm is a monopoly.

The competitive fringe's supply curve, $S(p)$, is the horizontal summation of the individual fringe firm's supply curves, as Figure 4.6 shows. That is, $S(p) = nq_f(p)$, where n is the number of firms and q_f is the output of a typical fringe firm.

[16] As drawn, each fringe firm produces essentially no output at $\bar{p}$. If the firms had the usual U-shaped average cost curves, however, they would produce a positive amount of output at that price.

The dominant firm's residual demand curve is the horizontal difference between the market demand curve and the competitive fringe's supply curve:

$$D_d(p) = D(p) - S(p).$$

In Figure 4.6b, the market demand curve (thin blue line) is above the residual demand curve (heavy blue line) at prices above $\bar{p}$ and equal to it at prices below $\bar{p}$. That is, the fringe firms meet some or all of the market demand if price is above $\bar{p}$, but they drop out of the market and leave all of the demand to the dominant firm if price falls below $\bar{p}$. At p^*, the quantity that the fringe supplies equals the quantity that the market demands, so the dominant firm has no residual demand.

The dominant firm maximizes its profits by picking a price (or equivalent, an output level) so that its marginal cost equals its marginal revenue. The dominant firm's marginal revenue curve (MR_d) is derived from its residual demand curve and has two distinct sections. If the competitive fringe produces positive levels of output, the dominant firm's residual demand curve lies below (and is flatter than) the market demand curve. The dominant firm's marginal revenue curve, MR_d, in this region is flatter than the marginal revenue curve in the region where the dominant firm's residual demand curve and the market demand curve are coincident. There is a discrete jump between the two sections of the marginal revenue curve at the point where the residual demand curve and the market demand curve meet.

The dominant firm behaves as a monopoly would with respect to the residual demand; it sets its price (or output) so that its marginal cost equals marginal revenue. Because the marginal revenue curve has two sections, there are two possible types of equilibria; which one occurs depends on the dominant firm's cost curves.

We now consider two types of markets:

1. The dominant firm charges a high price, so that it makes economic profits and the fringe firms also make profits or break even.
2. The dominant firm sets a price so low that the fringe firms shut down to avoid making losses. The dominant firm is now a monopoly.

The Dominant Firm–Competitive Fringe Equilibrium

The first type of equilibrium occurs if the dominant firm's costs are not substantially less than those of the fringe firms.[17] The dominant firm's marginal cost curve, MC_d, crosses the first downward-sloping segment of the marginal revenue curve, MR_d, in Figure 4.6b.

The dominant firm chooses to produce Q_d level of output at price p (the height of the residual demand curve at the output level Q_d). At the price level p, the difference between the market demand, Q, and the dominant firm's output, Q_d, is the competitive fringe's supply, Q_f (which is shown in Figures 4.6a and 4.6b). If the dominant

[17]A mathematical analysis of this case is presented at **www.aw-bc.com/carlton_perloff** "Dominant Firm and Competitive Fringe Model."

firm's costs are this high, it does not drive the competitive fringe out of business. Its own profits are maximized at a price so high that the fringe firms make positive profits.

In most markets, positive economic profits would attract new entrants. In this market, however, no new firms can enter (by assumption), so both the dominant firm and the competitive fringe firms can make positive profits forever. In Figure 4.6b, the dominant firm's profits are labeled π_d. The profits of a typical fringe firm are positive as well (because $p > \bar{p}$), and a typical fringe firm's profits are shown as π_f in Figure 4.6a. Because the dominant firm's average cost is lower than that of the fringe firms (minimum $AC_d < \bar{p}$), the dominant firm makes more profits per unit (average profits), and it also sells more units than an individual fringe firm, so it must make more total profits as well.

Thus, the dominant firm maximizes its profits by charging a price so high that it loses some of its market share to the competitive fringe. It does not make sense for the dominant firm to set its price so low that it drives the fringe out of business, even though that would increase the number of units of output the dominant firm could sell. After all, few good business people accept the argument, "I lose a little on every sale, but make up for it in volume."

The dominant firm makes lower profits than it would if it were a monopoly and the fringe did not exist. The fringe can only hurt the dominant firm and benefit consumers. For example, in 1993, NEC Corporation, which then controlled half of all personal computer sales in Japan, had to cut its prices roughly in half due to increased competition from U.S. fringe firms.

The Dominant Firm as Monopoly. Now, suppose that the dominant firm has extremely low costs compared to the fringe firms, so that its marginal cost curve is MC^*_d in Figure 4.6b. Notice that MC^*_d crosses MR_d in the lower part of its two downward-sloping sections. The dominant firm chooses to produce Q^*_d level of output at price p^* (the height of the residual demand curve at output level Q^*_d). Because p^* is below the fringe firms' shutdown point ($\bar{p}$ = their minimum average cost), the fringe firms produce nothing ($Q^*_f = 0$). As a result, market output, Q^*, equals the dominant firm's output, Q^*_d.

The dominant firm sets a monopoly price, and no competitive-fringe firm enters. The dominant firm meets all the demand of the market, unchecked by the fringe, and is thus a monopoly. The reason it has a monopoly is that MC^*_d intersects MR_d along the segment of MR_d that is the same as the marginal revenue curve associated with the market demand curve. That is, the monopoly price is below $\bar{p}$, so no fringe firm wants to produce.

A Model with Free, Instantaneous Entry

If unlimited entry is possible, a dominant firm cannot set as high a price as it can if entry is limited or prevented. This section retains all the assumptions made in the preceding section except that now an unlimited number of competitive-fringe firms may enter the market. Firms enter if they can make positive profits.

In this situation, fringe firms cannot make profits in the long run; they either break even or are driven out of business. If identical fringe firms produce at all, the market

EXAMPLE 4.9

China Tobacco Monopoly to Become a Dominant Firm

Established in 1982, the Chinese government's tobacco monopoly, the China National Tobacco Corporation, has been the most profitable corporation in the world, accounting for 12% of the Chinese government's revenues. It sells to China's 310 million smokers, a quarter of the world's smoking population, who consume 1,700 billion cigarettes a year—about 30% of global consumption.

By imposing a 230% tax rate on foreign cigarettes, and by imposing import quotas and restrictions (such as designating only a few sales outlets for imported cigarettes), the government limited legal foreign cigarette sales to less than 2% of total Chinese sales in the late 1990s. By 2003, their share was only 10%.

To appease the World Trade Organization (WTO), China has agreed to lift restrictions on the retail sale of imported cigarettes by January 2004, to reduce the tariff on cigarettes from the current 65% to 24%, and to phase out the tariff over the next two years.

Thus, the state's monopoly will be turned into a dominant firm. Government officials expect that the price of imported cigarettes will drop in half, and that they will gain a major share of the market.

Sources: Glenn Collins, "U.S. Tobacco Industry Looks Longingly at the Chinese Market, but in Vain," *New York Times*, November 20, 1998:A10; "China to Lift Restrictions on Retail Sales of Imported Cigarettes Next Year," *AFX European Focus*, February 11, 2003; "Remove of Foreign Tobaccos Retailing Licenses to Cut Prices by Half" (sic), *China News*, February 14, 2003:1; "Chinese Tobacco Industry Facing Mergers and Recapitalizations," *China Business Times*, February 17, 2003:1.

price ultimately can go no higher than a fringe firm's minimum average cost, so that fringe firms always just break even. After all, if they made positive profits, more firms would flood into the market and drive price down to the level where each earns zero economic profits. Because the dominant firm has lower costs than fringe firms, it makes positive profits, but its profits are lower than if entry did not occur.

Even with unlimited entry, the dominant firm can gain and hold indefinitely a large share of the market if it has some cost or other advantage (see Example 4.9). Another example is the Cheerleader Supply Co., which accounts for 60 percent of cheerleading uniforms and equipment sold in this country.[18] This is an industry with easy entry, and yet one firm has the lion's share of the market, presumably because it has superior products, a superior sales force, lower costs, or has generated goodwill with buyers.

The competitive-fringe firms' cost curves are the same as before. As more and more firms enter (n rises), the slope of the competitive-fringe supply curve becomes flatter

[18]According to its chief executive officer, Lawrence Herkimer, in Peter Applebome, "The World's Oldest and Fattest Cheerleader," *San Francisco Chronicle*, January 12, 1984:24.

FIGURE 4.7 Dominant Firm with Free, Instantaneous Entry by Fringe Firms

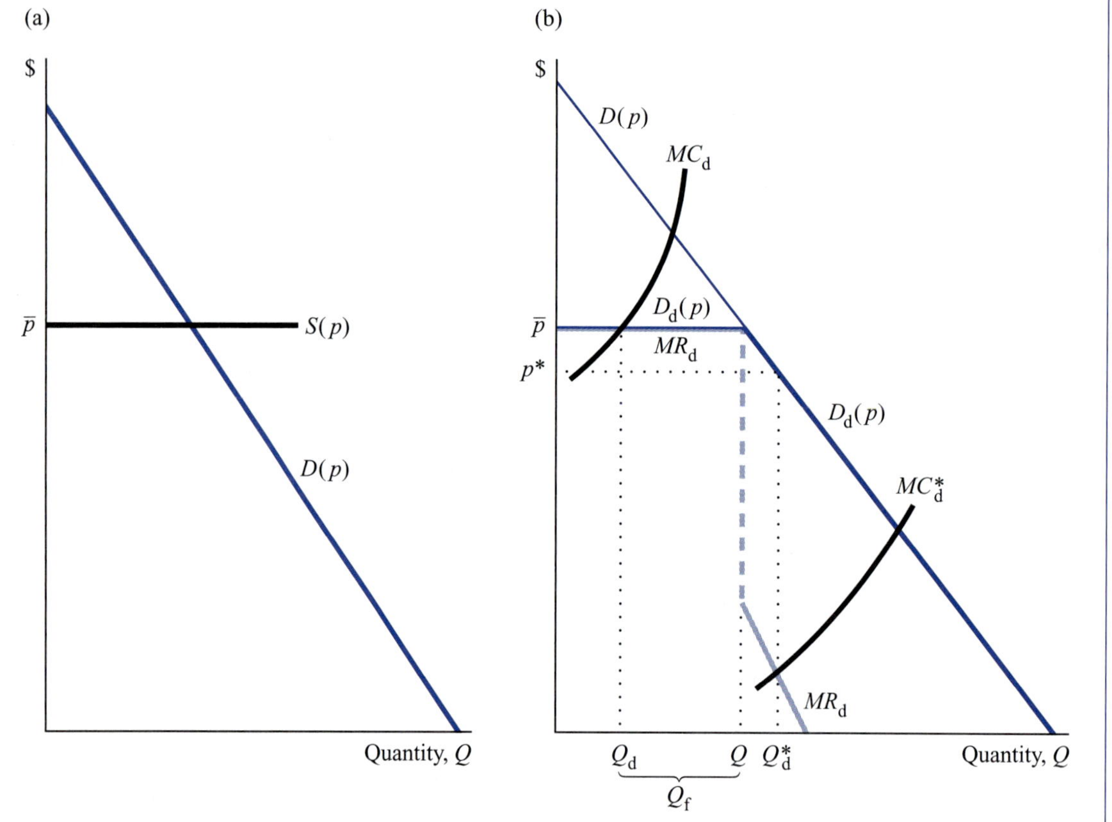

and flatter (it is n times the slope of a typical firm's supply, or MC, curve). As the number of firms grows large, the fringe's supply curve becomes essentially horizontal, as shown in Figure 4.7a. That is, as long as price is at least $\bar{p}$, the competitive fringe is capable of and is willing to supply any quantity that the market demands.

As shown in Figure 4.7b, the residual demand curve facing the dominant firm is horizontal at $\bar{p}$ so the corresponding marginal revenue curve is also flat (remember that in a competitive market a firm faces a horizontal demand curve, and hence its marginal revenue curve is identical to its demand curve at the market price). Below $\bar{p}$ the residual demand curve is the market demand, which slopes downward, so that the corresponding marginal revenue curve also slopes downward. Again, the marginal revenue curve corresponding to the residual demand curve jumps at the quantity where the kink in the residual demand curve occurs.

There are two possible equilibria. First, if the dominant firm's marginal cost is relatively high (MC_d in Figure 4.7b), so that it intersects the horizontal portion of the

MR_d curve, the price is $\bar{p}$, and the competitive fringe meets some of the market's demand. At this price, each fringe firm makes zero economic profits (because its average cost equals $\bar{p}$) and is indifferent between staying in business and leaving the market. How much is produced by the competitive fringe depends on the dominant firm's cost structure (that is, where MC_d intersects the horizontal marginal revenue curve), which determines the dominant firm's output, Q_d. Collectively, the fringe firms produce an output level $Q_f = Q - Q_d$, as Figure 4.7b shows.[19] It is possible that $Q_f = 0$ even though the presence of the fringe constrains price to equal $\bar{p}$.

Thus, if fringe firms flood into a market whenever positive profits can be made, the dominant firm cannot charge a price above the minimum average cost of a fringe firm. Although a dominant firm can make positive profits, competitive-fringe firms just break even. If the dominant firm's price would be above $\bar{p}$ in the absence of entry, consumers are better off if entry is possible because it results in lower prices.

The second type of equilibrium occurs if the dominant firm's marginal cost is lower (MC^*_d in Figure 4.7b), so that it hits the marginal revenue curve in the downward-sloping portion. Here, the price is so low that no fringe firm stays in the market when the dominant firm's costs are lower than the fringe firms' costs. This equilibrium (Q^*_d, p^*) is the same as discussed previously in the second no-entry equilibrium and is shown in Figures 4.6b and 4.7b. The dominant firm is a monopoly, and the potential supply of fringe firms is irrelevant.

SUMMARY

Monopoly or market power is the ability to price profitably above marginal cost. A single seller of a product, a monopoly, faces a downward-sloping demand curve and sets its price above marginal cost. As a result, less is purchased than if the market were perfectly competitive and society suffers a deadweight loss.

In some markets, however, there are benefits to monopoly. For example, the promise of future monopoly profits can spur a firm to develop new products or more efficient production techniques.

Not all firms that earn profits are monopolies, and not all monopolies earn profits. Just like a competitive firm, a monopoly can make either profits or losses in the short run. However, unlike a competitive firm, a monopoly can earn positive profits in the long run. A natural monopoly exists when it is efficient to have only one firm produce the market's output.

[19]Why don't fringe firms meet the entire demand at $\bar{p}$, instead of splitting it with the dominant firm? The answer is that the dominant firm has lower costs and can force some of the fringe firms out of the industry. Suppose that the dominant firm is producing its desired output of Q_d, and n fringe firms are producing $Q_f = Q - Q_d$. Now, if additional fringe firms enter this market, output exceeds market demand at $\bar{p}$. For the market to clear, the price must fall. Since the dominant firm is making positive profits, it stays in the industry. The fringe firms, however, start making losses (because they just break even at $\bar{p}$). Thus, some of the fringe firms must drop out of the industry until the price again rises to $\bar{p}$. Alternately stated, the dominant firm can always charge slightly below $\bar{p}$ to sell as much as it wants.

Monopsony is monopoly on the buying side. A firm with monopsony power sets lower prices and employs fewer resources than would prevail under competition. Like monopoly, monopsony imposes an efficiency cost on society. Monopsony power can persist only when resources are specialized in the long run.

A low-cost dominant firm has market power even though it competes with other firms. A profit-maximizing dominant firm does not attempt to drive out fringe firms at all costs. Its behavior depends on how great its cost advantage over fringe firms is and on how easily other firms can enter. If a large number of price-taking firms can enter the market whenever a profit opportunity occurs, and if they can produce at costs not much above those of the dominant firm, the dominant firm is unable to charge prices substantially above the competitive price. Even if fringe firms do not enter a market, the threat of their entry may cause a monopoly (in the sense that it is the only firm in the market) to set a lower price than it would in the absence of the fringe.

PROBLEMS

1. If the demand curve is $Q(p) = 10 - p$ and the marginal cost is constant at 4, what is the profit-maximizing monopoly price and output? What is the price elasticity at the monopoly price and output?

2. Suppose that the supply of football players is elastic at the lowest salary levels paid. Would a monopsony of football players restrict output?

3. If the demand curve is $Q(p) = 5/p$, what is the elasticity of demand? What is total revenue when $p = \$1$ and when $p = \$30$? If production costs \$1 per unit, and the smallest production level is 1 unit, how much should the monopoly produce?

4. If the demand curve is $Q(p) = p^{\epsilon}$, what is the elasticity of demand? If marginal cost is \$1 and $\epsilon = -2$, what is the profit-maximizing price?

5. Suppose the demand curve for corn is $Q(p) = 10 - p$. Suppose that one firm owns all five units of corn in the world and has zero marginal cost. Does a monopoly sell less output than would be sold in a competitive market in which 100 firms each own 0.05 units?

6. Suppose the Environmental Protection Agency sets new requirements that raise the (fixed) costs of reporting compliance with pollution control rules (Pashigian 1984). How would this change affect (a) the market price, (b) the number of fringe firms, (c) total output, and (d) the dominant firm's share of the market? *Hint:* What does an increase in fixed costs do to the average cost curve of a fringe firm?

7. By showing the behavior of both a monopoly and a dominant firm in the same graph, show that monopoly profits are greater than the profit of a dominant firm in the no-entry equilibrium (MC_d). Show how much consumers benefit from buying from a dominant firm-competitive fringe rather than from a monopoly. *Hint:* A firm's variable costs are the area under its marginal cost curve up to the relevant output.

8. How would the no-entry model diagrams (Figure 4.6) change if fringe firms had the usual U-shaped average and marginal cost curves? Assume that because of a barrier to entry, there are only n fringe firms. Describe the types of possible equilibria.

9. Would a profit-maximizing dominant firm ever produce more than if it were a monopoly? *Hint:* Show the behavior of both a monopoly and a dominant firm (in the no-entry model) on the same graph and note where the marginal revenue curves cross.

10. What effect does a binding minimum wage have on a monopsony labor market?

Answers to odd-numbered problems are given at the back of the book.

SUGGESTED READINGS

Stigler (1965) provides a good, nontechnical introduction to the dominant firm-competitive fringe model. Fisher, McGowan, and Greenwood (1983) is a very readable, controversial discussion of the important IBM antitrust case.

CHAPTER 5

Cartels

People of the same trade seldom meet together, even for merriment and diversion, but the conversation ends in a conspiracy against the public, or in some contrivance to raise prices. It is impossible indeed to prevent such meetings, by any law which either could be executed, or would be consistent with liberty and justice. But though the law cannot hinder people of the same trade from sometimes assembling together, it ought to do nothing to facilitate such assemblies; much less to render them necessary. —*Adam Smith*

In any market, firms have an incentive to coordinate their production and pricing activities to increase their collective and individual profits by restricting market output and raising the market price. An association of firms that explicitly coordinates its pricing or output activities is called a **cartel**. A cartel that includes all firms in a market is in effect a monopoly, and the member firms share the monopoly profits.

Cartels are more likely to occur in *oligopolistic markets*, where there are only a few firms, than in competitive markets. It is easier to reach and maintain an agreement on price or output when the number of firms is small. But even without an explicit agreement, firms may act so as to raise their collective profits. The factors that increase the likelihood that a cartel succeeds also affect whether oligopoly firms can elevate their prices above the competitive level. Thus, a study of cartels is also a study of oligopolies. In the next chapter, we use game theory to analyze oligopoly behavior.

Fortunately for consumers, although firms have an incentive to coordinate activities to restrict market output and raise prices, each member of the cartel has an incentive to "cheat" on the cartel agreement. Each cartel member wants to produce more output than is best for the cartel collectively. As a result, cartels tend to break apart even without government intervention.

When a cartel partially breaks apart so that some firms act outside of the cartel or when not all firms in the market join the cartel in the first place, the cartel may act like a dominant firm facing a competitive fringe of nonmember firms. As discussed in Chapter 4, entry of new fringe firms into a market can destroy the market power of a dominant firm or a cartel. Thus, only cartels that do not fall apart through lack of cooperation and that exist in markets in which entry is difficult can maintain market power for substantial lengths of time.

Four key questions are examined in this chapter:

1. Why do cartels form?
2. What factors cause some cartels to last and others to break up, even without government intervention?
3. How harmful are cartels?
4. What have governments done about cartels?

Why Cartels Form

United we stand, divided we fall.
Union gives strength. —*Aesop*

Why is Adam Smith correct that firms want to form cartels? The answer is that each individual firm wants to increase its own profit. But why should a firm's profit go up when the firms in a market form a cartel? After all, each competitive firm is maximizing its profit. How can the firms do better by forming a cartel if each is already maximizing its profit?

The answer involves a subtle argument. In a competitive market, each firm considers how much a reduction in its own output benefits it and ignores the gains to other firms, which benefit from a reduction in total market output to the extent that reduction raises the price. In contrast, a cartel takes into account the benefits to all its members of the reduction in each firm's output. Thus, a competitive market (in which each firm ignores the collective gain from its output reduction) produces more output than a cartel.

To illustrate the nature of this collective gain, consider two polar cases. First, suppose that a market is made up of many identical, competitive firms, each of which is a price taker. In contrast, suppose that all the firms join together to form a cartel and act as a monopoly. Figure 5.1a shows a typical firm's marginal cost curve. The sum of the individual firm's marginal cost curves is the market supply curve, which is shown in

FIGURE 5.1 Cartel

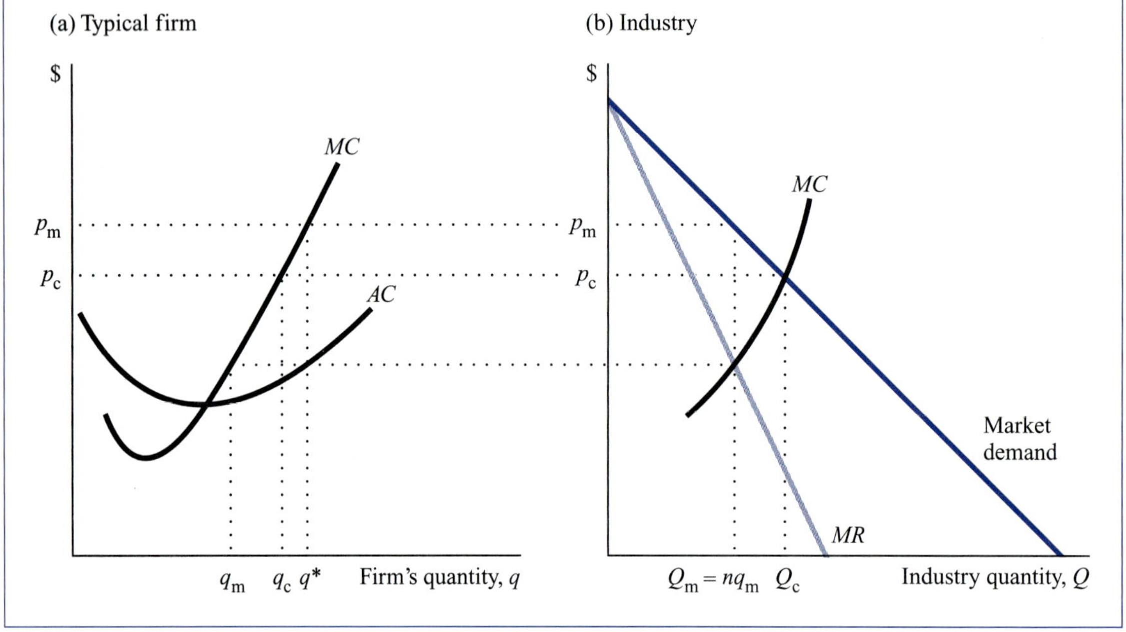

Figure 5.1b (labeled *MC*) along with the market demand curve. The competitive output, Q_c, is determined by the intersection of this supply curve with the market demand curve (Figure 5.1b), with each firm producing q_c units of output (Figure 5.1a) and the market price is p_c.

Why does it pay for the cartel to reduce output from the competitive level?[1] At the competitive output, the cartel's marginal cost is greater than its marginal revenue (Figure 5.1b), so it pays the cartel to reduce its output. Because the demand curve slopes downward, the marginal revenue curve lies below the demand curve, and marginal revenue is less than marginal cost at the competitive output Q_c. Thus, it pays for the cartel to reduce output from the competitive level—but by how much? It should lower output until its marginal revenue equals marginal cost, which guarantees that profits are maximized. The cartel increases its profits by lowering the aggregate cartel output to Q_m where *MR* equals *MC* (Figure 5.1b). The price rises to p_m. Because the cartel is made up of n identical firms, it requires each firm to reduce its output to $q_m = Q_m/n$. In this example, the identical firms share in the extra profits equally.

Why doesn't each competitive firm reduce its own output below the competitive level? At the competitive equilibrium, each competitive firm sets its marginal revenue

[1] As with a monopoly, the cartel can restrict output and let the demand curve determine price or raise price and let the demand curve determine output. The two approaches are equivalent.

equal to its marginal cost and has no incentive to further lower its output.[2] If it were to reduce its output by one unit, it would lose profits because the marginal revenue on the last unit produced (the price) would exceed its marginal cost. Thus, each competitive firm is maximizing its profits at the competitive output.

The gain in collective activity comes from the very slight slope to the competitive firm's demand curve. Although economists often say that each competitive firm acts as though it faces a horizontal demand curve—that it cannot raise its price by lowering its output—that is not absolutely correct. The demand curve does have a slight slope: A competitive firm that stops producing might raise the market price by a small amount.[3] That small slope can be ignored when talking about a single firm, but it cannot properly be ignored when talking about all firms collectively.

If all firms cut back by, say, 10 percent, the market price definitely rises; however, if only one firm cuts back by 10 percent, the effect on price is so small that it is hardly measurable. Each competitive firm decides that it doesn't pay to reduce its output significantly because its gain is less than its cost. If it reduces its output by one unit, its gain is the trivial amount by which price rises times the units it produces, whereas its loss is the price it would have received for this last unit.

A competitive firm ignores the good it does other firms by reducing its output and increasing the market price; it places no value on the gains of other firms. This gain by others is an *externality.*[4] Working cooperatively, the cartel members gain from the output reductions of each firm. When all firms belong to the cartel, all the gains from reducing output and raising price go to the cartel, which divides the gains among its members. Here, the externality created by each firm in reducing its output has been internalized by the cartel. As a result, it pays the cartel to reduce total output below the competitive level, even though it would not pay any competitive firm to reduce its output individually.

Creating and Enforcing the Cartel

> Socrates: *[Tell] me whether you think that a city, or an army, or a band of robbers or thieves, or any other company which pursue some unjust end in common, would be able to effect anything if they were unjust to one another?*
> Thrasymachus: *Of course not. . . .*
> Socrates: *[When] we say that any vigorous joint action is the work of unjust men, our language is not altogether accurate. If they had been thoroughly unjust, they*

[2]Because a price-taking competitive firm faces a horizontal demand curve, its marginal revenue curve is also horizontal and identical to the demand curve. Thus, the competitive firm's *MR* curve is horizontal at the competitive price p_c (where the market supply or *MC* curve hits the market demand curve in Figure 5.1b).

[3]See the discussion in Chapter 3 of the elasticity of demand facing a single competitive firm and Equation 3.1.

[4]An externality is a good (or bad) that is not priced by the market.

could not have kept their hands off one another. Clearly they must have possessed justice of a sort, enough to keep them from exercising their injustice on each other at the same time as on their victims. For the thorough villains who are perfectly unjust, are also perfectly incapable of action.[5]

Would you join a cartel if all the other firms in your market were forming one? Such behavior is usually illegal in the United States and many other capitalist countries, so, no doubt, you would refuse on moral and legal grounds. Suppose it was not a moral person like you who was being asked this question—suppose it was your slightly shady cousin. Would your cousin join an illegal cartel conspiracy?

Well, it depends. Your cousin's first thought is likely to be: "What's in it for me?" It should be obvious to him that it is in his best interest to let all the other firms in the market form a cartel that does not include his firm. Then the cartel would restrict output, driving up the price, while his firm could produce as much as it wanted. Of course, every other firm in the market makes the same calculation. Now suppose the other firms tell him that, unless his firm agrees, none of the others will join the cartel and restrict output. Your cousin now realizes that he can't have his cartel and produce as much output as he wants too. He can only obtain the higher price if his firm agrees to a reduction in output.

Your cousin then thinks: "What do I have to lose? If the cartel is caught by the government and convicted, my firm will have to pay a fine. But if the chance of being caught is small or the fine is low, it may be worth it to me." That is, if the expected loss from such a fine is low enough, your cousin joins the cartel.

But your cousin is always looking for an edge. Once he's joined the cartel, he says to himself: "Why shouldn't I cheat and produce more output than the cartel's agreement permits? After all, the cartel probably won't know who's producing the extra output." Of course, if all firms in the cartel think this way, the cartel will fall apart. The success of the cartel, then, turns on its ability to enforce its agreement.

Figure 5.1 illustrates why a firm has an incentive to cheat on the cartel's agreement. As explained above, the cartel members agree to restrict output to Q_m, which drives the price to p_m, the monopoly price. Figure 5.1a shows the cost curves of your cousin's firm, which is one of n identical firms in the market (and in the cartel). The cartel wants your cousin to produce $q_m = Q_m/n$ output: the output corresponding to his firm's share of the cartel output. But at the cartel's price, p_m, your cousin's firm can maximize its profits by producing q^* units of output (where its marginal cost curve equals p_m). Thus, although it is in the cartel's best interest for every firm to restrict output, it is in your cousin's best interest for every firm except his own to restrict output.

Cartels have little effect on prices if members do not cooperate. For example, in Kuala Lumpur, representatives of four pepper-producing countries decided that they would set a minimum price for black pepper. Even though the pepper cartel (Brazil, India, Indonesia, and Malaysia) produces more than 95 percent of the world's pepper

[5]Based on Plato, 1957, 37–8. The names of the speakers have been added and some material has been dropped.

and could raise the price, it has never been able to do so because its members keep undercutting the cartel's minimum price.[6]

Factors That Facilitate the Formation of Cartels

Once a cartel forms, the firms must agree to fix price (or equivalently, reduce output) if it is to be successful.[7] Why are there successful cartels in some markets but not in others? Unfortunately, we know a great deal about cartels that get caught, but very little about those that escape detection. As a result, it is not known whether the cartels that find themselves in court are unsuccessful or merely unlucky. Some evidence suggests that cartels that end up in court are actually unprofitable and hence, perhaps, atypical (Asch and Seneca 1976). Other evidence (Suslow 1998) suggests that cartels tend to form in less profitable industries.

Many characteristics of markets and firms that contribute to successful price-fixing conspiracies have been identified using studies of cartels that have ended up in court (Stigler 1964a; Hay and Kelley 1974). These characteristics may be roughly divided into those that allow a cartel to raise the market price in the first place and those that prevent the cartel agreement from breaking apart due to cheating by members. The following sections describe some of the major factors that facilitate the formation of cartels. Factors that lead to their survival are discussed in the next section. See Example 5.1 for a description of one of the most important cartels in American history.

Large firms may decide independently to behave as though they had a cartel arrangement without a formal meeting; that is, each one can cut its output and hope that the others will do likewise. Inevitably, in oligopolies, firms take their rivals' actions into account (as discussed in more detail in Chapter 6). When firms in an oligopoly coordinate their actions despite the lack of an explicit cartel agreement, the resulting coordination is sometimes referred to as **tacit collusion** or conscious parallelism.[8] Stigler (1964a) explains that a theory of oligopoly could be based on cartel theory even in the absence of explicit agreements.

---

[6]"Chaos in the Cartel: Pepper Producers Pick a Purchasers' Price." *San Francisco Chronicle,* August 8, 1983:49.

[7]Generally, price fixing is discussed rather than output reductions because it is believed to be more common. Other firms' prices are sometimes easier to observe than their output levels. In a study of antitrust cases from 1890 through 1969, Posner (1970, especially p. 400) found that only 1.6 percent of the cases had only explicit production or sales quotas.

[8]The use of the terms *tacit collusion* and *conscious parallelism* has led to confusion and added fuel to legal disputes. One ambiguity in the terms arises because the oligopoly price lies between the competitive and monopoly prices. Although many economists use these terms to mean that the oligopoly price is at the monopoly or cartel level, others use them to refer to the case where the noncartel price is elevated above the competitive price. A similar ambiguity arises with the term *collusion.* Economists often use the word to refer either to nonconspiratorial behavior (lawful actions where firms do not engage in explicit price fixing) or to conspiratorial behavior (illegal, explicit price fixing), but lawyers commonly use the term to refer only to conspiratorial behavior. A separate ambiguity in the law exists around the meaning of the word *agreement* (see Carlton, Gertner, and Rosenfield 1997).

EXAMPLE 5.1 *An Electrifying Conspiracy*

On a steamy Saturday, May 9, 1959, at 2:30 PM, reporter Julian Granger of the Knoxville *News-Sentinel* sat at his desk reading routine handouts from local publicity sources. The usual weekly newsletter from the Tennessee Valley Authority (TVA) announced that several contracts had been awarded. Pretty dull stuff.

But then Granger read that one contract had been awarded to Westinghouse for transformers for $96,760. The newsletter went on to note that "Allis-Chalmers, General Electric, and Pennsylvania Transformer quoted identical prices of $112,712." How could three companies bid prices that were identical to the penny under a system of secret, sealed bids?

Later in the release, he read that two other companies had quoted identical prices on a $273,200 contract. On yet another contract for conductor cable, there were seven identical bids of $198,438.24. Identical down to the 24¢.

Granger's story, which appeared on page 1 of the second section of the Knoxville *News-Sentinel* on May 13, 1959, drew little reaction. The lead of his second story on May 17, 1959, stated, "TVA purchasing records revealed today that at least 47 large and small American manufacturers have taken part in identical bidding on a wide variety of items in the past three years." He noted that the TVA had no choice in many cases but to award the contract on a chance drawing from a hat.

Could these identical bids have happened by accident? Oh, come now. Granger showed that some identical bids quoted the same delivered prices even though distances from delivery points varied by hundreds or thousands of miles for equipment you couldn't exactly weigh on a bathroom scale.

General Electric and Westinghouse, the two biggest electrical equipment manufacturers, had equal bids more frequently than other firms. Between 1946 and 1957, they raised prices 10 times on switching gear in a parallel pattern: The announcements of these increases came within a few days of each other.

After the second story, Granger went to local suppliers and got nowhere—they seemed afraid to talk. Granger did learn, however, that the Knoxville Utility Board had received a long series of identical bids from the electrical equipment manufacturers: up to 11 at one time. Their purchasing agent, Karl Strange, told Granger that he had noticed an increase in the practice since the end of World War II.

The Scripps-Howard papers reprinted the first two articles nationwide. On May 19, Senator Estes Kefauver inserted Granger's second story verbatim in the *Congressional Record* of the hearings before the Subcommittee on Antitrust and Monopoly.

Eight days before Granger's first story broke, Ralph J. Cordiner, Chairman of the Board of General Electric (GE), testified before the subcommittee on a bill to promote more vigorous competition in a variety of industries. He asked, "Is it assumed that companies in industries affected by this bill have the ability to 'administer' prices in a manner not responsive to market supply and demand?" He responded to his own question: "If so, the assumption is false, because these companies are just as much subject to competitive market conditions as any others." He continued, "In all instances the prices are completely subject to the force of competition in the marketplace and the value the customer believes he is receiving." He concluded that the then-current antitrust laws were "well enforced."

Exactly six months before Cordiner testified so sanctimoniously about competition, seven of his top executives met with their competitors in the Hotel Traymore in Atlantic City, New Jersey, to jack up the price of power switchgear assemblies ($125 million in annual sales). Until that time, the firms had an agreement that their sealed government bids would be divided by each of the conspiring companies in the following ratios: General Electric, 42 percent of the market; Westinghouse, 38 percent; Allis-Chalmers, 11 percent; and I-T-E, 9 percent.

Apparently, the initial conspirators made room for a major new entrant at this meeting. Federal Pacific, the newcomer to the cartel, was given permission to quote prices slightly lower than the others for a brief period in order to establish its assigned share of the market. GE and Westinghouse agreed to lower their shares to 39 percent and 35 percent, respectively, giving Federal Pacific 7 percent of the market. Over the next 12 months, at least 35 such meetings were held, with GE playing a prominent and active leadership role.

Senator Kefauver, the chairman of the Subcommittee on Antitrust and Monopoly, moved the hearings to Knoxville in September 1959. The hearings demonstrated that the prices of heavy industrial electrical equipment had increased 50 percent since 1951.

At the hearings, many examples of identical bids were presented. Even when the bids were not identical, the companies followed a rotation pattern, where one bid was low, one high, and the other two identical. The next time around, the order of the firms might change, but there would be one low, one high, and two equal bids. Presumably, the firms took turns winning the bidding in the proportions agreed to earlier. Apparently they agreed to alternate winning the bidding according to a *phase of the moon* formula: The firm to give the low bid was determined by the fullness of the moon.

The Philadelphia Antitrust Office spent 18 months tracking down evidence used to indict 29 manufacturers (practically the entire heavy electric industry) and 44 of their top executives. Attorney General William P. Rogers issued the first official announcement of the indictments on February 16, 1960.

According to the first indictments returned by a federal grand jury sitting in Philadelphia, Westinghouse, Allis-Chalmers, Federal Pacific Electric Company, GE, I-T-E, and many of these firms' top executives had engaged in a conspiracy at least since 1956. The defendants were accused of fixing and maintaining high prices, allocating the business among themselves, submitting noncompetitive, rigged bids, refusing to sell equipment to other manufacturers of electrical equipment, or raising prices to them so that they could not effectively compete.

Conspiracy in this industry was facilitated by the relatively small number of firms and the large market shares of the largest firms. Electrical manufacturing had a four-firm concentration ratio (sum of sales by the four largest firms divided by total industry sales) of over 50 percent compared to about 25 percent in all manufacturing. The concentration ratios were above 75 percent in all specific product areas involved and over 95 percent for turbogenerators, power transformers, power switchgear assem-

Continued

blies, distribution transformers, low-voltage power circuit breakers, isolated phase buses, bushings, and lightning arresters.

Eventually, 45 executives and 29 corporations were indicted. Most of them made no defense in the face of this overwhelming evidence. Generally, vice presidents and division managers took the fall. The seven men with the highest positions received jail sentences, but those were typically only on the order of 30 days. In addition, 24 people received suspended sentences. Total fines to firms reached nearly $2 million, while individual fines were $137,500.

In addition to the government suits, nearly 2,000 private suits were filed. General Electric settled its lawsuits for over $200 million (including $6.74 million to the TVA and $1 million to other federal agencies), and Westinghouse for more than $100 million. Total damages paid by all companies topped $400 million.

Many articles and books presented this story as a triumph of the system over evil conspirators, but this conclusion is hard to understand. Many, if not most, of the top directors of these firms were not personally indicted or punished, and the total fines were a small fraction of the monopoly profits the cartel earned over its life span. (Sultan (1974, 1975) argues that the conspiracy did not significantly raise prices; however, Bane (1973) and Lean, Ogur, and Rogers (1982) find that prices did rise.) According to a U.S. Congress report, this long-lasting conspiracy may have raised prices by nearly 10 percent. Other estimates have been over twice that for specific products. Electrical manufacturing accounts for about one-twelfth of total manufacturing and about 3 percent of all economic activity. About 30 percent of this manufacturing was electrical apparatus, which had $5 billion in shipments in 1958. The indictments referred to only about $1.75 billion of these annual sales (about 10 percent of all electrical manufacturing sales). Even assuming that prices were only 10 percent too high on only $1.75 billion worth of annual sales, purchasers paid roughly $175 million too much during each year of the conspiracy, which apparently lasted for decades. From the viewpoint of the firms involved, this experiment in cartel behavior probably looked like a great success, even after they were caught and punished.

The threat of penalties for illegal price fixing apparently was not viewed as a sufficient deterrent by GE and Westinghouse. These same firms have been charged and punished repeatedly since the Sherman Antitrust Act first went into effect in 1890. There were 13 U.S. Department of Justice antitrust cases and 3 Federal Trade Commission cases against GE and Westinghouse between 1911 and 1952. The government "won" all of these cases, obtaining convictions, *nolo contendere* pleas, or consent decrees in each (Walton and Cleveland 1964, 16–20).

Presumably, the conspirators should have learned to be more careful as a byproduct of the publicity, if not the fines, in the 1960s cases. However, GE and Westinghouse were accused of conspiring to fix prices on turbogenerators, starting with a new pricing policy GE announced in May 1963, just two and one-half years after they were found guilty in this bid-rigging case.

Sources: Fuller 1962; Walton and Cleveland 1964; and U.S. Congress, Joint Committee on Internal Revenue Taxation, *Staff Study of Income Tax Treatment of Treble Damage Payments under the Antitrust Laws* (Washington, DC: Government Printing Office, 1965), 39 (cited by Posner 1975).

Three major factors are necessary to establish a cartel. First, a cartel must be able to raise price above the noncartel level without inducing substantial increased competition from nonmember firms. Second, the expected punishment for forming a cartel must be low relative to the expected gains. Third, the cost of establishing and enforcing an agreement must be low relative to the expected gains.

The Ability to Raise the Market Price. Only if a cartel is expected to raise the price above the noncartel price and keep it high do firms join.[9] The more inelastic the demand curve facing a cartel, the higher the price the cartel can set and the greater its profits. If the cartel's demand curve is inelastic (relatively vertical at the current price), raising price can significantly raise revenues (that is, quantity demanded falls by a smaller percentage than price rises) and profits. In contrast, if a potential cartel faces an elastic demand curve (relatively horizontal), raising price causes revenues to fall (because quantity would fall by more than price increases, and profits may rise only slightly). See Example 5.2.

Entry by nonmember firms or *close substitutes produced in other industries* prevents a cartel from raising price. If the cartel controls only a small share of the relevant market, which includes all close substitutes, firms not in the cartel undercut the cartel and prevent it from raising the market price; that is, the demand curve facing the cartel is relatively elastic. Even if all firms initially in a market form a cartel and raise the price, the higher price may induce enough new firms to enter that the cartel is unable to keep the price high in the long run. That is, the long-run elasticity of demand facing the cartel is very high (especially relative to the short-run elasticity). Obviously, the longer the cartel can expect to keep the price high, the greater the current value of creating a cartel.

Low Expectation of Severe Punishment. Cartels only form if members do not expect the government to catch and severely punish them. Large expected penalties reduce the expected value of forming a cartel in the first place. Before they were made illegal in the United States in 1890, explicit cartels were much more common. During periods when the Department of Justice has been relatively lax in enforcing the laws, price-fixing conspiracies have been more prevalent (Posner 1970). Internationally, where cartels are legal, they have been more common than in the United States.[10] Some governments have created cartels (as discussed below).

As long as coordinating firms did not use unlawful acts of violence, intimidation, or fraud, British courts did not stop price fixing in modern times until 1956.[11] A survey

---

[9]If the noncartel price is close to the cartel price, then firms may not believe that joining the cartel is profitable given the legal liability they potentially face from belonging to a cartel.

[10]See the extensive discussion of the Organization of Petroleum Exporting Countries (OPEC) cartel at our web site at **www.aw-bc.com/carlton_perloff** "OPEC."

[11]The Restrictive Trade Practices Act (passed by Parliament in 1956) required that all contracts or agreements among suppliers in restraint of trade be reported to the Registrar of Restrictive Practices. This law has been modified substantially since then. In 1973, the Office of Fair Trading took over this responsibility and agreements among service industries had to be reported as well. This agency was empowered to challenge agreements that were contrary to the public interest. A special Restrictive Practices Court decides whether such agreements are prohibited. In contrast to U.S. law, this court can accept the argument that benefits outweigh damages and allow price fixing. A new Competition Act was passed in 1980 to facilitate investigations by the Office of Fair Trading.

EXAMPLE 5.2 *The Viability of Commodity Cartels*

Attempts have been made to cartelize the market for many of the major internationally traded commodities. Most of these initiatives have failed, however, as the cartels fell apart quickly or were unable to raise prices substantially.

Eckbo (1976) studied 51 formal international cartel organizations in 18 industries, with the earliest agreement in 1918 and the latest in 1964. He defined a cartel as successful if it raised the price at least three times the marginal production cost of the member with the highest cost. Only 19 cartels (37 percent) were successful by this criterion. One of them, the iodine cartel, lasted 61 years. The remaining successful cartels had formal agreements that lasted from 2 to 18 years, with a median lifetime of 5 years and a mean of 6.6 years. Only 5 of the 19 lasted 10 years or longer.

Of these successful cartels, 3 (out of 9 for which there is information) broke down for nonmarket reasons such as government intervention or war. Of those that collapsed for market-related reasons, 7 out of 16 (44 percent) had internal conflicts among cartel members, whereas 9 (56 percent) ended because of external forces such as competition from nonmembers (the usual case) or reactions by buyers.

Two factors that allow a cartel to persist and raise prices are that (1) it can detect and prevent cheating by members and (2) it faces a relatively inelastic residual demand curve at noncartel prices. The cartel's residual demand curve is likely to be inelastic if it has a relatively large share of the market, the market demand is not very elastic, and noncartel members have inelastic supply curves.

The longest-lived cartel in Eckbo's survey, iodine (1878–1939), made all sales through a central cartel office in London, which prevented members from cheating. Maintaining a cartel is not sufficient for success, however, if it cannot raise prices.

The Organization of Petroleum Exporting Countries (OPEC), the International Bauxite Association (IBA), and the Conseil Intergouvernemental des Pays Exportateurs de Cuivre (International Council of Copper Exporting Countries, or CIPEC) differ in their market power because of their different market shares and the residual demand elasticities they face. OPEC quadrupled the world oil price initially; IBA tripled the price of bauxite; but CIPEC has been unable to raise copper prices significantly.

When OPEC was formed, it had approximately two-thirds of the world's oil reserves and a similar fraction of the noncommunist world's oil production. By 1975, IBA accounted for 85 percent of total noncommunist world bauxite production. In contrast, CIPEC accounts for only about one-third of the noncommunist world's copper production. Of Eckbo's successful cartels, 15 out of 19 (79 percent) had four-firm concentration ratios over 50 percent. In 14 of them (74 percent), the cartels' share of total production exceeded 75 percent.

Of the 9 successful cartels about which we have enough information, 7 faced inelastic demand curves (elasticities less than 1 in absolute value). In 8 of the 9 cases, no short-term substitutes for the commodity were available outside the cartel, although for 7 cartels there were long-term substitutes—which may be why they eventually ended.

Pindyck (1977, 1979) shows that dynamic, long-run adjustments in commodity markets are also important. OPEC faces a relatively inelastic fringe supply. Despite major price increases, non-OPEC petroleum producers have not substantially increased their supply in the short to medium run. Similarly, the world demand for bauxite is extremely inelastic (up to a limit price), even in the long run.

In contrast, in the short run and even more so in the long run, secondary copper, which is produced from scrap, is very responsive to price. As a result, CIPEC faces a much larger long-run elasticity than short-run elasticity. If CIPEC were to raise its price very much, others would increase their production from scrap.

Given these differences, it is little wonder that OPEC and IBA could raise prices while CIPEC could not. These factors may also explain why still other natural resources have not been successfully cartelized. Pindyck holds that other minerals, such as iron ore, manganese ore, lead, tin, zinc, and nickel, would also face high long-run residual demand elasticities due to secondary supplies from scrap. Recently, IBA has suffered setbacks because Brazil and other producers have not restricted output. It continues as a research group.

Indonesia and Grenada produce 98 percent of the world's nutmeg and agreed to form a nutmeg cartel in 1987. For the 15 months before the formal agreement, however, Grenada operated informally under an Indonesian guideline. The two Countries claimed they did not intend to force prices higher but merely wanted to ensure that there is "no price cutting"—presumably from the informal cartel level. They were not worried about the impact of the cartel on demand. Nutmeg has no close substitutes; it has a distinctive taste, so bakers are unlikely to change their recipes appreciably.

One long successful cartel is the De Beers diamond cartel, which, throughout the twentieth century, has been the largest-selling agent of most of the world's diamonds. Even the Soviet Union, which was the second-largest diamond exporter after South Africa, sold all its diamonds through the De Beers cartel for the last quarter-century. The breakup of the Soviet Union threatened the stability of De Beers, though Russia apparently has returned to the cartel.

Traditionally, as new mines were developed, De Beers gave them sufficient market share so that they agreed to sell through De Beers and accept its production control system. When Tanzania decided to act independently, De Beers depressed the price for the quality of stones sold by Tanzania, forcing it to rejoin the syndicate.

Sources: Fisher, Cootner, and Bailey (1972); Eckbo (1976); Pindyck (1977, 1979); Fisher (1981); Alan J. Wax, "Spicy New Cartel Sets Nutmeg Prices." *San Francisco Chronicle,* May 25, 1987:20; Clyde H. Farnsworth, "OPEC Isn't the Only Cartel That Couldn't," *New York Times,* April 24, 1988: 3; "Diamonds: Friends Again," *The Economist,* March 2, 1996, 338:59–60.

of industrial trade associations carried out by the Political and Economic Planning agency in 1953–56 found that 243 of the 1,300 associations (19 percent) attempted to fix prices (Phillips 1972).

Low Organizational Costs. Even if a potential cartel could raise prices in the long run and not be discovered, it will not form if the cost of initial organization is too high. The more complex the negotiations, the greater the cost of creating a cartel. Four factors keep the cost low, facilitating the creation of a cartel: Few firms are involved, the market is highly concentrated, all firms produce a nearly identical product, and a trade association exists.

Setting up a secret meeting without the government's knowledge is relatively easy when there are few firms involved. Even if there are many firms in a market, the largest firms may meet and establish a cartel (dominant firm) that does not explicitly include the smaller fringe firms. Of the 606 Department of Justice price-fixing cases (1910–72) examined by Fraas and Greer (1977), the average number of firms involved in each case was 16.7, whereas the median was 8, and the mode was 4.[12] That is, a few cases involving a large number of firms raised the average, but the most common type of case involved 4 firms, and half the cases involved 8 or fewer firms.[13]

Of the Department of Justice price-fixing cases (January 1963–December 1972) studied by Hay and Kelley (1974), only 6.5% involved 50 or more conspirators.[14] The average number of firms in the remaining cases was 7.25. Although only 26% of the cases involved 4 or fewer firms, nearly half (48%) involved 6 or fewer firms, and 79% involved 10 or fewer firms.

Of the global cartels from 1990 to 2003 studied by Connor (2003), the median number of corporate participants was five. More than half (77%) of these cartels had six or fewer firms. Only 13% had 10 or more participants, but most of those were organized by quasi-official European trade associations.

Even where cartels are legal, as are many international cartels not involving U.S. firms, the number of firms is crucial. For example, a long period (1928–72) of successful cartelization by two countries of the world mercury market was followed by years

---

[12]If the number of firms involved in each case is arranged in ascending order, then the middle number is the median number of firms. If there were 5 cases with 2, 4, 5, 8, and 9 firms involved, the median number of firms would be 5. Imagine a graph that plots the cases so that the horizontal axis shows the number of firms involved and the vertical axis shows the number of cases involving a given number of conspiring firms. The mode is the highest point on the plot. The mode is the most common number of conspirators.

[13]The median number of firms involved varied by industry. In natural resources markets, the median number of firms was 13. The corresponding numbers were 7 in manufacturing, 11 in distribution, 15 in construction, 4 in financial institutions, 4 in transportation, and 8 in services.

[14]Hay and Kelley (1974) studied horizontal price-fixing conspiracies that were prosecuted by the U.S. Department of Justice Antitrust Division. Their study excluded price fixing by various professional groups (because they were not covert), but included virtually all other cases that were filed and won in trial or settled by *nolo contendere* ("no contest") pleas. Pleading *nolo contendere* is equivalent to pleading guilty for the purposes of sentencing but is not an admission of guilt by the defendant. When such a plea is accepted by the court, a trial is not necessary. Occasionally, courts accept such pleas over the objection of the Department of Justice.

of unsuccessful attempts at price fixing by a larger group of countries (MacKie-Mason and Pindyck 1986).

If a few large firms make most of the sales in a market, and if they coordinate their activities, they can raise price without involving all the other (smaller) firms in the market. For example, Spain and Italy, which controlled 80% of the world's production of mercury, formed a successful cartel that did not formally involve five other producers (MacKie-Mason and Pindyck 1986).

Empirical evidence supports the view that cartels are more likely in concentrated industries.[15] In 42% of the Department of Justice price-fixing cases studied by Hay and Kelley (1974), the four-firm concentration ratio (the sum of the market shares of the four biggest firms) was over 75%; in another 34% of the cases, the ratios were between 51 and 75%. Thus, in 76% of the cases, the concentration ratio was greater than 50%. Only 6% of the cases had concentration ratios less than 25%. The overall average was 67.7%.[16] Of the global cartels studied by Connor (2003), cartel members usually controlled over 90% of the market's sales. Moreover, when entry caused the cartel's share to drop below 65%, cartel activity typically ceased.

Similarly, the existing evidence shows that cartels are often found in smaller geographic areas. In the U.S. Justice Department price-fixing and other antitrust cases from the passage of the Sherman Act (1890) through 1969 studied by Posner (1970), nearly half (47.4%) the conspiracies were in local or regional markets, 37.6% were nationwide, and 8.7% involved foreign trade. The smaller the geographical area of a market, the more likely it is that a few firms have a large share of the business.

Firms have more difficulty agreeing on relative prices when each firm's product has different qualities or properties. Each time a product is modified, a new relative price must be established. It is easier for a cartel to spot cheating when all it has to examine is a single price. It is relatively difficult to detect price cutting that is achieved by an increase in quality; a firm could increase its quality and hold its price constant if it wanted to increase sales without explicitly violating the pricing agreement.

In virtually all the price-fixing cases studied by Hay and Kelley (1974), the product was relatively homogeneous across firms. In the few exceptions, complicated products or services were allocated on a job-by-job basis that facilitated coordination, or a single issue was isolated for the agreement. For example, a group of swimsuit manufacturers agreed to delay end-of-season discounts. Similarly, virtually all the recent global conspiracies (Connor 2003) involved homogeneous products.

---

[15]Scott (1991a) shows that multimarket contact can be important. Large conglomerates may be potential rivals in a number of markets simultaneously. They can communicate about all these markets at once. It is also potentially more costly to deviate from a cartel agreement in one because it risks destroying all the cartel agreements. To the degree that multimarket contacts are important, the degree of concentration in a single market may be misleading.

[16]To minimize the systematic bias from excluding cases for which the concentration measure could not be determined directly, if the number of firms was known, Hay and Kelley (1974) calculated minimum concentration ratios by assuming each firm had an equal share.

Trade associations, by lowering the costs of meeting and coordinating activities among firms in a market, facilitate the establishment and enforcement of cartels. Most industries have trade associations that meet regularly. Not all industries with trade associations necessarily form cartels. However, as Adam Smith observed, such meetings are conducive to price-fixing agreements, and trade associations are often the mechanism by which large groups coordinate activities. In the Hay and Kelley (1974) study of Department of Justice price-fixing cases, trade associations were involved in 7 out of 8 cases in which more than 15 firms conspired, and in all cases involving more than 25 firms. Overall, 29 percent of the cases involved trade associations. Fraas and Greer (1977) found that 36 percent of all price-fixing cases involved trade associations. Moreover, the median number of firms involved was 16 when there was a trade association, compared to 8 for all cases. Posner (1970) found that 43.6 percent of all antitrust cases involved trade associations.

Enforcing a Cartel Agreement

Even if a market consists of a small number of firms producing a homogeneous good with no close substitutes, has an inelastic demand curve, and faces no threat of entry, a cartel cannot succeed if members can and want to cheat on the agreement. Some of the factors that lead to the formation of a cartel also help it to detect cheating and enforce its agreement.

Detecting Cheating. Cartel agreements are easier to enforce if detecting violations is easy. Four factors aid in the detection of cheating:

- There are few firms in the market.
- Prices do not fluctuate independently.
- Prices are widely known.
- All cartel members sell identical products at the same point in the distribution chain.

With relatively few firms, the cartel may more easily monitor each one, and increases in one firm's share of the market (an indication of price cutting) are easier to detect. Further, moral (or immoral) suasion may be easier when there are only a few conspirators (See **www.aw-bc.com/carlton_perloff** "Broker").

Hay and Kelley (1974) found that most of the price-fixing conspiracies lasting 10 or more years were in markets in which there were few firms and the largest firms made most of the sales. When a large number of firms was involved, conspiracies were generally discovered very quickly, especially because details about some of the large-group organizational meetings often were printed in local newspapers. In contrast, Posner (1970) found that, of the detected cartels, large ones lasted as long as smaller ones. He found that 52 percent of conspiracies involving 10 or fewer firms had lasted for 6 or more years, whereas 64 percent of larger conspiracies persisted that long. Presumably, the more firms involved in a conspiracy, the more likely is discovery by the government. In general, conspiracies are uncovered through information provided by private parties rather than by Department of Justice investigations.[17]

If a market has frequent shifts in demand, input costs, or other factors, prices in that market have to adjust often. In that case, cheating on a cartel arrangement may be difficult to detect, because it cannot be distinguished easily from other factors that cause price fluctuations. Cheating is easier to detect if prices are known. Some cartels have arranged for firms to inspect each other's books. In Posner's (1970) study of antitrust cases, at least 6.2 percent of the cases involved exchange of information, whereas 4.3 percent involved policing, fines, and audits. Of course, books can be faked, so such inspections cannot prevent all violations of the cartel agreement.

In some cases, governments help. For example, they often report the outcome of bidding on government contracts, so that cheating is instantly observable by the cartel (see Example 5.3). A quarter of the cases Hay and Kelley (1974) examined involved some form of bid rigging.[18]

Example 5.1 describes a *phases of the moon* scheme used by manufacturers of electrical products to rotate the winning of sealed bids. No firm could hope to win out of turn because its treachery against the cartel would be instantly exposed when the government announced the winner.

Vincent (The Fish) Cafaro, a former member of the Genovese organized crime family, told senators the mob rigged bids in New York City, controlling the concrete industry and construction unions.[19] He said the contractors and unions that won construction jobs through bid rigging were required to kick back 2 percent to the "2 Percent Club," an organization run by the Genovese, Gambino, Lucchese, and Colombo families of New York City. He estimated that at least 50 percent of the highrise construction in New York had a mob connection and added, "Legitimate guys ain't got a chance" to win contracts for those buildings. According to Mr. Cafaro, the 2 Percent Club split up all of the jobs worth over $2 million. Contracts worth over $5 million went to mob-run companies.

---

[17]Of the cases studied by Hay and Kelley (1974), detection was due to grand jury investigation of another case in 24%; to complaint by a competitor in 20%; to complaint by a customer in 14%; to complaint by local, state, or federal agencies in 12%; and to complaint by current or former employees in 6%. Each of the following methods was responsible for detection in 4% of the cases: complaint by a trade association official, investigation of conduct or of performance by the Antitrust Division, report of a newspaper, and referral to the Antitrust Division by the Federal Trade Commission. Each of the following methods was responsible for 2% of the cases: complaint by an anonymous informant, merger investigation, and private suit.

[18]Hay and Kelley (1974) found some cases in which sales to government agencies were explicitly excluded from the agreement. Apparently cartel members believed that price fixing was more likely to be detected and prosecuted if directed against the federal government. In other cases, some market segments were excluded from agreements in order to reduce potential friction among cartel members. Fraas and Greer (1977) found that 19 percent of all cases over a longer period involved bid rigging. Posner (1970) determined that 7.4 percent of all cases involved sales to the government, and 6.7 percent involved other bidding cases.

[19]"Witness Says Mob Is into Highrises," *San Francisco Chronicle,* April 30, 1988:A7.

EXAMPLE 5.3 *Concrete Example of Government-Aided Collusion*

Members of a cartel have an incentive to undercut an agreed collusive price. If cartel members cannot detect such "cheating," the cartel is likely to fail. If a government agency publishes the prices each firm charges, it may facilitate the maintenance of a cartel, as appears to have been the case recently in Denmark.

Stigler (1964a) explained how the same factors that lead to a successful cartel also can result in successful tacit collusion. Many of the conditions necessary for successful tacit collusion in the ready-mixed concrete market were already in place prior to the government actions. The ready-mixed concrete market in Denmark consists of a relatively small number of firms. The two largest firms have plants throughout the country and compete with a number of smaller firms. Because ready-mixed concrete can be kept in a mixer truck for only about two hours after the mixing, it is typically shipped no more than 20 miles from the production site. As a consequence, relatively few firms compete in a given area: Usually fewer than 5 of the 115 plants in Denmark can serve a particular customer. Although the national four-firm concentration ratio is 57%, many local markets are monopolistic and the average market share of the largest firm in an area is 70%.

In 1993, the Danish antitrust authority started gathering and publishing firm-specific transaction prices for two grades of ready-mixed concrete. The government hoped that by providing buyers with price information, seller competition would be stimulated and price would fall.

According to Albæk, Møllgaard, and Overgaard (1997), the government's actions led to successful tacit collusive behavior: Prices rose and the variance in prices across firms was nearly eliminated. The average prices of the reported grades increased by 15–20% within less than a year (compared to an annual inflation rate of no more than 2%). No dramatic changes in costs or other factors explain this large increase (indeed wages, a major component of costs, fell during this period). Moreover, the variance in firms' prices dropped from about 30% around the average to only about 2–4%. Thus, it appears that the firms were able to set a higher price as a consequence of the government's information program.

When smaller contractors complained about the arrangement, they were given the right to split all jobs worth over $3 million. He said the Genovese family was "a very disciplined organization" with strict rules and capital punishment for serious violations.

Public availability of information can greatly simplify cartel enforcement. Publicly announcing price increases and decreases well in advance is one method of making price information available to all interested parties. An extreme, special case of sharing information occurs when a single sales agent or pool is used by all firms for all their sales, as was the case in 3 percent of the cases Fraas and Greer (1977) examined and in 6 percent of the cases studied by Posner (1970). Sales agents are commonly used in European cartels.

If some firms are *vertically integrated* (the same firm produces inputs, manufactures the product, and sells at the retail level), it may be difficult for the cartel to determine at what point in the distribution chain cheating occurs. In contrast, if all firms sell to the same type of customer (for example, at the retail level), cheating is easier to detect.

Cartels with Little Incentive to Cheat. A cartel may find enforcement easy under certain circumstances. Members have no incentive to cheat on the cartel agreement if their marginal cost curves are relatively inelastic, their fixed costs are low relative to total costs, their customers place small, frequent orders, or they have a single sales agent.

If a firm's marginal cost curve is nearly vertical, it has little to gain by cheating on the cartel agreement because it costs too much to substantially increase its output. In Figure 5.1a, if the marginal cost curve were nearly vertical, q^* would be close to q_c. Marginal cost curves are likely to be nearly vertical if firms are operating near their full capacities. Indeed, cartels may force their marginal cost curves to be more vertical by signing union contracts that require double wages for overtime work or using similar techniques (Maloney, McCormick, and Tollison 1979).[20]

Suppose a firm incurs a large fixed cost to build a plant in which it can produce at a constant marginal cost at any output level up to the plant's capacity. Such a firm has substantial unutilized capacity when demand falls (such as during a recession). It has an incentive to lower its price below the cartel level to stimulate its sales.

If there are many customers in a market who make small purchases, no firm has an incentive to lower prices below the cartel level. If it does so without announcing the price cut, other customers are unlikely to learn of the price cut; hence its sales will not rise. If the firm advertises its price reduction, the other cartel members will learn of the cut and retaliate. In contrast, when only a few customers place large, infrequent orders, a cartel has trouble detecting and preventing cheating.[21] Firms have an incentive to grant price reductions to large buyers to keep them as customers.

Legal cartels can try to prevent cheating by requiring that a single agent or organization sell output from all firms. For example, the iodine cartel, one of the longest-lived international cartels (61 years: 1878–1939), made all its sales through a central office in London (Eckbo 1976). See Example 5.4.

Methods of Preventing Cheating. Unless a cartel can detect violations of its price-fixing agreement and prevent reoccurrences, member firms engage in secret price cutting (or output expansions) that destroys the cartel. Although economists and lawyers understand a number of mechanisms that aid cartels in enforcing their agreements, the most successful cartel agreements and their enforcement mechanisms may be unknown. Here, we concentrate on six methods: fix more than just price, divide the market, fix market shares, use most-favored-nation clauses, use meeting-competition clauses, and establish trigger prices.

---

[20]So long as a cartel raises its marginal cost curve by more than its average cost curve, such actions increase profits (Salop, Scheffman, and Schwartz, 1984).

[21]Hay and Kelley (1974) argued that bid rigging and allocation of jobs among cartel members occur in industries in which orders are relatively large ("lumpy") compared to total sales.

EXAMPLE 5.4 *Relieving the Headache of Running a Cartel*

The major use for bromine in the late 1800s was as a headache remedy and sedative. The bromine industry was not concentrated and consisted of many small producers. Ordinarily, such an industry would not be a good candidate for a cartel because of the large number of producers.

In the early 1880s, the price of bromine fell by 40 percent. In 1885, the National Bromine Company ("bromine pool") was formed. It purchased the bromine produced by all manufacturers. The bromine pool then sold bromine to two independent distributors of chemicals, Powers and Weightman of Philadelphia and Malinckrodt Chemical Works of St. Louis, which were obligated collectively to buy the entire output of the pool. In turn, these two distributors sold to customers in their territories. The bromine pool required that manufacturers sell exclusively to it and that, if any manufacturer violated this provision, contracts with all other manufacturers could be terminated. Moreover, if a manufacturer entered the industry and did not contract with the bromine pool, contracts with other manufacturers could be terminated. The two distributors who were obligated by contract to purchase all the pool's output accumulated large inventories of bromine, which they threatened to dump on the market if any manufacturer failed to cooperate with the pool. Indeed, inventories were sold during price wars in 1886 and 1888 in order to punish competitors and to restore pricing discipline.

The distributors were much better able than individual manufacturers to monitor sales to customers and thus to detect whether any manufacturers were making secret sales. For their role in the cartel, the independent distributors took a significant share of the cartel profits. In 1892, this share was renegotiated to give a larger portion to manufacturers. (The original pool was replaced by W. R. Shields, which performed similar functions.)

The very successful bromine cartel lasted from 1885 to 1902. During its reign, the average price of bromine was about 25 percent higher than the average in the years before the cartel's formation.

There were only three periods of extended price wars over the cartel's roughly 20-year life span. The cartel ended because Dow Chemical Company developed a low-cost method of processing bromine in the 1890s. Dow initially signed contracts with the two bromine distributors that the bromine cartel had used as its exclusive distributors. But in 1902, Dow had grown so large that it decided not to rely exclusively on distributors to sell its products, and began selling directly to customers. The pool fell apart and the price of potassium bromide (the major bromine product) plunged 45 percent in two months. Undoubtedly, the demand by owners of small bromine-processing firms for potassium bromide as a headache remedy increased.

Source: Levenstein (1993).

To prevent cheating, successful cartels must do more than just set a price. Posner (1970, 400) finds that at least 14% of all Department of Justice antitrust cases involved explicit collusion on terms besides basic price (and this figure apparently does not include explicit rules on dividing the market, exchanging information, or sales quotas).[22]

Some cartels succeed in preventing cheating by assigning each firm certain buyers or geographic areas, which allows cheating to be detected easily. Fraas and Greer (1977) found that 26% of price-fixing cases involved market allocation schemes. Posner (1970) found that 7.8% of the antitrust cases involved an allocation of customers, 14.6% involved a division of territories, and 1.8% involved a division of product markets (or 24% overall). The two-country mercury cartel used a geographic division of markets: Spain supplied the United States, and Italy supplied Europe.

Another effective technique is for members of a cartel to agree to fix market shares (say, at their precartel levels). (See Example 5.5.) As long as market shares are easily observable, no firm has an incentive to cut its price. If it lowered its price, its share would increase, and other firms would retaliate. For example, cartel members who detect changes in the output levels of other firms could adjust their own output to maintain their proportionate shares of market output (Osborne 1976; Spence 1978a, 1978b). All firms expect this reaction, so no firm has an incentive to increase its own output only to earn lower profits after retaliation. As **www.aw-bc.com/carlton_perloff** "Conjectural Variations" discusses, fixing market shares can result in the cartel price.

A **most-favored-nation clause** in a sales contract guarantees the buyer that the seller is not selling at a lower price to another buyer (Salop 1986). A variant of such clauses was used in sales of large steam-turbine generators. The two major sellers, General Electric and Westinghouse (see Example 5.1), each used clauses in their contracts stating that the seller would not offer a lower price to any other buyer, current or future, without offering the same price decrease to the initial buyer. This rebate mechanism created a penalty for cheating on the cartel: If either company deviated from the agreement by cutting its price, it would have to cut prices to all previous buyers as well.

A **meeting-competition clause** in a long-term supply contract or in an advertisement guarantees the buyer that if another firm offers a lower price, the seller will match it or release the buyer from the contract (Salop 1986). Such a clause makes it difficult for a firm to cheat, because buyers will bring news of lower prices to the cartel. Thus, surprisingly, these clauses could be associated with high cartel prices rather than the low ones they seem to guarantee.

---

[22]Posner (2003, 51) notes, "The machinery [of cartelization] may include sales quotas, exclusive sales agencies, industry-wide price-fixing committees, the levying of penalties for infractions, provisions for the arbitration of disputes, the establishment of an investigative apparatus product standardization, allocation of customers, and the division of geographical markets."

EXAMPLE 5.5 *Vitamins Cartel*

In the 1990s, there was a massive worldwide cartel involving many different vitamins, including biotin, folic acid, and vitamins A, B1, B2, B5, B6, C, and E, among others. Vitamins have a wide variety of uses as additives to human and animal diets and in skin and healthcare products. The various vitamins are not substitutes for each other.

Vitamin production is highly concentrated among a few firms. At the time of the cartel, the three largest producers were Hoffman-LaRoche (which since has sold its vitamins business), which produced 40 to 50 percent of all vitamins; BASF, with a 20 to 30 percent share; and Aventis (formerly Rhone-Poulenc), with a 5 to 15 percent share. These major manufacturers produced many of the same vitamins. Over half of all vitamin sales were for vitamins A and E, which were sold by all three major producers.

Allegedly beginning in 1989, Hoffman-LaRoche, BASF, and Rhone-Poulenc held meetings to discuss allocations of market sales around the world so as to reduce competition, and soon thereafter other firms became involved in a worldwide cartel.

The cartel fixed market shares for each vitamin by country, agreed on price increases, specified target prices and minimum prices, and shared information to ensure that each firm was abiding by its allocation. Sometimes the firms explicitly discussed large individual customers and agreed on those customers' prices and how much of the customers' needs each manufacturer would supply.

The firms met regularly. There were four levels of meetings: the highest level involving senior executives who determined overall strategy and adherence to the agreements; the next level involving marketing executives about two or three times a year; another meeting (usually quarterly) involving marketing managers of individual products to monitor the implementation of the allocations; and finally, quarterly meetings of regional marketing managers to discuss pricing, implement price increases, and adjust allocations. The "budget meetings" in August were used to outline allocations for the coming year, together with price increases.

All cartel members could agree that if the market price drops below a certain level (called a **trigger price**), each firm will expand its output to the precartel level (Friedman 1971); that is, all firms will abandon the cartel agreement. In this case, a firm that cuts its price might gain in the extremely short run, but would lose in the end due to the destruction of the cartel by this predetermined punishment mechanism.

One reason to use trigger prices is that, in some markets, firms have difficulty distinguishing between cheating by other firms and random fluctuations in price due to fluctuations in demand or supply costs. It is possible, however, for cartels to modify their punishment methods to prevent cheating even when random shocks occur (Green and Porter 1984). If firms were to permanently revert to competitive behavior whenever they detected a fall in price, the cartel could be destroyed by a random fluctuation in

The price was usually raised in increments of 5 percent, and the effective date of a price increase was often April 1 of the next year. Hoffman-LaRoche typically initiated the price increases, with the other firms following suit. The detailed exchanges of sales information allowed the firms to monitor adherence to their sales allocation. If a firm had sold too much in a given year, it could be required to buy supplies from the other firms to restore the original sales allocation.

Although the exact amounts by which the cartel raised prices are subject to dispute, the increases during the cartel period were sizable. For example, the average price for vitamin A rose by 40 percent and that of vitamin E increased over 60 percent from 1990 to 1998. The price of vitamin C rose by about 30 percent during the identified cartel period and fell by 50 percent thereafter.

Starting in the late 1990s, Rhone-Poulenc participated in the U.S. Justice Department's corporate leniency program. The first cartel member to confess to the DOJ—if it is not a ringleader or enforcer in the conspiracy and if the DOJ is not aware of the illegal activity—is granted automatic amnesty. Rhone-Poulenc revealed the existence of the cartel and details about its operations so as to avoid antitrust fines. Subsequently other cartel members agreed to pay multimillion-dollar fines. These same firms had to pay fines to Canadian and European Union competition authorities as well.

The fines were substantially larger than had been collected in previous antitrust cases. The largest U.S. fines were \$500 million for Hoffman-LaRoche, \$225 million for BASF, and \$72 million for the Japanese company Takeda. Two Hoffman-LaRoche executives went to jail. The biggest Canadian fines were the \$48 million (Canadian) collected from Hoffman-LaRoche, the \$18 million from BASF, and the \$14 million from Rhone-Poulenc. The major European fines were €462 million for Hoffman-LaRoche, about €300 million for BASF, and €37 million for Takeda. Private antitrust settlements collected additional amounts from the cartel members.

Source: Official Journal of the European Communities, Commission Decision of 21 November 2001. (Case Comp/E-1/37.512—Vitamins.)

price (rather than price cutting by one firm). Instead, if the firms agreed to behave competitively only for a predetermined length of time and then to revert to the cartel behavior, a random fluctuation in price would not destroy the cartel permanently.[23]

One attraction of this scheme is that, even if the agreement temporarily breaks down, it can be reestablished without further meetings. In a market in which random

[23]If the firms revert to their precartel output level, the price falls to the precartel level as well. A more severe punishment, a price below the precartel level, may be used instead: With a lower price, it may be possible to shorten the punishment period. For an illustration of how cartel prices might be set to minimize cheating, see Davidson and Martin (1985). Where members of a cartel disagree on how to behave, some kind of voting mechanism may be used (Cave and Salant 1987).

price fluctuations can mask cheating on the cartel agreement by firms, such an agreement could lead to recurrent sharp declines in price and cartel profit levels. When a random drop in price occurs, cartel members punish themselves unnecessarily.

Nonetheless, this mechanism may be attractive to the cartel because, if the punishment period (when all firms produce large levels of output) is long enough, it is never in a firm's best long-run interest to cheat on the cartel. Thus, cartel members realize that the price only falls below the trigger price because of random fluctuations (because no firm ever engages in price cutting). The cartel must keep punishing itself, however; if it stopped, price cutting would occur.[24] Example 5.6 provides an example of the American rail-freight industry in the 1880s that may illustrate such behavior.

Cartels and Price Wars

Many observers, seeing large price fluctuations in a market, argue that the firms in that market are trying to form a cartel that keeps breaking apart. They conclude that government intervention is not required because competitive forces keep destroying the cartel. Yet, these fluctuations could be part of a rational, long-run cartel policy involving trigger prices, as discussed in the preceding section. This trigger-price argument holds that price wars occur more often during unexpected business cycle downturns (recessions and depressions) when price is likely to decline in response to lowered demand (Green and Porter 1984; Staiger and Wolak 1992). We expect then that cartels are more likely to terminate during a price war. Other economists argue that price wars should occur in periods of high demand (Rotemberg and Saloner 1986). They reason that the benefit from undercutting the cartel price is greatest during booms.

To see whether either or both theories are realistic, Valerie Y. Suslow (1998) investigates the stability of cartels over the business cycle by examining 72 international cartel agreements covering 47 industries during the period 1920–39.

Because major European countries had no systematic antitrust legislation prior to World War II, these cartels were legal and had formal written contracts. As of 1927, cartels were legal in Switzerland, whereas Belgium, France, Spain, Italy, and the Netherlands did not explicitly prohibit them. Under German law, cartels were legal; however, Germany passed antitrust legislation in 1923 that was designed to guard against abuses of economic power. In 1930, Great Britain adopted a resolution recognizing cartels as a fact of economic life, but calling for the *principle of publicity,* which required compulsory notification, registration, and publication of the cartel agreements. Other European countries followed Great Britain's policy in the mid-1930s. It was not until after World War II that France passed legislation to control cartel activity.

---

[24]Bernheim and Ray (1989), Evans and Maskin (1989), Farrell and Maskin (1989), and others point out that instead of going into a punishment phase, cartel members may renegotiate their cartel agreement. These papers indicate, however, that it may be possible to form agreements that avoid this renegotiation problem.

EXAMPLE 5.6

How Consumers Were Railroaded

During the 1880s, a cartel of U.S. railroads openly operated as the Joint Executive Committee (JEC). Prior to the Sherman Act of 1890, no law prohibited such a cartel. As Porter explains, the JEC appears to have used a trigger-price strategy (Green and Porter 1984).

The JEC agreement allocated market shares rather than the absolute quantities shipped. Each railroad set its rates individually, and the JEC office reported weekly accounts, so that each railroad could see the total amount transported. Because total demand was quite variable, each firm's market share depended on both the prices charged by all firms and unpredictable market fluctuations.

Entry occurred twice between 1880 and 1886 [the period Porter (1983a) studies]. In each case, the cartel passively accepted the entrants, allocated them market shares, and thereby allowed the cartel agreement to persist.

On a number of occasions, however, when the cartel thought that cheating had occurred, it cut prices for a time, and then returned to the cartel price. Porter finds that noncooperative periods averaged about 10 weeks in duration and occurred in 1881, 1884, and 1885. The 1881 and 1884 incidents each occurred about 40 weeks after a new firm entered. He notes, however, that these price wars were not triggered by an unexpected tapering off of demand.

Porter also finds that price was 66 percent higher and quantity was 33 percent lower in co-operative periods. As a result, the cartel as a whole earned about 11 percent more revenues in cooperative periods.

Sources: MacAvoy (1965); Ulen (1980); and Porter (1983a). See also Ellison (1994).

It should have been easier for these cartels to survive than for illegal ones in the United States. German, French, or British firms were participants in roughly half the cartels, and U.S. firms were involved in one-third of them. In the 1940s, U.S. firms were indicted for their participation in 10 of these international cartels.

According to Suslow, the median cartel lasted slightly more than 5 years; 75 percent lasted more than 2 years, and 20 percent lasted more than 10 years. There was an industry pattern. Of the single-episode cartels, 40 percent involved chemicals, with only 6 percent in metals. In contrast, 46 percent of the multiple-episode cartels involved metals, with only 17 percent in chemicals.

In the 42 cartel episodes in which the number of firms is known, 83 percent had 10 or fewer firms, 64 percent had 5 or fewer, and 39 percent had 3 or fewer. Of the 74 percent of the 39 cartels for which there is market-share information, each had a world market share of over 50 percent. Thus, as with U.S. cartels, these international cartels involved relatively few firms with large collective market shares.

TABLE 5.1 **Market Conditions Facilitating Global Price Fixing in Lysine, Citric Acid, and Vitamins A and E in the Early 1990s**

Market Conditions	Lysine	Citric Acid	Synthetic Vitamins A & E
High seller concentration (CR4[a])			
Global market	> 95%	> 80%	> 95%
U.S. market	> 97%	= 90%	100%
Few cartel participants	4 or 5	4 or 5	3
High cartel supply control	95–99%	65–70%	95–100%
Low buyer concentration (CR4)	< 30%	< 40%	< 20%
Homogeneous product	Perfect	High	High
High barriers to market entry:			
Large plant scales	$150 million+	$150 million	Probably
Sunk investment costs	Yes	Yes	Yes
Technology secret	Yes	Yes	Yes
Slow building of new plants	3 years+	3 years+	3 years+
Buyers' observation of market prices	None	Some	Little
Annual market growth	10%, steady	8%, steady	2–3%, steady

[a] CR4 is the share of sales of the four largest firms in the industry.

Source: Connor (2003).

Suslow estimates the probability that a cartel will fall apart at a specific time, given that it survives until that time. Controlling for other factors, she found that cartels are more likely to fail during business-cycle downturns (recessions and depressions).[25] Moreover, cartels that were alive during periods of growth were less likely to end than others. In general, greater volatility in aggregate economic activity over the lifetime of the cartel (frequent upswings and downturns) increases the probability of cartel breakdowns.

We have discussed several factors that help a cartel to form and to prevent cheating. Many large, successful cartels possess these properties. Table 5.1 (from Connor 2003) shows the presence of these market conditions in the lysine, citric acid, and vitamins A and E industries in the early 1990s, when each had an operating cartel. Entry plays a particularly important role (see de Roos 1999 on lysine).

[25]Hajivassiliou (1989) reaches similar findings based on his study of the 1880–86 U.S. railroad cartel. Porter (1983a) and Lee and Porter (1984) examine this cartel's behavior under the maintained assumption of the Green and Porter model. Town (1991) rejects both the Green and Porter and the Rotemberg and Saloner hypotheses for this cartel and concludes that price wars were not related to demand fluctuations.

Consumers Gain as Cartels Fail

Firms that follow a cartel's rules look with disfavor on firms that produce more than the cartel says they should. Violators of the cartel's rules may be called "cheaters" or worse by the firms that obey them. Consumers, however, benefit from such noncartel behavior. The violators of the cartel agreement produce more than the cartel wants, which lowers the market price.

A numerical example illustrates the effects of noncompliance by some firms (see Appendix 5A for details). The market in this example includes 50 identical firms. We assume that no more firms can enter this market.

Of the 50 firms, j firms do not follow the cartel's agreement to restrict output; they sell as much as they want. These firms are price takers. *The cartel is a dominant firm facing a competitive fringe,* as we studied in Chapter 4.

The residual demand facing the cartel is obtained by subtracting the fringe supply from the market demand. Figure 5.2b shows the residual demand curve (thick dark blue line) that lies below the market demand curve (thin blue line) at prices above the competitive firms' shutdown level ($p = 10$).[26] The residual demand curve has a kink

FIGURE 5.2 Imperfect Cartel

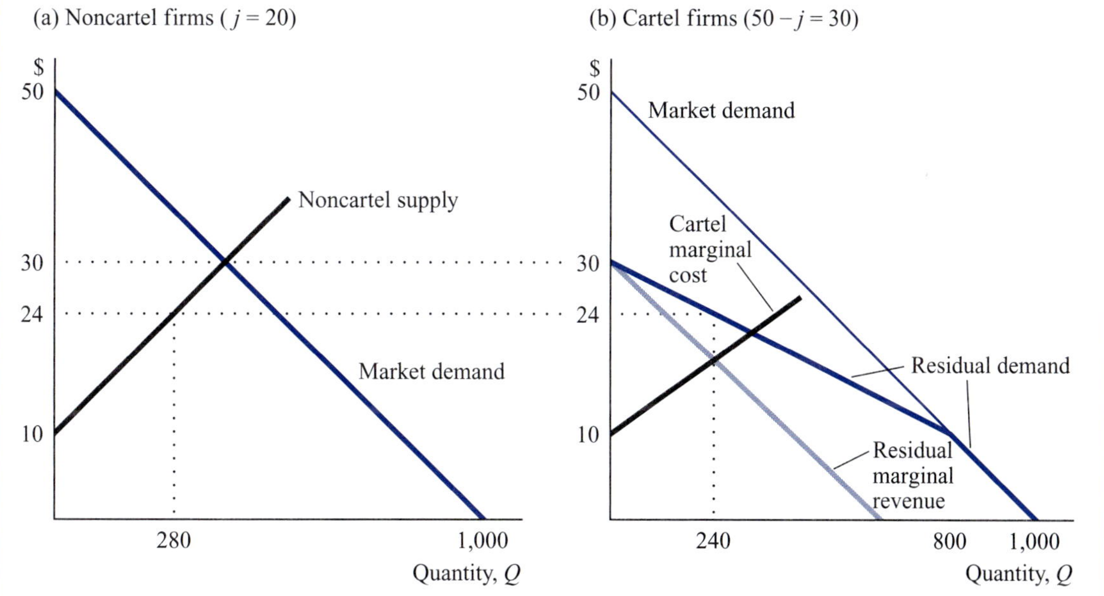

[26]Because each competitive firm's supply curve is $q = 10 + p$, it would lose money if it produced positive levels of output at prices below 10.

TABLE 5.2 **Market Variables Under Various Degrees of Cartelization (50 Firms)**

	Number of Noncartel Firms	Price (p)	Market Elasticity	Market Output	Industry Profits (π)	Consumer Surplus (CS)	Welfare ($CS + \pi$)
Monopoly	0	33.33	−2.00	333	6,667	2,778	9,445
	1	32.41	−1.84	352	6,524	3,094	9,618
	10	26.97	−1.17	461	5,318	5,304	10,622
	20	24.00	−0.92	520	4,360	6,760	11,120
	30	22.44	−0.81	551	3,743	7,591	11,337
	40	21.67	−0.76	567	3,391	8,027	11,418
	49	21.431	−0.75	571	3,267	8,162	11,428
Competition	50	21.429	−0.75	571	3,265	8,163	11,429

CS = Consumer Surplus is the triangle with area $(1{,}000 - 20p)^2/40$.
Cartel's Market Share (as a percentage) = 100 times the cartel's sales divided by total sales.
DWL = Deadweight Loss (competitive welfare − actual welfare).
Price Markup (as a percentage) = $100(p - MC)/p$.

in it at $p = 10$. Because cartel firms have the same cost functions as noncartel firms, the cartel cannot afford to produce at prices below $p = 10$ either, so the lower portion of the residual demand curve is not of interest. The profit-maximizing cartel chooses its output, 240, by setting its marginal revenue (the curve marginal to its residual demand curve) equal to its marginal cost, as shown in Figure 5.2b. This output determines the cartel price, 24. At that price, the noncartel firms' output is 280, as Figure 5.2a shows.

Table 5.2 shows what happens as the number of firms belonging to the cartel changes. The market is in competitive equilibrium when all 50 firms act independently and do not belong to the cartel ($j = 50$). The competitive market price is \$21.43, and consumer surplus and total welfare are maximized.

At the other extreme, if all the firms join the cartel ($j = 0$), the cartel is a monopoly. The monopoly price is \$33.33, or 56 percent higher than the competitive price. Only 333 units of output are produced by the market, or 58 percent as much as the competitive quantity, 571. However, each firm's profits of \$133.33 is more than double the competitive level, \$65.31. Consumer surplus is only about one-third as great, and total welfare is only 83 percent as great as under competition; that is, consumer losses are greater than the cartel gains. This loss to society, the *deadweight loss* to monopoly (see Chapter 4), is 18 percent of sales and 71 percent of consumer surplus (at the monopoly price).

DWL as % of Sales	Cartel's Market Share (%)	Price Markup (%)	Cartel Firm Output	Cartel Firm Profits	Noncartel Firm Output	Noncartel Firm Profits
17.9	100	50	6.66	133.33	—	—
15.9	94	48	6.72	128.02	22.41	251.10
6.5	63	36	7.27	96.95	16.97	143.99
2.5	46	25	8.00	80.00	14.00	98.00
0.7	32	16	8.89	71.08	12.44	77.38
0.1	18	8	10.00	66.70	11.67	68.09
0.0	2	1	11.27	65.32	11.431	65.33
—	0	—	—	—	11.429	65.31

As the cartel gains members, the incentive of a cartel firm to cheat also grows, because the discrepancy between a nonmember's profit and a cartel firm's profit increases. At every price, nonmembers earn more than cartel members, because nonmembers produce more yet sell at the same price as cartel members.

Consumers benefit if firms refuse to join the cartel. If only one firm refuses to abide by the cartel rules and is a price taker, market price is about 3 percent lower than the monopoly price, deadweight loss is 10 percent lower, and consumer surplus is 10 percent higher.

Table 5.2 also shows that it hardly pays for one firm to try to act as a price setter by itself. If one firm forms a "cartel" consisting only of itself (so that there are 49 noncartel firms), it faces a residual demand curve with only a slight slope. It can reduce its output from the competitive level of 11.429 to 11.27 units, thereby maximizing its profits, which rise by 1¢ from $65.31 to $65.32. The 49 noncartel firms, seeing the higher price and acting as price takers, increase their output to 11.431 units, causing profits to rise by a phenomenal 2¢ to $65.33—each noncartel firm's profits rise by more than those of the single-firm cartel. All firms' profits rise in this case because the expansion of output by the 49 noncartel firms does not completely offset the reduction in output by the single firm. Total market output falls from 571.43 to 571.38 units, causing the price to rise from $21.429 to $21.431. The welfare losses from such a limited cartel are small. The larger the market share of the cartel, the greater the efficiency cost. See Example 5.7.

EXAMPLE 5.7

The Social Costs of Cartelization

Posner (2003) estimates the social cost of several (mainly international) well-organized, overt cartels using his theory, discussed in Chapter 4, that all cartel profits are dissipated in rent-seeking activity. His results are shown in the table.

Industry	Cartel Price Increase (%)	Elasticity	Social Costs (as % of Industry's Sales)
Nitrogen	75	2.33	64
Sugar	30	4.33	35
Aluminum	100	2.00	75
Aluminum	59	3.63	56
Rubber	100	2.00	75
Electric bulbs	37	3.70	44
Copper	31	4.22	36
Cast-iron pipe	39	3.56	42

Note: These figures are based on the Appendix in Posner (2003). Apparently, two figures are given for aluminum because he has two estimates of the cartel price increase.

The elasticities are based on the cartels' price-increase data, on the assumptions that the industry is charging the profit-maximizing monopoly price and that the demand curve is linear. Because of these restrictive assumptions, Posner warns that these results should be viewed with some caution. Nonetheless, if these figures are anywhere near accurate, the social costs of these cartels are large.

Source: R. A. Posner, *Antitrust Law,* ©2003 by The University of Chicago. All Rights Reserved.

Price-Fixing Laws

Nothing is illegal if a hundred businessmen decide to do it.

—Andrew Young

In the late nineteenth century, cartels were legal and operated in several U.S. industries, including oil, powder, railroads, sugar, and tobacco. The Sherman Antitrust Act of 1890 was passed in response to this activity "to protect trade and commerce against unlawful restraints and monopolies" (see Chapter 19). In 1914, the Federal Trade Commission Act established the Federal Trade Commission (FTC), and its Section 5 holds that "unfair methods of competition are hereby declared illegal." This act is still used by the FTC in prosecuting antitrust violations, as is the Sherman Act by the U.S. Department of Justice.

The Sherman Act makes illegal conspiracies whose sole purpose is to raise price. For example, in the *Addyston Pipe and Steel* case in 1899, outright bid rigging and the dividing of the market into regional monopolies were found illegal.[27]

The *Trenton Potteries* case of 1927 and *Socony-Vacuum Oil Co.* case of 1940 determined that price fixing was a **per se** violation (the action by itself is illegal), regardless of whether the price set was above the competitive price.[28] These cases established that the violation is the *attempt* to charge the monopoly price; the government does not have to show that the defendants succeeded in their attempt (Posner 2003). Cartels formed solely to raise price are strictly prohibited.

Table 5.3 (based on Connor 2003) shows the number of price-fixing cases the DOJ filed over the period 1970–99, how many fines were collected, and the number in which individuals received prison sentences. Example 5.8 shows that U.S., Canadian, EC, and other antitrust authorities have heavily fined corporations engaged in global conspiracies since the early 1990s.

This approach to preventing price fixing is based on evidence of conspiracy rather than the economic effects of the conspiracy. The government seeks evidence of conspiracies (such as secret meetings in smoke-filled rooms) rather than economic evidence (such as price increases). Cases involving only tacit collusion (that is, without explicit communications between the parties) are not actionable under antitrust laws.

The current laws have been successful in eliminating overt (but not tacit) collusion. Posner (2003, 52) observes that the "elimination [of the cartel] is an impressive and remains the major, achievement of American antitrust." Increasingly, many other countries, especially those in Europe, actively try to prevent cartels.

TABLE 5.3 **Fines and Sentences in U.S. Department of Justice Price-Fixing Cases, 1970–1999**

Years	Number of Criminal Cases Filed	Cases in Which Fines Imposed	Cases in Which Prison Sentences Imposed
1970–1979	176	156	25
1980–1989	623	513	196
1990–1999	416	324	61

Source: Connor (2003).

[27] *Addyston Pipe and Steel Co. v. United States,* 175 U.S. 211 (1899). This citation is from the U.S. Reporter volume 175 and starts on page 211. The case was decided by the U.S. Supreme Court in 1899.

[28] *United States v. Trenton Potteries Co.,* 273 U.S. 392 (1927) established a per se rule. A later case, *Appalachian Coals, Inc. v. United States,* 288 U.S. 344 (1933), however, appeared to deviate from this per se rule. *United States v. Socony-Vacuum Oil Co.,* 310 U.S. 150 (1940) firmly established the per se rule.

EXAMPLE 5.8 *Prosecuting Global Cartels*

Between World War II and the 1990s, few private (non–government-run) global cartels were observed, although there were a number of government-organized cartels, as discussed in Example 5.2. The period since 1990 has seen an explosion of private international cartels that have been identified and prosecuted by antitrust agencies in North America and Europe. From 1993 through July 2003, antitrust authorities discovered (engaged in public investigation, handed down indictments, or imposed fines) 167 private cartels with corporate or individual participants from at least two countries. By July 2003, 128 were at least partially prosecuted, and public investigations were initiated for another 39. Moreover, approximately 35 secret U.S. grand-jury investigations of international cartels were ongoing.

Since the early 1990s, U.S., Canadian, EC and other antitrust authorities have heavily fined corporations engaged in global conspiracies. The prosecutions of 20 global (multicontinent) cartels after 1995 resulted in heavy fines in all cases and prison sentences in half. From 1996 through mid-2003, U.S., Canadian, EC and other antitrust authorities have imposed fines of over $5.3 billion on corporations engaged in international conspiracies.

Of the cartels, 31% operated in two or more continents, with most of them in North America, Europe, and Asia (covering 51% of affected sales); 20% had sales within more than one EU country (25% of sales); 26% operated in a single European country (13% of sales); 19% were only in the United States or Canada (11% of sales); and only six international cartels were discovered elsewhere.

Compared to previous international cartels, their markets encompassed more of the world, and hence the damages they inflicted were accordingly greater. Firms engaged in international cartels that were successfully prosecuted by the U.S. Department of Justice (DOJ) had sales that exceeded $55 billion. The DOJ collected over $900 million from international price fixers in 1999 alone—far more than it collected in the previous 108 years of U.S. antitrust enforcement.

For the 60 cartels for which he had adequate information, Connor (2003) reported that the cartels raised prices by an average of 28% (25% in organic chemicals and 35% in other industries). International cartel sales were concentrated in a few industries: 39% involved intermediate organic chemicals, 52% were other manufacturers (mostly metal, cement, plastics, graphite products) and the remaining 9% were in

SUMMARY

Firms have incentives both to form cartels and to cheat on the cartel arrangement. Firms want to join cartels if the cartel is capable of raising prices for sustained periods of time. Prices are more likely to be significantly elevated above the competitive level when the cartel controls a substantial share of the market's output, when it faces a relatively inelas-

construction, transport, finance, and other services. However, over 80% of sales in cartels discovered before 2000 involved food and agriculture.

The world's major antitrust agencies have responded to these threats to worldwide economic well-being by imposing unprecedented sanctions (1990–2003: $2.3 billion by the United States, €3.6 billion by the European Union). Of those corporations accused by the DOJ of criminal price fixing, fewer than 1% were foreign-based firms prior to 1995, whereas more than 50% were non-U.S. corporations after 1997. The DOJ has convicted cartel executives from 12 foreign countries, sending many to prison. Similarly, between 2000 and 2002, the EC fined 42 companies that were guilty of global price fixing, of which 55% were non-EU firms.

Executives were fined in 50% of cases and received prison sentences in 33% of U.S. cases. Sixty-two executives were fined, and 43 fugitives were indicted. The individual fines added up to $24.4 million, and four fines were greater than $350,000, but the median fine was only $50,000. Of the 62 executives fined, 30 received prison sentences averaging 11.1 months. Contrary to DOJ claims for all criminal price-fixing cases, Connor failed to find an upward trend in the length of prison sentences for participants in international cartels.

Canada prosecuted 18 cases between 1991 and 2003. Most of these cases followed U.S. actions. The initial Canadian prosecution started an average of eight months after a U.S. conviction. Canada fined 68 corporations $133 million (U.S.), almost all of which were non-Canadian. These fines were about 6% of the corresponding U.S. fines. Canada also fined four individuals a total of $600,000.

From 1990 to 2003, the EU prosecuted 35 cases, of which 16 were global cartels. The EU fined or granted amnesty to 259 corporations, of which 30% were located outside the EU. On average, EU decisions lagged U.S. prosecutions by 34 months. The EU fines were about 72% of comparable U.S. fines on the same cartel cases.

Although the antitrust agencies have acted more aggressively than in the past and are imposing larger fines, cartels continue to thrive. For the period 2000 through 2003, 23 international cartels were discovered on average per year, six times faster than a decade earlier. Apparently firms believe that the fines are merely a cost of doing business, as more than 50 corporations were members of multiple cartels (up to 13).

Source: Connor (2003).

tic demand curve, and when entry is limited. The expected rewards of forming illegal cartels are greater when detection by the government is unlikely and the fines are low.

Cartels fail due to cheating by member firms or by competition from firms outside the cartel. Individual firms have an incentive to cheat on a cartel agreement because they can make higher profits by increasing output or undercutting the cartel's price. A cartel can maintain its agreement only if cheating can be detected and adequately punished. Cartels have developed a number of techniques, including division of the market and complex contract clauses, in order to enforce their agreements.

When cartels succeed in raising prices, there is a loss of consumer surplus. The gain to the cartel is less than the loss to consumers: The difference is a deadweight (efficiency) loss. The fewer the firms that go along with the cartel agreement, the less market power the cartel has, and hence the less it harms consumers and society.

The U.S. government and many others have antitrust laws that penalize firms that form cartels. At least in the United States, price-fixing cartels have been vigorously prosecuted.

PROBLEMS

1. Suppose cartel members have lower (average and marginal) costs than noncartel firms. Draw the residual demand curve facing the cartel. (What assumptions are you making about entry?) Show on the graph the cartel's profit-maximizing output and price. Could the cartel drive the other firms out of business and still make a profit? Under what conditions?
2. In what way does a cartel consisting of only some firms in a market correspond to the dominant firm model described in Chapter 4?
3. Use a graph to show why an increase in the market demand elasticity reduces a cartel's monopoly power. Show how an increase in the market demand elasticity affects the elasticity of the residual demand curve.
4. (Problem based on Appendix 5A.) Show that the sum of a cartel's output plus the output of noncartel firms is less than the competitive output and that the corresponding price is higher than the competitive price.
5. (Problem based on Appendix 5A.) Show that a cartel's price falls as the number of noncartel firms (j) increases.

Answers to odd-numbered problems are given at the back of the book.

SUGGESTED READINGS

A good survey of modern thought on cartels is Jacquemin and Slade (1989). If you want to see how an actual cartel operates, go to **www.aw-bc.com/carlton_perloff**, Chapter 5, "A Cartel at Work." There, you will find a link (**www.usdoj.gov/atr/public/speeches/4489.htm**) to a speech given April 6, 2000 by James M. Griffin, Deputy Assistant Attorney General, Antitrust Division, U.S. Department of Justice, entitled "An Inside Look at a Cartel at Work: Common Characteristics of International Cartels," in which Griffin outlines how the international lysine cartel worked. The Department of Justice can supply you with an actual tape of the lysine cartel meetings. Contact the United States Department of Justice, Antitrust Division, Freedom of Information Act Unit, 325 Seventh Street, N.W., Suite 200, Washington, DC, 20530. Connor (2001) extensively analyzes global cartels since 1990.

APPENDIX 5A

The Effects of Cartel Size

This appendix derives the equations used in the example reported in Table 5.2, which shows how price and output vary with the number of cartel members. The total number of firms is assumed to be fixed at n—no further entry is possible.

The market demand curve is linear:

$$Q = a - bp, \tag{5A.1}$$

where a and b are positive constants, Q is market output, and p is the price. The elasticity of demand is

$$\epsilon = \frac{dQ}{dp}\frac{p}{Q} = 1 - \frac{a}{Q} = \frac{-bp}{a - bp}. \tag{5A.2}$$

Each firm has a linear marginal cost (MC) of

$$MC = d + eq, \tag{5A.3}$$

where q is the output of one of the n firms and d and e are positive constants. As a result, the competitive supply (the output produced at the point where marginal cost equals price) is

$$Q = nq = \frac{n(p - d)}{e}. \tag{5A.4}$$

Competitive equilibrium is determined by setting the right-hand sides of the quantity-demanded equation (5A.1) and the quantity-supplied equation (5A.4) equal, and solving for p_c (the equilibrium price). The equilibrium quantity, Q_c, can be found by substituting p_c into Equation 5A.1 or 5A.4. The equilibrium values are

$$p_c = \frac{ae + nd}{be + n}, \tag{5A.5}$$

$$Q_c = n\left(\frac{a - bd}{be + n}\right). \tag{5A.6}$$

Now suppose that $n - j$ firms in the market form a cartel and the remaining j firms ($j < n$) do not. As shown in Figure 5.2b, the residual demand, Q_r, is the market demand minus the noncartel supply, $Q_{nc} = jq$:

$$Q_r = Q - jq = a - bp - \frac{j(p - d)}{e}. \tag{5A.7}$$

The cartel acts as a monopoly with respect to its residual demand and sets its marginal revenue, MR_m, equal to its marginal cost. The cartel's revenues, R_m, may be found by solving Equation 5A.7 for p as a function of Q_r and multiplying that by Q_r to obtain

$$R_m = pQ_r = \left(\frac{ae + jd - eQ_r}{be + j}\right)Q_r. \tag{5A.8}$$

By differentiating R_m with respect to Q_r, we obtain the cartel's marginal revenue:

$$MR_m = \frac{ae + jd}{be + j} - \left(\frac{2e}{be + j}\right)Q_r. \tag{5A.9}$$

The cartel's marginal cost is

$$MC_m = d + \left(\frac{e}{n - j}\right)Q_m. \tag{5A.10}$$

The quantity the cartel chooses to produce, Q_m $(= Q_r)$, is determined by equating the cartel's marginal revenue, Equation 5A.9, and marginal cost, Equation 5A.10:

$$Q_m = \frac{(n - j)(a - bd)}{be + 2n - j}. \tag{5A.11}$$

By differentiating Q_m with respect to j, it can be shown that the cartel's output falls as the number of nonmember firms rises.

CHAPTER 6

Oligopoly

The Puritan's idea of hell is a place where everybody has to mind his own business.
—Wendell Phillips (attributed)

Although there is only one model of competition and one model of monopoly, there are many models of **oligopoly**: a small number of firms acting independently but aware of one another's existence. Unlike monopolistic and competitive firms, noncooperative oligopolists cannot blithely ignore other firms' actions.

As the only firm in an industry, a monopolist has no rivals. At the other extreme, individual competitive firms are too small to affect the industry's price, so each firm reasonably ignores the actions of any other; only the industry's collective actions matter to a competitive firm. In contrast, because there are only a few firms in an oligopoly, each firm knows that it can affect market price and hence its rivals' profits: Ford cannot and does not ignore Honda when making decisions. Thus, oligopoly differs from competition and monopoly in that a firm *must* consider rival firms' behavior to determine its own best policy. This interrelationship between firms is the key issue examined in this chapter. The factors discussed in Chapter 5 that influence a cartel's success also affect how oligopolistic rivals interact. For that reason, Stigler (1964a) regarded cartel theory as the basis for understanding the forces at work in any oligopoly.

Many industries are highly *concentrated* (see Chapter 8): A few firms make virtually all the sales. For example, the top four cereal manufacturers sell 90 percent of all breakfast cereals, and the top eight sell 98 percent. Only a handful of manufacturers produce many common consumer durables.

Where transportation costs or tariffs are so high that it is not cost-effective to ship a product outside of a small geographic region or local market, oligopolies are common. In countries with smaller markets (fewer consumers), many industries are oligopolistic.[1]

This chapter presents the best-known noncooperative oligopoly models. To keep the discussion as simple as possible, five strong assumptions are made:

1. Consumers are price takers.
2. All firms produce *homogeneous* (identical) products: Consumers perceive no differences among them.
3. There is *no entry* into the industry, so the number of firms remains constant over time.
4. Firms collectively have market power: They can set price above marginal cost.
5. Each firm only sets its price or output (not advertising or other variables).

The next chapter extends these models to consider *heterogeneous* (differentiated) products and entry of new firms. Chapter 14 discusses advertising, and Chapter 11 discusses other strategic actions beyond setting price or output.

The equilibrium price in an oligopoly market lies between that of competition and monopoly. In all of the oligopoly models, each firm maximizes its profits given its beliefs about how other firms behave: Each firm's expected profits are maximized when its *expected marginal revenue equals its marginal cost.* As in earlier chapters, a firm's marginal revenue depends on the *residual demand curve* facing that firm (the market demand minus the output supplied by its rivals). Indeed, the differences in the various oligopoly models are reflected in terms of differences in the residual demand curves facing firms.

All the oligopoly models may be seen as examples of noncooperative *game theory* (von Neuman and Morgenstern 1944), which uses formal models to analyze conflict and cooperation between **players** (strategic decision makers—firms in this chapter).[2] A **game** is any competition in which strategic behavior is important. Each firm forms a *strategy* or battle plan of the actions it will take (such as the prices it will set) to compete with other firms. Each firm's **payoff** (the reward received at the end of a game, profits) depends on the actions of all the firms.

The various oligopoly models differ in the type of actions firms may use (such as set prices or set outputs), the order in which they may take actions (such as which firm sets its price first), the length of the game (one-period model or many periods), and in other ways. Although there is extensive agreement among economists on the model of competition and the model of monopoly, there is no consensus on a single noncooperative oligopoly model. One reason for the lack of agreement is that market characteristics of real-world oligopolies differ substantially, so that the appropriate model varies by market.

Three of the best-known oligopoly models are the Cournot, Bertrand, and Stackelberg models. Firms set output levels in the Cournot and Stackelberg models, whereas

---

[1]Similarly, *oligopsonies* (few buyers) are frequently observed. For years, only two firms purchased most of the mussels caught in New England, and four firms bought most of the Pacific tuna.

[2]Another branch of game theory, cooperative game theory, is rarely used in modeling oligopolies. A notable exception is Telser (1972, 1978).

they set prices in the Bertrand model. All the firms act at the same time in the Cournot and Bertrand models, whereas one firm sets its output level before the others in the Stackelberg model. These differences in the actions firms use and the order in which they act result in different equilibria.

Similarly, some markets last for only one period and others last for many. For example, a *static* or *one-period* game model is appropriate when firms from all over the country meet only once at a one-day crafts fair. Such firms set their price or quantity that day and do not have an opportunity to observe how their rivals behave and then change their own behavior in the future.

A *multiperiod* game model should be used to analyze how two crafts shops that are located next to each other compete day after day for years. Where firms compete repeatedly over time, firms may adjust their beliefs about rivals' behavior over time and may use more complex strategies than in single-period models. For example, a firm's strategy might require it to set different output levels depending on how its rivals behaved in previous periods. One possible outcome of such a model is that firms may restrict output in early periods and then produce larger quantities in the last period.

Only sets of actions by a rival that are in the rival's best interests are considered **credible strategies** by a firm. For example, if one firm threatens to price below cost forever unless another rival leaves the market, that strategy is not credible because it would lead to the bankruptcy of the price cutter (see Chapter 11). In multiperiod games, more complex credible strategies are possible than in a single-period game.

After discussing the basic concepts of noncooperative game theory, this chapter presents the three best-known oligopoly models: Cournot, Bertrand, and Stackelberg. The chapter concludes by presenting experimental and empirical tests of various oligopolistic models that support the predictions of some of these models.

The key questions examined in this chapter are

1. What factors determine the oligopoly equilibrium? How does the equilibrium vary with the number of firms, the types of actions firms may take, and the order in which firms act?
2. Is the equilibrium price more likely to be closer to the monopoly price when markets last for more than one period?
3. Are the best-known oligopoly models consistent with experimental evidence?

Game Theory

When the One Great Scorer comes to write against your name—He marks—not that you won or lost—but how you played the game.

—Grantland Rice

Game theory analyzes the interactions between rational, decision-making individuals who may not be able to predict fully the outcomes of their decisions. Models of oligopoly can be viewed as games of strategies or actions (such as setting output, price, or advertising levels). Oligopolistic games have three common elements:

1. There are two or more firms (players).
2. Each firm attempts to maximize its profit (payoff).
3. Each firm is aware that other firms' actions can affect its profit.

The third element is the crucial one. Oligopolistic markets differ from competitive and monopolistic markets because each firm's actions significantly affect its rivals. For example, oligopolists may form cartels for the purpose of mutually beneficial actions; yet, because each firm's interests are different from those of other firms, the best outcome for a particular firm is not always in the collective best interest.

In competitive and monopolistic markets, firms do not act as if the actions of rivals affect their payoffs or as if other firms may have different objectives. Indeed, the competitive model may be viewed as a game against an impersonal mechanism (the market) rather than against other players with strategies.

The equilibrium payoffs are dictated by the number of firms, the rules of the game, and the length of the game. The major single-period oligopoly models differ as to the rules of the game. After showing how the best-known single-period models vary depending on the rules of the game and the number of firms, the chapter illustrates the effect of the length of a game by contrasting single-period games to multiperiod games of various lengths.

Single-Period Oligopoly Models

Early work on oligopoly theory concentrated on single-period, or static games. Such models are appropriate for markets that last for only brief periods of time, so that rival firms compete once, but never again. In such models, complex, long-run strategies and reputations for hard-nosed competition are irrelevant.

The three best-known single-period oligopoly models date from long before the introduction of game theory. These models can be interpreted as game theoretic models, and that is how this chapter presents them.[3] All well-known single-period oligopoly models use the concept of a Nash equilibrium, which we discuss before turning to the Cournot, Bertrand, and Stackelberg models.

---

[3]Earlier versions of these models were called *conjectural variation models* (see **www.aw-bc.com/carlton_perloff** "Conjectural Variation"). Game theorists view these conjectural variation models as unsatisfactory because they use dynamic stories to explain behavior in a single period. In the conjectural variations models, each firm chooses its price or output to maximize its profit based on its conjecture (hypothesis or expectation) about how each rival firm will respond to its actions (*variations*). For example, a firm may believe its rival will do nothing in response if the firm raises its price. A belief about a rival's reaction is called a *conjectural variation.* The conjectural variation approach has been used in empirical work (see **www.aw-bc.com/carlton_perloff** "Conjectural Variation" and Chapter 8). Another early static model, sometimes described as a conjectural variations model, that has an underlying, implicitly dynamic story is the kinked demand curve: see **www.aw-bc.com/carlton_perloff** "Kinked Demand."

Nash Equilibrium

John F. Nash (1951) defined the most widely used equilibrium concept. A set of strategies is called a **Nash equilibrium** if, holding the strategies of all other firms constant, no firm can obtain a higher payoff (profit) by choosing a different strategy. Thus, in a Nash equilibrium, no firm *wants* to change its strategy.

In the Cournot and Stackelberg models, firms' strategies concern setting quantities. In the Bertrand model, firms set prices. The Nash equilibrium concept is also useful when strategies include setting advertising or other variables in addition to output or price (see Chapter 11).

The Cournot Model

The French mathematician Augustin Cournot presented the first—and probably still the most widely used—model of noncooperative oligopoly in 1838. Cournot (1963) assumed that each firm acts independently and attempts to maximize its profits by choosing its output. The discussion starts with the *duopoly*, or two-firm, case and then considers what happens as the number of firms increases.

A Cournot Duopoly. Consider a market of melons in an isolated town:

- *No entry:* There are two firms and no entry by other firms is possible (these firms own the only good farm land anywhere in the area).
- *Homogeneity:* The firms produce identical (homogenous) melons, so the sum of their outputs equals industry output: $Q = q_1 + q_2$, where Firm 1 produces q_1 and Firm 2 produces q_2.
- *Single period:* This market and the two firms only exist for one period. The melons cannot be stored: They must be sold as soon as produced or they spoil.
- *Demand:* The market demand curve (Figure 6.1) is a linear function of price:

$$Q = 1{,}000 - 1{,}000p. \tag{6.1}$$

  For example, $Q = 0$ melons when $p = \$1.00$, $Q = 500$ when $p = \$0.50$, and $Q = 1{,}000$ when $p = 0$.
- *Costs:* Each firm has a constant marginal cost, MC, of production of 28¢ per melon and no fixed costs. Thus, its average cost is also 28¢. Each firm can produce enough output to meet the entire market's demand, as Figure 6.1 shows.

What strategy should Firm 1 use to choose its output level? The answer depends on its belief about Firm 2's behavior. If Firm 1 believes that Firm 2 will sell q_2 melons, it can determine the q_1 that will maximize its profit. Firm 1 can sell all but q_2 units of the amount demanded by the market; that is, it faces the *residual demand curve,*

$$q_1 = Q(p) = q_2, \tag{6.2}$$

which is the market demand curve from Equation 6.1, minus the expected output of Firm 2, q_2. As Figure 6.1 shows, the residual demand curve is obtained by shifting the market demand curve q_2 units to the left. Thus, because the market demand curve hits

FIGURE 6.1 Residual Demand Facing a Cournot Firm

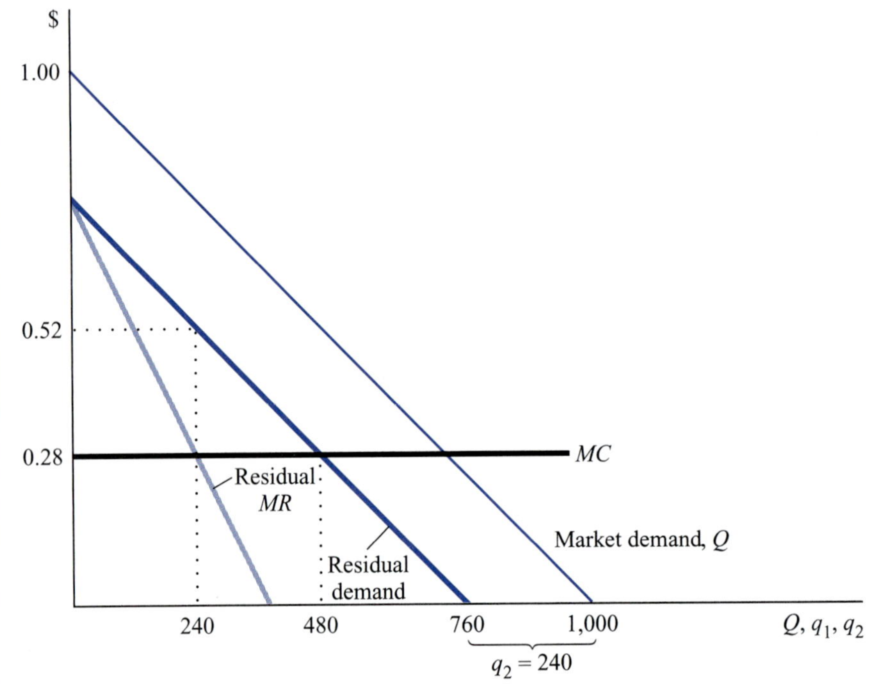

the horizontal axis at 1,000 melons, the residual demand curve hits the horizontal axis at $1{,}000 - q_2$. In the figure, q_2 is assumed to be 240 units.

Firm 1 has a monopoly over those consumers whose demands are not met by Firm 2. To maximize its profit, it sets q_1 where its marginal revenue curve based on the derived residual demand curve (residual *MR* in Figure 6.1) intersects its marginal cost curve. The profit-maximizing q_1 for various beliefs about q_2 are as follows:

If Firm 1 believes Firm 2 will sell q_2	Firm 1's profit-maximizing q_1 is
0	360
100	310
200	260
240	240
300	210
360	180
400	160
720	0

Rather than use a table, we can summarize the relationship between Firm 1's profit-maximizing quantity and Firm 2's quantity in an equation,

$$q_1 = R_1(q_2), \tag{6.3}$$

which is called a *best-response function* (or *reaction function*), which shows the best (highest profit) action (output) by a firm given its beliefs about the action its rival takes. To derive the best-response function, it is necessary to express the intersection between the marginal revenue curve and the marginal cost curve algebraically (see Appendix 6A for a mathematical derivation).

Firm 1's residual demand curve is linear, so its marginal revenue curve is also linear and has twice the slope of the residual demand curve: The MR curve hits the quantity axis at half the quantity of the demand curve (see Chapter 4). In Figure 6.1, where q_2 equals 240, the residual demand curve intersects the horizontal MC curve at $q_1 = 480$. In general, the residual demand curve intersects the marginal cost curve at $720 - q_2$. The marginal revenue curve corresponding to the residual demand curve crosses the marginal cost curve at half that value, or where $q_1 = 240$.[4] More generally, Firm 1's best-response function is

$$q_1 = R_1(q_2) = 360 - \frac{q_2}{2}, \tag{6.4}$$

as Figure 6.2 shows. If $q_2 = 0$, Firm 1 produces $q_1 = R_1(0) = 360$, the monopoly output level. The residual demand curve of a Cournot firm facing no competition is the market demand curve. Because the market demand curve intersects the marginal cost curve at 720, a monopoly's marginal revenue curve intersects the marginal cost curve at half that quantity, or 360. At the other extreme, Firm 1 does not cease production until $q_2 = 720$.

Firm 2's best-response function is derived in a similar way. The firms are identical (same costs, identical products), so Firm 2's best-response function is the mirror image of Firm 1's:

$$q_2 = R_2(q_1) = 360 - \frac{q_1}{2}. \tag{6.5}$$

Firm 2's choice of output depends on the output it expects Firm 1 to produce.

As Figure 6.2 and Table 6.1 illustrate, the two firms' best-response functions cross once at $q_1 = q_2 = 240$.[5] At the intersection of the best-response functions, if each firm believes that the other firm will sell 240 units, it wants to sell 240 units too.

Equilibrium. This point of intersection (240, 240) of the best-response functions is called a Cournot equilibrium. In the Cournot equilibrium, each firm sells the quantity

---

[4]If Firm 2 produces $q_2 = 240$, the residual demand curve facing the first firm is $q_1 = Q(p) - q_2 = (1{,}000 - 1{,}000p) - 240 = 760 - 1{,}000p$, or $p = 0.76 - 0.001q_1$. Thus, the first firm's revenue is $R = pq_1 = 0.76q_1 - 0.001q_1^2$, so its residual marginal revenue function is $dR/dq_1 = 0.76 - 0.002q_1$. Residual marginal revenue equals marginal cost where $0.76 - 0.002q_1 = 0.28$, or $q_1 = 240$.

[5]The intersection can be determined algebraically by simultaneously solving the two best-response function equations. Substituting Firm 1's best-response function $q_1 = 360 - q_2/2$ for q_1 in Firm 2's best-response function, $q_2 = 360 - q_1/2$, Firm 2's output is $q_2 = 360 - 1/2(360 - q_2/2)$. Simplifying, $q_2 = 240$. Substituting 240 for q_2 in Firm 1's best-response function, we learn that q_1 also equals 240.

FIGURE 6.2 Cournot Best-Response Functions

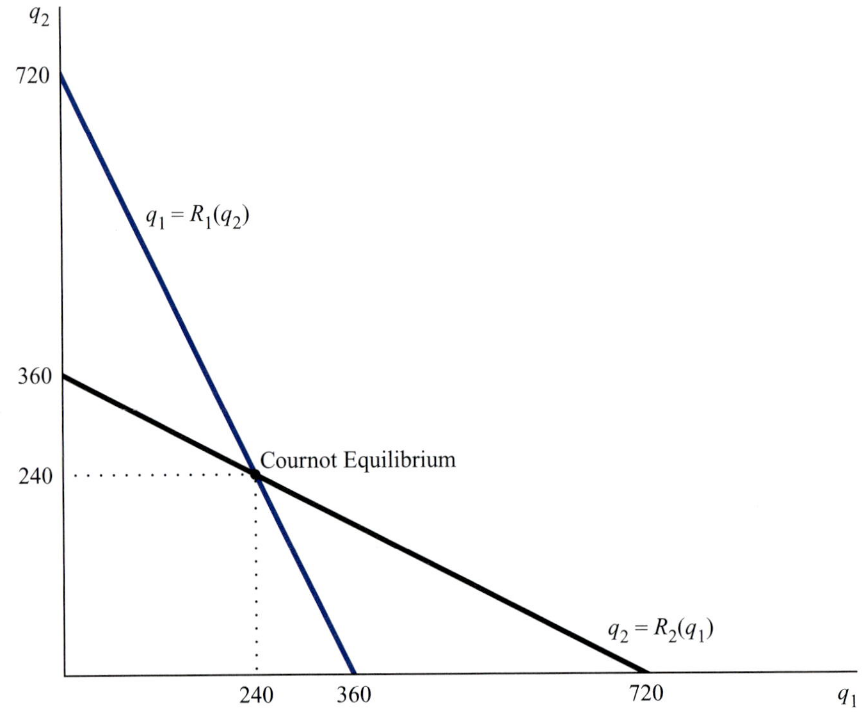

that maximizes its profits given its (correct) beliefs about the other firm's choice of output—the *best response* to the other firm's output level. Moreover, in equilibrium, each firm's beliefs about its rival's output is confirmed.

If each firm believes the other will produce 240 units and if each firm produces 240 units, neither firm wants to change its output. A firm is unwilling to produce at a point not on its best-response function because doing so would result in a lower profit. The only point where both firms are on their best-response functions is at the intersection of the best-response functions. A nonintersection point cannot be an equilibrium; an equilibrium point is one in which neither firm wants to change its behavior. In the Cournot equilibrium, total market output is 240 + 240 = 480 melons and the price is 52¢ per melon (Table 6.1).

In a single-period model in which firms only choose output levels, any output levels at which no firm believes it can increase its profits by increasing or decreasing its output are, by definition, a Cournot equilibrium, and no combination of outputs could be an equilibrium except a Cournot equilibrium. Thus, in a single-period model in which firms choose output levels independently, the Cournot equilibrium is not only realistic; it is the only plausible equilibrium (Friedman 1983, 32–3).

TABLE 6.1 **A Comparison of Oligopoly Equilibria: A Linear Demand and Constant Marginal Cost Example**

	Output			Profits ($)		
	Firm	Industry	Price (¢)	Firm	Industry	Consumer Surplus
Monopoly	360	360	64	129.60	129.60	64.8
Cournot Duopoly	240	480	52	57.60	115.20	115.2
Stackelberg Duopoly		540	46		97.20	145.8
Leader	360			64.8		
Follower	180			32.4		
Competition*		720	28	0	0	259.2
Cournot: n firms	$\frac{720}{n+1}$	$\frac{720n}{n+1}$	$\frac{100+28n}{n}$	$\frac{518.4}{(n+1)^2}$	$\frac{518.4n}{(n+1)^2}$	$\frac{259.2n^2}{(n+1)^2}$
Stackelberg: n firms		$\frac{360\,(2n-1)}{n}$	$\frac{28n+36}{n}$		$\frac{129.6\,(2n-1)}{n^2}$	$\frac{64.8\,(2n-1)^2}{n^2}$
Leader	360			$\frac{129.6}{n}$		
Followers	$\frac{360\,(n-1)}{n}$			$\frac{129.6\,(n-1)}{n^2}$		

Market demand: $Q = 1{,}000 - 1{,}000\,p$
$MC = 28$¢
*Efficient point, Bertrand equilibrium, Cournot equilibrium with unlimited number of firms.

The remaining question is how do firms form their beliefs? Is it reasonable that they each choose to believe that the other firm will produce 240 units? One practical answer is that experience often influences beliefs, but if we introduce experience, we are bringing a dynamic element into a supposedly static model. The failure to provide a theoretical basis for underlying beliefs is a criticism of the Cournot model and other static models.[6] This criticism led Stigler (1964a) to develop his analysis based on cartel theory (Chapter 5) and game theorists to develop multiperiod game models (discussed later in this chapter).

[6]One interesting response is provided by Daughety (1985), who describes the type of *infinite regress* reasoning firms might use. Firm 1's model of Firm 2 is subject to Firm 2's model of Firm 1's model and vice versa. That is, Firm 1's manager thinks about what Firm 2's manager is thinking: "I think that Firm 2's manager thinks that I think that Firm 2's manager thinks that I think . . ." Firm 2's manager thinks about Firm 1's manager's model similarly. Based on this type of reasoning, each firm chooses an output level. Daughety shows that the Cournot equilibrium is the only possible result of this type of reasoning.

EXAMPLE 6.1 *Do Birds of a Feather Cournot-Flock Together?*

Flocking birds must frequently look up (or *scan*) while feeding to see an approaching predator in time. Frequent scanning, however, decreases the feeding rate of individual birds. Because any bird can give the warning of impending doom (which greatly reduces the probability of death), it is in an individual bird's best interest for another member of the flock to scan (incur costs) while it eats constantly (benefits). Not surprisingly, as the size of the flock increases, each bird spends less time scanning and more time feeding.

Using high-speed cameras with telephoto lenses and trained predators that fly over the flock from time to time, scientists determined how members of a flock of yellow-eyed juncos behave (Pulliam, Pyke, and Caraco 1982). The scientists compared two game-theoretic models as explanations for this behavior. In the cooperative model, the birds work together, whereas in the selfish solution (analogous to the Cournot-Nash model), they operate independently. The following table compares the observed and predicted scanning rates (as percentages of time) under the cooperative and selfish models (using the most likely parameter estimates of each model—which explains why the numbers are different in the two models when there is only one bird in the "flock"):

		Predicted	
Number in Flock	Observed	Cooperative Model	Selfish Model
1	13.9%	15.9%	18.6%
2	7.85	6.2	3.4
3	6.22	5.9	0.6
4	6.02	5.5	0.0
5	5.87	5.2	0.0
6	5.66	4.9	0.0
7	5.58	4.7	0.0
8	5.59	4.5	0.0
9	4.88	4.4	0.0
10	4.65	4.0	0.0

In Cournot's equilibrium concept, no firm wants to change its output level given that the other firms produce at the equilibrium quantities. Because the Cournot equilibrium is a special case of the Nash equilibrium where firms have strategies over quantities, it is often referred to as a *Cournot-Nash equilibrium* or a *Nash-in-quantities equilibrium.* Example 6.1 describes a nonbusiness game in which the Nash generalization is apt.

A Comparison of the Cournot and Cartel Equilibria. The firms are worse off and the consumers are better off at the Cournot equilibrium than if firms act collusively as a cartel (monopoly). The cartel output is 360 and the cartel price is 64¢ (Table 6.1). The Cournot industry's output (480) is a third larger, and the price (52¢) is 19 percent lower than in the cartel equilibrium.

The predictions of the cooperative model do not differ in a statistically significant way from the observed values. A statistical test shows that the probability of the selfish (Nash) model is less than 0.005: It is virtually impossible that the observed scanning rates are the outcome of selfish behavior.

The scientists who conducted this study were surprised that birds behaved cooperatively. After all, a "selfish" bird—one that did not cooperate by sharing scanning duty—should have had an advantage over a "cooperative" bird. Thus, they expected selfishness to be an "evolutionary stable strategy."

After a little more thought, however, they concluded that the results made sense when the same players in a "game" meet again and again: "The only strategy evolutionarily stable to invasion may be to reciprocate in kind." That is, it is optimal to cooperate only as long as other birds cooperate. They called a bird that follows this conditional cooperative strategy a *judge.* A judge behaves like a cooperative bird if others are cooperative and like a selfish bird if others are not cooperative. They calculated the flocking "payoff" matrix for a flock of two birds with these three types of strategies, where the payoff (the numbers in the following table) is the probability that Bird 1 survives predator attacks for a day under adverse conditions.

		Bird 2		
		Cooperative	Selfish	Judge
	Cooperative	0.513	0.492	0.513
Bird 1	*Selfish*	0.528	0.503	0.503
	Judge	0.513	0.503	0.513

Notice that a judge does as well as a cooperative bird with another cooperative bird and better than a cooperative bird when paired with a selfish bird. As long as the birds are all cooperative or judges, we would expect to see cooperative behavior.

Consumers benefit from lower prices. The consumer surplus under the cartel is 64.8; the Cournot consumer surplus is 115.2 (Table 6.1). Thus, consumer surplus falls 44 percent if the Cournot firms form a cartel.

Lerner's price-cost margin, $(p - MC)/p$, is lower for a Cournot oligopoly than for a cartel. The cartel's price-cost margin is 56 percent, whereas the Cournot industry's margin is 46 percent—only 82 percent as large as the cartel's.

The Cournot firms have an incentive to form a cartel. The profit of Cournot Firm i is $(p - AC_i)q_i = (52¢ - 28¢)240 = \$57.60$. The sum of the profits of the Cournot firms, $\pi_1 + \pi_2$, is $115.20, but the cartel's combined profits are $129.60 (Table 6.1). Thus, if the firms form a cartel, their profits rise by 12.5 percent.

The maximum combined profits that two collusive firms can earn is $129.60. There are many ways to divide these monopoly profits: Firm 1 could earn $0 and Firm

FIGURE 6.3 The Profit Possibility Frontier

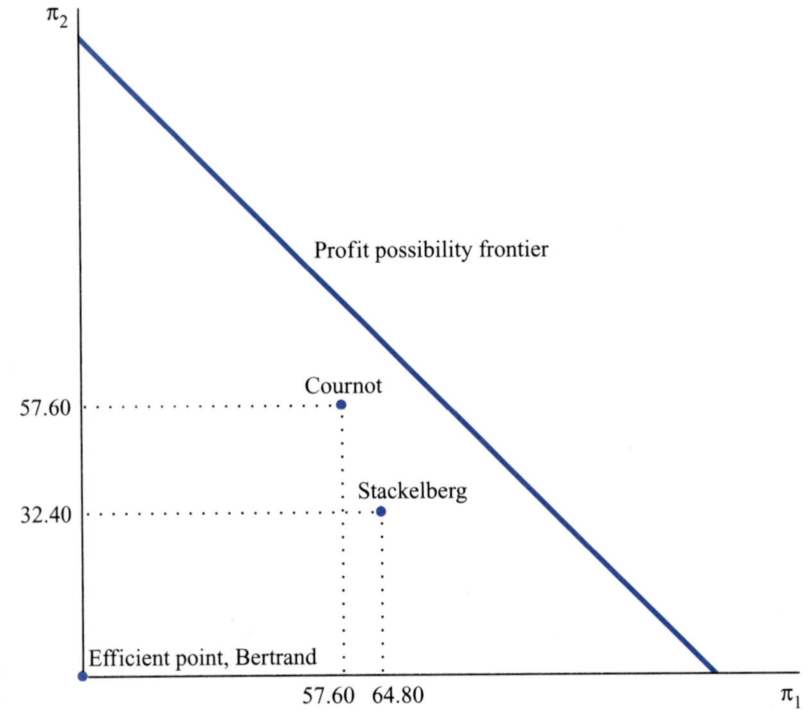

2 could earn \$129.60; each could earn half, \$64.80; Firm 1 could earn \$129.60 and Firm 2 could earn \$0; and so forth for any combination in which the sum of profits is \$129.60. The *profit possibility frontier,* $\pi_1 + \pi_2 = \$129.60$, in Figure 6.3 shows the highest profit one firm could earn, holding the profit of the other firm constant.[7]

Figure 6.3 also shows the Cournot equilibrium profit level, where each firm earns \$57.60, so $\pi_1 + \pi_2 = \$115.20$. The Cournot equilibrium lies well inside the profit possibility frontier, giving the firms an incentive to collude and increase their profits to the levels on the profit possibility frontier.

Comparison of the Cournot Equilibrium and the Social Optimum. How does the Cournot equilibrium compare to the social optimum where price equals marginal

[7]A profit possibility frontier is derived by holding Firm 1's profit constant at some level and then maximizing the profit of Firm 2 with respect to q_1 and q_2. In our example, the solution is

$$(q_1 - 1{,}080)q_1 + (q_2 - 1{,}080)q_2 - 2q_1q_2 + 259{,}200 = 0.$$

For any particular q_1, this equation simplifies into a quadratic in q_2. The relevant root is the smaller one. See Friedman (1983:22–7).

EXAMPLE 6.2 *Oligopoly Welfare Losses*

By exercising market power, oligopoly firms create deadweight loss, *DWL*. Bhuyan (2000) estimated the standard *DWL* triangle for 35 U.S. food manufacturing industries.* For all food industries, the *DWL* as a percentage of total sales was 5.5%. The percentage loss was as high as 33.4% for cereal preparation; 31.8% for soybean oil; 26.2% in flour and grain products; 17.5% in creamery butter; 10.4% for pickles, sauces, and salads; 10.2% in bottled and canned soft drinks; and 7.2% for malt beverages. The percentage losses were less than half a percent for canned specialties; dehydrated fruits, vegetables, and soup; rice milling; pet food; candy and confections; salted and roasted nuts and seeds; cottonseed oil; fresh or frozen seafood; and macaroni and spaghetti.

* Bhuyan (2000) also reports other measures of social loss. The higher profits from differentiated product oligopoly may induce firms to introduce new products that consumers value (as we discuss in the next chapter) and that may offset the loss from high prices.

cost (as in the competitive equilibrium)?[8] If both firms act as price takers at a price equal to the marginal cost of 28¢, they make zero profits per melon, so they are indifferent as to how many melons they produce. At a price of 28¢, 720 melons are demanded by the market (as determined by the intersection of the *MC* and market demand curves in Figure 6.1). If the firms split the total sales, each firm produces 360 melons. Consumer surplus is 259.2 (Table 6.1).

Thus, in our linear example, at the social optimum, twice as much output is produced as by a cartel and one-and-a-half times as much as by a Cournot duopoly. The competitive price is only 44 percent of the monopoly price and 54 percent of the Cournot price. At the social optimum output, consumer surplus is four times greater than under a cartel and two-and-a-quarter times greater than under a Cournot duopoly. The Cournot duopoly equilibrium, then, lies between the competitive and monopolistic equilibria. In linear examples such as this one, it is closer to the monopolistic equilibrium. See Example 6.2 for estimates of the welfare losses due to oligopoly in actual markets.

Three or More Cournot Firms. If there are n (≥ 2) identical Cournot firms, the same type of analysis can be used to derive the Cournot equilibrium, as Appendix 6A

[8]We compare Cournot to the social optimum rather than the competitive equilibrium because the competitive equilibrium requires a potentially unlimited number of firms, and there are only two firms in this market. In the socially optimal equilibrium, firms maximize profits subject to the constraint that price equals marginal cost (as in a competitive equilibrium). This equilibrium concept was introduced by Shubik (1959), who called it the *efficient point*. See Shubik with Levitan (1980) and Friedman (1983) for a discussion of the fixed costs consistent with the *efficient point*. Henceforth, we use the terms *social optimum* and *competitive equilibrium* interchangeably.

TABLE 6.2 **Cournot Equilibrium with Few and Many Firms**

			Firm		Industry	
	Number of Firms	Price (¢)	Output	Profit ($)	Output	Profits ($)
Monopoly	1	64	360	129.60	360	129.60
	2	52	240	57.60	480	115.20
	3	46	180	32.40	540	97.20
	4	42.4	144	20.74	576	82.94
	5	40	120	14.40	600	72.00
	6	38.3	102.9	10.58	617.1	63.48
	7	37	90	8.10	630	56.70
	8	36	80	6.40	640	51.20
	9	35.2	72	5.18	648	46.66
	10	34.5	65.5	4.28	654.5	42.84
	15	32.5	48	2.30	675	32.26
	20	31.4	34.3	1.18	685.7	23.51
	50	29.4	14.1	0.20	705.9	9.97
	100	28.7	7.1	0.05	712.9	5.08
	500	28.1	1.4	0.002	718.6	1.03
	1000	28.1	0.7	0.001	719.3	0.52
Competition	∞	28	~0	0.00	720	0.00

shows. Firm 1's best-response function is $q_1 = R_1(q_2, \ldots, q_n)$. If the other $n - 1$ firms produce an identical amount of output, q, then Firm 1's best-response function is $q_1 = R_1(q_2, \ldots, q_n) = 360 - q(n - 1)/2$. The other firms have similar best-response functions. As a result, the Cournot equilibrium quantity is $q = 720/(n + 1)$, and the equilibrium price is $p = (1 + 0.28n)/(n + 1)$.

Table 6.2 shows that the larger is n, the smaller is output per firm, whereas the larger is industry output, and the lower is price. The effect of additional rivals on quantity and price is initially very strong, but tapers off as the number of firms increases. If there are only 2 firms, the price is 86 percent above the competitive price. However with 10 firms, the price is only 23 percent above the competitive price, and with 50 firms it is only 5 percent above the competitive price. If the number of firms is extremely large, the output per firm, industry price, and industry output approach the socially optimal levels. Consumers are better off (lower prices, higher consumer surplus) and firms are worse off (lower profits) as the number of firms increases.[9]

In summary, the Cournot model includes monopoly and competition as extreme cases, and the Cournot equilibrium approaches the competitive one as the number of firms increases. See Example 6.3 on mergers.

[9]Ruffin (1971) discusses the conditions that must hold for the Cournot equilibrium price to converge to the competitive price as the number of firms grows large.

EXAMPLE 6.3 *Mergers in a Cournot Economy*

If all Cournot firms join together and behave as a monopoly, collective profits increase. Suppose only some of the Cournot firms merge (or coordinate actions as a cartel). The Cournot model has disturbing implications about the oligopolists' profits (given linear demand functions and identical constant marginal and average costs):

- In an industry with at least three firms (before mergers), if only two firms merge, their collective profits will fall.
- A merger of a larger number of firms *may* increase the size of the collective losses due to merger.
- For any given number of (premerger) firms, if a merger of firms causes collective losses, a merger by a smaller number of firms also causes losses. Similarly, if a merger of *k* firms causes gains, a merger by a larger number of firms also causes gains.
- If less than 80 percent of the firms merge, mergers will be collectively unprofitable.
- If any given share (less than 100 percent) of the firms in an industry merge, there is an initial industry size (number of firms) such that the merger causes losses.

These results imply that if the equilibrium is determined according to the Cournot model and firms maintain Cournot beliefs, then they will merge or form a cartel only if virtually all other firms in the industry join them. Alternatively, firms merge only if the firms do not maintain Cournot beliefs or the merger generates efficiencies.

Sources: Salant, Switzer, and Reynolds (1983) and Patinkin (1947). Compare Aumann (1973), Okuno, Postlewaite, and Roberts (1980), Farrell and Shapiro (1990), McAfee and Williams (1992), and Rothschild, Heywood, and Monaco (2000).

The Bertrand Model

Cournot's work was well ahead of its time. The first major challenge to his book came in 1883, 45 years after it was published. In this critique, Joseph Bertrand argued that it is hard to see who sets prices in oligopolistic markets if the firms do not set them. Cournot, by having firms choose output rather than price, fails to state explicitly the mechanism by which prices are determined (but, for that matter, so does a competitive model).

In Bertrand's model, firms set prices rather than output. If consumers have complete information and realize that firms produce identical products, they buy the one with the lowest price. In a Bertrand model, each firm believes its rival's price is fixed;

by a slight price cut, the firm is able to capture all its rival's business. In the Bertrand equilibrium discussed below, firms make zero profits and no firm can increase its profits by raising or lowering its price, which, when it exists, is equivalent to the social optimum (competitive equilibrium) discussed above.

An Example. To illustrate the Bertrand equilibrium, let us make the same assumptions as in the Cournot example: no entry, homogeneous products, single period, the same demand curve, Equation 6.1 (which we can rewrite as $p = 1 - 0.001Q$), and the same constant marginal cost of 28¢. The only important change is that firms now set prices rather than quantities. Each firm is willing to sell as much quantity as is demanded at the price it sets.

Suppose that Firm 1 charges a price p_1, which is greater than its marginal cost of 28¢. If Firm 1 makes any sales at all, it earns a positive profit. Because both firms produce identical products, however, all consumers buy from Firm 2 if p_2 is even slightly below p_1; none buy from Firm 2 if p_2 is above p_1; and consumers are indifferent between the two firms when $p_2 = p_1$. Thus, as Figure 6.4 shows, the residual demand curve (thick blue line) facing Firm 2 is zero when p_2 is above p_1, equals the market demand when p_2 is below p_1, and is horizontal at p_1. If both firms charge the same price,

FIGURE 6.4 A Bertrand Firm's Residual Demand Curve

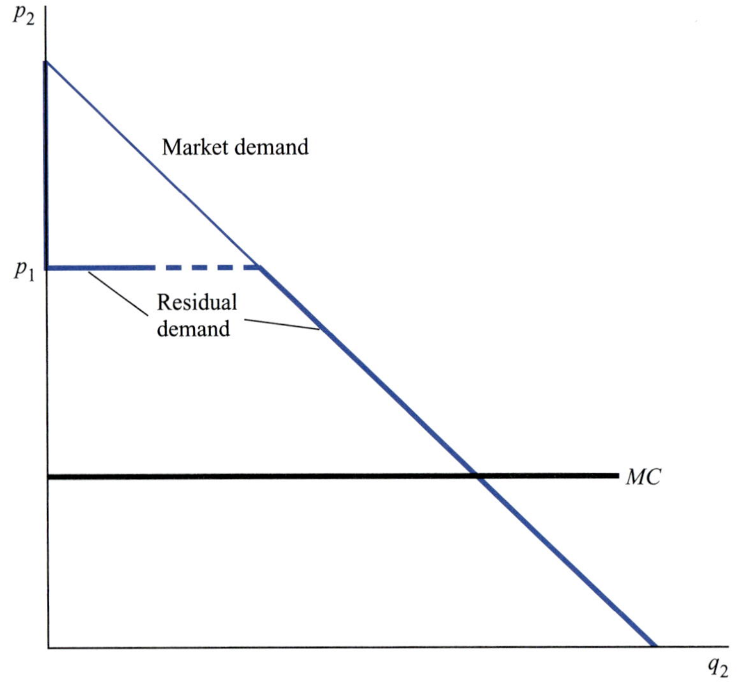

we assume that they split the total market demand. In Figure 6.4, where the demand facing Firm 1 is horizontal (at $p_2 = p_1$), half the horizontal line is dashed to indicate that Firm 1 sells only half the total amount demanded.

When both firms charge 28¢, neither firm profits by changing its price. If a firm lowers its price, it loses money (because price is then below marginal and average cost). If either firm raises its price, it makes no sales at all.

The only possible *Bertrand equilibrium* or *Nash-in-prices equilibrium* is $p = MC =$ 28¢.[10] Figure 6.5 illustrates this result using best-response functions in price space (the firms' prices are on the axes). Given whatever price, p_1, Firm 2 believes that Firm 1 will set, Firm 2 wants to set a price, p_2, that is slightly below p_1, as long as p_2 is greater than 28¢. That is, Firm 2's best-response function lies slightly below the 45° line (where the two prices are identical) through the point (28¢, 28¢). If Firm 1 sets p_1 below 28¢, Firm 2 does not respond because it cannot make a profit at any price. Similarly, Firm 1's best-response function lies slightly above the 45° line and above 28¢. The only intersection of these best-response functions (and hence the only equilibrium) is where price equals marginal cost.

FIGURE 6.5 Bertrand Best-Response Functions

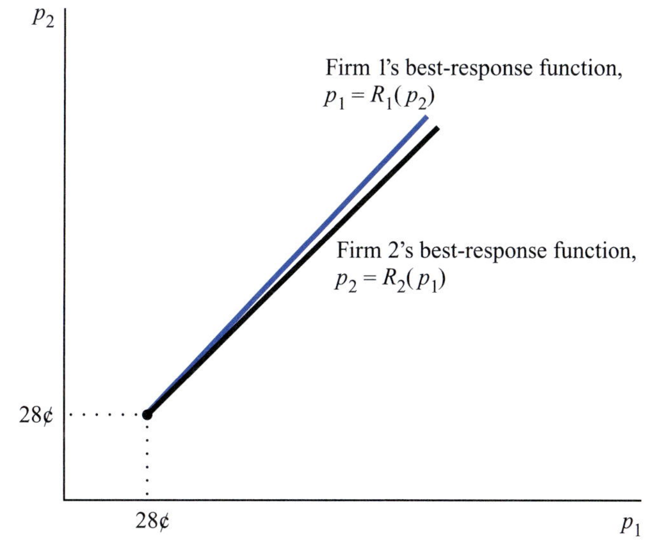

[10]This equilibrium can be obtained from other game-theoretic models. For example, Grossman (1981a) shows that if a firm's strategy is a supply function (the quantity supplied as a function of price rather than just the price itself), under weak conditions the competitive, or Bertrand, equilibrium is a Nash equilibrium. This outcome is the result of the threat of entry, which we consider in Chapter 11.

If both firms charge a price equal to marginal cost, they earn zero profits. Thus, the Bertrand equilibrium for homogenous goods is the same as the social optimum (competitive equilibrium), as shown in Figure 6.3. Consumers prefer the Bertrand equilibrium to the Cournot or cartel equilibria.

A Comparison of the Bertrand and Cournot Equilibria. In the absence of an auctioneer, it is difficult to imagine how prices are determined if firms set output (Cournot) rather than prices (Bertrand). As a result, some economists find Bertrand's model more attractive than Cournot's, because it explains how prices are set.[11]

Because price rather than output is the decision variable, the Bertrand firm's residual demand curve differs substantially from that of a Cournot firm. When goods are homogeneous and all firms charge the same price, a Bertrand firm's residual demand curve is kinked (Figure 6.4). By slightly lowering its price, a firm may increase sales from none of the market to all of the market. Such sudden shifts in sales are rarely observed in most industries. Rather, demand curves facing individual firms appear to be smooth (nonkinked), as in the Cournot model, so that each firm's output shifts slightly for small price changes. Thus, Bertrand's model of a homogeneous good may be more realistic in explaining who sets prices, but the nonkinked Cournot demand curve facing individual firms is more realistic.

The Cournot equilibrium is intuitively appealing: With a small number of firms, output and price lie between the competitive and monopolistic equilibria. In contrast, the Bertrand equilibrium is counterintuitive: So long as there are at least two firms, the Bertrand price is the competitive price (marginal cost).

This last result, however, depends on a number of strong assumptions: The output is homogeneous, the market lasts for only one period, and any firm can produce as much as it wants at constant marginal cost. If any of these assumptions is relaxed, the Bertrand price does not equal marginal cost. The next chapter shows that if firms differentiate their products, the Bertrand price is above marginal cost. Later in this chapter, we show that, if markets last for many periods, the equilibrium price is likely to be closer to the monopoly price (even if firms set prices rather than quantities). The next section shows that a price equal to marginal cost is not a Bertrand equilibrium if firms have limited production capacity.

Capacity Constraints in Bertrand's Model: Edgeworth's Model. In 1897, Francis Edgeworth showed that, if firms have limited capacity to produce, there is no single-price, static Bertrand equilibrium. To illustrate Edgeworth's point, suppose the previous Bertrand example is modified so that each firm's maximum output capacity is 360, which is half the amount demanded at a price equal to marginal cost. That is, each firm's

[11]A firm that must sell its product immediately and cannot store it, as in the melon example, must adjust its price rapidly, as necessary, or it will be stuck with useless output. On the other hand, a firm that cannot change prices quickly or can do so only at great cost—say, because it prints elaborate catalogs—may meet fluctuations in demand by varying output (see Chapter 17).

average and marginal cost curves are horizontal at 28¢ up to 360 units, and then the average and marginal cost curves are vertical (the cost of the next unit of output is infinite).

With limited capacities, is the original Bertrand equilibrium ($p_1 = p_2 = 28¢$, $Q = 720$) still an equilibrium? That solution is feasible given our assumptions, because, at those prices, the firms' combined output can just satisfy the market's demand of 720 units. That solution, however, is not an equilibrium.

For it to be an equilibrium, neither firm should want to change its behavior. At that proposed equilibrium, however, each firm wants to raise its price. In particular, suppose that Firm 1 believed that Firm 2 will charge $p_2 = 28¢$. What price should it set to maximize its profit?

As before, Firm 1 does not want to lower its price because it would suffer a loss if it charged less than marginal cost. If Firm 1 raises its price, all consumers want to buy from the second firm. Half the market, however, is unable to buy at that price because of the second firm's limited capacity. The first firm faces a positive residual demand from frustrated consumers who are unable to buy from Firm 2, as shown in Figure 6.6. The residual demand facing Firm 1 is the market demand minus the 360 units sold by Firm 2 (where only the portion above its marginal costs is of interest to Firm 1).

FIGURE 6.6 Bertrand Residual Demand When Firms Have Limited Capacity

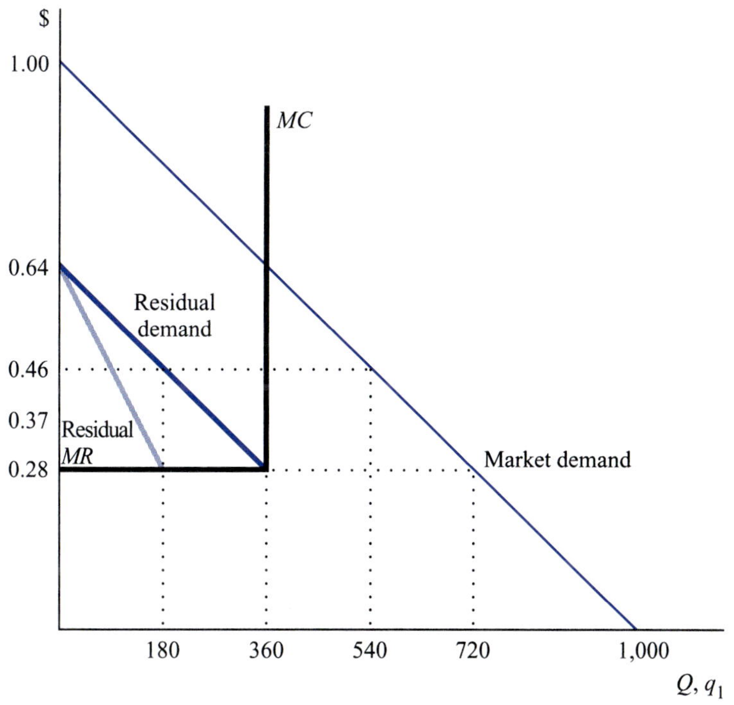

Firm 1 can maximize its profits by acting like a monopoly with respect to its residual demand. Its marginal revenue equals its marginal cost at a price of 46¢, and it makes positive profits (whereas Firm 2 makes no profits on its sales). Thus, the original Bertrand equilibrium is *not* an equilibrium if firms have limited capacity.

Is there an equilibrium price? Suppose that Firm 1 sets a price of 46¢. If Firm 2 sets a price slightly below 46¢, all consumers want to buy from it. Given its limited capacity, however, Firm 2 meets only two-thirds of the market demand. Firm 2 sells twice as much as Firm 1 at almost the same price, so its profits are double those of Firm 1.

By similar reasoning, if Firm 1 sets any price below 46¢ and above 37¢, Firm 2 will want to set a slightly lower one. If, however, Firm 1 sets a price at (or below) 37¢, Firm 2 would earn more by charging 46¢.[12] Thus, there is no single-price, static equilibrium.[13] See Example 6.4.

More generally, one can show that there is no static equilibrium if firms have extremely limited capacity, or, equivalently, their average costs rise rapidly at some relatively low output level (Shubik with Levitan 1980). If any firm can meet the entire market's demand, however, an equilibrium exists that is identical to the efficient solution.

The Stackelberg Leader-Follower Model

In many ways the saying "Know thyself" is not well said. It were more practical to say "Know other people." —*Menander*

Heinrich von Stackelberg (1952) presented the third important oligopoly model in 1934. In the Stackelberg model, firms set output, and one firm acts before the others.

The *leader* firm picks its output level and then the other firms are free to choose their optimal quantities given their knowledge of the leader's output. In some industries, historical, institutional, or legal factors determine which firm is the first mover. For example, the firm that discovers and develops a new product has a natural first-mover advantage.

---

[12]Each firm's owner makes the following calculation: If I drop my price to p, which is slightly below my rival's price, I can sell my maximum output, 360 melons. On the other hand, if I raise my price to 46¢, I can only sell 180 melons, but I make more per melon. At what price, p, are my profits the same as if I set my price at 46¢? To answer that question, I equate my profits at 46¢ to those at p and solve for p: $(46¢ - 28¢)180 = (p - 28¢)360$. That is, my profits are equal if I raise my price to 46¢ or lower it to 37¢.

[13]Technically, Edgeworth showed that there is no equilibrium in "pure strategies." There is no simple rule of the sort discussed in the Cournot and Bertrand models for firms to follow at all times that leads to equilibrium. Kreps and Scheinkman (1983), Dasgupta and Maskin (1986), and others show that mixed-strategy (see Appendix 6B) equilibria exist. Kreps and Scheinkman (1983) and Davidson and Deneckere (1986) also show that, if firms play a two-stage game in which they choose their capacity levels and then price according to Bertrand, the Bertrand equilibrium is the same as the Cournot equilibrium under certain circumstances. See also Allen and Hellwig (1986). Maggi (1996) presents a more realistic and elegant two-stage game that has the property that a solution in pure strategies always exists and varies, depending on the circumstances, between Bertrand and Cournot.

EXAMPLE 6.4 *Roller Coaster Gasoline Pricing*

In dynamic games, many outcomes are possible, including an "Edgeworth cycle" in which prices rise, then fall, and then rise again. Using the theoretical work of Maskin and Tirole (1988b), Noel (2001) examined pricing in Canadian retail gasoline markets. Noel discovered three patterns of pricing, the most prevalent being an Edgeworth cycle.

In about 40 percent of the cities he examined, Noel observed a pricing pattern in which the retail price spikes quickly above the wholesale (called the "rack") price and then slowly drifts down for the next 2–3 weeks; then, just before it reaches the wholesale price, the retail price quickly spikes up again. The steepness of the upward spike depends on the prevalence of lots of small firms.

The second most prevalent pattern is sticky prices, where retail prices change infrequently (every two months) even though the underlying wholesale price changes. This pattern was observed in markets with only a few retail firms. The third pattern is "normal" pricing where the retail price tracks movements in the wholesale price.

The average difference between the retail price and the wholesale price varies with the retail pricing pattern. The average difference was highest for normal pricing, next highest for sticky pricing, and lowest for Edgeworth pricing.

Source: Noel (2001).

An Example. Suppose one of the melon-producing firms from before is a follower firm (Firm 2) and the other is the leader (Firm 1). Firm 1 realizes that once it sets its output, q_1, the follower firm will use its Cournot best-response function to pick its optimal $q_2 = R_2(q_1)$.

The leader, therefore, picks q_1 to maximize its profit subject to the constraint that the follower firm chooses its corresponding output using its Cournot best-response function. In the Stackelberg equilibrium, the leader is better off and the follower is worse off than in a Cournot equilibrium. In short, *knowing how its rival will behave allows a leader to profit at the follower's expense.*

Because the firms have identical costs, Firm 1 knows the Cournot best-response function of Firm 2, $R_2(q_1)$, which Figure 6.7b shows. Consequently, the leader knows how much the follower will produce at any level of output the leader chooses. Thus, the leader can calculate the *total* production corresponding to any output level it chooses, and it chooses the level that maximizes its profits.

By subtracting the follower's output (as summarized by the follower's best-response function in Figure 6.7b) from total demand, the leader calculates its residual demand curve (Figure 6.7a). The leader picks its output, q_1, where its marginal revenue based on its residual demand curve equals its marginal cost. Firm 1 maximizes its profits by producing 360 melons (Figure 6.7a and Table 6.1). Firm 2 produces only 180 melons, which is determined by substituting 360 into Firm 2's best-response function (Figure 6.7b).

FIGURE 6.7 The Stackelberg Equilibrium

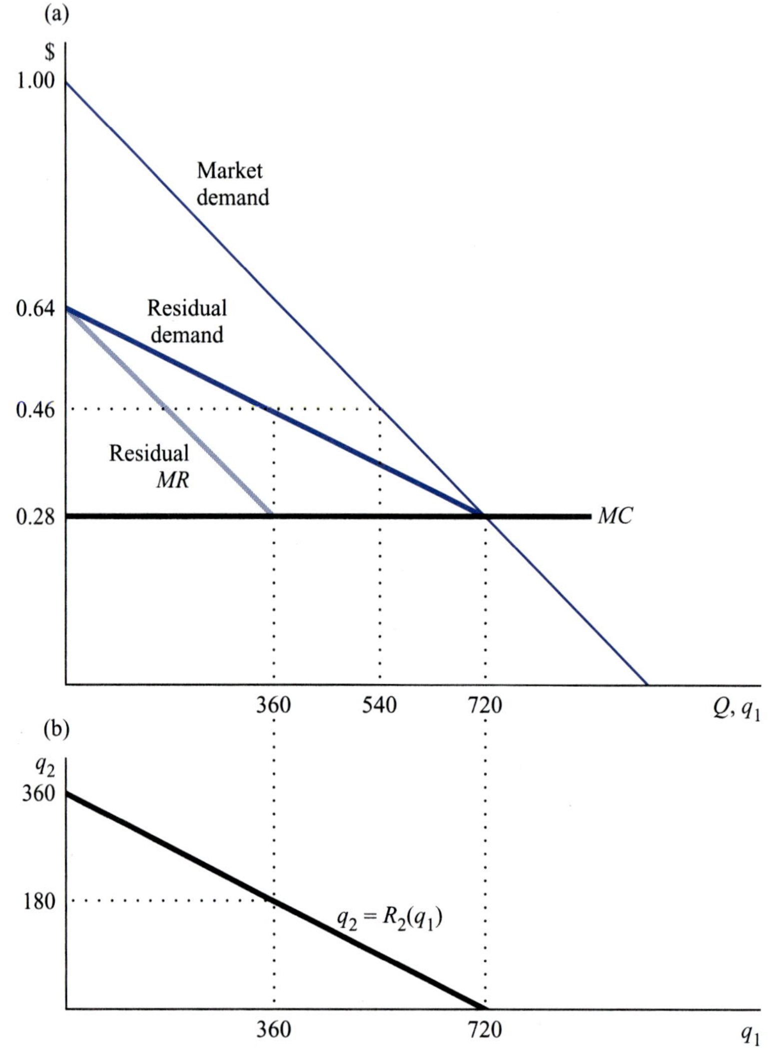

The Stackelberg game can be analyzed using the **extensive-form representation** of the game (or *decision tree*), which shows the order in which firms make their moves, each firm's strategy at the time of its move, and the payoffs. There are an infinite number of combinations of outputs the two firms can produce. Figure 6.8 shows only some of the output levels they can choose: the Stackelberg follower quantity (180), the Cournot quantity (240), and the Stackelberg leader quantity (360).

FIGURE 6.8 Extensive-Form Representation of Stackelberg Game

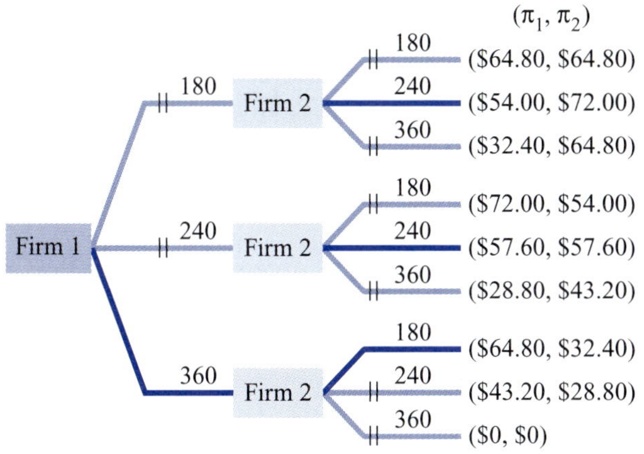

Each line represents an action, and each box is a point of decision by one of the players. Starting from the left of the diagram, Firm 1 picks its output level, then Firm 2 picks its output level, and the payoffs (Firm 1's profit first) are shown on the right. If Firm 1 chooses the Cournot quantity, 240, Firm 2's profit is maximized at $57.60 at the Cournot quantity, 240. A pair of straight lines are drawn through each of Firm 2's other two action lines, showing that Firm 2 does not want to choose those actions.

If Firm 1 chooses the Stackelberg leader quantity, 360, Firm 2's profit is maximized at $32.40 at the Stackelberg follower quantity, 180. Similarly, if Firm 1 produces 180 melons, of the three choices it has, Firm 2 produces 240.[14] Given the way Firm 2 will respond, Firm 1 realizes that its expected profit will be highest if it produces 360 melons, where it earns $64.80.

Stackelberg Equilibrium Compared to Other Equilibria. The Stackelberg leader produces more output (360 melons) and the follower less output (180) than would a Cournot firm (240), as Table 6.1 shows.[15] Total Stackelberg output (540 melons) is greater than the Cournot output (480), but less than the social optimum (competitive equilibrium) output (720). The Stackelberg price, 46¢, is higher than the competitive price, 28¢, but lower than the Cournot price, 52¢. As a result, consumer surplus is

[14]Given Firm 1 produces 180 units, if Firm 2 can pick any quantity, it produces 270 for a profit of $72.90.

[15]The Stackelberg equilibrium differs from the Cournot equilibrium because the leader acts first and the follower knows for certain its rival's output. That is, the leader's claim that it will produce a large quantity is *credible* because it has already done so. If the two firms were to act simultaneously (the Cournot game), one firm's claim that it will produce a large quantity may not be viewed as credible by a rival firm.

higher with a Stackelberg duopoly, 145.8, than with a Cournot duopoly, 115.2, but lower than the social optimum, 259.2.

The Stackelberg equilibrium lies inside the profit possibility frontier (Figure 6.3). The leader, Firm 1, makes a profit of \$64.80 and the follower, Firm 2, only makes half that, or \$32.40. Thus, total industry profits (\$97.20) are less than the combined profits in the Cournot (\$115.20) or collusive (\$129.60) equilibria.

A Comparison of the Major Oligopoly Models

The three major noncooperative oligopoly models make different assumptions about whether firms choose output or price and whether the firms choose simultaneously or sequentially. As a result, they predict very different firm and industry outputs, prices, profits, and consumer surpluses in equilibrium (Table 6.1).

If there is only one firm, all three models predict monopoly behavior. The more firms, n, in the industry, the closer the Cournot (Tables 6.1 and 6.2) and Stackelberg (Table 6.1) equilibria to the social optimum.

However, the Bertrand equilibrium with homogeneous goods is unaffected by the number of firms in the industry. As long as the market has at least two firms with unlimited capacity, the Bertrand oligopoly equilibrium is the same as the social optimum.[16]

Multiperiod Games

The most important recent development in game theory is the analysis of repeated, or multiperiod, games. This analysis shows that Stigler's (1964a) cartel theory analysis of oligopoly (Chapter 5) is closely related to multiperiod oligopoly models based on game theory.

In a multiperiod game, firms may use complex strategies in which they change behavior in one period depending on the outcome in previous periods. Repeated games where players know their rivals' previous actions and condition their actions in this period on those previous actions are often referred to as **supergames**.

The chief advantage of a multiperiod model is that it allows for more complex and realistic interactions between firms than a single-period model. For example, a firm can signal to another firm that it wants to avoid vigorous competition by lowering its output for a few periods. If the other firm responds by lowering its output, both firms can charge a higher price. If either firm increases its output, the other can retaliate for a while by raising its output (and lowering price) to punish the transgressor. Because of this ability to send signals and punish in multiperiod markets, firms that would produce at the Cournot-Nash level in a single-period model may further restrict output and make larger profits in a multiperiod model.

[16]However, with heterogeneous goods (discussed in the next chapter), the Bertrand equilibrium differs from the competitive equilibrium, and the number of firms in the industry affects prices.

This result can be illustrated using a specific game, known as the prisoners' dilemma game, that is repeated an infinite number of times. The results of repeating the game only a finite number of times are also considered, and some other recent work on multiperiod games is discussed.

Single-Period Prisoners' Dilemma Game

The game is up. —*Shakespeare*

Suppose in our Cournot example that firms were restricted to choose one of only two possible output levels: The firms can only produce the cartel output level (each produces 180 units) or the Cournot level of output (each produces 240). The two firms must act simultaneously. Their actions and their payoffs, which depend on the strategies both choose, are summarized in Figure 6.9a. The first firm's profit is shown in the upper right and the second firm's profit is shown in the lower left of each cell. If both firms choose to produce 240 units, each earns a profit of \$57.60; if both produce 180 units, each earns a profit of \$64.80. If the first firm produces 240 units and

FIGURE 6.9 Prisoners' Dilemma Game

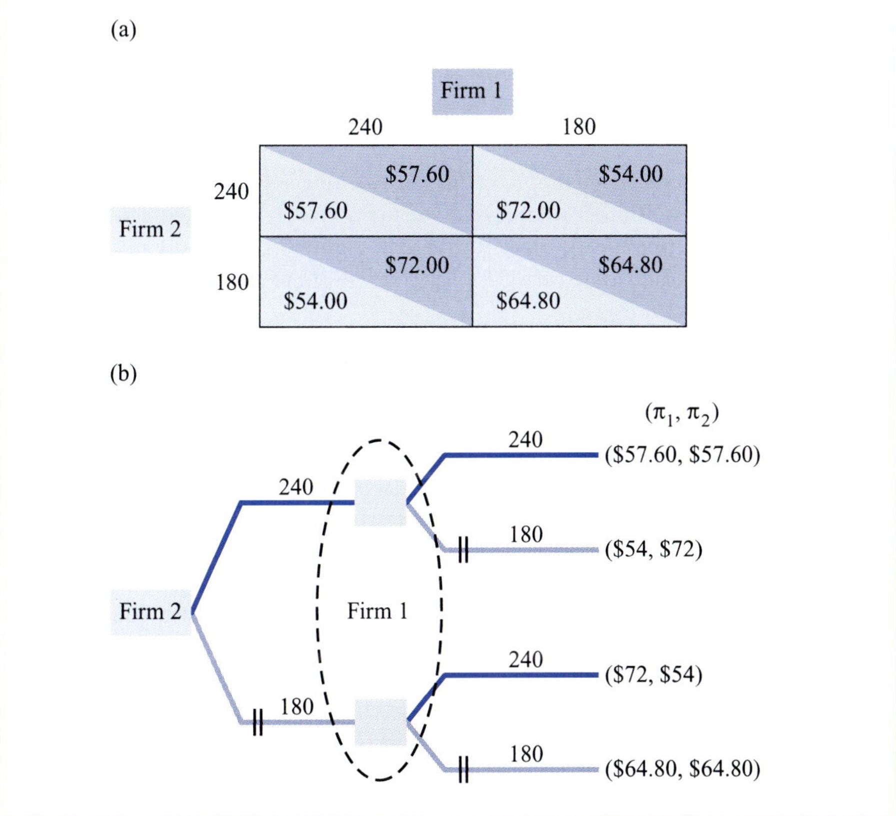

the second firm produces 180, however, the first firm earns $72, and the other only earns $54. A **normal-form representation** (or *strategic form*) of a game is a matrix, such as in Figure 6.9, that shows all the strategies available to each player (who must choose actions simultaneously) and the payoffs to each player for each combination of strategies.

Each firm must choose its action or strategy without knowing what the other firm will do. That is, the firms are engaged in a **game of imperfect information**, in which a firm must choose an action without observing the simultaneous (or earlier) move of its rival.

Figure 6.9b shows the options facing Firm 1. It is an extensive-form representation of this game. In this particular game tree, Firm 2 does not literally move before Firm 1: They move at the same time. As a result, Firm 1 is uncertain about Firm 2's (simultaneous) move. The dotted ellipse around Firm 1's two decision nodes (junction points or boxes in the game tree) indicates that Firm 1 cannot distinguish between the two nodes at the time it must decide on its strategy; that is, Firm 1 does not know which strategy Firm 2 will use. In the figure, Firm 1's payoff is listed first.

How should Firm 1 choose its strategy? The firm should reject any strategy that is *strictly dominated* by any other strategy. One strategy strictly dominates another if it produces as high or higher payoff than the other regardless of the action chosen by a rival firm. If one strategy dominates all other strategies regardless of the actions chosen by rival firms, the firm should choose this **dominant strategy**.

Although not all games have dominant strategies, this game does (see Appendix 6B for a game where players use random strategies). What strategy should Firm 1 choose? To answer that question, the manager of Firm 1 could use the following reasoning:

- If *Firm 2 chooses the high-output strategy* (240), and I choose it also, my profit is $57.60 (the first number in the payoff at the upper right of Figure 6.9b and the upper right number in the top left square in Figure 6.9a); if I use my low-output strategy (180), I only earn $54. I prefer $57.60 to $54, so *I'm better off with my high-output strategy.*
- If *Firm 2 chooses the low-output strategy* (180), then if I use my high-output strategy (240), my profit is $72; if I use my low-output strategy (180), my profit is only $64.80. Again, *I'm better off with my high-output strategy.*
- Therefore, *whichever strategy Firm 2 uses,* I'm better off using my high-output strategy. *The high-output strategy is a dominant strategy.*

The payoff table is symmetric, so the high-output strategy is also dominant for Firm 2. The double lines in Figure 6.9b drawn through each of the low-output action lines show that those actions are not chosen.

Both firms use the high-output strategy, and this strategy is a Nash equilibrium in strategies. Given the strategy of Firm 2, Firm 1 has no incentive to change its strategy and vice versa. Suppose in Figure 6.9a that Firm 2 produces 240 units. If Firm 1 changes from producing 240 units to 180 units, its profit falls from $57.60 to $54, so it does not want to change. Similarly, if Firm 1 produces 180 units, Firm 2 does not want to change its strategy. Because neither firm wants to change its strategy of producing 240 units if its rival also produces 240 units, both firms producing the large output is a Nash equilibrium.

This Nash equilibrium does not maximize the players' collective payoff. The two firms would be better off if they could cooperate and both use the high-price strategy. If both produce 180 units, combined profits are \$129.60; whereas, if both produce 240, combined profits are only \$115.20. If the game is only played once, its outcome is nonoptimal from the players' collective viewpoint. This game is called a prisoners' dilemma because both firms have dominant strategies that lead to a payoff that is inferior to what they could achieve if they cooperated.[17]

Infinitely Repeated Prisoners' Dilemma Game

If the single-period prisoners' dilemma game is repeated forever, the price in a given period is more likely to be higher than the price in a single-period game. For example, at a special event such as the Super Bowl, a souvenir firm may compete with others for a short period and then never see its rivals again. Such firms are relatively unlikely to succeed in charging a cartel price because each one knows it can cheat on any agreement with no fear of reprisal. In contrast, souvenir stands at popular tourist attractions that face each other over long periods are more likely to charge a relatively high price.

In the single-period prisoners' dilemma game, each firm took its rival's strategy as given and assumed it could not influence that strategy. If this game is repeated, however, each firm can influence its rival's behavior by *signaling* and *threatening to punish.* See Example 6.5.

Because both firms gain by a reducing output, they have an incentive to communicate to avoid the prisoners' dilemma problem, which stems from a lack of trust. Because antitrust laws make direct communications illegal, firms may try to communicate indirectly through their choice of strategy if (and only if) the game is repeated. For example, a firm can use a multiperiod strategy of setting a low quantity (or high price) and taking losses for several periods to signal its willingness to collude.

Similarly, a firm can threaten to punish its rival if it does not collude. (See Example 6.6.) To illustrate how penalties can be used to insure collusion, we use the quantity setting, single-period prisoners' dilemma game such as in Figure 6.9a. Each of the two firms in the industry can produce at different output levels in different periods. One possible strategy for a firm is to produce the Cournot-Nash level of output, q_n, each period ($q_n = 240$ in our example). If the other firm does the same, each earns the Cournot-Nash profits, π_n, each period (\$57.60). Alternatively, the firms can restrict output with each firm producing q_m, which is half the monopoly output, and earning a profit of π_m ($> \pi_n$) each period ($q_m = 180$ and $\pi_m = \$64.80$).

[17]Luce and Raiffa (1957) attribute the prisoners' dilemma game to A. W. Tucker. In the original version, two prisoners are accused of committing a crime. They are held in different rooms, so they are unable to communicate. Each prisoner has two choices of strategy: to talk or not to talk. If neither talks, each gets a one-year sentence on a minor charge. If both talks, each gets a five-year sentence. If one talks, but the other does not, the prisoner who confesses goes free, while the other gets a 10-year sentence. By the same reasoning as in the Figure 6.9a, both talk even though they are obviously better off if both keep quiet.

EXAMPLE 6.5 *Copying Pricing*

As every student knows, the way to learn something is to copy the relevant article and then absorb it through osmosis. As a result, copy shops often spring up near colleges. In the early 1970s, four firms in the Harvard Square area of Cambridge, Massachusetts, satisfied a large portion of the copy business of students from Harvard, MIT, Tufts, and other colleges in the area.

Initially, the smallest of the "big four" firms, Copy Cat Educational Services, Inc. (located in the J. August Clothing Store), charged much higher prices than its larger competitors. Then Jimmy Jacobs, the owner of the clothing store and copying service, lowered his prices to a level that the other firms contended was too low to make profits.

One competitor, Gnomon Copy, posted a sign in its window on the "Xerox Price Story." Gnomon charged that Jacobs "had sent word to the other Xerox services in Harvard Square that he was going to drive them all out of business . . . if they did not raise their prices to match his, which were then substantially higher than the going rate. . . . Now, Jacobs has carried out his threat."

Gnomon said it was meeting Copy Cat's price in Harvard Square in order not to lose customers, but that it would keep its prices at its other stores at their previous levels, which Gnomon considered "to be fair and reasonable." They urged customers to boycott Copy Cat, claiming, "You may pay a higher price today, but you will insure a viable competitive situation for the future."

Within hours of the posting of Gnomon's sign, according to Gnomon employees, Jacobs barged into their shop and said, "You call your boss and tell him he's got five minutes to take that down or I'll photograph it and use it in a libel suit." Upon reflection, Gnomon management decided it had not gone far enough and assigned an employee to hand out leaflets in front of Jacobs's copy center/clothing store. In turn, Jacobs filmed the leafleteers in the presence of a reporter, while a Gnomon salesperson was frantically searching for her camera to photograph Jacobs photographing everyone else. According to the reporter, "When the Gnomon salesperson ran out of notices, he began modeling his clothes. Mr. Jacobs laughed and kept filming."

The other firms did not lower their prices at first, and their business suffered. These other firms supported Gnomon's charge that Jacobs tried to get them to fix their prices at a higher level and had threatened to punish them by undercutting their prices if they did not cooperate. Jacobs said that he believed that all the firms had been charging too much and that he had decided to lower his prices, but only to a level where he could still make profits. He vigorously denied any attempt to fix prices.

Eventually prices in Harvard Square settled at a lower level, though cost changes may have been partially responsible. This example illustrates how firms try to influence their rivals' actions through their own price or output decisions and through communications when the game is played repeatedly.

Source: Vin McLellan, "Harvard Square: War of the Xerox Machines," *The Phoenix*, February 9, 1971.

EXAMPLE 6.6 *Car Wars*

In 1955, American passenger automobile production was 45 percent greater than it was in 1954 or 1956. Why?

Based on sophisticated econometric tests, Bresnahan (1987) contends that American automobile manufacturers' successful tacit collusion fell apart in 1955, but was reestablished in 1956. During the 1950s, major entry by foreign manufacturers had not yet occurred; thus, American manufacturers could collectively reduce output and increase price.

A casual perusal of automobile output for this period certainly indicates that 1955 was an unusual year. American automobile production from 1953 through 1959 was 6.13, 5.51, 7.94, 5.80, 6.12, 4.24, and 5.60 million cars. Thus, the 7.94 million cars produced in 1955 not only were substantially more than were produced in the adjacent years, 1954 and 1956, but also were substantially more than were produced in any year for the rest of that decade.

Not surprisingly, the large output in 1955 drove down the price of cars. Adjusting for quality, the price in 1955 was approximately 6 percent lower than in the adjacent years. The price fell by a smaller percentage than quantity increased, so that total expenditures rose. Automobile expenditures were (in billions of 1957 dollars) $13.9 in 1954, $18.4 in 1955, and $15.7 in 1956. In other words, consumers spent 32 percent more in 1955 than in 1954 and 17 percent more in 1955 than in 1956.

Firm 1 considers using the following two-part strategy:

- Firm 1 produces q_m output each period so long as Firm 2 does the same.
- If Firm 2 produces a different level of output in any period, t, then in period $t + 1$ and thereafter, Firm 1 produces q_n.

If Firm 2 believes that Firm 1 will follow this strategy, Firm 2 should produce q_m.[18] Firm 2 knows that it can make greater profits in period t by producing more than q_m in that period. If it does so, however, in the $t + 1$ period and every period thereafter, Firm 1 would produce q_n. As already demonstrated, when Firm 1 produces q_n, Firm 2 maximizes its profits by producing q_n also.

Thus, Firm 2 can earn unusually high profits in period t, but then it earns relatively low profits for the rest of the time. Unless Firm 2 puts very little value on future profits, it is in Firm 2's best interest to tacitly collude and produce q_m in each period.

In short, if the future matters significantly, the one-period gains from deviating from the monopoly output cannot compensate for the losses from getting π_n forever instead of π_m. Indeed, Firm 1 need not punish Firm 2 forever to induce it to cooperate; all it needs to do is produce q_n for enough periods so that it does not pay for Firm 2 ever to

[18]As in the single-period models, the question remains as to how firms form these beliefs. Unlike the single-period models, however, firms may form beliefs based on the history of the game in multiperiod models.

deviate. Thus, because strategies can involve signals and threats of punishment, firms are more likely to charge the monopoly price in multiperiod than in single-period games.

Types of Equilibria in Multiperiod Games

All repeated games do not result in high prices, however. The type of equilibrium in a repeated game depends on a player's ability to effectively threaten other players who are not cooperative. The effectiveness of a threat depends on the interest rate, the length of the game, and the credibility of the threat.

Credibility. At the beginning of a game, each firm chooses a strategy to maximize its present discounted profits. If interest rates are so high that profits in future periods are worth substantially less than profits in the current period, future punishment is inconsequential and hence has no effect on current behavior.[19] Lower interest rates, therefore, make the threat of punishment more effective. The more periods left in the game, the larger the total punishment that can be inflicted on a transgressor, because the punishment can be inflicted for more periods. However, if the threat is not credible, in the sense that Firm 2 does not believe that Firm 1 will actually inflict the punishment in future periods, then Firm 2 ignores the threat altogether.

The importance of credibility is illustrated by a two-period prisoners' dilemma example (where, now, firms can choose any output level—not just two possible levels). Suppose Firm 1 is a cartel member and announces that it will produce the collusive quantity, q_m, in Period 1 and the Cournot-Nash quantity, q_n, in the second period if Firm 2 will produce the collusive quantity in the first period. Firm 1 also announces (or signals somehow) that if Firm 2 produces more than q_m in the first period, Firm 1 will punish it by producing a very large quantity (greater than q_n), in the second period. If Firm 2 believes that Firm 1 will carry out its threat, and the potential losses in the second period are large enough, it produces q_m in the first period.

Firm 2, however, does not view Firm 1's threat as credible. Suppose Firm 2 does not produce q_m in the first period. There is now only one period left in the game. Firm 1 *can* punish Firm 2 in Period 2 by producing more than q_n, thereby lowering Firm 2's profits below the Cournot-Nash level. But will Firm 1 do that? Probably not, because it is not in Firm 1's best interests to do so in Period 2. Firm 1 can only harm Firm 2 by harming itself and lowering *each* firm's profits below π_n. In the second period, however, Firm 1 does not benefit from doing so. It is too late to affect Firm 2's behavior in the first period, and there are no future periods. Indeed, in Period 2, Firm 1 should act as though it is participating in a one-period game and produce q_n. Thus, Firm 2 does not view Firm 1's threat as credible; to carry it out would be like locking the barn after the horse is stolen.

A monopoly price in the first period is possible, however, if Firm 1 can make its threat credible by precommitting itself to punish Firm 2 in the second period. Ignor-

[19]If the interest rate is 10 percent, \$1 of profit in the first period is worth \$1, but \$1 of profit guaranteed in the second period is only worth 1/(1.1) ≈ 91¢ in the first period. The *present discounted* value of \$1 of profits in both the first and second years is \$1.91. With a high enough interest rate, profits in the future are essentially irrelevant to current decisions.

ing the legal issues, if Firm 1 writes a binding and enforceable contract in Period 1 that says it will forfeit an enormous sum of money if it does not punish Firm 2 in the second period if necessary, then its threat is credible.

Research in multiperiod games concentrates on equilibria that result from credible strategies and rules out other equilibria. Restrictions on possible equilibria are called **refinements**. One widely used refinement is to consider only **perfect Nash equilibria**: those Nash equilibria in which strategies (threats) are credible (Selten 1975). For example, in the two-period game in which Firm 1 threatens to punish Firm 2 in the second period if Firm 2 produces too much in the first period, the threat is credible only if the punishment is in Firm 1's best interest *in the second period.*

More generally, a strategy or threat is credible only if the firm will stick to that strategy in any **subgame**: a new game that starts in any period t and lasts to the end of the game. If the proposed strategies are best responses (Nash equilibria) in any subgame, these strategies are called a **subgame perfect Nash equilibrium** (or *perfect Nash equilibrium*).

One way to obtain a subgame perfect Nash equilibrium is to solve the game backward. We illustrate this technique for a two-period game. In the last period (the only interesting subgame), the strategy of each firm must be based on its one–period best-response function. That is, there is a Nash equilibrium in the second period in which the strategies are optimal in the sense that the players would have chosen them if the game were beginning in Period 2. In the second period, the Nash, or best-response, strategy for both firms is to produce q_n. Thus, Firm 1's only credible claim is that it will produce q_n in the second period. Because Firm 1's threat to punish in Period 2 is not credible, both firms also produce q_n in Period 1.

Now consider a game that lasts for a finite number of periods, T, greater than 2. To solve for a perfect Nash equilibrium requires working backward from the last period. In the last period, the firms produce q_n, by the preceding reasoning. Thus, Firm 1 cannot credibly threaten to punish Firm 2 for producing a large quantity in period $T - 1$. What happens in period $T - 1$? Effectively, it is now the last period. By the same reasoning, both firms produce q_n in that period. This reasoning can be repeated for $T - 2$, $T - 3$, and other earlier periods, with the conclusion that the firms produce q_n in each period. That is, the T-period game equilibrium simply repeats the single-period equilibrium T times (Selten 1978).

The intuition behind this argument is that firms cheat (produce more then q_m) in earlier periods because it is in their best interests to cheat in later periods—hence they do not have credible threats to produce q_m. As a result, any attempt to produce q_m in earlier periods unravels. The entire argument, then, depends crucially on the firms' cheating in the last period. The argument implicitly assumes that there is a *known,* fixed number of periods, T. All firms cheat in the last period, *if they know it is the last period.* If the period in which the game will end is not known until that period is over, a player is less likely to deviate from the cartel output level in that period. A game with a finite but unknown number of periods, so that players do not know which period is the final one, is therefore similar to a game with an infinite number of periods, and hence an enforceable cartel agreement is feasible.

To summarize, the subgame perfect Nash equilibrium depends on the number of periods in a multiperiod game and whether that number is known. First, we argued that producing the cartel output, q_m, each period is a subgame perfect Nash equilibrium in a game with an infinite number of periods. Then we showed that in a game with a known, finite number of periods, producing the Cournot-Nash output, q_n, in each period is a subgame perfect equilibrium. Finally, we contended that if the number of periods is finite but firms do not know which period is last until after it is over, then, again, the cartel equilibrium is a subgame perfect Nash equilibrium. Indeed, even without an explicit cartel agreement, the cartel equilibrium is a possible equilibrium as long as firms have the appropriate beliefs about each other's (credible) threats. These beliefs may be acquired by observing the history of a rival's behavior.

In a multiperiod game, a firm may have many strategies that involve different actions over time. In the previous example, Firm 1 could produce q_m in Period 1 and q_n thereafter if Firm 2 fails to produce q_m in Period 2. In general, Firm 1's output in any period can be a complicated function of its rival's output in previous periods. This multiplicity of strategies raises two problems for firms. First, it is unclear how firms know or form beliefs about their rivals' strategies if they are so complicated. That is why explicit communications in a cartel can be effective (see Farrell 1987). Second, with many possible strategies, there can be many possible Nash equilibria in strategies.

An infinite number of other subgame perfect Nash equilibria are possible in games with an infinite number of periods and little or no time discounting. The *folk theorem* (Friedman 1971, 1977; Fudenberg and Maskin 1986), which describes this set of subgame perfect Nash equilibria in infinitely long games, says, loosely, that any combination of output levels could be infinitely repeated so long as each firm's profits at those levels are at least as great as the minimum each firm could earn in a one-period game. As a result, in addition to the cartel solution, another perfect equilibrium in the infinitely repeated game is for each firm to produce the Cournot-Nash output, q_n, each period. Much current research is directed at further refining these results to provide better explanations of which equilibria occur. Without further refinements, almost any output level is a sustainable equilibrium, which makes this theory difficult to apply to actual industries.[20]

The folk theorem shows that in a dynamic setting almost any outcome can be sustained as an equilibrium as players follow strategies with punishment. Some of these strategies can be very simple. For example, in a dynamic "tit for tat" strategy, one player cooperates provided the other just did, but does not cooperate if the other player failed to cooperate on his last move. In experimental settings, this simple tit for tat strategy is frequently observed and leads to cooperation in the prisoners' dilemma game.

This chapter concentrated on games that assume no uncertainty about underlying economic conditions. Games in which firms are uncertain about rivals' actions or eco-

[20]However, with additional restrictions, one may be able to estimate a subgame perfect multiperiod model. For example, see Karp and Perloff (1989a, 1993a).

nomic conditions are even more complex.[21] Because such games have so many possible outcomes, economists studying them often place further restrictions or refinements on the possible equilibria to eliminate some possibilities.[22] Much of the current research in game theory is focused on games with uncertainty.

Experimental Evidence on Oligopoly Models

The various oligopoly models predict different equilibrium outcomes because they make alternative assumptions about how firms behave, the number of firms, the rules of the game (nature of the market), and the length of the game. Because all these models are logically consistent, one cannot choose between them on purely theoretical grounds. One can ask, however, whether their assumptions are reasonable or whether their predicted outcomes are consistent with actual market outcomes.

Chapter 8 discusses statistical studies of particular industries. Here, we discuss a number of experiments. Some economists conduct laboratory experiments to determine how college students behave under controlled conditions. Students play a game in which they set output or price for the firms each manages. Because the students keep their profits, they have an incentive to maximize profits in the experimental market. Postexperiment interviews indicate that a few students try to "win" the game by maximizing the difference in their profits relative to other players, rather than maximizing their own profits. The vast majority, however, do try to maximize their own earnings.

The experimental equilibria are compared to the various theoretically predicted equilibria. A survey of these experiments (Plott 1982, 1523) concludes that "three models do well in predicting market prices and quantity: the competitive equilibrium, the Cournot model, and the monopoly (joint maximization) model. Experiments help define the conditions under which each of these alternative models apply."

To give some idea of the results obtained, we discuss four representative, multiperiod game experiments. Virtually all simulation experiments use linear demand curves and a constant marginal cost.

---

[21] For example, in a multiperiod model in which Firm 1 does not know Firm 2's costs, Firm 1's beliefs about Firm 2's costs may affect how it behaves. Firm 1 may drop out of the market if it believes Firm 2's costs are much lower than its own. As a result, Firm 2 may attempt to convince Firm 1 that its costs are very low, perhaps by setting a very low price for several periods. Firm 1 uses the history of Firm 2's behavior in forming its beliefs about Firm 2's costs, taking into account Firm 2's attempts to mislead. Using the additional information about Firm 2's behavior that becomes available each successive period, Firm 1 updates its beliefs about Firm 2's costs. Firm 1 can combine the information about Firm 2's actual behavior with its prior beliefs to form a new estimate of the probability that Firm 2's cost is low by using Bayes's law from probability theory. An equilibrium in which firms form their beliefs using Bayes's law and in which each strategy is subgame perfect is called a *Bayesian perfect equilibrium*.

[22] For more detail on this and related topics, such as refinements and sequential equilibrium, see Harsanyi (1967–68), Kreps and Wilson (1982a, 1982b), Kreps and Spence (1984), Bernheim (1984), Pearce (1984), Tirole (1988), Shapiro (1989), Myerson (1991), Fudenberg and Tirole (1991), Binmore (1992), and Gibbons (1992). For theoretical and empirical research on dynamic oligopoly, see Maskin and Tirole (1988a, 1988b), McGuire and Pakes (1994), Ericson and Pakes (1995, 1998), and Fershtman and Pakes (2000).

Lave (1962), in work that started as a B.A. thesis at Reed College, conducted an experiment with undergraduates who participated in a repeated two-person, two-strategy, multiperiod prisoners' dilemma game. The players were placed so they could not see each other, making explicit communications impossible. Nonetheless, the vast majority of players were apparently able to communicate indirectly and thereby achieve the cartel solution. In various versions of the experiment, 75 to 100 percent of the outcomes were the cartel solution. As predicted theoretically, in the last period, when players knew the experiment was going to end, many (though not all) deviated from the cartel outcome because there could be no retaliation at that point.

Fouraker and Siegel (1963) conducted duopoly and triopoly (three-firm) experiments (compare Holt 1985). Each subject was given a payoff table showing that profits depended on a player's output choice and the output of the rival(s).

Each of 16 pairs of undergraduates played the game 25 times. Fouraker and Siegel used the players' decisions in the 21st period to evaluate the equilibrium. The duopoly outputs were distributed fairly uniformly over the range from slightly less than the collusive (cartel) level to the competitive (Bertrand) level. Five were closest to competition, 7 were closest to Cournot, 1 was between Cournot and cartel, and 3 were closest to the cartel equilibrium. The median output was the Cournot output.

In the triopoly game, however, the median output was only slightly below the competitive output. In 5 cases, the industry output was closest to Cournot, and in 6, it was closest to competition.

Fouraker and Siegel also conducted experiments in which subjects chose prices, as in the Bertrand game, instead of output levels. According to the payoff table, a player who chose a price above a rival's made no sales and suffered a small loss of profits.

When players had incomplete information (they knew whether their price was higher or lower than a rival's, but did not know the rival's profits), the price converged to the competitive equilibrium (or just above it) within 14 periods in 17 out of 18 cases. When duopoly players had full information (each knew all past prices and all players' profits), the results were more varied. In 6 cases, the market was at the competitive equilibrium by the 14th period, and in 3 more, the price was just above it. In 4 cases, the price was exactly midway between the competitive and the cartel price; in the remaining 4, it was at or adjacent to the cartel price.

In the triopoly case, whether players had incomplete or complete information, the market converged to the competitive level virtually every time. Thus, with full information, competitive behavior seems likely in three-person price games, but not in two-person ones. With incomplete information, competitive equilibrium is also more likely with three-person games.

One possible reason that competitive behavior was not observed in full-information duopoly games is that profits were near zero at the competitive level, so players had little to lose by choosing other strategies. Holt (1985) conducted a similar experiment of repeated duopoly games, in which the profits at the competitive or Bertrand equilibrium were positive.[23] He found that the outcomes were between cartel and Cournot, and closest to the Cournot outcome.

[23]This experiment differs from the Fouraker and Siegel experiment in a number of ways, most importantly in that it was constructed so that no possible strategy ensured a profit that always exceeded the positive competitive payoff. The end of the game was determined by the throw of a die, so as to avoid endgame effects.

Realizing that the repetition of the game favors cartel behavior, Holt tried a single-period experiment, which he felt would favor the Cournot equilibrium or possibly even more competitive behavior. Twelve experienced subjects engaged in a series of single-period games (with no guarantee as to which players were paired in a given game). In early games, the output choices were quite diverse, but eventually, virtually all the players chose the Cournot equilibrium output.

Holt concluded that in full-information duopoly games, whether or not there are multiperiod markets, the Cournot equilibrium is more likely than the competitive, or Bertrand, equilibrium. The only effect of experience and repeated games seems to be to raise prices.

Where explicit signaling is permitted, we would expect higher prices to be more likely. In a series of experiments, Friedman (1967) allowed players to transmit two written messages before privately making a price decision. Cartel outcomes were attained over 75 percent of the time. Further, 75 percent of these cartel agreements maximized each player's profits (with no side payments allowed). As should be expected, once the players succeeded in achieving the cartel solution, the probability of another cartel solution was 96 percent.

These experimental results have generally withstood the test of time and are still widely cited. There is now a large body of research on experimental methods and industrial organization. Based on his survey of the experimental literature, Holt (1995) drew the following conclusions. The one-period Cournot model often emerges as a good predictor of outcomes in one-period games. In multiperiod games with three or more sellers, the outcomes are often more competitive than a static Cournot model would predict. The price approaches the competitive level as the number of sellers increases if buyers and sellers propose prices simultaneously (a *double auction*) or if individual negotiations between each buyer and seller occur. Both these trading mechanisms result in lower prices than occur if sellers announce or post the prices at which they are willing to trade. Cooperation between players often increases as the number of times the game is repeated rises, but there has been no direct evidence that trigger-price strategies will result in cooperative outcomes without communications between players.

SUMMARY

Although most economists agree about the basic characteristics of oligopolistic markets, they do not agree about the best way to model these markets. Oligopoly models make very different assumptions about how firms behave; as a result, they make very different predictions about the nature of the equilibrium. Several conclusions can be drawn, however.

First, cartel outcomes are more likely in markets that last a long or uncertain period of time than in those that exist for only a short, known period of time. Experimental evidence supports the conclusion that cartel pricing is most likely to occur in repeated games. Explicit contact between firms increases the probability of achieving a monopoly price.

Second, most models (except the single-period, homogeneous-good Bertrand model) predict that the more firms in the industry, the more competitive is the equilibrium. The Bertrand model in which firms have constant marginal costs predicts the competitive equilibrium, regardless of the number of firms.

Third, experimental evidence indicates that the Cournot equilibrium is often (but not always) observed, especially in duopoly games. This evidence and the relative ease of using the model explain its continuing popularity.

Fourth, the reemergence of game theory has led to a better understanding of when strategies are credible to other firms. Research is ongoing to restrict the number of possible equilibria that can occur in multiperiod games with and without uncertainty.

All models in this chapter assume that the number of firms is fixed, firms produce homogeneous products, and firms maximize their profits by setting their expected marginal revenues equal to their marginal costs. The models differ only in the way in which firms calculate their expected marginal revenues. The next chapter extends these models to include product differentiation and the entry of new firms.

PROBLEMS

1. Under what conditions are the Cournot and Bertrand equilibria the same?
2. In the Cournot example in this chapter, fixed costs were assumed to be zero and marginal (average) costs were constant. What additional complications are raised if the cost functions have the usual U-shape?
3. What are the best strategies for Players 1 and 2 if each chooses between setting a low price or a high price and the payoffs are 5 if both firms charge the high price and zero for all other combinations of strategies? [*Hint:* Write down the 2 × 2 normal-form representation of this game and look for dominant strategies.]
4. What happens to price and output in the Cournot, Bertrand, and Stackelberg models if marginal costs increase by 10 percent?
5. For n = 2, 5, 10, 50, and 1,000, add columns to Table 6.2 for
   a. Market elasticity, ϵ, which equals $(dQ/dp)(p/Q)$.
   b. Lerner's measure of market power, $(p - MC)/p$.
   c. Consumer surplus.
   d. Social welfare = consumer surplus + industry profits.
   e. Deadweight loss (the amount by which social welfare is less than the optimum).

   Confirm that Lerner's measure of market power, $(p - MC)/p$, equals $1/(n\epsilon)$.
6. What is the relationship between the Stackelberg model and the dominant-firm-competitive-fringe model (Chapter 4)?
7. Using the data in Example 6.6, calculate the market demand elasticity for automobiles in the mid-1950s. For large changes in price and quantity, an *arc elasticity* is used. One common method of calculating an arc elasticity is to use the midway point between the two price-quantity pairs: (p, q) and (p^*, q^*). Thus, the formula for an arc elasticity is

$$\left(\frac{q - q^*}{q + q^*}\right) \Big/ \left(\frac{p - p^*}{p + p^*}\right).$$

   Is that number consistent with the theory that there was a profit-maximizing cartel in 1954? Why or why not?

Answers to the odd-numbered problems are given at the back of the book.

SUGGESTED READINGS

For a clear presentation of traditional oligopoly models and an introduction to game theory that is only slightly more technical than this textbook, see Shubik with Levitan (1980), Friedman (1983), and Ulph (1987). Williams (1966) has a good, relatively nontechnical discussion of simple games. Dixit and Nalebuff (1991) contains wonderful, nontechnical applications of game theory to a variety of economic problems. Binmore (1992) and Gibbons (1992) are relatively accessible game theory texts. Fudenberg and Tirole (1989) and Shapiro (1989) provide excellent surveys of oligopoly models. See Gaudet and Salant (1991) for a discussion of the effect of firms in related product markets.

Two short surveys of dynamic game issues are Kreps and Spence (1984) and Fudenberg and Tirole (1986b). Some of the relatively technical, recent textbooks on game theory are Shubik (1982, 1984), Friedman (1977, 1986), Mas-Collel, Whinston, and Green (1995), Tirole (1988), Fudenberg and Tirole (1991), and Myerson (1991).

APPENDIX 6A

A Mathematical Derivation of Cournot and Stackelberg Equilibria

This appendix uses calculus to derive the Cournot and Stackelberg equilibria prices and quantities for a general functional form and a linear example. Assume that there are n firms, where n is exogenously determined. The output of the ith firm is q_i and the total output, Q, is the sum of the (homogeneous) output of each firm: $Q = q_1 + \ldots + q_n$. The demand and cost functions are

	General Functional Form	Linear Example
Market demand	$p(Q)$	$p = a - bQ$
Firm's cost	$C(q_i)$	$C(q_i) = mq_i$

where a, b, and m are constants. In the example, demand is linear and marginal cost is constant. The competitive and monopoly solutions are

	General Functional Form	Linear Example
Competition	$MC \equiv C'(q_i) = p(Q)$	$m = a - bQ = p$
		$Q = \dfrac{a - m}{b}$
Monopoly	$MC = C'(Q) = p'(Q)Q + p(Q) = MR$	$m = a - 2bQ = MR$
		$Q = \dfrac{a - m}{2b}$
		$p = \dfrac{a + m}{2}$

where a, b, and m are constants.

To analyze a Cournot industry, one starts by examining the behavior of a representative firm. Firm 1 tries to maximize its profits through its choice of q_1:

$$\max_{q_1} \pi_1(q_1, q_2, \ldots, q_n) = q_1 p(q_1 + \cdots + q_n) - C(q_1). \tag{6A.1}$$

The first-order condition is $MR = MC$, or

$$p(q_1 + \cdots + q_n) + q_1 p'(q_1 + \cdots + q_n) \times \left(1 + \frac{\partial q_2}{\partial q_1} + \cdots + \frac{\partial q_n}{\partial q_1}\right) = C'(q_1). \tag{6A.2}$$

If the firms play Nash-in-quantities (Cournot), these partial derivatives, $\partial q_i/\partial q_1$, are zero. Thus, the first-order condition may be rewritten as

$$p(q_1 + \cdots + q_n) + q_1 p'(q_1 + \cdots + q_n) = C'(q_1). \qquad (6A.3)$$

Rearranging terms in Equation 6A.3, multiplying and dividing the right-hand side by n, and noting that $p' = \mathrm{d}p/\mathrm{d}Q$ and $Q = nq_1$ (given that all firms are identical), one obtains the Lerner Index,

$$\frac{p - C'}{p} = -\frac{1}{n}\frac{\mathrm{d}p}{\mathrm{d}Q}\frac{Q}{p} = -\frac{1}{n\epsilon}, \qquad (6A.3')$$

where the second equality holds because the elasticity of market demand, ϵ, is $(\mathrm{d}Q/\mathrm{d}p)(p/Q)$. The left-hand side of Equation 6A.3′ is Lerner's measure of market power: the ratio of the price markup over marginal cost to the price. If the market is competitive, then $p = C'$, and Lerner's measure is zero. The larger the measure, the greater the market power. With symmetric firms, the elasticity facing any one firm is $n\epsilon$. Notice that, holding the market elasticity constant, as the number of firms increases, Lerner's measure falls. As n approaches ∞, the elasticity facing any one firm approaches $-\infty$, so Lerner's measure approaches $1/\infty$ or 0, and the market is competitive (see, however, Ruffin 1971).

Equation 6A.3 shows how the profit-maximizing q_1 depends upon $q_2, \ldots, q_n$. One can rearrange this expression, solving for q_1, to derive Firm 1's best-response function:

$$q_1 = R_1(q_2, \ldots, q_n). \qquad (6A.3'')$$

With our linear example, the first-order condition for profit maximization 6A.2 is

$$MR = a - b(2q_1 + q_2 + \cdots + q_n) = m = MC. \qquad (6A.4)$$

In equilibrium, because all firms have the same cost function, $q_2 = q_3 = \cdots = q_n \equiv q$. Solving Equation 6A.4 for q_1, the best-response function 6A.3″ for the first firm is

$$q_1 = R_1(q_2, \ldots, q_n) = \frac{a - m}{2b} - \frac{n - 1}{2}q. \qquad (6A.5)$$

The intersection of the best-response functions determines the Cournot equilibrium. In the example, that occurs where $q_1 = q_i = q (i = 2, \ldots, n)$. Setting $q_1 = q$ in Equation 6A.5 and solving for q gives

$$q = \frac{a - m}{(n + 1)b}. \qquad (6A.6)$$

Total output, nq, equals $n(a - m)/[(n + 1)b]$. The corresponding price is obtained by substituting $Q = nq$ into the demand function:

$$p = \frac{a + nm}{n + 1}. \tag{6A.7}$$

Setting $n = 1$ in the last two equations yields the monopoly quantity and price. As n becomes large, the quantity and price approach the competitive levels. That is, using Equations 6A.6 and 6A.7, as n grows large, total output, nq, approaches $(a - m)/b$ and price approaches m.

Similarly, using Equation 6A.7, Lerner's measure of market power, $(p - C')/p$, equals $(a - m)/(a + nm)$. As n grows large, the denominator goes to ∞, so Lerner's measure goes to 0, and there is no market power.

A Stackelberg leader (say, Firm 1) takes the Cournot best-response functions of the follower firms as constraints. That is, its objective is

$$\max_{q_1} \pi_1(q_1, q_2, \ldots, q_n) = q_1 p(q_1 + \cdots + q_n) - C(q_1)$$
$$\text{s. t. } q_i = R_i(q_1, Q_i) \qquad i = 2, \ldots, n, \tag{6A.8}$$

where Q_i is the sum of the output of all the firms except Firm 1 and Firm i. Substituting the best-response functions into the profit expression for each q_i and differentiating with respect to q_1, we obtain the first-order condition for a profit-maximum.

For example, with a duopoly, the first-order condition for the Stackelberg leader is

$$p(q_1 + R_2(q_1)) + q_1 p'(q_1 + R_2(q_1))[1 + R'_2(q_1)] = C'(q_1), \tag{6A.9}$$

where R'_2 is the partial derivative of the best-response function of Firm 2 with respect to q_1. The follower's output is determined by setting the q_1 determined by Equation 6A.9 into the follower's best-response function.

In the linear example, each follower's best-response function is of the form of Equation 6A.5:

$$q_i = \frac{a - m}{2b} - \frac{(n - 2)q}{2} - \frac{q_1}{2}, \qquad i = 2, \ldots, n, \tag{6A.10}$$

where the output of the firms other than Firm i and Firm 1 is $(n - 2)q$. Because all the follower firms produce the same amount of output, q, the best-response function of the followers, Equation 6A.10, can be written as

$$q = \frac{a - m}{nb} - \frac{q_1}{n}. \tag{6A.10'}$$

The leader maximizes its profits, taking the best-response functions of the followers as given. The leader's first-order condition for profit maximization is given in Equation 6A.9. By differentiating Equation 6A.10′ with respect to q_1, one finds the slope of the followers' best-response functions, $dR_i/dq_1 = -1/n$, which we substitute into Equation 6A.9. That is, for every unit the leader firm's output rises, each follower firm's output falls by $1/n$, so the followers' collective output falls by $(n - 1)/n$. Thus, substituting the linear demand curve expression for p into Equation 6A.9 and solving for q_1, one obtains the output of the leader:

$$q_1 = \frac{a - m}{2b}. \tag{6A.11}$$

In this linear model, q_1 is independent of the number of follower firms and equals the monopoly output. The output for the $n - 1$ (≥ 1) follower firms is

$$q = \frac{a - m}{2bn}. \tag{6A.12}$$

Thus, $q_1 > q$ for any number of firms, n (≥ 2).

Total industry output is

$$Q = \frac{a - m}{2b}\left(\frac{2n - 1}{n}\right), \tag{6A.13}$$

which exceeds the Cournot market output of $[(a - m)/b][n/(n + 1)]$, using the Cournot q from Equation 6A.6. The market price is

$$p = \frac{a + m(2n - 1)}{2n}. \tag{6A.14}$$

Thus, as the number of firms, n, grows large, price and total quantity approach the competitive levels: $p \to m$ and $Q \to (a - m)/b$.

APPENDIX 6B

Mixed Strategies

In the text, only *pure* strategies, where a player picks a single price or quantity, were considered. Players, however, may use *mixed* strategies where they choose their actions randomly. For example, suppose Figure 6.9 were changed so that the payoff were:

		Firm 1: Low price	Firm 1: High price
Firm 2	Low price	Firm 1: 0; Firm 2: 2	Firm 1: 2; Firm 2: 1
	High price	Firm 1: 7; Firm 2: 0	Firm 1: 6; Firm 2: 6

Given these payoffs, Firm 2 wants to match Firm 1's price, but Firm 1 does not want to match Firm 2's price. Both of them setting a low price is not a Nash equilibrium because if Firm 2 believes Firm 1 will set a low price, it wants to set a high price. Nor is Firm 2 setting a low price and Firm 1 setting a high price a Nash equilibrium, because Firm 2 would want to change its behavior. Similarly, the other possible pairs of strategies are not Nash equilibria. The only possible Nash equilibrium is for the players to choose their actions randomly.

Let α be the probability that Firm 1 sets a low price and β be the probability that Firm 2 sets a low price. If the firms choose their prices independently, then $\alpha\beta$ is the probability that both set a low price, $(1 - \alpha)(1 - \beta)$ is the probability that both set a high price, $\alpha(1 - \beta)$ is the probability that Firm 1 prices low and Firm 2 prices high, and $(1 - \alpha)\beta$ is the probability Firm 1 prices high and Firm 2 prices low.

Firm 2's expected payoff, $E(\pi_2)$ is

$$\begin{aligned} E(\pi_2) &= 2\alpha\beta + (0)\alpha(1 - \beta) + (1 - \alpha)\beta + 6(1 - \alpha)(1 - \beta) \\ &= (6 - 6\alpha) - (5 - 7\alpha)\beta. \end{aligned}$$

Similarly, Firm 1's expected payoff is

$$\begin{aligned} E(\pi_1) &= (0)\alpha\beta + 7\,\alpha(1 - \beta) + 2(1 - \alpha)\beta + 6(1 - \alpha)(1 - \beta) \\ &= (6 - 4\beta) + (1 - 3\beta)\alpha. \end{aligned}$$

Each firm must form a belief about its rival's behavior. For example, suppose Firm 1 believes that Firm 2 will choose a low price with a probability β^e. If β^e is less than 1/3 (that is, Firm 2 is relatively unlikely to choose a low price), it pays for Firm 1 to choose the low price because the second term in $E(\pi_1)$, $(1 - 3\beta)\alpha$, is positive, so that as α increases, $E(\pi_1)$ increases. Because the highest possible α is 1, Firm 1 chooses the low price with certainty. Similarly, if Firm 1 believes β^e is greater than 1/3, it sets a high price with certainty ($\alpha = 0$).

If Firm 2 believes that Firm 1 thinks β^e is slightly below 1/3, then Firm 2 believes Firm 1 will choose a low price with certainty, and hence Firm 2 will also choose a low price. That outcome, $\beta = 1$, however, is not consistent with what Firm 1 expects (β^e is a fraction). Indeed, it is only rational for Firm 2 to believe Firm 1 believes Firm 2 will use a mixed strategy if Firm 1's belief about Firm 2 makes Firm 1 unpredictable. That is, Firm 1 uses a mixed strategy only if it is *indifferent* between setting a high or a low price. It is only indifferent if it believes β^e is exactly 1/3. By similar reasoning, Firm 2 will use a mixed strategy only if its belief is that Firm 1 chooses a low price with probability $\alpha^e = 5/7$. Thus, the only possible Nash equilibrium is $\alpha = 5/7$ and $\beta = 1/3$.

It can be shown that every game with a finite number of players, each of which has a finite number of pure strategies, has at least one Nash equilibrium, possibly in mixed strategies. Proofs are provided in the game theory texts cited in the recommended readings.

Many game theorists, however, do not like the concept of mixed strategies in static games. They believe that few people actually randomize over their pure strategies. It is hard to imagine a manager of a firm rolling dice to decide what price to charge tomorrow. One (weak) response to this objection is that the firms only have to *appear* to be unpredictable to each other.

A few mixed strategy models have been estimated. See, for example, Golan, Karp, and Perloff (2000).

CHAPTER 7

Product Differentiation and Monopolistic Competition

Good taste is better than bad taste, but bad taste is better than no taste.
—*Arnold Bennett*

In many markets firms engage in *monopolistic competition:* Firms have *market power,* the ability to raise price profitably above marginal cost, yet they make zero economic profits. Such a market structure combines attributes of monopoly (market power) and competition (zero economic profits). An industry has monopolistic competition if there is *free entry* and each firm faces a *downward-sloping demand curve.* If firms enter the industry whenever positive profits are available, each firm makes zero economic profits in the long run, as in a competitive industry. If a firm faces a downward-sloping demand curve, it has market power.

An important reason why a firm faces a downward-sloping demand curve is that consumers view its product as different from those of other firms in the industry. In previous chapters, we concentrated on industries with **homogeneous** or **undifferentiated** goods: Products are viewed as identical by consumers. That is, consumers view the products as *perfect substitutes* for each other. In many industries, however, products are typically **heterogeneous** or **differentiated**: Consumers consider products or brands of various firms to be imperfect substitutes. If consumers view brands in an industry as imperfect substitutes, a firm may raise its price above that of its rivals without losing all its customers.

The models analyzed in this chapter differ in two ways from the oligopoly models in Chapter 6. First, entry is impossible in an oligopolistic market (by definition), but firms can freely enter and exit an industry characterized by monopolistic competition. In this chapter, the number of firms is determined within the model by entry behavior rather than arbitrarily determined outside the model as in the oligopoly chapter. Second, in Chapter 6, we assumed that oligopolistic firms produce identical products, whereas in this chapter products differ across firms.[1]

In the models of Chapter 6, in which firms produced homogeneous goods, an increase in the number of oligopolists benefited consumers because the additional competition led to lower prices. If firms produce differentiated products, the entry of a new firm helps consumers for two reasons: It lowers prices and increases the variety of products from which to choose.

Both these effects are illustrated in models of monopolistic competition. There are two major types of monopolistic competition models with free entry and differentiated products. In one, the *representative consumer model,* all firms compete equally for all consumers who typically buy from each firm. This model might be used to study the restaurant market, in which firms produce differentiated products (such as different ethnic cuisines), but all compete for the same customers.

In the other, the *spatial* or *location* model, each consumer prefers products that have certain characteristics or are sold by firms located near him or her and is willing to pay a premium for these preferred products. Moreover, the consumer may not care greatly about the price of some other goods in the market. For example, a consumer whose favorite cereal is Kellogg's corn flakes is more sensitive to the relative price of Post's corn flakes than to the relative price of Nabisco's sugar-coated shredded wheat. The other brand of corn flakes is a much better substitute than other types of cereal.

These models differ in the type of demand each firm faces. In the representative consumer model, a firm's demand varies continuously with the prices of all firms. A small change in any one firm's price causes a relatively small change in the demand facing a firm. In the location model, as the cereal example suggests, the demand for one brand may be either independent of some other brand's price because they are not close substitutes, or highly dependent on another brand's price because they are close substitutes. Moreover, a firm may, at some very low price, gain a large number of extra consumers as it captures all the customers of another firm that produces a very similar product.

Either model can be used to study the welfare of consumers and firms by comparing the monopolistic competition equilibrium to the social optimum in terms of price and variety. This chapter asks whether there are too many or too few brands in the monopolistic competition equilibrium. The answer to this question depends on how much more consumers are willing to pay for greater variety (it is expensive to produce many types of products). Which would you prefer: a choice of three different-flavored soft drinks at 50¢ per drink or only one flavor at 25¢? The answers to such questions determine the optimal variety-price combination.

The first section of this chapter explains why product differentiation affects the demand curve facing a firm. Then the two most widely used models of monopolistic

[1]Differentiated products are sold in most oligopolistic markets. This heterogeneity was ignored in the previous chapter for simplicity. The analysis of differentiation in this chapter may be applied to those oligopoly models.

competition are discussed. Representative consumer models of monopolistic competition with both homogeneous and heterogeneous products are examined. The discussion shows how the homogeneous product, Cournot-Nash oligopoly model presented in the previous chapter changes when free entry is allowed and then describes how the equilibrium price in this model compares to the social optimum. Next, the model is modified to allow for product differentiation, and price and variety in the monopolistic competition equilibrium are compared to the socially optimal combination.

The discussion then turns to a location model. Product differentiation is inherent in location models, so no homogeneous product model is presented. Again, the welfare implications are examined. Finally, hybrid models that have elements of both models are used to explain why these two types of models have different properties.

The key questions in this chapter are

1. Why does product differentiation increase firms' market power?
2. What number of firms maximizes welfare if all brands are perfect substitutes (homogeneous)?
3. What number of firms maximizes welfare if consumers view brands as imperfect substitutes for each other?
4. What number of firms maximizes welfare if consumers only value some of the brands in the market?

Differentiated Products

The study of an industry of differentiated products is based on two key concepts. First, products are differentiated because consumers *think* they differ. That is, even though aspirin brands may be chemically identical, if consumers believe that the products differ and shop accordingly, then the products are effectively differentiated. For example, "commodity" beans (pintos, Great Northerns, and so forth) from Golden Grain/Mission sell for about 69¢ per pound at your local grocery, whereas those from Melissa's, which are in a pretty package, go for about $4.59 per pound.[2]

Similarly, many consumers strongly prefer Coke to Pepsi or vice versa, yet they have trouble differentiating them by taste. When regular cola drinkers were given samples of Coca Cola Classic, Pepsi, Diet Coke, and Diet Pepsi, only 37 percent could correctly identify the brand they said they preferred. Only 26 percent of diet cola consumers could identify their brand.[3]

---

[2]M. A. Mariner, "Consumers Are Willing to Pay a Lot for a Pretty Package," *San Francisco Chronicle,* April 30, 1997: Food 3.

[3]Consumer Union, "The Cola Wars," *Consumer Reports* 56, August 1991:518–25. In a similar study at Williams College ("Diet Cola Advertising Gets Put to the Test." *San Francisco Chronicle,* January 31, 1990:C1), only an "insignificant" number of subjects could consistently tell the difference between Diet Coke and Diet Pepsi. More than one-third of those professing a preference for one brand chose the other in the test.

Conversely, if consumers view chemically or physically different products as identical, then for economic purposes they are homogeneous: "The consumer is always right." See **www.aw-bc.com/carlton_perloff** "Spurious Product Differentiation: A Drug on the Market."

Second, the pricing of one brand exerts a greater constraint on another brand's pricing when the two brands are close substitutes than when they are not. For example, few would dispute that Pepsi Cola and Coca Cola are close substitutes. Indeed, Canada Dry Ginger Ale may also compete with Coke and Pepsi, because they are all soft drinks with sugar. But are soft drinks without sugar close substitutes? What about noncarbonated drinks like milk and water?[4] See Example 7.1.

An example of a market with homogeneous products is wheat: Consumers do not care which farm produced a particular bushel of wheat. It is harder to think of industries with a small number of firms whose products consumers view as perfectly identical, but there are a number of industries whose products consumers may view as nearly identical. Delivery services in a city may be viewed as quite similar. Different brands of beach balls may also strike most consumers as very close substitutes. An industry has relatively homogeneous products if consumers do not care which brand they buy.

There are two approaches to analyzing differentiation. In the standard consumer theory of basic microeconomics books, consumers have preferences regarding commodities: They choose between ice cream and cake or between brands of ice cream and cake. In an alternative formulation, consumers have preferences regarding the attributes, or characteristics, of commodities. For example, some consumers love chocolate, a characteristic of some ice creams and cakes. These consumers prefer either chocolate ice cream or chocolate cake to vanilla ice cream or white cake.

The Effect of Differentiation on a Firm's Demand Curve

A cynic is a man who knows the price of everything, and the value of nothing. —*Oscar Wilde*

In industries with undifferentiated products, the demand facing a particular firm depends only on the total supply of its rivals, whereas in an industry with differentiated products, the demand facing a firm depends on the supply of each of its competitors separately. For industries with either differentiated or undifferentiated goods, we can write the inverse demand curve facing Firm *i* as:

$$p_{\mathrm{i}} = D(q_1, \ldots, q_{\mathrm{n}}). \tag{7.1}$$

[4]The definition of a market is often a crucial issue in antitrust and merger cases (see Chapter 19). Often, expert witnesses in these cases contend that if products are "close substitutes," they are part of the same *market.* Throughout this book, unless otherwise noted, the term *market* is used loosely, without reference to legal definitions. This chapter assumes each firm's product is in the market being discussed, in the sense that at least some consumers view it as a substitute for at least some other products in the market. That is, it assumes the products are "adequately close" substitutes without defining what "adequately close" means.

EXAMPLE 7.1

All Water Is Not the Same

Until recently, few people thought of water as a product that could be differentiated. But with clever marketing, firms have convinced consumers that water is indeed a differentiated product.

In 2000, 5.0 billion gallons of bottled water were consumed (only about one-third of the consumption of carbonated beverages) and sold for $6 billion. By 2002, sales exceeded $7.7 billion. The many brands of bottled water appeal to different segments of the market and sell for very different prices:

Brand	Price per Quart (bottle size)	Source	2002 U.S. Wholesale Sales
Aquafina	$0.88 (1.5 liter)	Purified tap water	$838.0 million
Dasani	$1.58 (20 oz)	Purified tap water	$765.0 million
Poland Spring	$0.92 (24 oz)	Spring in Maine	$621.5 million
Deer Park	$1.32 (24 oz)	Springs in Florida, Maryland, & Pennsylvania	$311.1 million
Crystal Geyser	$0.77 (six pack of 1 liter bottles)	Springs in California & Tennessee	$270.0 million
Evian	$1.46 (1 liter)	Spring in the French Alps	$191.1 million

As the table shows, the best-selling brand, Aquafina, is moderately priced, while the second-place top brand, Dasani, costs nearly twice as much. Coca-Cola, Pepsi, Nestlé, and the other companies that sell bottled water each typically offer an array of different-price brands. Recently, water bottlers have added flavors in order to differentiate their products further. These flavored waters have become increasingly important, and their sales rose tenfold between 1999 and 2002.

Sources: J. Jordan and S. He, "Size Counts: The Economic Value of Bottled Water," *Choices*, September 22, 2002; International Bottled Water Association, "Marketing Statistics Gallonage by Segment," **www.bottledwater.org/public/gallon_byseg.htm**; "U.S. Soft Drink Sales Slow in 2002," Beverage Marketing Corporation of New York news release (July 24, 2003); Phil Lempert, "Navigating the Sea of Bottled Water," *Today Show*, June 17, 2003; prices are from peapod.com for Washington, DC, on August 27, 2003; source information comes from brand Web sites and Betsy McKay and Robert Frank, "Coke, Danone to Announce Venture—Pact to Market, Distribute Bottled Spring Water Could Challenge PepsiCo, Nestlé," *Wall Street Journal*, June 17, 2002:B5; sales data come from "Bottled Water Moves Up in the Rankings, Says Beverage Marketing Corporation," Beverage Marketing Corporation of New York news release (May 19, 2003).

That is, the price, p_i, that Firm i may charge depends on the quantity of its brand sold and the quantities of all other $n - 1$ brands. Where products are differentiated, this expression cannot be simplified. One can also write the demand curve facing Firm i as a function of the prices of each rival product, $q_i = \tilde{D}(p_1, p_2, \ldots, p_n)$.

If consumers view all products as identical, or perfect substitutes, however, the demand curve may be written more simply. Consumers are unwilling to pay more for one firm's product than another's. Thus, all firms must charge the same price, p, if all are to sell their products. With undifferentiated products, only total market output, $Q = q_1 + q_2 + \cdots + q_n$, matters in determining the price, p.[5] In this case, the inverse demand equation may be written as

$$p_i = p = D(q_1 + q_2 + \cdots + q_n) = D(Q). \tag{7.2}$$

As an example, suppose there are two firms in an industry. If the two products are viewed by consumers as identical, the price each firm may charge ($p = p_1 = p_2$) might be written as

$$p = a - bQ = a - b(q_1 + q_2) = a - bq_1 - bq_2, \tag{7.3}$$

where a and b are positive constants. That is, an increase in either firm's output reduces the market price—and hence the price for each firm—by an equal amount.

In contrast, if consumers view the products as imperfect substitutes, Firm 1's demand curve may be

$$p_1 = a - b_1 q_1 - b_2 q_2, \tag{7.4}$$

where $a > 0$ and $|b_1| > |b_2|$. That is, an increase in Firm 1's output has a greater effect on its price than an increase in Firm 2's output. Indeed, the more a firm succeeds in differentiating its product, the more insulated its demand is from the actions of other firms. For example, a change in the quantity sold or the price of Ripple or Thunder Bird, which are inexpensive wines in screw-top bottles, may have negligible effects on the price or demand for expensive wines.

Oligopolies or monopolistic competition markets may have differentiated goods, but, in a perfectly competitive market, products are not differentiated. If a firm's product is differentiated, it faces a downward-sloping demand function, which is inconsistent with a competitive firm's price-taking behavior.

Preferences for Characteristics of Products

In Lancaster's (1966, 1971, 1979) and Becker's (1965) consumer theories, consumers have preferences over the characteristics of commodities. Each commodity is a bundle of characteristics. For example, candy bars and ice cream vary in sweetness, temperature, texture, and so forth. Rather than comparing the products as such, consumers choose on the basis of the more fundamental characteristics.

---

[5] If the brands of two firms are perfect substitutes, a consumer's indifference curve for the goods is a straight line with a slope of -1. That is, a consumer is indifferent between having 20 units of Brand 1 and 0 units of Brand 2, or 10 units of each, or 0 units of Brand 1 and 20 units of Brand 2. The consumer's utility depends only on the sum of the output of the two brands.

To illustrate how products can be compared by examining their characteristics, suppose the only important characteristic of a soft drink is how sweet it is. Soft drinks are located in "sweetness" space:

Not Sweet ◄——————► Sweet

In this space, Schwepps Club Soda is located to the left of Classic Coke, which is to the left of Pepsi. That is, the sweeter products are, the further to the right they are located. Soft drinks, then, can be said to be located in a **characteristic space**: There is an axis showing the amount of each characteristic or attribute (here there is only one attribute, sweetness), and each brand can be located in this space according to its characteristics.

Of course, a product may have many characteristics: Cereal brands may differ by sweetness and "mouth feel." If those are the only important characteristics, then cereal brands can be located in a characteristic space that has sweetness on one axis and mouth feel (from soggy to crunchy) on the other.

The representative consumer model may use either the product or characteristic approach; location models inherently use a characteristic approach. We examine both models in turn.

The Representative Consumer Model

I alone am here the representative of the people. —*Napoleon Bonaparte*

The first monopolistic competition model was developed by Chamberlin (1933). In this **representative consumer model**, the typical consumer views all brands as equally good substitutes for each other; hence, brands are treated symmetrically. This representative consumer model can be used to examine industries with either differentiated or undifferentiated products. We start by examining undifferentiated product markets and then extend the analysis to markets in which products are heterogeneous. The analysis shows that whether or not products are differentiated, the equilibrium prices and number (variety) of brands in a monopolistic competition equilibrium are not generally socially optimal.

A Representative Consumer Model with Undifferentiated Products

In the simplest version of the representative consumer model, the various brands are homogeneous: All brands have the same characteristics. This model differs from the oligopoly models of the previous chapter only in the way the number of firms in the industry is determined. Both the oligopoly models and the monopolistic competition model determine the output of each firm. In both models, profit-maximizing behavior determines the output of each firm. That is, each firm chooses its output so that its

TABLE 7.1 **Comparison of Oligopoly and Monopolistic Competition Models**

Model	Profit Maximization by Individual Firms	Number of Firms (n) Determined by Entry
Noncooperative oligopoly	marginal revenue = marginal cost	No entry: number of firms is fixed at n
Monopolistic competition	marginal revenue = marginal cost	Free entry: firms enter until profit = 0, so n is endogenously determined

marginal revenue corresponding to its residual demand curve, MR_r, equals its marginal cost, MC.

Entry is treated differently in the two models. In the oligopoly models, the number of firms is arbitrarily determined outside the model: The existing firms, the government, or some other force prevents new entry. In Chamberlin's model, firms freely enter the industry as long as it is profitable for them to do so. This *entry condition* determines the number of firms in the industry within the model. The two conditions that determine the oligopolistic and monopolistic competition equilibria, profit maximization and entry, are shown in Table 7.1.[6]

The monopolistic competition model requires that firms face downward-sloping demand curves. Although product differentiation leads to such demand curves, high fixed costs can have the same result by limiting the number of firms that enter the industry, as the following example shows.

A Cournot Example. To illustrate how the monopolistic competition model with homogeneous goods differs from an oligopoly model, the Cournot-Nash model of a noncooperative oligopoly is modified to allow entry; otherwise the same assumptions are made as in the oligopoly example of Chapter 6:

- *Cournot equilibrium:* In equilibrium, no firm wants to change its output level, and each firm expects its rivals to produce at their actual level of output.
- *Homogeneity:* Output is homogeneous.
- *Demand:* The quantity that the market demands, Q, is a function of the market price, p:

$$Q = 1{,}000 - 1{,}000p. \tag{7.5}$$

- *Costs:* Each firm has a cost function of

$$C(q) = 0.28q + F, \tag{7.6}$$

[6]The shape of the marginal revenue curve referred to in Table 7.1 depends on the game (Bertrand or Cournot) being played.

where q is the firm's output and F is its fixed cost. As in Chapter 6, marginal cost is constant at 28¢.

The assumption of the oligopoly model in the previous chapter of a fixed number of firms is replaced by the **entry condition**: Firms enter the market when profits are positive and exit when profits are negative.

The marginal cost, MC, and average cost, AC, curves are shown in Figure 7.1. Marginal cost is a horizontal line at 28¢. The average cost may be calculated by dividing total cost from Equation 7.6, $C(q)$, by output. That is,

$$AC = \frac{C(q)}{q} = 0.28 + \frac{F}{q}.$$

Thus, average cost is the sum of average variable costs ($\$0.28 = [\$0.28\, q]/q$) and average fixed cost (F/q). As output grows, fixed costs are spread over more and more

FIGURE 7.1 Monopolistically Competitive Equilibrium

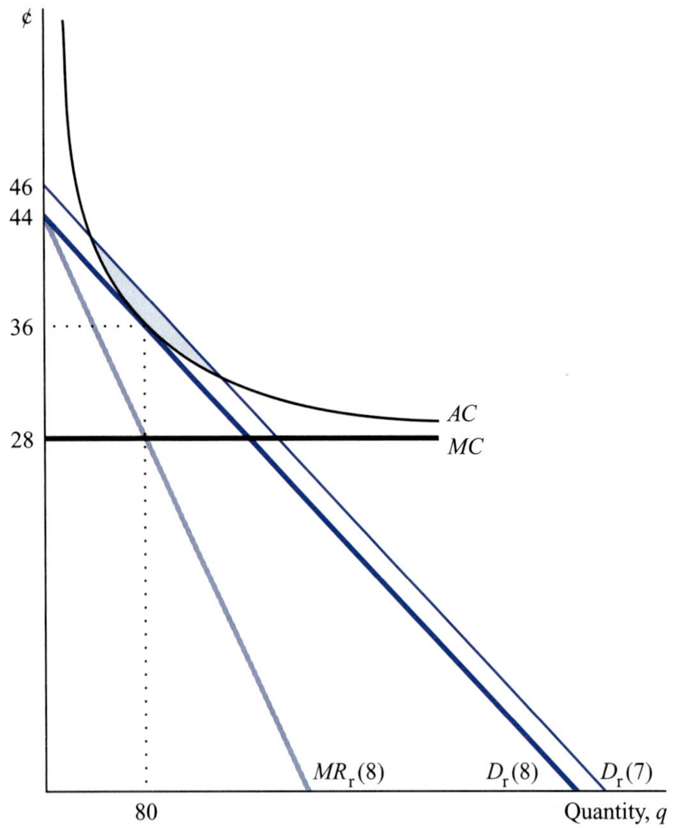

units, so average fixed costs fall, and the average cost consists primarily of average variable costs. As a result, AC is well above MC at low output levels and approaches MC (which is the same as average variable costs) as q gets large, as shown in Figure 7.1.

The entry condition says that firms enter the industry as long as profits are positive. Thus, firms enter the industry until economic profits are driven to zero:[7]

$$\pi = pq - C(q) = 0. \tag{7.7}$$

Thus, in long-run equilibrium, each firm makes zero profit overall; hence, it makes zero profit per unit, and each firm's average cost equals its price, $AC = p$.[8]

To determine the equilibrium number of firms, we use a two-step procedure. We first determine the Cournot equilibrium output for each possible number of firms (see Chapter 6). Second, we determine the number of firms by examining these equilibria and picking the one in which firms make zero profits.

To illustrate how the number of firms is determined in a monopolistic competition industry, suppose that each firm has a fixed cost of \$6.40. Thus, a firm enters this industry if profits are positive or, equivalently, if price is greater than average cost, $AC = 0.28 + 6.40/q$.

Table 7.2 shows market price, firm output, and profit for various numbers of firms. If there are initially five firms in the industry, each produces 120 units of output, and the market price is 40¢. Each firm makes a profit of \$8.00 [$= (p - AC)q = (\$0.40 - \$0.3333)120$].

If another firm enters, profit per firm falls to \$4.18. Because profits are still positive, more firms enter. Entry continues until eight firms are in the industry, and each one exactly breaks even. Because no firm is losing money, none has an incentive to leave the industry. No additional firm has an incentive to enter. As Table 7.2 shows, if a ninth firm enters, each firm loses \$1.22, so there is an incentive for firms to exit the industry. Thus, in this industry, the equilibrium number of firms is eight.

Graphic Analysis. This equilibrium can be determined graphically. Figure 7.1 shows the residual demand curve, $D_r(8)$, that each of the eight Cournot firms believes it faces, and the corresponding marginal revenue curve, $MR_r(8)$. The firm maximizes its profits by producing $q = 80$ units of output so that its $MR_r = MC$, as shown. It sells its output at the market price of 36¢. The firm's average cost curve is tangent to the demand curve (p = 36¢ = AC) where $q = 80$. As a result, the firm makes zero profit.

---

[7]The following discussion assumes that the profits of the last entrant are exactly zero. That condition does not always hold if there must be a whole number of firms. If there cannot be a fractional number of firms, profits may be positive in equilibrium, but if one more firm entered, all would make losses. Seade (1980) shows that the basic results discussed here hold even when one assumes that there must be a whole number of firms.

[8]We can write profit as $\pi = pq - C(q) = (p - C(q)/q)q = (p - AC)q$. Thus, if profit is zero, $\pi = 0$, then (dividing through by q) average profits must equal zero, $p - AC = 0$; hence, price equals average cost, $p = AC$. In our particular example, average profits are zero if $p = AC = 0.28 + F/q$.

TABLE 7.2 Cournot Monopolistic Competition Example with Different Fixed Costs (F)

			F = $6.40		F = $1.60	F = $0.00
Number of Firms	Price (¢)	Firm Output	Average Costs (¢)	Firm Profit ($)	Firm Profit ($)	Firm Profit ($)
1	64	360	29.8	123.20	128.00	129.60
2	52	240	30.7	51.20	56.00	57.60
3	46	180	31.6	26.00	30.80	32.40
4	42.4	144	32.4	14.34	19.14	20.74
5	40	120	33.3	8.00	12.80	14.40
6	38.3	102.9	34.2	4.18	8.98	10.58
7	37	90	35.1	1.70	6.50	8.10
8	36	80	36.0	0.00	4.80	6.40
9	35.2	72	36.9	−1.22	3.58	5.18
10	34.5	65.5	37.8		2.68	4.28
11	34	60	38.7		2.00	3.60
12	33.5	55.4	39.6		1.47	3.07
13	33.1	51.4	40.4		1.04	2.64
14	32.8	48	41.3		0.70	2.30
15	32.5	45	42.2		0.42	2.03
16	32.2	42.4	43.1		0.19	1.79
17	32	40	44.0		0.00	1.60
18	31.8	37.9	44.9		−0.16	1.44
20	31.4	34.3	46.7			1.18
100	28.7	7.1	118			0.05
500	28.1	1.4	473			0.002
1,000	28.1	0.7	918			0.001
∞	28	~0	~∞			0.00

Note: The negative profits shown in the table represent the profits that would occur if the number of firms indicated produced at their profit-maximizing (loss-minimizing) levels, given that exit was impossible and fixed costs were sunk. If costless (no sunk costs) exit is possible, these firms shut down to avoid making losses.

Figure 7.1 shows that if only seven firms are in the industry, it pays for a firm to enter. The demand facing one of the seven Cournot firms, $D_r(7)$, cuts the average cost curve, so that there is a shaded region where average costs are lower than the price on the residual demand curve. A firm that operates at a point within this region makes a positive profit because its price is above its average cost. As Table 7.2 shows, each of the seven firms maximizes its profit at 90 units of output, so the market price is 37, which is greater than each firm's AC = 35.1¢.

Lower Fixed Costs. How does this monopolistic competition equilibrium change if each firm incurs lower fixed costs? If fixed costs are $1.60, the new equilibrium has 17 firms (compared to eight when fixed costs are $6.40), as Table 7.2 shows.

Thus, the lower the fixed costs, the higher the equilibrium number of firms in a monopolistic competition industry. The reason for the increase in the equilibrium number of firms is that the lower the fixed costs, the higher the profits for any given number of firms in an industry. Additional firms must enter the industry to drive profits to zero.

How do we know that each firm's profit is higher (holding the number of other firms constant), the lower is its fixed cost? The reason is that a reduction in a firm's fixed cost does not affect its total revenues but does lower its total costs. Although fixed costs affect a firm's decision about whether to produce at all, they do not influence output levels if the firm actually produces. Each firm sets its output where $MR_r = MC$, and neither MR_r nor MC are affected by a change in the firm's fixed cost. A producing firm sells the same output regardless of the level of fixed costs, so its total revenues and total variable costs are not affected by a change in fixed costs. Total costs equal variable costs plus fixed costs, so holding variable costs constant and lowering fixed costs causes total costs to fall. Because total revenues remain constant as total costs fall, profits rise.

Graphically, with lower fixed costs, the average cost curve lies strictly below the one in Figure 7.1. For the new average cost curve to be tangent to a firm's demand curve, the demand must be lower as well. The only way to get a lower demand curve is to have more firms in the industry. It follows from this reasoning that if fixed costs fall to zero, the number of firms becomes unlimited, and this Cournot monopolistic competition industry becomes perfectly competitive, as the last column of Table 7.2 shows.

To summarize: High fixed costs cause price to be above marginal cost. Where there are no fixed costs, enough firms enter the industry to drive price to marginal cost: the competitive solution. See Example 7.2 on the effects of entry on price.

Welfare with Undifferentiated Products. How does this equilibrium compare to the social optimum in which welfare is maximized? Two welfare or efficiency problems arise with this monopolistic competition equilibrium. First, because price is above marginal cost, the industry produces too little total output: An extra unit of this product is worth more to consumers than it costs firms to produce it. Second, the number of firms is excessive when marginal costs are nonincreasing (constant or falling with quantity). Each additional firm must pay a fixed cost, F, so fixed costs to society are excessive.

EXAMPLE 7.2 *Entry Lowers Prices*

In the first year after United Airlines entered the short-hop market along the West Coast of the United States, prices plunged as much as 70 percent. The lowest fare United, Delta, and US Air were offering between San Francisco and Los Angeles in September 1994, before entry, was \$133. A year later, after United had entered the market, the lowest rate was \$39. Similarly, rates from San Jose to Seattle went from \$79 on Alaska Airlines and \$59 on Reno Air in 1994 to \$49 on all lines in September 1995 after United and Southwest entered this market. Entry was very likely responsible for these price declines, as the average fares across all U.S. pairs rose during this period.

FIGURE 7.2 First Best

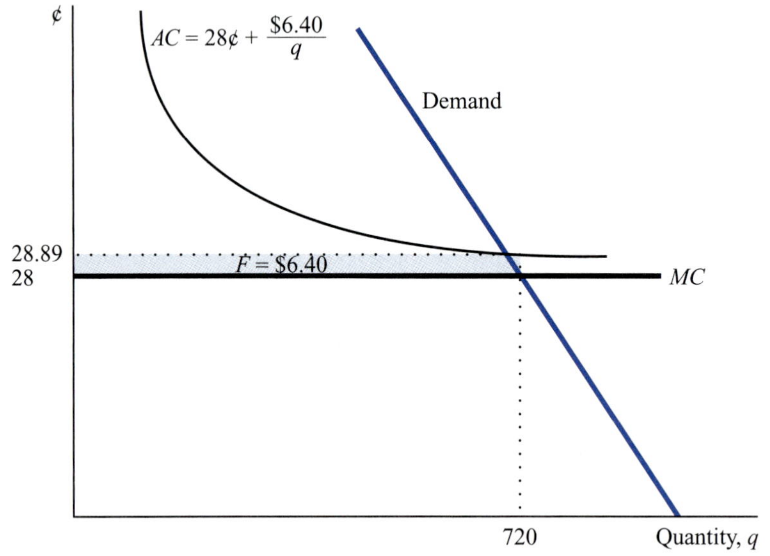

In the preceding example, each firm's cost function is $C(q) = mq + F$, where m is a firm's constant marginal cost. Here, society's optimal solution is to subsidize one firm to produce all the output and to require that price be set equal to marginal cost. The best possible solution (ignoring costs of administration) is referred to as the **first-best optimum** (see Appendix 7A).

Figure 7.2 illustrates the first-best solution. It shows a single firm's marginal and average cost curves and the market demand curve, based on the preceding example with fixed costs of \$6.40. In the proposed first-best equilibrium, the firm is regulated so that it sets its price equal to marginal cost, $m = 28¢$, and consumers purchase $q^* = 720$ units of output. The socially optimal output is 80 units (12.5 percent) more than the monopolistic competition output of 640.

At that price, the firm loses money because the price is less than the average cost ($p = \$0.28 < m + F/q^* = \$0.28 + \$6.40/720 = \$0.2889$). Thus, the government must subsidize the firm if it is to stay in business.[9] The shaded area in Figure 7.2 represents the subsidized loss $= F = \$6.40 = \$0.0089 \times 720 = (F/q^*)q^*$. The firm sells its product at its marginal cost or average variable cost, so it covers its out-of-pocket production expenses, but it does not recover its fixed costs.

[9]The government could raise the necessary revenues by taxing away the consumer surplus by charging consumers a fixed fee (to consume at all) and a price equal to the marginal cost for each unit consumed.

The consumer surplus at the social optimum is \$259.20.[10] If we define welfare as the sum of consumer surplus plus revenues minus costs, welfare at the social optimum is \$252.80. In contrast, in the monopolistic competition equilibrium, consumer surplus and welfare are \$204.80. Thus, welfare at the social optimum is 23.4 percent higher than in the monopolistic competition equilibrium.

If there is only one firm that can set its price however it likes, it will act like a monopoly, setting its p_m = 64¢ and selling q_m = 360 units. Its price is above its average cost (29.78¢), so it makes positive profits of \$123.20. Here, consumer surplus is \$64.80 and welfare is \$188. Thus, welfare in the monopolistic competition equilibrium is 8.9 percent higher and welfare at the social optimum is 34.5 percent higher than in the monopoly equilibrium.

When a single firm has a downward-sloping average cost curve, it is called a *natural monopoly* (Chapter 4) because one firm could fulfill all consumers' demands more cheaply than could two or more firms. Each firm could produce at the same marginal cost, but entry by an additional firm requires an additional expenditure of fixed costs, *F.* Thus, in the monopolistic competition equilibrium, not only is price above marginal cost, but if there are eight firms, too much has been spent in fixed costs. That is, one firm could produce the total monopolistic competition output for \$44.80 (= $7F$) less than eight firms could because of the savings on fixed costs. In this example, unnecessary fixed costs represent 20 percent of total industry costs.

Even if firms have U-shaped average cost (*AC*) curves, there are too many firms in a homogeneous Cournot equilibrium. With U-shaped curves, the equilibrium occurs where each firm's residual demand curve is tangent to its *AC* curve (profits are zero). Because the residual demand curve is downward sloping, this tangency occurs in the downward-sloping (increasing returns to scale) section of the *AC* curve. Thus, the firms operate at a smaller output than the output that minimizes their *AC.* That is, monopolistically competitive firms have "excess capacity." There are too many small firms producing the output compared to the social optimum: The same output could be more efficiently produced with fewer firms.

Typically, the government cannot regulate an industry so as to achieve a first-best solution and maximize society's welfare. For example, it may be politically infeasible to subsidize a monopoly such as a local electric company. In some industries, the government may be able to control the number of firms, but it may not be able to force them to produce more than the profit-maximizing quantity if it is unwilling to subsidize them. Many cities control the number of taxicabs, for example.[11] By choosing the optimal number of firms, the government can achieve the **second-best optimum**: the best possible outcome subject to a constraint that violates one of the conditions for a

---

[10]Consumer surplus equals the triangle under the demand curve above 28¢. If demand is $p = a - bq$, then consumer surplus at quantity q is $1/2[a - p(q)]q = 1/2[a - (a - bq)]q = 1/2bq^2$. In our example, consumer surplus is $0.0005q^2$.

[11]Many economists argue that the number of taxicabs is restricted to drive up the profits of those lucky enough to be allowed to operate (see the evidence in Chapter 20). That is, rather than trying to maximize social welfare, the government is trying to enrich existing cab companies.

first-best outcome. That is, welfare is raised to the highest level possible given that the government does not subsidize firms.

The government faces a trade-off. If it allows more firms to enter, it can drive the market price down, yet additional firms increase total expenditures on fixed costs. It can be shown (Appendix 7A) that, under some plausible conditions, there are too many firms in the monopolistic competition equilibrium. That is, welfare could be increased by restricting the number of firms.

By restricting entry, the government obtains the second-best optimum. Although welfare is not as high as in the first-best optimum, it is higher than in the unrestricted, monopolistic competition equilibrium. Table 7.3 shows the sum of consumer surplus and industry profits from Table 7.2, where $F = \$6.40$. The monopolistic competition equilibrium number of firms is eight, but the sum of consumer surplus and profits is maximized at three firms. By lowering the number of firms from eight to three, society reduces its expenditures on fixed cost (by $5F = \$32$) at the expense of a higher output price (46¢ instead of 36¢).

A Representative Consumer Model with Differentiated Products

The essence of the monopolistic competition model just discussed remains unchanged if all firms produce differentiated (heterogeneous) products. Profit maximization is still determined by $MR_r = MC$, and entry still occurs only so long as profits are positive. The only modification to the model of the previous section caused by product differentiation is that a firm's demand curve (and hence its MR_r curve) depends on the individual quantities produced by each of its competitors rather than on just the total quantity.

Adding product differentiation complicates the model. Each firm's demand curve may differ from another's so that it may not be sufficient to study a representative firm. It is possible, however, that although products are differentiated, the general form of the demand curves facing each firm is identical.

For example, all the firms in the industry could have demand curves of the form of Equation 7.4 where, due to product differentiation, a firm's price is more sensitive to changes in the quantity of its own product than to those of its competitors:

TABLE 7.3 Second-Best Optimum

Number of Firms	Price (¢)	Firm Output	Industry Profits ($)	Consumer Surplus ($)	Welfare ($)
1	64	360	123.20	64.8	188.00
2	52	240	102.40	115.20	217.60
3	46	180	78.00	145.80	223.80
4	42.4	144	57.34	165.89	223.25
5	40	120	40.00	180.00	220.00
6	38.3	103.9	25.08	190.34	215.42
7	37	90	11.90	198.45	210.35
8	36	80	0.00	204.80	204.80

Note: Parameters are the same as in Table 7.2, with fixed costs of $6.40.

$$p_i = a - b_1 q_i - b_2 \sum_{j \neq i} q_j, \tag{7.8}$$

where $\sum_{j \neq i} q_j$ means the sum of the output of all firms except Firm i.

The representative firm model with homogeneous products can be modified to handle this demand curve, and many of the qualitative results are the same as in the homogeneous model. For example, as each firm's fixed cost falls, the number of firms in the industry increases, and price may fall.

The primary impact of differentiation is that each firm faces a more steeply downward-sloping demand curve than it does otherwise, because other products are less close substitutes. This greater slope gives the firm more market power—the power to raise price profitably above marginal cost. See Example 7.3 on entry and product differentiation in the jeans market.

Welfare with Differentiated Products. The optimal welfare solution changes when products are differentiated.[12] In general, a monopolistic competition equilibrium with differentiated products has two problems: Neither the price nor the *variety* (number of brands) is optimal. As before, price is above marginal cost. However, there may be either too little or too much variety where products are differentiated.[13]

Two factors determine the variety in a monopolistic competition equilibrium. One of them leads to too few brands, but the other may lead to too many brands. The first factor is that highly desirable products may not be produced even though price is greater than firms' variable costs if fixed costs are so great that firms lose money. That is, consumer surplus would rise if more products were produced, but the high fixed costs keep the number of brands below the optimal level.

The second factor—the effect on other firms—is an offsetting force. When a firm introduces a new brand, it ignores the effect of its increased competition on the profits of other firms. When its product is a *substitute* for other brands, as Coke is for Pepsi, part of its profits come from these other brands. Because firms ignore these effects on other firms, they have a tendency to produce too many products at too low prices.[14] Because the two factors work in opposite directions, there may be too many or too few brands compared to the social optimum.

---

[12]Probably the first, and certainly among the best studies of welfare with differentiated products are Spence (1976) and Dixit and Stiglitz (1977). These models have been criticized by Pettingill (1979) and Koenker and Perry (1981), respectively. This section and the corresponding Appendix 7A are based, in part, on these articles and on unpublished lecture notes of Steven C. Salop, whom we thank.

[13]There is an analogous literature on the optimal amount of variety chosen by a single firm (Katz and Shapiro 1985; Farrell and Saloner 1985, 1986). A firm has to trade off the gains from standardization (such as economies of scale and compatibility with different manufacturers' products) against the benefits from variety.

[14]However, if products were *complements* such as bread and butter, there would be a tendency to have too few brands, with some prices too high because firms fail to account for the positive effect of their low prices and brands on the demand for other complementary products. Henceforth we assume brands are substitutes.

EXAMPLE 7.3

The Jeans Market

A lot of money is spent on jeans—and more every day. In 1996, sales of jeans in the United States grew 8 percent to $10.6 billion.

As the size of this market has ballooned over the last several decades, many firms have entered what used to be largely Levi's market. According to a survey of teenagers in the fall of 1996, 56% bought Levi's; 29%, Lee; 27%, Arizona; 21%, Guess; 19%, Gap; 18%, Calvin Klein; 16%, Bugle Boy; 15%, Wrangler; 13%, Union Bay; and 9% each, Chic and Tommy Hilfiger. Encouraged by the Gap's success and J. C. Penney's Arizona jeans, other large retailers started aggressively pushing their own private label jeans, such as Sears' Canyon River Blues.

In addition to entry by many new firms, greater product differentiation is occurring. Calvin Klein, Ralph Lauren, Donna Karan, and Tommy Hilfiger are spending substantial sums on promoting their designer jeans. Small startup firms, many based in Los Angeles, such as JNCO and Menace, sell offbeat cuts to younger consumers. These designer jeans sell for a premium over plain blue jeans.

Entry of new firms and product differentiation are important forces in this market. Increased competition has hurt the giant, Levi Strauss, which laid off about a thousand workers in 1997 after its share of the market fell 5 percentage points from the previous year, and suffered a drop in U.S. sales from $5.1 billion in 1999 to $4.1 billion in 2002. The other two largest jeans producers, Lee and Guess, also are shifting resources from manufacturing jeans. To combat their new rivals, the big three all engaged in new product differentiation and other actions to boost sales and profits.

Source: Jennifer Steinhauer, "Squeezing into the Jeans Market," *New York Times*, March 14, 1997:C1, C15; Alexandra Jardine, "As Levi's Celebrates Its 150th Birthday," *Marketing*, September 4, 2003.

If goods are homogeneous, as in the previous example, there are definitely too many firms because there is no benefit to having more than one firm that is regulated to set price equal to marginal cost, assuming such regulation is possible. However, variety is desirable with differentiated products. Thus, regulating the markets so that there is only one firm charging marginal cost is unlikely to be optimal. The following section considers this analysis in more detail, first illustrating that fixed costs tend to result in underproduction of certain types of goods, and then discussing how the optimal number of brands is determined.

Fixed Costs Lead to Too Little Variety. When firms operate in the increasing-returns-to-scale section of their average cost curves, they tend to produce too few products, all else the same. If a firm's marginal cost does not rise rapidly, and it has

FIGURE 7.3 When Does a Market Produce a Product?

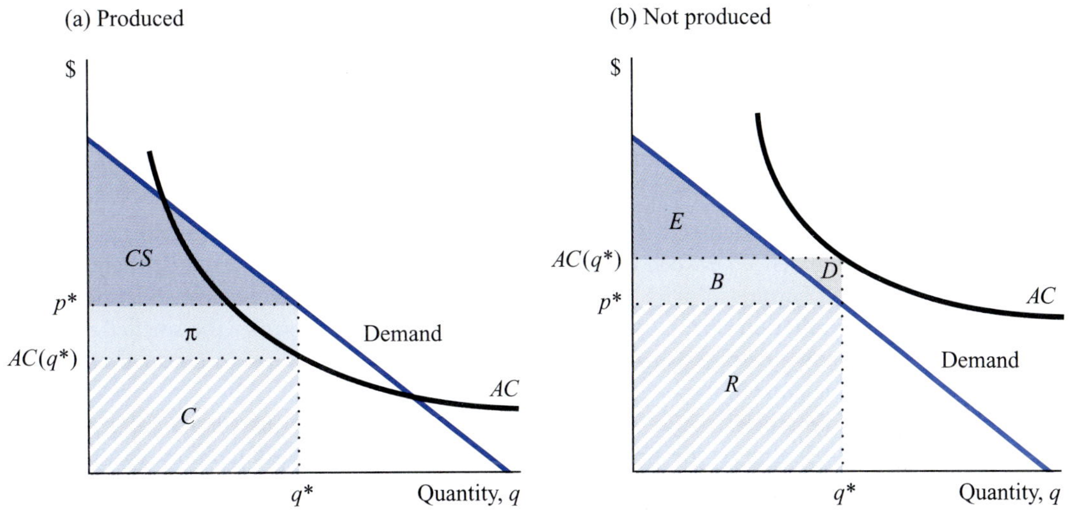

(a) Produced		(b) Not produced
$CS + \pi + C$	Social Benefit ($CS + R$)	$E + B + R$
$CS + \pi$	Welfare ($CS + R - C$)	$E - D$
CS	Consumer Surplus	$B + E$
$\pi + C$	Revenue	R
C	Cost	$R + B + D$
π	Profit	$-(B + D)$

large fixed costs, it operates in the downward-sloping, or increasing-returns, section of its average cost curve. Figure 7.3 illustrates why some desirable products are produced and others are not when the average cost curve is strictly falling.

In both diagrams in Figure 7.3, society is better off if the products are produced: Social benefit exceeds the social costs. In Figure 7.3a, the average cost crosses the demand curve, so it is profitable to produce. The firm's profit, π, is positive at quantity q^* because the average cost per unit is less than average revenue or price, p^*. Social benefit (the sum of consumer surplus, *CS*, and revenue, $\pi + C$) minus social (and private) cost (C) equals welfare ($CS + \pi$), which is positive.

In Figure 7.3b, the average cost curve is everywhere above the demand curve. Thus, total costs exceed total revenues at all output levels, so the product is not produced. It is, however, socially desirable to produce this product. Social benefit (consumer surplus, $E + B$, plus revenues, R) minus cost ($R + B + D$) equals welfare ($E - D$), which is positive because area E is greater than area D.

The reason the product is not produced, even though it is socially desirable to do so, is that the firm does not obtain the entire social benefit even though it pays the entire social cost. That is, the firm ignores consumer surplus when it makes its decision whether or not to produce. It would suffer a loss (negative profit, $B + D$) if it produced. Most customers would enjoy consumer surplus (the amount by which the product is worth more than p^*) if it were sold; whereas, the firm's price, p^*, is the value the marginal consumer (the one who has no consumer surplus) places on the good.[15] Thus, the example in Figure 7.3b shows that firms may not find it profitable to produce all goods that are socially desirable.

The product that is most likely to be produced is one for which the demand curve is a right angle: Consumers have an inelastic demand up to a cutoff price, p^*, at which their demand becomes perfectly elastic. With such a demand curve, there is no difference between total revenue and total social benefit, because there is no consumer surplus at price p^*. The firm's decision to produce or not is identical to society's criterion of total social benefit. Thus, all else the same, the smaller the ratio of consumer surplus to total revenues, the more likely is a firm to produce a socially desirable good.[16]

The crucial point is that this distortion—the underproduction of certain products—is due to the presence of fixed costs and the firm's inability to capture consumer surplus. For example, if there are no fixed costs and constant marginal costs, then average cost equals marginal cost. With constant marginal costs and no fixed costs, if it is socially optimal for a product to be produced, it pays for firms to produce it.

Optimal Diversity. The optimal equilibrium reflects the trade-off between product *variety*, the number of brands, and the *quantity* of each brand produced, which is determined by the price. For simplicity, assume that the number of brands, n, fully reflects the value of variety: The more firms or brands, the better off are consumers, all else the same. If all goods are produced with the same cost function and face the same demand curve, then the number of units of output, q, is the same for each brand in equilibrium. The essential facts about the equilibrium can be summarized by the number of brands, n, and the output per brand, q.

To illustrate the trade-off between variety and quantity, suppose the economy has 100 units of input, each unit of output can be produced at a constant MC of 1, and the fixed cost is 5. Table 7.4 shows some possible combinations of number of brands

---

[15] If a firm could perfectly price discriminate (Chapter 10), it could capture the entire consumer surplus. That is, it would charge each consumer the maximum that consumer would pay for the product, so that there would be no consumer surplus. Because its revenues would be larger than costs, the firm would find it profitable to produce. See also Romano (1991).

[16] For constant elasticity (ϵ) demand curves, $q = p^{-\epsilon}$, where $\epsilon > 1$, the higher the elasticity, the smaller the ratio of consumer surplus to revenues. Revenues are $R \equiv pq = p^{1-\epsilon}$, and consumer surplus is

$$CS = \int_p^\infty s^{-\epsilon} ds = \frac{p^{1-\epsilon}}{\epsilon - 1}.$$

Thus, the ratio of consumer surplus to revenues, $CS/R = 1/(\epsilon - 1)$, is decreasing in ϵ.

TABLE 7.4 **Variety and Quantity**

Number of Brands, n	Quantity of Each, q
1	95
2	45
3	28.33
4	20
5	15
6	11.67
7	9.29
8	7.5
9	6.11
10	5

and quantity (n, q). The **production possibility frontier** (*PPF*) is the feasible combinations of number of brands and quantity per brand that can be produced with society's total inputs (Figure 7.4 and Table 7.4).[17]

Society's preferences concerning the choice between quantity and variety are summarized by the indifference curves shown in Figure 7.4. Point $O = (q^*, n^*)$, the tangency between the *PPF* and an indifference curve, represents society's optimal choice. At any point on any indifference curve that lies below the indifference curve through point O, society is worse off. Points on indifference curves that lie above point O are above the *PPF* and hence cannot be produced. The point B on the *PPF* represents a possible monopolistic competition equilibrium. At that point, the industry is producing too few products, but more output per product than at the optimum. At point A on the *PPF*, the industry is producing more brands than at the optimum, but less output per brand.

Whether the monopolistic competition equilibrium is at a point like A, B, or O depends on the preference of the representative consumer and the production function. Appendix 7B discusses the factors that determine the relative position of the monopolistic competition equilibrium. In general, any of these outcomes is possible.

Conclusions About Representative Consumer Models

In the Chamberlinian representative consumer monopolistic competition equilibrium, price is too high and the number of firms is nonoptimal. With undifferentiated products, there are almost certainly too many firms. With differentiated products, there may be too many or too few firms.

[17]As Appendix 7B shows, the *PPF* in Figure 7.4, which equates total cost to total resources, is $(F + mq)n = (5 + q)n = 100$, where $F = 5$ is the fixed cost and $m = 1$ is the constant marginal cost. Equivalently, the *PPF* is $n = 100/(5 + q)$.

FIGURE 7.4 Optimal (*O*) and Monopolistically Competitive (*A* and *B*) Equilibria

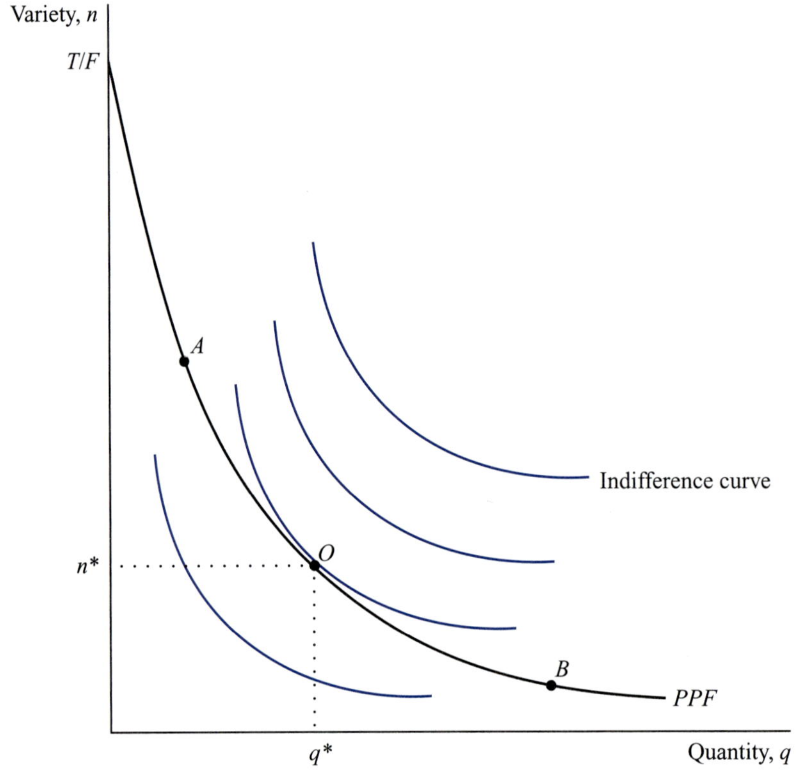

Typical representative consumer models assume that all products are equally good substitutes for each other. To apply such a model to the ice cream market, for example, one must believe that Breyer's ice cream competes equally with Häagen-Dazs and with Baskin-Robbins. That is, one must not believe that Breyer's is a closer substitute to Baskin-Robbins than to Häagen-Dazs. This extremely strong assumption makes the model relatively easy to use, but unrealistic in some markets.

Location Models

Brands compete more vigorously with brands that are close substitutes than with those that consumers view as less close substitutes. Consumers view certain brands as closer substitutes than others. For example, certain brands have a particular common characteristic that other brands lack: Some cereals are sugar coated and others are not. That is, each brand is "located" at a particular point in product characteristic space. As another example, products sold at nearby stores are close substitutes. That is, each firm is located at a particular address or point in geographic space.

Location *(spatial)* models are monopolistic competition models in which consumers view each firm's product as having a particular location in geographic or product (characteristic) space. The closer two products are to each other in geographic or characteristic space, the better substitutes they are. In these models, consumers also have locations in geographic or product space. It costs consumers more to shop at stores farther from home, or, alternatively, they receive less pleasure from products whose characteristics deviate from their ideal. Because firms or products only compete directly with others near them, each has some market power. The market power stems from the preference of consumers to make a purchase at the nearest firm or to purchase their preferred product.

The following discussion first examines the original location model and then uses a newer location model to analyze the impact of increased competition on the market equilibrium. Finally, the welfare implications of this equilibrium are analyzed.

Hotelling's Location Model

Hotelling (1929) developed a model to explain the location and pricing behavior of firms.[18] Although he concentrated on geographic space, his model can be used to study monopolistic competition by viewing products as being located in product or characteristic space. In Hotelling's location (spatial) model, products differ in only one dimension, such as the location of the stores that sell them. However, Lancaster (1966, 1971, 1979) and others have shown that this model can be extended to examine products that differ in more dimensions.

Consider a long, narrow city with only one street, Main Street, that is a fixed length. Consumers are uniformly distributed along this street, so that in any block there are an equal number. All consumers are identical except for location, and each consumer buys 1 quart of milk in each time period.

Two stores sell identical bottles of milk in this town. Store 1 is located a miles from one end of town (the left end in Figure 7.5), and Store 2 is located b miles from the other (right) end of town. Consumers have no preference for either store except that consumers prefer to purchase from the nearest store because each consumer faces a transportation cost of c per mile. That is, each consumer buys from the least expensive store, taking transportation costs into account. Consider Consumer i who lives at the location shown in Figure 7.5. She lives x miles from Store 1 and y miles from Store 2. Because x is less than y (see Figure 7.5), she goes to Store 1 to minimize her transportation costs. Only someone who lives exactly halfway between the two stores is indifferent as to which store to patronize.

Suppose that the government sets the price of milk. How should Store 1 choose its location to maximize its profits if Store 2 is already located b miles from the right end

[18] See also, Eaton (1976), D'Aspremont, Gabszewicz, and Thisse (1979), Novshek (1980), and Friedman (1983). For analytic simplicity, in the literature most representative consumer models assume firms play Cournot and most location models assume they play Bertrand, but either oligopoly concept can be used in either model.

FIGURE 7.5 Hotelling's Town

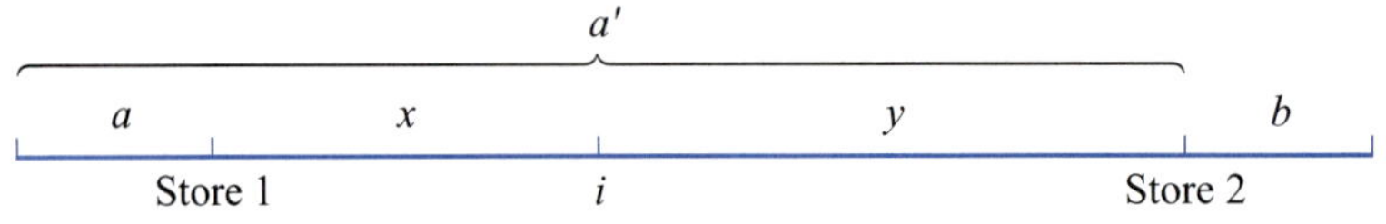

of the city and cannot change its location? Because consumers only care about how far they must travel, Store 1 wants to be the nearest store for the greatest possible number of consumers. Store 1 maximizes its profits by locating just to the left of Store 2, a' miles from the left end of the city. There, it gets all the customers to its left, which is the majority.

If Firm 2 could costlessly relocate after Firm 1 locates, however, it would move slightly to the left of Firm 1's new location. This process would be repeated until both firms were in the middle of the town, with each firm having half the customers. You may have noticed the propensity of firms to locate near each other in a variety of markets. For example, several gas stations often locate on the corners of a busy intersection.

Thus, if price is given, the location of two firms can be determined. This equilibrium is Nash in location strategies (see Chapter 6). That is, when firms are set at their equilibrium locations, no firm wants to change its location. Similarly, by fixing location and letting the firms vary prices, a Nash equilibrium in prices can be determined (similar to the Bertrand equilibrium discussed in the previous chapter).

Hotelling's model illustrates an important point: The properties of the Bertrand equilibrium discussed in the previous chapter hold only when two firms sell perfectly homogeneous products. In the Bertrand model with homogeneous products, if one firm undercuts the other, the high-priced firm loses all its customers. The same thing happens in Hotelling's town if both firms are permanently located in the center of town.

However, suppose that the two stores are permanently located some distance apart at a and b in Figure 7.5. If Store 1 charges less than Store 2, Store 2 still gets a number of customers. The reason is that Store 2 is much closer for several customers than Store 1, and some shoppers will pay more for the convenience.

Thus, Hotelling's model illustrates that the Bertrand equilibrium price equals the marginal cost only if the products are homogeneous (located at the same place in product or geographical space). In a more general model of differentiated products, firms with Bertrand expectations may charge different prices and all prices are above marginal cost.[19] In short, differentiation gives firms market power.

Unfortunately, it can be shown that when firms can costlessly change their prices *and* their locations (for example, reformulate their product), there is a *nonexistence of*

---

[19]Mergers of a subset of the firms in the industry have no effect in a Bertrand model with homogeneous goods, but are profitable for the merging firms in a Bertrand model with heterogeneous goods (Deneckere and Davidson 1985). Compare this result to those in Example 6.3.

equilibrium (D'Aspremont, Gabszewicz, and Thisse 1979).[20] This result is analogous to the Edgeworth example in the previous chapter, in which the two firms continuously change their behavior, never settling down to a single price (and location). The existence of an equilibrium, however, can be shown in modified versions of this model. One modification allows for nonlinear transportation costs. Another approach is studied next.

Salop's Circle Model

A circle is the longest distance to the same point. —*Tom Stoppard*

A number of models modify Hotelling's basic model so that an equilibrium exists. One of the most interesting and best known of these is Salop's (1979a) circle model, which introduces two major changes in Hotelling's model.

First, in this model, firms are located around a circle instead of along a line. The reason for this change is that a circle has no end-points. That is, a circle is roughly equivalent to an infinitely long line in that neither has end-points. It can be shown that a major cause of the nonexistence of equilibrium in Hotelling's model is the presence of end-points.

Second, Salop's model takes explicit account of a second, or outside, good. For example, the differentiated product might be brands (flavors) of ice cream (the products located around the circle), and the outside good might be chocolate cake, which is an undifferentiated product competitively supplied by another industry.

How Consumers Choose a Product. Assume that customers are uniformly located around the circle that is of unit circumference. For simplicity, each customer buys exactly one scoop of ice cream. A customer's location, t^*, represents that customer's most preferred type of ice cream. For example, suppose one location on the circle is chocolate ice cream, another vanilla, and a point between chocolate and vanilla is chocolate-chip ice cream. Each flavor of ice cream is a possible brand and is described by its location on the circle.

The pleasure (utility) a consumer gets from eating a scoop of a brand of ice cream located at t is

$$U(t, t^*) = u - c|t - t^*|, \tag{7.9}$$

where u is the utility from the consumer's favorite flavor of ice cream (the flavor located at the same point, t^*, along the circle as the consumer); $|t - t^*|$ (the absolute value of the difference between t and t^*) is the distance brand t is from the customer's favorite flavor t^*; and c is the rate at which a deviation from the optimal brand lowers the consumer's pleasure.

[20] A randomized (mixed strategy) equilibrium exists, where each firm chooses its action probabilistically.

FIGURE 7.6 Consumer's Utility Function

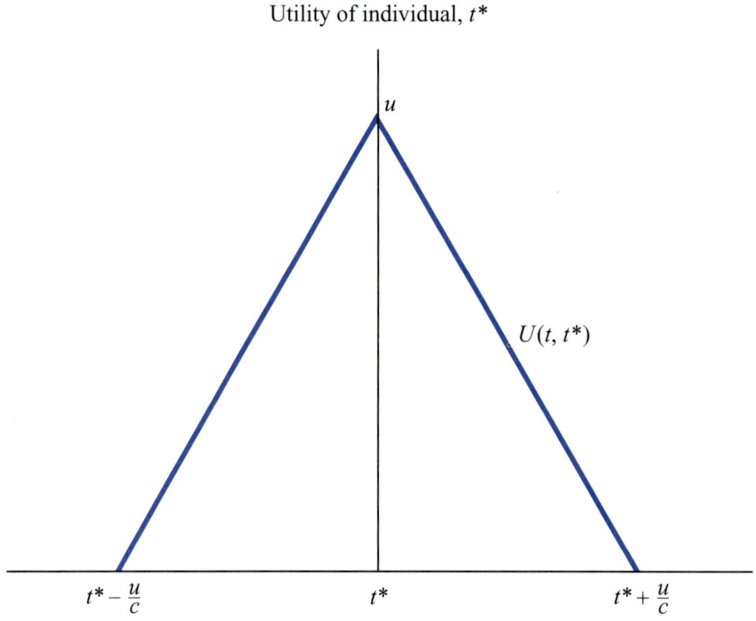

The consumer's utility function is shown in Figure 7.6, where a segment of the circle has been straightened out into a line. The figure shows that at $t = t^* + u/c$ and at $t = t^* - u/c$ the consumer has a utility of zero. The figure shows that the pleasure a consumer receives from a brand located either to the left or to the right of the optimal brand is lower than from the optimal brand.

Each consumer attempts to maximize consumer surplus, which is the difference between the consumer's pleasure from eating a brand located at t and the price: $U(t, t^*) - p$. In other words, if your favorite flavor of ice cream is chocolate, but chocolate chip ice cream costs half as much, you might buy the chocolate chip because the loss in taste or utility is less than the gain from buying the cheaper product. Thus, you purchase the *best buy:* the product with the greatest surplus—the best combination of price and quality.

Instead of buying one of the brands of ice cream, however, the consumer may decide to buy the outside good, chocolate cake, if it is a *better buy* in the sense that it gives more pleasure for a given amount of money. Suppose the surplus from the cake (pleasure from eating it less the price) is $\underline{u}$. The consumer only buys a scoop of the best-buy brand, i, of ice cream if its surplus is at least equal to $\underline{u}$:

$$\max_{i} \, [U(t_i, t^*) - p_i] \geq \underline{u}, \tag{7.10}$$

where the expression on the left side of the equation is the surplus from the best-buy brand of ice cream (maximize the surplus through choice of brand i), and the right side is the surplus from cake. That is, the consumer should only buy ice cream if the surplus from the best-buy brand of ice cream is at least as great as the surplus from cake.

If a consumer's ideal ice cream is produced (located at t^*) and sold at p^*, the greatest surplus the consumer can get is $u - p^*$. The consumer is only willing to buy that brand if its surplus is equal to or greater than that from cake: $u - p^* \geq \underline{u}$, or, rearranging terms, $u - \underline{u} \geq p^*$. As a result, the consumer has a *reservation price*, $v = u - \underline{u}$, which is the highest price that the consumer is willing to pay for that brand of ice cream.

Alternatively stated, a consumer buys a scoop of ice cream only if the *net surplus* from the best-buy brand, the surplus from the best-buy brand minus the surplus from cake, is positive:

$$\max_i [v - c\,|t_i - t^*| - p_i] \geq 0. \tag{7.11}$$

Equation 7.11 is obtained by subtracting u from both sides of Equation 7.10, substituting for $U(t, t^*)$ from Equation 7.9, and using $v = u - \underline{u}$.

Firms' Behavior. The symmetric equilibrium in this model depends on where firms are located and how they set price.[21]

All else the same, each firm wants to locate as far from its nearest competitors as possible. The further away other stores are from your store, the greater the market power you have with respect to the customers located near your store. As a result of trying to locate as far apart as possible, the stores locate equidistant from each other. If there are n ice cream brands located at equal distances around the circle, the distance between two brands is $1/n$ (because the circle is of unit circumference).

Salop starts his analysis by assuming that the stores are already located equidistant from each other and then asks what price each store charges. Suppose a typical brand (the one at the bottom of the circle) charges price p, and its two nearest competitors charge $\underline{p}$, as Figure 7.7 shows. How should the producer of the typical brand set price? The answer depends on how many brands there are. We first consider the case in which there are relatively few firms, and then consider a market with many more firms.

Monopoly Region. If there are relatively few brands, they do not compete with each other for the same consumers. Each brand is a local monopoly and sells to all consumers living close enough so that their net surplus is positive. That is, each monopoly sells only to consumers who receive more surplus from that brand than they get from cake.

[21]Economides (1986, 1989) examines existence of the full subgame-perfect equilibrium in the Hotelling, Salop, and two-dimensional space of characteristics models. His intuition is that the equilibrium price does not converge to marginal cost as the locations of two competing firms become nearly identical in the Hotelling model, so there is a strong tendency to undercut a rival's price when the locations are very close (see D'Aspremont, Gabszewicz, and Thisse 1979). If utility is quadratic in distance (or for a two-dimensional space even with linear utility), however, prices do converge to marginal cost as locations become nearly identical, which eliminates the undercutting and nonexistence problem.

FIGURE 7.7 Circular Market

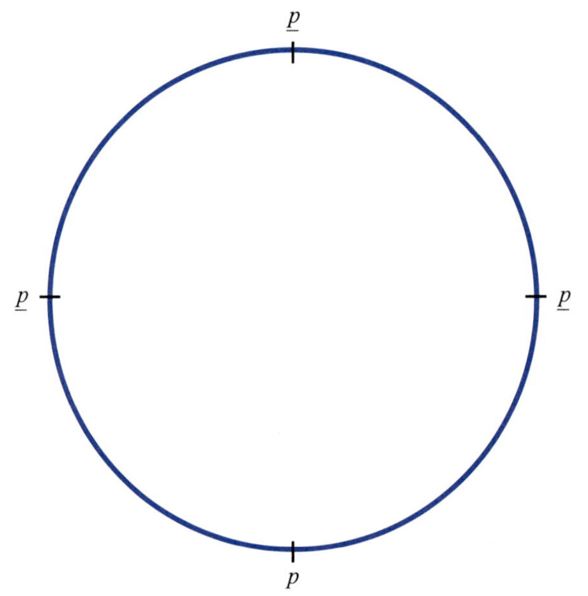

Consider a consumer located a distance $x = |t - t^*|$ from the brand at t with price p. The consumer is willing to buy that brand only if the consumer's net surplus is nonnegative: $v - cx - p \geq 0$ (using the expression for surplus in Equation 7.11). Thus, by rearranging this expression, the maximum distance, x_m, a consumer can be located from that brand and still buy it is

$$x_m = \frac{v - p}{c}. \tag{7.12}$$

This distance, x_m, is determined graphically in Figure 7.8a. The vertical axis in the figure is the net surplus from that brand and the horizontal axis is the distance, x, a consumer is from the most preferred brand (labeled with the price, p, which is assumed to be slightly more than $\underline{p}$) . The greater the distance, x, a brand is from the consumer's most preferred product, the lower the consumer's net surplus. When the brand is x_m distance from the consumer's most preferred location, the consumer's net surplus from that brand equals zero (where the net surplus line hits the x-axis) so that the consumer is indifferent between buying and not buying.

The brand captures all the consumers who are no further than x_m distance on each side of its location, or all the consumers in a $2x_m$ segment of the circle. If there are L consumers located uniformly around the circle, the monopoly demand facing this brand, q_m, is $2x_mL$, or, substituting for x_m from Equation 7.12:

$$q_m = \frac{2L}{c}(v - p). \tag{7.13}$$

FIGURE 7.8 Two-Market Structure

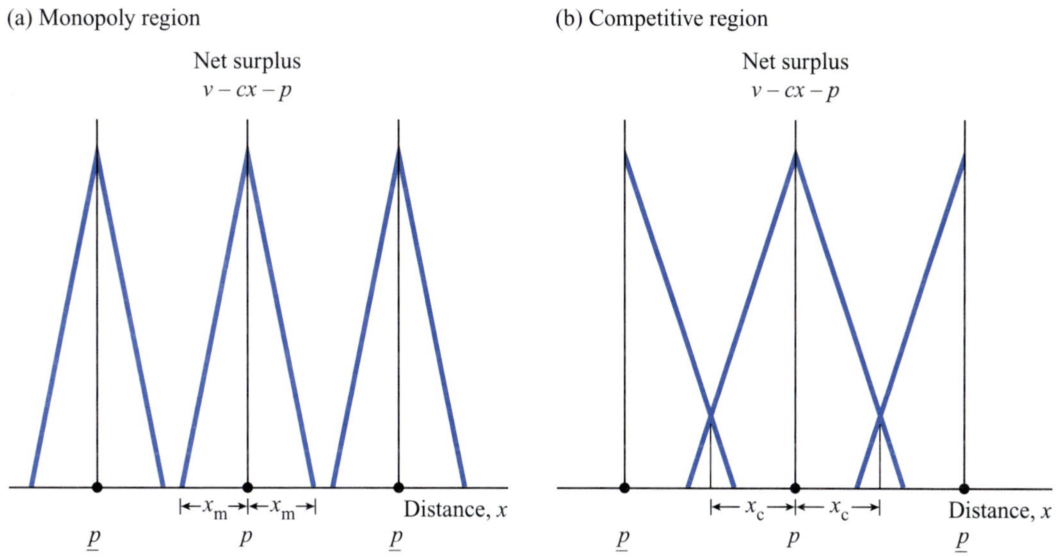

The monopoly quantity demanded of the firm, as shown in Equation 7.13, falls by $-2L/c$ as its price rises by \$1. If the firm sets its price equal to the reservation price, v, of the customer who most prefers this product, its sales fall to zero.

Competitive Region. If there are more firms, so that they are located closer together and compete for the same consumers, then each firm must take into account the price its rivals charge in setting its own price as in the homogeneous-good Bertrand model of Chapter 6. When firms compete with each other, a firm does not capture all the customers who prefer its ice cream to cake: It loses some to its two nearest rivals. Those customers located in the potential market of each of two brands buy from the one offering the highest net surplus.

Both of the typical brand's closest competitors are $1/n$ distance away and charge $\underline{p}$. How much does this brand sell if it sets its price at p? It captures all the consumers within a distance x_c, where x_c is the distance such that consumers get the same utility from this brand as from that of one of its closest rivals:

$$v - cx_c - p = v - c\left(\frac{1}{n} - x_c\right) - \underline{p}. \tag{7.14}$$

The left side of Equation 7.14 is the net utility from this brand, and the right side is the net utility from the other brand (because a consumer who is a distance x_c from this brand is $1/n - x_c$ distance from the rival brand). Figure 7.8b shows how the limit of the competitive region, x_c, is determined by the point where a consumer is just indifferent between the two goods—where Equation 7.14 holds with equality. Where the net surplus lines from two rival brands intersect, a consumer is indifferent between buying either brand.

FIGURE 7.9 Demand in Salop's Circle Model

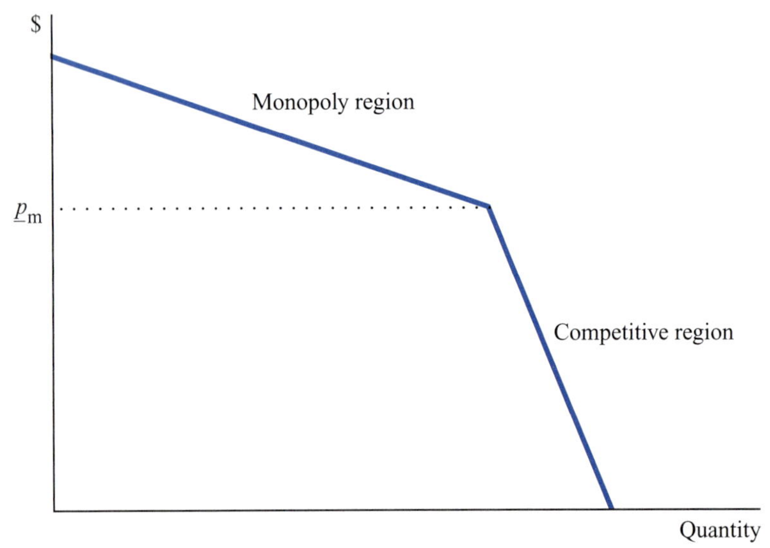

Solving Equation 7.14 for x_c, and noting that the quantity demanded of a competitive firm is $q_c = 2x_cL$, the competitive demand equation is

$$q_c = \frac{L}{c}\left(\frac{c}{n} + \underline{p} - p\right). \tag{7.15}$$

Thus, the competitive quantity demanded falls by $-L/c$ as p rises by \$1 (holding $\underline{p}$ constant). That is, the slope of the competitive demand curve is only half as steep as that of the monopolistic demand curve.

Types of Equilibria in the Circle Model. At high prices, the demand regions of the firms do not overlap. Each firm is a local monopolist. As the price falls, so that more consumers are interested in ice cream, the regions overlap, and competition between the firms begins. The monopoly and competitive demand regions are shown in Figure 7.9. At prices above $\underline{p}_m$ the demand region is monopolistic: A brand's customers do not consider buying any other brand. Below $\underline{p}_m$ the brand competes with its nearest neighbors.[22]

[22]As Equation 7.14 shows, at prices below $\underline{p} - c/n$, all of the customers between a given firm and its neighbor prefer buying from the low-priced firm, even if they do not like that brand as much. Consider the consumer located at the same point as the neighbor firm: a distance of $1/n$ from the low-priced firm. That consumer loses c/n utility by consuming the low-priced brand rather than the preferred brand. But the price saving is greater than that loss. This type of behavior is extremely aggressive (Salop calls it *supercompetitive*), because the low-priced firm captures all the new neighbor brand's contested customers. For simplicity, Figure 7.9 does not show this region.

Salop shows (in an argument analogous to the one used for the representative consumer models) that where firms have constant marginal and fixed costs, there exists a symmetric Nash equilibrium in which no firm wants to alter its price and no additional firms want to enter. That is, all firms charge the same price in equilibrium and are located $1/n$ distance from each other. Suppose that free entry is allowed and that firms can costlessly relocate so that they are equidistant from each other. Then, in a monopolistic competition equilibrium, the entry of one more firm causes all firms' profits to be negative. Example 7.4 discusses what happens when firms cannot costlessly relocate as new entry occurs.

EXAMPLE 7.4 *A Serial Problem*

In 1972, the U.S. Federal Trade Commission (FTC) charged the four largest U.S. manufacturers of ready-to-eat breakfast cereal (RTE cereal) with several antitrust violations, including conspiring through brand proliferation and differentiating similar products to prevent entry into the industry. Although the FTC failed to win its case, this argument is theoretically interesting.

Richard Schmalensee and F. M. Scherer used localized competition models to explain the FTC's argument. In such models, consumers choose cereals based on their characteristics, such as sweetness and "mouth feel." Each brand is located in a characteristic space. A given brand must compete for customers with other nearby brands located in that part of product space. If the company owning that brand can surround it with other similar brands of its own, then its brands compete with each other. For example, Kellogg's Corn Flakes and Special K may be very close substitutes.

If a firm creates enough of these surrounding, or *defensive*, brands, there may not be enough customers left for any other firm to profitably establish a brand in that area of product space, according to this brand-proliferation theory. Similarly, several firms could conspire to establish a large number of brands (more brands than are profit maximizing in the short run) in a given area of product space to prevent entry by new firms.

Whether the firms were conspiring or not, the top six firms had 95 percent of the sales of cereal. Moreover, between 1950 and 1972, the six leading producers introduced over 80 brands into distribution beyond test marketing.

In the early 1970s, however, "health" cereals started selling well. Because existing firms had not located in this area of product space, new firms (which included such giants as Colgate, International Multifoods, Pet, and Pillsbury) were able to enter. By mid-1974, these "natural" cereals had 10 percent of the market. But apparently, the previous positioning of these new firms did not prevent the established firms from entering this section of product space. As a result of the entry of the established firms and the decline in demand for that segment of the market from its 1974 height, all but one of the new entrants (Pet) was driven from that area of product space by late 1977.

Sources: Schmalensee (1978b), Scherer (1979), and (for a different view) Williamson (n.d.).

Changes in Costs and Welfare in the Circle Model. Salop shows that, as in the representative consumer models, in the competitive region, as fixed costs rise, there are fewer firms or brands, so price rises and equilibrium variety falls. In that region, as the constant marginal cost rises, price rises by an equal amount (all increases in costs are shifted to consumers), but equilibrium variety remains unchanged.

At the kink in the demand curve at $\underline{p}_m$ in Figure 7.9, however, an increase in either fixed or marginal cost reduces the number of firms (variety) but, perversely, lowers price (the kink shifts down and to the right in Figure 7.9). Thus, if the economy is at such a point, a tax that raises firms' costs lowers prices and decreases variety. Salop shows, however, that welfare rises, even if the proceeds of the tax are ignored.

Indeed, welfare in this circle market can be studied in the same manner as in the representative consumer models. Salop shows that the first-best optimal variety is less than the variety in either the monopolistic or competitive equilibria. With fewer brands, the savings in fixed costs exceed the losses due to higher prices. Thus, in the circle model's monopolistic competition equilibrium, there are unambiguously too many brands; whereas in the differentiated products, representative consumer model equilibrium, there can be too many or too few brands.

Salop shows that the second-best optimum, given the government's only regulatory policy is to control entry, is either the market equilibrium or complete monopoly. That is, the optimal entry policy is either free entry or entry restricted so that each brand has a complete monopoly market.

Hybrid Models

We have drawn the distinction between representative consumer models and location models. Although the vast majority of all monopolistic competition models fall cleanly into one or the other of these two categories, increasing use is made of hybrid models that combine some of the properties of each model.[23]

One of these hybrid models, Deneckere and Rothschild (1986), includes the circle model and a version of the representative consumer model as special cases of Bertrand equilibrium. Using their hybrid model, Deneckere and Rothschild show that prices are lower in a representative consumer model than in the circle model because there is more competition in a representative consumer model. They also show that adding another brand benefits relatively few consumers in the circle model, whereas consumers benefit substantially from the introduction of extra brands in the representative consumer model. It is for these reasons that there are too many brands in the equilibrium of the circle model, but there may be too many or too few brands in the equilibrium of the representative consumer model.

[23]Hybrid models based on the work of Anderson and de Palma (1992a, 1992b), Besanko, Perry, and Spady (1990), Deneckere and Rothschild (1986), Perloff and Salop (1985), and Sattinger (1984) are discussed in **www.aw-bc.com/carlton_perloff** "Hybrid."

Estimation of Differentiated Goods Models

The properties of the differentiated goods models we have described depend critically on the pattern of substitutability among the products. In recent years, advances in statistical techniques and more powerful computers have made possible the simultaneous estimation of demand functions for many brands within a single market.

Nonetheless, it remains difficult to simultaneously estimate the demand curves facing all the differentiated products in a market because of the large number of parameters that must be estimated. For example, there are at least 174 firms selling 230 brands and 613 different products of canned juices in U.S. grocery stores. If we had to estimate 613 simultaneous equations of the quantity demanded for each good conditional on 613 prices with one coefficient for each price in each equation, we would have to estimate at least 375,769 parameters. Even if we use utility theory to restrict these parameters, we would still have to estimate many thousands of parameters.

To reduce the number of parameters that must be estimated, researchers use restricted demand systems in which they impose relationships among the various demand curves, some of which stem from theory and others that are arbitrary, such as the functional form. Analysts use many different functional forms when estimating demand equations, such as logit, nested logit, and the almost ideal demand system, but they all have the purpose of imposing constraints on the pattern of substitution among the differentiated products in order to limit the number of parameters that have to be estimated.[24] Further, researchers frequently estimate demand curves for only the major products within a market.

Two approaches are used frequently. The traditional approach is to estimate a system of demand curves—one for each product—but to impose enough restrictions so that the parameters in the demand curves can be estimated (for example, Hausman and Leonard, 1997). An alternative approach is to use a logit or the more general random parameter logit (or probit) model, in which the econometrician tries to explain the fraction of sales for each product conditional on its characteristics (such as, flavor and size of container) as well as relative prices.[25] Researchers must be careful in making assumptions about the structure of the demand curves that they do not implicitly assume their conclusions by the manner in which they restrict the substitution patterns.

After estimating the demand system, researchers frequently want to make "what if" prediction about how changes in a market (such as a merger) will affect prices. To do so, they need a model of oligopoly behavior. Researchers usually lack information about marginal costs. However, by making strong assumptions, they can estimate marginal costs.

---

[24]See, for example, Baker and Bresnahan (1988), Trajtenberg (1989), Hausman, Leonard, and Zona (1994), Bresnahan, Stern, and Trajtenberg (1997), Hausman and Leonard (1997), Hendel (1999), and Peters (2003).

[25]See Berry (1994), Berry, Levinsohn, and Pakes (1995), Nevo (2000, 2001), and Petrin (2002).

EXAMPLE 7.5

Combining Beers

Consumers can choose from among many different brands and types of beer, the latter including premium, light (low calorie), and imported. Postulating a demand curve for each brand and type of beer, an analyst would have to estimate a very large number of parameters. Instead, Hausman, Leonard, and Zona (1994) postulate that there is a three-stage decision process to beer consumption. First consumers decide how much beer to consume in the aggregate. Then they decide what share of each type to consume. Finally, they pick the share of each brand for each type of beer. By specifying demand in this way, the analyst is reducing the number of demand parameters at the cost of imposing restrictions on demand substitution patterns.

The analyst then uses the estimated demand elasticities from this demand system to determine the markup of price over marginal cost based on the assumption that the firms engage in a Bertrand game and have constant marginal costs. A logical question to ask is what will happen to prices if two of the firms merge. To answer this question, the analyst rewrites the profit-maximizing equations describing the equilibrium with fewer firms. Previously, the two firms set prices independently. Now the new merged firm takes into account that it controls the pricing of products previously set by the other firm. Using this technique, Hausman et al. calculate that a merger of Coors and Labatts, two brewers of premium beers, would raise the Coors price by 4.4 percent and the Labatt's price by 3.3 percent. However, they also conclude that, if the merger results in a 5 percent gain in efficiency so that marginal costs fall by 5 percent, the merger will lead to lower, not higher, prices.

Unfortunately, usually they do not know marginal cost, so they use the assumptions that the firms maximize profit, engage in a Bertrand game, and have a constant marginal cost, m, to estimate the marginal cost. For example, the Lerner Index markup of price over marginal cost for a profit maximizing monopoly is $(p - m)/p = -1/\epsilon$ (Equation 4.3). This equation shows that the price markup depends only on the elasticity of demand, ϵ. Moreover, given that we can observe p and have estimated the demand equation and have an estimate of ϵ, we can use this equation to estimate m. This profit-maximizing condition generalizes for any profit-maximizing firm, even in markets with many differentiated products, given that one knows the type of game, such as Bertrand, that the firms play and all own and cross-price elasticities. Even in these generalized expressions, the price markup depends only on the own and cross-price elasticities of demand of all the products, so that again one can infer the constant marginal costs (see, for example, Hausman et al. 1994). Using this approach, researchers predict the price effects of a merger (see Example 7.5) and the value of new products (see Example 7.6).[26]

[26]In a comparison of how the various methods worked in predicting the effect of airline mergers, Peters (2003) found that estimation of the demand system combined with assumed oligopoly behavior did not perform significantly better than a "reduced form" estimation that directly relates prices to concentration (which Peters treated as an endogenous variable).

EXAMPLE 7.6 *Value of Minivans*

In 1984, Chrysler introduced the first minivan, the Dodge Caravan. The minivan was a successful innovation because it handled like a passenger car even though it was substantially larger than one. General Motors and Ford soon introduced their own minivans. Minivans' success came partially at the expense of station wagons, whose sales fell by over 60 percent during the next seven years.

How much was the introduction of the minivan worth to consumers? To answer this question, Petrin (2002) estimated the demand curve for minivans so as to calculate the increased consumer surplus that consumers receive. But even consumers who do not purchase the minivan can benefit if the minivan simulates competition and lowers the price of the car they do purchase.

Petrin estimated a random coefficient discrete choice demand system, which was pioneered by Berry et al. (1995). Here, the demand estimation allows for differences in tastes across individuals. In this approach, the researcher assumes that each individual chooses that product that yields him or her the highest utility, and that firms maximize profits in competition with others in Bertrand competition. Even though Petrin lacked information on purchases by individuals, he had data on the average income of a buyer of each type of car, which he used to better estimate his model.

Petrin calculated the amount of money consumers would have had to receive in the absence of minivans in order to attain the same utility as when minivans did not exist. He estimated that the average benefit per consumer over a four-year period was $1,247 with over 40 percent coming as benefits to non-minivan purchasers from increased competition. Petrin calculated, if one ignored taste heterogeneity, that the benefit would have been overestimated to equal $13,652. His best estimates of the benefits to consumers of minivans totaled $2.8 billion over a four-year period. However, his estimates ignore the negative externality—more deaths—imposed by minivans and sport utility vehicles on drivers of normal size cars and pedestrians (White 2002).

SUMMARY

This chapter examines product differentiation and monopolistic competition. Product differentiation creates at least some market power for a firm. The greater the perceived difference between two firms' products, the more each firm can charge.

If free entry is allowed, firms enter markets until profits are driven to zero. A monopolistic competition equilibrium is one in which firms face downward-sloping demand curves and earn zero profits.

There are two basic types of monopolistic competition models. In Chamberlin's representative consumer model, a typical consumer views all products as equally good substitutes for each other. Price is above marginal cost, and there may be too much or too little variety. Entry (due, for example, to a reduction in fixed costs) tends to reduce the prices of all firms.

Hotelling's location (spatial) model postulates that consumers' preferences and brands are located in product or geographic space. Consumers prefer brands near them. As a result, firms have some market power. The pricing behavior of other firms has little effect if the consumers who buy from a given firm do not like the products of those firms. In the localized competition circle model, price is above marginal cost, and there is unambiguously too much variety. New entry does not lower the price a given consumer pays unless a firm enters near the firm that the consumer patronizes because consumers are uninterested in brands that are very dissimilar to the ones they like best.

PROBLEMS

1. Compare the effect of a franchise tax (a lump-sum tax independent of the sales activity of the firm) on a monopolistic competition industry to its effects on a monopoly or competitive industry.
2. In an oligopolistic industry with homogeneous products and firms with Cournot expectations, must profits fall when a new firm enters? Why or why not? (For an answer, see Seade, 1980.)
3. Explain and illustrate the following claim: "In our example, a monopolistic competition industry with homogeneous products cannot be more than one firm away from the output sold at price equals marginal cost."
4. In Hotelling's town, if all firms are required to charge the same fixed price, describe the equilibrium location of three firms. Explain your answer. Now describe the equilibrium for four firms.
5. What is the effect of a cost-saving technological change on a monopolistic competition industry in which the cost curves facing each firm are $C(q) = mq + F$, where m is the constant marginal cost, and F is the fixed cost? *Hint:* A cost-saving technological change may be modeled as reducing m, reducing F, or reducing both.
6. Show graphically that if a firm's $MC = AC =$ a constant, it will produce a product if it is socially desirable for that product to be produced.

Answers to odd-numbered problems are given at the back of the book.

SUGGESTED READINGS

Friedman (1983) has a good survey and discussion of most of the models in this chapter. In the 1930s, there was a lively (and relatively nontechnical) debate between Chamberlin (1933) and Robinson (1934) and Kaldor (1935) concerning the necessary conditions for a firm to possess market power (the power to set price above marginal cost). For an excellent survey of the technical literature on product differentiation, see Eaton and Lipsey (1989).

APPENDIX 7A

Welfare in a Monopolistic Competition Model with Homogeneous Products

Why, a four-year-old child could understand this report. Run out and find me a four-year-old child. I can't make head or tail of it. —Groucho Marx

Two problems arise in a monopolistic competition equilibrium with homogeneous goods:[1]

1. Because price is greater than marginal cost, the industry produces too little output.
2. If marginal cost is constant, the industry bears excess fixed costs.

First-Best Optimum

All is for the best in the best of possible worlds. —Voltaire

Given constant marginal cost, the first-best optimum requires a single firm that charges a price equal to marginal cost, $p = m$, and a subsidy of the firm's losses. We illustrate this result using a simple, general equilibrium model. In this model, there is no important distinction between the partial and general equilibrium because the general equilibrium's income effect is the same as in the partial equilibrium.

The representative consumer's utility function is

$$U(Q, y) = u(Q) + y, \tag{7A.1}$$

where Q is the output of the monopolistic competition industry and y represents all other goods. Let y be produced at constant cost, and, by normalizing, let this constant cost equal 1 so that the competitive price is also 1.

The consumer maximizes his or her utility subject to the budget constraint

$$I = pQ + y, \tag{7A.2}$$

where I is the consumer's income and p is the price of a unit of Q. From Equation 7A.2, $y = I - pQ$. Substituting that expression for y into the consumer's utility function (Equation 7A.1), the consumer's utility maximization problem is

[1]Appendixes 7A and 7B draw heavily on Steven C. Salop's unpublished lecture notes, Dixit and Stiglitz (1997), and Spence (1976).

$$\max_{Q} u(Q) + I - pQ. \tag{7A.3}$$

The first-order condition for utility maximization is

$$u'(Q) = p. \tag{7A.4}$$

That is, the consumer picks Q so that marginal utility equals the marginal cost of Q, which is p. As a result, the consumer's demand function may be written as $p = p(Q) = u'(Q)$. Because marginal utility is positive, $p > 0$. The second-order condition, $u'' < 0$, implies there is diminishing marginal utility so that the demand curve is downward sloping: $p' < 0$.

If there are n identical firms in the Q-industry, each produces an equal amount of output, $q = Q/n$. The economy's resource constraint is

$$T = (nF + mQ) + y, \tag{7A.5}$$

where T is the total resources of the economy (maximum production), F is the fixed cost each Q-firm must sink to be in business, and $nF + mQ$ is the total cost of producing Q units of output. For example, if T is the total hours of labor available and y is leisure, then the total time spent producing output plus leisure equals T.

Society's problem is to maximize Equation 7A.1 subject to Equation 7A.5 through its choice of Q, y, and n. By substituting for y in Equation 7A.1 using Equation 7A.5, we may write this problem as

$$\begin{aligned} &\max_{Q,\, n} u(Q) + T - nF - mQ \\ &\qquad \text{s. t.} \quad n \geq 1, \\ &\qquad\qquad\quad Q > 0 \\ &\qquad\qquad\quad (p - m)\frac{Q}{n} - F \geq 0, \end{aligned} \tag{7A.6}$$

where the last condition is that each firm makes nonnegative profits so that they do not shut down. Equation 7A.6 says society should maximize the objective function, utility, $u(Q) + T - nF - mQ$, by choosing Q and n appropriately, subject to the restrictions that there is at least one firm ($n \geq 1$) and that some positive amount of Q is produced ($Q > 0$).

The Lagrangian may be written as

$$\mathcal{L} = u(Q) + T - nF - mQ - \lambda(n - 1) - \mu Q, \tag{7A.7}$$

with Lagrangian multipliers λ and μ. If any of the constraints are nonbinding (hold as a strict inequality), then the associated Lagrangian multiplier is zero.

The Kuhn-Tucker first-order conditions with respect to n and Q imply that[2]

$$n = 1, \tag{7A.8}$$

because $\mathcal{L}_n = 0$ implies that $-F = \lambda$, and

$$u'(Q) = m, \tag{7A.9}$$

because $Q > 0$. Thus, as shown in Figure 7.2, the first-best optimum requires the following:

- One firm produces all the output: $n = 1$, from Equation 7A.8.
- Because a positive amount of the monopolistic competition good is produced ($Q > 0$), price equals marginal cost, $u' = p = m$, from Equations 7A.9 and 7A.4.
- The single firm's losses are subsidized to prevent it from shutting down. The subsidy is necessary because the losses $= -F$.

This solution is that of a regulated natural monopoly (see Chapter 20). There are economies of scale everywhere; that is, the firm always operates in the downward-sloping portion of its average cost curve. For this solution to be optimal, funds for the subsidy must be raised in a nondistorting manner. Given a representative consumer, one efficient method of raising funds is a lump-sum tax.

Second-Best Optimum

Now assume that the government cannot achieve the first-best optimum because its actions are constrained:

- The government can control *only* the number of firms, n.
- The government cannot force the firms to produce more than the profit-maximizing quantity; that is, it may not subsidize firms.

In the second-best optimum, assuming firms play Cournot, each firm chooses its (positive) output level such that its marginal revenue equals its marginal cost:[3]

$$\frac{Q}{n} p'(Q) + p(Q) = m, \tag{7A.10}$$

where Q/n is the output of a single firm.

---

[2]The Kuhn-Tucker conditions are that $\mathcal{L}_n \le 0$, and if strictly less than zero, $n = 1$ (which occurs here); $\mathcal{L}_Q \le 0$, and if strictly less than zero, $Q = 0$ (not true here); $\mathcal{L}_\lambda \ge 0$, and if strictly greater than zero, $\lambda = 0$; and $\mathcal{L}_\mu \ge 0$, and if strictly greater than zero, $\mu = 0$.

[3]A single firm's revenue is $p(q^* + \underline{Q})q^*$, where q^* is its output and $\underline{Q}$ is the output of the $n - 1$ other firms. Differentiating revenue with respect to q^* using the Cournot assumption, and noting that in equilibrium $q^* = \underline{Q}/(n - 1) = Q/n$, we obtain Equation 7A.10.

Firms enter the industry if the marginal firm earns a nonnegative profit. That is, price is at least as great as average cost:

$$p(Q) \geq m + \frac{F}{Q/n}. \tag{7A.11}$$

Equations 7A.10 and 7A.11 determine Q and n.

To find out how much total output changes as the number of firms increases, we can totally differentiate Equation 7A.10:

$$\frac{dQ}{dn} = \frac{Q}{n}\left[\frac{p'}{(n+1)p' + Qp''}\right]. \tag{7A.12}$$

The denominator of this expression is negative by the second-order condition, so an extra firm increases industry output: $dQ/dn > 0$. A sufficient condition for the second-order condition to hold is $p'' \leq 0$. Because $p''(Q) = u'''(Q)$, p'' can have any sign in general;[4] however, for specificity, we assume $p''(Q) \leq 0$ in what follows.

As a result, increasing output through the market mechanism requires additional firms, and hence additional fixed costs. That is, output may be written as a function of the number of firms, $Q(n)$, where $Q'(n) > 0$. There is a trade-off between the total cost of production (more firms) and lower price (more output).

Society's problem is

$$\max_n \; u(Q(n)) + T - nF - mQ(n), \tag{7A.13}$$

subject to Equations 7A.10 and 7A.11. This problem differs from the problem in Equation 7A.6 in that society is maximizing with respect to n and not with respect to Q and n. Thus, this second-best optimization is constrained in the sense that society can only control Q indirectly through its choice of n.

Ignoring the constraint Equation 7A.11 for the moment, the first-order condition for welfare maximization is

$$(p - m)Q'(n) = F, \tag{7A.14}$$

where $u'(Q)$ is replaced with p using Equation 7A.4. This condition states that the difference between price and marginal cost times the change in output as n increases by one firm $[Q(n+1) - Q(n) \approx Q'(n)]$ equals fixed cost. The left side is the gain from more output from an extra firm, and the right side is the (fixed) cost from one more firm.

---

[4]See Seade (1980) for a discussion of how stability conditions rule out certain possibilities.

Equation 7A.14 is the appropriate optimality condition if the constraint in Equation 7A.11 is not binding. That is, industry profits are nonnegative for each of the n firms, where the government specifies n. We can show that profits are positive if the constraint does not bind. First, rewrite Equation 7A.14 as

$$p = m + \frac{F}{Q'(n)}. \tag{7A.14'}$$

For profits to be positive, we need $p = m + F/Q'(n) > m + F/[Q/n] = AC$, or

$$Q'(n) < \frac{Q(n)}{n} \quad \text{or} \quad \frac{nQ'(n)}{Q(n)} < 1. \tag{7A.15}$$

That is, the elasticity of *total output with respect to entry* is less than 1.

From Equation 7A.12,

$$\frac{nQ'(n)}{Q(n)} = \frac{p'}{(n+1)p' + Qp''}, \tag{7A.16}$$

so, because $p'' \leq 0$,

$$\frac{nQ'(n)}{Q(n)} \leq \frac{p'}{(n+1)p'} = \frac{1}{n+1}, \tag{7A.17}$$

or $nQ'(n)/Q(n) < 1$, as required. That is, if $p'' \leq 0$, the constraint that $p \geq AC$ (Equation 7A.11) is not binding. The free-entry equilibrium has too many firms (in the sense that the zero-profits constraint is not binding). Thus, society would benefit if it could costlessly restrict the number of firms to the optimal number.

APPENDIX 7B

Welfare in a Monopolistic Competition Model with Differentiated Products

The object of government is the welfare of the people.

—Theodore Roosevelt

We start by considering an economy with only a monopolistic competition industry. We then extend the model to include an outside good.

An Economy with a Single Monopolistic Competition Market

For simplicity, suppose that the degree of product variety is fully reflected by the number of different brands, n. If all firms have identical cost functions, in a symmetric equilibrium, each produces the same amount of output, q.

Each firm's cost function is $C = F + mq$, where C is total costs, F is fixed costs, and mq is the variable costs associated with output level q. Thus, both variable and marginal costs equal m.

Society's production possibility frontier (PPF) is the set of points (q, n) that can be produced with society's total resources, T:

$$(F + mq)n = T, \tag{7B.1}$$

where the left side of Equation 7B.1 is the total cost of n firms producing q units of output each. Equivalently, the PPF is $n = T/(F + mq)$, which is plotted in Figure 7.4. Totally differentiating this equation, we find that the slope of the PPF, $\mathrm{d}n/\mathrm{d}q = -mT/(F + mq)^2$, is negative, as shown in Figure 7.4. Using the numerical example in Table 7.4, $\mathrm{d}n/\mathrm{d}q = -100/(5 + q)^2$. Further, as q rises, the slope becomes less negative, $\mathrm{d}^2n/\mathrm{d}q^2 = 2m^2T/(F + mq)^3$, so that the PPF is concave, as shown in the figure.

Consumers have preferences regarding quantity, q, and variety, n. That is, they are willing to trade off some output of each brand for more brands. For example, the utility function over all *potential* brands, $i = 1, 2, \ldots, \infty$ is

$$U(q_1, q_2, \ldots, q_m, \ldots) = W\left(\sum_{i=1}^{\infty} u_i(q_i)\right). \tag{7B.2}$$

In the symmetric case with n firms in the industry, $u_i(q) \equiv u(q)$, for all i; $q_i = q$, for $i = 1, 2, \ldots, n$; and $q_i = 0$, for $i > n$, so we can rewrite Equation 7B.2 as follows:

$$U(q, q, \ldots, q, 0, \ldots, 0) = W(nu(q)). \tag{7B.3}$$

A consumer's indifference curve corresponding to utility level $\underline{w}$ is

$$W(nu(q)) = \underline{w}. \tag{7B.4}$$

The optimum output-variety combination, O = (q^*, n^*), is determined by the tangency of an indifference curve with the *PPF*, as shown in Figure 7.4. Points on lower indifference curves are less desirable and points on higher indifference curves are unobtainable because they lie above the *PPF*.

Points A and B on the figure represent possible market equilibrium. That is, one does not know if the monopolistic competition equilibrium lies to the left or the right of the optimum.

A Simple General Equilibrium Model

What is algebra exactly; is it those three-cornered things? —*J. M. Barrie*

To compare the market equilibrium to the optimum, an explicit general equilibrium model should be used. Figure 7.4 only considers the trade-off between output and variety of a monopolistic competition industry. If there is another good, y, one needs to consider the trade-off between the two industries. Again, we assume that the outside good, y, is produced at a constant cost equal to 1 and that its competitive price is 1.

The Optimum. If the utility function is additively separable in y, society's maximization problem is

$$\max_{q_i, y} W\left(\sum_{i=1}^{n} u(q_i)\right) + y \tag{7B.5}$$

subject to

$$y = T - \sum_{i=1}^{n} (mq_i + F).$$

If all firms are identical in the sense that they have the same cost function, $q_i = q$, society's problem may be rewritten as maximizing surplus:

$$\max_{q, n} W(nu(q)) + T - n(mq + F). \tag{7B.6}$$

There are two first-order conditions for a maximum. The first condition is obtained by differentiating Equation 7B.6 with respect to n, setting the derivative equal to zero, and rewriting it as:

$$W'u(q) = mq + F. \tag{7B.7}$$

This condition says that brands should be added until the marginal gain in welfare from an extra brand, $W'u$, equals the opportunity cost of the outside good ($mq + F$ is the cost of one more firm in terms of forgone consumption of the outside good).

The other first-order condition is obtained by differentiating Equation 7B.6 with respect to q, setting the derivative equal to zero, dividing through by n and rewriting it as

$$W'u'(q) = m. \tag{7B.8}$$

Equation 7B.8 says that each brand's output, q, should be increased until the marginal gain in utility from an extra unit of output, $W'u'(q)$, equals the marginal cost, m, of an additional unit of output. Using the same type of reasoning as in Appendix 7A, $p = W'u'(q)$. Thus, Equation 7B.8 says that price should equal marginal cost: $p = m$.

Equations 7B.7 and 7B.8 determine the optimal output per brand and number of brands (q^*, n^*). Dividing Equation 7B.7 by Equation 7B.8 and multiplying by $1/q$, we obtain

$$\frac{\dfrac{u(q)}{q}}{u'(q)} = \frac{\dfrac{mq + F}{q}}{m} = \frac{AC}{MC}. \tag{7B.9}$$

That is, at the optimum, the ratio of the average to the marginal utility equals the ratio of the average to the marginal costs.

If utility is concave ($u' > 0$, $u'' < 0$), average utility always exceeds marginal utility. As a result, Equation 7B.9 implies that average cost is greater than marginal cost at the optimum. That is, the optimum lies on the downward-sloping portion of the average cost curve. This condition is automatically met for the specific cost function we chose. It can be shown that this result holds even when average cost curves are U-shaped. Thus, firms should not produce at minimum average cost, as in a competitive industry. The optimum has more variety than would be the case if firms produced at full capacity (the bottom of a U-shaped average cost curve).

The Equilibrium. The equations that describe the Cournot monopolistic competition equilibrium are different from those that describe the optimum, Equations 7B.7 and 7B.8. We now derive the corresponding equations for the equilibrium.

The profits of a representative firm are

$$\pi = qW'u'(q) - mq - F, \tag{7B.10}$$

because $W'u'(q) = p$. Ignoring the integer problem, firms enter until profits are zero ($\pi = 0$) or revenue equals cost:

$$qW'u'(q) = mq + F. \tag{7B.11}$$

This equation differs from the corresponding condition for an optimum, Equation 7B.7, by having $qW'u'(q)$ instead of $W'u(q)$ on the left side.

By differentiating Equation 7B.10 with respect to q, we find that the Cournot firm maximizes profits where marginal revenue equals marginal cost, m:

$$W''(u'(q))^2nq + W'(qu''(q) + u'(q)) = m. \tag{7B.12}$$

The left side of this equation is different from Equation 7B.8, the condition for an optimum. Thus, because the conditions for an optimum (Equations 7B.7 and 7B.8) differ from those for the equilibrium (Equations 7B.11 and 7B.12), the optimum differs from the equilibrium.

These two sets of conditions are identical only if $W(\cdot)$ and $u(\cdot)$ are linear and $u' = u/q$. That case is uninteresting, however, because each brand is a perfect substitute for every other brand. Demands are therefore perfectly elastic, and no market equilibrium even exists. That is, prices are driven to marginal cost and profits are negative (due to fixed costs), as shown in Appendix 7A.

In general, it can be shown that the equilibrium may lie on either the left or the right of the optimum (in Figure 7.4). To determine the exact relationship, more structure on the utility function is required. A number of articles (Spence 1976; Dixit and Stiglitz 1977; and Koenker and Perry 1981) have worked out the relationship for particular utility functions similar to the one used here. These articles also show that price regulation with a zero-profit constraint leads to the market equilibrium.

CHAPTER 8

Industry Structure and Performance

Merely corroborative detail, intended to give artistic verisimilitude to an otherwise bald and unconvincing narrative. —*W. S. Gilbert*

Theories on competitive and noncompetitive markets hold that the less competition a firm faces, the greater its *market power*: the ability to set price profitably above marginal cost. Thus, market power (and hence price and profits) should be higher in industries with substantial entry barriers that reduce actual and potential competition. Economists conduct empirical investigations to test two of the implications of these theories:

1. How much market power do particular firms (industries) exercise?
2. What are the major factors that determine market power?

For many decades, economists have conducted *structure-conduct-performance* (SCP) studies that concentrate on the second question, which concerns the relationship between market performance and market structure. Market *performance* is the success of a market in producing benefits for consumers (for example, a market is performing well if prices are near the marginal cost of production). Market *structure* consists of those factors that determine the competitiveness of a market. Market structure affects market performance through the *conduct* or behavior of firms. Traditionally, SCP researchers presume that market power or performance can be measured relatively easily, and concentrate on the relationship between performance and structure.

In contrast, many economists now believe that readily available statistics often do *not* accurately reflect either market performance or structure. They rely on new data and techniques to better measure the degree of market power, and its relationship to market performance.

This chapter starts with a summary of the theories on the major market structures based on Chapters 3 through 7. Then, it turns to SCP research and discusses the traditional SCP studies' measures of performance and analyses of the relationship between performance and structure. The main findings are that many industries appear to depart considerably from perfect competition, yet the degree of this departure apparently is not strongly related to industry concentration (the share of sales made by the largest firms in the industry), which presumably reflects the structure of the industry. Finally, the chapter examines modern studies of market power.

Theories of Price Markups and Profits

The relationship between price, p, and marginal cost, MC, and the existence and persistence of economic profits depend on the market structure (Table 8.1). In a competitive industry composed of identical firms with free entry, price equals short-run marginal cost; short-run profits, π_{SR}, are either positive or negative; and long-run profits, π_{LR}, are zero, where capital is charged at its rental price based on the competitive return (or normal return) that capital earns in a competitive industry. Even if firms are price takers (competitive), each firm's profit equals zero in the long run only if each firm has equal access to the same technology and inputs. If some firms have lower costs than others, their profits will not be eroded completely by entry. Free entry guarantees only that the profit of the least profitable firm to enter (the marginal firm) equals zero in the long run.

In monopoly or oligopoly, price exceeds marginal cost, profit in the short run is either positive or negative, and long-run profit is either zero or positive. In monopolistic competition, price is above marginal cost and entry drives long-run profit to zero.

Based on the relationships summarized in Table 8.1, two important conclusions can be drawn. First, testing whether long-run profits are positive is a test of free entry, not of (perfect) competition. Free entry guarantees that long-run profits equal zero, but

TABLE 8.1 **Predictions Based on Market Structure**

	$p - MC$	π_{SR}	π_{LR}
Competition	0	+ or −	0
Monopolistic competition	+	+ or −	0
Monopoly	+	+ or −	+ or 0
Oligopoly	+	+ or −	+ or 0

p = price, MC = marginal cost (short run), π_{SR} = short-run profits, and π_{LR} = long-run profits.

not that price equals marginal cost: Firms in a monopolistically competitive industry may earn zero profit even though price is above marginal cost. To determine whether price exceeds marginal cost, one must examine price data, not profit data. Second, short-run profits reveal very little about the degree of competition in an industry because, in all market structures, short-run profits can be either positive or negative.

Although Table 8.1 shows only four market structures, many more structures are possible. Moreover, for any given market structure, industries can differ substantially. For example, an oligopoly with four firms may set prices differently than one with only two firms. Generally, one would expect price-cost margins and profits to vary with the number of rivals and the size of barriers to entry. It is this generalization that provides the foundation for the SCP approach.

Structure-Conduct-Performance

Edward S. Mason (1939, 1949) and his colleagues at Harvard introduced the structure-conduct-performance (SCP) approach, which revolutionized the study of industrial organization by introducing the use of inferences from microeconomic analysis. In the SCP paradigm, an industry's *performance*—its success in producing benefits for consumers—depends on the *conduct* or behavior of sellers and buyers, which depends on the structure of the market. The *structure* in turn depends on basic conditions such as technology and the demand for a product.

Because the nature of these connections is usually not explained in detail, many economists criticize the SCP approach for being descriptive rather than analytic. George J. Stigler (1968) and others argued that economists, rather than employ the SCP approach, should use price-theory models based on explicit, maximizing behavior by firms and governments. Others suggested replacing the SCP paradigm with analyses that emphasize game theory (von Neumann and Morgenstern 1944). We discuss modern approaches later in this chapter.

Most of the earliest SCP works were case studies of an individual industry (for example, Wallace 1937). The first empirical applications of the SCP theory were by Mason's colleagues and students, such as Joe S. Bain (1951, 1956). In contrast to the case studies, these studies made comparisons across industries.

A typical SCP study has two main stages. First, one obtains a measure of performance (through direct measurement rather than estimation) and several measures of industry structure. Second, the econometrician uses cross-industry observations to regress the performance measure on various measures of structure so as to explain the difference in market performance across industries. We first discuss the measurement of performance and structure variables and then examine the evidence relating performance to structure.

Measures of Market Performance

Measures of market performance try to provide an answer to our first key question as to whether market power is exercised in an industry. Two different measures that directly or indirectly reflect the profits or the relationship of price to costs are commonly used to gauge how close an industry's performance is to the competitive benchmark:

- The *rate of return,* which is based on profits earned per dollar of investment.
- The *price-cost margin,* which should be based on the difference between price and marginal cost, although, in practice, researchers often use some form of average cost in place of marginal cost.

A third measure, *Tobin's q,* is less commonly used. Tobin's q is the ratio of the market value of a firm to its value based on the replacement cost of its assets. (See **www.aw-bc.com/carlton_perloff** "Tobin's q" for more details.)

Rates of Return

A rate of return is a measure of how much is earned per dollar of investment. This section explains the relationship between economic profits and rates of return. The correct calculation of rates of return can be difficult, and sometimes compromises must be made that bias the final results. We discuss several different rate-of-return measures.

The Relationship Between Rates of Return and Economic Profit. The theories summarized in Table 8.1 make predictions about profit, and a rate of return is a measure of profit. The predictions in Table 8.1 refer to *economic* profit, which is revenue minus opportunity cost, not *accounting* profit (which is measured by accountants, using standard accounting principles). To test the predictions of Table 8.1, an economist's first step should be to adjust accounting profit to reflect economic profit before calculating the rate of return.

There are several important distinctions between economic and accounting profits. The main distinction concerns long-lived capital assets, like plant and equipment. Economic profit equals revenue minus labor, material, and an appropriate measure of capital cost. Measuring revenue, labor cost, and material cost is generally easy. The problem is measuring annual capital cost, which equals annual rental fees if all the capital assets were rented. The total rental fees equal the rental rate per unit times the number of units of capital. That is, the appropriate cost measure of capital is a *flow* (the price of renting capital per time period) and not a *stock* (the cost of capital, such as a machine, which lasts for many periods). If well-developed rental markets exist—for example, for used equipment—it is easy to calculate the relevant rental rate on capital and economic profits. When rental rates are not readily available, the economist must implicitly calculate a rental rate before calculating economic profit.

In the calculation of the implicit rental rate of capital used to determine long-run economic profits, capital assets should be valued at replacement cost, which is the long-run cost of buying a comparable-quality asset. If capital is valued at its replacement cost, then a low rate of return is a signal that no new capital should enter the industry. It does not mean that the firm should shut down or that it made an error in its past investment decisions. For example, a firm that bought machinery when it was cheap could earn a low rate of return based on the replacement cost and still have enjoyed a huge profit on its initial purchase. A high rate of return is a signal that new capital should enter the industry.

Researchers often divide economic profits by the value of the capital of the firm to obtain an earned rate of return on capital, which is a measure of profitability that controls for differences in capital across firms. There is a close relationship between economic profits, the earned rate of return on capital, and rental rates on capital. To develop this relationship requires an understanding of what a rental rate on capital really is: A rental rate must provide an owner of capital with a particular rate of return *after* depreciation has been deducted on the equipment.

Depreciation is the decline in economic value that results during the period the capital is used.[1] For example, if you rent your house for $1,000 a year, and the wear and tear on the house is $300 a year, then the depreciation is $300, and your net annual rental after accounting for the depreciation is $700. If the house is worth $10,000 initially, then your rate of return is 7 percent, and the depreciation is 3 percent. What matters to the investor is the return after depreciation has been deducted. For that reason, a rental rate (per dollar of capital) can be expressed as an earned rate of return, r, plus a rate of depreciation, δ.

Your profit is

$$\pi = R - \text{labor cost} - \text{material cost} - \text{capital cost},$$

where R is revenue and capital costs are the rental rate of capital times the value of capital. The value of capital is $p_k K$, where p_k is the price of capital and K is the quantity of capital. If the rental rate is $(r + \delta)$, then profit is

$$\pi = R - \text{labor cost} - \text{material cost} - (r + \delta)p_k K. \tag{8.1}$$

The earned rate of return is that r such that economic profit is zero. Setting π equal to 0 and solving for r in Equation 8.1 yields

$$r = \frac{R - \text{labor cost} - \text{material cost} - \delta p_k K}{p_k K}. \tag{8.1$'$}$$

Thus, the earned rate of return is net income divided by the value of assets, where *net income* is revenue minus labor cost minus material cost minus depreciation.[2]

The Relationship Between Rates of Return and Price. By how much would price or revenues have to fall in a highly profitable industry in order for that industry to earn a normal rate of return? To see how excess rates of return translate into price overcharges, suppose that a firm earns a rate of return r^* that is 5 percentage points higher than normal: $r^* = r + .05$. That is, the firm's invested capital earns excess rev-

[1] An accountant's definition of depreciation may be based on a formula involving historical cost and age. This measure of depreciation is likely to differ from an economist's measure of depreciation, which is based on opportunity cost.

[2] Another rate-of-return measure is the internal rate of return, which is that interest rate such that the discounted present value of cash flows equals zero. The value of the internal rate of return is that it concisely summarizes the return earned by a project lasting several years. When profitability is changing over time, it may be misleading due to its aggregate nature. Because an internal rate of return depends primarily on the observed cash flows each year (except for the initial and terminal value of the firm), it frees the economist from having to calculate the value of capital each year.

enues of 5 percent times the value of its capital above what it would earn if it were in a competitive industry. If the firm's revenue is R^*, then its rate of return is

$$r^* = [R^* - \text{labor cost} - \text{material cost} - \delta p_k K]/p_k K = \text{r} + .05.$$

Let R be the revenue that would yield a normal rate of return, r. The amount by which revenue must decline to yield the normal return is $R - R^*$, all else constant. Using Equation 8.1′ for r and the expression for r^*, we know that $r - r^* = -.05 = (R - R^*)/(p_k K)$. Multiplying both sides by $p_k K$, we find that $R - R^* = -.05 p_k K$. Thus, to get the normal rate of return, revenue would have to fall by 5 percent of the value of capital.

In many manufacturing industries, the ratio of the value of capital to the value of revenue is roughly 1. In such industries, revenues must fall by 5 percent in order for the industry to earn a normal return. Alternatively, all else constant, price needs to fall by 5 percent. Therefore, if a firm is earning a real rate of return 5 percent higher than the normal rate of return (which was roughly between 5 percent and 10 percent over the period 1948–1976), the competitive price is roughly 95 percent (= 1 − .05) of its current value. That is, industries that earn a rate of return 1.5 times higher than the return earned by competitive industries (say, 15 percent instead of 10 percent) have prices that are only 5 percent above those that generate a normal return. This price overcharge is the same as would occur if a monopoly faced an elasticity of −21. In other words, even large differences in rates of return on capital between concentrated and unconcentrated industries do not necessarily imply that prices in concentrated industries are much above the competitive level. In industries with a low ratio of capital to revenue, even large excess returns can translate into tiny price overcharges.

Pitfalls in Calculating Rates of Return. There are eight major problems in calculating rates of return correctly (see Fisher and McGowan 1983). First, capital is usually not valued appropriately because accounting definitions are used instead of the economic definitions. An economist measures the annual capital cost flow as the annual rental fee if all the capital assets were rented.[3] In contrast, the accounting value of capital, or *book value,* is based on the historical cost of the capital combined with accounting assumptions about depreciation. Capital should be valued at replacement cost (the long-run cost of replacing existing assets with comparable assets) to determine whether the rate of return is above the competitive level (in which case the firm or industry should expand) or below the competitive level (in which case the firm or industry should contract).[4] Because historical cost is often very different from the actual replacement cost of the capital, using the book value of capital rather than the economic value can severely bias the measurement of rate of return.

---

[3]See **www.aw-bc.com/carlton_perloff**, Chapter 2, "Turning an Asset Price into a Rental Rate."

[4]In all but dying industries, the current value of capital depends on replacement cost. In dying industries, the value of capital is permanently less than replacement cost. The low value of capital is a signal that the industry should not invest in new facilities. In an expanding industry, the current value of capital can exceed replacement cost. The high value of capital is a signal that the industry should invest in new capital. The speed (and cost) of adjustment determines how long the current value can differ from replacement cost.

Second, depreciation is usually not measured properly. Accountants use several fixed formulas to measure the depreciation of an asset. One common formula, called *straight-line depreciation,* assumes that the asset's value declines in equal annual amounts over some fixed period (the *useful life* of the asset). For example, a machine that costs $1,000 and is assigned a useful life of 10 years would incur $100 of depreciation annually for its first 10 years of life. If it lasts more than 10 years, it incurs no additional depreciation. The fixed formula's predictions of the amount of depreciation may be unrelated to the asset's decline in economic value, which is the measure of its economic depreciation. As a result, the estimate of the rate of return may be biased. (See **www.aw-bc.com/carlton_perloff** "Accounting Bias in the Rate of Return.")

Third, valuing problems arise for advertising and research and development (R&D) for the same reason as for capital: All have lasting impacts on either a firm's demand or its costs. The money a firm spends on advertising this year may generate benefits next year, just as a plant built this year provides a benefit next year. If consumers forget about an advertisement's message slowly over time, the advertisement's effect on demand may last for several years. If a firm *expensed* (initially deducted its entire cost of) annual advertising expenditures and then made no deductions in subsequent years, its earned rate of return would be misleadingly low in the initial year and too high in later years. A better approach is to calculate the advertising cost based on the interest rate and the annual decline in the economic value of the advertising. Unfortunately, it is difficult to determine the correct rates of depreciation for advertising expenses.

Similar problems arise with R&D expenditures. Research and development can have a long-lasting impact. In addition, because R&D is risky, we need to be careful in interpreting rates of return. For example, suppose that a firm's research to discover new products is successful one time in ten. If the firm's expected profit is zero, then the profit on the successful product must be high enough to offset the losses on the nine failures. It is misleading to conclude that there are excessively high profits based on an examination of the profit of the one successful product.

Fourth, proper adjustment must be made for inflation. The earned rate of return can be calculated as either a *real* rate of return (a rate of return adjusted to eliminate the effects of inflation) or as a *nominal* rate (which includes the effects of inflation). One should be careful to compare rates that are either all real or all nominal.

If one is using a real rate, income in the numerator of the rate of return should not include the price appreciation on assets from inflation—it should only include the gain in the value of assets beyond that due to general price inflation. For example, if capital is initially worth $100, annual income (before depreciation) is $20, and the annual depreciation rate is 10 percent (so depreciation is $10), then the earned rate of return is 10 percent [(20 − 10)/100]. If inflation was 20 percent during the year, the value of the capital at the end of the year equals $90 ($100 − 10 percent depreciation) times 1.2 (to adjust for inflation), or $108. The firm has incurred a "gain" of $18 on its capital, but it is illusory; it does not represent an increase in purchasing power because all prices have risen as a result of the inflation.

Fifth, monopoly profits may be inappropriately included in the calculated rate of return. This problem stems from using book value in the calculation, because book value sometimes includes *capitalized* (the present value of future) monopoly profit.

Suppose that the monopoly earns excess annual economic profits of $100 above the competitive rate of return and the annual interest rate is 10 percent. The owner of the monopoly sells the firm (and its future stream of monopoly profits) for $1,000 more than the replacement cost of its assets. The owner willingly sells the firm because that extra $1,000 will earn $100, or 10 percent, a year in a bank. The new owner makes only a competitive rate of return because the monopoly profit per year is exactly offset by the forgone interest payments from the extra $1,000. The extra $1,000 paid for the monopoly is the capitalized value of the monopoly profit, *not* the replacement cost to society of replacing the monopoly's capital. Thus, if the reported value of capital inappropriately includes capitalized monopoly profit, the calculated rate of return is misleadingly low if one wants to determine whether an industry is restricting output and is thereby earning an above-normal rate of return.

Sixth, the before-tax rates of return may be calculated instead of the appropriate after-tax rates of return. Corporations pay taxes to the government, and only what is left is of interest to individual investors. That is, after-tax rates of return govern entry and exit decisions. Competition among investors causes after-tax rates of return to be equated on different assets. If assets are taxed at different rates, the before-tax rate of return could vary widely even if all markets are competitive. For that reason, we should use after-tax rates of return and after-tax measures of profit, especially when comparisons are made across industries that are subject to different tax rates.

Seventh, rates of return may not be properly adjusted for risk. To determine whether a firm is earning an excess rate of return, the proper comparison is between the rate of return actually earned and the competitive **risk-adjusted rate of return**, which is the rate of return earned by competitive firms engaged in projects with the same level of risk as that of the firm under analysis. Investors dislike risk and must be compensated for bearing it: The greater the risk, the higher the expected rate of return.[5]

Eighth, some rates of return do not take debt into account properly. Researchers often use the rate of return to the stockholders as a measure of the firm's profitability. If a firm issues debt in addition to equity, both debtholders and equity holders (stockholders) have claims on the firm's income (Chapter 2). Because the assets of the firm are paid for by both debtholders and stockholders, the rate of return on the firm's assets equals a weighted average of the rate of return to the debtholders and the stockholders. The rate of return to debtholders is typically lower than the rate of return to stockholders, because debt is less risky than stock and debtholders get paid before stockholders when a firm is in financial distress. The return to stockholders increases with debt because the

[5]One commonly used approach to adjusting for risk is based on the Capital Asset Pricing Model. According to this model, the expected return on an asset equals the rate of return on risk-free investments (U.S. government Treasury bills are an example of a relatively risk-free investment) plus a number (called *beta*, the Greek letter β) times the difference between the market return (for example, return on the portfolio of all stocks) and the risk-free rate (Brealey and Myers 2003, Ch. 8). Beta reflects how closely the returns on one asset move with the returns on all other assets (the general economy). Risks that are related to movements in the general economy must generate higher returns than the riskless rate of return in order to attract investors.

income received by stockholders in a *highly leveraged* firm (one with a high ratio of debt to equity) is risky, so stockholders in such firms demand high rates of return.[6]

Therefore, it is improper to compare the rates of return to stockholders in two firms in order to measure differences in the degree of competition if the two firms have very different ratios of debt to equity. The debt/equity ratio has nothing to do with whether the firm is earning excess rates of return on its *assets*. Differences among firms in their rates of return to stockholders could reflect differences in competition facing firms or differences in their debt/equity ratios. Even though the rate of return calculated by dividing net income by assets differs from the rate of return from dividing income to stockholders by the value of stockholders' equity, they tend to be highly correlated (Liebowitz 1982b).

Comparing Rates of Return. To judge a rate of return, one must compare it to alternative rates of return. For example, if a firm has 100 units of capital each worth \$10, revenues of \$110, combined labor and material costs of \$10, and capital depreciation of 2 percent per year, then its earned rate of return is 8 percent per year: (110 − 10 − 20)/1,000. If investments in competitive industries yield a 5 percent rate of return, the firm is earning an *excess* rate of return.

There is an equivalent way to reach the same conclusion. If the rental rates on capital were based on the competitive rate of return of 5 percent, then the rental rate would equal 7 percent (5 percent plus depreciation of 2 percent). Calculating economic profit as revenue minus labor cost, material cost, and capital (rental) cost yields a *positive* economic profit of \$30 (110 − 10 − [.07 × 1,000] = 30). Thus, earning *positive* economic profit and earning *excess* rates of return (above the competitive or normal level) are equivalent ways of expressing the same idea. Excess economic profit exists if the earned rate of return exceeds the competitive rate.

Fraumeni and Jorgenson (1980) calculated the after-tax economic rate of return for a large sample of American industries over the period 1948–1976. In their calculations, they were careful to avoid many of the pitfalls described above. They found that over this period, the median manufacturing industry earned a nominal (unadjusted for inflation) rate of return of approximately 11 percent (Table 8.2). Over this same pe-

[6]Suppose that a firm initially has no debt and finances an investment with \$1,000 raised through sale of stock. Next year, the investment returns the \$1,000 plus either \$80 or \$200 with equal probability, so that stockholders' rate of return is either 8 percent or 20 percent, for an average return of 14 percent. Suppose, instead, that the firm raises the \$1,000 for the investment by issuing debt of \$500 that pays 10 percent interest and selling stock worth \$500. Debtholders must receive payment of interest before stockholders receive any income. Therefore, whether the firm earns \$80 or \$200, debtholders receive \$500 plus \$50 of interest. Stockholders receive \$500 plus either \$30 or \$150, so that the total amount paid to both debtholders and stockholders is \$1,000 plus either \$80 or \$200. Stockholders therefore earn either 6 percent (= 30/500) or 30 percent (= 150/500), for an average return of 18 percent, while debtholders earn 10 percent. Stockholders now earn a higher average rate of return and face a wider range of outcomes, even though the income potential of the firm is unchanged.

TABLE 8.2 **Average Annual Returns, 1948–1976**

Industry	Nominal Rate of Return	Own Rate of Return*	Nominal Rate of Return on Stockholders' Equity
Agriculture	.07	.04	
Crude petroleum	.12	.08	
Food	.10	.07	.10
Tobacco	.14	.11	.13
Textiles	.09	.06	.08
Chemicals	.13	.10	.14
Motor vehicles	.29	.25	.15
All manufacturing - median industry	.11	.08	.11
Railroads	.07	.03	
Telephone and telegraph	.15	.11	
Retail trade	.10	.07	

*The own rate of return subtracts from income the effects of increases in the price of capital for each industry. If the price of capital changes only with inflation, the own rate of return is a real (inflation-adjusted) rate of return.

Sources: Fraumeni and Jorgenson (1980); Federal Trade Commission, *Quarterly Financial Reports*, 1948–1976.

riod, the average rate paid on three-month U.S. government Treasury bills was roughly 3.6 percent, so the rate of return in manufacturing significantly exceeded the rate of return on Treasury bills, possibly to compensate for the increased risk.

Studies that calculate rates of return often differ in their methodologies and, because of data constraints, are commonly forced to calculate something other than economic rates of return. Nevertheless, they can still be valuable in investigating whether the rate of return in one industry is higher than that in another, as long as the biases in the calculated rates of return are similar across different industries. It is dangerous, however, to compare the absolute levels of rates of return from one study with the absolute levels of rates of return from another study if the studies follow different methodologies for calculating rates of return.

To illustrate the differences that can arise when different concepts are used to calculate rates of return, the last column of Table 8.2 presents the returns on the book value of stockholders' equity (the difference in the book values of assets and liabilities) published by the Federal Trade Commission (FTC).These rates of return are calculated as after-tax corporate income (which deducts interest payments on debt) divided by the stockholders' equity in the company. Table 8.2 shows that different methodologies can lead to different rates of return. For example, the nominal rate of return in motor vehicles is about 29 percent according to Fraumeni and Jorgenson (1980), but is 15 percent according to the FTC. Nonetheless, the relative rates of return between industries follow the same pattern using both methodologies. For example, tobacco earns a higher rate of return than textiles according to Fraumeni and Jorgenson as well as the FTC.

Price-Cost Margins

To avoid the problems associated with calculating rates of return, many economists use a different measure of performance, the Lerner Index or *price-cost margin*, $(p - MC)/p$, which is the difference between price, p, and marginal cost, MC, as a fraction of the price. The predictions in the first column of Table 8.1 about the relationship of price to marginal cost are stated in terms of the price-cost margin. Because the correlation between accounting rates of return and the price-cost margin can be relatively low (Liebowitz 1982b), it makes a difference which of these two performance measures is used.

The price-cost margin (Chapter 4) for a profit-maximizing firm equals the negative of the reciprocal of the elasticity of demand, ϵ, facing the firm:

$$\frac{p - MC}{p} = -\frac{1}{\epsilon}. \tag{8.2}$$

A competitive firm sets $p = MC$ because its residual demand price elasticity is negative infinity (it faces a horizontal demand curve).

Unfortunately, because a marginal cost measure is rarely available, many researchers use the price-average variable cost margin instead of the appropriate price-marginal cost margin.[7] Their approximation to the price-average variable cost margin is typically calculated as sales (revenues) minus payroll minus material cost divided by sales. That is, they tend to ignore capital, research and development, and advertising costs.[8]

This approach may lead to serious biases. Suppose that marginal cost is

$$MC = v + (r + \delta)\frac{p_k K}{Q}, \tag{8.3}$$

where r is the competitive rate of return, δ is the depreciation rate, and the cost of the labor and materials needed to produce 1 unit of output, Q, is v. Equation 8.3 describes a technology that requires K/Q units of capital (at a cost of p_k per unit of capital) to produce 1 unit of output. Using v in place of marginal cost can lead to serious bias, however, as can be seen by substituting MC from Equation 8.3 into Equation 8.2 to obtain

$$\frac{p - v}{p} = -\frac{1}{\epsilon} + (r + \delta)\frac{p_k K}{pQ}. \tag{8.4}$$

Thus, $(p - v)/p$ differs from the correct measure $(p - MC)/p = -1/\epsilon$ by the last term in Equation 8.4, $(r + \delta)p_k K/(pQ)$, which is the rental value of capital divided by the value of output.

[7] A few studies (Keeler 1983, Friedlaender and Spady 1980) estimate marginal cost based on cost functions.

[8] See Fisher (1987) for a critique of the typical price-cost margin. An even more serious error that is sometimes made is to use average total cost.

Measures of Market Structure

To examine how performance varies with structure, we also need measures of market structure. A variety of measures are used, all of which are thought to have some relation to the degree of competitiveness in an industry. We now describe some of the common measures of market structure.

Industry Concentration. In most SCP studies, industry concentration is the structural variable that is emphasized. Industry concentration is typically measured as a function of the market shares of some or all of the firms in a market.

By far, the most common variable used to measure the market structure of an industry is the four-firm concentration ratio, C4, which is the share of industry sales accounted for by the four largest firms. It is, of course, arbitrary to focus attention on the top four firms in defining concentration ratios. Other concentration measures are used as well. For example, the U.S. government also has published eight-firm concentration ratios, C8.

Alternatively, one could use a *function* of all the individual firms' market shares to measure concentration. The most commonly used function is the **Herfindahl-Hirschman Index**, HHI, which equals the sum of the squared market shares of each firm in the industry. For example, if an industry has three firms with market shares of 50, 30, and 20 percent, the HHI equals 3,800 (= 2,500 + 900 + 400). More attention has been paid to the HHI since the early 1980s, when the Department of Justice and Federal Trade Commission started using it to evaluate mergers. The government publishes HHI statistics by industry.

Typically, empirical studies produce similar results for both the HHI and a four-firm concentration index. It has been shown theoretically (Appendix 8A) that the HHI is the appropriate index of concentration to explain prices if firms behave according to the Cournot model.

Rather than aggregating information about the relative sizes of firms into a single measure, one could examine the effects of the market shares of the first, second, third, fourth, and smaller firms on industry performance. For example, one could determine whether increases in the market share of the second firm raise prices by as much as increases in the share of the leading firm. Using this approach, Kwoka (1979) showed that markets with three (relatively equal-size) firms are much more competitive than those with only two firms.

Table 8.3 shows three concentration measures—C4, C8, and HHI—for several manufacturing industries. Aside from concentration in individual industries, one can examine concentration in manufacturing in general. The 1997 Census of Manufactures reports concentration ratios for 470 manufacturing industries. In 1997, the concentration ratio of the four largest firms was below 40 percent in more than half of the industries, between 41 and 70 percent in about one-third of the industries, and over 70 percent in about one-tenth of the industries, based on value of shipments.

There are now more industries with low four-firm concentration ratios and fewer with high four-firm concentration ratios than in 1935. In 1935, about 47 percent of industries had a four-firm concentration ratio below 40 percent, and about 16 percent of industries had ratios above 70 percent. Since World War II, however, the distribution of concentration ratios in manufacturing has not changed much. Comparisons

TABLE 8.3 **1997 Concentration Ratios in Selected Manufacturing Industries**

Product Grouping	C4	C8	HHI*
Meat products	35	48	393
Breakfast cereal	83	94	2,446
Distilleries	60	77	1,076
Cigarettes	99	NR	NR
Men's and boy's suits and coats	42	56	846
Sawmills	15	20	87
Folding paperboard boxes	25	38	246
Book printing	32	45	364
Petroleum refining	29	49	422
Tires and inner tubes	68	86	1,518
Blast iron and steel mills	33	53	445
Household refrigerators and freezers	82	97	2,025
Motor vehicles and car bodies	87	94	NR
Computers	40	68	658

*Herfindahl-Hirschman Index for the 50 largest companies. *NR* indicates that the index is not reported.

Source: Census of Manufactures: Concentration Ratios in Manufacturing (2001, Table 2).

based on value of shipments, and not on the number of industries, produce similar conclusions.

Table 8.4 shows that there has not been a trend toward increasing aggregate concentration in the manufacturing sector based on *value added* (revenue minus the cost of fuel, power, and raw materials) accounted for by the largest firms. The table shows that aggregate domestic concentration has increased since 1947, but remained relatively constant between 1967 and 1992 and fell slightly in 1997. Moreover, these domestic concentration statistics overstate concentration because they ignore imports, which have grown in importance.

Most of what we know about concentration ratios concerns manufacturing industries, which comprised only about 14 percent of the GDP in 2001.[9] What about concentration in the other sectors of the economy? Unfortunately, data on concentration ratios are not readily available for most individual industries outside of manufacturing. It is generally believed that ease of entry keeps most of agriculture, services, retailing and wholesale trade, and parts of manufacturing and finance, real estate, and insurance relatively unconcentrated.

Unfortunately, concentration measures have two serious problems. First, many factors influence seller concentration measures. For example, profitability may affect the degree of concentration in an industry by affecting entry. One of the key questions

[9]Table B-12, Economic Report of the President, 2003.

TABLE 8.4 **Percent Aggregate Concentration in the Manufacturing Sector (measured by value added)**

Top Firms	1947	1954	1963	1967	1972	1977	1982	1987	1992	1997
50 largest	17	23	23	25	25	24	24	25	24	21
100 largest	23	30	30	33	33	33	33	33	32	29
200 largest	30	37	38	41	42	43	43	43	42	38

Sources: 1982, 1987, 1992, and 1997, *Census of Manufactures: Concentration Ratios in Manufacturing*, Table 1.

posed in the introduction concerns whether a less competitive market structure "causes" higher profits. A test of this hypothesis is meaningful only if structure affects profits, but not vice versa. That is, this theory should be tested using *exogenous* measures of structure, where exogenous means that the structure is determined before profitability and that profitability does not affect structure.[10]

Most commonly used measures of market structure are not exogenous. They depend on the profitability of the industry. For example, suppose that we use the number of firms as a measure of the structure of an industry, arguing that industries with more firms are more competitive. However, entry occurs in extraordinarily profitable industries if there are no barriers to such entry. Although, in the short run, an inherently competitive industry may have a small number of firms, in the long run, many additional firms enter if profits are high.

An exogenous barrier to entry is a better measure of structure than the number of firms. For example, if a government historically prevented entry in a few industries, those industries with the barrier should have higher profits, but the higher profits do not induce additional entry.

Most SCP studies have ignored the problem with obtaining exogenous measures of market structure. In particular, the commonly used concentration measures, such as C4, are definitely *not* exogenous measures of market structure.

The second serious problem is that many concentration measures are biased because of improper market definitions. The relevant *economic market* for a product includes all products that significantly constrain the price of that product (see Chapter 19). In order for industry concentration to be a meaningful predictor of performance, the industry must comprise a relevant economic market. Otherwise, concentration in an industry has no implication for pricing.

For example, the concentration ratio for an industry whose products compete closely with those of another industry may understate the amount of competition. If plastic bottles compete with glass bottles, the concentration ratio in the glass-bottle industry may reveal very little about market power in that industry. The relevant concentration measure should include firms in both industries. Similarly, firms classified in

[10]If measures of structure are determined by profitability, the measures are said to be *endogenously* determined. Failure to use exogenous measures of structure leads to what statisticians call the "simultaneous equations estimation problem."

one industry that can modify their equipment and easily produce products in another industry are potential suppliers that influence current pricing, but are not reflected in the relevant four-firm concentration ratio.[11]

Unfortunately, concentration ratios are published by the government for specific industries and products, and the definitions used do not necessarily coincide with relevant economic markets. Concentration measures are often based on aggregate national statistics. If the geographic extent of the market is local because transport costs are very high, national concentration statistics may misleadingly indicate that markets are less concentrated than is true. Some researchers use distance shipped to identify markets in which the use of national data is misleading: If the distance shipped is short, the concentration in the local market may be much different from the national market concentration.

Similarly, concentration measures are often biased because they ignore imports and exports. For example, the 1997 four-firm concentration ratio for U.S. automobiles was 80 percent. This figure indicates a very concentrated industry; however, it ignores the imports of British, Japanese, and German cars, which were over 23 percent of total 1997 sales in the United States. The use of improper concentration measures, of course, may bias the estimates of the relationship between performance and concentration.

Just as seller concentration can lead to higher prices, buyer concentration can lead to lower prices. When buyers are large and powerful, their concentration can offset the power of sellers. For that reason, several researchers include buyer concentration as a market structure variable explaining industry performance. The same type of market definition problems can affect this measure. However, this measure is more likely to be exogenous than is seller concentration.

Barriers to Entry. Probably the most important structural factor determining industry performance is the ability of firms to enter the industry (Chapter 4). In industries with significant long-run entry barriers, prices can remain elevated above competitive levels.

Commonly used proxies for entry barriers include minimum efficient firm size, advertising intensity, and capital intensity, as well as subjective estimates of the difficulty of entering specific industries. Chapter 3 makes a distinction between a long-run barrier to entry and the speed with which entry can occur. Most empirical studies do not distinguish these two concepts, and so any measure they use for entry barrier typically reflects both concepts.

Fraumeni and Jorgenson (1980) show that differences in rates of return across industries persist for many years. If there are no long-run barriers to entry or exit, rates of return across industries should converge. Their results indicate that there are long-run barriers, or that the rate of entry and exit is very slow so that convergence in rates of return is slow across industries, or that there are persistent differences across industries in the levels of risk that are reflected in rates of return.

---

[11] If the producers of some Product B could profitably switch production to Product A (Product B is a *supply substitute* for Product A), then the producers of Product B should also be considered in the market for Product A.

Again, many of the proxies to barriers to entry, such as advertising intensity, are not exogenous. Others, such as subjective measures, have substantial measurement bias.

Unionization. If an industry is highly unionized, the union may be able to capture the industry profits by extracting them through higher wages. Moreover, the higher wages would drive prices up. Therefore, unionization may raise prices to final consumers even though profits of the firms in the industry are not excessive. It is also possible that unions could raise wages and prices and also raise profits to the industry. By making it costly to expand the labor force, unions can prevent industry competition from expanding output and driving profits down. Unionization may not be exogenous if unions are more likely to organize profitable industries.

The Relationship of Structure to Performance

There are hundreds, if not thousands, of studies that attempt to relate market structure to each of the three major measures of market performance. This section first discusses the key empirical findings for each of the performance measures based on U.S. data.[12] Then, SCP studies based on data from other countries and on data for individual industries are examined. Finally, the section summarizes the major critiques of the results and their interpretation.

Rates of Return and Industry Structure. Joe Bain deserves credit for pioneering work that led to the voluminous literature on the relationship between rates of return and industry structure. Bain (1951) investigated 42 industries and separated them into two groups: those with an eight-firm concentration ratio in excess of 70 percent and those with an eight-firm concentration ratio below 70 percent. The rate of return (calculated roughly as income divided by the book value of stockholders' equity) for the more concentrated industries was 11.8 percent compared to 7.5 percent for less concentrated industries.

Bain (1956) classified industries by his subjective estimate as to the extent of barriers to entry. His hypothesis was that profits should be higher in industries with high concentration and high barriers to entry. The evidence that Bain presented is consistent with his hypothesis.

Brozen (1971) criticized Bain's findings for two reasons. First, as Bain recognized, the industries that Bain studied could be in disequilibrium. Brozen showed that the industries Bain identified as highly profitable suffered a subsequent decline in their profits, while the industries of lower profitability enjoyed a subsequent increase in profits. In fact, for the 42 industries of Bain's initial 1951 study, the profit difference of 4.3 percent that he found between the highly concentrated and less concentrated groups diminished to only 1.1 percent by the mid-1950s (Brozen 1971). Second, Brozen pointed out that Bain's use, in some of his work, of the profit rates of the leading firms, rather than the profit rate of the industry, could have skewed his results.

---

[12] See also **www.aw-bc.com/carlton_perloff** "Tobin's *q*" for a discussion of research using Tobin's *q*.

TABLE 8.5 **Average Profit Rates (selected industries)**

Eight-Firm Concentration Ratio over 70 Percent		Eight-Firm Concentration Ratio below 70 Percent	
Industry	Profit Rate (%)	Industry	Profit Rate (%)
Auto	15.5	Shoes	9.6
Cigarettes	11.6	Beer	10.9
Ethical drugs	17.9	Bituminous coal	8.8
Liquor	9.0	Canned fruits and vegetables	7.7
Steel	9.0	Average for all industries studied	9.0
Average for all industries studied	13.3		

Source: Mann (1966, 299).

Using 1950–60 data, Mann (1966) reproduced many of Bain's original findings (Table 8.5). Using the same 70 percent concentration ratio criterion as Bain used to divide his sample into two groups, Mann found that the rate of return for the more highly concentrated group was 13.3 percent compared to 9.0 percent for the less concentrated group.

Mann also investigated the relationship between profit and his own subjective estimates of barriers to entry. He found that industries with "very high" barriers to entry enjoy higher profits than those with "substantial" barriers, which in turn earn higher profits than those with "moderate to low" barriers. He confirmed Bain's predictions and earlier findings that concentrated industries with very high barriers to entry have higher average profit rates than concentrated industries that do not have very high barriers to entry.

There have been many econometric estimates of the relation between rates of return, concentration, and a variety of other variables, such as those measuring barriers to entry (see the surveys by Weiss 1974 and Schmalensee 1989). Econometric studies attempt to measure the effects of several variables on rates of return. Such an estimated relationship is called a *regression.* Regression studies provide not only an estimate of the effect of one variable on another but also a statistical measure of whether the estimated effect could be different from zero.

Based on his survey of many of these studies, Weiss (1974) concluded that there was a significant relationship between profit, concentration, and barriers to entry. Studies based on more recent data tend to find only a weak relationship or no relationship between the structural variables and rates of return. For example, Salinger (1984) found, at best, weak support for the hypothesis that minimum efficient scale in concentrated industries is related to rates of return.[13] He found no statistical support that

[13]Large capital requirements do not constitute a long-run barrier to entry unless other conditions, such as imperfect capital markets or sunk costs, are present (see Chapter 3).

his other entry barrier proxy variables (such as advertising intensity) are related to rates of return.

Econometric studies linking profit to market structure often conclude that measured profitability is correlated with the advertising-to-sales ratio and with the ratio of research and development expenditures to sales. These studies also commonly find that high rates of return and industry growth are related.

Some researchers have studied how the speed of adjustment of capital (and hence profit) is related to concentration. Capital-output ratios appear to rise with concentration, though less so recently than in the past. (Table 8.6). The full explanation for the correlation between capital-output ratios and concentration is not known. One possible reason for this result is that the plant of minimally efficient scale (the smallest plant that can operate efficiently) is so large relative to industry size that when economies of scale are important, only a few of them can fit into the industry. However, for most industries, minimum efficient scale (Chapter 2) is a small fraction of total industry demand.

It is possible that the more capital-intensive, concentrated industries use relatively more specialized capital. If so, their rates of adjustment of output should be slower than those of less concentrated industries because it is usually more difficult to adjust specialized capital than it is to adjust less specialized capital. If highly concentrated industries adjust more slowly than unconcentrated industries, that explains why high (or low) profits take longer to fall back to (rise to) the industry average in these industries (Stigler 1963, Connolly and Schwartz 1985, Mueller 1985). See Chapter 3 for studies of entry.

TABLE 8.6 **Capital-Output Ratios and Concentration**

	Average Capital/Output Ratio (Percent)	
Four-Firm Concentration Ratio	1963	1997
0–10	26.5	38.8
11–20	26.9	32.8
21–30	32.7	37.1
31–40	34.5	39.9
41–50	37.7	36.8
51–60	37.9	39.4
61–70	44.2	46.6
71–80	49.8	49.0
81–90	51.8	35.6
91–100	57.7	42.5

Source: 1963 series from Collins and Preston (1969, 272); 1997 series is based on authors' calculations using the 1997 *Census of Manufactures, Industry Series* and *Concentration Ratios in Manufacturing.* The numbers in Table 8.6 are based on gross book value of capital and, because of data unavailability, do not exclude depreciation.

Similarly, if concentrated industries take a long time to react to demand changes, then, all else equal, good economic news should raise the value of a company in a concentrated industry more than the value of a company in an unconcentrated industry. Lustgarten and Thomadakis (1980) find that good economic news raises the stock market values of companies in concentrated industries much more than those in unconcentrated industries, and bad economic news lowers their values more.

Price-Cost Margins and Industry Structure. Following Collins and Preston (1969), many economists examine the relationship across industries between price-average variable cost margins based on Census data and various proxies for industry structure, such as the four-firm concentration ratio and the capital-output ratio. A typical regression based on data from 1958 (Domowitz, Hubbard, and Petersen 1986, 7) is

$$\frac{p - v}{p} = \underset{(.01)}{.16} + \underset{(.02)}{.10}\, C4 + \underset{(.02)}{.08}\, \frac{p_k K}{pQ} + \text{other variables},$$

where $(p - v)/p$ is the price-average variable cost margin, v is a measure of average variable cost, $C4$ is the four-firm concentration ratio, and $p_k K/(pQ)$ is the ratio of the book value of capital to the value of output. The numbers in parentheses below each coefficient are standard errors, which are a measure of how precisely the coefficients are estimated.[14] The $p_k K/(pQ)$ term is necessary because price-average variable cost margins are used (see Equation 8.4).

The sensitivity of price to increases in concentration can be derived from this equation. According to the equation, if the value of capital to output, $p_k K/(pQ)$, is 40 percent (the average value across industries), the concentration ratio of the top four firms, $C4$, is 50 percent, and if other variables are zero, the predicted price-average variable cost margin is .24 ($\approx .16 + [.10 \times .5] + [.08 \times .4]$), or $p = 1.3v$. That is, price is 30 percent above average variable cost.

If this industry's four-firm concentration ratio doubles from 50 percent to 100 percent, the price-average variable cost margin rises to .29 or $p = 1.4v$. That is, price rises to approximately 1.4 times average variable cost, which is an increase in the price of only about 7 percent. Thus, even very large increases in concentration may raise price by relatively modest amounts.

Domowitz, Hubbard, and Petersen (1986) found that, for the time period 1958–1981, the differential in the price-average variable cost margins between industries of high and low concentration fell substantially over time. When they estimated a price-average variable cost equation with more recent data, the coefficient associated

[14]A commonly used method to express the confidence one has in a coefficient is to construct an interval (called a "95 percent confidence interval") for a coefficient that includes all values within roughly two standard errors of the estimated coefficient. The 95 percent confidence interval for the coefficient on $C4$ covers .06 to .14.

with the concentration ratio is much lower than its value in 1958. That is, the already small effect of concentration on price in 1958 shrunk in later years. Further, in the later period, a statistical test of the hypothesis that the concentration measure does not affect the price-average variable cost margin could not be rejected. In general, they found that the relationship between price-cost margins and concentration is unstable, and, to the extent that any relationship exists, it is weak, especially in recent times.

Instead of using industry average variable cost Census data to study the relationship between the price-average variable cost margin and industry structure, other investigators, among them Kwoka and Ravenscraft (1985), used Federal Trade Commission (FTC) data to investigate price-average variable cost margins at the individual firm level.[15] The studies using individual firm data showed that the link between higher concentration and higher price-cost margins is ambiguous. Some studies find that the link, if it exists at all, is very weak, whereas others discern no link at all. They also find that the presence of a large second or third firm greatly reduces the price-cost margin that can be earned. This discovery indicates that it is a mistake to use only four-firm concentration ratios to measure market structure.

Various studies report significant effects from other explanatory variables. Kwoka and Ravenscraft (1985) showed that industry growth has a significant and positive effect on price-average variable cost margins. Lustgarten (1975b) concluded that increased buyer concentration sometimes lowers price-cost margins. Comanor and Wilson (1967) reported that a higher advertising-sales ratio may raise the price-cost margin. Freeman (1983) showed that unions lower the price-cost margin.[16]

International Studies of Performance and Structure. Because international trade is more important in many other countries than it is in U.S. markets, the bias from ignoring imports and exports may be more substantial in studies based on data from those countries than on U.S. data. Concentration ratios based only on domestic concentration may not be economically meaningful as measures of market power. The relevant competition may well be from firms located outside a given country.

Nonetheless, despite differences across countries in sizes of domestic markets, domestic concentration ratios are correlated across countries (Pryor 1972). That is, an industry that is concentrated in the United States is also likely to be concentrated in the United Kingdom. However, the correlation is not perfect, as illustrated by Sutton (1989, 1998) for the U.S. and U.K. frozen food industries.

---

[15]The advantage of using the firm rather than the industry as the unit of observation is that the researcher can disentangle the effect of industry concentration on a firm's price-cost margin from the effect of the efficiency of that firm alone. For example, one firm's price-cost margin may be high either because the firm is particularly efficient (low cost relative to all other firms) or because all firms in the industry enjoy a high price (lack of competition in the industry). See Benston (1985) for a critique of studies that rely on the FTC data.

[16]Salinger (1984) and Ruback and Zimmerman (1984) also found that unionism has a significant negative effect on the profits of highly concentrated industries. Voos and Mishel (1986) showed that, although unions may depress the price-cost margin, the price is not significantly above the one that would prevail in the absence of a union.

Regardless of which country's data are used, most studies have difficulty detecting an economically and statistically significant effect of concentration on performance (Hart and Morgan 1977, Geroski 1981). However, Encoau and Geroski (1984) found that the United States, the United Kingdom, and Japan tend to have slow rates of price adjustment in their most concentrated sectors.[17]

Performance and Structure in Individual Industries. Most studies of SCP are based on cross-sectional data rather than data on a particular industry over time. There are two serious shortcomings in cross-sectional studies of the relationship between structure and performance across different industries.

First, it is unrealistic to expect the same relationship between structure and performance to hold across all industries. Suppose that one monopolized industry has a high elasticity of demand, and another monopolized industry has a low elasticity of demand. As Equation 8.2 shows, the price-cost margin in the industry with the high elasticity of demand is lower than the price-cost margin in the industry with the low elasticity of demand. Most cross-sectional studies fail to control for differences in demand elasticities across industries, thereby implicitly assuming that the elasticities are identical across industries.

Second, it is unlikely that the four-firm concentration ratios published by the U.S. Census Bureau correspond to the concentration ratios for relevant economic markets. If concentration ratios are not defined for the proper markets, one should not expect to find any correlation between performance and concentration across different markets.

To remedy these two problems, some studies focus on a single industry over time or across different locations. One can, for example, examine how performance in the industry changes over time because of changes in government regulation of entry. Two industry studies are reviewed here.

Airlines. The airline industry would appear to have low costs of entry between city pairs for airlines already in operation. All that is needed is to fly a plane from wherever it is to the new origin and destination pair. That is, the airline industry appears to be a contestable market. Despite the apparent ease of entry, however, studies of the airline industry consistently show that concentration in a city-pair market does influence fares.[18] Actual entry, not potential entry, is critically important in influencing airline fares.

Call and Keeler (1985), Bailey, Graham, and Kaplan (1985), and Graham, Kaplan, and Sibley (1983) found that fares are higher where concentration is high. They typically concluded that fares rise by roughly 6 percent if the four-firm concentration ratio doubles from 50 to 100 percent between two cities (Bailey, Graham, Kaplan 1985,

---

[17]The industrial organization of Japan is discussed in Caves and Uekasa (1976) and Miwa (1996).

[18]One interpretation of this result is that it is not so easy to construct an optimal airline network that flies passengers from "spoke" cities to "hub" cities where they can interconnect other hubs or spokes. Only in very dense markets with heavy end-to-end travel between city pairs (for example, Chicago–New York) with no interconnecting passengers (and hence no need for feeder traffic) are markets likely to be contestable. Carlton and Klamer (1983) discuss the economics of such networks. The limited numbers of gates, landing slots, and take-off slots at congested airports also limit the ease of entry.

165). Again, there is a statistically significant effect of concentration on performance, but it is of modest magnitude. Borenstein (1989) presented evidence that concentration at an airport (rather than on a particular route between two cities) can also lead to modest increases in fares.[19] Bamberger and Carlton (2003) find that route and airport concentration influence fares, but that this effect is much smaller when one accounts for connecting passengers. (Moreover, they find that the creation of hubs leads to output expansion, a clear benefit to consumers.) Weiher, Sickles, and Perloff (2002) show that the markup of airline fares over marginal cost depends primarily on whether one or two firms dominate a route.

Railroads. In contrast to the apparent ease of entry by airlines, it is now so costly to build a railroad that no one is likely to enter with a new large rail system. Therefore, the number of competitors can be taken as a completely exogenous variable if one focuses on commodities that are shipped only by rail and for which truck (or other) transportation is uneconomical. Studies have estimated the relationship between railroad rates as a function of distance, tons shipped, and concentration after the railroads were deregulated under the Staggers Act of 1980 and were given greater freedom to set fares.

MacDonald (1987) estimated that a railroad facing no competition can charge rates for transporting wheat that are 18 percent higher than when there is a competing railroad. When three railroads compete, rates fall by another 2 percent. These results are statistically significant, yet they indicate that rates do not go up all that much even for dramatic increases in concentration.[20]

Measurement and Statistical Problems. In summary, there is at best weak evidence of a link between concentration and various proxies for barriers to entry and measures of market performance. Are the theories concerning the relationship between performance and structure wrong, or are these studies flawed?

Although many SCP studies are well done, others are seriously flawed. Many of the negative findings in these studies may be due to two important problems. First, these studies commonly suffer from substantial measurement problems or related statistical problems. Second, and more important, most of these studies are conceptually flawed. Most suffer from a variety of measurement errors and other statistical problems that are difficult to correct. Many of these problems were discussed above. We analyze three additional ones here.

First, concentration measures and performance measures are frequently biased due to improper aggregation across products. Because most firms sell more than one product, any estimate of profits or price-cost margins for a firm reflects averages across dif-

---

[19]See also Hurdle et al. (1989), Borenstein (1992), Brueckner, Dyer, and Spiller (1992), and Evans and Kessides (1993).

[20]Although 20 percent is not small, it is less than one might expect as the difference between monopoly and competition among these firms. A 20 percent price overcharge is about what a monopolist would charge if it faced a demand elasticity of −6. The demand elasticity for rail transport of grain is believed to be considerably less elastic than −6.

ferent products. For a firm that makes products in many different industries, aggregate statistics can be misleading. For example, the Census assigns firms to industry categories based on the primary products produced and includes their total value of production under that industry category. The Census also tabulates statistics at the product level, based on data from individual plants. Because a plant is less likely than a firm to produce several products, product-level data are preferable because such data are less likely to have an aggregation bias than industry-level data.

Second, as discussed in the sections on measuring performance and structure, the performance and structural variables tend to suffer from other measurement errors. Some researchers include variables in addition to concentration to control for such measurement problems in an attempt to reduce these biases. For example, because most price-cost margins ignore capital and advertising, some economists include those two variables in their regressions of price-cost margins on concentration. The inclusion of these additional *explanatory variables* (those used to explain the measure of performance) may not eliminate the bias if they are measured with error or determined by industry profitability. For example, researchers frequently mismeasure advertising, and advertising may be more heavily used in highly profitable industries. The proper interpretation of the coefficients of variables such as advertising is that they reflect, in part, measurement error in the performance measure and not fundamental economic forces influencing "true" price-cost margins (based on marginal costs).

Third, many studies inappropriately estimate linear relations between a measure of performance and concentration. For example, if an increase in the concentration ratio has a smaller effect on performance above a certain level of concentration, the relationship between performance and concentration will flatten and resemble an S-shaped curve. This S-shaped curve can be approximated reasonably by a straight line only if the observed levels of concentration lie in the relatively straight portion of the curve. If concentration ratios vary from very low levels to very high levels, an estimate based on a presumed linear relationship may lead to incorrect results.

White (1976) and Bradburd and Over (1982) searched for critical levels of concentration below which price is less likely to increase as concentration increases, and threshold levels of concentration above which price is more likely to increase as concentration increases. They were only partially successful in finding such a level: There appears to be some evidence of an increase in price at four-firm concentration ratios above roughly 50–60 percent.[21]

Conceptual Problems. Many SCP studies have such serious conceptual problems that it is difficult to use them to test our second key question about the relationship between performance and structure. The two most common conceptual problems concern whether long-run performance measures are used and whether the structural variables are exogenous.

---

[21]Bradburd and Over (1982) present evidence that the effect of concentration on an industry's performance depends on levels of past concentration. As a highly concentrated industry becomes less concentrated, price remains higher than it would if the industry had never been highly concentrated.

The theories summarized in Table 8.1 predict how long-run profits vary with market structure. They say nothing about the relationship of short-run profits and market structure. Thus, an SCP study based on short-run performance measures is not a proper test of the theories.

The length of time it takes to reach the long run differs by industry. At any moment, some industries are highly profitable while others are not. Over time, some firms exit from the low-profit industries and enter the high-profit industries, which drives rates of return toward a common level. Stigler (1963), Connolly and Schwartz (1985), and Mueller (1985) find that high profits often decline slowly in highly concentrated industries. Only by analyzing both the level of profits (or other measures of performance) and the rate at which they change can the analyst distinguish between a long-run barrier to entry and the speed with which entry occurs (see Chapter 3). Most analyses do not make this distinction. This issue may be regarded as a problem in accurately measuring performance.[22]

The more serious conceptual problem with many SCP studies is that the structural variables are not exogenous. Many researchers, after finding a link between high profits (or excessive rates of return, or large price-cost margins) and high concentration ratios, infer improperly that high concentration rates are bad because they "cause" high profits. Profit and concentration, however, influence each other. An alternative interpretation of a link between profits and concentration is that the largest firms are the most efficient or innovative (Demsetz 1973, Peltzman 1977). Only when a firm is efficient or innovative is it profitable to expand in a market and make the market concentrated. In this interpretation, a successful firm attracts consumers, either through lower prices or better products. A firm's success, as measured by both its profits and its market share, is an indicator of consumer satisfaction, not of poor industry performance. One implication of this hypothesis is that a firm's success is explained by its own market share and not just by industry concentration, as found by Kwoka and Ravenscraft (1985).

If concentration is not an exogenous measure, then an estimate of the relationship between profits and concentration, which assumes that concentration affects profits and not vice versa, leads to what is referred to as a simultaneity bias. Weiss (1974), however, estimated the relationship between performance measures and concentration using statistical techniques designed to eliminate the simultaneity bias problem and found that the different estimation procedures make little difference in the estimated relationship.

Although the regression results may not change, their interpretation does. Even a correctly estimated relationship between performance and concentration is uninformative regarding causation. Concentration does not cause high profits; long-run barriers to entry do. These barriers lead to both high profits and high concentration.[23]

[22]The various measurement problems with performance may not be as serious as they first appear. Schmalensee (1989) used 12 different accounting measures of profitability in a SCP study. Strikingly, although these 12 measures are not highly correlated, many of his key SCP results held over all measures.

[23]Research on SCP continues. Noteworthy work includes Marvel (1978), Lamm (1981), Cotterill (1986), Schmalensee (1987, 1989), Cubbin and Geroski (1987), and especially Sutton (1991, 1998).

Modern Structure-Conduct-Performance Analysis

The original structure-conduct-performance literature sought to establish a systematic relationship between price and concentration. As we have noted, the criticisms of this approach are many, but perhaps the most significant criticism is that concentration itself is determined by the economic conditions of the industry and hence is not an industry characteristic that can be used to explain pricing or other conduct. The barrage of criticism has caused most research in this area to cease. But Sutton and his coauthors have developed an approach that builds on the structure-conduct-performance idea of looking for systematic patterns of competitive behavior across industries, and that at the same time addresses the endogenous determination of entry (Sutton 1991, 1998).

Sutton's research examines what happens to competition as market size grows. Does the market become less concentrated? Do other dimensions of the product—such as quality, promotional activity, and research and development—change? What are the fundamental economic forces that provide the bases for systematic answers to these questions across different industries? In answering these questions, Sutton analyzes markets in which the product is either homogeneous or heterogeneous and considers the cost of entering the market or altering certain attributes of products.

Theory

We divide our discussion of Sutton's theory into two cases depending on whether a firm's cost of entry is an exogenous sunk cost or an endogenous sunk cost. In the former case, each firm must spend some fixed amount, F, to enter the industry. In the latter case, the amount a firm must spend to enter the industry is variable and is chosen by the firm in an effort to affect the desirability of its product by influencing certain dimensions of the product.

Exogenous Sunk Cost. To illustrate his theory, Sutton examines markets with homogeneous and heterogeneous products. We start by considering a market in which the firms produce a homogeneous product and the only variable firms can compete on is price, not quality. Each firm incurs a fixed cost F and has a constant marginal cost m. At low prices, the industry demand curve is $Q = s/p$, where Q is industry quantity, s is a measure of market size (total expenditure, which is assumed to be determined independently of price), and p is price. That is, for low prices and given s, the market elasticity of demand is -1. At some high price p_m, the demand curve is perfectly elastic. Thus, a monopoly would charge a price of p_m in this market (see Chapter 4).

The final equilibrium and the change in equilibrium as the market size grows are determined by the form that competition takes. To fix ideas, Sutton considered three types of competition, each "tougher" than the next. The level of competition is lowest in a cartel in which all firms explicitly collude to set the monopoly price p_m and divide up the total cartel profit or monopoly profit among the n firms. Regardless of the number of firms, n, the price remains at p_m. Thus, profit per firm declines as n grows because the total monopoly profit is divided among more and more firms. At the equilibrium n, the total cartel profit is driven to zero.[24]

A more competitive market is a Cournot oligopoly. For any number of firms, n, the equilibrium Cournot price is $p(n) = m[1 + 1/(n - 1)]$.[25] Thus, the Cournot price p falls to m as n increases. The output per firm, q, equals $(s/m)[(n - 1)/n^2]$, while profit per firm is $[p - m]q - F$, which equals $s/n^2 - F$. Hence with free entry, n equals $\sqrt{s/F}$, at which point profit per firm is zero.

Finally, consider the toughest form of competition, Bertrand, where price equals m for any given $n > 1$. Here, the only free-entry equilibrium has one firm with positive profit. If a second firm enters, price is driven to marginal cost, so that profit is negative (because of the fixed cost), which leads to one firm's demise.

For each model of competition, Figure 8.1 shows how price changes as n increases. As the figure illustrates, for any given $n > 1$, price is lower as competition becomes "tougher," with Bertrand being the toughest and cartel being the least tough model of competition.

Figure 8.2 relates a measure of equilibrium industry concentration, $1/n$, to market size s for each model of competition, where by equilibrium market concentration, we mean that n such that total profit equals zero (or more accurately, if one additional firm enters, it will earn a negative profit).

Figure 8.2 reveals two interesting results. First, as expected, concentration falls as market size increases for all but the most competitive game (Bertrand). The intuition for this result is that larger markets can accommodate more firms.

The second result is counterintuitive: For any given market size, equilibrium market concentration is *higher*, the tougher the competition. Concentration is lowest for the cartel model, even though the cartel model has the highest price. The reason for this result is that tough competition leads to a low price, which discourages entry. This result illustrates that relying on concentration alone to make inferences about price and competitiveness can lead to erroneous conclusions.

The case of exogenous fixed costs with heterogeneous products has much less crisp results than the case of exogenous fixed costs with a homogenous product. In a model with heterogeneous products (such as the models in Chapter 7), the concentration in the market depends on the nature of the game, such as how many different products one firm may produce and whether a firm has an advantage if it can choose its products before other firms choose.

---

[24] Let the cartel profit be $\pi = [p - m]\, Q - nF$. The price that maximizes cartel profit is the same price that maximizes $[p - m]\, Q$. Define π_m as the maximum of $[p - m]\, Q$ (that is, it is the profit, ignoring fixed costs). Then, each firm's individual profit is $\pi_m/n - F$. In equilibrium where $\pi = 0$, the equilibrium n equals π_m/F.

[25] Each firm selects its output q_i to maximize its profit, which can be written as $p_i(\Sigma q_j)q_i - mq_i - F$, where $p_i(\Sigma q_j)$ is the inverse demand curve. Differentiating this expression with respect to q_i yields the first-order condition for each firm's optimal output level given its rival's output levels. Setting $q_i = q$ for all i yields the symmetric Cournot equilibrium (assuming that the resulting price is less than p_m). See Problem 6 at the end of the chapter.

FIGURE 8.1 Relationship Between Prices and Number of Firms Under Three Market Structures

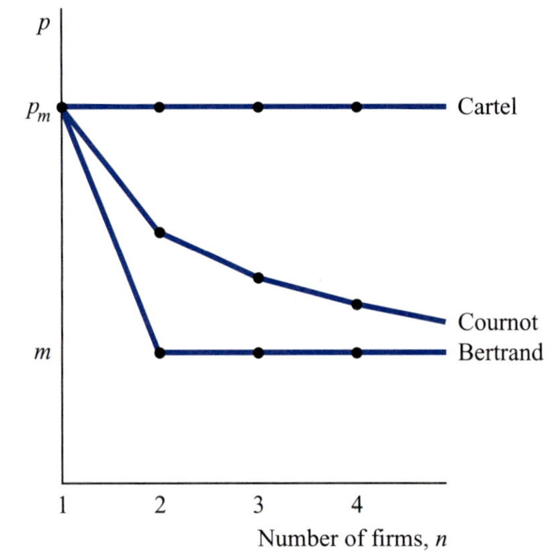

Sutton's main result for heterogeneous products is that the "toughness" of competition is, in general, diminished when one moves from a homogeneous to a heterogeneous product and so (analogous to the result that occurs in the case of a homogeneous product as competition weakens) the equilibrium concentration tends to fall

FIGURE 8.2 Relationship Between Concentration and Market Size Under Three Market Structures

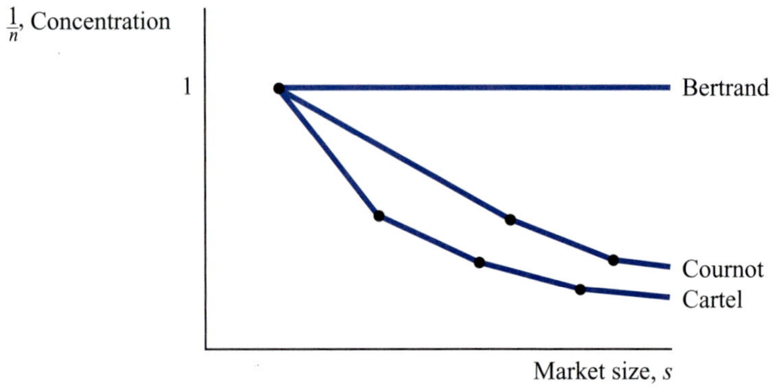

for any given market size s. However, unlike the case of a homogeneous product, there are many possible equilibrium outcomes for any given market size, s, and the best that an economist can derive is a *lower bound* on concentration for any given s. When this lower bound is low, there are very few empirical predictions one can make about equilibrium concentration because any equilibrium concentration is possible as long as it exceeds the lower bound.

The property that equilibrium concentration (or its lower bound) decreases with market size s depends on the assumption that fixed costs are exogenous and that product quality is given. Given this property, all else equal, concentration should be lower in big countries than in small countries, when market size is determined by the size of country.

Although this result holds for many industries, there are some industries that are highly concentrated in both large and small countries (Pryor 1972). How can this fact be explained? In examining this question, Sutton and his coauthors have substantially increased our understanding of the competitive process. We now turn to their findings.

Endogenous Sunk Costs. In most markets, firms compete not just on price but also along many other product dimensions, such as quality, reliability, research and development, and promotional activity. To fix ideas, let W be an index of quality, which we will broadly interpret to include information about the product. The key new assumption is that a firm may spend money to improve its product's W. For example, firms increase their expenditures on advertising, research and development, and engineering to increase W by raising the quality of the product or by heightening consumers' perception of its quality. Firms can compete for customers by spending money to improve product quality, lowering price, or both. Here we say that the firm has *endogenous* sunk costs because the firm decides how large an investment to make.

Paying to improve quality has two important effects. First, it raises the firm's fixed cost and perhaps its marginal cost of production if a higher-quality good costs more to produce. Second, it attracts customers who were previously buying a lower-quality good. These two effects can combine to completely reverse the results in the previous section, in which an increase in market size is associated with a decrease in equilibrium concentration. As market size s increases, firms have an incentive to compete by improving the quality W of their product. To raise quality, a firm must incur larger sunk costs, a circumstance that reduces the incentive for additional firms to enter the industry that otherwise arises from the larger s. As a result, as market size increases, concentration no longer necessarily falls. A given industry in different-size markets can remain highly concentrated, but bigger markets will have higher-quality products.

For this reasoning to hold, several assumptions need to hold. Consumers must value improvements in quality sufficiently so that they switch from lower-quality products to higher-quality goods. To establish the condition under which this assumption is so, Sutton uses a model of *vertical differentiation*. In this model, every consumer agrees on a ranking of products by quality, W, with all consumers preferring a higher-quality product to a lower-quality product.

Suppose that a consumer's surplus from a good of quality W equals $U = \theta W - p(W)$, where θ is a parameter reflecting the weight that consumers place on quality and $p(W)$ is the price of a product with quality W. Because consumers differ in θ, even though all consumers prefer more W to less, some consumers place such a low value on extra W that they are willing to pay very little extra money for a high W product, while other consumers so enjoy extra quality that they will buy a higher-quality good even if the price is relatively high. The optimal W for any consumer will depend on the price function $p(W)$, which reveals how prices rise as W rises and on the consumer preference, θ, for quality.

Sutton proves that as long as $p(W)$ and the marginal cost of producing a high-quality product do not rise "too fast" as W increases, then the equilibrium has three striking properties. First, the firms that produce the highest quality available in the market are the largest firms.

Second, an increase in market size leads to an increase in the quality of the best products in the market, with higher-quality products being chosen by consumers at higher prices and some lower-quality products disappearing from the market. Thus, the equilibrium quality rises as the market expands. Third, with higher quality and its attendant costs, fewer firms can afford to remain in the industry and concentration will remain high. Consequently, the property that a market remains concentrated as s increases continues to hold even where there is both horizontal and vertical differentiation as long as there is sufficient substitution between the vertical dimension (quality W) and the horizontal dimension over which consumers can have different preferences.

For both the endogenous and the exogenous sunk cost cases, the key empirical predictions about concentration and market size depend on the validity of certain assumptions. The most important assumption is that the form of the game—Bertrand, Cournot, or cartel—remains unchanged as market size increases. In a given market, this assumption may or may not be plausible. Moreover, neither Sutton nor anyone else has made significant progress in defining the industry economic characteristics that predict the form of the game that describes the competitive process. Therefore, analogous to the criticism of the earlier literature that concentration need not be exogenous, here we have the criticism that the form of the competitive game need not be exogenous.

Empirical Research

Sutton has produced two voluminous books of studies using data from six countries—France, Germany, Italy, Japan, the United Kingdom, and the United States—to test his theories, especially those concerning the endogeneity of advertising and technology. Sutton's empirical work helps explain why concentration is similar across different-size countries for some industries but not others. See Example 8.1.

In Sutton (1991), he tests his theoretical predictions about the relationship between concentration and market size for several industries in the food and beverage sector. He separates the industries into two types, one in which there is little advertising and the other in which there is significant advertising. The first industry type corresponds roughly to the use of exogenous sunk cost, while the second corresponds roughly to the case of endogenous sunk cost. For each type of industry, Sutton runs a regression

EXAMPLE 8.1

Supermarkets and Concentration

Ellickson (2000) applies Sutton's theory to the supermarket industry. In contrast to Sutton's focus on sunk costs associated with advertising or technology, Ellickson examines the role of sunk cost at the store level of building a large store and at the firm level of having the expertise and distribution systems to provide a wide variety of brands. Ellickson explains that these costs are important in distinguishing high-quality firms from low-quality stores, where he uses store size, existence of a deli or bakery, and existence of scanners and ATM machines to measure quality.

Ellickson examines the four-firm concentration ratio for supermarkets across 320 different metropolitan statistical areas (MSAs). Regardless of the size of the MSA, four or five firms that typically own multiple stores account for 70 to 80 percent of sales within each MSA. Moreover, concentration at the metropolitan level has remained high both over time and as the markets grew. Ellickson explains these results using Sutton's endogenous sunk cost theory. According to that theory, increases in market size should lead to higher-quality supermarkets but not more firms, which is exactly what Ellickson finds.

Further, consistent with the theory, the largest firm in each MSA provides a higher quality product than do the smaller firms. In addition, the quality of these largest firms differs across MSAs in exactly the way that the theory would predict: The firms in the largest markets have the highest quality.

Ellickson also examines how the industry has changed over time as MSAs have grown. The trend in the supermarket industry has been one of increasing concentration over time. For example, the average four-firm concentration ratio across 154 MSAs has grown from 45 percent in 1954 to 75 percent in 1998. Consistent with the theory, the number of products offered by each store has increased from 14,145 in 1980 to 21,949 in 1994, while average store size has been growing at the rate of 1,000 square feet per year.

of the form $C4 = a + b\ln(s/\sigma)$, where $C4$ is the four-firm concentration ratio and s/σ is the market size divided by the size of an efficient plant.[26] An econometric test of the theory is that b is negative for the first type of industry but zero for the second type. For his sample, Sutton indeed finds this result, which provides impressive empirical support for his theories.

Thus, Sutton's work increases our theoretical and empirical understanding of the relationship between concentration and competition. Still, there are two important caveats to Sutton's results. First, as his detailed analysis of each industry in each country reveals, the assumption that the competitive game is the same across

[26]Sutton actually uses a more complicated method because his theory predicts a lower bound to the relationship between concentration and market size.

countries is not always a particularly good one. There is little research so far explaining why in some countries competition in a particular industry is more intense than in others.[27]

Sutton uses the difference across countries in the competitive game for an industry to his advantage. Sutton identified industries and countries where competition is unusually intense and found, consistent with his theory, that the industry is more concentrated in those countries. He identifies countries with lax attitudes toward cartels and again, consistent with his theory, finds that those industries tend to have lower concentration levels.

The second caveat is that Sutton's theory predicts a lower bound to the relationship between market size and concentration. The reason for the lower bound is that there can be a multiplicity of equilibria, with some having greater concentration levels than the lower bound. The theory therefore is unable to help us much in predicting concentration in a particular country when the lower bound is low.

Although Sutton explains that this theory of lower bounds is the most one can say under general conditions, the analyst is left in the uncomfortable position of having a theoretical structure that may not narrow the possible equilibria very much. Sutton's detailed history of each industry shows that many idiosyncratic factors often are critical in explaining an industry's evolution. Thus his work provides a sobering lesson because it reveals the limits of theory to explain industrial structures.

Modern Approaches to Measuring Performance

An economist's guess is liable to be as good as anybody else's.

—Will Rogers

The SCP studies focus on our second question, concerning the relationship between performance and structure, and pay relatively little attention to the first question—how to measure performance. In contrast, most modern empirical approaches focus on measuring performance or market power. These studies start by rejecting the traditional measures of performance on the grounds that they are significantly flawed due to accounting difficulties. These approaches estimate market power using models based on formal theories of profit-maximizing behavior described in earlier chapters.

Researchers use both static and multiperiod models to estimate market power. Some economists rely directly or indirectly on observations of marginal cost and price; others look at the behavior of output or price to see if it is consistent with the competitive model. The following sections discuss some of these methods.

---

[27]One curious finding is that concentration tends to be slightly higher in the United States than in European countries. One explanation is that the United States has more intense competition, which Sutton's theory suggests should lead to higher levels of concentration.

Static Studies

Most modern studies based on static models can be divided into those that estimate marginal cost directly, those that estimate entire models of a market (thereby obtaining estimates of marginal cost and of the markup), and those that observe the relationship between changes in price and factor costs to test whether an industry is competitive.

Estimate Marginal Cost Using Cost Data. The most direct way to answer our first key question about the degree of market power in an industry is to calculate the price-cost markup directly.[28] Although price data are available for most industries, unfortunately, marginal cost data are generally not.

If information on total cost is available, however, an economist can estimate the relationship between observed total cost and observed total output and then calculate marginal cost. A price-cost margin is then simply calculated. Weiher et al. (2002) estimated marginal cost using total cost information and then calculated Lerner measures of market power directly.

Even total cost data, however, are rarely available. Studies that estimate cost functions frequently examine regulated industries because regulators force the firms to provide cost data. For example, Keeler (1983, 71) and Friedlaender and Spady (1980, Ch. 4) found that price exceeded long-run marginal cost by about 22 percent for rail service for bulk commodities in the Northeast during the late 1960s and early 1970s. Genesave and Mullin (1998) use cost data from a court case and find small markups.

Estimate the Markups Using an Industry Model. If cost data are not available, so that we cannot directly estimate marginal cost, *MC*, how can we calculate the price-cost markup? One method is to use assumptions about the shape of the demand and *MC* curves to infer the markup from observations on how the equilibrium price and quantity change over time.[29] This approach is called the new empirical industrial organization.

For many markets, we have enough information to estimate a demand curve. Figure 8.3 shows the demand curve, D_1, in a particular market. Suppose that we believe that the industry's marginal cost, *MC*, is constant, although we do not know its level. Currently, the market equilibrium, point E^* in Figure 8.3, is at price p^* and quantity Q^*. That equilibrium could be produced by a competitive industry with a relatively high marginal cost, MC_c, or by a monopoly with a relatively low marginal cost, MC_m

[28]Hall and Hitch (1939) conducted a series of interviews with businesspeople regarding their firms' pricing practices. Most claimed that they set price above marginal cost.

[29]See Bresnahan (1989) for a more extensive discussion and Corts (1999) for a critique that explains that these empirical methods depend on the validity of the conjectural variations model that is theoretically an inadequate model. Apparently the first modern study was Rosse (1970). Six other influential early studies are Iwata (1974), Applebaum (1979, 1982), Gollop and Roberts (1979), Just and Chern (1980), and Bresnahan (1981). The other major early conceptual work was Rohlfs (1974); however, it did not contain an empirical application.

FIGURE 8.3 Identifying Market Power

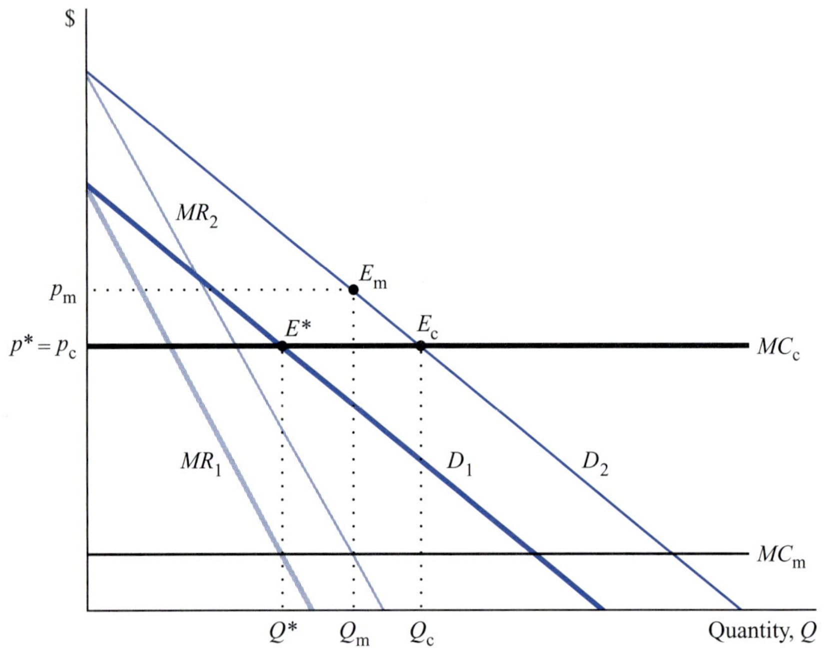

(which intersects the monopoly's marginal revenue curve, MR_1, at Q^*). With only this information, we cannot *identify* (determine) the marginal cost and price-cost markup.

However, if in the next period the demand curve shifts to D_2, which is to the right and parallel to D_1 in Figure 8.3, we can determine whether the industry is competitive or monopolistic. If the industry is competitive, the new equilibrium is at point E_c, so the price remains constant, $p_c = p^*$, and output increases substantially to Q_c. That is, by noting that the shift in demand does not change the price, we know that the industry marginal cost is MC_c and that Lerner's price-cost margin, $(p - MC_c)/p$, is 0.

If, instead, the shift in demand leads to a new equilibrium at point E_m, the price increases from p^* to p_m and the quantity increases only to Q_m. This increase in price is consistent with noncompetitive behavior. Thus, if we know *MC* is constant, an outward shift of the demand curve reveals whether the market is purely competitive. If the price does not change, the market is competitive; if the price increases, there is market power.

Economists use generalizations of this approach to estimate the degree of market power, Lerner's price-cost margin, and the marginal cost curve. Typically, they make specific assumptions about the shapes of the demand and marginal cost curves, which allow them to identify the price-cost margin by observing shifts in equilibrium price and quan-

TABLE 8.7 **Estimated Price-Cost Margins**

Study	Industry	$(p - MC)/p$
Bresnahan (1981)	Autos	.10–.34
Appelbaum (1982)	Rubber	.05
	Electrical machinery	.20
	Tobacco	.65
Porter (1983a)	Railroads (with cartel)	.40
Lopez (1984)	Food processing	.50
Roberts (1984)	Coffee roasting (largest firm)	.06
Spiller and Favaro (1984)	Large banks before deregulation	.88
	Large banks after deregulation	.40
Suslow (1986)	Aluminum	.59
Slade (1987b)	Retail gasoline	.10
Karp and Perloff (1989a)	Rice exports (largest estimate)	.11
Karp and Perloff (1989b)	Small black-and-white TVs in Japan	.58
Buschena and Perloff (1991)	Philippines coconut oil (post-1974)	.89
Wann and Sexton (1992)	Fruit cocktail	1.41
Deodhar and Sheldon (1995)	German bananas	.26
Genesove and Mullin (1998)	Sugar refining 1880–1914	.05
Hyde and Perloff (1998)	Australian retail meats	≈ 0

Sources: Articles cited and Bresnahan (1989, Table 1)

tity over time. One method is described in Appendix 8B.[30] Table 8.7 reports the estimated price-cost margins for several industries using these approaches. See Example 8.2.

Indirect Approaches. Some economists use the changes in price associated with changes in costs to test whether an industry is competitive without having to make detailed assumptions about the shapes of both the demand and the supply curves. If marginal cost shifts up by a certain amount in a constant-marginal cost market, the competitive price rises by the same amount because price equals marginal cost. For ex-

[30]Bresnahan (1989) surveys many of these studies, including Iwata (1974), Gollop and Roberts (1979), Spiller and Favaro (1984), Roberts (1984), and Applebaum (1979, 1982). Analogous techniques can be used to estimate monopsony power as well (Just and Chern 1980, Azzam and Pagoulatos 1990). Separate price-cost margins can also be estimated for individual firms, as shown in Spiller and Favaro (1984), Baker and Bresnahan (1985, 1988), Slade (1986, 1987a, 1987b, 1992), Gelfand and Spiller (1987), and Karp and Perloff (1989b). Any shock that shifts the relevant demand curve or marginal cost curve can be used to identify market power. For example, changes in taxes (Kolstad and Wolak 1983, 1985, 1986; Wolak and Kolstad 1988) or changes in the supply of a fringe (Buschena and Perloff 1991) help identify market power. Some of the more interesting applications (Bresnahan 1981, 1987) estimate market power based on spatial competition models (Chapter 7), taking explicit account of product differentiation.

EXAMPLE 8.2

How Sweet It Is

If we have data on marginal cost, MC, and market price, p, we can calculate the Lerner Index (Chapter 4) of market power, $(p - MC)/p$, directly. Unfortunately, such cost data are usually not available.

As a result, most new empirical industrial organization studies of market power identify the Lerner Index by using assumptions about the shape of the demand and marginal cost curves. Consequently, these estimates of market power are only as reliable as the (untested) assumptions about the shapes of the curves. Typically, these studies estimate the degree of market power using a parameter λ so that the Lerner Index is (Appendix 8B)

$$(p - MC)/p = -\lambda/\epsilon,$$

where ϵ is the estimated market demand elasticity. If the market is competitive, $\lambda = 0$ and there is no gap between price and marginal cost. If the market is monopolized, $\lambda = 1$. If λ is between zero and one, the degree of market power is between that of a competitive and monopolized market.

Genesove and Mullin (1998) have data on cost for the sugar refining industry. Consequently, they are able to see how well the estimation approach works compared to directly calculating market power using cost data.

The sugar refining industry became a highly concentrated industry as the result of acquisitions by the American Sugar Refining Company in the late 1800s. The largest firm accounted for over 60 percent of sales. Detailed cost data for this industry for 1880–1914 are available as a result of antitrust litigation. Genesove and Mullin use these data to calculate marginal cost directly, which they then use to calculate the Lerner Index. According to these calculations, a typical value of the Lerner Index during the 1880–1914 period is .05 (nearly perfectly competitive), while a typical value for λ is .1.

Next, Genesove and Mullin ignore their detailed cost data and use a technique similar to that described in Appendix 8B to estimate the demand curve, the marginal cost curve, and λ. Using this method, they estimate that $\lambda = .04$ and that the implied Lerner Index is .02. Although their econometric approach leads to a lower estimate of λ than does their cost method, the econometric method succeeds in correctly telling the researchers that, despite the high industry concentration, a monopoly ($\lambda = 1$) model is less consistent with the data than is a competitive ($\lambda = 0$) model.

ample, in a competitive market, a per-unit tax of \$1 raises price by \$1. By observing the relationship between the change in price and the change in costs (or some element of costs), one can test whether the industry is competitive.

Sumner (1981) examined the effect of tax differences across states on the price of cigarettes. He argued that if the retail prices of cigarettes differ between states by the amount of the tax differences, the market is relatively competitive. Bulow and Pfleiderer (1983) pointed out that it is possible to construct demand curves for which a monopoly does pass on costs on a one-for-one basis. Sullivan (1985) used a different method to avoid this criticism and confirms Sumner's finding of a significant degree of competition in cigarettes. Similarly, Ashenfelter and Sullivan (1987) used changes in excise taxes to identify market structure.

Hall (1988a) demonstrated another method of determining market power without making specific assumptions about the demand curve. He showed that, with constant returns to scale, shifts in costs are sufficient to identify market power.[31] When such an industry expands output in response to a shift in demand, the total value of its output (revenues) increases by exactly the increase in its total cost if the industry is competitive. If value rises by more than the additional cost, then price is above marginal cost and the industry is not competitive.[32]

Hall estimates very large markups, but subsequent work by Domowitz et al. (1988) and Roeger (1995) find much lower markups.[33] Roeger (1995) obtains markups ranging from 5 to 23 percent.

Multiperiod Studies

Almost all real-world markets last for many periods. A multiperiod model should be used to estimate market power if firms, in setting strategies, take previous behavior into account; if adjustment costs are significant, so that costs in this period depend on decisions in previous periods; or if demand today depends on past consumption. Economists use at least two types of multiperiod models to estimate market power: models of collusive behavior and models of behavior with costs of adjustment.

Collusion and Repeated Static Games. Stigler (1964a) argued that the opportunity and desire by oligopolistic firms to collude (at least tacitly) provides a basis for explaining all oligopoly behavior (Chapter 5). In this theory, prices below the monopoly

[31] Rosse and Panzar (1977), Panzar and Rosse (1987), and Shaffer (1982) showed how to test whether a market is competitive, oligopolistic, or monopolistic using information on shifts in revenue in response to shifts in factor prices. To estimate the actual degree of market power, however, one must have additional information or make some strong assumptions such as Hall's constant returns to scale assumption.

[32] Suppose that the industry has a demand curve with a constant elasticity of ϵ and a constant marginal cost. A monopoly sets price equal to $1/(1 + 1/\epsilon)$ times the constant marginal cost (as can be shown by rearranging Equation 8.2). If ϵ is -2, then the price is twice the marginal cost. If, holding ϵ constant, demand shifts out so that one more unit is sold, revenues rise by p, but total cost increases by MC, which is only half of p.

[33] Domowitz et al. (1988) do not find that concentration plays an important and statistically significant role in explaining the deviation between price and marginal cost. However, Shapiro (1987), using a variant of Hall's method, does find a strong relation between margins and concentration.

level are due to failures to enforce the cartel fully. In this story, market structure matters. For example, the more firms in an industry, the harder it is to detect cheating by any one firm, so more cheating occurs, and the average price is lower.

Game theorists model Stigler's insight as a supergame over repeated static games. In one version, random fluctuations in price due to fluctuations in demand or supply costs could make "cheating" by cartel members hard to detect because the price fluctuations could be due to either cheating or shifts in economic conditions. To prevent firms from cheating, all cartel members agree that if the market price drops below a certain level—a "trigger price"—each firm will expand its output to the precartel level for a certain period of time and prices will fall as a result. If firms expect other firms to stick to this agreement, a firm that cut its price might gain in the extremely short run, but would lose in the end because of the destruction of the cartel by this predetermined punishment mechanism (Chapter 5).

Porter (1983a), Lee and Porter (1984), and Ellison (1994) used this theory to estimate a model of 1880s railroad cartel behavior. Comparing high and low price periods, Porter finds that the cartel increased its rate by over 60 percent during periods of successful collusion. See Example 5.6.

Dynamic Models with Adjustment Costs. If firms have substantial adjustment costs from training new workers, from storage of inputs or outputs (inventories), or in accumulating capital, they must plan their actions over many periods if they are to maximize long-run profits. For example, if the firm must pay compensation to laid-off workers (an adjustment cost), the firm hires fewer workers in period t if it believes demand will be lower in period $t + 1$. Similarly, firms' costs may fall over time if there is **learning by doing** (costs fall with production because workers become more skilled at their jobs due to experience or as better ways of producing are discovered); actions by a firm in this period affect its costs and profits in later periods.[34]

Pindyck (1985) showed that, in a dynamic setting, a mechanical application of the Lerner Index for each period can be misleading. In the intertemporal case, neither the short-run demand elasticity nor the Lerner Index provides a meaningful measure of monopoly power. One solution is to discuss the steady-state price-cost margin (the margin that eventually would be reached and that would persist if there were no further cost or demand shocks) or to compare the path of price or quantity with respect to the path under the price-taking assumption.

The game-theoretic literature abounds with dynamic models of oligopoly that are too general to be usable in estimation. To estimate these models practically, further restrictions have to be imposed. Roberts and Samuelson (1988) use a dynamic oligopoly model with reasonably general functional forms to reject the hypothesis that the ciga-

---

[34]Analogous to dynamic models with adjustment costs are those where demand today depends on quantities in previous periods. Some marketing studies attempt to estimate demand curves with this property, as do studies of durable goods such as aluminum (Suslow 1986b). Similarly, in pumping oil, the costs today depend on how much was pumped in the past and price is expected to rise at the rate of interest (according to the Hotelling formula), so empirical studies of oil reflect these dynamic issues as well (Matutes 1985).

rette market is competitive. With their general functional form, however, they cannot estimate the degree of market power. Karp and Perloff (1989a, 1993a) used a dynamic oligopoly model with a linear demand curve and quadratic costs of adjustment to estimate steady-state price-cost margins for the international coffee and the international rice export markets. For recent work on dynamic oligopoly, see the references cited in Chapter 6, especially Ericson and Pakes (1995, 1998), Fershtman and Pakes (2000), and McGuire and Pakes (1994).

Value of Modern Approaches to Measuring Performance

The modern approaches have three major advantages over the SCP approach. First, they estimate the market performance rather than use an accounting proxy. Second, they use changes in exogenous variables (wages, taxes, demand growth) to explain variations in performance rather than endogenous variables such as concentration ratios and advertising. Third, they are based on maximizing models for individual industries so that hypotheses about behavior can be tested. Their key disadvantage is that many of these models require making detailed assumptions about the shapes of the supply and demand curves and about oligopoly behavior. Moreover, none of the modern approaches that we have discussed focuses on the use of cross-sectional variation across industries to make any predictions as to what factors cause competition to differ across industries. It was the search for such factors that was at the heart of the SCP approach and central to Sutton's approach.

SUMMARY

The empirical relationship between measures of performance, such as price-cost margins, and market structure, such as concentration and entry barriers, is not clear. Serious measurement problems can plague such structure-conduct-performance (SCP) studies. Accounting measures of performance may fail to measure economic profits or costs accurately, especially when long-lived capital assets are present. Concentration ratios for individual industries can be measured accurately, but make sense only when the individual industries constitute a relevant economic market. Finally, the measurement of barriers to entry is often subjective and typically fails to distinguish between long-run barriers to entry and the speed with which entry can occur.

Studies relating measures of industry performance to concentration and barriers to entry across industries suffer from several conceptual problems. A statistically significant relationship between concentration and performance would not necessarily imply that concentration caused price to be above the competitive level. An alternative explanation is that firms become large (concentration rises) because they are efficient. If so, within an industry, profits of the largest firms are higher than those of the smallest. The empirical results indicate either no effect or a small positive effect of concentration and barriers to entry on performance, but this effect is often statistically insignificant. Sutton and his collaborators have produced research that addresses many of the criticisms of the SCP approach and simultaneously uses industry information to make predictions about industry concentration.

Studies of individual industries can avoid many, though not necessarily all, of the conceptual problems of older SCP cross-sectional studies. Such studies tend to find a small but statistically significant effect of concentration on industry measures of performance, such as price.

Modern studies statistically estimate the price-cost margin for a particular industry rather than rely on accounting proxies. These studies have their own disadvantages: Researchers typically have to make detailed assumptions about demand, cost functions, or oligopoly behavior. Many of these industry studies find substantial margins. These methods have not yet been used to explore in detail the relationship of industry structure to the degree of deviation from perfectly competitive behavior.

PROBLEMS

1. Why do empirical researchers often include the advertising-sales and the capital-sales ratios in equations explaining performance?
2. An industry has a price of p^* and earns a rate of return r^* on its capital. The industry is characterized by a fixed-proportions production technology (a fixed proportion of labor and capital is required to make each unit of output—no substitution between labor and capital is possible). Let p and r be the price and rate of return, respectively, that would emerge if the industry were competitive. What is the relationship between $p^* - p$, $r^* - r$, and the capital-output ratio?
3. Concentration ratios are typically a firm's share of *domestic* production. If the United States engages in more international trade, will such concentration measures lose meaning? Could this effect explain the vanishing of the price-concentration effect over time?
4. (*Difficult*) Evaluate the following argument: "There exist demand curves for which a monopoly would pass along cost increases in price on a one-for-one basis. Therefore, nothing can be inferred about the competitiveness of an industry by comparing price changes to cost changes." In your evaluation, see if you can derive a demand curve with the stated properties (Bulow and Pfleiderer 1983).
5. Distinguish between zero profits and a price-cost margin that equals zero.
6. Suppose that the demand function is $Q = s/p$, where Q is the total quantity demanded, s is a measure of the size of the market, and p is the price of the homogeneous good. Let F be a firm's fixed cost and m be its constant marginal cost. If n firms compete in a Cournot model, calculate the price, p, a typical firm's output, q, and a typical firm's profit, π.

   a. Prove that:

      i. $p = m\left[1 + \frac{1}{n-1}\right]$,

      ii. $q = \frac{s}{m}\frac{n-1}{n^2}$, and

      iii. $\pi = s/n^2 - F$.

   b. If entry is free, what does n equal?

   c. What happens to equilibrium concentration, $1/n$, as s increases?

   d. What happens to equilibrium firm size as s increases?

Answers to odd-numbered problems are given at the back of the book.

APPENDIX 8A

Relationship Between the Herfindahl-Hirschman Index (HHI) and the Price-Cost Margin

An oligopoly consists of n identical firms that produce a homogeneous product. Each Firm i chooses its output, q_i to maximize its profits,

$$\pi_i = p(Q)q_i - mq_i,$$

where m is the constant marginal (and average variable) cost for each firm, and p, the price, is a function of total industry output, $Q = nq_i$.

The firms play Cournot (see Chapter 6), so each firm's first-order condition—which is obtained by setting the derivative of profits with respect to q_i equal to zero—is that marginal revenue equals marginal cost:

$$MR = p + q_i p' = m = MC, \tag{8A.1}$$

where p' is the derivative of price with respect to Q. Rearranging the terms in Equation (8A.1), this expression can be expressed in terms of the Lerner Index:

$$L \equiv \frac{p - m}{p} = -\frac{p'Q}{p}\frac{q_i}{Q} = -\frac{s_i}{\epsilon} = -\frac{1}{n\epsilon}, \tag{8A.2}$$

where $s_i \equiv q_i/Q = 1/n$ is the output share of Firm i and $1/\epsilon = (p'Q)/p$ is the reciprocal of the elasticity of demand. Because all firms are identical, Equation (8A.2) holds for every firm in the industry.

As Cowling and Waterson (1976) show, the industry average of firms' price-cost margins using share weights is

$$\sum_i s_i \frac{p - m}{p} = -\frac{\sum_i s_i^2}{\epsilon} \equiv -\frac{HHI}{\epsilon},$$

where HHI is the Herfindahl-Hirschman Index. That is, the HHI divided by the absolute value of the market demand elasticity equals the weighted average of the firms' price-cost margins.

APPENDIX 8B

Identifying Market Power

Under what conditions can the price-cost margin be determined if we cannot observe marginal cost directly? One approach to answering this question involves estimating a complete model of the market where the shapes of the demand and marginal cost curves are specified and profit-maximizing behavior is assumed.[1]

To illustrate this approach, suppose that an industry consists of a number of identical firms that produce a homogeneous product. The demand curve is $p(Q; Z)$, where p is the single price in the market, Q is output, and Z is another variable that affects demand, such as income or the price of a substitute.

Because industry revenues are $R \equiv p(Q; Z)Q$, we define the effective (or perceived) marginal revenue as

$$MR(\lambda) = p + \lambda p_Q Q,$$

where λ is a parameter to be estimated and $p_Q \equiv \partial p/\partial Q$. If the industry is monopolized, $\lambda = 1$ and effective $MR(1)$ is the usual MR measure: $p + p_Q Q$. If the firms in the industry are price takers, $\lambda = 0$ and effective $MR(0)$ equals price. Various other oligopolistic and monopolistically competitive market structures produce a λ that lies strictly between 0 and 1.

The profit-maximization or optimality condition is that effective marginal revenue equals marginal cost: $MR(\lambda) = MC$. As a result, λ is a measure of the gap between price and marginal cost. That is, the Lerner's Index is

$$L \equiv \frac{p - MC}{p} = -\frac{\lambda p_Q Q}{p} = -\frac{\lambda}{\epsilon},$$

where ϵ is the market elasticity of demand. This expression is very similar to those derived in Appendix 8A that depend on the number of firms, the market share, or the Herfindahl-Hirschman Index.

As an example, suppose that the demand curve has the particular linear form

$$p = \alpha_0 + \alpha_1 Q + \alpha_2 Z + \alpha_3 ZQ + \epsilon_1, \tag{8B.1}$$

[1]The following discussion of the role of market demand shocks in identifying market power is based on Just and Chern (1980), Bresnahan (1982), and Lau (1982).

so that the effective marginal revenue is

$$MR(\lambda) = p + \lambda p_Q Q = p + \lambda(\alpha_1 + \alpha_3 Z)Q. \tag{8B.2}$$

A profit-maximizing firm sets its effective marginal revenue equal to its marginal cost. If its marginal cost curve is linear in Q and factor price W,

$$MC = \beta_0 + \beta_1 Q + \beta_2 W + \epsilon_2,$$

its optimality equation, $MR(\lambda) = MC$, can be written as

$$p = \beta_0 + (\beta_1 - \lambda\alpha_1)Q - \lambda\alpha_3 ZQ + \beta_2 W + \epsilon_2. \tag{8B.3}$$

Using the appropriate statistical techniques, one can regress p on a constant, Q, ZQ, and W to obtain estimates of the coefficients in Equation 8B.3. By dividing the estimate of the coefficient on the ZQ term, $-\lambda\alpha_3$, from Equation 8B.3 by the estimate of α_3 from the demand Equation 8B.1, one obtains an estimate of the market structure parameter λ. The reason that one can identify λ is that the demand and MR curves rotate with Z due to the ZQ interaction term, which affects where the MR curve intersects the MC curve. Alternatively, if we know MC, we can use the information about price from the demand curve to determine λ. Rotating the demand curve leaves the level of demand unchanged at the rotation point, but changes the elasticity of demand. As the elasticity of demand changes, the price changes, which allows us to estimate λ.

If there is no ZQ term (that is, if $\alpha_3 = 0$) in the demand curve, λ may not be identified. The only remaining term with a λ in Equation 8B.3 is $(\beta_1 - \lambda\alpha_1)Q$. Although we know α_1 from the demand equation, that is not enough to identify λ because the estimated coefficient also depends on β_1 (the unknown slope of the MC curve).

The need for the demand curve to rotate is illustrated in Figure 8B.1.[2] Initially, the researcher observes the market equilibrium, E_1, price and quantity. The researcher estimates the demand curve D_1 (and, hence, can infer the marginal revenue curve, MR_1) but does not directly observe costs. The observed equilibrium, E_1, is consistent with a competitive industry structure and a marginal cost curve MC_c, where the equilibrium, E_1, is determined by the intersection of MC_c and D_1. It is also consistent with a cartelized market structure and a lower marginal cost curve, MC_m, where the quantity associated with E_1 is determined by the intersection of MC_m and MR_1.

[2] Lau (1982) shows that virtually any functional form for the demand curve leads to identification except the two most commonly used forms: linear or log-linear. If one wants to use a basically linear specification, one must add an interaction term, a squared term in output, or something else that adds some nonlinearity and allows the demand curve to rotate. Even if one does that, there is an additional serious problem with the linear specification: see Perloff and Shen (2001).

FIGURE 8B.1 Not Identified: Parallel Shift of the Demand Curve

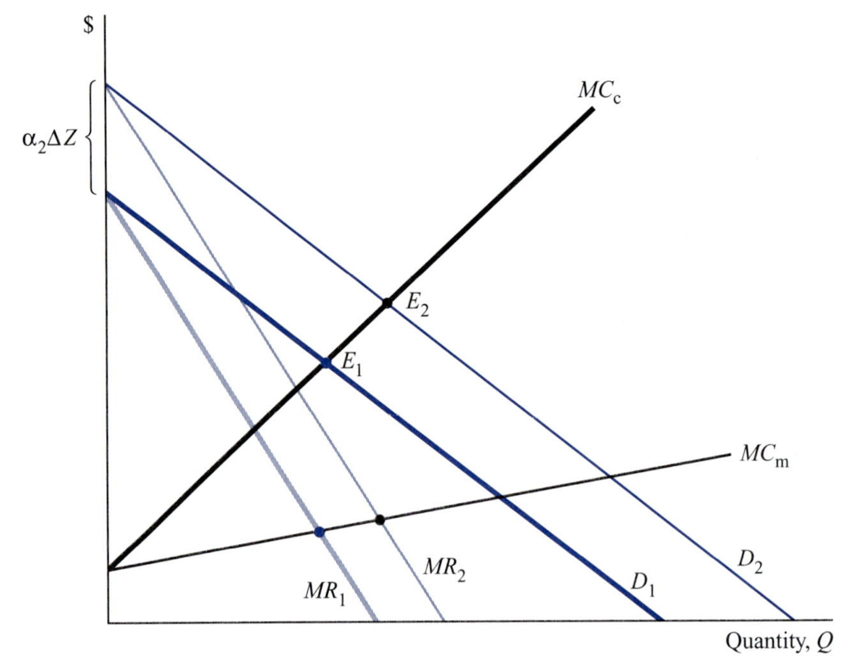

If $\alpha_3 = 0$, and Z increases by ΔZ, the intercept of the demand curve shifts up by $\alpha_2 \Delta Z$, as shown for the new demand curve, D_2. The new equilibrium, E_2, is still consistent with either of the two marginal cost curves. Thus, the researcher cannot determine from this shift in Z if the industry is competitive or cartelized.

In contrast, if $\alpha_3 \neq 0$, a shift in Z reveals λ. In Figure 8B.2, when Z increases, the new demand curve, D_3, rotates (for graphical simplicity, D_3 is rotated around the original equilibrium point). If the industry is competitive and the marginal cost curve is MC_c, the new equilibrium on D_3 remains E_1; whereas, if the industry is cartelized and the marginal cost curve is MC_m, the new equilibrium on D_3 is E_3. Thus, whether or not the equilibrium shifts reveals whether the market is competitive.

Anything (not just variables in the market demand curve) that causes the residual demand curve facing a firm to rotate can identify λ. For example, a dominant firm's residual demand curve is the market demand curve minus the supply of a competitive fringe. If the fringe supply curve rotates, the residual demand curve rotates even if the market demand curve does not. Similarly, a shift in an ad valorem tax rate, t, can identify the market structure.

As the chapter shows, information about the shape of the marginal cost curve also can help identify λ. It is possible to identify λ even if the demand curve does not rotate

FIGURE 8B.2 Identified: Rotation of the Demand Curve

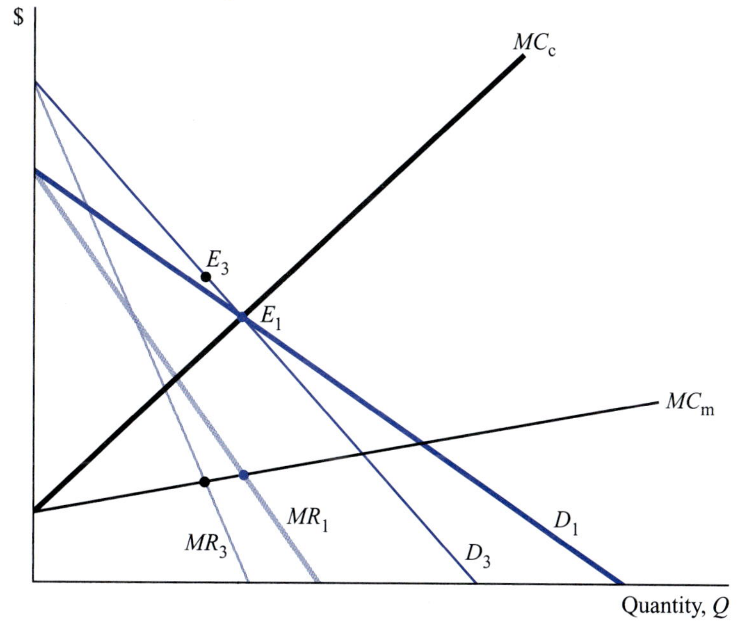

($\alpha_3 = 0$), if the marginal cost curve is constant in Q ($\beta_1 = 0$). Because $MC = \beta_0 + \beta_2 W$, marginal cost is a constant in any given period, but that constant shifts with the exogenous factor W over time causing price to change, which allows one to estimate the demand curve. The coefficient on the Q term in Equation 8B.3 is $\beta_1 - \lambda\alpha_1 = -\lambda\alpha_1$, so by knowing α_1 from the demand curve, one can identify λ.

PART THREE

Business Practices: Strategies and Conduct

CHAPTER 9

Price Discrimination

All . . . men have their price. —*Sir Robert Walpole*

Firms in a perfectly competitive market have no discretion in their pricing policies; they must take the market price as given. Most markets, however, are not perfectly competitive, and firms have some discretion over their pricing policies. In order to maximize profits, these firms may use **nonuniform pricing**: charging customers different prices for the same product or charging a single customer a price that varies depending on how many units the customer buys. When the price paid depends on the amount purchased, the price schedule is **nonlinear**. Price discrimination refers to any nonuniform pricing policy used by a firm with market power to maximize its profits. One common type of nonuniform pricing is **third-degree price discrimination**: A firm charges different customers different unit prices for the identical good. Not all price differences are due to price discrimination. For example, some price differences reflect variations in product characteristics or differential costs in supplying the product to various customers.

This chapter examines three main questions:

1. What are the common types of nonuniform pricing?
2. What are the necessary conditions for price discrimination to occur?
3. What are the welfare effects of price discrimination?

The next chapter analyzes more complicated methods of price discrimination, such as two-part tariffs and tie-in sales.

Nonuniform Pricing

In the models of competition, oligopoly, and monopoly discussed so far, the price per unit is the same for all customers. Many firms, however, set nonuniform prices. Numerous magazines offer student discount subscriptions. Many movie theaters offer discounts to senior citizens. The American Economic Association's membership fees vary with a member's income. Products are often packaged with discount coupons that entitle the bearer to purchase the product for a lower price next time. In effect, these coupons allow a firm to charge first-time users a higher price than repeat users. See Example 9.1.

This chapter deals with some simple types of price discrimination while Chapter 10 examines more complicated ones, such as:

1. **Two-Part Tariff:** A firm charges a consumer a fee (the first part of the tariff) for the right to buy as many units of the product as the consumer wants at a specified price (the second part of the tariff). For example, a health club may charge members an annual fee to join the club and additional fees for using particular facilities. Similarly, some amusement parks charge visitors an admission fee and additional fees for each ride.
2. **Quantity Discount:** A firm's price varies with the number of units of the good that a customer buys. Price discounts for large purchases are quite common. Electricity bills are frequently computed according to a *declining-block* schedule, in which the first units of usage incur one charge, and subsequent units incur lower charges.
3. **Tie-in Sale:** A customer can buy one product only if another product is also purchased. A common example of a tie-in sale is the purchase of a durable machine under the condition that the consumer also purchase from the seller all repair services or all repair parts. Firms may sell copy machines under the condition that customers also purchase related supplies (for example, developing chemicals) from the seller. Cameras could be sold under the condition that purchasers buy their film from the seller. Sometimes buyers have no choice and must buy film from the seller; for example, Polaroid cameras use only Polaroid film.[1]
4. **Quality Discrimination:** A firm offers consumers a choice of different quality products at the same price or at prices that do not fully reflect the quality differential. By offering a high-quality, high-priced product that appeals to consumers who place a high value on the product, and a low-quality, low-priced product that appeals to other consumers, a firm can *separate* the two types of consumers and charge high prices to those most

[1]A tie-in sale allows a firm to effectively charge higher prices to consumers who use more of the tied product. Because certain tie-in sales are currently a violation of antitrust laws, they were more common before the antitrust laws were passed. However, as Chapter 19 discusses, the law is unclear as to exactly what constitutes an illegal tie-in sale.

EXAMPLE 9.1 *Coupons*

One common means of price discriminating is to use cents-off coupons or to provide rebates to some but not all consumers. As we show later in the chapter, consumers who increase their purchases the most in response to a special low price (those whose demands are relatively elastic) are the ones who should receive the coupons. Marketing studies find that consumers who have a low cost of transportation (own cars), who have the space to store items (own homes), and who place a low value on time or who have flexible time schedules (a nonworking spouse without small children) are the most likely to take advantage of special promotions. By using coupons, manufacturers can provide discounts to people who are price sensitive and relatively likely to clip and use coupons, without providing discounts to other, typically wealthier people.

The number of coupons distributed was 100 billion in 1981, 200 billion in 1985, and 310 billion in 1994, but only 269 billion in 1995. According to the Promotion Marketing Association (PMA), marketers distributed 336 billion coupons in 2002. Of these, only 3.8 billion were redeemed (for $3.1 billion), the lowest rate since 1980. The average face value of a coupon was 81¢.

One recent innovation is the use of online coupons. Consumers downloaded 242 million coupons in 2002, 111% more than in 2001 but still a tiny fraction of all coupons. (Retailers are concerned that counterfeit coupons are being produced or exchanged over the Internet.)

The PMA reported in 2003 that 79% of all people in the United States use coupons. Coupon use increases with age, going from 71% for 18- to 24-year-olds to 84% for those 65 and older. Richer people are less likely to use coupons, with usage rates falling from 82% for people earning under $25,000 to 76% for those earning over $75,000.

Coupons are most likely to be used for household cleaners, followed by prepared foods, detergents, medications and home remedies, paper products, condiments and gravies, personal soap and bath additives, frozen prepared foods, cereal, and skin care preparations. More than four out of five (80.4%) of coupons were redeemed at grocery stores, with the rest handled by mass merchandisers (9.4%), drug stores (3.7%), and convenience stores (2.4%). The frequency of coupon use while shopping was 76% at grocery stores and 54% at mass merchandisers and drug stores.

Sources: Blattberg et al. (1978); Narasimhan (1984); Philip H. Dougherty, "Advertising: Redemption of Coupons," *New York Times,* July 13, 1988:C19; Eben Shapiro, "Consumers' Use of Shopping Coupons Is Up," *New York Times,* September 30, 1992:C12; George Lazarus, "Coupons Cruising at a Record Clip," *San Francisco Examiner,* October 4, 1992: E5; "Coupon Redemption Rate Down," *Editor & Publisher Magazine,* January 20, 1996:21; M. A. Mariner, "Disappearing Coupons," *San Francisco Chronicle,* January 29, 1997: Food 2; **www.pmalink.org/about/press_releases/release55.asp; www.couponmonth.com/pages/news.htm;** "Coupon Use Is Down," *Beacon Journal,* September 6, 2003; Bob Tedeschi, "E-Commerce Report," *New York Times,* March 17, 2003:C6.

willing to pay them. Therefore, the problem of what range of qualities a monopoly should produce is closely related to the theory of price discrimination.

Not every seller who charges a nonuniform price is price discriminating. There are many other explanations for prices to vary across consumers. (See Lott and Roberts 1991.) For example, a quantity discount may reflect cost savings from dealing with large orders that a manufacturer is passing on to consumers. This chapter and the next, however, focus on explaining how nonuniform pricing can be profitable for a firm with market power.

Incentive and Conditions for Price Discrimination

A firm price discriminates to increase its profits; however, a firm can price discriminate only under certain conditions. We now explain why price discrimination increases profits and what conditions are necessary for it to occur.

Profit Motive for Price Discrimination

Price discrimination is profitable because consumers who value the good the most pay more than if prices were uniform. To show why there is an advantage to price discriminating, we return to a monopoly that charges all customers a single price. The monopoly sets that price so that its marginal revenue equals its marginal cost (see Chapter 4).

Its marginal revenue—the increased revenue that results from selling an additional unit—is the sum of two effects. The first is the increase in revenue from selling one more unit, which is the price, p, that it receives for the last unit. The second is the decrease in revenue on all existing output, $Q\Delta p$, where Δp is the fall in price needed to induce the sale of one more unit.[2] If the monopoly could lower the price on *only* the one additional unit, it would do so as long as the price exceeded marginal cost. It would then earn its current profit plus an additional amount on the last unit. The monopoly would earn additional profit from this price discrimination.

All methods of price discrimination can be viewed as attempts to minimize this second effect on marginal revenue from expanding sales. This chapter and the next identify a variety of pricing policies that are designed to minimize the cost to the monopoly of trying to expand output at a lower price to a particular customer without simultaneously offering the same lower price to all consumers.

[2]Because total revenue equals $p(Q)Q$, for a small change in quantity, marginal revenue equals $p(Q) + Q(dp/dQ)$. In the text, dp/dQ is called Δp.

Conditions for Price Discrimination

Even though all firms would like to price discriminate, many are not able to do so. Three conditions are needed for successful price discrimination.[3]

1. A firm must have some *market power* (the ability to set price above marginal cost profitably); otherwise, it can never succeed in charging any consumer more than the competitive price.
2. The firm must know or be able to infer consumers' willingness to pay for each unit, and this willingness to pay must vary across consumers or units. That is, the firm must be able to *identify* whom to charge the higher price. Similarly, if each individual's demand curve slopes down, the firm may be able to charge a different price for the different units any one consumer purchases (such as $10 for the first unit and $5 for the second unit).
3. A firm must be able to *prevent or limit resales* by customers who pay the lower price to those who pay the higher price. Any attempt to charge one group a higher price than another is doomed to fail if resales are easy. If the group charged the lower price can resell to the other group at a lower price than the monopoly charges them, no one in the latter group would buy directly from the monopoly. Limiting resales is necessary for all types of price discrimination.

Resales

If a firm charges nonuniform prices, consumers who buy at a relatively low price may resell to those facing a relatively high price and thereby render useless the attempt to charge different prices. Similarly, if a firm offers quantity discounts for a product, it must ensure that the discount is not so great as to encourage high-volume purchasers to buy the product and then resell it to those who demand fewer units. There are at least seven reasons why reselling the good may be difficult or impossible for consumers:

Services. Most services cannot be resold. For example, a dentist may charge Lisa a very high price and Jackie a very low price, but it is impossible for Lisa to gain by having Jackie purchase the dentist's services for her. For that reason, price discrimination in services is more likely than price discrimination in industries with tradeable products (Kessel 1958). See Example 9.2.

Similarly, having seen an art show, one cannot transfer the experience to others. In 2001, when Steve Martin's art collection went on display in Las Vegas, the gallery in the Bellagio Hotel charged art lovers a hefty $12 per ticket unless they were Nevada residents, who were charged only $6.

---

[3]Price discrimination can be practiced by a single firm or a group of firms, such as a cartel. To keep the exposition simple, we discuss the actions of a single firm.

EXAMPLE 9.2 *Thank You, Doctor*

Movies and television shows often portray as great heroes doctors who charge poorer patients lower rates. In very old movies, the country doctor accepts a chicken as payment instead of charging cash. Are doctors selfless creatures or profit maximizers who engage in price discrimination? Certainly some doctors see indigent patients for no fees or trivial fees as an act of charity. Others, however, may be price discriminating.

The Association for Behavioral and Cognitive Therapy publishes a directory of its members who provide therapy in the San Francisco area along with the rates each charges. In the 1990–91 edition, 3 therapists merely state that they use a sliding scale, 10 others show a range, and 31 list a single rate. Many in the latter group often cut their listed fee for some patients.

Of those who listed an explicit range, one stated that he charged between $0 and $120 per session. All the others set their minimum rate at $40 or more. Their maximum rate averaged 1.8 times their minimum.

Warranties. A manufacturer can void a warranty if a product is resold. For example, a manufacturer could say that the warranty on a product is valid only for the first-time purchaser, which imposes a cost on a buyer who purchases a product from a previous buyer.

Adulteration. A manufacturer can adulterate a product to make it unfit for other uses. For example, alcohol is used for drinking (alcoholic beverages) and for medicinal purposes (rubbing alcohol). Suppose alcohol were produced by a monopoly that wanted to charge a higher price to those who drink alcohol and a lower price to those who use alcohol for medicinal purposes. The monopoly could prevent medicinal users from reselling to drinkers by adulterating the medicinal alcohol (adding ingredients that make it unfit for internal consumption yet preserve its medicinal qualities). This particular approach to eliminating resales would not work if medicine consumers were willing to pay more than drinkers, and the manufacturer wanted to prevent the resale of drinking alcohol for medicinal purposes.

Transaction Cost. If consumers incur any large transaction costs to resell the product, resales are less likely. For example, suppose some consumers are mailed coupons that entitle them to purchase a product at a lower price than others. The transaction costs of finding consumers without coupons are too high for it to be worthwhile for consumers with coupons to purchase the product and then resell the product. In many markets, storage costs, search costs, or other transaction costs are too high for any resales to occur.

Two important examples of transaction costs are tariffs (a government tax on imported goods) and transportation costs. A manufacturer that wants to charge a high price in the United States and a low price in Europe would have to worry about resale from Europe to the United States. However, a large tariff or transportation cost that must be paid by anybody importing the product from Europe to the United States reduces or eliminates resales.

Laws sometimes allow a company to charge more for its product in one country than in another by preventing others from shipping the good from the low-cost country to the other. That is, these laws prevent price arbitrage (reselling to profit from differential prices). See Example 9.3.

Contractual Remedies. A firm may contractually forbid resale as part of its terms of sale. For example, many universities and colleges arrange for students and faculty members to purchase computers at lower than market rates. To buy at this reduced rate, one might have to sign a contract that forbids resale. If restrictions on resale are not legally binding or not easily enforceable, such contractual clauses may not prevent resales.

Vertical Integration. Suppose a manufacturer wants to sell aluminum ingots to producers of aluminum wire at a lower price than it charges producers of aluminum aircraft parts. If the manufacturer did charge two different prices, the wire producers would resell their ingot to the aircraft producers. The ingot manufacturer may choose to produce aluminum wire. A firm that produces at more than one stage of a production process is said to be *vertically integrated.* The vertically integrated firm can charge final consumers of aluminum wire a low price (that is, effectively charge and pass along a low price for aluminum ingot to its own aluminum wire division) and still charge the aircraft producers a high price for aluminum ingot with no fear of resale. Resale does not arise for two reasons. First, the monopoly controls the actions of its aluminum wire division and does not allow it to resell the aluminum ingot. Second, it is cheaper for aircraft producers to purchase aluminum ingot rather than purchase aluminum wire and transform the wire back into ingots. Vertical integration prevents resale in a way similar to the adulteration argument given above. See Example 9.4.

Government Intervention. The government can enact laws that allow firms in a competitive industry to act collectively to prevent resale. For example, government regulations control how much of an orange grower's crop can be sold as fresh fruit and how much as processed (Appendix 9A describes government programs in agriculture that foster price discrimination). The remainder of this chapter assumes that a firm can prevent or control resale of its product and investigates the ways in which firms price discriminate.

Types of Price Discrimination

There are many methods for charging nonuniform prices. This section examines some of the simplest ones. The more complicated ones are discussed in the next chapter. We first study *perfect* or *first-degree* price discrimination, in which consumers are left with no consumer surplus (the value to consumers in excess of the purchase price). Then we

EXAMPLE 9.3

Halting Drug Resales from Canada

Pharmaceutical companies price discriminate across countries. The prices of many popular drugs are substantially lower than in the United States in virtually every other country in the world. Zoloft, an antidepression drug, sells for one-third the U.S. price in Mexico and about half in Luxembourg and Austria. Many well-known brand-name drugs sell in Canada for one-third to one-half the lowest price available in the United States.

These price differences reflect price discrimination by pharmaceutical firms. Sometimes the lower prices in other countries are due to differences in incomes, patent laws, and legal liabilities. However, frequently, regulations in other countries are responsible for the relatively low prices.

U.S. pharmaceutical companies are horrified about the possibility that resales—where drugs they exported from the United States at relatively low prices are reimported—will drive down U.S. prices. In 2003, the U.S. House of Representatives passed a bill to permit imports, but because it has not become law to date, such imports remain illegal. Nonetheless, U.S. senior citizens have taken many well-publicized bus trips across the Canadian and Mexican borders to buy drugs at lower prices; and many Canadian, Mexican, and other Internet sites offer to ship drugs to the United States. According to various estimates, only about 1 percent to 3 percent of U.S. drug expenditures went to imported drugs, but the fraction is growing.

Some drug companies, among them GlaxoSmithKline and Pfizer, are trying to reduce imports by cutting off Canadian pharmacies that ship south of the border. Wyeth and AstraZeneca report that they watch Canadian pharmacies and wholesale customers for spikes in sales volume that could indicate imports, and then restrict supplies.

The drug companies have also pressured the U.S. Food and Drug Administration (FDA) to help prevent imports. To date, the FDA has not enforced restrictions on purchases by individuals. However starting in 2003, the FDA took several steps to reduce imports. The FDA raised the specter that imported drugs were not as safe as those purchased in the United States (although it has provided little evidence to date to support that claim). The agency sent threatening letters to various state attorneys general saying that state agencies that imported Canadian prescription drugs would be violating federal law. It completed a sting operation targeting the supplier of Canadian drugs to the employee insurance program of the City of Springfield, Massachusetts (which reported it could save \$4 to \$9 million a year by ordering drugs through Canada). It took actions to close a chain of Canadian drugstores that ship drugs to the United States (Rx Depot has 85 stores in 26 states and operates other stores in Canada under the name Rx of Canada).

Sources: Tim Harper, "Canada's Drugs 'Dangerous'," *Toronto Star*, August 28, 2003:A12; Christopher Rowland, "FDA Sting Targets Medicine Supplier; Springfield Uses Firm to Get Canadian Drugs," *Boston Globe*, August 28, 2003:C1; Tony Pugh, "Canadian Online Pharmacies Struggle to Find Suppliers," *San Diego Union-Tribune*, September 7, 2003:A-3; Gardiner Harris, "U.S. Moves to Halt Import of Drugs from Canada," *New York Times*, September 10, 2003:C2.

EXAMPLE 9.4

Vertical Integration as a Means of Price Discrimination: Alcoa Shows Its True Metal

Alcoa had considerable monopoly power in the production of primary aluminum ingot from 1888 to 1930 due to tariffs that protected it abroad and by its control of bauxite lands at home. Further, the disruptions of World War I slowed entry of new firms.

The traditional view of why Alcoa forward integrated into processing activities (bought firms in these industries) was to demonstrate the technical and commercial feasibility of new aluminum products. Recent research indicates, however, that Alcoa probably vertically integrated in order to price discriminate.

Explicit price discrimination was not possible, because aluminum ingots are easy to handle and hence easy to resell. Alcoa overcame this problem by vertically integrating into some industries that purchased aluminum ingots.

Suppose that there are only two downstream industries (or groups of industries) that buy aluminum, and that Industry 1's demand for the product is less price-elastic than Industry 2's demand. Alcoa wanted to charge a higher price to Industry 1 than Industry 2. If it did so, however, Industry 2 firms would resell the aluminum to the high-price industry.

If Alcoa vertically integrated into the low-price industry (that is, Alcoa buys Industry 2), it could prevent resales by its own subsidiary. Moreover, because Alcoa supplied its subsidiary with its product internally, the only industry Alcoa explicitly sold ingot to was the high-price industry.

Alcoa only forward integrated into some industries that used primary aluminum. As predicted by this theory, Alcoa integrated into the high-elasticity industries. The five uses of aluminum listed in the following table represented more than 90 percent of Alcoa's output during most of this period. Of these uses, iron and steel production and aircraft manufacturing had the most inelastic demands because of a lack of good substitutes for aluminum in their production process. Alcoa did not integrate into these industries. Alcoa did integrate into the other, relatively elastic industries. Because there were many substitutes for aluminum in the manufacture of cookware (such as tin, glass, steel, iron, and so forth), electric cable (copper), and automobile parts (various metals), their demand for aluminum was relatively elastic.

Major Industries Using Aluminum

Industry	Elasticity of Demand for Aluminum	Integrated by Alcoa?
Cookware	Elastic ($\epsilon \approx -1.6$)	Yes
Electric cable	Elastic (copper substitute)	Yes
Automobile parts	Elastic ($\epsilon \approx -1.5$)	Yes
Iron and steel	Inelastic (no substitutes)	No
Aircraft	Inelastic (no substitutes then)	No

Source: Perry (1980).

study *third-degree* price discrimination, in which each group of consumers faces its own price per unit. Chapter 10 examines *second-degree* discrimination, in which the price per unit depends on the number of units purchased. In second-degree and third-degree price discrimination, the firm fails to capture all of the consumer surplus.

Perfect Price Discrimination

The purpose behind all methods of price discrimination is to capture as much consumer surplus (Chapter 3) as possible. **Perfect price discrimination** or **first-degree price discrimination** occurs when a monopoly is able to charge the maximum each consumer is willing to pay for each unit of the product.

Each Consumer Buys One Unit. Suppose that each consumer wants one unit of a product, but consumers are willing to pay a different amount for it, so that the demand curve slopes downward as shown in Figure 9.1. Assume that the firm knows the maximum amount that each consumer is willing to pay. If it can prevent resales, the firm charges each customer the maximum that person is willing to pay so the customer is left with no consumer surplus. The firm sells to any consumer who will pay at least as much as the firm's (for simplicity, constant) marginal cost, $MC = m$. That is, the perfectly discriminating monopoly sells Q^* units and the marginal consumer pays p^* as shown in Figure 9.1.

FIGURE 9.1 Competitive, Nondiscriminating Monopoly, and Perfectly Discriminating Monopoly

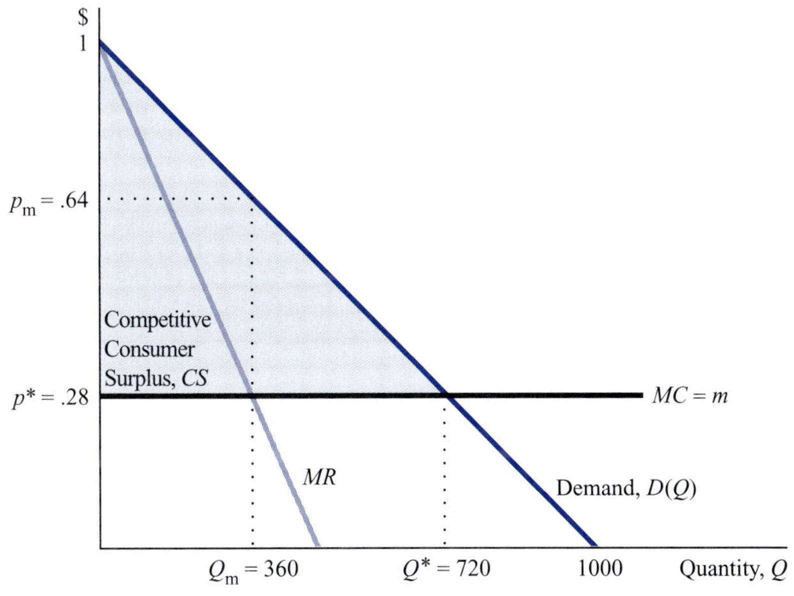

A competitive industry would also sell Q^* units and charge everyone a single price, p^*, which equals the marginal cost. Thus, a competitive industry and a perfectly discriminating monopoly charge the marginal consumer the same price, p^*, and sell the same total quantity, Q^*.[4] The difference is that the perfectly discriminating monopoly charges all but the marginal customer more than p^* so that there is no consumer surplus. Consumer surplus is maximized under competition (the area under the demand curve and above p^* in Figure 9.1) and eliminated (and captured) by a perfectly discriminating monopoly. Therefore, perfect price discrimination entails no efficiency loss (the price on the last purchase still equals marginal cost), but does affect the distribution of income.[5]

A nondiscriminating monopoly charges a single price, p_m, and produces Q_m, where its marginal revenue, *MR*, equals its marginal cost, *MC*, as shown in Figure 9.1. Consumers have a small amount of consumer surplus (the area under the demand curve and above p_m), which is smaller than the consumer surplus under competition. The perfectly discriminating monopoly produces more than the nondiscriminating, single-price monopoly. The single-price monopoly produces too little; it is inefficient.

The perfectly discriminating monopoly sells more than the nondiscriminating monopoly because it makes an incremental profit on each additional sale. By charging each consumer a different price, the perfectly discriminating monopoly avoids the adverse second effect on marginal revenue that a nondiscriminating monopoly faces. That is, the discriminating monopoly does not decrease revenues on the first units sold when it sells additional units at a lower price. The effect on marginal revenue of eliminating the second effect is that the demand curve becomes the marginal revenue curve.[6] The monopoly lowers price to only the additional customer and so gains that price as an increase in its revenues from selling one more unit.

Each Consumer Buys More Than One Unit

So far, we have assumed that customers differ in their willingness to pay and that each customer demands only one unit no matter how low the price. Now consider how perfect price discrimination works when consumers are identical but demand more units

[4]We ignore the effects of redistributing income through price discrimination. A discriminating monopoly earns higher profits and consumers have less income than under competition.

[5]However, see Edlin, Epelbaum, and Heller (1998) for a general equilibrium analysis.

[6]The perfectly discriminating monopoly picks Q so that its profit is maximized. Its profit is the area (revenues) under its inverse demand curve, $p(Q)$, less its costs, $C(Q)$:

$$\pi(Q) = \int_0^Q p(q)dq - C(Q).$$

Its first-order condition for an interior profit maximum is

$$p = p(Q) = C'(Q).$$

That is, profit is maximized at the quantity Q where price equals marginal cost. The second-order condition is that $p'(Q) - C''(Q) < 0$. That is, the slope of the marginal cost curve is greater than the slope of the demand curve.

as price falls. Suppose that each consumer is identical to all others and has the downward-sloping demand curve for the product. We now assume that the demand curve in Figure 9.1 reflects each consumer's curve rather than the market aggregate. Marginal cost is still assumed to be constant at m.

A perfectly discriminating monopoly charges a different price for each *unit* of the product that is sold and thus, by charging *quantity-dependent* prices, extracts all the consumer surplus from each customer. The monopoly charges a high price for the first unit consumed, a lower price for the next unit, and so on until it charges m, the marginal cost, for the last unit. That is, the monopoly sets its (marginal) price schedule equal to each customer's demand curve.

An alternative and equivalent method of perfect price discrimination would be to charge an optimal *two-part tariff,* where each customer pays a lump-sum fee for the right to purchase plus a per-unit charge of m for each unit consumed regardless of how many units each consumer purchases. If a customer's consumer surplus is CS (Figure 9.1) when price is m, then the monopoly sets the lump-sum fee equal to CS. The consumer is indifferent between buying or not because the monopoly captures all the consumer surplus. This pricing method yields the competitive output and generates the same profit for the monopoly as it would earn if it perfectly price discriminated. A similar approach used by unions is discussed in Example 9.5.

If each consumer has a downward-sloping demand curve but consumers differ, the monopoly charges each consumer m per unit consumed but charges each one a different lump-sum fee in order to extract all of the consumer surplus. Of course, a monopoly may not have detailed enough knowledge about each consumer's demand curve to design a pricing policy that captures all the consumer surplus of each consumer. If the monopoly lacks this detailed information, it may find it profitable to use the more complicated pricing policies described in the next chapter. However, sometimes it is possible to monitor customers to determine the values they place on products. For example, a firm that rents out copy machines may use a meter in the copy machine to keep track of the number of copies each customer makes and then set the rent depending on the number of copies made. This method of pricing maximizes profit if those who make the most copies value their machine the most.

Because perfect price discrimination requires detailed knowledge about individual buyers, it is more likely to occur (or be attempted) when one-on-one bargaining occurs. For example, a car salesperson may ask potential buyers about their jobs, where they live, and where else they have shopped in an effort to estimate the maximum they are likely to spend. Similarly, doctors may be able to successfully price discriminate if they can identify the wealthy people in their area (see Kessel 1958 and Example 9.2).

Different Prices to Different Groups

A firm that does not have enough information to identify each customer and determine what each one is willing to pay is unable to practice first-degree price discrimination and extract all consumer surplus. The firm may have, however, enough information to imperfectly price discriminate.

Suppose a firm can determine whether a particular customer belongs to one group rather than another where the demand elasticities for the aggregate demand curves of

EXAMPLE 9.5 *A Discriminating Labor Union*

A powerful labor union may be able to act as a perfectly discriminating monopoly and capture all the consumer surplus. Because it is difficult to charge different prices for each hour of labor services, unions use an alternative approach. The union sets both a wage and a minimum number of hours (Leontief 1946).

As shown in the diagram, if the labor market were competitive, a wage of w would be charged, and H hours of labor services would be sold. Purchasers of labor services would have consumer surplus equal to areas A and B. If, in contrast, all workers belong to a union, and the union acts like a perfectly discriminating monopoly, it charges a wage equal to the demand curve for each hour of labor services it sells (so that the wage for the last hour it sells is w), and it captures all the consumer surplus.

Alternatively, the union could set a single wage, w^*, and a minimum number of hours, H, and receive the same total amount of compensation. The union offers the firms the following choice: You may buy H hours of labor at w^* (so the total wage bill is Hw^*) or you may buy no hours at all. As shown in the diagram, if the union only set the wage at w^* and did not set a minimum number of hours, firms would purchase fewer hours (H^*). The only reason that the firms agree to buy so many hours at this wage is that the alternative is to buy no labor services at all.

As the diagram shows, the firms receive consumer surplus equal to area A for the first H^* hours, and then have negative consumer surplus (equal to area C) for the next $H - H^*$ hours. The union receives profits above the competitive level equal to areas B and C. If w^* is set appropriately so that area A equals area C, the union makes as much profit with this scheme as it would if it perfectly price discriminated.

The Longshoremen's union used this technique (U.S. Department of Labor 1975). Two-thirds of the union contracts in the transportation industry (excluding railroads and airplanes) had wage-employment guarantees in the early 1970s. In contrast, only 11 percent of union contracts in all industries had such guarantees.

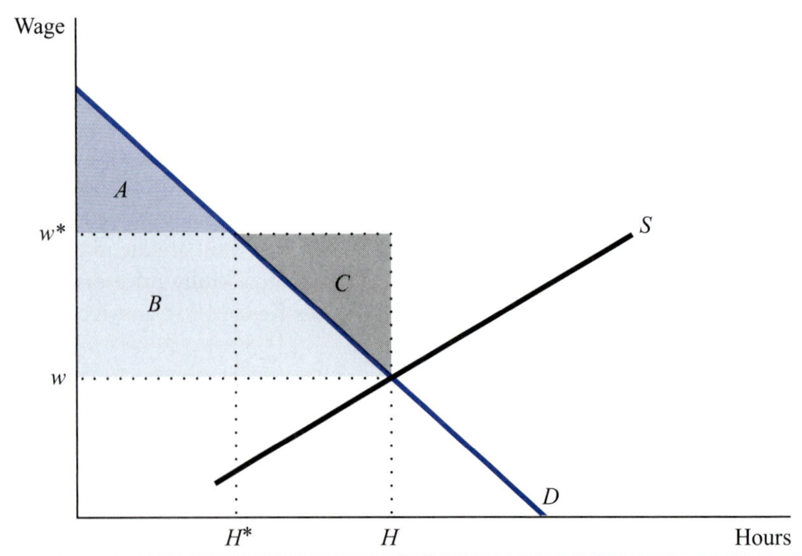

the two groups differ. If it is possible to prevent (or limit) resale between the two groups, and if the firm knows the aggregate demand curve of each group, then it is profitable to set different prices for the two groups. The monopoly is practicing **third-degree price discrimination**: It charges consumers in different groups different unit prices. For example, if high transaction costs prevent resale, a firm could charge consumers in California higher prices than those in New York.

If the monopoly has a constant marginal and average cost of m, its profit, π, is

$$\pi = [p_1(Q_1) - m]Q_1 + [p_2(Q_2) - m]Q_2, \tag{9.1}$$

where $p_1(Q_1)$, the inverse demand curve, is the price that the monopoly must charge Group 1 if it is to sell it Q_1 units and $p_2(Q_2)$ is, similarly, the inverse demand curve for Group 2. That is, p_1 depends only on the number of units sold to that group, Q_1 (and not Q_2) and $p_2(Q_2)$ depends on only Q_2. Total profit is $\pi = \pi_1 + \pi_2$, where π_i, the profit from sales to Group i ($i = 1, 2$) is $[p_i - m]Q_i$. That is, π_i is the profit per unit sold to Group i, $[p_i - m]$, times the number of units sold to that group, Q_i.

The monopoly maximizes its total profit (Equation 9.1) by maximizing its profits from sales to each of the groups separately. The monopoly charges the same price to every member of a given group. Thus, we can determine how the monopoly sets its price to each group by using the same method that we used for a nondiscriminating monopoly in Chapter 4. That is, the monopoly maximizes its profit when its marginal revenue from sales to Group i, MR_i, equals its marginal cost of producing that last unit, m:

$$MR_1 \equiv p_1\left(1 + \frac{1}{\epsilon_1}\right) = m, \tag{9.2a}$$

$$MR_2 \equiv p_2\left(1 + \frac{1}{\epsilon_2}\right) = m, \tag{9.2b}$$

where ϵ_i is the elasticity of demand for Group i, so that the marginal revenue for Group i equals $p_i(1 + 1/\epsilon_i)$ as discussed in Chapter 4.[7]

Because the marginal cost, m, is the same in both Equations 9.2a and 9.2b, it follows that the profit-maximizing monopoly equates marginal revenue across the two markets: $MR_1 = MR_2$. In the optimal solution, if the monopoly sells one less unit in Market 1 and one more unit in Market 2 or vice versa, revenues must be unaffected. Otherwise it would pay to reallocate sales between the two markets, which implies that

[7]The first-order conditions for a profit maximization are obtained by differentiating Equation 9.1 with respect to Q_1 and Q_2:

$$MR_i = p_i + Q_i p_i' = m = MC, \qquad i = 1, 2.$$

By multiplying and dividing by p_i, we obtain

$$MR_i = p_i\left(1 + p_i'\frac{Q_i}{p_i}\right) = p_i\left(1 + \frac{1}{\epsilon_i}\right).$$

FIGURE 9.2 Price Discrimination

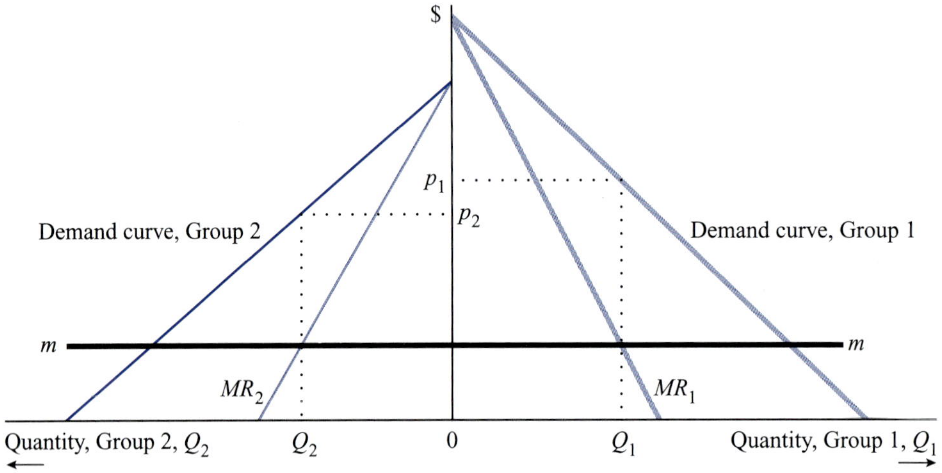

profits were not maximized. Equating the common marginal revenue to marginal cost yields maximum profits.[8]

The pricing decision of the discriminating monopoly is illustrated in Figure 9.2. The figure shows the demands of two consumer groups. The demand curve for Group 2 on the left side of the diagram is "flipped" so that it is read in the opposite direction from the Group 1 demand on the right side of the diagram. Setting the marginal revenue of each demand curve equal to a constant marginal cost m yields the optimal pricing and output decision (p_1, Q_1) and (p_2, Q_2).

We can rewrite Equations 9.2a and 9.2b as

$$\frac{p_1 - m}{p_1} = -\frac{1}{\epsilon_1}, \tag{9.3a}$$

$$\frac{p_2 - m}{p_2} = -\frac{1}{\epsilon_2}. \tag{9.3b}$$

[8]If marginal cost is not constant, cost varies with total output, so that Equation 9.1 is

$$\pi = p_1(Q_1)Q_1 + p_2(Q_2)Q_2 - C(Q_1 + Q_2),$$

where marginal cost is $C'(Q_1 + Q_2) = MC$. The optimal price and output for one consumer group depend on the optimal price and output of the other consumer group. The optimal pricing and outputs still satisfy Equations 9.2a and 9.2b:

$$MR_i \equiv p_i + Q_i p_i' = C'(Q_1 + Q_2) \equiv MC \quad \text{for} \quad i = 1, 2.$$

That is, the percentage markup of each Group i's price over its marginal cost, $[p_i - m]/p_i$, is inversely proportional to its elasticity of demand. The higher the group's elasticity of demand, the lower the price and the closer the price is to marginal cost. As a result, the group whose demand is relatively sensitive to price is charged a lower price. Equations 9.2a and 9.2b can be combined to show that the price ratio to the two groups depends on their relative elasticities:

$$\frac{p_1}{p_2} = \frac{1 + 1/\epsilon_2}{1 + 1/\epsilon_1}. \tag{9.4}$$

For example, if Group 1 has a nearly perfectly elastic demand ($\epsilon_1 \approx -\infty$) and Group 2 has a demand elasticity of -2, then $p_1/p_2 = 1/2$. Group 2, the group with the relatively inelastic demand, is charged twice as much as Group 1. Alternatively stated, a profit-maximizing discriminating monopoly provides a discount to the group that has the higher elasticity of demand. See Examples 9.1, 9.3, and 9.4.

Still another method of price discrimination is to make the price that the consumer pays depend on whether the consumer turns in a previous version of the product, as well as the identity of the manufacturer of that previous version (Fudenberg and Tirole 1998). For example, the price of the latest version of Microsoft's word-processing software, Word, may depend on whether the consumer's previous word-processing software was an earlier version of Word.

Other Methods of Third-Degree Price Discrimination

Firms can practice third-degree price discrimination in other, subtle ways. For example, in many markets some consumers are better informed than others about prices. One way a firm can charge different prices to consumers is to set a high list price (the price at which an item is marked or listed to sell). The firm charges the list price unless a customer complains that it exceeds the price of the product at other stores. In the event of a complaint, the store matches the lower price. This method of pricing causes uninformed consumers to pay higher prices than knowledgeable ones.[9]

Another example of third-degree price discrimination involves exploiting differences in the value customers place on time. High-wage, high-income people typically value their time more than low-wage, low-income people (and may have a more inelastic demand for certain goods). One clever way to price discriminate between these two groups is to make a special offer that requires consumers to spend time to take advantage of the offer. For example, suppose a store is willing to sell an item over the telephone at the regular price and mail the item to the consumer. The store runs a sale, but only gives the low price to consumers who take the time to come in and pick the item up at the store. This is an effective method of price discrimination in which consumers who place a high value on time receive the item by mail and pay the regular price, and consumers who place a low value on time pick the item up at the store and pay the low price.

[9]The moral of this story is don't be afraid to complain about high prices. Department stores often have a policy that they will not be underpriced by their rivals. Chapter 13 analyzes how a firm's behavior is affected by the presence of both informed and uninformed consumers.

A related method of price discrimination is to exploit differences in the willingness of consumers to wait to consume a new product. For example, some people insist on being among the first to see a new movie or own the latest electronic gadget. Early purchasers pay more than later purchasers if prices fall over time. Not all firms with market power can profitably price discriminate over time, however. If consumers know that prices will fall in the future, some postpone buying. Price discrimination over time will be profitable provided the number who are willing to wait for lower prices is not too large (Stokey 1979—see **www.aw-bc.com/carlton_perloff** "Discrimination Over Time").

Welfare Effects of Price Discrimination

There is no ambiguity about the welfare effects of perfect price discrimination. Output is at the efficient, competitive level, but consumers are poorer than they are under competition; therefore, perfect price discrimination does not distort efficiency but does affect the distribution of income.

The welfare effects of third-degree discrimination are more difficult to analyze. We do know that, as with first-degree discrimination, consumers wind up with less surplus than under competition. Moreover, from Equations 9.3a and 9.3b, we know that third-degree price discrimination prices exceed marginal costs, so they are not as efficient as perfect competition or perfect price discrimination.

Third-degree price discrimination, however, may be better or worse than nondiscriminating monopoly pricing from an efficiency viewpoint, depending on the shapes of the demand and cost curves. The closer imperfect price discrimination is to perfect price discrimination, the more likely it is that the price discrimination leads to a more efficient outcome than nondiscriminating monopoly pricing.

Three sources of inefficiency are present in third-degree discrimination. The first is the usual one associated with monopoly: Price exceeds marginal cost, which results in an output restriction and hence an output inefficiency.

The second is a consumption inefficiency. Because different consumers pay different per-unit prices for a product, each consumer's marginal willingness to pay is not the same, which results in an inefficiency because of unexploited opportunities for further trade. For example, suppose that resale is impossible and there are two consumers. Larry is willing to pay \$10 to consume the first unit and \$9 to consume the second unit for a total of \$19 to consume 2 units. If Larry is charged \$10 per unit, he consumes only 1 unit. Andrew is willing to pay \$7 to consume the first unit and \$4 to consume the second unit for a total of \$11 to consume 2 units. If Andrew is charged \$5 per unit, he consumes only 1 unit. At the margin, Larry values the product more than Andrew. Larry values an additional unit at \$9, and Andrew values the unit that he is consuming at \$7. In such a case it is more efficient for Larry to consume 2 units and Andrew none. For example, if Larry paid Andrew \$8 for his unit, both Larry and Andrew would be better off. Because resale is impossible, this trade does not occur, so there is inefficiency in consumption due to the price discrimination. Thus, if the discriminating monopoly produces the same (or less) output as the nondiscriminating monopoly, welfare is lower because there is no consumption inefficiency with the nondiscriminating monopoly since the monopoly charges all consumers the same price.[10]

A third source of inefficiency is that consumers may have to expend resources that do not benefit the firm to obtain a low price. For example, the consumer may have to wait in line or travel to a distant location to obtain the low price. One way to view this means of discriminating between groups of consumers is that the monopoly forces the consumer to buy a *bad* (such as the time waiting in line) in order to buy the good at a low price (Chiang and Spatt 1982).

Welfare may be higher with third-degree price discrimination than with a nondiscriminating monopoly if output is higher with discrimination. For example, suppose there are two groups of consumers and a nondiscriminating monopoly finds it optimal to set a price so high that one group buys no units. Then, because a discriminating monopoly serves both groups, output expands and consumers benefit in aggregate. In general, however, which type of monopoly leads to greater welfare is theoretically ambiguous and is an empirical question.[11] Competition can sometimes have unexpected price effects in cases where consumers differ. See Example 9.6.

The antitrust laws (Chapter 19) ban certain types of price discrimination. Apparently, it is not an antitrust violation to price discriminate among final consumers, but it is a violation to price discriminate among firms so as to affect their "competition" under the Robinson-Patman Act. Moreover, tie-in sales, which are closely related to a form of price discrimination, are illegal under certain circumstances. Given the ambiguous welfare effects of certain types of price discrimination, some economists question the desirability of a flat antitrust prohibition against these forms of price discrimination.

---

[10]Suppose Group 1 has an aggregate demand curve $Q_1 = a_1 - b_1p_1$ and that Group 2 has an aggregate demand curve $Q_2 = a_2 - b_2p_2$, where a_i and b_i ($i = 1, 2$) are numbers, and marginal cost is a constant, m. A discriminating monopoly chooses the profit-maximizing outputs $Q_1{}^*$ and $Q_2{}^*$, so that

$$Q_i^* = \frac{a_i}{2} - \frac{b_i m}{2}, \quad i = 1, 2.$$

A nondiscriminating monopoly picks a single price, p, and faces the demand curve for total quantity demanded, Q, given by $Q = (Q_1 + Q_2) = (a_1 + a_2) - (b_1 + b_2)p$ in the relevant range. If it is optimal to sell to both groups, the nondiscriminating monopoly chooses the profit-maximizing quantity

$$Q^* = \frac{a_1 + a_2}{2} - \frac{b_1 + b_2}{2}m,$$

so that $Q^* = Q_1^* + Q_2^*$. Hence, it follows that, in this case, output is the same with third-degree price discrimination and with simple monopoly. Welfare is lower with third-degree price discrimination than with a nondiscriminating monopoly because discriminating monopoly has a consumption inefficiency that simple monopoly does not.

[11]Schmalensee (1981b), Varian (1985), Katz (1987), and Ireland (1992) show that under special circumstances it is possible to make unambiguous welfare and output comparisons between simple monopoly and price discrimination, as we did in the previous footnote. Gale and Holmes (1993) examine welfare for airlines that use peak and off-peak pricing.

EXAMPLE 9.6

Does Competition Always Lower Price?

Grabowski and Vernon (1992) analyzed how a firm responds in its pricing to the retail sector when one of its brand name drugs comes off patent and faces competition from chemically equivalent drugs (generics). Before the patent expires, the firm takes advantage of its market power and sets a price above its marginal cost. After the drug comes off patent, the price will fall if all consumers regard generics as equivalent to the brand name drug. However, in their study of 18 major drugs whose patents had expired, Vernon and Grabowski noticed that, within two years of patent expiration, the market share of the firm with the previously patented product fell to about 50 percent, yet the price of the brand name drug *rose* by about 10 percent.

According to Grabowski and Vernon, there are two types of consumers, brand loyal and price sensitive. The brand-loyal consumers don't want to risk switching to another drug (even though it is chemically equivalent), while the price-sensitive consumers will switch if the generic price is lower than the price for the brand name drug. Prior to competition from generics, the firm sets one price to attract both the brand-loyal and price-sensitive consumers. When generics come into the market, the firm chooses not to meet the generic price (which is typically only 40 to 60 percent of the price for the brand name drug) and thereby forgoes sales to the price-sensitive segment. Once the firm does not have to attract the price-sensitive segment, it raises price to the remaining segment, the brand-loyal customers.

SUMMARY

Price discrimination occurs when a firm with market power uses nonuniform pricing to maximize its profits. Not all nonuniform pricing is due to price discrimination; some is due to cost differences.

For price discrimination to succeed, a firm must have some market power, know or be able to infer consumers' willingness to pay, and be able to prevent or control resales. In order to practice the types of price discrimination described in this chapter, firms must know quite a bit about individual consumers. For perfect, or first-degree, price discrimination, a firm must know each consumer's demand curve. For third-degree price discrimination, a firm must be able to identify the group that a consumer belongs to and must know the group's demand curve. Sometimes a firm does not have enough information to practice either first-degree or third-degree price discrimination. It must then use more complicated pricing methods to maximize its profits. These other pricing methods are examined in the next chapter.

Perfect price discrimination is efficient: The same quantity is sold as would be sold by a competitive industry. It leads to a redistribution of income where the monopoly obtains all the potential consumer surplus. Third-degree price discrimination is not as efficient as competition or perfect price discrimination. Compared to a nondiscriminating monopoly, it may be more or less efficient and have higher or lower welfare.

PROBLEMS

1. Suppose a firm has a monopoly in aluminum ingot and that it vertically integrates to produce its own aluminum wire, as discussed in the chapter. Will any independent aluminum wire producers remain? Could any wire producer afford to buy the aluminum ingot at the high price and compete successfully against the low-priced aluminum wire sold by the manufacturer of aluminum ingot?
2. Suppose there are two types of customers. Show diagrammatically that welfare can be either higher or lower under simple monopoly compared to discriminating monopoly.
3. It is often difficult to distinguish price discrimination from different prices for differentiated products. For example, if teachers recommend the magazines they read to students, they are helping to market the magazine. Because they save the magazine some marketing costs, it is profitable for the magazine to encourage teachers to subscribe by offering them a lower price. From the firm's viewpoint, a magazine sold to a teacher is a different product from a magazine sold to someone else. Can you explain a senior-citizen discount from movie theaters by appealing to this "different product" argument?
4. Suppose there are two groups of consumers and that it is optimal for a nondiscriminating monopoly to set $p = \$10$. At that price, no one from the first group chooses to purchase. Now, suppose the monopoly can price discriminate. Will total output expand? Why or why not?
5. Suppose a consumer wants just one unit of a good and is willing to pay at most \$10. Draw the demand curve and calculate the maximum consumer surplus that can be extracted. Suppose that there is a second consumer who also demands just one unit and is willing to pay at most \$9. A perfectly discriminating monopoly charges the first consumer \$10 and the second consumer \$9. Why is there no consumption inefficiency as occurs in third-degree price discrimination?
6. Would a price-discriminating monopoly ever produce less than a nondiscriminating monopoly?

Answers to odd-numbered problems are given at the back of the book.

SUGGESTED READINGS

Stole (forthcoming), Wilson (1993), and Varian (1989) provide an excellent survey of price discrimination. Borenstein (1985), Holmes (1989), Katz (1984), and Lederer and Hurter (1986) extend the analysis of third-degree price discrimination to market structures other than pure monopoly (such as monopolistic competition). Phlips (1983) covers a number of extensions to the basic theory and has some empirical applications.

APPENDIX 9A

An Example of Price Discrimination: Agricultural Marketing Orders

Federal and state governments mandate price discrimination in what would otherwise be competitive agricultural markets through the use of *marketing orders.* We first discuss how marketing orders permit farmers to price discriminate and then discuss the efficiency and welfare effects of these programs.[1]

Marketing Order Rules

Many marketing orders require farmers to participate in a *classified pricing* scheme, in which consumers in different markets are charged different prices. Typically, commodities are sold in at least two markets. In most marketing orders, the primary market is the fresh food (or domestic) market, in which the demand elasticity is relatively low and hence price is relatively high. The secondary market is the processed food (or export) market, in which the demand elasticity is relatively high and hence price is relatively low. Because processed foods cannot be converted back into fresh foods and it is costly to reimport exports, resales between the markets do not occur, so price discrimination is possible. How these market division schemes work varies across marketing orders.

One common scheme is a quantity restriction that dictates the share of a farmer's output that can be sold in the primary market. These *quantity share restrictions* increase prices in the primary market and lower them in the secondary market, where the extra output is sold. Examples include grade A milk, California almonds, Oregon-Washington filberts, Pacific Coast walnuts, California dates, and California raisins (Jesse and Johnson 1981). States that permitted quantity share restrictions in their marketing orders include California, Colorado, Georgia, South Carolina, and Utah (Garoyan and Youde 1975), though many of these programs have been dropped in recent years.

If there are no output restrictions, when classified pricing schemes are first introduced, they cause farms' profits to rise, which eventually induces entry and additional output. Output expands until the marginal farmers earn zero profits despite the price discrimination. Thus, in the absence of output restrictions, marketing orders produce a different equilibrium than would a price-discriminating monopoly or a competitive industry.

[1]We concentrate on the price discrimination aspects of marketing orders. Allegedly, Congress adopted marketing orders to help farmers act collectively to offset the monopsony power of milk processors (Novakovic and Boynton 1984). Modern defenders of marketing orders claim that they are "necessary" to stabilize prices or quantities, a view disputed by many agricultural economists (Jesse and Johnson 1981, Gardner 1984).

Efficiency and Welfare Effects of Marketing Orders

There are both gainers and losers under a price classification scheme, as is shown by a simplified model with fixed supply.[2] The marketing order allocates part of the total output to each of two markets: Class 1 (fresh) and Class 2 (processed), as shown in Figure 9A.1. By restricting output in the Class 1 market to Q_1, which is less than the competitive level, Q_1^c, the marketing order drives the price in the Class 1 market, p_1, above the competitive price, p_c. The excess output is sold in the Class 2 market, so Q_2 is greater than the competitive output Q_2^c, and the price in the Class 2 market, p_2, is below the competitive price, p_c.

Because the price in the fresh market is above the competitive price, $p_1 > p_c$, consumers of the fresh product lose consumer surplus equal to areas $A + B$. Farmers' profits on the Q_1 units they sell increase by area A $(= [p_1 - p_c]Q_1)$, so the net loss (the loss to consumers not offset by a gain to producers) in the fresh market is B.

Consumers of the processed product gain consumer surplus equal to area C due to the lower price, $p_2 < p_c$. Farmers' profits are lower on the Q_2 units of output they sell in the Class 2 market than if a competitive price were charged by areas $C + D$. The net loss in the processed market is D.

Consumers lose areas $A + B$ in the fresh market and gain area C in the processed market, for a net total loss of $A + B - C$. Farmers' profits increase. Farmers receive a *blend* (average) price $p_b = (p_1Q_1 + p_2Q_2)/(Q_1 + Q_2)$. The blend price is higher than the competitive price, or else there would be no point to engaging in such price discrimination. Farmers gain profits of A in the fresh market and lose profits of $C + D$ in the processed market, so their total net gains are areas $A - (C + D)$. Consumers lose more $(A + B - C)$ than producers gain $(A - C - D)$, for a net total loss of areas $B + D$. Thus, welfare is lower under a classified pricing scheme than under competition.

For simplicity, we assumed that supply was fixed and the only effect of the market allocation program was to redirect the product from the fresh to the processed market. More generally, where supply is not fixed, marketing orders, by increasing the effective price farmers receive (the weighted average of the fresh and processed prices), increase the amount supplied. Much of the extra supply is directed to the secondary market (to keep the price high in the primary market). Because the price in the secondary market is less than the competitive price (and hence marginal cost), the cost of this extra output exceeds its value to consumers. Thus, social loss can be even greater when supply curves are not vertical.

The social loss from most classified pricing programs is relatively small because the industries are small. There are, however, large social losses in dairy markets. Based on data from the early 1970s, Ippolito and Masson (1978) estimate that the effect of regulation was to raise the price of fresh (Class 1) milk 9.3 percent (at the farm level), to

[2]Ippolito and Masson (1978) and Berck and Perloff (1985) discuss static models. Berck and Perloff (1985) also show how the analysis changes in a dynamic model, where entry into the industry is slow. Cave and Salant (1987) model the voting behavior in agricultural marketing boards, which determine how marketing orders are run.

FIGURE 9A.1 Price Discrimination in Agricultural Marketing Orders

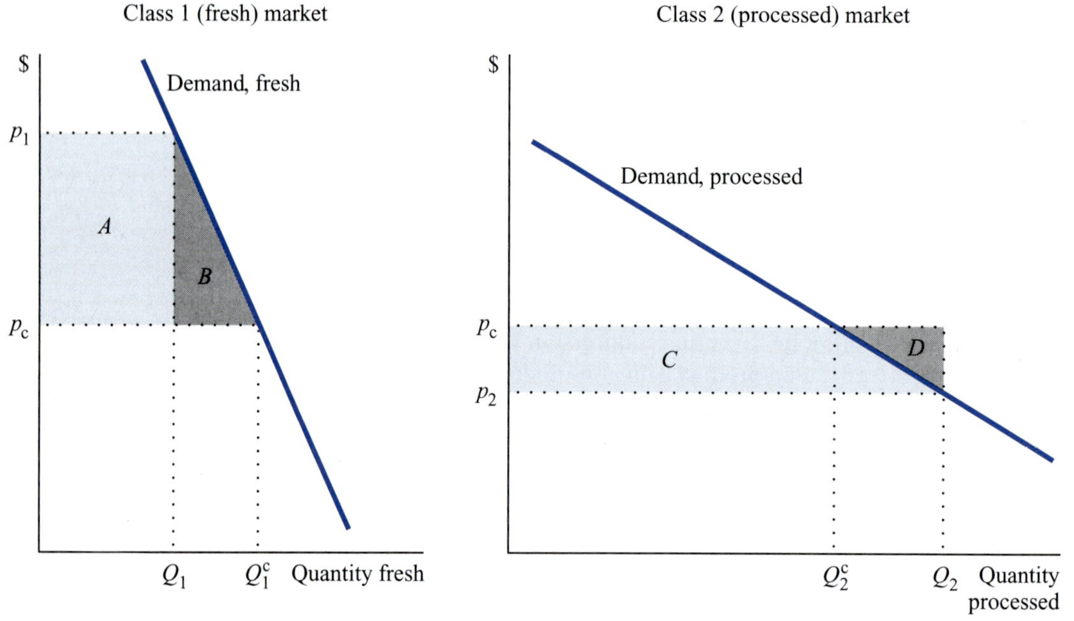

decrease the price of processed milk (used in products) (Class 2) by approximately 5.6 percent, and to increase the blend price facing regulated farmers by 3.7 percent. As a result, Class 1 consumption was 1.9 percent lower than it would have been without regulation, and Class 2 consumption was 9.6 percent higher. They calculate that the classified price regulation was equivalent to a tax on consumers of fresh milk of $333.8 million per year; and Class 2 users received a subsidy of $120.9 million. The producer profits on fresh milk increased by $210.6 million, and producer profits on processed milk fell by $105.2 million per year. Including the administration costs of running the program and the induced inefficiencies in transportation, they calculate that the total social cost was approximately $60 million per year.

Most other researchers, using other approaches, estimate larger costs. Kwoka (1977) estimates that the 1970 classified pricing and pooling schemes had an annual efficiency loss of $179 million. Heien (1977) calculates a total social cost of $175 million. LaFrance and de Gorter (1985) point out that these estimates are based on static analyses that ignore the time that it takes to build up a dairy herd. Using a dynamic model, they estimate that the social cost of the program is three times larger than the static estimates.

CHAPTER 10

Advanced Topics in Pricing

A fool and his money are soon parted. What I want to know is how they got together in the first place. —*Cyril Fletcher*

This chapter analyzes more complicated methods of price discrimination than were discussed in Chapter 9, such as nonlinear pricing, two-part tariffs, quantity discounts, tie-in sales, and quality choice. It shows how these common pricing methods increase profits of firms with market power that can control or prevent resale. The pricing methods in this chapter do not require that the firm have as much knowledge about consumers as was required to practice the methods described in Chapter 9.

The key points of this chapter are

1. Nonlinear pricing schemes can be used by a firm to price discriminate when the firm does not know the demands of individual consumers.
2. A firm can induce consumers to reveal which group they belong to through their choice from among several two-part tariffs.
3. The effectiveness of tie-in sales (where multiple goods must be purchased at the same time) in increasing profits depends on whether demands for these goods are related.
4. A firm with market power may use a variety of other policies to increase its profit above what it would earn if it charged everyone the same price.

Nonlinear Pricing

Nonlinear pricing occurs when a consumer's total expenditure on an item does not rise linearly (proportionately) with the amount purchased. That is, the price per unit varies with the number of units the customer buys. Methods of nonlinear pricing are used to practice *second-degree price discrimination*, where a firm

EXAMPLE 10.1 *Football Tariffs*

When the Raiders moved back to Oakland in 1995, they changed how they sold tickets to their football games. Under the new system, a fan paid a fee of between $250 and $4,000 for a personal seat license (PSL), which gave the fan the right to buy season tickets for the next 11 years at a ticket price per game ranging between $40 and $60. The Carolina Panthers introduced the PSL in 1993, and at least 11 NFL teams used a PSL by 2002. By one estimate, more than $700 million has been raised by the PSL portion of this two-part tariff.

that can prevent or at least control resale between individuals charges different consumers different prices, but the firm does not know the demands of each individual.[1] Rather, the firm makes use of its knowledge about the underlying distribution of demand in the population. This section first presents a simple type of nonlinear pricing schedule—a single two-part tariff—and then discusses the more general problem of nonlinear pricing, illustrating it with an example of a multiple two-part tariff.

A Single Two-Part Tariff

A firm that uses a *two-part tariff* charges consumers a lump-sum fee for the right to purchase goods and a usage charge per unit (see Chapter 9; also Oi 1971 and Schmalensee 1981a). For example, tennis clubs commonly charge a membership fee plus a usage fee that depends on how many hours one plays tennis. Many firms that rent copy machines pay a minimum rental fee plus a fee that depends on their usage of the machine. As a final example, suppose that a firm sells cameras whose use requires a special type of film (for example, Polaroid's instant-picture cameras). One can think of the purchase of the camera as the payment of a lump-sum fee and the film purchases as the payment of a usage-sensitive fee. Also see Example 10.1.

When a two-part tariff is used, a firm must somehow prevent resale. Otherwise, it would make sense for one customer to pay one fixed fee and purchase all the goods, and then resell them to everyone else, so that only one fixed fee is collected. For example, suppose that a firm requires $100 from each buyer plus a per-unit charge of $1. If Lisa and Daniel each buy 50 units, they each pay $150, for a total expenditure of $300. If, however, Lisa buys for both, the total expenditure is $200. Thus, Lisa and Daniel could each pay $100 and be better off. To prevent this, the firm could try to prevent Lisa from reselling to Daniel by making it costly to divide shipped orders. The remainder of this section assumes that firms use one of the methods discussed in the

[1] As Chapter 9 shows, nonlinear pricing can also be used to practice first-degree price discrimination when a firm knows each consumer's demand curve. A monopoly that uses second-degree discrimination cannot extract all consumer surplus, as it could if it were able to implement first-degree discrimination.

previous chapter to prevent resale. This section analyzes the case in which a firm can use only one two-part tariff; subsequent sections relax this restriction.

When consumers are identical, a two-part tariff can be used to extract all consumer surplus. This point was illustrated in Chapter 9 in the section "Each Consumer Buys More Than One Unit." Typically, however, there is more than one type of consumer, and the firm cannot distinguish among consumers. We assume that the firm knows that demands differ within the population but lacks specific knowledge of each individual consumer's demand. For example, from marketing surveys, the firm may be aware that 50 percent of its customers value its services greatly, whereas another 50 percent could easily switch to another product. Even though the firm knows the general distribution of demand, it may be unable to determine the group to which a particular customer belongs.

Suppose that there are only two types of consumers, and they have the demand curves of Figure 10.1. A Type 2 customer is willing to buy more at price p than a Type 1 customer and enjoys more consumer surplus ($T_2 > T_1$) than does a Type 1 customer. If a firm charging a price p per unit could identify each customer's type, it could also charge a Type 1 customer a fee of T_1 and a Type 2 customer a fee of T_2.

Suppose the firm must choose a single two-part tariff. It chooses a lump-sum fee, T, and a per-unit charge, p, so as to maximize profits. If p exceeds average variable costs, the firm earns positive net revenues from additional sales. If the firm is unable to distinguish consumer types and charges a single two-part tariff involving a per-unit charge of p, the lump-sum fee it charges cannot exceed T_1 if Type 1 consumers are to participate. For example, if the firm charges a lump-sum fee of T_2, Type 1 consumers refuse to purchase the product.

The firm faces a dilemma. If it charges a low price, it sells more of its product and can charge a higher lump-sum fee (as can be seen from Figure 10.1). On the other

FIGURE 10.1 Two Different Demand Curves

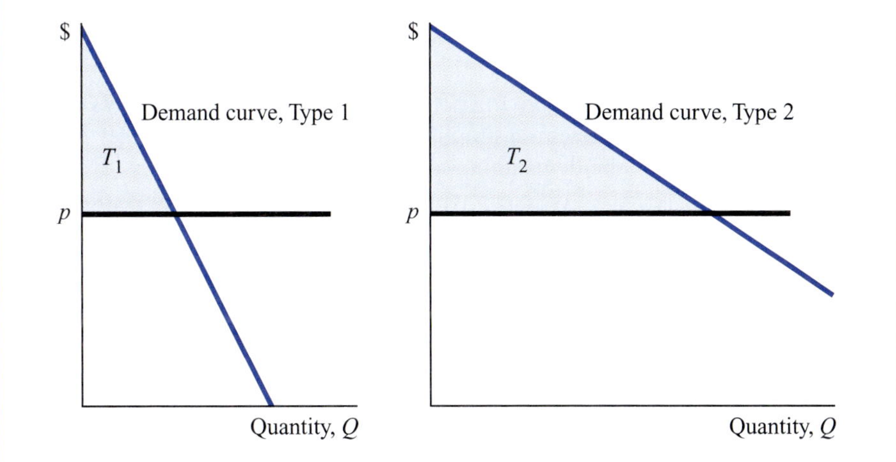

hand, its ability to charge a high lump-sum fee to extract the consumer surplus of Type 2 consumers is constrained by the Type 1 consumers' low willingness to pay. In many cases, the firm may make higher profits by concentrating on Type 2 consumers, letting Type 1 consumers choose not to purchase the product. The less similar Type 1 consumers are to Type 2 consumers, the more difficult it is for the firm to extract consumer surplus from Type 2 consumers with a single two-part tariff (see Appendices 10A and 10B).

The optimal two-part tariff typically generates more profits than a single price, because a single price is a special type of a two-part tariff: a two-part tariff with a zero lump-sum fee. The optimal two-part tariff generates less profit than perfect (first-degree) price discrimination, but may or may not generate less profit than third-degree price discrimination (where the firm charges a different price to each consumer group). However, unlike with third-degree price discrimination, a firm need not be able to identify which type a consumer is to use a two-part tariff.

One can think of a two-part tariff as consisting of a fixed charge for one product and a marginal charge for another. For example, the fixed charge could be the price of a camera, and the marginal charge that depends on usage could be the price of the film. Appendix 10A (and **www.aw-bc.com/carlton_perloff** "Two-Part Tariff for Two Products") shows that the usage-sensitive price (for example, the price of film) tends to exceed its marginal cost, but the fixed charge may well be below the marginal cost of the item (for example, the camera). In general, the fixed charge increases as the difference between the average quantity purchased and the quantity purchased by the marginal customer decreases, and as the elasticity of demand increases. The usage-sensitive price increases as the elasticity of demand decreases and as the difference between the quantities purchased by the average customer and the marginal customer increases.

Two Two-Part Tariffs

The two-part tariff just described is one of the simplest examples of a pricing structure in which the average price varies with output—which is a characteristic of any nonlinear pricing scheme. In general, the amount paid can vary with the amount purchased in any prespecified way: The price paid is a function of quantity, and the firm is allowed to choose any function it desires.

Finding the general nonlinear pricing policy that maximizes a monopoly's profits is complicated.[2] This section presents a simplified example to illustrate the key ideas.

Suppose a firm knows the demand curves of two types of consumers (Type 1 and Type 2) and the prevalence of different types of consumers in the population, but it does not know the type of any individual consumer. The firm can offer consumers a choice of two different two-part tariff schedules. Each consumer chooses or *self-selects* that schedule that corresponds to a higher level of utility. The two schedules are shown in Figure 10.2 as straight, black lines. The intercepts on the vertical axis are the fixed,

[2]See Katz (1983), Spence (1977b), Tirole (1988, Ch. 3), Wilson (1993), and Appendix 10B for more details.

FIGURE 10.2 Menu of Two-Part Tariffs

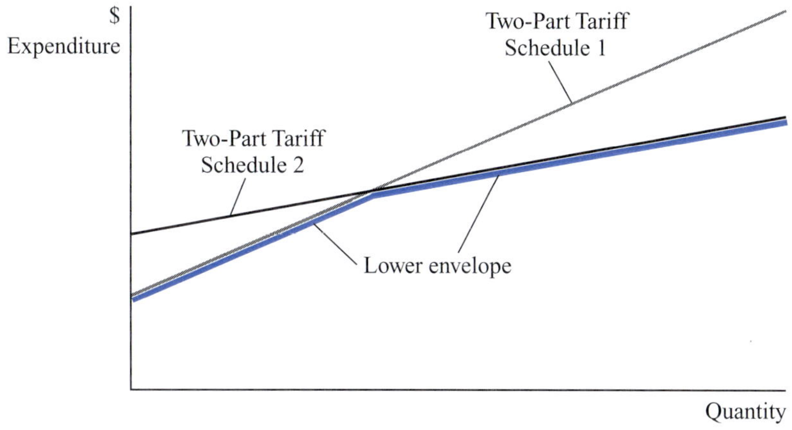

lump-sum fees, and the slopes of the curves are the constant marginal costs. From inspection, the consumer can purchase a small number of units for less money by choosing Two-Part Tariff Schedule 1 and a large number of units for less money by choosing Two-Part Tariff Schedule 2. Following this reasoning, consumers choose the lower "envelope" of the two curves, which is shown by a thick blue kinked line.

The firm chooses its two two-part tariff schedules to maximize its profits. The inability of the firm to identify the willingness of any individual customers to pay constrains its pricing policy. The firm provides a choice of two two-part tariffs in order to separate consumers into groups, so it can lower the price to one group without having to pass along the same low price to the other group. This motive is the same as in any price discrimination scheme (Chapter 9).

If the firm knew which consumers belonged to each group (and could prevent resale), the firm could design a two-part tariff for each group. From our earlier discussion of perfect price discrimination in Chapter 9, the optimal policy when the firm is knowledgeable is for the firm to charge each consumer a price equal to its marginal cost, m, and to extract the consumer surplus of each customer by charging a lump-sum fee. Thus, if in Figure 10.1, $p = m$, the firm charges a Type 1 consumer T_1 and a Type 2 consumer T_2.

Suppose the firm simply announced that it had two two-part tariffs: one of (T_1, m) and the other of (T_2, m), where the first number (T_1) in parentheses is the fixed fee, and the second (m) is the marginal price. If the two types of consumers have demand curves as shown in Figure 10.1, no consumer would ever choose the second two-part tariff, because T_2 exceeds T_1. That is, all consumers would choose the first two-part tariff. Because consumers always choose (self-select) the pricing structure that is best for them, the firm's ability to price discriminate is constrained. In this example, consumer unwillingness to choose higher price schedules rules out the possibility of perfect price discrimination. The firm designs its pricing structure to maximize profits subject to a **self-selection constraint**: a restriction on a firm's pricing structure such that consumers in any group do not prefer another group's two-part tariff schedule. We focus on an optimal solution in which the monopoly serves both types of consumers.

For example, suppose that Type 2 consumers demand more units than Type 1 consumers at every price, as shown in Figure 10.1. Then the firm's optimal policy is for the Type 2 consumers' fixed fee, T_2, to exceed the fee for Type 1 consumers, T_1; the marginal price facing Type 2 consumers, p_2, to be below that for Type 1 consumers, p_1, and to equal marginal cost (see Appendix 10B). By offering a low price to the large demanders, customers derive a large consumer surplus, which the firm captures through T_2. The high T_2 discourages the small-volume buyers (Type 1), who prefer to pay a higher marginal price on the smaller amounts they purchase. In other words, the high-volume purchasers (Type 2) value low prices much more than the low-volume purchasers (Type 1), which enables the firm to separate the two groups.

Restaurants provide one extreme example of the use of two two-part tariffs to separate consumers into groups. Many restaurants offer consumers choices of all-you-can-eat buffets (high T, $p = 0$) and an á la carte menu ($T = 0$, high p). Large eaters choose the buffet.

Figure 10.3 illustrates this example for Type 2 consumers. Even though the fixed fee T_2 is greater than T_1, a Type 2 consumer prefers (T_2, p_2) to (T_1, p_1) because the price is lower ($p_2 < p_1$) so that the remaining consumer surplus is higher under the second tariff. Similarly, Type 1 consumers prefer (T_1, p_1) to (T_2, p_2); their remaining consumer surplus is higher under the tariff (T_1, p_1) because they can take advantage of the low fixed fee.

FIGURE 10.3 How a Type 2 Consumer Fares Under the Two-Part Tariffs

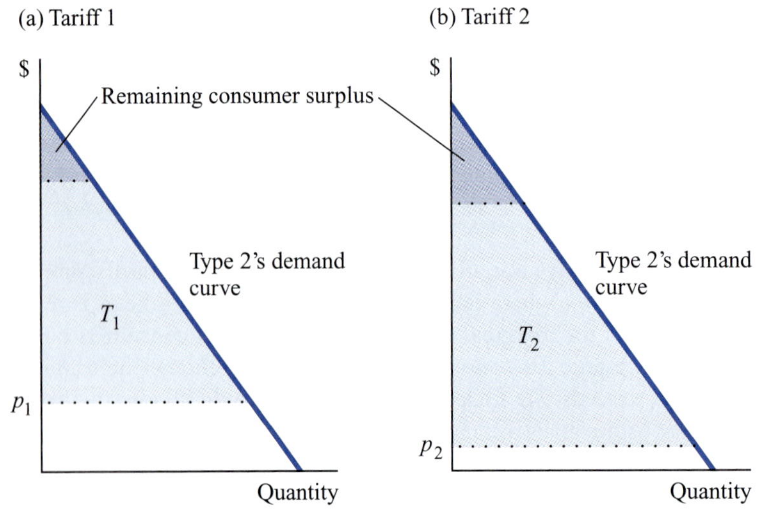

Type 2 consumers benefit from the presence of the Type 1 consumers. Without the Type 1 consumers, Type 2 consumers would receive zero utility. Consumer diversity helps consumers who have large demands. (See Appendix 10B.)

Tie-in Sales

A *tie-in sale* is one in which a consumer can buy one good only by purchasing another good as well. For example, if a supermarket sells you a pound of coffee on the condition that you also buy sugar, that would be a tie-in sale. Due to litigation growing out of legal restrictions governing the use of tie-in sales (see Chapter 19), there are many, well-documented examples of firms using tie-in sales.

Tie-in sales may be used to price discriminate. We use the term *price discrimination* quite broadly, in the sense that a tie-in sale enables a monopoly to increase its profit over and above what it would earn if the two goods were offered for sale individually at constant prices. As with all price discrimination schemes, the reason the tie-in can increase profits is that it enables a firm to charge more to consumers who value the good the most. Although tie-in sales can be used to price discriminate, it is important to recognize that there are many other reasons for tie-in sales that are unrelated to price discrimination.

General Justifications for Tie-in Sales

Tie-in sales may be used to increase efficiency, avoid price regulations, give secret price discounts, and to assure quality. After examining these motives in this section, we examine how tie-in sales can be used to price discriminate.[3]

Efficiency. Tie-in sales may be used to increase efficiency. For example, laced shoes are typically sold with laces; everyone who buys laced shoes needs shoe laces. As long as people's tastes for shoe laces do not differ dramatically, it is more efficient (that is, it lowers transaction costs) to sell laced shoes with standard shoe laces than to sell the shoe laces and shoes separately. In the extreme, every product can be thought of as composed of multiple products. For example, a radio consists of many individual components. The same is true of an automobile, which could be regarded as a package including an engine, tires, and a car body. Obviously, each of these products could be sold separately, but because consumers desire assembled products, they come tied together. See Example 10.2.

Another efficiency justification for tie-in sales is that they economize on the cost of grading individual units of a product. Instead of grading each unit separately, total search cost can be reduced if the buyer must purchase several items together. See Example 10.3.

Evade Regulations. Another common reason for tie-in sales is to evade price controls. Imagine that the government sets price controls on steel. Suppose the controlled

[3]In the next chapter, we analyze how tie-in sales can be used strategically to harm rivals.

EXAMPLE 10.2

You Auto Save from Tie-in Sales

Instead of purchasing an automobile already assembled—a tie-in sale—you could buy all the parts separately and assemble and paint the car yourself. Doing so would cost you substantially more, however. According to the *Journal of American Insurance*, the cost of buying an assembled 1988 Buick Skylark from a dealer was $12,568. The cost of purchasing the replacement parts for the car and the paint service was $40,280.

Source: Brendan Boyd, "By the Numbers," *San Francisco Chronicle*, March 3, 1989:B5.

price is below the market-clearing price (the price at which supply equals demand) by $5.00. One method of circumventing price controls is to sell steel at the controlled price but only on the condition that the consumer also pay $5.25 for a pencil that costs 25¢ to produce. In this way, the market-clearing price for steel is maintained, and the price controls are still met.

A variant of the preceding example is to use a tie-in sale to circumvent regulation. Some public utilities, such as electric utilities, are subject to rate regulation. If electric utilities were allowed to sell light bulbs and were also allowed to force consumers to buy light bulbs as a condition of receiving electric service, the electric utility could completely circumvent the rate regulation by charging a high price for light bulbs, unless the regulators also regulated the price for light bulbs.

Secret Price Discounts. Another motivation for tie-ins is to give a secret price discount. For example, a member of an oligopoly may want to give price discounts without rivals knowing about them (see Chapter 5). It may be able to keep its discounts se-

EXAMPLE 10.3

Stuck Holding the Bag

A large fraction of the world's diamonds is marketed by deBeers Consolidated Mines. A buyer is allowed to specify the average quality of diamond. The buyer is then given a bag containing several diamonds. The buyer has the right to reject or accept the bag in its entirety. A buyer who rejects a bag is not invited back. One rationale for this marketing procedure is that if buyers were allowed to investigate each stone in detail and reject any one stone, deBeers would have to spend resources to sort and grade the diamonds more carefully. The cost is avoided by the "take the bag or leave it" selling policy.

Source: Kenney and Klein (1983).

cret by selling a product at the oligopoly price but tying that sale to another product with a very low price. For example, a firm can give a 10 percent discount on a $100 price by giving as a gift to purchasers of the product another product that is worth $10. Alternatively, the firm could charge customers $10 less than they would have to pay if they purchased the tied product in the competitive market.

Assure Quality. Tie-in sales can assure quality. For example, Kodak claimed that it tied the development of its film to its film sales because it did not believe that independent developers could develop Kodak film as skillfully as could Kodak.[4] Kodak could have reasoned that if an independent developer made a mistake and produced poor pictures, the consumer would be unable to distinguish whether the film was bad or the developer was bad. The consumer might then be reluctant to purchase film from Kodak in the future.

Generally, a firm may assure quality by forcing customers to buy another of its products or services or to not use substitutes. When Searle introduced NutraSweet, a nonsugar sweetener, it claimed that it was natural and better tasting than other less expensive sugar substitutes, such as saccharin. Beverage manufacturers began using a blend of saccharin and NutraSweet in their diet sodas. Searle felt that the taste of the blend was not as good as NutraSweet alone, and, fearing that NutraSweet would be improperly judged, required that users of NutraSweet not use it as a blend.[5] Of course, both Kodak and NutraSweet may have had other motivations for their actions.

Tie-in Sales as a Method of Price Discrimination

A final reason for tie-in sales—the focus of the rest of this chapter—is to increase monopoly profit. That is, if a firm has a monopoly in a product, it may be able to increase its profits by tying another good to the sale of the monopolized good. Tie-in sales can be used to price discriminate in a variety of circumstances, and the way they work is analyzed differently depending on the circumstances. Therefore, after reviewing some general reasons for using tie-in sales as a method of price discrimination, we discuss their use in a variety of different circumstances.

There are two common types of tie-in sales. One is **bundling** (Adams and Yellen 1976) or a **package tie-in sale** and occurs when two or more products are sold only in fixed proportions. For example, a store requires that, if you buy one jar of coffee, you must buy one bag of sugar. Everyone who buys these products consumes them in these fixed proportions, or else they must dispose of part of one or the other product.

The other common type is a **requirements tie-in sale**, where customers who purchase one product from a firm are required to make all their purchases of another product from that firm. For example, IBM used to require that purchasers of its machines that used tabulating cards buy all of their tabulating cards, no matter how

[4]Kodak film was once sold only with development included. Purchasers simply mailed the film to Kodak for developing at no additional charge.
[5]*Newsweek,* January 28, 1985:57.

many, from IBM.[6] In such a requirements tie, different consumers might consume different relative amounts of the two products. For example, in the IBM case, a large accounting firm might consume many more tabulating cards than a small manufacturing firm. In some cases a requirements tie automatically occurs when the related product is only produced by the firm selling the other product. For example, Polaroid is the only firm that can sell film to fit the cameras it manufactures.

As with all methods of nonlinear pricing in which different consumers pay different prices for the same product, a firm can use a tie-in sale to price discriminate only if trades between consumers are prevented. For example, in the case of the (fixed proportions) package tie-in, the tie-in fails as a method of price discrimination if customers can break apart the package and resell the various products on the open market. Similarly, in the case of the requirements tie-in, the consumer must be unable to purchase the tied good elsewhere at the competitive price.

We now examine each of the two types of tie-in sales and the circumstances under which they increase profits, beginning with an analysis of a package tie-in where product demands are independent. Products have independent demands if the value a consumer places on one product does not depend on the consumption of the other product. We then turn to an analysis of products whose demands are related.

Package Tie-in Sales of Independent Products

To examine package tie-in sales of independent products, we first suppose that a firm has a monopoly in both products. Then we examine a firm that has a monopoly in only one of the two products.

Package Tie-in with Both Products Monopolized. Suppose a firm has a monopoly in both Product *A* and Product *B*. For example, a movie company, which sells movies to theaters, has two movies, *A* and *B*, which are in great demand. Would this monopoly earn higher profits if it sold *A* and *B* separately or as a package? The answer depends on the value that various consumers place on each of the two movies separately versus the value they place on the package (Stigler 1968c).

The monopoly sells to two types of consumers. Type 1 consumers are willing to pay at most \$9,000 to purchase *A* separately and \$3,000 to purchase *B* separately (see Table 10.1). Type 2 consumers are willing to pay at most \$10,000 for *A* separately and \$2,000 for *B*. The amount each group is willing to pay for *A* is independent of whether *B* is also purchased, and vice versa.

Suppose the cost of producing the products is zero, and the monopoly wants to maximize the revenues that it receives from selling to these two types of consumers. The monopoly has two choices: It can sell *A* and *B* separately or as a package. If it sells Product *A* separately, it maximizes revenue by charging a price of \$9,000. At that

[6] *IBM v. United States,* 298 U.S. 131 (1936). The machine performed numerical calculations mechanically based upon the holes in the cards that were placed into the machine. Customers who bought cards through IBM presumably paid a higher price than they would have if they bought from others.

TABLE 10.1 **Example of a Profitable Package Tie-in**

	Type 1 Consumers	Type 2 Consumers
Amount ($) willing to pay for *A*	9,000	10,000
Amount ($) willing to pay for *B*	3,000	2,000
Amount ($) willing to pay for *A* and *B* together	12,000	12,000

price, both types of consumers purchase Product *A*, and the monopoly receives $18,000. Similarly, in order to maximize the revenue from selling *B* separately, the monopoly sets a price of $2,000 and receives revenue of $4,000. Therefore, the total revenues received from selling *A* and *B* separately are $22,000.

Now, suppose that the monopoly decides to sell *A* and *B* as a package. Both Type 1 and Type 2 consumers are willing to pay $12,000 for the package. If the monopoly sells the package for $12,000, it sells to both consumers and receives $24,000. Therefore, in this example, profit (revenues) is maximized by tying the two goods together and selling them as a package instead of selling them separately. By selling the products as a package, the monopoly effectively is able to charge Type 1 consumers a higher price for *B* ($3,000) compared to that charged Type 2 consumers ($2,000) and a lower price for *A* ($9,000) compared to that charged Type 2 consumers ($10,000). In other words, when both Type 1 and Type 2 consumers buy the same package, they are placing different relative values on the components of the package. Thus, this tie-in sale is an example of price discrimination: The monopoly charges different prices to different customers for the same product.

By changing the numbers in Table 10.1, it is possible to show that a tie-in is not always the most profitable strategy. In Table 10.2, it is more profitable for the monopoly to sell the products separately than as a package. The maximum profit from selling the products separately is $20,000 ($18,000 for *A*, which is sold to both types of consumers, and $2,000 for *B*, which is sold to only Type 2 consumers), whereas the profit from selling *A* and *B* together (to both types of consumers) is only $19,000.

Let us return to the example in Table 10.1. Suppose someone purchases the packages of *A* and *B* together, breaks the package apart, and sells *A* and *B* separately in a resale market. The market-clearing price for *A* that induces the Type 1 and Type 2

TABLE 10.2 **Example of an Unprofitable Package Tie-in**

	Type 1 Consumers	Type 2 Consumers
Amount ($) willing to pay for *A*	9,000	10,000
Amount ($) willing to pay for *B*	500	2,000
Amount ($) willing to pay for *A* and *B* together	9,500	12,000

consumers to hold A is \$9,000. Similarly, the market-clearing price for B is \$2,000. Now if the Type 1 and Type 2 consumers realize that a resale market will develop after they purchase their packages and that the price of A will be \$9,000 and the price of B will be \$2,000, they will not be willing to purchase the package. Instead, they will wait until the resale market develops and purchase A and B separately for a combined price of \$11,000 rather than for the \$12,000 in the example. Thus, with a resale market, nobody purchases the package, and the attempt to practice price discrimination through a package tie-in does not work. That is, a resale market destroys the ability of a monopoly to charge effectively different prices for the same product and thereby destroys the ability to price discriminate through tie-in sales.

In the absence of a resale market, in the example in Table 10.1, a package tie-in resulted in a successful price discrimination because there is a negative relationship between what each type consumer is willing to pay for the two items. For example, Type 1 consumers put a relatively high value on B and place a relatively low value on A (see McAfee, McMillan, and Whinston 1989). As a result, there is relative heterogeneity between the two consumer types in their valuation of the individual products, but relative homogeneity in their valuation of the package.[7] See Example 10.4.

Mixed Bundling with Both Products Monopolized. Some firms give consumers a choice between buying a bundle and buying goods separately, which is called *mixed bundling* (Adams and Yellen 1976). You can buy a computer with bundled software or buy the hardware and software separately. Baseball teams sell season tickets and tickets to individual games.

If you ran a restaurant, you would want to know which of the following pricing methods would maximize your profit:

- *Individual pricing:* Customers order each item separately off an à la carte menu. A customer may order any appetizer, main dish, or dessert and may skip any course.
- *Pure bundling:* Customers can only purchase a fixed-price meal—a bundle—that includes all courses and offers limited choices (possibly only one) for each course.
- *Mixed bundling:* Customers may either order a fixed-price meal or order from an à la carte menu.

You'd first have to determine whether you can bundle at all. If you could bundle, then you'd have to determine which pricing method gives you the highest profit.

[7] Even when the valuations for A and B are not negatively correlated, bundling can be profitable. For example, suppose that there are two goods, A and B, each of which is valued by consumers at either \$7 or \$13. There are then four possible value combinations: (7, 7), (7, 13), (13, 7), (13, 13). Assuming that the products can be produced at no cost, if the goods are sold unbundled, the profit-maximizing price of each good is \$7, and four units of each good are sold for a total profit (revenue) of \$56. If the products are bundled, the profit-maximizing solution is to sell three bundles at \$20 each so that the total profit is \$60. See McAfee et al. (1989).

EXAMPLE 10.4 *Tied to TV*

In most areas of the United States, a monopoly provider of cable television offers consumers various service packages. Typically, the basic bundle of service includes local programming, TV network programming, and about seven additional cable network channels.

How should a cable provider decide which networks to include in its bundle? One answer is to choose them so as to be better able to price discriminate through bundling. Consumers differ in their valuations of individual networks. However, the cable provider may be able to bundle various networks so that consumers with varying tastes value the overall bundle relatively similarly. For example, a family's teenagers may watch MTV but rarely tune in to CNN News, while their parents may do the opposite. Thus, each household could value the bundle of MTV plus CNN News at the same price, even though they value each network differently. If so, the cable provider can charge a single price for the bundle that extracts most of the consumers' value, even though consumers differ greatly in their valuations of individual networks.

As more networks are added to the bundle, consumers who otherwise would have not purchased a particular network now purchase it as a part of the bundle. Moreover, the more networks in a bundle, the more likely it is that households value the bundle similarly, a preference that results in a more elastic demand curve. Crawford's (2001) empirical study of the bundling decisions of cable providers across the United States confirms these results. By combining several networks into a basic bundle service, a cable provider is able to increase its profit on average above unbundled sales by about 14 percent, according to Crawford's simulations. Consumers lose about 13 percent of the surplus they would have obtained in unbundled sales. Moreover, as price discrimination theory predicts, bundling together similar networks is less profitable than bundling dissimilar ones.

You can profitably bundle only if conditions on market power, resale, and tastes are met. We'll assume that restaurants are monopolistically competitive because their products are not perfect substitutes, so that you have some market power. Certainly you can ignore resale problems. A customer is unlikely to order the fixed-price dinner and then lean over to the person at the next table and offer to sell the appetizer.

It depends on your customers' tastes whether the condition is met that customers who put a relatively high value on one good place a relatively low value on another good. We illustrate how your decision depends on your customers' tastes in Figure 10.4.

For simplicity, suppose your restaurant only sells a main dish of halibut and a piece of pie for dessert. On the axes of the diagrams in the figure are the value or reservation price customers put on each good. In Figure 10.4a, your à la carte menu lists the price of both dishes at $8 each. Any customer in area *D*—who values the fish at more than

FIGURE 10.4 Customers and Mixed Bundling

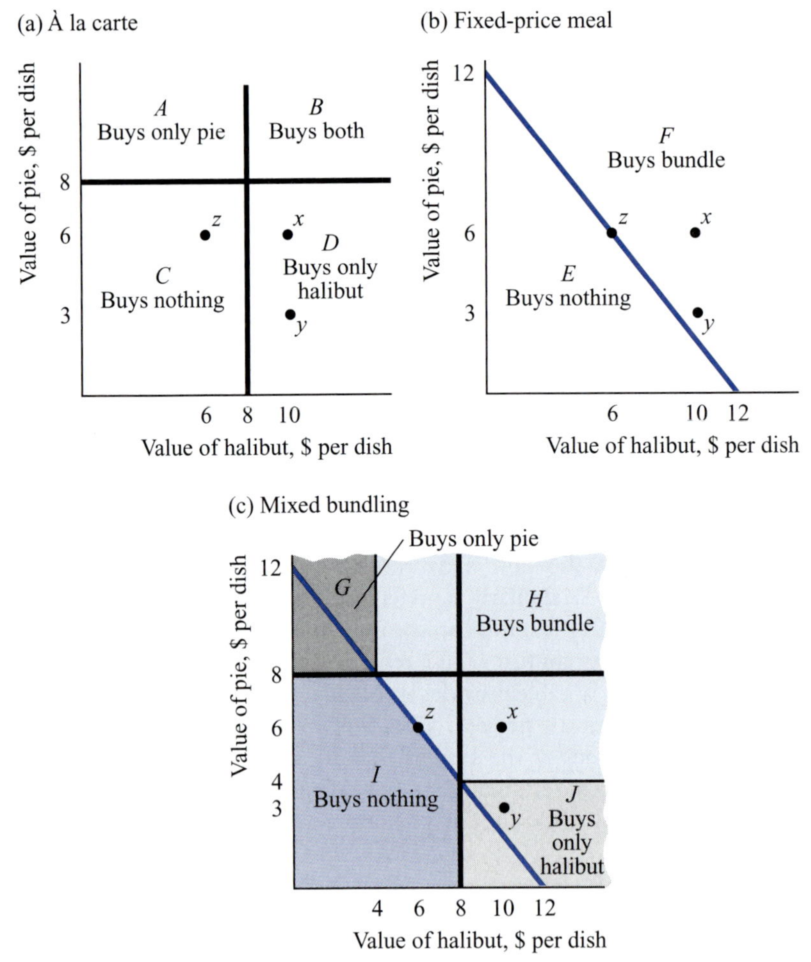

$8 and the pie at less than $8—comes to your restaurant just for the halibut. An example of such a set of tastes is point *x*, where a customer values the fish at $10 and the pie at $6. People whose reservation prices are in area *A* buy only pie, those in area *B* buy both, and those in area *C* buy neither (point *z* at $6 for halibut and $6 for pie).

Figure 10.4b shows how customers make decisions if you offer only a fixed-price meal of halibut and pie. The customer who values fish at $10 and pie at $6, point *x* in area *F*, buys the bundle at $12, because the customer was willing to pay $16 for the meal. As we saw in Figure 10.4a, this customer would not have been willing to buy the pie if each had been priced separately at $8, where buying both dishes cost $16. Any consumer in *F*, who values the bundle at more than $12, buys the bundle. A consumer who places a value on the bundle of less than \$12, area *E*, would not buy the fixed-price meal. The consumer at *z*, who bought neither good from the à la carte menu buys both from the fixed-price menu.

Figure 10.4c shows mixed bundling. A customer may buy either dish at \$8 each or buy the fixed-price meal bundle at \$12. The customer whose reservation prices are \$10 for fish and \$6 for pie, point *x* in area *H*, would still buy the fixed-price meal. The customer reaps \$4 of surplus from the fixed-price bundle (\$16 – \$12) but only \$2(= \$10 − \$8) of surplus from consuming only halibut.

If, however, this person valued pie at only \$3, point *y* in area *J*, the customer would buy only halibut at \$8. Because the customer places a value of \$13 on consuming both dishes, the consumer surplus from buying the bundle for \$12 is \$1(= \$13 − \$12). If the customer orders only the fish, the consumer surplus is \$2(= \$10 − \$8). Thus, the customer is better off ordering only the fish.[8]

By similar reasoning, consumers in area *G* buy only pie. Finally, consumers in area *I* do not patronize your restaurant because the price of the bundle exceeds the value to them and the price of each dish exceeds the consumers' reservation price.

Which pricing scheme gives you the highest profit depends on both how much your various customers are willing to pay for the two dishes and your costs of producing these dishes. For pure or mixed bundling to pay, your restaurant must sell more food than with individual pricing. Selling more, however, will increase profits only if revenue rises by more than costs.

Suppose you have only three types of customers—*a, b,* and *c*, with valuations of the two dishes in Figure 10.5—and that your cost of producing a dish is \$3 for halibut and \$2 for pie. If you price each dish separately, you maximize your profit by charging \$11 for the halibut and \$8 for pie. At these prices, Customers *a* and *b* buy only pie and Customer *c* buys only halibut. You earn \$6 = \$8 (price of pie) − \$2 (cost of pie) on each of the two servings of pie you sell and \$8 = \$11 − \$3 on the halibut, for a total profit of \$20. Because Customer *a* was willing to pay \$10 for a piece of pie and the price is only \$8, you are not capturing all the consumer surplus.

If you only sell a pure bundle, you charge \$12 and earn a profit of \$21 = (\$12 − \$5) × 3, where \$5 is the combined cost of producing both dishes. You make more by bundling than selling separately because customers who value one dish greatly put a lower valuation on the other. As a result, bundling allows you to sell more dishes. You sell two servings of pie and one of halibut with separate prices, whereas you sell three servings of pies and three of halibut with pure bundling.

Using mixed bundling, however, you can do even better. You set the bundle price at \$12, the price of halibut at \$10.99, and the price of pie at \$9.99. Customer *a* buys

---

[8]Let the reservation price for halibut be r_h, and that of pie be r_p. The price of halibut is p_h, the price of pie is p_p, and the bundle price is p_b. A consumer buys the bundle if

$r_h + r_p \geq p_b$ (the value of the bundle is greater than its price),

$r_p \geq p_b - p_h$ (the reservation value of pie is greater than the difference between the bundle price and the price of halibut), and

$r_h \geq p_b - p_p$ (the reservation value of halibut is greater than the difference between the bundle price and the price of pie).

FIGURE 10.5 Profitability of Mixed Bundling

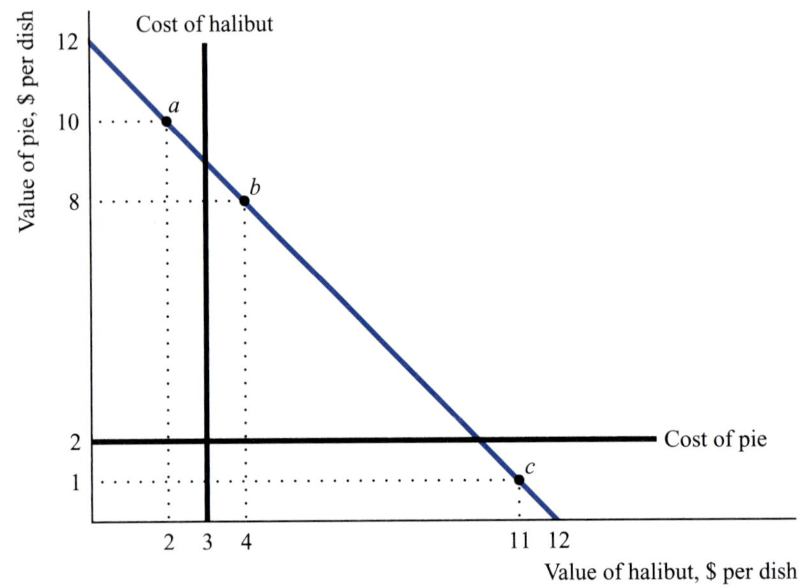

only the pie (the bundle costs $2.01 more and that customer only values halibut at $2), Customer *b* buys the bundle, and Customer *c* buys only the halibut (you sell two servings of pie and two of halibut). You make $7.99 each from Customers *a* and *c* and $7 from Customer *b* for a total of $22.98.

You sell more dishes with pure bundling—three of each—than with mixed bundling—two of each. The reason your profit is lower with pure bundling is that you're selling dishes to customers who value those dishes at less than your cost of production. With the pure bundle, Customer *a* values the halibut at $2, which is less than your cost of $3, and Customer *c* values the pie at $1, which is less than your cost of $2. As a result, selling those extra dishes doesn't benefit you. If you sell Customer *a* the bundle, you make $7 profit. On the other hand, if you sell Customer *a* the pie at $9.99, you make $7.99 profit. Thus, you benefit from discouraging that customer from buying the halibut. With mixed bundling you are capturing essentially all the consumer surplus.

With these same customers, if you had no cost of production, you would maximize profit by using pure bundling. With no cost of production, you want to sell lots of dishes. In general, depending on your customers' tastes and your costs of production, any of the three pricing methods could maximize your profit. See Example 10.5.

Package Tie-ins with Only One Product Monopolized. Now suppose that the firm is a monopoly of only Product *A* (with no marginal cost of production). Product *B* is competitively produced and sold at *m* (its constant marginal cost of production).

EXAMPLE 10.5 *Not Too Suite—Mixed Bundling*

Word processors and spreadsheets are separate computer-software products. During the 1990s, software producers shifted from selling word-processor and spreadsheet programs separately to selling them as part of a *suite* in which the two software products were bundled together. Consumers could still buy each component separately, so producers were engaged in mixed bundling.

Why did this mixed bundling occur? One answer is that it is efficient to buy a bundle to ensure that the component parts will work together: that is, to ensure quality. Another explanation uses price discrimination theory, saying specifically that mixed bundling would be profit maximizing if consumers who placed a high value on a word processing program (such as Microsoft Word) placed a low value on a spreadsheet program (such as Microsoft Excel), and vice versa.

Gandal (2003) finds that the empirical evidence supports the discrimination theory. In a survey of home PC users, 43% said that they used both programs, 50% used only one, and 7% used neither. Among business PC users, 63% said they used both programs, while 37% used only one. That is, a relatively large fraction of users use only one (but not both) pieces of software. Gandal's sophisticated estimation of consumer demand preferences using a discrete random choice model confirms that, in general, consumers with a high value for spreadsheets had a low value for word processors and vice versa, so that there is indeed a sizable negative correlation in demand for the two.

We continue to assume that the demands for Product A and Product B are independent, in the sense that consumers' valuation of Product A is unrelated to whether or not they also consume Product B and vice versa. Does it pay for the monopoly of A to tie Products A and B together in fixed proportions?

Before analyzing this example in detail, let us use common sense to guess the answer. Suppose that it were profitable for the monopoly to tie a competitive good B to the purchase of Product A. Because A and B are independent products, any competitive product could be tied to Product A to increase the monopoly's profit. In other words, a monopoly of, say, cars, might be expected to tie all sorts of unrelated products to the sale of cars. We rarely, if ever, see a monopoly tie a completely unrelated product to the sale of its own product. Because we do not observe that, it must generally not be profitable for a monopoly to tie an unrelated, competitively available product to the sale of its monopolized product.

Let us now analyze the example formally. Suppose that a monopoly of Product A uses a package tie-in and requires that for every unit of A purchased, one unit of Product B must also be purchased. The monopoly purchases B at the competitive price, m, inserts it into a package with A, and charges p^* for the package. The profit for every package sold is therefore $p^* - m$. This tie is not profitable if the monopoly would make more money if it sold Product A separately and charged $p^* - m$.

Two types of consumers consider purchasing the product. One type likes Product B. If those consumers do not obtain Product B in the package with Product A, they buy it elsewhere at price m. For these consumers, it is as if they are buying B at price m and paying $p^* - m$ for A. They are completely indifferent whether they pay $p^* - m$ for A and m for B separately or whether they buy A and B together in a package for p^*.

The second type of consumer values a unit of B at less than m (that is, this type of consumer is unwilling to buy B at the competitive price). If they buy the package, they are forced to consume more of Product B than they would have if they had been allowed to buy B separately at the market price, m. For example, a particular consumer may well end up getting B when, in fact, this consumer has absolutely no use for Product B and values it at zero. These consumers will purchase the package consisting of A and B at p^* only if they value A at p^* or above.

If A were sold by itself for $p^* - m$, more of this second type of consumer would purchase Product A than are willing to purchase the package at p^*. For example, consumers who place no value on B but a value of $p^* - m$ on A would buy A separately at $p^* - m$, but would refuse to buy the package at p^*. If the monopoly makes a per-unit profit of $p^* - m$ when the package is sold, and the same $p^* - m$ when A is sold separately (at price $p^* - m$), the monopoly's profits are higher if it sells A separately, because more units of A are sold. In other words, for any price for a package, p^*, a monopoly can always do better by selling A separately for $p^* - m$ than by selling the package for p^*. By packaging A and B together, the monopoly is throwing away sales by forcing some consumers to buy a package that includes a product that they do not value highly. As a result, some consumers who value A reasonably highly do not buy the package. Thus, a monopoly does not have an incentive to package its product in fixed proportions with a good that is competitively produced if the goods are independently demanded.[9]

Interrelated Demands

Very often the demands for goods are interrelated. For example, the value of a camera depends on the availability of film. The price of film influences the demand for cameras, and vice versa. This interrelationship of demand creates incentives to price discriminate through package tie-ins and requirements tie-ins. Before illustrating this point, let us first examine profit maximization with interrelated demands without tie-in sales.

[9]The case of a requirements tie with independent demand is more complicated than that of a package tie. Mathewson and Winter (1977) show that the use of a tie of a competitive and monopoly product with independent demands could be profitable. They give an example of a gas supplier to gas stations that tied the sale of gasoline to batteries and other accessories (which the gasoline supplier did not produce but sold with a markup) so as to "spread out the distortion" of the markup above the efficient transfer price across several products instead of just one.

Profit Maximization with Interrelated Demands. Suppose a firm has a monopoly in two products, *A* and *B*. If the demands are independent, the demand for *A* depends only on the price of *A*, and the demand for *B* depends only on the price of *B*. With interrelated demands, the demand for *A* depends on both the price of *A* and the price of *B*. Similarly, the demand for *B* depends upon the price of both *A* and *B*.

The constant marginal costs of production for Products *A* and *B* are m_A and m_B, the corresponding prices are p_A and p_B, and the corresponding demand curves are $D_A(p_A, p_B)$ and $D_B(p_A, p_B)$. The profit from selling *A* is:

$$\pi_A(p_A, p_B) = (p_A - m_A)D_A(p_A, p_B),$$

where $p_A - m_A$ is its profit per unit of *A* sold. Similarly, the profit from selling *B* is

$$\pi_B(p_A, p_B) = (p_B - m_B)D_B(p_A, p_B).$$

The monopoly's problem is to maximize profits from its sales of the two products, π, which depend on the two prices:

$$\begin{aligned} \pi(p_A, p_B) &= \pi_A(p_A, p_B) + \pi_B(p_A, p_B) \\ &= (p_A - m_A)D_A(p_A, p_B) + (p_B - m_B)\,D_B(p_A, p_B). \qquad (10.1) \end{aligned}$$

In choosing the optimal prices to charge, the monopoly not only considers its profits from the production and sale of *A*, π_A, but also takes into account how the price of *A* affects the profit from *B*, π_B, and vice versa. That is, a monopoly with interrelated products must take the interrelationship into account in determining its optimal prices.

Figure 10.6 illustrates the monopoly's problem. The demand curve for *A* shifts out as the price of *B* falls from \$5 to \$4. By altering price p_B, the monopoly may be able to shift out its demand curve for *A* in such a way that it can extract a large enough profit from the extra sales of *A* to more than offset any decline in its profit from its sales of *B*.[10] (If p_A changes, D_B would also shift.) Thus, a monopoly of two complementary products may set at least one price higher than would separate monopolies and one price lower.[11]

[10]To choose the profit maximizing p_A and p_B, the monopoly sets the derivatives of profits, π, in Equation 10.1 with respect to each price equal to zero:

$$\frac{\partial \pi}{\partial p_A} = \frac{\partial \pi_A}{\partial p_A} + \frac{\partial \pi_B}{\partial p_A} = 0,$$

$$\frac{\partial \pi}{\partial p_B} = \frac{\partial \pi_A}{\partial p_B} + \frac{\partial \pi_B}{\partial p_B} = 0.$$

These conditions are different from the conditions that would result if, instead of a single monopoly that controls both p_A and p_B, there were two monopolies, one setting p_A and one setting p_B. Those conditions are $\partial \pi_A/\partial p_A = 0$ and $\partial \pi_B/\partial p_B = 0$, assuming Bertrand behavior.

[11]With substitutes, a single monopoly will generally charge higher prices than separate monopolies that ignore their (negative) price effect on each other's profit.

FIGURE 10.6 Interrelated Demands

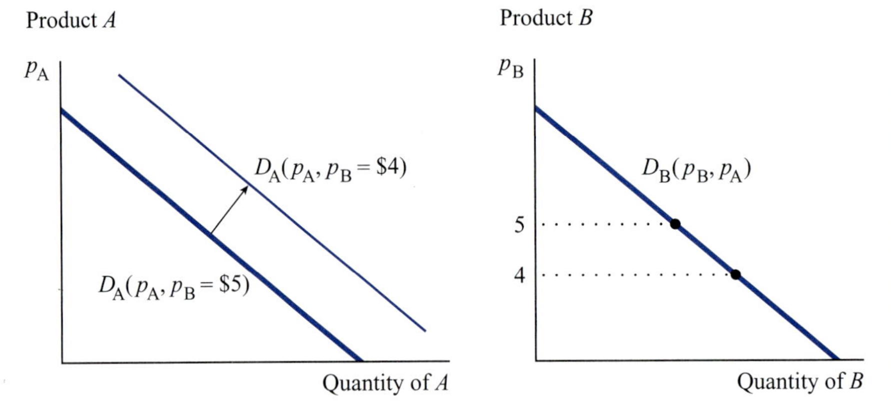

Indeed, it may pay to set p_B below its production cost in order to sell *A* at a higher price. This result is similar to that from a two-part tariff. For example, one could interpret the sale of a camera and film as a two-part tariff in which the lump-sum fee is paid for the camera and the usage fee is paid for the film. As we explained above with respect to the two-part tariff, it could be profitable to charge a price below cost for the camera. We now investigate both package tie-ins and requirements tie-ins when demands are interrelated.

Package Tie-ins with Interrelated Demands. If demands are interrelated, package tie-ins are one method that a monopoly can use to avoid inefficient behavior by consumers and hence increase its profit. For example, automobiles are made from aluminum and steel. The automobile manufacturers' willingness to pay for aluminum depends on the price of steel. Therefore, if output can be produced using variable proportions of the two inputs, the demands for the two inputs are interrelated.

Suppose that the automobile and steel industries are competitive, but that aluminum is provided by a monopoly. The automobile manufacturers choose a combination of aluminum and steel based on the ratio of a monopoly aluminum price to a competitive steel price. Because the price of aluminum is relatively high (higher than the competitive price), they use relatively too much steel and too little aluminum, so that automobile production is inefficient. More disturbing to the aluminum monopoly, relatively little aluminum is purchased.

The aluminum monopoly could force the car manufacturers to sign contracts that require them to use relatively more aluminum in the manufacture of cars. For example, it could force them to use the efficient proportion of aluminum to steel (the ratio that would be chosen if all industries were competitive). The monopoly could impose this restriction by requiring that car manufacturers purchase the efficient amount of steel from the aluminum monopoly, which could purchase the steel on the competitive market. Of course, as with all tie-in sales, if the tie-in is to work, it must be impossible for the consumer, in this case the car manufacturer, to purchase steel secretly on the open market; that is, the consumer must not be able to undo the package tie-in.[12]

Requirements Tie-ins with Interrelated Demands. Perhaps the most common type of tie-in is a requirements tie-in in which consumers buy one good and are then required to make all their purchases of some other related good from the same manufacturer. Chapter 19 examines several examples that have arisen in litigation. One famous case involved the A. B. Dick Company, which had a patent monopoly to sell mimeograph machines.[13] A. B. Dick required that customers who bought mimeograph machines also buy all their ink from A. B. Dick, which did not have a monopoly in ink. Another famous tie-in case was mentioned earlier: the IBM tabulating card case, in which IBM required purchasers of its machines to buy all their tabulating cards from IBM.

In the typical requirements tie, the firm sets a price for the first good and charges a high price (above the competitive price) for the related good. Consumers with large demands effectively pay more for the first good than consumers with small demands. For example, a person who bought a tabulating machine and 100 tabulating cards effectively paid a higher price for the machine than someone who bought only 10 cards. Therefore, a critical element for a requirements tie to maximize profit is that consumers differ in their demand for the related good. We now examine in more detail why requirements ties may be profitable.

Suppose that a firm develops a new machine that automatically sews buttons on shirts. Prior to the development of the machine, buttons were sewn by hand onto shirts, and the labor cost was 1¢ per button. There are many shirt manufacturers. Suppose a large manufacturer sews on 10,000 buttons per year. That manufacturer is willing to pay $100 per year for the machine because its saves $100 from reduced labor costs. Another manufacturer that uses only 1,000 buttons would pay at most $10 for the machine per year.

To keep the example simple, suppose that a machine lasts for only a year and that the total number of buttons that each manufacturer sews on shirts during a year is unchanged by this invention. The demand curve for the machine, $D_M(p_M, p_B)$, depends on the price of the machine, p_M, and the price of buttons, p_B. The price of buttons is 5¢ for the solid demand curve in Figure 10.7a.

Suppose that the monopoly of the machine decides to allow firms to use the machine for free provided they purchase all their buttons from the machine monopoly for

[12]An alternative approach is for the aluminum monopoly to take over the automobile industry (vertically integrate) so as to eliminate this inefficiency in production and increase the demand for aluminum and its profit (see Chapter 12). With interrelated demands, a package tie-in sale enables a monopoly to achieve the same increase in profit that it could achieve through vertical integration. Note also that the monopoly could achieve the same result as with the package tie-in by using a requirements tie-in in which the relative prices charged for aluminum and steel were in the same ratio as their marginal costs. Such prices will lead to an efficient use of aluminum and steel.

[13]*Henry v. A. B. Dick Co.*, 224 U.S. 1 (1912). A mimeograph machine produced copies of an original stencil using ink.

FIGURE 10.7 Shifts in Demand for Machines and Buttons as a Result of Tie-in

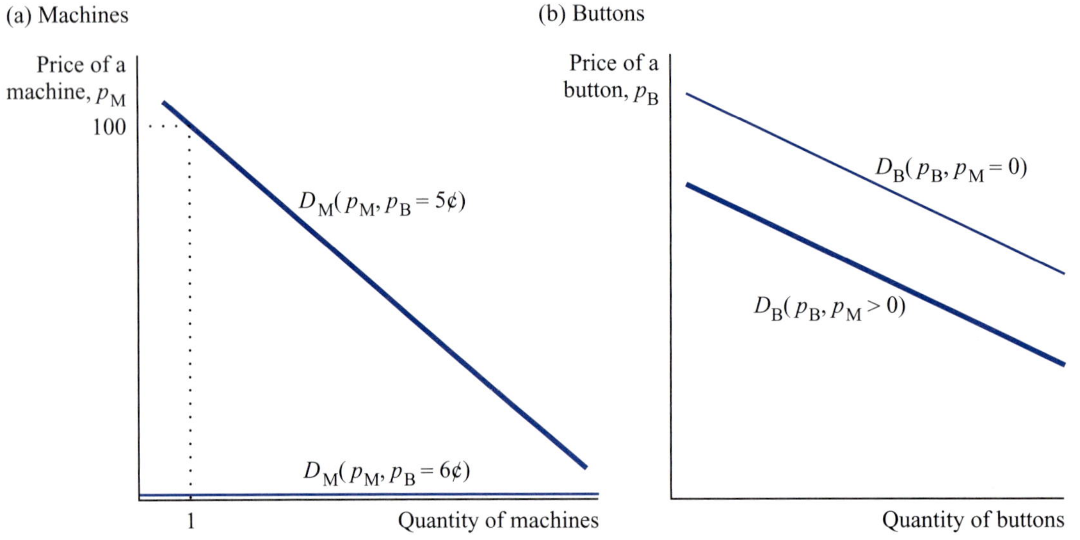

p_B = 6¢ (or perhaps a shade less), which is 1¢ above the competitive price. In other words, the monopoly ties the sale of buttons to the sale of the machine and charges a 1¢ premium (or a shade less) on each button. Any firm that has a use for the machine agrees to these conditions because the machine saves 1¢ per button.

As a result of this tie-in, the largest users of buttons pay a higher effective price for the machine. For example, the firm that uses 10,000 buttons effectively pays $100 for the machine; however, the firm that uses only 1,000 buttons pays only $10 for it. Thus, a tie-in between buttons and machines enables the monopoly of the machine to charge customers effectively different prices for the machine, charging the most to those who value the machine the most. This tie-in enables the monopoly to extract all consumer surplus from under the demand curve. That is, it allows the monopoly to achieve perfect price discrimination.

We can relate this example of a tie-in between a machine and buttons to the earlier examination of interrelated demand curves. If the monopoly charges 6¢ per button and captures all the consumer surplus, customers are unwilling to pay anything for a machine (the demand curve for the machine becomes the black line that lies on top of the horizontal axis in Figure 10.7a).

The adoption of the machine makes the demand curve for buttons shift out. As Figure 10.7b illustrates, if the machine is given to the user for free, the demand curve for buttons shifts up by one penny above where it was before the machine existed. (The thick blue line in Figure 10.7b can be thought of as the demand for buttons when the price of machines is set so high that no one purchases a machine, while the thin blue line is the demand for buttons when the price of the machine is zero.) As the price of the machine rises, the demand curve for buttons eventually falls to the initial demand curve.[14] Thus, the tie-in, which sets $p_M = \$0$ and $p_B = 6¢$, shifts down the demand curve for the machine and shifts up the demand curve for buttons relative to where they would be if $p_M > 0$ and $p_B = 5¢$. The tie-in allows the firm to perfectly price discriminate, so it is more profitable than setting any single positive price for the machine and not selling buttons (or selling them at the competitive price).

The preceding example is special in the sense that each firm has a pre-established demand for buttons and that it costs each firm the same to sew buttons on by hand. It is more likely that each firm has some flexibility over how many buttons it purchases and that the firms differ in the values they attach to sewing on buttons by machine. In response to a tie-in sale of a machine and buttons in which users are overcharged for buttons, some users might reduce their use of buttons. If so, the tie-in does not allow perfect price discrimination as in the simpler example. However, the tie-in may still be the most profitable approach even if all consumer surplus cannot be extracted. The tie-in can be regarded as a two-part tariff in which the machine's price is a lump-sum payment and the price of buttons is a per-unit charge. The tie-in sale cannot achieve perfect price discrimination for the reason discussed earlier that a two-part tariff cannot generally achieve perfect price discrimination,[15] that is, the firm is unable to separately identify and charge each consumer the most that consumer is willing to pay.

In the examples in this section, the tie-in serves to meter usage. Alternatively, the firm may meter usage explicitly. For example, IBM could have installed a meter to measure the number of cards each of its customers punched on the IBM machines. Customers could purchase cards anywhere, but the price they paid IBM for the machine would depend on their measured card usage. The choice between using a tie-in or an explicit meter depends on the relative costs of the two methods. Meters may be costly, and they may be easy to unhook, trick, or break. Tie-ins, on the other hand, may be hard to police (for example, customers could buy cards elsewhere), and they could distort efficient use. Photocopiers, telephones, and electric utilities often use explicit meters to monitor usage.

We have seen how a tie-in sale between two goods can raise the profit of a monopoly. More generally, a monopoly might require not just one good but several to be used in conjunction with its monopolized good. A monopoly could also specify that particular inputs must *not* be used with its monopolized goods.

---

[14] The decisions of whether to purchase the machine and how many buttons to buy are made simultaneously. No one would pay to purchase the machine and pay an extra 1¢ per button. The higher the price of the machine, the less buyers are willing to pay per button.

[15] If the number of buttons used per shirt is variable, and if, in response to an increase in the price of buttons, some shirt manufacturers use fewer buttons, the machine owner may wish to specify as a condition of purchase the minimum number of buttons that can be sewn on per shirt.

Quality Choice

Imagine a monopoly that produces several goods of differing quality—for example, a monopoly of cars of high, medium, and low quality. Goods of different qualities are typically related on the demand side because consumers can substitute among them. If the qualities of the goods are prespecified, the monopoly's decision about pricing them is the same as the one already examined in the discussion of interrelated demands. However, if the monopoly must also decide on the qualities of the goods to be produced, then it takes the demand interrelationship into account not only when it decides how to price the various quality goods, but also when it decides on the qualities of the goods it offers for sale (Mussa and Rosen 1978). Thus the monopoly's decisions about levels of quality are influenced by the same forces that influence the choice of nonlinear pricing schemes.

For example, the automobile monopoly may choose to produce only very high-quality and very low-quality cars. By not providing close substitutes for the high-quality cars, the monopoly may be able to extract more profit from selling them than it could if it also produced medium-quality, moderate-priced cars that were good substitutes for the high-priced, high-quality cars. The reason is that the firm can charge a high price for the high-quality car and not worry about consumers substituting to the low-priced, low-quality car because it is not a good substitute.

In summary, when consumers prefer different levels of quality, a monopoly manipulates the qualities of goods produced in the market in order to extract consumer surplus. The monopoly follows the principles already studied regarding price discrimination and chooses the quality spectrum so as to charge a high price to those who value the good the most, and a low price to those who value it the least, without having to pass along the low price to those who value the good the most (see Mussa and Rosen 1978; see also **www.aw-bc.com/carlton_perloff** "Quality Choice of a Monopoly").

Other Methods of Nonlinear Pricing

This chapter discusses only some of the many possible pricing schemes that monopolies can adopt as they attempt to maximize profits. A few other pricing schemes are quite common and deserve mention.

Minimum Quantities and Quantity Discounts

Many sellers specify that their product can be bought only in certain minimum amounts. Such a restriction causes pricing to be nonlinear. The average price per unit consumed is very high for small quantities and is lower after consumption reaches the minimum purchase level. A similar effect is achieved by granting quantity discounts.

Selection of Price Schedules

Sometimes consumers must choose the pricing schedule that will govern their purchases *before* they know how much they will purchase. For example, some telephone companies require consumers to select a pricing schedule at the beginning of the month. Some consumers elect to pay a large fixed fee and have unlimited calling; others elect to pay a modest lump-sum fee that entitles them to make calls and pay extra for calls in excess of a certain amount. At the end of the month, a consumer may discover that the pricing schedule not chosen would result in a lower bill. By requiring customers to specify in advance the pricing schedule they will face, monopolies can discriminate between those who can accurately predict their demands and those who cannot. Those who cannot accurately predict may overpay relative to those who can predict accurately.

In contrast, electricity companies generally do not require customers to choose a pricing schedule in advance. Instead, consumers of electricity typically face a declining block schedule where high prices are charged for the initial usage and lower prices are charged thereafter. Because this schedule applies to all consumers, the bill at the end of the month is independent of the customers' ability to predict their demands.

Another related example involves the purchase in advance of a fixed amount of a product for a lower price than for smaller, as-needed purchases. For example, many commuter railroads sell individual tickets at much higher prices per ride than monthly passes. If consumers misestimate how frequently they will travel, the railroad profits from their mistake.

Premium for Priority

If consumers differ in their desires to obtain a good quickly, a firm can charge more for rapid delivery. For example, a common pricing strategy for new goods is to price high initially and then to lower price over time. Airlines often charge more for tickets ordered one day in advance than for those ordered several weeks in advance. One possible reason for this pricing behavior is that business people, who often travel on short notice, have a less elastic demand than tourists, who do not travel on short notice. In general, when obtaining a good is uncertain, it may be possible to price discriminate by charging different prices for different probabilities of obtaining the good (Harris and Raviv 1981, Maskin and Riley 1984).[16] If, however, customers impose different costs on the firm (as is likely for customers who order in advance), labeling the price differences as price discrimination may be misleading.

[16]The welfare implications of such pricing schemes are very complex. For example, Gale and Holmes (1992) show that advance-purchase discounts offered by an airline can lead to an efficient allocation of capacity between peak and off-peak flights when it is not possible to operate a spot market on the day of a flight. Moreover, the socially optimum discount may be either larger or smaller than that offered by the monopoly.

Auctions

Some firms use auctions to sell valuable assets, such as art, antiques, off-shore oil leases, and Treasury bills. The purpose of an auction is to obtain the maximum revenue from buyers when the seller does not know which buyers value the goods the most. The objective is to design a pricing mechanism that induces the consumers with the greatest willingness to pay to bid high prices.

What is the best way to conduct an auction to obtain the maximum revenue? Should it be an auction in which bids start low and rise until there is no one willing to bid any higher (**English auction**)? Should it be an auction in which the price starts out very high and is slowly lowered until one person agrees to buy at that price (**Dutch auction**)? Should a minimum bid be specified? The answer to these questions is, under plausible assumptions, surprisingly simple. If buyers maximize expected consumer surplus and have independent valuations of the item in the auction, (such as idiosyncratic tastes for a painting) Dutch and English auctions yield the same expected revenues, and it is optimal to set minimum bids.[17]

This result does not hold when the buyers share a common value for an item, as in a case where the item will be resold to consumers, such as an auction for wholesale oil that is eventually resold to final consumers. Here bidders must guard against placing too high a bid because they overestimate the common value (eventual resale price). Such excessive bidding is called the winner's curse because the auction winners are likely to have overpaid owing to their belief that they are better able to estimate the expected market value of the item than other bidders. See Example 10.6.

SUMMARY

If a firm with market power lacks detailed knowledge about the demands of individual consumers, it cannot charge different prices to different consumers so as to maximize its profit. Instead, the firm must offer the same pricing policy to all consumers and let them choose (self-select) how much to pay and consume. However, a firm can earn a higher profit than if it set a single price by using nonlinear pricing policies. Many nonlinear pricing policies—such as a menu of two-part tariffs—induce different consumers to behave differently from each other and to pay different prices.

Tie-in sales work similarly to two-part tariffs and other nonlinear price schemes. They cause different consumers to pay different prices. Both package and requirements tie-in sales increase a firm's profit under appropriate circumstances.

Other pricing policies in addition to nonlinear price schedules are widely used. These policies allow a firm with market power to earn a higher profit than if it charged a single price to everyone. These policies include quality choice, auctions, priority of delivery, and minimum purchase orders.

[17] McAfee and McMillan (1987) and Klemperer (1999, 2001) survey the results from the large literature on auctions.

EXAMPLE 10.6

Price Discriminating on eBay

The online firm eBay conducts auctions on millions of items. In a typical eBay auction, the seller sets a minimum bid and then buyers submit their bids up to their maximum willingness to pay. If a new bidder places a bid that exceeds the current highest bid, then the new highest bid listed on eBay's computer is the previous highest bid plus an increment (50¢ for low-price items). Thus, the auction allocates the good to the highest bidder at a price equal to the maximum willingness to pay of the second-highest bidder, plus an increment.

A seller in an auction is a monopoly and wants to obtain the highest price. How should the monopoly set the minimum bid? Bulow and Roberts (1989) answer this question using the principles of price discrimination.

In an ascending (English) auction, the high bidder wins at a price just above that of the next highest bidder. That means that if no one else bids, the high bidder obtains the good for the minimum bid. Thus, the seller has an incentive not to set an extremely low minimum bid. However, the disadvantage of a relatively high minimum bid is that it dissuades some bidders from entering the auction (forcing the eventual winner to pay a higher price). So, the seller should set the minimum bid taking account of this trade-off.

Bajari and Hortacsu (2003) use sophisticated econometric techniques to analyze eBay auctions for collectible coins. Because many collectors resell their coins to other collectors, they should all place a common value on any given coin. In a common value auction, the winning bidders should worry that they have overbid—suffered from the *winner's curse*—because they overestimated this common value. Sophisticated bidders should therefore reduce their bids in common value auctions as the number of bidders increases.

Bajari and Hortacsu find that in a typical auction, the minimum bid is set on average at about 70 percent of the current retail market value of the collectible coin. They also find that more bidders enter the auction when the minimum bid is low. For example, they estimate that about four to five bidders show up when the reserve price is zero, but only two enter if the minimum bid is set at 80 percent of the retail price. Bidders do recognize the winner's curse and reduce their bids by 3.2 percent for each additional bidder in the auction. Finally, they estimate that the optimal minimum bid that maximizes expected seller revenue is about 10–20 percent below the current retail price. They conclude that sellers on eBay are doing a pretty good job of setting minimum bids in order to capture the consumer surplus of the high bidder.

PROBLEMS

1. Suppose a firm gives coupons to selected consumers that entitle them to price discounts. Why might the firm limit the number of coupons that a customer can use on a single purchase?

2. Look at Appendix 10A and **www.aw-bc.com/carlton_perloff** "Derivation of the Optimal Two-Part Tariff," which discusses the optimal two two-part tariffs to charge. Explain intuitively why it is optimal to charge a price equal to the marginal price of m to the consumer with the highest willingness to pay.

3. A person who consumes X units of Good 1 and Y units of Good 2 derives utility of $Y + 10X$. Suppose the person has \$100, the price of Y is \$1, and the nonlinear expenditure for purchasing X units of Good 1 is X^2. What X maximizes that person's utility?

4. Suppose a manufacturer sells a button-fastening machine that saves a firm the labor cost of 1¢ per button sewn on shirts. Suppose firms differ in the total number of buttons they sew on. The manufacturer sells its machine with a requirements tie-in that requires a purchaser to buy all its buttons from the manufacturer. Suppose the manufacturer can install a meter that measures how many buttons each machine sews. If the manufacturer can charge according to the use measured on the meter, is there any advantage to the tie-in? Would it be sensible to outlaw tie-in sales but allow the manufacturer to charge according to the metered use?

5. Let the demand for Products 1 and 2 be $q_1 = 10 - 2p_1 + p_2$ and $q_2 = 10 + p_1 - 2p_2$, where q_i is the quantity of Good i and p_i is the price of Good i. Assume production costs are zero. Calculate the prices that two separate monopolies would charge when each regards the other's price as beyond its control. Calculate the prices that a single monopoly of both goods would charge.

6. A monopoly produces and delivers goods to consumers who are located at varying distances from the factory. It costs m per unit to produce the good and \$1 per mile to transport a unit of the good. Resales are impossible. Calculate the price that a monopoly charges consumers at location t if demand is $q_t = a - bp_t$, where q_t and p_t are the quantity and price at location t. How does p_t change as t increases? Who bears the freight cost?

7. In Figure 10.5, if your costs of production are \$1 each for halibut and pie, which pricing scheme—individual pricing, pure bundling, or mixed bundling—maximizes your profit?

Answers to odd-numbered problems are given at the back of the book.

APPENDIX 10A

The Optimal Two-Part Tariff

The following problem illustrates the forces that determine the optimal two-part tariff. Let p be the per-unit usage price, T the lump-sum fee, N the number of demanders, and Q the total amount of the product demanded. The quantity demanded, Q, is a function not only of p (price) but also of the lump-sum fee (T). Imagine that consumers can be indexed by the parameter α. The higher is α, the more consumers are willing to pay for the product. Let $f(\alpha)$ be the number of consumers of type α.

The parameter α varies between $\underline{\alpha}$ and $\overline{\alpha}$. For any choice of p and T, there is a critical level, α^*, such that consumers whose α exceeds α^* (who value the product more than α^* type consumers) purchase the product. Consumers whose α is below α^* choose not to purchase the product. The consumer of type α^* is called the *marginal* consumer. Let $S(p, \alpha)$ be an α-type individual's consumer surplus at price p in the absence of a fixed fee, T. Then the marginal consumer (the consumer who is indifferent between buying and not buying) is one whose surplus equals the lump-sum fee:

$$S(p, \alpha^*) = T. \tag{10A.1}$$

For the marginal consumer, the surplus obtained from paying price p is exactly equal to the lump-sum fee, T, so that the total surplus from the purchase is zero. The number of consumers who purchase the product (the number of consumers whose α is greater than α^*, which from Equation 10A.1 depends on p and T) is

$$N(p, T) = \int_{\alpha^*}^{\overline{\alpha}} f(\alpha)\mathrm{d}\alpha. \tag{10A.2}$$

If $q(p, \alpha)$ is the demand curve of an α-type consumer, then the total amount demanded as a function of p and T equals the sum of all the demands of consumers whose α exceeds α^*:

$$Q(p, T) = \int_{\alpha^*}^{\overline{\alpha}} q(p, \alpha)f(\alpha)\mathrm{d}\alpha. \tag{10A.3}$$

If marginal cost is constant and equals m, then the firm's profit is

$$\pi = N(p, T)T + (p - m)Q(p, T), \tag{10A.4}$$

where $(p - m)$ is the profit per unit and NT is the total of the lump-sum fees collected. The firm maximizes its profit by choosing p, the price, and T, the lump-sum fee, optimally. The discussion at **www.aw-bc.com/carlton_perloff** "Derivation of the Optimal Two-Part Tariff," shows that the first-order condition for the determination of price is

$$\frac{p - m}{p} = -\frac{1}{\epsilon}\left(1 - \frac{q^*}{\bar{q}}\right), \tag{10A.5}$$

where $q^* = q(p, \alpha^*)$ is the demand of the marginal consumer, $\bar{q} = Q(p, T)/N$ is the average quantity demanded across all consumers who purchase (those with a $\alpha \geq \alpha^*$), and ϵ is the price elasticity of demand of consumers who purchase the good:

$$\epsilon = \int_{\alpha^*}^{\bar{\alpha}} \frac{q}{Q} \frac{p}{q} \frac{\partial q(p, \alpha)}{\partial p} f(\alpha) d\alpha. \tag{10A.6}$$

Notice that ϵ differs slightly from the usual price elasticity of demand, which accounts for the change in α^* as p rises.

Equation 10A.5 would be the same as the optimal first-order condition of a simple monopoly ($[p - m]/p = -1/\epsilon$) were it not for the last term in the parentheses on the right side. That term is the ratio of the purchases of the marginal user (that is, the demand of the α^* consumer) to the purchases of the average user in the marketplace times $1/\epsilon$. The ratio $q^*/\bar{q}$ is less than 1 if, as in the usual case, the marginal purchaser buys less of the good than does the average purchaser.

Suppose that all consumers are identical, so that q^* equals $\bar{q}$. Equation 10A.5 becomes

$$(p - m)/p = 0, \tag{10A.7}$$

which implies that price should equal m. That is, if all consumers are identical, it is optimal to charge each consumer marginal cost. All of the profits then come from the lump-sum fee, T, as discussed in the chapter.

In the usual case, the marginal consumer (who is indifferent between buying and not buying) demands a lower quantity than other consumers so that q^* is less than $\bar{q}$. (The demand curve of the marginal consumer lies below that of other consumers.) Therefore, the term in parentheses on the right side of Equation 10A.5 is positive. Thus, in the usual case, price exceeds m. For the usual case, the usage-sensitive price is closer to m as ϵ increases in absolute value and as consumer diversity, as measured by the difference between 1 and the ratio of the marginal to average purchase, declines.

It is possible, however, that it is profitable for the usage charge to be below unit cost if consumers who get extensive surplus from the product at a given price buy only small amounts (e.g., 5 units), whereas the marginal consumers who get very little surplus buy large amounts (e.g., 15 units). This case is illustrated in Figure 10A.1. The intuition in this unusual case is that it is profitable for the firm to lower the price below m in order to raise the lump-sum charge to both types of consumers.

The optimal policy cannot involve a negative value for T, which would mean that people are *paid* a lump-sum amount for the right to consume the good whether or not

FIGURE 10A.1 Unusual Configuration of Demand Curves

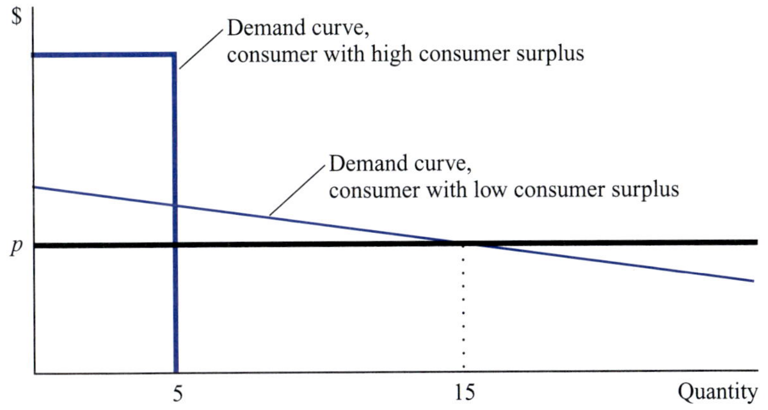

they consume it. Obviously, if any manufacturer offered to pay people whether or not they consumed the good, everybody would sign up and bankrupt the manufacturer.[1] Hence, in the optimal solution, the lump sum, T, is positive or zero. A two-part tariff generally produces higher profits than a single-price policy because a single price is a special case of a two-part tariff in which the lump-sum fee is zero.

[1]This conclusion is overstated if the costs associated with collecting a gift (for example, time) are very large.

APPENDIX 10B

Nonlinear Pricing with an Example

With nonlinear pricing, Consumer *i* faces the following problem:

$$\max_{q_i, y_i} u_i(q_i, y_i) \quad \text{s.t. } E(q_i) + y_i = I_i, \tag{10B.1}$$

where $E(q_i)$ is the total expense when q_i units are consumed of Good 1, y_i represents all other goods whose per-unit price is normalized to 1, I_i is the consumer's income, and u_i is the consumer's utility function.

The maximization problem facing a firm that wishes to offer a nonlinear pricing schedule that maximizes its profit is to

$$\text{choose } E(\cdot) \text{ to maximize } \sum_i [E(q_i) - mq_i], \tag{10B.2}$$

subject to the constraint that each consumer *i* maximizes as in Equation 10B.1, $i = 1, \ldots, N$, where m is the constant marginal cost, and q_i is the amount consumed by consumer *i*.

The firm chooses the $E(q)$ to maximize profit, which equals the sum of the profits made by selling to each consumer, subject to the condition that each consumer maximizes his or her utility. (Each consumer who purchases Good 1 must be better off by doing so than by forgoing consumption of the good entirely.)

The solution to the problem posed in Equation 10B.2 is complicated (Katz 1983; Spence 1977b; Tirole 1988, Ch. 3). Rather than present the general solution, we illustrate some of the key ideas that arise in nonlinear pricing through an example where the firm can only use two-part tariffs.

Consider the problem discussed in the chapter of a firm that faces two consumers, Consumer 1 and Consumer 2, and offers two two-part tariffs (T_1, p_1) and (T_2, p_2). If it costs m to produce one unit of the good, and if Consumer 1 chooses (T_1, p_1) and Consumer 2 chooses (T_2, p_2), then profit equals

$$T_1 + (p_1 - m)q_1(p_1) + T_2 + (p_2 - m)q_2(p_2), \tag{10B.3}$$

where $q_i(p_i)$ is the demand curve of Consumer *i*. The key additional requirement of the equilibrium in this problem is that Consumer 1 prefers (T_1, p_1) to (T_2, p_2) and vice versa for Consumer 2. Let $U_i(T, p)$ be the utility of Consumer *i*, which depends on T and p. The self-selection constraints are

$$U_1(T_1, p_1) \geq U_1(T_2, p_2), \tag{10B.4}$$
$$U_2(T_1, p_1) \leq U_2(T_2, p_2).$$

Let $S_i(p)$ be the consumer surplus of Consumer i at price p in the absence of a lump-sum fee. Then utility can be written as $U_i(T, p) = S_i(p) - T$. The pricing problem facing the firm is

$$\max_{T_1, p_1, T_2, p_2} \quad T_1 + (p_1 - m)q_1(p_1) + T_2 + (p_2 - m)q_2(p_2)$$

$$\begin{aligned} \text{s.t.} \quad & S_1(p_1) - T_1 \geq S_1(p_2) - T_2 \\ & S_2(p_1) - T_1 \leq S_2(p_2) - T_2 \\ & S_1(p_1) - T_1 \geq 0 \\ & S_2(p_2) - T_2 \geq 0. \end{aligned} \tag{10B.5}$$

The objective function in Equation 10B.5 is the total profit that the firm earns from charging a lump sum, T_1 and T_2, and charging price p_1 when quantity q_1 is consumed, and price p_2 when quantity q_2 is consumed. The constraints in Equation 10B.5 are the consumers' self-selection constraints. The first constraint guarantees that Consumer 1 has more utility with a tariff (T_1, p_1) than with the tariff (T_2, p_2). The second constraint guarantees that the utility of Consumer 2 at (T_2, p_2) is greater than at (T_1, p_1). These two constraints guarantee that Consumer 1 chooses (T_1, p_1). and Consumer 2 chooses (T_2, p_2). The last two constraints in Equation 10B.5 guarantee that both consumers have positive utility.[1]

To illustrate the principles involved in nonlinear pricing, suppose that the demand of Consumer 2 is $\lambda(> 1)$ times larger than the demand of Consumer 1: $q_2(p) = \lambda q_1(p)$. That is, the demand curve of Consumer 2 lies strictly to the right of the demand curve of Consumer 1.

Figure 10B.1 shows the indifference curves of consumers in (T, p) space—that is, the combinations of T and p that leave a consumer indifferent. As T falls, p rises along an indifference curve; consumers trade off a higher T for a lower p. They receive higher utility as they move toward indifference curves closer to the origin. Along an indifference curve, when p falls, the amount by which T rises depends on the amount that consumers purchase. Those who purchase a large amount of the good are willing to pay a much higher fixed fee as the per-unit price of the good falls. Therefore, as Figure 10B.1 shows, the indifference curve for Consumer 2 is steeper than the indifference curve for Consumer 1 when the curves cross.

The equation of the indifference curve for $U_2 = 0$ is $T_2 = S_2(p)$, and that for $U_1 = 0$ is $T_1 = S_1(p)$. Along its zero utility curve, a consumer must pay a fixed fee exactly equal to surplus. Along the indifference curve at which Consumer 2 is just indifferent $(U_2 = 0)$ between purchasing the good or not, Consumer 1 does not

[1] It is possible that the optimal solution involves satisfying only one consumer type and that the other consumer type does not consume the good. We consider only the possibility in which it is profit maximizing for the firm to serve both types of consumers because this chapter has already examined the profit-maximizing two-part tariff when only one homogeneous group is involved.

FIGURE 10B.1 Indifference Curves in (T, p) Space for Type 1 and Type 2 Consumers

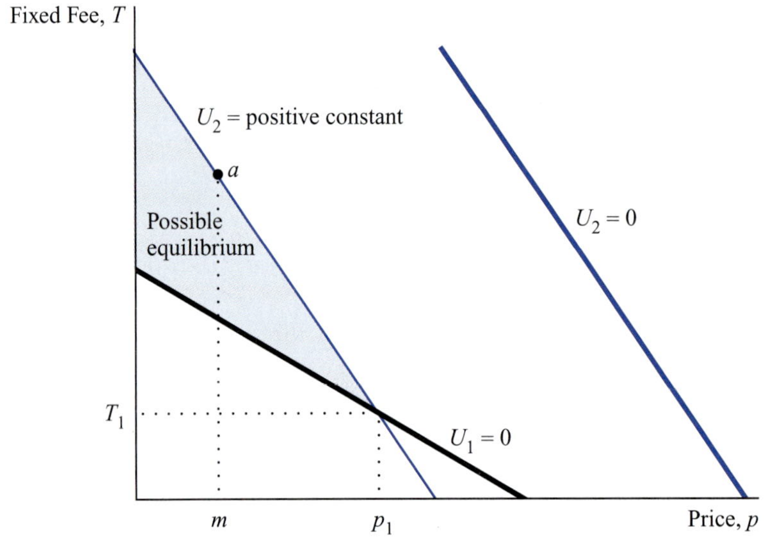

purchase the good. Consumer 1 does not purchase because, at any price p, the surplus enjoyed by Consumer 2 is higher than it is for Consumer 1 and Consumer 2 is just indifferent between buying and not. Therefore, Consumer 1 would rather forgo consumption of the good than pay a fixed fee.

The monopoly's optimal solution to Equation 10B.5 involves driving the utility of at least one of the two consumer types down to zero. If both types have positive utilities, the monopoly can raise the fixed fees, continue to sell its product, and still make more money. Thus, the monopoly raises the fixed fees until at least one type's utility is driven to zero.

Which type will that be? Suppose it were Consumer 2 whose utility is driven to zero. That means that Consumer 2 is on its zero utility curve in Figure 10B.1. Where, then, could Consumer 1 be? Consumer 1's utility is negative along the $U_2 = 0$ curve; therefore, the only (T, p) combinations that will keep Consumer 1 in the market are those that lie below the $U_2 = 0$ curve. But if there were a two-part tariff (T, p) that lay below the $U_2 = 0$ curve, Consumer 2 would prefer that point to the one on the $U_2 = 0$ curve. Thus, Consumer 2 cannot have zero utility in the optimal solution provided that both Consumer 1 and Consumer 2 are purchasing. By this reasoning, in the optimal solution involving both consumer types, the utility of Consumer 1 must be zero.

Thus, (T_1, p_1) lies on the curve $U_1 = 0$. Where is (T_2, p_2)? The answer is that (T_2, p_2) cannot lie below the curve $U_1 = 0$. Otherwise, Consumer 1 would prefer that two-part tariff to its own. The self-selection constraints guarantee that the utility of Consumer 2 at its two-part tariff cannot be less than the utility at (T_1, p_1). Hence, (T_2, p_2) can only lie within the shaded region of Figure 10B.1. The monopoly wants to extract as much surplus as possible from Consumer 2 and still satisfy the self-selection constraints. The monopoly achieves the goal by moving as far upward as it can for any p_2 and still remain in the shaded area in Figure 10B.1. Therefore, (T_2, p_2) lies along the upper part of Consumer 2's indifference curve that passes through (T_1, p_1). Consumer 1 would always prefer to remain at (T_1, p_1) rather than at any (T_2, p_2) point that lies above the $U_1 = 0$ curve and along the U_2 curve through (T_1, p_1) and Consumer 2 is indifferent between (T_1, p_1) and points on its indifference curve through (T_1, p_1), and, for simplicity, we assume that Consumer 2 chooses (T_2, p_2) if indifferent between (T_1, p_1) and (T_2, p_2).

These insights help solve the problem in Equation 10B.5. We have established two results. First, the utility of Consumer 1 is zero in the optimal solution so that $T_1 = S_1(p)$. Second, the utility of Consumer 2 at (T_1, p_1) must equal its utility at (T_2, p_2). Based on these two results,

$$S_1(p_1) - T_1 = 0, \tag{10B.6a}$$

$$S_2(p_1) - T_1 = S_2(p_2) - T_2. \tag{10B.6b}$$

We can solve for T_1 and T_2 in terms of p_1 and p_2 from Equations 10B.6a and b and substitute into Equation 10B.5 to reexpress the problem facing the firm as

$$\begin{aligned} \max_{p_1, p_2} \; & S_1(p_1) + (p_1 - m)q_1(p_1) + S_2(p_2) - S_2(p_1) \\ & + S_1(p_1) + (p_2 - m)q_2(p_2). \end{aligned} \tag{10B.7}$$

By assumption, for any p, $\lambda q_1(p) = q_2(p)$, and therefore $\lambda S_1(p) = S_2(p)$. As a result, we can rewrite Equation 10B.7 as

$$\begin{aligned} \max_{p_1, p_2} \; & S_1(p_1) + (p_1 - m)q_1(p_1) + \lambda S_1(p_2) - \lambda S_1(p_1) \\ & + S_1(p_1) + \lambda(p_2 - m)q_1(p_2) \\ \equiv \; & (2 - \lambda)S_1(p_1) + SP(p_1) + \lambda S_1(p_2) + \lambda SP(p_2), \end{aligned} \tag{10B.8}$$

where $SP(p_i) = (p_i - m)q_1(p_i)$ is the "standard profit" that a single price monopoly facing demand curve $q_1(p_i)$ earns at price p_i. The function $SP(p)$ reaches a maximum at p^*, as shown in Figure 10B.2, which is the price that a standard, single-price monopoly would charge. To the left of p^*, the slope of $SP(p)$ is positive, and to the right of p^*, the slope of $SP(p)$ is negative.

We are now ready to determine the p_1 and p_2 that maximize Equation 10B.8. The first-order conditions are

FIGURE 10B.2 Monopoly Profit

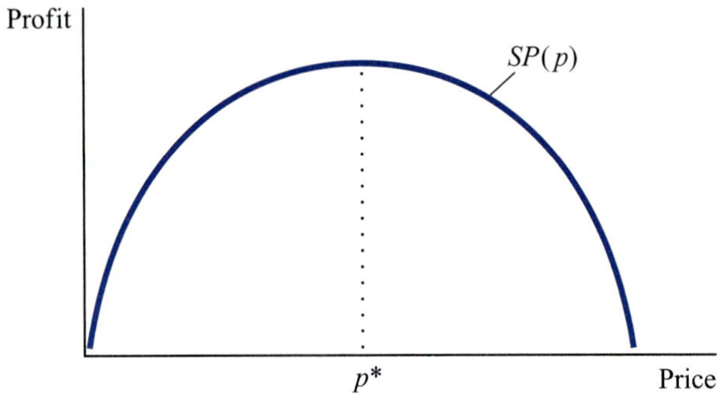

$$(2 - \lambda)\frac{dS_1(p_1)}{dp_1} + \frac{dSP(p_1)}{dp_1} = 0, \tag{10B.9a}$$

$$\frac{dS_1(p_2)}{dp_2} + \frac{dSP(p_2)}{dp_2} = 0. \tag{10B.9b}$$

Because $dS_1/dp_1 = -q_1(p_1)$ and $dS_1/dp_2 = -q_1(p_2)$,[2] we can write Equation 10B.9a as

$$\frac{dSP(p_1)}{dp_1} = (2 - \lambda)q_1(p_1), \tag{10B.10a}$$

$$\frac{dSP(p_2)}{dp_2} = q_1(p_2). \tag{10B.10b}$$

From Equation 10B.10a, if $\lambda > 2$, the optimal p_1 is such that the slope of $SP(p_1)$ is negative; that is, p_1 exceeds p^*. According to Equation 10B.10b, p_2 should be chosen where the slope of $SP(p)$ is positive; hence p_2 is less than p^*. In other words, when the demand of Consumer 2 is large ($\lambda > 2$) relative to that of Consumer 1, Consumer 1 is charged a very high price—indeed, a price above the simple profit-maximizing price—so that Consumer 2 can be charged a low price and a high lump sum. Although profit is forgone by charging Consumer 1 a price above p^*, the extra profit from Consumer 2 more than compensates. Consumer 1's price is high so that the

[2] As price falls by $1, the additional surplus equals the quantity consumed (ignoring income effects).

(T_1, p_1) tariff is not attractive to Consumer 2, so Consumer 2 is willing to pay a high T_2. By using two two-part tariffs, it is possible to separate Consumers 1 and 2 and limit the problem of having to pass along the low p_2 to Consumer 1 and the low T_1 to Consumer 2.

When $1 < \lambda < 2$, at p_1, the slope of $SP(p)$ is positive by Equation 10B.10a so that $p_1 < p^*$. As Figure 10B.1 shows, $p_2 < p_1$; hence, $p_2 < p_1 < p^*$.

The most efficient method of price discrimination against Consumer 2—and one that does not interfere with self-selection by Consumer 1—is to set price at marginal cost and charge a high lump-sum fee. Hence $p_2 = m$ in the profit-maximizing solution,[3] and the optimal (T_2, p_2) combination therefore is a point like *a* in Figure 10B.1.

In summary, the optimal tariff depends on how large λ is. The per-unit price to Consumer 1 always exceeds that to Consumer 2, and the fixed fee to Consumer 1 is always less than that to Consumer 2. The per-unit price to Consumer 2 equals marginal cost. The presence of Consumer 1 constrains the T_2 and p_2 that Consumer 2 can be charged. The larger the relative demand of Consumer 2 (higher λ), the more profitable it is to forgo profits on Consumer 1 (that is, charge p_1 in excess of p^*) in order to charge a high lump-sum fee and low per-unit price to Consumer 2. Consumer 2 is better off when Consumer 1 is present in the market. From the solution to Equation 10B.5, we know that $U_2(T_2, p_2) > 0$, but, if Consumer 2 were the only customer, the optimal two-part tariff would extract all consumer surplus so that U_2 would be zero. Consumer diversity helps those with the greater willingness to buy the good. In contrast, Consumer 1's utility is completely unaffected by the presence of Consumer 2.

[3]We obtain this result by differentiating Equation 10B.7 with respect to p_2, setting the result equal to 0, and noting that $\partial S_2(p_2)/\partial p_2 = -q_2(p_2)$. This result of no marginal distortion for Consumer 2 is analogous to the results concerning optimal taxation in Mirrlees (1971).

CHAPTER 11

Strategic Behavior

Do unto others before they do unto you.

This chapter analyzes actions taken by firms to reduce competition by actual and potential rivals. These actions are loosely called *strategic behavior,* and they can be more complicated than simply setting prices or quantities. For example, the first firm in a market could build a gigantic plant so as to leave little room for potential rivals to enter.

This chapter first defines strategic behavior and then examines both noncooperative and cooperative strategic behavior. We explore the differences between cooperative and noncooperative strategic behavior and discuss the legal treatment of strategic behavior under U.S. antitrust laws.

The key questions examined in this chapter are

1. Under what conditions does a firm benefit from using noncooperative strategic behavior?
2. When do oligopolists benefit from using cooperative strategic behavior?
3. Should antitrust laws forbid all actions that appear to be noncooperative or cooperative strategic behavior?

Strategic Behavior Defined

Strategic behavior is a set of actions a firm takes to influence the market environment so as to increase its profits. The **market environment** comprises all factors that influence the market outcome (prices, quantities, profits, welfare), including the beliefs of customers and of rivals, the number of actual and potential rivals, the production technology of each firm, and the costs or speed with which a rival can enter the market.[1] By manipulating the market environment, a firm may be able to increase its profits. As in the theory of oligopoly, the equilibrium in models of strategic behavior crucially depends on what one rival believes another rival will do in a particular situation. This chapter describes how a firm can influence the conditions of rivalry and thereby affect the outcome of the rivalry.

We examine two types of strategic behavior: noncooperative and cooperative. Although the distinction between noncooperative and cooperative behavior is not sharp, for expositional purposes it is helpful to consider them separately. **Noncooperative strategic behavior** encompasses the actions of a firm that is trying to maximize its profits by improving its position relative to its rivals. Noncooperative strategic behavior generally improves the profits of one firm and lowers the profits of competing firms. **Cooperative strategic behavior** comprises those actions that make it easier for firms in a market to coordinate their actions and to limit their competitive responses.[2] Cooperative strategic behavior raises the profits of all firms in a market by reducing competition.

A firm's blowing up its rival's store is an example of noncooperative strategic behavior. On the other hand, a scenario in which two rivals who are distrustful of each other sit down in a room to work out a price-fixing agreement is an example of cooperative behavior. Their subsequent behavior (for example, attempts to cheat on the price-fixing agreement) may be noncooperative.

Antitrust laws, which attempt to limit the undesirable acquisition of market power, are used to attack certain types of strategic behavior. The first and perhaps most important U.S. antitrust law, the Sherman Act, was passed in 1890. Section I of the Sherman Act prohibits all contracts, combinations, and conspiracies in restraint of trade. Section I is used to attack explicit cooperative behavior, such as a price-fixing agreement. Section II of the Sherman Act prohibits attempts to monopolize. Section II has been used to attack noncooperative strategic behavior, such as pricing below cost to drive rivals out of business.

Noncooperative Strategic Behavior

All business sagacity reduces itself in the last analysis to a judicious use of sabotage. —*Thorstein Veblen*

A firm engages in noncooperative strategic behavior to harm its rivals and thereby benefit itself. Firms use many techniques to prevent rivals from entering a market, to drive rivals out of a market, or to reduce the size of a rival. Some of these strategies are designed to allow a firm to scare off potential rivals by changing rivals' beliefs about how

[1] The term *market environment* is slightly more inclusive than the term *market structure* because the latter, as commonly used, does not include beliefs of market participants.

[2] The term *cooperative* does not necessarily imply that the firms have an *explicit* agreement to undertake the behavior.

aggressively the firm will behave in the future. Two conditions must be met for a noncooperative strategy to be successful:

1. *Advantage:* The firm must typically have an advantage over the rivals. For example, the firm may be able to act before its rivals. That is, a firm must be able to do unto its rivals before they can do unto it.
2. *Commitment:* The firm must demonstrate that it will follow its strategy regardless of the actions of its rival.

If two firms are identical, both firms are in an equal position to threaten each other. For a strategy to work, then, one firm must have an advantage that allows it to harm the other firm before that firm can retaliate. Asymmetry between firms allows one firm to make a commitment that makes its threatened behavior believable.

For a firm's strategic behavior to work, its rivals must believe that the firm will remain committed to its strategy for as long as necessary. For example, an incumbent firm may announce that it will do something drastic (such as produce large quantities of output, a tactic that drives price down) if another firm enters its market. Talk is cheap, however, so the rival does not believe the incumbent's claim unless it is rational for the incumbent to follow this strategy after entry occurs.[3] For the incumbent firm's claim to be a **credible threat**, its rivals must believe that its strategy is rational in the sense that it is in the firm's best interest to continue to employ it. By making a commitment that does not allow it to change its strategy even if it wants to later, a firm can make its threat credible.

This section begins by analyzing four well-known strategies: predatory pricing, limit pricing, investment to lower costs, and raising rivals' costs. These strategies may work where barriers to quick entry and exit prevent another identical firm from using the same strategies. Without these barriers there can be no asymmetry among firms, and these strategic behaviors do not work. Next, the text examines why incumbents may have a natural advantage over later entrants. The section concludes with a discussion of antitrust policy toward such behavior.

Predatory Pricing

A dead man can't bite. —*Plutarch*

A firm engages in **predatory pricing** by first lowering its price in order to drive rivals out of business and scare off potential entrants, and then raising its price when its rivals exit the market. In most definitions, the firm lowers price below some measure of cost (legal definitions are discussed below). That is, the firm incurs short-run losses to obtain long-run gains.

What does a firm have to do to drive its rivals out of business? It has to convince its rivals that it is willing to drive price below their costs and keep it there until they leave

[3]Talk may be cheap, but it can be effective in allowing one rival to communicate a complicated strategy to another rival and in making it possible for a firm to develop a reputation for telling the truth. See Farrell (1987).

the market. This strategy is likely to be successful only if the firm can survive low prices longer than its rivals can. In many cases, however, the firm has no ability to convince its rivals that it is willing to maintain low prices for as long as it takes to drive them out of business.

If the firm succeeds in driving out its current rivals and then raises its price, new rivals may enter the market, and the incumbent must again lower its price to drive out those firms. For the predation to be successful, potential entrants must believe that it does not pay to enter this business because of the incumbent's pricing behavior. Only then can the incumbent raise its price to the monopoly level with no fear of inducing entry.

If the predator succeeds in forcing its rivals into bankruptcy, it should try to gain control of their assets or see that they are permanently withdrawn from the market. Otherwise, when the incumbent raises its price, a rival could again use those assets or another firm could buy the assets and compete. Even if a rival's assets are purchased by a firm in another market, they could always be redeployed to compete against the predator.

This discussion of predatory pricing begins by examining a model of identical firms in which predation is unlikely to be successful. Next, we consider a model in which one firm has an advantage over its rivals so that predation may be a profitable policy. Then, we look at how courts identify predatory pricing, and conclude with a review of the empirical evidence.

Predation with Identical Firms. Does the model of predatory behavior make sense if firms are identical? During the period of predation, the predating firm loses much more money than an equally efficient rival. The predatory firm must meet all demands at the low price in order to maintain the low price, but the rival is free to reduce its output in order to minimize its losses. As a result, the predation is unlikely to succeed.

To illustrate this result, suppose that there are only two firms, an incumbent and a recent entrant, in the market with identical cost functions, as shown in Figure 11.1. The incumbent firm lowers the market price to p^* so as to inflict losses on its rival and drive it out of business. For the market price to be p^*, q^* units of output must be sold, as shown by the market demand curve in Figure 11.1.

If the rival does not exit the market, it produces q_e units, where p^* equals its marginal cost, and suffers a loss equal to area *A* in the figure. To keep the price at p^*, the incumbent must produce $q_i \equiv q^* - q_e$ units so that total market output is q^*. Thus, the incumbent produces at a higher marginal and average cost than its rival and suffers losses equal to area *A* plus area *B*. As a result, the incumbent's loss is greater than that of its rival by an amount equal to area *B*.

Consumers gain during the period of predation because they are able to purchase the product at price p^*, which is less than the duopoly price. If the predation is successful, consumers lose after the rival is driven out of business because the price rises to the monopoly level (which is greater than the duopoly price).

The major problem with this story of predatory pricing, when firms have identical cost functions, is that it is just as reasonable to suppose that the entrant can threaten the incumbent as to suppose the reverse. With no differences between the firms, why should any firm believe that another firm is willing to suffer losses greater than those of its rival for as long as necessary to drive the rival from the market?

FIGURE 11.1 Predation

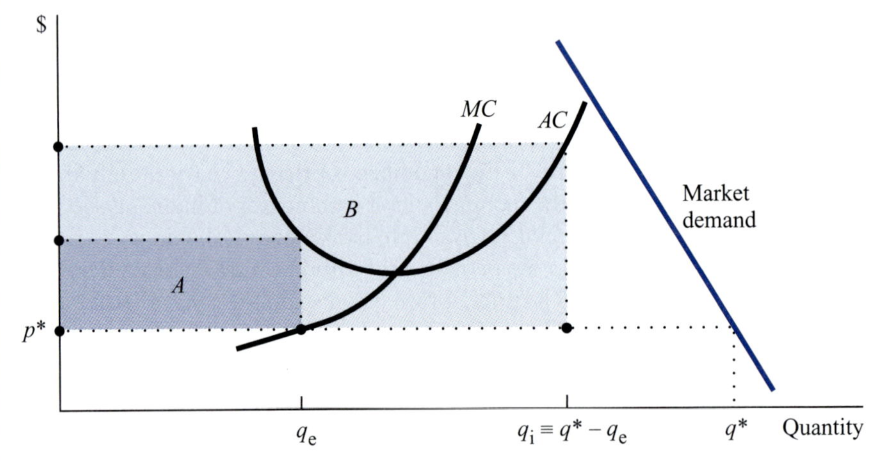

For predation to work, the rival must believe that a firm will keep price low for as long as it takes to drive the rival out of business. Because the incumbent's proposed action is not viewed as rational by its rival, it is not viewed as a credible threat. See Example 11.1.

If an entrant did fear that its entry would precipitate a price war and drive prices below cost, it could avoid this problem in several ways. First, it could try to talk the in-

EXAMPLE 11.1

Supreme Court Says Alleged Predation Must Be Credible

In 1986, the Supreme Court reached an important decision regarding predatory pricing in *Matsushita Electric Industrial Co., Ltd. v. Zenith Radio Corporation et al.*, 106 S. Ct. 1348 (1986). A group of U.S. manufacturers claimed that certain Japanese firms had conspired for 20 years to sell consumer electronic products in the United States at prices below cost in an effort to drive the U.S. producers out of business.

The Supreme Court concluded that it was unlikely that any firm or group of firms would willingly inflict losses upon itself for 20 years in order to drive firms out of business eventually. Only a firm that made a very poor calculation of the discounted present value of the costs and benefits of the predatory strategy would predate for so long. The Supreme Court ruled that predation was not the reason for the low prices and that other explanations, such as legitimate competition, better described the reasons why the Japanese were able to price below American producers.

cumbent into merging, thereby enabling itself to charge a high price immediately and avoid the costly period of predation. U.S. antitrust laws, however, prohibit mergers to monopolize as well as predatory pricing (see Chapter 19).

A second approach is for the entrant to obtain contracts with buyers to set the price in advance of entry. A drop in the incumbent's price would not hurt it because its sales would be at the prespecified price. Buyers should be willing to sign fixed-price contracts at prices below the monopoly price that the incumbent initially charges.[4] Of course, it is not always possible to line up enough customers in advance on fixed-price contracts, especially when each customer is small. However, when there are large customers who realize that the entrant will prevent the incumbent from exercising market power, the entrant should have an easier time signing up customers in advance.

A third approach, as mentioned above, is for the rival to reduce its output during periods of predation to minimize the harm. In some markets, a rival can exit a market costlessly and redeploy its assets to another market during a period of predation. When the incumbent raises its price, the rival reenters the market. Exiting and entering can be repeated as long as necessary so that the predation can never inflict significant losses on the rival.

For example, suppose that the incumbent produces desks. The rival enters the market, and in response to its entry, the incumbent lowers the price of desks below cost. Suppose that the rival can quickly and profitably switch its factory to make tables instead of desks. As long as it is relatively inexpensive for the rival to switch between the manufacture of desks and the manufacture of tables, the incumbent cannot drive the rival out of business or credibly threaten to do so.

The rival can easily change industries if it does not have large *sunk costs* (costs that cannot be recovered once a business has been entered—see Chapter 2). Thus, if the rival has minimal sunk costs, an incumbent can have no hope in succeeding with predatory strategies because it has no way to impose costs on its rival. That is, in perfectly *contestable markets* (those in which instantaneous entry and exit at no cost disadvantage are possible), predation can never succeed.

Thus, the rival can avoid or mitigate the harms of predation in at least three ways. It can merge with the incumbent, sign long-term contracts in advance of the predation, or reduce its output during the period of predation.

Predation Where One Firm Has an Advantage. The reason that predation is unlikely to succeed where firms have identical costs is that the predating firm suffers greater losses than its intended victims. Thus, for successful predation to occur, the predating firm needs an inherent advantage over its rivals.

Not all differences between the predating firm and others, however, lead to successful predation. Many early studies of predatory pricing described the incumbent as a large firm and its rival as a small firm and argued that large firms can afford losses during predatory periods better than small firms. This assumption is questionable: Why

[4]Conversely, an incumbent facing the threat of entry may sign long-term contracts with buyers that limit entry of some lower-cost firms (Aghion and Bolton 1987).

wouldn't somebody lend to a small firm if it is not believable that the large firm will continue to incur losses forever?

Moreover, such a theory does not explain why other large firms fail to enter. For example, if small firms are at a disadvantage in competing with large firms, competition among large firms will ultimately dominate the economy. Therefore, predation should not necessarily lead to monopoly profits even when small firms are ineffective competitors.

More recent models of predatory behavior explain that differences in firms' beliefs about their rivals can result in successful predation.[5] For example, suppose that a firm can be either a high-cost firm or a low-cost firm and that only the firm knows its own costs with certainty. In response to entry, an incumbent firm may lower its price for one of two reasons. First, if the incumbent is a low-cost firm, the price decline might simply represent vigorous price competition that is profitable for the low-cost incumbent firm to pursue. Even if its new price is below the entrant's cost, it may be above the incumbent's cost. Second, if the incumbent is a high-cost firm, it may engage in predatory pricing.

The difference between this model and the previous models of predation is that it provides a possible explanation (that the firm has low costs) of why it is profit maximizing for an incumbent firm to drop its price in response to entry. The other firm, after observing the incumbent's pricing behavior, infers whether the incumbent firm is likely to have low or high costs. The lower its cost, the more likely the incumbent firm is to meet entry with very low prices.

As a result, an incumbent can acquire a reputation of being a low-cost firm by responding to entry with very low prices. Its pricing history is used by other potential entrants as an indicator, albeit not a perfect indicator, as to whether the incumbent firm has low or high costs. Because its pricing history is only a rough indicator, a high-cost firm might be able to price predate and convince potential entrants that it is really a low-cost firm. Of course, pricing histories can be used as an indicator of a firm's costs only if high-cost firms use low prices less frequently than do low-cost firms.

An entrant with no associated pricing history cannot influence the incumbent's beliefs about its costs, so there is a natural asymmetry between the firms. Because the entrant has no prior history whereas the incumbent has a history, the incumbent's beliefs about the entrant may differ from the entrant's beliefs about the incumbent. In this model, predatory pricing may be plausible. Pricing below cost for a high-cost firm turns out to be a rational strategy if it is able to create the illusion that it is a low-cost firm, and thereby deter entry.

Although these recent models show that it is possible to construct believable models of predatory pricing, it is still true that the practice is costly to an incumbent firm.[6] Moreover, the counterstrategy in which entrants contract with customers at a fixed price in advance may preclude successful predation.

---

[5]See, for example, Williamson (1977), Selten (1978), Ordover and Willig (1981), Easterbrook (1981), Kreps et al. (1982), Kreps and Wilson (1982a), and Milgrom and Roberts (1982b).

[6]See **www.aw-bc.com/carlton_perloff** "Spatial Predation" for a discussion of models where location is used to preempt rivals.

Finally, an entrant may have a reputation. For example, a firm's reputation in one market may carry over to any new market it enters. If so, there may be little asymmetry between the incumbent and the entrant, and hence little hope of successful predation.

Legal Standards of Predation. An extensive economic and legal literature suggests several standards for determining whether a firm is practicing predatory pricing. Many courts have adopted a rule proposed by Areeda and Turner (1975): A firm's pricing is predatory if its price is less than its short-run marginal cost. The logic behind this test is that no firm ever profitably chooses to operate where price is less than short-run marginal cost unless it is motivated by strategic concerns.[7] One possibility, if price is below short-run marginal cost, is that the firm is trying to drive rival firms out of business in order eventually to maximize profits. Pricing below short-run marginal costs would not make sense without some prospect of benefits in the future.

Areeda and Turner further suggest using average variable cost as a proxy for short-run marginal cost if data limitations prevent the determination of short-run marginal costs.[8] A strength of the Areeda-Turner rule is that it explicitly recognizes that pricing below average total cost is not, by itself, proof of predatory behavior. Indeed, price often is below average total cost in competitive industries such as agriculture due to short-run demand or supply fluctuations. (See Example 11.2 for a case in which the pricing-below-average-cost rule was used.)

Many economists and lawyers have responded to the article by Areeda and Turner. Some authors have suggested the use of long-run marginal cost, others have argued for the use of average cost, and still others have advocated observing price patterns over time or the amount produced over time to determine whether predation is actually occurring.[9]

Unfortunately, most of the suggested tests for predation can be difficult to implement, for two reasons. First, the data needed to determine short-run marginal production costs or even average variable production costs are often difficult to obtain. Second, other factors having nothing to do with price predation may explain violations of the tests.

It is common for a firm, upon entering a market, to attract consumer attention by running price promotions. During the start-up phase of a business, many firms give away their products as samples. Giving away a product may be a very effective promotional device to build business for the future, and it reflects rational, profit-maximizing behavior. This behavior appears to violate the Areeda and Turner rule and most other predation tests.

---

[7]In a one-period model, a profit-maximizing firm sets marginal revenue equal to marginal cost so that price is greater than or equal to marginal cost. If a firm is maximizing profits over time, however, it may operate at a price below short-run marginal cost, as is discussed below, even without a predatory strategy.

[8]In a multiproduct setting, the courts must use definitions that allow tests for predation involving only some of the many products that a firm produces. One standard, for example, could be that the price of one product could not be less than the average incremental cost of the product: the change in total cost from producing q units of a product divided by q, holding output of all other products at some prespecified level (Appendix 2A). This standard was used in *MCI Communication Corp. v. AT&T*, 708 F.2d 1081 [7th Circuit], cert. denied, 486 U.S. 891 [1983].

[9]Easterbrook (1981) and Posner (2001) discuss several of these alternative tests.

EXAMPLE 11.2 *Evidence of Predatory Pricing in Tobacco*

A firm may practice predatory pricing to force its rivals to sell their firms to it at a low price. By so doing, a firm can acquire its rivals cheaply and gain market power.

The Tobacco Trust allegedly engaged in predatory pricing against its rivals around the turn of the century. During the period 1881–1906, the Tobacco Trust acquired over 40 rivals and gained control of large shares of plug tobacco, smoking tobacco, snuff, and fine-cut tobacco sales. Frequently, the Tobacco Trust would identify a rival that it wished to buy and then introduce a competitive brand at a low price. The low profits would induce rivals to sell out to the Tobacco Trust at a low price.

For example, in 1901, the Tobacco Trust's American Beauty brand of cigarettes in North Carolina competed with a similar product of the Wells-Whitehead Tobacco Company of Winston, North Carolina. The American Beauty price was $1.50 per thousand, which was exactly equal to the required tax; it was therefore definitely below production costs. The Tobacco Trust claimed that the low price was an introductory offer. In 1903, the Tobacco Trust purchased its rival.

A detailed analysis of the value paid for the rivals purchased by the Tobacco Trust between 1881 and 1906 shows that predatory pricing had a large negative effect on the purchase price paid. Predation lowered the acquisition costs by about 25 percent.

As a result of violations of the antitrust laws, the Tobacco Trust was ordered dissolved and was broken into several separate firms (primarily American Tobacco, Liggett and Myers, and Lorillard) in 1911. By the 1920s, three firms dominated the cigarette industry, Reynolds (Camel brand), Liggett and Myers (Chesterfield brand), and American Tobacco (Lucky Strike brand).

In a famous antitrust suit (*American Tobacco Co. v. United States,* 328 U.S. 781 [1946]), these three firms were charged with explicit collusion to charge low prices to drive rivals out of business. During the Great Depression, the three major cigarette manufacturers increased their prices despite declining costs. New firms entered in response to this profit opportunity and sold, for roughly 5¢ less than the brands of the three major manufacturers, what were called *10-cent brands.* Between 1931 and 1932, the new brands increased their market share from below 1 percent to 23 percent.

In early 1933, the three major manufacturers dropped their wholesale prices by about 20 percent so that their retail prices were only slightly higher than those of the 10-cent brands, whose share fell to around 6 percent. The evidence suggests that these prices were not below the average total costs of the major cigarette companies. The 10-cent brands maintained a significant market share until the 1940s, when they disappeared. Even though price exceeded average cost and the 10-cent brands survived, the Court found that the companies had violated the antitrust laws by conspiring to lower prices with the intent to drive the 10-cent brands out of business.

Sources: Burns (1986), Tenant (1950, 43), Koller (1971), and *American Tobacco Co. v. United States,* 328 U.S. 781 (1946).

For most firms, a price of zero is lower than short-run marginal cost. A reasonable alternative view, however, is that the price of zero is a short-run promotional activity and is an investment designed to attract future customers. The price after the promotional period should be above the appropriate marginal cost measure where the price cut is treated as a promotional activity or cost. Just as investments in plant and equipment would not be expensed but would instead be amortized over time, so too should price promotions. Unfortunately, making such calculations can be difficult.

Similarly, a profit-maximizing firm may provide a product at a loss in the short run so as to signal the market that it will provide that product in the future. A firm may be concerned that potential customers may buy a rival's product and be unwilling to switch later, when it can produce cost-effectively. Pittman (1984) argues that IBM should have expected to make losses when it introduced its supercomputer but did not introduce the machine to engage in predatory pricing. Rather, IBM was signaling potential customers that it would provide supercomputers then and in the future.

Similarly, price can appear lower than short-run marginal cost when there is *learning by doing*: A firm's cost of production decreases as it produces more because it learns how to produce the product more efficiently. Because of this effect, a firm's costs are initially high but decline over time. By setting a very low price initially, the firm makes many sales and thereby accumulates experience that will enable it to lower its costs in the future. Even if the current price is lower than its current production costs, the prospect of reducing costs in the future by accumulating knowledge today justifies the lower price as an important investment for the firm. Again, the low price today should be viewed as an investment for the future. The short-run marginal cost of production that ignores future cost savings is not the relevant cost measure when a firm is involved in dynamic learning over time. Instead, one should look at the marginal production cost today plus (the present discounted value of) the change in production cost in the future that results from increased production today.

Most lawsuits alleging predatory pricing are brought by a firm against its rival. These rival firms may be complaining not about prices below cost but about price competition from a more efficient firm. If a firm is more efficient than another, one would expect the efficient firm to charge lower prices and take over the market. Indeed, the price could be below the inefficient firm's cost but equal to or above that of the efficient firm.

Therefore, predatory pricing suits could be a strategy by a less efficient firm to protect its market position. The evidence in a predatory pricing case of a lowering of price that inflicts losses on rivals is exactly what one expects when a more efficient firm competes in a market. If vigorous enforcement of predatory pricing laws prevents efficient firms from lowering their prices out of fear of a predatory pricing suit, it harms rather than helps consumers.

For this reason, Easterbrook (1981) suggests that the courts should not consider a predatory pricing suit until after a firm has been driven from business *and* the alleged predator has raised its price. Only then could one be sure that it was predation and not vigorous competition that drove the rival out of business.

Evidence on Predatory Pricing. Given all the theoretical difficulties with successful predatory pricing, it is not surprising that economists and lawyers have found few instances of successful price predation in which rivals are driven out of business and prices then rise. Although predation is frequently alleged in lawsuits, careful examination of these cases indicates that predation in the sense of pricing below cost usually did not occur.

For example, one of the most widely cited examples of price predation was the creation of Standard Oil. Supposedly, Rockefeller bought small, independent oil refineries after having lowered price to drive them out of business. McGee (1958), in his careful examination of this historical period, rejects that view and concludes that Rockefeller's rivals were bought out on rather favorable terms.

Koller (1971) reviews the available records in predatory pricing cases since 1890. Of the 26 cases for which adequate data existed, Koller finds evidence of below-cost pricing in 7 cases. Of these, only 4 represented successful predation, in that the rival vanished. Of these, 3 involved mergers.[10] A review of several predation cases illustrates that the evidence for predation in most cases is very weak and that defendants win over 90 percent of the time (Hurwitz et al. 1981). Isaac and Smith (1985) show that predation is rare in experimental settings.

The theory of predatory pricing relies on the incumbent's creation of a reputation for being a fierce competitor. The criticism of that theory is that it is unclear how such a reputation can be established and why rivals should believe it.[11] However, any theory that rests on a postulated set of beliefs cannot be logically *proven* wrong. Therefore, it is a mistake to think of price predation as inconceivable (see Example 11.2 and Weiman and Levin (1994), Genesove and Mullin (1997), and Morton (1997)).

Limit Pricing

Anybody can win unless there happens to be a second entry. —*George Ade*

A firm is **limit pricing** if it sets its price and output so that there is not enough demand left for another firm to enter the market profitably. Early models of limit pricing were developed by Bain (1956), Modigliani (1958), and Sylos-Labini (1962). In the early limit-pricing models, the potential entrant believes that the incumbent firm will not change its output after the new firm enters. Therefore, a firm contemplating entry believes that total market output will equal its own output plus the current output of the incumbent. The extra output causes price to fall. In this model, the incumbent firm, given these beliefs by the potential entrant, chooses its output level and its associated price in such a way as to remove the incentive of a firm to enter.

Suppose that both the incumbent and a potential entrant have the same average cost, *AC*, curve (Figure 11.2). If the incumbent firm produces q_i units (and will continue to do so in the face of entry), then the demand curve facing an entrant equals the

[10] Mergers that lead to significant increases in market power are illegal under U.S. antitrust laws; thus, if successful predation requires a merger to exercise market power, there is no need for a law aimed at predatory pricing, because merger policy can be used to protect consumers.

[11] See Lott (1999), who argues that government enterprises, not private firms, are more likely to engage in predation.

FIGURE 11.2 Limit Pricing

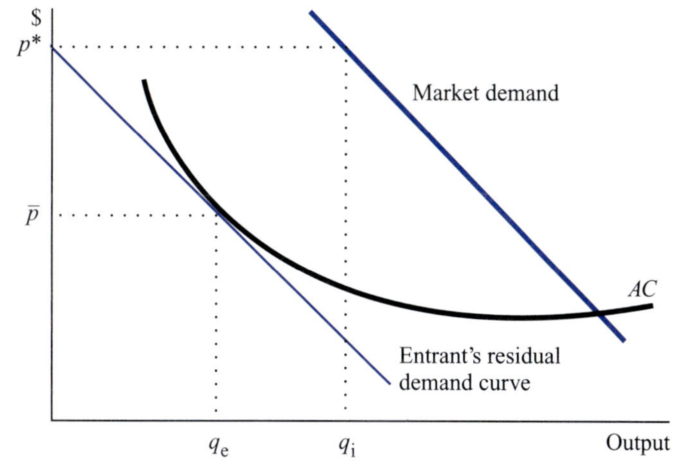

market demand curve minus q_i. If the entrant believes that the incumbent will continue to produce q_i units of output, it believes its residual demand curve is the total demand curve minus q_i units.

If the potential entrant chooses not to enter, then the incumbent firm sells its q_i units for p^*, as Figure 11.2 shows. If instead the new firm enters the market and produces q_e units of output, then total market output equals $q_e + q_i$, and the market price is $\overline{p}$. Because of the incumbent's choice of q_i, $\overline{p}$. is just equal to the average cost for the potential entrant of producing q_e units, and the entrant is indifferent between entering and not (so presumably it does not enter).

If q_i is chosen so that the residual demand curve facing the potential entrant is just below (or equal to) its average cost curve, then the entrant cannot produce a quantity such that it earns a positive profit in this market. As Figure 11.2 shows, the incumbent can sell q_i at p^*, which is above its average cost of production, yet not induce entry. That is, the potential limit price $\overline{p}$ prevents entry. Indeed, the incumbent does not have to produce q_i to deter entry; it needs only to convince the potential entrant that it will produce q_i if entry occurs.

Limit Pricing with Identical Firms. The main problem with this model of strategic behavior is the same as in the model of predatory pricing: Why should an entrant with identical costs believe that the incumbent will carry out its threat to produce q_i units after entry occurs? It is not profit maximizing for the incumbent to continue to produce q_i in the event of entry. Thus, its threat to do so is not credible with identical firms.

Because both the incumbent and the potential entrant have identical costs, it is difficult to see how one firm could scare another based on assumed behavior after entry.

It is as plausible to believe that a potential entrant can scare an incumbent into exiting by threatening to enter and produce q_i as it is to assume that the incumbent can deter entry through limit pricing.

Further, as in the case of predatory pricing, a counterstrategy for the entrant would be to enter the market with existing fixed-price contracts already in hand. An entrant could induce customers to sign such contracts at a price slightly less than p^*, a price far above its minimum average cost.

Limit Pricing Where One Firm Has an Advantage. In order to make limit pricing believable and effective, an incumbent firm must pursue a strategy in which it is optimal for it to produce the q_i units at the limit price $\bar{p}$ after entry.[12] If the two firms have identical average cost curves, it is not believable that an incumbent would keep its output unchanged in the face of large-scale entry by another firm. The key to making limit pricing believable is for the incumbent firm to somehow manipulate the market environment when entry occurs so that the incumbent has the incentive to produce q_i units.

For example, suppose that in the first stage of a game between an incumbent and a potential entrant, the incumbent builds its plant. Only in the second stage can the potential entrant decide whether to build a plant so it can enter the market.

Further, suppose that the incumbent can construct its manufacturing facility so that it only can produce exactly q_i units.[13] Given such a plant, the potential entrant has no doubt that the incumbent will produce q_i units of output whether or not entry occurs. If the potential entrant knows that the incumbent has built such a plant, it will not enter. The incumbent has successfully practiced limit pricing: It has *committed* itself so that its threat to produce q_i units is believable.[14]

There is an inherent asymmetry in this model between the incumbent and the potential entrant. The incumbent chooses its investment first so that it can commit to produce q_i units of output whether or not entry occurs, whereas the entrant is not able to precommit to an output level before the incumbent acts. This fundamental asym-

---

[12]See, for example, Spence (1977a, 1979), Dixit (1979, 1980), Salop (1979b), Milgrom and Roberts (1982a), Fudenberg and Tirole (1983), Bulow, Geanakoplos, and Klemperer (1985b), Eaton and Ware (1987), Gilbert and Lieberman (1987), and Waldman (1987). Many of these papers stress the role of the incumbent's maintaining excess capacity. LeBlanc (1992) points out that a firm may choose between using limit pricing and predatory pricing. The stronger (relative to the entrant) incumbent is more likely to choose predatory pricing; and the weaker one, limit pricing. For intermediate cases, a combination of the two methods may be used. For an empirical analysis of entry deterrence, see Geroski (1991). For an analysis of limit pricing in an oligopoly setting, see Bagwell and Ramey (1991) and Martin (1995).

[13]More reasonably, it might build a large plant with very low marginal costs at q_i.

[14]Committing to a fixed capacity in the future becomes more difficult if capital depreciates over time because the incumbent may be unable to maintain the natural asymmetry that arises from moving first. With rapid depreciation, the incumbent's advantage erodes rapidly. Both the incumbent and the new entrant may be on equal footing in terms of their ability to precommit to replace capacity as it wears out.

FIGURE 11.3 Extensive-Form Representation of Limit Pricing Game

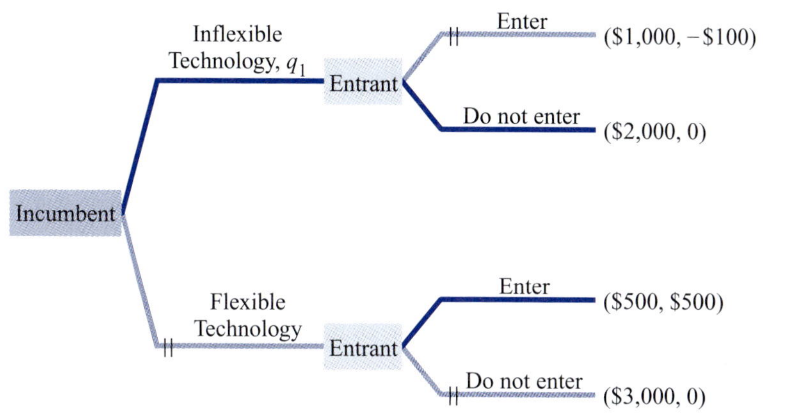

Note: The incumbent's profit is the first in the pair of payoffs.

metry is exploited by the incumbent to make its strategic behavior believable.[15] The incumbent manipulates the underlying environment (its ability to produce) in such a way as to give itself an advantage over the potential entrant.

The incumbent spends money in the first stage of this game to limit its productive options. That is, without such an investment, the incumbent could produce a wide range of output instead of only q_i units. At first glance, the incumbent is *purposefully shooting itself in the foot* by reducing its production options. Rather than only harming itself, however, the incumbent benefits from this restriction. The restriction makes believable the incumbent's threat to produce q_i units in the face of entry, so the potential entrant does not enter.

In general, a firm can benefit if it can precommit (limit its future options). By making commitments that render its threats credible, a firm raises its profit even though it restricts its future options.

Figure 11.3 illustrates this example of limit pricing using an *extensive-form representation* of the game (Chapter 6) that shows the sequence of all the possible actions and outcomes for both firms. Each line represents an action, and each box represents a decision point. The outcomes of actions are shown in parentheses, where the incumbent's profits are listed first. In the first stage of the game, the incumbent chooses between two production technologies: a flexible one that allows a wide range of output to be produced, and an inflexible one that can produce only q_i, where q_i is an output level that deters entry. In the second stage, the potential entrant decides whether to enter.

[15]Another way the incumbent might make a commitment is to sign a contract that penalizes it if it fails to produce q_i. However, because such contracts usually are not legally enforceable, they do not make the incumbent's threat credible.

To determine its optimal strategy in the first stage, the incumbent solves the game backward starting from the top right of the diagram. The potential entrant has to decide whether to enter. If the incumbent chose the inflexible technology and must produce q_i, the potential entrant earns \$0 if it does not enter and loses \$100 if it does enter. Thus, the potential entrant chooses not to enter. The two lines across the *Enter* line of action show that this strategy is ruled out.

Next the incumbent considers the bottom right corner of Figure 11.3. If the incumbent chose the flexible technology, the potential entrant earns a profit of \$500 if it enters and \$0 if it does not. Therefore, two lines block the action *Do not enter.* By this reasoning, the incumbent infers how the entrant would behave conditional on the incumbent's decision in the first stage of this game.

As a result, in the first stage, the incumbent decides whether to produce with the flexible or inflexible technology. If the incumbent chooses the inflexible technology, the entrant does not enter, so the incumbent earns a profit of \$2,000. If the incumbent chooses the flexible technology, the potential entrant enters, so that the incumbent earns a profit of only \$500. Thus, choosing the inflexible technology is more profitable.[16] Hence, the two lines across the *flexible technology* option block that line of action. The solution of choosing the inflexible technology is *subgame perfect* (see Chapter 6) because the threat to produce q_i is credible.[17]

Even if the incumbent chooses the flexible technology, it can still threaten a potential entrant that it will produce q_i if it enters. In so doing, the incumbent is trying to have it both ways: deterring entry through its threat and having a flexible technology if entry does not occur. Unfortunately for the incumbent, its threat is not credible without the commitment. The potential entrant knows that if it enters, the incumbent can make more money acting like a duopolist and reducing output below q_i than it can producing q_i. That is, the threatened post-entry strategy of producing q_i is not subgame perfect. Thus, the only way the incumbent can prevent entry is by committing to the inflexible strategy.

Dynamic Limit Pricing. If a firm sets prices (or quantities) over time so as to reduce or eliminate the incentives of rivals to enter a market, it is practicing **dynamic limit pricing.**[18]

Although a dominant firm may be able to set an extremely high price and maintain it in the short run, it may choose not to do so. A very high price attracts additional fringe firms, causing the market price to fall. Conversely, if a dominant firm

---

[16]If there were no threat of entry, the incumbent would prefer the flexible technology because its profit is higher (\$3,000) than with the inflexible technology (\$2,000). However, as the example shows, the inflexible technology is better for the incumbent when entry can occur.

[17]A Nash equilibrium in strategies is subgame perfect if the original strategies are Nash equilibria (best responses) in any subgame (a new game that starts in any period *t* and lasts to the end of the game). That is, no player wants to change strategies in a later period.

[18]See **www.aw-bc.com/carlton_perloff** "Dynamic Limit Pricing," Judd and Petersen (1986), Kamien and Schwartz (1971), De Bondt (1976), Gaskins (1971), Baron (1973), Stigler (1965), and Berck and Perloff (1988, 1990).

keeps its price very low to prevent entry, it has very low profits in both the short and the long run. Thus, a dominant firm that faces the threat of entry must trade off high profits in the short run against the entry of more competition and lower profits in the future.

It is often in the dominant firm's best interest to set a high price at first and then slowly to lower the price as entry occurs. Although the high price increases the rate of entry, profits today are worth more to the dominant firm than are profits in the future (given positive interest rates).

Because of this pricing behavior, it is common for dominant firms to lose market share over time (Example 11.3). When U.S. Steel was created in 1901, its share of the steel ingot market was thought to be 66 percent, but by 1982, its share had fallen to 19 percent.

EXAMPLE 11.3

The Shrinking Share of Dominant Firms

Generally, a dominant firm's share of an industry's sales shrinks over time. Consider 13 unregulated major industries in which firms compete on a national or international basis. Using the *Fortune 500* rankings to determine the leading firm in each industry, Pascale (1984) traced these firms' shares of industry sales over a 20-year period:

Industry Share Trends in 13 Key Industries

		Industry Share		
Leading Firm	Industry	1962	1982	Percent Change
Sears	Mass-market retailing	5	5	0
International Harvester	Farm tractors	24	18	−25
U.S. Steel	Finished steel	26	19	−27
Goodyear	OEM tires	29	27	−7
General Electric	Electrical appliances (refrigerators)	40	53	+33
RCA	Color TVs	49	20	−59
Boeing	Commercial wide-body jet aircraft	51	60	+18
General Motors	Passenger cars	52	46	−12
General Electric	Generators	59	61	+3
IBM	Mainframe computers	60	68	+13
Kodak	Photographic film	85	65	−24
Harley-Davidson	Motorcycles	100	36	−64
Xerox	Plain copiers	100	42	−58

Of these 13 leading firms, eight lost share, and one firm's share remained unchanged over the period. Three firms lost over half of their share of industry sales (RCA, Xerox, and Harley-Davidson), including both firms that made essentially all their industry sales in 1962.

EXAMPLE 11.4 *And Only a Smile Remained*

[The Cheshire Cat] vanished quite slowly, beginning with the end of the tail, and ending with the grin, which remained some time after the rest of it had gone.
—Lewis Carroll

Laszlo Jozsef Biro took out a patent on a ball-point pen in Paris in 1939. During World War II, he moved to Argentina, where his company, Eterpen S.A., started producing and selling the pens in 1943. Unlike a conventional fountain pen, it had a miniature socket that held a ball bearing, it used a special ink that dried almost instantly, and it held enough of this unconventional ink to work for months without refilling.

Also unlike a fountain pen, this pen could work at high altitudes without the risk of leakage. As a result, the U.S. Air Force was interested. It sent pens to various American manufacturers, saying it might want to buy ten thousand or so of them. The big three pen manufacturers—Parker, Sheaffer, and Eversharp—looked into the patent rights and discovered that Eberhard Faber, a pencil manufacturer, had obtained them but had run into difficulties producing the pens. Eversharp obtained the rights in 1945.

Eversharp redesigned the pen for mass production and instituted an advertising campaign to prepare the public for this new "miracle pen." This advertising greatly benefitted Milton Reynolds, who ultimately beat Eversharp to the market.

Reynolds had seen the pen in South America. When he found that he was too late to buy the rights from Biro, he developed ways around Biro's patent. What was unique about the Biro pen was its pressure-feed system that regulated the ink supply. Reynolds developed a different system that used gravity.

The Reynolds International Pen Company started production on October 6, 1945. A major New York department store, Gimbel's, advertised extensively, claiming that the pen was guaranteed to write for two years without refilling, to write under water and at stratospheric altitudes, and to make a clear impression on six to eight carbons. These claims made Gimbel's price of $12.50 (the maximum price allowed by the wartime Office of Price Administration) seem, if not a bargain, at least not the most staggering extravagance of all time.

With the initial cost of production around 80¢ per pen, healthy profits were realized when Gimbel's sold 10,000 pens (worth about a third of the store's average total daily sales volume) on the first day of sale, October 29, 1945. This success encouraged Reynolds to expand production; by early 1946, his 800 employees were producing 30,000 pens per day.

There are many examples of new industries in which a product is introduced at a high price that soon falls to a competitive level. When an industry is new, one or a few firms have large market shares and face relatively few competitors. Only over time do new entrants drive down the price. A particularly striking example from the early days of the ball-point pen industry is given in Example 11.4.

Production could not keep up with orders, and gift certificates were printed. By March 1946, Reynolds had banked \$3 million. During one 10-day period, he deposited \$1.5 million from orders of pens yet to be made. By February 1946, Reynolds had an after-tax profit of \$1,558,607.81.

These enormous profits encouraged entry. Gimbel's rival department store, Macy's, sold the Biro pen for \$19.98. It, too, did well, encouraging still more entry. Late in April, Eversharp finally entered the market with a \$15 pen. The July 1946 *Fortune* magazine reported that Shaeffer was going to sell a pen at \$15. Eversharp then announced plans to sell a retractable pen at \$25.

Meanwhile, Reynolds introduced a new model with a retractable point protector that cost 60¢ per pen to produce but sold at the original price of \$12.50. By late in the summer of 1946, his pens were being sold in 37 other countries (with prices in Hong Kong reaching \$75). As profits remained high, still others entered.

The Ball Point Pen Company of Hollywood ignored a patent infringement suit and sold a \$9.95 version. Another manufacturer, David Kahn, announced plans to sell a pen for less than \$3. In October, Reynolds introduced a new pen that cost 30¢ to produce and sold for \$3.85.

Approximately 100 manufacturers were producing pens by Christmas 1946, some selling for as little as \$2.98. Reynolds again introduced a new model, priced at \$1.69, but Gimbel's sold it for 88¢ in a price war with Macy's. At one point, Gimbel's changed prices five times during shopping hours. Reynolds then introduced a new, two-color model priced at 98¢ that was still highly profitable.

By mid-1948, some ball-point pens were selling for 39¢ and cost between 8¢ and 10¢ to produce. The price of some pens fell to 25¢ by 1951, and soon after, pens were available at 19¢. By this time, the large number of firms in the industry had driven the price down to the point where no unusual economic profits were being earned. Reynolds's market share went to zero and the firm stopped producing new pens in the United States.

This example shows that if a firm has no cost advantage or other advantage, it cannot maintain a large share of the market in the long run. Nonetheless, even a short-lived period of dominance can be highly lucrative. It is estimated that in a single month Reynolds earned profits as high as \$500,000, or about 20 times his original investment of \$26,000.

Sources: Lipsey and Steiner (1981) and Thomas Whiteside, "Where Are They Now?" *New Yorker,* February 17, 1951:39–58.

Investments to Lower Production Costs

In models of oligopoly behavior, the market outcome typically depends on the costs of the competing firms (Chapter 6). That is, the costs of each firm are part of the market environment that determines the outcome of the competition among the firms. In the following model, an incumbent firm manipulates the market environment to its advantage. We consider two examples where one of the firms has an advantage so that its strategy may be successful. In the first, one of the firms can engage in research and development (R&D) to lower its costs in a later period. In the second example, one firm lowers its cost through learning by doing.

Investing in R&D. Suppose that there are two time periods and two firms with identical initial cost functions. In Period 1, the incumbent firm is a monopoly and can invest in research and development (R&D) that will lower its costs in Period 2. In Period 2, the second firm may enter. The asymmetry in this model results from the assumption that only the incumbent firm, not the entrant, can invest in R&D to lower its costs. This asymmetry arises naturally when one firm is in a market before another firm.

Does the incumbent firm have an incentive to invest in R&D in order to lower its costs in Period 2? To illustrate the strategic choices of the incumbent firm, consider a specific example where the duopolists use Cournot strategies (Chapter 6) in Period 2.[19] In Period 1, the incumbent firm incurs $1 of fixed costs and has a constant marginal cost of $6. If the incumbent makes no investments in R&D in Period 1, then its fixed and marginal costs are the same in Period 2. The costs of the entrant in Period 2 are the same as the costs of the incumbent in Period 1. The linear market demand curve is $q = 12 - p$.

To decide whether to engage in R&D in Period 1, the incumbent needs to compare its profits in the equilibria with and without R&D. Table 11.1 shows the price and profits conditional on whether entry occurs in Period 2 and on whether the incumbent invests in R&D.

First, consider the equilibrium where the incumbent does not invest in R&D and the second firm enters in Period 2. In Period 1, the incumbent firm is a monopoly and equates marginal revenue based on the market demand curve to its marginal cost. It charges a price of $9 and produces 3 units, resulting in a profit of $8 in Period 1.[20] In Period 2, the incumbent and the entrant face the same cost conditions and play Cournot. In the equilibrium in Period 2, each firm produces 2 units at a price of $8 and earns a profit of $3.[21] Thus, the incumbent's total profit for the two periods is $11

[19]Although the quantitative results depend on the particular oligopoly behavior, the general insights from this model hold for all standard oligopoly models. The key feature of the example is that the incumbent's behavior in Period 1 influences the equilibrium in Period 2.

[20]The incumbent's profit in Period 1 is its total revenue minus its total cost: $\pi_i = q_i(12 - q_i) - (1 + 6q_i)$. The first-order condition for profit maximization is $12 - 2q_i - 6 = 0$, or $q_i = 3$. Consequently, p is $9 and π_i is $8.

[21]In Period 2, the incumbent maximizes its profit, $\pi_i = q_i[12 - q_i - q_e] - (1 + 6q_i)$. Consequently, the incumbent's best-response (reaction) function (see Chapter 6) is $q_i = 3 - q_e/2$. The entrant maximizes $\pi_e = q_e[12 - q_i - q_e] - (1 + 6q_e)$, so its best-response function is $q_e = 3 - q_i/2$. In the Cournot equilibrium (Chapter 6), which is determined by the intersection of these best-response functions, $q_i = q_e = 2$, $p = 8$, and $\pi_i = \pi_e = 3$.

TABLE 11.1 **Strategic R&D Investment: Monopoly in Period 1, Cournot Competition in Period 2**

	Period 1	Period 2	Total Profit in Periods 1 and 2
Entry			
No R&D investment	Profit of incumbent = \$8	Profit of incumbent = \$3	\$11
		Profit of entrant = 3	3
	Price = 9	Price = 8	
R&D investment	Profit of incumbent = 8 − 7.01 = 0.99	Profit of incumbent = 10.11	11.10
		Profit of entrant = 0.77	0.77
	Price = 9	Price = 7.33	
No Entry			
No R&D investment	Profit of incumbent = 8	Profit of incumbent = 8	16
	Price = 9	Price = 9	
R&D investment	Profit of incumbent = 8 − 7.01 = 0.99	Profit of incumbent = 15	15.99
	Price = 9	Price = 8	

(assuming, for simplicity, that the discount rate is zero). These results are summarized at the top of Table 11.1.

Now suppose that the incumbent firm invests in R&D in Period 1 and the rival enters in Period 2. For an investment of \$7.01, the incumbent can lower its marginal cost next period by \$2 (with certainty, for simplicity). If the incumbent makes the investment, it earns less money in Period 1. If it does not invest, it earns \$8 in Period 1, whereas if the incumbent invests, it earns \$8 − \$7.01 = \$0.99 in Period 1. The investment causes the incumbent's marginal cost to fall from \$6 to \$4 in Period 2. In the Cournot equilibrium in Period 2, the incumbent produces 3 1/3 units, the entrant produces 1 1/3 units, and the price equals \$7.33.[22] The incumbent's profit in Period 2 is \$10.11 (see Table 11.1).

Combined with its profit of \$0.99 in Period 1, its total profit for the two periods is \$11.10, which exceeds the \$11 that it earns if it does not invest in R&D in Period 1. Thus, given entry in Period 2, the incumbent earns more by investing in R&D because its reduced earnings in Period 1 are more than offset by the increased earnings in Period 2. Moreover, consumers are better off when Firm 1 invests in R&D because the price in Period 2 is lower when R&D occurs.

Now, suppose that entry does not occur in Period 2. Would it still be profitable for the incumbent to invest in R&D? If the firm makes no investment in either period, it earns its monopoly profit of \$8 in each of the two periods, for a total profit of \$16. If the firm invests in R&D, its monopoly profit in Period 1 is \$0.99 and its monopoly

[22]The incumbent chooses q_i to maximize its new Period 2 profit, $\pi_i = q_i(12 - q_i - q_e) - (1 + 4q_e)$. Its new best-response function is $q_i = 4 - q_e/2$. The entrant's best-response function remains $q_e = 3 - q_i/2$. The best-response functions intersect at $q_i = 3\frac{1}{3}$ and $q_e = 1\frac{1}{3}$.

FIGURE 11.4 Extensive-Form Representation of R&D Game

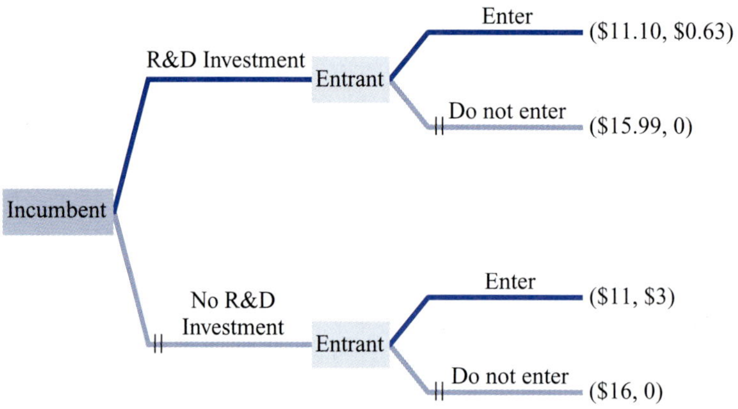

Note: The incumbent's profit is the first in the pair of payoffs.

profit in Period 2 is $15 (Table 11.1).[23] That is, it earns $7.01 less without the investment in Period 1 and earns $7 more in Period 2. Its total profit is $15.99, which is less than the $16 it would earn if it does not invest. Thus, it should not invest.

Figure 11.4 shows the extensive-form representation of this R&D game. The diagram illustrates that regardless of whether Firm 1 invests in R&D, its rival will enter the market (the double lines block the *Do not enter* action lines). As a result, it pays for the incumbent to invest in R&D: It earns $11.10 over the two periods instead of $11.

The incumbent makes an investment in Period 1 to alter the environment of Period 2 in its favor. This strategic behavior is attractive to the incumbent due to the asymmetry that allows it to act before the entrant. This example is similar to the Stackelberg model (Chapter 6) in that the incumbent benefits from being able to act before its rival and credibly committing itself to produce a relatively large output. In this example, the incumbent's ability to invest in R&D benefits both consumers and the incumbent. Without the threat of entry, the incumbent would not invest in R&D.

Learning by Doing. If the incumbent can reduce its costs in Period 2 through learning by doing in Period 1, it can gain an advantage over its rival that enters in Period 2. The incumbent has an incentive to sell more than it otherwise would in Period 1 to gain experience and lower its cost relative to that of its rival in Period 2. To increase its sales in Period 1, the incumbent must sell at a lower price than it otherwise would.

[23]If the incumbent invests in R&D, its monopoly profit in Period 2 is $q_i(12 - q_i) - (1 + 4q_i)$. Its first-order condition requires that it equate its marginal revenue to its marginal cost by setting q_i equal to 4. As a result, p is $8, and its profit is $15.

Thus, its profit in Period 1 is lower than it would be if it ignored the benefit of increased production on its costs in Period 2. Learning by doing, then, can be thought of as an investment that enables the firm to earn more in subsequent periods.

In a learning-by-doing model, the advantage of being able to go first depends on how much a firm can lower its cost relative to that of its rival and how long it takes to learn. If learning is either extremely rapid *or* extremely slow, the advantage of having a head start is not very great. When learning is very rapid, late entrants can quickly catch up with the incumbent. Conversely, when learning is very slow, the head start a firm gets does not matter very much. In the intermediate cases in which learning is neither very rapid nor very slow, the strategic importance of learning by doing is greatest for increasing profits (Spence 1981a). Indeed, if the learning-by-doing cost advantage is substantial enough, the second firm may choose not to enter the market.

Raising Rivals' Costs

A firm may benefit from strategic behavior that raises its rivals' costs.[24] In oligopoly models (Chapter 6), a firm's profit depends on its costs relative to those of its rivals. If a firm can costlessly raise its rivals' costs relative to its own, it can increase its profit at the expense of its rivals. In order to affect a rival's costs, usually a firm must have some market power or political power. This section examines a firm's strategies that raise its rivals' costs relative to its own and also those that raise everyone's costs. Then it discusses strategies that an entrant may use.

Raising the Rivals' Relative Costs. A firm clearly benefits if it can raise only its rivals' costs. Indeed, a firm may benefit from actions that raise its own costs if they raise its rivals' costs by more. The firm could use a direct method or one of several indirect methods.

Direct Methods: A firm may directly raise its rivals' costs if it can interfere with its rivals' production or selling methods. To take an extreme case, an unethical firm could blow up a rival's plant or sabotage a rival's machines. Both actions would raise its rival's costs, reduce competition, and raise the profit of the unethical firm practicing this strategic behavior (assuming that the firm is not caught). If the unethical firm must spend money to raise its rival's costs, then it must balance its increased expenditures for sabotage against its benefit from raising its rival's costs.

In 1993, British Airways (BA) admitted in court to playing dirty tricks on a smaller rival, Virgin Atlantic Airways (VAA) and is paying $2.5 million to settle a libel suit by the owner of VAA. BA's staff tapped into VAA's computers to obtain names and numbers of their passengers; phoned or met VAA passengers and falsely claimed that their flights were delayed or overbooked, and offered inducements to fly with BA; broke into homes and cars of VAA staff; hired a consultant to dig up dirt on VAA's owner and to plant negative news stories; and withdrew cooperation in maintenance and

[24]See Salop and Scheffman (1987), Krattenmaker and Salop (1986), Riordan and Salop (1995), and the papers in Salop (1981).

training.[25] No wonder Richard Branson, Chairman of VAA, once said that competing with BA was "like getting into a bleeding competition with a blood bank."[26]

The French government may have hidden microphones on Air France flights to Paris to gather information about American firms' marketing and technical plans.[27] The French Foreign Ministry portrays alleged spying as an essential way for France to keep abreast of international commerce and technology. The French may have won a billion-dollar contract to supply jet fighters to India by getting inside information on competing bids. The FBI also reported a French scheme to infiltrate foreign offices of IBM and Texas Instruments, perhaps to obtain information for the largely government-owned Compagnie des Machines Bull. Theft lowers a firm's costs relative to its rivals and is equivalent in its effects to raising a rival's relative costs.

Another example of a direct method is to make it difficult for a rival to gather information. For example, if an entrant conducts a marketing experiment to see whether its product is liked in certain locations, the incumbent can counteract the experiment by offering huge promotional discounts in those locations, making it more difficult for the entrant to judge consumer acceptance of its product relative to the incumbent's product (Fudenberg and Tirole 1986a).

Interference Through Government Regulation: A firm may raise its rivals' costs through government regulation. Many government regulations "grandfather" (exempt from regulation) existing firms and make it more onerous for new firms to operate in a market. For example, some environmental regulations impose more stringent requirements on new equipment than on old equipment and thus favor existing firms over entrants. By supporting government regulation so that a new rival cannot adopt their production techniques, incumbent firms can preserve and protect their market position and make it more costly for entrants to compete.

Tie-ins of Other Products: Sometimes an incumbent produces two products that must be used together, whereas the entrant produces only one of these products. Examples of products that complement each other are a camera and film or a computer and peripheral devices (printers, floppy drives, and so forth). Where products must be used together, the incumbent can disadvantage the entrant either through a contractual tie whereby the consumer must purchase both products together from the incumbent or through a product design decision that makes the entrant's product incompatible or difficult to use with the incumbent's other product. For example, a computer manufacturer could use a nonstandard plug to connect a printer. Even if a product's design reduces the amount consumers are willing to pay for it, the increased profits that come from hampering a rival may offset the loss (Farrell and Saloner 1986a,

---

[25]Paula Dwyer, "British Air: Not Cricket," *Business Week,* January 25, 1993:50–1; "Tactics and Dirty Tricks," *The Economist,* January 16, 1993:21–2.

[26]*London Times,* September 20, 1984.

[27]Larry Reibstein, Christopher Dickey, and Douglas Waller, "Parlez-Vous Espionage?" *Newsweek,* September 23, 1991:40.

Matutes and Regibeau 1988, Whinston 1990). See Example 11.5. Appendix 11A provides a detailed analysis of the strategic use of complements with applications to network industries (e.g., railroads, computers). Even where the products are independent, a tie-in can so reduce demand that rivals cannot efficiently produce (see Nalebuff forthcoming).

Raise Switching Costs: An incumbent can make it difficult for consumers of its product to switch to an entrant's product in the future (Schmalensee 1982; Klemperer 1987, 1990; Segal and Whinston 1996). That is, the incumbent may be able to raise the entrant's marketing costs to attract customers. For example, appropriate design may make it impossible to use computer programs written for one computer on another computer. Although the design may make the incumbent's product less desirable, it also serves to raise the switching costs to its consumers. As a result, a potential entrant faces a lower demand than it would otherwise, which reduces its incentive to enter.

Raising Wages or Other Input Prices: An incumbent firm that uses a different production technology than its rivals may be able to raise their costs disproportionately by raising the cost of an input to all firms in the market. If, for example, the rival uses more labor per unit output than does the incumbent firm, the incumbent's costs rise less from an increase in the wage rate than do the entrant's. Although total profits in the *market* must go down when wages rise, the market share of the less labor-intensive firm can increase by enough that its profits rise. This strategic behavior takes advantage of the natural asymmetry in production and assumes that the incumbent can influence market wages.

An incumbent may be able to increase wages by supporting union activities (Williamson 1968). For example, all the U.S. automobile manufacturers face a single union. Each time the union contract comes up for renewal, the union negotiates with (and strikes if necessary) one of these firms, and the others accept the outcome of these negotiations. A single firm, then, could negotiate an unusually high wage rate.

Similarly, an incumbent firm may be able to raise wages through direct market purchases. If the incumbent can purchase enough of the labor in a market to drive up the market wage, it has monopsony power. It can strategically use that market power to increase the costs of other firms more than its own if the other firms are more labor intensive.

To illustrate how raising a rival's costs can raise an incumbent firm's profits even if its own costs go up, consider the case of an incumbent that uses less labor per unit output than does a rival. Suppose that the incumbent has a constant marginal (and average) cost of m until its capacity, $\hat{q}_i$, is reached, whereupon its marginal cost is infinite, as Figure 11.5 shows. There are many rivals, a competitive fringe, all with the same constant marginal cost, m_1, as the figure illustrates.

In the absence of strategic behavior, the equilibrium price in the market is m_1, and it is optimal for the incumbent to produce at capacity, $\hat{q}_i$, where it earns profits equal to $(m_1 - m)\hat{q}_i$. Suppose now that the incumbent can raise the market wage rate. Because the incumbent's technology is different from everyone else's, the wage

EXAMPLE 11.5

Strategic Behavior and Rapid Technological Change: The Microsoft Case

In some markets, the product design of the primary product (such as a CD player) as well as that of complementary products (such as CDs) can change rapidly. In such settings, there is scope for strategic behavior in which a firm with market power in the primary product uses complementary products to increase its power in the primary market (see Appendix 11A). A recent government antitrust suit aimed at Microsoft attacks such behavior.

The government alleged in this case that Microsoft has market power in the market for personal computer operating systems, its primary product, because Microsoft's Windows operating system is the dominant system in use. The government charged that to preserve and enhance its power, Microsoft bundled its operating system together with its browser (software used to interact with the World Wide Web), a complementary product. The government then alleged that, as a consequence, the demand for Netscape's rival Internet browser declined substantially, and Netscape was forced to stop charging for its browser.

Although end users may benefit from obtaining free browsers, the government was concerned that potential competitors to Microsoft's Windows operating system might be driven out of business. Netscape's browser worked with all major operating systems, including Windows. Although Netscape's browser was designed initially to allow users to read Web pages, the government argued that Microsoft was concerned that Netscape's browser would evolve into an alternative "programming platform." According to the government, Microsoft executives worried that, in time, Netscape would add to its product "application programming interfaces" that software developers could use to write application programs. Such interfaces would pose a threat to Microsoft if they allowed application programs to run on all the operating systems that work with Netscape because that would erode the advantage that Windows had of having more application programs than other operating systems. The success of Netscape's browser would aid competition in operating systems, which might lead to a decline in Microsoft's dominance of operating systems. In its defense, Microsoft argued that the integration of its browser with Windows led to efficiencies that would be unattainable were the products sold separately and not integrated into a single program. The court ruled that Microsoft violated the antitrust laws.

Note: Carlton served as a consultant to Sun Microsystems, which sued Microsoft on related grounds.

Source: Carlton (2001), Carlton and Waldman (2002), and *U.S. v. Microsoft,* 253 F. 3d 34. See also Evans et al. (2000).

increase will have a different effect on m_1 than on the incumbent's marginal cost. Consider an extreme example in which the marginal cost of the incumbent firm does not change, and the marginal cost of rivals increases from m_1 to m_2. The equilibrium price rises from m_1 to m_2, the incumbent's optimal level of production is

FIGURE 11.5 Raising a Rival's Costs

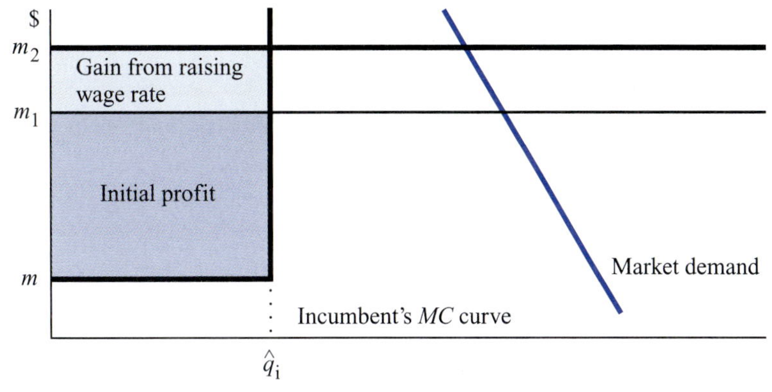

unchanged at $\hat{q}_i$, and its profit increases to $(m_2 - m)\hat{q}_i$, as Figure 11.5 shows. By behaving strategically and raising the costs of the competitive fringe from m_1 to m_2, the incumbent is able to increase its profit. Moreover, even if the wage increase raises the incumbent's costs, it may still be profitable for the incumbent to raise wages as long as the cost increase is smaller than the gain in Figure 11.5.

Another way to raise rivals' costs is to make distribution of the product more costly. If an incumbent can control most of the distributors (such as wholesalers or retailers), it can raise the cost of their rivals (Ordover, Saloner, and Salop 1990, Salop and Riordan 1995).

Raising All Firms' Costs. It may pay for the incumbent to raise the costs of all firms. A natural asymmetry often exists between an incumbent and potential entrants, in that the incumbent has already made expenditures (that is, sunk costs) that make it unlikely that it would exit the market.[28] Having made these expenditures before anyone else, the incumbent is committed earlier than anyone else to remaining in the market and derives a strategic advantage from this commitment. This strategic advantage creates incentives for the incumbent to spend more money to keep entrants out of a market than they are willing to spend to get into it (Salop 1979b, Gilbert 1989), as shown in the following example, illustrated in Figure 11.6.

Before entry the incumbent earns a monopoly profit, $\pi_m = \$100$. With entry the incumbent and entrant together earn duopoly profits, $\pi_d = \$80$, which are less than π_m because they cannot collude perfectly. If the incumbent and entrant equally share the duopoly profits, the entrant would pay $\pi_d/2 = \$40$ to enter, whereas the incumbent would pay $\pi_m - \pi_d/2 = \$60$ to keep the entrant out.

[28]Ghemawat and Nalebuff (1985) discuss the strategic issues that arise when a firm considers exiting a declining industry. Lieberman (1990) presents an empirical analysis.

FIGURE 11.6 Extensive-Form Representation of the Raising Costs Game

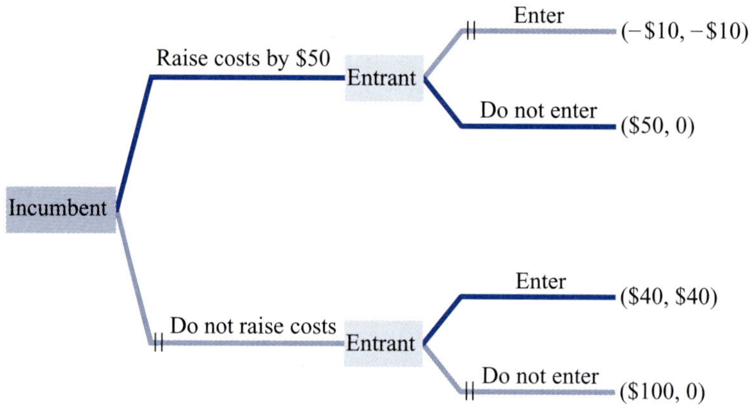

Note: The incumbent's profit is the first in the pair of payoffs.

This asymmetry is natural. Because π_m always exceeds π_d, it is always worth more to the monopoly to keep the entrant out than it is worth to the entrant to enter.

If the incumbent can raise the entrant's costs as well as its own by $50, the incumbent's profit is $50 if entry does not occur and its loss is $10 if entry occurs. With these increased costs, its rival loses $10 if it enters, so it does not enter. Because a profit of $50 exceeds the $40 that the incumbent would earn if it does not engage in strategic behavior, the incumbent has an incentive to raise costs for both its rival and itself by $50.

One way the incumbent could raise costs would be to support government legislation that raises both its own and its rival's costs by $50, for example, legislation regarding pollution controls. Alternatively, the $50 could be spent on advertising. Suppose that advertising does not change total consumption but does affect the relative market shares of firms within a market. A rival must match the advertising expenditures of the incumbent if anyone is to purchase the rival's product. Given the assumed asymmetry in this example, the incumbent can commit to spending on advertising first. As the example shows, the incumbent can gain by behaving strategically to raise both its own and its rival's costs.

Another implication of this natural asymmetry between an incumbent and a rival is that the incumbent is willing to bid more than an entrant for the right to a scarce resource that would enable entry (see Example 11.6). For example, suppose that only one distribution outlet is available to an entrant to market a product. Returning to the preceding numerical example, the incumbent firm is willing to bid $60 in order to purchase that distribution channel. An entrant would be willing to bid only $40. Moreover, the incumbent, which presumably already has a channel of distribution, would simply be purchasing the additional distribution outlet in order to foreclose its use by the entrant—it might not actually use the outlet. This strategy would deter

EXAMPLE 11.6 *Value of Preventing Entry*

In the 17th century, the Dutch were mad for tulips. After extensive experimentation, a Dutch shoemaker succeeded in producing the most sought-after specimen: a black tulip. He sold this marvel to a grower from Haarlem for 1,500 florins—a fortune. Immediately, the buyer threw it to the floor and stamped it to a pulp. That grower had already produced a black tulip of his own and wanted to prevent competition.

Why did no one outbid the Haarlem grower? The bulb was worth more to a monopolist than to others, because monopoly profit exceeds duopoly profit. If many such bulbs could be created, this policy of preventing entry would not be practical.

Source: Don Paarlberg, "Economic Pathology: Six Cases." *Choices,* 1994:17–21.

entry and guarantee that the incumbent's profit would be more than it would be if entry were allowed to occur. The scarcity of distribution channels is critical in this example. If distribution were easy to obtain, the incumbent could not profitably foreclose entrants by purchasing all distribution channels (Salop and Scheffman 1987).

Many antitrust suits allege that incumbent firms buy up industry supplies of scarce resources in an effort to prevent rivals from using them. For example, it was alleged that Alcoa (which had a monopoly in aluminum) signed contracts with power companies containing a provision that prevented the power companies from supplying power to any other firm for the purpose of making aluminum.[29]

Similarly, a firm may strategically obtain *sleeping patents*: patents that, once obtained, are "put to sleep" and not used (Gilbert 1981). By so doing, the firm prevents its rivals from obtaining and using these inventions.

Advantage of Entrants. Although an incumbent often has a natural advantage that it can exploit in its strategy, sometimes the entrant has an advantage. For example, a large firm with many locations or many products may not want to cut its price everywhere when confronted by new competition in only one location or in just one product. A large firm that has more to lose than a smaller firm if price falls may prefer to let an entrant develop a small foothold rather than engage in a price war. Thus, a firm that enters and remains at a small scale can compete without fear of retaliation.

If a large firm has stores at many locations that all charge the same price (perhaps because of economies of scale in national advertising), and another firm enters in just one of these locations, the large firm may abandon that location rather than lower its prices everywhere. Of course, if the large firm believed the small firm (or other entrants) would continue to expand, it might choose to fight vigorously.

[29] *United States v. Aluminum Co. of America,* 148 F.2d 416 (1945). Lopatka and Godek (1992) dispute this allegation.

If the large firm decides to fight, one alternative to reducing its uniform price is to introduce a new brand, sometimes called a **fighting brand**, whose price is low and whose availability is limited to those areas where a (small) rival is successful. In this way, the large firm can engage in competition without lowering price to all its customers. See Example 11.2.

Similarly, a firm that produces many substitute products views price competition in one product as costly because such competition also affects its revenues from other products. Conversely, a firm that produces complementary products does not find a price war in one product as costly if lost profits in one product are offset by increased profits in others. A firm has less to fear about competitive reaction to its aggressive pricing policy when its rival produces several substitute products, is relatively large, and believes that the entering firm only wants to occupy a small market niche (Bulow et al. 1985a, Fudenberg and Tirole 1984).[30]

Welfare Implications and the Role of the Courts

It is difficult to determine whether strategic behavior raises or lowers welfare. Moreover, it is difficult to distinguish competitive from strategic behavior.

Some strategic behavior lessens competition and harms consumers. For example, successful predatory pricing that leads to market power in the long run has no socially redeeming virtues.

Other types of strategic behavior, however, can produce socially desirable results. For example, even if R&D investments are a strategic action, consumers may ultimately benefit from lower prices. Even when strategic behavior leads to monopoly, consumers may benefit. Indeed, patents are designed to create monopolies because the incentive of monopoly profits encourages firms to develop new knowledge (see Chapter 16). These examples suggest that the welfare implications of strategic behavior need to be considered case by case. Strategic behavior may be socially undesirable in one set of circumstances and socially desirable in another.

In practice, it may be difficult to distinguish between strategic behavior and desirable competitive behavior. For example, passing along cost savings through lower prices, investing in R&D in order to lower costs, gathering marketing information, and arranging distribution channels for a product are all desirable features of competition that are difficult to distinguish from strategic behavior.

U.S. antitrust laws (Chapter 19) allow the government to intervene if it believes that firms are taking actions that lessen competition. The antitrust laws also give private plaintiffs who are the victims of such behavior the right to sue. The difficulty of distinguishing between beneficial competition and undesirable strategic behavior presents government enforcement agencies and the courts with a problem. Too little enforce-

---

[30]Bernheim and Whinston (1990) and Whinston (1990) provide examples of how multimarket contact and other devices can signal likely competitive responses. Products are called *strategic complements* if an aggressive action in one product induces an aggressive reaction (such as a firm's meeting its rival's price cut) and *strategic substitutes* when the reaction is dissimilar (a firm reduces output in response to a rival's expansion). See Bulow et al. (1985a).

ment leads to bad behavior and monopoly power, whereas too vigorous enforcement may deter firms from pursuing desirable forms of competition for fear that this competition will be misinterpreted. For example, if attempts to compete through lower prices trigger lawsuits for predatory pricing, then firms that lower prices for purely competitive reasons risk being sued for predatory pricing. Thus, the proper role of enforcement agencies and the court in dealing with strategic behavior is not easy to define.

When designing proper enforcement policies, one should consider the costs of making an error. The success of strategic behavior depends on the asymmetry between the firm practicing the strategic behavior and the firm that is its target. If a new firm can eventually model itself after an incumbent firm (for example, adopt its technology to remove any asymmetries in the use of labor), then strategic behavior is doomed to fail. In such cases, even if the courts fail to prevent its exercise, strategic behavior leads only to temporary market power that is eventually eroded as firms learn how to imitate the incumbent. (Of course, such market power causes more harm the longer it takes for new firms to enter.) In contrast, if the courts falsely condemn desirable behavior as strategic, this harm is not eliminated by future actions by firms.

Cooperative Strategic Behavior

Cooperative strategic behavior comprises those actions that rival firms take in their own self-interest that raise the oligopoly price closer to the monopoly level. The theory of cooperative strategic behavior relies on cartel theory (Chapters 5 and 6), which holds that oligopoly profits depend on the ability of each member of the cartel to assure the others that it is not trying to steal its rivals' customers.[31] The greater the mutual assurance that firms are not stealing each other's customers through lower prices, the easier it is for them to succeed in charging a price above the competitive level.

In Chapter 5, we examined several practices that can facilitate collusion (see also Salop 1986). Here we consider several additional practices and examine their treatment under the antitrust laws.

Practices That Facilitate Collusion

Oligopolies employ a variety of cooperative strategic actions to elevate price (for example, by facilitating collusion). Chapter 5 discusses the use of most-favored-nation and meeting-competition clauses in contracts, information sharing, dividing the market, and other methods. The following are some other important approaches.

Uniform Prices. If all of a firm's customers are charged exactly the same price, then it is costly for the firm to try to steal a rival's customers by offering them a slightly lower price. The reason is that the slightly lower price, by assumption, must also be offered to

[31] Explicit agreement is not necessary for an oligopoly to succeed in raising price above competitive levels (Chapters 5 and 6).

all of the firm's existing customers (this approach may be implemented through a most-favored-nation clause in contracts; Edlin 1997). This uniformity of price lowers the firm's gain from stealing away the rival's customers. Moreover, if all of the firm's customers pay identical prices, it is easier for a rival to learn when a firm has lowered price.

The question arises then as to what forces a firm to charge a single price to all consumers. One answer is government legislation. The Robinson-Patman Act requires that firms charge identical prices to customers who buy identical products.[32] Firms sometimes use this law as a justification for not granting selective discounts to particular customers. Therefore, the Robinson-Patman Act may facilitate collusion.

Penalty for Price Discounts. A more dramatic way of reducing a firm's incentive to steal another firm's customers by lowering price is for each firm to adopt a policy whereby any lower price is passed on not just to the firm's current customers (as occurs with a uniform price to all customers), but to all of its past customers over some time period. For example, if a firm signs a contract with buyers that entitles them to receive any price discount that occurs in the next year, then the firm has a great disincentive to lower price. Its rivals know that this firm is not likely to discount price because of the cost of applying the discount to past customers.

Advance Notice of Price Change. Cartels have difficulty maintaining a pricing arrangement when prices change (Chapter 5). At the time of a price change, firms distrust each other because each is likely to be selling at different prices.

Suppose that it is clear that the prices in an oligopoly that is not a cartel should rise. Which firm should increase the price? Some industries have a natural price leader, but many others do not. The first firm to raise price is at a serious disadvantage because it loses sales from its relatively high price. Of course, if rivals eventually match the higher price, all firms are better off with the higher prices. Nonetheless, if the firm that initiates the increase suffers a loss relative to its rivals who follow slowly, then no firm wants to be the price leader.

One way around this problem is to use advance notice of price increases, a tactic that allows other firms in the market to decide whether to go along with the price increase before it becomes effective. If rivals decide not to go along, the firm that announced the price increase can rescind it. In such a circumstance, firms need never find themselves selling at different prices in the market, and the disincentive to raise price is eliminated.[33]

Using the same logic, at times of decreased demand, the firm initiating the price decline gains relative to its rivals who take time to respond to the price cut. Thus, each firm

[32]The relevant portion of the Robinson-Patman Act applies if customers are firms that compete against each other and if the effect of the price discrimination is to substantially lessen competition.

[33]In industries in which price increases are announced in advance, firms compete over how much buying to allow before a price increase takes effect. Some firms have policies of allowing customers to buy an extra month's supply at the old price. More usually, the amount of buying at the old price is variable and differs over time and across firms.

has an incentive to cut its price first. Advance notice of price decreases mitigates this incentive by ensuring that no firm gains an advantage from taking the lead in cutting price.

Several industries give advance notice of price increases, and some have been the subject of lawsuits and investigations. For example, in the 1990s the Department of Justice investigated the major airlines' use of advance notices of fare changes and alleged that the airlines' communication of their pricing intentions led to elevated prices. The case was settled with the airlines agreeing to cease the practice, despite consumer groups' support of the practice. However, there is no evidence that cessation of the advance price announcements had any effect on fares (see Carlton, Gertner, and Rosenfield 1997, and Borenstein 2003).[34] Also see Example 11.7.

Information Exchanges. Information exchanges between firms can facilitate cartels or promote efficiency. One way a firm can convince rivals that it is not trying to steal customers through a price discount is to announce the identity of its new customers and the price and quantity terms offered. The firm makes this announcement so that when a customer shifts suppliers, a price war is not triggered by rivals who believe incorrectly that the shift was due to a lowered price. Another method of conveying information is disseminating publicly what the firm's strategy is so that rivals will not misinterpret the firm's actions and can coordinate with the firm's strategy. See Farrell (1987).

There may also be legitimate efficiency reasons for industry members to exchange information. When a centralized market does not exist, disseminating price information can improve market efficiency (see Example 11.8). Moreover, firms can monitor their own efficiency better if they can compare their costs to those of other firms.

Delivered Pricing. A delivered pricing system specifies the total delivered price (inclusive of freight) that a buyer must pay as a function of the buyer's distance from a specified location (a *basing point*), but not of the location of the seller. A delivered pricing system can be created by specifying the total delivered price as the sum of a going market price at the basing point plus freight from that point. For example, steel used to be sold with Pittsburgh as the basing point. If an Ohio steel mill shipped steel to Chicago, the price the buyer paid equaled the going price of steel in Pittsburgh plus freight from Pittsburgh to Chicago. The freight charges were calculated from standard published rate schedules.

At first glance, delivered pricing systems seem so bizarre that they inspire suspicion. Indeed, many economists believe that delivered pricing is an odd mechanism adopted only to facilitate collusion.[35] It facilitates collusion because it prevents competing firms from secretly granting discounts disguised as low freight charges. Forcing all firms to charge the same freight and same price makes it easy to detect deviations from a collusive price agreement.

---

[34]Carlton served as an expert for the airlines, and Borenstein served as an expert for the Department of Justice.

[35]See Thisse and Vives (1992) on how such a pricing scheme can arise in a static game only under somewhat contrived circumstances, but how it can be an effective punishment in a repeated game.

EXAMPLE 11.7 *The FTC versus Ethyl et al.*

In 1979 the FTC brought an antitrust suit [*E. I. du Pont de Nemours & Co. v. FTC*, 729 F.2d 128 (2d Cir., 1984)] against four producers (du Pont, Ethyl, Nalco, and PPG) of an additive to leaded gasoline. The FTC charged that certain business practices of these four firms had the effect of facilitating collusion in the industry. Some of the practices that the FTC attacked were the use of 30-day advance notice of price increases (not decreases) to buyers, most-favored-nation clauses, and public press announcements of all price changes. Although the evidence indicates that this industry did not behave perfectly competitively, the real issue was not the competitiveness of the industry but rather whether the practices decreased the competitiveness of the industry.

The primary economic theory of the FTC was that the industry practices eliminated uncertainty in the industry and improved the ability of rivals to match each other's prices. Empirical tests of the effect of some of the practices are possible. For example, public press announcements of price changes had ceased in the industry. Yet there appeared to be no difference in the speed with which rivals were able to match each other's prices before and after the cessation of the press announcements. Even though the advance notice provision applied only to price increases and not to decreases, rivals matched each other's price decreases as rapidly as they matched their price increases.

The trial record indicates that because many of the practices were adopted at a time when only one firm was in the industry, their adoption was not intended to facilitate collusion. Thus, these practices also might serve an efficiency function. For example, buyers might value advance notification of price increases so they could plan better. Moreover, some of the issues in the case, such as an attempt to ban public notice of price announcements in the *Wall Street Journal*, raised issues of free speech. The FTC ruled against the industry; however, the Second Circuit Court of Appeals overturned that verdict.

Note: Carlton appeared as an expert in this case on behalf of Nalco Industries.

The pricing system that many economists predict should emerge with competition is called **FOB pricing**: The buyer pays a *free-on-board* (FOB) price, where the seller loads the good onto the transport carrier at no cost to the buyer, plus the actual freight.[36] Under such a system, the freight charge varies with a buyer's location, and

[36]Because prices reflect costs in competition, economists expect purchasers to pay for FOB pricing and for actual freight under competition. In fact, firms in competitive industries often use delivered pricing because it is simple and saves on administrative costs. For example, firms may use uniform delivered pricing as long as freight does not vary much among customers. Typically, furniture stores include delivery in the price of an item, provided that customers live reasonably close to the store. Some firms have zone pricing, in which buyers who live in a firm's region pay lower freight charges than those in more distant regions. It appears that uniform delivered pricing is often followed as long as the variation in freight charges among customers is 10 percent or less (Carlton 1983c).

EXAMPLE 11.8

Information Exchanges: The Hardwood Case

In the *Hardwood* case [*American Column and Lumber Co. et al. v. United States,* 257 U.S. 377 (1921)], a group of lumber mills were accused of violating the Sherman Act. These producers ran the American Hardwood Manufacturers Association, which, under their *Open Competition Plan,* collected and disseminated price and production information. The number of mills in the industry was large—about 9,000 mills in 20 states. Participation in the Open Competition Plan was voluntary, and 465 mills participated (representing 30 percent of output).

Although monitoring output and prices can facilitate collusion, collusion can be difficult with such a large number of independent firms in the industry. Even though information-sharing arrangements are particularly suspect when the number of firms in the industry is small enough to make collusion likely, the Supreme Court ruled that the information exchange violated Section I of the Sherman Act, and the information dissemination ceased. Alexander (1988) contends that the information exchange had no anticompetitive impact on market output and instead was likely an attempt to disseminate valuable but costly information to a competitive industry.

sellers can cut price by undercharging for freight (which rivals cannot easily observe). In such a pricing system, firms at different locations generally quote different prices to a buyer, so that enforcing a collusive agreement about price is difficult.

Underlying this story is the implicit assumption that colluding firms detect cheating by observing deviations from an agreed-upon price schedule. Another way firms detect cheating is by monitoring shifts in market share: If firms see that a rival is inexplicably gaining customers, they suspect cheating. When this latter method of detecting cheating is used, delivered pricing may be less effective than FOB pricing in facilitating collusion.

A great disadvantage to collusion through the use of delivered pricing is that it fails to allocate the market to sellers. For example, suppose that there are two sellers of steel—one in Chicago and the other in Pittsburgh. If Pittsburgh is the basing point for delivered pricing, it might be profitable for either a Chicago or a Pittsburgh steel mill to sell steel near Chicago. In such a case, no inference of cheating would follow if the Pittsburgh mill were seen selling in the Chicago area. If the firms instead adopted FOB plant pricing plus freight, the market would be clearly divided: Consumers closer to Chicago would buy from Chicago, and those closer to Pittsburgh would buy there.

Figure 11.7 illustrates that FOB pricing creates a clean market division precisely because firms charge most buyers different prices. As the figure shows, suppose that each firm agrees to charge the same FOB price at its plant and to charge actual transportation charges. The price lines represent the price that a buyer at any location must pay. They rise as one moves away from the location of each firm to show that transportation costs rise with distance. All customers to the west of Cleveland buy from Chicago, and all customers to the east of Cleveland buy from Pittsburgh.

If the Pittsburgh steel mill were seen selling in the Chicago area, one would infer that it was not adhering to the FOB pricing agreement. In contrast, under delivered

FIGURE 11.7 FOB Pricing Divides the Market

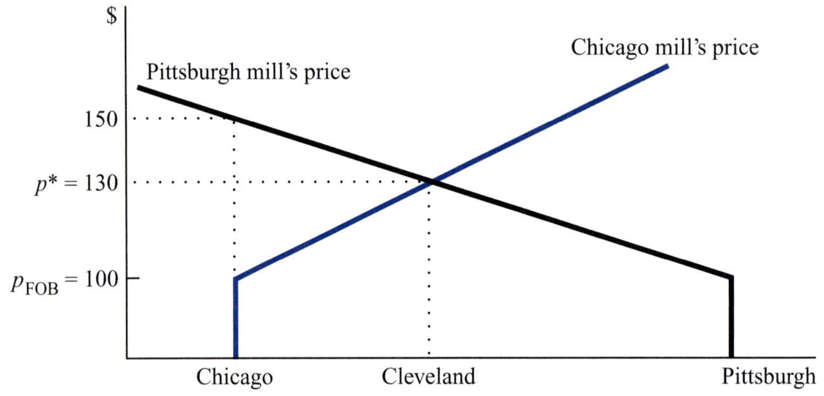

pricing, all firms charge the same price, and there is no neat market division. Moreover, under delivered pricing, the Chicago firm could be selling in Pittsburgh and the Pittsburgh firm could be selling in Chicago so that there is a lot of inefficient cross-hauling of the product. In general, the greater the distance between the firms and the more important the transportation charges, the better FOB pricing is as a means of market allocation and collusion compared to delivered pricing (Carlton 1983).

There is an important difference between delivered pricing and FOB pricing. In an equilibrium with FOB pricing, all firms must charge the *marginal* buyer the same price ($130 at Cleveland in Figure 11.7). At points other than Cleveland, however, the firms located at Pittsburgh and Chicago charge *different* prices under FOB pricing but not under delivered pricing. Despite this difference between delivered and FOB pricing, it is sometimes possible for the two pricing systems to look alike.

Suppose that many steel consumers are located in both Pittsburgh and Chicago, but that initially all of the many steel mills are in Pittsburgh. In a *competitive* equilibrium, if it costs $100 to produce a ton of steel, a buyer in Chicago pays $100 plus freight, say $50, from Pittsburgh, for a final price of $150. If a very small steel mill opens in Chicago, how will the equilibrium change? At any price below $150, the Chicago steel mill has more business than it can possibly handle because it is a very small mill. Therefore, there is no reason for the Chicago mill to charge below $150! In this competitive equilibrium, the Chicago mill charges what appears to be a delivered price based on Pittsburgh freight. Yet it is the competitive equilibrium. The small Chicago mill earns a rent because it has chosen such a desirable location.

Failure to understand that price-taking firms at some locations (like Chicago in the example) can charge $150 could lead one to mischaracterize a competitive FOB pricing arrangement as collusive delivered pricing. As more steel mills locate in the Chicago region, they will eventually be unable to sell all their steel in Chicago at $150, and they will start selling outside of Chicago (say, Cleveland). When that occurs, the

FOB price can no longer equal $150 in Chicago. If the FOB price is $150 in Chicago and the Chicago mill adds freight to Cleveland, the price to Cleveland exceeds the FOB price at Pittsburgh plus freight (of $30) from Pittsburgh, and no Chicago steel would be sold in Cleveland (see Figure 11.7). Therefore, the new competitive equilibrium must involve an FOB price below $150 in Chicago. Eventually, competitive entry of steel mills in the Chicago region will drive the Chicago price down to a marginal cost of $100. Buyers close to Pittsburgh buy from Pittsburgh, and those close to Chicago buy from Chicago.

The intensity of government scrutiny of spatial pricing schemes has varied over time. In *FTC v. Cement Institute* (333 U.S. 683 [1948]), the FTC alleged that a conspiracy among cement producers was facilitated by the use of delivered pricing with basing points. The FTC won the case, but subsequent political pressure from businessmen led to congressional hearings that seemed to stop the FTC from bringing many more cases.

More recently, pricing policies in the lumber industry were attacked in *Boise Cascade v. FTC* (63 F.2d 323 [9th Cir. 1980]). All plywood used to come from the Pacific Northwest. Beginning in the early 1960s, some plywood was shipped from the South. Initially, little southern plywood was shipped, but eventually significant amounts were shipped. The price of southern plywood always equaled the price of the wood plus freight, where the freight fee was based on shipping charges from the Pacific Northwest. Although it follows from the logic of the steel example (Figure 11.7) why the price of southern plywood was initially quoted in this way, it is harder to explain why these policies continued as the southern plywood industry grew.

The lumber firms practicing the policy claimed that it was just a convenient device to facilitate comparisons of price quotes from the South and the Pacific Northwest. They also claimed that the southern FOB price was different from the Pacific Northwest FOB price. The implication was that each FOB price was determined by the forces of supply and demand, and the resulting pricing equilibrium was the competitive FOB pricing equilibrium predicted by the reasoning in our steel example. For example, suppose that the true competitive price of southern plywood to a buyer in New York is $200, consisting of two parts: $100 of true freight plus $100 of true FOB price. If the freight from the Pacific Northwest is $150, then the quoted price for southern plywood is $50 FOB plus $150 freight, for a total price of $200. The court decided that the pricing scheme did not represent illegal collusive behavior. Gilligan (1992) shows that the subsequent replacement of the peculiar pricing scheme with FOB pricing caused the price to fall in the South but not in the Northwest.

In summary, the method of spatial pricing used can affect the ability to collude. Although using delivered pricing can facilitate collusion, it does not always do so. In some settings, delivered pricing can lead to greater competition than FOB pricing. Moveover, delivered pricing can be more efficient (reduced transaction costs) than FOB pricing, and therefore can appear in competitive industries.

Swaps and Exchanges. Firm C, located in Chicago, has a customer in Boston, and Firm B, located in Boston, has a customer in Chicago. To minimize shipping costs and service their customers, Firm C "swaps" or "exchanges" one unit of its output in Chicago for one unit of Firm B's output in Boston. Although this arrangement may appear odd, it is common in industries where the product (such as chemicals, gasoline, and paper) is relatively homogeneous and transport costs are high. A swap is not equivalent to two independent buy-sell transactions. Indeed, there are typically no prices involved in swaps, and the final customer transacts with only one of the firms.

Swaps have often been attacked as a facilitating device in antitrust cases. The theory is that swaps are a mechanism to divide the market, allow rivals to communicate, and prevent competition from occurring, yet still allow firms to service distant clients. Swaps also can make it difficult for a small entrant to service distant customers because the new entrant has few locations that it can use to engage in swaps.

Although this explanation is theoretically possible, there are other rationales for swaps. Swaps can be an enforcement mechanism to guarantee timely delivery in industries where supply availability is key. Firm C is reasonably assured that it can rely on Firm B in Boston as a supply source for its Boston customer because it knows that Firm B relies on it for deliveries in Chicago. If Firm B fails to deliver to Firm C's customer in Boston, then Firm C will not deliver in Chicago for Firm B. Frequently, firms closely monitor their swaps to make sure that Firm C and Firm B are "in balance" and don't "owe" any product to the other for long periods.

Cooperative Strategic Behavior and the Role of the Courts

Cooperative strategic behavior, requiring, as it does, that firms all choose similar actions, seems superficially easier to identify and condemn than other types of strategic behavior. After all, any agreement or practice that tends to reduce competition is likely to harm society. The problem is that many practices may be chosen not to restrict competition but for efficiency reasons (see Example 11.7).

For example, advance notice of price changes might benefit consumers even though it could also facilitate collusion. A policy that condemns practices reached through agreement to limit competition seems correct. A policy that condemns business practices, however chosen (for example, at the insistence of the buyer), that conceivably could affect collusion, is probably too broad and would leave firms in a quandary as to which of their policies would be subject to antitrust scrutiny. The result might be to deter firms from adopting efficient practices that their customers desire.

SUMMARY

Strategic behavior is an attempt by a firm to influence the market environment in which it competes. This environment includes the beliefs of rivals and customers, the technologies and costs of the firms, and the knowledge of customers. For noncooperative strategic behavior to be successful, the strategy must be believable to rivals. Asymmetry among firms is a key ingredient of successful strategic behavior.

Predatory pricing is a costly policy for a firm to follow. There have been only a few documented cases of successful predatory pricing in which price was below some measure of cost. Other noncooperative strategies, such as price cuts down to (but not below) cost, strategic R&D, and raising rivals' costs, might well be more profitable, and one should expect them to be used more often than predatory pricing.

Cooperative strategic behavior requires firms to act similarly and is a direct application of the theory of oligopoly studied in Chapters 5 and 6. Any practices that firms can use collectively to reduce uncertainty about each other can facilitate collusion.

The proper legal posture toward strategic behavior is complicated. Some strategic behavior helps consumers, for example, by encouraging investments. Other types of strategic behavior harm consumers. Even successful strategic behavior can maintain market power only until entry occurs. Strategic behavior is therefore likely to be harmful only in industries in which entry is difficult.

Distinguishing the good strategic behavior from the bad can be difficult for both economists and courts; hence, great care should be used in applying antitrust laws against apparent strategic behavior. Society faces a trade-off between too little enforcement, which leads to market power, and too much enforcement, which deters healthy competition.

PROBLEMS

1. In several industries, firms engage in *swaps*. For example, a paper firm with a plant in California and a customer in New York swaps one ton of paper with another paper firm with a plant in New York and a customer in California. Often, the customers have many plants located throughout the country. Provide an efficiency explanation for swaps. Provide an anticompetitive explanation. [*Hint:* Consider why assignment of multiplant customers to firms might make monitoring a cartel easier.]
2. Draw an extensive-form representation of the predation game discussed above where the potential entrant is unsure about the incumbent's marginal cost. [*Hint:* See Chapter 6 for an example with uncertainty.]
3. If a firm has debt, it must pay interest to the debtholders. Suppose that there is a blot on a manager's record if the firm he or she operates goes bankrupt. Discuss whether the use of a high ratio of debt to equity among all firms in a market could be a practice that facilitates collusion. Consider the consequences if firms issue debt in different years and if interest rates vary from year to year.
4. Using a model of price predation, explain why driving a rival into bankruptcy does not, by itself, enable the predator to charge monopoly prices. [*Hint:* What happens to the assets of the bankrupt firm?]
5. Suppose that the Japanese firms in Example 11.1 were indeed predating for 20 years in the hope that in the 21st year and thereafter they could charge a monopoly price. Suppose that the annual loss is \$1 million for each of the first 20 years, and let π_m be the annual flow of monopoly profits thereafter. If the interest rate is 10 percent, calculate how high π_m would have to be in order for the predation strategy to be profitable. [*Hint:* The discounted present value of the 20 years of annual loss is

$$\frac{1}{r}\left[1 - \left(\frac{1}{1+r}\right)^{20}\right],$$

and the discounted present value of an annual profit of π_m beginning in year 21 is

$$\frac{\pi_m}{r}\left(\frac{1}{1+r}\right)^{20},$$

where r is the interest rate.]

Answers to odd-numbered problems are given at the back of the book.

SUGGESTED READINGS

Gilbert (1989), Ordover and Saloner (1989), Tirole (1988), and Wilson (1992) provide excellent overviews of modern theories of strategic behavior.

Farrell and Klemperer (2003) survey the literature on switching costs and network effects.

APPENDIX 11A

The Strategic Use of Tie-in Sales and Product Compatibility to Create or Maintain Market Power with Applications to Networks

In this appendix, we study the strategic incentive to use tie-ins and product compatibility decisions to create or maintain market power. (In Chapter 10, we studied the use of tie-in sales as a method of price discrimination.) We apply these strategic concepts to network industries.

Tie-in Sales

A tie of product *B* to the sale of product *A* can, under certain circumstances, affect the market power of a monopoly producer of *A* in the market for either *A* or *B*. By tying the sale of product *B* to *A*, the monopoly producer of *A* can reduce the size of the market available to the rival producers of *B*. If *B* is not produced in a constant returns environment with competition, then the tie can affect the market structure of product *B* (Whinston 1990) and benefit the monopoly producer. With constant returns to scale in the production of *B*, such a tie would not benefit the monopoly producers under certain conditions (see Chapter 10).

For example, suppose that local residents share their island with a hotel.[1] The residents frequent two local tennis clubs, each of which also serves some of the hotel's guests. If the hotel builds a health club and ties the guests to that club (for example, by allowing free use of the facilities), such an action may deprive the local clubs of the necessary size to support themselves, causing the hotel to become the monopoly owner of a tennis club on the island. This result depends critically on the presence of scale effects in the provision of tennis clubs. This "foreclosure of competition" for product *B* has been the traditional antitrust concern with tie-in sales. Nalebuff (forthcoming) shows that a monopoly of good *A* may sell its product tied to another independent good *B* so as to prevent rivals from achieving sufficient scale to enter the market for *B*.

Tie-in sales can also have an effect on competition in the market for *A* and can enable a monopoly supplier of *A* to maintain or even extend its market power into new products (Carlton and Waldman 2002). For example, suppose that consumers are willing to consume products *A* and *B* only if they can consume them together, and

[1]We thank R. Gertner for this example.

that one firm is a monopoly supplier of *A* and uses product *B* as a complementary good. By tying *B* to *A*, the monopoly producer of *A* monopolizes *B*. So far, the story is the same as our earlier one. However, now imagine that another firm wishes to enter the market and compete in producing *A*. That firm, even if it is an especially efficient entrant, can be deterred from entering because it will have no supply of product *B* at least initially.

The original monopoly remains the monopoly producer of *A* by using tying to control (or raise the cost of) key complementary products that entrants to produce *A* require. Indeed, the firm that controls *B* can prevent entry into any new market *A** that requires *B*, and in this way can swing its original monopoly of *A* into one for *A**. This scenario is most likely in a market where technology changes rapidly so that the market size for *B* does not remain large for extended periods, where sunk costs (such as R&D costs) are large relative to the scale of the market for *B*, and where entry into *B* takes a long time (without these conditions, firms will enter the market for *B*).

One possible example of such strategic behavior comes from the computer industry. Suppose that one firm is the only producer of an operating system for personal computers. All software is therefore designed to work with this (and only this) operating system. A new device, a hand-held computer, is invented that could use many different operating systems. However, because the available software works only with the monopoly's operating system, the monopoly has an advantage in selling the operating system for the new device and could thereby become the monopoly supplier of the operating system for the new device.

Product Compatibility

Many systems consist of complementary products *A* and *B* that work together: A stereo and its headphones, a computer and its printer, and a camera and its film. Should a manufacturer of computers produce printers that are compatible with its competitors' computers or not?

To demonstrate the role that compatibility plays, we consider two situations. Initially, two firms each manufacture products *A* and *B*. The unit costs for the first firm are \$1 for *A* and \$2 for *B*, while those for the second firm are \$2 for *A* and \$1 for *B*. With Bertrand competition on each component, the price of *A* is \$2, and the price of *B* is \$2, so that the total system price is \$4.

In contrast, suppose that each firm produces a version of product B that will not work with a rival's product *A*. Now consumers are only willing to buy *A* and *B* together from one firm. The Bertrand system price for both products is \$3.

This numerical example illustrates a general, if somewhat counterintuitive, principle: Product incompatibility may lead to more vigorous competition. When there is product compatibility, a cut in the price of one component stimulates demand for that component but does not stimulate demand to the same extent for the complementary component produced by the same firm (because some consumers use the complementary component produced by the other firm). In contrast, if firms produce products that are incompatible with rivals' products, a firm's price cut in one component automatically increases demand for its complementary component. Hence, the gain to price cutting is greater with product incompatibility, and the consequence is more vigorous competition and lower prices. Accordingly, firms may choose compatibility in order to avoid competition.[2]

If the various components produced by rival firms are not identical but differ in their characteristics, then the ability to mix and match will lead to a greater variety of products, and this greater variety of products stimulates demand and benefits some consumers. Moreover, with compatibility, the more efficient firm for each component will wind up producing that component. Matutes and Regibeau (1988, 1992) show that full compatibility maximizes social welfare, ignoring the costs to achieving compatibility.

Networks

In the last decade, interest in what has been labeled "network industries" has increased greatly. Loosely speaking, these are industries in which activities in one part of the network affect other parts. An example is a phone network, whose consumer value depends on the number of consumers hooked up to the network. The literature often stresses the failure of competition to work in network industries but unfortunately has not always been precise in tracing the failure of competition to the network feature. In this section, we first define network effects and then discuss strategic use of tie-in sales and product design in networks.

A physical network consists of pathways connecting nodes. Good examples are a railroad network (tracks connect stations), a telephone network (wires connect phones), and an electricity grid (wires connect generators and users). In the operation of such a network, there can be interactions between the various parts of the network. For example, the cost of shipping electricity on one path depends on the electricity loads on the other paths. The cost of shipping by rail from A to B depends on the amount of other traffic on the track between A and B and whether that traffic can be easily shifted to another track.

In such networks, Koopmans and Beckman (1957) showed that the use of prices alone does not necessarily lead to the optimal use of the network among decentralized firms, each owning different parts of the network. If the network is a single firm, that firm will internalize these network interactions and have an incentive to operate its network efficiently. Hence, there is an incentive for a single firm to operate a network. The problem that arises here is identical to Coase's insight that a firm is created when it can produce and allocate goods more efficiently than can a market (Chapter 12). A firm controlling a network can achieve scope economies by virtue of its superior allocation ability compared to a decentralized price system attempting to coordinate independent parts of one network (Carlton and Klamer 1983). The recent widespread consolidation into large national networks in the airline, railroad, and telecommunication industries vividly illustrates these forces.

---

[2]The idea that product incompatibility can increase the vigor of price competition has a direct implication for the incentive to use tie-in sales. A tie-in sale effectively creates product incompatibility, thereby intensifying competition, with the result that entry can be deterred (see Whinston 1990).

Even though there are efficiency gains from a national network, offsetting problems occur due to monopoly. Whether a network industry is a natural monopoly depends on how costs change as the network gets larger. Just as there can be many competing multiproduct firms, so too can there be many competing national networks.[3]

It may be impossible for any one firm to establish a property right in some network. No one firm can take over part of Chicago's roads and allocate cars over its streets. Moreover, there are circumstances in which networks aren't physical and exclusion from the network cannot occur. For example, imagine three people: *A*, *B*, and *C*. *A* and *B* wish to speak together, as do *B* and *C*. The trio form a "network." If *A*, *B*, and *C* all learn English, that is more efficient than if *A* and *B* learn English while *B* and *C* learn French. Yet no one person or firm owns the "right" to set language standards. (Of course, countries often do try to influence language choice.) When standards are adopted voluntarily and no one can exert property rights over their use, the familiar economic problem of an inefficiency due to an unpriced resource can result.

Networks Where the Type of Interaction Depends on Size

The recent literature focuses on two effects in networks where the type of interaction depends on size. In the "direct" network effect, the benefit to a network user depends directly on how many other users are hooked up to the network, as in a telephone network. In the "indirect" network effect, the benefit to a user arises indirectly because the number of users of the network affects the price and availability of complementary products. For example, an increase in the number of computer users of Windows (an operating system) leads to the development of additional software that is compatible with Windows. Let us examine each of these two effects in some detail. See Dranove and Gandal (2003) and Saloner and Shepard (1995) for empirical measurement of network effects.

Direct Network Effect. The value that a phone user places on the phone network rises with the number of people that user can call. Moreover, the decision of additional users to join such a network benefits existing users, who can now communicate with the new subscribers.

It is sometimes suggested that, because a new user provides a benefit to old users, there is an externality and a market failure. That need not be true. The theory of clubs (Buchanan 1965) was developed to deal with cases in which the size of a firm influences the quality of its product. In such a case, a competitive firm has the appropriate incentive to choose the efficient size[4] of its customer base—provided that the size is finite. Although there is a benefit to size, there may also be costs; hence, the optimal

[3]A complication arises when it is desirable for networks to interact. Then, the separate networks can no longer be regarded as independent competitors. Moreover, strategic denial of interconnection could occur in an attempt to inflict costs on a rival. See Laffont, Rey, and Tirole (1998a, 1998b).

[4]A variant of this point arises in Chapter 17, where we discuss a firm's incentive to create the optimal composition of heterogeneous consumers when the heterogeneity of consumers influences the firm's costs (Carlton 1991).

network size can be finite. The firm will generally charge both a variable user fee and a membership fee.

If the optimal size of the network is infinite, then the market may have a natural monopoly. Even here, competition can occur among a few networks and be a stable equilibrium outcome as long as the scale economies are not too great. Indeed, the new technologies in telephony have allowed competition among several phone networks to become a reality for many communications products.

Indirect Network Effect. The indirect network effect arises when the benefit of size leads to increased variety or lower pricing of complementary products. Such an effect occurs typically because of scale economies in production of the complementary product so that lower costs and more competitors go along with bigger markets. As more people use a particular operating system, more software is developed for that operating system. This type of effect is the same as occurs in nonnetwork industries: As more people play tennis, there could be increased variety and lower prices for tennis balls.[5]

Networks and Strategy

We now examine how tie-in sales and product design can be used strategically in network industries. The analysis can become quite complicated for several reasons.[6]

First, since price competition in our example is reduced and profits are elevated under product compatibility, an incentive is created for new firms to enter the industry or for firms to engage in R&D to produce better-quality products. In other words, the suppression of price competition due to product compatibility leads to an offsetting benefit caused by the increased incentive for nonprice competition. Even when theory can guide us about the presence of these trade-offs, the empirical magnitude of the trade-offs is uncertain and is an area for future research. In assessing these trade-offs, we need to keep in mind the key point that the social rate of return to innovation typically exceeds the private rate (Chapter 16).

Second, in network industries, competing networks can "tip" so that if one network overtakes the other, the other becomes insignificant. For example, the VHS (video recorder) recording format overtook and put out of business the rival Beta recording

[5]Some people contend that this indirect network effect necessarily creates a market failure because the lowered price of the complementary product is not considered by the primary users of a network. This inference is not correct for at least two reasons. First, given the usual assumptions of how markets work, one can show that this indirect effect leads to precisely the correct market incentives. Second, even if the conditions for efficiency fail, the empirical relevance of such resulting inefficiencies is a matter of debate. See Liebowitz and Margolis (1994). The alleged failure of competition when indirect effects are present is related to claims that standard setting can be inefficient.

[6]There is an enormous literature of networks and strategic behavior. See Farrell and Saloner (1985, 1986a), Economides (1988a), Katz and Shapiro (1985b, 1994), and the special issue of the *International Journal of Industrial Organization* (1996) on networks, especially the Economides (1996) article. For a discussion of strategic issues related to the Microsoft case, see Carlton (2001), Carlton and Waldman (2002), Evans et al. (2000), and Whinston (2002), and the references they cite.

format. In such settings, strategic behavior to prevent a rival from prospering has enormous competitive benefits. A firm can become and remain dominant by using the standard setting process to impede rivals or by creating unnecessary product incompatibilities, such as making it difficult for rivals to use complementary products.

Third, the expectation of future network size influences the desirability of buying a product today that will last into the future. A key marketing claim of a firm that produces a durable good is that new complementary products for its network will be available and that its network will be larger in the future. Advance announcements of future new products can harm a rival if those announcements are believed. Computer firms frequently announce that a new software product will be available next year in order to dissuade consumers from buying a rival's product today. Sometimes these announcements turn out to be false: The alleged product is nonexistent "vaporware."

A firm can try to convince consumers of the availability of future products and of its future size by signing contracts in advance with providers of complementary products, or by licensing in advance its intellectual property to others. If the expectation of size is important to consumers, then in such a network industry, there can be multiple equilibria with differing numbers of competitors.

Fourth, the expectations of future network circumstances can be affected by how fast the network is growing and how costly it is for consumers to switch networks. If consumers are locked into their network, the network might find it profitable to concentrate on introducing new products that appeal only to new consumers (unless price discrimination can be used). This could lead to excessive product introduction, especially in rapidly growing networks. Conversely, in a stable environment, a network might fail to introduce a new, desirable technology that benefits its locked-in customers, unless it can charge for the innovation, resulting in sluggish technological change. One way to avoid this problem is with pricing that depends on whether one is a new or an old customer: New purchasers of the latest version of a software program are often charged more than existing customers who are upgrading.

CHAPTER 12

Vertical Integration and Vertical Restrictions

Outside the firm, price movements direct production, which is coordinated through a series of exchange transactions on the market. Within a firm, these market transactions are eliminated and in place of the complicated market structure with exchange transactions is substituted the entrepreneur-coordinator, who directs production. It is clear that these are alternative methods of coordinating production.
—*Ronald Coase (1937)*

A firm that participates in more than one successive stage of the production or distribution of goods or services is **vertically integrated**. Nonvertically integrated firms buy the inputs or services they need for their production or distribution processes from other firms. A nonintegrated firm may write long-term, binding contracts with the firms with which it deals, in which it specifies not only price, but also other terms or forms of behavior. Contractual restraints on nonprice terms are called **vertical restrictions** (or restraints). For example, manufacturers commonly restrict their distributors by limiting their sales territories, setting inventory requirements, and, where legal, setting the minimum retail price they can charge.

Some firms choose to vertically integrate and perform all production and distribution activities themselves. Most firms partially vertically integrate. For example, they may produce goods, but rely on others to market them. A restaurant that bakes its own pies instead of buying them ready-made is partially integrated.

Some firms are not vertically integrated but buy from a small number of suppliers or sell through a small number of distributors. These firms often write complex contracts that restrict the actions of those with whom they deal. These vertical restrictions can approximate the outcome from vertically merging. Other firms buy in the open market from any number of anonymous firms. For example, they may buy wheat from a wheat broker without knowing who grew it or using any formal long-term contracts. Such firms place no restrictions on their suppliers.

An example of an integrated firm is Perdue, a prominent chicken supplier.[1] In the 1950s, Frank Perdue began to mix his own feed rather than buy what he felt was an inferior commercial mix. In 1961, he bought a soybean plant to make feed. In 1968, he bought the first Perdue processing plant so that his firm could kill, dress, and deliver chickens to market rather than rely on meat packers. In 1969, Perdue started appearing in his own television ads.

A firm's decision to vertically integrate, write complex contracts with vertical restrictions, or rely on markets is a basic strategic decision. It affects the subsequent pricing and promotional behavior of that firm and other related firms. Chapter 2 notes that a firm may choose to vertically integrate because it is cost effective to do so. This chapter expands on that analysis and examines vertical restrictions. Vertical restrictions between manufacturers and distributors are of particular interest and have been the subject of lengthy antitrust litigation. This chapter explores the procompetitive as well as the anticompetitive reasons for such restrictions.

The analysis begins by examining why some firms vertically integrate, whereas others do not. That analysis provides a story of the life-cycle of firms, in which they integrate at certain times and not at others. We then examine how some firms use vertical restrictions to achieve many of the advantages of vertical integration. Finally, we present some empirical evidence on franchising, an increasingly important vertical relationship, and the motives for vertical integration and vertical restrictions.

We analyze four key issues:

1. Why do firms vertically integrate? Why not rely on the market (other firms) to supply inputs and distribute products?
2. What should public policy be toward vertical integration? We know that horizontal mergers sometimes have anticompetitive effects; is the same true for vertical mergers?
3. Why do some manufacturers establish vertical restraints that give their distributors some of their monopoly power?
4. What should public policy be toward vertical restraints? Do these restrictions necessarily hurt retailers and consumers?

The Reasons for and Against Vertical Integration

If you want something done right, do it yourself.
He is a slave of the greatest slave, who serves nothing but himself.

Most of the reasons that firms choose to vertically integrate have to do with reducing costs or eliminating a market externality. Firms choose the least costly approach: Only

[1] Glenn Plaskin, "How Perdue Found Success," *San Francisco Chronicle*, January 27, 1993:B4.

EXAMPLE 12.1

Outsourcing

Whether a firm performs a task itself or relies on the market depends on the relative costs. A firm may find that it can save money by having outsiders provide services that the firm originally performed. This divestiture of activities is called *outsourcing*.

Many industries use outside firms for specific activities, such as payments. A 2003 Payroll Manager's Report survey found that more than half the firms surveyed outsourced payroll activities. Also in 2003, Accenture, a consulting firm, reported that two-thirds of U.S. retail and commercial banks with assets of at least $3 billion outsourced one or more business functions.

Outsourcing is particularly common in high-tech industries. Ingram Micro Inc., the world's largest wholesale distributor of computers, builds and distributes personal computers for rival firms that sell one-third of U.S. computers, including Acer, Apple, Hewlett-Packard, and IBM. U.S. high-tech firms are expected to outsource 1 in 10 jobs to low-cost emerging markets by the end of 2004. Worldwide, one-fifth of major firms are outsourcing their programming projects—often to India. The motive is cost savings. A programmer in Ireland may cost the firm up to 10 times as much as a comparably skilled programmer in India. Other countries that are effectively bidding for software work include Canada, China, Mexico, the Philippines, Russia, and Singapore.

Governments also rely on outside firms. Accenture reported in 2003 that 90 percent of government executives in 23 governments in Asia, Europe, North America, and South America outsource various functions. New Jersey purchases its welfare processing from an Arizona firm with a call center in Bombay, India. An advisory panel urged the Japanese government to outsource part of the management of a test module for the International Space Station to cut costs.

Even colleges and universities use outside firms for services such as janitorial, accounting, and teaching. Indeed, we once investigated the outsourcing of pithy sayings for this book, but decided against it when we considered the possible pithfalls.

Sources: Saul Hansell, "Is This the Factory of the Future?" *New York Times,* July 26, 1998, Section 3:1, 12, 13; Jon Surmacz, "Offshore Outsourcing Still Popular Despite Political Tensions," *CIO Metrics,* July 17, 2002; "Two-Thirds of U.S. Banks Outsource One or More Functions," *Business Wire,* February 24, 2003; "Vast Majority of Government Executives Report Outsourcing 'Important' or 'Critical' Activities, Accenture Report Finds," *Financial News,* May 15, 2003; "Exclusive ONR Survey," *2003 IOMA Payroll Manager's Report,* June 2003; "Cheap Labor at America's Expense," *Insight on the News,* June 9, 2003:32; "Japan to Outsource Management of Space Module Kibo," *BBC Monitoring International Reports,* June 25, 2003; "One Out of 10 Jobs at US Tech Firms to Go Offshore by 2004," *Agence France Presse,* July 29, 2003.

if a firm can perform most of the necessary production steps less expensively than if it relied on other firms does it vertically integrate. In general, a firm needs a good reason to vertically integrate because integration can involve substantial costs. In some cases, firms can avoid integration by having outside firms perform some functions for them (Example 12.1) or by using detailed contracts (Example 12.2).

EXAMPLE 12.2 *Preventing Holdups*

As Central and Eastern European countries convert from communism to capitalism, they are confronting serious transition problems. Communist Central and Eastern European countries had relatively few large, highly vertically integrated firms. The transition to capitalism has caused disruptions of traditional exchange systems, and the restructuring of firms both upstream and downstream has led to serious contracting problems.

One major problem is that contract terms are hard to enforce in these countries at this time. When contract terms cannot be enforced (or are not fully specified), holdup problems occur, typically leading to underinvestment in relation-specific capital.

Gow and Swinnen (1998) carefully examined sugar processors in Slovakia. A typical holdup problem is delayed payments by food processors to farmers. By delaying payment, processors effectively obtained interest-free loans and reduced their indebtedness due to high rates of inflation. According to surveys in 1994 and 1995, the average delay in payments for delivered products was 94 days—77 days for commercial farms and more than 100 days for state farms.

Faced with these adverse conditions, some farmers left the market, while others reduced their investments in land, equipment, and seed. Consequently, the amounts of beet sugar available to processors fell.

Given the large number of farmers involved, vertical integration was not feasible, even with foreign direct investment. Instead, long-term contracts and the establishment of trust through long-term relationships are used by Juhocukor a.s. in Slovakia to deal with holdup problems and to encourage investment in relationship-specific assets. Juhocukor a.s. is a subsidiary of Eastern Sugar BV, a firm that also owns operations in other Central and Eastern European countries, including the Czech Republic and Hungary. In 1993, Eastern Sugar BV purchased a 51 percent stake in

There are at least three possible costs of vertical integration. First, the cost of supplying its own factors of production or distributing its own product may be higher for a firm that vertically integrates than for one that depends on competitive markets, which serve these needs efficiently. Second, as a firm gets larger, the difficulty and cost of managing it increase. The advantage of dealing with a competitive market is that someone else supervises production. Third, the firm may face substantial legal fees to arrange to merge with another firm. For example, lawyers may be used to defend the merger before the U.S. Federal Trade Commission or the U.S. Department of Justice.

Because of these costs, firms vertically integrate only if the benefits outweigh the costs. Six major advantages to integrating are[2]

---

[2]See Perry (1989) for an excellent survey that discusses these and other explanations.

Juhocukor a.s. from Slovakia's privatization program. Later, it increased its holding to 76 percent and started a four-year development program to inject capital.

Before the takeover, Juhocukor a.s. had a reputation for late payments to farmers. To ensure sufficient high-quality sugar beet deliveries and to stimulate farm investment, the new management made three changes. First, it paid contracts on time at a price above that of the rest of the market and paid a premium for high sugar content. Second, it started a development program that included increasing processing and production productivity; made available high-quality seeds, fertilizer, and harvesters to farmers; and extended financing to growers. Third, it initiated a two-year information and media campaign directed at farmers and the agricultural community, explaining what the firm's long-term contract offered and how the contract would be beneficial for growers.

In short, the new management worked to establish credibility in a number of ways. By providing prompt payments and above-market prices, it showed that it was not going to engage in further holdup behavior. The new firm also signaled that it wanted long-term contracts and relationships with farmers based on mutual trust. By making large investments in its own plant, it signaled it was in the business for the long haul. Similarly, the firm could only benefit by helping supply farmers with financing and providing information, better-quality seeds, fertilizer, and harvesters if it continued to buy from the farmers in the long run. Finally, the firm increased quality by offering premiums and penalties for quality variations in sugar content of the beets.

The program worked. From 1992 to 1997, the amount of land the firm had under contract rose by 91 percent, yields per hectare increased by 140 percent, sugar content rose 119 percent, and total sugar production climbed 234 percent. These increases were not in response to market conditions as market prices were stable during this period, and the increases were large compared to those of other firms, which have since attempted to imitate these programs, with limited success.

1. *Lower transaction costs:* A firm may lower its transaction costs by vertically integrating. For example, the transaction costs of buying from or selling to other companies are avoided.
2. *Assure supply:* A firm may vertically integrate to assure itself a steady supply of a key input. To do so, the firm may *vertically integrate backwards,* buying or building the capacity to produce that input. Delivery problems may thus be reduced, because it is often easier to exchange information within a firm than between firms.
3. *Correct market failure:* A firm may vertically integrate to correct market failures due to externalities by internalizing those externalities. For example, by owning or controlling all its restaurants, McDonald's can ensure a uniform quality, which results in a positive reputation (externality). Wherever their travels bring

them, consumers know that they can expect a certain minimum quality at any of this chain's restaurants.

4. *Avoid government rules:* A firm may be able to avoid government restrictions, regulations, and taxes by vertically integrating. Examples of government interventions include price controls, regulations that restrict profit rates (see Chapter 20), and taxes on revenues or profits.
5. *Gain market power:* A firm may vertically integrate to better exploit or to create market power. For example, a sole supplier of a vital input may *vertically integrate forward,* buying the manufacturing firms, so as to monopolize the final product market and thereby increase its monopoly profits. Similarly, a firm may try to buy its sole supplier to increase combined profits. By vertically integrating, a firm may create or increase its monopoly profits by being able to price discriminate, eliminate competition, or foreclose entry.
6. *Eliminate market power:* A victim of another firm's market power may vertically integrate to eliminate that power. For example, around the turn of the century, dairy farmers contended that they faced a single processor that bought their milk at a low, monopsonistic price. To raise the price of milk, dairy farmers vertically integrated forward to form their own processors.

Integration to Lower Transaction Costs

A key reason why a firm performs productive activities itself rather than relying on other firms has to do with *transaction costs,* such as the expenses associated with writing and enforcing contracts (Williamson 1975, 1985; Alchian and Demsetz 1972; Klein, Crawford, and Alchian 1978). When such costs are high, a firm may engage in **opportunistic behavior**: taking advantage of another when allowed by circumstances. Each side may try to interpret the terms of a contract to its advantage, especially when terms are vague or even missing.

If contracts are simple (for example, a transaction involving one bushel of a specific variety of corn in Chicago on a particular date), opportunistic behavior is unlikely. The more unpredictable the future and the more complicated the contract, however, the harder it is to specify contractual terms. People have *bounded rationality:* a limited ability to enumerate and understand all future possibilities. In complicated contracts, it is often too difficult to specify all possible contingencies, and a signed contract may contain provisions that turn out to be undesirable to one of the parties.

Opportunities for exploitation are greater when one firm is dependent on another. For example, to respond to a sudden increase in demand, an automobile manufacturer needs more supplies. If there is only one supplier of a critical part, that supplier can raise its prices, and the auto manufacturer has nowhere to turn in the short run. Even when such complications and dependencies can be foreseen, it may be difficult to structure a contract that completely removes the incentives for either firm to behave opportunistically toward the other. For example, the Intel Corporation designs and sells many embedded control-function semiconductor chips, which are customized to do one job quickly and well. But buyers who start using these chips in their products have only one source because Intel does not allow other companies to produce the new chips. As one observer noted, "If they can get customers to make the transition, they now have captives."[3]

A firm chooses to perform activities itself rather than to rely on the market when transaction costs are likely to be high. Vertical integration transforms the monitoring problem from monitoring between firms to monitoring employees within the firm. Within a firm, a boss can coordinate the decisions of different divisions and can monitor workers in ways that are not possible when firms are completely independent. On the other hand, an employee on a fixed salary may work less hard than an owner of a subcontracting firm.

The desirability of integrating increases as the transaction costs of using the marketplace rise. There are four types of transactions in which transaction costs are likely to be substantial enough to make vertical integration desirable. They involve *specialized assets, uncertainty* that makes monitoring difficult, *information,* or *extensive coordination.*

Specialized Assets. A **specialized asset** is tailor-made for one or a few specific buyers. To illustrate why the use of specialized assets provides a reason to integrate, consider a supplier that has custom-designed its facility to suit a particular buyer's needs. That supplier will be at the mercy of the buyer should any disputes arise subsequent to the construction of the supplier's plant. In this case, we expect to see vertical integration because of asset specificity, which takes three main forms involving specific physical capital, specific human capital, and site-specific capital (Williamson 1985, 95–96).

Specific physical capital includes buildings and machines that can be used for only one or a few buyers. As an example, suppose that specific dies (molds used to make parts) are needed on a machine press to produce a particular part for one buyer. If the supplier that owns the machine press also owns the dies, there is a chance for opportunistic behavior: The supplier can raise the price, and the buyer may find it prohibitively expensive to switch suppliers in the short run. If the buyer owns the dies and has other firms bid to provide the machine-press services, no opportunistic problems arise. In this case, complete vertical integration is not necessary. Only partial or **quasi-vertical integration** (or quasi-integration), where the firm owns the specific physical asset (the dies) and not the entire supplying firm, is required to avoid opportunistic behavior. If the machine press itself is unique, however, this method cannot be used, and vertical integration may be necessary.

Ownership by the buyer diminishes the incentive for opportunistic behavior on both sides. For example, automobile manufacturers that rely on outside suppliers for

[3]Michael Slater, editor of *Microprocessor Report,* quoted in Don Clark, "Intel Corp. Planning New Chip Campaign," *San Francisco Chronicle,* April 2, 1988:B1, B20.

custom-made components often own the specialized dies needed to make them. Monteverde and Teece (1982) found that the more specialized the die, the more likely an automobile company is to own it.[4]

A firm may need workers, such as engineers, who are specially trained in how the firm operates (*specific human capital*) to produce a particular product. If it uses outside contractors as opposed to its own employees, opportunistic behavior is possible. For example, a contractor who knows that a firm is facing a deadline may demand more money. Vertical integration in the form of an employment relationship can avoid such problems.

If successive stages of a production process must be located adjacent to each other (that is, they involve *site-specific capital*), vertical integration is likely. The reason is that if a manufacturing firm stops demanding the input of a supplying firm, that supplying firm must relocate, which can be extremely costly. Opportunistic behavior can be avoided by integrating. The empirical section at the end of this chapter discusses three studies of the importance of specific physical assets and site-specific capital in the automobile and airplane manufacturing industries and in manufacturing as a whole.

When a firm relies heavily on one supplier for specialized products, not only is it at risk from opportunistic behavior by the supplier, but also a rival may try to interfere strategically with its supply. For example, in 1990, Conner Peripherals Inc., a disk-drive manufacturer, sued Seagate Technology Inc., a rival disk-drive manufacturer with half the market, charging that Seagate had blocked Conner's supplies of a critical component. Conner had bought thin film heads from Imprimis Technology Inc., the dominant supplier of the three thin film head vendors. After Seagate acquired Imprimis, it cut off Conner as a customer, according to Conner's complaint.[5]

Uncertainty. As an example of the second transaction-cost reason for vertical integration, *uncertainty,* suppose that a buyer cannot determine how long a durable machine will last. The best way to predict quality (life expectancy) may be to observe the method by which the machine is constructed. If an outside firm cannot monitor quality controls on construction, it may vertically integrate where quality is crucial.

Transactions Involving Information. The third transaction-cost reason for vertical integration concerns transactions involving information. It may be difficult to structure a contract that gives the supplying firm the appropriate incentives to develop the information. For example, if one firm pays another firm a fixed fee to obtain information on newly developing markets, the hired firm does not have an incentive to work hard at the margin to uncover all the information, and the buyer has

[4]See also Masten (1984), who shows that asset specificity influences asset ownership in the aircraft industry, Anderson and Schmittlein (1984), who examine asset specificity and the decision of a firm to have its own sales force, and Crocker and Reynolds (1993), who study how asset specificity influences procurement procedures of the Air Force.

[5]Ken Siegmann, "Conner Sues Seagate over Component Cut-Off," *San Francisco Chronicle,* April 19, 1990:C1. Roxanna Li Nakamura, "Conner Sues Seagate for Contract Reneging," *InfoWorld,* April 30, 1990.

no way of determining whether the supplier did a good job. Disputes on payments may well arise and be difficult to resolve. Such problems can be avoided by vertical integration.

Extensive Coordination. The fourth transaction-cost reason to vertically integrate is to facilitate extensive coordination, as in industries with networks such as airlines and railroads. A railroad depends heavily on developing feeder traffic for its through-routes. Although it might be possible to devise a price system for feeder traffic on each link in the network, such a system would be very complicated. As a result, there is an incentive for railroads to merge to deal with these coordination problems (Carlton and Klamer 1983).

Technological conditions alone do not explain the vertical integration of a firm. For example, a common case of vertical integration is a steel mill that produces its own pig iron. The molten pig iron is run directly into the steel furnace. Although it is inefficient to allow the pig iron to cool down and then ship it to a steel furnace where it must be heated again, it is not necessary that one firm produce both pig iron and steel: Two firms can locate side by side. However, because pig iron production and steel production are so interrelated, there is a potential for opportunistic behavior if two separate firms are involved. Therefore, vertical integration often arises when production processes at different stages are closely interrelated. (See **www.aw-bc.com/carlton_perloff** "Biotech Firms.")

Integration to Assure Supply

A common reason for vertical integration is to assure the supply of important inputs. Timely delivery of an item is of concern to businesspeople, yet standard models of market behavior ignore this topic. Assurance of supply is important in markets where price is not the sole device used to allocate goods (see Chapter 17). Nonprice allocation occurs in a wide range of common situations. For example, a bakery frequently runs out of bread by the end of the day and yet does not raise its price. Instead, late-arriving customers cannot buy the bread. Similarly, grocery stores frequently run out of produce without raising prices. In many producer-good industries, good customers often get the product during "tight" times, and other customers must wait. It is the marketing department, not customer responses to short-run price movements, that allocates goods. Such rationing has occurred in many industries, including paper, chemicals, and metals. Toyota and Dell Computers stress the use of *just-in-time* deliveries of inputs to minimize inventory costs while ensuring timely delivery.

When rationing is a possibility, there is an incentive to vertically integrate in order to raise the probability of obtaining the product. A firm has an incentive to produce its own supplies to meet its predictable level of demand and to rely on other firms for supplies to meet its less stable demand. Outside suppliers respond to this risky environment by raising prices. This arrangement, in which outside suppliers bear the risky demand, may not be the most efficient system for reliably providing the product, but may provide a strong incentive for a firm to vertically integrate (Carlton 1979b).

Integration to Eliminate Externalities

A firm may integrate to internalize externalities. If all Radio Shack stores carry the same products, maintain certain standards of service, and provide advice on the use of their products, a regular customer who moves from one city to another knows what to expect from a Radio Shack in the new city. That is, there is a positive reputation externality. A consumer who likes one of the outlets knows that the others are similar. Thus, it is in the chain's best interest to maintain high uniform standards. A bad store can harm the business of all distributors and lower the profit of the firm, Tandy, that supplies the products sold by these distributors. Thus, Tandy has an incentive to integrate forward into distribution (own Radio Shack stores) to control this externality.

Integration to Avoid Government Intervention

The only thing that saves us from the bureaucracy is its inefficiency.
—Eugene McCarthy (former U.S. senator and presidential candidate)

Firms may vertically integrate to evade or avoid government price controls, taxes, and regulations. A vertically integrated firm can avoid *price controls* by selling to itself. For example, the federal government has controlled prices on steel products on several occasions since World War II: It set a maximum price that could be charged for steel. Under binding price controls, a firm that buys steel is unable to purchase all the steel that it wants at the controlled price because producers choose to ration steel rather than supply as much as is demanded at the controlled price. A firm that badly needs more steel for its production process may find that it pays to purchase the company that supplies it with steel. Because transactions within a company are unaffected by price controls, a buyer who really wants steel can get it by purchasing a steel company and producing all the steel it needs. Purchasing a steel company is thus a simple way to avoid price controls (see Example 12.3). Indeed, if there are no

EXAMPLE 12.3 *Own Your Own Steel Mill*

A legal case, *Perlman v. Feldmann* (219 F.2d 173 [1955], cert. denied), illustrates the incentive for vertical integration in the presence of rationing. Feldmann controlled a majority of the stock of Newport Steel Corporation, which produced steel products. In 1950, steel supplies were becoming tight, apparently due to fear of Korean War price controls. Feldmann arranged for the sale of a controlling interest of Newport's stock to the Wilport Corporation, a user of steel. Wilport, by obtaining controlling interest, would be able to control the allocation of steel (to itself) in times of shortages.

The plaintiff in this case was a shareholder who complained that the high price Feldmann received for his shares (\$20 versus \$12 for noncontrolling shares) represented a value that other shareholders were entitled to because it represented the value of steel at uncontrolled market prices. The Court ruled that Feldmann was not entitled to receive the entire value of the right to control allocation, but only his pro-rata share of that value. Even though Feldmann was allowed only his pro-rata share, his activities reflect the incentive created by price controls to vertically integrate.

transaction costs to buying steel companies, and if owners of steel mills are entitled to steel in proportion to their ownership, then price controls on steel are completely ineffective because all users vertically integrate by acquiring ownership interests in steel mills.

Similarly, *taxes* encourage vertical integration. Depending on where firms are located, they may be subject to different taxes. For example, tax rates differ by state as well as by country. A vertically integrated firm may be able to shift profits from one location to another simply by changing the *transfer price* at which it sells its internally produced materials from one division to another. (See **www.aw-bc.com/carlton_perloff** "Oil Depletion Allowance," for an example.) By shifting profits from a high tax jurisdiction to a low tax jurisdiction, a firm can increase its profits. The Internal Revenue Service is, of course, aware of such shifting and insists that firms use internal transfer prices that reflect prices in the marketplace (see Chapter 18).

Government *regulations* create incentives for a firm to vertically (or horizontally) integrate when the profits of only one division of a firm are regulated. For example, the profits that local telephone companies earn on local services are regulated, but their profits on other services, such as selling telephones in competition with other suppliers, are not regulated. If a telephone company can shift profit from its regulated division to its unregulated division, it can effectively avoid the regulation of its local telephone service.

For example, suppose that such a firm is able, through accounting conventions, to transfer costs from its unregulated division to its regulated division, thus lowering its reported profits in the regulated line of business and raising them in the unregulated line. At the next rate hearing, the telephone company may argue that it is entitled to increase its rates to raise its profits in its regulated business. By shifting profits from the regulated to the unregulated division, the telephone company can thus increase its overall profits. The fear that profits would be transferred from a regulated business to an unregulated business, and the difficulty of detecting such transfers, motivated the U.S. government to control the entry of local telephone companies into unregulated businesses after it dismantled the phone monopoly.[6]

Integration to Increase Monopoly Profits

God helps them that help themselves. —*Benjamin Franklin*

A firm may be able to increase its monopoly profits in two ways by vertically integrating.[7] First, a firm that is a monopoly supplier of a key input in a production process used by a competitive industry may be able to vertically integrate forward, monopolize the production industry, and increase its profits. Or a firm that is a buyer may benefit from acquiring its sole supplier. Second, a vertically integrated monopoly supplier may be able to price discriminate.

[6]Even if some avoidance of regulation does occur, there may be offsetting efficiencies to society from allowing the telephone company to enter new businesses. See Chapter 20 on regulation and **www.aw-bc.com/carlton_perloff** "The Breakup of AT&T."

[7]As discussed in Chapter 11, another reason for vertical integration is strategic. A firm that controls scarce inputs could put its rival at a disadvantage.

Vertical Integration to Monopolize Another Industry. In some cases, a monopoly supplier of an input can increase its profits by vertically integrating to monopolize the producing industry. When does it pay to forward integrate to extend monopoly power? The answer depends on the production process, as the following model illustrates.

In the industry illustrated in Figure 12.1, consumers purchase Q units of a competitively produced good at price p. The competitive industry produces that good using a production function, f, that depends on inputs of energy, E, and labor, L:

$$Q = f(E, L) \tag{12.1}$$

These inputs are sold to competitive firms at prices e and w (wage), respectively. The firms that supply the inputs in the production process are referred to as the **upstream firms**, and the firms that produce the good are called **downstream firms**. (In the past, firms often located along a river, and the upstream firms used the flow of the river to take their products downstream on boats or barges to the processors, who in turn sent it downstream to consumers.)

We make five assumptions about the market in Figure 12.1:

1. *Constant returns to scale:* The production function, $f(E, L)$, exhibits constant returns to scale. That is, if both inputs are doubled, output doubles.
2. *The inputs are produced at constant marginal cost:* The producing firms can buy as much labor, L, as they want at a wage of w (the supply curve of labor is horizontal at w). Energy, E, is produced at a constant marginal cost of m.
3. *Monopoly upstream:* This is the only upstream firm that supplies energy, and it does not fear that entry by other firms will eliminate its monopoly.

FIGURE 12.1 Vertical Organization of an Industry

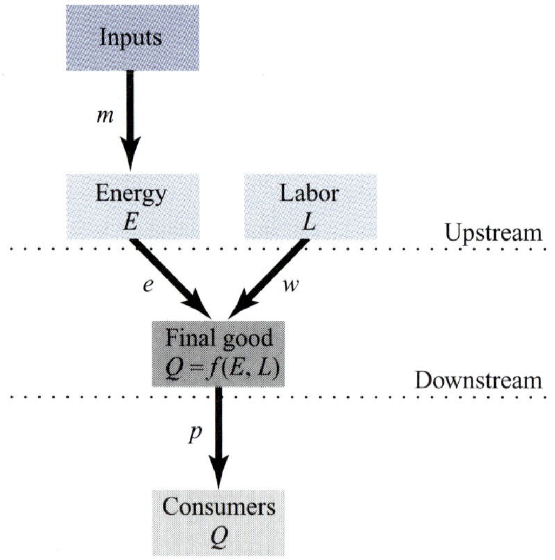

4. *Competition downstream:* The downstream industry is competitive. We relax this assumption later.
5. *Costs of vertically integrating:* Certain costs are associated with vertically integrating, such as negotiation and legal fees. Thus, unless there are benefits from vertically integrating, the firm does not integrate.

Under what additional conditions does it pay for the monopoly supplier of E to vertically integrate forward and take over the downstream production? The answer depends on whether the industry has a fixed-proportions production or a variable-proportions production function. In a **fixed-proportions production function**, the inputs are always used in the same proportions, so the proportions used are independent of relative factor prices. In a **variable-proportions production function**, one factor can be substituted for another to some degree, so the ratio of factors used is sensitive to relative factor prices.

Given the four assumptions, there are two key results:

1. If the downstream production process uses fixed proportions, the upstream monopoly does not have an incentive to vertically integrate. It makes the same profit whether it integrates or not.
2. If, alternatively, the downstream production process uses variable proportions, the monopoly has an incentive to vertically integrate. It integrates if its increase in profits exceeds the cost of integration.

The following sections examine fixed proportions and variable proportions in turn and then present a numerical example to illustrate how the two cases differ.

Fixed-Proportions Production Function. In a fixed-proportions production process it is impossible to substitute one input for another. Producing firms buy cardboard boxes from one input market and cakes from another input market. The production industry takes one box and one cake and produces a "cake in a box," which it sells. If the cost of a cake doubles while the cost of a box remains unchanged, the production firm still uses the same proportions of cakes and boxes (one of each), because it cannot substitute boxes for cakes.

Graphically, such a production process has an *isoquant* (a curve that shows the various combinations of the inputs that produce a given output level) in the shape of an L, as Figure 12.2 shows. The isoquant illustrates the various combinations of cakes and boxes that can be used to make one cake in a box. If the firm has two boxes and one cake or one box and two cakes, it can make only one cake in a box.

The figure also shows an isocost line (the various combinations of the inputs that cost a given amount) where the prices for cakes and boxes are equal (1 to 1), and another isocost line where a cake costs three times as much as a box (3 to 1). Regardless of the relative price of the two inputs, the cost-minimizing combination of inputs is to use one unit of each to make one cake in a box: Both isocost curves hit the isoquant at the point (1, 1) in Figure 12.2.

Now we can compare the profits that the energy monopoly makes if it vertically integrates and if it does not. For simplicity, suppose that it takes 1 unit of E and 1 unit of L to make 1 unit of Q.

FIGURE 12.2 Fixed-Proportions Isoquant and Isocost Curves

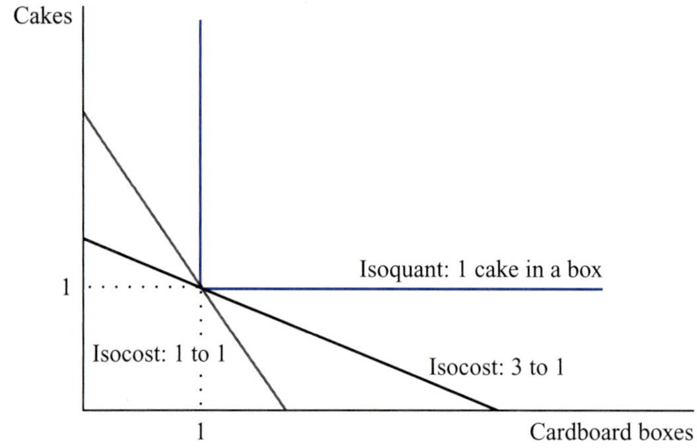

The integrated monopoly's cost of producing a unit of Q is $m + w$. That is, it takes 1 unit of E, which costs the firm m to make, and 1 unit of L, which can be hired at a cost of w. Figure 12.3a shows this per-unit, or marginal, cost, $MC_Q = m + w$. Also in the figure is the inverse demand curve for the final product, $p(Q)$, which shows the price that consumers are willing to pay to buy Q units of the product, and the corresponding marginal revenue curve, MR_Q.

The integrated monopoly maximizes its profits by producing Q^* units of output so that its marginal cost equals its marginal revenue: $MC_Q = m + w = MR_Q$. It uses $E^* = L^*(= Q^*)$ units of inputs. It charges p^* and makes a profit (box in Figure 12.3a) of

$$\pi^* = [p^* - (m + w)]Q^*. \tag{12.2}$$

We can contrast the vertically integrated industry to one in which the energy monopoly supplies a competitive industry. The nonintegrated energy monopoly's marginal cost of producing E, MC_E, is m and is shown as a thick black line in Figure 12.3b. It faces an inverse demand, $e(E)$, for its product from the competitive industry, shown in the figure as a thick blue line. This line shows the highest price, e, that the competitive industry pays for E units of energy. The corresponding marginal revenue curve is MR_E (the thick light blue line).

The output market demand curve of Figure 12.3a is shown in Figure 12.3b as a thin blue line for comparison. Both sets of curves can be shown in the same diagram because both sets of curves are scaled the same (it takes 1 unit of E to produce 1 unit of Q).

The demand curve facing the upstream monopoly can be derived from the demand curve facing the competitive downstream industry. The monopoly views its demand curve as the highest price it can charge the downstream firms for a given quantity of E.

FIGURE 12.3 Fixed-Proportions Production Function

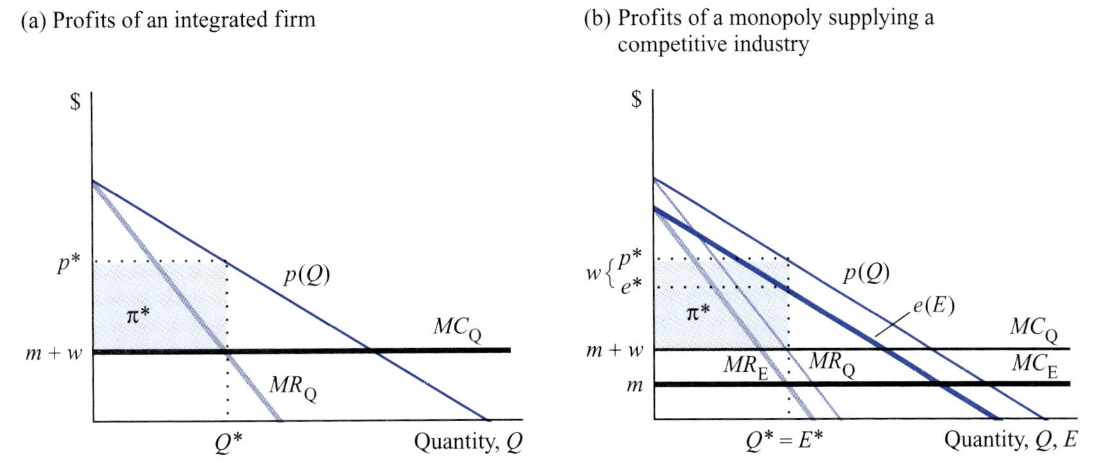

The price a competitive downstream firm receives for a unit of its output is p. To produce that unit of output, it must spend w for a unit of labor. Thus, the most it will pay for a unit of E is $e = p - w$. As a result, the demand curve facing the input monopoly equals the demand curve facing the competitive industry minus w. As shown in the figure, the monopoly's demand curve, $e(E)$, is just the industry's demand curve, $p(Q)$, shifted down by w.[8]

The energy monopoly sets its output at E^* to equate its marginal revenue, MR_E, with its marginal cost, $MC_E = m$. Thus the energy monopoly maximizes its profit, $[e(E) - m]E = [(p(E) - w) - m]E$, which is identical to what the vertically integrated firm maximizes, Equation 12.2, because $E = Q$. It charges m. As the diagram shows, $E^* = Q^*$. That is, the industry output and the amount of energy used are the same whether the industry is vertically integrated or not. The energy monopoly's profit (box in Figure 12.3b),

$$\pi^* = (e^* - m)E^* = [(p^* - w) - m]E^*,$$

is the same as before. The monopoly now receives only e^* (which is $p^* - w$) instead of p^* per unit sold, but its costs are only m instead of $m + w$ per unit produced.

[8]The competitive downstream industry price, p, equals the marginal cost, $MC(Q) = e + w$. That is, $p = e + w$. The price (demand function) is decreasing in Q, and e (the price the monopoly charges) is decreasing in E. Because $Q = E$, this price equation can be rewritten as $p(E) = e(E) + w$, or, $e(E) = p(E) - w$. That is, the derived demand curve facing the upstream monopoly equals the demand curve facing the competitive industry minus the cost of a unit of labor.

Thus, because the upstream firm earns the same profit whether it integrates or not, if there is any cost to integration, it chooses not to integrate. What is the intuition behind this result? When the nonintegrated monopoly raises its price for a unit of E by \$1, the marginal cost of the downstream firm ($m + w$) rises by \$1, so the price to consumers also goes up by \$1. That is, the energy monopoly can perfectly control the final price consumers pay without vertically integrating. Not only can it raise the price, but also it captures all the resulting profits. None go to the competitive industry, which merely passes on higher energy costs to consumers. The reason that the nonintegrated monopoly can control the downstream price perfectly is that the downstream firms cannot substitute away from the input produced by the monopoly.

Variable-Proportions Production Function. The preceding intuition suggests that the results are different if the competitive downstream industry faces a variable-proportions production function, with which the downstream industry substitutes away from the input monopoly's product if the price rises.

Figure 12.4 shows the isoquant of a variable-proportions production function. Unlike the fixed-proportions production function, it is a smooth curve, showing that the products are (imperfect) substitutes. As a result, as the relative costs of the inputs change, as shown by a shift in the slope of the isocost line, the firm substitutes more of the now less expensive input for the more expensive input. With a variable-proportions production function, if the upstream energy monopoly increases its price to the competitive downstream industry, firms in that industry substitute more labor for the monopoly's product. If the monopoly raises its price by a dollar, the price of the final good no longer necessarily increases by a dollar, and the amount of E used falls by relatively more than Q does.

Consider an extreme case where the two inputs are perfect substitutes in the production process. Here, the isoquant is a straight line. For example, downstream food processing firms (manufacturers of crackers and other similar products) view palm oil and coconut oil as perfect substitutes, so the isoquant is a straight line with a slope of -1. If a monopoly in palm oil increases its price above that of coconut oil, all the downstream firms switch to coconut oil. Thus, an upstream monopoly cannot raise the price of palm oil above that of coconut oil.

In short, if downstream firms have some ability to substitute between inputs (variable-proportions production process), the upstream monopoly does not have complete control over the downstream industry. Every time it raises its price, the downstream industry substitutes away from its input and this substitution, though it constrains the market power of the monopoly, leads to inefficient production, because efficiency requires the slope of the isoquant to equal the slope of the isocost line. That slope equals the ratios of the inputs' marginal costs. Downstream firms are using too much L and too little E. This inefficiency means that there are less profits for the monopoly to seize.

If the upstream firm integrates forward so that it monopolizes the downstream industry, it has complete control and can use the inputs in the most efficient combination. Thus, its profits increase. If profits increase by more than the cost of vertical integration, the firm vertically integrates. At **www.aw-bc.com/carlton_perloff** "Fixed

FIGURE 12.4 Variable-Proportions Isoquant and Isocost Curves

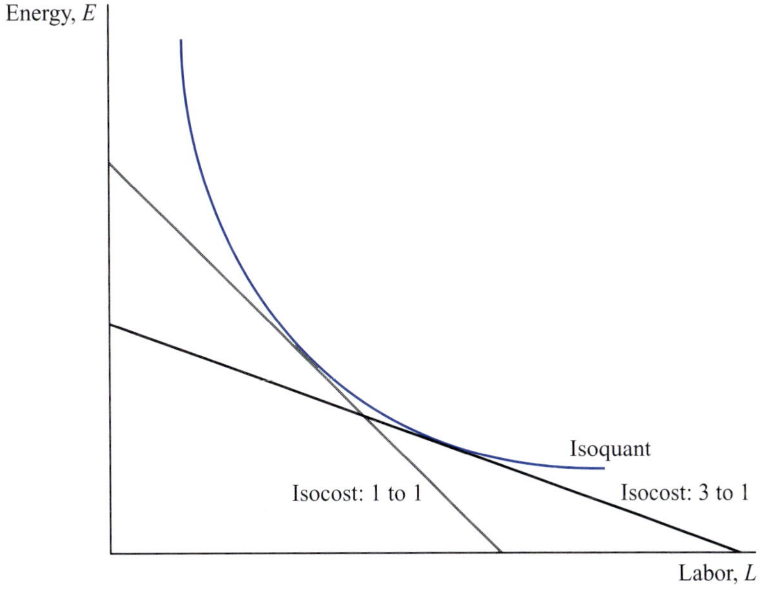

vs. Variable Proportions," we provide a detailed numerical example that illustrates that vertical integration can raise the profit of an upstream input monopoly if the production process of downstream firms uses variable proportions, but not if it uses fixed proportions. We also explain that with variable proportions, the price to consumers can go up or down depending on whether the efficiency effect overwhelms the increased market power (see Mallela and Nahata 1980).

Price Discrimination. A monopolistic supplier may vertically integrate so that it can successfully price discriminate. Chapter 9 explains that an essential element for successful price discrimination is the ability to prevent resale of the product by those who pay a low price to those who pay a high price. If resale cannot be prevented, it is impossible to price discriminate. Vertical integration can be used to prevent resale.[9]

For example, aluminum ingot is used in many products (see Example 9.4). For simplicity, suppose that aluminum ingot is used to produce only aluminum wire and aircraft. There are good alternatives for aluminum wire in electric cables, such as copper, but there are no good alternatives to aluminum in airplanes. As a result, the elasticity

[9]Carlton and Perloff (1981) show that preventing vertical integration eliminates the ability of firms with market power to price discriminate and hence affects the rate at which a nonrenewable resource such as oil is exhausted.

of demand for aluminum ingot by wire manufacturers is much higher than it is for airplane manufacturers. Thus, it is profitable to charge a higher price for aluminum ingot to airplane manufacturers than aluminum wire producers.

If the aluminum monopoly charges a higher price to airplane manufacturers without integrating, the aluminum wire producers can purchase aluminum ingot at a relatively low price and resell to the airplane manufacturers at a lower price than the monopoly charges. To prevent this resale, the aluminum monopoly can vertically integrate forward and become the only producer of aluminum wire. It can then charge a very high price for aluminum ingot to the aircraft manufacturers, without worrying about resales from wire manufacturers. By transforming the product from aluminum ingot to aluminum wire, the vertically integrated firm prevents resales.

Integration to Eliminate Market Power

Just as a firm can increase its monopoly profit by vertically integrating, another firm can reduce or eliminate monopoly power by vertically integrating. Suppose, for example, that only one firm sells an input that is essential for your production process. If that firm is charging you a high, monopoly price, you should determine whether it is cost effective for you to vertically integrate backward and produce that product yourself. You could, for example, build a new production plant to produce that input.

If, instead of building a new plant, your firm tries to buy its supplier, it faces the same issues analyzed in the previous section. The combined profit of the buying and supplying firm rises only if there are variable proportions in production. If there are fixed proportions, there is no gain from integration. In this case, the purchase of a monopoly supplier by a buyer affects neither total profit nor the profits of individual firms. Presumably, the monopoly supplier will sell its firm for the discounted present value of the future monopoly profits, so the buyer winds up paying the same total monopoly overcharge whether or not vertical integration occurs.

The Life Cycle of a Firm

If you want to make an apple pie from scratch, you must first create the universe. —*Carl Sagan*

Firms vertically integrate if the benefits outweigh the costs. Stigler (1951) and Williamson (1975), building on Adam Smith's theorem that "the division of labor is limited by the extent of the market," used the ideas discussed in the preceding section to develop a theory of the life cycle of firms. They explain why firms rely on markets during certain periods, whereas during other periods, they vertically integrate.

If the demand for a product is small, so that the collective output of all the firms in the industry is small, each firm must undertake all the activities associated with producing the final output itself. Why don't some firms specialize in making one of several inputs that they then sell to another firm to assemble the final product? The answer is that when the industry is small, it does not pay for a firm to specialize in one activity even if there are increasing returns to scale. A specialized firm may have large setup (fixed) costs. If the specialized firm produces large quantities of output, the average setup or fixed cost per unit is small. In a small industry, however, the setup costs per unit are large, so that, if specialized firms are to earn a profit, the sum of the specialized firms' prices must be higher than the cost of a firm that produces everything for itself.

As the industry expands, it may become profitable for a firm to specialize, because the per-unit transaction costs fall.[10] That is, as the industry grows, firms *vertically disintegrate.* When the industry was small, each firm produced all successive steps of the production process, so that all firms were *vertically integrated.* In the larger industry, each firm does not handle every stage of production itself but rather buys services or products from specialized firms.

For example, in the 1860s, Birmingham, England, was the leading production center of the small-arms industry.[11] Virtually all of the 5,800 people working in this industry were located in a small district near St. Mary's Church. The firms were localized because large numbers of firms specialized in particular processes, so parts frequently had to be transported from one workshop to another. The typical master gun manufacturer owned a warehouse rather than a factory or workshop. These entrepreneurs purchased semifinished parts from "material-makers," such as barrel makers, lock makers, sight stampers, trigger makers, ramrod forgers, gun-furniture makers, and bayonet forgers. The gun maker then sent the parts to a succession of "setters-up," or specialized craftsmen, who assembled them into guns. For example, jiggers worked on the breech end; stockers dealt with the barrel and lock and shaped the stock; barrel strippers prepared the gun for rifling and proofing; and hardeners, polishers, borers and riflers, engravers, browners, and finally the lock freers adjusted the working parts.

As an industry matures further, new products often develop and reduce much of the demand for the original product, so that the industry shrinks in size. As a result, firms again vertically integrate.

In 1919, 13 percent of manufacturing companies studied had two or more establishments making successive products, where the product of one was the raw material of the next (Stigler 1951, 135). In 1937, successive functions were found in 10 percent. Similarly, in 1919, 34.4 percent of all complex central offices had successive establishments (companies with establishments in two or more vertically related industries); in 1937, only 27.5 percent did. Studies prior to 1970 found no overall trend in vertical integration after 1929 (Adelman 1955, Laffer 1969, Livesay and Porter 1969). Tucker and Wilder (1977) also find little variation in their vertical integration indices from the mid-1950s to the early 1970s. However, Maddigan (1981) concludes that "major" firms became more vertically integrated from 1947 to 1972. O'Huallacháin (1996) documents a small decline in vertical integration over the period 1977–1987, although there was significant variation across industries.

---

[10]A specialized firm cannot charge for its product a price that is higher than the minimum average cost of the product if one of the nonspecialized firms produces it itself.

[11]This discussion is based on G. C. Allen, *The Industrial Development of Birmingham and the Black Country, 1860—1927,* (London: 1929), 56–7 and 116–7, cited by Stigler (1951).

Vertical Restrictions

I don't trust him. We're friends. —*Bertolt Brecht*

A manufacturer that contracts with a distributor to sell its product may place vertical restrictions on the distributor's actions beyond requiring it to pay the wholesale price for the product. These vertical restrictions are determined through contractual negotiations between the manufacturer and the distributor. The manufacturer places these restrictions so as to approximate the outcome that would occur if the firms vertically integrated. Examples of restrictions include requirements that the distributor sell a minimum number of units, that distributors not locate near each other, that distributors not sell competing products, and that distributors charge no lower than a particular price.

Why are restrictions used instead of vertical integration? Manufacturers often rely on independent firms to distribute their products rather than doing their own distribution, because the costs of monitoring employees at distribution outlets exceed the costs of using independent firms. For example, the distribution outlets may be far apart, making it costly for managers to travel to them and spend time becoming familiar enough with local market conditions to be able to judge the efficiency of a particular distribution outlet.

Every manufacturer, regardless of whether it is a monopoly or a competitive firm, wants its product distributed at the lowest possible costs. The manufacturer also wants the distributors to price and sell in a manner that is best for the manufacturer.

Economists describe the relationship between a manufacturer and a distributor as a **principal-agent** relationship: The *principal* hires the *agent* to perform an action in a manner that the principal cannot fully control. Here, the manufacturer (principal) contracts with distributors (agents) to sell its product. The manufacturer cannot perfectly observe the sales effort of the distributors and realizes that they may try to take advantage.

For example, distributors may advertise less than they contracted to do, in order to save money and *free ride* on the manufacturer's reputation. **Free riding** occurs when one firm benefits from the actions of another without paying for it. Free riding is an externality. Where free riding is possible, each distributor has an inadequate incentive to advertise; it prefers to rely on the efforts of others and does not do its share. These principal-agent problems are often addressed through vertical restrictions that the manufacturer places on the distributor beyond requiring it to pay the wholesale price for the product.

Economists and the courts initially were uneasy about vertical restrictions because several such restrictions—for example, forbidding the distributor to lower its price or sell competing products—appear to restrain competition and should not occur in a perfectly competitive market. But this observation may only tell us that the economic models of perfect competition, in which distribution is taken to be a costless activity, are not applicable here. Simple models of competition ignore the cost of sales efforts. Where it takes resources to distribute a product, a manufacturer must pay somebody to do it and wants to control how the distribution takes place. Thus, models of perfect competition that ignore the cost of distribution do not provide good intuition for markets that rely on substantial sales effort.

In the following sections we identify a number of problems that arise when vertical integration is impossible, and describe the vertical restrictions that are used to deal with these problems. We then discuss the pro- and anticompetitive implications of these vertical restrictions.

Vertical Restrictions Used to Solve Problems in Distribution

Four problems commonly arise when distribution is costly and a manufacturer retains a distributor to retail its products:

1. There is a double monopoly markup (also called double marginalization) by successive monopolies in manufacturing and distribution.
2. Some distributors may free ride (not do their share in promoting the good) on other distributors.[12]
3. Some manufacturers may free ride on other manufacturers.
4. There may be a lack of coordination among distributors that leads to externalities.

We discuss each problem in order, along with the vertical restrictions designed to deal with each.

Double Monopoly Markup. If the manufacturer and the distributor are both monopolies, each adds a monopoly markup (the difference between its price and its marginal cost is positive), so consumers face two markups instead of one. This double markup provides an incentive for firms either to vertically integrate or to use vertical restrictions to promote efficiency and thereby increase joint profits. We first illustrate the losses due to the double monopoly markup and then show how vertical restrictions can be used to prevent these losses where vertical integration is not practical.

An Example of the Loss from a Double Monopoly Markup. To illustrate the effect of a double markup, we contrast a market in which a manufacturer is vertically integrated into distribution to one with two successive monopolies. Both consumers and firms lose from the double markup.[13]

Suppose that the vertically integrated, monopolistic manufacturer-distributor faces the downward-sloping demand curve, D_1, for its product in Figure 12.5a. The firm produces Q^* units so as to equate its marginal cost of production, m, and its marginal

---

[12]Most of the existing literature on vertical restraints emphasizes the role of free riding. However, Winter (1993) presents a more general way to explain why manufacturers want to use vertical restraints.

[13]Suppose that a retailer buys a good from the manufacturer and then resells it. The retailer has no additional costs other than the price it pays the wholesaler, and faces a constant elasticity of demand with elasticity ϵ_1. Because it has monopoly power, the retailer sets its price, p_1, equal to $\mu_1 p_2$, where p_2 is the manufacturer's price for the good and $\mu_1 = 1/[1 + 1/\epsilon_1] > 1$ is the usual monopoly markup (Chapter 4). The manufacturer sets its price, p_2, equal to $\mu_2 m$, where $\mu_2 = 1/[1 + 1/\epsilon_2] > 1$, ϵ_2 is the demand elasticity facing the manufacturer, and m is its constant marginal cost. Thus, $p_1 = \mu_1 \mu_2 m$ and there is a double monopoly markup over the manufacturing cost of $\mu_1 \mu_2$, which is greater than either μ_1 or μ_2 alone.

FIGURE 12.5 Monopolies in Both Manufacturing and Distributing

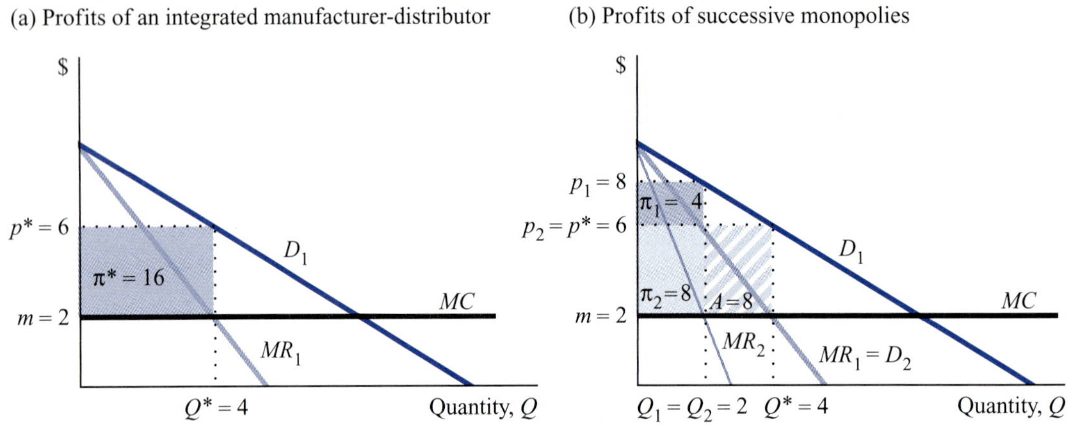

revenue, MR_1. For graphic simplicity, we assume that the costs of distribution are zero. The firm's profit, π^*, the blue shaded area in the figure, equals the monopoly markup per unit (the difference between the sales price, p^*, and the cost per unit) times the number of units, Q^*.

Now suppose that the monopolistic, upstream manufacturer uses a monopolistic, downstream firm to distribute its product. Because each firm adds a monopoly markup to its per-unit costs, there is a double monopoly markup. Here, the distributor faces the same downward-sloping demand curve, D_1, and marginal revenue curve, MR_1, as in Figure 12.5a. The manufacturer charges the distributor a wholesale price, p_2, per unit. The distributor treats this wholesale price as its marginal cost. It maximizes its profits by selling Q_1 units, such that its marginal cost, p_2, equals its marginal revenue, $MR_1(Q_1)$, which is a function of Q_1, as shown in Figure 12.5b. Because distribution costs are assumed to equal 0 and demands are linear, $p_2 = p^*$.

The number of units of the manufactured good the distributor demands depends on the manufacturer's wholesale price, p_2, and is determined by the intersection of the MR_1 curve with the horizontal line at p_2. This demand curve facing the manufacturer, D_2, equals the distributor's marginal revenue curve, MR_1. The manufacturer maximizes its profits by choosing its output level, Q_2, so that its marginal cost, m, equals its marginal revenue, MR_2 (the curve marginal to D_2).

Figure 12.5b shows the resulting double markup. The manufacturer charges p_2, which is above its marginal cost of m; the distributor charges p_1, which is above its marginal cost of p_2. Because the marginal revenue is less than price, $p^* = p_2 < p_1$. Consumers facing the double markup buy less output, Q_2, than when there is an integrated firm, Q^*. As a result, they are worse off. Using the demand curve, $p = 10 - Q$, and setting marginal cost, m, equal to 2, $p^* = p_2 = 6$ and $p_1 = 8$.[14] Thus, consumers pay a third more ($8 instead of $6) due to the successive monopoly markup than they would pay if the firms were integrated. They buy half as many units: $Q_1 = Q_2 = 2$ instead of $Q^* = 4$.

The firms' collective profits are also lower. The profits of the integrated firm are $\pi^* = 16$. With the successive monopolies, the retailer's profits, π_1, are 4 and the manufacturer's profits, π_2, are 8. As Figure 12.5b shows, π^* equals π_2, plus Area A, the profits lost due to reduced sales from the higher price. Total profits drop by Area $A - \pi_1 = 8 - 4 = 4$. That is, the total profits of the successive monopolies are 25 percent lower than those for the integrated firm.

Vertical Restrictions to Reduce Double Markups. Thus, both consumers and firms are worse off with successive monopolies than when there is a single, integrated monopoly. These losses provide a strong incentive to integrate.[15] It is not always practical to do so. For example, where the manufacturer is Japanese and the distributor is French, it may be too costly for the Japanese firm to vertically integrate into distribution. One alternative is to use vertical restrictions.

The problem with the successive monopolies is that the distributor has an incentive to restrict output and raise price. The manufacturer does not want its distributor to restrict output further—or, equivalently, to increase its price, p_1, above the wholesale price, p_2—because profits from the distributor's markup go to the distributor, not the manufacturer. The manufacturer wants as efficient a distribution system as possible (that is, with the smallest distributor's markup).

Ideally, the manufacturer wants to induce competition at the distribution level in order to drive p_1 to the wholesale price, p_2. There are many instances, however, when it is not possible to have competition in distribution, so the manufacturer is stuck with a monopolistic distributor. Before discussing why competition at the distribution level may be impossible, we examine three vertical restrictions that manufacturers can use to induce a monopoly distributor to behave more competitively.

Where it is legal, the manufacturer may be able to impose contractually a *maximum retail price*, $\bar{p}$, that the distributor can charge. By so doing, a manufacturer prevents a distributor from raising its price much above the wholesale price, p_2. As a result, the distributor sells more units. If $\bar{p}$, is set equal to p_2, the distributor behaves like a competitive firm, sells Q^* units, and the outcome is the same as with an integrated firm. If the distributor does not accept this restriction, and $\bar{p}$ is set between p_1 and p_2, then a

---

[14]In this example, $p_1 = D_1(Q_1) = 10 - Q_1$, $MR_1 = 10 - 2Q_1 = p_2 = D_2(Q_2) = 10 - 2Q_2$, and $MR_2 = 10 - 4Q_2$. Equating marginal cost and marginal revenue for the upstream firm, $m = 2 = 10 - 4Q_2 = MR_2$, implies that $Q_2 = 2$, so $p_2 = 10 - (2 \times 2) = 6$. As a result, $p_2 = 6 = 10 - 2Q_2 = MR_1 = 10 - 2Q_1$, $Q_1 = 2$, and $p_1 = 10 - 2 = 8$.

[15]If the integrated firm produces as efficiently as the separate firms, then integration makes consumers and the firm better off. Even if the integrated firm is less efficient, the desirable effect of eliminating one of the monopoly markups may outweigh this negative effect. It is possible, however, that some vertical mergers are privately profitable but not socially desirable, and that some socially desirable mergers are not privately profitable (Ross 1990).

quantity between Q_1 and Q^* is sold. Such restrictions were common in the United States before 1976, when a change in the law made it illegal for manufacturers to control the retail prices of independent distributors.

A manufacturer uses **quantity forcing** if it imposes a *sales quota* on a distributor; that is, the distributor must sell a minimum number of units. With this restriction, a manufacturer does not have to restrict a distributor's price. Sales quotas induce distributors to expand their output by lowering their prices. Many automobile dealerships and computer retailers have sales quotas.

Another tactic is for a manufacturer to adopt a more complicated pricing scheme than merely charging a distributor p_2 per unit of output. A manufacturer can use a two-part pricing scheme, as described in Chapter 10. It charges the distributor one price for the product and a second price for the right to sell the product. For example, the manufacturer sells the **franchise** rights, or rights to sell the product (often together with a brand name) to the distributor, for a *franchise fee.*

Why would a manufacturer want to set two prices? Suppose that instead of charging the distributor a price per unit of p_2, which is greater than its marginal cost, m, the manufacturer charges its marginal cost. Here, the distributor equates marginal revenue to its marginal cost, m, and sells Q^* units, which is the same outcome as with a vertically integrated firm. Thus, by setting $p_2 = m$, the manufacturer prevents the second monopoly distortion.

If the manufacturer charges m per unit, however, it earns zero profits, and the distributor earns all the monopoly returns. But the manufacturer may make positive profits from its franchise fee. Indeed, as long as there are many *potential* distributors, the use of a franchise fee allows the manufacturer to earn the same profits as it would earn if it were vertically integrated into distribution. The manufacturer can offer for sale the *right* to be the sole distributor of its product with a contractual guarantee that the wholesale price to the distributor is m per unit. The largest franchise fee a distributor is willing to pay is the value of the monopoly profits, π^*, as shown in Figure 12.5a. If a large number of firms want the monopoly franchise rights, competitive bidding ensures that the franchise fee equals the present value of the monopoly profits. Thus, the manufacturer can achieve the equivalence of vertical integration by charging a franchise fee and charging the marginal cost for its product.

In summary, if there is only one distributor, the problem of double monopoly markups may occur. If vertical integration is not feasible, vertical restraints such as maximum retail prices, quotas, or franchise fees may reduce or eliminate the problem. See Examples 12.4 and 12.5.

Free Riding Among Distributors. In a typical distribution arrangement, several independent firms distribute one manufacturer's product. Each distributor benefits from the promotional activities of other distributors without having to pay for them. The following sections identify several situations where free riding by distributors is likely to occur and then discuss some vertical restraints that may minimize free riding.

Where distributors must make substantial expenditures (for advertising, showrooms, training a sales staff, training purchasing agents, maintaining quality) to sell a

EXAMPLE 12.4 *Double Markup*

Do both food manufacturers and grocery retailers exercise market power in setting prices, so that consumers face a double markup? In the past, many industry observers believed that food manufacturers had substantial market power whereas supermarkets were relatively passive, competitive firms. Recently, though, industry experts report that supermarkets have acquired greater bargaining power relative to manufacturers. The explanations for this shift include the growing importance of private label brands (brands carrying the store's own label) and the increased concentration at the retail level (the average four-firm concentration ratio is 70 percent in the 100 largest metropolitan areas). The resulting increase in retailer market power and competition for limited shelf space has prompted manufacturers increasingly to pay slotting allowances to retailers to get their new products displayed.

Yogurt provides an interesting test of whether a double markup occurs. Dannon and General Mills together account for 62 percent of national yogurt sales, and private labels have 15 percent. Thus, the larger manufacturing firms may have market power as well as retailers.

Villas-Boas (2002) tested the double markup hypothesis for grocery store sales of yogurt. She used her yogurt demand curve estimates to compute price-cost margins for retailers and manufacturers under various models of vertical contracting between manufacturers and retailers in the supermarket industry. These models included double markup pricing, a vertically integrated model, and a variety of alternatives: strategic supply scenarios, allowing for collusion, nonlinear pricing, and strategic behavior with respect to private label products. On the basis of statistical tests, she rejected the double markup hypothesis. She concluded that manufacturers' wholesale prices are close to their marginal costs and that retailers have market power in the vertical chain. This result is consistent with two explanations: Manufacturers lack market power, or they exercise it by engaging in some form of second-degree price discrimination (nonlinear pricing) in which their marginal price equals their marginal cost.

Sources: Ellickson (2000), Sexton et al. (2002), Villas-Boas (2002), and Ward et al. (2002).

product, free riding is likely, because some of that sales effort helps other distributors. A distributor that cannot reap the full benefits of its sales efforts has an incentive to reduce those efforts and thereby sell less of the manufacturer's product. Free riding, therefore, is a problem that arises because distributors are not compensated *separately* for sales efforts; instead, they are compensated for sales efforts on behalf of a particular product only when they sell that product.

Suppose that one distributor heavily *advertises* a manufacturer's product that is also carried by another distributor. The first distributor creates a demand for the product, which benefits both distributors, but the second distributor incurs no cost at all. Unless something is done, the first distributor may have little incentive to advertise, because it does not capture the full benefits of its advertising.

EXAMPLE 12.5

Blockbuster's Solution to the Double Marginalization Problem

Before 1998, distributors of video movies exercised market power by selling tapes to video rental stores at a fixed price of about $65 to $70 regardless of the title. Retailers would decide how many tapes to stock and what price to charge. To the extent that retailers also exercised market power, customers rented fewer movies due to the double markup, and movie distributors' profits fell correspondingly.

As we have seen in this chapter, one solution to the double marginalization problem is to have distributors charge retailers a low per-unit fee (marginal cost) and then capture all subsequent profit in a separate fee. One mechanism to do this would be a revenue sharing contract combined with a unit fee per tape. Blockbuster introduced such a contract in 1998, and other video rental firms quickly followed suit. A typical contract sets the revenue sharing percentage at between 40 and 60 percent with a per-unit tape charge of $8 to the retailer.

Using detailed data on video rental stores, Mortimer (2002) estimates that the sum of retailers' plus distributors' profits increased from 3 to 6 percent as a result of this more efficient contracting and that consumers benefited substantially. She estimates that the rental price declined from $4.64 to $4.08 and that the average number of tapes in a store's inventory rose from 20.1 to 24.2 for the most popular films. For the next most popular category of movies, prices fell from $3.47 to $3.01 and the average inventory per title rose from 9.7 to 11.7. Mortimer concludes that revenue sharing would have an even more dramatic effect if all video rental firms adopted it. For the most popular category of movie, she estimates that the rental price would fall from $4.08 to $2.88.

There are many examples of free riding other than advertising. Selling many durable goods (for example, automobiles, stereo equipment, and appliances) requires a large showroom to display products, so that consumers can select the best model to satisfy their particular needs. Showrooms, of course, cost money, as does the inventory on display. If only one distributor has a well-stocked showroom, all customers go to that showroom to decide which product to buy, but they can buy from other distributors with less fancy showrooms and smaller inventories. These distributors can charge a lower price than the first distributor because their costs are lower. Thus, no dealer has an incentive to maintain a well-stocked showroom.

There was a clear example of this behavior near the Berkeley campus of the University of California. A discounter opened a store next door to a retailer that sold stereo equipment in a fancy, well-stocked showroom with carpets and attractive lighting. The discounter piled its merchandise in its original boxes on a linoleum floor under minimal lighting. The store had a crude, handwritten sign in the window that said, "Go next door, see which equipment you want, then come here for a lower price."

Another example of free riding occurs when a distributor's *sales staff* must be well trained in order to sell a product. Computer salespeople are a good example. If one distributor has highly trained salespeople, customers go to that store and learn a great deal about the product. Some of them subsequently may buy from a distributor (often a mail-order house or an Internet firm) without a trained staff, at a lower price. Discount distributors can sell at lower prices because they do not incur training costs. Again, the first distributor has a reduced incentive to maintain a well-qualified staff.

Still another example of free riding concerns *certification.* Here, there are no explicit services—only a distributor's reputation that its product line is of high quality. For example, certain department stores are known for carrying only high-quality, trendy clothes. Presumably, they have built this reputation by hiring qualified staff who are able to spot trends in fashion as well as to recognize high-quality clothes.

Other stores that carry the same merchandise as that stocked by the "certifying" fashion store reap a benefit: Their goods have been certified by the fashionable store as being of high quality and trendy. The other stores are free riding on the reputation of the certifying store and do not invest in building up their own reputations. This free riding creates a dilemma for the manufacturer (Marvel and McCafferty 1984). If the manufacturer sells to only the highest-quality stores, it may not get large enough distribution of its product. If it sells to every store, high-quality stores may be unable to capture an adequate return on their reputations.

A final example of free riding occurs when the *reputation of the product,* which the dealer can affect, influences the overall demand for the product. For example, imagine a chain of independently owned food shops all selling under the same brand name (say, McDonald's, Burger King, or Wendy's). The brand name carries a certain reputation that attracts buyers. If one shop decides to chisel on quality and to produce a lower quality than the other shops, the brand's reputation declines and all distributors suffer. The chiseling firm loses reputation, but if customers primarily rely on brand reputation and not an individual store's reputation, the decline in demand facing the chiseling store may be more than offset by the decline in that store's cost. For example, if the store is located on an interstate highway and has little repeat business, it may be profitable for the store to lower its quality and to free ride on the brand's reputation.

Manufacturers encourage sales efforts by distributors to increase the demand for the product, thereby increasing the manufacturer's profits. Because free riding reduces the incentive of distributors to promote a manufacturer's product, manufacturers use a variety of vertical restrictions to deal with the free-riding problem. Several of these restrictions create a *property right* in the sales efforts that distributors expend on behalf of a manufacturer. That is, these restraints are designed so that distributors reap much of the benefits from their sales effort.

One of the most common vertical restraints is an **exclusive territory**, in which only a single distributor may sell a product within a region: The distributor obtains monopoly rights to customers who buy within its territory. Exclusive territories usually involve a promise by the manufacturer that other distributors will not be allowed to locate within a certain distance of the existing distributor. For example, a distributor of Cadillacs may have a clause in its contract with General Motors (GM) that prevents

EXAMPLE 12.6

Free Riding on the Web

The rise of the Internet as an important sales channel creates several free-rider problems. For example, suppose that Harry's Camera Store has an exclusive territory for a given brand of camera. The exclusive territory provides an incentive for the retail outlet to have a trained sales staff who can explain the camera's features to a customer. However, if the customer, after visiting the store, finds that she can buy the camera at a lower price from a store on the Internet, then the Internet store's free riding reduces Harry's incentive to provide a strong sales effort. Ultimately, Harry's no longer has an exclusive territory.

With the rise of the Internet, auto dealers became concerned about the ability of auto manufacturers to bypass them and possibly to free ride off them through Internet sales. As a result of effective political actions, auto dealers have long benefited from state laws that protect their exclusive territorial rights. The dealers used these laws to convince GM and Ford to abandon plans to sell directly to customers on their own Internet sites. Liquor and insurance dealers have also used state laws to thwart manufacturers from directly selling over the Internet.

But what happens when dealers can't prevent a manufacturer or other retailers from setting up their own Web sites? For goods where free riding is likely to be a problem, the manufacturer has an incentive to try to prevent it. Therefore, one should not expect any bargains at a manufacturer's Web site or that of other authorized retailers for products where free riding could cause problems.

Carlton and Chevalier (2001) find this result in their study of perfume and DVD players. For perfume brands with exclusivity—a restriction on the number of retail outlets—manufacturers control free riding by using only retail Internet sites that do not discount or by avoiding using retail Internet sites and instead selling only at their own high-price Internet site.

Similarly, the two DVD manufacturers with the largest U.S. sales, Sony and RCA, charge prices at their own Web sites that are about 5 percent higher than prices on their authorized retailers' Web sites. Unlike the case of fragrances, there were several Web sites of unauthorized retailers where one could buy DVDs at discount prices. In an effort to control free riding, DVD manufacturers have been devoting increasing efforts to restricting the availability of their product through these unauthorized retailers.

GM from opening any other Cadillac dealership within a radius of several miles of it. By granting a geographic monopoly to the distributor, the manufacturer insulates it from competition. This insulation may be essential if the distributor is to reap the benefits of its sales efforts (see Example 12.6). Of course, creating market power for the distributor creates the problem of a double monopoly markup. Thus, the manufacturer may have to impose other vertical restrictions as well.

A second type of vertical restraint manufacturers use to stimulate sales efforts is to *limit the number of distributors*. The effect of this limitation is similar to that of exclusive territories. That is, price competition is limited, and more of the gain from sales efforts accrues to the distributor that makes the efforts. Again, the manufacturer must contend with the problem of a double monopoly markup due to the market power it confers on individual distributors.

Another method of controlling free riding is a **resale price maintenance** agreement where a manufacturer sets a *minimum* price that retailers may charge.[16] Such agreements create an incentive for retailers to compete for customers in other dimensions, such as sales effort. For example, if the wholesale price the distributor pays is \$10, and the minimum resale price is \$20, each dealer has an incentive to spend up to \$10 to attract customers. Thus, up to \$10 per unit is invested in advertising, training sales staff, or fancy showrooms. Minimum price restrictions channel competition among distributors toward sales effort and away from price cutting. They lead to more sales effort than occurs without them.

Many countries ban resale price maintenance. The practice was outlawed by Canada in 1951, Sweden in 1954, Denmark in 1955, the United Kingdom in 1965 (though exemptions may be requested), and the United States in 1976. Where legal, however, resale price maintenance is widely used.[17] One study estimates that, before resale price maintenance was banned in the United Kingdom in 1965, 44% of consumer expenditures on goods were on price-maintained items. Other studies indicate that the rate was 25% to 40% by 1960. A Canadian study estimates that 20% of goods sold in grocery stores and 50% of goods sold in drug stores were price maintained. In Sweden, 30% of consumer goods were covered by resale price maintenance. Another study indicates that, before the ban, coverage in the United States varied from 4–10% of retail sales.

A fourth approach to dealing with free riding is for the manufacturer to *advertise on behalf of its distributors.* If the manufacturer takes over the sales effort and handles the advertising, it does not have to worry about free riding among distributors, who can only free ride on the sales efforts of other distributors. A manufacturer that advertises and stimulates demand for its product can charge each distributor for that service through higher wholesale prices or a higher franchise fee. The problem with the manufacturer's assumption of the marketing and advertising function is that the appropriate advertising and marketing may differ by locale, and a local distributor may be better informed than the manufacturer about the best strategy for its area. If local distributors have no comparative advantage in marketing, the manufacturer should vertically integrate, all else equal.

One solution to this information problem is cooperative advertising, in which the manufacturer agrees to pay some of the distributors' advertising costs. The cooperative

---

[16]See Overstreet (1983) and Yamey (1966) for detailed discussions of several instances of resale price maintenance. See Telser (1960) for a discussion of why manufacturers want resale price maintenance agreements, which used to be allowed in the United States under what were called *fair trade laws.* See Mathewson and Winter (1984), Marvel and McCafferty (1984), Perry and Porter (1986), and Klein and Murphy (1988) for further discussions of vertical restraints to deal with free riding.

[17]See the survey of studies in Overstreet (1983, 113, 152–6). The following numbers on the percentage of goods covered by resale price maintenance agreements are based on his summary. There is an extensive discussion of various countries' laws in Yamey (1966).

arrangement can place the responsibility for choosing the advertising in the hands of the knowledgeable party, the local distributor, and the advertising subsidy from the manufacturer to the dealer helps prevent the free-riding problem from eroding the distributor's incentive to advertise.

A fifth approach to the free-rider problem is for the manufacturer to monitor each dealer's sales effort and compensate each accordingly, perhaps by rewarding dealers by sending them larger or more timely shipments when demand is unexpectedly high. This monitoring is costly.

Free Riding by Manufacturers. It is also possible that competing manufacturers can free ride off the efforts of each other. Suppose that two competing manufacturers both use the same distributor to sell their product and that one manufacturer conducts a massive advertising campaign to entice consumers to go to the distributor to buy its product. The second manufacturer benefits from the increased customer flow. In fact, because the free-riding manufacturer does not advertise, it has lower costs than the advertising manufacturer and can sell at a lower price. The distributor then can (correctly) tell a customer who is enticed into the store by the advertising of the first manufacturer, that the second manufacturer's product is a much better deal at a lower price. See **www.aw-bc.com/carlton_perloff** "Requiring Exclusivity."

Another example of free riding among manufacturers occurs when one manufacturer trains its distributors to repair or sell its product. To the extent that such training is costly and can be applied to other products, a second manufacturer can free ride on these training expenditures by using the same distribution outlets as the first manufacturer. Again, the free rider has lower costs and can outcompete the manufacturer that pays for the training.

A final example of free riding among manufacturers occurs when one manufacturer provides a list of potential customers to a distributor. If the distributor also sells the competing products of a second manufacturer, the second manufacturer benefits from the first manufacturer's customer list. These examples of free riding among manufacturers are similar in their effects to free riding among distributors. If the free riding is unchecked, manufacturers have reduced incentives to advertise, provide training for distributors, and develop customer lists. The solution to these free-rider problems is to create a system that allows manufacturers to obtain the full reward for their sales efforts. One common solution, exclusive dealing, is for manufacturers to forbid their distributors to sell the products of competing manufacturers (Marvel 1982).

Externalities Due to a Lack of Coordination Among Distributors. A manufacturer that relies on independent distributors that compete with each other usually wants to coordinate or restrict the ways in which they compete. For example, distributors often compete with each other on location (see Chapter 7 on monopolistic competition). The optimal location from a manufacturer's viewpoint may differ from the one that emerges under monopolistic competition by independent retailers.

A manufacturer wants to ensure that its goods are available wherever consumers are likely to buy. For example, by selling at unprofitable locations, the manufacturer may prevent buyers from trying other products, and thereby develop brand loyalty. This strategy can raise profits elsewhere, and hence total profits. Because an independent dealer sells only where its profits are nonzero, a conflict arises between the locational desires of the manufacturer and its independent distributors.

Competition among distributors depends on how each distributor thinks the others will react to its behavior. This competitive interaction among dealers can lead to a price and service quality that are different from what the manufacturer prefers. As shown in Chapters 6 and 7, price and quality vary depending on rivals' behavior toward each other, so it is unlikely that any particular oligopolistic outcome is consistent with the manufacturer's desires. Again, a conflict arises between the manufacturer's desires and the outcome of competition among distributors.

For example, suppose that a monopoly distributes its product using competing retailers whose sales efforts are important. Even in the absence of free riding, the incentive of the retailers to sell the product is inadequate from the monopoly's perspective because the competitive retailers make little on each additional sale (unlike the monopoly). Similarly, the retailers are less likely than the monopoly to want to stock inventories and bear the risk of unsold goods. That is why many book publishers allow stores a refund on unsold goods (Kandel 1996). In summary, by controlling competition among all dealers, a manufacturer can profitably coordinate their pricing, sales efforts, and locations and achieve higher profits than those that result from uncoordinated decision making among competing distributors. Table 12.1 summarizes the main problems arising in distribution, and the possible solutions for a manufacturer. Example 12.7 examines these issues in the alcoholic beverage industry.

The Effects of Vertical Restrictions

In general, manufacturers use various combinations of vertical restrictions to reduce the problems of double monopoly markup, free riding, and competitive interactions. These restrictions typically limit the amount of competition that can occur in a market and, at the same time, encourage additional efforts to sell the product.

A restriction on competition is something that an economist abhors, as it may increase market power. On the other hand, an increase in sales efforts is something that an economist applauds. So, should an economist conclude that vertical restraints are desirable or undesirable? There is no clear-cut answer to this question, but one can make several observations about the trade-off between restrictions and additional sales effort. In the following sections we describe markets where vertical restrictions benefit both firms and consumers, where the effects are ambiguous, and where vertical restrictions harm consumers. Finally, we note the implications of banning vertical restrictions.

Desirable Effects of Vertical Restrictions. Vertical restrictions that benefit both firms and consumers are unambiguously desirable. It is often in a manufacturer's selfish interest to use vertical restrictions that help consumers. Any manufacturer, even one with substantial market power, wants its product distributed at the lowest cost. Distribution is viewed by the manufacturer as an input necessary to make a sale, just as a raw material is an input in the manufacturing process. A monopolistic manufacturer

EXAMPLE 12.7

Brewing Trouble: Restricting Vertical Integration in Alcoholic Beverage Industries

Regulation has spawned strange vertical relationships within the U.S. alcoholic beverage industry, often creating monopolies and affecting vertical relationships. The Twenty-first Amendment to the U.S. Constitution, which ended Prohibition in 1934, states in section 2 that "the transportation or importation into any state, territory, or possession of the United States for delivery or use therein of intoxicating liquors, in violation of the laws thereof, is hereby prohibited." This passage has been interpreted as giving the states permission to continue restricting the marketing of alcoholic beverages. (See, however, Example 3.3.)

Almost all states have laws that create a three-tier distribution channel: suppliers (brewers, vintners, and importers); wholesalers; and retailers (liquor stores and restaurants). Allegedly, the original purpose of the laws was to prevent vertical integration in the industry, which might lead retailers to push the house brand beyond acceptable social limits. The Federal Alcohol Administration (FAA) Act was designed to prevent such marketing abuses. The FAA Act forbids practices that induce retailers to carry only one supplier's brands, and prevents suppliers from having ownership interest in retailers, although it does permit them to own retailers outright.

Starting in the 1970s, wholesalers have successfully backed various laws that enrich them. Twenty-three states require suppliers to sell only to locally licensed wholesalers and prohibit suppliers from having any interest in a wholesale or retail establishment. In addition, 18 "control" states (and one Maryland county) monopolize the distribution of alcoholic beverages and sell them at the wholesale and often at the retail levels. Consequently, almost all alcoholic beverages must be handled by wholesalers, because suppliers cannot directly deal with retailers. Thus, these laws prevent vertical integration and make the middlemen a powerful (and profitable) force between suppliers and retailers.

tries to distribute the product as efficiently as possible, just as it tries to produce the good at the lowest cost.[18] Thus, although in some cases vertical restrictions can be used for anticompetitive purposes, a number of economists argue that many, if not most, vertical restrictions benefit consumers by lowering prices or increasing services.

Vertical restrictions may lower prices either because they increase the output of existing firms or because they encourage new firms to enter markets. Vertical restrictions that allow a firm to promote its product more effectively and that lead to more output sold at a lower price help both firms and consumers. For example, competition among

[18]For examples of instances when vertical restrictions are procompetitive, see several of the case studies in Lafferty, Lande, and Kirkwood (1984) and Ippolito (1991).

Many state laws protect wholesalers from being "fired" by suppliers. All states except Alaska and Hawaii (which has a more general law) have franchise termination laws specifically covering some or all of beer, wine, and spirit distribution. These laws increase the double markup problem by precluding suppliers from enforcing provisions designed to limit downstream markups by ending a franchise relationship with a wholesaler. The consequence has been an increase in wholesaler markups, which often account for 18 to 25 percent of the price of wine to retailers and 15 to 25 percent of the price of liquor—percentages that exceed those typical in comparable industries.

At least prior to 1977, federal antitrust law prohibited establishing exclusive territories unless they were mandated under state law. Now 24 states mandate exclusive dealing, which gives wholesalers regions in which they are monopolies. Even in states without a monopoly wholesaler, laws make entry difficult, so there are only a small number of wholesalers. California has only two distiller liquor wholesalers, Young's Market and Southern Wine & Spirits. These two firms also control 70 percent of wine distribution. In Massachusetts, two firms control 43.5 percent of alcohol distribution and the top four control 65.3 percent. Some suppliers, such as Joseph E. Seagram & Sons, wanted wholesalers who could distribute their products over entire states and regions. Apparently they reasoned that large distributors would have lower costs and that wholesalers could avoid spillover and free-riding effects in promoting brands and maintaining quality. However, restricting the number of wholesalers increases their market power. A study by the New York City Department of Consumer Affairs found that beer prices rose 30 percent in the year that Miller Brewing and Anheuser-Busch set up exclusive agreements.

Sources: Fortune, December 9, 1985:135; Jordan and Jaffee (1987); Whitman (2003); **www.nabca.org**.

different brands is heightened if competing firms can effectively promote their products. That is, although competition among dealers of the same brand is restricted, competition across brands is encouraged, because the vertical restrictions stimulate sales efforts for each brand. Vertical restrictions also may make entry easier, which leads to lower prices. Without vertical restrictions, new products that rely heavily on sales efforts have difficulty breaking into a market.

In many cases, consumers view the *relevant product* as both the good and the service provided with it. Consumers who cannot get full use from a good without instruction from the retailer suffer if the good is sold without service. For example, it may pay for a neophyte photographer to buy a camera from a local store that provides instructions on how to use it. Although the camera can be purchased at a lower price from a mail-order distributor, the extra service from the local store may be worth the difference in price.

TABLE 12.1 Problems That Arise in Distribution and Manufacturers' Responses

Problems in Distribution	Manufacturers' Responses
Double monopoly markup	Encourage competition among distributors Sell at marginal cost and charge a franchise fee Establish sales quotas or maximum prices
Free riding among dealers	Establish exclusive territories or restrict the number of dealers Establish minimum price (resale price maintenance) Take over the marketing effort Monitor and subsidize or pay for dealers' sales effort
Free riding among manufacturers	Impose exclusive dealing on dealers
Lack of coordination among dealers leading to externalities	Use a combination of the policies above

In such cases, the good-with-service is really an entirely different product than the good without service. Vertical restrictions allow the good to be sold with service (sales effort). Without the restrictions, the price is lower, but fewer services are provided.

Ambiguous Effects of Vertical Restrictions. Whether a vertical restriction is desirable depends on the same factors that influence the social desirability of product choice. Imagine two groups of buyers: those who know how to use a good (experienced users) and those who do not (beginners). With no training provided, experienced users buy the good at $10 and beginners do not purchase it. With vertical restrictions that allow beginners to receive instruction, both groups buy the good for $11. The experienced users are worse off with the vertical restrictions because they spend more per unit but do not benefit from the availability of training. The beginners, however, are better off because if they purchased the good, it must be worth at least $11 to all of them, and some may receive consumer surplus.

Training is not the only useful sales effort. Showrooms are also useful—for example, to automobile, camera, computer, and stereo buyers. Without showrooms, potential customers could not easily examine the various products before purchase. Many, if not most, consumers would prefer to pay a slightly higher price and have a chance to test-drive a car before purchasing it.

Vertical restrictions, just like vertical integration, can be used to price discriminate. Suppose that consumers in California have an inelastic demand for some product, and consumers in Illinois have an elastic demand. The manufacturer wants to charge a high wholesale price to the distributor in California and a low price to the distributor in Illinois. If the manufacturer tries to do so, however, the independent Illinois distributor may be able to profitably resell in California the product it buys from the manufacturer. By granting exclusive territories to the independent distributors in exchange for no resale agreements, the manufacturer can charge a low wholesale price in Illinois and a high price in California. As explained in Chapters 9 and 10, however, imperfect price discrimination has ambiguous welfare effects and can increase or decrease welfare compared to simple monopoly pricing.

A growing literature shows that a variety of vertical contracts (or vertical integration) possibly impairs competition. From our earlier discussion, we know that a monopoly producer of good *A* gains nothing if it vertically integrates into a competitive downstream market for good *B* that is produced in fixed proportion to *A*. Moreover, if the market for *B* is not competitive so that a further markup is added to the price of *B*, then vertical integration (or a vertical contract involving nonlinear pricing) into *B* eliminates the inefficiency of the double markup, and consumers benefit. Thus with fixed proportions, vertical contracts (or vertical integration) do not harm and may benefit consumers.

However, there are at least two possibly offsetting effects. First, as we have already shown, if the production process has variable proportions, an input monopoly gains market power by vertically integrating forward (which tends to raise the price), even though it produces more efficiently (which tends to lower the price), so that the price may rise or fall. Second, if firms in market *B* differentiate their products then the input monopoly may not be able to constrain the final price for *B*, and hence the price will remain excessively high even if the input monopoly integrates forward. Again, it is unclear whether price will rise or fall with vertical integration. However, the reader is reminded that in calculating social welfare, gains in efficiency frequently swamp increases in deadweight loss. The principles for why these two conditions alter the desirable effects of vertical integration are at the heart of several papers on the possible harmful effects of vertical contracts and vertical integration. The theoretical possibilities of harm in these models depend on very specific and hard-to-verify conditions and, with slight changes in assumptions, the theoretical possibility of harm disappears. There have been few, if any, attempts to empirically document the validity of these conditions in any industry.[19] It is a fruitful area for research.

Undesirable Vertical Restrictions. In some cases, vertical restrictions (and vertical integration) can be used for anticompetitive purposes. For example, they may be used to cartelize an industry or to prevent entry, or otherwise harm rivals by raising rivals' costs (Chapter 11).[20]

---

[19] Rey and Stiglitz (1995) illustrate how competing manufacturers can use exclusive contracting with distributors to lessen the intensity of competition among the manufacturers. Ordover et al. (1990) explain how vertical integration (or its equivalent achieved through vertical contracts) can harm competition for differentiated products. See also Bernheim and Whinston (1998), Chen (2001), Rey and Tirole (1986), Riordan and Salop (1995), and Segal and Whinston (2000a).

[20] Salinger (1988), Riordan (1998), Ordover, Salop, and Saloner (1990), Hart and Tirole (1990), and Riordan and Salop (1995) discuss whether vertical mergers can harm competition. However, see Carlton (1990) and Reiffen and Vita (1995) for a critique of this literature. In the absence of transaction costs (or legal impediments to contracting), if there is an incentive for a vertical merger that harms consumers, then there is an incentive for the same result to be achieved by a vertical contract in the absence of the merger. Hence, it is only when such contracting cannot occur that one should worry about the anticompetitive consequences of a vertical merger. Those anticompetitive effects are similar to the ones discussed here in relation to vertical contracting.

Vertical restrictions can lead to either distributors' or manufacturers' cartels. A group of dealers can impose vertical restraints that lead to monopolization. For example, suppose that a particular group of dealers alone can distribute a product. They may force the manufacturer to grant exclusive territories, leading to local monopolies and restricted competition among dealers. As discussed in Chapter 5, allocating territories is an effective way to cartelize and results in higher consumer prices. This outcome is likely only if entry into distribution is difficult, so that the manufacturer has no choice but to assist in the creation of the dealer cartel.

Vertical restrictions (or vertical integration) can also help to perpetuate a cartel of manufacturers. Suppose that a group of manufacturers wants to collude. It may be difficult for them to observe the price that each is charging its dealers if they are not vertically integrated into distribution. If they all agree to charge the same price at retail, however, and enforce this agreement with vertical restrictions (such as resale price maintenance) on dealers, it is easier for them to detect if any manufacturer cheats on the agreement by lowering price, because it is easier to observe retail prices than wholesale prices.

Vertical restrictions (or vertical integration) may be used to increase the difficulty of entering an industry. For example, Chapter 11 shows how an incumbent can make it difficult or impossible for a rival to enter by tying up scarce distribution channels. Exclusive dealing is one way for manufacturers to tie up distribution. Under such agreements, both parties to the contract agree to rely only on each other, not on other firms. Such strategic behavior can successfully raise the cost of entry only if the channels of distribution are limited.

Rasmussen et al. (1992) and Segal and Whinston (2000) explain how a manufacturer can become a monopoly by tying up distribution without having to pay for it. Imagine that there are 100 dealers (no more can enter) and that a manufacturer needs at least 30 dealers to enter profitably. By signing exclusives with 71 dealers, the incumbent firm can foreclose entry of a rival and can become a monopoly. How much will the monopoly have to pay the dealer for this privilege? Nothing! As long as each distributor thinks that at least 71 other dealers will sign with the monopoly, dealers will rush to sign an exclusive agreement for free.[21]

Banning Vertical Restrictions

Even where vertical restrictions are undesirable, in some cases little is accomplished by banning them. If vertical restrictions are outlawed, a manufacturer has an incentive to vertically integrate and handle its own distribution, so that it can impose the desirable restrictions. It would be counterproductive to enact a law preventing contracts between independent firms when a firm could easily avoid such prohibitions by vertically integrating and distributing the product itself.[22] Only where the cost of vertically inte-

---

[21]Carlton and Waldman (2002), Nalebuff (forthcoming), Whinston (1990), and Stephandis and Choi (2001) show that, in other situations where scale matters, vertical restrictions can foreclose the market to competition. See Carlton (2001) for a more detailed discussion.

[22]Sometimes vertical integration is banned. See Barron and Umbeck (1984) and Blass and Carlton (2001) for an analysis of the costly consequences of a ban on oil companies owning their own gas stations.

grating is much higher than the cost of imposing vertical restrictions does a ban on vertical restrictions effectively end such practices.

In summary, although manufacturers impose vertical restrictions to increase their profits by generating more sales efforts, consumers may either gain or lose. Courts have recognized the value of increasing competition by encouraging promotional efforts. The courts have tried to bar certain vertical restrictions such as those that enhance or create a dealer or manufacturer cartel or raise costs of entry. Unfortunately, even where vertical restrictions are undesirable, forbidding them does not prevent the associated harms unless vertical integration is more expensive than the vertical restrictions. See Chapter 19 and **www.aw-bc.com/carlton_perloff** "Vertical Relations Antitrust Laws" for details on the relevant U.S. laws concerning vertical integration and vertical restrictions.

Franchising

One special type of vertical relationship is that between a *franchisor* and a *franchisee* (Caves and Murphy 1976, Rubin 1978). The franchisor, a firm such as McDonald's, sells a proven method of doing business to the individual franchisee (the owner of a McDonald's outlet) or sometimes sells only the right to carry the franchisor's brand. Franchises include fast food outlets, car repair centers, service stations, auto dealers, and soft-drink bottlers. A franchisor that provides a total system of doing business is called a *business-format* franchisor. Most franchises—with the exception of gas stations, auto dealers, and soft-drink bottlers—are business-format franchises.

Franchising has been growing in importance. From 1975 to 2003, the number of U.S. franchise outlets has increased from about 220,000 to more than 580,000.[23] According to one estimate, 40 percent of U.S. retail sales take place at franchise outlets.[24] Table 12.2 shows the 10 fastest growing franchises in the United States in 2003. Number one on the list, Subway, now has 17,000 locations in 75 countries.

The business-format franchisor provides the franchisee with training and other assistance, which often includes advice on purchasing, pricing, choice of location, accounting procedures, and advertising.[25] The franchisee agrees to run the business in the manner stipulated by the franchisor, who continues to monitor the franchisee's performance to make sure that it abides by the franchisor's methods. The franchisor's vertical restrictions greatly limit the way a franchise is run, though federal antitrust and state laws often limit aspects of franchisor control (see Chapter 19). (See Brickley, Dark, Weisbach 1991 for an analysis of how franchisors have responded to various

[23] *The 1986 Franchise Annual* and *The 2003 Franchise Annual*, Lewiston, N.Y.: Info Press. The *Franchise Annual* excludes some types of franchises, such as auto dealerships and gasoline stations. The reported numbers would be much higher if such omitted franchises were included.

[24] "Franchising in the United States," *AP Newswire*, July 6, 2002.

[25] This assistance does not result in generally lower failure rates for franchises compared to nonfranchises. Instead, the evidence suggests similarities in failure rates with the failure rate for small franchises being somewhat higher in the initial years, but lower in later years than that of independent firms (Bates 1995, Stanworth et al., 1998).

TABLE 12.2 **Fastest-Growing Franchises in the United States in 2003**

Franchisor	U.S. Franchises	Company-Owned Outlets	Franchise Fee	Royalty Fee on Sales
Subway (sandwiches)	15,257	1	$12,500	8%
Curves (women's fitness & weight loss)	4,671	0	$24,900	$395/month
7-Eleven Inc. (convenience stores)	3,761	2,547	varies	varies
McDonald's (hamburgers)	11,465	8,094	$45,000	12.5% +
Jani-King (commercial cleaning)	7,843	33	$8,600–$16,300	10%
Taco Bell Corp. (Mexican quick-service food)	5,363	1,331	$45,000	5.5%
Quizno's Franchise Co. (sandwiches)	2,000	0	$25,000	7%
Super 8 Motels Inc. (economy lodging)	1,987	0	varies	5%
Jackson Hewitt Tax Service (income tax preparation)	3,709	516	$25,000	15%

Source: EntrepreneurMag.com.

laws restricting their actions.) Franchisee agreements can typically be terminated by the franchisor. As compensation to the franchisor, the franchisee usually pays a franchise fee plus a percentage, or royalty, on sales, which is usually in the range of 0–10 percent.

The franchisor-franchisee relationship requires each party to rely on the efforts of the other—efforts that may be difficult to observe. Because a franchisor has difficulty monitoring how well a franchise is run, it provides incentives to the franchisee by letting the franchisee keep the bulk of extra profits. Thus, the franchisee has an incentive to work harder than a salaried employee of the franchisor would.

In cases where it is not difficult to monitor the behavior of the franchisee, the franchisor may own the outlet itself. Many franchisors own and operate a substantial fraction of their outlets. In the United States, about 13% of franchisor sales come from company-owned outlets excluding such heavily franchised sectors as auto dealerships and gas stations (*2003 Franchise Annual*). Car dealerships are 100% franchised, and gasoline stations 85% franchised, while fast-food restaurants are 79% franchised, and convenience stores are 82% franchised (Hadfield 1990, *2003 Franchise Annual*). Company-owned outlets tend to be larger than independent franchises and typically are located closer to a regional headquarters of the franchisor than independent franchises. There appears to be a long-run tendency for the proportion of company-owned outlets to decline as the franchisor continues to expand (Martin 1988, Brickley and Dark 1987). Lafontaine (1992) finds that the incidence of franchising is greater when there is an incentive or monitoring problem at the franchise level. Consistent with LaFontaine's findings, Shephard (1993) and Blass and Carlton (2001) find that gas stations are more likely to be company operated the higher the volume of gasoline sold and if the station has no repair bays.

After entering into the agreement, the franchisee expects the franchisor to continue to offer services and to make sure that the other franchisees maintain the reputation of the brand. If the franchisor sells franchises to inept people, the brand name declines in value and so does the business of each franchisee—even those run efficiently. By linking the franchisor's fee to a percentage of sales, as is typical, the franchisor has an incentive to continue to assist and monitor franchisees and to ensure that they succeed. If total sales fall, the franchisor's fee falls.

A more difficult question is why the franchisor's fee depends on sales and not profits. After all, it is profits, not sales, that franchisees and franchisors want to maximize. One answer is that it is easier to measure sales rather than profits (which, for example, requires a determination of depreciation). Another answer, which is difficult to verify, is that a fee based on sales, and not profits, better induces the franchisor to monitor other franchisees and preserve the brand's reputation.

Because an independent franchise sets its own retail prices, it is possible to examine whether prices at company-owned franchises are lower than at independent franchises due to the elimination of double marginalization. LaFontaine (1995) compared prices between company-owned and independent franchises for identical products at Arby's, Dairy Queen, KFC, McDonald's, Wendy's and other fast food franchises in the Pittsburgh and Detroit areas. She found that prices at company-operated franchises were 2 percent lower on average. Her results that prices are lower at company-owned franchises are consistent with similar results on gas pricing by Barron and Umbeck (1984) and Shephard (1993).

Empirical Evidence

There are many theories as to why firms vertically integrate or impose vertical restrictions. Real-world evidence illustrates how significant the explanatory power of the various theories is in predicting where vertical integration and vertical restrictions occur. We examine first the evidence on vertical integration and then that on vertical restrictions.

Evidence on Vertical Integration

Most existing studies of the reasons for vertical integration focus on the transaction costs or market power theories discussed in this chapter. Williamson's (1975, 1985) transaction costs or specific assets theory holds that when either firm in a vertical relationship must invest in a specific asset (one with no alternative use), vertical integration may be used to avoid opportunistic behavior. Opportunistic behavior typically involves reneging on implicit or explicit contracts or promises, with the intent of extracting a larger share of the rents generated by the transaction. The firm does whatever is least expensive—vertically integrates or relies on markets—taking into account possible opportunistic behavior by other parties. The market power theory holds that firms vertically integrate to increase profits or eliminate market power. This section discusses empirical studies that examine why firms produce some products internally but obtain others through market procurement.

Monteverde and Teece (1982) examine quasi-integration by automobile manufacturers. They explain why, in some cases, a manufacturer owns a machine necessary to produce a part, rather than buying the part from another firm that owns the machine. For example, suppose the machine that makes a specialized part that can only be used by the manufacturer must be custom built. If another firm owns that machine, it is at the mercy of the manufacturer, which could suddenly announce it is no longer willing to buy the parts, making the machine virtually worthless. This opportunistic behavior can be avoided if the manufacturer vertically integrates backward and owns the other firm. A less extreme solution is quasi-vertical integration, in which the manufacturer owns only the machine, not the other firm. The other firm runs the machine for the manufacturer and charges an hourly rate.

Monteverde and Teece (1982) examine a sample of manufactured components from two divisions of a major U.S. automobile supplier, all of which require special machinery and cannot be purchased on the open market. Monteverde and Teece test whether the possibility of opportunistic behavior leads to quasi-integration. Opportunistic behavior is likely if the value of the specialized asset to the downstream firm is much higher than for its next most valuable use. To illustrate this point, suppose the machine that makes a specialized part can be converted easily to produce parts for other firms. In that case, the opportunities for exploitation of this firm by the manufacturer are much less than if there is no other use for the machine. Opportunistic behavior is more likely the higher the tooling cost (the cost of producing the special machines to produce the part) and the more specialized the part (the higher the cost of converting the machine to its next best use). Monteverde and Teece's empirical evidence confirms that quasi-integration is more likely in these circumstances.

Different firms make very different decisions, however. For example, GM buys 57 percent of its parts from its own divisions, whereas Chrysler buys only 30 percent from its own divisions.[26]

Masten (1984) studies vertical integration in the aerospace industry. Firms can either make various components used in the industry themselves or buy from others. As in the previous study, integration is more likely when specialized assets are used. Masten employs two measures of asset specificity. The first, *design specificity,* reflects whether the item is used exclusively by this company (highly specialized), is easily adaptable for use by other aerospace firms (somewhat specialized), or is used in other industries (relatively standard). For example, transistors and resistors are standard items, and hybrid circuits designed for specific firms are highly specialized. The second, *site specificity,* reflects whether having the product produced nearby reduces costs. Masten also measures the complexity of the product: The more *complex* the product, the more things that can go wrong, and the greater the possibility of opportunistic behavior.

Masten's statistical analysis shows that products that are highly complex and highly design specific are more likely to be produced internally, but that site specificity, at

---

[26]David Woodruff and Zachary Schiller. "Smart Step for a Wobbly Giant." *Business Week,* December 7, 1992:38.

least in this industry, is not an important factor. If the product is both design specific and complex, there is a 92 percent probability that it is produced internally. If it is design specialized but not complex, there is a 31 percent probability of internal production. The probability drops to 2 percent or less if it is not design specialized, regardless of whether or not it is complex. Thus, design specialization appears to be the most important factor. Other studies showing the importance of asset specificity include Spiller (1985), Weiss (1992), Crocker and Reynolds (1993), Minkler and Park (1994), Whyte (1994), and Wimmer and Garen (1997).

Lieberman (1991) examines the importance of asset specificity, market power, and assurance of supply as explanations for vertical integration in the chemical industry. His study is a rigorous test of Carlton's (1979a) theory on the importance of supply assurance. Lieberman finds strong support for the importance of both asset specificity and supply assurance, but not market power, as reasons for vertical integration.

Evidence on Vertical Restrictions

Most of the empirical studies of vertical restrictions concentrate on the effects of resale price maintenance. This section examines resale price maintenance as well as other types of vertical restrictions.

Most of the studies presented to Congress in 1975, when it was debating making resale price maintenance illegal, found that maintained prices were from 16 to 19 percent higher than those in states that did not enforce fair trade laws. A Library of Congress study estimated that consumers paid between $1.66 billion and $6.23 billion more on retail transactions covered by fair-trade laws than in free-trade states. Thus, families in fair-trade states may have paid $150 more per year for maintained prices (Shepard 1978).

Several studies of resale price maintenance have compared the periods before and after the federal law in 1976 that banned the practice.[27] By looking at prices and output in the two periods, these studies try to test whether resale price maintenance helps or harms consumers. The difficulty with such studies is that it is not clear whether the behavior of prices and output allow one to distinguish the case where resale price maintenance is harmful from the case where it is helpful. For example, if resale price maintenance is anticompetitive, prices should fall and output should rise after the ban. But the same may be true even when resale price maintenance is procompetitive. The reason is that if the resale price maintenance promotes sales effort and promotional activity, then some of the effect of that sales effort and promotional activity will remain in the short run. Once resale price maintenance is not allowed, prices should fall as firms compete, and output should rise. But eventually the benefit of past promotional efforts will subside and free riding will reduce additional sales promotions, with a re-

[27]Although federal law prohibits resale price maintenance, manufacturers can legally pressure distributors to control the retail price. For example, manufacturers can suggest a retail price, can choose to deal with retail stores that do not discount, and can structure promotional incentives so that retail stores do not charge less than the manufacturer-specified minimum advertised price.

sulting decline in output. The price will be lower, but so will promotional activity, so output may be higher or lower than before the repeal of the resale price maintenance. Thus whether a ban benefits consumers may depend on the value that consumers place on sales services.

A study by Shepard (1978) of the 18-month period following federal repeal of resale price maintenance (January 1976 to June 1977) suggests that consumers saved \$6.5 billion more in fair-trade states. The prices of discount firms are estimated to have fallen 11.6% relative to the prices they were forced to charge in December 1975, and specialty store (nondiscounter) prices fell by only 1.8%. Price differentials between discounters and nondiscounters in furniture, apparel, and tools became very large, 20–30%. Nonprice competition probably fell as a result. A survey of retailers in California, a fair-trade state, found that nondiscount specialty stores discounted some product lines sold at nearby discount outlets. Moreover, 15% of surveyed retailers claimed that they or their rivals had reduced their advertising budgets following repeal. This claim is supported by average advertising linage purchased by retailers in major newspapers in the 108 largest U.S. cities. In 1975, prior to repeal, mean advertising in the 82 fair-trade cities was 13.2% higher than in free-trade cities. In 1976, after repeal, advertising in these cities was only 12.7% higher.

Ornstein and Hanssens (1987) consider whether resale price maintenance of liquor increased or decreased welfare. Presumably, if resale price maintenance increases efficiency in distribution, it increases output and thereby raises consumer surplus.[28] They compare states with resale price maintenance to others for the period 1974–1978. They find that the presence of resale price maintenance lowers per capita consumption by 8%, holding other factors constant. They also compare the effects in California counties for eight years prior to the repeal and in 1984. The repeal of the law had a significant negative impact on liquor store license values of between 23% and 25%. This large loss is consistent with the belief that resale price maintenance was used to establish prices above the competitive level. It is also consistent with the view that resale price maintenance was used to create some profits in the distribution sector in order to encourage sales effort.

Using a cross-state analysis, Ornstein and Hanssens estimated the welfare loss from resale price maintenance, ignoring the negative externalities from drinking. Based on estimates of the price elasticity of demand for liquor that range from -0.5 to -1.5, their estimates of the direct welfare loss range from \$2.5 to \$7.5 million. The wealth transfer from consumers to firms was more substantial: \$226.6 million in 1978, or 4.5% of estimated retail sales in the affected states. Given the data difficulties associated with the estimates, Ornstein and Hanssens say that these figures should be viewed as suggestive only.

[28]More liquor sold at a lower price increases consumer surplus from direct consumption. More consumption, of course, could cause substantial harm, such as from drunk driving. These indirect harms are not included in the welfare calculations that follow.

Ippolito (1991) and Overstreet (1983) study several industries that used resale price maintenance. They conclude that the evidence favors the hypothesis that resale price maintenance is used to facilitate sales effort and not to facilitate a cartel among dealers or manufacturers.

In addition to studies of resale price maintenance, there have been studies of other types of vertical restrictions. For example, Ekelund et al. (1987) analyze the effect of exclusive territories on the price of beer. They conclude that, when account is taken of state advertising restrictions on price, there is no evidence that exclusive territories raise price.

Mueller and Geithman (1991) examine the effect of the distribution system used by Sealy, a manufacturer of mattresses. In 1968, Sealy instituted a new licensing agreement designating each licensee's former exclusive sales territory as an "area of primary responsibility" (APR). When a licensee sold outside its APR, it had to pay the owner of the invaded APR a "passover payment" and "warranty repair charge." Consequently, distributors made few sales outside of their APRs. As a result of a private antitrust action, this practice was found to be a restraint of trade. Starting in 1981, Sealy licensees began selling in others' APRs. Sales outside of retailers' own APR went from 0.9% in 1980 to 4.6% in 1985.

Mueller and Geithman conclude that the licensing system created market power for local dealers, to the detriment of Sealy. When this system ended, consumers enjoyed substantial discounting. Apparently, no free-rider problem leading to reduced advertising resulted. Local and national advertising rose above their 1980 levels. Eckard (1994) questions Mueller and Geithman's interpretation of the evidence and notes that, inconsistent with a diminution of local dealers' market power, Sealy's profit fell after 1980.

There is a need for more empirical studies to identify both desirable and undesirable vertical arrangements. Although many theoretical papers show how vertical restrictions can be either harmful or helpful, the evidence from U.S. antitrust case law provides at best weak support that the effects are harmful. Thus Easterbrook (2002) argues that it would be a mistake for courts to take a harsh attitude toward vertical arrangements.

SUMMARY

Vertical integration occurs for the same reasons that firms are created in the first place. Although firms may vertically integrate to increase monopoly profits, they also have many efficiency-related motives. When firms decide not to vertically integrate, they may impose vertical restrictions on the firms with which they deal. It is often in the best interest of a manufacturer to use vertical restrictions to give limited monopoly power to distributors. By doing so, the manufacturer induces the distributors to put forth more sales effort. These vertical restrictions can stimulate product sales and promote competition. In certain circumstances, vertical integration and vertical restrictions may be used for purely anticompetitive reasons. Although there are exceptions, in general, it is difficult to show that either vertical integration or vertical restrictions decrease welfare.

PROBLEMS

1. Show that it is more efficient (larger joint profits) for a franchisor to collect from a franchisee a royalty that is a percentage of profits rather than sales. Why do most franchisors collect royalties as a percentage of sales?
2. Suppose a monopolistic upstream firm sells to a number of downstream firms, and one of these is a monopoly in its retail market. If vertical integration is impractical, what might the government do to reduce the distortions from the double monopoly markup?
3. If a pure profits tax (a percentage of the economic profits) is collected at the retail level, does a downstream monopoly's incentive to vertically integrate change? Does the incentive change if the tax is collected at both upstream and downstream levels? Does a sales tax (at the retail level) affect the incentive to vertically integrate?
4. A monopolistic producer uses a dealer network, in which it limits the number of dealers and restricts them to exclusive territories, to sell its product in another country. Some importers buy the product in the other country and sell it in the United States. Such imported products are said to be sold on the *gray market*. Explain why the manufacturer might not act to prevent such gray market sales.
5. A woman wants to present a friend with a gift and, as an inside joke, wants to present it inside an empty red-and-white-striped barrel of Kentucky Fried Chicken. She tries to buy the empty carton from a fast food chain that sells Kentucky Fried Chicken and is told that it costs $10! The barrel full of chicken costs $10.99. The reason is that the corporate headquarters keeps its inventory on the amount of chicken sold by the number of cardboard containers sold.[29] To ensure an accurate count, the parent firm may have required the franchisees to purchase cartons only from it. Should society bar the franchisor from requiring such purchases by franchisees? Why does the franchisor want to use this method? How can the franchisee try to get around this restriction?
6. One possible measure of the degree of vertical integration is the ratio of value added (sales minus material and energy costs) to sales. Contrast this measure for a mining firm and for a car producer.

Answers to odd-numbered problems are given at the back of the book.

SUGGESTED READINGS

See Perry (1989) on vertical relations and Katz (1989) on vertical contractual relations for excellent, relatively nontechnical surveys of the entire literature. The classic articles on vertical integration are Coase (1937) and Stigler (1951). The two books by the leading proponent of the transaction costs approach, Williamson (1975, 1985), are relatively nontechnical and are fascinating reading. Blair and Kaserman (1983) is a clear but more technical analysis. Telser (1960) is the first article to present the modern rationale for vertical relations and is nontechnical. A clear discussion of that topic is White (1985). See Martin (1988), Hadfield (1990, 1991), Gallini and Lutz (1992), Lafontaine (1992, 1995), Katz and Owen (1992), and Brickley (1999, 2002, forthcoming) for recent work on franchising. Preston (1994), Noll and Owen (1994), Warren-Boulton (1994), and Guerin-Calvert (1994) use economics to analyze five important cases involving vertical arrangements.

---

[29]Clark DeLeon, "The Colonel: That Will Work, Won't It?" *Philadelphia Inquirer,* December 30, 1980:2-B.

PART FOUR

Information, Advertising, and Disclosure

CHAPTER 13

Information

There is no absolute knowledge. . . . All information is imperfect. We have to treat it with humility. —*J. Bronowski*

This chapter examines the problems that arise from limited consumer information. Consumers often do not know which store sells a good at the lowest price or how quality varies across brands. Providing consumers with information about product prices, attributes, or quality alters their purchasing behavior and thereby affects market structure. The results of recent research on markets in which consumers have limited information are startling and contradict the strongest conclusions from the standard economic models based on perfect consumer information. In markets in which consumers have limited information, high-quality products may not be supplied, some of the desirable effects of perfect competition vanish, and firms may have an incentive to reduce consumers' information.

The five major questions addressed in this chapter are

1. What is the effect if consumers have limited information about product quality?
2. What is the effect if consumers have limited information about prices charged by stores?
3. If some consumers have full information and others only limited information, is the full-information equilibrium obtained?
4. Do firms have an incentive to lower consumer information so as to price discriminate?
5. When does providing consumers with more information lower the equilibrium price?

The chapter begins by showing that if consumers have limited information about a product's quality, one of two serious problems occurs: Either the market does not exist, or, if it does exist, the quality produced is different (usually lower) than would occur in a world of perfect information.[1] For example, often only the lowest-quality products are produced. Providing information through experts, standards, and certification is socially desirable if the benefits to consumers outweigh the costs of collecting and disseminating the information. Warranties or guarantees may also eliminate problems due to limited information.

Next, we show that imperfect consumer information about prices may eliminate a market, enable even small firms to set their prices above marginal cost, or lead to the charging of a variety of prices for a homogeneous good. That is, with imperfect consumer information about price, perfect competition is impossible. In this sense, the *law of supply and demand* and the *law of a single price* do not hold in markets with limited information.

Then, we consider that firms may purposely raise consumers' costs of search in order to obtain market power. For example, a firm may charge different prices for the same good at various locations or under different brand names so as to make it difficult for consumers to find the low-priced brand. Finally, we show that improving consumer information can sometimes lower average price.

Why Information Is Limited

Research by psychologists, economists, marketing experts, and others reveals that consumers have imperfect knowledge of prices and qualities in the marketplaces where they shop. There are five chief reasons for this limited knowledge (Federal Trade Commission 1978).

First, information varies in reliability. Not all "information" is accurate, and hence a rational consumer should not rely equally on information from all sources. Information that was once correct may become dated and therefore inaccurate.

Second, there is a cost to collecting information. It does not pay for consumers to collect information beyond the point where the marginal benefit equals the marginal cost of collecting it. For example, going to several stores to determine which one has the lowest priced candy bar almost certainly does not make sense. See Example 13.1 and **www.aw-bc.com/carlton_perloff** "Sources of Consumer Information."

Third, consumers can remember and readily recall only a limited amount of information (see **www.aw-bc.com/carlton_perloff** "Do Consumers Know How Much

[1]Many economists call the limited information equilibrium *nonoptimal* or *inefficient* or say that it is a *market failure.* Because it is common terminology, we will refer to departures from perfect competition as inefficient. However, this terminology is inaccurate because it implies that a problem exists that can and should be fixed. It is costly to provide perfect information, and the costs of providing perfect information may exceed the benefits. Thus, even though such departures from a perfect world are commonly referred to as nonoptimal, it may not be optimal or even possible to correct this "inefficiency" or "market failure."

EXAMPLE 13.1

Genetically Modified Organisms: Do Consumers Not Care or Not Read?

All Western countries strictly regulate the labeling of food products.The labels must be informative in the sense that they are accurate and useful descriptions of the ingredients or characteristics of the product. Although the labels may not be explicitly misleading, producers have an incentive to stress only positive characteristics on the labels, putting the unfavorable qualities in small type. Consequently, regulators impose strict conditions on the size, color, and positioning of information on packages.

A key factor that is handled differently across countries is whether a food product contains genetically modified organisms (GMOs). European countries require a disclosure about GMOs in lettering that is at least as large as those in the list of ingredients. Surveys indicate that European consumers are hostile to products containing GMOs. However, Noussair, Robin, and Ruffieux (2001) conducted an experiment that suggests that this hostility may not translate into buying behavior.

Their experiment shows that consumers don't react to labeling, probably because they do not even notice it, and hence do not realize that the product contains GMOs. Using people from Grenoble, France, the experimenters conducted Vickery auctions to determine the consumers' willingness to pay. In these auctions, each participant simultaneously submits a bid independently. The good goes to the highest bidder at an amount equal to the second-highest bid. According to theory, each bidder has a dominant strategy to bid an amount equal to his or her actual willingness-to-pay.

In period 1 of the experiment, four chocolate bars without packaging were auctioned, including two identical bars, called *S* and *U*. Each subject received a taste of the four products. Then an auction was held. In the second period, the subject saw the original packaging (without the price but with the list of ingredients). The package for *S* listed corn, and that for *U* listed "genetically modified corn." A second auction was conducted. In the third period, the subjects were shown a magnified and projected list of ingredients from the packaging and were invited to read the list of ingredients.

In the first two periods, the average bid for products *S* and *U* were essentially equal. However, in the third period, the average bid for the GMO product, *U*, was only 75 percent as high as that for the non-GMO product, *S*. Moreover, 80 percent of the subjects were willing to pay a positive price for *U*. Thus, although the reported hostility to GMO products exists, apparently most people will still buy the products and will generally pay as much for them as non-GMO products, as they do not read the labels carefully.

They Pay?"). They are, of course, more likely to retain and recall relatively important information.

Fourth, it is often efficient for consumers to use simplified rules to process information. That is, they rationally use only some of the information they have collected because it is costly to process it. A customer may check a restaurant bill to see if any nonordered items were included, but may not check the addition. A sensible consumer processes information up to the point where the marginal benefit equals the marginal cost of processing more information (this behavior is called *bounded rationality*).[2]

Fifth, some consumers do not have sufficient education or intelligence to process available information on all products correctly. For example, some quite intelligent people do not know how to determine the quality of various computers or industrial organization textbooks, the healthfulness of foods, or the probability that a house plant will survive in their yard. Others lack the math skills to compare the cost of buying a car by paying for it outright to the cost of making a relatively small payment each month for years. See Example 13.2.

Limited Information About Quality

Lord Bowen's definition of hard work: *answering yes or no on imperfect information.*

Consumers frequently do not know how quality varies across brands in markets for the services of professionals (doctors, lawyers, plumbers, electricians, and economists), processed foods, used goods, and complex mechanical or electronic products. There is **asymmetric information**: One party (seller) to a transaction knows a material fact (the quality of the good) that the other party (buyer) does not. Asymmetric information about quality can have either of two undesirable results: An equilibrium may not exist, or, if the equilibrium exists, resources are used less efficiently than they would be if there were perfect, symmetric information.

The Market for "Lemons"

Probably the best-known study of the way limited information can disrupt a market is Akerlof's (1970) classic analysis of the market for "lemons." Akerlof shows that, where sellers have perfect information and consumers have extremely limited information, a market may not exist, or only the lowest-quality product may be sold.

For example, in the used car market, the seller (current owner) has learned over time if the car rarely needs repairs (a good car) or frequently needs them (a "lemon"), whereas, at best, a potential buyer knows the probability of getting a good car. If buyers cannot distinguish between good and bad used cars, the cars sell for the same price.

Bad Products Drive Out Good Products. Bad cars are overvalued and good cars are undervalued in this market. For example, suppose that consumers believe that half the used cars in the market are lemons that consumers value at $100 and the other half are good cars that they value at $200. Consumers are risk-neutral: They are indifferent

[2]Simon (1957, 1959), Cyert and March (1963), and Williamson (1964).

EXAMPLE 13.2

Understanding Consumer Information

The "fat-free" label isn't misleading! The fat is free. We only charge for the other ingredients.

Many consumers do not understand potentially valuable information:

Unit Pricing: A shopper can use unit pricing information in grocery stores to determine which brands or sizes are relatively inexpensive per unit. In 300 post-shopping interviews in 1975, 39% of shoppers claimed to use unit pricing frequently, and another 32% occasionally. Only about 19% said that they seldom or never used shelf tags for price comparisons, and 10% admitted that they had never noticed the tags. Thus, over 7 out of 10 customers said that they occasionally used unit pricing, whereas only 22% rated unit pricing as "not helpful."

The other consumers may not use unit pricing because they cannot process the information. One experiment found that understanding of the unit price information increased with education. The percent who understand the unit price information was 48 for those completing grade school, 71 for those with some high school, 75 for high school graduates, 81 for those with some college, and 83 for college graduates.

Insurance Cost: Surveys show that the model life insurance cost-disclosure format adopted by the National Association of Insurance Commissioners is incomprehensible to the average consumer. Only 38% of life insurance purchasers knew that a policy's index number could be used to compare the costs of life insurance policies. Only 21% knew that the lower the policy's index number, the lower its cost, and 61% said that they did not know how to use an index number.

Brightness of Light Bulbs: Since 1970, the Federal Trade Commission has required the disclosure of brightness information for light bulbs. Five years after the rule was promulgated, most consumers did not understand the concept of "lumens," which measure brightness. In a survey of 168 people, only one mentioned lumens as a pertinent factor in selecting light bulbs.

Nutrition: According to a 1991 Harris Poll, 22% of people say that they have trouble understanding food label information. Moreover, although the Food and Drug Administration requires that nonstandard food items be labeled, many consumers (including the authors of this text) find it hard to understand the meaning of certain terms. For example, if a product is not the real thing and is nutritionally inferior to the real thing, it must be called *imitation.* If the product is not real but is nutritionally equivalent, it may be called a *substitute.* The terms *salt free, no salt, no salt added, unsalted,* and *without salt* may be misleading to many consumers. These phrases mean that no salt has been added during processing, but the original product may be very high in salt or sodium.

Sources: The Progressive Grocer, October 1975:48; D. McCullogh and D.I. Padberg, "Unit Pricing in Supermarkets," *Search: Agriculture* 1971:1:18, Table 22; Federal Trade Commission (1979, 93–4); Sheldon Margen and Dale Ogar, "To Your Health: The Writing on Food Labels Often Confuses," *San Francisco Chronicle,* October 22, 1986:FF4; Sheldon Margen and Dale Ogar, "To Your Health: Labels on Our Food Don't Tell the Whole Story," *San Francisco Chronicle,* October 29, 1986:FF3; Associated Press, "20% Confused by Food Labels," *San Francisco Chronicle,* March 12, 1991:B4.

between having a dollar and having something that has a 50 percent probability of being worth nothing and a 50 percent probability of being worth \$2. Then the value to a typical consumer of a randomly selected car is \$150 $(= 1/2 \times 100 + 1/2 \times 200)$. That is, the buyer is willing to pay more than the value of a bad car (\$150 > \$100) because the car might be good, but the buyer is not willing to pay the full value of a good car (\$150 < \$200) because the car might be a lemon.

In such a market, bad cars drive out good cars. Although an owner of a bad car is delighted to sell it for more than it is worth, an owner of a good car is unwilling to sell it for less than its value and keeps it. Thus, in a market with only two types of cars, only the bad cars are sold. Because only bad cars are sold, buyers know they are getting lemons and will only pay the value of a lemon, \$100. *There is no market for good-quality used cars.*

This example can be extended to many qualities of cars, but the result is the same. The lowest-quality cars eventually drive all other cars out of the market by the same sort of reasoning.[3]

This type of problem also arises in markets for insurance and for home repair. The price of health insurance increases with age because older people are more likely to need health insurance. Healthy senior citizens, however, may not find medical insurance attractive because the premiums are too high. As in the used car example, there is **adverse selection**: As the price of an insurance policy rises, only the worst risks buy the policy. If individuals can determine their own health better than insurance companies, insurance companies sell a disproportionate number of policies to the least healthy members of society.

Similarly, suppose that some roofers use high-quality materials and others use low-quality materials. If homeowners cannot tell the honesty of a roofer for many years (for example, bad materials break down in 5 years and good materials last 10 years) and must pay bad and good roofers the same amount, then bad roofers may drive out the good ones, whose costs are higher. In each of the examples, high-quality goods that would be sold if buyers and sellers had symmetric information are not sold if there is asymmetric information. Consumers are therefore deprived of the ability to consume certain products.

Asymmetric Information Lowers Quality. Although not all markets with asymmetric information degenerate so that only the lowest-quality item is sold, there is always inefficiency in these markets relative to a world with perfect information: Quality levels are too low (Leland 1979a, 1979b). Unfortunately, these inefficiencies relative to a perfect world usually cannot be remedied by government intervention, because providing perfect information is often prohibitively expensive.

These low-quality inefficiencies are due to an *externality* in which a firm does not completely capture the benefits from selling a higher-quality product. When a seller

[3]The Akerlof model applies better to insurance and similar markets where people cannot easily switch between being buyers and sellers. Kim (1985) shows that when people can decide whether to be a buyer or a seller, the results may differ.

provides a relatively high-quality product, the average quality in the market rises, so buyers are willing to pay more for *all* products. That is, the high-quality seller shares the benefits of its high-quality product with sellers of lower-quality products by raising the average price to all. Because the price based on average quality is less than the cost of producing the higher-quality product, a firm is unwilling to produce and sell it.

Solving the Problem: Equal Information

I only ask for information. —*Charles Dickens*

The problem of bad products driving out good ones results from the asymmetry of information. Where information is symmetric, markets are more likely to exist. We consider two types of symmetric information: Either both sides costlessly know the quality of a product, or neither knows.

If both buyers and sellers know the quality of used cars, prices reflect the true values of cars. Good-quality cars sell for more than bad-quality cars. The market is perfectly competitive and there are no inefficiencies.

If sellers know no more than buyers (as with new cars), then good and bad cars are sold at a price that reflects an average of the two qualities. That is, the price does not reflect the true value of a given car, but it does equal the expected value. Where there is symmetric but imperfect information, markets do not vanish.

Whether it pays for consumers (or sellers) to obtain information, however, depends on the costs of obtaining it as well as its benefits. Where costs of obtaining information are relatively low, consumers obtain the information and markets function smoothly; if costs are high, the information is not gathered and inefficiency results.[4]

One possible solution to the asymmetric information problem is to require sellers to make disclosures (Chapter 14). Consumers also obtain information in at least five other ways.

Guarantees or Warranties. By providing credible *guarantees* or *warranties*, sellers of high-quality goods credibly convey the information to consumers that their products are of high quality. By providing consumers with information, such firms are able to charge higher prices that reflect the higher quality of their goods.

[4]In some markets, price may convey the information necessary for consumers to infer relative qualities of different products; in others, price is not a good indicator. See Grossman and Stiglitz (1980) and Cooper and Ross (1984). Ginter, Young, and Dickson (1987) survey studies of the relationship between price and quality in many different types of markets (clothing, cameras, shoes, food, small appliances, and others) and find that the correlation between price and quality is almost always low (in all studies, the average correlation was less than 0.29). On the other hand, price does correlate well with some major purchases of durable goods (Gerstner 1985; Tellis and Wernerfelt 1987; and Curry and Reisz 1988). Smallwood and Conlisk (1979) and Chan and Leland (1982) contend that high prices should be correlated with high quality when there are informed consumers. Bagwell and Riordan (1991) show that when quality is fixed, a high price can signal high quality if a higher-quality good costs more to produce. Klein and Leffler (1981) argue that high prices signal high quality as a payoff for the repeated choice of the high-quality good by consumers. These theoretical issues are discussed in more detail below and in the next chapter.

EXAMPLE 13.3 *Counterfeit Halal Meat*

Many Muslims—including a quarter of the 6–8 million Muslims in the United States—only eat food prepared according to strict Islamic guidelines called Halal. Unfortunately, many stores are selling counterfeit Halal. Halal meat is expensive, and retailers commonly mislabel other meats so as to pass them off as Halal.

One solution is legal intervention. Several states have passed laws making it a crime to sell food falsely labeled as Halal. And in England, Wales, Northern Ireland, and the Irish Republic, authorities have raided vendors peddling fake Halal.

Another approach is the use of a guarantee. Mohammed Patel, a Chicago grocer, put a sign in his store window: "If you prove our meat is not Halal, we will give you $50 thousand." The sign greatly increased his business.

Sources: Charles Osgood, "Laws to Stop Counterfeit Halal Foods," August 19, 2003; **wcbs880.com/siteSearch/osgood_story_231115949.html; www.ehn-online.com/cgi-bin/news/news1/EpVyykuAyFLWiuELJf.html; www.muslimconsumergroup.com/news.htm**.

However, guarantees only convey this information if they are credible. For example, an established dealer's guarantee on a used car is more credible than a guarantee from an individual. A guarantee is valuable only if the buyer believes that the seller can be found and made to honor it in the future.[5] See Example 13.3.

Typically, guarantees are provided only if the life of a product does not depend heavily on how consumers use it. Otherwise, buyers have an incentive to use the product relatively carelessly and rely on the seller to fix problems under the warranty. A *moral hazard* is an incentive for a consumer to behave carelessly when the product is covered by a guarantee that the seller will fix all problems (even those caused by the consumer).

Liability Laws. Liability laws may serve the same function as explicit warranties. If consumers know that liability laws or contract laws force the manufacturer to make good on defective products, then the manufacturer need not list its obligations in a warranty. The problem with relying on legal recourse rather than explicit warranties, however, is that the precise obligations of the manufacturer may be ambiguous, and as a result, the transaction costs (such as going to court) may be high. Thus, manufacturers may find that explicit warranties are still necessary.

Reputation. A store or manufacturer may rely on its reputation to signal that its goods are of high quality. A store that expects repeated purchases by a consumer if it

[5] A Federal Trade Commission study found that only 4.8 to 14.8 percent of consumers carefully study guarantees and warranties before purchasing; thus, in many markets, they may be provided for reasons other than to signal quality before purchase (Crocker 1986).

provides high-quality products has a strong incentive not to provide defective products. In general, in markets where the same consumers and firms deal regularly, a reputation is easy to establish. In markets where items are purchased infrequently, reputations are harder to establish.

Experts. A disinterested party, an expert, may be able to provide consumers with reliable information. For example, if a potential purchaser of a used car can take it to a mechanic and get it appraised, then any information asymmetry may be eliminated.

Consumer groups may publish expert comparisons of different brands, as in Consumers Union's *Consumer Reports.* Objective information supplied by outside organizations is rare because information is a *public good* (a good that, if it is supplied to anyone, can be supplied to others at no extra cost). Information is socially valuable if it is worth more (say, to consumers) than it costs to provide it. Although socially valuable information may exist, it is possible that no firm can profitably provide it because it cannot capture all the benefits. Consumers Union does not capture the full value of its information through subscriptions because subscribers to its magazine, *Consumer Reports,* lend their copies to friends, libraries stock the magazine, and newspapers report on its findings. As a result, Consumers Union does not engage in as much research as it otherwise would.

Standards and Certification. The government, consumer groups, industry groups, or others may provide information in the form of *standards* and *certification.* A **standard** is a metric or scale for evaluating the quality of a particular product. For example, the "R-value" of insulation tells how effectively it works. **Certification** is a report that a particular product has been found to meet or exceed a given level on a standard.

Standard Setters: Industry groups may set their own standards and get an outside group or firm, such as Underwriters' Laboratories (UL) or Factory Mutual Engineering Corporation (FMEC), to certify that their products meet specified standard levels. Often standards are set to guarantee conformity across brands. For example, a VHS video-recorder owner is assured that a VHS tape manufactured by another firm works in that machine.

Government agencies may require manufacturers to disclose information about their products, such as the energy consumption of an electric appliance or the potentially harmful side-effects of certain drugs. Governments may set and enforce minimum quality standards by requiring that professionals be licensed and that drugs be effective or by testing the products directly. For example, in 1988 the U.S. Food and Drug Administration (FDA) tested 115,000 condoms for defects, rejected 30 million imported condoms as defective, and ordered the recall of 3 million domestic condoms.[6] Governments also may set fines to guarantee that firms meet standards or liability rules requiring firms to recompense consumers if products malfunction.

[6]Robert M. Andrews, "His Job: Condom Tester," *San Francisco Chronicle,* February 9, 1990:B6. The FDA works with manufacturers to ensure that latex condoms are not damaged. An average of 996 out of 1,000 spot-checked condoms must pass a water test for leaks. Under pressure from the FDA, one manufacturer recalled 57 million condoms in 1997. All but one U.S. producer has had a recall as of 2003.

Effect of Standards: Unfortunately, standards and certification may either help or hurt. They are harmful if their information is degraded or misleading, or if they are used for anticompetitive purposes. Where consumers are inexpensively informed of the relative quality of all goods in a market, the information is unambiguously useful. Often, however, information is degraded.

For example, although quality may vary along a continuous scale, it may be the case that only a high- versus a low-quality rating is used. With such standards, products are likely to be made so that they have either the lowest-possible quality (and hence cost of manufacture) or just barely a high enough quality level to obtain the high-quality rating.

Such high–low rating schemes are often combined with the exclusion of low-quality goods or services. For example, many state and local governments license professionals, and only those meeting some minimum standards are granted licenses and allowed to practice. In most states dozens, if not hundreds, of professions and crafts are licensed, such as electricians, plumbers, dentists, psychologists, contractors, and beauticians. In California, as of 1991, nearly one in four workers holds a professional license, including approximately 400,000 cosmetologists, 300,000 contractors, and 200,000 private investigators.

Licensing has two offsetting effects (Leland 1979a, 1979b). First, the restrictions raise the average quality in the industry by eliminating low-quality goods or services. Second, these restrictions raise the prices consumers pay. The number of people providing services is reduced because the restrictions screen out some potential suppliers. Moreover, consumers are unable to obtain the lower-quality and less expensive goods or services. As a result, welfare may go up or down depending on whether the increased-quality or the higher-price effect dominates. Only by setting the standard properly and changing it as necessary can welfare be raised. It is debatable whether such restrictions can be set properly and cost-effectively by government agencies.

A better solution than trying to set the best possible standard is to provide consumers with objective information on the relative quality of each brand or professional, and let them judge whether the price savings justifies purchasing a low-quality good or service. Restrictions on supply may be superior to providing such information only if consumers are unable to understand more subtle grading systems or if it is too costly for consumers to train themselves to use this information.

A further problem with licensing and mandatory standards and certification is that they can be used for anticompetitive purposes, such as erecting entry barriers to new firms and products. For example, many model plumbing and building codes required that pipes be made of copper or a few other types of materials and have certain dimensions (Federal Trade Commission 1978, 162–63). As a result, manufacturers of plastic pipe faced problems in introducing their products.[7] These mandatory standards in building codes impeded the diffusion of innovations (Oster and Quigley 1977).

[7]One reason for the building-code restriction on plastic pipes is that they can be installed more quickly and by less skilled labor than copper pipes can. As a result, plumbing unions supported the restrictive codes in order to increase the demand for their skilled labor.

A similar problem arises because many professions license themselves, under government auspices. Thus, doctors, lawyers, electricians, and others may set their own licensing standards. These groups may define standards that prevent entry of professionals from other states or those who have just finished their education, so as to keep the wages of currently licensed professionals high. Here, licensing is very likely to be socially harmful, because it excludes qualified professionals and raises consumers' costs. Unfortunately for economists, their profession is not licensed, so they cannot act in this anticompetitive manner to limit supply and raise their wages.

Evidence on Lemons Markets

The lemons market theory has been tested with both empirical and experimental evidence. The evidence is used to examine whether a lemons market problem exists and whether various proposed solutions work.

Empirical Evidence. Empirical evidence is used to determine whether the lemons problem occurs in used car markets and whether laws requiring sellers to disclose all known defects to buyers eliminate the lemons problem. Lacko (1986) analyzed Federal Trade Commission telephone survey data on used cars purchased between October 1978 and January 1980 to answer these questions. One test of the lemons problem is to see if quality varies by type of seller. If warranties, reputation, or friendship can prevent the lemons problem, then dealers or friends and relatives should provide better-quality cars than those purchased from a stranger through an ad.

To test this hypothesis, a statistical analysis was used that controlled for the age, mileage, and repair record of the used cars. For used cars 1–7 years old, few differences in quality were found by type of seller (through an ad, friend or relative, new and used car dealer, used car only dealer, or someone of whom the buyer had heard). With older cars (8–15 years old), average quality differed significantly by seller. Cars purchased from friends and those purchased from a new and used car dealer were rated higher. Cars purchased from friends or relatives were statistically significantly less likely to need a repair than those purchased through an ad. Finally, compared to cars purchased through an ad, repair expenditures were \$418 lower for cars purchased from a friend or relative, \$533 lower if purchased from a new and used car dealer, and \$449 lower if purchased from someone the buyer had heard of from others.

The survey data were used to test the effectiveness of a Wisconsin law requiring the disclosure of defects in used cars sold by car dealers. The Wisconsin defect–disclosure law did not have a statistically significant effect on quality (compared to cars sold in other states). One possible reason is that it applied only to car dealers, for whom the lemons problem was not severe.

Thus, there is little evidence of a lemons market problem for used cars less than 8 years old, but there is evidence of the problem for cars 8 to 15 years old. Apparently, reputation or loyalty helps prevent the lemons problem. You can buy higher-quality cars from friends, relatives, or people you know slightly than you can through ads. New and used car dealers also provide higher-quality cars, presumably to maintain their reputations.

All 50 states and Washington, D.C., have lemon laws (**autopedia.com/html/Hotlines_lemon2.html**). However, consumers do not always take advantage of them. For example, in the first 13 months Connecticut's lemon law was in effect, only 40 autos were returned out of 113,000 registered cars (Smithson and Thomas 1988). See Example 13.4.

Experimental Evidence. The Federal Trade Commission sponsored an experimental study of markets where buyers have less information than sellers (Lynch et al.

EXAMPLE 13.4 *Certifying Thoroughbreds*

Unlike buyers, horse breeders know a thoroughbred's full medical history, temperament, and physical attributes as well as other valuable information. Such information is valuable because the difference between low-quality and high-quality horses is substantial. Less than 1 percent of thoroughbreds win the top-stakes races, and many earn nothing from racing.

An owner of a thoroughbred has three choices: keep the horse and race it or sell at either a certified or noncertified public auction. A breeder "nominates" a horse for a certified auction by paying a nonrefundable fee to the auction house and providing information such as the horse's pedigree. The auction house physically inspects the horse and permits only the high-quality horses to be auctioned. In contrast, at a noncertified sale, auction houses sell all nominated horses. About one in five horses sold at auction is certified.

Typically, buyers are allowed to inspect horses before all sales and may perform minimally intrusive tests such as x-rays and sonograms. By eliminating low-quality horses, certified auctions allow buyers to save resources by inspecting only relatively high-quality horses.

Certification, by providing a minimum quality standard, may reduce but not eliminate adverse selection. Wimmer and Chezum (2003) conducted several tests of whether certification, by providing consumers with more information, reduces the lemons problem.

For example, they find that noncertified horses' post-sale racetrack earnings per race is less than the earnings of certified or retained thoroughbreds, controlling for other observable characteristics. Similarly, they estimate the effect of adverse selection on prices in noncertified sales and find that the expected price on the basis of observable characteristics is $88,259 at certified sales, whereas the expected price is only $9,253 at noncertified sales. Controlling for observable characteristics, they estimate that 87 percent of the difference in the price of a randomly selected horse at a certified sale to one at a noncertified sale is attributable to the seller's selection process. Thus, they conclude that certification reduces the lemons problem by providing buyers with information.

1986). College students played the roles of buyers and sellers, and two types of quality were offered: low-quality items (lemons) and high-quality items. In some experiments, sellers were not identified; that is, they did not have a brand name. In other experiments, the sellers were identified by number or brand names. Sellers were allowed to advertise in some experiments by making a claim about the quality of the item offered. In some cases sellers were allowed to make false claims, whereas in other experiments, only true claims were allowed. The key results were

- Without brand names or advertising, virtually only lemons were sold. This result confirms Akerlof's prediction.
- Where only truthful claims were permitted, the market behaved almost perfectly efficiently. High-quality products were supplied whether or not brand names were allowed.
- Reputations alone were not enough to overcome the lemons problem. That is, when sellers had brand names but were not restricted to truthful claims, virtually only lemons were sold.

This last result is surprising because one would expect that reputation alone could solve the lemons problem. Perhaps the value of brand names in this experiment was not sufficient to establish a reputation for truthfulness because the long-term gain from a favorable reputation was not sufficiently high.

Limited Information About Price

The person who succeeds will be the person with the best information.
—Disraeli

Firms can obtain market power from consumers' lack of knowledge about prices and quality. Limited information can lead to a monopolistic price in what would otherwise be a competitive market. See Example 13.5.

For example, suppose that many stores in an area sell the same good. If one store raises its price above the level of others, and all consumers know it—that is, consumers have *full information*—that store loses all its business. As a result, the store faces a demand curve that is horizontal at the going market price, and has no market power. The market price is the full-information competitive price, p^c.

In contrast, suppose that some or all customers do not know that other stores charge lower prices: Consumers have *limited information* about price. Now, a store can raise its price without losing all its sales (Diamond 1971).[8] The store faces a downward-sloping demand curve and has some market power. As shown in the following model, if there is a single price in the market, it is higher than p^c. However, there may be either no market or a multiple-price equilibrium (stores sell at different prices).

[8]Probably the first paper to make this point clearly was Scitovsky (1950). Diamond (1971) was the first to present a formal mathematical analysis. Salop (1976) and Stiglitz (1979) provide excellent, relatively nontechnical surveys of the early literature.

EXAMPLE 13.5 *Price Dispersion and Search Costs in the Talmud*

The Talmud, written by Jewish scholars about 1,500–1,800 years ago, consists of laws together with interpretations and discussions. In one section, the rabbis analyzed the consequence of price dispersion. One group of rabbis proposed that if a buyer paid more than one-sixth above fair market value (a term that is never precisely defined), the buyer could demand a cancellation of the sale and a full refund. A buyer's right to demand the refund is limited to the time it takes the buyer to show the merchandise to another knowledgeable person, such as another seller.

Rabbi Tarfon of Lod disagreed with the proposal and instead suggested that the buyer could demand cancellation of the sale and a full refund only if the buyer paid more than one-third above fair market value. Lod was a center for trade, and initially the merchants of Lod supported Rabbi Tarfon's ruling.

They changed their minds, however, when Rabbi Tarfon announced that a buyer had a full day to exercise his rights. Apparently, the merchants believed that with the great number of merchants in Lod, search costs were so low that, in less than a day, an overcharged buyer easily could find a seller who would agree that the buyer had been overcharged.

Source: The Talmud, Steinsalz Edition, 1990, Random House, Volume III, Part III, Tractate Bava Metzia: 99–100.

The Tourist-Trap Model

A typical tourist, Lisa, arrives in a small town filled with souvenir stands. Each stand sells mugs with the town hall painted on it. Lisa wanders by one of these stands, sees some mugs, and decides to buy one. She has but a short time before her bus leaves, and she does not expect to return to this town again. Thus, she does not have time to check the prices at each souvenir stand, and she cannot use information obtained through even a limited search in the future.

If there are many such tourists, what prices do the stands charge for these mugs? To answer this question, we make four assumptions for specificity:

- All firms (souvenir stands) have the same costs and sell the identical product.
- All consumers have identical demand functions.
- A guidebook provides each consumer with the general distribution of prices (how many stands charge each price), but does not give the particular price each stand charges.
- The tourist's cost of going to a stand to check the price or to buy is c, which reflects the tourist's time and expenses (taxi rides).

Thus, if Lisa goes to two souvenir stands, her search costs are $2c$. If she buys a mug at the second stand at price p, her total cost is $p + 2c$. The least a mug will cost her is $p + c$, because she must visit at least one stand to buy a mug.

Fixed Number of Firms. Initially, assume that there are a fixed number of souvenir stands, n. How much does each one charge for the mug? We start by considering whether each stand charges the full-information, competitive price, p^c, which equals the constant marginal cost.

Breaking the Full-Information, Competitive Equilibrium: To determine whether the full-information, competitive equilibrium (price equals marginal cost) price holds when consumers have limited information, we need to determine if any firm has an incentive to deviate from that price. If firms benefit from deviating from this proposed equilibrium, they **break the equilibrium**; that is, the proposed equilibrium is not an equilibrium.

If all other stands charge the full-information, competitive price p^c, it pays for a deviant firm to set a higher price. The deviant firm can profitably charge $p^* = p^c + \epsilon$, where ϵ is a small, positive number, and not lose its customers.

For example, Lisa walks up to the stand and sees that the mug sells for p^*. Her guidebook tells her that all the other souvenir stands charge p^c. "What amazingly bad luck," she thinks to herself (or something to that effect), "I've hit the only expensive stand in town." She is annoyed and considers going elsewhere because she knows with certainty that any other stand will charge her less. Nonetheless, she does not go to another stand if the price in this stand, p^*, is less than the price at another stand *including* the additional cost of getting to that stand: $p^* < p^c + c$. That is, she does not go to another stand if the cost of search, c, is greater than ϵ, the price markup.

Thus, it pays for the deviant stand to raise its price by an amount just less than the cost of additional search. As a result, the proposed equilibrium where all stands charge the full-information, competitive price p^c can be broken: *The full-information, competitive price equilibrium is not an equilibrium when consumers have limited information about price and positive search costs.*

Is all stands charging p^* an equilibrium? No, that proposed equilibrium can also be broken, as we can show by using the same type of argument. If a deviant stand raises its price to $p^{**} = p^* + \epsilon = p^c + 2\epsilon$, it is not worthwhile for a tourist unlucky enough to enter that stand to search further. Thus, p^* is not the equilibrium price. Along similar lines, all stands charging p^{**} cannot be an equilibrium.

So what is the equilibrium price? We know that the equilibrium price cannot be less than p^c, because firms would lose money selling for less than the full-information, competitive price. Similarly, we have shown that it cannot be p^c or a price slightly above p^c because firms have an incentive to raise prices.

There is a remaining possibility that we have not rejected. If all stands charge the monopolistic price p^m, no stand would want to charge a higher price. *If there is a single price equilibrium, it can only be at* p^m. At prices below p^m, firms have an incentive to raise prices.

When Lisa learns the price at the souvenir stand, she decides whether to buy. If the price is set too high, the stand loses sales and hence profits (marginal revenues exceed marginal costs). Only when the price is set so that the stand's marginal revenue equals its marginal cost, the monopolistic price, is its profit maximized. Even if the stand could charge a higher price without losing all its sales, it has no incentive to do so.

The only remaining question is whether a stand would like to charge a lower price than p^m if all other stands are charging p^m. If not, then p^m is the single-price equilibrium. If it does want to charge a lower price, there is no single-price equilibrium.

It can pay a deviant stand to lower its price only if the decrease is substantial enough to induce consumers to search for this low-price stand.[9] If search costs are c, and if the stand lowers its price by less than c, then consumers have no incentive to search for this low-price stand. Thus, the stand makes less on each sale, and its profits must fall. It may pay, however, for a stand to deviate by dropping its price by more than c. If there are few stands, consumers may search for this low-price stand. Although the stand makes less per sale than the high-price stands, its profits may be higher due to greater volume. Here, there is no single-price equilibrium.

If there are many stands, consumers do not search for the low-price stand because their chances of finding it are slight. As a result, when a large number of stands makes searching for a low-price stand impractical, the proposed single-price equilibrium at p^m is an equilibrium.[10]

Reducing Search Costs: Can reducing search costs lower the equilibrium price? Strangely, the equilibrium price does not change as long as search costs are positive and there is a single-price equilibrium.

Suppose that the government or a private firm sells firm-specific price information. As a result, the cost of search (learning the price at a single store) falls from c to $c/2$. We can repeat the previous analysis because nothing depends on the size of c, as long as c is positive. A deviant firm can still raise its price by $\epsilon < c/2$ and break any proposed single-price equilibrium at a price less than p^m.

Thus, *lowering search costs has no effect on the single-price equilibrium until search costs fall to zero.*[11] If search costs fall to zero, consumers have full information, so the only possible equilibrium is at p^c, which equals marginal cost.

Nonexistence of the Single-Price Equilibrium: Where search costs are positive, can the proposed single-price equilibrium where all firms charge the monopolistic price p^m be broken? The answer depends on the shape of consumer demand curves, the number of firms in the industry, and the search costs.

As already noted, if the number of firms is small, the single price equilibrium at p^m may be broken by firms cutting price. An even more striking result is that, for demand curves of certain shapes, consumers visit no stores and buy nothing if firms charge p^m. The market does not exist (Stiglitz 1979, 340). Suppose that each tourist wants at most one mug and will buy the mug only if the price is no more than p^u. That is, a

---

[9]We continue to use the assumption of the model that consumers know the distribution of prices but not which particular stand has the lowest price. This latter assumption is, of course, unrealistic if there are only a few stands.

[10]It may be possible for firms to advertise that they have low prices and thereby overcome the high search-cost problem, as discussed in the next chapter.

[11]See, however, Stahl (1989), who presents a model in which oligopolistic pricing varies smoothly between marginal cost pricing and monopoly pricing as the search cost changes.

tourist's demand curve is a vertical line at a quantity of 1 up to a price p^{u}. Given this demand curve, $p^{m} = p^{u}$.

To go to even one stand, a consumer must incur a search cost, c. As a result, the full cost of a mug, the price plus the search cost, is $p^{m} + c$. Thus, the full cost of shopping for the mug, $p^{m} + c = p^{u} + c$, exceeds the maximum value the consumer places on the mug, p^{u}, so the consumer does not shop at all!

In attempting to take advantage of the tourists, the souvenir stands set their prices so high that consumers do not find it worthwhile to shop. Thus, if consumers have this type of demand curve, p^{m} is not an equilibrium, and there is no single-price equilibrium.

If no single price equilibrium exists, the only possible equilibrium is for firms to charge different prices. In this simple tourist-trap model, however, the lowest-price firm has an incentive to raise its price by the reasoning above. Thus, there is no possible multiple-price equilibrium; there may be no equilibrium. We discuss multiple-price equilibria in a more complicated model after the following examination of the effects of entry.

Free Entry. With a small number of stands, each of which charges the monopoly price, each one may earn large profits. If there are no barriers to entry, these profits attract new stands. As new stands enter the industry, the number of tourists going to any one souvenir stand falls, and profits fall. Entry continues until profits are driven to zero. A *monopolistically competitive* equilibrium results: Price is above marginal cost, but each firm's profits are zero.[12]

In contrast to a market where consumers have full information, the additional entry does not necessarily lower price if consumers have limited information. Additional entrants must sink some costs (buy a souvenir stand), so society can be worse off with free entry: Consumers do not gain from entry, all monopoly profits are dissipated in excess entry (firms earn zero profits), and social expenditures on sunk costs rise.

Indeed, under certain circumstances, reducing the number of firms may increase *effective* competition. For example, if there is a large number of firms, it does not pay for any one firm to cut its price from p^{m}. If several stands merge to form a chain of souvenir stands and collectively lower prices, however, they may be able to induce individuals to search for one of the stands in this low-price chain (Stiglitz 1979, 340). Thus, by reducing the number of independent stands (though not necessarily the number of souvenir stands), effective competition may be increased and price lowered.

This reasoning suggests a result that is the exact opposite of that for a market where consumers have full information. *With imperfect consumer information,* competition may be socially wasteful because of entry costs, so that *welfare may rise as the number of firms falls.*[13]

[12]If consumers' demand curves are downward sloping, the equilibrium resembles that of the standard monopolistically competitive industry. Price is above marginal cost (at the quantity where marginal revenue equals marginal cost), and the demand curve is tangent to the average cost curve (so that profits are zero).

[13]Some of the surprising results of the tourist-trap model change when there are repeated transactions. We discuss the roles of repeated transactions and reputations in more detail in the next chapter.

★The Tourists-and-Natives Model

If it's tourist season, why can't we shoot them? —*Steven Wright*

Our analysis of the tourist-trap model raises two questions about markets in which consumers have limited information about price. First, is there a model in which a multiple-price equilibrium is possible? That is, is there an equilibrium where stores charge different prices for the identical good so that there is a **price dispersion**? Second, if some consumers are fully informed, even though others have limited information, can there be a full-information equilibrium where price equals marginal cost?

Both questions can be examined by modifying the tourist-trap model so that there are two types of consumers. A persistent price dispersion requires that at least some consumers be unable or unwilling to learn which stands charge the low price.[14] The discussion below shows that where some consumers are fully informed and others have limited information, there is either a multiple-price equilibrium (Example 13.6) or a single-price equilibrium at marginal cost.

Consider a market in which all firms have identical costs, but there are two types of consumers with different search costs. Natives are *informed* consumers and have zero search costs. They know the entire distribution of prices in the market. Tourists are *uninformed* consumers who have search costs of c. For example, natives in a town might know the prices charged by each restaurant, but a tourist has to spend time (search costs) to learn the price at any given restaurant.

Natives buy only at low-price stores. Thus, even if tourists do not know the distribution of prices charged by different stores, the shopping behavior of the natives may drive the market price to the full-information, competitive price p^c. For price to be driven to marginal cost, there must be a substantial number of knowledgeable consumers.

In a rigorous version of this model, Salop and Stiglitz (1977) show that with many informed and many uninformed consumers, a single, competitive-price equilibrium may exist, but it is also possible that there is a single-price equilibrium at a higher price, or a multiple-price equilibrium. To illustrate their result, we add the following assumptions:

- Of the L consumers in this market, the natives, αL, are informed and the tourists, $(1 - \alpha)L$, are uninformed.
- Each consumer buys 1 unit of the good as long as the price is no higher than p^u.
- There are n firms.

[14]Stigler (1961) shows that if there is a price dispersion, consumers search for low prices, and that if the search is costly, they do not conduct sufficient searches to learn the entire price distribution. A number of papers present models where firms have different costs, and random changes affect the market so that the store with the lowest price keeps changing, and hence consumers cannot easily learn the identity of the low-cost store in a given period. The explanation that follows assumes that the firms have identical cost functions and there are no random changes. See Reinganum (1979) for an analysis where firms' costs differ.

EXAMPLE 13.6 *Price Dispersion*

Prices for many goods vary substantially across stores. Some of the variation reflects differences in the stores' characteristics, such as location. The rest of the price dispersion reflects an individual store's pricing strategies (including temporary sales).

Price variations vary by goods and across cities. We calculated the ratio of the highest to the lowest observed price during 1999 for a large (67.6 oz.) bottle of Coca-Cola and for a large (64 oz.) container of Tropicana Pure Premium orange juice. The table shows how this ratio varies across grocery stores and the number of stores for which we have data by city.

	Coke		Tropicana Orange Juice	
City	Ratio	Stores	Ratio	Stores
Atlanta	1.6	6	1.3	6
Boston	1.6	3	1.3	3
Cedar Rapids, IA	1.6	12	1.4	12
Chicago	1.9	8	2.0	8
Detroit	1.1	3	1.0	3
Denver	1.8	4	1.4	4
Eau Claire, WI	6.4	11	1.9	8
Grand Junction, CO	1.5	10	1.5	10
Houston	2.0	7	1.3	3
Kansas City	1.5	6	1.4	6
Los Angeles	1.6	8	1.6	8
Memphis	1.3	5	1.4	5
Midland, TX	2.9	9	1.4	7
Minneapolis/St. Paul	1.6	3	1.7	3
New York	2.2	8	1.5	8
Philadelphia	1.8	3	1.4	3
Pittsburgh	1.9	3	1.8	5
Pittsfield, MA	1.6	12	1.6	7
Rome, GA	1.4	3	1.2	3
St. Louis	1.3	7	1.7	7
San Francisco/Oakland	2.2	4	1.7	4
Seattle/Tacoma	2.8	5	1.6	3
Tampa/St. Petersburg	1.6	3	1.4	3
Visalia, CA	2.5	16	1.6	10

Maynes and Assum (1982) found that consumers' perception of the degree of price dispersion was most accurate for items with relatively small actual price dispersion, such as many food items and heating oil. Consumers tended to underestimate the spread of prices for high-dispersion items such as consumer durables.

Sources: Maynes and Assum (1982) and authors' calculations.

This model has several possible equilibria, such as the full-information, competitive price equilibrium and a two-price equilibrium. Under what circumstances can the full-information, competitive price equilibrium be broken? In this proposed equilibrium, all firms set the same price p^c, and each is assumed to obtain an equal share of the consumers, so it sells $q^c = L/n$ units of output. Suppose that a deviant firm raises its price to $p^* = p^c + \epsilon$. By the same reasoning as in the tourist-trap model, this firm obtains no informed customers but still gets its share of uninformed customers, as long as $\epsilon < c$. Thus, the firm's sales fall to $(1 - \alpha)q^c$.

Many Informed Consumers. If there are many informed consumers, it does not pay for a firm to deviate by raising its price above p^c. As shown in Figure 13.1, the demand curve facing the deviant firm consists of four parts. If the firm's price is above p^u, its sales are zero.[15] If its price is between p^u and p^c, it sells $q^u = (1 - \alpha)q^c$ units, because it loses all its informed customers. If its price equals p^c, its sales are q^c. If its price is slightly below p^c, all the informed consumers shop there as well as its share of the uninformed consumers, so its sales are $\alpha L + (1 - \alpha)q^c$. The deviant is uninterested in charging less than p^c, because that price is below its average cost, so that it makes negative profits.

With the demand curve as shown in Figure 13.1, it does not pay for the deviant to raise its price, because it loses money. Although it receives more per sale ($p^u > p^c$), it makes so few sales that its costs exceed its revenues: At q^u, its average cost is above p^u.

The proposed equilibrium at p^c cannot be broken. There are so many informed consumers that a store charging more than p^c loses so much business that it loses money. Thus, *if there are enough informed consumers, all consumers are charged the full-information, competitive equilibrium price.*

Few Informed Consumers. In contrast, if there are relatively few informed consumers, a deviant firm can raise its price without losing many customers. Let q^a be the quantity such that the average cost equals p^u, $AC(q^a) = p^u$, as Figure 13.2 shows. It pays for a firm to deviate if $q^u = (1 - \alpha)L/n = (1 - \alpha)q^c > q^a$ or

$$\alpha < 1 - \frac{q^a}{q^c}. \tag{13.1}$$

In Figure 13.2, at q^u the deviant firm's average cost is less than p^u, so it makes a profit if it charges p^u. Because the firm would earn zero profit at p^c, it has an incentive to raise its price. Thus, *if there are relatively few informed consumers* (α is relatively small),

[15] It is implicitly assumed in Figure 13.1 that the deviant raises its price to p^u. As explained in the discussion of the tourist-trap model, the deviant charges ϵ more than the price other firms are charging, or p^u (the maximum price a consumer is willing to pay), whichever is less. For it to be profitable for the deviant firm to charge p^u, search costs, c, must be large enough that $p^c + c \geq p^u$.

FIGURE 13.1 Single-Price Market

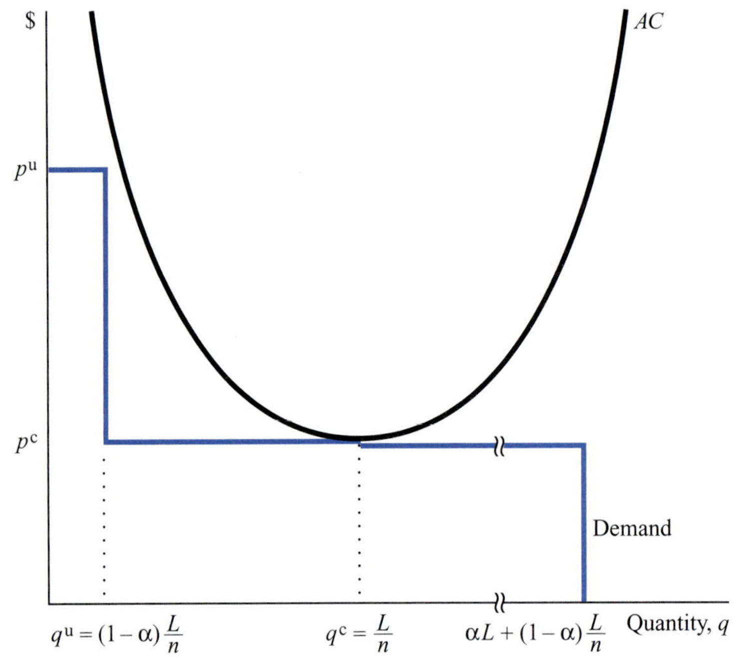

it pays to deviate, and *the proposed full-information, competitive price equilibrium is broken.* Equation 13.1 shows that the number of informed consumers needed to produce a single-price equilibrium depends on the shape of the average cost curve and the maximum price consumers are willing to pay, p^u.

There cannot be an equilibrium where all firms charge p^u. A firm can lower its price to any amount less than p^u and obtain all the informed consumers. It profits because it has more sales at a price that is almost as high as p^u.

Can there be a multiple-price equilibrium? Given our assumptions, a *two-price equilibrium is possible, but there cannot be an equilibrium with more than two prices.*

Suppose that there is a three-price equilibrium with some stores charging $p^1 = p^u$; others charging p^2, $p^u > p^2 > p^c$; and the rest charging $p^3 = p^c$. The stores charging p^2 make no sales to informed customers. They have, on average, the same number of uninformed customers as stores charging p^u, but they make less money than those stores. As a result, if a store charging p^2 raises its price, it loses no customers and earns higher profits, so that this proposed three-price equilibrium can be broken.[16] Thus, it does not make sense for a store to charge less than p^u and more than p^c.

[16]This reasoning holds even if $p^1 < p^u$ and $p^3 > p^c$.

FIGURE 13.2 Breaking the Single-Price Equilibrium

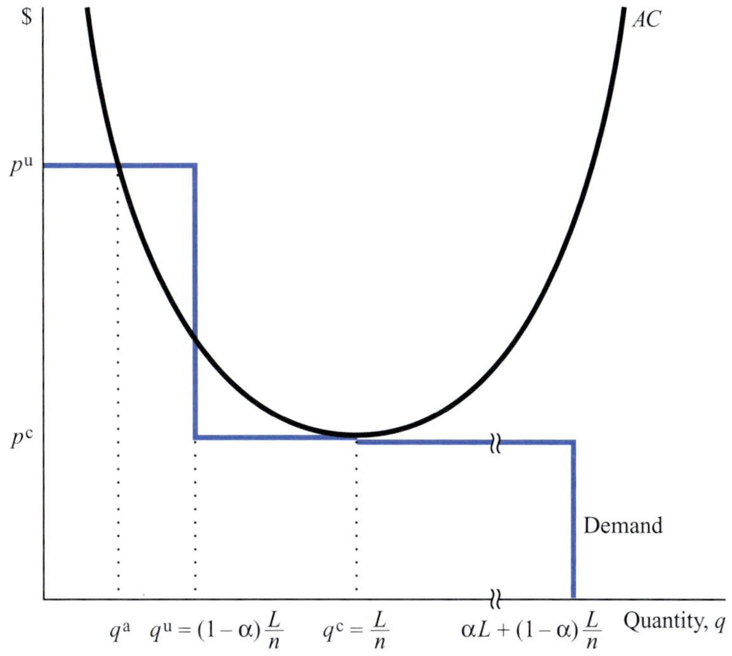

By similar reasoning, we also can reject equilibria with even more prices. Thus, the only possible multiprice equilibrium is a two-price equilibrium.[17]

If there is a two-price equilibrium, the low-price firms charge p^c and the high-price firms charge p^u. All the informed customers shop at the low-price stores, and the uninformed consumers shop randomly. Thus, the low-price stores' share of the market is greater than the proportion of informed consumers.[18] Appendix 13A calculates the number of firms in the equilibrium and the fraction of each type of firm.

[17]With other, less restrictive assumptions, there may be many different prices in a market. For example, if consumers know about some but not all firms, firms may charge a full range of prices (Butters 1977). Rothschild (1974) provides a good survey of search theories, which explain price distributions. Where there are many prices charged, as the number of firms increases, the cost of obtaining information may rise. As a result, some firms may charge higher prices as new firms enter. A study of the prices of primary-care physicians' services in 92 metropolitan areas concludes that factors that increase search costs, such as the number of providers, increase average prices (Pauly and Satterthwaite 1981).

[18]Thus, consumers who go to large stores and buy brands with large shares of the market may be acting rationally (Smallwood and Conlisk 1979). If uninformed consumers observe market shares, they become informed. It is possible, however, that if consumers use share as a signal, then the first entrant in a market may maintain its high share solely as a result of its historical monopoly rather than its superior product.

All firms must make the same profits, or a firm has an incentive to change its pricing policy. The low-price stores make zero profits because $p^c = AC(q^c)$, as Figure 13.3 shows. Thus, in equilibrium, the high-price stores must also make zero profits. Suppose instead that they make positive profits (as Figure 13.2 shows). Then, either new firms enter the market as high-price stores, or low-price stores start charging high prices. As the number of high-price stores increases, each one sells less (as the uninformed consumers are spread over more stores). The number of high-price stores increases until profits are driven to zero when each firm is charging its profit-maximizing price, as Figure 13.3 shows.

To summarize, where only a relatively small number of customers are informed, there may be a two-price, monopolistically competitive equilibrium.[19] The low-price stores charge a price equal to marginal cost (the full-information, competitive price),

FIGURE 13.3 Two-Price Equilibrium

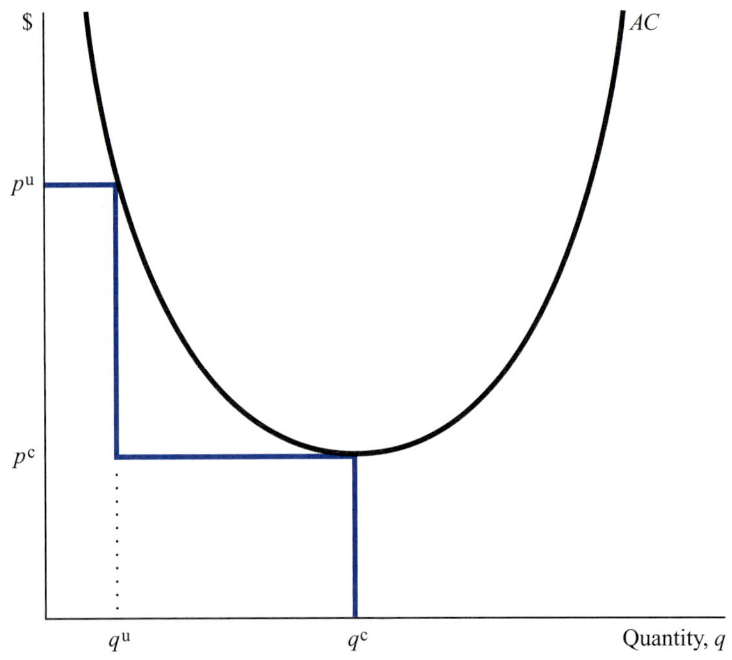

[19]Albrecht, Lang, and Vroman (2002) extend this result to examine the price and quality effects of increasing the fraction of fully informed consumers. In equilibrium there may be three firm types: high-price/high-quality, low-price/low-quality, and high-price/low-quality. The last of these takes advantage of the uninformed by mimicking the high-quality firm's price, but provides low quality. Increasing the share of informed customers harms the uninformed by altering the mix of firms.

and the high-price stores charge their profit-maximizing price. See Example 13.7. Both types of stores make zero profits in equilibrium because of entry. All the informed consumers and some of the uninformed consumers shop at the low-price stores, so these stores have a disproportionately large share of the market. In **www.aw-bc.com/carlton_perloff** "Monopoly Price Dispersion," we show that a monopoly may create *noise* in a market—charging different prices for nearly identical products or for the same product at different stores—as a means of sorting consumers so as to price discriminate.

Providing Consumer Information Lowers Price

It is a great nuisance that knowledge can only be acquired by hard work. It would be fine if we could swallow the powder of profitable information made palatable by the jam of fiction. —*W. Somerset Maugham*

It seems intuitively obvious that providing consumers with comparative price information should lower the average price observed in the market. Yet, as the tourist-trap model shows, lowering the cost of search has no effect as long as the cost is positive. That result may not be as perplexing as it first appears because merely decreasing the cost of search does not provide consumers with extra information. Indeed, in the tourist-trap equilibrium, no further searches occur when the costs of search are lowered, so consumer information does not increase.

An information program that actually provides consumers with comparative price information may, then, have an effect where merely lowering the cost of search does not. The following discussion first summarizes theoretical arguments that supplying more consumer information results in a lowered equilibrium price and then presents some empirical evidence that supports this conclusion.

How Information Lowers Prices

At least two types of models show that improving information can lower prices. First, as the tourists-and-natives model with many firms shows, as more consumers become informed, the market share of low-price firms increases. Indeed, as most consumers become informed, all stores charge the low, competitive price. A second model described at **www.aw-bc.com/carlton_perloff** "Information and Price Dispersion" shows that, where information is provided that allows consumers to better estimate true prices, the average price may fall. This latter model explains the existence of a single-price equilibrium, where the price lies between the monopolistic and the full-information, competitive price (marginal cost).

In the second model, consumers, who want to shop at the lowest-price store but do not know which store has the lowest prices, gather information. They collect information by visiting various stores, reading advertisements, watching commercials, and asking friends (see Example 13.7). Consumers form estimates based on available information

EXAMPLE 13.7 *Tourist Cameras*

Many economists predicted that the Internet, by providing consumers with low-cost searches through the use of shop-bots (Web sites that compare prices across firms), would lead to competitive pricing for many manufactured goods. Unfortunately, this prediction has not panned out so far.

If electronic markets were highly competitive, we would expect either one price or perhaps a trade-off between price and services or fees. We would anticipate that firms that provide extra service, offer guarantees, or charge low shipping rates and other fees would set higher prices to cover their extra costs. But neither hypothesis is true for a popular Olympus digital camera or a Hewlett-Packard flatbed scanner (Baylis and Perloff 2002).

Indeed, it appears that there are "good" firms and "bad" firms out there in the ether. Good firms offer both low prices and superior services, while bad firms charge higher prices and provide fewer services and guarantees.

For example, for the Olympus digital camera, sites that provide a return guarantee—an unconditional offer to return the good for a refund—charged about $42 less than firms that did not. Moreover, many of the high-price sites charged lump-sum handling fees and membership fees—an average of $11.66 for the camera—that were not charged by the low-price firms.

This outcome is consistent with the Salop-Stiglitz (1977) model showing that firms may charge informed and uninformed consumers different prices. Some uninformed customers (tourists) in the 2002 study have a positive cost of searching for the lowest-price firm in that they do not know how to use shop-bots, while informed customers (natives) face virtually no cost to search. If there are enough uninformed customers, some firms will charge high prices and make relatively few sales to uninformed customers, while other firms will charge low prices and sell to informed customers and lucky uninformed customers.

Indeed, some Web sites appear to be designed to make searching costly. On one Web page, the potential customer chooses "cameras," on another page the brand, and on yet another page a specific model. Some sites require going through as many as nine pages to reach a particular camera. One possible explanation is unintentional bad design. An alternative explanation is that the site was purposely designed to select for those customers with low search costs or low time preference. Such a practice makes sense if the firm charges those customers a low price and charges a higher price at another site that is easier to search. Indeed, many firms have multiple sites under differing firm names. On sites where it takes more than three pages to get to the desired product from the home page, firms charged $48.25 less for the Olympus camera.

of the prices at each store and then choose the store they estimate has the lowest price (Perloff and Salop 1986).

Because consumers do not know the prices exactly, however, a store may raise its price without losing all its customers. That is, the demand curve facing each store changes from being perfectly elastic under full information to being less elastic under limited consumer information. As consumers become more knowledgeable, the demand curve facing a firm becomes more elastic. Thus, if consumers gain more information, prices may fall.

An Example: Grocery Store Information Programs

Does providing consumers with information increase the market shares of relatively low-price stores, lower the average market price, and reduce the variance in prices across stores? A 1974 experiment by the Food Price Review Board of Canada was designed to answer these questions for grocery stores.[20]

There were three phases in the experiment. During Phase 1 (a 17-week period), supermarket price information was collected in both the control city, Winnipeg, and the experimental city, Ottawa-Hull. Only during Phase 2 (a 5-week period) was the information on grocery store prices in Ottawa-Hull published in newspapers and mailed to some consumers, whose behavior was then monitored in detail. At no time was price information disseminated in the control city, Winnipeg. In the final phase (6 weeks), price information was again collected in both cities but not disseminated.

Average food prices declined in Ottawa-Hull by 1.5% during the first week of Phase 2, by 3.0% the following week, and then remained steady for the next three weeks. During the first week following the end of Phase 2, prices dropped an additional 2.5%. Thus, the total decline over this 6-week period was 7.1%. Prices in the control market declined by 0.6% during Phase 2. Thus, prices in the experimental city fell relative to prices in the control city by 6.5% during the 6-week period that included the first week of Phase 3 (see Figure 13.4).

During the experimental period, prices at the higher-price stores (and chains) fell more than those at initially low-price stores. The difference in price index levels between high- and low-price stores dropped from a maximum of 15% during the preinformation period to a low of 5.4% at one point in Phase 2. The difference for chains fell from a maximum of 7.3% to a low of 3.1%. The average range of prices during the 12-week period prior to the information program was 9.71% compared to 7.83% during Phase 2.

A consumer survey found that 43% of the consumers in the test market indicated that they had changed stores as a direct result of the comparative price program. As a result of this shift, the top four corporate chains increased their share of the market from 74% to 81%. Lower-priced chains increased their share relative to others.

Average retail food prices in the test market began to rise within two weeks after the termination of the information program and increased 8.8% by the end of the research period. One interpretation of these results is that during the information period, a once-and-for-all drop in average prices occurred. With the end of the information program, prices increased to their preinformation levels. It appears that stores realized that the experiment would be short-lived and were particularly aggressive in trying to

---

[20]Devine and Marion (1979) and Devine (1978). Lesser and Bryant (1980) critique Devine and Marion (1979), who respond in Devine and Marion (1980).

FIGURE 13.4 Consumer Price Index for Food Consumed at Home, May 1974–March 1975 (May 1974 = 100)

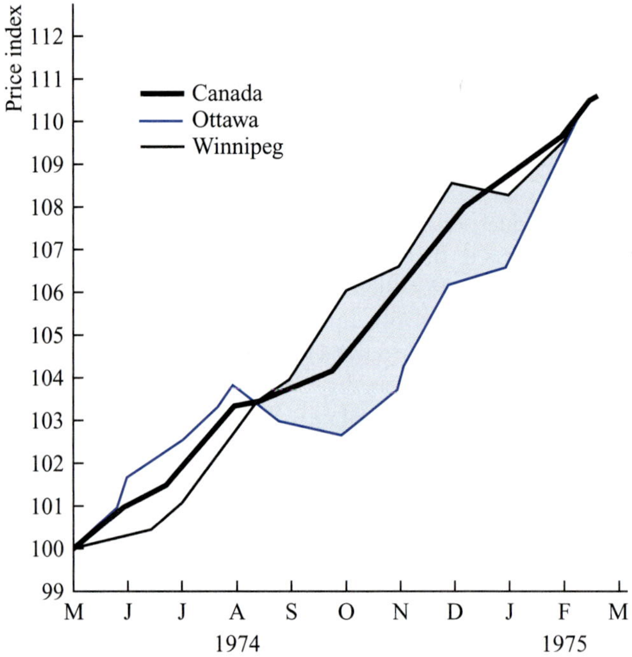

Note: Observations are made once a month during the first two weeks of each month.

Source: Devine and Marion (1979) from Statistics Canada.

convince consumers that they had relatively low prices while the program was in effect. Apparently, to maintain low prices, information must be continuously supplied.

A back-of-the-envelope calculation of the welfare gain (the change in the sum of consumer surplus plus profits) indicates that it could significantly exceed the costs of collecting the information. The basic results of this experiment were largely duplicated in another experiment conducted in the province of Saskatchewan in October 1975 to determine the long-run effects of an information program (Devine 1978).

A similar experiment was conducted in the United States by Purdue University and the U.S. Department of Agriculture in four pairs of U.S. cities (Boynton et al. 1981, McCracken, Boynton, and Blake 1982). Relative prices declined by 0.2 to 3.7 percent in the experimental compared to the control markets. In three of the four experimental cities, a statistically significant decline in the prices of the 26 items, which were individually reported, was found. In all four experimental cities, a statistically significant decline in the total (100-item) index was found.[21]

Thus, a number of studies have shown that providing consumers with information can lower average price. When the information programs are ended, however, the average price tends to rise to its original level. Providing information to consumers may increase welfare (see **www.aw-bc.com/carlton-perloff,** "Warnings that Affect Markets" and "Cost-Benefit Analysis of Providing More Accurate Information").

SUMMARY

There are five major results from models in which consumers have limited information about quality or prices. First, if consumers have limited information about the quality of a product, either there is no market or, where the market exists, quality levels are usually lower than the levels produced if consumers have full information. Expert information, reputation, standards, and certification may provide consumers with information about quality and hence rectify these problems; however, standard setters can behave anticompetitively.

Second, where consumers have limited information about prices, no equilibrium may exist or, if it exists, even small firms may set prices above marginal costs. In this sense, the law of supply and demand does not hold. Indeed, with this type of limited information, it is possible for welfare to be higher with fewer firms than with many.

Third, when some consumers know the prices at all stores and others must incur search costs to determine the price at any given store, two types of equilibria are possible. If there are enough informed consumers, the equilibrium price equals marginal cost. If there are relatively few informed consumers, a two-price equilibrium is likely, where some stores charge a high price and others charge marginal cost, even though the good is homogeneous. The law of a single price does not hold.

Fourth, with differently informed consumers, price discrimination is possible. A monopoly may charge different prices at its different stores in order to price discriminate between informed and uninformed consumers.

Fifth, lowering the cost of gathering information may not lower average prices. For example, in a single-price equilibrium, reducing search costs for all consumers may have no effect. In contrast, providing consumers with the location of the lowest-price store is likely to lower average price.

Thus, markets with limited information differ from those with perfect information. Providing information or lowering the cost of obtaining information may not always increase welfare when the costs of providing the information or lowering the search

[21]Perhaps the strongest evidence that this information program had an effect is that a number of stores covered in this study banned the price reporters (Don Yaeger, "U.S. Price Study Goes on Despite Two-City 'Lockout,' " *Supermarket News*, February 11, 1980:1). In some cities, the indexes were challenged by the stores (Don Yaeger, "Purdue Price Study to Be Ended Early," *Supermarket News*, February 25, 1980:1, 34).

costs are taken into account. The next chapter examines the incentives of individual firms to inform or misinform consumers by using advertising and the effects of such advertising.

PROBLEMS

1. Explain why the first-year depreciation of new cars is so high. (If you buy a new car and try to sell it in the first year—indeed, in the first few days after you buy it—the price that you get is substantially less than the original price.)
2. Suppose that there are two types of firms. All firms have U-shaped average cost curves, where n firms have average costs of $AC(q)$ and m firms have average cost curves of $AC(q) + k$. There are two types of consumers: The natives have zero search costs, and the tourists have very high search costs. Describe the resulting equilibrium.
3. Suppose that two economists write a textbook. Their publisher offers them royalties on sales of the book equal to α percent of the sales revenue. The economists are concerned. They believe that such a royalty system causes the publisher to sell less than the joint profit-maximizing number of copies of the book. Demonstrate this reasoning. They believe that a royalty in the form of a lump-sum payment, L, or δ percent of profits does not cause the publisher to publish too few books. Why do they agree to the α percent royalty? *Hint:* One explanation concerns asymmetric information on the part of the publisher concerning costs of publication.
4. Determine the equilibrium prices, quantities, and number of high- and low-price stores in the tourists-and-natives model if consumers have downward-sloping, linear demand curves: $q = a - bp$, where a and b are positive constants.
5. A firm spends a large amount on advertising that informs consumers of the brand name of its bananas. Should consumers conclude that its bananas are likely to be of higher quality than unbranded bananas? Why or why not?

Answers to odd-numbered problems are given at the back of the book.

SUGGESTED READINGS

Two nontechnical papers that give a good overview of many of the issues covered in this chapter are Salop (1978) and Beales, Craswell, and Salop (1981). More technical articles on uncertainty, information, and welfare are Colantoni, Davis, and Swaminuthan (1965), Allen (1981), and Kahnemann, Slovic, and Tversky (1982). Important work on the value of information includes Lave (1963), Gould (1974), and Antonovitz and Roe (1986). Work on search and strategic behavior by firms includes Wilde and Schwartz (1979) and Varian (1980). The role of information in oligopolistic or monopolistic competition is discussed in Shapiro (1982), Wolinsky (1986), and Ross (1988). Stiglitz (1989) provides an excellent survey of the pre-1990 literature.

APPENDIX 13A

Market Shares in the Tourists-and-Natives Model

In the two-price equilibrium in the tourists-and-natives model, the low-price stores, β fraction of the n stores, charge p^c and sell q^c, whereas the high-price stores, $1 - \beta$ fraction, charge p^u and sell q^u. The high-price stores only sell to their share of the $(1 - \alpha)L$ uninformed consumers, $(1 - \alpha)L(1 - \beta)$, so each high-price firm sells

$$q^u = \frac{(1 - \alpha)L(1 - \beta)}{n(1 - \beta)} = \frac{(1 - \alpha)L}{n}. \tag{13A.1}$$

The share of total sales of a high-price store is

$$1 - \beta = \frac{q^u}{L} = \frac{1 - \alpha}{n}. \tag{13A.2}$$

Each low-price store sells to its share of the αL informed consumers and to its share of the $(1 - \alpha)L\beta$ uninformed consumers who are lucky enough to find a low-price store:

$$q^c = \frac{\alpha L + (1 - \alpha)L\beta}{n\beta}. \tag{13A.3}$$

The share of total sales of a low-price store is

$$\beta = \frac{q^c}{L} = \frac{\alpha + (1 - \alpha)\beta}{n\beta}. \tag{13A.4}$$

In equilibrium, the low-price stores get all the informed consumers and some of the uninformed consumers (the lucky tourists), so their share of the market is greater than the proportion of informed consumers: $\beta > \alpha$.

In equilibrium, the low-price and high-price firms make zero profit due to entry. Let q^a be the quantity at which average cost equals p^u. In equilibrium, $q^a = q^u$, so that

$$q^a = \frac{(1 - \alpha)L}{n}. \tag{13A.5}$$

Similarly, q^A is the quantity at which average cost equals p^c, so

$$q^{\mathrm{A}} = q^{\mathrm{c}} = \frac{\alpha L + (1 - \alpha)L\beta}{n\beta}. \tag{13A.6}$$

Thus, q^{a} and q^{A}, Equations 13A.5 and 13A.6, are two equations in two unknowns, β and n. Solving Equation 13A.5 for n yields

$$n = \frac{(1 - \alpha)L}{q^{\mathrm{a}}}. \tag{13A.7}$$

Substituting from Equation 13A.7 into 13A.6 and rearranging terms,

$$\beta = \frac{\alpha q^{\mathrm{a}}}{(1 - \alpha)(q^{\mathrm{A}} - q^{\mathrm{a}})}. \tag{13A.8}$$

The two-price equilibrium is characterized by n and β (Equations 13A.7 and 13A.8). The βn low-price stores sell $q^{\mathrm{A}} = q^{\mathrm{c}}$ (Equation 13A.6) units at p^{c}, and the $(1 - \beta)n$ high-price stores sell $q^{\mathrm{a}} = q^{\mathrm{u}}$ (Equation 13A.5) at p^{u}.

CHAPTER 14

Advertising and Disclosure

Advertisements contain the only truth to be relied on in a newspaper.
—*Thomas Jefferson*

Advertising is a racket . . . its constructive contribution to humanity is exactly minus zero.
—*F. Scott Fitzgerald*

Advertising has many purposes. An advertisement may inform consumers that a firm has a new product or the lowest price, or it may help to differentiate the firm's product from that of its rivals. A firm uses advertisements to inform consumers of its product's strengths but not its weaknesses. Firms grudgingly disclose some facts to consumers, enthusiastically advertise other claims, and hide yet other product attributes. This chapter examines the motives for advertising and for truthful or untruthful disclosure.

In 2003, Microsoft spent nearly one-fifth of a billion dollars on a single advertising campaign to induce users to upgrade to its latest version of Microsoft Office. As Table 14.1 shows, the firm with the highest advertising budget in the United States, General Motors, spent \$3.65 billion in 2002 to advertise automobiles and trucks. The second-largest advertiser, AOL Time Warner, spent \$2.92 billion to promote its media empire. Number 3, Procter & Gamble, dropped \$2.67 billion trying to induce customers to buy its soaps, cleaners, and other products. The U.S. government spent \$1.08 billion and was the 24th-largest advertiser.

Advertising as a percentage of sales varies widely, as Table 14.1 shows. For example, Verizon, the 14th-largest advertiser, allocated only 2.4 percent of its sales revenues to advertising, whereas L'Oreal, which is the 20th-largest advertiser, spent 26.3 percent.

U.S. advertisers account for more than half of the world's advertising expenditures (53.7 percent). Total expenditures on advertising in the United States are

TABLE 14.1 **Twenty-five Leading National Advertisers**

	Rank	U.S. Advertising in 2002 ($ millions)	Advertising as a Percentage of U.S. Revenue (%)
Automotive			
Daimler Chrysler	6	2,032	2.8
Ford Motor	5	2,252	2.1
General Motors	1	3,652	2.6
Honda	18	1,193	3.1
Toyota	13	1,553	3.0
Electronic and Office Equipment			
Sony	11	1,621	8.2
Entertainment and Media			
AOL Time Warner	2	2,923	9.0
Viacom	16	1,260	6.1
Walt Disney	7	1,803	8.7
Food, Restaurants, Soft Drinks			
Altria	17	1,206	2.7
McDonald's	15	1,336	24.6
Nestle	25	1,073	5.8
PepsiCo	21	1,114	6.7
Government			
U.S. government	24	1,083	n.a.
Personal Care			
L'Oreal	20	1,118	26.3
Procter & Gamble	3	2,673	12.6
Unilever	10	1,640	14.2
Pharmaceutical			
GlaxoSmithKline	12	1,554	9.7
Johnson & Johnson	8	1,799	8.0
Merck	19	1,158	2.4
Pfizer	4	2,566	12.4
Retail			
J. C. Penney	22	1,108	3.4
Sears, Roebuck	9	1,661	4.5
Telephone			
SBC Communications	23	1,092	2.5
Verizon	14	1,528	2.4

Source: Advertising Age Web site http://adage.com/dataplace/archives.

six times higher than in Japan (second place) and ten times more than in Germany (third place).[1]

Advertisers pay for television and radio broadcasts. It is hard to imagine life without Saturday morning cartoons supported by toy and cereal ads. Firms may also influence magazine and newspaper reporting by threatening to remove advertising.[2] Advertising may provide 50 percent of the revenues of magazines and 80 percent of newspapers. United States junk mail constitutes one out of every six pieces of mail worldwide.[3] Advertising on the Internet is increasing exponentially.

Another recent trend is to tie movie advertising campaigns with related products manufactured by other firms. Dr Pepper cans carried ads for the movie *X2: X-Men United.* Another film, *The Matrix Reloaded,* had promotional tie-ins with Coca-Cola (PowerAde), General Motors (Cadillac), Heineken, and Samsung. PowerAde sports drinks were sold in oddball bottles inspired by the movie. Movie makers also sell "product placements" to manufacturers—for a fee, a firm's product will be prominently displayed within the movie. According to Jeff Bell, vice president for the Jeep division, because scenes in the script for *Lara Croft Tomb Raider: The Cradle of Life* "show Lara using Jeeps as a tool for her to achieve her heroic, adventurous endeavors," Jeep signed a cross-marketing agreement with Paramount, the film's studio.[4]

Despite the pervasive role of advertising in our daily lives, standard models of competition ignore promotional efforts. This chapter incorporates those efforts into models of competitive and noncompetitive behavior.

We start our discussion by considering how product types affect the informational content of advertising, contrasting advertisements that inform with those that attempt to persuade without using many facts. Next we examine the profit-maximizing advertising level, and then we consider whether the profit-maximizing level of advertising is socially optimal. The effects of advertising on prices, entry barriers, and consumer welfare are described.

We then consider when firms advertise truthfully and when they lie, and discuss the optimal level of enforcement of truth-in-advertising laws. Finally, we analyze a firm's decision to disclose or hide information. Although a firm may have strong incentives to tell consumers about the high quality or low prices of its products, it may hesitate to disclose facts about weaknesses in those products, such as side effects and bad repair records. Indeed, as Chapter 13 shows, a firm may gain market power by reducing consumers' information. In many cases, however, it is in the firm's best interest to disclose information. Although truth-in-advertising laws encourage truthful disclosures, we show that mandatory disclosure laws may have a perverse effect.

---

[1] http://adv.asahi.com/english/market/advertising.html.

[2] A health magazine allegedly offered to report favorably on two diet products for $25,000 (Robert J. Samuelson, "The End of Advertising?" *Newsweek,* August 19, 1991:40).

[3] L. M. Boyd, "Grab Bag," *San Francisco Chronicle,* January 23, 1993:C20.

[4] Stuart Elliott, "Summer Movie Tie-Ins Coming Early and Often," *New York Times,* April 30, 2003:C1 and C5.

The four key points made in this chapter are

1. The purpose of promotion is to increase sales by shifting consumers' tastes or informing them of opportunities.
2. Although some types of advertising are harmful, many other types are welfare improving. Even where moderate advertising is helpful, however, there may be excessive advertising.
3. Skepticism by consumers discourages false advertising. Partial enforcement of antifraud laws may increase the amount of both truthful and false advertising.
4. When antifraud laws are fully enforced, firms generally have an incentive to disclose relevant information to consumers. Under some circumstances, however, mandatory disclosure laws reduce the extent of such disclosures.

Information and Advertising

Advertising may convey hard facts, make vague claims, or try to create a favorable impression of a product. Some advertisements list a store's prices. If consumers learn that a firm has the lowest prices in town, the demand for its products increases. In contrast, other advertisements merely show a product being used in a pleasant setting. An attractive person consuming a soft drink near a waterfall may convey to consumers the impression that this product is refreshing. By convincing consumers that its product has certain desirable traits, a firm can differentiate its product from others. As its product becomes differentiated, a firm may face a higher and less elastic demand curve, so that it can charge a higher price and earn greater profits (see Chapter 7). For example, one heavily promoted brand of bleach sells at a much higher price than many other physically identical bleaches.

Promotions

Advertising can be subtle and indirect or it can hit you over the head with its bluntness. Advertising is only one of many ways to promote a product; firms also use price discounts and sales staffs. When it is hard to describe a product, a firm may include a discount coupon in its advertisement to encourage consumers to try the product. In addition to advertising in newspapers, on radio, and on television, firms may advertise indirectly by establishing a brand name or otherwise establishing a positive reputation.

For example, some agricultural firms now sell their fruits and vegetables under brand names (Example 14.1). Unlike sellers of unbranded produce, these farmers are trying to develop a reputation for producing a particular (presumably high) quality of produce. Such branding can help overcome the "lemons" problem discussed in Chapter 13. Although this chapter concentrates on advertising, most of the discussion applies equally well to other types of promotions.

EXAMPLE 14.1

Branding and Labeling

Most fruits and vegetables are sold without a brand name. Consumers assume that a tomato is a tomato and that there is little variability in quality across firms. That is, these markets competitively provide perfectly homogeneous products. Recently, however, several firms (Natural Pak Produce Inc., Campbell Soup Co., and Dart & Kraft Inc.) have started selling branded tomatoes.

Consumers are willing to pay more for products that they believe are superior. Sunkist oranges, Dole pineapples, and Chiquita bananas have gross profit margins 10 percent to 60 percent higher than generic produce. When introduced, one brand of tomato sold at about $1 per pound, or 30¢ more than unbranded tomatoes.

There are risks associated with building a brand. Unless firms can provide better produce consistently, consumers may eventually hold a brand's name against it. After all, why pay more for a product that's no better than the unbranded produce? Further, even if consumers view the product as superior and pay a premium for it, the premium may not be high enough to cover the extra costs of producing higher quality and establishing a brand name. Castle & Cooke, Budd Co., and other smaller firms did not recoup their investment on branded cauliflower, grapes, and broccoli.

Similarly, labeling can be used to promote products. Consequently, producers will fight for the right to restrict the use of these names.

In 2003, the European Union (EU) listed 41 wines, cheeses, and other products that it wants protected by a global trade pact. The EU agricultural commissioner claimed that geographical indicators are a quality guarantee and prevent confusion among consumers. The EU accuses producers in other countries of abusing (using) the names of its delicacies. It wants to create a global register of geographically defined products that would prevent producers from other areas from using the names.

The United States and Canada are among other countries resisting this proposal, which would restrict products labeled as beaujolais, champagne, chianti, and medeira wines; feta, gorgonzola, and roquefort cheese; Parma ham and mortadella sausages; and others. Similarly, India wants to protect darjeeling tea, Sri Lanka defends its ceylon tea, and Guatemala claims its Antiguan coffee.

In some countries, local producers have registered these names as their trademarks. Italian Parma ham cannot be sold in Canada because the trademark "Parma ham" is reserved for a ham produced in Canada.

Sources: Christopher S. Eklund, "Will a Tomato by Any Other Name Taste Better?" *Business Week,* September 30, 1985:105; Naomi Koppel, Associated Press Worldstream, June 11, 2003.

"Search" Versus "Experience" Goods

The informational content of advertising depends on whether consumers can determine the quality of a product prior to purchase (Nelson 1970, 1974). If a consumer can establish a product's quality by inspection before purchase, the product has search qualities. Examples are furniture, clothing (determining style), and other products whose chief attributes can be determined by visual or tactile inspection. If a customer must consume the product to determine its quality, it is said to have experience qualities. Examples are processed foods, software programs, and psychotherapy.[5]

Advertising provides direct information about the characteristics of products with search qualities; advertisements for search products often include photographs. In some cases a consumer cannot directly observe a physical attribute, but it can be concisely described. For example, food and drink advertisements may claim that their products are low in calories. In contrast, for experience goods, the most important information may be conveyed simply by the presence of the advertising; some advertisers do little more than mention the name of the firm to enhance the firm's reputation. Such advertisers hope that consumers infer the quality or reputability of a firm by the frequency of its advertising and the expense involved: Fly-by-night firms may be less likely to advertise in expensive publications or on national television.

Some firms claim that all their products are excellent. Their advertisements contend that if you have experienced and liked one of their products, you will like all of them (Duncan Hines, Green Giant). Such advertisements may do little more than show the company's name; they do not describe the properties of each of its products. Alternatively, a firm may try to convince consumers that its product is different from and superior to other, similar brands—that is, it may attempt to differentiate its product from competing brands (for example, Bayer vs. generic aspirin, Clorox vs. generic bleach, Coke vs. Pepsi, Tide vs. all other laundry detergents).

Informational Versus Persuasive Advertising

Some economists distinguish between informational advertising, which describes a product's objective characteristics, and persuasive advertising, which is designed to shift consumers' tastes. For example, informational advertising may cite the price of a product, compare the advertising store's price to its rivals' prices, describe the features of the product, or list its uses. Persuasive advertising may explicitly or implicitly make claims aimed to stimulate a purchase, such as "Smoke these cigarettes to look more mature and sexier."

Some companies may use persuasive advertising to try to change consumers' perceptions of their product (reposition their brand in product space) when they cannot truthfully change their informative advertising. For example, Dr Pepper's share of soft drinks grew by about a tenth in 1992 over 1991 when the firm altered the product's image. In the 1970s and 1980s, the brand's ads said that Dr Pepper was a misunder-

[5]Some economists identify a third category, in which the quality of some goods cannot be determined even after consumption. Darby and Karni (1973) call these *credence* goods. Examples include many repair services and medical care, where the consumer must rely on the provider's assurances that the work was done properly. See also Becker and Murphy (1993), who treat advertising as a complementary good to the consumed good, and Becker (1996), for an analysis of the formation of tastes.

stood beverage, and appealed to those consumers who wanted to stand out in a crowd and who craved "much more" than a cola. Not surprisingly, this policy relegated Dr Pepper to a narrow segment of the market. Then Dr Pepper discovered that many of its consumers were cola drinkers, and realized that by insulting colas they were attacking their own customers. They went from saying drink Dr Pepper because you don't like cola to saying drink it as an alternative to cola because you drink so much cola.

It seems reasonable that producers of search goods are more likely to use informational advertising and that experience-goods producers are more likely to use persuasive advertising, but this division is not perfect. The advertising/sales ratio for products classified as experience goods is three times greater than that for products classified as search goods, and the difference is statistically significant (Nelson 1974, 738–40). A possible inference is that images (used in persuasive advertising) are forgotten more quickly than facts (used in informative advertising). Thus, consumers may learn and remember that a particular good has fewer calories (is "less filling") in one or a few exposures to an advertisement, but may need to be bombarded with repeated exposures to be convinced that a product "tastes great."

Such empirical evidence must be viewed with caution, however, because it is difficult to classify products as either experience or search goods or as using either informational or persuasive advertising. If your younger brother's self-image depends on the need to be "cool" and he sees an ad showing a cool person such as a well-known actor or singer using a particular brand of sunglasses, he may interpret the advertisement as being informative (see Example 14.2).[6] It tells him and his friends that this particular brand of sunglasses is cool. You, on the other hand, may view such testimonial advertising as persuasive, having little informational content.

Profit-Maximizing Advertising

All advertising is designed to increase the demand for a firm's product whether facts are used or merely smoke and mirrors. An increase in informative or persuasive advertising expenditures from α to α' causes an outward shift of the demand curve facing a firm from $D(Q, \alpha)$ to $D(Q, \alpha')$, as shown in Figure 14.1.[7] The firm chooses its output, given its advertising expenditures, by setting its marginal revenue with respect to quantity, $MR(Q, \alpha)$, equal to its marginal cost, MC, which we assume equals average cost (for simplicity).[8]

The outward shift in the demand curve increases profits (not adjusted for advertising expenditures) for two reasons. First, profits increase by area B and area C because

[6]Celebrity endorsements have a long, proud history. Buffalo Bill Cody hawked Kickapoo Indian Oil in the mid-nineteenth century, and Honus Wagner allowed his autograph to be imprinted on a Louisville Slugger bat in 1905.

[7]The following analysis ignores the effects of the firm's advertising and quantity decisions on other firms. Empirical evidence suggests, however, that the amount of advertising is influenced by market structure (Weiss, Pascoe, and Martin 1983). Lambin (1976) finds that advertising by rivals lowers a firm's market share roughly by as much as its own advertising increases it. Dorfman and Steiner (1954) was one of the first articles to model advertising's effects on demand.

[8]That is, $MR(Q, \alpha) \equiv \partial R(Q, \alpha)/\partial Q$, where R, revenues, equals $D(Q, \alpha)Q$.

EXAMPLE 14.2 *Celebrity Endorsements*

The celebrity is a person who is known for his well-knownness.
—Daniel J. Boorstin

Do celebrity endorsements work? Certainly some advertisers believe they do, given how much they spend hiring well-known shills. Former high school basketball star LeBron James inked a four-year promotional deal with Nike for $100 million even before he started playing basketball for the Cleveland Cavaliers. A 1999 study at Illinois State University concluded that approximately one-fifth of all television advertising features a well-known individual from the worlds of sports, television, movies, or music.

However, academic and industry studies indicate that the effectiveness of celebrity ads is mixed. Industry lore suggests that celebrity ads are particularly effective in Japan, Korea, and Taiwan. Probably the biggest advertising battle in 2004 will be between two male-potency drugs, Levitra and Viagra, as former NFL coach Mike Ditka goes up against baseball slugger Rafael Palmeiro. In contrast, a third male-potency drug, Cialis, will not use a celebrity—instead, Lilly, the maker of Cialis, will stress that its drug lasts longer.

Firms can select from a range of celebrities with vastly different fees for ads and personal appearances. As of 2003, daytime stars (such as Kamar De Los Reyes and Kassie DePaiva) are often available for two- to three-hour personal appearances for between $5,000 and $10,000. Sports figures (such as Jim Palmer, Mike Ditka, and Mary Lou Retton) cost between $10,000 and $35,000, compared to some sports stars (Mark McGwire, Joe Montana, and Magic Johnson) whose time runs in the $50,000 to $100,000 range. Some television, film, and recording stars (Jennifer Aniston, Faith Hill, and Jim Carrey) may cost more than one-quarter of a million dollars.

Of course, when a firm builds an advertising campaign around a star and that star stumbles in public, the firm can be left with egg on its face, as Hertz found when O. J. Simpson was accused of murder. More subtly, Nike received bad press when its top representative, Tiger Woods, admitted that he was switching from his Nike golf club to a Titleist to improve his game. One way to reduce such risks of embarrassment is to use a group of celebrities. In Great Britain, Nike gathered some of the world's greatest soccer players for its campaign.

Sources: "Celebrity Scares," *Marketing Week*, August 7, 2003:23; "Asking the Right Questions Before You Hire a Celebrity Spokesperson," *PR News*, May 19, 2003; "Companies Need to Forge Brands," *Korea Herald*, September 3, 2003; Matt Schiering, "Celebrity Endorsements," *Brandweek*, September 15, 2003; Luke Timmerman, "Ads for Viagra Competitor Cialis to Focus on Results, Not Celebrities," *Seattle Times*, October 10, 2003.

the firm increases its sales from Q to Q'. This extra profit is $(p' - AC)(Q' - Q)$, where AC is the average (and marginal) production cost, so $(p' - AC)$ is the profit per unit. Second, the firm makes more profits on the Q units it used to sell, area A. Because price rises from p to p', its profits on the first Q units increase by $(p' - p)Q$.

FIGURE 14.1 Advertising

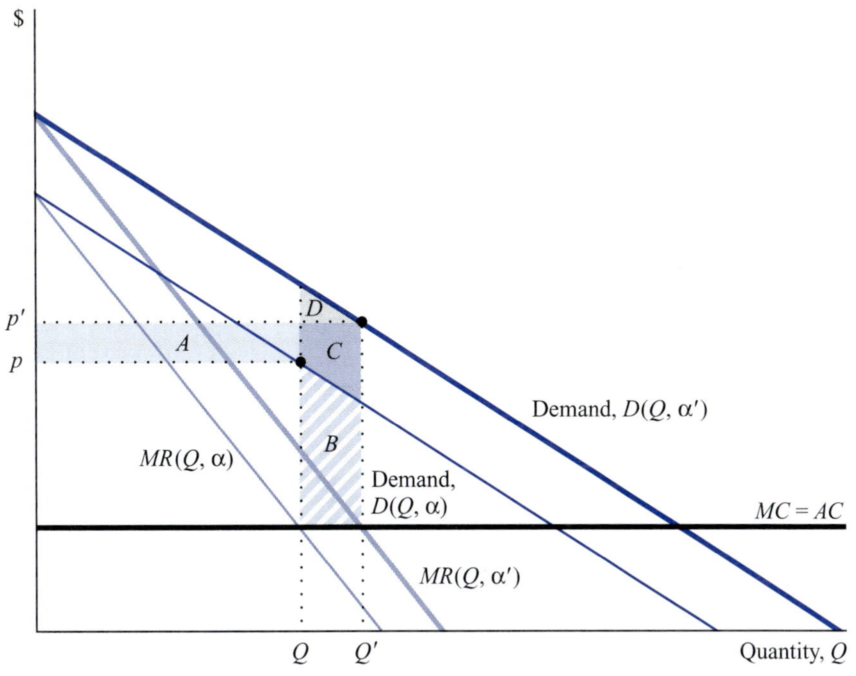

Thus, profits (ignoring advertising costs) increase by the sum of areas *A*, *B*, and *C* due to the extra advertising.

If the extra expenditure on advertising, $E = \alpha' - \alpha$, is less than or equal to the increase in profits, $A + B + C$, the extra advertising pays. If profits rise by more than the advertising expenditures, then advertising expenditures should be increased even more. A profit-maximizing firm sets its advertising expenditures so that the last dollar spent on advertising increases its profits, excluding advertising costs, by exactly one dollar (Appendix 14A). That is, the firm maximizes its profits by setting the marginal cost of advertising equal to the marginal benefit. (Example 14.3 illustrates that groups of producers may fail to do so.)

The lower the cost, the more advertising in a society. In ancient Egypt, some entrepreneurs used criers to announce ship and cargo arrivals. By 1630, printing lowered the cost of advertising sufficiently that wide-scale public advertising became common. More recently, the development of radio and television again lowered advertising costs. Today, the largest advertisers spend over a billion dollars a year on advertising, thus ensuring that we are constantly exposed to it.

The perfect competition model ignores selling costs and assumes that firms can sell all they want at the market price. In fact, most firms do incur selling costs. Usually, firms with market power incur promotional expense to cause their demand curves to shift outward or become more inelastic, so that they can sell more at higher prices.

EXAMPLE 14.3 *Milk Advertising*

State and federal milk-marketing programs fund over $200 million annually for generic milk advertising and promotion. There is a mandatory assessment of 15¢ per hundredweight on all milk marketed for commercial use in the contiguous 48 states. Of that 15¢, at least one-third goes to national advertising and promotion programs, and the rest goes to qualified local promotion programs.

Liu and Forker (1988) assume that consumers forget at a constant rate, so that there is an incentive to continue advertising. They estimate, for New York City, that a 1 percent permanent increase in advertising causes the demand for milk to rise and reach a new higher level in about six months. The long-run demand elasticity with respect to advertising is 0.0028. With current levels of advertising, 18.27 pounds of milk are consumed per month per capita. If advertising were only 10 percent of historical levels, all else the same, consumption would fall 1.5 percent to 17.99 pounds per month per capita. They calculate that the profit-maximizing level of advertising (where marginal benefit equals marginal cost; see Appendix 14A) is about 55 percent of the historical level. Depken, Kamerschen, and Snow (2003) find that U.S. milk advertising is less than the profit-maximizing level.

Similarly, Suzuki et al. (1994) examine the effect of comparable Japanese generic milk promotion on sales. They estimate that the marginal rate of return to promotion is 6.04 in 1981 and 4.33 in 1989, so the Japanese milk marketing boards need to advertise more to maximize profits. Hill, Piggott, and Griffith (2001) report that the Australian dairy industry underinvests in generic milk promotion.

However, it is possible for a firm to advertise and still face a very elastic demand curve. For example, such a firm may act as a price-taker, but needs to advertise to inform customers where its store is located. That is, advertising need not be inconsistent with price-taking behavior. Moreover, competing firms may jointly advertise to increase demand for a homogeneous product. For example, California farmers spend more than $100 million annually on advertisements (Carman, Green, and Mandour 1992). Advertising for dancing raisins represents 5.8 percent of California raisin crop value.

Effects of Advertising on Welfare

> *Advertising may be described as the science of arresting human intelligence long enough to get money from it.* —*Stephen Leacock*

Many social commentators attack advertising. Yet the Federal Trade Commission (FTC), which is supposed to protect consumers, opposes groups that want to forbid advertising, arguing that some advertising benefits consumers. This section examines research on the effects of advertising on welfare. Substantial empirical evidence indicates that advertising about prices can increase competition and raise welfare. In some cases, nonprice advertising can overcome the lemons problem discussed in Chapter 13. Theoretical models differ, however, as to whether advertising always promotes welfare.

Price Advertising Increases Welfare

Advertising that provides price information tends to lower the market price. Truthful advertising lets consumers know where to buy at the lowest price. Because it is costly, firms do not advertise unless the costs are at least covered by the additional revenues from an increase in demand.

If relatively low-price stores advertise their prices and attract more customers, these stores gain in size and the average price in the market falls (Smallwood and Conlisk 1979). In the tourists-and-natives model (Chapter 13), if tourists can gather information only by visiting local stores, the cost of information gathering may be sufficiently high to create a two-price equilibrium in which some stores charge natives the low price and others charge tourists the high price. If, however, relatively low-price stores can advertise in the local paper, the tourists' cost of gathering information falls, more consumers become informed, and the market share of low-price stores increases. If enough consumers become informed, all stores may charge the low price. Thus, without advertising, no store may find it profitable to charge the low price; but with advertising, all stores may charge the low price.[9]

Many empirical studies show that advertising about price lowers the average price consumers pay for products such as drugs (Cady 1976), eyeglasses (Benham 1972; Example 14.4), liquor (Luksetich and Lofgren 1976), toys (Steiner 1973), and retail gasoline (Maurizi 1972). Other studies show that although advertising can lower the price of legal and optometric services, it may also cause quality to fall in such markets (Arnould 1972, Muris and McChesney 1979, Kwoka 1984, Schroeter, Smith, and Cox 1987).

Because advertising can lower price in a market, it is in the interest of professional groups to ban advertising. Until Supreme Court decisions stopped them, doctors, dentists, and lawyers prevented advertising on the grounds that it was unprofessional.

Advertising to Solve the Lemons Problem

In some markets, firms cannot profitably sell high-quality products because consumers are unable to distinguish between high-quality and low-quality products, as in the lemons model (Chapter 13). If firms can use guarantees or warranties to signal high

[9]Butters (1977) shows that the less expensive is advertising or consumer search, the lower is the average price in a market. He also demonstrates that a free market generates the optimal amount of advertising and the maximum possible welfare. Stigler and Becker (1977) and Nichols (1985) also conclude that competing firms buy the socially optimal quantity of advertising. Stegeman (1991) argues that where consumers receive price information only through advertising, under certain conditions, competitive firms advertise less than is socially optimal.

EXAMPLE 14.4 *Social Gain from Price Advertising*

In the past, some states forbade price advertising for eyeglasses. Benham (1972) shows that eyeglass prices in 1963 were substantially higher in states that banned advertising than in those that had no restrictions. Adjusting for differences across states in income, age, sex, and family structure, the cost of eyeglasses was $7.37 higher in states with complete advertising restrictions. Because the average price was $26.34 in states with no restrictions, the restrictions increased the average cost by 28 percent.

There was only a $1.32 difference (which was not statistically significant) among states that had restrictions on price advertising but not other forms of advertising and those that had no restrictions. Thus, complete bans on advertising have a more significant effect on price.

A Federal Trade Commission study (Bond et al. 1980) also reports that prices were lower in cities that allowed advertising than in those that did not. Moreover, they found that the quality of the glasses was the same in both sets of cities. In cities without advertising bans, even optometrists who did not advertise charged an average of $20 less for an exam and glasses than did their counterparts in cities that banned advertising.

In the late 1970s, the Federal Trade Commission (FTC) enacted a trade regulation prohibiting states and trade organizations from restricting price advertising for eyeglasses and related services. The basis for this rule was the economics literature showing that such restrictions increase average price (see Ippolito 1986).

More recently, a court decision eliminated Rhode Island's ban on liquor price advertising in 1996. The Rhode Island Liquor Stores Association opposed ending the ban. By comparing Rhode Island prices to those in Massachusetts, Milyo and Waldfogel (1999) find that stores that advertise reduce price by more than 20 percent on those items that they advertised, and cut prices on products advertised by rivals. Nonadvertising firms did not lower prices in response to advertising by rivals. Milyo and Waldfogel conclude that ending the advertising ban had little effect on overall liquor price levels.

quality, the lemons problem can be avoided. Similarly, advertising may solve the lemons problem if it signals quality.[10]

Suppose, for example, that a firm wants to start selling a high-quality experience good. The firm believes that if consumers try its product, they will like and purchase it repeatedly. That is, the firm's incentive to provide high-quality goods is to induce repeat

[10]Nelson (1974), Schmalensee (1978a), Klein and Leffler (1981), Shapiro (1983), Wolinsky (1983), Kihlstrom and Riordan (1984), Milgrom and Roberts (1986), and Rogerson (1986). For a different view see Allen (1984). Bagwell and Riordan (1991) point out that high and relatively slowly declining prices also signal a high-quality product. High prices result in a loss of sales volume that is more damaging for lower-cost, lower-quality products.

sales (Klein and Leffler 1981, Shapiro 1983, Rogerson 1986). The firm hopes to make large profits by signaling its high quality and getting consumers to try its product.

To keep this example simple, let us make two additional assumptions. First, assume that consumers can find out about a product's quality only by trying the good; otherwise, the firm could produce a few items, give them away to some consumers, and rely on word of mouth to sell its product (Dodson and Muller 1978). Second, assume that the firm's marginal and average variable costs of production are the same as those of firms that produce low-quality goods (we drop this assumption later in this chapter). As a result, if the high-quality firm sells more units than low-quality firms sell at the same price, it makes higher profits on these sales.

The high-quality firm has a greater incentive to advertise than does the low-quality firm. The high-quality firm's advertising leads to repeated sales, whereas the low-quality firm's advertising leads to sales only in the current period. Because both types of firms have the same costs of production and advertising and because the rewards to advertising are greater for the high-quality firm, it engages in more advertising.[11]

When Advertising Is Excessive

It is against the law to advertise on tombstones in Roanoke, Virginia.

Newspaper columnists and social philosophers often argue that there is too much advertising because it induces consumers to buy goods they do not "need." This argument has been formalized to show that where products are differentiated, firms engage in more than the socially optimal amount of both persuasive and informative advertising. We explain why this conclusion may not always hold.

★Advertising for a Single Product. Until recently, most economists concluded that very little could be said about the welfare effects of persuasive advertising.[12] They reasoned that if advertising changes consumers' tastes (as reflected by consumers' utility functions), then there is no fixed basis for comparing welfare before and after advertising.

Suppose that an advertisement convinces many consumers that using a cologne makes them more attractive, and thus results in more sales at a higher price. Are consumers better off? The price is higher than before, but some consumers are receiving more pleasure from using the cologne than before. Most social commentators who are not economists say that the consumers just "think they are better off," and hence argue that their greater pleasure after advertising is spurious and should be discounted. Economists, however, typically argue that consumers are the best judges of their own tastes. Unfortunately, it is difficult to compare consumers' pleasure before and after advertising if the scale on which the pleasure is measured has changed.

---

[11]Rogerson (1986) discusses some complications in this type of model. Fluet and Garella (2002) and Linnemer (2002) show that whether firms use price or advertising to signal quality depends on the type of competition between the firms and the knowledge of consumers.

[12]For an earlier debate on the welfare effects of advertising, see Kaldor (1949–50) and Telser (1966).

In a clever but controversial article, Dixit and Norman (1978) argue that strong welfare conclusions can be drawn. They use the two natural extremes of consumers' preadvertising and postadvertising tastes (utilities) as the basis for their conclusions. For example, if you believe that advertising is pure deception, you could use preadvertising tastes in evaluating welfare. If instead, you believe that postadvertising tastes represent the consumers' true interest, you should use those tastes. If on the basis of both sets of tastes one gets the same welfare results, then Dixit and Norman argue that the results hold regardless of one's underlying assumptions about the appropriate set of tastes.

We start by examining the welfare effects of advertising on a monopoly and its customers. The monopoly has a constant marginal cost of production. Advertising is supplied at constant cost, so that advertising agencies do not receive unusual profits, and hence the advertising cost is the same for both the firm and society. As a result, the welfare analysis can ignore the advertising agencies; they receive zero profits regardless of the amount of advertising.

Let α be the initial level of advertising that is increased to a new level α'. We refer to α as the *preadvertising* level and α' as the postadvertising level. In Figure 14.1, the additional advertising expenditure, $E = \alpha' - \alpha$, causes the demand curve to shift outward to $D(Q, \alpha')$. That is, at any given price, consumers demand more output postadvertising. If output falls, welfare definitely falls, and no further analysis is necessary. We assume, then, that the equilibrium price, p', and quantity, Q', are higher in the postadvertising monopolistic equilibrium than in the original equilibrium (with price p and output Q), as shown in Figure 14.1.

As an initial standard, we use the preadvertising preferences of consumers, as reflected by the preadvertising demand curve with α advertising, $D(Q, \alpha)$. In the postadvertising equilibrium, consumers appreciate this product more than before, so consumers buy $Q' - Q$ more units. The additional consumer surplus from these extra units is the area under the preadvertising demand curve between Q and Q', because we are evaluating welfare at the preadvertising level. The cost of producing these extra units is the area under the marginal (and average) cost curve between Q and Q'. Thus, the net social gain from these extra units, area $B - E$, is the difference between the extra consumer surplus and the cost of producing them less the cost of the additional advertising, E.

Using the postadvertising preferences as our standard, consumer surplus increases by the area under the postadvertising demand curve between Q and Q'. Thus, the change in welfare is the increase in consumer surplus above the marginal cost curve, $B + C + D$, minus the additional cost of advertising, E. That is, using the postadvertising preferences, welfare changes by $B + C + D - E$, instead of just $B - E$, using the preadvertising preferences. For small amounts of advertising, C and D are generally very small relative to B, so that there is little difference in the change in welfare between the two standards.

In either case, the gain to advertising is the area under the *relevant* demand curve (either the pre- or postadvertising demand curve) between Q and Q' and above the marginal cost curve, less the additional advertising expenditures, E. That is, we are measuring the social value of a change in output from Q to Q' using the relevant standard.

The outward shift of the consumers' demand curve due to additional advertising increases the monopoly's profits for two reasons, as discussed above. First, the monopoly sells $Q' - Q$ more units of output. Second, the monopoly sells each unit of output at a price that is $p' - p$ dollars more per unit than before. Thus, the monopoly's profits increase by the sum of areas A, B, and C, less the cost of advertising, E. The increase in price due to the advertising makes firms better off by raising profits, $A + B + C - E$, but makes consumers worse off by raising the cost of the original output, $A = (p' - p)Q$. The change in welfare, using either standard, approximately equals the increase in profits to the monopoly less the extra expenditures, A, by consumers.

Using the preadvertising preferences, welfare cannot rise unless the monopoly finds advertising profitable. The change in welfare, $B - E$, is less than the increase in profits, $A + B + C - E$.[13] Thus, unless an increase in advertising increases profits, welfare cannot rise. Alternatively stated, profitability is a *necessary* condition for additional advertising to increase welfare; it is not a *sufficient* condition, because profits could go up $(A + B + C - E > 0)$, and yet welfare could fall $(B - E < 0)$.

Using postadvertising preferences, the change in welfare is $B + C + D - E$. For a small increase in advertising, C and D are small relative to A and B. Again, welfare cannot increase unless profits, $A + B + C - E$, are positive. Thus, using either set of preferences, profitability is a necessary condition for welfare to rise.

In equilibrium, the monopoly increases advertising until the extra expenditure on advertising, E, exactly equals the marginal increase in profits net of advertising, $A + B + C$. That is, in equilibrium, the change in the monopoly's marginal profits, net of the additional advertising expenditures from one more dollar of advertising, is zero. Because the change in welfare is marginal profits (which are zero in equilibrium) minus the extra consumer expenditures due to advertising (which are positive), the marginal change in welfare is negative for the last advertising dollar. Regardless of the welfare standard—preadvertising or postadvertising preferences—a marginal increase in advertising causes welfare to fall by approximately area B, the extra consumer expenditures. That is, advertising is excessive: *At the equilibrium, a small decrease in advertising increases welfare.*

Dixit and Norman (1978) show that these results hold in oligopolistic and monopolistically competitive markets as well. They conclude that in all these markets:

- A small increase in advertising raises welfare only if the firm finds it profitable. There cannot be too little advertising, because if society benefits from the advertising, the firm finds it profitable to provide it.
- Reducing advertising from the profit-maximizing level raises welfare. This result holds even using the postadvertising preferences of consumers.

[13]The change in welfare is approximately the difference between the extra profits of the monopoly, $A + B + C - E$, and the higher cost to consumers for the original output, A, or $B + C - E$. For small changes in advertising expenditures, C is small relative to B, so that $B + C - E$ approximately equals $B - E$, the change in welfare. Area A represents a transfer of wealth from consumers to the monopoly and hence does not affect total welfare: The monopoly's gain offsets the consumers' loss.

That is, it is possible that a low level of profitable advertising maximizes welfare, but that firms advertise at a higher level. Even at that excessive level, however, welfare may be higher than with no advertising.

Two serious criticisms of Dixit and Norman's (1978) conclusions have emerged.[14] First, as Fisher and McGowan (1979) explain, in general, one should not examine welfare on the basis of just preadvertising or just postadvertising preferences. Suppose that an improvement in the product's quality, instead of advertising, shifted demand. Dixit and Norman's analysis would imply that there is an overinvestment in product quality. The reason for this counterintuitive result is that Dixit and Norman compare welfare before and after advertising using either the preadvertising or postadvertising preferences for both equilibrium outcomes. If the preadvertising equilibrium based on the preadvertising preferences is compared to the postadvertising equilibrium based on the postadvertising preferences, the welfare effects of advertising are ambiguous. If advertisements (or quality improvements) change preferences (consumers' willingness to pay), the utility levels of consumers pre- and postadvertising cannot be directly compared. Here it is inappropriate to use just one or the other set of preferences to evaluate the welfare effects.

Second, Shapiro (1980) explains that if advertising serves to inform consumers that a product exists rather than to shift tastes, there is too little advertising. In Shapiro's example, some consumers are unaware of the product before it is advertised. After exposure to advertising, they become aware of the product and purchase it, but no consumer tastes have changed. Unless the monopoly can price discriminate, it advertises too little, because it bears the full cost of advertising but does not receive the full benefits (it does not capture all the additional consumer surplus).[15] The welfare effects of advertising are also ambiguous when the advertising concerns differentiated goods (see **www.aw-bc.com/carlton_perloff** "Advertising and Differentiated Products"). Example 14.5 discusses the welfare effects of advertising for sin goods.

Advertising as a Barrier to Entry. Dixit and Norman (1978) and Grossman and Shapiro (1984) do not argue that all advertising is harmful; they contend only that there is too much of some types in certain circumstances. Many people, however, argue that persuasive advertising is anticompetitive and should be banned.

Persuasive advertising is said to be anticompetitive for two reasons (Bain 1956, Comanor and Wilson 1974). First, advertising may cause some consumers to conclude mistakenly that physically identical brands differ, an effect called **spurious product differentiation**. For example, some people pay a premium for branded bleaches that are chemically identical to many generic brands. Because buying behavior depends on consumers' perceptions of products rather than on the products' physical characteristics, advertising can lead to higher prices for some brands than for others. It is not clear

---

[14]Dixit and Norman (1979, 1980) respond to these criticisms.

[15]See Shapiro (1980) for a graphic analysis. A similar point is made by Diamond and Rothschild (1978). Shapiro (1980) and Dixit and Norman (1980) also debate the welfare effects when advertising affects consumers differently. See also Becker and Murphy (1993).

EXAMPLE 14.5 *Welfare Effects of Restricting Alcohol Ads*

Governments often try to discourage "sinful" activities, such as drinking, smoking, and gambling. Rather than ban these activities outright or tax them, governments may limit advertising.

To prevent more government interference in their industries, firms may voluntarily restrict ads. For example, U.S. distilled spirits producers voluntarily banned the use of radio ads starting in 1936 and television ads starting in 1948. However, as distilled spirits producers have recently lost market share to beer and wine firms, this compact has collapsed. Crown Royal whiskey broke the voluntary ban by broadcasting a television commercial in June 1996. After other distillers did likewise, the Distilled Spirits Council of the United States voted unanimously to rescind its voluntary ban on November 7, 1996. With the end of the voluntary ban, a lively public debate has raged as to whether state or federal governments should ban such ads.

Alcohol advertising bans are widely supported because of the belief that ads promote alcohol consumption and abuse. In Europe, 6 percent of all deaths among people under 75 and 20 percent of all acute hospital admissions are related to alcohol use. Nonetheless, advertising of alcoholic beverages is widespread. According to *Advertising Age,* in 2003, U.S. beer, wine, and liquor firms spent $1.7 billion on advertising, which represents nearly 15 percent of their sales.

Studies in the United States, Canada, and various European countries in the late 1980s and early 1990s found that advertising had little effect on the total market demand for alcoholic beverages (although advertising might strongly affect the sales of the advertised product). Consequently, some people concluded that, because bans of television or billboard ads would not affect total demand, they would have little effect. However, such bans may affect competition within the beverage industry, the demand for other products, and the use of advertising in other, nonbanned media.

Based on their study of the relationship between alcohol advertising bans and alcohol consumption in 20 countries, Saffer and Dave (2002) report that alcohol advertising bans decrease alcohol consumption. They conclude that such bans reduce alcohol consumption by 5–8 percent. Tremblay and Okuyama (2001) note that eliminating alcohol advertising bans tends to increase price competition, which can lead to greater alcohol sales.

Nelson (2003) finds, not surprisingly, that a restrictive law that applies to only one beverage (or one form of advertising) results in substitution toward other beverages (or nonbanned media). In particular, he finds that laws banning price advertising of distilled spirits lead to lower consumption of spirits and wine but higher consumption of beer. He also finds that, if a government wants to restrict alcohol consumption, advertising bans may be less effective than requiring that alcohol be sold by a monopoly or by raising the legal drinking laws.

Sources: Tremblay and Okuyama (2001), Saffer and Dave (2002), and Nelson (2003).

whether consumers are fooled in these cases by claims that a particular brand is superior in some unspecified way. For example, advertising may cause consumers incorrectly to become concerned that some generic brands are weak or contaminated and thus find it worth paying the premium for a branded good to avoid this (false) worry.

Second, some economists argue that advertising by firms already in an industry may make entry by new firms more difficult. A potential entrant must advertise extensively to overcome the goodwill created by an incumbent firm's advertising, whereas the incumbent incurred no such introductory advertising expense when it entered the market. Such a barrier to entry increases the market power of incumbent firms, and they charge higher prices as a result. The importance of this entry barrier depends on how long-lasting the effects of advertising are. The empirical evidence is not completely clear. Some researchers, among them Ayanian (1983), find that the effects of advertising for some goods last for several years, whereas other researchers, such as Boyd and Seldon (1990), find that advertising effects are gone within a year.

If the incumbent has no advantage over a potential entrant in advertising, the advertising does not restrict entry even if the incumbent has built up goodwill through its past efforts (Schmalensee 1974). If a potential entrant can advertise as effectively as an incumbent, eventually it will be on an equal footing with the incumbent. The potential entrant, foreseeing that day, is not deterred from entering, and there is no long-run barrier to entry as defined in Chapter 3 (see also von Weizsäcker 1980). Moreover, in many cases the entrant incurs lower advertising costs than the incumbent, especially if the incumbent has already persuaded consumers that the product is desirable. On the other hand, if (as in Chapter 11) the second entrant faces higher marketing costs than the first, there is a barrier to entry. Because there are theoretical arguments on both sides of this issue, the debate can be resolved only with empirical evidence. There are almost as many empirical studies claiming that advertising is not anticompetitive as there are studies showing that it is, however.

Many studies examine whether concentration ratios are related to advertising.[16] Studies finding that advertising increases concentration (Mann, Henning, and Meehan 1967, Ornstein et al. 1973, Strickland and Weiss 1976) are no more common than those finding that it either has no effect or lowers concentration (Telser 1964, 1969, Ekelund and Maurice 1969, Ekelund and Gramm 1970, Vernon 1971, Edwards 1973). Whether these studies actually test that advertising causes barriers to entry is open to question (Schmalensee 1976). For example, Weiss, Pascoe, and Martin (1983) infer that market structure, as measured in part by concentration ratios, determines advertising/sales ratios. The connection between concentration ratios and market power is tenuous at best, and the direction of causality between concentration ratios and advertising is not clear. Indeed, it is likely that both are determined simultaneously rather than that one determines the other.[17]

---

[16]Telser (1964) was probably the first to do so. Many of these studies are reviewed in Ornstein (1977) and Comanor and Wilson (1979).

[17]Lambin (1976) and Schmalensee (1973) attempt to measure separately the effects of advertising by firms on their own demand curves and on the industry's demand curve. Unfortunately, their data do not allow them to measure these effects precisely.

Another approach (Comanor and Wilson 1974, Miller 1969, Weiss 1969) examines the relationship between various accounting measures of profit and advertising. Again, the causality of any such relationship is open to question. Moreover, if advertising is long-lived in the sense that advertising today affects purchasing decisions in the future, then short-run profitability differences associated with advertising may be misleading.[18] Firms may incur costs today, lowering current profits, that raise profits in the future. Ayanian (1983) estimates that the average stock of advertising (the cumulative effect of many advertisements) typically lasts seven years. After adjusting profits for the stock of advertising, he concludes that advertising does not cause entry barriers that result in unusual profits.

As we previously discussed, a number of studies show that informative advertising about prices can lower the average price in a market. Persuasive advertising, by enabling new firms to differentiate their products, can sometimes facilitate entry. Thus, even if it could be shown that persuasive advertising can create barriers to entry, restricting advertising would also reduce its desirable effects of facilitating entry.

False Advertising

Advertising is legalized lying. —*H. G. Wells*

False advertising is illegal. If enforcement is lax, however, firms can advertise for years in a false, deceptive, or misleading manner with few, if any, penalties. This section considers the circumstances under which firms are most likely to engage in false advertising and whether truth-in-advertising or antifraud laws are desirable. The results are surprising: Under some circumstances, antifraud laws can lead to more false advertising.

Limits to Lying

The truth is the safest lie.

Why don't all firms lie in their advertising? One answer is that most consumers are hard to fool (Nelson 1974, Schmalensee 1978a).[19] Nelson (1974, 749) proposes a consumer decision rule that usually prevents a consumer from being deceived: "[B]elieve an advertisement . . . when it tells about the functions of a brand; do not

---

[18]Lambin (1976, 97) reports that the elasticity of sales with respect to advertising expenditures usually is greater in the long run. The short-run elasticity for electric shavers is 0.229 (a 1 percent increase in advertising expenditures leads to a 0.229 percent increase in sales), but the long-run elasticity is over twice that, 0.597. Similarly, the short-run and long-run elasticities for cigarettes are 0.154 and 0.752; for detergents, 0.055 and 0.659; and for soft drinks, 0.057 and 0.415.

[19]But not always: A 1945 *Fortune* magazine article reported that at least 10 men had written letters proposing marriage to Betty Crocker, the fictional spokesperson for a food company.

believe the advertisement when it tells how well a brand performs that function." The functions of a brand are easily tested before purchase (search qualities), whereas the performance can be confirmed only after purchase (experience qualities). A firm's claim that it sells king-size beds is much easier to confirm than the claim that the bed will last for 50 years. Thus, the first claim is more plausible than the second.

False advertising is more likely for experience goods than for search goods. For example, in a six-month period, all 58 Federal Trade Commission cases of deceptive advertising about product attributes concerned experience qualities rather than search qualities (Nelson 1974, 750). A false claim about a search good leads to no additional purchases if the claim can be inexpensively checked prior to purchase. Making such a false claim only damages a firm's reputation. As a result, firms have no incentive to make such a claim. In contrast, they may have an incentive to lie about experience goods, because the lie may prompt consumers to make a trial purchase.

Nonetheless, the amount of false advertising about experience goods may be minimized by high-quality firms' incentives to advertise the truth.[20] A consumer who tries and enjoys a high-quality item is likely to make repeated purchases, whereas a consumer disappointed by a low-quality product does not buy it again. Thus, the benefit to having a consumer try its product is greater for a high-quality firm than for a low-quality firm if both have the same costs. As a result, high-quality firms should advertise more than low-quality firms do, so that even the *amount* of persuasive advertising may be a signal of quality.

This argument appears sound as far as it goes: High-quality firms have a greater incentive to advertise extensively than low-quality firms do, assuming that both have the same costs. In many, if not most, markets, however, low-quality or fraudulent firms have relatively low costs. A fly-by-night firm can sell a worthless product that is almost costless to produce, so that its costs are substantially below those of a high-quality firm. The fly-by-night firm makes larger profits on its initial sales because it makes higher profits per unit; however, it expects no repeat business and has no expectation of surviving for very long. In such markets, therefore, it is unclear whether a high-quality firm with a relatively high cost of production advertises more or less (Schmalensee 1978a, Kihlstrom and Riordan 1984, Milgrom and Roberts 1986) than a low-quality firm.

We would expect high-quality products to be advertised more if the variable costs of the high-quality firm are no higher than those of low-quality firms and if consumers cannot learn about a product's quality except through consumption (Shapiro 1983, Rogerson 1986).[21] However, if the high-quality firm has relatively high costs, a large

[20]The conditions under which advertising can serve as a signal of quality are discussed in Nelson (1974), Schmalensee (1978a), Klein and Leffler (1981), Shapiro (1983), Wolinsky (1983), Allen (1984), Kihlstrom and Riordan (1984), Milgrom and Roberts (1986), and Rogerson (1986, 1988).

[21]If potential consumers can learn about quality through word of mouth from others who have tried the product, a high-quality firm need only sell a small amount of output at low introductory rates to convince consumers that it has an outstanding product, and hence it has no incentive to advertise extensively.

amount of advertising may not signal high quality.[22] Thus, either high-quality or low-quality firms may advertise more, so extensive advertising is not necessarily associated with high quality. For example, Kotowitz and Mathewson (1986) do not find evidence in either automobiles or whole-life insurance that greater advertising indicates better buys or signals higher quality.

The advertising industry claims to police itself to some degree. The American Association of Advertising Agencies, representing agencies that produce 80 percent of television and print advertising, established a children's advertising review unit in 1974. Since then, it has persuaded companies to modify or discontinue 270 commercials that had the potential to mislead or confuse children.[23]

Antifraud Laws

An advertisement for a carburetor to save gasoline ended with: ". . . If not satisfactory, money will be returned." When some customers complained, they were told, "So far, all money we have received has been satisfactory."[24]

A company that sells an unsafe or otherwise substandard product typically can produce at lower cost than can firms producing a safe or standard product. Such a firm may engage in deceptive advertising that implies that its products are safe and useful in order to induce consumers to buy. Although there may be no repeat sales from satisfied customers, the company may still make money if its costs are low enough. One approach to dealing with deceptive ads is to prosecute unscrupulous firms under antifraud laws.

Paradoxically, more deception may occur when an antifraud law is moderately enforced than when it is not enforced at all (Nelson 1974, 749–51). Suppose, for example, that the law prohibits the mislabeling of the fabric content of clothing. If the law is almost always enforced, consumers believe that a clothing label is usually correct, thereby giving a manufacturer an incentive to mislabel. That is, if consumers believe that labels are generally accurate, false labels may fool them (see **www.aw-bc.com/carlton_perloff,** "Taking Candy from Babies"). In contrast, in the absence of any enforcement, consumers generally do not trust clothing labels.[25] Here, deceptive labels do little harm because no one believes them. As a result, firms have little incentive to make deceptive claims.

Does it follow that we should not have antifraud laws? Such a conclusion is too strong. These laws induce firms to make more information available to consumers. If a firm knows that consumers do not believe its claims in the absence of an antifraud law,

---

[22]Even here, however, extensive advertising signals quality under some circumstances (Milgrom and Roberts 1986).

[23]Anthony Ramirez, "Advertising: Campaigns for Children Criticized," *New York Times,* July 18, 1990:C9.

[24]L. M. Boyd, "Grab Bag," *San Francisco Chronicle,* April 2, 1988: C12.

[25]Eaton and Grossman (1986b) show that a firm may have an incentive to disclose information accurately if its product is very different from the products of its rivals.

it does not bother making any. Thus, there is a trade-off between having more claims (and perhaps more information) and having more deception.

The government must determine the optimal level of enforcement, taking into account the cost of enforcement. The optimal level of enforcement lies in the middle range between no enforcement and testing all claims.

Disclosure Laws

Do you promise to tell the truth, the whole truth, and nothing but the truth?

Disclosure laws require firms to reveal truthfully to consumers certain information about their products. Antifraud laws require only that any information voluntarily disclosed by firms be truthful. A firm advertises primarily to inform consumers about the desirable properties of its products, but it may also disclose their undesirable properties, such as side effects of drugs, for various reasons. For example, the firm may provide appropriate warnings as protection against liability suits, or it may decide that full disclosure is profit-maximizing. In some markets, the government requires firms to make disclosures about all *material* facts: all the good and bad factors that should influence the decision to buy the product.

As discussed in Chapter 13, a market for lemons may develop if high-quality sellers cannot practically differentiate their products from those of low-quality sellers, with the result that consumers remain uninformed. Here, however, we consider markets in which high-quality sellers have both an incentive and the ability to distinguish their products.[26]

Recall from the previous chapter that when statements about a product's quality can be established at low cost after the sale, firms not only tell the truth but provide warranties or guarantees to establish that they are telling the truth. For example, if a firm states that its box of oranges contains six oranges, a consumer can verify this claim upon opening the box, at virtually no cost.

When statements about a product's quality are costly to convey to consumers or costly to verify after the sale, firms do not offer standard guarantees. For example, it is difficult for a car maker to describe the quality of an automobile's construction and difficult for a consumer to verify this quality even after purchase. We do not expect to see a guarantee that all the parts of an automobile are of high quality and were properly assembled. It is relatively easy, however, to determine whether or not the car breaks down. If high-quality cars have a lower probability of failure than low-quality cars, a car maker can use guarantees covering breakdowns instead of direct guarantees of construction. We now consider the need for and effects of disclosure laws under various assumptions about the buyers and sellers.

[26]The following discussion is based on Grossman and Hart (1980), Milgrom (1981), and especially Grossman (1981b).

EXAMPLE 14.6 *Restaurants Make the Grade*

Los Angeles County health inspectors have graded restaurants on their hygiene for many years. Prior to 1998, restaurants did not generally choose to reveal their hygiene ratings. Beginning in 1998, it became mandatory for restaurants to post their hygiene ratings as either an A (the restaurant received a score of 90–100), B (80–89), C (70–79), or lower. Jin and Leslie (2003) find that this campaign to better inform consumers has had substantial effects. Mandatory disclosure raised hygiene scores by an average of 5.3%. Restaurants receiving an A saw their revenues increase by 5.7%, those receiving a B saw their revenues rise by 0.7%, while those receiving a C saw their revenues decrease by 1%. An analysis of hospital admission records revealed that admissions for food-related disorders dropped by 13.3%, even though non-food-related admissions increased by 2.9%. In short, the mandatory information disclosures increased welfare.

Firms may have an incentive to reveal product information when buyers are knowledgeable about the sellers' ability to obtain information about the product through testing or other means. It is also possible that firms may fail to test for fear of being forced to disclose unfavorable results. (See **www.aw-bc.com/carlton_perloff** "Product Disclosure.")

Empirical Evidence. Disclosure laws are common in financial markets, housing markets, and other markets where the quality of products is complex and sellers have substantially more information than buyers. We now examine two markets—securities and used cars—where disclosure laws are used. See Example 14.6 for an important example in another market.

Federal securities legislation was designed to prevent the overpricing of new stock issues resulting from buyers' ignorance about the undesirable attributes of these new stocks (Benston 1973, Hilke 1984). Stigler (1964b) and Jarrell (1981) compare the rates of return and the associated risks of investing in new issues before and after the 1933 Securities Act that imposed stringent disclosure requirements. They find, at most, small differences in relative performance across periods, although one researcher determines that fewer risky new stocks were available after the disclosure requirements.[27]

Another type of study examines the purchase of consumer durables. Consumers may differ in their ability to determine quality before purchasing, in their bargaining power, and in the gains they provide to firms when they are satisfied. McNeil et al. (1978) find that the poor pay more for used cars, are less likely to receive redress for defects they discover after purchase, and are less satisfied and more likely to believe

[27]Hilke (1984), commenting on these studies, questions whether the mandatory disclosure requirements of the 1933 Securities Act significantly increased disclosure requirements.

that something was misrepresented. This study also finds that the adoption of disclosure regulations in Wisconsin did not help. In short, there is little evidence to show that disclosure laws have been useful in either financial or used car markets.

SUMMARY

Firms have an incentive to inform consumers about the strengths of their products and to try to shift their tastes. In addition to advertising in newspapers and on radio and television, firms may advertise indirectly by creating brand names or otherwise establishing positive reputations.

A firm determines the profit-maximizing amount of advertising by setting the marginal cost of advertising equal to the marginal benefit stemming from increased sales. Existing empirical studies find that firms generally spend more on advertising for experience goods (goods that the consumer must try in order to determine if they are desirable) than on search goods (goods that consumers can instantly appraise).

The welfare effects of advertising are complex and depend on the type of product and type of advertising. Advertising about prices of homogeneous products typically lowers the average price that consumers pay, as demonstrated in studies of eyeglasses and other products. However, these studies show only that some advertising is desirable; they do not show that firms engage in the socially optimal amount of advertising. When persuasive advertising changes consumers' utility, one cannot determine if there is too much or too little advertising.

Advertising that leads to the spurious differentiation of goods and results in higher prices for consumers is harmful. Advertising may also create a barrier to entry, but the evidence supporting this view is mixed. Thus, the effects of advertising on consumer welfare are generally ambiguous. In some markets, advertising can make entry easier for a firm without a reputation, but it can also lead to the creation of market power.

Skepticism by consumers discourages false advertising. Paradoxically, antifraud laws can increase the amount of both truthful and false advertising. Society must therefore trade off the cost of enforcing antifraud laws and the harm of false advertising against the benefit from an increase in truthful advertising in order to determine how strictly to enforce these laws.

When antifraud laws are fully enforced, firms generally have an incentive to disclose relevant information to consumers. Surprisingly, under some circumstances, mandatory disclosure laws can reduce the extent of such disclosures by reducing the incentives for firms to acquire information. Existing empirical studies of mandatory disclosure laws fail to reveal a beneficial effect in securities and used car markets.

PROBLEMS

1. Use a graph to illustrate Shapiro's (1980) critique of the Dixit and Norman (1978) argument that if a monopoly's advertising only informs consumers that a product exists rather than shifting tastes, there is too little advertising. Assume that demand is linear and marginal costs are constant.

2. What is the profit-maximizing rule for advertising if advertising depreciates (that is, consumers forget about it over time if not reminded)?
3. What happens if a firm advertises, but only some people see the ads? *Hint:* Consider the tourists-and-natives model in Chapter 13.
4. A manufacturer uses vertical restraints in its contract with its dealer network (see Chapter 12) to encourage dealers to advertise locally. Under what conditions are such vertical restraints socially desirable?
5. Using the model in Appendix 14A, suppose the inverse demand curve facing a monopoly is $p = a + \alpha - bQ$, where α is the amount of advertising, and the cost function is mQ. Determine the optimal level of advertising and output.

Answers to odd-numbered problems are given at the back of the book.

SUGGESTED READINGS

The following are relatively nontechnical (or have nontechnical sections). To get a good overview of the older literature on advertising, see Schmalensee (1973) and Comanor and Wilson (1974, 1979). More recent work includes Bagwell (2001), Ekelund and Saurman (1988), and Leahy (1997).

APPENDIX 14A

Profit-Maximizing Advertising

Suppose that the price a firm may charge, p, is a function of its output, Q, and advertising, α. That is, its inverse demand curve is

$$p = p(Q, \alpha). \tag{14A.1}$$

Its revenues, then, are

$$R = p(Q, \alpha)Q \equiv R(Q, \alpha). \tag{14A.2}$$

The firm's costs are the sum of its production costs, $C(Q)$, and its advertising costs, α, where \$1 of advertising costs \$1.

In a one-period model that ignores the effect of advertising on future purchasing behavior, the firm maximizes its profits through its choice of quantity and advertising levels:

$$\max_{Q,\, \alpha} \pi = R(Q, \alpha) - C(Q) - \alpha. \tag{14A.3}$$

The two first-order conditions are

$$\pi_Q = R_Q - C_Q = 0, \tag{14A.4}$$

$$\pi_\alpha = R_\alpha - 1 = 0, \tag{14A.5}$$

where $R_Q \equiv \partial R/\partial Q$, $R_\alpha \equiv \partial R/\partial \alpha$, and $C_Q \equiv \partial C/\partial Q$. The optimal Q and α must simultaneously satisfy Equations 14A.4 and 14A.5. According to Equation 14A.4, output should be chosen so that marginal revenue from an extra unit of output, R_Q, equals the marginal cost of producing an extra unit, C_Q. According to Equation 14A.5, the firm should advertise until the marginal revenue resulting from an increase in advertising, R_α, equals the marginal advertising cost, 1.

PART FIVE

Dynamic Models and Market Clearing

CHAPTER 15

Decision Making Over Time: Durability

Time is nature's way of keeping everything from happening at once.

This chapter is the first of two that analyze firms' decision making over time. Here, we examine markets for goods that last for several time periods—**durable goods**. Examples of durable goods include light bulbs, automobiles, washing machines, and X-ray machines. In the United States, expenditures on durable goods are about 10 percent of all personal consumption expenditures and half of all sales of goods.[1]

Manufacturers of durable goods must decide how long their products should last. By spending more money initially, a manufacturer can make the product last longer. Manufacturers' decisions about durability depend on several factors. In particular, manufacturers consider whether consumers only care about the flow of services from the durable good (such as light from a light bulb or transportation from a car) or whether they also care about the durability of the good that provides the service (consumers prefer to drive a new rather than an old car). This chapter answers two questions about durability:

1. Does market structure affect the durability of products? For example, does a monopoly produce as durable a product as a competitive firm?
2. Does it matter whether a monopoly rents or sells its goods?

How Long Should a Durable Good Last?

In the long run, we are all dead. —*John Maynard Keynes*

When buying a durable good, consumers consider how long it should last and its resale value in future years. For example, manufacturers of high-quality, expensive cars often argue that consumers are better off buying their cars than less

[1] 2003 *Economic Report of the President* (Tables B-2 and B-9).

expensive, lower-quality ones because the better cars last longer and can be resold for a higher percentage of their initial purchase price in any future year.

A firm must trade off higher initial manufacturing costs against a product with a longer life that it can sell at a higher price. The firm's optimal policy is to increase initial expenditures up to the point where the marginal cost of greater durability equals the marginal benefit from a higher sales price. The firm's decision may be influenced by a number of factors, including its market power and the presence or absence of a resale market. We start by examining a competitive firm's decision and then a monopolistic firm's decision where consumers care about only the flow of services from the durable good.

Competitive Firm's Choice of Durability

I'm not afraid to die. I just don't want to be there when it happens.

—*Woody Allen*

Consider a competitive light bulb manufacturer's trade-off. The firm manufactures a light bulb that lasts N periods under normal use. A light bulb that is N periods old is just as useful—provides as much light—as a new one. At the end of N periods, the light bulb dies and must be replaced; it does not pay to fix it.[2]

When one says that a light bulb is useful, one refers to the *service*—the light of a specified intensity—that the light bulb provides. The light bulb is a machine or capital asset: something that lasts for many periods and that provides a service in each period.[3]

The manufacturer must decide how durable to make the light bulb; that is, the manufacturer must choose N. Suppose that the constant marginal cost of manufacturing a light bulb that lasts N years is $C(N)$. The more durable (long-lived) is the light bulb, the higher the cost of manufacture but the less frequently the bulb wears out. Thus, the firm faces a trade-off between durability and manufacturing cost. The competitive firm must pick the optimal trade-off because if it cannot produce efficiently, other firms will drive it out of business.

What is the cost of providing the light service from one light bulb forever? In the first period, the bulb costs $C(N)$. No replacement is needed until N periods later, at which time $C(N)$ dollars must again be spent to replace the bulb. Thereafter, every N periods, the bulb must be replaced at a cost of $C(N)$ dollars.

Costs in the future, however, are less important than costs today because future dollars are worth less. For example, if the interest rate is 10 percent, a dollar today is worth \$1.10 next period. Alternatively stated, a dollar next period is worth only

[2]A light bulb differs from many other products in that light from an older light bulb is the same as light from a new one until it suddenly dies. The main results of this section, however, do not depend on this special property of light bulbs. They do depend on the assumption that consumers do not care about the life of the light bulb in the sense that light from a bulb that lasts one year is equivalent to consumers as light from two bulbs each of which lasts six months.

[3]The light bulb, a machine, is a *stock*, which has no time dimension. The service is a *flow*, which has a time dimension: the amount of light *per period*.

\$0.91 (1/1.1) today. To calculate the present value of a stream of future expenditures, then, we *discount* expenditures in the future. Thus, if one is committed to pay \$1 this year and \$1 next year, the *present value* of this commitment, assuming a 10 percent interest rate, is \$1 + \$0.91 or \$1.91. Therefore, the present value of the cost of providing one light bulb's worth of service forever is the cost of producing it today, plus the discounted cost of producing another after N periods, plus the discounted cost of producing another in $2N$ periods, and so on.[4]

Figure 15.1 illustrates the effect of interest rates on the cost of providing one light bulb's worth of service forever. The present value of costs is plotted as a function of N, the durability of the bulb, for a particular cost function.[5] One line is the present value of costs for an interest rate of 10 percent, and the other for a rate of 20 percent. A competitive firm picks the durability, N, that minimizes the present value of the costs of providing 1 unit of light bulb service forever. If the interest rate is 10 percent, the present value of cost is minimized at $N = 13$ years. If the interest rate is 20 percent, it is minimized at $N = 7$ years. Thus, the higher the interest rate, the less durable the bulb should be because the future savings from delaying replacement of the bulb diminish, whereas the cost of making the good more durable is borne currently and not discounted.

The Monopoly's Choice of Durability

The meaning of life is that it stops. —*Franz Kafka*

Does a monopoly make a different decision regarding durability than a competitive firm? Suppose only one company can produce light bulbs. Its choice of durability may depend on whether it rents or sells the product. We start by analyzing this problem if the monopoly rents; that is, it sells light services rather than light bulbs. The sales problem is analyzed later.

Renting. Let $Q(R)$ be the number of units of light services that consumers demand in each period if the rental price is R. This demand curve, $Q(R)$, does not change over time. If the monopoly rents the bulbs in each period at price R, it receives a continuous flow of revenue equal to $RQ(R)$ in each period. In contrast, the monopoly's costs of producing $Q(R)$ units per period are not incurred continuously. To provide $Q(R)$ units per period, the monopoly must initially produce $Q(R)$ bulbs, then produce another $Q(R)$ bulbs N periods later, and so on.

The monopoly chooses a rental price, R, and a durability, N, that maximize profits, where profits equal the discounted present value of rentals minus production costs. The choice of durability, however, does not concern consumers. Consumers only care about the rental cost of the light service. How long the bulb lasts is irrelevant to con-

[4]Interest may be compounded continuously rather than just once a year. With continuous compounding and an annual interest rate of 10 percent, the present value of \$1 next year is $\$1e^{-.1} \cong 90¢$. In the following, except where otherwise noted, continuous compounding is used.

[5]The cost function is $C(N) = N^{\alpha}$, where $\alpha = .487$ in Figure 15.1. See **www.aw-bc.com/carlton_perloff** "Optimal Durability Under Competition and Monopoly" for a mathematical treatment.

FIGURE 15.1 Present Value of Costs of Providing One Unit of Service Forever

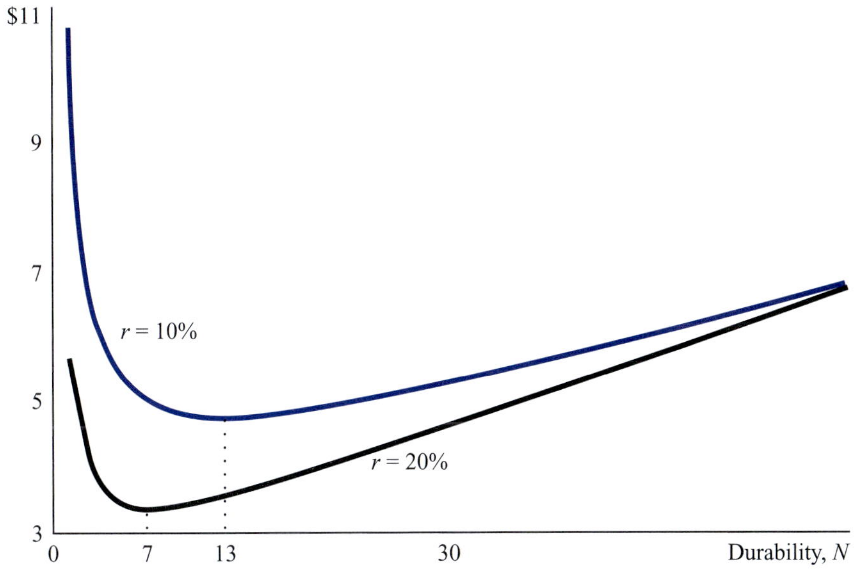

sumers if the monopoly instantly replaces burned-out bulbs with new ones. As a result, the monopoly should choose the N that minimizes the discounted present value of the cost of producing $Q(R)$ units of service forever. Given constant returns to scale, the N that minimizes total cost also minimizes the cost of producing one unit.

Thus, both a competitive firm and a monopoly choose the same N, which is the one that minimizes the cost of producing a unit of light service forever. This result is not surprising because both a monopoly and a competitive firm always produce so as to minimize costs. If the choice of durability affects only costs, both competitive and monopolistic firms choose the same durability. If there are no scale economies and durability does not affect demand for the service, *the optimal durability is identical for a monopoly and a competitor.*[6]

[6]See **www.aw-bc.com/carlton_perloff** "Optimal Durability Under Competition and Monopoly." Schmalensee (1979a) and Liebowitz (1982a) surveyed the durability literature. Swan (1970) was the first to show that a monopoly chooses the same durability as competitive firms under constant returns to scale (cost is increasing in durability but constant per unit with respect to the level of output). Sieper and Swan (1973) relaxed the constant-returns-to-scale assumption by introducing a fixed-capacity cost. They show that durability is independent of market structure in the long-run equilibrium (though not necessarily in the short run). Kamien and Schwartz (1974) showed that with rising average-cost curves, a monopoly chooses a lower durability than competitive firms. However, Swan (1977) noted that if the monopoly has access to the same technology as the competitive industry (many plants), then the independence result continues to hold. More recently, Abel (1983) found that the independence result holds under weaker conditions than constant returns to scale, but that without constant returns to scale, the independence result need not hold. We show later that when the product is sold instead of rented, the monopoly may opt for a shorter-lived product.

TABLE 15.1 Time Pattern of Revenues and Costs

Period	1	2	3	4	...	N	$N+1$	$N+2$	$N+3$	...
Rental revenue per unit	R	R	R	R	...	R	R	R	R	...
Sales revenue per unit	$R\lambda$	0	0	0	...	0	$R\lambda$	0	0	...
Costs per unit	$C(N)$	0	0	0	...	0	$C(N)$	0	0	...

Once the optimal N is chosen, the monopoly must choose how many bulbs, Q, to rent. The monopoly sets marginal revenue equal to marginal cost so as to maximize profits. A competitive firm chooses its output level so that its marginal cost equals price. Thus, although both the competitive industry and the monopoly choose the same durability, the monopoly produces fewer units at a higher price.

Selling. Whether the monopoly rents or sells does not affect this analysis *if the monopoly can convince consumers that it will stick to a particular pricing policy in the future.* We assume that aggregate demand is constant over time. Table 15.1 shows the pattern of revenues and costs for the monopoly over time. The top line shows the rental revenues. The firm receives rents of R in each period for each bulb. The bottom line shows the monopoly's expenditures over time to produce the bulb; the firm has chosen R and N to maximize profits.

Now suppose the monopoly, instead of collecting rent R in each period, allows the rents to accumulate and only collects the rent every N periods. The monopoly collects rents of $R\lambda$, where $R\lambda$ is the present value of the rental for N periods collected all at once rather than every period for N periods.[7] For example, if the rent, R, is \$1 per period, the duration, N, is 3 periods, and the interest rate is 10 percent, then the present value of the rent for 3 periods is $R\lambda = \$1 + \$0.9048 + \$0.8187 \cong \$2.72$. Only \$2.72 is collected rather than \$3 because rent in the future is worth less than rent today.

Both the monopoly and consumers are indifferent between a rent of \$1 per period and a payment collected every three periods of \$2.72 if transaction costs are negligible and *consumers believe that prices will not change in the future.* The monopoly is indifferent between receiving the payment of \$2.72 every three periods or a rent of \$1 each period. The monopoly has no incentive to charge a sale price different from \$2.72 if that is derived from the profit-maximizing rental. A lower or higher price would reduce profits.

As a result, if the bulb is sold rather than rented, the monopoly sells it for $R\lambda$, which is equal to the present value of the rental stream. The present value of the profits from both selling and renting is the same. Because the costs are the same in both

[7]The discount factor with continuous compounding is $\lambda = (1 - e^{-rN})/(1 - e^{-r})$, where r is the annual interest rate.

cases, and (by construction) the present value of revenues collected over N periods is the same, the results of the rental analysis also hold for the sales case and the monopoly chooses the durability that minimizes costs, just as in the competitive case.

Costly Installation and Maintenance

We have just shown that under certain conditions, durability is the same under competition as it is for both a monopoly that rents and a monopoly that sells. When installation is costly or better maintenance can extend a product's life, however, durability can differ across these market structures.

Costly Installation. Suppose that it is costly to install a light bulb. For example, suppose that a maintenance person must change the bulb. If the costs are the same for each consumer, both the monopoly and the competitive firm choose the same durability that minimizes the full cost of changing the bulb, including the installation.

In contrast, suppose that the costs of installing light bulbs vary across consumers, so that the total costs of buying and installing a light bulb differ across consumers. Those consumers with relatively high replacement costs prefer relatively expensive, long-lived bulbs. In contrast, those with relatively low costs prefer relatively inexpensive, short-lived bulbs. Here, durability affects the demand for the service and, since consumers are heterogeneous, the results of the previous section no longer apply. Durability is an attribute of the product that the monopoly can use to segregate consumer groups. In this case, the problem becomes choice of quality. The analysis in Chapter 10 shows that the monopoly typically produces a different range of durabilities than does a competitive industry.

Maintenance. Let us now make the problem more realistic. Suppose that the durability of the product is determined by consumer behavior as well as by the manufacturer. ("If I had known that I was going to live this long, I would have taken better care of myself.") For example, a consumer may be able to use labor to maintain a machine, such as a car, so that it lasts longer. The consumer purchases labor in a competitive market and combines the labor with the machine to produce machine service.

Many different combinations of machines of a particular durability and labor services can be used to produce a steady flow of machine services. If the price of a machine is relatively high, consumers maintain it longer to economize on the number of times the expensive machine must be purchased. For example, when the price of new cars increases, consumers keep their old cars longer.

This problem is analogous to the case of vertical integration with variable proportions discussed in Chapter 12. A monopoly provider of a machine does not want its consumers substituting away from the machine and toward labor. Firms may try to prevent this substitution by contracts that place vertical restraints on consumers. For example, a firm may *tie* maintenance to the purchase of the machine.[8] Maintenance is also tied to the machine if a firm refuses to sell the machine and instead only rents it with maintenance included.

---

[8]Epple and Raviv (1979) show these results also hold when durability is stochastic (varies randomly around an average).

EXAMPLE 15.1 *United Shoe*

United Shoe, which had over 80 percent of the shoe-making equipment market, originally only leased certain machines. As a result of losing an antitrust case [*U.S. v. United Shoe Machinery Corporation,* 110 F. Supp. 295 (1953)], United Shoe was forced to offer its equipment for sale. The United Shoe case is often cited as an example of how a monopoly of a durable good such as shoe-manufacturing equipment only wants to lease and not sell its product.

Based on their examination of the facts of this case, Masten and Snyder (1993) contend that the court's conclusions and subsequent economic analyses are wrong about United Shoe's motivation for its leasing policy. They believe that the lease-only policy was a response to the need to obtain prompt repair. Complicated shoe-making machinery was subject to breakdowns and required continuous service and development. If a firm bought such a machine, it might worry that United Shoe would not provide reliable service.

United Shoe's lease contracts created an automatic incentive for repair. If the machine failed, United Shoe received no lease payment until it repaired the machine. This penalty created incentives for United Shoe to repair the machine quickly—which is what the customer wants when a crucial machine fails.

Masten and Snyder point to two pieces of evidence that support their view. First, they find that it is not true that United Shoe only leased machinery. Indeed, of the 343 machine types it manufactured, United Shoe offered 42 for sale only, 122 for either sale or lease, and 179 for lease only. Thus, a theory based on the desire of a durable good monopoly only to lease does not explain the company's behavior.

Second, they found that United Shoe's lease-only policy was primarily used for expensive, complicated machines that were critical to the buyer's production. This pattern is consistent with using lease-only contracts where providing quick service is essential.

In a famous antitrust case, United Shoe was charged with attempting to monopolize the market for machines that manufacture shoes. One of United Shoe's tactics that was attacked was its refusal to sell certain machines outright. Prior to losing an antitrust case, United Shoe only leased some of its machines with maintenance included. One possible explanation for this *lease-only* policy is that it prevents consumers from maintaining their machines longer than is desirable from the firm's point of view. See Example 15.1.

This maintenance example suggests those conditions where market structure will influence the durability choice. When the consumer can alter the lifetime of his machine in response to the price of a new machine, there will be a consumer optimization decision that will constrain a monopoly that sells but not one that rents. The reason is that there is no consumer optimization decision in the rental case. For example, as goods age, their operating costs often increase. Consumers will choose to stick with their low-quality old goods longer as the price of new goods rises. This ability of consumers to substitute can constrain a monopoly that sells and cause it to behave differently than a monopoly that rents (Rust 1986).

Renting Versus Selling by a Monopoly

It is better to buy a quart of milk by the penny than keep a cow.

—James Howell

Even if machines do not require maintenance, a monopoly may prefer to rent rather than to sell. In the preceding example, in which the monopoly and consumers were indifferent between renting and selling, we assumed that the consumers believed that the monopoly would stick to a particular pricing policy in the future. If, however, the monopoly cannot convince consumers that it will do so, it can make more money by renting than by selling. Indeed, where the monopoly must sell the durable good, it may lose much (or even all) of its market power. To illustrate this result, the following sections first examine the effect of consumers' ability to resell the product, then consumers' behavior, and finally the monopoly's behavior.

Resale Market

Until now, we have assumed that consumers keep a machine until it dies. This section examines the effect on a durable goods monopoly if consumers can resell the machine.

Consider a monopoly that produces a nondurable good (a good that is completely consumed in one period) and sells Q^* units at \$10 to those who value the product the most. Even if those Q^* consumers may resell the product, there are no further transactions because, by assumption, those Q^* consumers who valued the product most already own it, and no one else is interested in bidding the product away. The market price remains at \$10. The ability to resell leaves the optimal pricing unchanged.

As long as the consumers who value the machine the most do not change over time, the same result holds for durable goods. Suppose a monopoly sells durable machines with a lifetime of N and that it is profit maximizing to sell Q^* units every N periods. That is, customers consume Q^* units of machine service (for example, light) each period. The initial consumers of the machines are those who value it the most, and by assumption they continue to be the ones who value it the most, so there are no resales. The opportunity for resales leaves the optimal (sales) solution unaffected.

Suppose now that the overall demand curve for the machine services each period does not vary over time, but the consumers who value the machine the most change. In this case, there are resales from owners who now place less value on the machines to consumers who now value the machines highly but do not own them. Because Q^* machines (the monopoly's optimal number) are available each period, the value consumers place on consuming the product per period (the implicit rental price) is unchanged over time because, by assumption, aggregate demand is unchanged. The initial sales of the machine reflect the discounted present value of these consumer values. As in Table 15.1, resale does not affect R (the implicit rental price), so the solution is the same as in the case where the identity of those who value the good the most is unchanged.

We illustrate these results with a light bulb example. Consumers are willing to pay \$1 per period per light bulb, the interest rate is 10 percent, and the monopoly's optimal solution is to produce 50 light bulbs that last 3 periods. The present value of a bulb given a rental of \$1 for 3 periods is \$2.72(= \$1 + \$.90 + \$.82).

Now suppose that consumers' desires change over time so that resales occur each period but that overall demand for services each period is unchanged. If an initial owner in the first period sells the bulb a year later to another consumer, then the discounted value in the initial period from the resale in the beginning of the second period is \$1.72.[9] That is, after reselling the bulb, the initial owner has spent \$2.72 − \$1.72 = \$1 for the use of the bulb for one year, which equals the rental rate for one year. It is, of course, of no interest to the monopoly if this resale occurs because the total demand it faces has not changed: The same number of bulbs are demanded in each period as when consumers' desires were unchanging. With a resale market of used goods, the optimal solution to the monopoly's problem is the same whether consumers' preferences change or do not change because the full monopoly profits are obtained in the initial sales of the light bulb.[10] The presence of a resale market does constrain the price that can be charged by the monopoly in the periods subsequent to the initial sale. See Example 15.2.

Without a resale market, when the consumers who value the good the most change over time, the monopoly cannot obtain as high profits as it would if the same consumers always valued the good the most. For example, suppose you want the use of a refrigerator during this school year only. If you cannot resell it, you are not willing to pay as much for it as you would if you planned to keep it for its entire product life. Resales help both consumers and the monopoly by effectively lowering the cost of providing each unit of service to consumers and by allowing the monopoly to capture the value of subsequent resales in the initial purchase price.

A resale market is different than a recycling market. To show the distinction, we examine an aluminum monopoly. The aluminum is sold to fabricators who sell aluminum pots to consumers. Suppose consumers discard aluminum pots when they get old. A recycling firm finds the pots. The pots are melted to create aluminum. This recovered aluminum is sold in a *secondary market* that competes with the original monopoly. Consumers are not willing to pay as much for the aluminum as they would if they could resell it. The secondary market constrains the monopoly, but consumers' willingness to pay is lower than when *they* receive the value of the recycled pot.

---

[9]The original owner receives \$1.9048 in the second period, so the discounted value of this resale in the initial period is \$1.72.

[10]One qualification to this result is that the optimal rental solution (that prevents resale) does not require the monopoly to reduce output over time. A sales policy cannot always duplicate a rental policy when cutbacks in output are required over time. Moreover, if consumers differ, preventing resale can sometimes allow price discrimination.

The importance of a secondary market was debated in a famous antitrust case involving Alcoa. Alcoa was the sole supplier of aluminum ingot; however, aluminum products can be recycled to obtain aluminum ingot. The legal question became whether Alcoa had market power even though it did not control the secondary scrap market directly. The recycling market constrained the price Alcoa could charge in subsequent periods for its aluminum. When demand is growing over time, the constraint of the secondary market on the monopoly's pricing is an empirical issue (see Example 15.3 and Martin 1982). If demand is growing extremely rapidly so that the supply of the resold material does not account for a large fraction of demand, then there is little constraint on the monopoly. Academic analyses of the Alcoa case (Example 15.3) find that Alcoa was little constrained by the secondary market due to growing demand.

We can now understand how a monopoly that sells may have an incentive to intervene in the used good market, buy up and discard used goods, and thereby reduce the supply of used goods. Alternatively, the monopoly may produce a durable good with a shorter life. Suppose consumers do not regard new and used goods as perfect substitutes. Then control of (or intervention into) the used good market can better allow a monopolist who sells to price discriminate. (Fudenberg and Tirole 1998, 1999, Waldman 1997, and Hendel and Lizzeri 1999a). A renting monopoly automatically can control the ratio of new and used goods, but this is not true for a monopoly that sells. Accordingly, intervention in the used good market can enable the monopoly that sells to reduce the availability of used goods and charge a higher price for new goods by eliminating the substitutable used goods. Therefore, laws or actions by the monopoly may raise the transaction costs of using the resale market, thereby limiting the competition the monopoly faces from secondhand sales. (In contrast, the Internet may lower these transaction costs, in so doing exacerbating the monopoly's problem.) Many developed countries have laws requiring that artists receive a share of the proceeds of any resale. To the degree that they are enforced—typically only for major artists at auction sales in a few European countries—these laws discourage resales (Perloff 1998, Solow 1998).

Recent literature considers the effect of leasing when there is also an adverse selection problem, where the resellers of a durable good know its quality but potential buyers do not (see the lemons model in Chapter 13). See Example 15.4.

★Consumers' Expectations Constrain the Monopoly

We should all be concerned about the future because we will have to spend the rest of our lives there. —*Charles Francis Kettering*

When resales are possible, the price that consumers are willing to pay for a durable good depends on both the value of the services of the durable good during the period the consumer owns it and the resale value at the end of that period. That is, consumers' expectations about the future resale price affect the initial price. For example, if you buy a house, the amount you are willing to pay depends in part on how much

EXAMPLE 15.2

The Importance of Used Goods

In 1985, Deere & Co. proposed acquiring the farm machinery division of Versatile Co., a Canadian company. Deere & Co. is one of the world's largest manufacturers of a variety of tractors. Versatile was one of the largest producers of four-wheel-drive (4WD) tractors, which have power in all four wheels.

Versatile and Deere were the top two North American producers of 4WD tractors in 1985 and were of roughly equal size; between them, they had a substantial share of the sales of new tractors. There were only two other major producers of 4WD tractors. Just a few years earlier there had been double the number of firms, but the precipitous collapse of the farm economy reduced the 1985 demand for 4WD tractors to about 30 percent of that in 1981, from about 14,000 units to about 5,000 units.

Tractors are a durable good, and 4WD tractors are especially durable, lasting anywhere from 15 to 30 years. There is a well-organized market for used tractors, and many farmers can substitute between new and used equipment. As a result, there is a close relationship in the price movements of new and used goods.

If new and used goods are substitutes, then market shares based on new sales have limited meaning. Even if a firm suddenly becomes a monopoly of new sales, but new sales account for only a small fraction of total tractors in use, the monopoly could not raise the price of new tractors significantly.

The rental rate of tractors is determined by the intersection of the supply curve of tractor services with the demand curve. The price equals the discounted present value of future rentals. In any year, the supply of tractor services equals the services available from the new stock plus those available from the old stock. The supply of services from the old stock equals the (depreciated) service left in tractors sold in previous years. The supply curve in year t can be written as a function of the year and the rental rate, R:

$$S(R, t) = S_{\text{o}}(R, t) + S_{\text{n}}(R, t),$$

where $S_{\text{o}}(R, t)$ is the old supply at rental rate R in year t and $S_{\text{n}}(R, t)$ is the new supply at rental rate R in year t.

If we ignore maintenance, the rental rate, R, does not affect the supply from previous years, so we need not write the supply from previous years as a function of the rental rate. An econometric analysis indicates that the annual depreciation rate was

you think you will receive when you sell it years later. This section analyzes the effects of consumers' price expectations on a monopoly.

Products that are likely to be fads, and hence worthless in the future, tend to sell for less today than products that will remain valuable. In general, consumers' price expectations depend on what they believe about the demand curve and the output of a mo-

about 8 percent per year. Because 92 percent of the previous year's supply is available in a given year, the supply in 1985 was

$$S_o(1985) = .92\ S_n(1984) + .92 \times .92\ S_n(1983) + \cdots.$$

Based on this formula and the data on sales, the ratio of new tractors to existing stock in 1985 was less than 10 percent. Because older tractors dominate the stock of tractors in use and are likely to do so for years to come, even a monopoly of new tractors could not profitably and significantly reduce total industry supply (and hence significantly raise prices) for several years.

The U.S. Department of Justice, in deciding whether to permit mergers, is concerned primarily about the effect of a merger on prices. Thus, the Department of Justice is likely to permit a merger that creates a firm with a large market share but no ability to raise prices.

The Department of Justice felt that the Versatile acquisition posed anticompetitive problems. The Department of Justice understood the constraining effect of used equipment but felt that it was not significant enough to prevent price from rising over the foreseeable future. In deference to the Canadian government's plea that otherwise Versatile would exit the industry, the Department of Justice said it would allow the acquisition if there were no other potential buyer. The transaction was never completed.

The analysis suggests that any durable good with a low depreciation rate and a large outstanding stock might be hard to monopolize, at least initially (Carlton and Gertner 1989). For example, in the automobile industry, the depreciation rate (23 percent) is about three times higher than that for tractors. Thus, all else the same, a monopoly in automobiles could raise prices sooner than one in tractors because used goods constrain the market for a shorter time in the automobile industry.

Moreover, it can be shown that in a durable good industry, competition among oligopolists is likely to be more intense than in a nondurable good industry (Carlton and Gertner 1989). The intuition behind this result is that a firm that makes an extra sale today is taking current and future rentals from rivals, increasing the incentive to make sales today relative to that for a nondurable good.

Note: Carlton worked as a consultant to Deere & Co.

Sources: Farm and Industrial Equipment Institute. *State of the Industry 1985 Update* and *The State of the Industry 1978–1980;* Canadian Firm and Industrial Equipment Institute. *Industry Outlook* 1986; U.S. Department of Agriculture, Economic Research Service. *Outlook and Situation Report,* August 1985.

nopoly in subsequent periods, because demand and output levels determine the resale price.

The constraining effect of consumers' expectations leads to a surprising result, sometimes called the **Coase Conjecture** (Coase 1972): A durable goods monopoly that sells its product has less market power—indeed, in the extreme case, no market

EXAMPLE 15.3 *The Alcoa Case: Secondhand Economics*

In 1945, Judge Learned Hand, writing for a panel of three judges, found the Aluminum Company of America (Alcoa) guilty of monopolizing the domestic aluminum market. The case turned, in large part, on the court's finding that the relevant market consisted only of domestic aluminum production and net imports of primary ingot. The court held that secondary aluminum, which is obtained by remelting aluminum scrap, was *not* part of the market even though secondary aluminum is a close substitute for primary aluminum. Judge Hand's reasoning was that Alcoa controlled the secondary production through its domination of primary production. Essentially, he contended that the existence of secondary aluminum producers did not substantially curtail Alcoa's monopoly profits from the sale of primary aluminum.

Several economists have examined whether Judge Hand was correct. Gaskins (1974) estimated the demand for aluminum and the supply of secondary aluminum and used other data to simulate the long-run effects of having a secondary market. He compared simulations with and without a secondary market, and he obtained two key results. First, the presence of a secondary (recycling) market causes a durable goods monopoly to set a higher price initially. Second, because the demand for aluminum was growing over time, the constraining effect of the secondary market was small.

For one set of parameters, he found that the initial price was 6 percent above the monopoly price without a secondary market and nearly 3.5 times larger than the competitive price (long-run marginal cost). The long-run monopoly equilibrium price with a secondary market was 14 percent less than the monopoly price without a secondary market, but 2.8 times higher than the competitive price. According to the simulations, the monopoly price with a secondary market falls slowly over time, so that it takes 100 years for the price to fall within 5 percent of its long-run equilibrium value.

Swan (1980), using different models, conducted other simulations that reached the same conclusion: Alcoa's predicted price was only slightly below the monopoly price without a secondary market and well above the competitive price (based on Alcoa's own cost figures).

power—when compared to a monopoly that rents the durable good.[11] The intuition behind this result is that a monopoly that sells has an incentive to cut price in the future, whereas such behavior does not occur if the monopoly only rents. We now illustrate this result through a series of examples.

[11]See Stokey (1981), Bulow (1982), and Gul, Sonnenschein, and Wilson (1986) for proofs of the Coase Conjecture under various conditions. Bagnoli, Salant, and Swierzbinski (1989) show that the Coase Conjecture proof of Gul, Sonnenschein, and Wilson (1986) depends on a continuum of consumers (two neighboring consumers are virtually identical) and that, with discrete demand types, the Coase Conjecture can fail.

Gaskins explained why the first-period price is higher than the short-run monopoly price. His argument has three steps. (1) Initially, there is no stock of aluminum, so there is no secondary market. Later, for a given stock of aluminum in the world, the higher the price for aluminum, the more it pays to convert scrap aluminum to pure aluminum, so the supply of secondary aluminum is increasing in price. (2) When maximizing the present discounted profits, a firm must trade off short-run versus long-run profits. Thus, the firm must be concerned that higher production in the short run will lead to a larger stock of aluminum later and hence more competition from the secondary market. (3) Therefore, in the initial period, the primary-producer monopoly sells even less than the short-run profit-maximizing level of output and charges a price that is higher than the monopoly price.

Gaskins concluded that Judge Hand's contention that monopoly control of primary production is nearly equivalent to a pure monopoly in its welfare implications was approximately correct in this case. That is, leaving out the secondary market did not substantially bias the results. Including the secondary market still would have left Alcoa with a large market share and would have led to the same conclusion. Because in other cases the secondary market can constrain pricing in the primary market, it is, in general, a mistake to ignore it (Fisher 1974).

Suslow (1986b) argued that, because new and used aluminum are not perfect substitutes, Alcoa's market power was not as constrained by the fringe as it would have been were they perfect substitutes. Similarly, she noted that there are lengthy recycling lags, so Alcoa faced limited recycling in its early years. She estimated that before 1940, Alcoa's markup of price over its short-run marginal cost was 59 percent. That is, she concluded that the "Alcoa problem" was not very important to Alcoa.

Technical Note: In the simulations of Gaskins and Swan, Alcoa is assumed to be able to set its pricing in the initial period and to stick to that pricing. Thus, these results differ from the more appropriate model that assumes Alcoa changes its policy over time. See the discussion in this chapter on consumer expectations and Suslow (1986a).

Examples Where Consumers Do Not Expect Price Cuts. First, suppose that a monopoly produces a nondurable good that lasts for only one period. There are no costs of production. The demand curve for the services of the good is

$$Q(R) = 20 - R \tag{15.1}$$

where R is the rental price and $Q(R)$ is the amount demanded at rental rate R. In this one-period market, the optimal policy for the monopoly is to charge \$10 and sell 10 units.[12] The monopoly's profits (revenues) are \$100. It makes no difference whether

[12]The monopoly's profits are equal to its revenues, which are $20R - R^2$. The first-order condition for profit-maximization is $20 - 2R = 0$, or $R = 10$.

EXAMPLE 15.4

Leasing Under Adverse Selection

Car manufacturers must consider the effect of the used car market on their future sales. People who highly value quality buy new cars, which they eventually resell to lower-valuation consumers. As our discussion of the lemons model (Chapter 13) illustrates, adverse selection occurs in used car markets because the seller, who has driven and maintained the car, is likely to know more about the quality of the car than potential buyers do. Indeed, Emons and Sheldon (2002) find that the predictions of the lemons model are true: Used car buyers in Switzerland are less informed than sellers, and sub-average cars are traded by private sellers (although not necessarily by dealers).

If all leased cars were returned to dealers, sellers (dealers) of used leased cars would not have better information than potential buyers because no self-selection would have occurred in which only the worst-quality used cars were sold. Because leasing, but not selling, new cars avoids adverse selection in the used car market, we would expect that the price for used cars that were leased would exceed that of used cars that originally were purchased new (Hendel and Lizzeri 2002, Waldman 2003). That expectation is confirmed by the data on prices. Consequently, a monopoly seller of new cars could lease to avoid the inefficiency in used car markets that results from asymmetric information. Such a monopoly earns more money from leasing a new car and then reselling than it would from selling the new car and leaving the initial buyer with the problem of reselling a used car subject to the lemons problem.

Consumers can choose between buying and leasing a car. Those who lease make an additional choice: to buy the car at the end of the lease period or to return it. Auto-leasing contracts typically specify a rental rate and an option price at which the used good can be bought at the end of the lease period. This price need not have any connection to the expected price of a used car.

By making these choices, consumers segment the market. Whether consumers buy, lease without buying, or lease with buying provides information that influences the degree of adverse selection in the used car market. Strikingly, higher-income consumers are more likely than lower-income consumers to lease (contrary to what the

the monopoly rents or sells because there are no future periods: Renting is identical to selling.

Suppose this durable good lasts for two periods and that the demand curve for services (rather than for the good itself) is Equation 15.1 in each of the two periods and zero thereafter. If the monopoly only rents the good and the demand curve for services remains constant, the optimal policy is for the monopoly to rent 10 units of the good in Period 1 for \$10 and 10 units in Period 2 for \$10, producing all 10 units in Period 1 and no units in Period 2. With this policy, the monopoly earns \$200 total (assuming the interest rate is zero for simplicity).

popular press frequently claims, arguing that lower-income people prefer the lower cash flows from leasing).

Hendel and Lizzeri (2002) predict that leased cars will have a higher turnover rate than purchased new cars because owners of leased cars value having the latest model car, and because the resale market for leased cars avoids the serious adverse selection problem of the typical used good market. In fact, people who lease cars are more likely to return the car at the end of the lease period than are owners likely to sell on the used car market after two or three years. Only one-quarter of leased cars are bought at the end of the contract. Because most lease contracts mature in two or three years, a large percentage of leased cars are sold in the used market by the time they are three years old. In 1996, formerly leased cars were 42% of all "premium" used cars: those two to four years old. Nearly 20% more leased cars were resold in this period than owned cars. As a result, used cars that were leased were of better quality than used cars of the same vintage that were not leased.

In a lemons market where owners resell their cars, we may expect that used cars offered for sale are worth less than the average used car price. In contrast, by setting a post-lease purchase price higher than the market-clearing price in the used market, the manufacturer can make sure that its resold leased cars are worth more than the average used car price.

The share of consumers leasing new cars has risen substantially over time: About 3.5% leased new cars in 1985, 7.3% in 1990, 24.2% in 1995, and 31.5% in 1998 and 2002, according to CNW Marketing/Research. Hendel and Lizzeri note that the increased popularity of leasing is partially explained by recent improvements in durability. The incentive of a manufacturer to lease rises as its good becomes more durable, because by improving the resale market value (by mitigating the adverse selection problem), the manufacturer can considerably increase the full value of a new good (which includes its initial lease price plus its resale value).

Sources: **http://www.eere.energy.gov/vehiclesandfuels/facts/2003/fcvt_fotw269.shtml**, Hendel and Lizzeri (2002), and Waldman (2003).

Now consider the optimal sales policy *if consumers do not expect a price cut in the second period and the monopoly can commit to selling nothing in the second period.* The monopoly sells 10 units at the beginning of Period 1 for \$20. Consumers are willing to pay \$20 per unit to buy because, according to Equation 15.1, consumers are willing to pay \$10 per period per unit in Periods 1 and 2. The monopoly earns \$200 in Period 1 and no revenue in Period 2. This argument is the same as the one made previously with respect to Table 15.1. Thus, the optimal sales policy is equivalent to the optimal rental policy and gives the monopoly \$200 in profits.

Consumers Expect Future Price Cuts. For the optimal rental policy and the optimal sales policy to be equivalent, the monopoly must sell 10 units in Period 1 and nothing in Period 2. Is such a policy believable? We now show that the monopoly has an incentive to produce in the second period, so that the price in Period 2 is less than in Period 1, and rational consumers anticipate this fall in price.

Consider the demand curve the monopoly faces in Period 2. Because only one period remains at the beginning of Period 2, a consumer willing to rent the good for R in Period 2 is willing to pay R to purchase the good. That is, in the last period there is no difference between the sales price and the rental price for a durable product. Therefore, the demand curve the monopoly seller faces in Period 2 equals the demand given in Equation 15.1 minus the 10 units that are already in the marketplace. This residual demand curve in Period 2 is shown in Equation 15.2, where R_2 is the rental rate that is equivalent to the selling price of the good in Period 2, and $Q_2(R_2)$ is the number of additional units beyond those already sold in Period 1 that the monopoly sells in Period 2 for R_2:

$$Q_2(R_2) = (20 - R_2) - 10 = 10 - R_2. \tag{15.2}$$

Given this residual demand curve in Period 2, will the monopoly decide to produce zero units in Period 2? The answer is clearly no. The monopoly faced with the demand curve of Equation 15.2 sets $R_2 = \$5$, sells $Q_2 = 5$, and receives revenues of \$25 in Period 2.[13] Thus, the monopoly has an incentive to produce a positive amount in Period 2. The sales policy in which the monopoly produces 10 units in Period 1 and 0 units in Period 2 is not credible to consumers, who recognize that the monopoly has an incentive to produce a positive amount in Period 2.

Won't these sales in Period 2 be good for the monopoly? Surprisingly, the answer is no if consumers anticipate this behavior. But why? If the monopoly can sell 10 units in Period 1 for \$200 and then sell 5 more units in Period 2 for an additional \$25, the monopoly earns a total of \$225, which is more than the previous \$200. Unfortunately for the monopoly, this calculation is wrong.

A monopoly that only rents is unconstrained in setting profit-maximizing rental fees. In the calculation above, the highest total profit it can earn is \$200; hence, earning more is impossible, because \$200 *is* the profit-maximizing solution. The problem with the reasoning in the sales calculation is that no one is willing to pay \$20 per unit in Period 1 if the monopoly is going to sell the same unit in Period 2 for only \$5.[14] In other words, consumers in Period 1 are only willing to pay $R_1 + R_2$ for a machine,

---

[13]The monopoly's profit is $\pi_2 = (10 - R_2)R_2$. From the first-order condition with respect to R_2, $R_2 = 5$. Substituting 5 for R_2 into Equation 15.2, $Q_2 = 5$.

[14]We assume that consumers are rational and have perfect foresight about the monopoly's behavior in Period 2. If consumers are myopic and do not expect the monopoly to produce in the second period, then consumers' expectations not only do not constrain the monopoly, but benefit the monopoly, which can earn profits of \$225. That is, the monopoly's maximized profit is \$200 if consumers cannot be fooled but more if they can. For example, if consumers are gullible, the monopoly can tell them that the price will rise next period to induce them to pay more initially. Indeed, profit is unbounded if consumers believe everything they are told.

where R_1 is the implicit rental value they place on the machine in Period 1 (\$10) and R_2 is the rental value in Period 2 (\$5). No consumer values the good at \$10 in Period 2 if it can be purchased for only \$5. If the monopoly produces additional units in Period 2, so that R_2 equals \$5 instead of \$10, consumers are only willing to pay \$15 (rather than \$20) to purchase the good in Period 1. Thus, the total amount the monopoly earns from sales is actually $\$15 \times 10 + \$5 \times 5 = \$175$, which is less than the \$200 it would earn if it only rented.

This example illustrates an important point: When the monopoly sells the good rather than rents it, it has an incentive to produce and sell a positive number of additional units in Period 2. These additional sales drive the price down in Period 2 below what it would have been had no additional units been produced. This lower price, in turn, causes consumers to lower the amount they are willing to pay for the good in Period 1. Moreover, consumers recognize the monopoly's incentive to produce in Period 2 and *expect* such additional production to occur. Their expectations influence their behavior in Period 1.

If the monopoly rents, it faces no constraints from consumers' price expectations. It can produce more in later periods without affecting the rental rate in the first period, because consumers do not care about future production. It is not optimal for the monopoly to produce and rent additional units in Period 2: If it tries to rent more units in Period 2, the rental rate is driven down below the profit-maximizing level.

Thus, a monopoly that must sell the good is actually constrained in a way that does not occur in the rental case. When selling, the monopoly cannot credibly commit to producing zero units in Period 2, in contrast to the rental case. It cannot credibly commit in the sales case because consumers know that it is *not* optimal for the monopoly to produce nothing in the second period, whereas that policy is optimal if the monopoly only rents.

Because the rental solution was an unconstrained profit maximization, a monopoly earns as high or higher profits from renting as it does from selling. The monopoly is harmed in the selling case by being unable to credibly restrain itself from producing in the future. In other words, the monopoly suffers from being able to produce additional units in Period 2 profitably because this extra production lowers price in the initial period. United Shoe Company, IBM, and Xerox all initially only rented some of their durable products; however, they are now legally required to sell them (Bulow 1982, 318). (But see Example 15.1.)

There are several methods whereby a monopoly can overcome the problem caused by consumers' expectations. Before discussing them, however, let us return to the problem of the monopoly that must sell a durable good in a two-period world and determine its *second-best* policy (its "optimal" policy given that it must sell rather than rent).

The Monopoly's Optimal Sales Policy. To determine the monopoly's second-best sales policy, we work backwards starting in Period 2 (see Appendix 15A for more detail). Suppose the monopoly sells Q_1 in Period 1. Then, the residual demand curve facing the monopoly in Period 2 is

$$Q_2(R_2) = 20 - R_2 - Q_1, \tag{15.3}$$

which is a generalization of Equation 15.2, where we replace the number 10 with Q_1. The monopoly solves for the optimal rental rate, R_2, that maximizes profits, where demand depends on the quantity sold in Period 1.

The residual demand curve in Figure 15.2 hits both the R_2 and Q_2 axes at $20 - Q_1$. The marginal revenue curve, *MR*, corresponding to this residual demand curve hits the Q_2 axis at half the distance from the origin, $10 - 1/2Q_1$, as does the demand curve, because the demand curve is linear. Because costs (and hence marginal costs) are zero, profits are maximized where $MR = 0$. As the figure shows, that occurs where $R_2 = Q_2 = 10 - 1/2Q_1$. Total profits in Period 2, π_2, are shown as the shaded box in the figure. Thus, output, rents, and profits in the second period all depend on output in the first period, Q_1. The monopoly wants to maximize the present value of profits in the two periods combined, which are equal to profits in Period 1 plus profits in Period 2 (assuming the interest rate is 0, so that profits in Period 2 are not discounted). That is, the present value of profits (*PVP*) is

$$PVP = \pi_1 + \pi_2 = (R_1 + R_2)Q_1 + R_2Q_2. \quad (15.4)$$

The sales price in Period 1 equals the rental rate in that period plus the rental rate in Period 2. The sales price in Period 2 equals the rental rate in that period. The rental rate in Period 2 depends on the total amount consumed in Period 2, $Q_1 + Q_2$.

Having shown that the monopoly's choice of R_2 and Q_2 depends on Q_1, we now examine how profits depend on Q_1. Because R_1 depends on Q_1 (Equation 15.1), *PVP*

FIGURE 15.2 Profits in the Second Period

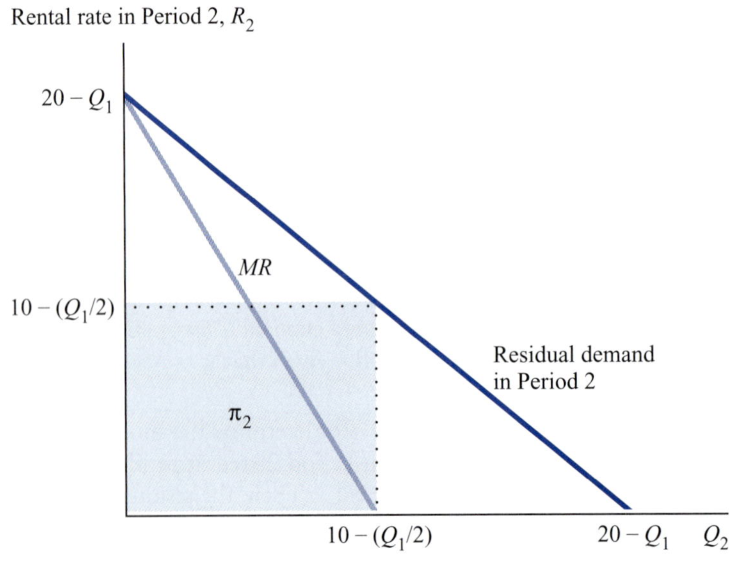

TABLE 15.2 Profits in a Two-Period Model

Sales Period 1, Q_1	Rental Rate Period 1, R_1	Sales Period 2, Q_2	Rental Rate Period 2, R_2	Profits Period 1, π_1	Profits Period 2, π_2	Present Value of Profits, $PVP = \pi_1 + \pi_2$
1	19	9.5	9.5	28.5	90.25	118.75
2	18	9	9	54	81	135
3	17	8.5	8.5	76.5	72.25	148.75
4	16	8	8	96	64	160
5	15	7.5	7.5	112.5	56.25	168.75
6	14	7	7	126	49	175
7	13	6.5	6.5	136.5	42.25	178.75
8	**12**	**6**	**6**	**144**	**36**	**180**
9	11	5.5	5.5	148.5	30.25	178.75
10	10	5	5	150	25	175
11	9	4.5	4.5	148.5	20.25	168.75

$\pi_1 = (R_1 + R_2)Q_1$
$\pi_2 = R_2 Q_2$
$Q_2 = 10 - 1/2 Q_1$

(Equation 15.4) can be expressed in terms of only Q_1. Table 15.2 shows how profits vary with Q_1. Where $Q_1 = 8$, the present value of profits is maximized at \$180.

This *PVP* of \$180 is higher than the \$175 that is obtained when $Q_1 = 10$. Setting $Q_1 = 10$ leads to higher profits in the first period than when $Q_1 = 8$, but profits in the second period are enough lower that *PVP* is lower when $Q_1 = 10$. However, this *PVP* of \$180 is lower than the rent-only *PVP* of \$200.

The Paradox. The preceding analysis demonstrates that a monopoly's profits are lower when it sells rather than rents. The reason selling is less profitable is that the monopoly produces too much in the later periods. In our example, the monopoly is better off committing to produce nothing at all in the second period. Unfortunately for a monopoly that sells the machine, that policy is not credible. Consumers realize that the monopoly will produce in Period 2 and hence the price in Period 2 will be below that in Period 1, so they will pay less in Period 1 than if they expected no production in Period 2. This problem with consumer expectations does not arise in our example when the monopoly only rents because the expectation is credible that the monopoly that rents will not expand output in the future.

In our two-period sales example, the price in Period 2 is below that in Period 1. When the two-period sales example is extended to cover many periods (Appendix 15A), the monopoly's price falls in each subsequent period. It can be shown that the price falls to zero as the number of periods increases. A monopoly's behavior, where it sells continuously over any given time span, can be approximated by a model with a finite number of many short time periods. As the length of the periods shortens, the number of periods increases. The model suggests that the price will be driven to zero quickly by this increase in periods (Appendix 15A). It therefore follows that a monopoly that sells a durable good can never receive a price above the competitive price (zero in our example) even for a short period of time. One way to think about this puzzling result is that if the monopoly cannot credibly commit to a policy of no further production, it is as if the monopoly is a different firm in each future period. With an infinite number of future periods, it is as if there were an infinite number of competitors. Thus, the monopoly of the future is competing with the monopoly of today, and this competition immediately drives the price down to the competitive level.[15]

This result is indeed bizarre and arises, in part, from the extreme assumption that has been made about the cost conditions. It is not the assumption that costs are zero that turns out to be critical. The results hold for any (constant) positive level of marginal costs. The critical assumption is that the output level can be increased costlessly as fast as the monopoly desires. If consumers know that the monopoly cannot expand output costlessly, then consumers can credibly believe that output in the future is constrained and therefore the price can remain above the competitive price for some time. This insight leads to a variety of policies that a monopoly can undertake to get around the expectations problem.

How the Monopoly May Solve Its Expectations Problem. We have just shown that a durable goods monopoly that sells its product loses monopoly power when consumers form their own expectations as to the monopoly's future behavior.[16] A monopoly can only overcome this problem by credibly committing itself not to take advantage of certain profitable opportunities in the future. There are at least five ways the monopoly may avoid the expectation problem (Bulow 1982, 329–31).

First, the monopoly can refuse to sell the product and only *rent* or lease it. Renting or leasing may reduce or avoid the expectation problem (Bulow 1982) (see Example 15.5). Durable goods are frequently leased. A third of the capital equipment used by U.S. corporations is leased.

Second, the monopoly may try to convince consumers that it will limit the number of units it produces, which will prevent the future price from falling. If consumers are aware that a monopoly faces an upward-sloping marginal cost curve, they know that the monopoly will produce fewer units than it would if it faced a horizontal marginal cost curve.[17] Consequently, if a monopoly has a choice of two technologies, it may

---

[15]We ignored depreciation of the durable good in our discussion. Bond and Samuelson (1984), Suslow (1986a), and Karp (1996) examine the durable goods monopoly problem with depreciation.

[16]For a discussion of durable goods and oligopoly, see Ausubel and Deneckere (1987), Gul (1987), and Carlton and Gertner (1989).

[17]Kahn (1986) shows that if the monopoly sells an infinitely durable product with an increasing marginal cost of production, the sales policy results in a lower level of stock (that is, cumulative sales) than the socially optimal level, but that the monopolistic stock asymptotically approaches the socially optimal long-run solution. If the good is not infinitely durable, the asymptotic stock under the monopoly sales policy is less than the socially optimal long-run solution.

EXAMPLE 15.5 *Sales Versus Rentals*

A monopoly has an incentive to rent to avoid problems due to consumer expectations about future prices (the Coase Conjecture problem). In contrast, a firm with rivals may want to sell. Increased sales, like greater durability, allow the firm to lock up consumers today (prevents them from buying from rivals in the future). Thus, we would expect that the more competition a firm faces, the greater its sales/rental ratio.

Both IBM and Xerox substantially increased their sales/rental ratios (where rental includes returns from both renting and services) from 1968 to 1983 as their competition apparently increased. This ratio for IBM rose from 0.46 in 1966 to 1.38 in 1983. The ratio for Xerox rose from 0.28 in 1968 to 0.85 in 1983. Various factors in addition to increased competition may have contributed to the increased use of sales.

Source: Bulow (1986), Carlton and Gertner (1989).

choose a less efficient technology with a steeper marginal cost curve (Karp and Perloff 1996). In the extreme case where the monopoly's marginal cost curve is vertical, it can produce at most a fixed number of units. For example, an artist may commit to producing only a limited number of a particular lithograph (each explicitly numbered) by destroying the plate used to produce it.

Third, if the firm cannot explicitly contract to control its future production, it may attempt to acquire a *reputation* for never lowering price. For example, De Beers, the South African diamond monopoly, claimed it had a policy of never reducing the nominal price of its diamonds (although it apparently has on occasion). See **www.aw-bc.com/carlton_perloff** "A Diamond Price Is Forever?"

Fourth, because the problem of expectations arises only for durable goods, the monopoly can produce *less durable* goods. The monopoly can use **planned obsolescence**—purposely making a durable good short-lived—as a way of limiting its ability to lower its price in the future (Bulow 1986, Waldman 1993, Fishman and Rob 2000, and Kumar 2002). Having new models each year, as with automobiles or high-fashion dresses, may be examples of planned obsolescence; however, the costs of redesigning products frequently limit the monopoly's ability to use this technique. Microsoft and other software firms can relatively easily upgrade their products. See Example 15.6.

Fifth, the monopoly can *guarantee* to buy back products from any consumers at the price they paid for it. This *buy-back* provision protects the consumer in case the monopoly expands output and thereby lowers price in the future. This policy is not feasible where consumer abuse may lower the value of a product, as with automobiles, or if the products cannot be easily transferred, as with railroad tracks. Similarly, a monopoly may use other contractual clauses, such as best-price or most-favored-nation provisions to reassure customers about future prices (Butz 1990).

Thus, there are a number of ways in which a durable goods manufacturer may precommit itself to assure consumers that goods purchased today will not drop in value tomorrow. A durable good monopoly can maintain its market value by renting or by

EXAMPLE 15.6 *Lowering the Resale Value of Used Textbooks*

A monopoly or oligopoly producer of a durable good can reduce competition from used goods by producing new, superior products over time. Successful textbooks are revised (and, we hope, improved) relatively frequently, typically at three- or four-year intervals. As we were working on this textbook's revision, the fourth edition, we used an Internet book-price search site to check the prices of the third edition. The (then current) third edition had a U.S. list price of $98. Used copies of the third edition in good-to-excellent shape sold for between $50 and $90. In contrast, used (or even unused) copies of the second edition sold for between $7.50 and $65. Thus, the issuance of a new edition reduced the resale value of an older edition.

The publisher gains from issuing a revised textbook because it contains new material that makes it more valuable than the older edition, a feature that allows the publisher to charge more for the newer edition than it could charge for the older one. However, because frequent revisions lower students' expectations about the resale value of a text, the publisher knows that frequent revisions lower the price that students are willing to pay for a new edition, ignoring the improvements. A publisher must consider the trade-off between these two offsetting effects when deciding how frequently to revise a text. Finally, some books are classics that students never want to part with. Our advice to you is to save this invaluable book for use as a reference (or paperweight) and not even consider reselling it!

selling "with strings attached." What is striking in this case is that the strings bind the monopoly, not the consumers, and that the monopoly likes it that way.

SUMMARY

The future isn't what it used to be.

Market structure usually does not affect the durability of a good when durability, by itself, is not important to consumers and when firms are not constrained by consumer expectations. Firms choose the durability that minimizes the cost of providing the services. This result does not hold if consumers have preferences for a specific durability (such as new model cars).

Generally, a monopoly is better off if it can rent its product than if it must sell it. When the monopoly must sell the product with no strings attached, consumers can invest more in maintenance, so they purchase fewer durable goods in the future. Moreover, rational consumers expect that a monopoly will produce more units in the future, thereby lowering both future prices and resale values, and as a result, the initial purchase price. A monopoly that sells recognizes that a resale market can increase the willingness of buyers to pay for a new good, but that it can also limit the monopoly's ability to price discriminate between consumers who want the new good and those who want the used good. Under certain conditions, a monopoly that sells a durable good may make no monopoly profits at all. It is therefore in the monopoly's best interest to *credibly* commit itself not to expand future output and not to lower prices in the future. If it can do so, it can make monopoly profits from selling as well as from renting.

PROBLEMS

1. Use Example 15.2 to calculate the elasticity of demand facing a monopoly producer of four-wheel drive tractors, assuming it rents in the future but has sold units in the past, of which 20 units remain. Show how the elasticity is affected by the ratio of new to used equipment.
2. Explain how the analysis in Problem 1 is affected if farmers can maintain tractors forever.
3. Explain how the analysis in Problem 1 is affected if farmers never sell or buy used tractors (that is, transaction costs are too high for a used tractor market to develop).
4. Explain how the analysis in Problem 1 is affected if an investment tax credit (which lowers a firm's taxes in proportion to the amount spent on new capital) encourages overconsumption of tractors.
5. Explain how the analysis in Problem 1 is affected if four-wheel-drive tractors are close substitutes for other types of tractors.
6. Suppose the cost of producing a machine that lasts N periods is $C(N) = N^{1/2}$. If the interest rate is 5 percent, what duration should the firm plan for its machine? Describe the conditions determining whether it should modify its behavior if consumers can maintain the machine for one extra period for \$1. Does your answer depend on whether the manufacturer rents or sells the machine?
7. Why does an artist destroy a lithograph plate after making a fixed number of copies?

Answers to odd-numbered problems are given at the back of the book.

SUGGESTED READINGS

See Schmalensee (1979a) and Liebowitz (1982a) for surveys of the early durability literature. Waldman (2003) provides a nontechnical discussion of modern durable good theory.

APPENDIX 15A

Multiperiod Durable Goods Monopoly

A monopoly that sells, rather than rents, a durable good in many periods earns less than one that only rents, as discussed in the chapter. Here, we determine the output and price in each period. We start by considering a two-period world.

Two Periods

A monopoly sells a durable good. For simplicity, we assume that

- There is no cost of production (so marginal cost equals 0).
- The interest rate equals 0.
- The duration of the good is given and equals two periods.
- Resales are allowed.
- Total demand for services is unchanged over the two periods and equals

$$Q_i = 20 - R_i, \tag{15A.1}$$

where Q_i is the output sold in Period i and R_i is the rental rate in that period.

In order to determine the monopoly's optimal policy, we must work backwards starting in Period 2. Suppose that the monopoly sells Q_1 in Period 1. Then the residual demand curve facing the monopoly in Period 2 is

$$Q_2(R_2) = 20 - R_2 - Q_1. \tag{15A.2}$$

The monopoly solves for the rental rate in Period 2, R_2, that maximizes profits, where demand depends on the quantity sold in Period 1.

Because there is, by assumption, no cost of production, the monopoly's profits in Period 2 are equal to its revenues,

$$\pi_2(R_2, Q_1) = R_2 Q_2(R_2) = R_2(20 - R_2 - Q_1). \tag{15A.3}$$

Notice that profits in the second period are a function of the rental rate in Period 2 and output in Period 1: $\pi_2(R_2, Q_1)$.

Differentiating Equation 15A.3 with respect to R_2, setting the resulting partial derivative equal to zero, and rearranging terms gives the profit-maximizing rental rate in the second period:

$$R_2 = \frac{20 - Q_1}{2}. \tag{15A.4}$$

This same result is shown in Figure 15.2. By substituting Equation 15A.4 into Equation 15A.2, we find that the profit-maximizing output in the second period is

$$Q_2 = \frac{20 - Q_1}{2}. \tag{15A.5}$$

By substituting for R_2 and Q_2 in Equation 15A.3 (using Equations 15A.4 and 15A.5), we find that profits in Period 2 are

$$\pi_2 = \frac{(20 - Q_1)^2}{4}. \tag{15A.6}$$

Thus, output, rents, and profits in the second period all depend on output in the first period, Q_1.

The monopoly wants to maximize the present value of profits in the two periods. The present value of profits, *PVP*, equals profits in Period 1 plus discounted profits in Period 2 (we assume that the interest rate equals 0, so profits in Period 2 are not discounted), or

$$PVP = \pi_1 + \pi_2 = (R_1 + R_2)Q_1 + R_2 Q_2, \tag{15A.7}$$

because the sales price in Period 1 equals the rental rate in Period 1 plus the rental rate in Period 2. By substituting for π_2 from Equation 15A.6 into Equation 15A.7 and noting that demand in the first period is $Q_1 = 20 - R_1$ or $R_1 = 20 - Q_1$, we obtain

$$PVP = \left[(20 - Q_1) + \frac{20 - Q_1}{2}\right]Q_1 + \frac{(20 - Q_1)^2}{4}. \tag{15A.8}$$

Equation 15A.8 expresses the present value of profits as a function of just Q_1. Once Q_1 is determined, Q_2 is determined from Equation 15A.5, and in turn, the rental and sales rates for both periods are determined.

To maximize the present value of profits, we must differentiate Equation 15A.8 with respect to Q_1 and set that derivative equal to zero. Simplifying that expression shows that the Q_1 that maximizes the *PVP* is 8. Substituting $Q_1 = 8$ into the other equations shows that $R_2 = 6$, $Q_2 = 6$, $R_1 = 12$, $\pi_2 = 36$, $\pi_1 = 144$, and $PVP = 180$ (which is less than the present value of the optimal rental profits of 200).

Infinite Number of Periods

Suppose, now, that the monopoly sells in each of T periods, where T is arbitrarily large. It is possible to show that the rental rate in period i is

$$R_i = \beta_i R_{i-1}, \tag{15A.9}$$

where $\beta_i < 1$ is a constant for Period *i*. From Equation 15A.9, it follows that the rental rate in Period *i* can also be expressed as a function of the rental rate in the initial period, R_0:

$$R_i = (\beta_i \beta_{i-1} \beta_{i-2} \cdots \beta_1) R_0. \tag{15A.10}$$

The product of the β's must approach zero as *i* grows large (Stokey 1981). Because the length of a time period is arbitrary, if the time periods are very short, so that there are many periods within any given time interval, the rental rate immediately falls to zero by this reasoning.[1] A striking implication of this result is that a monopoly of a durable good with zero cost of production receives a price of zero—the competitive price. See, however, Kahn (1986) for a model where marginal cost is upward sloping and Bagnoli et al. (1989), where consumers are heterogeneous.

---

[1] A situation where a monopoly sells continuously over a given time interval can be approximated by a model with many short time periods. The approximation improves as the length of the time periods falls so that the number of periods grows large.

CHAPTER 16

Patents and Technological Change

The Congress shall have power . . . to promote the progress of science and useful arts, by securing for limited times to authors and inventors the exclusive right to their respective writings and discoveries.
—*U.S. Constitution, Article 1, Section 8*

Patents, which give the inventor or creator of a new product an exclusive right to sell it, have both desirable and undesirable effects. The chief benefit is that the possibility of obtaining monopoly profits encourages more inventive activity. Without patents or other similar incentives, there may not be enough inventive activity. The chief disadvantage is that new products may be sold at excessively high (monopoly) prices if no close substitutes are available.

Were it not for these exclusive rights, it might not pay for a drug company to invest large sums to discover a drug that cures cancer or prevents heart attacks. But once the drug is discovered, setting the price many times higher than the manufacturing cost puts the drug beyond the reach of many consumers who would gladly pay a competitive price—or even all their wealth—for it.

This chapter begins by discussing the various methods of granting inventors and other creators exclusive rights to encourage their work. The remainder of the chapter concentrates on answering five questions relating to patents and imperfect competition:

1. If there were no patents or other government incentives, would there be too little research and development (R&D)?
2. If there is too little research, should the patent system be used to encourage research rather than other incentives, such as prizes, research contracts, and joint ventures (research projects conducted collectively by several firms)?
3. Given that we keep the patent system, how long should patent protection last to obtain the best possible trade-off between incentives to invest and the harms from monopoly?

4. Are monopoly profits higher if a patent holder produces the invention or licenses it to others for production?
5. How does the structure of a product market affect the incentives to conduct research and the timing of innovations?

Patents, Copyrights, and Trademarks

The protection of intellectual property is needed to create incentives for creative efforts. These efforts are, in large part, responsible for the inventions and other technological advancements that are important for economic growth. Indeed, there is a strong correlation between a country's income and the strength of its laws protecting intellectual property (Ginarte and Park 1997). Patents, copyrights, and trademarks are three important types of protection for intellectual property. The three types of protection differ in what they cover and how long they last. A fourth type of intellectual property right is a trade secret, such as the formula for Coca-Cola, where the invention is protected simply by keeping it a secret.

Patents

A **patent** provides an inventor with exclusive rights to a new and useful *product, process, substance,* or *design.* New products include machines (mechanisms with moving parts) or manufactured articles (without moving parts) such as tools. New processes or methods include chemical processes for treating metal or for manufacturing drugs, mechanical processes for manufacturing goods, or electrical processes. New substances include chemical compounds and mixtures; this concept covers the composition of matter. New forms of animals and plants can also be covered. New designs include the shapes of products where the shapes serve a functional purpose

The first U.S. patent act, written by Thomas Jefferson, was designed to give "liberal encouragement" to human ingenuity and was passed by Congress in 1790. The first patent was awarded in that year to Samuel Hopkins for making potash used to produce fertilizer, soap, and other products. Another early patent was Eli Whitney's cotton gin in 1794. Other U.S. patent holders include Abraham Lincoln for inflatable chambers that could lift boats over shallow water (1849); Mark Twain for a self-pasting scrapbook (1873) and for a history game (1885); Hedy Lamarr (as Hedwig Keisler Markey) and George Antheil (a film score composer) for an anti-jamming device to foil Nazi radar; Danny Kaye for a party noisemaker (1952); John Dos Passos for soap-bubble gum (1959); and Edwin E. (Buzz) Aldrin, Jr., (who walked on the moon) for a space station (1993). The record number of U.S. patents by the big three—Thomas Edison, 1,093, Edwin Land, (founder of Polaroid), 533, and Jerome Lemelson, roughly 500 and growing (**www.lemelson.org/about/patents.php**)—are not threatened by these celebrities, however.

Approximately 100,000 applications are submitted to the U.S. Patent and Trademark Office each year, and more than 5 million patents have been granted since 1790. Table 16.1 shows how the number of applications to, and patents issued by, the U.S.

Patent and Trademark Office grew from three patents granted in 1790 to 166,039 in 2001. Biotechnology and computer software patents doubled between 1990 and 2000 (Gallini 2002). The share of U.S. patents by foreign residents has increased substantially. Foreigners received only about 2% of all issued U.S. patents in 1850. That share increased to 4.2% in 1875, rose to 14.1% in 1900, dipped to 10.2% in 1950, and has been roughly 50% since 1975, reaching 51.3% in 2001. Japanese residents received 19% of all U.S. patents in 2001, followed by Germans with 6.5% and Taiwanese with 3.6%.

Corporations are responsible for most patents. For the ninth consecutive year, International Business Machines Corporation (IBM) led all organizations in patents in 2001, followed by NEC and Canon. The top 10 patenting organizations include two U.S. corporations, seven Japanese corporations, and one corporation from the Republic of Korea. The U.S. government was sixteenth among top patenting organizations. Independent inventors' share of all patents issued to U.S.-resident inventors was 19.1%.

In the United States since 1994, patents generally provide 20 years of protection from the filing date for these inventions. Exceptions include patents for new designs, which last 14 years from the date the patent issues. The 2004 fee for a patent is $385 for small entities (independent inventors, small businesses, and nonprofit organizations) and $770 for large ones. Small entity patent holders must pay maintenance fees after 3.5 ($455), 7.5 ($1,045), and 11.5 years ($1,610). The corresponding fees for large entities are $910, $2,090 and $3,220, respectively.

To obtain a patent, the inventor must prove that the invention is *useful* (especially for new chemicals), *novel,* and *nonobvious* (you cannot patent a slight modification of something known to everyone in the business); must publicly describe the innovation;

TABLE 16.1 **U.S. Patent Applications and Grants**

	Applications	Total Grants	Grants to Foreigners
1790	n.a	3	n.a
1800	n.a.	41	n.a.
1825	n.a.	304	n.a.
1850	2,193	884	20
1875	21,638	13,291	563
1900	39,673	24,656	3,483
1925	80,208	46,432	5,347
1950	67,264	43,039	4,408
1975	101,014	72,000	36,271
2000	295,926	157,495	78,869
2001	326,508	166,039	85,170

n.a. / not applicable

Source: **http://patents.uspto.gov/web/offices/ac/ido/oeip/taf/h_counts.htm**

and, if appropriate, must provide a working model. Two percent of patent applications are granted in Israel, 5% in Ireland, 11% in China, 12% in Canada, 14% in the United Kingdom, 16% in Germany, 25% in France, and 44% in the United States.[1]

The U.S. Patent and Trademark Office issues three categories of patents: utility or mechanical patents, design patents, and plant patents. The most common patents are utility patents (and are normally what people mean when they say "patent"). They cover many types of inventions, such as mechanical devices, chemical compositions and processes, manufacturing methods, computer software, biotechnology, and business methods. Design patents cover only the ornamental appearance of a useful product. Plant patents protect types of plants such as flowers, fruits, shrubs, and vines.

Not all these inventions could be patented in the past. The courts extended patentability to genetically engineered bacteria in 1980, software in 1981, and business methods and financial service products in 1998.[2] These extensions have led to some very strange patents on business methods that seem obvious, such as Amazon.com's one-click Internet ordering process and Priceline.com's reverse auction method for booking products such as airline tickets on the Internet.

The 1999 Inventors Protection Act requires that all patent applications filed in the United States and abroad be made available for public inspection 18 months from the earliest domestic or foreign filing date. This rule should create a more certain environment for conducting research and development by reducing the concerns of potential inventors that someone has already patented the ideas on which they are working (Gallini 2002).

Copyrights

Only one thing is impossible for God: To find any sense in any copyright law on the planet!
—*Mark Twain*

Copyrights give their creators the exclusive production, publication, or sales rights to artistic, dramatic, literary, or musical works. Examples include articles, books, drawings, maps, musical compositions, distinctively designed items, or photographs. Copyright law covers original "works of authorship" as long as they are "fixed" in a "tangible medium," such as a book or a computer hard drive as may occur when a paper is posted on the Web. Computer software on floppy disks and music on records are other examples of works preserved on tangible media. Filing for copyright registration costs $30.

Whereas patents protect function and purpose (ideas, devices, mechanisms, methods, and means), copyrights cover artistic expression. Indeed, copyright law (§102(b)) states that

> In no case does copyright protection for an original work of authorship extend to any idea, procedure, process, system, method of operation, concept, principle, or discovery,

---

[1]World Intellectual Property Organization: **www.wipo.int/ipstats/en/publications/a/pdf/patents.pdf**.

[2]*Diamond v. Chakrabarty*, 447 U.S. 303, 206 U.S.P.Q. (BNA) 193 (1980); *Diamond v. Diehr*, 450 U.S. 175 (1981); *State Street Bank and Trust v. Signature Financial Group*, 149 F. 3d 1368 (Fed Cir. 1998).

regardless of the form in which it is described, explained, illustrated, or embodied in such work.

In the United States, since 1998, copyrights to businesses last 95 years (or 120 years from when the work was created if that period is shorter), whereas copyrights to individuals last for life plus 70 years. Many countries provide protection for different lengths of time. For example, in Japan copyright protection lasts 50 years after the death of the artist and recordings are also protected for 50 years. Copyrights have exceptions, such as the *Fair Use Doctrine,* which allows individuals to make copies for their own use of a short passage from a book.[3] *International copyrights* are reciprocal arrangements extending copyright protection to citizens of other participating countries. The United States has reciprocal relations with more than 100 countries, whereby a foreign author receives *national treatment*: The author's works are protected under the same rules as are a native author's.

Trademarks

Trademarks are words, symbols, or other marks used to distinguish a good or service provided by one firm from those provided by other firms. A trademark may be registered with the Patent Office in the United States.[4] Examples include Kodak film, Exxon gasoline, Apple computers, Clorox bleach, Bib the Michelin Man who symbolizes tires for the Michelin Company, and a stylized penguin that symbolizes paperback books published by Penguin Books. The one millionth trademark registered with the U.S. Patent Office is for Sweet 'N Low. Unlike copyrights and patents, trademarks do not expire after a fixed term, although a firm may lose its trademark protection. For example, if a word comes to signify all products in an industry, it no longer distinguishes a particular brand and the trademark protection ends.

To keep from losing its trademark, General Foods stresses "Sanka-*brand* decaffeinated coffee," so that Sanka will not come to describe all decaffeinated coffee. Xerox placed ads that say in part: "Once a trademark not always a trademark. . . . We need your help. . . . Whenever you use our name, please use it as a proper adjective in conjunction with our products and services: e.g., Xerox copiers or Xerox financial services.

[3]There may be another strange copyright exemption. In a recent case, *BV Engineering v. University of California, Los Angeles,* 858 F.2d 1394 (9th Cir.), a federal appeals court concluded that state institutions can "violate the federal copyright laws with virtual impunity" due to the immunity clause in the 11th Amendment to the Constitution, which prohibits suits against states for damages, and parts of the Copyright Act, which has sections that exempt states. Apparently a copyright holder can get an injunction against officials of state institutions to stop violating copyrights, but no damages can be collected. Congress tried to eliminate this loophole, but apparently was overruled by the courts.

[4]A *trademark* is literally a mark such as a word or logo that represents a product. A *service mark* is a mark for a service rather than a product. A *common law trademark* is a mark that is not formally registered but has accrued minimal rights through use. *State registration* of a trademark or service mark provides better protection than the common law, but is only useful within that state. A *trade name* is the name a firm uses to do business.

And never as a verb: 'to Xerox' in place of 'to copy,' or as a noun: 'Xeroxes' in place of 'copies.' With your help and a precaution or two on our part, it's 'Once the Xerox trademark, always the Xerox trademark.'" Examples of trademarks that have become generic names are aspirin, cellophane, cornflakes, dry ice, escalator, high-octane, kerosene, linoleum, mimeograph, nylon, raisin bran, shredded wheat, thermos, trampoline, and yo-yo (Landes and Posner 1987).

Distinctions Between Patents, Copyrights, and Trademarks

The remainder of this chapter concentrates on patents. Copyrights can be analyzed similarly to patents, as protection designed to encourage creation. Trademarks, too, can be analyzed as providing protection by encouraging firms to develop reputations that convey information to consumers, allowing them to identify which products they like and dislike (Landes and Posner 1987).

One important distinction between patents and copyrights is that copyrights protect the particular expression of an idea, whereas patents protect any tangible embodiment of the idea itself. Two versions of the same story told in two different ways (*Romeo and Juliet* and *West Side Story*) can be copyrighted. A patent, however, prevents others from using an application of an idea in their products.

Therefore, patents allow greater exclusivity and, presumably, more monopoly power. Patents, though, are more difficult to obtain than copyrights. As the following discussion shows, a society's patent policy reflects a trade-off between more stimulus to invention and more monopoly power. Because the greater the monopoly power, the sooner one can accumulate large profits, it is not surprising that society sets patent terms shorter than those for copyrights.

Incentives for Inventions Are Needed

If you took away everything in the world that had to be invented, there'd be nothing left except a lot of people getting rained on. —Tom Stoppard

Many economists and policy makers believe that without patents or other government incentives, there would be too little research. According to Jones and Williams (1998) and Mansfield (1998), the estimated private rate of return to R&D is far less than the social rate of return. The chief reason is that inventions are fundamentally new information, and information is a public good.[5] If I eat a hot dog, you can't eat that same hot dog. However, if I possess some information, you can possess and benefit from that same piece of information. Thus, my knowledge of the information doesn't prevent you from using it. If some consumers of the information can obtain it costlessly (for example, you can read a book in a library), the producer of the information has

[5] See also, for example, Arrow (1962). When secrecy about a discovery can be maintained, this problem may be eliminated (Taylor and Silberston 1973, ch. 9; Kitch 1975; and Cheung 1982).

less incentive to produce it than if everyone had to pay for it. Why would anyone be willing to incur the entire expense of developing new information, processes, or products if people could benefit from them for free? Although some people like inventing for its own sake or as a service to humanity, many current inventors and firms undertake research for the pecuniary rewards.[6] Thus, if they could not benefit from their new developments, this latter group would not engage in research.

Eliminating most such research would harm society because it has social value. New manufacturing methods lower the costs of producing existing products and allow society to produce more output with the same amount of input. New products increase productivity (for example, improved seeds with higher output or better quality) or give pleasure (videocassette recorders). Indeed, society becomes dependent on many new inventions. For example, 46% of Americans say they do not know how they could get along without Scotch tape.[7] Although 11% of Americans say the wheel is the greatest invention of all time, 10% say the automobile is.[8] How would our world survive without perforated toilet paper, invented in the 1880s by English manufacturer Walter James Alcock; the zipper, designed for boots and shoes by Chicago engineer Whitcomb L. Judson, who filed for a patent in 1893; or the Barbie doll, developed by Ruth Handler in 1959?[9] Of course, not everyone believes all new products are desirable: 67% of Iowans think music videos are among the "least useful changes" in modern life.[10] Further, 0% of American car owners keep gloves in their glove compartments.[11]

To create new products, many firms invest large amounts of money. For example, IBM Corp. spent $4.75 billion in 2002, or 5.9 percent of revenues. However, R&D expenditures as a percent of revenues vary substantially across firms: In 2002, Chevron Texaco (oil) invested 0.2% of its revenues in R&D; Hewlett-Packard (equipment, computers) invested 5.8%; Microsoft (software), 15.2%; Advanced Micro Devices (microprocessor chips), 30.3%; Biogen (biotechnology), 32%; and Genentech (biotechnology), 22.9%.[12] Of the 71,000 U.S. corporate-owned patents issued to Americans in 2000, universities held only 4.4%.[13]

---

[6]John Walker (the inventor of matches) and Pierre and Marie Curie (the discoverers of a process for isolating radium) never took out patents because they believed that their inventions should belong to all of humanity. Recently, much computer software, such as Linux, is *open source,* in which innovators make software code publicly available (Lerner and Tirole 2002a).

[7]Roper Organization, as cited in Lapham, Pollan, and Etheridge (1987).

[8]R. H. Bruskin, as cited in Lapham, Pollan, and Etheridge (1987).

[9]Irving Wallace, David Wallechinsky, and Amy Wallace, "The Column of Lists: Anonymous Inventions," *San Francisco Chronicle,* August 10, 1988:B3.

[10]Des Moines Register and Tribune Company, as cited in Lapham, Pollan, and Etheridge (1987).

[11]Runzheimer International, as cited in Lapham, Pollan, and Etheridge (1987).

[12]Data from individual firms' 10-K forms. These comparisons may be somewhat misleading. For example, oil companies appear to do little R&D because their value added as a fraction of sales is low. Oil companies appear more R&D-intensive if we compare R&D to value added or scientists to total employment.

[13]U.S. Patent and Trademark Office, **www.uspto.gov/web/offices/ac/ido/oeip/taf/univ/asgn/table_1.htm**.

U.S. investment in knowledge—defined as the sum of investment in R&D, software, and higher education—was almost 7% of gross domestic product (GDP) in 2000, well above the share for the European Union or Japan.[14] The average for Organization for Economic Cooperation and Development (OECD) countries (large developed nations) was 4.8% of GDP, of which almost half was for R&D. OECD countries spent $645 billion on R&D in 2001, with the United States accounting for 44% of the OECD total, the European Union 28%, and Japan 17%. More than 30% of total business R&D is in the service sector in Norway, Denmark, Australia, and the United States, but less than 10% falls in this sector in Germany and Japan. High-technology industries invested more than 52% of total manufacturing R&D in 2000: over 60% in the United States, 47% in the European Union, and 44% in Japan. As of 2000, gross domestic expenditure on R&D is over 4% of GDP in Israel; between 3% and 4% in Sweden and Finland; between 2% and 3% in the United States, Korea, and most OECD countries; and between 1% and 2% for Canada and the United Kingdom. While 37% of U.S. and 34% of Japanese citizens have post–high school education, only 21% do so in the European Union, according to the OECD.

The United States apparently puts more resources into pure research, rather than commercial applications, than other countries, receiving more Nobel prizes in the sciences since 1950 than all the other countries in the world combined. However, the percentage of defense R&D was 14% in the United States in 2001, compared to virtually nothing in other OECD countries.

Imitation Discourages Research

Men often applaud an imitation and hiss the real thing. —*Aesop*

Without a patent, anyone could use new information, and *imitations* of new inventions could be sold legally. Suppose you discovered a cure for AIDS. You could sell your new drug for large sums of money if a patent gave you exclusive rights. Without a patent, other companies could duplicate your drug, and competition would drive the price to the competitive level. You would incur all the research costs, but not all the private benefit (profits). For example, Ford's innovation of an assembly line was quickly duplicated by others. Every firm wants to copy others' inventions, and no firm wants to go to the expense of inventing anything itself. Thus, without patents, consumers could buy new inventions at competitive prices, but there would be few new inventions. Indeed, society tries to reduce the number of certain types of new inventions by not offering patent protection. For example, in the United States, you cannot patent a gambling device such as a slot machine.

Even with patents, the return to the inventor of a new invention may be less than its value to society. For example, although Xerox earns substantial returns from its plain paper copier, other companies, upon seeing Xerox's success, were able to invent similar but not identical products. They were able to capture some of Xerox's plain pa-

---

[14]OECD, STI Scoreboard 2003. **www.oecd.org/dataoecd/41/0/17130709.pdf**.

per copier business in spite of existing patents. During a 10-month period in 1974, 16 companies, including IBM, Kodak, 3M, Addressograph-Multigraph, Bell & Howell, GAF, Litton, and Pitney-Bowes, obtained 390 patents in the field of xerography (Scherer 1981, 292). In many cases, then, competitors can "invent around" a patent, lowering the patent's value to its inventor.[15]

In 1992, an appeals court judge ruled that reverse engineering (disassembly) is "fair use" of software. The court ruled that[16]

> Disassembly of copyrighted object code is, as a matter of law, a fair use of the copyrighted work if such disassembly provides the only means of access to those elements of the code that are not protected copyright and the copier has a legitimate reason for seeking access.

Reverse engineering is used by software manufacturers to create applications that are compatible with certain hardware or that imitate functions of other software programs.

Moreover, many patents and copyrights are not enforced (Example 16.1). Mansfield et al. (1982) estimate that imitators' costs average only 65% of innovators' development costs. A survey of high-level R&D managers in 129 lines of business finds that even for major new or improved products, many firms are capable of duplicating an innovation (Levin, Klevorick, Nelson, and Winter 1987). In 2% of the cases, no firm is capable of duplication; however, in 19% of the cases, 1 or 2 firms are capable of duplicating; in 57% of the cases 3 to 5 firms are capable; in 20%, 6 to 10 firms; and in 3%, more than 10 firms. For a typical new product, the corresponding numbers are 1%, 4%, 26%, 49% and 20%. That is, for a typical new product, in 70% of the cases, 6 or more firms can produce an imitation.

Work on copying innovations can start quickly. Information about R&D programs in manufacturing industries is in the hands of at least some rivals within 12 to 18 months after the development decision is made (Mansfield 1985). Information spreads due to movements of employees between firms, formal and informal communications among engineers and scientists at various firms (especially at professional meetings), reports of input suppliers and customers, and reverse engineering of new products.

Even if the patent restrictions can be circumvented, patents increase the cost of imitation, as Table 16.2 shows. At the very least, they typically delay the time when imitators enter the market. Mansfield (1968) reports that in the United States, the time between the first use of a major innovation and the time when 60% of all related products have imitated the innovation can be as short as a month (see Example 11.4) or a year (packaging beer in tin cans), or as long as several decades (by-product coke oven for steel mills and continuous annealing of tin-plated steel). Of 48 firms interviewed, the median estimate of the increase in the cost of imitation due to patents is

[15]To prevent entry by rivals, defensive *sleeping patents* may be obtained by the original inventor. These similar patents are not used but prevent others from patenting these similar products. See Gilbert and Newbery (1982), Chapter 11, and the following discussion.

[16]Shawn Willett, "Appeals Court Judge Rules Reverse Engineering Is Fair Use of Software," *InfoWorld,* November 2, 1992, 14:24.

EXAMPLE 16.1 *Piracy*

A patent, copyright, or trademark is of little value if the right is not enforceable. Protecting intellectual property, such as music and computer software, from unauthorized copying has proved difficult. Music and software publishers have responded in many ways to the threat of piracy. For example, they have sued companies such as Napster that facilitate copying and have instituted copy protection schemes. So far, these attempts to prevent copying have had at best limited success anywhere in the world. By some estimates, 90% of movies, music, and software in China comprises illegal copies that are sold for a fraction of the original price—one-fifth for many new DVDs. Worldwide use of music-sharing services such as Napster and Kazaa flourished, at least before a series of lawsuits by publishers in 2003. These lawsuits apparently had some success in the United States. According to one survey, the share of computer users who employed file-sharing programs to download music fell from 29% in the spring of 2003 to 14% by late 2003.

Music and software publishers claim that they suffered piracy losses in excess of $17.6 billion in 2002. However, it is possible that consumers who use pirated copies eventually decide to purchase legitimate copies of that work or other related works. Thus, the effect of piracy on legitimate demand is an empirical question. Hui and Png (2003) examine this question using data from 28 countries for music CDs from 1994 through 1998. They conclude that publishers' losses from theft outweigh the positive effects of piracy. Adjusting for the positive effects, they conclude that the industry's 1998 loss was 42% of the industry estimate, or 6.6% of sales.

However, Hui and Png note that, were it not for the piracy, publishers would have increased prices, so that the industry suffered additional forgone revenue losses. For example, in response to unrelenting online piracy, Universal Music Group, the world's largest record company, announced in 2002 that it would sell 43,000 downloadable songs without monthly fees or copying restrictions and in 2003 that it would cut prices on its CDs by as much as 30% to lure consumers back to stores. Thus, although piracy hurts producers, the implications of piracy for overall welfare are ambiguous.

Sources: Joseph Kahn, "The Pinch of Piracy Wakes China Up on Copyright Issue," *New York Times*, November 1, 2002:C1, C5; Benny Evangelista, "Universal to Sell Songs Online for 99 Cents," *San Francisco Chronicle*, November 20, 2002:B2; Hui and Png (2003); Amy Harmon, "Universal to Cut Prices of Its CD's," *New York Times*, September 4, 2003:C1, C2; Nick Wingfield, "Online Swapping of Music Declines in Wake of Suits," *Wall Street Journal*, January 5, 2004:B4.

11% overall, 30% in ethical drugs (pharmaceuticals without advertising directed at consumers), 10% in chemicals, and 7% in electronics and machinery (Mansfield et al. 1982).

Similarly, the Levin, Klevorick, Nelson, and Winter (1987) survey finds (Table 16.3) that the cost of duplicating an innovation as a percentage of the innovator's cost

TABLE 16.2 **Estimated Percentage Increase in Imitation Cost Due to Patents for 33 New Products in the Chemical, Drug, Electronics, and Machinery Industries**

Percent Increase in Imitation Cost	Number of Products	Percent of Cases Studied
Under 10%	13	39%
10–19%	10	30%
20–49%	4	12%
50–99%	0	0%
100–199%	3	9%
200% and more	3	9%
Total	33	100%

Source: Mansfield (1984).

TABLE 16.3 **Cost of Duplicating an Innovation as a Percentage of the Innovator's R&D Cost: Frequency Distribution of Median Responses**

Type of Innovation	Less Than 25%	26%–50%	51%–75%	76%–100%	More Than 100%	Timely Duplication Not Possible
Major new process						
Patented	1	5	19	66	26	10
Unpatented	5	10	55	49	6	2
Typical new process						
Patented	2	15	61	41	6	2
Unpatented	8	43	58	14	4	0
Major new product						
Patented	1	4	17	63	30	12
Unpatented	5	13	58	40	7	4
Typical new product						
Patented	2	18	64	32	9	2
Unpatented	9	58	40	15	5	0

Note: Each row adds to 127, reflecting the 127 lines of business surveyed.

Source: Levin, Klevorick, Nelson, and Winter (1987, Table 8, 809).

was higher for patented than unpatented major or typical processes or products. They also show that on average it takes longer to duplicate a major new product if it is patented than if it is not. As a result, even though obtaining a patent requires revealing information to potential imitators, many firms obtain patents.

Patents Encourage Research

By imposing costs on potential imitators, patents can give market power to patent holders. The resulting profits can be a strong inducement to be the first to invent a new product.

A rational inventor engages in costly research up to the point where the expected marginal return from more research equals its marginal cost. If the inventor's return is less than society's, the inventor tends to underinvest in research. Patents may permit inventors to capture a large share of the benefits (internalize the externality) associated with the production of knowledge by insulating them from competition. By granting these exclusive rights through patents, society encourages more inventions in some industries (see Example 16.2 and **www.aw-bc.com/carlton_perloff** "The Importance of Patents Varies by Industry"). However, even when patents protect the inventor from imitation, the patent holder's monopoly profit is less than the full social benefit (unless the patent holder can price discriminate). Thus, although patents encourage additional research, they may induce less than the optimal level.

Alternatively, patents may also encourage too much innovation (Hirshleifer 1971, Mansfield et al. 1977). For example, suppose an improved method of weather prediction is developed that allows accurate prediction of crop yields after all planting decisions have been made. The inventor can make a fortune speculating on future farm prices. Despite the profits from speculation, there may be little efficiency gain to society from the new forecasting technique.

Patents Encourage Disclosure

Disseminating new ideas is valuable to society (see Example 16.3). The sooner a good new idea is adopted, the quicker society benefits. Moreover, one idea can lead to others. Thus, policies that increase the diffusion of inventions are desirable.

Some countries' patent laws encourage disclosure of new discoveries sooner than other countries' laws. To obtain a patent, an inventor must demonstrate that the invention is novel and nonobvious. By providing patent protection to inventors, society obtains two valuable results: greater incentives for additional research and development and an acceleration of innovation through disclosure of inventions.[17] Section 112 of the patent law states that

> the specification shall contain a written description . . . in such full, clear, concise and exact terms as to enable any person skilled in the art . . . to make and use the same.

Such disclosure can increase the pace of invention as one inventor builds on the work of another. For example, the government maintains a "microbe zoo" in Rockville, Maryland, where, for $70 (or $40 for nonprofit organizations), virtually anyone with a college degree in science can buy a vial of the same genetically altered cells that Genentech developed at a cost of $200 million to produce TPA, a clot-dissolving drug designed to

[17]This section is based on Scotchmer and Green (1990).

EXAMPLE 16.2 *Patents Versus Trade Secrets*

In exchange for a patent and its protection, an inventor's ideas are exhibited for the entire world to see. Consequently, rather than patent and reveal their new ideas, many firms keep the details of their innovations secret. Moreover, some countries do not have patent systems covering all ideas.

Are patents crucial for inventive activity? Are trade secrets a good substitute? To answer these questions, Moser (2003) collected data from exhibition catalogues for two nineteenth-century world fairs on technology: the Crystal Palace Exhibition in London in 1851, with 13,876 exhibits in 30 industries, and the Centennial Exhibition in Philadelphia in 1876, with 19,076 exhibits in 344 industries. National committees picked the most innovative products for exhibition. Products displayed at the exhibitions were economically useful (that is, commercial) innovations. Only a fraction of innovations are patented, and not all patents lead to economically useful innovations. Indeed, many of these products were not patented in either the home country or the country where they were exhibited.

Many economists (such as Nordhaus 1969 and Gilbert and Shapiro 1990) contend that strong patent laws raise the number of innovations that are made within a country. One might infer from these arguments that countries without patent laws should display few important new technologies. However, countries without patent laws brought many important innovations to the fairs and received a disproportionate share of medals for outstanding innovations.

Switzerland had the second-highest number of exhibits per capita among all countries that visited the Crystal Palace Exhibition. Swiss inventors, who concentrated on watch making and specialized steel making for scientific and optical instruments, kept their innovations secret rather than patent them. This strategy was successful because their potential English competitors found these innovations to be difficult to reverse engineer. Had the Swiss inventors obtained patents, their rivals would have learned their most important secrets.

Moser does not find evidence that patent laws increased levels of innovative activity but does report strong evidence that patent systems influenced in which industries innovative activity occurred. In countries without patent laws, inventors concentrated on industries where secrecy was effective relative to patents. Because the manufacture of scientific instruments became mechanized during this period, progress in this industry required innovations in manufacturing machinery, which critically depended on patent protection. Inventors in countries without patent laws began to specialize in food processing, another industry where secrecy was effective. The share of Dutch innovations in food processing rose from 11 percent to 33 percent after the abolition of the Netherlands' patent laws in 1869 under pressure from the Free Trade party. Moser concludes that introducing forceful and effective patent laws in countries without patents may have a stronger influence on changing the direction of innovative activity than on raising the number of inventions.

Source: Moser (2003).

EXAMPLE 16.3

Monkey See, Monkey Do

Some of humans' closest relatives also invent. In 1953, a young female macaque monkey in the south of Japan invented an improved method of food preparation when she washed a muddy sweet potato in a stream before eating it. Some monkeys quickly imitated her behavior, and it became the norm in her immediate group in fewer than 10 years. By 1983, all Japanese macaques used this method.

This Einstein of monkeys innovated again in 1956. She invented a new technique of throwing handfuls of mixed sand and wheat grains upon the sea and then skimming the floating cereal from the surface. By 1983, virtually all Japanese macaques were using her method.

Thus, monkeys can invent, can learn from others by observing, and are willing to replace old methods with superior processes. However, the diffusion of inventions—adoption by others—takes time. In these cases, full diffusion took three decades.

Sources: Kawai, Watanabe, and Mori (1992); Hall (forthcoming).

prevent heart attacks.[18] The purchaser can use the vial for research purposes, but may not violate Genentech's patent and sell the product in competition with Genentech. The TPA-producing cells are just one of more than 8,000 patented life forms at the American Type Culture Collection. For $560, a firm may make a deposit consisting of six vials of living materials. The fee covers 30 years of storage. By depositing here, a company partially meets the patent requirement to supply enough information to allow a skilled specialist to reproduce its invention. It has been estimated, however, that only 1 percent of recombinant DNA patents need a deposit today; the general scientific community has a good understanding of the technology so that a written description is sufficient. For a $100 fee, a depositor obtains a list of all the people requesting a sample of its patented organism, which may be useful to check for patent infringement.

Some firms do not patent discoveries so that their competitors will not learn about them. These firms must protect their secret knowledge (*trade secrets*) from leaking out to others, as can occur when employees take a job with a competitor. It is illegal for employees to reveal trade secrets of their former firms. To the degree that firms use the patent system, there is greater disclosure than would occur with trade secrets.

The United States, under the 1951 Invention Secrecy Act, blocks patents from being issued and, in some cases, prohibits the inventors from selling or licensing their technology to anyone except the government if it believes doing so could threaten national security. Nearly 6,000 inventions are still covered today, even with the end of the Cold War. Most are nonnuclear technologies that the government does not want to see exported, including computer hardware, advanced ceramic materials, laser systems, and others.

[18] Sabin Russell, "'Microbe Zoo' Stores Life Forms," *San Francisco Chronicle,* May 23, 1988:C1, C5.

Competing firms may make similar discoveries at virtually the same time, although two or more applications for nearly identical inventions represent only about 1 percent of all U.S. patent applications.

The novelty requirement greatly affects possible profits and the incentive to disclose. The more extreme the requirement that an innovation differ from previous ones, the harder it is to obtain a new patent, and the longer the owner of a current patent can earn monopolistic profits. As a result, the more stringent the novelty requirement, the greater the reward to a patent and hence the greater the incentive to engage in research. On the other hand, the less frequently patents are issued, the less likely one can obtain a patent, so the lower the incentive to engage in research. Moreover, the less frequently patents are issued, the less disclosure there is, which tends to slow research by others. Thus, the stringency of a novelty rule affects the trade-off between rewards and incentives and has an ambiguous effect on the incentive to engage in R&D.[19]

★Patents, Prizes, Research Contracts, and Joint Ventures

Most of the economic research on how to encourage inventive activity has centered on choosing the optimal patent system. But why should society only use patents? Why not use other incentives such as *prizes* and *government research contracts*?[20] For example, the government could offer a cash prize to the first person who discovers a cure for AIDS, or it could give research contracts to firms or individual researchers to work on an AIDS cure. Alternatively, the government could relax antitrust prohibitions (as the U.S. government has done) to allow firms to coordinate research activities through research **joint ventures.**

The following example illustrates how patents, prizes, research contracts, and joint ventures affect research effort. (See **www.aw-bc.com/carlton_perloff** "Patents, Prizes, and Research Contracts" for the corresponding mathematical analysis.) Suppose there is an industry for research with the following properties (as illustrated in Table 16.4):

- There are an unlimited number of identical firms that can each undertake one research project. The number of firms currently in the industry, and hence the number of projects undertaken, n, is shown in the first column of Table 16.4.
- Each research firm can conduct one research study at a constant marginal (and average) cost: $m = 1$. Thus, the total cost of research for n firms is $C(n) = nm = n$ (Column 6).
- The more firms actively searching for a particular invention, the higher the probability that at least one of them will discover it. Thus, $\rho(n)$, the probability

[19]Scotchmer and Green (1990) show that a weaker novelty rule is better than a stronger rule in some markets, but they do not claim that their result holds in all markets. They argue, however, that first-to-file is better than first-to-invent in virtually all cases.

[20]The following comparison of prizes, research contracts, and patents is based in large part on Wright (1983).

TABLE 16.4 **Costs and Benefits of Research Programs**

Number of Projects, *n*	Expected Marginal Social Benefit	Expected Payoff with a Prize = *B*	Probability of Success, *p*(*n*)	Expected Social Benefit, *Bp*(*n*)	Social Cost, *C*(*n*)	Net Social Benefit, *Bp*(*n*) − *C*(*n*)
1	4.14	4.60	0.18	4.60	1.00	3.60
2	3.38	4.17	0.33	8.35	2.00	6.35
3	2.76	3.80	0.46	11.41	3.00	8.41
4	2.25	3.48	0.56	13.91	4.00	9.91
5	1.84	3.19	0.64	15.94	5.00	10.94
6	1.50	2.93	0.70	17.61	6.00	11.61
7	1.23	2.71	0.76	18.97	7.00	11.97
8	**1.00**	**2.51**	**0.80**	**20.08**	**8.00**	**12.08**
9	0.82	2.33	0.84	20.98	9.00	11.98
10	0.67	2.17	0.87	21.72	10.00	11.72
11	0.54	2.03	0.89	22.32	11.00	11.32
12	0.44	1.90	0.91	22.81	12.00	10.81
13	0.36	1.79	0.93	23.22	13.00	10.22
14	0.30	1.68	0.94	23.54	14.00	9.54
15	0.24	1.59	0.95	23.81	15.00	8.81
16	0.20	1.50	0.96	24.03	16.00	8.03
17	0.16	1.42	0.97	24.21	17.00	7.21
18	0.13	1.35	0.97	24.35	18.00	6.35
19	0.11	1.29	0.98	24.47	19.00	5.47
20	0.09	1.23	0.98	24.57	20.00	4.57
21	0.07	1.17	0.99	24.65	21.00	3.65
22	0.06	1.12	0.99	24.71	22.00	2.71
23	0.05	1.08	0.99	24.77	23.00	1.77
24	0.04	1.03	0.99	24.81	24.00	0.81
24.84	0.03	1.00	0.99	24.84	24.84	0.00
25	0.03	0.99	0.99	24.84	25.00	−0.16

$m = 1$, per-firm cost of a research project

$B = \$25$

$\alpha = 0.031$

$p(n) = (1 - e^{-\alpha n})$, probability of success with n projects

of (at least one) success (Column 4), is an increasing function of the number of firms, n.

- Research takes place in period $t = 0$. If the discovery is made in that period, society benefits in subsequent periods ($t = 1, 2, \ldots$). For simplicity, we assume that research does not take place in subsequent periods if the discovery is not made in the initial period.
- If successful, the research will allow production of a new product at a constant marginal cost. If the present value of the potential benefit to society (the

present value of the consumer surplus at the competitive price) from a successful invention is $B = \$25$, then the expected social benefit of having n firms race to make the discovery is $B\rho(n)$: the benefit times the probability of success (Column 5).

The analysis begins by determining the optimal number of firms racing to be the first to make the discovery. Next, we suppose that the government has as much information as firms about all possible research projects and ask how many firms would race under five possible government incentive programs: no government incentives, government research programs, government prizes, legal joint ventures (research projects funded by two or more firms), and patents. Finally, we examine how the analysis changes if the government has less information than research firms have.

Determining the Optimal Number of Firms

Society should choose the number of firms racing to make discoveries that maximizes expected *net social benefit* (Column 7 of Table 16.4), which is the expected social benefit, $B\rho(n)$, minus the social cost, $C(n) = nm = n$. In our example, net social benefit is maximized at 8 firms, as shown in Table 16.4 (bold row) and Figure 16.1a.

Figure 16.1a shows that both the social costs of a research program, $C(n) = n$, and the expected social benefits, $B\rho(n)$, increase with the number of research programs. When there are few firms, adding one more firm substantially increases the probability of success. However, in this example, as more firms join the race, the probability of success approaches 1 (certainty), so that adding more firms to the race has little effect on expected benefits. Thus, expected social benefits first rise rapidly and then level off. The thin blue line in Figure 16.1a is the expected net social benefit, $B\rho(n) - C(n)$, which equals the gap between the expected social benefits and social costs. The gap between social benefits and costs and the height of the net social benefits curve is maximized at 8 firms.

Another way to describe that result is to say that the marginal (social) cost equals the marginal social benefit at 8 firms (see Figure 16.1). The marginal social cost of one more research program is $m = 1$, which is the height of the marginal cost curve in Figure 16.1b and the slope of the cost curve in Figure 16.1a. The marginal benefit curve in Figure 16.1b equals the slope of the expected benefit curve in Figure 16.1a. The gap between expected benefits and costs is greatest in Figure 16.1a at $n = 8$—where the slope of the benefit and cost curves are equal (in Figure 16.1b).

Suppose that one more firm undertakes a research project. The expected benefit increases by 0.9 from 20.08 to 20.98 (Table 16.4), but the marginal cost of that extra research project is 1, so net benefits fall by 0.1 (= 1 − 0.9), from 12.08 to 11.98.[21]

[21] The marginal benefit, the derivative of $B\rho(n)$ with respect to n, at $n = 8$ only approximately equals the benefits at $n = 9$ minus the benefits at $n = 8$.

FIGURE 16.1 Costs, Expected Benefits, and Net Social Benefits from R&D

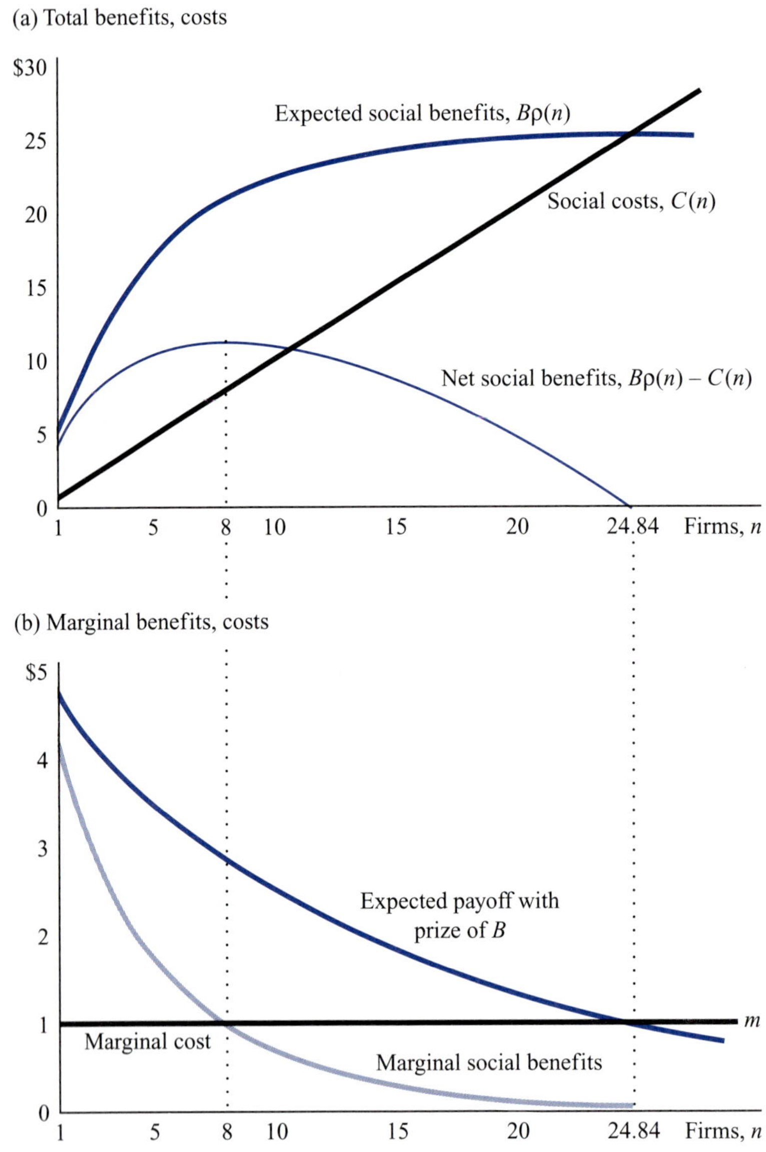

No Government Incentives

Is it progress if a cannibal uses knife and fork? —*Stanislaw Lem*

In the absence of patents and other incentives to invent, few, if any, inventions may be produced. If once a discovery is made everyone can copy it, then the new product is sold at a competitive price, and the inventor makes no economic profits. If inventors bear the full private and social cost of research ($m = 1$) but receive no private financial benefits from their inventions, the profit-maximizing solution for inventors is to engage in no research.

Government-Financed Research

A government can encourage more research by subsidizing research costs. The U.S. government, for example, has given 20 percent tax credits for R&D expenditures. These credits have increased over time. For example, a 1992 U.S. Tax Court decision permits companies to use stock options for engineers (incentives for workers) in calculating R&D tax deductions. India provides both tax breaks and special duty-free export zones for its software makers.

More directly, the government can pay firms to conduct research. In the preceding example (Table 16.4), the government can ensure that the optimal number of research projects is undertaken by offering eight research contracts to the lowest bidders and retaining the rights to successful products. Competitive bidding drives the price to $m = 1$. Assuming that the firms engage in energetic research even though payments are independent of success, this approach leads to the optimal solution. Of course, the government can only pick the optimal number of firms if it knows the true research costs and expected benefits. With adequate information, this approach is efficient if the research is funded efficiently (for example, the government raises the money through nondistorting taxes, such as lump-sum taxes).[22]

In 2002, the federal government paid for 28 percent of the estimated $264 billion spent on R&D in the United States. Defense was 15 percent of the total R&D. Private industry paid 65 percent.[23]

Japan's Ministry of Economy, Trade, and Industry (METI—formerly MITI) finances laboratories that produce commercial products. Often a discovery is licensed to as many Japanese firms as possible. Other times, it is licensed to one firm for three to five years to develop the technology and then licensed broadly. METI spent 0.57 trillion yen in 2001, between one-eighth and one-half of Japan's R&D expenditures.[24] Other Japanese agencies, such as the Japan Research Development Corp., provide additional support.

Mansfield (1984), based on a study of 25 major firms in chemical, oil, electrical equipment, and primary metals industries in the United States, concludes that without government support, these firms would have funded only between 3 percent and

---

[22]In recent years, however, there have been complaints that, although the U.S. government funded the medical research, monopoly rights were given to a single company. For example, the National Institutes of Health spent $30 million developing Taxol, an anticancer drug, and then gave Bristol-Myers Squibb Co. exclusive commercial rights in 1991. Tim Smart, "How Many Times Must a Patient Pay?" *Business Week*, February 1, 1993:30–1.

[23]U.S. National Science Foundation: **www.nsf.gov**.

[24]**www.nsftokyo.org/rm97-06.html#mitibgt; www.meti.go.jp/policy/tech_research/indicator/english(h13.10).pdf**.

EXAMPLE 16.4 *Joint Public-Private R&D*

Many research projects at land-grant universities in the United States and other public institutions are jointly funded by the public and private sectors. One fear is that the private funding distorts research away from maximizing the public good to maximizing private returns.

A case study of Canadian malting barley, which is used in the production of beer, illustrates how sources of funding affect research. Research is funded by the Canadian government, universities and associated research institutions, and by the Brewing and Malting Barley Research Institute (which is funded by private firms). The contribution from private firms was 28.3 percent of the total in 1951, but fell to 6.7 percent by 1981.

Research can improve the yield or quality of barley. Ulrich, Furtan, and Schmitz (1986) calculate the public (social) return and the private (industry) return. They conclude that the social rate of return would be at least 40 percent higher if only yield research were funded. The (relatively small) grants and liaison work from the private sector, however, are likely to keep public research institutes concentrating on a research path that produces both yield and quality improvements. The private sector's best strategy is to provide just enough funding to encourage the "right kind" of publicly funded research. They calculate that every $1 spent by the private sector costs the public sector $25.74 from distorted research that reduces social welfare.

Thus, the interaction between the public and private sectors can cause two problems. The problem that economists have traditionally worried about is that public investment in research displaces private investment. The private sector's share of R&D expenditures on barley has fallen substantially over time. A second problem is that relatively small private contributions may distort public research programs. At least with barley, the social loss from this distortion is large.

20 percent of the energy R&D that they performed with government support. Lichtenberg (1987) finds that, for the entire private sector, federal R&D expenditures do not statistically significantly raise or lower private-sector expenditures. Thus, the government can increase the total amount of research by offering government contracts because its funding does not reduce private research efforts by an equal amount (however, see Example 16.4). A reduction in private research is even less likely if the government funds research that private industry would otherwise ignore.

Prizes

I can forgive Alfred Nobel for having invented dynamite, but only a fiend in human form could have invented the Nobel Prize.

—George Bernard Shaw

The government, with little risk, can induce firms to engage in research by offering prizes for successful research because if no one makes the discovery, the government has no cost. Even if anyone can copy the discovery once the prize is awarded, a large

EXAMPLE 16.5 *Prizes*

Prizes are used to spur research. Three important historical examples are the development of the chronometer, the introduction of canning, and the invention of celluloid. A more recent example concerns refrigerators.

In 1713, prizes were offered in England to encourage the discovery of the measurement of longitude at sea. One of the important discoveries was that of Mayer, who was able to accurately predict the moon's position, which allowed a calculation of a ship's longitude. For this discovery, Mayer's widow received £3,000. Awards of £10,000, £15,000, and £20,000 were offered for a chronometer that measured longitude to within 60, 40, and 30 minutes respectively. In 1762, 49 years later, John Harrison claimed the £20,000 award. Payment was completed in 1773. By 1815, £101,000 in prizes had been awarded.

In 1795, Napoleon's Society for the Encouragement of Industry offered a prize of 12,000 francs for a method of food preservation that could be employed by the military. Fifteen years later, in 1810, Nicolas Appert received the prize for his method of food canning that used heat treatment of food in sealed champagne bottles.

In the 1860s, John Wesley Hyatt invented celluloid, the first synthetic plastic. By doing so, he won a $10,000 prize in a contest to develop a substitute for ivory billiard balls.

Electrical utilities, due to government regulation (see Chapter 20), often want to discourage electrical consumption at the margin. Refrigerators account for about a fifth of household electricity demand. In 1992, 25 electrical companies offered a prize of $27.5 million for the best design for a new refrigerator that runs on 25 percent less electricity than the government standard and uses no chlorofluorocarbons (a refrigerant blamed for damaging the ozone layer). They received 500 responses. In 1993, Whirlpool won.

Sources: Wright (1983, 704); Stigler (1986); Morris (1991).

enough prize can induce firms and inventors to undertake research (see Example 16.5). If the government sets the prize properly, the optimal number of firms race to win it; setting a higher prize, however, stimulates excessive research.

Optimal Prize. A firm undertakes a research project in an attempt to win a prize if its expected winnings are at least as great as its costs.[25] The number of firms racing to win the prize is determined by the size of the prize. To induce the optimal number of firms, n^*, to compete for a prize, the government must set the prize so that if n^* firms race to be first, each firm's expected earning equals its research costs.

[25]For simplicity, this example assumes that firms are risk-neutral and are willing to take a fair bet. That is, they participate in a gamble if their expected winnings equal their expected costs. Moreover, if there is a tie, the prize is either split equally or awarded randomly to one of the successful firms.

The probability that at least one firm makes the discovery is $\rho(n)$. If each of the n firms believes it has an equal chance of winning, then its expected gain is $\rho(n)/n$ times the prize. From the preceding analysis, we know that at the optimal number of firms, $n^* = 8$, the cost of a research project, $m = 1$, exactly equals the expected marginal social benefit of having n^* firms race to make the discovery. The optimal prize, then, is determined by dividing the expected marginal social benefit at $n^* = 8$, which is 1, by a firm's probability of winning, $\rho(8)/8$. Using the numbers in Table 16.4, the optimal prize is $9.96 = $1/(.80304/8).[26]

With this prize, each firm's expected winnings are the same as the expected marginal social benefits for $n = 8$ shown in Table 16.4. With $n = 8$, each firm's expected winnings are $1.00, which equals its costs. A ninth firm considering joining the race calculates that its expected winnings are $0.93 ($9.96 $\times$ $\rho(9)/9$), or less than its cost of $1.00, and decides that it is not worth joining the race. As a result, only the optimal number of firms, 8, compete for the prize. Net social benefit is maximized at $12.08. As long as the government has the necessary information to set the prize optimally, and as long as the prize is financed without distortions, prizes can efficiently induce innovation.

Too High a Prize and the Common-Pool Problem

It might appear reasonable to set the prize equal to the social value of the discovery, $B =$ $25, rather than $9.96. That prize is so high, however, that too much research is undertaken.

The *Expected Payoff with a Prize* $= B$ column in Table 16.4 shows a firm's expected benefit from engaging in research if the prize is $25. If 24 firms engage in research, the probability, $\rho(24)$, that at least one will be successful is 99.24 percent, so the probability that a particular firm wins the prize is 0.9924/24 = 4.13 percent. As a result, each firm's expected prize is $25 times 4.13 percent, or $1.03, as shown in Table 16.4. With 25 firms competing, each firm's expected earnings are $0.99 (less than the cost of a research project). Thus, if there can only be a whole number of firms racing for the prize, 24 firms compete.

That much research is excessive because the competition dissipates almost all of the rents from research. Table 16.4 shows that the net social benefit when $n = 24$ is $0.81: The social cost of the research nearly equals the expected benefits. This problem is analogous to the overfishing or *common pool* problem (see **www.aw-bc.com/carlton_perloff** "Commons"). Each firm considers its private return rather than the social return when deciding whether to undertake research. If there can be a fractional number of research projects, 24.84 projects are undertaken, and net social benefits are completely dissipated. Figure 16.1b shows the expected returns from each research project, which are equal to the marginal cost, $1.00, when there are 24.84 projects. In

[26]The prize equals $B\rho'(n^*)/[\rho(n^*)/n^*]$, where $B\rho'(n^*)$ is the expected marginal social benefit from having n^* compete, and $\rho(n^*)/n^*$ is the probability that one of the n^* firms will be the first to make the discovery. See **www.aw-bc.com/carlton_perloff** "Patents, Prizes, and Research Contracts."

contrast, the expected marginal benefit to society from having the last project is only about 3¢, as shown in Table 16.4.

To summarize, when the prize is set at $9.96, only 8 firms compete, and the probability that at least one will make the discovery is only 80 percent. When the prize is set at $25, 24 firms compete and the probability rises to 99 percent. Increasing the probability by these extra 19 percentage points, however, requires that the social cost of the research rise from $8 to $24, or 300 percent. Thus, raising the probability by 19 percentage points does not pay. With a prize of $9.96, net social benefit is maximized at $12.08, whereas with a prize of $25, net social benefits are essentially eliminated.

Relaxing Antitrust Laws: Joint Ventures

The reason there is too little research without additional incentives, such as prizes and government research contracts, is that there is an externality if an inventor cannot capture the full value of a new discovery. In the absence of patent laws, each firm interested in producing a new product prefers to copy the discovery of another firm that paid to develop the product. As a result, each firm may wait for others to bear the cost, and little research is undertaken.

If all the firms in an industry, however, agree to share the cost of development in a research joint venture, this externality problem can be avoided. Firms may fear, however, that such joint research activity may lead to antitrust prosecutions. When the firms meet to agree on funding the research and sharing existing knowledge, the government may suspect that they also conspire to set the price for the new product at the monopoly level. Many policy makers and economists argue that antitrust laws and policies should be changed to encourage joint research activities (but not joint price setting).[27] The National Cooperative Research Act of 1984 tried to reduce firms' fears of antitrust penalties by lowering the damages a joint venture must pay if it is convicted of an antitrust violation. One provision of this act is that registered joint ventures cannot be sued for punitive damages and treble damages under the antitrust laws.

When several patents covering a single process are owned by multiple firms, a firm may be inhibited from engaging in R&D for fear that its invention may be worthless unless it can license the other relevant patents on reasonable terms. In such situations, firms may form a patent pool, in which they agree to cross-license patents to each other at reasonable rates (Lerner and Tirole 2002b). However, firms with competing patents can use patent pools to collude and can either exclude or charge a monopoly price to firms outside the pool (Gilbert 2002).

The U.S. Department of Justice (DOJ) has approved patent pooling in a number of antitrust cases (Gallini 2002). For example, in 1997, the DOJ allowed the pooling of patents for the MPEG-2 video compression technology, which involved nine patent holders and 27 patents. Similarly, the DOJ permitted pooling of Digital Versatile Disk (DVD) technologies in 1998 and 1999.

---

[27]See, for example, Ordover and Willig (1985), Grossman and Shapiro (1986), Brodley (1990), Jorde and Teece (1990), and Shapiro and Willig (1990).

It is unclear, in the preceding example, whether a joint venture finances the optimal number of research projects. On the one hand, a joint venture may be able to avoid needless duplication of research projects, and hence its costs of research may be lower than when there is competition. On the other hand, if the joint venture cannot capture the full expected social value, $B\rho(n)$, the joint venture undertakes too little research, because it bears the full social cost.[28] Except when it can act as a discriminating monopoly, a joint venture typically captures less than the full social value of a new product, which includes consumer surplus. Moreover, in an industry where research can be easily copied by firms outside the joint venture, the joint venture may capture little of the social value of a discovery. Joint ventures are unlikely to generate substantial research in such markets.

Joint ventures in technological fields, where R&D costs are high, are becoming increasingly common in the United States. Under the National Cooperative Research Act, 111 cooperative endeavors were registered between January 1985 and June 1988 (Jorde and Teece 1988). Joint ventures are more common in Japan and Europe.

International joint ventures are increasingly common. For example, in 1992, Toshiba, IBM, and Siemens announced they would collaborate in developing advanced memory chips and, on the same day, Fujitsu and Advanced Micro Devices said they would jointly manufacture flash memories (which are used for data storage instead of disk drives). From April 1991 to July 1992, at least seven technology alliances to produce memory chips were formed between U.S. and Japanese firms.

Patents

Patents, which grant exclusive rights to successful inventors, also induce research. Unlike prizes or government research contracts, however, patents lead to distortions due to monopoly pricing. Thus, they are less efficient than optimal prizes or research contracts if the government has sufficient information to induce the optimal amount of research. There are reasons to use patents, however, because the government typically has limited information. In any case, patents are an extremely common method of inducing research throughout the world. For example, the former Soviet Union, which one might expect to rely on government-directed research, issued one and one-half times as many patents as the United States.[29]

Value of a Patent. Suppose that the first successful firm receives a patent granting exclusive rights to sell the product. Does this reward of monopoly profits induce the optimal number of firms to conduct research? To determine how many firms engage in

---

[28]If the firms currently in the industry can obtain patent protection for a discovery they jointly finance, they can make it more difficult for other firms to enter the industry. This barrier to entry stems from the patent and not from the joint venture. Without such patent protection, firms are less likely to undertake a joint venture, because new entrants can profit from their discoveries.

[29]L. M. Boyd, "The Grab Bag," *San Francisco Examiner,* July 24, 1988: "This World" section, 7. An important U.S. example of an industry affected by patents is discussed at **www.aw-bc.com/carlton_perloff** "A Bell Patent Monopoly."

a **patent race**, in which several firms compete to be the first to make the discovery and be granted the patent, one needs to find out how much the patent is worth.

Continuing to use the same example, we add four assumptions to calculate the value of the patent:

1. The demand in each period for the new product is linear:

$$p = 6 - 5Q,$$

where p is the price and Q is the number of units sold.
2. The marginal (and average) cost of production is 1.
3. If two firms make a discovery simultaneously, they split the patent rights.
4. The interest rate, r, is 10 percent.

A firm that obtains exclusive rights under a patent acts like a monopoly and maximizes its profits by setting marginal revenue equal to marginal cost. In the example, the monopoly charges price $p_m = \$3.50$, sells $q_m = 0.5$ units and makes annual profits of $\pi_m = \$1.25$. With monopoly pricing, the annual consumer surplus is \$0.65, which is one-fourth the consumer surplus of a competitive industry. These calculations show how much monopoly rights to sell the new good are worth per year. How much the patent is worth over time depends on how long it lasts. We consider two cases: a patent that lasts forever and one that lasts for only a few years.

Permanent Patent. If a patent lasts forever, the patent holder earns monopoly profits forever. These large potential rewards may induce many firms to race to win the patent, resulting in excessive research effort.[30]

If the patent lasts forever, and the interest rate $r = 10$ percent, the present value of the patent is $\pi_m / r = \$12.50$. That is, the present value of a stream of monopoly profits at the rate of \$1.25 every year forever is \$12.50. The present value of a permanent patent, in our example, is 50 percent (= \$12.50/\$25) of the net social value of the invention if the product were sold at competitive prices.

Each firm has an equal chance of obtaining the patent, so the expected return to a firm undertaking research is \$12.50 times the probability that it makes the discovery first, $\rho(n)/n$. A firm joins the patent race so long as its research costs, $m = 1$, are less than its expected benefits from winning the race.

In the example, 11.22 research projects are undertaken given permanent patent rights (see **www.aw-bc.com/carlton_perloff** "Patents, Prizes, and Research Contracts") if fractional projects are possible, or 11 if fractional projects are impossible.

[30]There is a large literature on patent races. Early articles include Usher (1964) and Barzel (1968). A later literature—Loury (1979), Dasgupta and Stiglitz (1980), Lee and Wilde (1980), Reinganum (1982)—which is surveyed in Reinganum (1984), investigates *poisson* patent races, in which the probability that a firm makes a discovery first depends only on its current R&D expenditures and not on its experience to date. An even more recent literature, where experience matters, is discussed later in this chapter.

Thus, in the example, a permanent patent leads to excessive research: 40 percent more research projects than the optimal number 8.[31]

Finite Patent Length. By having patents last shorter periods of time, t, the government can reduce the incentive for excessive research. Having exclusive rights for only t years reduces the present value of the flow of monopoly profits; thus, the expected private benefit to each firm is lower, so fewer firms engage in research.

Unlike a prize or a research contract, a patent causes a pricing distortion—a monopoly price—after a discovery. The government is faced with a trade-off: the longer the patent, the greater the inducement for research but the larger the cost due to more research projects and the monopoly loss. Given that the government uses patents, then, it should choose the length, t, to maximize expected net social benefit, taking into account monopoly pricing. Table 16.5 and Figure 16.2 show the net social benefits corresponding to various patent lengths, t.[32] Both show the number of projects and associated net social benefits if fractional numbers of projects are possible and if only whole numbers of projects are possible.

As shown in Table 16.5, if fractional numbers of projects are possible, net social benefit is maximized when $t = 11.4475$, there are $n = 6.004$ projects, and net social benefit = \$8.608908. If there can only be whole numbers of projects, the best solution is $t = 11.4408$, $n = 6$, and net social benefit = \$8.608906. If t is set at 15.94, there are 8 projects, and net social benefit is \$8.08.

Because of the distortions associated with patents, society only wants approximately 6 projects rather than the 8 desired with prizes or research contracts. To get 8 projects rather than 6 using patents, the length of time for the grant of exclusive rights must be increased 39 percent from 11.44 to 15.94. An increase in the number of projects from 6 to 8 only increases the probability of success from 70 percent to 80 percent (Table 16.4), which does not fully offset the additional costs. The net social benefit falls 6.2 percent, from \$8.61 to \$8.08 (Table 16.5).

Prior to the patent law change of 1995, patents lasted 17 years in the United States. (Since then, they last 20 years.) Why 17 years? The length of patent protection, in the first piece of legislation passed after the Constitution was signed into law by George Washington in 1790, was related to the length of an apprenticeship, which lasted for 7 years.[33] Some in Congress wanted to offer patent protection for the length of two apprenticeships. Other representatives, however, wanted to allow the patent to be renewed after 14 years for another 7 years. Congress decided to split the difference and offer a single term of 17 years.

Setting a fixed length for a patent for all types of products probably means that monopoly power is granted for too long a period for some types of products and too short

---

[31]This result stems, in part, from the particular probability function used in the example: $\rho(n) = 1 - e^{-\alpha n}$, where $\alpha = .2031$. If we choose $\alpha = 0.1342$, the optimal number of projects is 9, but a permanent patent leads to 8.51 projects, which is fewer than the optimal number.

[32]We assume that the patent holder does not price discriminate. See, however, Hausman and MacKie-Mason (1988), who discuss the social desirability of price discrimination by patent holders and the effect of such discrimination on the optimal length of a patent.

[33]Michael Schrage, "Patent System Outmoded," *San Francisco Examiner,* November 3, 1991:E-14.

TABLE 16.5 **Optimal Patent Length**

	Fractional Firms Possible		Fractional Firms Impossible	
Length of Patent, t	Number of Projects, n	Net Social Benefit	Number of Projects, n	Net Social Benefit
5.35	0.50	$1.66	0.00	$0.00
5.71	1.00	3.10	1.00	3.20
6.53	2.00	5.35	2.00	5.35
7.47	3.00	6.91	3.00	6.91
8.56	4.00	7.91	4.00	7.91
9.00	4.35	8.14	4.00	7.84
9.87	5.00	8.44	5.00	8.44
10.00	5.09	8.47	5.00	8.42
11.00	5.74	8.60	5.00	8.29
11.4408	**6.00**	**8.608906**	**6.00**	**8.60891**
11.4475	**6.004**	**8.608908**	**6.00**	**8.60793**
12.00	6.31	8.59	6.00	8.53
13.00	6.82	8.51	6.00	8.41
13.40	7.00	8.47	7.00	8.47
14.00	7.26	8.39	7.00	8.39
15.94	**8.00**	**8.08**	**8.00**	**8.08**
19.51	9.00	7.48	9.00	7.48
25.36	10.00	6.72	10.00	6.72

FIGURE 16.2 Net Social Benefit Varies with Patent Length

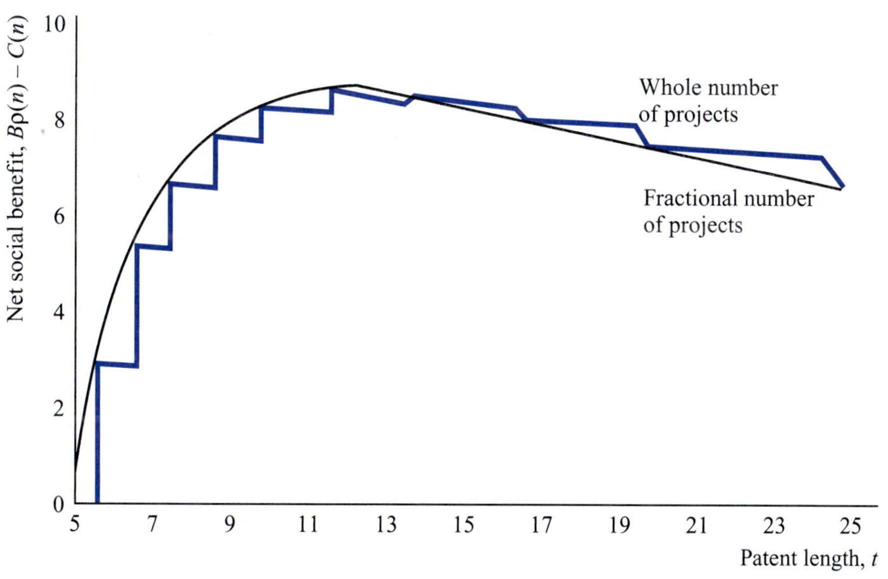

EXAMPLE 16.6

Mickey Mouse Legislation

Mickey Mouse was going to enter the public domain in 2003, when the Walt Disney Company's 1928 copyright on the original Mickey Mouse character was set to expire. In response to intense lobbying by Disney and other corporations, congressional lawmakers passed a Mickey Mouse bailout law, the Sonny Bono Copyright Term Extension Act of 1998. This law increased copyright protection by at least 20 years for all "original works of authorship" such as books, songs, and graphical art copyrighted since 1923. Thus, this Mickey Mouse legislation extended Disney's rights to Mickey to 2023.

What is the logic behind this legislation? We grant monopoly power (a bad) to creators to encourage the production of new art or other inventions (a good) and hope that the net effect is positive. However, once the work has been created, granting additional monopoly power by extending the copyright period is unambiguously harmful. This act provided a huge windfall to holders of existing copyrights, including publishing conglomerates (such as AOL Time Warner) and movie studios (such as Disney) at the expense of the public.

The act also provides that any work copyrighted from 1978 on has copyright protection for the author or artist's life and the next 70 years (an increase from 50 years). Works copyrighted prior to 1978 are protected for 95 years. In contrast, the original 1790 legislation set the length of a copyright at 14 years with an option to renew for another 14 years.

The well-known images of Uncle Sam and Santa Claus were created by the nineteenth-century cartoonist Thomas Nast. Had Nast created under the Sonny Bono rules, everyone from the U.S. Department of Defense to retailers would be paying his estate royalties for these images, or, more likely, these images would not currently be an important part of our culture. Keeping works out of the public domain prevents others from using and extending original concepts, as Disney did when it drew on the work of the brothers Grimm to produce *Cinderella* and *Snow White.*

In 2002, a legal challenge to the Copyright Term Extension Act, *Eldred v. Ashcroft*, 57 U.S. 1160 (2003), reached the U.S. Supreme Court. Eric Eldred wanted to allow

a time for others.[34] Moreover, because, for some products, firms must obtain regulatory approval before the products can be sold, the effective patent life is shortened. To partially compensate for this problem, the Drug Price Competition and Patent Term

[34]Nordhaus (1969), however, argues that 17 years is close to optimal for many industries. Compare DeBrock (1985) and Dasgupta and Stiglitz (1980). See Gilbert and Shapiro (1990), who discuss the optimal coverage of a patent. Caves, Whinston, and Hurwitz (1991) examine what happens to prices of drugs when patents expire. They show that prices often remain high for some drugs, perhaps indicating that the monopoly power extends beyond the patent life.

people free access on his Web site to literary works such as Robert Frost poems and F. Scott Fitzgerald's novel *The Great Gatsby*, whose copyrights would have expired were it not for the great giveaway. His lawyer, Stanford Law School professor Lawrence Lessig, argued that the retroactive extension of copyright protection (but not the extension of protection to new works) violated the sense, if not the literal words, of the Constitution's grant to Congress of authority to "promote the progress of science" by issuing copyrights for "limited times." Fifteen economists from across the political spectrum, including the Nobel laureates Milton Friedman and Kenneth Arrow, wrote a brief supporting the challenge. At the hearing, Justice Sandra Day O'Connor said, "It is hard to understand how, if the overall purpose of the Copyright Clause is to encourage creative work, . . . some retroactive extension could possibly do that." As many people have, she concluded "One wonders what was in the minds of the Congress." Unfortunately, the Supreme Court rejected this challenge in 2003 in a 7–2 vote (O'Connor voted with the majority), apparently on the grounds of precedence: Congress has made this mistake of retroactively extending copyright protection many times in the past, including 11 times in the last 40 years.

Luckily, EU copyright protection lasts only 50 years. Consequently, copyright protection of a treasure trove of 1950s jazz (Ella Fitzgerald), opera (Maria Callas), and early rock 'n' roll (Elvis Presley) albums has expired or will expire soon. As these recordings enter the public domain in Europe, any European recording company can release albums that previously have been sold exclusively by a particular label. U.S. record companies are calling for EU countries to extend copyright terms, or failing that, for the United States to block imports of records still covered under U.S. copyrights that last 95 years.

Source: Amy Harmon, "Debate to Intensify on Copyright Extension Law," *New York Times*, October 7, 2002:C1; Amy Harmon, "Challenge in Copyright Case May Be Just a Beginning," *New York Times*, October 14, 2002:C4; Seth Shulman, "Freeing Mickey Mouse," *Technology Review*, November 2002:81; Anthony Tommasini, "Labels Ready for Battle on Copyright," *San Francisco Chronicle*, January 3, 2003:B2; Linda Greenhouse, "20-Year Extension of Existing Copyrights Is Upheld," *New York Times*, January 16, 2003:A22; **http://eldred.cc/eldredvashcroft.html; http://cyber.law.harvard.edu/openlaw/eldredvashcroft**.

Restoration Act of 1984 extends patent lives of pharmaceuticals to offset the delays in introducing new drugs as a result of regulatory requirements (Grabowski and Vernon 1986). In 1991–1992, Procter & Gamble asked Congress to extend its patent for the fat substitute olestra, which was due to expire in 1994, because the Food and Drug Administration was slow to approve it (some argue that Procter & Gamble delayed in submitting safety studies). Upjohn and U.S. Bioscience Inc. have also tried to extend patent claims through private bills before Congress. See Example 16.6 with respect to copyrights.

The time it takes to obtain a patent from the U.S. Patent Office differs across industries. According to the U.S. General Accounting Office, companies must wait an average of four years to obtain a patent in genetic engineering, compared to three years for other aspects of biotechnology, and an average of 18 months for all other types of patents.[35]

Where the pace of invention is rapid, the length of a patent may be irrelevant because new products eliminate the demand for older ones, even though the latter still have patent protection. In many European countries, patent lengths vary because patent holders must pay annual fees to maintain their monopoly rights under patents and may choose to let their patents lapse after a few years (Example 16.7).

Government Uncertainty

The example in Tables 16.4 and 16.5 demonstrates that if the government has as much information as research firms, it can set prizes or research contracts so as to induce the optimal level of research, maximizing net social benefit. When the government has full information, patents and joint ventures are less desirable than prizes or research contracts because they distort pricing. With prizes or research grants, after the discovery is made, the new product is sold at competitive prices, and consumer surplus is maximized.[36] For the life of a patent, a new product is sold at a monopolistic price, which leads to too few sales. However, if inventors have more information before they start inventing than do government officials, as seems likely, then patents and joint ventures may be superior.

Suppose the government sets a prize, research contract, or patent length before the value of an invention is known. If the researcher believes correctly that the invention is worth more than the value the government has set, then the patent may induce more research than the prize or government contract. Of course, if the length of the patent is very short, then prizes or research contracts, even if set too low, may be superior.[37]

In general, it is difficult for anyone, even the potential inventor, to predict the value of an invention beforehand. Indeed, even after it is invented, its value may be quite uncertain because demand is hard to predict or because of legal uncertainties about the ownership of the patent. For example, the inventor of the shoelace made $2.5 million on his patent, whereas the inventor of the safety pin earned only $400.[38] It is estimated that fewer than 1 of every 50 patent holders makes money from his or her patent.[39]

Patent Holders May Manufacture or License

A patent gives the inventor the monopoly on an idea for a fixed period of time. The patent holder may produce the product (or use its new process) or **license** (permit) others to produce it in exchange for a payment called a **royalty**. We will now show that

---

[35] *San Francisco Chronicle,* "How Slow Patent Process Hurts Biotechnology Firms," July 19, 1990:C2.

[36] If the inventor can obtain a patent on the government-financed research, however, this advantage is lost. Such patenting occurs in Australia (Tisdell 1974).

[37] Wright (1983) identifies the conditions under which patents, prizes, or research contracts are likely to be best in a world of uncertainty. Patents are likely to be best when the probability of success is low and the elasticity of supply of research is relatively high.

[38] L. M. Boyd, "The Grab Bag," *San Francisco Examiner,* March 27, 1988: "This World" section, 7.

[39] L. M. Boyd, "The Grab Bag," *San Francisco Examiner,* September 6, 1987: "Sunday Punch" section, 7.

EXAMPLE 16.7 *European Patents*

In many countries, unless patent holders pay an annual renewal fee, they lose their monopoly rights under the patent. A firm only renews a patent if the expected returns to one more year of exclusive rights exceed the cost of renewing. Pakes (1986) estimates the distribution of the value of holding patents in France and Germany and shows how this distribution changes over the lifetime of a patent. This information tells us the value to patent holders of the proprietary rights created by the patent in each year after the patent has been issued.

There is no renewal fee in France until a patent is 2 years old, 3 years old in Germany, or 5 years old in the United Kingdom. A patent can only be renewed until it is 16 years old in the United Kingdom, 18 in Germany, and 20 in France. Renewal fees are relatively low in all three countries in the early years, but increase significantly faster in Germany in later years.

The estimated average annual net profits from a patent, based on renewal data for the 1950s, 1960s, and 1970s, for France and Germany for the first five years, are (in 1980 $US):

Year	France	Germany
1	$380	$1,609
2	1,415	3,401
3	1,432	3,225
4	1,339	2,899
5	1,193	2,641

In France, the average annual initial net profit from a patent is $380. In that year, one-fifth of the French patent holders discover a use for the patent, allowing them to increase subsequent returns. Over 6 percent find that their patented ideas cannot be profitably exploited, so they do not pay the renewal fee in the second year. The rest renew, maintaining the option of patent protection while continuing to look for profitable uses. The average annual net profit on remaining patents rises to $1,415. The next year, another 9 percent fail to renew, and the average annual net profit increases to $1,432. Learning about profitable uses of the patent decreases over time, so that by the fifth year, virtually no more learning takes place, and obsolescence starts dominating learning. The average annual net profit on remaining patents falls to $1,193.

In contrast, the average initial net profit of German patents, $1,609, is much higher than French patents. One reason may be that 93 percent of French applicants are granted patents, whereas only 35 percent of German applicants are granted patents. As a result, fewer Germans bother to apply for patents of questionable value. A second factor is that French data contain all applicants, but the German data include only successful ones. The average annual net profit of German patents is $3,401 in the second year, $3,225 in the third, $2,899 in the fourth, and $2,641 in the fifth.

These results show that most patents have very low initial annual net profits. Indeed, most patent holders do not find a use for their patents within the first few years, and hence do not renew the patent after the first few years. Of those who do find a use for a patent, typically, they find it within the first few years. (See Schankerman, 1998, and Lanjouw, 1998, for more recent evidence on European patent renewals.)

a profit-maximizing inventor is indifferent between being the only seller of the product and licensing others to produce and sell it, so long as the product market was competitive prior to the invention.[40]

A Model of Licensing. Suppose a market was originally competitive and all firms produced at constant (marginal and average) cost m. The competitive price of the good was m, and Q units were sold. Now suppose someone develops a new process that allows the same good to be produced at a lower cost, $\underline{m}$, as shown in Figure 16.3a.

If the firm that owns the new patent decides to sell the product itself, it is essentially a low-cost dominant firm that faces a competitive fringe (Chapter 4).[41] The lowest price it considers charging is $\underline{m}$: Any lower price leads to losses. The highest price it can charge is m: Any higher price allows the fringe to undercut its price. Suppose that it is optimal for the dominant firm to charge just slightly less than m to prevent the fringe from making any sales. The profits from the invention are the difference between the old cost and new cost times the number of units sold. This amount is labeled *Royalties* in Figure 16.3a.

Now suppose the firm considers licensing other firms to use the new technology. The firm charges a royalty per unit of output sold by the other firms (*royalty rate*).

What royalty rate maximizes the firm's profits? To answer this question, we must determine the derived demand for a patent license: the maximum price a producer is willing to pay for a license. Figure 16.3a shows an example for a run-of-the-mill or minor invention that only slightly reduces the cost of production. The derived demand for licenses is the difference between the residual demand curve facing the patent holder and the cost of producing under the new process, $\underline{m}$. That is, the maximum royalty a competitive firm will pay for a license is the difference between the competitive price and the cost under the patented process. Thus, for the first Q units (the amount sold by a competitive industry), the competitive price is m, so the maximum royalty is $m - \underline{m}$, which is labeled the *Derived demand for license* in Figure 16.3a. If more units are sold, the value of the license drops, illustrating that the derived demand curve slopes down beyond Q units. Indeed, at Q^*, the value of a license is zero, because the competitive price equals the cost of production under the new process.

The profit-maximizing royalty occurs where the marginal revenue (MR) from selling one more license equals the marginal cost of a license. The marginal cost of a license is zero. Thus, the profit-maximizing royalty is determined by the intersection of the marginal revenue curve for a license with the quantity axis. In the case shown, that occurs at quantity Q and a royalty rate $r = m - \underline{m} = p - \underline{m}$. That is, the profit-maximizing royalty is the *total* per-unit savings from using the new process. This amount equals the earnings if the firm did not license the product, but sold it itself.

[40] This section focuses on only a small aspect of licensing. Gallini (1984), Gallini and Winter (1985), and Katz and Shapiro (1985a, 1986) discuss these and other important issues. For example, Gallini (1984) and Gallini and Winter (1985) note that, under certain circumstances, licensing may reduce inefficient R&D expenditures.

[41] This graphic presentation follows Arrow (1962), McGee (1966), Nordhaus (1969), and Dasgupta and Stiglitz (1980).

FIGURE 16.3 License Royalties

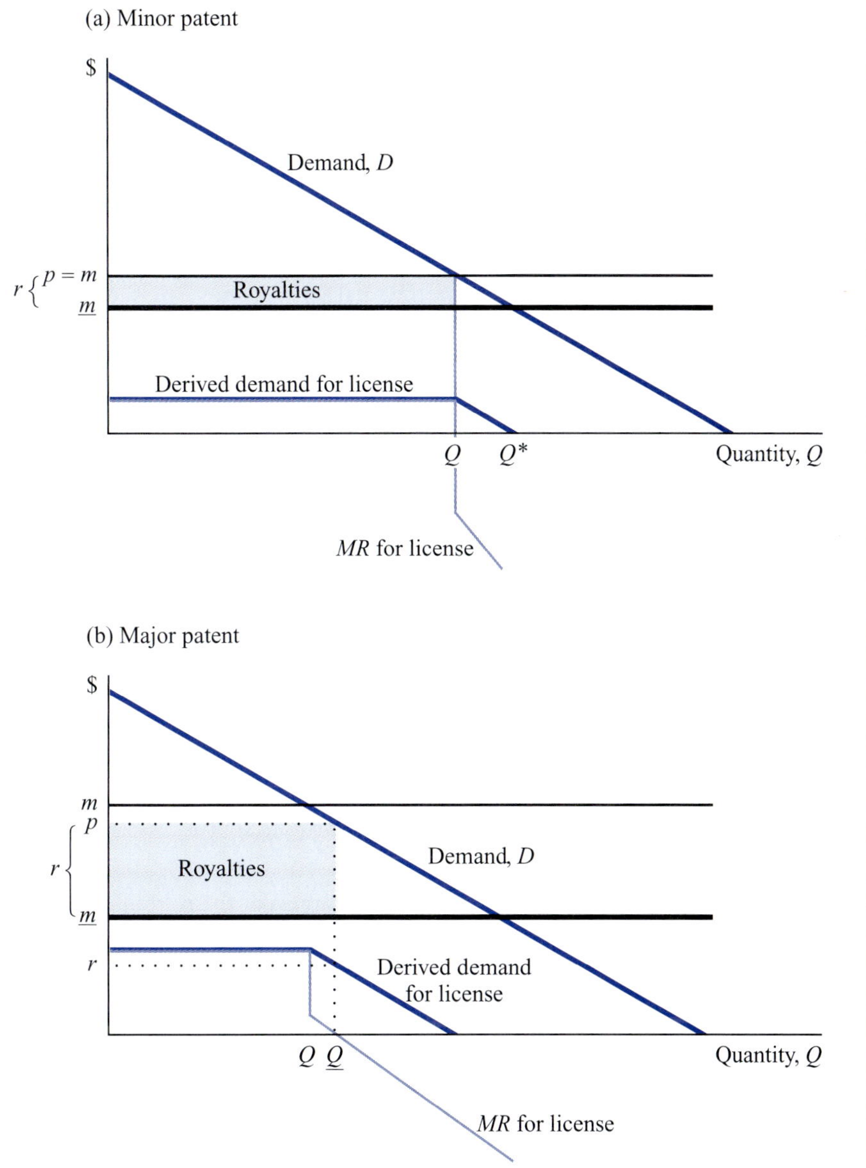

Figure 16.3b uses the same types of curves to examine the case of a major new process that produces a dramatic fall in costs. Here, the marginal revenue for the derived demand for licenses equals zero at $\underline{Q}$. The profit-maximizing price, p, lies between m and $\underline{m}$. As a result, the royalty rate $(r = p - \underline{m})$ is less than the cost reduction $(m - \underline{m})$, but $\underline{Q} > Q$ licenses are sold.

There are two conclusions from this analysis. First, if the inventor can produce as efficiently as others, the inventor is indifferent between selling the product and licensing it because the competitive fringe restricts the monopoly equally in both cases. Licensing is likely (and more profitable than not licensing) when licensees have lower manufacturing costs than the inventor. Licensing provides an important mechanism through which new discoveries can be implemented throughout the world (see **www.aw-bc.com/carlton_perloff** "International Licenses").

Second, the inventor captures all the gains to society of minor discoveries, but not of major discoveries. With minor discoveries, consumers continue to buy the same quantity at the same prices, so they are unaffected by the discovery. With major discoveries, price falls and quantity rises so that consumer surplus rises. So, with major discoveries, the inventor's gain is less than the total social gain.

Examples of Royalties. Licensing and the collection of royalties is very common. We discuss the licensing by two well-known companies and royalties collected by the record industry.

IBM has extensive and fundamental patents on all phases of computing. For example, it has a patent covering computer screen behavior such as when a cursor is on the last position on the last line of the computer display and you hit the carriage return/line feed button, the screen scrolls upward by one line. IBM has licensed its patents for over thirty years. By 1990, IBM claimed to have licensing agreements with 90 percent of PC manufacturers worldwide, collecting 1 percent to 3 percent of the selling price of all PCs. Other firms avoid paying royalties by signing cross-license agreements giving each firm access to the other's patents.

Record companies tried for years to obtain a royalty on analog tape recorders and blank audio cassettes that could be used to duplicate their records. With the arrival of the new digital audio tape and compact cassettes in 1991, they tried again. Under an agreement between digital audio technology companies and the recording and the consumer electronics industries, all digital audio tape recorders sold in the United States would be equipped with a special "serial copy management system" chip that would let owners make personal copies of songs but prevent them from making copies of copies that could be distributed commercially. In addition, the industry group agreed to a 3 percent royalty on blank digital audio tape and cassettes and 2 percent royalty on digital audio tape recorders. Congress ratified this agreement in the Audio Home Recording Act of 1992.[42]

Eliminating Patents

Support for patents is not universal. An energetic global debate is raging about patents in general and pharmaceutical patents in particular. At the end of the 1980s, at least 40 developing countries did not grant patents for pharmaceutical product innovations

[42]Michael Schrage, "Innovation: Cough It Up, Music Lovers (You Thieves)," *San Francisco Examiner,* September 1, 1991:E7; "Audio Recording Bill for Digital Machines Is Cleared by Senate," *Wall Street Journal,* October 8, 1992:B3.

(Lanjouw and Cockburn 2001). However, under the 1995 Agreement on Trade-Related Intellectual Property Rights (TRIPS), members of the World Trade Organization (WTO) must recognize and enforce product patents in all fields of technology, including pharmaceuticals, by 2005. One argument for doing so was that it would induce pharmaceutical companies to develop new drugs for poor countries (for example, to deal with tropical diseases). Many low-income countries opposed the agreement, predicting that establishing patent systems similar to those in the United States and Europe would raise the price of life-saving drugs and threaten the health of their people. The developing nations apparently accepted this agreement in exchange for future trade concessions on their export goods, such as textiles and apparel.[43]

What is the likely effect of adding drug patent protection in India? India led the opposition to the TRIPS agreement. Prior to 2003, India did not recognize pharmaceutical patents. Domestic Indian firms produced versions of many pharmaceuticals that were under patent in other countries.

Chaudhuri, Goldberg, and Jia (2003) estimate what would happen in the short run if the Indian pharmaceutical market for systemic antibacterials (antibiotics) had been under patent protection in India as they were in the United States. They calculate that the total annual welfare losses to the Indian economy from the withdrawal of the four domestic product groups would be approximately $713 million (U.S. dollars), or about 118 percent of the sales of this segment of the market in 2000. Forgone consumer surplus represents almost all of this welfare loss. Lost domestic producer profit is roughly $50 million (7 percent), and the profit gain to foreign producers is only about $57 million per year. However, these calculations ignore the effects on future inventive activity. Presumably, the effect of patents in India on inventive activity is much less than the effect of U.S. or European patents.

Hughes, Moore, and Snyder (2002) ask what would happen in the long run if the U.S. government abruptly ended patent protection for current and future pharmaceuticals. Although increased access to current drugs would yield large benefits to current consumers, these benefits would come at a loss of future consumer benefits due to a reduction in the flow of new drugs as pharmaceutical firms reduced their R&D. To determine which effect is likely to dominate, Hughes et al. simulate the effects of this change in policy, which they call "Napsterizing" pharmaceuticals (Napster helped individuals obtain copyrighted music for free over the Internet).

While people of goodwill can debate the reliability of such simulations, the authors use as much available evidence as they can to produce reasonable estimates. To determine the price effects, they include evidence on the effects of the entry of generic drugs on the price of branded and generic products. They also note that the prices of branded drugs do not fall to the price of generics after generics enter; hence drug firms would still have some incentive to innovate. They conclude that, for each extra dollar in consumer benefit due to greater access to the current stock of drugs, future consumers would lose three dollars in present-value terms from reduced future innovation.

[43]The Unitesd States did not respect British copyrights when the United States was a net importer of intellectual property in the nineteenth century. The United States signed a bilateral copyright agreement only after the literary balance of trade changed in its favor (Ethier 2003).

Market Structure

The incentives to conduct research, the timing of innovations, and the nature of patent races are all determined by the market structures in the product and research industries. Joseph Schumpeter (1950) initiated modern research about the effects of market structure on innovation by stressing the role of economic agents in technological progress. In the Schumpeterian view, there is a positive relationship between innovation and market power, and large firms are more innovative than small firms.[44]

The Schumpeterian argument is that innovation is more important than price competition because it is a more effective means of gaining an advantage over competitors. Two connections exist between market structure and innovation. First, patents allow one to gain market power by innovating. Second, a firm with market power may be able to prevent entry and imitation through defensive patents, or maintain its power through the introduction of new products.

The two key questions considered in the remainder of this section are:

1. Does a competitive industry or a monopoly have a greater incentive to invent?[45]
2. Which type of industry innovates faster?

We first demonstrate that if firms do not have to worry about others inventing the product first, a competitive firm has a greater incentive to invent than a monopoly. Then we illustrate that a competitive firm sometimes innovates too quickly, and certainly more quickly than a monopoly. Finally, we show that a monopoly that must worry about a potential rival entering its market by inventing has an incentive to innovate to prevent entry. This threat of competition gives the monopoly a greater incentive to invent than a competitive firm. Thus, which type of market structure provides a greater incentive to invent depends on whether a patent race is possible.

Market Structure Without a Patent Race

Suppose that a firm, which is uniquely suited to innovate, believes that, if it does not invent a new process, no other firm will. If the firm is initially in a competitive market, it is likely to have a greater incentive to invent a cost-saving process than if it is a monopoly. The basic intuition is that the competitive firm earns profits from its new process over more units than does a monopoly (Arrow 1962).

Let us stick to the minor cost-reducing invention from the preceding section. We assume that a royalty fee is collected from each firm that produces the product in the final goods market and consider two contrasting market structures. In one, the inventing

[44]See Schumpeter (1950), Galbraith (1952), Nelson and Winter (1982), Kamien and Schwartz (1982), and Geroski (1991). See also **www.aw-bc.com/carlton_perloff** "Size and Innovation."

[45]We restrict attention to a monopoly and to a competitive industry consisting of identical firms. In any industry, of course, the firms may be heterogeneous and may pursue divergent R&D policies (Scott 1984, 1991b).

firm is initially part of a competitive market; in the other, the inventing firm is already a monopoly in the product market, and barriers to entry prevent future competition.

If the product market is competitive and the competitive price before invention is m, after invention the price is $\underline{m} + r$, where r is the per-unit royalty rate, as shown in Figure 16.4. For a minor innovation, the new price, $\underline{m} + r$, equals m, as discussed above. Thus, the competitive price and quantity, Q, are the same before and after the invention. In contrast, a monopoly sets marginal revenue equal to marginal cost. Figure 16.4 shows the original price, p_m, corresponding to the original cost m, and the new price $\underline{p}_m$ corresponding to the new cost $\underline{m}$. The corresponding quantities are Q_m, and $\underline{Q}_m$.

As a result of the innovation, the monopoly earns more on the original Q_m units and makes a profit on the extra $\underline{Q}_m - Q_m$ units, so its profits must rise. Its original costs were mQ_m = areas $A + B$. After the discovery, its costs are $\underline{m}\underline{Q}_m$ = areas $B + E$. Thus, the change in its cost is $(A + B) - (B + E) = A - E$. Its revenues increase by the area under the marginal revenue curve between Q_m and $\underline{Q}_m$, or areas $D + E$. Thus, its profits rise by $(D + E) + (A - E) = D + A$.

This diagram shows that a monopoly gains less from the invention than an inventor in a competitive industry. The optimal royalty level for the inventor in the competitive market is $r = m - \underline{m}$. Thus, in a competitive market, the inventor earns $rQ = (m - \underline{m})Q$ = areas $A + D + F + G$ in Figure 16.4. In other words, the gain to the inventor in the competitive industry is $F + G$ more than the gain to the monopoly. Indeed, on just the first $\underline{Q}_m$ units, the competitive inventor earns $A + D + F$, whereas the monopoly only earns $A + D$. The royalties on the $Q - \underline{Q}_m$ extra units sold in a competitive industry are "gravy." Thus, in this example, an industry with a product-market monopoly provides less of an incentive to conduct research than a competitive industry.

Even the gain to the competitive industry, however, is less than the full social benefit, $A + D + F + G + H$, the area bounded by the lines at m, $\underline{m}$, and the demand curve that could be achieved if output is $\underline{Q}$. Thus, the competitive market provides less of an incentive for research than is socially optimal, but more of an incentive than does a product-market monopoly.

It is important to stress that, in this example, the innovator does not fear a patent race. Later in this chapter, we examine how the incentives to innovate depend on market structure when there is a patent race.

Optimal Timing of Innovations

Things have never been more like the way they are today in history.
—Dwight David Eisenhower

If only the first firm to produce and patent an innovation can collect royalties on it, competing firms have a strong incentive to be the first to invent. This incentive may be so strong that competitive firms innovate before a monopoly would. A monopoly does not have to worry about being in a patent race, so it innovates at whatever rate it considers optimal.

FIGURE 16.4 Gains to Discoveries Vary with Market Structure

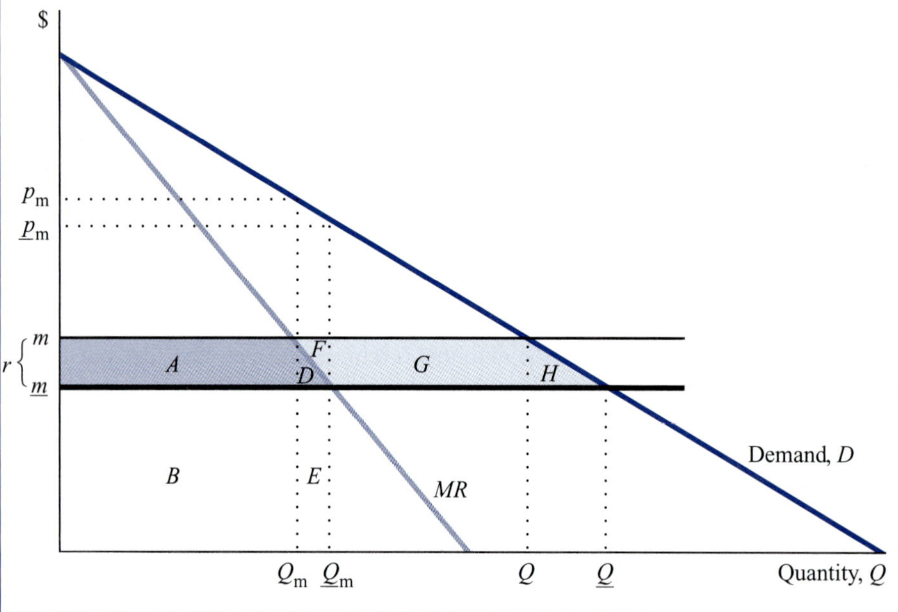

Decades ago, several firms had the knowledge and ability to construct a supersonic transport (SST). Nonetheless, actual production took an enormous investment. In the race between Americans, the British-French *Concorde* team, and the Russians, the SST may have been produced too soon. Indeed, the SST was never profitable.

To illustrate that competing firms may innovate before monopolies, consider a new example (Table 16.6):[46]

- The knowledge to make a minor innovation is costlessly available, but it takes an investment of $2,000 to put it into operation. Once developed, the innovation can be used forever at no additional cost.
- This minor innovation saves $1 per unit of output in a particular production process. As previously discussed, the inventor sets the royalty rate for use of the innovation at $1. For simplicity, we assume the inventor can earn the royalty forever.
- In year 1, 60 units are demanded at the market price. With price held constant, demand grows, and output increases by 10 units each year. This growth in

[46]The following example is based on Barzel (1968). See Kamien and Schwartz (1982, ch. 4) for a rigorous version of a similar model.

TABLE 16.6 **Earning Streams from Four Alternative Investment Policies of Investing $2,000**

Year	Innovate Immediately	Invest Elsewhere	Innovate in Year 5	Innovate in Year 15
1	$60	$200	$200	$200
2	70	200	200	200
3	80	200	200	200
4	90	200	200	200
5	100	200	100	200
6	110	200	110	200
7	120	200	120	200
8	130	200	130	200
9	140	200	140	200
10	150	200	150	200
11	160	200	160	200
12	170	200	170	200
13	180	200	180	200
14	190	200	190	200
15	200	200	200	200
16	210	200	210	210
17	220	200	220	220
18	230	200	230	230
19	240	200	240	240
20	250	200	250	250
•	•	•	•	•
•	•	•	•	•
•	•	•	•	•
Present value	$1,600	$2,000	$2,000	$2,263.33

demand makes the innovation progressively more profitable. By year 15, demand has grown to 200 units.

- The interest rate is 10 percent.

There are four alternative earning streams. First, the inventing firm could put the innovation into effect immediately (the second column of Table 16.6). Because 60 units are sold in that year and the royalty rate is $1 per unit, the firm earns $60 that year, and in each successive year it earns $10 more. The present discounted value of these earnings, at 10 percent interest, is $1,600, which is less than the initial investment of $2,000.

The second strategy (column 3) is to invest the $2,000 elsewhere and earn 10 percent interest, or $200, forever. The present discounted value of this strategy is $2,000.

The third strategy (column 4) is to put the $2,000 in the bank earning 10 percent interest until the fifth year, when the innovation is activated. The firm earns $200 in years 1–4, $100 in year 5, $110 in year 6, and so forth. The present discounted value of these earnings is $2,000.

The final strategy has the largest present value: The firm leaves the $2,000 in the bank until year 15, when it puts the innovation into service. The present discounted value of this stream of earnings is $2,263.33. Making the switch from the bank to innovating at either an earlier or later year produces a lower present discounted value of earnings. The present value of earnings from the fourth option is the highest. As Table 16.6 shows, that strategy has as high or higher earnings than any of the other strategies in each year.

The optimal time to innovate is when the present value of the savings due to the innovation equals the present value of the alternative earnings of the original investment. That is, innovation should occur when the marginal revenues (from royalties) become large enough to cover the marginal cost of the forgone interest ($200). A monopoly facing this schedule uses that strategy.

Competitive firms may not behave like the monopoly, however, because they race to be first. Suppose you own a firm that can produce the innovation. You know that if you are the first to produce and patent it, you will collect royalties forever. Moreover, you know that if you are the first to innovate and your innovation occurs in year 15, your profits from the royalties will be maximized. You may not be able to wait until year 15, however. You know that it is profitable to innovate from any year after the fifth. You also know that if you wait, someone else may innovate first. If, in an attempt to be first, you innovate in year 5, you are indifferent between making the investment and leaving your money in the bank.

Thus, given the schedules in Table 16.6, a competitive industry is likely to innovate before a monopoly. A firm with a monopoly on information introduces the innovation at the time that is optimal for it. In this example, with a permanent patent, a competitive industry overinvests in research, as previously shown, and the research occurs *too soon.*

In general, the year a firm chooses to innovate depends on a variety of factors, such as the cost and demand functions and the number of rival firms. The innovation time of a competing firm is immediately after the zero profit introduction time (Kamien and Schwartz 1982). It is possible to construct examples in which competitive firms innovate before or after monopolies. One reason for this ambiguity is that monopolies charge more for the new product than competitive firms, so they face different benefit schedules in general from the innovation.

So far, we have shown that competitive firms may conduct research more quickly than a monopoly that is not involved in a patent race. The analysis of rates of adoption of new technologies is similar (see **www.aw-bc.com/carlton_perloff** "Adoption of a New Technology: Optical Scanners"). We now turn our attention to the case where a monopoly faces a patent race.

Monopolies in Patent Races

Suppose a monopoly fears that a potential rival will invent a new, similar product and enter the monopoly's market. Both firms have an incentive to invent the new product. If the monopoly gets there first, it maintains its monopoly power. If the potential rival is first to invent, it competes with the incumbent and duopoly results. Thus, the rewards are asymmetric: The monopoly stands to lose more from failing to be first than the rival. The rival loses only its R&D expenditures, whereas the monopoly loses its R&D expenditures and some of its monopoly profits.

Not losing is the monopoly's primary aim; it does not care particularly if it makes or implements the new discovery—it only cares that its rival does not. Indeed, if the monopoly makes the discovery first, it may let its patent "sleep." That is, a monopoly may patent related products so as to prevent anyone else from doing so and then not use the new patents (see **www.aw-bc.com/carlton_perloff** "Compulsory Licenses and Sleeping Patents" and Example 16.8).

Suppose someone invents a product that is slightly superior to the one the monopoly is currently selling. The monopoly is willing to bid more for the patent than a potential rival. The monopoly can use the new invention to maintain its monopoly power, whereas the rival only can use it to become a duopolist. Thus, the monopoly is willing to bid more than the potential rival, up to the difference between monopoly and duopoly profits. An incumbent firm also may have an advantage making new discoveries because of experience (see **www.aw-bc.com/carlton_perloff** "Learning by Doing, Innovation and Market Structure").

Unfortunately for the monopoly, it is not always able to bid for new inventions. The monopoly gets the patent if it invents first; otherwise a potential rival obtains it. If the potential rival could sell the patent to the monopoly, the potential rival would earn more than if it competes as a duopolist, but antitrust laws are intended to prohibit such practices.

How then can a monopoly maintain its monopoly power? Or, restated, how can the monopoly guarantee it is the first to invent (Gilbert and Newbery 1982, Kamien and

EXAMPLE 16.8 *Patent Thicket*

During the 1970s, the federal courts viewed computer programs as mathematical algorithms, which cannot be patented under U.S. law. One could patent systems that used software, but only if the novel aspects of the invention did not reside entirely in the software. Congress decided to protect computer programs under copyright law. Starting with a Supreme Court decision in *Diamond v. Diehr*, 450 U.S. 175 (1981), a series of court and administrative decisions by the U.S. Patent and Trademark Office made it dramatically easier to patent software-related inventions. Now, software patents are 15 percent of all patents.

Most software patents were acquired by manufacturing firms and large firms, with only 6 percent held by software publishers. Bessen and Hunt (2003) test whether software patents and R&D are substitutes or complements. They find that software patents substitute for firm R&D and are associated with lower R&D intensity. They conclude that firms primarily use software patents to create a strategic "patent thicket" to limit the ability of competitors to enter the market or to protect themselves from potential hold-ups.

TABLE 16.7 **Effectiveness of Alternative Means of Protecting the Competitive Advantages of New or Improved Processes and Products**

	Averages*	
Method of Appropriation	Processes	Products
Patents to prevent duplication	3.52	4.33
Patents to secure royalty income	3.31	3.75
Secrecy	4.31	3.57
Lead time	5.11	5.41
Moving quickly down the learning curve	5.02	5.09
Sales of service efforts	4.55	5.59

*Based on a survey of 650 high-level R&D managers of a cross-section of U.S. firms. Each manager answered on a 1–7 scale, where 1 = not at all effective and 7 = very effective.

Source: Levin, Klevorick, Nelson, and Winter (1987, Table 1, 794).

Schwartz 1982, Fudenberg et al. 1983, and Harris and Vickers 1985)? One way is to obtain such a big head start in a patent race that all potential rivals drop out of the race. A firm with a relatively short head start can discourage its rivals from entering a patent race. A trailing firm with no chance of catching up should drop out of the race immediately. In this case, the monopoly can maintain its market power, but it may be forced to innovate faster than it prefers. Alternatively, if the trailing firm has a good chance to gain the lead ("leapfrog" ahead), then it should stay in the race.

A survey of high-level R&D managers in U.S. firms, however, suggests that, in many cases, patents are not an important means of protecting a competitive advantage, as shown in Table 16.7 (Levin, Klevorick, Nelson, and Winter 1987). Patents were rated the least effective mechanisms of appropriating the returns from a competitive advantage for new processes. Secrecy, lead time, moving quickly down the learning curve (gaining experience that leads to lower production costs), and sales or service efforts were all rated higher. Patents ranked above secrecy, but below lead time, moving quickly down the learning curve, and sales or service efforts for new products. These averages across all industries, however, do not give the full picture. Patents were considered to be effective for protecting new products in inorganic chemicals, organic chemicals, drugs, and plastic materials. Thus, patent races are relatively less likely for new processes and relatively more likely for new products in certain industries with high levels of R&D.

SUMMARY

This chapter examines five questions concerning patents and technological progress and reaches the following conclusions. First, without patents or other government incentives to conduct research, there is typically too little R&D and hence too little technological progress. Too little effort is put into R&D because information externalities prevent inventors from capturing the values of their discoveries in the absence of property rights. Patents, prizes, government research contracts, and joint ventures can help overcome this problem.

Second, although patents encourage inventive activity, they cause monopoly pricing distortions. By adjusting the length of a patent, governments can trade off more inventive activity versus more efficient pricing. Shortening the length of a patent reduces the harms from monopoly pricing but also reduces the incentive to invent. Many, if not most, governments rely primarily on grants of monopoly power for a fixed maximum number of years in the form of patents to encourage research. In some cases, welfare may increase with changes in the lengths of patents, greater use of prizes or research contracts, and possibly from compulsory licensing of unused patents.

Third, government prizes and research contracts stimulate R&D and do not have the same drawback as patents and joint ventures—monopoly pricing. Patents, however, may come closer in stimulating the optimal amount of R&D if the government lacks the information or ability to set prizes or research contracts properly. The government may be unable to set them properly if it has less information than researchers about the value of potential new discoveries or the likelihood of making a discovery.

Fourth, a patent holder achieves the same profits by being the sole producer of the product as it does by licensing it and receiving royalties if production costs are the same across manufacturers. The patent holder can capture all the social benefits from many minor cost-saving inventions, but not from major ones.

Fifth, market structures affect rates of research. If there is only one innovator, then a monopoly may innovate more slowly than would a competitive firm. When either a competitive firm or a monopoly faces a patent race, it innovates more rapidly than it otherwise would. A firm can prevent a patent race, however, if it can obtain a sufficient lead in research. A monopoly wants to preempt other firms from engaging in a patent race, because patents are worth more to it than to competitive firms. If the monopoly makes the discovery first, it receives its monopoly profits, whereas if the competitive firm makes the discovery first, it must compete with the former monopoly and earn duopoly profits. It is unclear on theoretical grounds whether greater monopoly power would stimulate innovation in a particular industry and, instead, is an empirical question.

PROBLEMS

1. What is the effect of a sales (revenue) tax on the incentive to invent under a patent system?
2. What is the effect of a profits tax on the incentives to invent?
3. Graphically illustrate (using the benefit and cost curves in Figure 16.1) the effect of a longer patent life on the incentive to invent.
4. If the government could only observe prices, quantities, and royalty rates (but did not know the demand curves or the marginal cost curves), could it determine if a royalty was for a minor or major patent?
5. Using an argument similar to that for monopolistic competition, show that firms operate on the downward-sloping section of their average cost curves for inventive activities.

Answers to odd-numbered problems are given at the back of the book.

SUGGESTED READINGS

Arrow (1962) and Barzel (1968) are important early papers that are relatively nonmathematical. For good surveys of innovation theory, see Kamien and Schwartz (1982) and Reinganum (1989). An interesting collection of empirical research on patents is contained in Griliches (1984). Griliches (1990) surveyed recent work on the significance of patent statistics and Mairesse (1991) surveyed econometric studies on the relationship between R&D and productivity. Novos and Waldman (1984) examined copyrights, and Landes and Posner (1987) and Economides (1988b) analyzed trademarks. Wright (1983) discussed patents and alternatives. Katz and Shapiro (1987) analyzed the problems patents raise where licensing or imitation is possible. The *Rand Journal of Economics,* Vol. 21, 1990, had a special issue on patents and technology. Riordan (1992) discussed how regulation affects technology adoption with an application to cable television.

A new literature discusses the role of piracy of computer software, music, and other intellectual property. See, for example, Shy and Thisse (1999) and Banerjee (2003).

In recent years, the U.S. patent system has undergone a number of major changes. For an interesting viewpoint on the effects of these changes, see **www.bustpatents.com**, which argues that many U.S. patents are invalid—particularly software and biotech patents. Jaffe (2000) and Gallini (2002) provide superb surveys of the changes in the patent system and their effects. Gallini and Scotchmer (2001) survey recent theoretical literature, while Landes and Posner (2003) provide a comprehensive treatment of the economic foundations of intellectual property law.

CHAPTER 17

How Markets Clear: Theory and Facts

Fortune is like the market, where many times, if you can stay a little, the price will fall.
—*Francis Bacon*

Earlier chapters assumed that **market clearing**—the equilibration of the quantities supplied and demanded—occurs exclusively through the price mechanism.[1] Price alone determines how much consumers buy and firms sell. In many, if not most, markets, however, more than just price adjustments are used to allocate goods. This chapter examines the evidence on how goods are allocated to customers and presents some recent theories that explain some of the evidence.[2]

The chapter begins with a brief review of three simple, traditional theories about how markets clear. These theories focus on price as the mechanism for achieving resource allocation and investigate how the price-clearing function is altered depending on whether the market is a competitive one, an oligopoly, or a monopoly. We then provide evidence on what is known about price behavior. The evidence varies sufficiently from the predictions of the simple theories that it raises serious questions about their usefulness for explaining price behavior in many markets.

Next, we examine a variety of alternative theories that help explain some of the observed puzzles in the data on price. In particular, we present a general theory of market behavior without relying on price as the exclusive market-clearing mechanism. Finally, features of market structure other than the degree of market concentration are used to show how market structure matters in explaining the response of various industries to shocks in either supply or demand. Because the failure of markets to clear through price changes is a key assumption in several macroeconomic theories, the issues discussed in this chapter have received widespread attention from macroeconomics (such as Mankiw and Roemer 1991).

[1] One exception was the discussion of search in Chapter 13.

[2] This chapter is a revised version of Carlton (1989).

The five key points in this chapter are

1. Simple theories, which hold that price alone clears markets, are inconsistent with the evidence in many markets.
2. Other mechanisms that clear markets include adjusting consumption and inventories over time, altering quality and rationing.
3. Firms are slow to change prices because of transaction costs and other factors.
4. Long-term relationships between firms affect which mechanisms are used to clear markets.
5. How markets react to demand and cost shocks depends on more than just the degree of market concentration.

How Markets Clear: Three Simple Theories

This section briefly reviews the three most important simple models of the ways in which markets operate. These models form the background against which the next section analyzes the evidence on prices. Only by understanding where the models fail can economists develop better models.

Competition

The standard competitive model assumes that price adjusts so as to equate supply to demand.[3] The amount by which price must adjust depends not only on the size of the shifts in either supply or demand but also on the shape of the supply and demand curves. There are no unsatisfied demanders nor any sellers who wish to sell but cannot. All sellers receive and all buyers pay the same price, price changes are perfectly correlated across different buyers, and the transaction cost is zero.

Oligopoly Models

No single model of oligopoly behavior is universally accepted today. However, most models of oligopoly assume that there are no unsatisfied demanders or sellers who want to sell but cannot at whatever price is set, that price changes are passed along to all buyers simultaneously, and that it is not costly to transact in the market. In most models of oligopoly, prices behave differently than in a competitive market.

Many oligopoly theories predict that price is unresponsive to some cost fluctuations. Any time an oligopolistic firm changes its price, it faces a risk that it will trigger a price war. Hence, firms are reluctant to change price.

Monopoly

A monopoly equates marginal revenue to marginal cost. Thus, the monopoly price exceeds marginal cost. As in the models of competition and oligopoly, there are no un-

[3]How prices adjust to a new equilibrium is normally not explained. For example, which firm first changes its price and why? See Arrow (1959).

satisfied demanders at the market price, and the cost of allocating goods (the cost of using a market price to allocate goods) is assumed to be zero. The theory assumes that price changes across different buyers are perfectly correlated.

The theory explains how a monopoly reacts to shifts in either supply or demand. For example, if marginal cost changes, the new price is determined by the intersection of the new marginal cost curve with the marginal revenue curve.

It is commonly stated that a monopoly's price varies less than the competitive price in response to changes in costs. This conclusion is based on the assumption that demand curves are linear, so that any change in marginal costs translates into a change in the monopoly price that is *less* than the change in marginal costs. In the competitive case, because price equals marginal cost, the changes in price and marginal cost are equal. For example, if the demand curve is

$$Q = 9 - p,$$

and (constant) marginal cost equals $1, the monopoly price is $5. If marginal cost rises from $1 to $3, the monopoly price goes up from $5 to $6. That is, price rises by one-half of the increase in marginal cost. In contrast, if this industry were competitive, price would increase by the same amount as marginal cost.

It is also possible to construct examples in which the monopoly's price varies more than the competitive price in response to cost changes. For example, if the monopoly faces a constant elasticity of demand curve and has a constant marginal cost, its price equals a constant markup above marginal cost. Because the markup exceeds 1, it follows that the price increases by more than the increase in marginal cost. For example, if the elasticity is -2, the monopoly's price is $2 if its marginal cost is $1. If marginal cost rises to $3, the optimal price rises to $6, so the increase in price, $4, exceeds the increase in marginal cost, $2. If the industry were competitive, the price would increase by the same amount as marginal cost.

These examples regarding price variability show that the relation of price changes to cost changes varies with the shape of the demand curve. Therefore, it is not possible to make any general statements about the variability of price in relation to the variability of cost based on whether a market is competitive or monopolized. Moreover, because oligopolies range from almost competitive industries to almost monopolized industries, no general statements can be made for oligopoly. (For small cost changes, however, some theories of oligopoly suggest that prices may remain unchanged.)

Empirical Evidence on the Role of Price in Allocating Goods

Both casual observation and formal surveys on prices provide evidence on the role that price plays in clearing markets. This evidence is used to examine both the rigidity of prices and the movement of prices over the business cycle.

The Rigidity of Prices

Casual evidence shows that prices are more rigid than most simple theories suggest and that consumers are sometimes unable to find the good. Consumers know that if there are three cars ahead of them at the gas station, the price of gasoline at the pump will not rise; rather, they will have to wait to get their car filled up. In fact, for many items commonly purchased, prices stay fixed for some time once they are set. Consumers know that it is not unusual to go to the supermarket to buy a product and find that the product is not in stock.

Newspaper articles often describe how some companies have difficulty assuring themselves of supply during periods of high demand. Histories of business (Chandler 1977) explain in detail that many firms vertically integrate, not necessarily to get a lower price for a product, but simply to get the product on a reliable basis. Waiting for delivery of a good and being unable to purchase a good when one wants it are typical rather than atypical experiences in many markets. In periods of tight supply, preferred customers get delivery, whereas new customers are often unable to assure themselves of a supply at the same price as steady customers. Indeed, short-term customers may be unable to get the product at all.

Such observations suggest that, in many markets, price is not the sole mechanism used to clear the market. None of the simple theories of the previous section are able to explain the existence of unsatisfied demanders, yet they appear to be an observed feature of many markets.

Early Price Surveys. Frederick Mills (1927) conducted one of the earliest studies regarding the flexibility and behavior of prices. Mills examined numerous price statistics

FIGURE 17.1 Frequency of Price Change

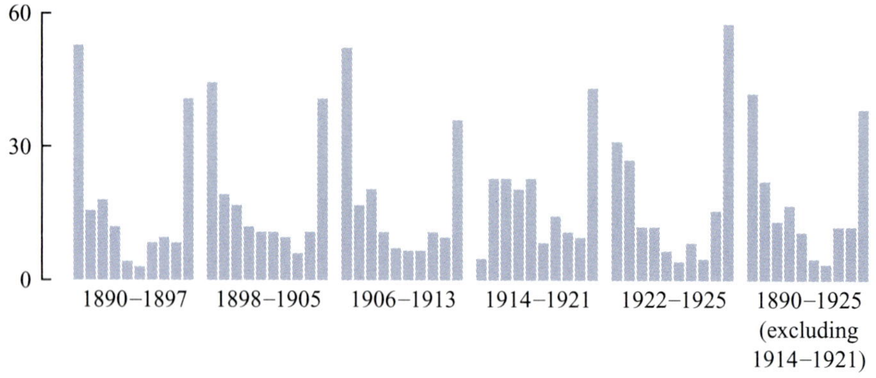

The horizontal axis measures frequency of price change. Frequency increases as one moves to the right within any one time period. The vertical axis measures the number of commodities of any given frequency.

Source: Mills (1927, 371)

gathered by the U.S. Bureau of Labor Statistics (BLS) for frequency of change and amplitude of change. His work represents an outstanding contribution to our knowledge of price behavior.

Figure 17.1 presents some of Mills's findings regarding the frequency of price change over various time periods. The diagrams show that the distribution across markets of the frequency of price changes is U-shaped; that is, there are many products whose prices change frequently, and many whose prices change infrequently.

It is possible that supply and demand are in equilibrium in all industries and that what Mills is showing reflects simply the distribution of shocks to various supply and demand curves. So, for example, there are many markets in which shocks and the resulting price changes are frequent and also many markets in which shocks and the resulting price changes are few. Another possibility is that in some markets prices change frequently and are the exclusive device used for market clearing, whereas in other markets prices do not vary frequently, and something else is working to clear those markets. **Price rigidity** is said to occur when prices do not vary in response to fluctuations in costs and demand.[4]

The next noteworthy study of prices was by Gardiner Means in 1935. Unlike Mills, Means had an enormous effect not only on economists but also on policy makers. His influence persists to this day. Means claimed that the traditional economists' models could not explain price behavior in many markets. He suggested that the Great Depression occurred because in many markets the laws of supply and demand had been "repealed," and prices no longer fluctuated to clear the markets. Means's arguments attracted widespread attention. His explanation for the Great Depression, which was inexplicable to most economists, was based on a breakdown in market clearing, which formed the basis for all economists' beliefs.[5] Means's hypotheses challenged the profession, and although (as explained later) his inferences were misguided, they were motivated by the inability of the simple theories to explain price behavior in many markets.

[4]Rigid prices are of interest, not because of the rigidity itself, but because the rigidity suggests that prices may not be clearing markets. Even if prices were perfectly indexed to inflation and hence were always changing, it would be troubling if there were unsatisfied buyers, a fact that would indicate that price was not clearing markets.

Inefficient resource allocation occurs in the simple models when the *marginal* price (the price of an additional unit) fails to clear markets. A contract that specifies a fixed quantity at a fixed price is *not* a rigid price that can induce inefficiency because the price of an additional unit is the price of buying that unit in the marketplace. When the quantity term is left open, the contract price is the marginal price; and, therefore, the rigid price has efficiency effects.

[5]Keynes and other macroeconomists developed theories to explain the Great Depression based on an assumption that wages (not final goods prices) failed to fluctuate to clear markets. Wage rigidity, however, is probably less important than price rigidity, so that the reliance by macroeconomists on wage rigidity is misplaced (Garman and Richards 1992). Evidence of how real wages (wages adjusted for inflation) behave over the business cycle can help one determine whether wages are stickier than prices. If prices are stickier than wages, real wages should be procyclical (rise during booms and fall during bad times); whereas, if wages are stickier than prices, real wages should be countercyclical (fall during booms and rise during busts). Real wages are procyclical (Zarnowitz 1985).

Means's theory was that many markets have **administered prices:** Prices are under the control of firms and not subject to the laws of supply and demand. Under this view, firms, for unexplained reasons, chose not to vary prices to clear markets. Means claimed that price changes in administered markets are much less frequent than in competitive markets and that when price changes occur, they are much larger. According to Means, because administered markets have long stretches of unchanging or rigid prices, prices fail to clear markets, resulting in a disequilibrium such as the Great Depression.

Means did not contend that administered prices were restricted to markets with high concentration, and there was confusion as to what he meant by an administered price. A voluminous and contentious literature developed that attempted to give structure to Means's arguments and test them.[6] This literature confirms that something unusual is going on in the behavior of some prices.[7]

The earlier work of Mills (1927), which attracted much less attention than that of Gardiner Means, does not indicate a significant increase in price rigidity from the 1890s to the mid-1920s (Figure 17.1). We are unaware of any study that shows greater rigidity of prices right after 1929. Means was correct in asserting that economists had inadequate theories for predicting the flexibility of prices, but the phenomenon he was talking about was not confined to the period of the Great Depression. Indeed, as shown below, the phenomenon of rigid prices characterizes the U.S. economy today.

Later Studies. The major criticism of Means's work is that it relies on price statistics gathered by the U.S. Bureau of Labor Statistics (BLS). A study done by McAllister (1961) for a Congressional Committee on Price Statistics shows that the BLS data typically do not reflect price discounts. Moreover, an examination of the way in which the BLS gathered price statistics shows that the number of firms reporting prices to the BLS varies from market to market. The more firms reporting price, the more likely is the observation of some flexibility in an average price. This is especially true when products are heterogeneous.

Recognizing the inadequacies of BLS price statistics, Stigler and Kindahl (1970) collected data on individual transaction prices based on actual transactions between buyers and sellers. Although the Stigler-Kindahl data undoubtedly contain reporting errors, they are probably the best source of information on pricing behavior available to economists today. Stigler and Kindahl construct indices of prices (averages of individual prices) for individual commodities and find that their price indices move much more smoothly than those of the BLS: Price indices based on actual transaction prices are much more flexible than those based on BLS data. Stigler and Kindahl conclude that the BLS data are misleading. Although Stigler and Kindahl do not explicitly claim

[6]See Beals (1975), Lustgarten (1975), Qualls (1979), Scherer (1980, Ch. 13), Weiss (1977), and Weston and Lustgarten (1974), and the references they cite.

[7]See, for example, Weiss (1977), but see Stigler and Kindahl (1973) for a different point of view.

that their findings are completely in accord with any of the simple theories of market clearing, they do suggest that their work goes a long way toward explaining the unusual findings of investigations based on BLS data.

Stigler and Kindahl recognize that there are some puzzling features even in their own data set. For example, they note that the typical pattern is for buyers and sellers to remain in contact with each other for long periods of time, even for transactions involving apparently homogeneous goods. That is, buyers and sellers view their relationship with each other as a valuable way of doing business and believe that the relationship is worth preserving. As shown later, this insight can be used to explain a great deal of what appears to be unusual pricing behavior.

Not only do the Stigler-Kindahl prices move more smoothly than the BLS data, the prices have different general trends from the BLS indices during some time periods. The BLS data are primarily based on price quotations for immediate delivery. The Stigler-Kindahl data are based on prices from long-term relationships between buyers and sellers. Therefore, it is likely that the BLS indices reflect fewer long-term contracts than the Stigler-Kindahl indices do (Stigler and Kindahl 1970, 6). A comparison of the Stigler-Kindahl and BLS price indices shows that during booms, spot prices (prices for immediate delivery) rise relative to long-term contract prices.[8]

Another interesting feature noted by Stigler and Kindahl is that although most of the transactions last a long time and may be pursuant to a contract, they seem to specify neither a price nor in many cases a quantity. Thus, it is not true that most contracts rigidly set both the price and the quantity terms in a marketplace (Williamson 1975).

Weiss (1977) weighs the evidence of Stigler and Kindahl against the evidence put forward by Means (1935, 1972). Although recognizing the difficulty of giving theoretical content to Means's hypothesis, Weiss concludes that the evidence on pricing does appear unusual in the sense that the simple theories do not do a good job of explaining pricing behavior.

Carlton (1986) reanalyzes the Stigler-Kindahl price data. Unlike Stigler and Kindahl, Carlton does not construct indices of prices to examine how a price index behaves over time, because indices can mask interesting behavior. For example, if new buyers pay different prices than old buyers, an index of prices may seem to be perfectly flexible even though most contracts are characterized by rigid prices. Yet, it is surely important to know whether price is being used to allocate goods to some buyers and not to others, and whether some other mechanism, such as a seller's knowledge of each buyer's requirements, is being used to allocate goods.

Carlton examines how often a price changes once it has been set to an individual buyer. The degree of price rigidity—the average length of time during which prices are unchanged—differs greatly across industries: from roughly 6 months in household appliances to over 18 months in chemicals (Table 17.1). There are several instances of

[8]There have been only a few attempts to explain this difference in behavior of the two types of prices: Stigler and Kindahl (1970), Carlton (1979a), and Hubbard and Weiner (1989).

TABLE 17.1 Price Rigidity by Industry

Industry	Average Duration of Price Rigidity (Months)
Steel	17.9
Nonferrous metals	7.5
Petroleum	8.3
Rubber tires	11.5
Paper	11.8
Chemicals	19.2
Cement	17.2
Glass	13.3
Truck motors	8.3
Plywood	7.5
Household appliances	5.9

Source: Carlton (1986, Table 1).

transactions in the Stigler-Kindahl data in which the price paid by a buyer does not change for periods of well over five years.[9]

The evidence in Table 17.1 could be consistent with the simple theories under some extreme assumptions. For example, one could argue that in industries with very rigid prices, the supply and demand conditions are virtually stable over time, whereas in the other industries with flexible prices, the supply and demand conditions change frequently. The duration of the rigidity in some prices to individual buyers is so long that this explanation is not credible.

One can also examine the correlation (co-movement) of price changes across different buyers of an identical commodity using the Stigler-Kindahl data. In all of the simple theoretical models of market clearing, price changes across different buyers of the same commodity should be highly correlated. Although price changes are highly correlated in some markets, there are several markets in which price changes appear to be poorly correlated across buyers.

One of Carlton's findings is a strong positive relationship between industry concentration and price rigidity. The more highly concentrated an industry, the greater the likelihood that its prices remain unchanged for long periods of time. Recall that the simple models make no predictions relating price rigidity to the amount of concentration in a market.[10]

[9]Cecchetti (1985) analyzes newsstand prices of magazines and finds that they changed infrequently, every seven years, on average, in the 1950s and every three years, on average, in the 1970s. See also Kashyap (1995).

[10]Although the theory of oligopoly can justify price rigidity in the face of small cost changes, as the industry becomes more concentrated and the oligopoly becomes more powerful, the oligopoly should behave more like a monopoly, and monopoly prices should not be rigid, according to the simple theory.

EXAMPLE 17.1 *Price Rigidity—It's the Real Thing*

In 1886, John Pemberton, a pharmacist, mixed together a dark, sugary syrup and produced Coca-Cola, one of the most successful products of all time. He and his partner, Frank Robinson, planned to sell this "medicine" (it originally contained as medicinal ingredients coca leaf and kola nut) by the glass. Instead of charging a high price typically associated with patent medicines, they charged 5 cents per glass. By the 1950s—when Coke was sold primarily in 6.5 ounce bottles instead of as a fountain drink—the price was still 5 cents! Thus, Coke prices were rigid for over 70 years.

Why did they remain rigid, and how did Coca-Cola control the retail price? Levy and Young (2002) believe that the prime reason for this rigidity was an implicit understanding that Coca-Cola had with its loyal consumers. Coke heavily advertised the nickel price, and consumers believed that neither Coke's price nor its quality would change. In addition, given the widespread use of vending machines, it would have been costly to reconfigure machines to accept something other than nickels (and a price increase to 10 cents was considered too high). Even though Coke often had no legal means to enforce a 5-cent retail price, it accomplished its goal by its massive advertising campaigns promoting nickel Coke.

In summary, detailed examinations of the Stigler-Kindahl data reveal price behaviors that are inconsistent with the simple models of market clearing. These findings do not necessarily prove that markets are operating inefficiently. Rather, they prove that the simple models of price clearing are inapplicable to certain markets. See Example 17.1.

Bils and Klenow (2002) examine BLS prices for consumer products using unpublished BLS data on products in 350 detailed categories of consumer goods and services. They find that about half of the prices remain in effect for more than five months. The prices of one-quarter of the consumer goods change on average each month, with the frequency highest for durable goods (32%), moderate for nondurable goods (29%), and lowest for services (20%). They also find that during inflationary periods, there is a large drop in the relative price of sticky-price goods relative to that of flexible-priced goods, and that this change in relative prices causes a significant shift in consumption away from sticky-price goods. There appears to be a strong negative relationship between price rigidity and whether the product is closely related to a primary input (Means found that the agricultural sector had much greater price flexibility than manufacturing in the 1930s), and a strong positive correlation between price rigidity and industry concentration. This latter result disappears when one controls for whether the product is a primary input.

International Studies. Gordon (1983), Encaoua and Geroski (1986), and others analyze the different degrees of price flexibility in various countries. Encaoua and Geroski (1986) use a detailed database to estimate the relationship between price, cost, and concentration across several countries (Canada, Japan, Sweden, United Kingdom, United States) and commodities. They find, in general, that the higher the degree of concentration in a market, the slower is the adjustment of price to cost changes.[11] They show that the more an industry is characterized by new entry and competition (measured by imports), the more likely it is that prices rapidly adjust to cost changes. They also find that price flexibility varies across countries; Japan, for example, has more flexible prices than the United States. Understanding the reasons for the different flexibility of prices across countries remains an important task.

Movements in Prices and Price-Cost Margins over the Business Cycle

There have been many empirical investigations of the relationships among price, price-cost margins, business cycles, and concentration.[12] Here we describe several recent studies, which reach different conclusions, so this area remains one of active research.

Domowitz, Hubbard, and Petersen (1986a, 1986b, 1987) examine the behavior of manufacturing prices in the United States over the period 1958–1981, using data on over 400 industries. They draw three interesting conclusions. First, price-cost margins (which theoretically equal the ratio of price minus marginal cost to price) in concentrated industries are *procyclical:* They rise in booms and fall in recessions (see also Qualls 1979). Second, price-cost margins in relatively unconcentrated industries tend to be *countercyclical:* They fall in booms and rise in recessions. Third, extensive unionization, which is more common in concentrated industries, keeps wages in those industries relatively stable over the business cycle.

They explain their finding of procyclical margins in concentrated industries by showing that costs, in particular real wages, are more rigid in those industries. That is, during a boom, a firm in a concentrated industry experiences a price increase that is accompanied by only a modest cost increase, so that the gap between price and (marginal) cost rises. Unions provide one explanation for the greater rigidity of wages in concentrated industries because unionization and concentration are positively correlated.

This finding of procyclical margins in concentrated industries has important implications about how concentrated markets work. A firm raises its price-cost margin only if its demand curve becomes less elastic. There is no apparent reason why industry demand elasticities should decrease in booms. Therefore, some other explanation is needed to explain procyclical margins in concentrated industries. Possible explanations could rely on either oligopolistic interdependence (for example, incentives to cheat on the oligopoly price in booms versus recessions) or on the long-term relationship of the buyer and seller.

Some researchers draw conclusions opposite to those of Domowitz et al. For example, Bils (1987) finds that marginal cost is procyclical and that, in general, margins are countercyclical. He finds no effect of concentration on this relationship; however, his investigation of the concentration effect relies on fewer observations than does the work of Domowitz et al. Bils takes special care to measure marginal as opposed to av-

[11] Domberger (1979) finds the opposite for the United Kingdom.

[12] See Chapter 8 and Schmalensee (1989) for a survey of some of these studies.

EXAMPLE 17.2 *How Much Is That Turkey in the Window?*

Chevalier, Kashyap, and Rossi (2000) examine fluctuations in price-cost margins for grocery store items that are subject to seasonal surges in demand. For example, what happens to margins on turkeys at Thanksgiving or on beer on the Fourth of July? They find that margins generally fall on seasonal items during their peak demand period because stores compete to attract customers by advertising low prices on popular seasonal items. MacDonald (2000) finds the same result and concludes that price declines are greater in markets with several rivals than where a single firm dominates.

erage variable cost. In contrast, Domowitz et al. use average variable cost in their measure of margins. If marginal cost is rising, then the true price-cost margin (the one based on marginal cost) could be unchanging or even falling over the business cycle, even though Domowitz et al. measure an increasing margin. Although the different definitions of costs may not completely explain the discrepancy between Bils and Domowitz et al., it reconciles at least part of the discrepancy.

Additional evidence against procyclical mark-ups in concentrated industries comes from Chevalier (1995) and Chevalier and Scharfstein (1995). Chevalier (1995) documents that when supermarket firms acquire a lot of debt and therefore see their likelihood of bankruptcy rise, they tend to raise prices especially in a concentrated industry where there presumably is more ability to set price. The empirical results of Chevalier and Scharfstein (1995) support the view that margins are countercyclical and that margins in concentrated industries and in markets where many firms face a significantly elevated likelihood of bankruptcy in recessions tend to be more countercyclical than the typical margin. See Example 17.2.

A final piece of contradictory evidence to procyclical margins comes from Mills (1936). Mills studies the behavior of margins during the period before and during the Great Depression and finds them to be strongly countercyclical. Although Mills does not investigate the relationship of margins to concentration, his strong finding across all industries does contrast with the finding of Domowitz et al. of only a tendency for countercyclical behavior of margins, and that tendency occurs only in unconcentrated industries.

Explaining the Evidence

The evidence on price behavior reveals that some markets are well described by the simple models of market clearing, but others are not. Markets differ greatly in price flexibility, with the degree of concentration being an important determinant of flexibility. In some markets, price changes to one buyer are uncorrelated with those to another buyer, suggesting that other factors, such as a seller's knowledge of a buyer, are involved. In many markets, long-term relationships between buyers and sellers are important.

There are several approaches (starting with Tucker 1938) to reconciling economic theory and the observed evidence. One approach is to extend and improve the simple theories. That approach can be quite fruitful, and we describe some of the most useful extensions. However, extensions to the simple theories help resolve only some of the inconsistencies between the theory and the evidence. The remainder of this section explores alternative theories that are useful in explaining the evidence.[13]

Extensions to the Simple Theory: The Introduction of Time

The expositions of the simple theories stress price as the market-clearing mechanism and ignore the possibility of delaying consumption or production to a later time, which is known as **intertemporal substitution**. It is a straightforward extension of the simple competitive model to date goods and treat a good at one date as different from the same good at a different date (Debreu 1959, ch. 7). In a dynamic model, a customer faces many substitutes to consuming a product today—not only other products, but also the same product consumed in the future. Similarly, a supplying firm can substitute production today for production tomorrow by holding inventories.

The introduction of time into any of the simple models of competition, oligopoly, or monopoly makes them more realistic by emphasizing the importance of intertemporal substitution on both the demand side and the supply side. The following sections describe how each of the three simple theories is altered by the introduction of time.

Competition. The demand curve for a product at a particular time depends not only on current price but also on consumers' perceptions about what the price of the product will be in the future. If consumers are willing to wait at least a short time to consume the product, then the price today cannot deviate very far above the price expected to prevail in the future without inducing consumers to cease purchasing today and wait to do so in the future. That is, the price elasticity of demand for purchases today (all else equal) is very high.

Similarly, the supply curve at a particular time depends not only on the current price but also on future expected prices. Intertemporal substitution affects the willingness of firms to supply the product today at a given price. Firms recognize that an alternative to producing and selling today is to produce today, hold goods in inventory, and sell them tomorrow. The ability of a firm to decide on the optimal time path of production and the optimal employment of factors of production, one of which is inventory, affects the shape of the short-run marginal cost curve.

[13]We do not explore the importance of risk aversion in explaining price rigidity. Empirical work indicates that it is not important (Carlton 1986). See Polinsky (1987) for a detailed study of risk aversion and pricing. Blinder et al. (1998) provides a good summary of several theories of price rigidity and explores their applicability based on surveys of businessmen.

In the competitive equilibrium, a separate price is determined for each commodity at each date at which it may be consumed. Anything that changes production cost, today or in the future, or demand, today or in the future, affects all prices over time. Thus, a shock to demand today affects the price of a good not only today but also in the future. As a result, shocks to supply or demand today may be absorbed primarily by something other than prices today. For example, an increase in demand today may have a small effect on prices today and in the future, but may shift a significant amount of consumption from today to the future.

The important insight from this view of competition is that even though prices are equating supply and demand, only small price changes may be necessary to equilibrate the market. Quantity shifts among different goods (in particular, the same good consumed at different periods of time) may bear the brunt of the adjustment, and not price.[14]

If there are large shifts in the timing of consumption as demand or supply conditions change, the data should reveal large swings in delivery lags (the lag between the placement and shipment of an order). Zarnowitz (1962, 1973), Maccini (1973), and Carlton (1983b) stress the importance of delivery lags as market-clearing phenomena. Many markets are characterized by large fluctuations in delivery dates and small fluctuations in price. For example, Table 17.2 presents measures of the variability (the standard deviation of the logarithm of a variable is a measure of the variability of the percent change in that variable) of price and delivery lags for several major manufacturing industries. As the table shows, the measure of variability of delivery lags is 1.6 to 8.3 times larger than the measure of variability in price for many industries. Thus, the insight of the dynamic competition theory—that the price fluctuations that clear markets may be lower than those predicted by a simple model that ignores the importance of intertemporal substitution—is consistent with the evidence.

Carlton (1985) estimates the importance of price and delivery lags in determining demand. As Table 17.2 shows, for many markets, the fluctuations in delivery lags also can be important in equilibrating demand and supply. For example, according to Table 17.2, an increase of one standard deviation in the logarithm of the price of steel causes demand to fall by about $.43 (= .03 \times 14.36)$ percent while an increase of one standard deviation in the logarithm of delivery lags causes demand to fall by about $.20 (= .25 \times .78)$ percent.

Nadiri and Rosen (1973), Haltiwanger and Maccini (1988), and Topel (1982) estimate the time paths by which firms adjust factors of production in an attempt to meet fluctuations in demand. These studies explicitly recognize that firms can vary price, inventories, labor, and other factors of production to achieve their desired sales. Such studies of intertemporal substitution in production provide a better understanding of the behavior of price over time. For example, if it is costless to store inventories, price cannot

[14] If goods are described by a vector of characteristics, then in response to a perturbation in either supply or demand, not only does the quantity consumed and the price of the good change but also its characteristics can change (Rosen 1974). For example, in response to an increase in the demand for bus transportation during rush hour, each bus may be much more crowded than during nonrush hours. That is, a less desirable product has been substituted, and prices have remained unchanged.

TABLE 17.2 **Price and Delivery Lag Fluctuations**

Industry	Standard Deviation of Log of Price	Standard Deviation of Log of Delivery Lag	Median Delivery Lag (months)	Demand Elasticity of Price	Demand Elasticity of Delivery Lag
Paper and allied products	.05	.08	.46	−1.37*	−.40*
Steel	.03	.25	1.95	−14.36*	−.78*
Fabricated metals	.03	.18	3.06	−1.75	−.30*
Nonelectrical machinery	.04	.25	3.63	−3.50*	−.35*
Electrical machinery	.05	.10	3.86	−1.60*	−.64*

*Indicates that the estimated coefficient is statistically different from zero using a commonly applied statistical criterion.

Source: Carlton (1983b, Table 1), and Carlton (1985).

be expected to increase. If price were expected to increase, there would be an incentive to sell less today and hold more inventory for the future, driving current price up. If price were expected to fall, then firms would sell their current inventory today, tending to drive price down. Therefore, the possibility of inventory holding tends to stabilize price.

A firm's choice of production technology influences its ability to engage in intertemporal substitution, affects the firm's supply curve, and thereby affects the speed with which supply can respond to changes in demand (Stigler 1939). Mills and Schumann (1985) investigate which firms adopt a production technology that is flexible in the sense that the firm can, at low cost, vary its production over a wide range of outputs. Mills and Schumann find that small firms typically have more flexible production technologies than large firms. It would follow, then, that small firms expand relative to large firms during booms.

In summary, a dynamic competition theory explains how markets respond to shocks without large changes in current prices. Instead of large price changes, large shifts over time in the quantities consumed or produced may occur as firms or consumers take advantage of intertemporal substitution.

Oligopoly. The introduction of time affects oligopoly models for many of the same reasons just discussed for the competitive model. That is, the ability of consumers to substitute across time periods and the ability of firms to produce across different time periods affect how the market responds to changes in supply or demand. In Chapters 5 and 6, we discussed the pricing implications of several different models of oligopoly over time. In Rotemberg and Saloner (1986) and Rotemberg and Woodford (1991), price wars break out in booms, whereas in Stigler (1964a) and Porter (1983b) and Green and Porter (1984), price wars break out in downturns in business activity or when economic uncertainty increases, as in inflationary times (Vining and Elwertowski 1976).[15] The empirical evidence discussed in Chapter 5 does not support the Rotemberg and Saloner model's prediction of when cartels break apart.[16]

Monopoly. The introduction of dynamic elements into the study of monopoly raises the same issues about intertemporal substitution in demand and supply discussed for competition. For example, a monopoly that can hold inventory takes into account the relation among the marginal revenue curves at different points in time in setting its price. As a result, the monopoly chooses a more stable price policy than the simple models of monopoly would suggest (Amihud and Mendelson 1983, Blinder 1982, Phlips 1983, and Reagan 1982).

The introduction of time raises an additional element in the case of monopoly (or perhaps among firms in an oligopoly) that does not arise in the case of competition. A monopoly is concerned not only with the influence of today's price on current demand, but also with its influence on future demand (Chapter 15 analyzes this effect for a durable goods monopoly). For example, an increase in the price of steel scrap may lead some steel producers to alter their plans for building new steel furnaces, and this in turn affects the future demand for steel scrap. To the extent that consumers adjust their future behavior in response to price changes today, a monopoly takes that adjustment into account in setting price. In contrast, a competitive firm has no control over its price today or in the future and, therefore, cannot respond to incentives to influence future demand.

For example, if costs rise unexpectedly in the short run but the monopoly knows that the increase is only temporary, the monopoly may not raise its price and pass these costs on to consumers for fear that they will misinterpret the current price increases as permanent and react to them in such a way that their long-run demand declines. Therefore, a monopoly may have an incentive to absorb temporary cost increases so that the current price is a good indicator to consumers of the future price.

Fixed Costs of Changing Price

If a fixed cost must be incurred every time a price is changed, a firm will not vary prices continuously as predicted by a simple market-clearing model under either competition or monopoly. Instead, an established price will remain fixed until a new price can exceed the old one by an amount sufficient to justify incurring the fixed costs (Barro 1972).[17]

---

[15]Carlton (1983a) discusses the effects of inflation on price behavior. Inflation raises information costs and can lead to greater use of standardized commodities with more flexible prices.

[16]In addition to studying the effect of successful collusion on pricing, intertemporal models in the presence of market power have been used to study inventory behavior (Rotemberg and Saloner 1989) and the pricing trade-offs that arise when a firm with an established client base seeks to attract new customers (Chevalier and Scharfstein 1995).

[17]Rotemberg and Saloner (1987) show that a duopoly with a fixed cost of price adjustment has more flexible prices than a monopoly under certain conditions.

This theory clearly accounts for price rigidities, but to be believable, it must explain the source of the fixed costs of changing a price. For example, it may cost money to publish a new catalog, print a new menu, or change the price of items already on the shelf.

Aside from the costs of having to relabel items, send out new catalogs, or print new menus, there is another reason that firms might be reluctant to change prices and might act as if they faced fixed costs for doing so. Some customers decide which firm to buy from only after comparing the price of that firm to the prices of other firms. As long as they believe nothing has changed, customers remain with the initially chosen firm. If they interpret a change in price by the firm as a signal that market conditions have changed, they may decide to search again to see if the chosen firm still has attractive prices. (See Ball and Cecchetti 1988.)

If the fixed costs of changing prices are high, then small price changes do not occur. Carlton (1986) tabulates the smallest observed price changes across a wide variety of products sold at the intermediate level of manufacturing and finds that, for the large majority of commodities examined, the smallest price changes are quite small. These small price changes in many goods suggest that, at least for these goods, the fixed costs of changing prices is small.[18] In contrast, Levy et al. (1997) find that the cost of price changes in supermarkets equals 35 percent of net margins. (See Example 17.3. See also Lach and Tsiddon 1996.)

Implications of an Unchanging Price for Inventories

Because prices for many products, once set, do not change for some time (Cecchetti 1985, Carlton 1986), there is a risk that consumers will be unable to buy products temporarily. The standard theories never consider the possibility that a product may be unavailable. Yet unavailability of a product is a fact of life in many markets.

Mills (1962) examines the behavior of a monopoly that must set price and production before observing demand. The optimal policy for a risk-neutral monopoly is to have enough output available so that the expected price received equals marginal cost. The expected price equals the price charged times the probability that a customer arrives and purchases the output.[19] The optimal inventory-holding policy of the firm depends on the markup of price above marginal cost. The closer price is to marginal cost, the smaller the optimal inventory; conversely, the higher the markup, the larger the optimal inventory. The incentive to hold inventory declines as the markup falls because the profit from making a sale falls, while the cost of holding unsold goods remains unchanged. What is interesting about this relationship is that the probability of *stock-outs* (shortages) increases as the market price falls relative to marginal cost.

[18]We use the word *suggest* because it is possible that we observe small price changes only when the new supply and demand conditions are expected to persist for a long time. The evidence could then be consistent with significant fixed costs of changing prices that cause prices to remain rigid for temporary shifts in supply and demand, but not for permanent ones. Although this explanation is possible, we have seen no evidence to support it.

[19]Imagine a newspaper vendor whose retail price is p, wholesale price is c, and that faces a random number of customers each day. If $F(S)$ is the probability that fewer than S customers will arrive in any day, then to maximize its profit, the risk-neutral vendor chooses S so that $p[1 - F(S)] = c$.

EXAMPLE 17.3 *The Cost of Changing Prices*

Economists who study price formation frequently comment that rigid prices reflect a relatively high cost of changing price. But what exactly are those costs? To answer this question, Zbaracki et al. (2003) followed one large industrial firm's price making process for its 8,000 products.

They divided costs into three kinds: physical, managerial, and customer. *Physical costs* include the cost of having to print and send out new prices, commonly called *menu costs. Managerial costs* include gathering the information needed to change prices and analyzing it. *Customer costs* reflect the effort of disseminating the new prices to customers and subsequent negotiations about price. This particular company began its price analysis in the summer and produced new list prices in November.

The study revealed that nearly a quarter of the cost (23%) of any price change is the time spent by managers in analyzing pricing and in communicating the price policy to the sales force. For example, company personnel involved in sales, marketing, finance, and pricing all spent considerable time on the pricing analysis before customers were informed about the new prices. By far, the most costly part of any price change (73%) is the time spent by managers and sales representatives meeting with customers and then renegotiating prices. The least costly part of the price change (4%) is the physical cost of the change.

Overall, the total cost of changing price accounted for 1.2% of the company's revenue, 6% of its operating cost, and 20% of its net margin. Although the firm changed more than 8,000 list prices, there were many more price changes because of individual price negotiations. The cost of per-price change ranged between $22 and $122. This estimate is considerably larger than estimates by some of the same authors for retail supermarkets and drugstores, primarily because of the large component involving customer interaction for this industrial company.

In Carlton (1977, 1978, 1984b, 1991), Deneckere and Peck (1995), DeVany and Saving (1977), and Gould (1978), consumers judge a firm not only by its pricing policy but also by its inventory policy. Consumers care not only about the price but also about the probability that a good is available. Inventory policy affects the probability that a firm has the good available. Some consumers prefer to shop at high-price stores that run out of goods infrequently, whereas others prefer to shop at stores that charge low prices but may run out of goods frequently.

Because a firm must maintain a relatively large inventory to satisfy customers whose demands fluctuate a great deal, the variability of consumers' demand for a product affects a firm's costs. Thus, the cost function of the firm depends on the demand characteristics of consumers. The simple separation between supply curves and demand curves is lost in these models.

If variability of demand influences a firm's costs, the firm wants to charge different consumers different prices based on their respective variability of demand. These price differences do not represent price discrimination; they reflect cost differences. Prices to consumers differ according to each consumer's variability of demand, even if each purchases the same quantity of a physically identical product in the long run. Moreover, if the variability of one customer's demand changes, then the price to that consumer would change while the prices to other consumers remain unchanged. The result would be a low correlation of price changes across consumers—a finding that characterizes many markets.

Prescott (1975), Eden (1990), and Dana (1999, 2001) use alternative models in which firms set prices before demand is revealed and customers can visit all stores before consuming, instead of visiting just the one store that the customers think is most likely to satisfy their demands. Imagine a road frequented by tourists driving into town looking for a hotel. The number of tourists varies from day to day. Prices are set each morning before any tourists arrive and cannot be changed during the day. The lowest-price hotels fill up first, so that the equilibrium involves a price distribution with the higher-price hotels renting all rooms less often than do the lower-priced ones, but every hotel earns zero expected profit. When demand is high, the prices paid rise on average because more high-priced rooms are rented. Thus, average price varies, even though the prices of all hotels are unchanged over time.

Now suppose that some travelers can book with a hotel in advance. Hotels prefer advanced bookings because reservations assure the hotel that its rooms are booked. Consequently, hotels use a pricing system similar to that of airlines, in which those customers who book early face different prices than those who are unable to book in advance. Dana (1998) shows that such pricing can lead to inefficiency.

Asymmetric Information and Moral Hazard

In many economic transactions, buyers and sellers have different information. Does the introduction of this kind of asymmetric information affect the equilibrium in a market? As discussed in Chapter 13, Akerlof (1970) showed that the answer is yes.

Akerlof's model can be extended to show how equilibrium may be characterized by either excess demand or supply (Stiglitz 1976, 1984). For example, suppose a firm wishes to hire one worker of a particular skill level. The firm obviously wants to pay as little as possible for such a worker. However, if the firm advertises a low wage, the people who apply for the job are likely to be low-quality workers. The higher the wage rate offered, the higher the average quality of the applicant. The average quality rises with the wage because higher-quality workers (in addition to the lower-quality workers who applied at the lower wage) apply for a job as the wage rises. Therefore, when a firm has difficulty measuring worker quality in advance, it sets a wage high enough to attract more than one applicant.[20] Equilibrium, therefore, involves setting a high wage and having an excess supply of labor apply to the firm.

---

[20]See also Keeton (1980) and Stiglitz and Weiss (1981) for examples in which interest rates remain rigid in models with asymmetric information.

Toward a General Theory of Allocation

This section sketches a theory that explains some of the puzzling evidence on price behavior that has already been reviewed. The theory relies on the simple insight that if it is costly to use a price system, then alternative allocation mechanisms may develop.[21]

The Cost of Creating a Market That Clears by Price Alone

Simple theories of market clearing ignore the cost of creating a market in which price allocates goods to buyers. Presentations of the standard theory often pretend that a fictional auctioneer adjusts prices to clear markets. Few markets, however, have auctioneers.

The markets that probably come closest to the textbook model of competitive markets are financial markets, such as futures markets. In a futures market, transactions for the right to buy or sell in the future occur. For example, Daniel agrees to buy and Lisa agrees to sell 1 bushel of wheat on April 1 of next year at an agreed-upon price and location. It is costly to run a futures market. Aside from the actual physical space required, there is the time cost for all those who participate in the market. For example, at the Chicago Board of Trade, there are floor traders and employees of the brokerage firms, as well as the members of the associated clearinghouses. The users of futures markets must somehow pay all the people who work either directly or indirectly in making the transactions for customers.[22] These payments can take several forms, such as direct commissions to those who transact, or bid-ask spreads to traders. If the trader buys at one price (called the bid price) but sells at a higher price (called the ask price), the trader can make a profit (the bid-ask spread) even in a steady market.

An important cost of making markets is the time cost of the actual customers (Becker 1965). A market in which customers had to spend large amounts of their own time in order to transact could be inefficient. The purpose of a market is not merely to create transactions, but to create transactions at the lowest cost.

Because the creation of markets is itself a productive activity that consumes resources, it makes sense to regard the making of markets as an industry. Just as there is competition to produce a better mousetrap, so too there is competition to produce better and more efficient markets (Carlton 1984a). The New York Stock Exchange competes with the NASDAQ market and the Chicago Mercantile Exchange competes with the Chicago Board of Trade. Creating successful markets is difficult (see Example 17.4).

Heterogeneity of the Product

The heterogeneity of the product is perhaps the most critical characteristic in determining whether an organized market (for example, one with an auctioneer) can be created that clears by price alone. If buyers prefer to buy at different firms, or at different

---

[21]The theories in this section are developed in detail by Carlton (1991). See also Okun (1981) and Williamson (1975).

[22]Markets also benefit nonusers by providing price information, thereby creating a free-rider problem.

EXAMPLE 17.4

Creating Futures Markets

It is difficult to create a successful futures market. Futures markets are markets that clear by price alone, and such markets exist for only a handful of commodities. Because there are definitely social benefits to the creation of such markets, and because at least some of these benefits can probably be privately appropriated, the paucity of such markets emphasizes that it must be costly to create them.

The table shows the average failure rates of new, successfully introduced futures markets (those listed in the *Wall Street Journal*) in the United States. The table indicates that about 40 percent of all futures markets fail by their fifth year. The making of successful markets is a risky activity, and, as the operators of exchanges well know, it is hard to predict which markets will succeed and which will fail.

Death Rates of Futures Markets

Age (Years)	Probability of Dying at the Given Age or Less
1	.16
2	.25
3	.31
4	.37
5	.40
10	.50

Source: Carlton (1984a).

times, or have different preferences for quality, it becomes more difficult to create an organized market that clears by price alone. Attempts to do so in the face of widespread product heterogeneity lead to markets with only a few traders in any given product, and the traders will not be able to pay for the cost of running the market (Telser and Higgenbotham 1977).

Suppose that each buyer can purchase either a standardized product or one specifically designed for the buyer. The advantage of a specially designed product is that it can satisfy the idiosyncratic needs of the buyer. The disadvantage is that the buyer is forced to transact in a less liquid (higher transaction cost) market. If there are few firms that can supply the buyer, the transaction costs rise. The greater the benefits from custom designing a product to one's own specifications, the less likely it is that a market can be created that clears by price alone. Indeed, in the extreme case, in which every buyer demands a slightly different product, it is impossible for traders to trade with each other without engaging in the time-consuming task of enumerating each product's characteristics, and the incentive to create an organized market is small.

Market Clearing in the Absence of Organized Markets. When an organized market does not exist, firms cannot costlessly discover the market clearing price, and they must rely on other methods to determine how to allocate their products to buyers. One alternative is for firms to post prices and for consumers to search over firms (see Chapter 13).

Another alternative is for firms to hire salespeople whose task is to become knowledgeable about the demands of individual customers. Even if it is difficult for the firm to set the market-clearing price, it may be possible to identify those customers who should obtain the goods so that goods can be efficiently allocated.[23] The firm could first use price to screen out those buyers who value the goods the least and then could use its knowledge of each buyer's needs to decide which of the remaining buyers should receive the goods. So, for example, it would not be uncommon during times of tight supply for steady customers to receive delivery while new customers wait. It would also not be unusual for buyers and sellers to enter into long-term relationships so that they could better understand each other's needs. See Example 17.5. Japanese firms frequently use this approach.

If price is not the sole mechanism to allocate goods, prices may remain rigid even though goods are being efficiently allocated. Although rigidity of prices implies inefficiency in any of the simple models in which price is the exclusive mechanism for efficient resource allocation, rigidity does not necessarily imply inefficiency in a world in which price is but one of many methods firms use to allocate goods. A theory that combines price with nonprice methods of allocation has five major implications:[24]

Knowledge of Needs: The longer the buyer and seller deal with each other (the better they know each other), the less need there is to rely on price to allocate goods efficiently. A seller's knowledge of a buyer's need can be a substitute for an impersonal (auction) market that clears by price alone. For example, a seller may know that a particular buyer's demand is greatest during the summer season and will ensure a large enough supply during that period to satisfy the buyer.

Different Treatment of Long-term Customers and Short-term Customers: The length of time over which a buyer and seller do business becomes a characteristic of the transaction and can make one buyer different from another in the eyes of the seller. A customer who regularly buys one unit every week is purchasing a different *product* than does the customer who purchases a unit only once. Therefore, observing differences in price movements to different buyers who buy identical physical commodities at one instant may reveal nothing about allocative efficiency; prices for different "products" should be expected to move differently from one another. The evidence that indices of spot prices and long-term contract prices do not always move together (Stigler and Kindahl 1970) is consistent with this implication, as is the evidence that the correlation of price movements across buyers of the same product is often low.

---

[23]For example, imagine that a firm with a capacity of 100 units has only two buyers, who are known to be identical but whose level of demand is not precisely known. If the firm is operating at capacity (that is, each buyer's demands are high at the stated price), then the efficient allocation is obvious (50–50), even if the exact market-clearing price is not known (Carlton 1991).

[24]Additional implications regarding behavior during periods of price controls, speed of price adjustment, behavior of price indices, and the role of marketing departments are discussed and tested in Carlton (1986, 1991).

EXAMPLE 17.5 *Oh Say, Does That Star-Spangled Banner Yet Fly?*

In the aftermath of the terrorist attacks of September 11, 2001, patriotic spirit flourished in the United States as Americans united to cope with the tragedy. One outcome of this patriotic fervor was a huge and unexpected increase in the demand for the American flag. How did flag manufacturers and retailers respond?

The answer is that the major flag retailers and flag makers did not raise prices, and the flag makers had to ration their scarce supply of flags. All of the flag makers faced excess demand from flag retailers for their flags. The flag makers delivered flags to flag retailers who were their previous customers. They did not supply new retailers who wanted to capitalize on the sudden jump in the demand for flags. Because the supply of flags was limited, manufacturers limited the number of flags that their traditional retail flag store customers could buy, typically in proportion to their historical purchases. Naturally, potential buyers were dissatisfied. "What we tried to do was make the dissatisfaction uniform throughout our customer base," reported Valley Forge, a flag supplier. Neither established flag retailers nor flag suppliers raised prices for fear that doing so would generate ill will among customers. According to Flag Zone, a retailer, "Nobody raised prices." If any flag supplier had jacked up the prices that it charged Yankee Doodle Flag Co., that retailer announced that it would cease doing business with that manufacturer in the future.

In addition, flag makers used various means to increase their output in the face of unprecedented demand. For example, Valley Forge reduced the number of flag styles it supplied from more than 100 to 12. Another company used printed rather than embroidered stars in order to raise production.

Source: Jeff Bailey, "Lessons for Small Firms from a Spike in Sales," *New York Times*, December 31, 2002:A11.

Different Prices for Customers: The pattern of a buyer's demand over the business cycle or, alternatively, the co-movement of one buyer's demands with those of other buyers is crucial information for the seller because it permits the seller to plan capacity to match customer needs. Even though two buyers purchase the same cumulative amount of the identical commodity, they may be charged different prices and have their prices change differently simply because they have different buying patterns over time. Moreover, the evidence on different price movements for different buyers of the same product is consistent with this observation.

Turnover and Price Rigidity: Rapid turnover of customers prevents the use of long-term relationships in which a seller's knowledge of customers is used to allocate goods. Industries with significant new entry or with customers that have little firm or brand loyalty should rely on price as the primary mechanism to allocate goods.

Firms Object to New Futures Markets: The establishment of a new futures market disrupts the traditional pricing policies of existing firms in an industry. These firms often complain about the introduction of the new futures market. For example, the aluminum futures market was established in the late 1970s. Aluminum producers opposed its establishment (*American Metal Market*, January 6, 1978, 9). If the allocation of goods is a productive activity that requires resources, then a futures market acts as a competitor to the marketing departments of firms in the industry. Futures markets create marketing information. Without futures markets, other agents, such as salespeople, must create this marketing information and be compensated for doing so. If a futures market is established, there is increased competition in marketing, and the value of marketing skills declines. Therefore, it is natural for firms that were successfully performing the marketing function before the introduction of the futures market to complain about the increased competition.

Market Structure Is More Than Concentration

Industrial organization economists often examine how market behavior differs as concentration in a market changes.[25] However, there are many other features of market structure that matter a great deal in explaining how markets behave and, in particular, how they respond to shocks in either supply or demand. For example, the previous sections show that market operation is significantly influenced by the ability of consumers and suppliers to substitute over time, and by the market's reliance on price to allocate goods.

This section presents two illustrations of market characteristics that influence an industry's responses to shifts in either supply or demand.[26] The two illustrations involve whether an industry holds inventories and whether an industry has a fixed price in the face of random demand. For simplicity, we treat these characteristics as given and proceed to analyze the subsequent industry behavior; however, these characteristics may depend on underlying economic conditions.

Produce-to-Order Versus Produce-to-Stock

Industries are organized in two basic ways: **produce-to-order**, where firms wait for orders and then produce, or **produce-to-stock**, where firms produce first, hold inventories, and then sell the inventoried products (Zarnowitz 1973, Belesley 1975). Our economy has probably increased its reliance on industries that produce to order versus

[25]This experiment only makes sense if concentration in a market is an exogenous variable. Concentration, however, is an endogenous variable and is influenced by the relative efficiency of firms (Demsetz 1973, Peltzman 1977, Sutton 1991, 1998, and Chapter 8). See Schmalensee (1985) for a different viewpoint.

[26]Other characteristics that influence the industry's response to shifts in either supply or demand include the ability of the industry to plan (Carlton 1982), the degree of vertical integration, (Carlton 1983a, Wachter and Williamson 1978), the importance of new products (Shleifer 1986), and the possibility of search (Lucas 1981, Diamond 1982).

those that produce to stock, especially with the relative growth of the service sector in recent times. In recent years, Japanese firms have emphasized the use of *just-in-time* deliveries of factors to minimize the maintenance of inventories.

An industry that produces to stock can satisfy customers more quickly and can take greater advantage of economies of scale than an industry that produces to order. On the other hand, an industry that produces to order eliminates the cost of inventory holdings of the final good (though not necessarily of inputs), can custom design products to closely match buyers' specifications, and can, perhaps, use flexible technologies to compensate for its lack of inventory holdings of the final output. The need to cut or raise prices significantly in order to clear markets often is greater in produce-to-stock industries than in produce-to-order ones. Moreover, the transmission of shocks to other sectors of the economy or into the future depends on whether an industry produces to stock (that is, holds inventories). For example, if either firms or final consumers hold inventories, a temporary increase in demand is at least partially accommodated by a decrease in inventory that, next period, will lead to an increase in production to replenish these stocks. If inventory is not being held, the increase in demand may only drive up current prices, with little, if any, increase in production in the current or subsequent periods.

Transmission of Shocks in Industries with Fixed Prices

In many industries, once prices are set, they do not change for some period of time. The production of the goods must occur before demand is observed, and therefore there is some risk that firms will run out of the good. The ratio of inventory to average demand depends on the ratio of price to cost (Carlton 1977). The reason is that the opportunity cost of a lost sale rises with price, so that the incentive to hold inventories increases with price. If price exceeds cost by a large amount, the amount of goods produced exceeds the amount demanded, on average. If, in contrast, price is close to cost, inventory on hand is small relative to the average level of demand, and the firm frequently runs out of stock.

Carlton (1977) also shows that in response to an increase in the riskiness of demand, firms increase their inventory holdings when price significantly exceeds marginal cost and decrease them when price is close to marginal cost. Firms that operate with little extra inventory are not able to cushion demand shocks. Therefore, when prices are temporarily unchanging and demand becomes riskier, an economy is more vulnerable to disruption (stock-outs) from shocks the closer prices are to marginal costs.

Economists have investigated the aggregate macroeconomic implications of models involving fixed costs of price changes (Akerlof and Yellen 1985, Mankiw 1985, Blanchard and Kiyotaki 1987).[27] This work shows that the need to adjust prices may be less important for a firm with market power (price above marginal cost) than for the economy as a whole. The firm's decision to change price in response to a demand change depends on whether the resulting increased profit, which depends on the gap between the new marginal revenue and marginal cost, offsets the fixed cost of the price change. Society's increased welfare from the price change depends on the gap between

[27]See also Dreze (1975), Fischer (1977), Hall (1978), Malinvaud (1979), Rotemberg (1982), and Phelps and Taylor (1977).

price (not marginal revenue, which is lower) and marginal cost and the fixed cost of the price change. If the firm was initially maximizing profits, so that marginal revenue equals marginal cost, then for small changes in demand the firm has no incentive to lower price even if society would benefit. Therefore, a firm's incentive to incur a cost to change price and society's incentive to do so may diverge.[28]

SUMMARY

The empirical evidence about price behavior is sufficiently inconsistent with the simple theories of market clearing that economists are now exploring more sophisticated theories. Prices for some products are much more rigid than any of the standard theories predict.

In markets in which prices do not adjust rapidly, temporary shortages occur. Other mechanisms besides price adjustments clear these markets. For example, consumers may postpone consumption or firms may adjust their inventories over time. Firms are slow to change prices because of transaction costs and for other reasons.

New theories account for some of the more puzzling features of market clearing. These theories recognize that intertemporal substitution matters, that marketing is a costly activity, and that price adjustments in conjunction with nonprice methods are often used for allocation.

The nature of the relationships between buyers and sellers helps determine the best method to clear the market. The creation of new futures markets may alter which methods are used. The way markets react to demand and cost shocks depends on many factors in addition to the degree of concentration in the market.

PROBLEMS

1. Suppose a bakery must bake bread at a constant unit cost of production of \$1 before it observes the demand for bread. It will have either 100 or 50 customers, and each outcome is equally likely. Each customer demands one loaf of bread, provided the price is \$5 or less. What are the optimal price and number of loaves if the bakery is a monopoly? Suppose the most consumers would pay for a loaf of bread is \$1.50. How do your answers change?
2. Suppose an industry produces to order. What economic conditions would have to change for it to become a produce-to-stock industry?
3. Suppose that a firm has an upward-sloping marginal cost curve. Illustrate how the price-marginal cost margin behaves as price increases. How does the price-average cost margin change as price increases?
4. Is the establishment of an organized auction market more likely to benefit small firms or large firms?
5. Suppose two customers pay different prices for the identical physical product. Give a sufficient condition such that it is reasonable for an analyst to conclude that there is no price discrimination.

Answers to the odd-numbered problems are given at the back of the book.

[28]A closely related point is that in the presence of distortions between price and marginal cost, the value of an output expansion can be greater to society than to a firm (see Harberger 1971). Hart (1982) and Hall (1988a) apply this principle in a macroeconomic setting.

PART SIX

Government Policies and Their Effects

CHAPTER 18

International Trade

Free trade, one of the greatest blessings which a government can confer on a people, is in almost every country unpopular.
—Thomas Babington, Lord Macaulay 1824

Increasingly, industrial organization theory has been applied to international trade problems.[1] There are at least two reasons. First, international trade topics such as trade in branded products, dumping, the use of tariffs, subsidies, and quotas, and transfer pricing within a multinational firm are closely related to analogous problems in industrial organization. Second, interest groups that want either protection from foreign competition or subsidies from taxpayers use industrial organization theories to provide a patina of intellectual rigor to their pleas. Unfortunately, many of the policies governing international trade are contrary to the economic interest of consumers, and many laws cannot be justified on efficiency grounds by economic theories.

This chapter addresses four major issues:

1. Trade between countries may result in product differentiation, predatory pricing, price discrimination, or free riding.
2. Tariffs, quotas, and subsidies are used to create or battle monopolies.
3. Strategic trade policies are used to help domestic oligopolists compete with foreign rivals.
4. Trade policies help some groups and hurt others.

Reasons for Trade Between Countries

There are many reasons for trade between countries. The most important reason, the theory of *comparative advantage,* is that it is cost-effective for the countries to trade. After briefly discussing the theory of comparative advantage, we

[1]See, e.g., Krugman (1989).

turn to explanations for trade that are based on industrial organization theories: trade in differentiated products, free riding, and dumping (selling abroad at prices below costs or domestic prices).[2] Although the theory of comparative advantage explains much of the volume of trade between countries, the studies in Feenstra (1988) and others find that the theory does not explain other patterns of trade, especially those involving trade in similar products.

Comparative Advantage

Traditionally, the existence of trade between countries has been explained using the theory of comparative advantage. According to this theory, a country exports those products it can produce relatively inexpensively and imports those goods that it can produce only at relatively great expense.[3]

To illustrate this theory, suppose that the United States and Japan initially do not trade, and each country is in competitive equilibrium, in which price equals marginal cost. The United States produces and sells rice at \$1 per bag and televisions at \$10 per set. Japan produces rice at 200¥ (yen) and televisions at 1,000¥. If the United States were to produce one fewer television set, it could produce 10 extra bags of rice. Japan could produce one more television set at the cost of only 5 bags of rice. Thus, the two countries combined could produce the same number of television sets and have 5 extra bags of rice if they reallocated their resources in this manner. Both could gain if the United States shipped rice to Japan and Japan shipped television sets to the United States (assuming no transportation costs).

This argument that there is a *gain to trade* does not depend on absolute productivity levels. The argument would still hold if one Japanese worker could produce more of both goods than an American worker, or vice versa. The argument turns on only the *relative* costs of the goods in the two countries.

An **exchange rate** is the price of one currency in terms of another currency. In the previous example, if the exchange rate is 200¥ per dollar, a bag of rice sells for the same price in both countries, but a Japanese television set sells for half the price of an American set, so that Japanese sets would be shipped to the United States. If the exchange rate is 100¥ to the dollar, a television set costs the same in both countries, but a bag of U.S. rice sells for half as much as Japanese rice, so that U.S. rice would be shipped to Japan.[4]

The relative advantage of countries in producing, for example, food or clothing depends on the technology of each country and on each country's endowment of land, labor, and other resources. A country with a lot of labor and little capital finds it to its

---

[2]In addition, firms may have an incentive to ship products to other countries to avoid taxes. See **www.aw-bc.com/carlton_perloff** "International Transfer Pricing."

[3]We discuss this traditional explanation for trade only briefly. See any basic trade textbook, such as Krugman and Obstfeld (1997), Caves, Frankel, and Jones (1999, ch. 3), or Houck (1986) for more details.

[4]Trade models must have a constraint that links the value of imports and exports. In such models, there is an equivalence between taxes on exported and imported products (Lerner 1936). This chapter abstracts from several general equilibrium issues that link together expenditures on exports and imports.

advantage to export labor-intensive products and import capital-intensive products from countries with lots of capital and little labor. Given the United States' highly trained labor force, we would expect it to export goods and services requiring knowledgeable workers to countries that do not have a highly trained workforce.

Intra-Industry Trade in Differentiated Products

Trade of similar goods between similarly developed countries has grown rapidly.[5] For example, the United States both imports and exports automobiles, processed foods, clothing, and many other goods. That is, not only do countries with different endowments of factors of production trade one type of good for a very different good, but also countries with similar endowments of factors trade similar goods.

Models of differentiated products can explain this latter type of trade between countries. It does not make sense, of course, to have two-way trade in an undifferentiated product such as short-grain rice: One country should only export and the other country should only import. In contrast, countries may both import and export differentiated goods. Some Americans want to buy British cars and some British consumers want to buy American cars.

By applying the representative consumer model of differentiated products (Chapter 7) to international trade, we can show that consumers may benefit from such trade. Suppose consumers in each of two countries demand a variety of differentiated products (each produced by a different firm) and value variety. Because of scale economies (Chapter 7), only a finite number of different products get produced in each country.

Without international trade, the equilibrium number of products is, say, n in each country. If the two countries trade, the size of the combined market expands and each country can still produce n different products, but together, consumers in each country can choose between $2n$ different products. Thus, consumers are better off because they face a wider choice.

Free Riding, International Price Differences, and Gray Markets

The value of a dollar in terms of the German mark, the Japanese yen, or other currencies—that is, the exchange rate for the dollar—changed substantially over the last two decades. For example, \$1 was worth 203 yen at the end of 1980, 251 yen at the end of 1984, 136 yen at the end of 1990, and 107 yen at the end of 2003. The change in exchange rates greatly affects the incentives to trade between the United States and other countries.

Suppose that \$1 is worth 1 Japanese yen initially. Two identical products might sell for \$1 in the United States and 1 yen in Japan. Now suppose that the exchange rate changes so that a dollar becomes more valuable: \$1 is worth 2 yen or, equivalently, 1 yen is worth \$.50. A Japanese retailer could ship the product to the United States and receive \$1 or 2 yen, instead of receiving 1 yen from selling the product at home. Firms that ship products between the two countries to make a profit cause the price in the

[5] Helpman and Krugman (1985, 1989), and Helpman (1988).

United States to fall (because the supply there rises) and the price in Japan to rise (because the supply there falls). This process, called *arbitrage,* drives the prices in the two countries into equality at the new exchange rates. For example, if the product is produced only in the United States and the competitive supply curve is horizontal, the U.S. price remains at $1, but the Japanese price rises to 2 yen ($1 at the new exchange rate).

In the mid-1980s, the prices of many products did not behave as expected in several countries as exchange rates fluctuated and the dollar became more valuable. Many prices remained at their initial levels rather than changing in response to exchange rate fluctuations. Even if the foreign and U.S. prices were roughly equivalent initially, after the exchange rates changed they were no longer equivalent. For example, Mercedes cars, Nikon cameras, and French perfume sold for much higher prices in the United States than in foreign countries when prices are expressed in a common currency using prevailing exchange rates.

Apparently these manufacturers prevented arbitrage from equilibrating the prices in different countries. Some manufacturers only permit authorized dealers to handle their products. Any authorized dealer that imports the product from Europe instead of buying it from the manufacturer could lose its authorization. The foreign goods shipped to the United States outside of normal channels (those authorized by the manufacturer) of distribution are called *gray market* goods. Efforts to prevent gray markets by camera manufacturers are discussed in Example 18.1.[6]

Two possible explanations can be given for the rise of gray markets: one based on international price discrimination and the other on costs of promotion and free riding. Suppose that the price elasticity of demand for a product is initially the same in the United States and in a foreign country, but the demand becomes relatively less elastic in the United States as the dollar appreciates in value. A manufacturer with market power would price discriminate, charging more in the United States and attempting to prevent resale of its goods from foreign distributors to U.S. distributors. If the manufacturer cannot prevent resales, a gray market forms.

Although the price discrimination explanation is logically possible, it is doubtful that it can explain much of the behavior during this period. Why should the U.S. price elasticity of demand increase as the exchange rate rises? Surely the demand for all goods did not simultaneously become less elastic in the United States. Moreover, in several of the affected industries, there are many competitors, so that significant market power seems unlikely.

An alternative explanation based on international free riding may be more plausible. A distinguishing characteristic of most, if not all, of the products with gray markets was that they were heavily promoted using advertising or other sales efforts.

Suppose that some product, say cameras, is manufactured in Japan. Cameras are a promoted product in which the reputation of the camera is created and established in a consumer's mind. Promotion typically involves advertising as well as in-store

[6]Fargeix and Perloff (1989) show that under certain circumstances, manufacturers may oppose tariffs designed for their protection and instead may prefer gray markets.

EXAMPLE 18.1

Gray Markets

During the early to mid-1980s, the dollar rose substantially in value relative to other major trading currencies. This increase led to some dramatic differences across countries in the prices of branded goods in terms of dollars. For example, a Mercedes-Benz that sold for about $24,000 in Los Angeles cost only $12,000 in Munich, Germany. Rolex watches cost $600 in Zurich, Switzerland, but $1,800 in New York. Similar price differentials were observed in the markets for cameras and perfume. These large international price differences led to gray markets.

As a result of gray market imports, authorized U.S. distributors faced competition from goods purchased abroad and sent to the United States without the consent of the manufacturer. For example, an authorized dealer sold an Olympus camera in the United States for about $240, whereas the U.S. gray market price was $190 for the same camera. Distributors and manufacturers spent considerable effort to track down and limit the unauthorized shipments from abroad, but frequently were not successful.

Due to the gray market, some customers paid a lower price but were not always able to benefit from promotion and sales efforts of authorized U.S. distributors. Some customers became dissatisfied. For example, several manufacturers provide warranties on cameras sold by authorized U.S. distributors, but not for physically identical cameras sold through the gray market. When customers with gray market cameras needed warranty service, they often were rudely surprised to learn that, based on the serial number of their camera, they were not entitled to the U.S. warranty. Occasionally, to preserve goodwill, the manufacturer would foot these repair bills. Numerous articles in newspapers warned consumers of the potential problems with buying gray market goods.

By the late 1980s, however, the value of the dollar had fallen relative to the currency of most of our trading partners. Because of the lowered value of the dollar, the concern with the gray market in the United States disappeared.

The increased value of the yen relative to the dollar, however, created incentives for goods in the United States to be shipped to a Japanese gray market. For example, in 1988, a Canon camera sold for $340 in New York and for a dollar-equivalent price of $462 in Japan. Cameras sold in the gray market in Japan were selling for 30 to 40 percent less than similar cameras sold through authorized distribution channels.

Source: Larry Armstrong, "Now, Japan Is Feeling the Heat from the Gray Market." *Business Week,* March 14, 1988:50–51; Sylvia Porter, "Gray Market Goods Cause Consumer Problems." *The Dispatch,* July 15, 1985:11; Grace Weinstein, "Gray Market Discounts: Be Careful." *Good Housekeeping,* September 1, 1985:251; Maks Westerman, "The $7 Billion Gray Market: Where It Stops, Nobody Knows." *Business Week,* April 15, 1986:86–87.

demonstrations.[7] The amount and effectiveness of promotion varies by country. Indeed, if the reputation of the product, which is created by promotion, differs in the two countries, the camera in the United States is not the same product as the camera in Japan. As a result, differences in price may not reflect price discrimination. Indeed, the price differences might only reflect the different costs of promotion in the two countries.

To illustrate this theory, suppose a Japanese manufacturer faces the same elasticity of final demand, ϵ, in the United States and Japan, so that there is no possibility of traditional price discrimination. The manufacturer incurs a constant marginal and average cost m to produce the product and uses one distributor in each country to sell the product to customers and to promote the product or train consumers to use it. The manufacturer provides each distributor with an incentive to provide sales effort by giving the distributor an exclusive territory, in this case a country (Chapter 12). The manufacturer charges the distributor its marginal cost, m, for the product and extracts all distributor profits using a franchise fee (which gives the distributor the exclusive right to sell the product).

To keep the example simple, assume, initially, that both U.S. and Japanese distributors must incur a promotional or training expenditure of E dollars per unit and E yen per unit respectively and that initially \$1 equals 1 yen. The distributor maximizes its profit by setting its marginal revenue equal to its marginal cost. Equivalently, its monopoly price markup (Lerner's Index) equals the negative of the reciprocal of its elasticity of demand,[8]

$$\frac{p - (m + E)}{p} = -\frac{1}{\epsilon}, \tag{18.1}$$

where all relevant prices and costs are in yen. In the United States, the optimal retail price is determined by

$$\frac{p - (fm + E)}{p} = -\frac{1}{\epsilon}, \tag{18.2}$$

where p and E are in dollars, m is in yen, and f is the exchange rate (initially $f = 1$) converting yen to dollars. If $m = 1$, $E = 1$, and the elasticity of demand, ϵ, equals -2, then $p = 4$ in each country.

---

[7]For example, to many consumers, a sophisticated camera becomes useful and valuable only if camera store personnel are sufficiently trained (at great expense) so that they can inform the consumer about the product. A camera sold by trained personnel is a different product than one sold by personnel without training. We expect the price of a camera to be higher in countries where consumers have access to an expensive distribution system with trained sales people than in countries with no distribution system.

[8]The distributor's profit is $\pi = [p(q) - (m + E)]q$ minus a (fixed) franchise fee. Thus, its first-order condition is $p'q + p = (m + E)$, or marginal revenue equals marginal cost. This expression can be rewritten as

$$\frac{p - (m + E)}{p} = -\frac{p'q}{p}.$$

Noting that $p'q/p = (dp/dq)(q/p) = 1/\epsilon$ we obtain Equation 18.1, which is equivalent to Equation 4.3.

Suppose an unauthorized American distributor can import the product and sell it in a gray U.S. market. The unauthorized firm would free ride on the efforts of the authorized firm and would provide no promotional or training efforts. For example, the authorized dealer could provide a showroom where consumers could try out the product or provide training in using it. The unauthorized dealer could send its customers to the showroom to see the product.

The authorized Japanese distributor has an incentive to sell to the unauthorized U.S. distributor. By doing so, the Japanese distributor can avoid incurring the (Japanese) promotion charge of 1 yen and the unauthorized American distributor can free ride off the promotion efforts of the authorized American distributor. The authorized Japanese distributor could profitably sell to an unauthorized American distributor for, say, 3 yen, and the unauthorized American distributor could profitably sell to customers for \$3.50, which is less than the authorized U.S. distributor's monopoly price of \$4.

Similarly, the authorized American distributor has an incentive to sell to an unauthorized Japanese distributor, who can free ride on the promotional efforts of the Japanese distributor. Thus, bilateral international trade occurs because of international free riding. Indeed, there is an incentive for this bilateral trade to occur even if there is no difference in the retail price between the two countries in the absence of gray markets. This free riding harms the manufacturer because it erodes the incentive of its authorized distributors to promote the product, and it can ultimately harm consumers by reducing or eliminating promotional and service activities by distributors (Chapter 12).

There are two additional implications of free riding in an international context that do not arise in the domestic story. First, the optimal U.S. price varies as the exchange rate, f, changes. By solving Equation 18.2 for p, we find that the optimal U.S. price is $(fm + E)\epsilon/(1 + \epsilon)$. The production cost, m, is fixed in yen because the product is produced in Japan; however, p varies as the exchange rate, f, changes. The percentage change in the U.S. price in response to a change in f becomes smaller when the fraction of manufacturing cost to total cost becomes smaller.[9] For many heavily promoted products, the actual manufacturing cost is such a small fraction of total cost that one may see little price variation in the optimal U.S. price in response to changes in the exchange rate. Thus, if manufacturing costs are a small share of total costs, free riding provides an explanation for why the price of highly promoted internationally traded products did not vary much in response to large exchange rate fluctuations.

Second, the incentive to free ride increases as the promotional expense increases (Chapter 12). Even if initially E dollars equals E yen, after a large exchange rate movement in which the dollar becomes more valuable (f falls), the E dollars of U.S. promotion is much more valuable than the E yen of Japanese promotion and the profitable

[9]The percentage change in price with respect to a change in the exchange rate is $(dp/df)/p = m/(fm + E)$. If $f = 1$ initially, the percentage change equals the share of manufacturing costs in total costs.

incentive for the authorized Japanese distributor to ship to a free-riding, unauthorized U.S. distributor increases. Therefore, we expected to see more authorized Japanese distributors shipping goods to the United States in the 1980s than in the 1990s. Moreover, it is not just the Japanese distributor who has the incentive to ship to the United States. As f falls from its initial value of 1, the Japanese retail price $(m + E)\epsilon/(1 + \epsilon)$ is lower (when converted to dollars) than the U.S. retail price. This differential creates an incentive for any entrepreneur to buy at retail in Japan and ship to the United States.[10]

Indeed, in the mid-1980s, many people bought products in Japan at retail and resold them in the United States. Similarly, Japanese retail stores shipped the products to unauthorized U.S. distributors. Typically, these imported gray market goods were sold by U.S. discount retail stores at lower prices than were charged by authorized U.S. distributors.

Manufacturers feared that the free riding by these discount stores, together with the reduced price, would erode the incentives for their authorized U.S. distributors to promote the product. The manufacturer wants to control the free riding and will spend money to monitor the efforts of its authorized distributors and make sure that its authorized distributors are not participating in the gray market. However, it is much more difficult for a manufacturer to prevent Japanese customers (or retail stores) from selling to the United States.

In the mid-1980s, many manufacturers asked the U.S. government to protect their trademark on the branded products that they promoted by refusing to allow any unauthorized foreign trade in their branded goods unless the brand name was removed. In most cases, the manufacturers were unsuccessful.

Dumping

Certain types of price differentials across countries are prohibited. Under international law, a firm is **dumping** if it sells its product abroad at a price below its domestic price or below its actual costs. For example, if a Japanese firm sells steel in the United States for $250 a ton, but sells it at $300 a ton in Japan, that firm is said to be dumping steel in the United States.

In justifying laws against dumping, many argue that dumping is typically a strategic act designed to harm rival firms. There are many explanations for dumping.[11] We focus on three: predatory pricing, price discrimination, and reciprocal trade for spatial reasons. We then discuss the legal aspects of dumping.

---

[10] If retail stores in addition to distributors engage in sales promotion, the example becomes more complicated (see *An Analysis of Gray Markets,* Lexecon Report, 1985, in which Carlton participated), but the basic conclusion is unchanged. Free riding creates incentives for Japanese retail customers, Japanese retail stores, and Japanese distributors to ship to the United States in the example in the text.

[11] We have seen how free riding can give rise to foreign sales at prices below domestic prices. Ethier (1982) contends that dumping may result as a response to cyclical conditions. When domestic demand is low, firms may choose to sell abroad at a low price rather than lay off their employees. See also Davies and McGuinness (1982), Bernhardt (1984), Brander and Krugman (1984), Hillman and Katz (1986), Gruenspecht (1988a), Berck and Perloff (1990), and Dick (1991).

Predatory Dumping. If a firm sets an extremely low price in a foreign country so as to engage in predatory pricing (Chapter 11) against that country's firms, it is said to be engaged in **predatory dumping**. Firms in the United States frequently claim that a dominant firm (or entire industry acting collectively) in a foreign country sells its product in the United States at a price below the minimum average cost of the U.S. domestic firms, which drives them out of business. Once the domestic industry is destroyed, the foreign firm is free to raise its price in the United States to a monopoly price.[12]

This story of predatory dumping has the same logical problems that we discussed in Chapter 11. Why should the foreign firm be willing to incur losses for as long as necessary to destroy the U.S. industry? Why don't the U.S. firms retaliate or, better yet, encourage U.S. customers to consume massive amounts of goods so as to bankrupt the foreign firm? What prevents the U.S. firms from reentering the market once the foreign firm raises its price? The U.S. Supreme Court has recognized explicitly these logical problems in a case involving a charge of predatory dumping where it ruled that predation was not plausible (see Example 11.1).

If a foreign firm that is identical to U.S. firms tries to predate, it probably will fail and go bankrupt. However, a foreign country could tax its citizens to provide a subsidy to its firm to enable it to charge predatory prices in the United States. Charging low prices for extended periods of time might then be feasible for the foreign firm. A government, unlike a private firm, need not be constrained by economic rationality (Lott 1999). Nonetheless, when the price eventually rises, U.S. firms may be able to reenter the market. If there is little chance of success in subsequently raising price, the foreign country that is subsidizing the predation is providing a gift to U.S. consumers.

If a foreign firm has lower costs than U.S. firms, it can successfully drive them out of business but still set price above its costs. Once the U.S. firms are driven out of business, the foreign firm can raise its price to the point where U.S. firms are indifferent between reentering the market and not. That is, the foreign firm can limit price (Chapter 11).[13] Were a low-cost U.S. firm to engage in this action, it probably would not be violating any antitrust law. Indeed, we want to encourage efficient firms to take over markets because consumers can only benefit. Putting foreign policy concerns aside, it is difficult to see why efficient foreign firms should be treated differently than efficient domestic firms.

Discriminatory Dumping. If a firm charges a lower price in a foreign market than in the domestic market so as to price discriminate, it is engaging in **discriminatory dumping** (Viner 1923) and thereby violating antidumping laws. Suppose a Korean monopoly sells at home and in the United States. If demand is less elastic in Korea than in the United States, it is profit-maximizing for the monopoly to price discriminate and charge a lower price in the United States. In the absence of the price discrimination, the price will typically rise to Americans and fall to Koreans as long as both

[12]For example, the *Economist* (April 5, 1986: 82) reports: "To a man the American ragtrade believes that Crompton was driven out of business by Japanese dumping. They say that the day after Crompton filed for Chapter 11 bankruptcy the Japanese raised their prices on rival goods by 50 percent."
[13]Berck and Perloff (1990) show that it is not optimal for a low-cost foreign firm to predate in the sense of pricing below its marginal cost while driving competitive fringe domestic firms out of business.

American and Korean customers continue to be served. American consumers benefit, Korean consumers are hurt, and the monopoly benefits from the price discrimination.

Were it not for international trade barriers and transport costs, such price discrimination could never exist. Without trade barriers and transportation costs, entrepreneurs would ship goods from low-price countries to high-price countries (arbitrage) until prices are equated in both countries. That is, price discrimination is impossible unless resale can be prevented (Chapter 9).

In our example, U.S. consumers clearly benefit from price discrimination. Why then would the United States want to complain about discriminatory dumping? U.S. consumers benefit from such price discrimination; however, U.S. producers are harmed. Even though the gain to U.S. consumers exceeds the loss to U.S. producers, producers may bring actions against foreign firms under U.S. laws to prevent U.S. consumers from receiving such a benefit (Dixit 1988a).

Reciprocal Dumping. In a variant of the price discrimination story, firms in different countries engage in reciprocal dumping (Brander and Krugman 1983) where each firm dumps in the other's country. This story is based on a model of spatial competition (Chapter 7).

Suppose there is a single firm in each country. Without international trade, each firm charges the (same) monopoly price, p_m, in its own country. If trade is allowed, each firm sells in the other country if the cost, T, to ship a good to the other country is low enough so that $p_m - T$, exceeds marginal cost, m. If the firms invade each other's country, then, in each country, the domestic firm has a cost advantage over its foreign rival.

In equilibrium, the domestic firm sells more than the foreign firm at a price, p, that is lower than p_m because competition between the two firms drives prices down from the monopoly level. Moreover, the price a firm receives at home, p, is more than the net price, $p - T$, it receives from sales in the foreign country. That is, both firms are price discriminating in the sense that they receive different net prices from sales to different consumers. This reciprocal price discrimination or dumping benefits consumers in *both* countries by lowering prices below the monopoly level, although consumers are still paying more than the competitive price.

This shipping of identical goods in both directions (cross hauling) is clearly inefficient. It makes no sense for society to incur the transport costs of importing a foreign-produced product if that product can be supplied locally. Inefficient cross hauling arises only because of the noncompetitive market structure, but does result in lower prices to consumers.

Legal Standards for Dumping. Dumping is defined under the General Agreements on Tariffs and Trade (GATT) as selling a product "at less than its normal value."[14] Dumping is said to occur if a product is exported from Country 1 to 2 and

[14]GATT is a set of rules agreed to by many nations that controls the terms of trade between these nations. One purpose is to limit "trade" wars in which countries wind up adopting protectionist measures that dampen trade and harm all countries involved. In 1995, the World Trade Organization (WTO) was formed to promote international trade and incorporated GATT into its rules. It has about 150 member countries.

1. the price of the exported product in Country 2 is below the price of the comparable product in Country 1, or
2. if no such comparison can be made, the price of the exported product in Country 2 is below either (a) the price of a comparable product exported from Country 1 and sold in any other country, or (b) the cost of producing and selling the product.

Individual countries pass antidumping laws that are consistent with the GATT. In the United States, the International Trade Administration (ITA) within the U.S. Department of Commerce is responsible for administering the law in the United States. The U.S. International Trade Commission (ITC), an independent federal agency, conducts independent investigations into injury from dumping. The Court of International Trade and, if requested, the Court of Appeals for the Federal Circuit determine whether the ITC and ITA act in conformity with the antidumping statutes.

The antidumping laws are the most frequently used tool to limit competition from imports into the United States (Horlick 1989, 102). Between 1995 and 2002, 292 antidumping petitions were initiated with the ITA and ITC against firms in 48 countries around the world.[15] The per year rate of filing of cases was 36.5 compared to 22.9 cases per year in the 1970s (Sun 1993). Domestic firms bring actions under these laws frequently because the penalties in dumping cases are often very high and thereby offer sizable protection from foreign competition. For example, in March 2002, the U.S. imposed tariffs of between 8 and 30 percent on a wide range of steel products (Francois and Baughman 2003).

For the cases filed in the United States from 1995 to 2002, 14 percent were filed against Chinese firms, 9 percent against Japanese firms, 7 percent against South Korean firms, 5 percent against Taiwanese firms, and 4 percent each against German and Indonesian firms. Table 18.1 shows the pattern of dumping investigations in several countries.

Of the U.S. cases initiated during the period 1995–2002, 65.8 percent had antidumping duties assessed. Presumably, many cases filed have little merit. Whereas 76 and 75 percent of the suits against Chinese and Taiwanese firms, respectively, resulted in the imposition of an antidumping measure, only 38 percent of the cases against German firms had such a result.

Over time, governments have increasingly used antidumping cases to protect local industries (Finger and Flate 2003). Before 1994, the number of antidumping proceedings initiated by industrial (developed) countries far exceeded the number initiated by developing countries. Since 1994, that pattern has reversed as developing countries have increasingly protected their local industries. For example, between 1995 and 2002, industrial countries (Australia, Canada, the European Union, Iceland, Japan, New Zealand, Norway, Switzerland, and the United States) conducted 819 antidumping investigations, and developing countries (all other countries, excluding those 27 countries defined by the United Nations to be transition economies) brought 1,144.

---

[15]The World Trade Organization Web site has statistics on antidumping initiations and measures for the period 1995–2002 disaggregated by both reporting and affected country.

TABLE 18.1 **Number of Dumping Case Investigations Initiated**

	Year								
Country	1995	1996	1997	1998	1999	2000	2001	2002	Total
Argentina	27	22	14	8	24	45	26	14	180
EC	33	25	41	22	65	32	29	20	267
India	6	21	13	27	65	41	79	79	331
South Africa	16	33	23	41	16	21	6	4	160
United States	14	22	15	36	47	47	76	35	292
Other	61	101	137	121	138	102	146	124	930
Total	157	224	243	255	355	288	362	276	2160

Source: WTO website: **www.wto.org/english/tratop_e/adp_e/adp_stattab2_e.pdf**.

In contrast in the earlier 1987–1994 period, the corresponding numbers were 1,150 and 445. Moreover, if one adjusts for the amount of imports on the theory that more imports will lead to more antidumping actions, the intensity with which some developing countries (such as Argentina, India, and South Africa) use antidumping proceedings is far above the norm. Interestingly, the developing economies not only initiated more dumping proceedings than industrial economies over the period 1995–2002, but they also were the target of dumping proceedings more frequently than the industrial countries.

The United States defines dumping as "sales at less than fair value." The definition of fair value is extremely complex.[16] The U.S. antidumping laws mandate that a foreign firm's home price not be used as a basis of comparison if the home price is below fully allocated cost plus a reasonable profit. This provision has allowed U.S. antidumping actions to focus not on a comparison of the U.S. price with the home country price, but rather on a comparison of the U.S. price with the "full" cost plus reasonable profit (an 8 percent margin). About 60 percent of all U.S. dumping actions have used this standard since 1980 (Horlick 1989, 136). Curiously, while the below-cost justification is increasingly used in antidumping cases, the U.S. Supreme Court has sharply reduced the applicability of the doctrine in predatory pricing cases (Chapter 19 and Example 11.1).

[16]For example, Section 722(d)(1)(C) of the Tariff Act of 1920, as amended, 19 U.S.C. Section 1677a(d)(1)(C), and Section 353.10 of the antidumping regulations provide that, in determining whether the price in the United States is less than the price in the home country, the International Trade Administration of the U.S. Department of Commerce shall increase the U.S. price by: "the amount of any taxes imposed in the country of exportation directly upon the exported merchandise . . . which have been rebated, or which have not been collected, by reason of the exportation of the merchandise to the United States, but only to the extent that such taxes are added to or included in the price of such or similar merchandise when sold in the country of exportation. . . ." Such rules, of course, make these comparisons difficult (Karp and Perloff 1989b).

In cases where the below-cost standard is not used, the price of a particular transaction in the United States is usually compared to the average price in the home country to determine whether dumping occurred. Such a comparison is bound to find at least some offending individual U.S. sales as long as there is some price dispersion, as is typical for most products. For example, suppose that the average price in both the foreign country and the United States is $5. However, in each country half the sales occur at $6 and half at $4. There could still be a finding of U.S. sales below fair value, because half of all U.S. sales are below the average home price of $5. No offsetting credit is given for U.S. prices above $5. These offending sales are subject to a duty equal to the dumping margin based on the average price.

A second element of any U.S. antidumping proceeding is the showing that material injury to the U.S. industry (*not* to U.S. consumers) results from the dumping. From an economic viewpoint, the sale of a foreign product in the United States must reduce U.S. domestic sales from what they otherwise would be. Despite the apparent simplicity of this concept, whether an "injury" occurred is often vigorously debated. The injury is usually interpreted as lower prices, output, investment, employment, and profits than would exist in the absence of dumping. The "materiality" requirement presumably requires that the effects are significant, not trifling.

A typical element of any dumping proceeding is to show that the imports were the "cause" of injury to U.S. industry. As a logical matter, events other than dumped imports influence an industry, and those other events should be considered when evaluating whether the injury caused by the dumped imports to the domestic industry was material.

The lack of economic logic underlying the desirability of antidumping laws combined with the lack of economic logic associated with parts of the administration of the antidumping laws probably results in a significant harm to U.S. consumers that is only partially offset by a small gain to U.S. producers.[17] The antidumping laws are often used to protect U.S. industries from competition and can be viewed as a successful use of government to protect powerful U.S. industries. If current practices continue, the cost to the United States will climb as the potential for international trade increases.

Tariffs, Subsidies, and Quotas

Tariffs, subsidies, and quotas serve to insulate a domestic market from international trade and may help domestic firms compete with foreign rivals.[18] We examine their use first in competitive markets, then in noncompetitive markets, and finally in markets in which there are positive externalities. We conclude the section with an evaluation of the evidence on the success of strategic international trade policies.

[17]A number of studies examine the effects of antidumping laws on exporting firms and conclude they are trade distorting (Webb 1987, Gruenspecht 1988a, Leidy and Hoekman 1990, and Staiger and Wolak 1991a, 1991b).

[18]See any of the standard texts on trade, such as Krugman and Obstfeld (1997) and Caves, Frankel, and Jones (1999), or Bhagwati and Ramaswami (1963).

Competition

The domestic industry is competitive. The domestic demand curve is $D(p)$ and domestic supply curve is $S(p)$. If there is no international trade, the equilibrium price is p_0 and the quantity consumed is Q_0 in Figure 18.1a.

FIGURE 18.1 (a) Effect of Tariff, t^*, that Eliminates Imports
(b) Effect of a Subsidy of t^*

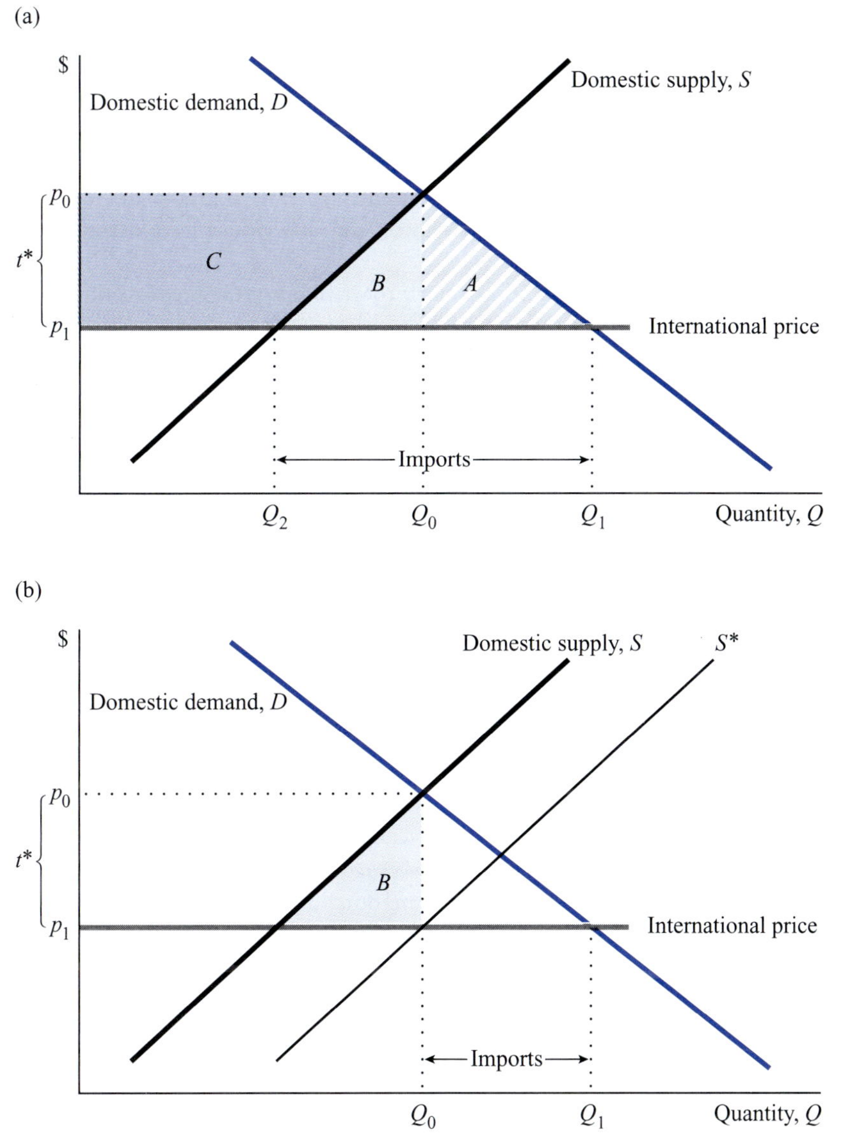

Suppose that the rest of the world's competitive supply of the product is perfectly horizontal at the world price, p_1, which is below p_0. If trade occurs, the equilibrium domestic price is p_1 and the amount consumed is Q_1, which is larger than Q_0. Domestic production falls from Q_0 to Q_2. Imports make up the difference between the amount consumed, Q_1, and the amount produced domestically, Q_2.

Domestic consumers are better off with international trade because they consume more at lower prices. Domestic society saves resource costs because it spends only p_1 for the output it now imports instead of the higher price it used to pay. Those extra resources can be used to produce other valuable products. The net gain to the domestic country from international trade is the triangle formed by the sum of the areas labeled A and B.

Suppose that the domestic industry convinces its government to impose a *tariff* (a tax on imports) of t^* equal to or greater than $p_0 - p_1$. Foreign producers faced with such a tariff do not sell in this country, and the no-trade equilibrium is reestablished at a price p_0 and quantity Q_0. Domestic producers gain extra producer surplus, C in Figure 18.1a. Consumers lose consumer surplus equal to $A + B + C$. The net loss to society is the triangle $A + B$. A straight ban on imports would have exactly the same effect.

Suppose that instead of instituting a tariff to drive out foreign competition, the domestic government subsidizes the domestic industry by an amount, t^*, that equals $p_0 - p_1$. The effect of the subsidy is to shift the domestic supply down by t^* to S^* in Figure 18.1b. The equilibrium results in a price of p_1, domestic consumption of Q_1, domestic supply of Q_0, and imports of $Q_1 - Q_0$. Consumers prefer this equilibrium to the one in Figure 18.1a in which the tariff eliminates all trade because p_1 is less than p_0. Domestic producers are in exactly the same position as before in the no-trade equilibrium.

The deadweight loss in Figure 18.1b, B, is less than the deadweight loss from preventing trade in Figure 18.1a, $A + B$. Thus, a country can help its producers as much by using a subsidy as by preventing imports, yet create less deadweight loss.

Suppose that the domestic industry is not politically powerful enough to obtain the tariff $t^* = p_0 - p_1$, but instead receives a lower tariff t. The tariff t does not eliminate all imports, as Figure 18.2 shows. The domestic price equals $p_1 + t$, the quantity consumed is Q_3, the quantity domestically produced is Q_4, and imports equal $Q_3 - Q_4$. The deadweight loss to domestic society from the imposition of the tariff equals the sum of areas E and F. The tariff revenues collected are equal to the tariff times the imports, $t(Q_3 - Q_4)$.

What happens if the domestic industry persuades its government to impose a quota of $Q_3 - Q_4$ instead of the tariff? The same outcome as in Figure 18.2 results with one important exception. Instead of the domestic government collecting tariff revenues from foreign producers as in Figure 18.2, foreign suppliers earn extra revenues equal to the amount of the former tariff revenues.

By using quotas instead of tariffs, the domestic country enriches foreign suppliers. Because foreign suppliers reap a reward, the foreign governments could auction off the right to export to the domestic country. Thus, foreign governments could earn the tariff revenues formerly received by the domestic government.

FIGURE 18.2 A Tariff, t, that Reduces Imports

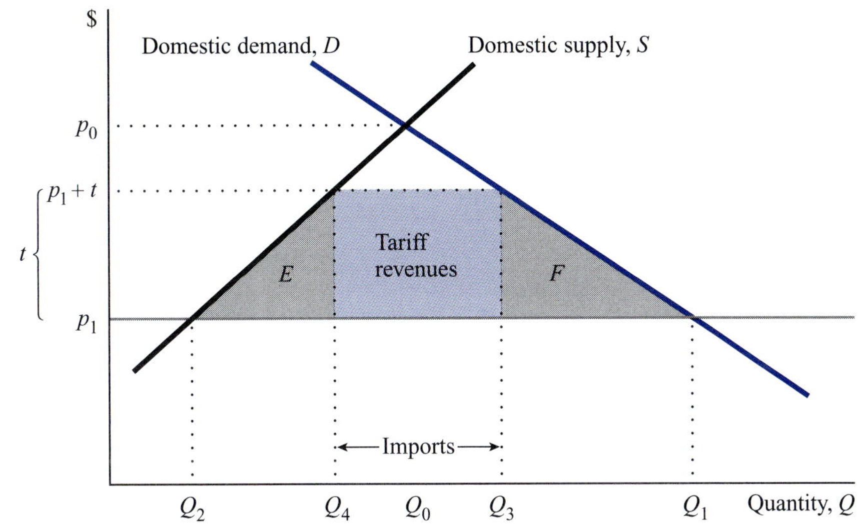

Quotas are one way for a country to provide benefits to either foreign suppliers or foreign governments and at the same time benefit domestic producers. Example 18.2 shows another way to benefit foreigners.

Creating and Battling Monopolies

Governments may attempt to increase domestic welfare or the profits of domestic producers by creating domestic monopolies or battling foreign monopolies.[19] We consider four cases. First, a government can help a domestic industry become a monopoly to the detriment of domestic consumers by preventing foreign competition. Second, a government can help domestic firms act like a monopoly to the rest of the world. Third, a government can help foreign producers restrict output, creating market power that hurts domestic consumers, through the use of an import quota. Fourth, a government can help its consumers by undermining a foreign monopoly.

Creation of Domestic Monopoly. Suppose a firm is the only domestic producer of a product for which there is a competitive world market. The domestic firm wants to be insulated from foreign competition so that it may exercise market power in the domestic market. In Figure 18.3, in the absence of world trade, the domestic producer sets a monopoly price p_m and sells Q_m, which is determined by the intersection of its

[19]Results for monopsony are similar. See Example 18.2.

EXAMPLE 18.2 *Timber Wars and Retaliation*

In the mid-1980s, U.S. lumber and timber producers complained to the U.S. International Trade Commission (ITC) and the U.S. Department of Commerce that Canada was subsidizing its lumber sales and causing material harm to U.S. producers. In late 1986, the Department of Commerce issued a preliminary finding that Canada was providing a 15% subsidy to its lumber producers and the ITC made an initial determination of harm to U.S. producers. Prior to the final ITC decision, a 15% countervailing duty was levied by the United States on Canadian imports, which would be refunded if the final ITC decision was favorable to Canada.

Canadian lumber is an important industry in Canada, accounting for about 4% of its gross national product. Canada exports about 60% of its lumber to the United States and accounts for about 30% of total U.S. supply. The Canadians weren't happy about the U.S. action. Canada's Minister of International Trade termed the duty "total harassment" and threatened retaliation. Canada imposed a 67% duty on U.S. corn shipments to Canada. The duty on Canadian lumber was scheduled to start on December 30, 1986. Negotiations with Canada continued in late 1986 to try to soothe the Canadians. The agreement that was reached was that the 15% duty (to be collected by the United States) would be replaced by a 15% Canadian export tax (to be collected and kept by Canada). The Canadian tax on corn remained.

Had the United States established a tariff without inducing a response from Canada, that duty could have been regarded as the United States trying to exercise its monopsony power. By taxing Canadian output, the United States could capture some monopsony rents. U.S. consumers would be harmed, but U.S. producers would benefit and the U.S. government would earn tariff revenues. The resolution of the lumber controversy resulted in Canada's imposing an export tax on lumber sales to the United States.

Who won as a result of the trade war? The U.S. lumber producers and the Canadian government were the big winners, and the U.S. consumers and the U.S. government were the big losers. Kalt (1988) estimates (in U.S. dollars) that under either a 15% U.S. tariff or a 15% Canadian export tax, U.S. lumber producers gained $416.8 million and U.S. lumber users lost $556.9 million. If it set a tariff, the U.S. government's tariff revenues would have been $340.5 million; however, it received no revenues from the Canadian export tax. The combined loss to the United States and Canada combined from either the tariff or the tax was $22.5 million. With the tariff, the United States would have gained $200.4 million and Canada would have lost $223.0 million. Instead, with the export tax, Canada gained $117.6 million and the United States lost $140.1 million.

marginal cost, *MC*, curve and its marginal revenue, *MR*, curve (which corresponds to the domestic demand curve, *D*).

For simplicity, assume that foreign producers have a perfectly elastic (flat) supply curve at p_1. If trade is allowed, the domestic price is p_1 and the total quantity consumed is Q_c, in Figure 18.3. The domestic firm, which has no market power in the

FIGURE 18.3 A Comparison of a Tariff to a Quota for a Domestic Monopoly

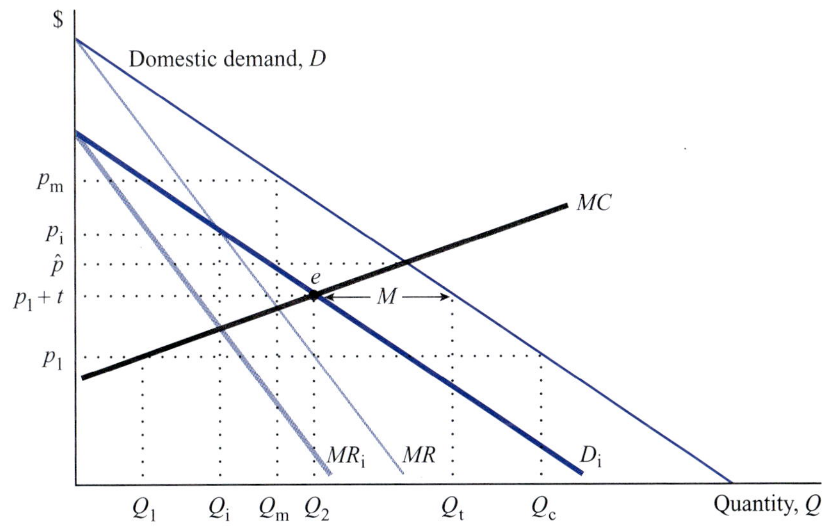

presence of world trade, sells Q_1, where its *MC* curve hits the foreign supply curve at p_1.

If the government imposes a tariff *t*, the equilibrium is *e*, where the domestic producer sells Q_2 units at $p_1 + t$. If, as shown, *t* is small enough that $p_1 + t$ is less than $\hat{p}$ (which is determined by the intersection of *D* and *MC*), *M* units of the good are imported because the quantity demanded, Q_t, exceeds the amount the domestic producer is willing to supply, Q_2. However, if *t* is so large that $\hat{p} < p_1 + t < p_m$, no goods are imported even though the price at which the domestic firm sells is constrained by the threat of imports. If *t* is so large that $p_1 + t$ exceeds p_m, the threat of imports imposes no constraint at all on the monopoly.

Now suppose that instead of a tariff, a quota is set so that only *M* units of the good can be imported (the quantity imported if the tariff is set at *t*, as in Figure 18.3). Is a tariff of *t* a superior policy? Or, is an import quota set equal to *M* better? Or are the two policies equivalent?

The domestic supplier prefers the import quota. An import quota of *M* shifts the demand curve facing the domestic producer to the left to $D_i = D - M$. By construction, the new demand curve D_i includes the tariff equilibrium point *e*.

However, the monopoly does not want to operate at *e* and sell Q_2 units with an import quota. The monopoly wants to sell Q_i units, which is determined by the intersection of its *MC* and its new marginal revenue curve, MR_i (which corresponds to the demand curve D_i). The monopoly charges p_i, which is greater than the price under the tariff system, $p_1 + t$. Therefore, this import quota provides less of a constraint on the monopoly than the tariff policy.

The type of foreign trade restriction influences the effectiveness of foreign competition in restraining a monopoly. Indeed, certain types of import quotas may *not* restrain the domestic price at all. For example, suppose that the quota rule limits foreign sales, Q_f, to be no more than a fixed percentage, α, of domestic sales, Q_d. That is, $Q_f = \alpha Q_d$.

The domestic monopoly sets Q_d to maximize its profit,

$$\pi = [p(Q_f + Q_d) - m]Q_d,$$

where $p(Q_f + Q_d)$ is the inverse demand curve expressing price as a function of total output, $Q_f + Q_d$, and m is its constant marginal cost. Given the import restriction, the monopoly's profit may be written as

$$\pi = [p(Q_d(1 + \alpha)) - m]Q_d.$$

To maximize its profit, the monopoly chooses Q_d so that

$$\frac{p - m}{p} = -\frac{1}{\epsilon}, \qquad (18.3)$$

where ϵ is the price elasticity of demand.[20] The monopoly sets its output such that its Lerner Index equals the negative of the reciprocal of the demand elasticity, which is the standard monopoly markup rule (Equation 4.3).

Thus, the monopoly's price is identical to what it would be if international trade were banned! The monopoly sells less as a result of the foreign sales, but, surprisingly, these additional foreign sales exert no downward pressure on the price. The reason is that the monopoly effectively controls the output of foreign suppliers because Q_f is tied to Q_d. Recognizing this link, the monopoly is able to restrict industry output so as to achieve the monopoly price.[21]

Thus, the nature of tariff or quota restrictions has a significant effect on the competitive constraints that foreign firms place on domestic firms.[22] Whether foreign sales

---

[20]The monopoly's first-order condition is $p'[1 + \alpha]Q_d + [p - m] = 0$. Rearranging terms, and noting that $1/\epsilon = p'Q_d(1 + \alpha)/p$, we obtain the expression in the text.

[21]Maximizing $[p(Q_d) - m]Q_d$ yields the same optimal p as maximizing $[p([1 + \alpha]Q_d) - m](1 + \alpha)Q_d$. Letting $(1 + \alpha)Q_d = Z$, this second objective is of the same form as the first one, $[p(Z) - m]Z$. Thus, the Q_d that maximizes the first objective is the same as the Z that maximizes the second objective, and the optimal price is the same for the two objective functions. The domestic monopoly maximizes the first objective function when $\alpha = 0$ (no trade). When $\alpha > 0$, the domestic monopoly maximizes the second objective function times a constant, $1/(1 + \alpha)$, hence the optimal price is independent of α.

[22]One implication of this result is that a government agency should take tariffs and quotas into account when evaluating a potential merger between two U.S. firms because these trade restrictions affect the amount of competitive pressures imposed by foreign firms on the merging firms. The April 1997 *Department of Justice and FTC Horizontal Merger Guidelines* have a separate section (Section 1.43—Special Factors Affecting Foreign Firms) that explicitly recognizes the need for evaluating the particular trade restrictions surrounding foreign trade in order to evaluate the constraint that foreign competition places on U.S. firms.

have a significant effect on price depends on the form of the quota or tariff. Example 18.3 illustrates an attempt to restrict foreign competition and raise domestic price through the use of quotas.

Creation of a Monopoly That Sells Abroad. In the examples we have examined so far, the tariff or quota policies reduce the domestic country's welfare because the losses to domestic consumers exceed the gains by the domestic producer. We now consider a policy that increases domestic welfare.

One country contains all the producers of a product that is sold only to consumers in other countries. These producers compete with each other so that the world price p_0 is competitive. The government recognizes that it could behave as a monopoly and efficiently cartelize the domestic industry by levying an export tariff of t so that the price the firm receives, p_1, plus t equals the monopoly price, p_m, in Figure 18.4. Effectively, the government is taxing the rest of the world. The domestic government, which is concerned only with its own citizens' welfare, does not mind that its tariff harms foreign consumers.

The domestic (exporting) country's gain from tariff revenues ($t \times Q_m$) is a rectangle, $A + B$ in Figure 18.4. The tariff reduces domestic producers' exports from Q_0 to Q_m. As a result, domestic producers lose producers' surplus equal to $B + C$.

The exporting country as a whole benefits from the tariff because the tariff revenues exceed the producers' losses. The rectangle A must exceed the triangle C, or p_m is not the monopoly price. If there were no tariff and the producers formed a cartel, the equilibrium price and exports would be the same as with the tariff, but the producers, rather than the government, would benefit from restricting exports.

Another method to effectively cartelize the domestic industry is to impose export controls. If industry output is restricted to the monopoly quantity Q_m, in Figure 18.4, the industry receives the monopoly price, p_m. Unlike with an export tariff, those domestic producers who are lucky enough to get a production quota keep the monopoly profits. As with an export tariff, the domestic country as a whole gains at the expense of foreign consumers.

Creation of a Foreign Monopoly. Just as export controls may create a domestic monopoly, import controls may create a monopoly of foreign suppliers. If the United States restricts imports of a particular good using a quota, it drives up the domestic price. If the United States slightly restricts imports, foreign profits rise. As the government restricts imports further, foreign profits rise until the imports are at the monopoly level (which is equivalent to creating a foreign cartel). Further restrictions reduce profits from the cartel level. A complete ban on imports eliminates foreign profits. Quotas help foreign and domestic producers but harm U.S. consumers by driving up the domestic price (see Example 18.4).

Combating a Foreign Monopoly. If the government of Country 1 uses an export tariff or quota so that its firms sell to consumers in Country 2 at a monopoly price, Country 1 benefits if Country 2 does not retaliate. Country 2 may be able to retaliate

EXAMPLE 18.3

Foreign Doctors

Controlling foreign supply benefits domestic suppliers of medical services. The American Medical Association (AMA) has exerted control over the number of doctors in the United States for many decades. During the 1960s, the American Medical Association's control of the number of domestic graduates weakened. At the same time, the immigration laws were changed; as a result, many more foreign doctors were able to practice in the United States and the percentage of new doctors who were foreign rose from roughly 15 percent in the 1960s to about 40 percent in the early 1970s. With these two sources of increased supply, the number of doctors per capita rose by almost 50 percent between 1965 and the early 1980s. Noether (1986) estimates that the increased supply reduced the annual income of doctors by about $23,000 in 1981 dollars.

In 1996, the Institute of Medicine (part of the National Academy of Sciences) issued a doctor-written report that urged federal and state governments to restrict the entry of foreign-trained doctors into the United States. The doctors were alarmed that the number of active physicians in the United States rose from 308,487 (151.4 per 100,000 population) in 1970 to 627,723 (245 per 100,000) in 1992.

They concluded that this increase was due to an influx of foreign-trained doctors because the annual number of graduates from U.S. medical schools has been stable at 17,000 over the past couple of decades. Hospital demand for residency interns each year exceeds the 17,000 figure by 6,000 to 7,000, and these doctors—who work 80 weeks for $25,000 to $30,000 a year—are foreign-trained and mostly foreign-born.

The 12 members of the committee unanimously recommended that the government curb the inflow of foreign-trained physicians. The doctors' warning on foreign physicians was based on a concern that rising numbers of immigrants will depress opportunities for U.S.-born doctors and consequently could "demoralize U.S. physicians."

Thus, the reason the report gives for why we should prevent immigration is that the foreign influx will leave some doctors in a bad mood. The doctors warn that the resulting drop in doctors' earnings—from an average of $150,000 a year—may convince potential U.S. medical students that a medical career is "a poor personal investment." Apparently, not many potential students have this fear: The 1999 total of 45,365 applicants to U.S. schools was about 50 percent higher than five years previously.

(At least this commission's recommendations are less sweeping than those of other recent commissions. The Pew Charitable Trusts Health Professions Commission called for closing one in five U.S. medical schools and sharply shrinking the number of doctors, nurses and pharmacists.)

Sources: Noether (1986); Keith M. Rockwell, "Medical Panel Sees a Crisis in U.S.—Too Many Foreign Doctors." *Sacramento Bee,* February 12, 1996: B7; Stuart Auerbach, "Blue-Ribbon Panel Calls for End of Subsidies for Foreign Doctors." *Houston Chronicle,* January 24, 1996: A5.

FIGURE 18.4 A Tariff Leads to a Monopoly Price

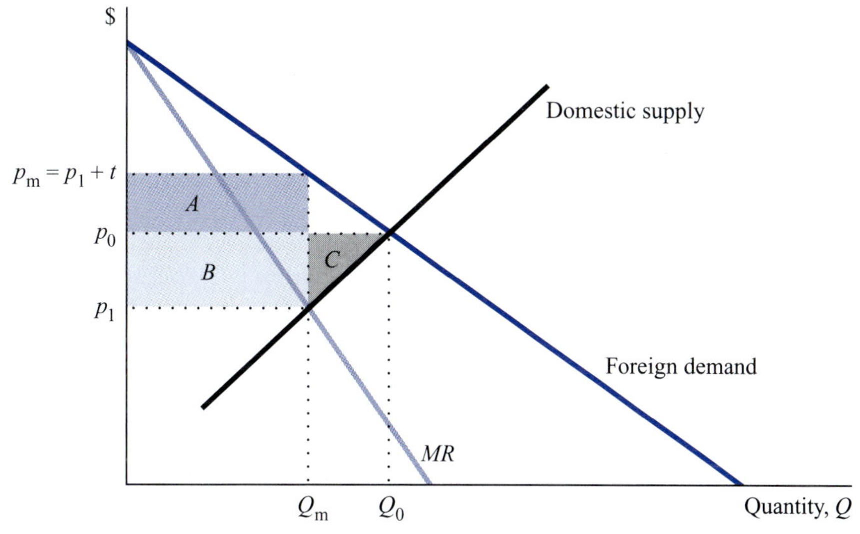

in several ways. It may go to war, exercise monopsony power, or cartelize one of its industries that exports to Country 1. Collectively, both countries are better off in a world of free trade at competitive prices than in a world with trade at *distorted* prices.

One way that an importing country could deal with a foreign cartel is to make its country's demand curve perfectly elastic at the competitive price by imposing a price ceiling at the competitive price. If it does not know the exact competitive price but only a likely range, it may try to make the demand curve very elastic in that range by imposing a nonlinear tariff. The nonlinear tariff is very high for prices above the range believed to contain the competitive price. The foreign monopoly would then choose to operate in the desired range.

If the importing country decides to levy a simple tariff on the foreign monopoly, its actions have two effects. First, the quantity sold falls and the domestic price rises, which harms consumers in the importing country. Second, it raises tariff revenues, which helps the country in general. Depending on the shape of demand, a tariff could help the country. In general, there is always either an optimal tariff or a subsidy that raises the welfare of an importing country facing a foreign monopoly.

The subsidy case is interesting because it suggests that it is sometimes optimal for the country to subsidize foreign production! As an example, suppose that the demand curve in the importing country has a constant elasticity of demand of -2. If the foreign producers set price to maximize their profits, price equals twice marginal cost (Equation 18.3). A subsidy paid to the foreign monopoly of \$1 per unit lowers price in the importing country by \$2. Domestic consumers gain more per unit than the cost of

EXAMPLE 18.4 *Being Taken for a Ride: Japanese Cars*

The Japanese share of car sales in the United States increased from under 10 percent in 1975 to over 20 percent by 1980. In response to this dramatic increase, quotas were placed on Japanese imports into the United States beginning in 1981. As a result, by 1987, Japan's share remained at about its 1980 share.

The quota raised prices, which hurt U.S. consumers and helped Japanese and U.S. auto manufacturers. By restricting the U.S. sales of Japanese cars, the quota raised the price of Japanese cars in the United States by over $2,000 per car in 1985. Due to the reduced competition from Japanese cars, the average price of a U.S. car increased by over $750. Both of these price increases harmed U.S. consumers. Applying these estimates to sales between 1980 and 1986, U.S. consumers paid an extra $80 billion as a result of the quotas.

The increase in the price of Japanese cars increased the profits of Japanese manufacturers. The U.S. quota helped the Japanese car producers act like a cartel and restrict output. The same output restrictions could have been achieved if the United States had levied a tariff, with the important difference that the extra profits would have gone to the U.S. government in the form of tariff revenues rather than to the Japanese producers.

The U.S. producers benefitted by the increase in their prices. Real profits increased steadily in the early to mid-1980s. Auto workers also gained. Wages in the auto industry were about 40 to 50 percent above the average manufacturing wage in the 1970s. That premium rose to about 50 to 60 percent in the early 1980s.

Source: Crandall (1987).

the subsidy at the current level of consumption so that the subsidy could generate a net welfare gain to the importing country, especially if consumption is already large.

Another possible response to a foreign monopoly is for the importing country to announce it will make no purchases at the monopoly price. The monopoly might respond that it will make no sales except at the monopoly price. The question then comes down to who can make the more credible commitment, the monopoly or the importing country.

Strategic Trade Policy

Recent work applying oligopoly theory to international trade has generated lots of attention from policy makers.[23] These models show that if a government can help its firms make binding commitments, these firms can compete more effectively with their

[23]See Helpman and Krugman (1985, 1989), Krugman (1989), and Baldwin (1992) for good surveys of this literature.

foreign rivals. The government is said to be using a strategic trade policy. Governments use many different types of strategic trade policies (see **www.aw-bc.com/carlton_perloff** "Strategic Trade Policies").

We have already seen the gain from commitment in some of the models of oligopoly in Chapters 6 and 11. For example, if a Stackelberg-leader firm can commit to an output level before its rival, it picks a relatively large output, which induces the follower firm to pick a relatively small output level. The leader makes a higher profit than the follower because its early commitment gives it an advantage.

In contrast to the Stackelberg model, in the static Cournot model, firms have to choose their output levels at the same time and firms cannot make credible commitments, so no one firm can convince the others that it will produce a large output. If the two firms are identical, they produce the same Cournot output. Although firms are unable to make credible commitments, a government may be able to commit its firm to produce a large quantity and thereby cause its firm to act like a Stackelberg leader.[24]

A duopoly example illustrates the strategic use of trade policy. Country 1 and Country 2 each have a firm that exports to countries other than Country 1 or Country 2. In the absence of government intervention, these firms behave as Cournot duopolists. We make the following assumptions:

- *No entry:* No other firms can enter.
- *Homogeneity:* The firms produce identical products, so that the sum of their outputs equals industry output: $Q = q_1 + q_2$, where Firm 1 (in Country 1) produces q_1 and Firm 2 (in Country 2) produces q_2.
- *Demand:* The inverse demand curve in the other countries is linear:

$$p = 46 - q_1 - q_2.$$

- *Costs:* The firms produce at constant marginal cost equal to 10.

The best-response functions of these firms are shown in Figure 18.5 and formally derived in Appendix 18A. The Cournot equilibrium is $q_1 = q_2 = 12$ and $p = 22$. Each Firm i earns a profit, π_i, of $144 (= [p - 10]q_i)$.

Now, suppose that the government in Country 1 can give Firm 1 a subsidy of s per unit without fear that the other government will retaliate. This subsidy encourages Firm 1 to produce more output—to be a more aggressive competitor. For example, if Firm 2 continues to produce 12 units and Firm 1 expands its output to 13 units, price falls to 21, and Firm 1's profit falls to 143 (from 144). If s is greater than 1, it pays for Firm 1 to expand its output by at least one unit.

The best-response function of Firm 1 (see Appendix 18A) is

$$q_1 = 18 - \frac{1}{2}q_2 + \frac{1}{2}s.$$

[24]Because the gain comes from the ability to commit, a government can help domestic firms remain large by taxing adjustments so as to make it costly for the firm to shrink (Karp and Perloff 1992, 1993b). The advantages to a government of these taxes over export subsidies are that they make rather than cost money and they do not violate the rules of the WTO.

FIGURE 18.5 Effects of Export Subsidy on Cournot Duopoly

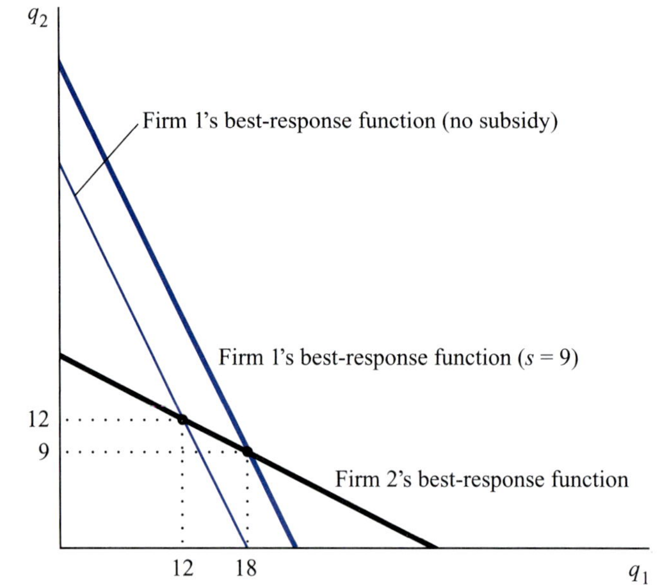

The larger the subsidy, the more Firm 1 produces for any given level of q_2. That is, the best-response curve of Firm 1 shifts to the right by $s/2$ (as Figure 18.5 shows for $s = 9$).

With the subsidy, the new equilibrium occurs at the intersection of Firm 2's original best-response function and Firm 1's subsidized best-response function. In the new equilibrium, $q_1 = 18$ and $q_2 = 9$. Firm 1's before-subsidy profit is $162 (= q_1 \times [p - 10])$, plus it receives a subsidy of $162 (= q_1 \times s)$, so that its after-subsidy profit is $\pi_1 = 324$. The subsidy is a transfer from the government to the firm. Assuming the subsidy can be paid without creating deadweight loss, the welfare (profit minus the subsidy) rises to Country 1 at the new equilibrium.

The government wants to choose the subsidy to maximize domestic welfare. Table 18.2 shows output, profits, and welfare in Country 1 $(= \pi_1 -$ subsidy payments) for several different values of s. Welfare in Country 1 is maximized at $s = 9$. As the table shows, Firm 1 would be delighted to receive an even larger subsidy than the one that is optimal for Country 1.[25] The subsidy raises Firm 1's profit from the free trade level,

[25]Indeed, when the per-unit subsidy exceeds the marginal cost, the first would like to produce an unlimited quantity and not even bother to sell it. In Table 18.2 where $s = 12$, we assume that the government limits the subsidy to Firm 1 at $q_1 = 20$, which is determined by the intersection of the relevant best-response functions.

TABLE 18.2 **Effect of an Export Subsidy**

	Country 1			Country 2		
s	q_1	π_1	Welfare	q_2	π_2	p
0	12	144	144	12	144	22
3	14	196	154	11	121	21
6	16	256	160	10	100	20
9	18	324	162	9	91	19
12	20	400	160	8	64	18

increases welfare in Country 1, harms Firm 2 and lowers welfare in Country 2, and helps consumers in importing countries because the price falls.

By choosing $s = 9$, the government in Country 1 enables Firm 1 to act like a Stackelberg leader. This equilibrium is the same as would occur if Firm 1 could commit before Firm 2 and act like a Stackelberg leader. That is, the government in Country 1 understands exactly how the game is played between Firms 1 and 2 and chooses the subsidy to manipulate the equilibrium to achieve the outcome that is best for Country 1.

Although the results from the model are logically correct, one can question the reasonableness of some of the assumptions.[26] Three assumptions are particularly crucial.

First, Government 1 must be able to act before the firms act. In this model, Firm 1 cannot act before Firm 2, but its government can.

Second, our example assumed that the firms play Cournot. Were the firms to engage in a different game, Government 1 would have to use a different policy. For example, if the firms play Bertrand and produce differentiated products, the optimal policy for Government 1 would be a tariff.

Third, nothing prevents Government 2 from retaliating (Karp and Perloff, 1995a). Government 2 could subsidize Firm 2. If both governments intervene, instead of having a game of strategy between firms, we have a game of strategy between countries. Although predicting political behavior is certainly more complicated and adds an interesting twist to an analysis of international competition, the empirical insights of game theory are few even when only firms are involved, so it is too much to expect

[26]Spencer and Brander (1983), Dixit (1984), Brander and Spencer (1985), Eaton and Grossman (1986a), Carmichael (1987), Cheng (1988), Gruenspecht (1988b), Markusen and Venables (1988), Neary (1991), and Karp and Perloff (1995a, 1995b) show that the optimal policy varies substantially with the assumptions used, such as the type of game played, the choice variables used by firms, the number of firms, barriers to entry, the exogeneity of costs, whether the firms or the government act first, whether the firms sell to domestic consumers, and whether the foreign government intervenes. See Maggi (1996) for a model where the results are less sensitive to these assumptions.

anything more than limited insights when we add political behavior to the already complicated environment.

We know from our earlier study of strategic behavior of firms that being able to credibly commit is a necessary feature of any subgame perfect equilibrium. That insight suggests that countries that engage in strategic behavior must somehow bind themselves to their proposed actions if the strategic behavior is to be effective. Countries may find it difficult to commit to long-term policies.

Most economists who have developed these strategic trade models argue strongly against their use. For a country to optimally choose such a policy, it must know how all the firms in the world will react and how other governments will behave. It must be able to credibly act first and commit to its policy indefinitely. If other countries also use strategic trade policies, it is likely that all countries will be harmed. Strategic trade policies are inherently "beggar thy neighbor" policies. It is for this reason that the WTO tries to constrain subsidies in general and explicitly forbids the use of most export subsidies (except for agriculture).

Most economists support the elimination of trade barriers. But countries can be very reluctant to overcome the political pressure to protect their powerful businesses, even though the protection may harm their own citizens. In September 2003, the WTO considered the reduction of agricultural subsidies and tariffs in developed economies. These subsidies and tariffs make it difficult for farmers in developing countries to sell their products. For example, large U.S. subsidies to U.S. cotton farmers are estimated to have reduced world prices by 20 to 40 percent, to the detriment of cotton farmers in developing countries.[27] Japan protects its rice farmers by levying high tariffs (600 percent) on rice imports, harming Japanese consumers and foreign rice farmers.

In return for lowering their protection of agricultural goods, the developed nations wanted to pursue agreements regarding competition law, investment procedures, transparency in government procurement, and increased trade—all designed to facilitate trade and foreign investment. The World Bank estimated that a successful negotiation would have raised global annual income by about $500 billion in about 10 years. Unfortunately, negotiations completely broke down as each side refused to compromise and reduce their protection of certain powerful domestic interests in their own countries.

Industries with Positive Externalities

Countries are often urged to adopt trade policies in order to assist industries that generate positive benefits to other domestic industries when the industries are not compensated for the benefits they generate (externalities). For example, research conducted in one industry may stimulate research in other sectors. An industry that generates such externalities does not expand output enough to equate the marginal social benefit

---

[27]Hoekman (2000); "The WTO Under Fire," *The Economist,* September 20, 2003, 26–28; Gretchen Peters, "In Cancun, A Blow to World Trade," *Christian Science Monitor,* September 16, 2003, p. 6.

to marginal cost because the firms cannot charge for the knowledge they generate. Thus, countries want to stimulate research beyond the levels that markets produce. They may use patents, prizes, or direct grants to induce firms to engage in the socially optimal amount of research (Chapter 16).

Typically, the lack of social efficiency arises because of a *domestic* distortion between marginal cost and social marginal benefit. Too little research is inherently bad—it does not matter whether the firm sells at home, sells abroad, or imports. However, arguments about externalities are often used to justify protectionist measures such as tariffs or import restrictions. The argument is that if domestic firms did not have to worry about foreign competition, they would spend more on research and generate benefits for the domestic economy. Often proponents of the measures urge that a newly emerging industry that will generate externalities needs to be protected, at least initially, until it achieves a certain scale.[28]

Even if subsidizing research in industries that create positive externalities is a good idea, trying to achieve that goal using trade policies is questionable. At best, trade policies are an indirect (and hence inefficient) solution. At worse, the distortions (monopoly pricing, trade wars) created by such policies offset the gains from additional research. A subsidy, import tariff, or quota on international trade protects an industry from competition and allows the industry to survive even if it becomes inefficient. Moreover, there is a danger that industries with powerful political support will receive subsidies or import protection rather than those industries that create many positive benefits.

Thus, as in the case of strategic intervention in trade, as a theoretical matter, subsidies or protection from foreign competition may be welfare enhancing. However, it does not follow that such policies must increase welfare. An examination of the evidence is required. Moreover, even if these policies are welfare increasing, direct subsidies are likely to achieve the same end without the accompanying distortions of trade policies.

Empirical Evidence on Intervention in International Trade

Based on the theories we have just reviewed, there are many motivations for trade policies. Some empirical evidence exists on why trade policies are used and whether they benefit the entire country or only certain interest groups.

Why Trade Policies Are Used. There are two views of why intervention in trade occurs. One view is that tariffs, subsidies, and import quotas are designed to protect certain interest groups such as domestic producers or workers at the expense of others. Another view is that these interventions are designed to increase overall domestic welfare.

[28]Firms in new industries with rapidly evolving technology areas may benefit from learning by doing (per-unit production cost falls as more is produced). These industries often petition for protection from foreign competitors until they become "established," at which time they supposedly will generate lots of spillover knowledge for the rest of the economy. For example, Japan adopted such a protectionist policy (preventing imports) in order to encourage its semiconductor industry to develop.

For example, a country may use an export tariff to help its producers monopolize an industry or use quotas to protect domestic industries that generate positive externalities.

As the strategic trade example in Table 18.2 shows, domestic firms may want to be subsidized beyond the point that is optimal for the country as a whole. Many firms and industries throughout the world lobby their governments for trade protection or subsidies.

Evidence suggests that trade restrictions are primarily used to aid domestic producers, especially in developed countries. There is little evidence that developed countries impose export tariffs to monopolize trade (Baldwin 1992). However, developing countries often try to form cartels among themselves (with varying degrees of success) to raise their output prices (Baldwin 1992).

If tariffs or quotas are pure payoffs to well-connected interest groups, they are more likely in certain circumstances. First, if they are payoffs, tariffs and quotas are likely in concentrated industries because they are easy to organize to lobby the government.[29] Second, where the victims of the higher price are many and small and thus it is costly to organize them, there should be limited opposition to such payoffs. For example, where there are many consumers instead of only a few, such payoffs are more likely (Godek 1985). Third, the call for protection should be greatest in industries where the country has little or no comparative advantage. For example, the United States has a comparative advantage in trade involving skilled labor and a comparative disadvantage in trade involving unskilled labor. Accordingly, we expect low-skilled workers to call for trade protection for the industries in which they work.[30] Although free trade increases welfare in both countries, certain groups, such as low-skilled workers in the United States, lose unless they are compensated.

Godek (1985) finds evidence consistent with each of these predictions. Godek further shows that quotas become increasingly important the larger the total protection from foreign competition the industry receives.[31] The use of quotas has greatly increased in the last two decades. One possible reason is that quotas can be viewed as a payoff to foreign producers (or countries), who keep the revenue that would have been collected by the domestic government under a tariff. If so, foreign producers must have become increasingly important interest groups that domestic governments want to please.

If trade restrictions insulate an industry from competition, we should expect to see domestic firms entering the protected industry. Because the industry is insulated from competition, inefficient firms can survive (Horstmann and Markusen 1986). There is evidence in support of this hypothesis in Canada and in less-developed countries (Eastman and Stykolt 1960, Harris 1984, Harris and Cox 1984, Caves 1989, Baldwin 1992).

---

[29]Frequently, quotas are requested to prevent foreign competition from undermining domestic cartels or government-imposed production restrictions. See Vercammen and Schmitz (1992) for a welfare analysis.

[30]Trade can be thought of as increasing competition among the factors of production of different countries. If all factors of production could costlessly migrate, they would compete with each other. Migration of goods is an alternative way the factors of one country compete with factors of another. Free trade in goods can be a complete substitute for the free migration of factors sometimes. As such trade occurs, the wages of workers in industries where the United States has little or no comparative advantage fall.

[31]Quotas may also be used because they are less likely than tariffs to trigger retaliatory measures under WTO rules (Sykes 1999).

The Effects of Trade Restrictions in Specific Industries. Researchers conduct empirical studies and simulations for various industries to determine who benefits from subsidies, tariffs, and quotas. Based on a study of the auto industry, Dixit (1988b) concludes that any gains to the United States from strategic tariffs or subsidies are relatively small. Baldwin and Krugman (1988a) study whether Japanese restriction on imports helped the development of random access memory (RAM) chips by the semiconductor industry. They find that, without the Japanese policy, no Japanese industry would have developed and the U.S. industry would have expanded greatly. They also conclude, however, that Japan did not benefit from this policy because Japanese production was more costly than U.S. production would have been. The Japanese policy therefore harmed both Japan and the United States. Baldwin and Krugman (1988b) find similar results for France, Germany, the United Kingdom, and Spain's Airbus (Example 18.5).[32]

Studies of only one industry ignore general equilibrium effects: An expansion of one sector of the economy must cause a contraction in another sector because total resources are limited. Harris (1984) and Harris and Cox (1984) used general equilibrium models to analyze the effects of liberalizing trade between Canada and the

EXAMPLE 18.5 *Wide-Body Aircraft*

France, Germany, the United Kingdom, and Spain own Airbus, which manufactures wide-body aircraft. Boeing is Airbus's main competitor. The industry for wide-body aircraft is characterized by high sunk cost, economies of scale, long product life, and learning by doing. Boeing claims that the owners of Airbus provide large subsidies that make it difficult for Boeing to compete. Airbus responds that the U.S. industry receives a subsidy from the U.S. government in the form of military contracts.

There is considerable controversy over how much subsidy Airbus receives. Using a model similar to the Cournot subsidy example in the text, Baldwin and Krugman (1988b) simulate the effects of the Airbus subsidy under a variety of assumptions. They find that Airbus significantly stimulated competition to the benefit of consumers worldwide. They also show that the United States was a net loser from the policy because the decline in Boeing's profits offset the increase in consumer surplus. They find that the European countries may have been net losers after paying the subsidy.

Irwin and Pavcnik (2001) estimate the demands for Boeing and Airbus aircraft. Based on these estimates, they conclude that the 1992 U.S.–E.U. agreement on trade in civil aircraft that limits subsidies resulted in a 3 percent increase in aircraft prices. This increase is consistent with a 7.5 percent increase in marginal costs after the subsidies were eliminated.

[32]Later, the British had second thoughts about using strategic trade policy. Former Prime Minister John Major told the United States that governments usually are unsuccessful when they try to manage industrial policies to encourage specific industries and that the U.K. policies had seriously damaged their economy. Craig Forman, "The Hidden Dangers of Industrial Policy." *Wall Street Journal,* March 1, 1993:1.

EXAMPLE 18.6

Steeling from U.S. Consumers

In March 2002, President George W. Bush imposed tariffs on steel after a Section 201 ("safeguard") investigation under the U.S. Trade Laws. The U.S. steel industry had hit hard times, with at least 35 firms declaring bankruptcy since 1998. The industry complained that a surge of cheap foreign imports had contributed to its difficulties. To protect the industry and give it time to reorganize, President Bush imposed tariffs ranging up to 30 percent on steel imports, to last for three years.

Although politically popular among steel producers, the measure was understandably unpopular among steel consumers, as the price of steel rose. One study done by the U.S. International Trade Commission (ITC) estimated that Bush's actions cost U.S. consumers more than $680 million annually. Strangely, the ITC concluded that the tariffs did not drastically hurt many steel-consuming businesses, although Francois and Baughman (2003) disagree.

The WTO ruled in 2003 that the U.S. actions violated international trade laws, even those that allow governments to help domestic industries suffering from an increase in imports. The European Union threatened to impose duties of up to 30 percent on more than $2 billion of U.S. exports. The U.S. removed the tariffs soon thereafter.

Sources: Elizabeth Becker, "In Glare of Politics, Bush Weighs Fate of Tariffs on Steel," *New York Times*, September 20, 2003:C1; Jonathan Weisman, "Tariffs Help Lift U.S. Steel Industry, Trade Panel Reports," *Washington Post*, September 21, 2003:A12; "Panel Says Tariffs on Steel Did Little Harm," *Chicago Tribune*, September 20, 2003:1; "U.S. Steel Tariffs Ruled Illegal, Sparking Potential Trade War," *Wall Street Journal*, November 11, 2003; Neil King Jr. and Carlos Tejada, "Bush Abandons Steel Tariff Plan," *Wall Street Journal*, Dec. 5, 2003:A3; Francois and Baughman (2003).

United States. They predicted that Canada's gross national product would increase about 8 to 12 percent with free trade.

Some governments claim to use trade policies to aid industries that either generate externalities or will do so once they thrive. Such policies are welfare improving only if the government is correct that the industry has (or will have) positive externalities and the appropriate subsidy or other policy is used.

As a practical matter, the government may choose to subsidize industries based on their political power rather than on their potential to generate positive externalities (see Example 18.6). The experience of other countries indicates the danger of government subsidies. For example, as one press account noted,[33]

> Strategic trade has not always served America's competitors well. Take Japan's $2.5 billion failure in the aluminum business in the 1970s. Or its government's misguided rush into steel just as low-paid Koreans and Brazilians mastered their arc furnaces. Japanese taxpayers have also taken baths on two recent flashy government-sponsored flops: artificial computing intelligence and high-definition television.

[33]Sylvia Nasar, "The Risky Allure of Strategic Trade." New York Times, February 28, 1993: Section 4, 1.

Although certain groups or even an entire country may benefit from trade restrictions, a strategic trade policy could trigger retaliation and a trade war. Trade wars often harm all countries. By ending trade, trade wars force countries to produce goods that they cannot produce efficiently. Kindleberger (1986) argues that the protectionist trade policies during the 1930s significantly contributed to the severity of the Great Depression.

If countries recognize that their actions can precipitate a trade war, and that such trade wars will harm all countries, then they might choose to bind themselves by treaty not to engage in such behavior. In fact, the rules of the WTO influence how countries trade with each other and how they respond to new tariffs or subsidies. That is, rules of the WTO can be viewed as a (weak) mechanism by which countries bind themselves not to engage in a trade war.

SUMMARY

Models of industrial organization explain certain types of trade. Models of differentiated products and scale economies explain why countries often conduct trade in products within the same industry. Free riding can also explain the volume of trade between countries for heavily promoted branded products. The free riding typically becomes most severe when exchange rate movements create large differences in the dollar equivalent retail prices for the same physical good in different countries. Models of price discrimination also explain the incentive to trade and charge prices abroad that differ from those charged domestically. There are many explanations for dumping, such as price discrimination and predatory pricing. The laws governing dumping tend to help domestic producers and harm domestic consumers.

There are many reasons motivating intervention in international trade. Many times, restrictions on international trade help domestic producers at the expense of domestic consumers. It is theoretically possible for trade intervention to help the entire country. In some cases, one country can take advantage of the collective market power of either its producers or its consumers. One country can also assist an industry that generates lots of spillover benefits to the economy. Finally, one country can assist its firms in making binding commitments that benefit its industry in the outcome of an oligopoly game. The empirical evidence suggests caution to anyone who believes that governments can actually pursue trade policies that benefit the entire country rather than protect producers from competition and harm consumers.

PROBLEMS

1. Can there be free riding and a gray market even if the retail prices in two countries are the same? If so, who would be engaged in shipping the product abroad?

2. Use a diagram to illustrate the net gain to a country from taxing a foreign monopoly.

3. Suppose Firm 1 in Country 1 produces Good 1 and Firm 2 in Country 2 produces Good 2. Both goods are sold only to consumers in other countries. The demand curves for the two goods are

$$q_1 = 15 - 2p_1 + p_2,$$
$$q_2 = 15 + p_1 - 2p_2.$$

Calculate the Bertrand equilibrium assuming that marginal cost is zero. Now suppose that Country 1 and Country 2 each place a \$3 export tax on their domestic firms. What are the new equilibrium prices and profits for Firms 1 and 2?

4. A competitive industry with an upward-sloping supply curve sells Q_h of its product in its home country and Q_f in a foreign country, so that the total quantity that it sells is $Q = Q_h + Q_f$. No one else produces this product. There is no cost of shipping. Using graphs, show the prices and quantities in the two countries. Now, the foreign government imposes a binding quota, Q^* ($< Q_f$ at the original price). What happens to prices and quantities in both the home and foreign markets? Finally, suppose the foreign government acts as a monopsony, and show how prices and quantities change in the two countries.

5. Suppose that all the buyers for a particular product live in Country 1, and all the firms that manufacture that product are in Country 2. The foreign supply curve is $Q = p$. The demand curve is $Q = 18 - p$. What is the competitive equilibrium? If Country 1 levies an import tariff, t, of \$2, what are the new equilibrium price, quantity, and tax revenues? What is the equilibrium if Country 1 acts like a monopsony? What is the welfare-maximizing tariff for Country 1 (in the absence of retaliation)?

Answers to odd-numbered problems are given at the back of the book.

APPENDIX 18A

Derivation of the Optimal Subsidy

Firm 1 in Country 1 and Firm 2 in Country 2 sell a homogeneous good to the rest of the world. They face an inverse demand curve of

$$p = a - b(q_1 + q_2), \tag{18A.1}$$

where a and b are positive constants, q_1 is the output of Firm 1 in Country 1 and q_2 is the output of Firm 2 in Country 2. Each firm has a constant marginal cost of production, m. In the absence of government intervention, the firms play Nash in quantities.

The government of Country 1 subsidizes Firm 1 at s per unit. Firm 1's profit is

$$\pi_1 = pq_1 - mq_1 + sq_1 = [a - b(q_1 + q_2)]q_1 - mq_1 + sq_1, \tag{18A.2}$$

where the second equality is obtained by substituting for p using Equation 18A.1. No subsidy is provided in Country 2, so Firm 2's profit is

$$\pi_2 = [a - b(q_1 + q_2)]q_2 - mq_2. \tag{18A.3}$$

Firm 1's Cournot best-response function is determined by differentiating π_1 in Equation 18A.2 with respect to q_1 and setting this expression equal to zero. After rearranging terms, this condition is

$$q_1 = (a - m + s - bq_2)/(2b). \tag{18A.4}$$

Similarly, Firm 2's best-response function is

$$q_2 = (a - m - bq_1)/(2b). \tag{18A.5}$$

The Nash-in-quantities equilibrium is obtained by solving Equations 18A.4 and 18A.5 simultaneously for q_1 and q_2 (the intersection of these two best-response functions):

$$q_1(s) = (a - m + 2s)/(3b), \tag{18A.6}$$

$$q_2(s) = (a - m - s)/(3b). \tag{18A.7}$$

[To find the presubsidy, Cournot equilibrium, set $s = 0$ in Equations 18A.6 and 18A.7.] For the particular values used in the chapter, $a = 46$, $b = 1$, and $m = 10$, $q_1(s) = 12 + 2s/3$ and $q_2(s) = 12 - s/3$. As s increases, q_1 increases and q_2 falls.

The government in Country 1 sets s to maximize its welfare, which is π_1 minus the subsidy, sq_1 (this transfer is a gain to the firm that is offset by an equal loss to the government). In choosing s, Country 1 must take into account the firms' equilibrium response to s, which is given in Equations 18A.6 and 18A.7. Thus, Country 1's problem is

$$\begin{aligned} \max_s \pi_1 - sq_1(s) &= (a - b[q_1(s) + q_2(s)] - m)q_1(s) \\ &= (a - m - s)(a - m + 2s)/(9b) \end{aligned} \tag{18A.8}$$

Setting the derivative of Equation 18A.8 with respect to s equal to zero, we find that the net-welfare-maximizing $s = (a - m)/4$. For our particular values, $s = 9$. Substituting this value into Equation 18A.6, we find that Firm 1 produces $q_1 = 18$. This solution is the same one we would obtain if Firm 1 could commit first and act like a Stackelberg leader.

CHAPTER 19

Antitrust Laws and Policy

The first thing we do, let's kill all the lawyers. —*William Shakespeare*

The U.S. government uses **antitrust laws** to limit the market power exercised by firms and to control how firms compete with each other. The antitrust laws do not make monopoly illegal, but they control how firms attain and maintain their market power. This chapter describes the antitrust laws and how they affect efficiency. It is not intended as a complete course in antitrust law; it is designed to provide an overview of the most important developments and issues in federal antitrust policy.[1]

The chapter first describes the major antitrust statutes and their major objectives. As with most laws, a literal reading of the statutes does not convey how the laws have been applied. Our discussion of court decisions concentrates on market power, which is a central focus of the antitrust laws.

The chapter then examines the two major areas of antitrust law applications. The first deals with agreements among competitors, such as price-fixing agreements and agreements to merge. The second deals with the actions of a single firm that may harm rivals. These actions involve strategic behavior such as predatory pricing, vertical relationships among firms, and tie-in sales. Next, the chapter reviews the antitrust doctrines on price discrimination. The chapter concludes with an overall economic assessment of the effect of the major antitrust doctrines on firm organization.

[1]See Posner and Easterbrook (1980), Posner (1976a), Bork (1978), Areeda and Turner (1978, 1980), and Areeda (1986) for more detailed examinations of antitrust issues. The presentation and analysis of the cases in this chapter rely heavily on Posner and Easterbrook (1980) and its supplements. Although states have antitrust laws, we concentrate on federal laws.

The seven main points we make in this chapter are

1. The interpretation of U.S. antitrust laws varies over time.
2. Antitrust laws should promote efficiency.
3. Monopoly is not prohibited, but certain activities that could lead to a firm's acquiring or exercising monopoly power are banned.
4. Price fixing is generally prohibited.
5. Certain agreements among competitors, vertical relations between firms, and various other strategic acts may increase or decrease welfare; hence, they should be evaluated on a case-by-case basis.
6. A few antitrust laws, such as the prohibition on price discrimination that allegedly reduces competition among customers, almost always lower welfare.
7. Prohibiting certain activities and not others can lead to inefficient organizations of firms.

The Antitrust Laws and Their Purposes

The antitrust laws are simple to state but have proved difficult to apply. Indeed, the Supreme Court has changed its interpretation of these laws several times. This section describes the laws, their enforcement, and their purposes. It explains who can sue under the antitrust laws and how damages are paid.

Antitrust Statutes

The three major statutes governing antitrust policy are the Sherman Act (passed in 1890), the Clayton Act (1914), and the Federal Trade Commission Act (1914). Additions, deletions, and amendments to these statutes have been made over the years.

Even prior to the passage of the Sherman Act, however, legal principles governed competition among firms. Under the common law (the precedents based on court decisions in the absence of explicit statutes), price-fixing among firms, though not illegal, was unenforceable: A court would not enforce a contract in which one firm agreed with a competitor to fix prices. Similarly, agreements not to compete that accompanied the sale of a business or an employment relationship were also unenforceable if they were judged "unreasonable." Agreements among workers either to fix wages or to strike were often held to violate the law. Practices by which firms attempted to exclude competitors (for example, predatory pricing) were not considered to violate the law unless accompanied by additional illegal actions such as fraud (Posner and Easterbrook 1980, 18).

The antitrust statutes were passed at a time of great upheaval in American industry. Around 1890, when the Sherman Act was passed, large firms became increasingly common with the birth of the modern American corporation and the creation of very large firms through mergers and scale economies. Adjusting for the size of the economy, the merger wave in the 1890s and early 1900s was the largest in our history (Chapter 2).

The *Sherman Act*, the first federal antitrust legislation, was, in part, a response to these changes in the U.S. economy. Section 1 of the Sherman Act states that

> every contract, combination in the form of trust or otherwise, or conspiracy, in restraint of trade or commerce among the several States, or with foreign nations, is declared to be illegal. . . .

That is, Section 1 forbids explicit cartels.

Section 2 states that

> every person who shall monopolize or attempt to monopolize, or combine or conspire with any other person or persons, to monopolize any part of the trade or commerce among the several States, or with foreign nations, shall be deemed guilty of a felony. . . .

Although one might read Section 2 as prohibiting monopoly, courts have interpreted it differently. As explained later, it is not a crime to be a monopoly as long as the monopoly does not commit "bad acts."

The courts' interpretation of the Sherman Act left doubt as to whether the Act prohibited certain industry behavior. As a result, in 1914, legislators passed additional antitrust legislation: the Clayton Act and the Federal Trade Commission Act. The *Clayton Act* is directed primarily against four specific practices. Section 2 of the Clayton Act (amended in 1936 by the Robinson-Patman Act) prevents price discrimination that lessens competition. Section 3 prohibits the use of tie-ins and exclusive dealing when the result is to lessen competition. Section 7 (amended in 1950 by the Celler-Kefauver Act) prohibits mergers that reduce competition. Section 8 deals with the creation of interlocking directorates among competing firms (that is, the control of competing firms by interrelated boards of directors). The Clayton Act also allows an injured party to recover **treble damages** (three times actual damages) plus attorneys' fees.[2]

The *Federal Trade Commission Act* created a new government agency, the Federal Trade Commission (FTC), which enforces antitrust laws and adjudicates disputes under the antitrust laws under the Federal Trade Commission Act in addition to other activities. The main antitrust provision of the FTC Act is Section 5, which prohibits "unfair" methods of competition. The FTC's other main responsibilities include consumer protection and the prevention of deceptive advertising.

It is common for an antitrust complaint to list violations of several of the antitrust statutes simultaneously. So, for example, an antitrust complaint regarding tie-in sales could list violations of both the Sherman Act and the Clayton Act.

Enforcement

Both the FTC and the U.S. Department of Justice (Justice Department) are responsible for administering the antitrust laws. A suit brought by the Justice Department is adjudicated in federal court, whereas an action brought by the FTC is heard and decided by an administrative law judge at the FTC and then reviewed by the Federal

[2] A profit-maximizing firm has an incentive to violate antitrust laws if the expected punishment is less than the expected gain. If the probability of being caught is less than one (certainty), a fine equal to the damage caused may not discourage this activity. Thus, larger (treble) damages are used. See, however, Salant (1987), who argues that trebling damages may have undesirable effects if buyers anticipate receiving damage awards.

Trade Commissioners.[3] After the FTC has completed its proceedings, defendants can appeal adverse decisions to the federal courts.

An action brought by the FTC can result in a *cease and desist* order, which prohibits specific acts. A suit brought by the Department of Justice can result in a similar type of order, an *injunction.* The Department of Justice can also bring a criminal suit, which may result in criminal fines or jail sentences. Aside from its enforcement responsibilities, the Department of Justice can sue to recover the cost of the suit plus the damages that arise when the U.S. government is a victim of an antitrust offense. A private individual or firm can bring an antitrust suit and, if victorious, receive treble damages plus the cost of the suit including attorneys' fees. Such private litigation comprises a significant share of antitrust litigation (White 1989).

Goals of the Antitrust Laws

Most economists believe the antitrust laws *should* have the very simple goal of promoting efficiency. That is, they should prevent practices or amalgamations of firms that would harm society through the exercise of market power.

Some analysts, however, argue that the actual objective of these laws is not efficiency, and that these laws were passed to help certain groups and harm others. For example, some argue that the antitrust laws are designed to help small firms that compete with large firms, whether or not efficiency is increased. In particular, the antitrust laws against price discrimination were passed in response to political lobbying by many small firms that were complaining of larger firms' ability to secure lower prices in their purchases of supplies (Ross 1984).

A group of firms that obtains a general exemption from the antitrust laws can reduce competition and thereby benefit. Many groups have succeeded in obtaining exemptions from the antitrust laws. Workers who unionize in order to raise their wages are specifically exempted from the antitrust laws, as are certain agricultural groups and export associations. Although certain regulated industries such as insurance have obtained antitrust exemptions, regulated industries are generally subject to the antitrust laws. Moreover, as Chapter 20 shows, legislators often try to protect certain groups from competition that is legal under the antitrust laws. It is legal for firms to attempt to influence legislation in order to protect themselves from competition and insulate themselves from antitrust liability (but see Example 19.1).[4]

[3]The FTC can also bring an action in federal court to obtain a preliminary injunction preventing consummation of a merger.

[4]This lobbying is protected by what is called the Noerr-Pennington doctrine: *Eastern Railroad Presidents Conference v. Noerr Motor Freight, Inc.*, 365 U.S. 127 (1961) and *United Mine Workers of America v. Pennington*, 381 U.S. 637 (1965). We cite cases primarily from the U.S. Reporter (U.S.), Federal Reporter (F.2d), and the Supreme Court Reporter (S. Ct.), which are standard legal references. For example, the Pennington citation appears in vol. 381 of the U.S. Reporter starting at page 637, and that case was decided by the Supreme Court in 1965. A case is first decided in a District Court. It can then be appealed to the Court of Appeals in the relevant region (called a Circuit Court) and after that to the Supreme Court.

EXAMPLE 19.1

Using the Government to Create Market Power: Misuse of the Orange Book

Under the Noerr-Pennington doctrine, firms have the right to petition the government for legislation and then to take advantage of that legislation. That is, a firm has the legal right to lobby for legislation that will make it difficult for others to compete with it, even though such legislation will harm consumers. Recently, the Federal Trade Commission (FTC) has succeeded in reining in firms' ability to misuse government might to create market power.

The FTC has paid particular attention to misuses related to drug approvals. If a firm wishes to make a generic version of a branded drug, it can submit an abbreviated application for a new drug and rely on previous testing of the branded drug in order to obtain approval from the Food and Drug Administration (FDA). The FDA asks makers of branded drugs to list in its "Orange Book" any patents that still apply to their drugs. The FDA will grant an automatic 30-month delay to the introduction of a generic drug that the manufacturer of a branded drug claims violates a patent listed in the "Orange Book." The FDA does not investigate whether the patents listed in its Orange Book are in fact valid. Therefore, it is possible for the manufacturer of a branded drug to list a patent that is invalid or inapplicable and to use it to delay the introduction of a generic rival.

The FTC claimed that Bristol-Myers misused FDA procedures to prevent competition from generic rivals for three of its best-selling drugs, with the result that consumers for these anxiety-preventing and cancer treatment drugs were deprived of generic competition that commonly drives down drug prices by more than 50 percent. The FTC claimed that, among other things, Bristol-Myers filed a false patent to block entry, and that it acquired another patent for the purpose of preventing generic entry. The combined sales of the drugs that Bristol-Myers sought to protect exceeded $1.5 billion in the year before generics entered. The FTC and Bristol-Myers settled the case with Bristol-Myers agreeing to restrictions on its conduct.

Source: John Wilke, "Bristol-Myers Settles Patent-Law Abuse," *Wall Street Journal*, March 10, 2003.

The view that the guiding principle of the antitrust laws should be efficiency, rather than the taking of resources from one group and granting them to another, has gained increasing acceptance among legal and academic scholars. One appeal of such a simple proposition is that it provides a clearer guide as to what antitrust policy should be than does the alternative view of helping "deserving" groups.

Even if one accepts the proposition that the goal of the antitrust laws is to promote efficiency, economists often have difficulty determining which practices result in inefficient behavior. For example, suppose that two firms merge and the resulting reduction in competition causes price to rise. That sounds bad. However, suppose that, as a result of the merger, the merged firm develops a new and better product or provides the same product but offers better services or develops a lower-cost method of production than before. That sounds good. Should the antitrust laws ban all mergers if they significantly eliminate competition, or should they also pay attention to the potential efficiency gains and balance the two?

To see how the trade-off between an increased price and increased efficiency in other dimensions can be compared, suppose that, as a result of a merger, a firm raises its price from \$1 to \$1.10 because of the elimination of competition, which causes a deadweight loss (a triangle in Figure 19.1). Suppose that the merger also enables the firm to operate more efficiently and lower its constant marginal cost from \$1 to \$0.90, which results in a greater productive efficiency (a rectangle in Figure 19.1).

If the triangular area representing the deadweight loss from the price increase is smaller than the rectangular area of efficiency gain, the merger is, on balance, good for society. The relative size of these two areas depends on the particular circumstances. The larger the quantity sold in the marketplace, the more important the efficiency gains, and the larger the area of the rectangle compared to the triangle. Even small reductions in costs per unit can result in efficiency gains that swamp deadweight loss in importance.[5]

For example, suppose that the initial quantity is 100 units (initial equilibrium point F), and the postmerger quantity is 90 (equilibrium point E). Because the efficiency savings are 10¢ per unit, the efficiency gains are \$9. The deadweight loss from the price increase is approximately 50¢ ($= -1/2 \times 10¢ \times [-10] \cong -1/2 \Delta p \Delta Q$). Thus, the efficiency gains outweigh the deadweight loss.

These types of calculations can be complicated, and it is a matter of debate whether courts should be charged with making such calculations in deciding the legality of a merger (Williamson 1968–69). The current policy statement of the Department of Justice and the Federal Trade Commission, the *Horizontal Merger Guidelines*, explicitly recognizes the importance of efficiency gains in evaluating mergers. However, these guidelines suggest in general that a merger would be challenged if it has an anticompetitive effect (a price increase) even if there is an offsetting efficiency gain.

Most other antitrust authorities also forbid mergers that raise price even if total efficiency (producer surplus plus consumer surplus) rises. Two notable exceptions are Australia and New Zealand, countries that rely heavily on international trade and for which efficient export industries are a key to economic prosperity. Lyons (2002) shows how a merger standard that prohibits efficiency-enhancing mergers that increase price can lead to greater efficiency than one that allows mergers as long as the merger increases efficiency. The reason is that if a firm is prevented from undertaking one efficiency-enhancing merger (a merger in which price rises), it may engage in another

[5]An efficiency gain, which depends on the total quantity produced, tends to swamp the deadweight loss, which depends on the restriction in output resulting from the merger if the output restriction is a small percentage of the total quantity produced. Notice that Figure 19.1 is based on the assumption that the price is initially set competitively. Were the price initially set higher, the deadweight loss would be a trapezoid comprising a triangle plus a rectangle whose width is 10 units and its height equals the initial gap between price and marginal cost.

FIGURE 19.1 Production Efficiency vs. Market Power Harm

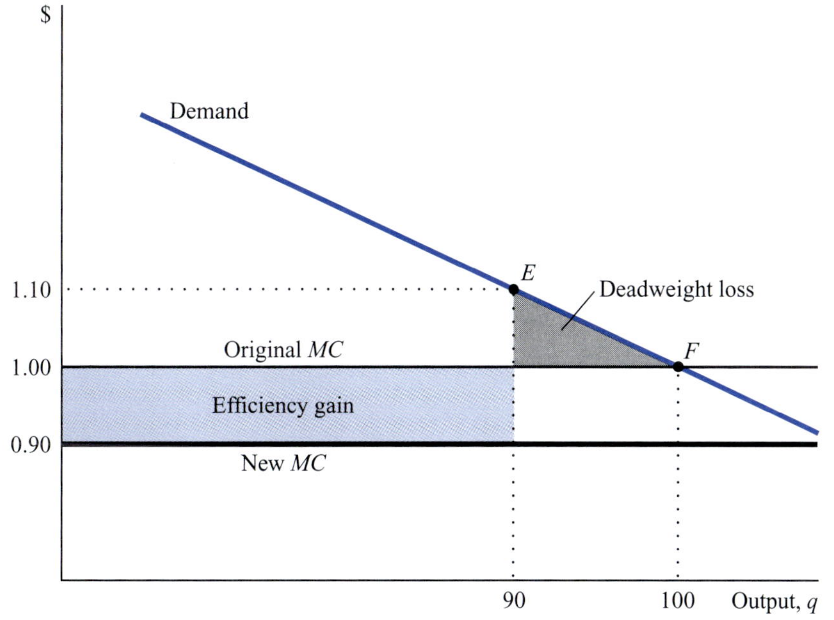

merger that ultimately creates greater efficiency for society (even though profit to the merging firm will be lower).

Requiring courts to apply sophisticated economic analyses to evaluate behavior may be unrealistic. Moreover, the courts must often deal with economic problems that economists have not yet analyzed. Courts don't have the luxury of taking as much time as necessary to solve a problem. Still, it is hard to argue that economic knowledge should be ignored. Use of economics in antitrust proceedings has increased worldwide. As a result, litigation is more complicated because economic analysis can now be the centerpiece of a case, and different countries can have conflicting analyses. (See Example 19.2.)

Who May Sue?

Individuals and firms, in addition to the Department of Justice and the FTC, can bring antitrust suits. Deciding who has legal standing, which is the right to bring a suit, is complicated. Only a party that suffers an injury that the antitrust laws were designed to prevent is permitted to sue. For example, suppose that if two firms merge, they will become very efficient and reduce price. Rival firms would be harmed by the merger, yet they have no legal standing to sue to block the merger under the antitrust laws because the goal of the antitrust laws is to generate low prices to consumers.[6]

---

[6] *Brunswick Corp. v. Pueblo Bowl-O-Mat, Inc.*, 429 U.S. 477 (1977) and *Cargill Inc. v. Monfort of Colorado*, 197 S. Ct. 484 (1986).

EXAMPLE 19.2

Conflict Between European and U.S. Antitrust Authorities: GE-Honeywell

In October 2000, General Electric (GE) announced plans to merge with Honeywell. GE manufactures many products, including aircraft engines for commercial aircraft. Honeywell does not produce aircraft engines, but does make products used in aviation such as weather radar, engine accessories, braking equipment, aircraft lighting, and environmental control systems. Thus, the merger would not involve both firms producing the same product or raise vertical supply relations issues because the merging firms manufactured only complementary products. How then could this conglomerate merger present an antitrust issue?

As we saw in Chapter 11, when a single firm prices two complementary products, it takes into account that lowering the price on one product will stimulate demand for the other. This demand effect creates an incentive for the firm to set lower prices for both products than would be set if each product were sold by a different firm. Thus, one should expect lower prices and consumer benefits from the GE-Honeywell merger due to more efficient pricing. Using this reasoning, U.S. antitrust authorities did not challenge the merger.

Because GE and Honeywell have large worldwide sales, their merger also fell under the scrutiny of European antitrust authorities. European authorities disagreed with U.S. authorities and prevented the merger in July 2001. The European authorities reasoned that, because the combined firm would have an incentive to lower prices, it would "dominate" the market, and hence the merger should be prevented. This convoluted reasoning is a throwback to earlier U.S. antitrust history when regulators viewed the creation of large, efficient firms as undesirable because it would drive less efficient rivals out of business even though the greater efficiency would benefit consumers. Most economists would argue that the protection of competition, not competitors, should be the focus of antitrust law.

This failed merger and the conflict among antitrust authorities has spawned efforts to harmonize antitrust enforcement and standards. Such harmonization is one of the goals of the International Competition Network, a recently formed organization comprising all major antitrust authorities. Preventing foreign antitrust authorities from repeating past mistakes of U.S. antitrust policy would be a major contribution of this organization.

Source: Nalebuff (2004) in Kwoka and White (2004).

Suppose that several manufacturing firms engage in a conspiracy to raise prices and that they sell their products to a retail department store, which then sells them to final consumers. The retail department store is not engaged in any conspiracy and simply applies the usual retail markup to the price it is charged. Who should be allowed to sue the manufacturers who are engaged in the conspiracy? The department stores, which are direct purchasers from the conspiring parties, certainly have the right to sue. Do final consumers (indirect purchasers) have a right to sue? It would be double counting to allow both consumers and retailers to collect damages from the same overcharge. In *Illinois Brick*, the Court limited the right of indirect purchasers to sue.[7] One possible justification for this decision is the difficulty of determining all of the potential indirect and direct parties who would be entitled to sue and to obtain duplicative damages for the same price overcharge from the plaintiffs (Landes and Posner 1979).

Suppose that individual consumers are the direct purchasers of a product from firms that have engaged in a conspiracy. Would an individual purchaser have the incentive to sue if all that could be recovered was the price overcharge on the product, trebled, plus attorneys' fees? Usually no. In an effort to create greater incentives to bring suits, courts allow attorneys to file class-action suits on behalf of all consumers. Attorneys are entitled to legal fees, and this provides an incentive for them to bring such suits. Of course, attorneys have an incentive to bring too many such cases if they are overcompensated.

Economic Theory of Damages

Economists use their theories to recommend the optimal amount of damages that a guilty defendant should pay. Although economic theory is widely used to determine antitrust liability, it is less commonly used to determine optimal damages.

The economic theory of damages starts from the proposition that the purpose of damages is to deter inefficient activity but not to be so burdensome as to deter efficient activity. For example, suppose that any time a firm was convicted of illegally conspiring with another firm, the firms' managers were executed. As will be shown, it is not so easy to determine when an agreement among firms is an illegal one. If the penalty were death (or otherwise extremely harsh), many firms might be dissuaded from activity that could be perfectly lawful and beneficial, such as the creation of a trade association that sets product safety standards. The optimal penalty is one that balances the beneficial and the nonbeneficial aspects of deterrence.

An optimal penalty reduces the incentive to engage in illegal activity. For example, suppose that, if a group of firms conspire, they can raise their profits by \$100. If this conspiracy could be detected with certainty and at no cost by enforcement officials, then a penalty of \$100 would suffice to deter the activity. Of course, deterrence is not perfect, and it takes resources to discover illegal activity. Because the firms know that they may not be caught, a penalty higher than \$100 may be necessary to deter cartel behavior. For example, suppose that price-fixing conspiracies are detected in only one-third of all cases. Then, as a first approximation, charging a penalty of \$300 should be enough to deter the illegal activity.[8]

An additional complication arises with an international cartel. If the purpose of a damages award is to deter, then the damages should deprive the cartel of its full profits.

[7] *Illinois Brick Company v. Illinois,* 431 U.S. 720 (1977). The word *court* spelled with a capital *C* refers to the Supreme Court of the United States.

[8] For more on optimal damages in antitrust cases, see Landes (1983) and White (1989). According to Landes, the optimal penalty equals the harm the firms impose on others, adjusted for the probability of detection.

But if some foreign country does not have an antitrust law, the cartel can earn excessive profits in that country unless foreign consumers can sue for damages in the United States or other countries with antitrust laws. The possibility of bringing suit in another country raises complicated jurisdictional issues that remain unsettled.[9]

Suppose that a group of firms is convicted of violating the antitrust laws. How should the penalties be apportioned among the firms? Should one defendant pay all of the damages, or should there be some sharing rule? In particular, suppose that of the two defendants to a lawsuit, one defendant settles with the plaintiff (for example, pays the plaintiff $100 to be dismissed from the lawsuit) before the case goes to trial. At the trial, the damage award to the plaintiff is several times the amount of the settlement. Should the remaining defendant be forced to pay the entire amount? The Court has ruled that an antitrust defendant is not entitled to **contribution**, which is a payment to a guilty defendant from other culpable parties.[10] This decision has been criticized on the grounds that it appears unfair. However, the incentive to settle will be greatest if, once the settlement is achieved, no further liability can be assumed, and therefore a large damage award can be avoided. Thus, this rule greatly increases the incentive to settle, with a resulting savings in litigation costs (Easterbrook, Landes, and Posner 1980).

The Use of U.S. Antitrust Laws

U.S. antitrust laws have been used increasingly to prosecute price-fixers, and penalties have increased.[11] From 1890 through 1974, the Justice Department brought 1,000 civil and 723 criminal cases (Posner 1976, 25). The penalty in a criminal case can be a jail sentence, but the penalty in a civil case cannot. Since World War II, Democratic and Republican administrations have brought cases at roughly the same rate (Posner 1970, 411–12). The Department of Justice wins most of the cases it brings. In every five-year period since 1910 studied by Posner (1970, 381–82), the Department won at least 64% of all its cases; since 1925 it has won at least 78%; and since 1955 it has won at least 85%.[12]

The Department of Justice loses few criminal cases (Posner 1970). Since 1890, 57% of the cases have been disposed of on *nolo contendere* ("no contest") pleas, 21% on other convictions, and only 22% resulted in acquittals and dismissals. The recent

---

[9]See *S.A. Emparagran, et al. v. F. Hoffman-La Roche, Ltd. et al.*, 315 F.3d 338 (D.C. Circuit, 2003). The case is before the Supreme Court in 2004.

[10]*Texas Industries, Inc. v. Radcliff Materials, Inc.*, 451 U.S. 630 (1981).

[11]Cases brought by states under their own antitrust laws were extremely infrequent prior to the 1970s. In recent years, a few states have made increasing use of their antitrust laws, but state cases are still uncommon.

[12]Posner (1970, 384) also shows that the Department of Justice has won 74% of its cases before the Supreme Court, the Federal Trade Commission has won 75%, and private claimants have won 63%. Averaged across the three groups, 70% of these cases before the Supreme Court were won by the plaintiffs.

conviction rates have been even higher (Snyder 1990). During the early 1990s, the conviction rates exceeded 90%. These high success rates may indicate that the Department only tries sure cases or that defendants plead *nolo contendere* and pay small fines (avoiding the costs of long court battles and the risks of losing). One advantage of a *nolo contendere* plea for a defendant in a government case is that it does not provide evidence of collusion that can be used subsequently in a private antitrust action seeking treble damages.

The penalties imposed by the federal antitrust laws have historically been relatively small. The FTC's only remedy is an injunction called a *cease-and-desist order,* which prohibits the behavior but does not penalize the firm for engaging in it. The maximum fine under the original Sherman Act was $5,000 and the maximum prison sentence was one year. The maximum fines were increased to $50,000 in 1955. In 1974, they were increased to $100,000 for individuals and $1 million for corporations. In the 1950–1959 period, the fines in the Justice Department's cases averaged $40,000 (0.08% of the sales involved in the conspiracy), whereas from 1960 to 1969 they averaged $131,000 or 0.21% of the sales involved in the conspiracy (Posner 1970, 1976). Gallo et al. (1994) estimate that fines averaged 1% of the present value of conspiracy sales from 1985 to 1993. The maximum fines are currently $10 million for a corporation and $350,000 for an individual. However, the fines can be increased up to twice the violator's gain or twice the victims' loss (Berkman 1997). Beginning in 1997, fines levied on individual firms and total fines across all firms increased enormously. The Department of Justice collected total criminal fines of less than $50 million per year between 1990 and 1996. However, from 1997 to 1999, total fines rose from $205 million to over $900 million per year, but they declined to $102.5 million in 2002, and to $64.2 million in 2003. The largest fines on individual firms were $500 million for Hoffman-La Roche and $225 million for BASF (1999 vitamin price-fixing case); $135 million for SGL Carbon, $134 million for Mitsubishi, and $110 million for UCAR Carbon (1999, 2001, and 1998 cases, respectively, concerning the fixing of the price of graphite electrodes used in steel furnaces); and $100 million for Archer Daniels Midland (1997 lysine and citric acid price-fixing case).[13] In addition to fines, a guilty firm must recompense private individuals, firms, and government bodies who prove in court that they were damaged from the price-fixing conspiracy. Individuals and firms are entitled to treble damages plus attorneys' fees, and the U.S. government receives damages plus attorneys' fees.

Prison sentences are rare in federal antitrust cases. There were none during the period from 1890 to 1909. From 1910 to 1974, there were 33 cases in which a prison sentence was imposed, roughly one every other year (Posner 1976, 33). Prior to 1925, most of those jailed were union organizers and officers. Until after World War II, most prison sentences for price fixing were restricted to cases involving violence. The maximum jail sentence was increased to three years in 1974. The average prison term over the period from 1955 to 1993 was about three months (Gallo et al. 1994).

[13]U.S. Department of Justice, "Sherman Act Violations Yielding a Fine of $10 Million or More," January 23, 2003: **www.usdoj.gov/atr/public/criminal/202532.htm.**

In 2002, of the 36 individuals sentenced in antitrust cases, 19 were sentenced to incarceration time for a cumulative total of 10,501 days (16 individuals were sentenced to other confinement such as house arrest or a halfway house for a total of 3,607 days).

Private Litigation

Private actions brought by individuals or firms harmed by anticompetitive behavior were rare for price-fixing cases until the electrical conspiracy of the early 1960s (see Example 5.1). In the next two decades, private actions, including class-action suits, increased substantially. These private actions, which often follow federal suits, can substantially increase the cost of conspiracy, because treble damages plus attorneys' fees may be collected.[14] For the period from 1937 to 1954, there was an average of 104 private cases per year; for the period from 1955 to 1959, the average increased to 229 cases per year. From 1960 to 1964, 1,919 cases were filed concerning electrical equipment, causing the yearly average to rise to 671 cases. For fiscal years ending June 30th, the number of private civil antitrust suits fell from 1,457 in 1980 to 1,100 in 1984 to 638 in 1989 (Salop and White 1986, Abere 1991).

Market Power and the Definition of Markets

The antitrust laws concentrate on controlling the creation and maintenance of market power. This section defines market power, discusses how to measure it, and points out that it is sometimes difficult to measure market power accurately. Some economists and lawyers argue that one should define a market and then calculate the market share of the firm under analysis as an approximation of its market power, where a high market share is interpreted as an indicator of market power. This section describes the principles that should be used to define a market and provides a background against which cases can be interpreted.

Market Power

A firm (or group of firms acting together) has market power if it is profitably able to charge a price above that which would prevail under competition, which is usually taken to be marginal cost. This ability to set price above marginal cost implicitly uses the model of perfect competition as a benchmark against which to measure the behavior of firms. If this definition is applied literally, probably every firm in the United States has at least a tiny bit of market power. The model of perfect competition is an extreme one that describes few, if any, actual industries. Therefore, presumably, when courts find that a firm has market power, they must mean the firm has a substantial

[14]According to Posner (1970, 372), in the period from 1956 to 1960, at least 278 private cases were preceded by a Department of Justice judgment, while in the period from 1961 to 1963, 880 cases followed such judgments.

amount of market power for some significant period of time. Unfortunately, the courts have not stated how much market power is needed. Does a price 5 percent above marginal cost for two years reflect substantial market power? Or 10 percent above for one year?

It is difficult to measure marginal cost and therefore difficult to measure the deviation between price and marginal cost, even if the courts stated how substantial a deviation must be to constitute significant market power. An alternative approach is to estimate the price elasticity of the residual demand (the market demand net of the quantity supplied by other firms) facing an individual firm (or group of firms). This elasticity of residual demand facing a firm summarizes the ability of a firm (or group of firms acting together) to exercise market power. The price-cost margin equals the negative of the inverse of the elasticity of demand (Chapter 4): $(p - MC)/p = -1/\epsilon$, where p is price, MC is marginal cost, and ϵ is the elasticity of residual demand.[15]

If the elasticity is large, the firm has little market power. Most empirical estimates of demand curves for individual firms selling branded products rarely find the absolute value of price elasticities to be higher than 5 to 10 (Telser 1972, 274–306). Using the price-cost margin formula, if the elasticity is -5, price is 25 percent above marginal cost; if the elasticity is -10, the price is 11 percent above marginal cost.

Whether a firm currently has market power is a much different question from whether, as a result of a merger, it could acquire and exercise *additional* market power. The first question, whether price is already elevated significantly above competitive levels, can be answered directly by comparing price and marginal cost or indirectly by looking at the elasticity of demand facing the firm. The second question, whether price will rise significantly above its current level as a result of the merger activity, can be answered directly by predicting how price will change or indirectly by predicting how the elasticity of demand facing the firm will change as a result of the merger.

For example, suppose a firm makes a differentiated product, Product A. The residual demand curve for A can be estimated as a function of the price of Product A and the price of another firm's substitute product, Product B. If the direct elasticity of A at current prices is very large, then the firm producing A has no market power. In a merger case, economists attempt to predict how the elasticity of each product will change as a result of the merger. For example, suppose the firms producing A and B want to merge. The merger between the firms will allow the merged firm to set prices jointly, and the analyst can calculate the resulting prices based on the demand curve facing the merged firm (Baker and Bresnahan 1985, Hausman et al. 1994). The

[15] In a static model, the elasticity of residual demand completely summarizes a firm's market power and determines its pricing. In a dynamic model, this simple relationship does not hold because the profit-maximizing price depends on the responses of consumers and firms over time. Moreover, in dynamic oligopoly models, the equilibrium depends on the game played by rivals. Another approach to measuring market power involves calculating the long-run rate of return. See Chapter 8 for a discussion of the caveats of using this approach.

merger increases market power if the postmerger prices are higher than the premerger ones.[16]

Sometimes economists cannot estimate a price elasticity accurately because the data are inadequate or unavailable. In an attempt to reach some workable solution to the problem of determining market power, analysts and the courts often define a market and then construct a measure of market share. If the market share of the firm (or firms) under analysis is high, the suggestion is that market power exists. In a merger case, the Justice Department or the FTC looks at whether there will be a significant increase in concentration as a result of the merger. There is no agreement as to exactly what share (or change in share) is "high," but many economists regard a share in the range of 30 to 50 percent as too low to indicate significant market power in an industry with a competitive fringe comprising the remainder of the market.

Market shares are imperfect indicators of market power, so additional analysis of the economic conditions is necessary before one can reach a conclusion about market power. For example, if entry is easy, then the industry pricing is severely constrained regardless of whether an existing firm has a large market share. Similarly, the presence of factors that make it difficult to maintain a cartel is relevant (Chapter 5).

Market Definition

In merger or other antitrust cases, economists are often called on to define a market. Were it not for these cases, it is doubtful whether such a large body of economic research would have developed on defining markets.

Alfred Marshall (1920, 324) defined a market as an area in which "prices of the same goods tend to equality with due allowance for transportation costs." Since Marshall's time, economists and lawyers have refined the definition of a market. A **market definition** specifies the competing products and geographic area in which competition occurs that determines the price for a given product. Clearly Coke and Pepsi are in the same market. But is Dr Pepper or Canada Dry Ginger Ale in that market? Is milk?

How the market is defined often determines the outcome of antitrust cases. For example, in determining whether to permit a merger, the government and the courts examine the market shares of firms, which are viewed as proxies for the firms' actual or potential market power. A firm's market share depends crucially on the market definition. Coke's share of its market will be much larger if the market is defined as colas than if it is defined as all soft drinks or all drinks. Example 19.3 discusses how the government applies the principles of market definition in its antitrust enforcement policy toward mergers.

[16]A merger simulation typically estimates demand curves; assumes that firms engage in a particular game (such as Bertrand); calculates marginal cost by using observed prices and estimated elasticities; and predicts new prices assuming that the merged firm coordinates pricing among the products it controls. See Example 7.5 and see Carlton (2003, 2004a) for a discussion and critique of this approach.

EXAMPLE 19.3 *The Merger Guidelines*

The government policy on the definition of markets is contained in the *Horizontal Merger Guidelines* that the Department of Justice and the Federal Trade Commission (FTC) issued in 1992. These *Merger Guidelines* set forth the principles that the government uses to define relevant economic markets in its enforcement of the antitrust laws regarding merger activity. These guidelines were slightly revised in 1997.

According to the *Merger Guidelines*, the government's first step in reviewing a proposed merger is to properly define the market. The *Merger Guidelines* specify that a market is the smallest group of products and the smallest geographical area such that a hypothetical monopoly of all those products in the area could raise price by a certain amount (for example, 5 or 10 percent) above any prevailing or likely future levels. One problem with this definition is that according to the definition, a small group of firms could constitute a market even though fringe firms existed that produced the identical product. Stigler and Sherwin (1985) raise other objections as well.

After defining the market, the *Merger Guidelines* require that the government determine whether the proposed merger will greatly increase concentration (and hence, presumably, market power). Concentration is measured using a Herfindahl-Hirschman Index (HHI), which is the sum of the squared market shares (expressed as percentages) of firms in the industry. The *Merger Guidelines* do not regard a merger between two firms as raising concerns about competition if the postmerger HHI in the industry is below 1000. If the postmerger HHI is between 1000 and 1800, the merger does raise concerns if the change in the HHI resulting from the merger is 100 points or more. If the industry's postmerger HHI is over 1800, the merger raises concerns about competition if the change in the HHI resulting from the merger is 50 points or more.

For example, suppose that an industry consists of four firms, each with a 25 percent market share, and two of the firms want to merge. The initial HHI is $2500 (= 25^2 + 25^2 + 25^2 + 25^2)$, and the postmerger HHI is 3750 $(= 50^2 + 25^2 + 25^2)$. Because the postmerger HHI exceeds 1800 and the change in the HHI exceeds 50, concerns about competition are raised according to the *Merger Guidelines.*

The application of the *Merger Guidelines* implicitly assumes that after a merger, the firms involved will be able to maintain their premerger market shares and the merged firm will enjoy a market share equal to the sum of the premerger shares of the firms that are merging. When this assumption is not reasonable, the analysis should be modified in order to properly reflect the merged firms' market share. The *Merger Guidelines* recognize that other factors (such as ease of entry) in addition to market concentration influence market behavior. Both the Department of Justice and the FTC consider those factors before deciding to challenge a merger.

The Extent of the Product Market. A proper definition of the product dimension of a market should include all those products that are close demand or supply substitutes.[17] Product B is a *demand substitute* for A if an increase in the price of A causes consumers to use more B instead. Product B is a *supply substitute* for A if, in response to an increase in the price of A, firms that are producing B switch some of their production facilities to the production of A.[18] In both cases, the presence of B significantly constrains the pricing of A, provided that an increase in the price of A would result in either a significant decline in the quantity of A consumed as consumers switch from A to B or a significant increase in the supply of A as firms switch production from B to A.

The degree of substitution between products depends on the current prices of the two products. For example, A and B may be highly substitutable at a high price for A, but not at a low price for A. Even a monopoly may raise its price sufficiently above competitive levels so that eventually it faces some competition from other products. Just because a monopolized product faces close demand substitutes at the monopoly price, it does *not* follow that the firm producing the product has no market power (though it may not be able to raise its price further). It is only if the substitution possibilities are so large as to generate a highly elastic residual demand that the monopoly has no significant market power. Because it is difficult to determine which products to include in the market definition, market shares may be only a crude indicator of market power.

The *Cellophane* case illustrates these difficulties in defining a market.[19] The Court investigated whether du Pont had market power in the pricing of cellophane. The Court reasoned that du Pont lacked market power because, at the current market prices, a user of cellophane had many substitutes, such as paper bags, and du Pont's share of the market including these substitutes was not large. There was also evidence, however, that price substantially exceeded marginal cost. Based on the foregoing discussion, it was an error to include other wrapping materials in the market definition because they did not prevent the exercise of market power and constrain the price of

---

[17]The relevant economic market is not necessarily the same as the *market* that a salesperson might refer to. Substantial confusion has sometimes resulted when market definition is based on memos written by marketing personnel. For that reason, some antitrust lawyers advise companies to instruct marketing personnel to avoid the use of the word *market* in memos.

[18]The relationship between the demand elasticity facing a firm and supply and demand substitutes can be illustrated using the model of a dominant firm facing a competitive fringe (see **www.aw-bc.com/carlton_perloff** "Dominant Firm and Competitive Fringe Model" and Landes and Posner 1981). One can derive that

$$\epsilon_d = \frac{Q}{Q_d}\epsilon - \frac{Q_f}{Q_d}\eta_f,$$

where ϵ_d is the residual demand elasticity facing the dominant firm, ϵ is the market demand elasticity, Q is the market quantity, Q_d is the quantity sold by the dominant firm, Q_f is the quantity supplied by the fringe, and η_f is the supply elasticity of the fringe. As the absolute value of ϵ increases (more demand substitutes) and as η_f increases (more supply substitutes), and as the dominant firm's share (Q_d/Q) falls, ϵ_d rises in absolute value and the dominant firm has less market power.

[19]*United States v. E.I. du Pont de Nemours & Co.*, 351 U.S. 377 (1956).

cellophane to competitive levels. If, however, instead of asking whether du Pont had market power, the Court had investigated whether a proposed merger would raise the cellophane price, its market definition might have been appropriate.

In the *Brown Shoe* case, the Supreme Court articulated a laundry list of criteria that can be used to define markets.[20] It said: "The boundaries of such a submarket may be determined by examining such practical indicia as industry or public recognition of the submarket as a separate economic entity, the product's peculiar characteristics and uses, unique production facilities, distinct customers, distinct prices, sensitivity to price changes, and specialized vendors." The application of this laundry list of criteria has not led to precision in defining a market for antitrust purposes.[21]

Numerous methods are used to identify the good substitutes for a particular product. One is to interview producers in the industry who presumably know both their customers and their potential competitors from other industries.

If Products A and B are in the same economic market, then their prices should tend to move closely together. Therefore, a reasonable *first* step in defining economic markets is to examine the price correlations (a statistical measure of how closely prices move together) among different products that are under consideration for inclusion in the same product market.[22]

Although no standard levels of correlation have been established to determine if two products are in the same market, the available data may often be used to develop such standards. For example, suppose that everybody agrees that two different types of plastic materials are in the same economic market. One could compute the correlation between their prices and use it as a benchmark to determine whether some third plastic material belongs in the same economic market with the other two products.

The direct price elasticity—*not* the cross-elasticity of demand—determines market power. The **cross-elasticity of demand** is the percentage change in quantity demanded in response to a 1 percent change in the price of another product. There is a lot of discussion in court decisions as to the importance of cross-elasticity of demand in defining markets. Courts often use the term loosely to indicate that products are substitutes. There is a relationship between cross-elasticity and direct elasticity,

[20]*Brown Shoe Company v. United States,* 370 U.S. 294 (1962).

[21]The courts, in addition to defining economic markets, have occasionally attempted to define economic *submarkets* that are contained within an economic market. Presumably, competition between two products in the same economic market is more intense if the two products also belong to the same submarket. The distinction between *market* and *submarket* is not very useful, and we will not refer to it or even attempt to give an economic definition of the term *submarket.*

[22]Price correlations are a useful first step in defining markets; however, high correlations need not always indicate that two products are in the same market. For example, dissimilar products made from similar inputs may have high price correlations. Similarly, low correlations need not always indicate that products are not in the same market, provided large quantity shifts accompany the relative price shifts. If the price of one product rises, but the price of a good substitute does not, the quantity demanded of the first product sharply declines.

however. All else the same, the larger a cross-elasticity of demand, the larger in absolute value is the direct elasticity of demand.[23]

To intelligently discuss a cross-elasticity, one must specify whether it is the cross-elasticity of Product A with respect to the price of Product B or vice versa. Although these two different cross-elasticities are usually not distinguished in court decisions, they are not equal in general.[24] The relevant cross-elasticity of demand when the question is whether the market for Product A should include Product B is the cross-elasticity of demand for Product A with respect to the price of Product B.

The Extent of the Geographic Market. The geographic limit of a market is determined by answering the question of whether an increase in price in one location substantially affects the price in another. If so, then both locations are in the same market. The process of determining these limits proceeds along the same lines as discussed for the product market definition and involves similar reasoning. For example, consider the consumption of oranges in Chicago. Oranges are shipped to Chicago from outside the city limits. The geographic areas that ship to Chicago (or could profitably do so if price rose slightly) are in the same economic market as Chicago because they contain orange producers whose output significantly influences the price of oranges in Chicago. Notice that these same orange producers could also significantly affect the price of oranges in Milwaukee. Thus, Milwaukee and Chicago could be in the same economic market, and the price of oranges in Chicago would generally be closely related to the price of oranges in Milwaukee.[25]

Cooperation Among Competitors

This section explores the restrictions that the antitrust laws place on cooperation among competitors. We first examine explicit agreements to set price or output and then explicit agreements that lead to new products being produced, as well as informa-

[23]This result follows because the sum of the direct elasticity plus all cross-elasticities of demand equals 0. Let the cross-elasticity of demand of Product A with respect to the price of B be $\epsilon_{AB} \equiv (\partial Q_A/\partial p_B)(p_B/Q_A)$, where Q_A is the (income-compensated) demand for A, and p_B is the price of *B*. Then, $0 = \epsilon_{AA} + \sum_B \epsilon_{AB}$, where ϵ_{AA} is the own (direct) price elasticity of demand for product A (Henderson and Quandt 1980, 31–33). The cross-elasticity of demand is positive for substitutes, and the direct price elasticity is negative. The direct elasticity can be large even if no individual cross-elasticity is large.

[24]From demand theory, $\partial Q_A/\partial p_B = \partial Q_B/\partial p_A$. This last relationship does not imply that the cross-elasticities of demand (defined in the previous footnote) ϵ_{AB} and ϵ_{BA} are equal (Henderson and Quandt 1980, 30).

[25]See Carlton (2003, 2004a), Landes and Posner (1981), Scheffman and Spiller (1987), and Stigler and Sherwin (1985) for further analysis of market definition and its use in antitrust cases.

tion sharing among rivals. We then analyze oligopoly behavior in which firms behave similarly, though not as a result of explicit agreements. Finally, we examine mergers among competitors.

Price-Fixing and Output Agreements

The Court's views on price-fixing and output agreements are that an agreement whose sole purpose is to eliminate competition and raise prices above competitive levels—that is, a "naked" agreement to eliminate competition—is illegal. No inquiry as to the reasonableness of the price set is necessary to reach the conclusion that the agreement violates the law. When no additional inquiry is necessary to analyze the facts of a situation in order to determine the legality of the conduct, the conduct is said to be *per se* illegal. Therefore, it is often said that price-fixing and output-fixing agreements are per se violations of the antitrust laws.[26] Example 19.4 discusses the approach that other countries have taken toward such agreements among competitors.

Soon after the passage of the Sherman Act, the courts considered two cases of firms that cooperatively set prices and allocated customers. In *Trans-Missouri Freight Association,* a group of competing railroads entered into agreements about what rates to charge.[27] The railroads claimed that the rate agreements resulted in reasonable rates that prevented ruinous competition. The Court rejected these arguments and instead ruled that "the claim that the Company has the right to charge reasonable rates and that therefore it has the right to enter into a combination with competing roads to maintain such rates cannot be admitted. . . . Competition will itself bring charges down to what may be reasonable. . . ."

After the decision limiting their ability to fix rates, railroads continued to push for the ability to set their rates and avoid competition. They were ultimately allowed to do so by legislation. The Staggers Act of 1980 eliminated many of the restrictions on competition. Apparently as a result, many railroad mergers followed.

Considered at almost the same time as *Trans-Missouri,* the *Addyston Pipe* case also involved price fixing.[28] A group of manufacturers of cast-iron pipe met to set price terms in certain geographic areas. Their defense was that the prices they set were fair and reasonable and restrained the deleterious effects of ruinous competition. The

[26]It is ironic that an agreement among two small competitors in a very competitive industry where the two together cannot affect the market price is a per se violation of the antitrust laws while a merger of the two firms is legal. If agreements among competitors can never generate efficiencies, then it lowers enforcement costs to ban both effective and ineffective agreements to fix price among competitors. However, just like mergers, agreements among competitors can generate efficiencies, so it is peculiar to distinguish between the two, unless one could claim that efficiencies are more likely from a merger than from a price-fixing agreement. As we discussed in Chapter 5, it is often unclear what the word *agreement* means. Here, we refer to explicit communication among firms about what specific price to charge or output to produce. See Carlton, Gertner, and Rosenfield (1997).

[27]*United States v. Trans-Missouri Freight Association,* 166 U.S. 290 (1897).

[28]*United States v. Addyston Pipe & Steel Co.,* 175 U.S. 211 (6th Cir. 1899).

EXAMPLE 19.4

Antitrust Laws in Other Countries

Many countries took a much different view toward agreements among competitors than that taken in the United States. For example, Germany, Japan, and the United Kingdom allowed the formation of cartels that the government believed would promote efficiency. Although competition was generally viewed as desirable, these countries also believed that in certain circumstances it would not lead to efficiency. For example, West Germany and Japan both allowed for cartelization so that firms could reduce capacity during periods of excess capacity. Audretsch (1987) showed that in West Germany, prices rose during the cartelization period and fell after the cartel dissolved.

In addition to having their own laws, countries belonging to the European Union (EU) are also governed by antitrust provisions under the Treaty of Rome as well as by the European Commission Merger Regulation. The main antitrust provisions under the Treaty of Rome are Articles 85 and 86. Basically, Article 85 prevents anticompetitive harms resulting from contracts (such as those that restrict distribution terms) or from agreements (such as cartels). Similarly, Article 86 prevents anticompetitive harm from "abuse of dominant position" (such as from predatory pricing). The EU now uses its antitrust laws to question mergers and its competition policy to prevent price fixing and other similar activities. Thus, the EU laws now more closely resemble U.S. law in enforcing competition. The eastern and central European countries, formerly in the Soviet bloc, are adopting laws similar to those of the European Union.

The International Competition Network, an organization comprised of the antitrust authorities of over 85 countries, was recently formed to promote the development of antitrust laws throughout the world.

Sources: Audretsch (1987) and Swann et al. (1974).

Court reaffirmed its rejection of this type of argument. Several months after the adverse decision, all of the defendants merged into a single firm. The government did not challenge the merger. Therefore, the firms were able to achieve through merger what they were unable to achieve through horizontal agreements. These two early important price-fixing cases both involved industries with high fixed costs that made claims of ruinous competition.[29]

Nearly three decades later, the Court reinforced the prohibition against price fixing in *Trenton Potteries.*[30] The firms that manufactured and distributed 82 percent of the

[29] It is possible in high-fixed-cost industries for no equilibrium to exist without additional restrictions on competition (see **www.aw-bc.com/carlton_perloff** "Theory of the Core"). See Bittlingmayer (1982) for an analysis of the *Addyston Pipe* case from this point of view.

[30] *United States v. Trenton Potteries Co.*, 273 U.S. 392 (1927).

bathroom fixtures produced in the United States attempted to set list prices and urged adherence to these prices. Without investigating whether the agreement could successfully affect prices, the Court ruled that the reasonableness of price was no justification for price fixing.

During the 1930s, there was a widespread belief that the forces of competition were, in large part, the cause of the Great Depression. In 1933, in an apparent response to the current thinking of the time, the Court contradicted its previous rulings on price fixing and ruled in *Appalachian Coals* that a price-fixing cartel could be desirable if it prevented financial ruin. This anomalous decision was overruled by the Supreme Court in 1940. In *Socony-Vacuum,* the Court reaffirmed its previous views regarding price agreements among competitors.[31] In that case, a group of oil producers formed an organization designed to raise prices in order to rescue the industry from its serious financial plight. The Court ruled that "the elimination of so-called competitive evils is no legal justification" for such programs.

The reduction in the number of cartels is likely the most important achievement of U.S. antitrust laws. Cartels can significantly raise prices to consumers. So, for example, bid rigging conspiracies led to a price increase of about 6.5 percent for milk (Porter and Zona 1999; see also Pesendorfer 2000), 19 percent for highway construction in North Carolina (Brannman and Klein 1992), and 23–30 percent in Defense Department auctions for frozen fish (Froeb, Koyak, and Werden 1993). (See Chapter 5 and Connor 2003 for many additional examples involving international cartels in citric acid, vitamins, and other goods.) Consumers benefited greatly from the prosecution and elimination of these cartels.[32]

Not All Agreements Among Competitors Are Illegal

Although it is true that an agreement whose sole purpose is to fix prices or restrict output is a per se violation of the antitrust laws, it is not true that every agreement that results in prices being fixed is illegal per se. The Supreme Court has indicated that if the price fixing is ancillary to achieving another procompetitive purpose, then the agreement may well be deemed lawful. In such situations, it is necessary to investigate whether the price-fixing agreement is necessary to achieve the procompetitive purpose that underlies an agreement.

The Court long ago recognized that competitors sometimes must cooperate for the sake of efficiency and that this cooperation could involve pricing. Rather than applying a per se rule of illegality to such agreements, the courts apply a *rule of reason* analysis, in which the reasonableness of the cooperation is analyzed. One famous early case in which the rule of reason is eloquently articulated is *Chicago Board of Trade.*[33] In that

---

[31] *United States v. Socony-Vacuum Oil Co.,* 310 U.S. 150 (1940). This case is also referred to as *Madison Oil* because it was tried in Madison, Wisconsin.

[32] In contrast to these findings, Sproul (1993) found that Department of Justice prosecutions between 1973 and 1985 had little effect on prices. However, Sproul used less detailed data than those used in the studies cited in the text.

[33] *Board of Trade of City of Chicago v. United States,* 246 U.S. 231 (1918). *Standard Oil Co. of New Jersey v. United States* 221 U.S. 1 (1911) is the first case to employ a rule of reason.

case, members of the Board of Trade (who compete with each other to buy and sell contracts involving grains) agreed among themselves that after the Board had closed, no member of the Board of Trade could transact in a certain type of grain at a price other than the closing price that day. The Board of Trade was open during the early part of each day, and during that time, members transacted at prices that were determined by their willingness to buy or sell. The last price of the day was the closing price. The rule that no members could trade after the Board had closed except at the closing price made it more difficult for members to transact after closing, because supply and demand were likely to have moved the equilibrium price away from the closing price. The effect of this rule, therefore, was to create an incentive for members who wanted to trade to do so when the Board was open.

An organized exchange provides a valuable service. It amalgamates the information flows of buyers and sellers in such a way as to create a market price. An exchange is compensated for its activities by charging in some way for each trade that occurs. If one could costlessly observe the prices at the Board of Trade without having to pay any fees to it, one could free ride on the informational activities at the Board of Trade. By waiting to trade until after hours, one could use the information generated during the trading session by the Board of Trade yet avoid paying any fee. Therefore, this rule had two effects. First, it created an incentive to conduct more trades during the day on the exchange, making the market a larger one that can process more information. Second, it reduced the free-riding problem by discouraging trading after hours.

The Court ruled that this agreement was not a per se violation of the antitrust laws. The opinion, written by Justice Brandeis, said that

> Every agreement concerning trade, every regulation of trade, restrains. . . . The true test of legality is whether the restraint imposed is such as merely regulates and perhaps thereby promotes competition or whether it is such as may suppress or even destroy competition.

Thus, the Court clearly believed that a cooperative agreement among rivals about pricing can promote competition sometimes.

In *Broadcast Music, Inc. (BMI),* the Supreme Court investigated the way in which music is licensed.[34] Copyright owners of musical scores have property rights to their material. No one is allowed to use that material without permission and the payment of the agreed-upon fees. For example, any time a copyrighted song is played on the radio or on television, the copyright owner of that musical score must be compensated. It would be very costly for television and radio stations to locate and pay the copyright owner of each of the musical scores that it uses. Similarly, it would be very difficult for individual copyright owners to constantly monitor radio and television to determine if their musical scores were being performed.

To get around these horrendous transaction problems, two organizations were formed. One is the American Society of Composers, Authors, and Publishers (ASCAP) and the other is Broadcast Music, Inc. (BMI). Copyright owners belong to one

[34] *Broadcast Music, Inc. v. Columbia Broadcasting System, Inc.*, 441 U.S. 1 (1979).

or both of these organizations and rely on them to collect revenues on their behalf. These organizations monitor musical productions and issue blanket licenses that enable the licensee to use any song listed in the blanket license. Fees for blanket licenses are ordinarily flat dollar amounts or percentages of total revenues. Therefore, ASCAP and BMI do fix prices in some sense, and they are, of course, organizations of competitors, handling the many songwriters.

The Supreme Court realized that ASCAP and BMI were providing an important service that lowered transaction costs and that the only way they could provide it was to set the price. In this sense, then, both BMI and ASCAP were performing procompetitive functions, and, by lowering transaction costs, they were expanding the amount of consumption that could occur. The Supreme Court therefore recognized that the per se rule was not appropriate here; instead, it decided that a rule of reason was necessary to analyze the reasonableness of the restraint. This case emphasized that cooperative agreements regarding price need not always violate the antitrust laws. (See Carlton and Klamer 1983, Halverson 1988, and Example 19.5 for an alleged price-fixing case involving not-for-profit colleges and universities.)

Information Exchanges Among Competitors

A common and natural form of association among competitors is a trade association, which is an organization composed of firms in similar businesses. Trade associations often collect information on the industry that is valuable to its members. Of course, trade associations can also serve as a vehicle by which prices are fixed (Chapter 5). However, it is important to recognize the legitimate information-generating services that trade associations can provide, such as revealing cost information to their members, or even revealing transaction prices to market participants, provided there is not collusion.

In the *Hardwood* case, the Court investigated the activities of the American Hardwood Manufacturers' Association, which had about 400 members.[35] The association engaged in gathering and reporting information about the sales, production, inventory, and pricing activities of each member and making such information available to the members. Moreover, at their meetings, members frequently discussed business conditions and the suitability of increases or decreases in industry production in light of these conditions. This behavior is consistent with that of a cartel. A cartel with 400 members, however, would be a difficult one to police and is therefore not likely to be successful in raising price for long. Therefore, it is likely that the exchanged information probably improved the knowledge of market conditions without increasing price. Nonetheless, the Court ruled that these activities were illegal (see Example 11.8).

Justice Brandeis disagreed with his colleagues on the Supreme Court about the *Hardwood* case. He explained that had there been a centralized market, much of the information collected by the trade association would have been automatically available. The provision of information was viewed by Brandeis as a beneficial, procompetitive effect of the trade association.

[35] *American Column & Lumber Company v. United States,* 257 U.S. 377 (1921).

EXAMPLE 19.5

Colleges and Antitrust: Does Your School Belong to a Cartel?

In the 1950s, some Ivy League schools met and agreed not to offer aid to star athletes except on the basis of the financial need of the athlete. Soon, the agreement was extended to cover star students. By the 1980s, twenty-three elite schools in the Northeast were participating in this agreement, which was called the Overlap agreement. Under the Overlap agreement, each school would (1) agree to provide aid to students only on the basis of need, (2) adopt similar procedures to define need, and (3) meet to examine the actual awards made to each student who was admitted to at least two of the schools participating in the Overlap agreement and adjust aid offers if they differed.

The schools claimed that the Overlap agreement allowed them to conserve their financial resources to concentrate aid on poor students so as to achieve the twin goals of (1) having admission decisions based only on merit, and (2) guaranteeing full financial aid (based on need) to every admitted student. Few schools outside of those participating in the Overlap agreement adhered to these twin goals. The schools also claimed that their Overlap policies were fully consistent with federal education policies, which, for the most part, forbid the use of federal funds for scholarship aid if the aid is not based on need.

In 1991, the U.S. Department of Justice sued the eight members of the Ivy League and MIT under Section 1 of the Sherman Act. The Department of Justice claimed that the Overlap agreement was a per se illegal price-fixing agreement designed to raise each school's revenue. All the Ivy League schools agreed to stop the behavior and the suit against them was dropped. MIT refused to settle and went to trial.

Although colleges might want to cooperate to raise their own revenue and thereby harm students, they also might want to cooperate to achieve a social goal such as helping poor students. After all, one of the objectives of a not-for-profit college is to benefit students. Carlton presented an econometric study of average tuition paid by all students that revealed that there was no evidence to support the view that average tuition was higher as a result of the Overlap agreement. There was no question, however, that the Overlap agreement caused some students to pay higher tuition and others to pay lower tuition than they would have otherwise paid.

The court ruled that a per se approach should not be used because of the not-for-profit nature of colleges. The court found that the Overlap behavior did result in a violation of the antitrust laws because it restrained competition—specifically, the bidding for star students. Curiously, the Department of Justice did not attack the agreement not to bid for star athletes. The case was reversed on appeal and sent back to the district court for further review. Soon after the initial district court decision, Congress passed legislation to make it legal for the schools to continue to abide by most of the Overlap agreement that had been judged illegal. The case was settled with the schools being allowed to engage in most of the conduct covered by the Overlap agreement. However, the schools never reinstituted the Overlap conduct. Subsequent research by Hoxby (2000) confirmed the predictions of the original econometric model that Overlap did not cause an increase in average tuition.

Source: Carlton, Bamberger and Epstein (1995) and Bamberger and Carlton (2004). Carlton served as an expert witness for MIT.

A few years later, the Court again examined another trade association, the Maple Flooring Manufacturers' Association, with twenty-two members who accounted for roughly 70 percent of the total production of hardwood-type floors.[36] The association provided information on costs, freight, quantities sold, and prices received by individual members, and held meetings at which various industry members exchanged views about the state of the industry. The Court ruled that this activity was not a violation of the antitrust laws and cited the procompetitive benefits that result from a free flow of information and having industry participants apprised of market conditions. Using the economic theories about number of participants developed in our discussion of cartels, it appears that the trade association was much more likely to act successfully as a collusive device in the *Maple Flooring* case than it was in the *Hardwood* case. Despite this, the Maple Flooring Association was exonerated, but not the Hardwood Association.

Several decades later, the Court investigated exchanges of price information among producers of corrugated containers.[37] One competitor would request information from another on the most recent price that it had offered. The industry was concentrated, with the defendants accounting for about 90 percent of the shipments of corrugated containers from plants in the southeastern United States. After examining the economic factors of the industry including its concentrated structure, the Court concluded that the exchange of information was anticompetitive.

The discussion of oligopoly theory in Chapters 5 and 6 shows that exchanges of information can assist in collusion. For this reason, courts have paid careful attention to the activities of trade associations. At the same time, the courts recognize that information is a scarce commodity and that its dissemination can often be valuable. Evaluating these two offsetting effects is difficult.

Oligopoly Behavior

Noncooperative oligopoly prices may be above the competitive level because firms recognize their mutual interdependence and find it in their interests not to drive prices to competitive levels. The question the courts had to address was whether such pricing and other oligopoly behavior can be regarded as the result of an agreement among competitors that violates the antitrust laws. The enforcement of the antitrust laws often focuses on explicit agreements among competitors. The prosecution effort centers on showing evidence of an agreement (for example, incriminating documents) rather than on showing the effects of an agreement (for example, higher prices).

The Court addressed the question of when one could infer that a conspiracy or agreement had been made among competing firms in *Interstate Circuit*.[38] The Court said, "In order to establish agreement, it is compelled to rely on inferences drawn from the course of conduct of the alleged conspirators." The Court ruled that similarity in behavior was enough to constitute evidence of an agreement.

---

[36] *Maple Flooring Manufacturers' Association v. United States*, 268 U.S. 563 (1925).

[37] *United States v. Container Corp. of America*, 393 U.S. 333 (1969).

[38] *Interstate Circuit, Inc. v. United States*, 306 U.S. 208 (1939).

In the *American Tobacco* case, the Court examined in detail the behavior of the cigarette industry in the 1930s.[39] List prices of the three major companies (the "Big Three"), Reynolds, American, and Liggett & Myers, were identical most of the time. During the height of the Depression, the cigarette companies all raised their prices even though their costs fell.

After prices rose, new competitors entered the cigarette industry and were able to sell their brands for 10¢, which was less than the 15¢ charged for the brands of the three majors. The market shares of the Big Three started to erode, and they had lost roughly 22 percent of total cigarette sales by 1932. The Big Three responded by cutting prices, and sales of the 10¢ brands fell considerably: The market share of the 10¢ brands was reduced to around 6.5 percent by 1933. The three major cigarette companies used their influence to make sure that no retail store sold the brands of the Big Three for more than 3¢ above the price of the 10¢ brands. See Example 11.2.

The Court found that the similarity of conduct among the three major companies provided a basis to infer that an unlawful conspiracy had occurred:

> Where the circumstances are such as to warrant a jury in finding that the conspirators had a unity of purpose for a common design and understanding, or meeting of minds in an unlawful arrangement, the conclusion that a conspiracy is established is justified.

After *American Tobacco,* it was unclear exactly what type of oligopoly behavior would be subject to the antitrust laws. Was merely parallel behavior, in which firms who recognize each other's interdependence act similarly, a violation of the antitrust laws?

In a series of cases, the Court aggressively attacked oligopoly behavior involving delivered pricing (see Chapter 11). However, in 1954 the Court indicated a change in direction. In the *Theatre Enterprises* case, the Court addressed the question of parallel behavior of movie theaters.[40] A newly refurbished theater sought to obtain the rights to run first-run feature movies from several distributors. The distributors refused because they already had theaters lined up for their first-run features. The Court ruled that

> business behavior is admissible circumstantial evidence from which the fact finder may infer agreement . . . but this Court has never held that proof of parallel business behavior conclusively establishes agreement or, phrased differently, that such behavior itself constitutes a Sherman Act offense.

In other words, the common action of the distributors in refusing the movie theater the right to run first-run movies did not constitute a violation of the antitrust laws. This case is often interpreted to mean that parallel behavior ("conscious parallelism"), the kind that naturally results from a few firms' competition with each other in an oligopoly, cannot by itself lead to an antitrust violation; there must be some additional offense ("conscious parallelism plus") for the behavior to constitute an illegal action.

---

[39] *American Tobacco Company v. United States,* 328 U.S. 781 (1946).
[40] *Theatre Enterprises Inc. v. Paramount Film Distributing Corp.,* 346 U.S. 537 (1954).

The view that parallel behavior alone is not sufficient for an antitrust violation has been reaffirmed in several recent cases that the Federal Trade Commission has brought unsuccessfully, in which it has alleged that either markets are so-called shared monopolies (firms choose not to compete for the same customers and instead have local monopolies)[41] or are not competitive because of certain business practices adopted independently by each firm. For example, in *du Pont,* the FTC charged that the noncollusive adoption of certain common business practices, such as notification to buyers of price increases, the use of a most-favored nations clause (see Chapters 5 and 11), the use of uniform delivered pricing, and public announcements in the press all constituted business practices that facilitated noncompetitive pricing.[42] The Court of Appeals for the Second Circuit rejected such arguments as indicating violations of the antitrust laws:

> The mere existence of an oligopolistic market structure in which a small group of manufacturers engage in consciously parallel pricing of an identical product does not violate the antitrust laws.

Mergers

Prohibitions against price fixing would have little effect without limits on mergers. The antitrust laws try to prevent the creation of additional market power through mergers of competitors. The issue in a merger case is not whether the industry is currently competitive, but whether it will become less competitive as a result of a merger. Because mergers can generate efficiencies, a merger policy that overdeters merger activity imposes a significant cost on society. Conversely, too lenient a policy leads to the creation of additional market power. We first discuss mergers among competitors and then among potential competitors.

Mergers of Competitors. In an early decision, *Northern Securities Company,* the Supreme Court investigated the creation of a holding company that would control two large, competing railroads: The Great Northern Railroad Company and the Northern Pacific Railway Company.[43] The creation of this holding company, which would exercise control over these two previously competing railroads, was deemed to violate the antitrust laws. The *Northern Securities* decision in 1904 coincided with the end of the widespread merger movement in the early 1900s (see Chapter 2).

Soon after the *Northern Securities* decision, the Court reached another decision involving market power acquired through merger. In *Standard Oil,* the Court investigated the creation of the Standard Oil Company and the practices it followed in

---

[41] *FTC v. Kellogg et al.,* Docket No. 8883, 99 FTC Reporter 8, 1982. The FTC eventually dismissed the case. See Schmalensee (1978b) for an analysis of this case.

[42] *E.I. du Pont de Nemours & Co. v. FTC,* 729 F.2d 128 (2d Cir. 1984). This case is also sometimes called the *Ethyl* case because Ethyl was a participant. See Example 11.7 and Hay (1999).

[43] *Northern Securities Company v. United States,* 193 U.S. 197 (1904).

acquiring businesses related to petroleum products.[44] John D. Rockefeller and others were the defendants. One charge was that the defendants

> purchased and obtained interest . . . and entered into agreements with . . . various persons . . . engaged in purchasing, shipping, refining, and selling petroleum and its products . . . for the purpose of fixing the price of crude and refined oil and the produce thereof, limiting production thereof, and controlling the transportation therein, and thereby restraining trade . . . and monopolizing interstate commerce.

Another charge was that refineries that refused to enter into the agreement were driven out of business through a variety of predatory tactics such as low prices. Other charges included unfair practices against competing pipelines, contracts with competitors, espionage, and division of the United States into districts and limiting the amount of competition in each district. The Court ruled that the actions indicated "a conviction of a purpose and intent" to monopolize, and it ordered the dissolution of the combination. This case is famous because the Court refused to apply a per se ban to mergers among competitors and introduced the rule of reason, in which one had to investigate whether the resulting effect of the merger was an unreasonable restraint of trade.

In the *United States Steel* case, the Court seriously retreated from vigorously applying the antitrust laws to enjoin merger activity.[45] The case involved the creation of the United States Steel Company through the merger of approximately 180 independent firms. U.S. Steel produced 80 to 90 percent of the entire steel output of the country. The Court refused to find the creation of U.S. Steel illegal, and seemed to indicate that because U.S. Steel, unlike Standard Oil, did not engage in improper behavior, the combination was lawful.

Dissatisfaction with the Supreme Court's treatment of mergers (especially in light of a failure to block another acquisition)[46] led Congress to pass the *Celler-Kefauver Act* in 1950, which strengthened Section 7 (on merger activity) of the Clayton Act. In *Brown Shoe,* the Supreme Court applied the new standards of the amended Section 7 of the Clayton Act to block a proposed merger between G.R. Kinney Company and Brown Shoe Company.[47] Both were manufacturers and retail sellers of shoes. The language of the Court's decision indicated that a combined share of 5 percent in a city was excessive, taking into account the trend toward increasing concentration in this industry. The Court also issued its famous laundry list of criteria for defining a market, which we discussed in the section on market definition.

The Court continued its hard line on mergers by stopping a merger among banks in *Philadelphia Bank.*[48] The merged firm would have had less than 40 percent of de-

---

[44] *Standard Oil Company of New Jersey v. United States,* 221 U.S. 1 (1911). McGee (1958) analyzes this case.
[45] *United States v. United States Steel Corporation,* 251 U.S. 417 (1920).
[46] *United States v. Columbia Steel Company,* 334 U.S. 495 (1948).
[47] *Brown Shoe Company v. United States,* 370 U.S. 294 (1962). Peterman (1975) analyzes *Brown Shoe.*
[48] *United States v. Philadelphia National Bank,* 374 U.S. 321 (1963).

posits in the Philadelphia area. The Court also rejected a consideration of the efficiency benefits of a merger.

The Supreme Court took its strictest stance in enforcing Section 7 of the Clayton Act in *Von's*.[49] Von's Grocery Company sought to acquire Shopping Bag Food Stores, another retail grocery company operating in Los Angeles. Their combined sales accounted for only 7.5 percent of all sales in Los Angeles, yet the Supreme Court prevented this acquisition. Shortly thereafter in 1968, the Department of Justice issued very strict guidelines on which firms could likely merge without challenge (see **www.aw-bc.com/carlton_perloff** "1968 Merger Guidelines").

The more recent 1984, 1992, and 1997 Merger Guidelines (Example 19.3) recognized the potential efficiency gains from mergers. These guidelines apparently are a response to the earlier rejection by the government and the Court to using proposed efficiency gains from mergers as a defense to justify a merger that increases concentration in a market. The application by the Department of Justice and the FTC of the current merger guidelines, which recognize the value of efficiencies, suggests that efficiencies alone generally do not provide sufficient justification for a merger in which prices are expected to rise. Efficiencies, however, can provide a justification for a merger that results in increased concentration if the efficiencies would lead to lower prices.

One defense that courts have allowed in merger cases is the *failing-firm defense,* in which the firms explain that if the proposed merger is not allowed, one of the firms will go out of business. If the proposed transaction is the least anticompetitive one that can prevent the assets from leaving the industry, the Department of Justice or FTC will not challenge the merger. However, if the failing firm goes bankrupt but the creditors continue to operate the firm, then the bankruptcy does not affect competition and there is no reason to allow a failing-firm defense.

The failing-firm defense can be regarded as a recognition that current market shares may not reflect the future importance of the competitor that will vanish as a result of the merger. If a firm will go out of business unless it merges with others, then the fact that it currently has a high market share is irrelevant in considering whether the merger should go through or not. Merger policy should be forward-looking, and it is really the future competitive significance of the merging firms that is important in understanding whether a merger is anticompetitive.[50] This principle is recognized by the Supreme Court in several cases in which it finds that current market shares may be inaccurate indicators of the future competitive significance of a firm.[51]

---

[49] *United States v. Von's Grocery Company*, 384 U.S. 270 (1966).

[50] Suppose that there are three firms in an industry with market shares of 30%, 30%, and 40%, and that the one with 40% is failing. If it fails, the remaining firms will have 50% and 50%. If, instead, the failing firm is acquired by one of the remaining firms, the shares will be 70% and 30%. Thus, if a merger occurs, concentration as measured by the Herfindahl-Hirschman Index (HHI) increases (see Chapter 8). The comparison of the HHIs is *irrelevant* however, if the output level is not held constant. If, as a result of the acquisition, more assets remain in the industry and output is permanently higher, then consumers are better off even if market concentration increases from what it would have been if no acquisition had occurred, the failing firm had failed, and its assets had exited the industry.

[51] *United States v. General Dynamics Corporation*, 415 U.S. 486 (1974).

Thus, the criteria for analyzing mergers used by the Court and the government have evolved considerably since the Celler-Kefauver Act in 1950. As the Court has eliminated some of the inconsistencies in its opinions in defining markets, and as economists and lawyers have become more sophisticated about defining markets and understanding the effects of market concentration, government policy toward mergers has become more systematic. A merger such as that attacked in *Von's* would probably not be attacked today. Moreover, both the FTC and Department of Justice address their concerns about lack of competition resulting from a proposed merger by allowing the merging firms to restructure the proposed transaction to remedy competitive concerns (such as by selling some assets to a new entrant). They have used this "fix it first" policy extensively since the 1980s.

Mergers of Potential Competitors. Suppose two firms that do not currently compete in the same market wish to merge. Can the merger be blocked if the government thinks it is likely that the two firms would have competed in the future? Logically, there is nothing wrong with blocking a merger if it will improve future competition. Practically, it is very difficult to determine which firms are potential competitors. The decisions of the Court have evolved over time so that a merger between potential competitors is now much less likely to be challenged as anticompetitive.

An early case involving a merger between potential competitors was *El Paso Natural Gas.*[52] El Paso Natural Gas sought to acquire the assets of Pacific Northwest Pipeline Corporation. Both companies operated large natural gas pipelines. Only one of them, El Paso, delivered natural gas into California, a market in which the government contended competition would be lessened if the acquisition occurred. Even though Pacific Northwest had never sold gas in California, on several occasions it had attempted to obtain the necessary regulatory approval to deliver gas into California. Indeed, Pacific Northwest had conducted lengthy negotiations with a large customer in southern California. The result of these negotiations was to heighten competition, even though El Paso eventually won away the customer. The Court ruled that although Pacific Northwest was not a successful seller in California, it was indeed a competitor: "Unsuccessful bidders are no less competitive than the successful ones." The acquisition was barred. Because Pacific Northwest had actually bid for business, it seems more reasonable to regard this case as one between actual rather than potential competitors.

Another important case involving potential competition was *Procter & Gamble.*[53] Procter & Gamble Company acquired Clorox Chemical Company, which was the leading manufacturer of household liquid bleach and had about 50 percent of U.S. sales. Procter & Gamble did not manufacture or sell bleach, but was a major manufacturer and seller of many other household products. The Court decided that the acquisition should be blocked because Procter & Gamble was a likely entrant into the liquid-bleach market. As a result of the decision, Clorox was divested in 1969 (12 years after the original merger).

---

[52] *United States v. El Paso Natural Gas Company*, 376 U.S. 651 (1964).

[53] *Federal Trade Commission v. Procter & Gamble Company*, 386 U.S. 568 (1967).

The potential competition doctrine was again used by the Supreme Court in *United States v. Falstaff Brewing Corporation.*[54] Falstaff, one of the nation's largest brewers, sought to acquire Narragansett, which was the largest brewer in the New England area—an area in which Falstaff did not compete. The government argued that the merger should be enjoined because Falstaff was a likely entrant into the New England area. The district court had found that Falstaff had no intentions of otherwise entering the New England area, but the Supreme Court ruled that Falstaff may have affected competition in New England anyway because Falstaff might have been perceived as a potential entrant into the New England area and therefore might have restrained prices. The district court subsequently found that Falstaff was not perceived as a potential entrant. Although logically a perceived potential competitor could influence the market, a perceived potential competition doctrine depends on the state of mind of the competitors and not on any easily verifiable facts. Therefore, even though the doctrine is logically consistent, it turns out to be extremely complex to litigate such a case, which is based on the opinions of competitors who may be interested in preventing a merger that would result in the creation of an efficient competitor and rival.

The Supreme Court significantly constrained the application of the potential competition theory in *Marine Bancorporation.*[55] The government challenged a proposed merger between a commercial bank in Seattle and one in Spokane: two banks that were not direct competitors even though both were located in the same state. The government challenged the merger on the grounds that the acquiring bank would have found an alternative and more competitive means for entering the Spokane area. The Court was unconvinced that an alternative method of entry would achieve the same procompetitive effects as this acquisition. It appears, then, that the Court's decision requires a showing that first, the potential competitor has some unique advantage to entry, and second, that this means of entry would allow the potential competitor to enter and prosper. Since the *Marine Bancorporation* decision, the potential competition doctrine has not fared well (Posner and Easterbrook 1980, 531). Of course, if markets are broadly defined, there is little need for a potential competition doctrine because the potential competitors are considered part of the market.

Exclusionary Actions and Other Strategic Behavior

So far, this chapter has described how antitrust laws are designed to prevent agreements between competing firms, such as a price-fixing conspiracy or a merger, that can lead to the creation of market power. This section examines actions by a single firm (or firms acting collectively) that may help it maintain its monopoly or facilitate its acquisition of market power at the expense of its rivals. These **exclusionary actions** are used

[54] *United States v. Falstaff Brewing Corporation*, 410 U.S. 526 (1973). See also *United States v. Penn-Olin Chemical Co.*, 378 U.S. 158 (1964).

[55] *United States v. Marine Bancorporation Inc.*, 418 U.S. 602 (1974).

by a firm to eliminate rivals from a market or harm them, thereby either helping to maintain or create a monopoly. These actions, or bad acts, include predatory pricing, denial of key products to rivals, vertical relationships among firms, and tie-in sales. Many of these practices are a violation of Section 2 of the Sherman Act. Hence, antitrust cases alleging these actions are often called *Section 2 cases.*

Section 2 of the Sherman Act forbids firms' exclusionary conduct (bad acts) that adversely affect competition. A recurrent problem in Section 2 cases is that the Court has been unclear exactly how vigorously a dominant firm can respond to new competition. Moreover, economists cannot usually say with certainty which types of strategic behavior lead to benefits for consumers when competitors are harmed (Chapter 11). For example, a firm may strategically invest before other firms can enter an industry. Such a policy can benefit consumers even if it prevents potential competitors from entering the market. Thus, blanket prohibitions of such behavior may be harmful in some industries.

Section 2 litigation can be costly (as can all complicated litigation). One example of costly litigation is the IBM case in which the government sought to force IBM to break itself up into several firms. The government claimed that IBM practiced numerous policies designed to exclude competition. The legal fees as well as the time of IBM and government employees probably put the litigation cost in the area of hundreds of millions of dollars. The government eventually dropped the case.[56]

How vigorously should courts use Section 2 to constrain the action of firms? The answer turns on specific attributes of a market. Where entry can occur quickly, market power may be short lived, and there may be no need for Section 2 litigation. Over-vigorous enforcement of Section 2 cases, in addition to reducing market power, could dissuade firms from pursuing certain efficient policies that would benefit consumers. This efficiency loss could be large and would not diminish over time. Striking the right balance in Section 2 cases remains a difficult problem for the courts. We now examine strategic behavior by a firm with respect to both rival firms in its market and vertical relations.

Competition Between Rivals

In general, competition benefits consumers; however, some forms of competitive behavior can reduce competition, as Chapter 11 shows. This section reviews some of the main types of behavior between rivals that the Court has found to violate the antitrust laws. We begin with a general discussion of some famous cases in which the Court deemed certain behavior undesirable and then discuss the specific examples of predatory pricing and denial of key products to rivals.

Competitive Behavior Deemed Undesirable by the Court

One of the most famous Section 2 cases is *Alcoa.*[57] Alcoa produced and sold aluminum ingot and also fabricated the aluminum ingot into many finished and semifinished goods. In part because Alcoa owned or licensed many of the critical original

[56]See Fisher, McGowan, and Greenwood (1983) for a description of this lengthy litigation from IBM's perspective. See Houthakker (1985) for a different view.
[57]*United States v. Aluminum Company of America*, 148 F.2d 416 (1945).

patents, no firm could effectively compete with Alcoa prior to 1909. In the government's 1945 case, it alleged that, after 1909, Alcoa maintained its market power through a series of exclusionary tactics, among them (1) the signing of power contracts that forbade the power companies to sell power to anyone else who made aluminum; (2) explicit price-fixing agreements with foreign producers of aluminum to prevent imports into the United States; (3) a price squeeze, in which the price of aluminum ingot was raised to independent aluminum-sheet fabricators, who were then unable to make a profit fabricating the sheet and selling it in competition with Alcoa at the prices Alcoa was setting for aluminum sheet; and (4) a strategy of expanding capacity with the intention of eliminating competition. Alcoa remained the sole domestic producer of aluminum until 1945.

One of Alcoa's defenses was that the profit it earned was not very high. The court ruled that whether profits are high or low is irrelevant: "[Congress] did not condone good trusts and condemn bad ones; it forbade all."[58] The court stated that *the mere acquisition of a monopoly by itself was not necessarily illegal.*

Despite this view, which implies that efficient firms that grow should not be penalized, the court looked with disfavor on Alcoa's policy of anticipating demand and building capacity for it in advance:

> It was not inevitable that it should always anticipate increases in demand for ingot and be prepared to supply them. . . . It insists that it never excluded competitors; but we can think of no more effective exclusion than progressively to embrace each new opportunity as it opened.

The court's reasoning is perplexing. It is difficult for an economist to distinguish evil capacity expansion from desirable capacity expansion that occurs as a result of foresight.

The court also ruled that "The monopolist must have both the power to monopolize, and the intent to monopolize." By stressing intent, the frame of mind of the violator becomes relevant in an antitrust suit. Endless litigation can result when someone's frame of mind, rather than the actual effects of the economic actions, is the subject of the litigation. The court further ruled that Alcoa's price-squeeze policy was unlawful.[59]

---

[58]The *Alcoa* case was decided by a court of appeals rather than the Supreme Court; the Supreme Court was unable to hear the case because of a conflict of interests involving several of the Justices. The Court of Appeals for the Second Circuit was designated as the court of last resort for the *Alcoa* case, and Judge Learned Hand wrote the decision.

[59]A fascinating issue in the *Alcoa* case was the definition of the market. Aluminum ingot, once it is made into fabricated aluminum, can be recycled as scrap aluminum. Scrap aluminum competes with primary ingot for many uses. The question arose as to whether the secondary market should properly be considered as part of the market in which virgin aluminum ingot competes. The court ruled that secondary aluminum should not be part of the market definition and concluded that a market share for virgin ingot of 90 percent would definitely indicate monopoly power; 67 percent might indicate monopoly power; but 33 percent would not. Secondary and primary products definitely compete with each other, but such competition need not erode the initial market power in the primary product. Once the primary product is sold, there may be no further monopoly profits to be made, because the secondary market does constrain the *subsequent* pricing of primary aluminum, even though it does not constrain the initial price. (See Chapter 15, "Renting Versus Selling by a Monopoly.") Another issue in the definition of the market involved whether imports should be included in the market. The court correctly decided to include them.

The Court remanded the case to the district court for reconsideration. The main antitrust divestiture order facing Alcoa, resulting from the antitrust litigation, was one regarding its Canadian properties. During the time period of the district court's reconsideration, the United States government sold off aluminum facilities built for it during World War II and thereby set up Reynolds and Kaiser as two competitors to Alcoa. The monopoly on aluminum that Alcoa enjoyed in the United States disappeared. By 1958, Alcoa's share of primary aluminum ingot capacity had fallen to 35 percent.

The *Alcoa* decision had far-reaching implications for dominant firm behavior. It was unclear if there was anything a dominant firm could do to avoid being charged with consciously seeking to maintain control of the market. Further, it was unclear how one would determine whether its monopoly condition was "thrust upon it," maintained by clever but legal business practices, or maintained by practices that the courts would find illegal.

In *United Shoe,* another major Section 2 case, the government charged that United Shoe maintained its market share of 75 to 85 percent of American shoe machinery primarily through the practice of refusing to sell its equipment, agreeing only to lease it.[60] The government maintained that United Shoe, by only leasing its equipment, created barriers to entry. The reason was that because United repaired its own equipment, there were no independent repair organizations that a competitor could rely on; therefore, if a competitor sought to enter the field, it would have to also provide repair services. The Court also ruled that the leasing system under which United leased the machines for 10 years would "deter a shoe manufacturer from disposing of a United machine and acquiring a competitor's machine." The Court ruled that the leases were "so drawn and so applied as to strengthen United's power to exclude competitors." Although the Court recognized the superiority of many of United's products and services, it felt that the leasing system contributed to its market power. The Court required United to offer for sale any machines that it leased. *United Shoe* appears to illustrate the important concept presented in Chapter 15 that a monopoly would prefer to lease rather than sell its machines; however, see Example 15.1.

The Court's views on the 10-year period of the lease are troublesome. If leases come up for renewal over time, and if there can be competition to obtain the customer whose lease has expired, then it is unclear why competition is reduced by the leases. Only if the slow turnover of customers prevents a rival from attaining some critical mass necessary for its survival as an efficient competitor would there seem to be an antitrust concern.[61] Even in that case, one would also want to consider any benefits that arise as a result of the long-term nature of the contract.

In *Griffith,* the Court considered the buying practices of chains of motion picture theaters.[62] These motion picture theaters paid for the movies through rentals that were based on the total attendance of the entire chain, rather than at any particular

---

[60] *United States v. United Shoe Machinery Corporation,* 110 F. Supp. 295 (1953). This citation refers to the Federal Supplement, a standard legal reference in which the opinions of the district courts appear.

[61] Aghion and Bolton (1987) analyze models in which long-term contracts can create anticompetitive harm by allowing the buyers to act collectively as a monopsony.

[62] *United States v. Griffith,* 334 U.S. 100 (1948).

theater. That meant that if a chain had a theater in a town in which it was competing with a single, independent theater, the chain could obtain the same movie at a lower price than the single theater. The Court ruled that this placing of single competitors at a disadvantage was a violation of Section 2 of the Sherman Act. The Court also ruled that the effect of the action rather than the intent of the actor was a reasonable focus of inquiry.

In *Berkey,* the Court of Appeals for the Second Circuit examined the duty that a monopoly has toward its rivals.[63] In 1972, Kodak, the dominant firm in the markets for cameras and for film, introduced the 110 pocket Instamatic camera and a film format to fit that camera. Berkey was a manufacturer of cameras and a processor of film. One of Berkey's claims was that because Kodak refused to predisclose the format of its 110 film, Berkey was unable to manufacture cameras to fit the 110 format film until well after its introduction. Berkey claimed that Kodak's dominance in both film and cameras required it to predisclose to its competitors any changes in film format that would affect competition in the camera market. The court ruled that predisclosure was not a duty imposed on a dominant firm by the antitrust laws. The court recognized that the antitrust laws, especially Section 2, do not forbid monopolies. The court reiterated that the standard for a Section 2 offense is the possession of market power and the willful acquisition or maintenance of that power, as distinguished from growth or development as a consequence of a superior product, business acquisition, or historic accident.[64]

Predation. One of the classic bad acts is predatory pricing (Chapter 11); however, there is a danger of confusing predatory pricing with aggressive competition. The *Utah Pie* case involved a claim of predatory pricing.[65] Utah Pie Company sold frozen dessert pies in Utah. Continental Baking Company, Carnation Company, and Pet Milk Company sold pies in competition with Utah Pie. The Salt Lake City market was the scene of dramatic price competition, and there was evidence to show that prices of the defendants' products were lower in Salt Lake City than they were elsewhere. Evidence suggested that the prices of the defendants' products, at least some of them, were below their direct cost plus an allocation for overhead. There was evidence that one of the defendants had employed an industrial spy to infiltrate the Utah Pie plant to obtain information. The Court ruled that such price discrimination eroded competition and, therefore, was predatory and in violation of the law.[66]

In *Telex,* the Court of Appeals for the Tenth Circuit investigated IBM's pricing behavior with regard to peripheral devices (such as disk drives) that plugged into an IBM

---

[63] *Berkey Photo, Inc. v. Eastman Kodak Company,* 603 F.2d 263 (2d Cir. 1979) cert. denied, 444 U.S. 1093 (1980).

[64] See also *United States v. Grinnell Corp.,* 384 U.S. 563 (1966).

[65] *Utah Pie Company v. Continental Baking Company,* 386 U.S. 685 (1967). Elzinga and Hogarty (1978) provide an economic analysis of this case.

[66] The language of *Utah Pie* suggests that price discrimination can violate Section 2, even if prices exceed average cost. As discussed in Chapter 11, fully allocated cost is an inappropriate standard to use in determining if prices are predatory.

central processing unit.[67] Telex claimed that IBM violated the antitrust laws by its decision to slash prices on its peripheral devices in order to compete with Telex. The court found that because the price was not below IBM's production costs, there were no grounds to the complaint.

In *Matsushita,* the Supreme Court again investigated a charge of predatory pricing.[68] This case involved a claim that certain Japanese manufacturers engaged in predatory pricing over a 20-year period. The Court recognized the irrationality of such a scheme—it would obviously be unprofitable to lose money for 20 years—and dismissed the case (Example 11.1). Alleged predatory behavior must be credible to be found to violate the law.

In *Brooke Group v. Brown and Williamson Tobacco* (113 S. Ct. 2578 (1993)), Liggett (Brooke), which pioneered the development of low-price generic cigarettes, charged that Brown and Williamson introduced its generic cigarettes at predatory prices. The Court held that a successful predation claim required proof that price was set below some measure of cost and the alleged predator had a reasonable likelihood of recouping its losses from predating. The Court found that the market structure for the sale of generic cigarettes would not allow Brown to recoup any predatory losses. The Court ruled that with no possibility of recouping its losses, even below-cost pricing does not support a claim of predatory pricing. Because the parties agreed to use average variable cost as the measure of costs, the Court declined to rule on what the appropriate cost measure should be in predation cases. Thus, there still is no Supreme Court precedent on that important issue.

Refusals to Deal and Essential Facilities. When a group of firms collectively decide to boycott or refuse to deal with a rival, thereby denying the rival access to certain markets, their actions can violate Section 1 in addition to Section 2. For example, in *Eastern States,* the Court condemned the actions of a group of retail lumber dealers who refused to deal with any wholesale lumber dealers who also sold at retail.[69]

Frequently, the courts have treated collective action involving a refusal to deal with certain firms as a per se violation. Two recent cases may indicate a change in view. In *Northwest Wholesale Stationers, Inc. v. Pacific Stationery and Printing Company,* the Court refused to apply the per se rule to a case involving an agreement among competitors.[70] This case involved the expulsion of one member from a cooperative buying agency (a group of firms that buy products as one purchaser). The Court determined that the cooperative buying agency, through an agreement among competitors, did not necessarily engage in a per se violation by expelling the plaintiff and refusing to deal with that firm. The Court ruled that in the absence of proof that the cooperative

[67] *Telex Corp. v. International Business Machines Corp.,* 510 F.2d 894 (1975).

[68] *Matsushita Electric Industrial Co. v. Zenith Radio Corporation,* 106 S. Ct. 1348 (1986).

[69] *Eastern States Retail Lumber Dealers Association v. United States,* 234 U.S. 600 (1914).

[70] *Northwest Wholesale Stationers, Inc. v. Pacific Stationery and Printing Company,* 105 S. Ct. 2613 (1985).

had market power or unique access to a critical resource necessary for effective competition, it was not appropriate to treat the conduct as a per se violation, and instead it had to be subjected to a rule of reason.[71]

In deciding refusal to deal cases, courts often emphasize the role of **essential facilities:** scarce resources that a rival needs to use to survive. For example, a trucking firm that owns the sole bridge leading to an island owns a facility that is essential to rival trucking firms that deliver to the island. Under the essential facilities doctrine, the owner of the essential facility must sometimes make the facility available to competitors.

In *Terminal Railroad,* all the railroad bridges in St. Louis were owned by a group of railroads.[72] The concern was that this control could allow the owning railroad companies to harm rival railroads (Reiffen and Kleit 1990). The Court ruled that the owning group had to provide access to rival railroads on reasonable terms.

Collective action receives close scrutiny under our antitrust laws because of the danger that competitors will agree to restrict competition. For that reason, many joint ventures that limit entry (such as sports leagues) face antitrust concerns regarding exclusionary acts that would not arise in the context of a single firm. Under *Colgate,* a single firm supposedly can decide with whom it deals.[73] But that doctrine has not always been followed and even single firms may have a duty to deal with rivals. For example, in *Aspen Ski Company v. Aspen Highland Skiing Corporation,* 472 U.S. 585 (1985), the Court ruled that an owner of three ski mountains had to continue its historical practice of cooperating with the owner of a fourth mountain in issuing lift tickets that allow skiers access to all four mountains. The reasoning seems to put a higher burden on a monopoly that once dealt with a rival than one that never did. In *Kodak,* the Court reiterated its view in *Aspen* that a monopoly may refuse to deal with its rivals "only if there are legitimate competitive reasons for the refusal."[74] See Carlton (2001) for further analysis.

The context of many cases involving refusals to deal and essential facilities is that one firm owns a scarce resource that its rivals need in order to compete. These cases, therefore, have a vertical element and can best be viewed in the context of the models of Chapter 11 involving raising rivals' costs or the natural advantage of an incumbent. For example, by denying access to or by raising the toll on the only bridge to an island, the railroad that owns the bridge can put its rival at a competitive disadvantage.

There are two noteworthy features about forcing one firm to provide supplies to its rival. First, the Court must be concerned that the firm with the scarce resource does not charge too high a price; otherwise, no rival will be able to compete even if it has

---

[71]See also *Federal Trade Commission v. Indiana Federation of Dentists,* 106 S. Ct. 2009 (1986).

[72]*United States v. Terminal Railroad Association of St. Louis,* 224 U.S. 383 (1912). See also *Otter Tail Power Co. v. United States,* 410 U.S. 366 (1973).

[73]*United States v. Colgate & Co.,* 250 U.S. 300 (1919).

[74]*Eastman Kodak Co. v. Image Technical Services, Inc.,* 112 S. Ct. 2091 (1992) n. 32. Recent cases such as the FTC's suit against Intel and the Department of Justice's case against Microsoft have raised antitrust concerns about the way in which an allegedly powerful firm can deal with its customers when those customers are also its rivals in some products.

access to the scarce resource. Second, a firm with monopoly power is usually allowed to charge any price it likes. It is unclear why that principle should be different here for the single firm that owns the scarce resource just because the scarce resource is an input for its rival.

Vertical Arrangements Between Firms

So far, the section has described how one firm (or a group of firms acting collectively) can harm a competitor through bad acts. The antitrust laws also characterize certain types of vertical relationships among noncompeting firms, typically a manufacturer and a distributor, as bad acts that harm competitors. We now analyze vertical integration and vertical restraints (resale price maintenance, exclusive territories, and exclusive dealing). The area of the law dealing with vertical relationships has changed significantly, and certain aspects of the law appear to be inconsistent with economic theories. See Carlton (2001) for a detailed analysis.

Vertical integration and vertical restrictions are not necessarily anticompetitive (Chapter 12). Even when a manufacturer is a monopoly, it is not at all clear that the vertical restrictions it may impose on a distributor reduce consumer welfare. It is not possible to prove definitively that vertical integration or restrictions always improve society's welfare, but neither is it possible to prove that a monopoly's choice of quality or any other product dimension always improves consumer welfare. Moreover, it is typically costly to examine a particular case of a vertical relation or quality choice, and, even after lengthy examination, it may still be difficult to reliably predict the effect of the vertical relation or quality choice on consumer welfare. Few argue that the antitrust laws should be used to control how a monopoly chooses quality or manufactures its product, yet there is usually no greater justification for interfering in the monopoly's choice of distribution than for interfering in its choice of quality or production.

In some markets, however, vertical integration or restrictions reduce competition and harm society, and those are the ones the antitrust laws should try to prevent. We now discuss those situations.

Exclusive dealing can harm society if it prevents or impedes rivals from obtaining distribution of their product. The same is true for vertical integration into distribution. However, as long as other efficient methods of distribution are available to rivals, neither exclusive dealing nor vertical integration restrain the entry of rivals.

Other vertical restrictions, such as exclusive territories, can have anticompetitive effects if they are forced on a manufacturer by a dealer cartel. That is, the exclusive territories could be part of an agreement among competing dealers on how to allocate territories.[75] Only if the dealers have monopsony power, however, does such a claim make sense (Chapter 12). No manufacturer would willingly take part in such a conspiracy of its dealers, because it would raise the manufacturer's distribution costs.

Antitrust policy toward vertical relationships has implications for the ability of a firm to price discriminate. Vertical integration and restrictions may enable price dis-

[75] Vertical integration and vertical restrictions can also be used by manufacturers to facilitate collusion by making it easier to detect cheating on a cartel of manufacturers (see Chapter 5).

crimination to take place (Chapter 9). For example, a manufacturer that wants to charge different prices in New York and California could do so if it prevents resale between the two states by requiring its distributors to sell only in their own territories. Because it is unclear whether society is, in general, harmed or helped by imperfect price discrimination (Chapter 9), it seems unwise to apply a per se ban. Moreover, to examine every instance of price discrimination under a rule of reason would be costly, and even after the analysis, it probably would be difficult to predict reliably the welfare effects of the discrimination.

Vertical Integration: The Court's early views on vertical relations in general and vertical integration in particular were unclear at best. Apparently, the Court was concerned with *foreclosure of competition.* For example, if a firm that manufactures shirts vertically integrated backward into producing buttons, the firm would have foreclosed competition in the button market because other button manufacturers could now no longer sell to that firm.

In *Yellow Cab,* the Court suggested that vertical integration through merger might be per se illegal.[76] However, soon thereafter, it reached the opposite (and more reasonable) conclusion in *Columbia Steel* that "it is clear to us that vertical integration, as such without more, cannot be held violative of the Sherman Act."[77]

The next major vertical integration case was *du Pont.*[78] Since 1920 (or earlier), du Pont, a major supplier to General Motors of automotive finishes and fabrics, had owned a 23 percent stock interest in General Motors. The U.S. government brought suit, claiming that the vertical relationship violated the antitrust laws. Although it was unclear how consumers would be adversely affected by this vertical ownership, the Court ruled that du Pont's ownership violated the antitrust laws.

It appears that since the *du Pont* case, enforcement policy toward vertical mergers has been in line with the reasonable economic logic of *Columbia Steel.* The vertical guidelines of the Department of Justice (repudiated by the Clinton administration) emphasized that vertical integration alone is not objectionable; instead, they focus on whether the vertical integration could be used to increase market power.

Although the FTC and the Department of Justice are less hostile to vertical integration than in the past, the courts have not always concurred. For example, in *Fotomat,* the Court of Appeals for the Seventh Circuit ruled against a franchisor that sought to open outlets in competition with its own franchisee.[79] It is difficult to understand why vertically integrating forward into distribution is an antitrust violation simply because independent dealers face additional competition.

Vertical Restraints: Using contracts, a firm may impose vertical restraints on another firm instead of vertically integrating to directly control that firm. Were vertical

---

[76]*United States v. Yellow Cab Co.,* 332 U.S. 218 (1947).

[77]*United States v. Columbia Steel Company,* 334 U.S. 495 (1948).

[78]*United States v. E.I. du Pont de Nemours & Company,* 353 U.S. 586 (1957).

[79]*Photovest v. Fotomat Corp.,* 606 F.2d 704 (7th Cir. 1979).

restraints to be outlawed but vertical integration allowed, firms would have an increased incentive to vertically integrate. Important vertical restraints include resale price maintenance, exclusive territories, and exclusive dealing.

Resale Price Maintenance: A manufacturer may set a minimum (or maximum) price that retailers may charge, called *resale price maintenance,* because the manufacturer wants to control the retail price at which its product is sold to consumers (Chapter 12). In 1911, the Court addressed whether a manufacturer could place pricing restrictions on its distributors. In *Dr. Miles,* John D. Park, a distributor, refused to enter into a contract that established minimum prices at which Dr. Miles's drug products could be sold.[80] The Court ruled that this pricing agreement was illegal because it suppressed competition among dealers and was equivalent to the fixing of price.

This ruling was unpopular, and the antitrust laws were eventually amended to allow resale price maintenance for certain products. In 1937, Congress passed the Miller-Tydings Resale Price Maintenance Act and in 1951, the McGuire Act. These acts gave manufacturers the right to set retail prices free of any antitrust liability provided the states had a *fair-trade* statute that allowed resale price maintenance (which would allow products to be sold at a "fair" price). Many states passed such fair-trade laws. In states without fair-trade laws, it was easier for one distributor to free ride on the promotional efforts of other distributors, because resale price maintenance is one way to control free riding (Chapter 12). The laws allowing resale price maintenance were repealed in 1975, and all resale price maintenance again became per se illegal.

The procompetitive logic of resale price maintenance is that resale price maintenance is one way for a manufacturer to induce its distributors to promote its products (Chapter 12). This logic was not understood by most economists prior to the 1960s. Since the 1960s, economists have discussed the competitive benefits of restraints that manufacturers want to place on the distributors of their products. These economists make no distinction between pricing restrictions and other restrictions that manufacturers might want to place on their distributors. Both can promote competition and prevent free riding (Posner 1981). Resale price maintenance can be anticompetitive, however, if it facilitates collusive behavior.

With the repeal of the laws permitting resale price maintenance in 1975, manufacturers can no longer set price floors for distributors.[81] However, a recent decision by the Supreme Court may indicate relaxation of this ban.[82] The Court analyzed a case in which a retailer that had cut prices had its supply terminated. The retailer claimed that termination occurred because of the price-cutting and that the termination constituted a violation of the antitrust laws. Although the Court stated that vertical agreements on resale prices are illegal per se, it ruled that because there was no agreement on price among the other competing retailers and the manufacturer, there was no violation of

---

[80] *Dr. Miles Medical Company v. John D. Park & Sons Company,* 220 U.S. 373 (1911).

[81] The setting of maximum prices is judged under the rule of reason. See *State Oil v. Kahn,* 522 U.S. 3 (1997).

[82] *Business Electronics Corporation v. Sharp Electronics Corporation,* 485 U.S. 717 (1988).

the antitrust laws. Therefore, although apparently the Court did not overrule its per se prohibition on vertical price fixing, its decision in this case reaches the conclusion of many economists that a manufacturer's control of pricing should not necessarily be an antitrust violation.

Exclusive Territories: A manufacturer may find it profitable to assign a geographic area, an *exclusive territory*, to one of its dealers and not allow its other dealers to locate in that area (Chapter 12). Exclusive territories provide dealers with incentives to promote the product and prevent one dealer from free riding on the promotional efforts of another. Exclusive territories can also adversely affect competition if they facilitate a cartel. Obviously, a territorial restriction on the ability of a manufacturer's dealers to compete literally restricts competition, even though the purpose of the territorial restriction may be to promote competition and the sale of the product.

In 1963, the Court addressed the issue of territorial restrictions in *White Motor.*[83] A truck manufacturer limited the territory in which its distributors could sell the product. The Court ruled that such territorial restrictions do not necessarily violate the antitrust laws and their legality should be determined only after examining their effects.

In *General Motors,* the Court investigated the location clauses that General Motors had in its dealers' contracts that prevented dealers from moving from one territory to another.[84] General Motors also tried to prevent its dealers from reselling cars to discount dealers, who sold them without the same promotional activities as other dealers. The Court ruled that the efforts of General Motors "to eliminate sales of new Chevrolet cars by discounters was to protect franchise dealers from real or apparent price competition." Accordingly, the Court ruled that this behavior violated the antitrust laws.

In *Schwinn,* the Court ruled that exclusive territories "are so obviously destructive of competition that their mere existence is enough."[85] This important case made the use of exclusive territories a per se violation of the antitrust laws.

In *Sealy* and *Topco,* the Supreme Court interpreted territorial restrictions as agreements to limit competition among rivals.[86] In both cases, groups of firms combined and agreed to territorial restrictions as part of an effort to promote their products and a common trademark and to avoid free-rider problems. The Court held that in both cases, these agreements were per se violations of Section 1 of the Sherman Act. However, to the extent that in both cases the territorial restrictions were necessary to develop a new trademarked product, it would seem that the subsequent ruling in the *BMI* case (agreements among firms are acceptable if they are necessary to provide the product) would mean that the *Sealy* and *Topco* cases would, if examined now, be analyzed under the rule of reason and not viewed as per se violations.

---

[83] *White Motor Company v. United States,* 372 U.S. 253 (1963).

[84] *United States v. General Motors Corp.,* 384 U.S. 127 (1966).

[85] *United States v. Arnold, Schwinn & Company,* 388 U.S. 365 (1967).

[86] *United States v. Sealy, Inc.,* 388 U.S. 350 (1967) and *United States v. Topco Associates Inc.,* 405 U.S. 596 (1972).

In 1977, the Court overruled *Schwinn* in *GTE Sylvania.*[87] Sylvania imposed locational restrictions on its distributors. The Court recognized that vertical restrictions improved the ability of a manufacturer to sell its product and provided a way to overcome certain free-rider problems (Chapter 12). Therefore, the Court overruled *Schwinn's* per se prohibition against territorial restrictions and instead instituted a rule of reason under which vertical restrictions should be judged.

In *GTE Sylvania,* the Court's reasoning was based on the promotion of interbrand competition (competition among different products) at the expense of restricting intrabrand competition (competition among dealers of the same product). The use of this distinction is misleading. Vertical restrictions can indeed promote interbrand competition by making it profitable for dealers to promote and service each product, but it is not obvious that there is an undesirable effect on intrabrand competition. Although it is true in the literal sense that exclusive territories restrict the ability of one distributor to compete with another distributor, it is not true that a single manufacturer uses exclusive territories to restrict competition solely to raise the retail price and inflict an anticompetitive injury on consumers (Chapter 12).

After all, a manufacturer can raise the retail price (assuming no constraint from other products) by raising the wholesale price even without vertical restrictions. Through its control of the wholesale price, the manufacturer affects the retail price everywhere its product is sold. Rather than allowing the manufacturer to control only price, vertical restrictions give the manufacturer more control over promotional activities and service. By instituting a rule of reason criterion in *GTE Sylvania,* the Court acknowledged that vertical restraints can promote competition. See Example 19.6.

Exclusive Dealing: The Court has also analyzed *exclusive dealing* in which a manufacturer prevents its distributors from selling competing brands. Exclusive dealing allows manufacturers to overcome a different type of free-riding problem than the one overcome through the use of exclusive territories (Chapter 12). Exclusive territories address free riding of one dealer on the efforts of another; exclusive dealing addresses free riding of one manufacturer on the efforts of another. Exclusive dealing can also be used to raise entry barriers of rivals by raising distribution costs.

In 1922, the Supreme Court refused to enforce a manufacturer's contract with a retailer that forbade the retailer to sell brands of other manufacturers.[88] In 1949, in *Standard Stations,* the Court again addressed the problem of exclusive dealing.[89] Standard Oil of California required its independent dealers to purchase petroleum products and automobile accessories only from it. Rather than applying a rule of reason, the Supreme Court concluded that it would be too great a burden to show that competition had actually been diminished by the exclusive dealing and therefore it ruled that "Section 3 [of the Clayton Act, which forbids exclusive dealing] is satisfied by proof that competition has been foreclosed and a substantial share of the line of com-

---

[87] *Continental TV Inc. v. GTE Sylvania Inc.*, 433 U.S. 36 (1977). See Preston (1994).

[88] *Standard Fashion Company v. Magrain-Houston Co.*, 258 U.S. 346 (1922).

[89] *Standard Oil Company of California v. United States*, 337 U.S. 293 (1949).

EXAMPLE 19.6 *The FTC Plays with Toys 'Я' Us*

Toys 'Я' Us told toy manufacturers that if an *identical* toy were sold to warehouse clubs (very large stores that sell, often in bulk, at low prices), Toys 'Я' Us would consider not carrying those particular toys. The FTC charged that this policy was designed to eliminate rival toy retailers in an effort to restrict competition.

Toys 'Я' Us responded by claiming that they had no market power in toy retailing and that their policy was designed to limit free riding on their promotional activities by warehouse stores. It is difficult to predict which toys will be the Christmas season's big hits. Typically, toy manufacturers do not raise the price of the hits. Instead, the manufacturers ration them to retail toy stores. An allocation of hits can be viewed as a payment by the manufacturers to toy stores that engage in extensive promotional activities, provide showroom services, and sell toys year round.

Toys 'Я' Us engages in promotion and collaborates with manufacturers in designing toys. It stocks several thousand individual toy items in each store throughout the year, even though over 60 percent of toy sales occur in the last quarter of the year, the Christmas season. In contrast, warehouse clubs engage in little or no promotional activities and typically stock 100 to 150 toy items only at the end of the year.

Toys 'Я' Us had about a 20 percent share of retail toy sales, while warehouse clubs had less than 5 percent. According to statistical evidence presented at trial, Toys 'Я' Us did not have a statistically significant ability to raise retail prices even in areas where it faced only one major rival.

Despite this evidence, Toys 'Я' Us lost the case. Its market share of toys has continued to fall and was about 17.5 percent in 2003.

Note: Carlton served as an expert witness for Toys 'Я' Us.

Source: Carlton and Sider (1999); George James, "For Toys 'Я' Us, A Time to Rebuild," *New York Times,* January 14, 2004:1.

merce affected." Justice Jackson dissented, arguing that the Court had made an error in economic reasoning and that exclusive dealing can be "a device for waging competition."[90] The Court's future treatment of exclusive dealing will presumably incorporate its *GTE Sylvania* decision, in which it recognized that vertical restrictions can promote competition sometimes.

Litigating Vertical Restraint Cases. In many cases, a distributor complains that a vertical agreement between some distributors and a manufacturer is intended to eliminate or prevent competition by other distributors. Plaintiffs phrase the complaint in

[90]See also *Tampa Electric Company v. Nashville Coal Company,* 365 U.S. 320 (1961).

this way so as to characterize the behavior as a conspiracy involving price-fixing or output restrictions. The reason for this is that plaintiffs hope to apply the per se rules of the antitrust laws against price and output agreements and to obtain treble damages. If only breach of contract or other contract law violations were alleged, for example, they would receive only single damages. Thus, a terminated dealer may claim that the termination violates the antitrust laws rather than contract law in order to recover greater damages.

One example of an attempt to turn a vertical restriction case into a conspiracy case is *Klor's*, concerning the inability of a Klor's appliance store to obtain supplies from the same sources as its competitors.[91] Klor's was located close to a Broadway Hale department store, which distributed appliances. Many well-known brands of appliances were sold to Broadway Hale, but not to Klor's. Klor's claimed that there was a conspiracy among Broadway Hale and the appliance manufacturers to drive it out of business. Klor's claimed that Broadway Hale used its market power to prevent manufacturers from selling to Klor's. Broadway Hale's defense indicated that numerous other retailers located close to Broadway Hale also sold the appliances of major manufacturers. The important economic question is whether Broadway Hale had sufficient buying power over the manufacturers to prevent them from selling to Klor's. If it did not, then a likely alternative explanation for the manufacturers' behavior is to control free-rider problems (see Chapter 12).

Price Discrimination

Many forms of price discrimination have been challenged under the antitrust laws. For example, predation can involve a firm's charging a lower price in a market where it faces a rival than in another market where it does not. Such price discrimination that harms direct competitors is called *primary-line price discrimination* (see for example, *Utah Pie*). A second form of price discrimination, *secondary-line price discrimination,* is one that leads to harm among the customers. The Robinson-Patman Act forbids both types of price discrimination. A third form of price discrimination that is restricted under antitrust laws is tie-in sales. This section discusses secondary-line discrimination and tie-in sales.

Price Discrimination Under Robinson-Patman

The Robinson-Patman Act prohibits a firm from price discriminating if it harms competition among the firm's customers (secondary-line discrimination). The Robinson-Patman Act (which amended Section 2 of the Clayton Act in 1936) was passed in response to political pressure from small retail stores (for example, grocery stores) that complained that larger chains were able to purchase supplies on more favorable terms

[91] *Klor's, Inc. v. Broadway Hale Stores Inc.*, 359 U.S. 207 (1959).

and thereby charge lower prices (Ross 1984). Many economists view the Robinson-Patman Act as special-interest legislation designed to protect small firms from competition from larger, more efficient firms that would be able to purchase supplies at low cost in the absence of the Act (Posner 1976b, Ross 1984).

One consequence of the Robinson-Patman Act is higher prices to consumers, who are deprived of the benefits of economies of scale in purchasing that the chain stores would otherwise be forced by competition (among themselves) to pass along to consumers (Ross 1984). The Robinson-Patman Act has led to substantial litigation (although government litigation has waned recently) and has also distorted pricing in many markets (Elzinga and Hogarty 1978). This law has harmed consumers. Although the FTC has brought relatively few cases in recent years, private actions are still brought.

Tie-in Sales

The antitrust laws have been used to prevent a firm from using *tie-in sales* in which the sale of one product is conditioned upon the purchase of another. The courts often characterize tie-in sales as a way of denying competitors the opportunity to make sales. Tie-in sales can arise for efficiency reasons or because a firm has some market power in one market and by the use of tie-in sales is able to earn higher profits than if it could only charge for one product (Chapter 10). Tie-in sales, then, can be a variant of price discrimination. They raise the return to being a monopoly in an industry. They do not necessarily create greater inefficiency losses and could result in output expansion. However, as discussed in Chapter 11, tie-in sales can also be used strategically as a tool to harm rivals. Curiously, courts have focused on cases more closely related to price discrimination.

Aside from the price discrimination motive, many products are naturally and efficiently tied together or bundled. For example, a car consists of many component parts, as does a radio. Consumers would be extremely unhappy if the government prohibited such efficient bundling of components. There are, however, some cases where tie-ins are anticompetitive. For example, tie-in sales could be used to raise entry costs (by tying repair to a machine, no independent repair shops arise and entrants are disadvantaged). However, the courts do not focus solely on these types of cases in their decisions to prohibit tie-in sales.

In early cases involving patented products, the Supreme Court ruled that tie-in sales were indeed legal. For example, in *A. B. Dick,* the Court did not find fault with A. B. Dick's practice of selling its patented mimeograph machines with a requirement that only ink purchased from A. B. Dick Company, as well as other supplies made by A. B. Dick, could be used.[92] Such a tie-in could enable A. B. Dick to identify and extract more money from those who used the machine most intensively (Chapter 10).

The Clayton Act, passed in 1914, contained a section outlawing tie-in sales that had the effect of reducing competition. Soon thereafter, the Court overruled the *A. B.*

[92] *Henry v. A. B. Dick Company,* 224 U.S. 1 (1912).

Dick case in *Motion Picture Patents.*[93] In two subsequent cases, the Supreme Court refused to alter its prohibition against tie-ins. In another, *IBM,* the United States attacked IBM's practice of selling key-punch machines with the requirement that the purchaser use only IBM tabulating cards.[94] IBM granted a special exception to the government that allowed it to use tabulating cards of its own manufacture provided the government paid an extra 15 percent rent. The Supreme Court used the government's experience to reject IBM's claim that its reputation would be damaged unless its tabulating cards were used because otherwise its machines might malfunction.

In *International Salt,* the Court investigated the requirement by International Salt Company that its purchasers use salt provided by International Salt in some machines that International Salt provided.[95] As in *IBM,* the Court rejected International Salt's claim that its reputation would be damaged if low-quality salt were used, with resulting damage to its machines. The Court ruled that since a substantial amount of the salt market was "foreclosed" to competitors, the tie-in was per se illegal.

In *Northern Pacific,* the Court ruled that the Northern Pacific Railway Company's requirements that lessees of certain lands be required to use its railway to ship under certain conditions was a per se violation:[96]

> Tying agreements serve hardly any purpose beyond the suppression of competition. They deny competitors free access to the market for the tied product, not because the party imposing the tying requirement has a better product or a lower price, but because it has power leverage in another market.

The Court found that the defendant possessed substantial economic power and concluded that the tie-in was illegal. In *Fortner II,* the Court stated that "for a tie-in to be illegal, the seller must have some advantage not shared by his competitors in the market for the tie-in product."[97]

Another important case involving tie-ins is *Hyde.*[98] A hospital had contracted for the provision of anesthesiology services from a private firm. The hospital agreed to use only that firm in the provision of anesthesiology services to its patients. An anesthesiologist sued and charged the hospital with tying anesthesiology to its other hospital services. The Court states that the requirements for an illegal tie are (1) the existence of two products, (2) market power in one product, and (3) *forcing.* By forcing, the Court means that products get sold together that would not be sold together without the tie. The Court said, "It is far too late in the history of our antitrust jurisprudence to question the proposition that certain tying arrangements pose an unacceptable risk of stifling competition. . . ." The Court did not find that

[93] *Motion Picture Patents v. Universal Film Manufacturing Co.,* 243 U.S. 502 (1917).

[94] *IBM Corporation v. United States,* 298 U.S. 131 (1936).

[95] *International Salt Company v. United States,* 332 U.S. 392 (1947). See Peterman (1979) for an economic analysis of this case.

[96] *Northern Pacific Railway Company v. United States,* 356 U.S. 1 (1958).

[97] *United States Steel Corporation v. Fortner Enterprises, Inc.,* 429 U.S. 610 (1977).

[98] *Jefferson Parish Hospital District No. 2 v. Hyde,* 466 U.S. 2 (1984). Lynk (1994a) analyzes this case.

the questioned conduct was illegal, apparently because the hospital lacked market power.

Kodak is an important tie-in case.[99] Kodak sells photocopiers in competition with many other firms. Kodak also provided Kodak parts and service to its customers. Kodak refused to supply certain parts to independent repair shops and was charged with illegally tying the sale of its photocopiers with its parts and service. Kodak asked that the case be dismissed because both sides agreed that Kodak faced lots of competition in the initial sale of photocopiers. If there is competition initially, then customers will not buy from Kodak if they know that they will be overcharged on repair parts and service. The Court rejected Kodak's argument. According to the Court, even if Kodak lacked market power initially in photocopiers, it is theoretically possible that either consumers are uninformed or that they are unable to forecast their repair cost. Essentially, the Court ruled that any equipment manufacturer could be considered a monopolist of its own unique repair parts and that a factual investigation is necessary to resolve a tie-in case even if there are hundreds of competing manufacturers of equipment. The Court failed to explain how any consumer would benefit if Kodak were forced to sell repair parts to independent repair shops at a price that Kodak could choose.

The courts' rulings regarding tie-in sales, especially those between franchisors and franchisees, have been inconsistent with the economic theory described in Chapter 12. A franchisor may place many types of restrictions on a franchisee in order to obtain certain desired economic performance. The franchisor also needs to be compensated for its efforts. One method by which a franchisee can compensate the franchisor is through various tie-in sales. For example, the franchisor could require that it be the sole supplier of napkins to the franchisee in lieu of charging a franchise fee based on sales. This conduct, however, has been attacked as a means to foreclose competition in napkins, using antitrust laws that ban tie-in sales.[100]

Effects of Antitrust Laws on the Organization of Unregulated and Regulated Firms

When laws prohibit firms from taking particular actions, firms seek alternate routes to accomplish their objectives. Because the antitrust laws inhibit agreements between independent firms both horizontally and vertically, some firms merge or simply grow large and do everything themselves. Thus, the antitrust laws can encourage firms to

[99]*Eastman Kodak Co. v. Image Technical Services, Inc.*, 112 S. Ct. 2072 (1992). See Calkins (1993) and Carlton (2001) for analyses of this case. See also the discussion of the Microsoft case, Example 11.5.

[100]See, for example, *Siegel v. Chicken Delight Inc.*, 448 F.2d (9th Cir. 1971) cert. denied, 405 U.S. 955.

merge or grow larger than would otherwise occur. For example, Bittlingmayer (1985) explains that many firms merged around the turn of the century when antitrust laws first forbade agreements among firms but did not forbid mergers.

Similarly, some of the decisions of the Supreme Court to forbid certain types of contractual vertical restrictions create an incentive for vertical integration.[101] Several states have responded by adopting statutes that prevent certain manufacturers from integrating forward into distribution. For example, several states prevent oil companies from owning and operating their own gasoline stations.

The antitrust laws, as already mentioned, affect how a franchisor can deal with a franchisee. The effect of the antitrust laws (and several state franchise laws) is to transfer certain rights from franchisors to franchisees and to make the franchise arrangement less attractive as a method of distribution (Smith 1982). If laws make it difficult for franchisors to control franchisees' actions, the incentive to use this mode of organization is diminished. Where antitrust laws encourage firms to alter their organizational form, it is likely that the new form will be less efficient.

Antitrust laws can have a large impact on regulated firms. The intersection of antitrust law and regulation is a complicated and contentious subject. Courts do not accept the argument that regulation immunizes a firm from antitrust actions because it is under the watchful eye of a regulator. Indeed, it was application of the antirust laws that eventually forced the break-up of the AT&T phone monopoly in the early 1980s.[102]

However, courts do accept the principle that regulation can immunize some actions of a regulated firm, especially when those actions are essential to the regulatory purpose. See for example, *Silver v. New York Stock Exchange*, 373 U.S. 341. In a case in 2003 (*in re: Stock Exchanges Options Trading Antitrust Litigation*, 317 F.3d 134), the Court ruled that the antitrust laws could not be used to attack the exchanges where options are traded for certain behavior because their actions were closely monitored by the Securities and Exchange Commission, the regulatory body charged with overseeing the operations of U.S. financial markets.

If a regulator imposes on a regulated firm a duty to deal with its rivals, then the rivals will be more formidable competitors. If a regulated firm misbehaves toward its rivals, should it be subject to antitrust sanctions or only to sanctions imposed by the regulator? The Supreme Court has recently ruled that the antitrust laws do not apply in cases where a firm is forced by regulation to deal with its rivals when it would not have done so in the absence of regulation.[103]

---

[101] Alternatively, firms could use devices whose legality turns on legal technicalities. For example, a distributor may sell a good on consignment (which means that the manufacturer, not the distributor, owns the good) rather than owning the good and reselling it. The restrictions that can be placed on consignment sales can differ from those on nonconsignment sales.

[102] *U.S. v. AT&T Co.*, 552 F. Supp. 131 (1982). See also **www.aw-bc.com/carlton_perloff** "The Breakup of AT&T."

[103] See *Goldwasser v. Ameritech Corp.* 222 F.3d 390 (Seventh Circuit 2000) and *Verizon Communications Inc. v. Law Offices of Curtis V. Trinko,* 540 U.S. (2004).

SUMMARY

The major federal antitrust statutes are the Sherman Act, the Clayton Act, and the Federal Trade Commission Act. The interpretation of these statutes has varied considerably over time. There has been an increasing emphasis on the use of economic analysis in deciding what the antitrust laws should prohibit. Economists stress using antitrust laws to achieve efficiency.

It is a common mistake to think that the antitrust laws prohibit monopoly. They do not; however, they do prohibit certain actions that could allow a firm to acquire or maintain monopoly power.

Many antitrust cases revolve around whether a firm has market power, which is the ability to set price profitably above the competitive price. It is often difficult to assess directly whether a firm has market power. Courts and economists often use market share as a rough guide to whether a firm has market power. For this calculation of market share to be meaningful, the market must be properly defined. The market definition should include all those products whose presence significantly constrains the price of the product under analysis.

The courts use both per se rules and rules of reason. A per se rule prohibits certain acts without regard to the effect of the acts. For example, a price-fixing conspiracy whose sole purpose is to raise price is a per se violation. A rule of reason requires an investigation of the effect of the challenged conduct. Vertical restraints, other than on price, are now judged under a rule of reason.

The antitrust laws severely limit the types of cooperative behavior in which competitors can engage. For example, any attempt to fix price or limit output so as to harm consumers is a per se violation. That is, even unsuccessful attempts to fix price violate the law. There are some instances, however, where the courts allow cooperative behavior, even with respect to price, if the cooperative behavior is essential to producing the product. Mergers among competitors can be prevented if the effect of the merger is to create additional market power. Curiously, two firms with no market power are allowed to merge even though those same two firms would violate the law if they remained independent but spoke to each other and set price together.

The antitrust laws also constrain actions designed to hamper a firm's rivals. For example, strategic behavior, such as predatory pricing, designed to drive a rival out of business is illegal. The problem with antitrust enforcement in this area is that it is difficult to distinguish vigorous competition from strategic behavior that harms consumers. Overzealous enforcement could deprive consumers of the benefits of competition.

An important application of the antitrust laws has been to vertical relations between firms. The Court's reasoning has often been confused and has relied on a foreclosure of competition doctrine in which one firm that, say, vertically integrates into steel production is said to foreclose other steel producers from selling steel to the first firm.

There is a variety of reasons why a firm vertically integrates or imposes vertical restraints on its distributors. Many, but not all, of these reasons promote competition. Recently, the Court has recognized the possible procompetitive effect of nonprice vertical restrictions, but still regards vertical restrictions on price as a per se violation.

It is impossible to prove that vertical restrictions always benefit each consumer. The welfare effect of some vertical restrictions is ambiguous. Even after careful study, an analyst may be unable to decide whether a particular vertical restriction harms consumers. A vertical restriction may help some consumers and harm others. But the same could be said of the choice of product quality. There is often no greater justification for controlling how a manufacturer distributes its product than there is in dictating the quality of product that the monopoly produces.

There are, however, cases where vertical integration or restrictions harm consumers. Where the vertical integration or restrictions significantly impede or foreclose entry by rivals or where they allow distributors or manufacturers to act like a cartel, they harm consumers.

The welfare effects of price discrimination and tie-in sales designed to achieve price discrimination are generally ambiguous. As in the case of certain vertical restrictions, it is often costly and difficult to determine conclusively whether consumers are harmed in a particular situation. Pursuing strenuous general antitrust enforcement in areas with ambiguous welfare effects is unwise.

Using the antitrust laws to control some activities but not others can lead firms to adopt inefficient organizational forms. For example, if antitrust laws do not allow certain vertical restrictions but do allow vertical integration, firms may choose to vertically integrate to achieve their goals even if vertical integration is more costly than relying on vertical restrictions. Application of the antitrust laws to regulated industries can have large impacts on its market structure.

PROBLEMS

1. In *United Shoe*, the Court ruled that the 10-year leases adversely affected competition, in part, because they prevented other competitors from selling to a customer who had a United Shoe lease. Such a claim can be made of any contract. Identify circumstances where a long-term lease impedes competition.
2. Suppose Firm A is the only one that can sell in New York. Firm A faces competition elsewhere in the country. If Firm A can price discriminate, will the prices in New York differ from those elsewhere? Will there be a high correlation of price movements between New York and elsewhere? Is there one geographic market or two?
3. Suppose there are some industries in which the competitive equilibrium does not exist (the core does not exist—see **www.aw-bc.com/carlton_perloff** "Theory of the Core"). Should firms in these industries be allowed to collude under the antitrust laws?
4. Where demand curves are compensated (adjusted for income effects), it can be shown that

$$\frac{\partial Q_j}{\partial p_i} = \frac{\partial Q_i}{\partial p_j},$$

where Q is the quantity demanded, p is the price, and subscripts indicate the products i or j. Suppose $p_i = p_j$, but $Q_i = 100Q_j$. What are the relative sizes of the two relevant cross-elasticities of demand? Why does it matter which one is used in the analysis of market definition?
5. It can be shown that

$$\frac{p_i}{Q_i}\frac{\partial Q_i}{\partial p_i} = -\sum_{j \neq i} \frac{p_j}{Q_i}\frac{\partial Q_i}{\partial p_j},$$

where Σ is a summation sign (sum over all products j other than product i), p is price, and Q is the compensated demand. Explain how this relation can be used to relate the elasticity of demand to cross-elasticities of demand. Use the formula to determine which cross-elasticity an analyst investigating market power in Product A should examine to determine whether Product B constrains the pricing of Product A.

Answers to the odd-numbered problems are given at the back of the book.

SUGGESTED READINGS

Kwoka and White (2004) is an easy-to-read collection of articles providing economic analysis of some recent antitrust cases. Interesting books on the economics of antitrust law include Posner (2001), Posner and Easterbrook (1980) with subsequent supplements, and Williamson (1987). The Areeda and Hovenkamp (1997) treatise on antitrust provides an exhaustive analysis of antitrust issues. Pittman (1992) discusses merger law in Central and Eastern Europe, as do numerous, Web sites sponsored by the International Competition Network. Carlton (2004b) discusses the lessons foreign countries have learned from U.S. antitrust experience.

CHAPTER 20

Regulation and Deregulation

If it moves, tax it.
If it still moves, regulate it.
If it stops moving, subsidize it. —*Ronald Reagan*

Government regulation of firms may increase welfare in markets that are not perfectly competitive. Unfortunately, actual regulation often deviates considerably from optimal regulation and exacerbates market inefficiencies.

A prime example of an inefficient market is a monopolized industry, which charges too high a price. Optimal regulation can force a monopoly to set the competitive price. However, if a monopoly is badly regulated, shortages occur, or the monopoly is encouraged to produce inefficiently. Even where regulations are properly applied, the cost of administering them may exceed the benefits.

In addition, some regulations create problems where none would otherwise exist. For example, federal and state government marketing orders permit otherwise competitive firms to price discriminate and restrict output (Appendix 9A).

Regulation of monopolies is only one type of regulation commonly seen in Western economies. For example, in Germany, the hours that firms may stay open are strictly limited. Large U.S. regulatory agencies with budgets over $200 million per year are listed in Table 20.1, the largest of which is the Transportation Security Administration, which was created in 2001 in response to the 9/11 tragedy. The Environmental Protection Agency (EPA) controls pollution. The Occupational Safety and Health Agency (OSHA) protects workers. The Consumer Product Safety Commission (CPSC), the Federal Trade Commission (FTC), and the Food and Drug Administration (FDA) protect consumers (see also Example 20.1). The regulation of advertising and disclosure laws by the FTC and others is discussed in Chapter 14.

TABLE 20.1 **U.S. Regulatory Agencies with Budgets of at Least $200 Million in Fiscal Year 2002**

Agency	Year Created	Budget ($ Millions)	Responsibility
Social Regulation			
Consumer Safety and Health			
Department of Agriculture			
Animal and Plant Health Inspection Service	1972	948	Meat and poultry packing plants
Food Safety and Inspection Service	1981	808	Meat, poultry, and egg products
Department of Health and Human Services			
Food and Drug Administration	1906	1,574	Safety of food and drugs (since 1906) and cosmetics (since 1938); effectiveness of drugs (since 1962)
Department of Justice			
Bureau of Alcohol, Tobacco, Firearms, and Explosives	1972	795	Alcohol, firearms, and explosives
Transportation			
Department of Homeland Security			
Coast Guard	1915	2,127	Vessel safety
Transportation Security Administration	2001	4,080	Airport baggage screening
Department of Transportation			
Federal Aviation Administration	1958	1,436	Airline safety and air traffic control
Federal Motor Carrier Safety Administration	2000	367	Motor carrier safety, including transport of hazardous materials
National Highway Traffic Safety Administration	1970	242	Automobile safety; automobile fuel economy (since 1975)
Job Safety and Other Working Conditions			
Department of Labor			
Employment Standards Administration	1972	247	Legally mandated wages and working conditions
Mine Safety and Health Administration	1977	254	Safety and health in mining, especially coal mines
Occupational Safety and Health Administration	1971	446	Industrial safety and health
Equal Employment Opportunity Commission	1964	320	Job discrimination
National Labor Relations Board	1935	226	Unfair labor practices by unions or employers

(continued)

TABLE 20.1 **U.S. Regulatory Agencies with Budgets of at Least $200 Million in Fiscal Year 2002 (continued)**

Agency	Year Created	Budget ($ Millions)	Responsibility
Social Regulation			
Environment			
Department of Agriculture			
Forest and Rangeland Research	N.A.	290	Vegetation management and protection
Department of Interior			
Fish and Wildlife Service	1940	283	Fish, wildlife, plants, and their habitats
Office of Surface Mining Reclamation and Enforcement	1977	454	Coal mines
Environmental Protection Agency	1972	4,758	Air, water, and noise pollution
Energy			
Nuclear Regulatory Commission	1975	553	Nuclear materials and commercial nuclear reactors
Economic Regulation			
Finance and Banking			
Department of the Treasury			
Comptroller of the Currency	1863	417	National banks
Federal Deposit Insurance Corporation	1933	593	Banks and thrift institutions
Federal Reserve System			
Federal Reserve Banks	1913	471	State-chartered member banks and bank holding companies
Industry-Specific Regulation			
Department of Agriculture			
Agricultural Marketing Service	1972	219	Cotton, fruits and vegetables, livestock and seed, poultry, and tobacco
Federal Communications Commission	1934	333	Interstate telephone and broadcasting (since 1934); cable television (since 1968)
General Business			
Department of Commerce			
Patent and Trademark Office	1825	1,144	Patents and trademarks
Securities and Exchange Commission	1934	489	Public security issues and security exchanges, and public utility holding companies

Sources: Dudley and Warren (2003), **www.multied.com/Civics/Index.html**; various government agency Web sites.

Spending at 60 U.S. federal social and economic regulatory agencies was approximately $26.2 billion in 2002, almost five times what it was in 1970, after adjusting for inflation (Dudley and Warren 2003). The regulatory system was staffed by about 133,000 people, up from less than 70,000 in 1970 and 122,000 in 1980. The economic regulation

EXAMPLE 20.1 *Pizza Protection*

On average, each American adult and child eats seven pizzas a year. To protect these consumers, 310 separate rules, filling over 40 pages of federal documents, govern what goes on a pizza and how these toppings may be described on labels and menus. A few of these rules are

- *Crust:* There must be 2.9 milligrams of thiamine, 24 milligrams of niacin, and at least 13 (but not more than 16) milligrams of iron in each pound of flour.
- *Mozzarella cheese:* The cheese must contain at least 30%, but no more than 45%, fat and must be made from pasteurized cow's milk.
- *Anchovies:* Imports from Spain, Portugal, and Morocco must be packed in oil and in a solution of at least 12% salt.
- *Green peppers:* Salt preservatives, such as calcium chloride, in canned green peppers must not exceed .026% of the food's weight.
- *Onions:* Only if the onions come from the bulb of the plant rather than the stalk may canned onions be used.
- *Beef:* Fat must constitute no more than 30% of ground beef.
- *Italian sausage:* To be called that, sausage must be uncured and contain at least 85% meat. If more than 13% extenders are used, sausage must carry the notice "texturized soy flour added."

These regulations affect the final product in many ways. For example, the labeling division of the U.S. Department of Agriculture (USDA) initially concluded that the frozen trendy pizza of famous Los Angeles chef Wolfgang Puck could not be called a pizza because it did not have tomatoes on it. Puck said, "I think it's ridiculous that some bureaucrat in Washington thinks they are going to tell us what a pizza is. Tomato sauce has a cheap image on pizza and we decided to have fresh ingredients." Nonetheless, Puck agreed to add some tomato chunks to the basil-pesto sauce. The USDA also discovered that the "country sausage" on the label was made in the City of Commerce, which is not a rural area. Puck agreed to change the label to "Spago's Original Sausage and Herbs." Today, a dozen agencies enforce 35 different laws concerning food safety.

Sources: "The Pizza Principles," *San Francisco Examiner,* June 6, 1982: "This World" Section, 15; Garchik, Leah. "Federal Ruling on Pizza Without Tomatoes." *San Francisco Chronicle,* November 11, 1987: A10, Jennifer Kabbany, "Armey Targets Waste in Federal Agencies," *Washington Times,* February 12, 1999.

spending is split between finance and banking (39%), industry-specific regulation (17%), and general business (44%). The annualized real growth rate in regulation spending under the current Bush administration (based on its 2004 budget request) is 9.40%, far more than under the Clinton (1.88%), previous Bush (5.26%), and Reagan (1.34%) administrations. Congress created the Transportation Security Administration in November 2001, adding more than 56,000 new employees as airport baggage screeners.

This chapter focuses on regulations that directly affect price, quantity, quality, or entry. We begin by considering the objectives of the regulators and then look at the regulations that make monopolistic industries more competitive and those that make competitive industries more monopolistic. Finally, the chapter considers the effects of recent deregulation efforts.

The main questions examined in this chapter are

1. What are the objectives of regulators?
2. Under what conditions is regulation most likely to raise welfare?
3. What types of regulation are most likely to lower welfare?
4. What has been the effect of deregulation?

The Objectives of Regulators

Man is the only animal that laughs and has a state legislature.

—Samuel Butler

There are two contradictory views about regulation and its effects. One view holds that government should and can regulate to correct market inefficiencies. The opposing view is that either the government lacks the information necessary to regulate optimally or that special-interest groups pressure legislatures and regulators so that regulations create market inefficiencies.

Market Inefficiencies

The most common justification for regulation is to correct a deviation from perfect competition, a market inefficiency. As discussed at length throughout this book, there are many causes of market inefficiencies. Commonly observed causes of market inefficiencies include monopoly power, externalities such as pollution, uncertainty, and various forms of opportunistic behavior.

Williamson (1975) contends that market imperfections are caused by human and environmental factors. Human factors that are likely to lead to market inefficiencies include bounded rationality and opportunism. Environmental factors include small numbers of firms and uncertainty. For example, *bounded rationality* limits people's ability to analyze and deal with uncertain or complex situations. Thus, market inefficiencies are more likely where transactions are complex or the outcome is uncertain. Opportunism leads to problems when there are few buyers or sellers (market power) or asymmetric information.

Unfortunately, the same factors that make market inefficiencies frequently make correcting the inefficiencies difficult. Moreover, not all inefficiencies can be corrected even by optimal government intervention. For example, if the inefficiency stems from limited information, the government may not be able to obtain and disseminate the relevant information cost effectively. That is, the world would be better off with full information, but that is not a viable option.

Correcting Market Inefficiencies

Consumer advocates such as Ralph Nader argue for regulations that are designed to promote or protect the public welfare.[1] Legislators pass such laws believing that government can increase welfare.

Of course, even such people of goodwill differ as to the appropriate objectives for government actions. There are two chief alternative points of view:

- Many, if not most, economists argue that the chief objective of government regulation should be to promote *economic efficiency* by eliminating market inefficiencies (Schmalensee 1979b; Kahn 1970, 1975).
- Other economists and consumer advocates argue that regulation should be used to *redistribute income.*

Although some economists believe that regulations can be used to redistribute income (Feldstein 1972a, 1972b), others believe that trying to use regulation to redistribute income is difficult, and possibly counterproductive (Kahn 1975, Peltzman 1976). As Schmalensee (1979b, 23) concludes, evaluating distributional issues may be possible in principle but is extremely difficult in practice. Thus, for the rest of this chapter, we concentrate on the use of regulations to promote economic efficiency.

Capture Theory and Interest-Group Theory

But who would guard the guards themselves? —*Juvenal*

One cynical—or realistic (depending on your viewpoint)—explanation for regulation is **capture theory**: The firms in an industry want to be regulated because they can then "capture" (persuade, bribe, or threaten) the regulators, so that the regulators do what the industry wants. Regulation, according to this theory, protects firms from competition. Although these economists typically believe that the appropriate objective of regulation is to correct market inefficiencies, they think that even if an appropriate law were passed, the affected industry would subvert the purpose of the law by capturing the regulators.

A generalization of this theory is that various interest groups are affected differently by regulation and compete to influence legislation. Those that are the best organized and most affected by regulation spend the most money attempting to promote their own interest through legislation and sympathetic regulators. In this more general **interest-group theory**, firms, consumers, or other groups can influence a regulatory body (Stigler 1971; Posner 1971, 1974; Peltzman 1976, 1989; Becker 1983). In some cases, one consumer group benefits at the expense of another (see Example 20.2).

A prime example of this self-interest theory is occupational licensing. Here, the regulated occupations—such as plumbers, electricians, doctors, lawyers, and beauticians—lobby for licensing laws and set the rules themselves (Example 20.3, Chapter 13).

[1] See Joskow (1974) on the efforts environmentalists direct at electric utility regulation.

EXAMPLE 20.2

Cross-Subsidization

Many public utilities cross-subsidize rates. For example, they price discriminate, charging one group higher rates than another for identical services. The high-price users are said to be cross-subsidizing the low-price users. In another common form of price discrimination, two groups pay the same rate, even though the cost of providing the service is more to the subsidized group. For example, urban and rural phone rates are often the same, even though the costs of providing the service in rural areas are higher.

Regulators often force a public utility to cross-subsidize. Why? One explanation is that a powerful group of consumers takes advantage of a less powerful group through pressuring the regulators to subsidize them.

The hypothesis that regulators impose cross-subsidies was tested using data from a period when there still were several unregulated states. Industrial users consume larger amounts of electricity than residential customers and are relatively few in number, so they can more effectively lobby regulators. Thus, under this hypothesis, the ratio of the residential price to the industrial price is higher in regulated states. Presumably, any cost differences in providing the services to the two groups are not substantial across regulated and unregulated states.

As predicted, in 1917, the average ratio of the residential price to the industrial price was 1.616 in regulated states and 1.445 in unregulated states. Thus, the relative price residential consumers paid was 12 percent higher in regulated states. The corresponding ratios in 1937 were 2.459 in regulated states and 2.047 in unregulated states, so that the relative price for residential customers was 20 percent higher. In short, regulators forced residential users to subsidize industrial users.

Sources: Stigler and Friedland (1962). See Faulhaber (1975) for a precise definition of cross subsidy.

Not surprisingly, the regulations typically make entry into these occupations difficult, thereby raising the wages of regulated occupations.

Industries may capture regulatory bodies directly or indirectly. First, firms in an industry may lobby legislatures to be regulated (Noll 1989). Occupational licensing, and the regulation of railroads, trucking, and inland water shipping are often presented as examples. Second, firms in an industry may capture the staff of the regulatory agency.

There are at least three reasons why regulatory agencies are likely to become captured (Asch and Seneca 1985, 316–17). First, regulatory commissions are usually staffed by experts on the regulated industry who, typically, worked in the industry or related government agencies and hence tend to be sympathetic to the interests of firms within the industry (see **www.aw-bc.com/carlton_perloff** "Building Codes"). Second, regulatory staff members often expect to receive attractive jobs in the industry after leaving the regulatory agency. After all, their services are valuable to firms because they are experts on regulations. These prospective job candidates may act as sympa-

EXAMPLE 20.3 *Legal Monopolies*

Lawyers throughout the world obtain market power by restricting entry into the profession and fixing prices. In virtually all of the member countries (most European and Scandinavian countries, Australia, Canada, Japan, New Zealand, and the United States) of the Organization for Economic Cooperation and Development (OECD), lawyers must earn a degree from a recognized law school and obtain a license in order to practice their trade. They are often also required to join the bar association or law society, as in the Netherlands.

As an OECD (1985, 35) report notes,

> Control of the licensing process by Bar Associations may in most countries operate, directly or indirectly, to limit the numbers of new entrants to the legal profession. Requirements that candidates be of "good conduct" allow for subjective decisions as to who will be permitted to practice.

In the United States and other countries, bar associations have authority over the grading of exams. Because practicing lawyers make up the bar association, it is not surprising that, although applicants for the bar exam are graduates of accredited law schools, the average failure rate is 25 to 30 percent.

Many countries also have quotas for entrance to law schools. For example, there are only 150 places annually for solicitors in Ireland. Some countries, such as Belgium and France, have quotas on the number of entrants and practitioners of certain public legal functions.

The geographic mobility of lawyers is limited in most OECD countries. These limits allegedly ensure that lawyers are familiar with local laws and regulations. In the United States, lawyers must be licensed in each state in which they practice. Reciprocity between states is limited. In the United Kingdom, there is reciprocity, after three years of practice, between Scotland, Northern Ireland, England, and Wales. In Canada, there are restrictions on practicing in other provinces. Indeed, in Alberta, provincial regulations prevent local lawyers from practicing with lawyers from other provinces.

Traditionally, most OECD countries have barred lawyers from advertising (which increases price competition), seeking free publicity in the media, and other means of attracting new business. However, in recent years, several countries, including Denmark, Sweden, and the United States, modified or rescinded advertising restrictions. Other countries still have restrictive rules, such as Belgium, the United Kingdom, Finland, Germany, Japan, Norway, and Spain.

Fee schedules, otherwise known as price fixing, are common in OECD countries. Typically the fees are set by the bar association, often under government authority. Ireland sets fees by statute and association rules. Fees are set locally or regionally in Canada. Germany sets upper limits. The courts or other authorized bodies in Australia set fee schedules. Some countries, such as the United Kingdom, however, do not set fees. Government competition officials have challenged fee scales in Denmark and France, and court decisions have sharply restricted fee setting by lawyers in the United States. Thus, some of lawyers' most monopolistic practices have eroded.

Source: Organization for Economic Cooperation and Development (1985).

thetic regulators of the industry. Third, because regulatory commissions often have limited resources, they may rely on well-financed regulated firms to cover many of their expenses. These expenses may then be "reimbursed" in the form of higher allowed profits to the regulated firms.

Of 174 people appointed and confirmed to the Civil Aeronautics Board (CAB), Federal Communications Commission (FCC), or Interstate Commerce Commission (ICC) by the end of 1977, 48% had some precommission experience in a related public sector, whereas 21% previously held related private-sector jobs (Eckert 1981). Of the 142 commissioners whose postcommission jobs are known, 51% took private-sector jobs in the regulated industry, and 11% of ex-commissioners took related public-sector jobs. These jobs, deaths in office, and retirements account for 70% of all commissioners. In short, commissioners were twice as likely to come from the related public sector as the related private sector. However, they were nearly five times as likely to leave their jobs for related private-sector jobs than for related public-sector jobs. Almost half (49%) of the commissioners who were patronage appointees went to work for the regulated industry, whereas only a third of the regulators who came from the private sector did so (Spiller 1990).

A spectacular example of the capture of a regulatory body by railroads occurred when trucks first started competing with railroads for long-distance freight-moving business in the early 1930s (Stigler 1971, 8). Texas and Louisiana placed a 7,000-pound payload limit on trucks serving two or more railroad stations (and hence competing with railroads), but applied a 14,000-pound limit to trucks serving only one station (and hence not competing directly with railroads).

Of course, not all regulations benefit regulated firms.[2] Where several agencies regulate a single industry, capturing regulators is more difficult. For example, many agencies have jurisdiction over genetically altered products created by the new biotechnology industry: the Environmental Protection Agency (EPA), U.S. Department of Agriculture (USDA), Food and Drug Administration (FDA), Occupational Safety and Health Administration (OSHA), and the National Institutes of Health (NIH). Any of these may decide that certain risks are unacceptable and ban a product. In addition, the National Environmental Policy Act (NEPA) of 1969 empowers courts to review agency actions that will have a "significant impact" on the environment.[3] Moreover, in some industries, both federal and state agencies may regulate.

Djankov et al. (2002) examine the relationship of regulation to a country's economic development using data from 85 countries. They calculate the time and cost required for a legitimate business to obtain all the necessary permits to enter an industry.

---

[2]For example, Isé and Perloff (1997) show that granting exclusive rights to portions of the electromagnetic spectrum gave billions of dollars in extra profits to television stations, but Federal Communications Commission rules prohibiting cigarette advertising and restricting station ownership, programming, and syndication reduced these profits by about a third.

[3]Peter W. Huber, "Biotechnology and the Regulation HYDRA," *Technology Review* 1987:57–65. Following a study by the White House Office of Science and Technology in June 1986, some order in the system emerged. Where one agency has statutory authority, the report establishes a lead agency and provides for coordinated regulatory review. At least one interagency group was also established.

The time to enter varies widely, from a low of two days in Australia and Canada to a high of 152 days in Madagascar. Costs also vary significantly, from less than half a percent of annual per capita income in the United States to more than 4.6 times annual per capita income in the Dominican Republic. Countries with onerous entry requirements have lower income, less competition, more corruption, and a larger illegal sector than countries with low entry requirements. Moreover, countries with greater regulation have lower-quality products and poorer environments. In short, their evidence overwhelmingly rejects the public interest theory of regulation.

The rest of this chapter ignores the original or declared intent of the enabling legislation and the objectives of individual regulators, and concentrates on the market effects of specific types of regulations. We start with regulations designed to create competition and then examine regulations designed to decrease competition.

Making Monopolies More Competitive

In most monopolized industries, resources are not efficiently allocated because the monopoly price is greater than marginal cost. This distortion is often used to justify regulating all monopolies. The danger in this reasoning is the failure to understand how a firm becomes a monopoly. There are three cases where regulation is unnecessary or harmful.

First, firms have an incentive to develop a new product, make a new discovery, or obtain a more efficient technology than anyone else so as to become a monopoly. Regulation that removes this incentive to innovate without replacing it with other incentives may be harmful (see Chapter 16). Second, if a market is competitive or *contestable* (Baumol, Panzar, and Willig 1982)—entry and exit are costless and instantaneous—there is little or no need to regulate because market pressures eliminate monopoly power. Third, the cost of regulation may be so high or regulators so inept that society is harmed by regulations.

Where a monopoly is not likely to be eliminated quickly by entry and where it does not serve as an incentive to innovate, government intervention may be useful. In particular, a monopoly created by an arbitrary restriction on entry usually results in a serious market failure. The case for regulation is especially strong if the government chooses to allow only one firm in an industry (Kahn 1970, 1975; Schmalensee 1979b; and Joskow and Noll 1981). These monopolies typically have one of two causes. Either they are created by a government, which blocks entry by other firms, or they are the result of the cost structure in the industry.

The problem of monopoly is inherent in industries in which it is efficient for only one firm to provide all the output because of economies of scale. When a single firm can produce the market quantity at lower cost than two or more firms, it is called a *natural monopoly* (Chapter 4). Natural monopolies always occur when a firm has a declining long-run average cost curve, but they can occur in other circumstances as well, as discussed below. Competition among several firms is inefficient in such a market, but an unregulated natural monopoly is also inefficient because it sets the price above marginal cost. Concern over the pricing of (possible) natural monopolies provides one justification for the regulation of many public utilities such as telephone service, electricity, and natural gas. There are several approaches to regulating such monopolies. One approach is direct government ownership. Alternatively, several different price or rate-of-return regulations have been used to increase the competitiveness of such markets. After examining these types of regulations, we consider some of their unintended side effects.

Government intervention need not take the form of regulation. For example, if a monopoly is created through the merger of many firms, then the appropriate response is to restore competition (or prevent monopoly through mergers), rather than to regulate. In general, the antitrust laws are designed to prevent actions that reduce competition, whereas regulation can be used to control natural monopolies. Let us now discuss the various types of regulations of natural and other monopolies.

Government Ownership

One approach to regulating a natural monopoly is to have the government own it and set prices to maximize welfare rather than profits. Most governments own many monopolies.

Public ownership of utilities is common in the United States. Seventy-five percent of the population use publicly owned water, and 20% get their electricity from publicly run firms. In the United States, 28% of the employees in the utility sectors (electricity, gas, water, and sanitation) are public employees, compared to 20% in Japan, 43% in West Germany, and 60% in Switzerland (Schmalensee 1979b, 85). In most countries, postal services are publicly owned. The British government owned many industries at one time or another in the post–World War II period, although it has led the divestiture movement in recent years. Venezuela's state-owned oil company, Petróleos de Venezuela S.A., contributed 63% of the government's budget in 1996 and 50% in 1997.[4]

Unfortunately, there is little evidence that government monopolies behave optimally. Often, government-owned firms are less efficient than privately owned firms (Example 20.4). Managers have less of an incentive to maximize profits under public ownership (Williamson 1967). Pashigian (1976) finds that public urban transit systems have lower profit rates than private ones. There is little evidence that government-owned firms set prices to maximize welfare.[5]

Privatizing

Because the government does not tend to run businesses efficiently, there has been a worldwide trend in recent years to privatize many state-owned monopolies. For example, Khadafy privatized Libya's camel industry, transferring 6,000 government-owned camels to the private sector, to save millions of dollars per year in subsidy costs.[6]

---

[4]Larry Rohter, "Hasta la Vista, Oil Kings," *New York Times*, April 17, 1999:B1, B14.

[5]However, see DeAlessi (1974), who surveys much of the earlier literature. He also notes that rates to various classes of customers vary between publicly and privately owned utilities. See also Peltzman (1971) who finds that, although municipal utilities charge lower prices on average, this difference is due to the government firms' tax exemptions.

[6]Jonathan Marshall, "Taking Lessons from Khadafy," *San Francisco Chronicle*, October 23, 1995:E1, E2.

EXAMPLE 20.4 *Public, Monopolistic, and Competitive Refuse Collection*

In some cities, public monopolies collect household refuse, whereas, in other cities, either private monopolies or unregulated firms that compete with each other provide this service. All three market organizations are common. New York City has a public monopoly; Boston pays a private firm to collect refuse; and Portland, Oregon, has private firms collect from some, but not all, households in an area.

If there are scale economies in collecting refuse, then a monopoly can collect it at lower unit cost, so that refuse collection is a natural monopoly. If there are no scale economies, then competition among many firms keeps the competitive price as low as possible. Some scale economies are expected in collecting refuse because it should be cheaper for one firm to collect from all the houses on a block than for two firms to collect from, say, every other house.

Using data from 340 public and private firms in as many cities across the United States, Stevens (1978) estimates cost functions, holding service levels constant and taking market structure as given. She draws four main conclusions:

1. There are economies of scale for cities with populations of less than 20,000 (or cities served by fewer than four trucks).
2. In all cities, the competitive arrangement is from 2% to 48% more costly than the private monopoly arrangement, perhaps due to higher billing expenses and the extra costs due to nonexclusivity within a market area.
3. For cities with populations up to 50,000, the price charged by the private monopoly is equivalent to the cost of the public monopoly.
4. For larger cities, public monopoly or the competitive arrangement are from 27% to 37% more expensive than the private monopoly.

One reason for this last result is that labor productivity in a public monopoly is lower than that of the private monopoly, and this difference increases with city size. The mean crew size for the public monopoly is 3.26 compared to 2.15 for the comparable private monopoly. Similarly, the public monopoly uses trucks with smaller capacity: 20.63 cubic yards compared to 27.14.

More recent studies and studies from around the world confirm these results. Dijkgraaf and Gradus (2003) report 15% to 20% cost savings for contracting out refuse collection in the Netherlands. Reeves and Barrow (2000) estimate that in the Republic of Ireland, cost savings for contracting out refuse collection are around 45%, primarily due to real efficiency gains.

Great Britain led the way in Europe. The Thatcher government started by privatizing British Gas in 1986, creating a free market for the first time as of 1996 whereby consumers could choose their gas supplier. Gas prices in real terms were 35% lower in 1999 than in 1986. As of January 1, 1998, France's four-centuries-old art and antiquities auction monopoly ended (as they lost business to London and New York). The dismantling of communism in the former Soviet Union and Eastern Europe has led to massive efforts to privatize former government monopolies (Shleifer and Vishny 1999).

Megginson and Netter (2001) survey the effects of the worldwide movement away from state-owned enterprises (SOEs) over the last 20 years, especially in developing countries. During this period, the fraction of world income produced by SOEs declined from 10% to 6%, while that same fraction in low-income countries fell from 16% to 7%. Private firms are more efficient by about 2%, require fewer workers, are less likely to engage in cross-subsidization of different consumer groups, are less likely to rely on government subsidies, write long-term contracts at lower cost, and rely much less on debt than do SOEs. How well privatization works in specific cases depends on a host of factors. For example, efficiency improves, especially if the privatized firm faces competition or if substantial deregulation occurs. Regulation may be necessary for privatized firms that are natural monopolies, and the form of regulation largely determines the success of the privatization. As we discuss later in this chapter, regulation that creates incentives for cost cutting can significantly improve efficiency. Experience with privatization in which there are many small shareholders and where labor has a powerful voice in the control of the firm, or where incumbent managers retain control, has been poor compared to instances where a new management comes in and has concentrated ownership. Laws protecting shareholder rights and corporate governance can be an important factor in achieving a successful privatization.

Franchise Bidding

Governments may privatize monopolies by selling them, using **franchise bidding**: A government sells the right to a monopoly to the highest bidder.[7] Thus, instead of having the government give monopoly rights to firms (as in the assignment of television and radio station rights in the United States), the government captures the monopoly rents through a bidding process. Franchise bidding was used for water supply and funeral services in France for over 100 years. Bidding was also used in New York City around the turn of the century (Schmalensee 1979, 71).

The government may use bidding to capture the monopoly profit from a private monopoly, as Chicago and San Francisco do to a large extent with private towing companies and many cities do when they grant monopoly rights to operate stores at airports. Alternatively, the government may require, as a condition of bidding, that the firm operate so as to increase welfare over the monopoly level.[8] For example, in deciding to whom to award the franchise, a government agency could consider not only the fee for the right to operate that a bidder will pay, but also the price that the bidder will charge consumers. If bidders are forced to charge these low prices, monopoly profits are eliminated (Demsetz 1968; Posner 1972; Baumol et al. 1982). That is, instead of awarding the franchise to the highest bidder for a lump-sum payment (which allows

[7]John Stuart Mill introduced this approach in 1848 (Schmalensee 1979, 68–73).

[8]Analogously, Spiller (1988) discusses allowing potential regulators to bid for jobs, as they eventually will be rewarded or "bribed" by the regulated industry.

the government to capture the expected monopoly profits), the franchise is awarded to the firm that offers to produce in the manner that is best for consumers (see **www.aw-bc.com/carlton_perloff** "Cable Television"). A century ago, railroad franchises were awarded to firms offering to charge the lowest rates (Chadwick 1859).

Under the Local Government Act of 1988, local U.K. governments put refuse collection services out to bid rather than using a government agency as they had previously done. The lowest bid wins, and the winner must provide services at the bid rate. Gomez-Lobo and Szymanski (2001) find that the larger the number of bids, the lower the cost of service, controlling for other factors. Compared to having only one bidder, two bidders lower the cost by about 7 percent and four bidders by about 13 percent. (Given that the British government elected in 1997 abolished this bidding procedure, Gomez-Lobo and Szymanski predict that local authorities' refuse collection expenditures will rise.)

Traditionally, the Federal Communications Commission (FCC) allocated the frequency spectrum to specific uses (radio, television, mobile phones, law enforcement, public defense), and then assigned licenses by comparative hearings or, beginning in the 1980s, lotteries. Total FCC fees for renewals and for lotteries in 1991 were $46.6 million. For example, comparative hearing fees for a new applicant for land-mobile services was $6,760 in 1991. Some lottery winners of cellular telephone licenses never intended to provide services and sold their licenses at enormous profit to firms that did, including one payment of $41 million in 1990 for a Cape Cod, Massachusetts, service area. In 1993, Congress passed a bill to auction off, for the first time, part of the frequency spectrum for new personal communication services such as smaller handheld telephones and pagers. By the end of 2003, the auction proceeds exceeded $41.8 billion.[9]

Franchise bidding, although it may transfer monopoly profits to governments, does not necessarily result in efficient pricing (Telser 1969, Williamson 1976, Schmalensee 1979b, Williamson 1985). Efficiency requires that a firm set price equal to marginal cost, but if the firm is a natural monopoly, it may lose money at that price (Chapter 4). As a result, none of the bidders for a natural monopoly are willing to price efficiently (unless they are allowed to price discriminate, use nonlinear prices such as access fees plus usage fees or are subsidized). Moreover, this approach does not eliminate the need for regulation: The government may need to confirm regularly that the winning firm is keeping its agreement and not raising prices or reducing service.[10] A further problem is that the economic environment changes over time, so that the initial agreement may not be desirable in the future. Thus, repeated bidding may be required, and the incumbent may gain an advantage in subsequent bidding because of its experience (Williamson 1976, 1985).[11]

---

[9]See: **http://wireless.fee.gov/auctions/summary.html**.

[10]Ellingsen (1991) points out that buyers may also lobby to control prices. Bidders for a monopoly, anticipating such actions, would bid less than otherwise.

[11]But see Zupan (1989) and Prager (1990), who analyze cable TV franchises and find that opportunistic behavior by the incumbent may not be a serious problem.

Riordan and Sappington (1987) propose an optimal policy to maximize expected consumer welfare where potential firms possess imperfect information about production costs. They recommend awarding the franchise to the producer with the lowest expected costs, but allowing prices to exceed realized marginal costs to encourage more competitive bidding.

Price Controls

Governments frequently use **price controls**—limits on how high firms may set prices—to attempt to control inflation or to keep prices in a particular industry low. The discussion here concentrates on the effects of price regulation on a monopoly.

Many methods are used to control prices. Many countries use direct controls, taxes, or subsidies that affect the prices that monopolies charge. In most Western countries, special agencies often regulate the prices of monopolies. Typically, a regulatory board sets the price explicitly or must approve one proposed by a monopoly.

In the following example, the board fixes the maximum price that the monopoly may charge. We start by examining the effect of price regulation on a monopoly with increasing marginal costs, and then examine the effect of regulation on one with constant or decreasing marginal costs.

Price Regulation of an Increasing Marginal Cost Monopoly. Price regulation of a monopoly has efficiency and redistribution effects. A moderate reduction in a monopoly's price increases the quantity sold and raises efficiency. An excessive reduction in price creates shortages and can decrease the quantity sold. Lowering prices also redistributes wealth from the monopoly to consumers. As a result, monopolies dislike price regulations and consumers generally applaud them.

Figure 20.1 shows the demand and marginal revenue curves facing a monopoly with an upward-sloping marginal cost curve. In the absence of regulation, the monopoly profitably charges price p_m and sells Q_m units of output, which is determined by the intersection of the marginal revenue and marginal cost curves (Chapter 4).

The deadweight loss (*DWL*) to society is the shaded triangle below the demand curve, above the marginal cost curve, and to the right of Q_m. This deadweight loss reflects the loss in both consumer and producer surplus due to the relatively few units of output sold. If this market were competitive, the competitive price, p_c, would equal marginal cost and consumers would purchase a larger quantity, Q_c. Thus, the inefficiency of monopoly is due to setting the price p_m above the marginal cost and restricting output below Q_c.

If the regulatory board sets the maximum price that the monopoly may charge, $\underline{p}$, above p_m, so that the monopoly is not constrained, the regulation has no effect.[12] We first show that if $\underline{p}$ is set equal to marginal cost (the competitive or efficient price), welfare is maximized. Then we show that if a lower $\underline{p}$ is set, shortages may occur.

---

[12]There is no need to regulate unless there is a market failure. Thus, there is no reason to regulate a competitive market. In this section, we assume that the market is not competitive.

FIGURE 20.1 Efficient Price Regulation

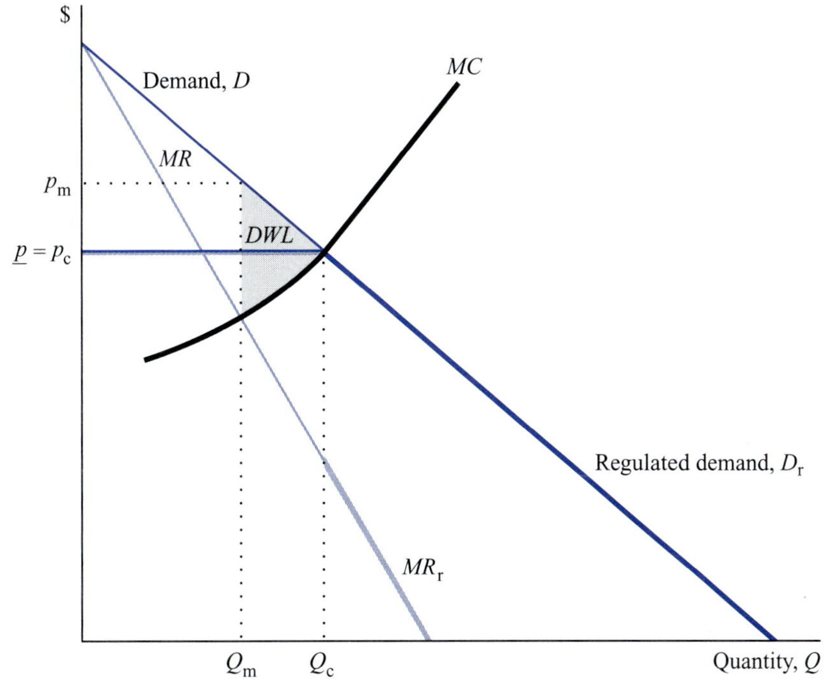

If the regulatory board sets $\underline{p} = p_c$, the deadweight loss is eliminated, as we now show. Because it can no longer charge a price higher than p_c, the monopoly's regulated demand curve (thick blue line in Figure 20.1), D_r, is horizontal at p_c until it hits the original demand curve at Q_c, and is downward sloping thereafter.

The monopoly's regulated marginal revenue curve, MR_r, corresponding to this new demand curve, is horizontal and equal to the new demand curve, where the new demand curve is horizontal.[13] Where the demand curve slopes down, the marginal revenue curve also slopes down. Indeed, for this portion of the demand curve, the marginal revenue curve is the same as in the unregulated case, as shown by the thickened line on the relevant portion of the downward-sloping marginal revenue curve. At Q_c, the marginal revenue curve is discontinuous.

[13]Its marginal revenue curve is horizontal for the same reason that a competitive firm's marginal revenue curve is horizontal: The corresponding demand curve is horizontal. Along a horizontal demand curve, additional units can be sold without lowering price, so the marginal revenue equals the average revenue or price. Mathematically, marginal revenue equals $d[p(Q)Q]/dQ = p'(Q)Q + p(Q)$, where $p(Q)$ is the inverse demand curve, $p(Q)Q$ is total revenue, and $p'(Q)$ is the (negative) slope of the demand curve. If the demand curve is horizontal at $\underline{p}$, $p(Q) = \underline{p}$ and $p'(Q) = 0$, so marginal revenue equals $p(Q) = \underline{p}$.

The regulated monopoly sets marginal revenue equal to marginal cost to determine its optimal price. If the monopoly in Figure 20.1 is regulated, its marginal revenue, MR_r, equals its marginal cost, MC, at Q_c rather than at Q_m as in the unregulated case. If the monopoly sells one fewer unit, it loses profit because its revenue falls by more than its costs. If it sells one more unit, its revenue increases by less than the increase in its costs. Its profits are lower than without regulation, but the monopoly is still maximizing its (regulated) profits.

In summary, if $\bar{p}$ is set at p_c, the efficient (competitive) solution is obtained, and deadweight loss is eliminated because price equals marginal cost. As Kahn (1970, 65) says, "The central policy prescription of microeconomics is the equation of price and marginal cost."

This type of regulation is not desirable or feasible unless three additional conditions are met. First, the monopoly must make positive profit, or else it refuses to produce.

Second, the cost of running the regulatory board should be less than the social gain (the elimination of the deadweight loss). Unfortunately, the cost of administration is often high. For example, Gerwig (1962) finds that the cost of regulating natural gas prices in interstate commerce was about 7 percent of the base price of the gas.

Third, the regulatory board must have enough information to set its regulations optimally. Often, the regulatory board has trouble setting $\underline{p}$ at p_c because the board does not know either costs or demand exactly. Thus, even if the board wants to set $\underline{p} = p_c$, it may set $\underline{p}$ too high or too low.[14] If the board chooses a $\underline{p}$ between p_m and p_c, the monopoly sells at that price, by the same reasoning as above.[15] Consumers are better off than in the unregulated case—they buy more units at a lower price—but not as well off as when the regulated price is set at p_c.

If the board sets too low a price, the price regulation introduces a new problem. If the price is so low that the firm shuts down (as would occur in the long run if price were below the minimum of the monopoly's average cost curve), then consumers can buy nothing, so all consumer surplus is lost. Figure 20.2 illustrates a less extreme case where the monopoly does not shut down. The demand and cost curves are the same as

[14]A number of methods to induce firms to truthfully reveal the relevant information have been devised (for example, Baron and Meyerson 1982, Riordan 1984). Regulators offer a choice of contracts to a monopoly that possesses private information about its marginal cost of production. Once the firm chooses the optimal *incentive compatible* contract, it maximizes its profit by producing the optimal quantity. According to the *revelation principle*, for any indirect regulatory mechanism (even one where the firm misrepresents its privately held information about its costs), there exists a mechanism that achieves the regulator's objective as successfully and that induces truthful revelation of the key information. When a regulator must induce a firm to reveal information, the regulator usually cannot achieve the same outcome (price and quantity) as when the regulator already and independently knows the relevant information. See Laffont and Tirole (1993).

[15]The regulated demand curve is a horizontal line at $\underline{p}$ until it hits the original demand curve at some quantity $\underline{Q}$ where ($Q_m < \underline{Q} < Q_c$), and is then downward sloping. The corresponding marginal revenue curve is horizontal up to $\underline{Q}$, then falls vertically until it hits the downward-sloping section, as in Figure 20.1. The marginal cost curve intersects the marginal revenue curve in its vertical section, so the monopoly sets price equal to $\underline{p}$ (see Problem 2).

FIGURE 20.2 Price Regulation That Causes a Shortage

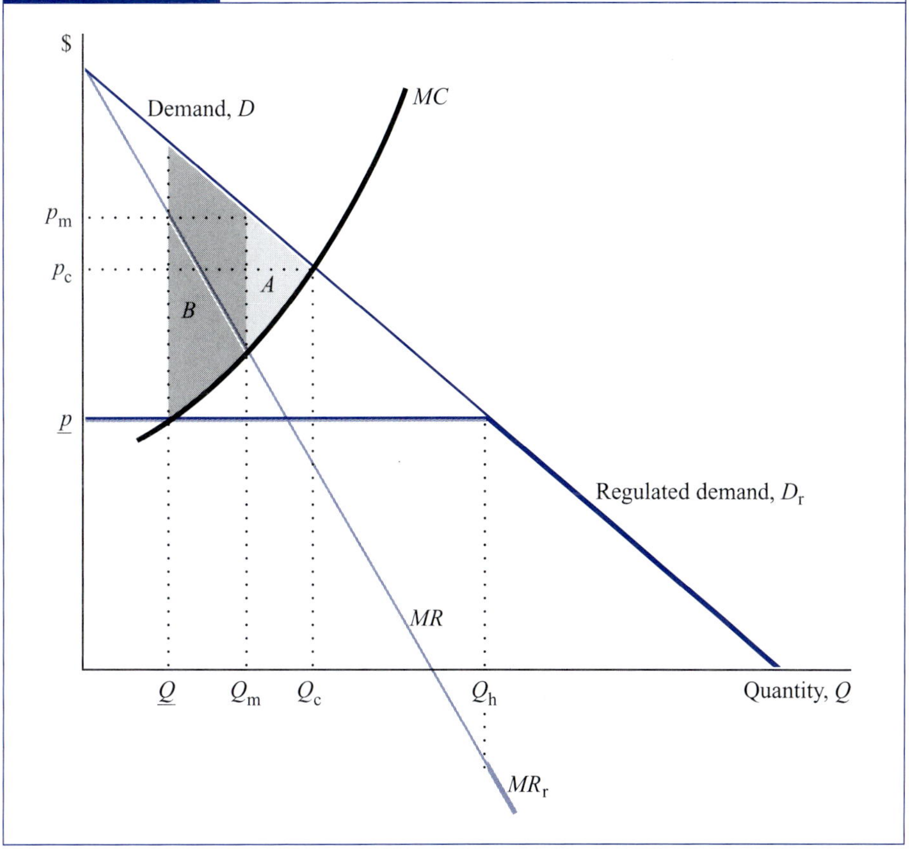

in Figure 20.1, but $\underline{p}$ is set below p_c. The monopoly's new effective demand curve is horizontal at $\underline{p}$, and thereafter is downward sloping. Where the demand curve is horizontal, the marginal revenue curve is horizontal and is the same as the demand curve.

The monopoly maximizes its profit if it charges $\underline{p}$ and sells $\underline{Q}$. Consumers want to purchase $Q_h(>\underline{Q})$ units at this price. If the monopoly sells any more units, it loses money on each unit. As a result, there is a shortage of $Q_h - \underline{Q}$ units. Which consumers are lucky enough to buy at this low price depends on how the monopoly allocates its output. It could use a first-come, first-served policy, or discriminate on any other basis except price. Some consumers are better off than in the unregulated case, because they buy the good at a very low price. However, other consumers are worse off because they are unable to buy the good at all.

In Figure 20.2, there is greater deadweight loss than in the unregulated case. The deadweight loss from unregulated monopoly pricing is area *A* in Figure 20.2 (the area labeled *DWL* in Figure 20.1). The deadweight loss from setting $\underline{p}$ is area *A* plus area

B.[16] This increased deadweight loss results because $\underline{p}$ is much lower than p_c. If it were only slightly below p_c, only small shortages would occur, and the deadweight loss would be less than in the unregulated case.

The regulatory board should consider raising $\underline{p}$ if the monopoly chooses to shut down rather than operate at that price or if shortages occur. Of course, the board must be sure that the monopoly is not trying to trick it by causing a shortage even though $\underline{p} \geq p_c$.

To summarize, the effect of price regulation depends on where $\underline{p}$ is set:

- If $\underline{p} \geq p_m$, the regulation has no effect in a static model: price $= p_m$, quantity $= Q_m$, and there is deadweight loss.
- If $p_m > \underline{p} > p_c$, then price $= \underline{p}$, output lies between Q_m and Q_c, and deadweight loss is reduced but not eliminated.
- If $\underline{p} = p_c$, then price $= \underline{p}$, quantity $= Q_c$, and there is no deadweight loss.
- If $\underline{p} < p_c$, then price $= \underline{p}$, quantity demanded is greater than Q_c, but quantity supplied is less than Q_c. The deadweight loss may be greater or smaller than in the unregulated case.

Thus, the regulatory board can increase consumer surplus and welfare if it forces the monopoly to price at $\underline{p} = p_c$. If it guesses wrong and sets a $\underline{p}$ so low that shortages occur, it should raise $\underline{p}$. If the cost of running the regulatory board is extremely high, the best solution is to disband the board and not to regulate.

Price Regulation of a Natural Monopoly. A firm is a natural monopoly if it can produce the market quantity at a lower cost than can two or more firms (Chapter 4). A natural monopoly often has falling average costs and constant or falling marginal costs in the region in which it operates. Figure 20.3 shows a natural monopoly with constant marginal cost and falling average cost.

If the natural monopoly is not regulated, it charges p_m, sells Q_m units, and makes a large profit (because price is well above average cost). If the regulatory board sets $\underline{p} = p_a$, the price determined by the intersection of the average cost curve and the demand curve, the monopoly sells Q_a units and makes no profit. Consumers benefit from such regulation because they buy more output at a lower price.

Regulatory boards may try to set $\underline{p} = p_a$ because they know that if they set $\underline{p}$ lower, the monopoly will stop operating. Nonetheless, setting $\underline{p} = p_a$ leads to inefficient pricing because p_a is above marginal cost, *MC*. The consumer is paying more than it costs to produce the last unit of output. The efficient solution is to set $\underline{p} = p^* = MC$ and sell Q^* units. Because average costs are always falling with larger scale, there is only room for one efficient firm in this industry.

---

[16] We assume that those with the greatest willingness to pay obtain the goods at price $\underline{p}$. This outcome would occur if, for example, people wait in line for the good and those who value the good the most are willing to wait the longest and so line up first. We ignore the cost of standing in line in Figure 20.2.

FIGURE 20.3 Price Regulation of a Natural Monopoly

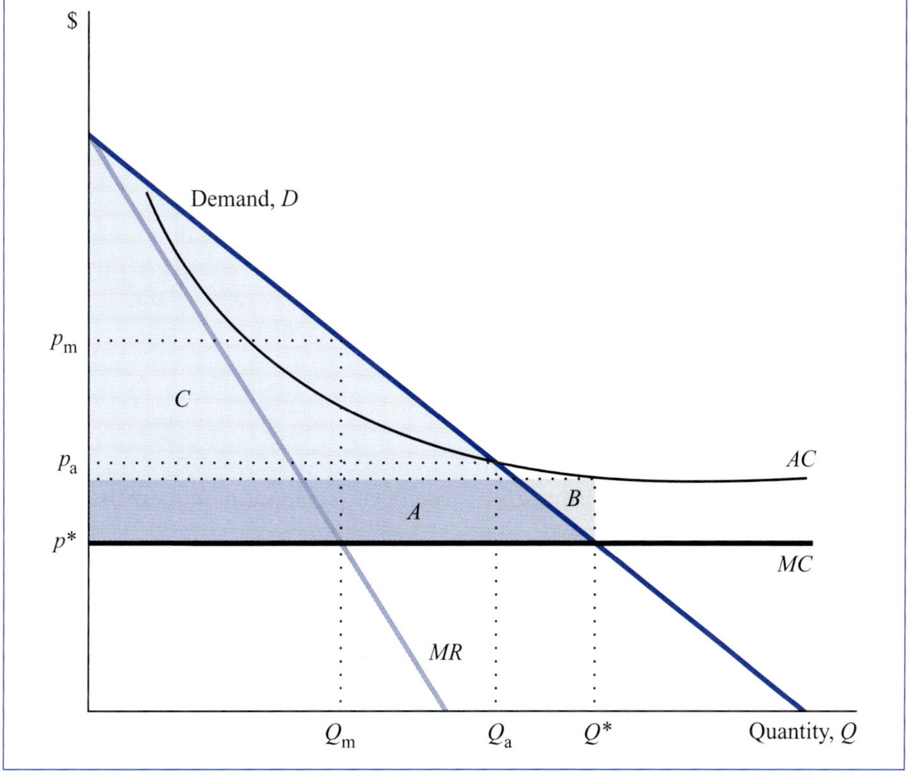

If $\underline{p} = p^*$, price is below average cost, so the monopoly loses money. Its lost profit equals $A + B$ in Figure 20.3.[17] The monopoly prefers to shut down rather than take losses.

Society could keep the monopoly operating at p^* by subsidizing it by an amount equal to the lost profit, $A + B$. At $\underline{p} = p^*$, consumer surplus, $C + A$, minus firm losses, $A + B$, equals $C - B$. If administration costs are low, welfare is maximized at p^* if welfare is defined as consumer surplus plus firm profit (or loss) minus the regulatory board's administrative costs.[18]

If it is possible to subsidize the monopoly using efficiently raised tax revenue, welfare is maximized with price equal to marginal cost and a subsidy. The subsidy is a

[17]The monopolist is covering its variable costs, because p^* = average variable cost, but not its fixed costs, F. As drawn, its costs are $C(Q) = mQ + F$, where m is its constant marginal costs and average variable costs. At $p^* = m$, its profit is $\pi(Q^*) = p^*Q^* - mQ^* - F = -F$.

[18]At any higher price, the increase in profit is less than the loss of consumer surplus (see Problem 1).

transfer of wealth from the monopoly and nonusers to consumers of the product and, as such, has no efficiency implications. Unfortunately, governments rarely, if ever, raise taxes efficiently. Most commonly used taxes, such as income and sales taxes, drive a wedge between price and marginal cost. Thus, subsidies typically have a real resource cost. We commonly see second-best regulations that set price at p_a rather than p^*.

An alternative way to keep the monopoly operating, and operating efficiently, is to allow it to price discriminate. Some consumers dislike this solution because it transfers income from them to the monopoly and treats consumers unequally.[19]

If a firm produces many products, the analysis of optimal regulation is more complicated. The regulatory prices that maximize consumer welfare subject to the requirement that revenues cover costs is called **Ramsey pricing**, after Frank P. Ramsey (1927), who first derived this result. This solution is similar to optimal monopoly price discrimination. Essentially, the optimal prices are the monopoly prices scaled down so that total revenue exactly equals costs (Baumol and Bradford 1970, Sharkey 1982).[20]

Sustainability of Natural Monopolies. Strangely, a natural monopoly may not be immune to profit-seeking entry (Faulhaber 1975; Baumol, Bailey, and Willig 1977; Panzar and Willig 1977b; Baumol et al. 1982; Sharkey 1982). Even if it is most efficient for one firm to produce the entire industry output, such a firm may not be able to simultaneously prevent entry, satisfy consumer demand, and cover its costs. A natural monopoly that can prevent entry is said to be **sustainable**.[21]

A single-product natural monopoly is sustainable at every output if and only if there are economies of scale at all outputs (Sharkey 1982, 88–90). That is, a natural monopoly with increasing returns to scale (as in Figure 20.3) that has a strictly falling average cost curve is immune to entry. A natural monopoly with a U-shaped long-run average cost curve may not be immune.

To illustrate the problem of sustainability, consider a monopoly with a U-shaped average cost function as in Figure 20.4. The demand curve crosses the average cost curve at a price of \$1.10 and 110 units of output. Suppose that the monopoly is regulated to produce at that price, so that it makes no profit. In this second-best regulation,

---

[19]Around the turn of the century, economists started advocating a form of price discrimination called *time-of-day* pricing (see Hausman and Neufeld 1984). Since the 1970s, time-of-day (or *peak-load* pricing) and *seasonal* pricing have been widely used in regulating U.S. public utilities such as electric power and telephones (Weiss 1981). Differentiating rates over time has been particularly common in California, New York, and Wisconsin (Weiss 1981). This type of pricing is different than standard price discrimination because the costs different consumers impose on the system vary over time.

[20]See **www.aw-bc.com/carlton_perloff** "Ramsey Pricing" for a mathematical presentation.

[21]A natural monopoly is sustainable (Baumol, et al. 1977; Sharkey 1982) if, given a cost function C and a demand function D, there is a price p and an output $Q = D(p)$ such that $pQ = C(Q)$ and $p^*Q^* < C(Q^*)$ for all $p^* < p$ and all $Q^* \leq D(p^*)$. A slight modification of this definition also applies if Q is a vector of different products.

FIGURE 20.4 Sustainability

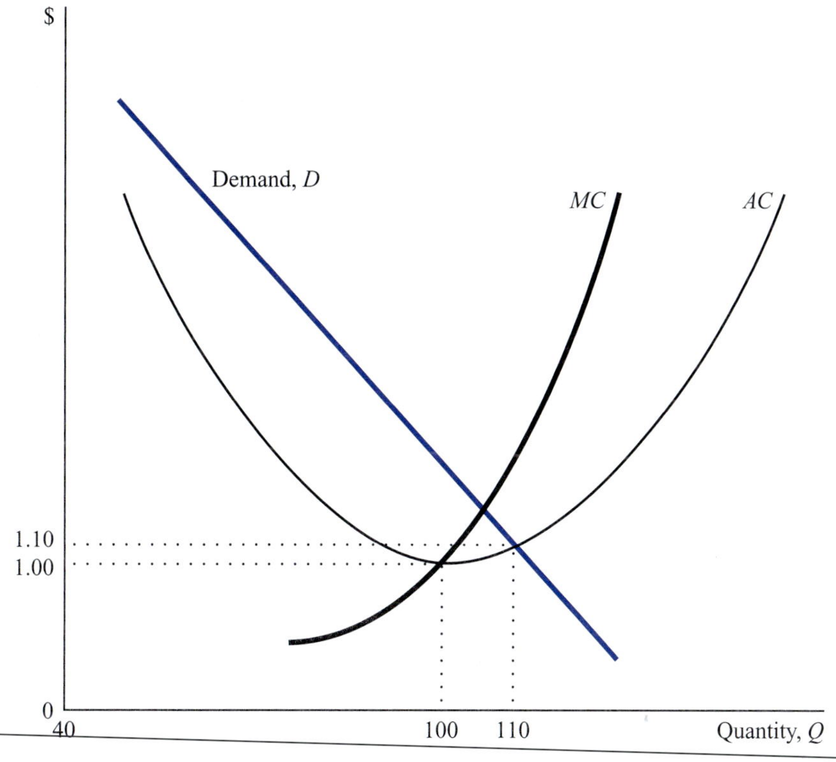

the firm can charge only one price for its product, and the regulators cannot subsidize the firm. This type of regulation is inefficient—price is below marginal cost—so society is less well off than with first-best (marginal-cost pricing) regulation.

Another firm can enter profitably if it has the same cost function as the monopoly. It could produce 100 units and charge a price between \$1 and \$1.10. Although the natural monopoly could respond, this entry shows that the original regulated equilibrium is not a sustainable equilibrium.

If, instead, the demand curve in Figure 20.4 crosses the average cost curve at or to the left of the minimum point (\$1 and 100 units), then the monopoly is sustainable. In that case, the average cost curve is strictly falling at the equilibrium; hence, the firm is operating in the region of increasing returns to scale, as in Figure 20.3.

It is difficult to derive necessary and sufficient conditions to guarantee sustainability where the monopoly produces many products.[22] However, it is likely that a natural

[22] See, for example, Baumol et al. (1977). The problem is even more difficult when there are several firms, although some progress on sustainability with oligopoly has been made (Braeutigam 1984).

monopoly, earning zero profits, will be immune from entry if the monopoly may use a nonlinear pricing scheme (Chapter 10), the monopoly can respond rapidly to entry, and any potential entrant must sink substantial costs to enter.

Of course, regulators can solve the sustainability problem by forbidding entry and thereby protecting the natural monopoly. However, entry may be desirable—especially if the entrant is more efficient than the natural monopoly, which may become lax in a protected market.

Entry by a new competitor into a market with a natural monopoly does not guarantee efficiency because it is efficient to have only one firm producing. Competition of potential entrants may provide a check on a firm's behavior, but even here there can be problems. Suppose that each potential entrant competes by announcing the price it would charge if it were the sole firm. Further suppose that average cost declines everywhere with output. Because the average cost curve is falling, marginal cost must be below average cost, so setting price equal to marginal cost yields losses. In this case, there is no way to set price equal to marginal cost and earn zero profits. One possible solution is to have each firm announce a *two-part price* consisting of a fixed charge plus a usage charge. The usage charge could be based on marginal cost, and the fixed fee could be chosen to yield zero profits. Another solution is to have the firm charge an average cost that is above marginal cost, but there is a deadweight loss due to the gap between price and marginal cost.

Even if it were possible to determine what pricing scheme to use to earn zero profits, a related problem is that no monopoly is content to earn zero profits if greater profits are possible. Once a firm has been established as the natural monopoly, it is likely to develop advantages over potential entrants who can then no longer adequately constrain prices. Therefore, regulation of the price of the natural monopoly may be necessary to protect consumers, even though regulation is often difficult and creates its own problems.

Although it is theoretically possible that natural monopolies are unsustainable, there is little empirical evidence in most regulated industries showing that sustainability problems might justify regulators forbidding entry.

However, regulators may create sustainability problems. For example, suppose that regulators decide to charge high prices for long-distance telephone calls and use the extra revenues to subsidize local service. This pattern of pricing prevailed prior to the breakup (divestiture) of AT&T. Given this cross subsidy, where the revenues earned from one product are used to pay for the cost of providing another, there is an incentive for alternative providers of long-distance service to enter and charge a lower price, even if they have higher costs than the natural monopoly (Faulhaber 1975). Indeed, before the breakup of AT&T, firms offering only long-distance service entered the market and underpriced AT&T (see **www.aw-bc.com/carlton_perloff** "Price Umbrella").

If regulators insist on cross subsidizing, they must prevent entry.[23] In 1984, entry was permitted in the telephone industry (indeed the number of companies offering long-distance service, excluding wireless service providers, increased from 321 in 1993

[23]For a variety of views on this policy, see Baseman (1981), comments by Baumol (1981, 361–64), Panzar (1981, 365–69), and Brock and Scheinkman (1983).

to 1072 in 2002), thereby reducing cross subsidization.[24] Of course, if a monopoly is protected against entry and its prices or profits are regulated, its incentives to hold down prices and produce efficiently are reduced.

Regulatory Lag. Inducing regulated firms to produce efficiently may be a problem. Regulated firms are not rewarded when they achieve lower costs because their regulated price is lowered accordingly. For this reason a number of economists argue that regulatory lag, a delay in instituting and enforcing regulations, is desirable (Baumol 1967, Williamson 1971, Bailey 1973, Wendel 1976). They reason that if regulators are slow to react, then regulated monopolies earn increased profits when costs fall, and the short-term gains give them an incentive to cut costs. In the 1960s, intervals between electric power rate cases were long, although possibly for other reasons (Joskow 1974).

Obviously, there are mechanical problems in determining the best interval of time between setting new prices because there is a trade-off between lower costs in the long run and the lowest possible price at any given time. Insisting on the lowest possible price could so deprive a firm of incentives to behave efficiently that consumers are harmed in the long run.

Regulatory lag may be unattractive during periods of rapid increases in the costs of factors of production, as with energy costs in the 1970s. Under those conditions, delays in allowing prices to rise cause regulated firms to lose money for long periods of time. When regulators finally act, they may be tempted to grant extremely large price increases to make up for these lost profits, resulting in prices that were too high in some periods and too low in others.

Regulators often intervene only when pressured by the firm or consumers (Joskow 1974). From 1963 to 1967, when declining fuel prices and improvement in technology reduced costs for electric utilities, there were only 17 electric utility rate cases, so prices did not fall quickly. During the rapid inflation of 1973–77, however, there were 119 rate cases (Braeutigam and Quirk 1984). Many utilities reported that they voluntarily reduced rates in the 1960s, so the asymmetry in regulation may not be quite as extreme as it appears at first. Fitzpatrick (1987) uses a statistical model to show that the utilities "voluntarily" lowered their prices to keep consumers from complaining to rate commissions and demanding even greater rate reductions.

A variant of price regulation is *price cap* regulation, where a maximum price that can be charged is set and not changed for several years. During the period when the maximum price cannot be changed, the regulated firm has an incentive to lower its costs because it keeps the resulting profits (Symposium on Price Cap Regulation 1989). Such price cap regulation is especially common for local phone rates in the United States and the United Kingdom.

Price Regulation May Not Lower Price. Although lowering the price set by a monopoly is desirable, there is considerable doubt that regulatory boards do lower prices.

[24] Federal Communications Commission, "Statistics of the Long Distance Telecommunications Industry," Industry Analysis and Technology Division, Wireless Competition Bureau (May 2003).

The regulation of electrical rates provides an example. Today most states have commissions to regulate rates of electric utilities, but only 6 states had such commissions prior to 1910, and only 29 adopted commissions between 1910 and 1920 (Stigler and Friedland 1962). By 1937, 39 states had regulating commissions. Thus, using historical data, we can test whether regulatory boards lower prices.

The average price per kilowatt-hour (KWH) was 1.88¢ in regulated states and 3.20¢ in unregulated states in 1917, or 41 percent lower in the regulated states. However, this comparison is not terribly informative because the rates were relatively low in the regulated states before regulation went into effect.

Stigler and Friedland's statistical analyses separate the effects of regulation from those of variations in urban population, per capita income, and the proportion of energy from hydroelectric sources. They analyzed data for the years 1912, 1922, 1932, and 1937, and found that only in 1937, after controlling for other factors, did regulation have a statistically significant effect on price, lowering it by 9.7 percent.

Possibly, the reason that more dramatic effects are not found when the average price of electricity is examined is that regulation only helps certain classes of consumers (Example 20.2). Based on statistical analyses for subgroups, in 1932, regulation did not statistically significantly lower the price of electricity to either domestic or commercial and industrial customers. In 1937, regulation did not statistically significantly lower price to domestic customers, but statistically significantly lowered the rates for commercial and industrial customers by 8.8 percent. Apparently regulation helped commercial and industrial users at the expense of households.

Thus, it appears that regulations did not lower electricity prices in the first several decades they were in place, with the possible exception of lowering prices for businesses in 1937. It is possible that utilities in unregulated states kept their prices down to prevent regulation.

If regulation does lower price, it must lower the profitability of the monopoly. Similarly, if regulatory boards act slowly, regulatory lag keeps prices from keeping pace with cost increases, lowering profitability. Thus, an alternative test of the effect of regulation is whether the stock values of the electric companies in regulated states were lower than in unregulated states. Statistical analyses that control for the growth in sales do not show a statistically significant effect of regulation on stock prices.[25]

The Stigler-Friedland study led to a massive outpouring of research on the effects of regulation. Generally, those numerous studies confirm Stigler and Friedland's thesis that regulation often does not lower price. This confirmation is all the more striking in light of a subsequent data error found in the original Stigler-Friedland study, which when corrected shows electricity rates to domestic consumers lower in regulated states by about 25 percent (not under 5 percent as originally reported), though the results are still statistically insignificant (Peltzman 1993).

Some studies of electrical utilities in later periods do find statistically significant effects of other types of regulations, such as rate-of-return regulation. We now turn to this very common form of nonoptimal, indirect price regulation.

---

[25]Schwert (1981) criticizes this approach, however, for failing to control for changes in risk.

★Rate-of-Return Regulation

Don't get the idea that I'm knocking the American system. —*Al Capone*

In the United States, regulatory boards often used rate-of-return (ROR) regulation to limit the rate of return to capital of utility monopolies, such as electric and gas companies, instead of controlling prices directly. Although ROR regulation may help consumers, it does not encourage firms to behave efficiently. One commonly cited inefficiency, called the Averch-Johnson effect, is the tendency to overinvest in capital (Averch and Johnson 1962).

The effects of ROR regulation can be illustrated using a model of a public utility that uses labor, L, and capital, K, as inputs to produce electric power.[26] If unregulated, this monopoly restricts output but uses labor and capital to produce that output as efficiently as possible. That is, the firm hires workers up to the point where the last dollar spent on labor adds \$1 to revenues, and similarly for capital. The firm chooses its output level through its choice of labor and capital so as to maximize its profits at the monopoly level.[27]

A firm's ROR is usually defined as a ratio of its profit (revenue minus operating cost, including capital depreciation), π, to the value of the capital stock, $p_k K$:

$$ROR = \frac{pQ - wL - uK}{p_k K}, \tag{20.1}$$

where w is the wage the firm pays to hire one unit of labor, u is the user cost of capital (the cost of using or renting the capital for one period),[28] and p_k is the purchase price of a unit of the capital stock.[29]

One reason for the use of the ROR is to facilitate comparisons of profits across different-sized firms. For example, a firm with a big factory may have a higher profit level than one with a smaller factory, but they may have identical RORs if their profits per square foot of factory are equal.

---

[26]For a mathematical analysis, see **www.aw-bc.com/carlton_perloff** "Averch Johnson," which is based on Takayama (1969). The corresponding graphic analysis follows Zajac (1970) and Baumol and Klevorick (1970). However, in our graphs, the firm is assumed to be a natural monopoly, whereas in their diagrams, a decreasing-returns-to-scale production function is implicitly assumed.

[27]The relation between output and labor and capital is described by a production function: $Q = f(L, K)$. Profit is a function of output, so that profit is also a function of labor and capital: $\pi(Q) = \pi(f(L, K))$. By choosing L_m units of labor services and K_m units of capital services, the firm maximizes its profit at the monopoly level, $\pi_m(f(L_m, K_m))$.

[28]The user cost of capital (**www.aw-bc.com/carlton_perloff** "Turning an Asset Price into a Rental Rate") is $u = (r + \delta - \dot{p}_k/p_k)p_k$, where r is the interest rate, δ is the depreciation rate of the capital (the rate at which the capital stock is used up), $\dot{p}_k$ is the change in the price of the capital asset over time (the derivative with respect to time), and $\dot{p}_k/p_k$ is the appreciation rate of the stock of capital (the percentage change in the price of the capital asset over the period).

[29]Some analysts (for example in Table 20.2) alternatively define the ROR by replacing u in Equation 20.1 with the depreciation rate of capital.

Given the definition in Equation 20.1, an ROR of zero is a normal or competitive rate of return (that is, no unusual economic profit). An unregulated monopoly generally has a higher ROR than competitive firms. Many regulatory boards limit the ROR of monopolies to a *fair rate of return,* a phrase that is not usually clearly defined. Some boards may set this rate at the average ROR in the unregulated sectors of the economy. Table 20.2 shows the rates of return in a number of regulated industries in the mid-1970s, before the recent deregulation movement.

A regulated firm may lower its ROR from the monopoly level either by lowering its profit or by increasing its capital (or both). Moreover, if the allowed rate of return is above the competitive return, then the firm earns more by investing more in capital. Thus, as Averch and Johnson (1962) point out, a regulated firm has an incentive to increase its capital relative to the amount of labor it uses (and thereby produce inefficiently) in order to maximize its profits. That is, the monopoly could produce at lower cost using a lower capital/labor ratio. Normally a firm buys labor and capital in proportions that minimize the cost of producing a given level of output. However, with ROR regulation, capital has an additional value to the firm. The more capital, all else the same, the lower the ROR (see Equation 20.1), so that the firm can have a higher level of profit and keep its ROR below the specified level. This overcapitalization result is illustrated in the following numerical example.

An Example. The local monopoly power company produces electricity using labor and capital. Suppose that the inverse demand curve facing the firm is

$$p(Q) = 100 - Q, \tag{20.2}$$

where p is the price and Q is the quantity of electricity sold.

The wage, w, and the user cost of capital, u, are \$168. The interest rate, r, is 10 percent, and there is no depreciation. The price of capital is \$1,680.

The quantity of electricity that the firm can produce is a function of the labor and capital inputs it uses:

$$Q = f(L, K) = LK. \tag{20.3}$$

This production function exhibits increasing returns to scale. If both labor and capital are doubled, output, instead of doubling, rises fourfold: $(2L)(2K) = 4LK = 4Q$. That is, this firm is a natural monopoly, with downward-sloping average and marginal cost curves, as Figure 20.5 shows.

Table 20.3 shows how much output the firm can produce with various levels of labor and capital. If the monopoly is unregulated, it maximizes its profit at \$288 by using 6 units of labor and 6 units of capital to produce 36 units of output.

Because the wage of labor equals the per-unit cost of capital and the production function is symmetric in L and K, the least expensive way for the firm to produce is to use labor and capital in equal proportions, so the ratio of capital to labor equals one ($K/L = 1$). For example, at the profit-maximizing level of 36 units of output, the firm uses 6 units each of labor and capital. If the firm uses equal amounts of labor and capital to produce 36 units of output, its factor costs are \$2,016 = $wL + uK = (168 \times 6) + (168 \times 6)$. If, for example, the 36 units of output were

TABLE 20.2 **Rates of Return (%) in Regulated Industries, 1974–1977**

Industry	On Book Value of Assets[a]	On Investors' Value[b]
Electricity	8.3	5.8
Gas transportation	9.7	5.7
Gas utilities	10.9	6.1
Telephone	8.7	5.8
Railroad transportation	6.0	4.2
Airline transportation	5.0	3.7
Motor-freight transportation	7.9	6.1
Market return	5.8	
Unregulated service industries		6.6

[a]The rate of return is the book-value weighted average of retained earnings plus dividends plus interest payments divided by the book value of assets.

[b]The rate of return on investors' value is the market-value weighted average of all interest and dividends plus price appreciation divided by the market value of all securities (such as stocks and bonds) for that industry.

Source: MacAvoy (1979, Table 2.13 and Appendix C).

produced using 4 units of labor and 9 units of capital, the firm's costs would be $\$2{,}184 = (168 \times 4) + (168 \times 9)$, which is 8.33% higher (Table 20.3).

The levels of capital and labor that maximize profit do not maximize ROR (Table 20.3). For example, where profit is maximized, $K = 6$, $L = 6$, $K/L = 1$, and the ROR is 2.86%. In contrast, where $K = 5$ and $L = 7$, the ROR is higher at 3.08%, although the profit is only \$259.

If the regulatory board sets the fair rate of return at 1.61%, the monopoly tries to maximize its profit subject to the constraint that its ROR is less than or equal to 1.61. It must lower π or raise K or both.

The monopoly can satisfy this regulatory constraint by raising capital from $K = 6$ to $K = 8$, lowering labor from $L = 6$ to $L = 5$. By so doing, the firm increases its output by 11.1% (from 36 to 40 units). To sell this extra output, it must drop its price from \$64 to \$60. Its profit falls from \$288 to \$216. Thus, by lowering profits and raising capital, the firm lowers its rate of return from 2.86% to 1.61%, the fair rate of return.

The regulated firm is producing inefficiently because its capital/labor ratio is 1.6 instead of 1. It costs the firm \$2,184 to produce 40 units of output using $L = 5$ and $K = 8$. It costs the firm only \$2,125 (2.8% less) to produce 40 units of output using 6.32 units each of labor and capital.

As predicted, the firm responds to the regulation by overcapitalizing.[30] Consumers are better off because the price is lower. Consumer surplus rises by 23% and welfare

[30]Several economists have argued that rate-of-return regulation may lead to undercapitalization rather than overcapitalization if firms maximize sales revenue instead of profits (Bailey 1973, Ch. 5) or because of dynamic considerations (Gilbert and Newbery 1988, Dechert 1984).

FIGURE 20.5 Rate-of-Return Regulation

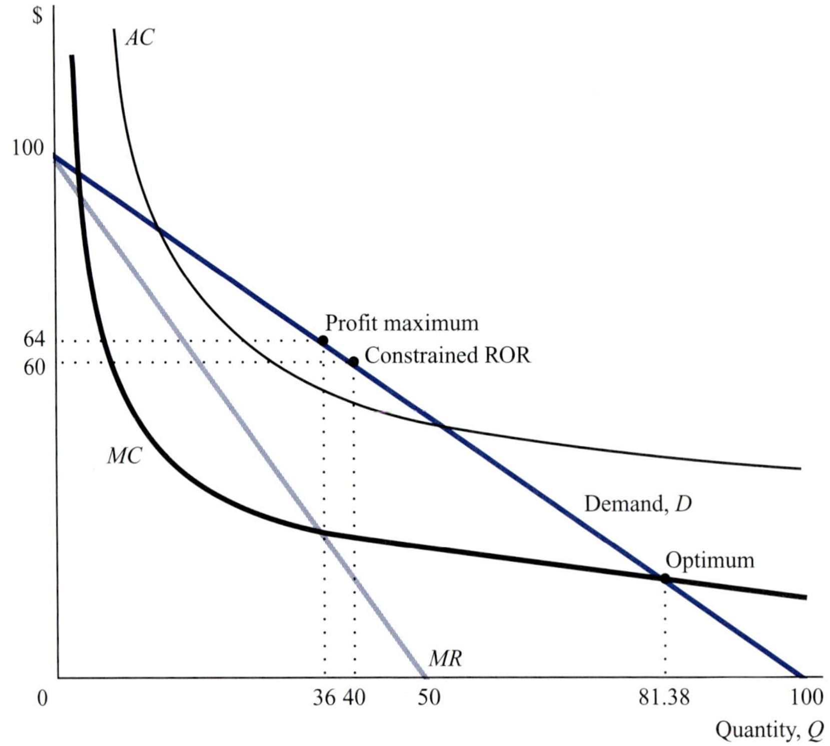

(consumer surplus plus producer surplus or profit minus administrative costs) rises by 8.5% if the regulatory board's administrative costs are negligible.

Graphical Analysis. Figure 20.5 shows the three equilibria that appear in bold text in Table 20.3. The unregulated, profit-maximizing equilibrium ($Q = 36$) is determined by setting marginal revenue equal to marginal cost. The ROR-regulated equilibrium has more output ($Q = 40$), so consumers are better off. The welfare-maximizing solution ($Q = 81.38$) occurs where price equals marginal cost. The least-cost way to produce 81.38 units is to use 9.02 units each of capital and labor. Although production and consumption are efficient in the welfare-maximizing solution, the firm must be subsidized by $1,515.40 (Table 20.3), because price is below average cost (Figure 20.5).

In this example, the best type of regulation more than doubles output obtained under the fair-rate-of-return regulation: 81.38 versus 40. Could the fair-rate-of-return

TABLE 20.3 **Rate-of-Return (ROR) Regulation**

Capital (K)	Labor (L)	Output (Q)	Price (p)	Profit (π)	Capital/Labor (K/L)	Rate of Return (ROR)	Consumer Surplus (CS)	Welfare (W)
5	4	20	80	88	1.25	1.05%	200.0	288.0
5	5	25	75	195	1.00	2.32	312.5	507.5
5	6	30	70	252	0.83	3.00	450.0	702.0
5	7	35	65	259	0.71	3.08	612.5	871.5
5	8	40	60	216	0.62	2.57	800.0	1016.0
5	9	45	55	123	0.56	1.46	1012.5	1135.5
6	4	24	76	144	1.50	1.43	288.0	432.0
6	5	30	70	252	1.20	2.50	450.0	702.0
6	**6**	**36**	**64**	**288**	**1.00**	**2.86**	**648.0**	**936.0**
6	7	42	58	252	0.86	2.50	882.0	1134.0
6	8	48	52	144	0.75	1.43	1152.0	1296.0
6	9	54	46	−36	0.67		1458.0	1422.0
7	4	28	72	168	1.75	1.43	382.0	560.0
7	5	35	65	259	1.40	2.20	612.5	871.5
7	6	42	58	252	1.17	2.14	882.0	1134.0
7	7	49	51	147	1.00	1.25	1200.5	1347.5
7	8	56	44	−56	1.14		1568.0	1512.0
7	9	63	37	−357	0.78		1984.5	1327.5
8	4	32	68	160	2.00	1.19	512.0	672.0
8	**5**	**40**	**60**	**216**	**1.60**	**1.61**	**800.0**	**1016.0**
8	6	48	52	144	1.33	1.07	1152.0	1296.0
8	7	56	44	−56	1.14		1568.0	1512.0
8	8	64	36	−384	1.00		2048.0	1664.0
8	9	72	28	−840	0.89		1592.0	1752.0
9	4	36	64	120	2.25	0.79	648.0	768.0
9	5	45	55	123	1.80	0.81	1012.5	1135.5
9	6	54	46	−36	1.50		1458.0	1422.0
9	7	63	37	−357	1.29		1984.5	1627.5
9	8	72	28	−840	1.12		2592.0	1752.0
9	9	81	19	−1485	1.00		3280.5	1795.5
9.02	**9.02**	**81.38**	**18.62**	−1515.4	**1.00**		**3311.4**	**1796.5**
10	10	100	0	−3360			5000.0	1640.0

Notes: The ROR is not shown if it is negative.

$w = u = 168$.

r = interest rate = 10 percent.

In calculating the welfare measure, consumer surplus plus profit, we assume that administrative costs are zero.

type of regulation achieve close to the optimal level of output? No, it cannot, as long as a positive fair rate is set. As Table 20.3 and Figure 20.5 show, profit is negative at the welfare maximum; hence, the rate of return is negative as well.

Despite its inefficiency, ROR regulation may increase welfare if the loss from inefficiency in production is offset by the gain from greater output and lower prices.[31] However, optimal direct price regulation can lower the price without inducing production inefficiencies, so optimal direct price regulation is preferable theoretically.

Empirical Evidence. Three empirical studies from the early 1970s found that ROR regulation substantially affected electric utilities (Courville 1974, Petersen 1975, Spann 1974). For example, Courville (1974) estimated an average overcapitalization of nearly 12 percent. These studies have been criticized on technical grounds (McKay 1977).

Other studies fail to find overcapitalization (Smithson 1978) or find evidence of undercapitalization (Baron and Toggart 1977). In short, the empirical evidence on overcapitalization is mixed. However, there is a general consensus that production under ROR regulation is likely to be inefficient. Regulators in the United States have been moving away from ROR regulation in recent years; however, this type of regulation is still common in other countries.

Quality Effects

There we were, one foot on a bar of soap and the other in the gutter.
—Commander Pursey, M.P. (attributed)

Even if price controls and ROR regulation lower prices, they may cause some vexing problems. For example, they may alter the quality of the product regulated or reduce the variety of products from which a consumer may choose (Archibald 1964, Stigler 1968d, White 1972, **www.aw-bc.com/carlton_perloff** "Drugs"). Unless more sophisticated regulations than pure price and entry controls are used, society must choose between two unattractive alternatives: high price and high quality versus low price and low quality.

For the purposes of this discussion (based on White 1972), suppose that quality is a second output of a firm. For example, if a firm's primary output is air transportation, the second output could be in-flight meals or in-flight movies.

The second output (quality) of the firm influences the demand for the firm's primary output and may be jointly produced and consumed. For example, a consumer may be more likely to fly on a given airline, all else the same, if a meal is served on board. Moreover, an in-flight meal can be consumed only while simultaneously flying, by definition.

[31] See Klevorick (1971), Bailey and Coleman (1971), and Sheshinski (1971).

Price and entry restrictions affect the number or tastiness of meals (or other similar quality measures).[32] Suppose, initially, that airlines are unregulated and that travel and meals can be purchased separately. The number of flights demanded, Q_F, and the quantity of meals demanded per passenger per trip, Q_M, vary with the price of a flight, p_F, and the price of a meal, p_M:

$$Q_F = Q_F(p_F, p_M),$$
$$Q_M = Q_M(p_F, p_M).$$

The total quantity of meals demanded is $Q_M Q_F$. Assume, also, that the average and marginal cost of producing a trip, m_F, or a meal, m_M, are constants.

If there are a substantial number of airline firms, then the industry is competitive. The price of basic transportation and of meals equal the corresponding marginal costs: $p_F = m_F$ and $p_M = m_M$. If each industry is monopolized, prices are likely to be higher than the corresponding marginal costs: $p_F > m_F$ and $p_M > m_M$.

A competitive industry provides a wide choice of quality levels. Flights with 1, 2, 3, or more meals are offered, where flights with more meals (or better tasting meals) cost more. For example, first class costs more than coach because first class provides better meals, bigger seats, and so forth. A monopoly may provide a different choice of qualities than a competitive industry (see the discussion of bundling, Chapter 11).

If regulatory authorities forbid new entry and set a single price, p_F^*, that must be charged regardless of the level of quality provided, the demand for flights depends only on the fixed price and the level of meals, $Q_F = Q_F(p_F^*, Q_M)$.

Firms can only attract business from their competitors by providing higher quality flights; they cannot compete on price. If an extra meal generates positive profits, the firm increases the number of meals. Each firm adds meals until the added profits made on each customer are driven to zero. That is, the net revenue from each passenger, $p_F^* - m_F$, from basic transportation just equals the marginal cost of providing that number of meals, $Q_M m_M$.

Thus, regulated competitive firms increase quality as long as they can profitably take customers from their competitors. This competition drives profits to zero because meals are provided at constant marginal cost. Because only one price, p_F^*, is charged, each firm chooses the same quality level: $Q_M = (p_F^* - m_F)/m_M$. In contrast to the unregulated case, no variability in quality is observed across flights within a given market.

A regulated monopoly offers a lower level of quality per passenger than a regulated competitive industry, holding the regulated price constant. Each regulated competitive

[32] White (1972) shows that analogous results are obtained for other quality variables such as luxurious waiting rooms or in-flight films. Schmalensee (1977) and Panzar (1979) discuss other quality measures of airlines, such as load factors and flight frequencies. See also Douglas and Miller (1974).

firm believes that the increase in the number of seats sold as the number of meals is increased is infinite: The demand curve facing the competitive firm is horizontal. In contrast, the regulated monopoly knows that the industry demand curve slopes downward, so that increasing meals increases seat sales by a limited amount. As a result, the regulated competitive firm has a greater incentive to increase quality than the monopoly.[33]

There are five main results of this analysis. First, a regulated competitive industry offers more quality per passenger than does a monopoly holding the regulated price fixed. Second, as a result, a regulated competitive industry sells more seats than a monopoly. Third, the higher the regulated price, p_F^*, the higher the quality provided by the competitive industry, because the rewards to attracting more business are higher. Fourth, regulation of a competitive industry harms fliers by eliminating different quality levels. Regulation of a monopoly may help or hurt fliers because the loss of variety in quality may be offset by a lower price. Fifth, raising the price of a regulated competitive industry does not increase profitability, because firms increase quality to compete until all extra profits are dissipated.[34]

With the Airline Deregulation Act of 1978, some of these hypotheses could be tested. For example, there should be more variety in quality level and probably a lower overall quality level now than before deregulation. The empirical evidence, discussed later in the section on airline deregulation, supports these hypotheses.

Making Competitive Industries More Monopolistic

Governments often regulate competitive industries, making them less competitive and lowering welfare. Governments may regulate poorly because of mistakes or because legislatures or regulators are captured by special-interest groups.

---

[33]The profits of a regulated firm, if its price per seat is regulated and it cannot charge for meals is

$$\pi = (p_F^* - m_F)Q_F - m_M Q_M Q_F.$$

The firm determines the optimal number of meals by differentiating π with respect to Q_M and setting this first derivative equal to zero:

$$\frac{d\pi}{dQ_M} = (p_F^* - m_F)\frac{\partial Q_F}{\partial Q_M} - m_M Q_M \frac{\partial Q_F}{\partial Q_M} - m_M Q_F = 0.$$

Rearranging terms, the profit-maximizing number of meals is

$$Q_m = \frac{p_F^* - m_F}{m_M} - Q_F \bigg/ \frac{\partial Q_F}{\partial Q_M}.$$

This expression holds for both regulated competitive and monopolistic firms. For competitive firms, however, $\partial Q_F/\partial Q_M = \infty$; whereas, a regulated monopoly faces a finite $\partial Q_F/\partial Q_M$. As a result, Q_M is bigger for a regulated competitive firm, all else the same.

[34]Several authors argue that regulated firms often have strong incentives to provide high-quality products, especially if quality is capital-intensive. See Schmalensee (1979b, 33), Kahn (1970, 21–26), and Spence (1975). See Crew and Kleindorfer (1978) and Telson (1975) on utilities choosing excessive levels of reliability. See Panzar (1979) on regulating monopolistic competition markets.

Earlier chapters present several examples in which regulations make markets more monopolistic. Many occupations—such as electricians, realtors, lawyers (Example 20.3), and doctors—are or have been empowered by governments to establish restrictions on entry, fix prices, and in other ways convert competitive industries into monopolies. Agricultural marketing orders (Appendix 9A) allow farmers to act collectively to reduce total crop production and to price discriminate. In some industries, laws allowed advertising about prices to be forbidden (Example 14.4). This ban on advertising gave firms information-based monopoly power and resulted in higher prices. Example 20.5 discusses how rent control can create inefficiencies as well as redistribute income. This section examines two types of government intervention that harm consumers and reduce efficiency: restrictions on the number of firms in an industry and agricultural regulations, such as price supports and quantity controls.

EXAMPLE 20.5 *Rent Control*

Regulation can reduce the efficiency of competitive markets. In many cities around the world, government agencies regulate apartment rental rates, using *rent controls* to keep rental rates below the competitive level. As a result, the demand for housing exceeds the supply.

Rent control transfers wealth from owners to renters. It also reduces the incentive to build new rental housing, exacerbating the shortage in the long run. Similarly, owners have less of an incentive to maintain rental housing, so it deteriorates faster than otherwise.

Rent control is common throughout much of the world. Large percentages of housing in Britain, Sweden, Mexico City, New York City, Berkeley, and San Francisco have been covered by rent control. In the United States, some 200 cities, including nearly 50 in California, have some type of rent control. However, California state law ended rent control in five California cities in 1999.

Olsen's (1972) empirical study finds that in New York City in 1968, occupants of rent controlled housing consumed 4.4 percent less housing services and 9.9 percent more nonhousing goods than they would have consumed in the absence of rent control. As a result, their real income was 3.4 percent higher, and poorer families received larger benefits than richer ones. The cost of rent control to landlords, however, was twice its benefit to the tenants.

Using data from New Jersey, Epple (1987) finds that the greater the rate of population increase, the more likely a community is to have rent control. Long-time renters are more likely to obtain rent-control units, so they benefit more from rent control than new arrivals. He also concludes that rent control is more likely in communities with more durable rental structures, which allow wealth to be more successfully transferred to renters when suppliers' ability to reduce supply is limited.

Sources: Olsen (1972); Epple (1987); Ray Tessler, "Rent Control Wins Decision in High Court," *San Francisco Chronicle,* February 25, 1988:1; and "Rent Control in Berkeley, Four Other Cities to End Jan. 1," **www.sfgate.com,** December 22, 1998.

Limiting Entry

Every decent man is ashamed of the government he lives under.
—*H. L. Mencken*

In many industries, governments restrict entry. For example, occupational licensing laws often allow current, licensed members of an occupation to write the licensing exam (Example 20.3). If they write a difficult exam, or grade unreasonably, potential entrants can be denied licenses. Automobile dealers are required to obtain a "Certificate of Need" before opening a new dealership in 18 states (Oliver 1988). Similarly, potential competitors to the U.S. Postal Service are not allowed to deliver mail to individuals' mailboxes. There are also restrictions on entry in industries as diverse as international air travel, taxicabs, health care, and public utilities. This section concentrates on government control of the number of business licenses (rights to operate in an industry), which restricts entry.[35]

By restricting entry into an industry, a government creates artificial scarcity and raises prices to consumers. The higher prices cause a transfer of wealth from consumers to firms in the industry. That is, the government creates property rights—the right to operate a firm in the industry—and often transfers these rights to a few, lucky individuals.

When the restrictions to entry are first created, governments often provide these rights or business licenses at no charge to all the firms already in the industry, which are said to be *grandfathered.* New firms are prohibited from entering the industry without business licenses. Unless the government creates additional licenses, a potential entrant can only obtain a license from a license-holder who is willing to leave the industry. As a result, the number of firms in the industry stays constant.

Any rents from these licenses go to the original owners. That is, an owner sells a license for the present discounted value of the future stream of profits. Thus, new entrants do not make excess profits on their investments, although consumers continue to pay high prices. Only those lucky enough to get the original licenses benefit.

Presumably, lobbying by firms leads to legislatures limiting the number of business licenses. Economists often refer to such lobbying efforts as *rent seeking:* the expenditure of resources to obtain government-created monopoly profits. It is worth lobbying for additional profits (rents) up to the point where the marginal cost from more lobbying equals the expected marginal gain.[36]

There are many examples of governments restricting entry by limiting business licenses. In California, a law allowing only one fish farm resulted in that firm earning a 1,200 percent return on capital in its first year. Another proposed law in California

---

[35]Some label such restrictions "barriers to entry." We use the term "restriction to entry" instead because we earlier defined a "long-run barrier" as an advantage that one firm has over other firms that enables it to earn excess profits in the long run. If the government requires all firms to pay a (market-determined) license fee, the government restricts entry by raising costs but does not create a long-run barrier (as we defined it) that favors some firms over others.

[36]Pittman (1988) shows that rent seeking is most likely in concentrated industries.

EXAMPLE 20.6 *Brewing Trouble*

The California Legislature overwhelmingly passed a bill to grant monopolies to beer distributors. The bill required breweries to sell beer to only a single wholesaler in any given area. Ninety percent of the beer sold by breweries to California wholesalers is under exclusive dealer contracts. Nonetheless, wholesalers wanted to make the practice state law to prevent major retailers from buying directly from breweries, perhaps to control free riding on distributors' promotional efforts. Wholesalers also feared that the courts would use antitrust laws to reject exclusive distribution contracts.

Consumer groups, large store chains, and the state's attorney general opposed the bill. Common Cause and the Consumers Union branded the bill as the worst special-interest measure of the year. When Indiana, New Jersey, and New York adopted similar laws, beer prices increased 10 to 20 percent, or 25 to 50 cents per six-pack.

Why did it pass easily? Although we don't know for sure, wholesalers were extremely generous in their campaign contributions to Republicans and Democrats alike. Of the 120 members of the state Assembly and Senate, 116 reported receiving in excess of $530,000 collectively.

The governor vetoed the bill.

Sources: Steve Wiegand, "Beer Distributors' Monopoly Bill Okd," *San Francisco Chronicle*, August 28, 1987: A10, and "Veto the Beer Bill," *San Francisco Examiner*, August 30, 1987: A18.

reflected an attempt to monopolize beer wholesaling (Example 20.6). In some states, one must have a liquor license to sell liquor, and restrictions on licenses may drive the free market price of a license over $100,000.

One well-known example of an industry with entry restrictions is taxicabs. Some city governments in virtually every country in the world limit the number of taxicab licenses. (Partially offsetting the anticompetitive effects of these restrictions to entry are price controls on rates that cabs charge.) Entry into the taxicab market is often restricted by requiring each cab to have a medallion (a physical business license) and then limiting the number of medallions. In most years, new cabs cannot enter the market unless they buy a medallion from an existing owner. As a result, the original owners capture the present value of future excess profits by charging high prices for their medallions. In the mid-1980s, it cost $100,000 to own a taxi in New York City and $140,000 in Boston, but only the cost of a jalopy in Washington, D.C. (Oliver 1988). By 1993, the price of a medallion in New York City reached $182,000, and by 2004 had reached $225,000.

A 1984 study for the U.S. Department of Transportation estimated that the annual extra cost to consumers from restrictions on the number of taxicabs throughout the United States was $800 million. This amount is an underestimate of the total lost consumer surplus, because it does not include lost waiting time and other inconveniences associated with having relatively few cabs. However, some people argue there are offsetting benefits. Other taxicab regulations are often used to offset, at least partially, the bad effect of the entry restriction, and to justify the entry restriction. Typically, a medallion owner is subject to a number of restrictions, including price and safety regulations, which may benefit consumers.

Local monopoly power of cabs can be kept in check, at least partially, by the threat of losing a medallion. Imagine that you arrive in a strange city and there is only one cab within sight. You are tired and hungry and the rain is coming down hard. The cab driver says, "I'll take you to your hotel for five times the amount on the meter." As angry as that makes you, you may still take the cab. However, if your report of this incident could cause the driver to lose the medallion, the driver would be hesitant to make such a demand.

Most of these justifications for regulation fail to explain why the number of cabs must be limited to the point where a medallion is worth hundreds of thousands of dollars. One justification for entry limitation is that, because an additional cab raises search costs of other taxis to find riders, there is excessive entry, as in fisheries (Gallick and Sisk 1984). However, it is difficult to believe that most cities operate optimally, given the high values of medallions. Presumably the main purpose of these regulations is to transfer wealth from riders to medallion owners. One explanation for why wealth is transferred in this way is the interest-group theory: Medallion owners lobby strongly for these restrictions.

An alternative explanation is that the type of regulation is determined in large part by the incentives facing regulators (Eckert 1973). The taxi industry tends to be regulated by either municipal agencies or independent commissions. Municipal agencies are run by bureaucrats who impose rules and require supervision of the industry so as to justify large salaries and staffs. Independent commissioners, in contrast, have part-time appointments. Supervising large staffs, dealing with exceptions, and so forth would require more of their time. Moreover, as they tend to be appointed for a limited term, long-run returns in bigger staffs from more regulations would aid only their successors.

Commissioners often find that they can reduce their level of regulatory effort if they only have to deal with a single "responsible" firm. Equivalently, the market may be divided into exclusive territories through regulation, creating local monopolies. Thus, according to this hypothesis, commissions prefer monopolies or market divisions more than do agency bureaucrats. Of 6 cities that Eckert studied with commissions, 5 (83.3 percent) had monopolies or market divisions. Of the 27 cities he studied with agencies, only 5 (18.5 percent) had monopolies or market divisions.

Regardless of commissioners' motives, however, cab riders lose and long-time medallion owners gain. However, these transfers are trivial compared to those in agriculture.

Agricultural Regulations: Price Supports and Quantity Controls

Most standard microeconomic textbooks point to agricultural markets as examples, possibly the only examples, of perfectly competitive markets. After all, agricultural markets are typified by a large number of small firms. Unfortunately, in virtually every country in the world, governments intervene in these markets and reduce their efficiency, driving them from the competitive equilibrium.

Why do governments engage in policies that promote inefficiency and harm consumers? One common explanation is that the government wants to transfer income to the agricultural sector but does not want to do so openly and directly by just giving farmers money. To accomplish this transfer of income, price supports and quantity controls are used.

Price Supports. During the Great Depression in the United States, farmers were struck early and hard. In response, the Federal Farm Board was established in 1929 to buy and sell farm output in order to ensure "orderly agricultural marketing."[37] The objective was to achieve *parity* in relative prices or incomes between agriculture and other sectors compared to the levels achieved in 1910–14. The board used **price supports**: By buying when prices would otherwise be low, it prevented prices from falling below certain levels called support prices. By buying large quantities at high prices, it created large stockpiles and exhausted its available funds.

Figure 20.6 shows why. Farm price supports induce farmers to produce more than would be produced by a competitive market.[38] The competitive equilibrium is determined by the intersection of the demand curve and the supply curve, *S*. The competitive price is p_c and the competitive quantity is Q_c. If the government guarantees farmers a support price of $p_s > p_c$, consumers are only willing to buy $\underline{Q}$ units. Thus, the government must buy the rest of the total amount supplied, $Q_s - \underline{Q}$, and store it. The government cannot sell it domestically as long as the price remains at p_s.

This program is a very inefficient way to transfer income to farmers: It costs consumers and taxpayers much more than farmers receive. Under this program, farmers' incomes rise by $A + B + C$ in Figure 20.6. This total area represents the extra income from selling more units (Q_s rather than Q_c) at a higher price (p_s rather than p_c) less the cost of producing the extra units (the area under the aggregate supply curve from Q_c to Q_s). At the higher price, consumer surplus falls by $A + B$. The government pays $p_s(Q_s - \underline{Q})$, which equals $B + C + D$, for the extra crop and then pays to store the surplus (assuming that the government has no alternative use for the crop). Thus, the net loss to society is $B + D$ plus the cost of storage, which is the loss to consumers ($A + B$) plus the loss to the government ($B + C + D +$ storage) minus the gain to farmers ($A + B + C$).

[37]Apologists for our agricultural policy usually justify it on the grounds that it stabilizes prices. By maintaining a high price, prices are more stable (fluctuate less from year to year) than they would be otherwise. Eliminating uncertainty, proponents of such stabilization maintain, increases farmers' welfare. Why this market needs stabilizing more than manufacturing and other markets, and why this type of stabilization should be achieved through government intervention is a mystery to us, so we do not discuss it further here.

[38]During most of the history of the U.S. farm supports, explicit price supports have not been used. Rather, the Commodity Credit Corporation (CCC) makes "nonrecourse" loans with the farmer's potential crop as collateral. That is, if the farmer does not pay back the loan, the agency keeps the crop but has no further recourse to the farmer's assets if the crop does not cover the loan. If agricultural prices are below the implicit price set by the loan, the farmer defaults on the loan and the CCC claims the crop. This technique is equivalent to a formal price support but involves more paperwork.

FIGURE 20.6 Price Supports

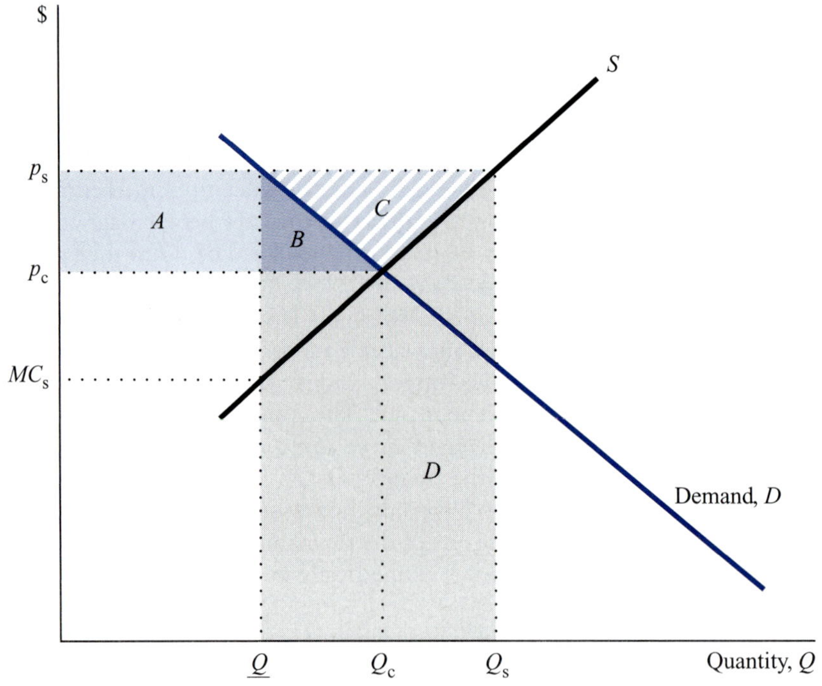

Three distortions are created by this program. First, there is excess production. Farmers produce Q_s instead of the competitive quantity, Q_c, which is excessive because consumers do not want to consume all of it at the price p_s. Second, there is inefficiency in consumption: Consumers pay p_s for $\underline{Q}$ units of output. The marginal cost of producing that output is MC_s. Thus, the consumer is paying a price above marginal cost: $p_s > MC_s$. Third, the government is paying to store the excessive output, which is produced but not consumed. There may be a future benefit if the output is later consumed before it rots.

Because these programs are very costly to governments, the United States and other governments have moved away from straight price supports. For example, they may impose quantity restrictions (see **www.aw-bc.com/carlton_perloff** "Agricultural Quantity Restrictions").

The Cost of Agricultural Support Programs. Most countries use price supports and other means to keep agricultural prices high domestically. The European Community (EC) uses price supports for grains, dairy, livestock, and sugar; deficiency payments for oilseeds; production quotas for sugar; export refunds for grains, dairy, and livestock; and various import tariffs and quotas.

In some countries, government farm subsidy payments exceed the amount farmers receive from consumers for the products. The Organization for Economic Co-Operation and Development (OECD) collects information about such subsidies in its member nations, which include most European and Scandinavian countries, Australia, Canada, Japan, South Korea, Mexico, New Zealand, and the United States.[39] Farmers in OECD countries received $231 billion in subsidies in 2001, down from an average of $239 billion during the period 1986–88. These subsidies were 31 percent of the amount consumers paid in 2001 and 38 percent in 1986–88. Total subsidies to agriculture, which includes subsidies for general services (e.g., marketing and promotion, infrastructure), totaled $311 billion (1.3% of GDP) in 2001, compared to an average of $302 billion (2.3% of GDP) over the period 1986–88.

The European Union had the largest producer subsidies to agriculture, $93 billion in 2001. Producer subsidies were $49 billion in the United States and $47 billion in Japan. Among OECD nations, Switzerland's farm subsidies constituted the largest fraction of consumer payments. Their $4.2 billion of producer subsidies were 69 percent of the value of production: The Swiss government gives the farmer more than two dollars for every dollar a farmer earns from the market. Producer subsidies as a fraction of farm production have generally declined since the mid-1980s. For example, New Zealand's producer subsidies averaged 11 percent of total value in 1986–88 but only 1 percent in 2001.

The cost of these supports to the average taxpayer is substantial. As of 2001, the average citizen in the European Union pays $281 a year in total subsidies to agriculture, although the payments rise to $650 a year for the typical Swiss citizen. Japanese citizens spend $467 per person, South Koreans pay $417 each, Americans pay $346, Canadians $168, Mexicans $81, Australians $61, and New Zealanders $37.

Deregulation

In markets in which regulation is harmful rather than helpful, deregulation makes sense. In the last two decades, many major industries were deregulated (Table 20.4), especially during the Carter and Reagan administrations.[40] Industries that were partially or totally deregulated include airlines, interstate trucking, railroads, banking and savings and loans (limits on interest rates), television, and telephones. Unfortunately, there has been little deregulation in agriculture. Other countries are also deregulating. For example, the British now allow cable television companies into the telephone business while the United States now allows telephone companies to enter the cable business.[41]

Typically, there are strong supporters and opponents of any proposal to deregulate an industry. Indeed, deregulation campaigns create some strange bedfellows. Support-

[39] *Agricultural Policies in OECD Countries: Monitoring and Evaluation,* Organization for Economic Co-Operation and Development, 2002.

[40] Conversely, many new regulations were instituted. The number of final rules published in the Federal Register averaged 7,347 in the Carter administration, fell to 5,335 in the Reagan administration, fell even further to 4,405 in the George H. Bush administration, and then rose somewhat to 4,671 under the Clinton administration. In the first two years of the George W. Bush administration, the number of final rules averaged 4,150 (Crews 2003).

[41] "Now You're Talking," *The Economist,* July 25, 1992:69–70. For detailed analysis of the effects of deregulation in telephones, see Cole (1991), Crandall (1991), MacAvoy (1992), Economides (1999), and Cave and Crandall (2001).

TABLE 20.4 Major U.S. Deregulation Decisions

1968	The Supreme Court permits non-AT&T equipment to be connected to the Bell System.
1969	MCI is permitted to connect its long-distance network to local phone systems.
1970	Interest rates are deregulated on bank deposits of $100,000 or more.
1972	The Federal Communications Commission (FCC) establishes a domestic satellite open skies policy.
1975	The Securities and Exchange Commission ends fixed brokerage fees for stock market transactions.
	Rate bureaus for railroads and trucking firms are prohibited from protesting independent rate filings.
1976	The Railroad Revitalization and Regulatory Reform Act of 1976 partially deregulates railroads and makes rate setting more cost-based.
1977	Deregulation of air cargo gives airlines more freedom in pricing.
1978	Congress partially decontrols natural gas.
	The Occupational Safety and Health Administration revokes 928 "nitpicking" rules.
	The Civil Aeronautics Board is phased out, eliminating controls over airline entry and prices.
	The Environmental Protection Agency permits emissions trading.
1980	The FCC removes most federal regulation of cable TV and of equipment on consumers' premises.
	The Motor Carrier Act eliminates barriers for new entry and permits operators to establish fares and routes with little oversight by the Interstate Commerce Commission.
	The Depository Institutions law phases out interest rate ceilings and permits savings and loans to offer interest-bearing checking accounts.
	The Staggers Rail Act enables railroads to adjust rates without government approval and enter into contracts with shippers.
1981	President Reagan decontrols crude oil prices and petroleum allocations.
	The FCC removes many radio regulations.
1982	A new bus regulatory statute allows intercity bus companies to change routes and fares.
	The Garn-St. Germain Act allows savings and loans to make more commercial and consumer loans and removes interest-rate differentials between banks and savings and loans.
1984	As part of an antitrust settlement, AT&T agrees to divest local operating companies.
	Individual ocean shipping companies are allowed to offer lower rates and better service than shipping "conferences."
1990	Clean Air Act of 1990 allows for a free market in pollution.
1992	Energy Act lifts most of the restrictions on independent power producers, allowing them to sell power to utilities at market rates.
1994	Riegle-Neal Interstate Banking and Branching Efficiency Act of 1994 allows bank holding companies to own banks in states other than their home state without forming lower-tier bank holding companies and allows banks to own branches across state lines (except in Texas and Montana).
	The Trucking Industry Regulatory Reform Act effectively eliminates all state oversight of intrastate trucking operations.
1996	Telecommunications Act of 1996 allows increased competition in communications markets, relaxes ownership restrictions on the number of broadcast stations that can be owned by a single entity, and ends (March 1999) price regulation of cable television rates.
	California governor Pete Wilson signs legislation to open up California's electricity market to competition.
1998	The Ocean Shipping Reform Act loosens regulations, such as allowing shippers and ocean carriers to negotiate and reach confidential service contracts and eliminates tariff filing requirements for individual carriers, but retains antitrust immunity for shipping conferences.
1999	The Gramm-Leach-Bliley Act loosens restrictions on banks' ability to underwrite securities and permits banks to underwrite insurance policies.
2003	The Federal Communications Commission sets new rules loosening restrictions on media ownership, such as one that allows the same company to own newspapers and broadcast stations in the same city and another that allows a company to own up to three television stations and eight radio stations in the largest markets. Pending litigation has blocked implementation of the rules.

Sources: Weidenbaum (1987); Lee, Baumel, and Harris (1987); Lown et al. (2000); Tang and Ma (2002); various newspapers.

ers of deregulation typically include many, but certainly not all, economists, some regulators, and some consumer groups. Opponents typically include some economists, many regulators, some consumer groups, the regulated firms, and unions that work for those firms.

Supporters of deregulation want to remove regulations that set prices and restrict entry. Proponents claim that deregulation increases efficiency and lowers prices. They point to two types of efficiency gains from removing the distortions created by price regulations. The first is a result of letting the market rather than regulators set relative prices. For example, many transportation and telephone regulations cross-subsidized people and firms in rural areas at the expense of other consumers. Deregulation, by allowing these rates to adjust, increases consumption along major transportation routes or phone usage in urban areas and decreases it on minor routes and in the boondocks, increasing efficiency. Even though society may collectively benefit from deregulation, some consumers may lose from these adjustments.

Second, proponents claim that deregulation lowers prices overall. In many industries, regulated prices are set well above marginal costs. Because prices are regulated but service levels may not be, regulated firms compete by increasing product quality or the frequency of their service, thereby driving their costs up to the level of the regulated prices, rather than allowing prices to fall to low-cost levels. Moreover, to the degree that regulated prices are cost-based, firms have little incentive to cut costs. Further, because regulators restrict entry, deregulation leads to lower prices due to increased competition from new entrants. Thus, proponents believe that deregulation lowers prices by ceasing to prop up prices artificially, allowing quality or service levels to fall from their high levels, and increasing the number of firms.

Opponents argue that most regulated industries are inherently oligopolistic. As a result, they claim, deregulation causes prices to shoot through the ceiling because smaller firms are driven out of business and remaining ones often collude. They also contend that, without controls, service and quality fall. Opponents also object that small communities lose service under deregulation because, without the cross-subsidization, it is unprofitable to provide the same level of service as under regulation. The deregulators counter that if it is unprofitable to serve these areas, they should not be served.

In most industries, deregulation has occurred slowly over time. Slow deregulation has created inequities and inefficiencies in some markets. Under the 1978 Natural Gas Policy Act, prices on natural gas wells differed by the time of discovery, with "old" gas still regulated and "new" unregulated.

In other industries, partial deregulation caused other problems. Many controls on savings and loans and banks were removed in 1980, and insurance on accounts was more than doubled. The insurance was provided by three federal entities: the Federal Deposit Insurance Corporation (FDIC), the Federal Savings and Loan Insurance Corporation (FSLIC), and the National Credit Union Share Insurance Fund (NCUSIF).

These insurers were exposed to risks by bank and savings and loan owners and managers, yet did not charge insurance premiums that varied according to the risk exposure (White 1988). Banks and savings and loans could take extremely high risks, knowing that the insurers would protect the depositors if they failed, but they could keep the high returns if they succeeded.

Aside from the failure to charge risk-based premiums, the regulation of banks was governed by the use of accounting conventions whereby the market value of the assets of a bank could bear no relation to the accounting value used for regulatory purposes. In 1982, the estimated market value of the net worth of the savings and loan industry was negative $100 billion or lower (White 1991, 77), yet federal agencies closed relatively few financial institutions.

In addition to deregulation, there were many other reasons for the plight of the financial institutions, including unexpected changes in interest rates (White 1991). Finally, especially when real estate values declined in the 1980s, many financial institutions were declared insolvent. According to the Federal Home Loan Bank Board, 520 savings and loan institutions were declared insolvent in 1987, and 434 in 1988, compared to 43 in 1980. From 1981 to 1987, there was nearly a fivefold increase in the number of thrifts declared insolvent.

Nonetheless, in several major industries, decontrol was rapid and fairly complete. Although all evidence is not in yet, many studies of deregulation in these industries find overall efficiency gains. The following sections examine deregulation in three transportation industries—airlines, trucking, and railroads—in more detail. Example 20.7 examines deregulation in electricity markets, while Example 20.8 examines deregulation in telecommunications. Peltzman and Winston (2000) and Winston (1993) provide an overview of the effects of deregulation across a broad range of industries.

Airlines

In 1938, Congress established the Civil Aeronautics Administration, which later became the Civil Aeronautics Board (CAB). The CAB controlled the interstate airlines industry, including entry by airline companies, air routes, fares, and agreements between airlines. The CAB also provided subsidies to promote air transportation. By the late 1970s, however, the CAB started to deregulate the industry and permitted free entry of any certified carrier to a few selected routes. Several major airlines were initiating suits against the CAB for violating its congressional mandate by allowing too much competition when Congress passed the Airline Deregulation Act of 1978 (Borenstein 1992).

Many economists and others believed that the CAB kept pricing far above competitive levels. Indeed, in the early 1970s, intrastate flights in California that were not regulated had prices that were about 40 percent less than fares in comparable eastern interstate markets, primarily due to flying fuller planes (Breyer 1982).

Proponents of deregulation argued prices would fall as a result of deregulation. They claimed that a deregulated airline travel market is contestable. That is, because planes can be moved easily to different locations, there are many potential entrants on each route, even though the number of actual competitors is small. Indeed, because regulators prevented entry, entry should be facilitated by deregulation. They also claimed that deregulated firms would offer better mixes of quality and be more responsive to the fluctuating desires of the public.

President Carter's chairman of the CAB, Alfred Kahn, an expert on the economics of regulation, was a forceful advocate of airline deregulation. When airlines were first deregulated, he observed, "I have more faith in greed than in regulation."[42]

[42] *New York Times,* October 7, 1980.

Opponents included the major airlines and their unions.[43] They feared economic harm. Some opponents argued that the airlines would become unsafe. Despite these objections, President Carter signed the Airlines Deregulation Act in 1978, which took pricing and route decisions from the CAB and allowed airlines to make these decisions. The CAB rapidly implemented the Airlines Deregulation Act, permitting entry routinely. The Act eliminated the CAB at the end of 1984.

To deal with one of the largest fears about deregulation, however, service to smaller communities was guaranteed for 10 years. The Essential Air Service Program, designed to cover a 10-year "phased transition" to a completely unregulated and unsubsidized market, cost $71 million to subsidize 202 communities in the continental United States in its first year of operation. By 1987, only 102 communities were being subsidized at a cost of $21 million.[44]

The deregulation of airlines had several major effects. Fares fell and passenger travel increased; industry profits fell; the airline industry developed hub-and-spoke networks and became increasingly concentrated; productivity increased; more price and quality choices became available to consumers; and there was no decline in safety. Morrison and Winston (1986) estimate the annual benefits from airline deregulation to be about $6 billion (in 1977 dollars).[45]

Average fares paid (in real terms) dropped by about 20 percent from 1980 to 1989, although fares rose in the late 1980s. The number of passenger miles flown by U.S. carriers more than doubled from the late 1970s to 1990.[46]

The long-term fall in prices lowered the profits of airlines. Price wars caused rates of return to be very low or negative. Several carriers exited the industry (Braniff, Midway, Pan Am, Eastern) and several continued operating under protection of the bankruptcy code (America West, Continental, TWA, United, and US Air). (See Borenstein and Rose 2003.) Airline workers suffered a 10 percent loss in relative earnings following deregulation (Card 1998).

Airlines developed extensive hub-and-spoke networks, sometimes by merging with other carriers (Brueckner and Spiller 1991). (The successful low-cost airline Southwest Airlines is a notable exception to the development of hub-and-spoke networks.) Following deregulation, there was new entry. But there were also several subsequent exits

[43]Spiller (1983) points out that, based on history during the regulatory period, some airlines could be predicted to profit from deregulation and others to lose. Moreover, potential entrants expected to gain from deregulation. As a result, some firms favored deregulation.

[44]According to a Department of Transportation (DOT) analysis, without the subsidies, about 70 of the 102 communities would not have air service. Of the 70, however, 43 serve fewer than five passengers a day and 33 are within 75 highway miles of airports with scheduled, unsubsidized flights. At the end of 1987, Congress voted to extend the subsidy, which still exists. Jack Anderson, "The High Cost of Air Travel," *San Francisco Chronicle*, December 1, 1987:A23.

In fiscal 1989, Congress appropriated $25 million for the program—$6.6 million less than necessary to maintain the existing level of support. DOT announced cutbacks eliminating service to up to 56 communities in as many as 39 states, but exempting Alaska and Hawaii because air service is often the only feasible transportation mode in those states. "Subsidy Cuts Threaten Rural Air Service," *San Francisco Chronicle*, January 4, 1989:A10.

[45]See also Kahn (1988), Meyer et al. (1987a, b), and Moore (1986).

[46]Gene Koretz, "Why Booking Air Travel Isn't Lifting Airlines," *Business Week*, October 12, 1992:24.

EXAMPLE 20.7

Deregulating Electricity: California in Shock

Until recently in California, regulated local monopoly utilities produced and distributed electricity. California had one of the United States' highest electricity rates. In 1996, in an effort to improve efficiency, the state legislature passed a "deregulation" bill that separated generation from transmission and distribution. The bill permitted independent generators to compete to produce power, a change that ideally would have increased competition and market efficiency. However, the industry remained highly regulated in many ways, for example, through explicit price controls on wholesale prices during many periods.

In the short run, the electricity supply curve is virtually horizontal up to the point where production capacity is reached, where it becomes nearly vertical. The figure (based on Borenstein 2002) shows California's thermal-generation supply curve for August 2000. The electricity wholesale demand curve is inelastic (nearly vertical) in the short run because retail prices are generally fixed; however, the wholesale demand

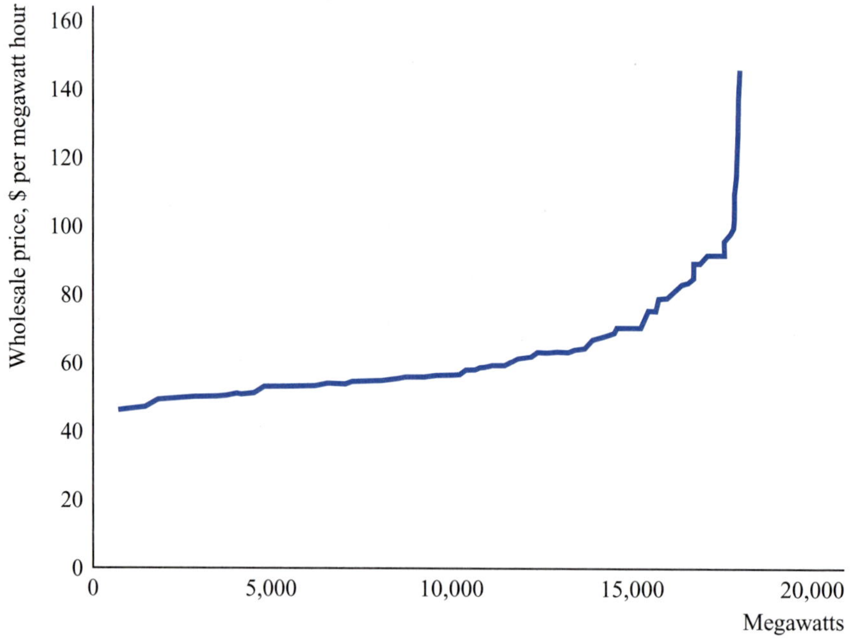

and at least 24 mergers. Thus, the initial influx of new carriers after deregulation was offset by exits and mergers, so that the industry became more concentrated, especially along routes that are not heavily traveled. The four-firm concentration ratio for the

curve shifts to the right substantially in warm weather and during daytime hours. A small rightward shift of the demand curve in the horizontal portion of the supply curve has little effect on the wholesale price. However, if the demand curve is near the full-capacity quantity, a small shift in the demand curve can create large swings in the wholesale price. In this situation, if even one generator significantly cuts back the power it supplies, it can have a powerful effect on price.

When demand for electricity exceeds available supply (too many people flip on a switch), the system can fail partially or totally. Modern systems adopt procedures to shed demand (ration customers) so as to avoid system failure. In California in 2000, the system operator mandated partial shutdowns on several occasions to prevent a catastrophic system failure.

In 2000, California's wholesale energy prices started to soar. By the spring of 2001, the wholesale price of energy was more than 10 times its value in the previous year. To make matters worse, the retail price of electricity was regulated, so that utilities were sometimes forced to sell at retail at about 6¢ per kilowatt-hour when they were buying electricity at a wholesale rate of 10¢. The state's largest utility, Pacific Gas and Electric, filed for bankruptcy. The state stepped in and entered into long-term contracts for wholesale power that it then made available to the utilities. Soon thereafter, the price of natural gas (an input into electricity generation) fell, leaving California in the unfortunate position of having signed long-term contracts at prices that may have been double the expected wholesale price.

There have been many analyses of the causes of the California crisis, and these point to several contributing factors in addition to the capacity problem. Two other important factors are that the government continued to regulate retail prices and continued to forbid long-term contracting by utilities. Because households and most firms faced fixed retail prices, they had no price incentive to cut back consumption during crisis periods. Utilities could not sign long-term supply contracts for wholesale power, and so they could not use these contracts to mitigate short-run fluctuations in prices due to hot weather, higher natural gas prices, or other causes. Moreover, if utilities could have contracted in advance, they would not have been so much at the mercy of any one generator or group of generators in the short run.

Unfortunately, many people have drawn the false conclusion from the California crisis that deregulation is harmful. Actually, there was substantial regulation before and after the change in 1996, and most of the worst problems in 2000 stemmed from continuing or new regulation and fixed capacity rather than from the very limited deregulation itself.

Sources: Borenstein (2002), Joskow (2000a).

domestic airline industry was 56.2 percent in 1977, 64.8 percent in 1987 (Borenstein 1992), 55 percent in 2000, and 54 percent in 2003 (authors' calculations). Thus, the domestic industry is now slightly less concentrated than before deregulation. A study

EXAMPLE 20.8

International and U.S. Deregulation in Telecommunications

In 1980, most countries had state-owned telecommunications companies, with the exception of North American nations. By 1998, data from 167 countries indicated that 42 percent had replaced state ownership with some form of partial or total private ownership together with regulation. The first big event was British prime minister Margaret Thatcher's decision in the early 1980s to privatize British Telecom, to reject the U.S. model of rate of return regulation in favor of price cap regulation, and to introduce competition. Along with privatization, many countries have allowed various forms of competition, with the necessary interconnections that competitors require being under regulatory control.

Most existing evidence is consistent with the view that privatization and competition have each been important sources of efficiency and growth in telecommunications. Privatization, where profit-maximizing firms replace a government entity, leads to lower costs. But regulation plus competition is also needed to ensure that consumers reap the rewards of the improved efficiency. For example, one study finds that between 1990 and 1998, privatization together with competition caused output to rise by over 17%, with each contributing about equally. Similarly, privatization together with competition caused investment per capita to rise over the 1990–98 period by more than 40%. In each case, there is an interaction between privatization and competition that shows that competition makes privatization more effective in instilling efficiency.

In the United States, partial deregulation of telecommunications has led to significant benefits to consumers. The break-up of the nationwide AT&T phone monop-

of individual airports, however, indicates that the Herfindahl-Hirschman Index (HHI) at the top 100 airports was lower, on average, in 1989 than in the late 1970s.[47] Although concentration at hub airports did increase, concentration at nonhub airports declined so that on average, concentration at individual airports fell.[48] This finding is similar to Morrison and Winston's (1990) finding that the number of effective competitors on individual routes rose by about 30 percent between 1978 and 1988. Bailey and Williams (1988) show that in certain local markets, one or a few airlines have virtual monopolies. Bailey, Graham, and Kaplan (1985) and Hurdle et al. (1989) conclude that city pairs are not generally perfectly contestable (price is above marginal cost), so that high concentration on some routes does lead to higher fares.

Deregulation also led to greater efficiency, which helped lower prices (Sickles et al. 1986). A comparison of U.S. airlines to those in other countries also reveals a substan-

[47]Borenstein (1989, 1990) and Berry (1990) show that average price rises with airport concentration. Bamberger and Carlton (1993) show that average price rises as an airline adds more of its own feeder traffic on a route. Call and Keeler (1985) and Moore (1986) show that entry lowers prices.

[48]Based on a tabulation of originating passengers; see Bamberger and Carlton (2003).

oly in 1984 spurred the creation of competition in long-distance telephony. AT&T's share of long-distance calls, which exceeded 90% in 1984, fell to 65% by 1990 and to 38% by 2000. Corresponding to improvements in technology and to increased competition from rivals such as MCI and Sprint, average long-distance rates fell from 55 cents per minute in 1984 to 27 cents per minute in 1990 and to 12 cents per minute in 2000. The 1996 Telecommunications Act attempted to create competition in local telephony by requiring the incumbent local phone providers to make some of their facilities available to rivals. As of December 2002, the share of local lines handled by nonincumbent phone providers (called Competitive Local Exchange Carriers, or CLECs) was 13.2%, of which only about 3% was provided by CLECs using their own equipment.

Competition from wireless providers of phone services has deepened competitive pressures on both local and long-distance rates. Roughly half of the U.S. population have cell phones. Moreover, the Internet holds out the possibility of providing competition using the Voice Over Internet Protocol (VOIP), and cable can now provide phone service. Thus an industry that once was a monopoly that provided local and long-distance phone service over traditional phone lines is rapidly becoming an industry with many players using a variety of rapidly developing technologies to provide consumers with local and long-distance phone service. In such an industry, regulation can distort or delay the introduction of new technologies, to consumers' detriment. According to one estimate, the FCC's delay in authorizing cellular service in the 1990s imposed annual costs of about $34 billion (in $1994) over a 10-year period.

Sources: Statistics of the Long Distance Telecommunications Industry, FCC May 2003; *CTIA Wireless Industry Indices,* April 2003; *FCC Trends in Telephone Service,* May 2002; Hausman (1997b); Li and Xu (2002).

tial increase in efficiency from deregulation (Caves et al. 1987). In the postregulation period, the rate of growth in productive efficiency for U.S. airlines was at least as high as before deregulation, whereas the rate of growth for airlines in other countries declined by nearly 40 percent. Assuming the United States would have had the same experience as in other countries had deregulation not occurred, deregulation lowered U.S. airline unit costs by 10 percent by 1983, a saving of over $4 billion.

A full continuum of price/quality choices is now offered (Bailey and Williams 1988). In particular, in contrast to the regulated period, low-price, low-quality service is now offered. Improved service is also available for higher fares (Moore 1986). Overall, however, service has declined—there are greater travel delays, longer travel times, and more lost luggage. Many, if not most, of these problems stem from greater congestion in hub cities and relatively fewer air traffic controllers, due to lack of action by Congress and the Department of Transportation (Moses and Savage 1987). Not only do price and quality now vary more, but there appears to be more price discrimination (Borenstein and Rose 1989).

There are now more types of fares, and they change more frequently. Under regulation, there were relatively few rates, which changed infrequently. In the old days, the

Airline Tariff Publishing Co., a cooperative venture owned by the airlines to process changes in ticket prices, considered 25,000 daily fare changes a large number. By 1988, 40,000 to 60,000 changes were not unusual, and in one week, nearly 600,000 were processed.[49]

Despite the congestion, especially at hub airports, the failure to provide traffic controller support at the level of the previous era, and the failure to increase the number of Federal Aviation Administration (FAA) inspectors, the long-term trend in improvement in airline safety continued after deregulation.[50] During the 1972–78 period, there were 2.35 accidents per 100,000 flight hours, whereas from 1979–86, there were 1.73 per 100,000 hours (Weidenbaum 1987). However, Rose (1989), using a statistical study that controls for a number of factors, finds that lower profitability is correlated with higher accident and incident rates, particularly for smaller carriers. Thus, the safety record after deregulation may become uneven across airlines as variability in profitability increases. In contrast, Kanafani and Keeler's (1989) statistical analysis shows no difference between the safety of new entrants and established carriers. McKenzie and Womer (1991) find, if anything, that safety increased marginally after deregulation.

Overall, consumers have benefited significantly from airline deregulation. Consumers fly more at lower prices on aircraft that apparently are as safe as during the regulated period.

However, concerns about competition among airlines continues. In 1998, the U.S. Department of Transportation (DOT) released a study showing that the number of city-pair markets where at least two airlines compete for passengers declined by 28 percent since 1992. According to this study, the cost of a one-way ticket for travel under 500 miles is on average $165 at airports without competition and $75 at airports with competition. In 1999, the Department of Transportation and the Department of Justice investigated the possibility of predatory actions by established carriers aimed at entrants, and the Department of Justice unsuccessfully sued American Airlines for predation (140 F. Supp. 2d 1141(2001)).

International airline competition is more regulated than domestic airline competition. By the early 1990s, talks were underway between nations on international deregulation.[51] See Example 20.9 on European airline deregulation.

Ground Transportation

The 1887 Act to Regulate Commerce created the Interstate Commerce Commission (ICC), an independent agency of the U.S. government. The ICC was the first regulatory commission in the United States. Over time, it was given jurisdiction over freight

[49]Martha M. Hamilton, "Airline Pricing: Highly Complex, Hotly Competitive," *Washington Post,* November 20, 1988:H1, H16.

[50]Although the number of flights has significantly increased since deregulation, the number of FAA inspectors has increased by only 2, according to the FAA (cited in Lapham, Pollan, and Etheridge 1987).

[51]Andrea Rothman, Seth Payne, and Paula Dwyer, "One World, One Giant Airline Market?" *Business Week,* October 5, 1992:56–57.

EXAMPLE 20.9 *European Deregulation of Airlines*

Europe trailed the United States in deregulating airlines. In 1992, the European Union lifted most restrictions on the routes airlines could fly within Europe and what they could charge. The European Community agreed to allow unrestricted competition throughout the community starting on April 1, 1997. With the end of regulation, a few low-price, no-frills airline services became available in Europe for the first time. Entrants included Debonair and Easy Jet in the United Kingdom, Denim Air in Holland, Air Liberte and Air Jet in France, Virgin Express in Belgium, and Air One and Azzurra Air in Italy. However, many carriers, such as Air France, remain state owned and are just starting to cut their operating costs. They survive due to government subsidies: Iberia received $705 million from the Spanish Government in 1995 and Air France received $4 billion.

High landing fees (which make up 5 to 10 percent of airline costs) and limits on landing slots help restrict further entry. As a result, fares remained very high relative to those in the United States.

One study by American Express found that fares within Europe are roughly twice as high as those for comparable distances in the United States. For example, the Washington to New York route is 216 miles, while London to Paris is 211 miles, yet a one-way trip over the European route costs over a third more. More striking, a flight from Copenhagen to Oslo (311 miles) costs 3.3 times as much as one between Houston and New Orleans (302 miles). It remains to be seen how long it will take for Europe to benefit from deregulation in the form of lower prices.

Sources: "Why Heathrow Is Hell," *The Economist,* 336(7929) August 26, 1995:47–48; Dirk Beveridge, "'No Frills' Airline Service Finally Gets to Land in Europe," *San Francisco Chronicle,* March 3, 1995:D2; Richard W. Stevenson, "Still Worlds Apart on Air Fares," *New York Times,* December 20, 1995:C1, C2; John Tagliabue, "American Aces of the Foreign Sky," *New York Times,* June 6, 1997:C1, C2.

service transportation, now including railroads, trucking companies, bus lines, freight forwarders, water carriers, oil pipelines, transportation brokers, express agencies, telegraph, telephone, wireless, and cable companies.

The Transportation Act of 1920 gave the ICC the power to fix rates that would yield "a fair return upon the aggregate value of the railway property of the country." The ICC's price regulations led to more uniform pricing by railroads and essentially eliminated price wars. The ICC also had power to approve or block mergers. Indeed, it was supposed to plan the consolidation of railroads into a small number of integrated systems. The Motor Carriers Act of 1935 gave the ICC control over pricing and entry into the bus and trucking industries. The licenses required to operate were valuable, indicating significant restraints on entry. The ICC-certified general freight carriers could discuss and agree on rates, which were then presented to the ICC for approval (Moses and Savage 1987). As a result, firms competed on quality. There was also substantial cross-subsidization. The Motor Carrier Act of 1980 (trucking) and the

Staggers Act of 1980 (railroads) continued the movement toward deregulation of surface transport, which began in the late 1970s.

Trucking. Trucking deregulation led to entry, improved safety, greater efficiency, a drop in union drivers' wages, and lowered trucking rates. Keeler (1989) finds that deregulating trucking allows efficient firms to expand, where previously their routes were limited. As a result, efficient firms now expand to optimal size, taking advantage of economies of scale. The largest firms (those with over 5% of the market) increased their collective share of the market from 11.6% to 20.8% of the market from 1980 to 1984.

Keeler (1989) calculates that deregulation reduced trucking rates from the start and that the effect grew stronger over time, presumably as entry occurred and firms became more efficient, so that rates were ultimately reduced by 22% from what they would have been with regulation. In related research, Ying and Keeler (1991) estimate that deregulation cut rates 22% by 1983.

Boyer (1987) does not find a statistically significant effect on real trucking rates. He finds, though, that deregulation's effect on shares of freight (over rail, for-hire motor carrier, and other surface modes) was statistically significant. In the first four years of deregulation, the for-hire motor carrier industry gained 5.6 points and the private (unregulated) carriers lost 7.1 points (Boyer 1987, 412–14).

Rose (1987) shows that, before deregulation, union drivers captured up to 75% of total industry rents (profits in excess of the usual rate of return), but nonunion drivers did not capture a significant share of regulatory rents. After deregulation, there were substantial reductions in union wages. The union markup over nonunion wages fell from 50% to less than 30%, implying that union workers lost, in aggregate, between $950 million and $1.6 billion. The individual union driver's compensation fell by between 10% and 20% of what it would have been if the 50% wage differential had been maintained.

Safety improved under deregulation (Moses and Savage 1987). Adjusting for changes in the quality of goods carried, an accidents index fell substantially from 100 in 1978 to 69 in 1985. An index of auto fatalities in truck-related accidents per mile of automobile usage also fell by 21% from 1978 to 1985. These reductions occurred despite the higher accident record of new firms. New firms in 1985 had 0.246 accidents per million miles, whereas firms established in 1980–81 had an accident rate of 0.167 in 1985.

Deregulation by states trailed federal action. For example, prior to 1990, it cost $123 to send a ton load from Reno to San Francisco, but $136 (11 percent more) to send it across the bridge from Oakland to San Francisco. In 1990, the California Public Utilities Commission relaxed its hold on rates, allowing truckload shipping costs to fall 10%. Still, 20 other states maintained controls, which, according to studies prepared for the U.S. Department of Transportation, cost between $3 billion and $8 billion a year. A federal law ended state regulation of trucking in 1994.

Railroads. Deregulation of the railroads started with the Railroad Revitalization and Regulatory Reform Act of 1976 (4-R Act), which called for more competition and cost-based rate setting. The Staggers Rail Act of 1980 further deregulated the industry, giving firms substantial freedom to set rates. In combination with administrative actions by the ICC, this legislation gives railroads virtually unlimited rights to lower rates, and companies that are not "market dominant" can raise them. In practice, the

ICC only exercises rate-setting powers over certain bulk commodities where railroads are not subject to truck competition. Trucking competition is taken as evidence that railroads are not dominant in a market (Boyer 1987).

Lee, Baumel, and Harris (1987) show a statistically significant decrease in the rate per ton-mile for Class I (large) railroads of 18% during the 4-R years and 23% in the first four years after the Staggers Act.[52] By 1990, the rates for transporting all types of commodities (except primary forest products) fell up to 34% from the 1980 levels (Friedlaender et al. 1992).

Because more than one-third of total railroad costs are fixed (including tracks, rights-of-way, and locomotive power), railroad lines are often natural monopolies (Willig and Baumol 1987, 29). If, during regulation, prices had been set equal to marginal costs, railroads would have suffered losses. Willig and Baumol (1987, 30–31) argue that the ICC "undermined competition through protectionist rules, froze rail business into inefficient and outdated patterns, interfered with and delayed private decisions, and, ironically, virtually precluded the financial viability of railroads. . . . The commission protected rival transport modes from price competition by setting inflated floors below which individual rates were not permitted to fall. . . . The railroads were generally unable to abandon services—even services with such limited demand that there was no prospect of profitable operation."

Thus, many of the gains from deregulation are likely to come from letting more efficient firms expand, by allowing firms to abandon unused track, and by eliminating cross subsidization. The studies to date typically find that deregulation had modest to large positive efficiency effects. Boyer (1987) calculates gains of at most $93 million, whereas Barnekov and Kleit (1988) estimate that deregulation created billions of dollars worth of efficiency gains. Stansell and Hollas (1988) also find a significant drop in industry costs in the postregulation period. Lee et al. (1987) find that operating expenses per ton-mile fell by 17% during the 4-R years and 29% during the first four years of the Staggers Act. McFarland (1989) concludes that the annual rate of growth in labor productivity increased by about 0.9% annually after deregulation. Deregulation also had dramatic effects on the mode of transit used (Boyer 1987). Unlike trucking, where labor earnings for union workers fell sharply after deregulation, Peoples (1998) finds little effect on wages in railroads.

Deregulation decreased rail's share (compared to that of motor vehicles) by 5.2 points during the first four years of deregulation. After a decade of deregulation, the number of Class I railroads fell from 37 to 14, rail employment fell 52%, and rail route mileage dropped 29% (Friedlaender et al. 1992).

The chief fear about deregulating railroads was that monopoly prices would be charged, at least in some markets. Although the 1980 Staggers Rail Act allows higher rates in less competitive markets as long as they are "reasonable," some carriers may be charging monopolistic rates. (In a natural monopoly, even monopoly prices may not generate supracompetitive rates of return.) For example, an Interior Department study finds that rates charged utility buyers by the one railroad serving much of the Wyoming and Montana coal fields were "monopolistic"—a charge denied by the

[52]See Boyer (1987) for an alternative view.

railroad. Yet when a competitor ran a spur line to one section, rates there fell by 20%.[53]

One test of whether railroads earn monopoly profits is to compare the ratio of a railroad's market value to the replacement cost of its assets, a measure called Tobin's q (Chapter 8), to that of other nonfinancial firms (McFarland 1987). This test finds that railroads do not earn supracompetitive profits, and that their Tobin's q is lower than for other nonfinancial firms. Rates of return remained low during the first decade of deregulation (Friedlaender et al. 1992).

In summary, deregulation has changed the trucking and railroad industries. Deregulation has eliminated many of the harms resulting from previous regulation and has resulted in more efficient and lower-price industries.

SUMMARY

How many economists does it take to screw in a light bulb?
Economist: None, the market will do it.
Consumer Advocate: None, the regulators will do it.

Optimal regulation, if feasible, can eliminate market inefficiencies and increase welfare. Nonetheless, due to problems of limited information, uncertainty, sustainability, human frailties, and institutional weakness, regulators often apply regulations badly or use regulations that create harmful distortions in order to help special-interest groups. It is difficult to find an example of optimal regulation, although there are many examples of markets in which nonoptimal regulations help.

Particularly disturbing are regulations that convert efficient, competitive markets into inefficient monopolistic markets. In some extreme examples, the regulations appear designed to redistribute wealth from consumers to special-interest groups that have successfully pressured or captured legislators or regulators. In some of these examples, such as agriculture, the social losses are enormous.

The recent trend toward deregulation is an attempt to remove particularly harmful regulations and "let markets work." In recent years, regulators and legislators who recognized these harms have improved or eliminated regulations in several markets. As a result, in many, if not most, of these markets, consumers gained on average as prices fell, output increased, cross-subsidization ended, the rate of entry increased, and production efficiency increased.

PROBLEMS

1. In Figure 20.3, prove that welfare, defined as consumer surplus plus profit, is higher at $\underline{p} = p^* =$ marginal cost than at $\underline{p} = p_a =$ average cost, even though it is necessary to subsidize the monopoly. [*Hint:* At p_a, profit is zero, so that $(p_a - p^*)Q^* =$ fixed cost $= A + B$ (in the fig-

[53]Chris Welles with Seth Payne, France Seghers, and Tom Ichniowksi, "Is Deregulation Working?" *Business Week*, December 22, 1986:50–55.

ure) because $p^* =$ average variable costs. You should show that welfare increases by a triangular area in the figure.]

2. In a figure such as 20.1 or 20.2, show the effect of regulating a monopolist's price at a level strictly between p_m and p_c.
3. A government providing an agricultural price support may impose an acreage quota on farmers. What effect would an acreage quota have on the supply curve and on the government's expenses?
4. Which of the following two agricultural policies will cost the government (taxpayers) more? (a) A program with price supported at $p_s (> p_c$, the competitive price) and with a quota equal to the competitive output level, Q_c. (b) A target price program in which farmers sell Q_c units at the competitive price, p_c, and the government gives them a subsidy equal to $(p_s - p_c)Q_c$. [*Note:* The elasticity of demand for most agricultural goods is inelastic.]
5. Suggest an alternative agricultural policy that eliminates the inefficiencies in price-support or quota programs and yet transfers an equivalent amount of income to farmers. Why is your program better?
6. Several years ago, MCI started competing with Bell Telephone by offering lower rates on long-distance calls. Many people thought that Bell's long-distance service was a natural monopoly. Nonetheless, MCI may have been able to cover its costs. Is that possible? Should MCI's entry have been encouraged or prohibited by regulators? Why or why not? (When MCI started, it only provided service to a limited number of areas. Although MCI's pricing was not constrained, Bell was required to use distance-based pricing.)
7. Under rate-of-return regulation, a firm that earns too high a rate of return must give some of it back to ratepayers, but a firm that fails to earn the target rate of return bears the shortfall itself. Explain how this asymmetry affects a firm's incentive to innovate. Is rate-of-return regulation more or less appropriate for an industry undergoing technological change?
8. Compute an example of the effects of rate-of-return regulation (similar to Table 20.3) where the production function is Leontief: $Q = \min(L, K)$ and labor and capital cost are the same. (This production function implies that efficient production involves equal amounts of labor and capital. It takes 1 unit of each to produce 1 unit of output, and 2 units of each to produce 2 units of output.) What effect does rate-of-return regulation have on output, profits, consumer surplus, and capital/labor ratio? [*Note:* This question can be answered without using mathematical analysis or calculating a table.]

Answers to odd-numbered problems are given at the back of the book.

SUGGESTED READINGS

This chapter only scratches the surface of the economics of regulation. Viscusi, Vernon, and Harrington (2000) is a good undergraduate text, and Spulber (1989) is a good graduate text. Joskow and Rose (1989), Peltzman (1989), Winston (1993), and Viscusi (1996) provide clear discussions of the effects of economic regulation and deregulation. Joskow (2000b) is a collection of classic articles on regulation and its reform. Peltzman and Winston (2000) contains recent studies of the deregulation of the airline, railroad, telecommunications, and electric power industries in the United States. Economides (1999) analyzes the impact of the 1996 Telecommunications Act. MacAvoy (2000) discusses the regulation and deregulation of natural gas. Gonenc and Nicoletti (2000) and Williams (2002) discuss international airline deregulation. Cummins (2002) contains a collection of articles on deregulation in the property-liability insurance industry. Braeutigam (1989) discusses the regulation of natural monopoly. Laffont and Tirole (1993) provides an advanced theoretical treatment of incentives under regulation.

Bibliography

Abel, Andrew B. 1983. "Market Structure and the Durability of Goods." *Review of Economic Studies* 50:625–37.

Abere, Andrew. 1991. "An Economic Analysis of Nuisance Suits in Private Antitrust Litigation." Ph.D. dissertation. Columbia University.

Abiru, Masahiro. 1988. "Vertical Integration, Variable Proportions and Successive Oligopolies." *Journal of Industrial Economics* 36:315–25.

Adams, William J., and Janet L. Yellen. 1976. "Commodity Bundling and the Burden of Monopoly." *Quarterly Journal of Economics* 90:475–98.

Adelman, Morris A. 1955. "Concept and Statistical Measurement of Vertical Integration," in George J. Stigler, ed., *Business Concentration and Price Policy.* Princeton, NJ: Princeton University Press.

Aghion, Philippe, and Patrick Bolton. 1987. "Contracts as a Barrier to Entry." *American Economic Review* 77:388–401.

Akerlof, George A. 1970. "The Market for 'Lemons': Quality Uncertainty and the Market Mechanism." *Quarterly Journal of Economics* 84:488–500.

Akerlof, George A., and Janet L. Yellen. 1985. "A Near-Rational Model of the Business Cycle, With Wage and Price Inertia." *Quarterly Journal of Economics* 100(Supp.): 823–38.

Albæk, Svend, Peter Møllgaard, and Per B. Overgaard. 1997. "Government-Assisted Oligopoly Coordination? A *Concrete* Case." *Journal of Industrial Economics* 45:429–33.

Albrecht, James, Harald Lang, and Susan Vroman. 2002. "The Effect of Information on the Well-Being of the Uninformed: What's the Chance of Getting a Decent Meal in an Unfamiliar City?" *International Journal of Industrial Organization* 20:139–62.

Alchian, Armen A. 1959. "Costs and Outputs," in Moses Abromovitz et al., eds., *The Allocation of Economic Resources.* Stanford, CA: Stanford University Press.

Alchian, Armen A., and Harold Demsetz. 1972. "Production, Information Costs and Economic Organization." *American Economic Review* 62:777–95.

Alexander, Donald L. 1988. "An Empirical Test of Monopoly Behavior: An Application to the Hardwood Case." *Applied Economics* 20:1115–27.

Allen, Beth. 1981. "Generic Existence of Completely Revealing Equilibria for Economies with Uncertainty When Prices Convey Information." *Econometrica* 49:1173–99.

Allen, Beth, and Martin Hellwig. 1986. "Bertrand-Edgeworth Oligopoly in Large Markets." *Review of Economic Studies* 53:175–204.

Allen, Franklin. 1984. "Reputation and Product Quality." *Rand Journal of Economics* 15:311–27.

Amihud, Yakov, and Haim Mendelson. 1983. "Price Smoothing and Inventory." *Review of Economic Studies* 50:87–98.

Anderson, Erin, and David C. Schmittlein. 1984. "Integration of the Sales Force: An Empirical Examination." *Rand Journal of Economics* 15:385–95.

Anderson, Simon P., and André de Palma. 1992a. "The Logit as a Model of Product Differentiation." *Oxford Economic Papers* 44:51–67.

Anderson, Simon P., and André de Palma. 1992b. "Multiproduct Firms: A Nested Logit Approach." *Journal of Industrial Economics* 40:261–76.

Andrade, Gregor, and Erik Stafford. 2001. "New Evidence and Perspectives on Mergers." *Journal of Economic Perspectives* 15:103–20.

Antonovitz, Frances, and Terry Roe. 1986. "A Theoretical and Empirical Approach to the Value of Information in Risky Markets." *Review of Economics and Statistics* 68:105–14.

Applebaum, Elie. 1979. "Testing Price-Taking Behavior." *Journal of Econometrics* 9:283–99.

Applebaum, Elie. 1982. "The Estimation of the Degree of Oligopoly Power." *Journal of Econometrics* 19:287–99.

Archibald, G. C. 1964. "Profit-Maximizing and Non-Price Competition." *Economica* 31:13–22.

Areeda, Phillip E. 1986. *Antitrust Law,* Vols. 6 and 7. Boston: Little, Brown and Co.

Areeda, Philip E., and Herbert Hovenkamp. 1997. *Antitrust Law: An Analysis of Antitrust Principles and Their Application.* Multiple volumes. Aspen Publishers.

Areeda, Phillip E., and Donald F. Turner. 1975. "Predatory Pricing and Related Practices Under Section 2 of the Sherman Act." *Harvard Law Review* 88:697–733.

Areeda, Phillip E., and Donald F. Turner. 1978, 1980. *Antitrust Law,* Vols. 1–5. Boston: Little, Brown and Co.

Arnould, Richard J. 1972. "Pricing Professional Services: A Case Study of the Legal Services Industry." *Southern Economic Journal* 38:495–507.

Arrow, Kenneth J. 1959. "Toward a Theory of Price Adjustment," in Moses Abromovitz et al., eds., *The Allocation of Economic Resources.* Stanford, CA: Stanford University Press.

Arrow, Kenneth J. 1962. "Economic Welfare and the Allocation of Resources for Invention," in National Bureau of Economic Research, *The Rate and Direction of Inventive Activity.* Princeton, NJ: Princeton University Press.

Asch, Peter, and J. J. Seneca. 1976. "Is Collusion Profitable?" *Review of Economics and Statistics* 68:1–12.

Asch, Peter, and Rosalind Seneca. 1985. *Government and the Marketplace.* New York: Dryden.

Ashenfelter, Orley, and Daniel Sullivan. 1987. "Nonparametric Tests of Market Structure: An Application to the Cigarette Industry." *Journal of Industrial Economics* 35:483–98.

Audretsch, David. 1987. "The Effects of Legalized Cartels in West Germany." Berlin: International Institute of Management.

Auerbach, Alan J., ed. 1988a. *Mergers and Acquisitions.* Chicago: University of Chicago Press.

Auerbach, Alan J., ed. 1988b. *Corporate Takeovers: Causes and Consequences.* Chicago: University of Chicago Press.

Auerbach, Alan J., and David Reishus. 1988. "The Effects of Taxation on the Merger Decision," in Alan J. Auerbach, ed., *Corporate Takeovers: Causes and Consequences.* Chicago: University of Chicago Press.

Aumann, Robert. 1973. "Disadvantageous Monopolies." *Journal of Economic Theory* 6:1–11.

Ausubel, Lawrence, and Raymond J. Deneckere. 1987. "One Is Almost Enough for Monopoly." *Rand Journal of Economics* 18:255–74.

Averch, Harvey, and Leland L. Johnson. 1962. "Behavior of the Firm Under Regulatory Constraint." *American Economic Review* 52:1052–69.

Ayanian, Robert. 1983. "The Advertising Capital Controversy." *Journal of Business* 56:349–64.

Azzam, Azzeddine M., and Emilio Pagoulatos. 1990. "Testing Oligopolistic and Oligopsonistic Behaviour: An Application to the U.S. Meat-Packing Industry." *Journal of Agricultural Economics* 41:362–69.

Bagnoli, Mark, Stephen W. Salant, and Joseph E. Swierzbinski. 1989. "Durable-Goods Monopoly with Discrete Demand." *Journal of Political Economy* 97:1459–78.

Bagwell, Kyle, ed. 2001. *The Economics of Advertising.* Cheltenham, UK: Edward Elgar Publishing.

Bagwell, Kyle, and Garey Ramey. 1988. "Advertising, Coordination, and Signaling." Northwestern University, Center for Mathematical Studies in Economics and Management Science, Discussion Paper 7897.

Bagwell, Kyle, and Michael Riordan. 1991. "High and Declining Prices Signal Product Quality." *American Economic Review* 81:224–39.

Bailey, Elizabeth E. 1973. *Economic Theory of Regulatory Constraint.* Lexington, MA: D.C. Heath.

Bailey, Elizabeth E., and Roger D. Coleman. 1971. "The Effect of Lagged Regulation in an Averch-Johnson Model." *Bell Journal of Economics* 2:278–92.

Bailey, Elizabeth E., and Ann F. Friedlaender. 1982. "Market Structure and Multi-product Industries." *Journal of Economic Literature* 20:1024–48.

Bailey, Elizabeth E., David R. Graham, and Daniel P. Kaplan. 1985. *Deregulating the Airlines.* Cambridge, MA: MIT Press.

Bailey, Elizabeth E., and John C. Panzar. 1981. "The Contestability of Airline Markets During the Transition to Deregulation." *Law and Contemporary Problems* 44:125–46.

Bailey, Elizabeth E., and Jeffrey R. Williams. 1988. "Sources of Economic Rent in the Deregulated Airline Industry." *Journal of Law and Economics* 31:173–202.

Bain, Joe S. 1951. "Relation of Profit Rate to Industry Concentration: American Manufacturing, 1936–1940." *Quarterly Journal of Economics* 65:293–324.

Bain, Joe S. 1956. *Barriers to New Competition: Their Character and Consequences in Manufacturing Industries.* Cambridge, MA: Harvard University Press.

Bain, Joe S. 1959. *Industrial Organization.* New York: John Wiley and Sons.

Bajari, Patrick, and Ali Hortacsu. 2003. "The Winner's Curse, Reserve Prices, and Endogenous Entry: Empirical Insights from eBay Auctions." *Rand Journal of Economics* 34:329–55.

Baker, Jonathan B., and Timothy F. Bresnahan. 1985. "The Gains from Merger or Collusion in Product-Differentiated Industries." *Journal of Industrial Economics* 33:427–44.

Baker, Jonathan B., and Timothy F. Bresnahan. 1988. "Estimating the Elasticity of Demand Facing a Single Firm." *International Journal of Industrial Organization* 6:283–300.

Baldwin, Robert E. 1992. "Are Economists' Traditional Trade Policy Views Still Valid?" *Journal of Economic Literature* 30:804–29.

Baldwin, Robert E., and Paul R. Krugman. 1988a. "Market Access and International Competition: A Simulation Study of 16K Random Access Memories," in Robert

Feenstra, ed., *Empirical Methods for International Trade.* Cambridge, MA: MIT Press.

Baldwin, Robert E., and Paul R. Krugman. 1988b. "Industrial Policy and International Competition in Wide Bodied Jet Aircraft," in Robert E. Baldwin, ed., *Trade Policy Issues and Empirical Analysis.* Chicago: University of Chicago Press.

Ball, Laurence M., and Stephen J. Cecchetti. 1988. "Imperfect Information and Staggered Price Setting." *American Economic Review* 78:999–1018.

Bamberger, Gustavo E., and Dennis W. Carlton. 2003. "Airline Networks and Fares," in *Handbook of Airline Economics.* New York: McGraw-Hill.

Bamberger, Gustavo E., and Dennis W. Carlton. 2004. "Antitrust and Higher Education" in John E. Kwoka, Jr. and Lawrence J. White, eds., *The Antitrust Revolution,* 4th ed., Oxford, England: Oxford University Press, 2004.

Bane, Charles A. 1973. *The Electrical Equipment Conspiracies: The Treble-Damages Actions.* New York: Federal Legal Publications.

Banerjee, Ajeyo, and E. Woodrow Eckard. 1998. "Are Mega-Mergers Anti-Competitive? Evidence from the First Great Merger Wave." *Rand Journal of Economics* 29:803–27.

Banerjee, Dyuti S. 2003. "Software Piracy: A Strategic Analysis and Policy Instruments." *International Journal of Industrial Organization* 21:97–127.

Barnekov, Christopher C., and Andrew N. Kleit. 1988. "The Costs of Railroad Regulation: A Further Analysis." Bureau of Economics Working Paper 164. Washington, D.C.: Federal Trade Commission.

Baron, David P. 1973. "Limit Pricing, Potential Entry, and Barriers to Entry." *American Economic Review* 63:666–74.

Baron, David P., and Roger B. Myerson. 1982. "Regulating a Monopolist with Unknown Costs." *Econometrica* 50:911–30.

Baron, David P., and Robert A. Taggart. 1977. "A Model of Regulation under Uncertainty and a Test of Regulatory Bias." *Bell Journal of Economics* 8:151–67.

Barro, Robert J. 1972. "A Theory of Monopolistic Price Adjustment." *Review of Economic Studies* 39:17–26.

Barron, John, and John Umbeck. 1984. "The Effects of Different Contractual Arrangements: The Case of Retail Gasoline Markets." *Journal of Law and Economics* 27:313–28.

Barzel, Yoram. 1968. "Optimal Timing of Innovations." *Review of Economics and Statistics* 50:348–55.

Baseman, Kenneth C. 1981. "Open Entry and Cross-Subsidization in Regulated Markets," in Gary Fromm, ed., *Studies in Public Regulation.* Cambridge, MA: MIT Press.

Bates, Timothy. 1995. "Analysis of Survival Rates Among Franchise and Independent Small Business Startups." *Journal of Small Business Management* 33:26–36.

Baumol, William J. 1967. "Reasonable Rules for Rate Regulation: Plausible Policies for an Imperfect World," in Almarin Phillips and Oliver E. Williamson, eds., *Prices: Issues in Theory, Practice, and Public Policy.* Philadelphia: University of Pennsylvania Press.

Baumol, William J. 1981. "Comments," in Gary Fromm, ed., *Studies in Public Regulation.* Cambridge, MA: MIT Press, 361–64.

Baumol, William J., Elizabeth E. Bailey, and Robert D. Willig. 1977. "Weak Invisible Hand Theorems on the Sustainability of Prices in a Multiproduct Monopoly." *American Economic Review* 67:350–65.

Baumol, William J., and David F. Bradford. 1970. "Optimal Departures from Marginal Cost Pricing." *American Economic Review* 60:265–83.

Baumol, William J., and Alvin K. Klevorick. 1970. "Input Choices and Rate-of-Return Regulation: An Overview of the Discussion." *Bell Journal of Economics* 1:162–90.

Baumol, William J., John C. Panzar, and Robert D. Willig. 1982. *Contestable Markets and the Theory of Industry Structure.* New York: Harcourt Brace Jovanovich.

Baylis, Kathy, and Jeffrey M. Perloff. 2002. "Price Dispersion on the Internet: Good Firms and Bad Firms." *Review of Industrial Organization* 21:305–24.

Beales, Howard, Richard Craswell, and Steven Salop. 1981. "Efficient Regulation of Consumer Information." *Journal of Law and Economics* 24:491–539.

Beals, Ralph E. 1975. *Concentrated Industries, Administered Prices, and Inflation: A Survey of Empirical Research.* Washington, D.C.: Council on Wage and Price Stability.

Becker, Gary S. 1965. "A Theory of the Allocation of Time." *Economic Journal* 75:493–517.

Becker, Gary S. 1983. "A Theory of Competition Among Pressure Groups for Political Influence." *Quarterly Journal of Economics* 98:371–400.

Becker, Gary S. 1996. *Accounting for Tastes.* Cambridge, MA: Harvard University Press.

Becker, Gary S., and Kevin M. Murphy. 1993. "A Simple Theory of Advertising as a Good or Bad." *Quarterly Journal of Economics* 108:941–64.

Belesley, David A. 1975. *Industry Production Behavior.* Amsterdam: North-Holland.

Benham, Lee. 1972. "The Effect of Advertising on the Price of Eyeglasses." *Journal of Law and Economics* 15:337–52.

Benston, George J. 1973. "Required Disclosure and the Stock Market: An Evaluation of the Securities Exchange Act of 1934." *American Economic Review* 63:1323–55.

Benston, George J. 1985. "The Validity of Profits-Structure Studies with Particular Reference to the FTC's Line-of-Business Data." *American Economic Review* 75:37–67.

Berck, Peter, and Jeffrey M. Perloff. 1985. "A Dynamic Analysis of Marketing Orders, Voting, and Welfare." *American Journal of Agricultural Economics* 67:487–96.

Berck, Peter, and Jeffrey M. Perloff. 1988. "The Dynamic Annihilation of a Rational Competitive Fringe by a Low-Cost Dominant Firm." *Journal of Economic Dynamics and Control* 12:659–78.

Berck, Peter, and Jeffrey M. Perloff. 1990. "Dynamic Dumping." *International Journal of Industrial Organization* 8:225–43.

Berkman, Harvey. October 20, 1997. "Justice Seeking Stiffer Price-Fixing Sanctions: The $10 Million Maximum Fine Would Increase Tenfold." *National Law Journal* 20:A1.

Berle, Adolph A., Jr., and Gardiner C. Means. 1932. *The Modern Corporation and Private Property.* New York: Macmillan.

Bernhardt, Dan. 1984. "Dumping, Adjustment Costs and Uncertainty." *Journal of Economic Dynamics and Control* 8:349–70.

Bernheim, B. Douglas. 1984. "Rationalizable Strategic Behavior." *Econometrica* 52:1007–28.

Bernheim, B. Douglas, and Debraj Ray. 1989. "Collective Dynamic Consistency in Repeated Games." *Games and Economic Behavior* 1:295–326.

Bernheim, B. Douglas, and Michael Whinston. 1990. "Multimarket Contact and Collusive Behavior." *Rand Journal of Economics* 21:1–26.

Bernheim, B. Douglas, and Michael Whinston. 1998. "Exclusive Dealing." *Journal of Political Economy* 106:64–103.

Berry, Steven T. 1990. "Airport Presence as Product Differentiation." *American Economic Review* 80:394–99.

Berry, Steven T. 1992. "Estimation of a Model of Entry in the Airline Industry." *Econometrica* 60:889–918.

Berry, Steven T. 1994. "Estimating Discrete Choice Models of Product Differentiation." *Rand Journal of Economics* 26:242–52.

Berry, Steven T., James Levinsohn, and Ariel Pakes. 1995. "Automobile Prices in Market Equilibrium." *Econometrica* 63(4):841–90.

Besanko, David, Martin K. Perry, and Richard H. Spady. 1990. "The Logit Model of Monopolistic Competition: Brand Diversity." *Journal of Industrial Economics* 38:397–415.

Bessen, James, and Robert M. Hunt. 2003. "An Empirical Look at Software Patents." Federal Reserve Bank of Philadelphia Working Paper 03–17.

Bhagwati, Jagdish, and V.K. Ramaswami. 1963. "Domestic Distortions, Tariffs and the Theory of Optimum Subsidy." *Journal of Political Economy* 71:44–50.

Bhuyan, Sanjib. 2000. "Corporate Political Activities and Oligopoly Welfare Loss." *Review of Industrial Organization* 17:411–26.

Bils, Mark. 1987. "The Cyclical Behavior of Marginal Cost and Price." *American Economic Review* 77:838–55.

Bils, Mark, and Peter Klenow. 2002. "Some Evidence on the Importance of Sticky Prices." National Bureau of Economic Research Working Paper 9069.

Binmore, Ken. 1992. *Fun and Games.* Lexington, MA: D.C. Heath and Company.

Birch, David. 1987. *Job Creation in America: How Our Smallest Companies Put the Most People to Work.* New York: The Free Press.

Bittlingmayer, George. 1982. "Decreasing Average Cost and Competition: A New Look at the Addyston Pipe Case." *Journal of Law and Economics* 25:201–29.

Bittlingmayer, George. 1985. "Did Antitrust Policy Cause the Great Merger Wave?" *Journal of Law and Economics* 28:77–118.

Blair, Roger D., and David L. Kaserman. 1983. *Law and Economics of Vertical Integration and Control.* New York: Academic Press.

Blanchard, Oliver, and Nabuhiro Kiyotaki. 1987. "Monopolistic Competition and the Effects of Aggregate Demand." *American Economic Review* 77:647–66.

Blass, Asher, and Dennis W. Carlton. 2001. "The Choice of Organizational Form in Gasoline Retailing and the Cost of Laws That Limit That Choice." *Journal of Law and Economics* 44:511–24.

Blattberg, Robert, T. Buesing, P. Peacock, and S. Sen. 1978. "Identifying the Deal-Prone Segment." *Journal of Marketing Research* 15:369–77.

Blinder, Alan S. 1982. "Inventories and Sticky Prices: More on the Microfoundations of Macroeconomics." *American Economic Review* 72:334–48.

Blinder, Alan, S., Elie R. D. Canetti, David E. Lebow, and Jeremy B. Rudd. 1998. *Asking About Prices: A New Approach to Understanding Price Stickiness.* New York: Russell Sage Foundation.

Bond, Eric W., and Larry Samuelson. 1984. "Durable-Good Monopolies with Rational Expectations and Replacement Sales." *Rand Journal of Economics* 15:336–45.

Bond, Ronald S., John E. Kwoka, Jr., John J. Phelan, and Ira Taylor Whitten. 1980. "Staff Report on Effects of Restrictions on Advertising and Commercial Practice in the Professions: The Case of Optometry." Bureau of Economics, Federal Trade Commission. Washington, D.C.: U.S. Government Printing Office.

Borenstein, Severin. 1985. "Price Discrimination in Free Entry Markets." *Rand Journal of Economics* 16:380–97.

Borenstein, Severin. 1989. "Hubs and High Fares: Dominance and Market Power in the U.S. Airline Industry." *Rand Journal of Economics* 20:344–65.

Borenstein, Severin. 1990. "Airline Mergers, Airport Dominance, and Market Power." *American Economic Review* 80:400–4.

Borenstein, Severin. 1992. "The Evolution of the U.S. Airline Industry." *Journal of Economic Perspectives* 6:45–73.

Borenstein, Severin. 2002. "The Trouble with Electricity Markets: Understanding California's Restructuring Disaster." *Journal of Economic Perspectives* 14:191–21.

Borenstein, Severin. 2004. "Rapid Price Communication and Coordination: The Airline Tariff Publishing Case," *The Antitrust Revolution*, 4th ed., John E. Kwoka and Lawrence J. White, 4th edition, Oxford University Press.

Borenstein, Severin, and Nancy L. Rose. 1989. "Price Discrimination in the U.S. Airline Industry." MIT working paper.

Borenstein, Severin, and Nancy Rose. 2003. "The Impact of Bankruptcy on Airline Service Levels." *American Economic Review* 93:415–19.

Bork, Robert H. 1966. "Legislative Intent and the Policy of the Sherman Act." *Journal of Law and Economics* 9:7–48.

Bork, Robert H. 1978. *The Antitrust Paradox: A Policy at War with Itself.* New York: Basic Books.

Borrus, Michael, Laura D'Andrea Tyson, and John Zysman. 1986. "Creating Advantage: How Government Policies Shape International Trade in the Semiconductor Industry," in Paul R. Krugman, ed., *Strategic Trade Policy and the New International Economics.* Cambridge, MA: MIT Press.

Bound, John, Clint Cummins, Zvi Griliches, Bronwyn H. Hall, and Adam Jaffe. 1984. "Who Does R&D and Who Patents?" in Zvi Griliches, ed., *R&D, Patents, and Productivity.* Chicago: University of Chicago Press, 21–54.

Boyd, Roy, and Barry J. Seldon. 1990. "The Fleeting Effect of Advertising." *Economics Letters* 24:375–79.

Boyer, Kenneth D. 1987. "The Costs of Price Regulation: Lessons from Railroad Deregulation." *Rand Journal of Economics* 18:408–16.

Boynton, Robert D., Joseph N. Uhl, Brian F. Blake, and Vicki A. McCracken. 1981. "An Analysis of the Impacts of Comparative Foodstore Price Reporting on Price Structures and Consumer Behavior." Purdue University Agricultural Experiment Station Research Bulletin 968 (August).

Bradburd, Ralph M., and Mead A. Over, Jr. 1982. "Organizational Costs, 'Sticky Equilibria', and Critical Levels of Concentration." *Review of Economics and Statistics* 64:50–58.

Bradley, Michael, Anand Desai, and E. Han Kim. 1988. "Synergistic Gains from Corporate Acquisitions and Their Division Between the Stockholders of Target and Acquiring Firms." *Journal of Financial Economics* 21:3–40.

Braeutigam, Ronald R. 1984. "Socially Optimal Pricing with Rivalry and Economies of Scale." *Rand Journal of Economics* 15:127–34.

Braeutigam, Ronald R. 1989. "Optimal Policies for Natural Monopolies," in Richard Schmalensee and Robert Willig, eds., *Handbook of Industrial Organization.* Amsterdam: North-Holland.

Braeutigam, Ronald R., and James Quirk. 1984. "Demand Uncertainty and the Regulated Firm." *International Economic Review* 25:45–60.

Brander, James A., and Paul R. Krugman. 1983. "Intra-Industry Trade in Identical Commodities." *Journal of International Economics* 15:313–21.

Brander, James A., and Paul R. Krugman. 1984. "A 'Reciprocal Dumping' Model of International Trade." *Journal of International Economics* 15:313–21.

Brander, James A., and Barbara J. Spencer. 1985. "Export Subsidies and International Market Share and Rivalry," *Journal of International Economics* 18:83–100.

Brannman, Lance E., and J. Douglass Klein. 1992. "The Effectiveness and Stability of Highway Bid-Rigging" in David B. Audretsch and John J. Seigfried, eds., *Empirical Studies in Industrial Organization: Essays in Honor of Leonard W. Weiss.* Norwell, MA: Kluwer Academic Publishers, 61–75.

Brealey, Richard A., and Stewart C. Myers. 2003. *Principles of Corporate Finance.* New York: McGraw-Hill.

Bresnahan, Timothy F. 1981. "Departures from Marginal-Cost Pricing in the American Automobile Industry." *Journal of Econometrics* 17:201–27.

Bresnahan, Timothy F. 1982. "The Oligopoly Solution Concept Is Identified." *Economics Letters* 10:87–92.

Bresnahan, Timothy F. 1987. "Competition and Collusion in the American Automobile Oligopoly: The 1955 Price War." *Journal of Industrial Economics* 35:457–82.

Bresnahan, Timothy F. 1989. "Studies of Industries with Market Power," in Richard Schmalensee and Robert D. Willig, eds., *The Handbook of Industrial Organization.* Amsterdam: North-Holland.

Bresnahan, Timothy F., and Peter C. Reiss. 1988. "Do Entry Conditions Vary Across Markets?" *Brookings Papers on Economic Activity* 1:833–82.

Bresnahan, Timothy F., and Peter C. Reiss. 1990. "Entry in Monopoly Markets." *Review of Economic Studies* 57:531–53.

Bresnahan, Timothy F., and Peter C. Reiss. 1991. "Entry and Competition in Concentrated Markets." *Journal of Political Economy* 99:977–1009.

Bresnahan, Timothy F., Scott Stern, and Manuel Trajtenberg. 1997. "Market Segmentation and the Sources of Rents from Innovation: Personal Computers in the Late 1980s." *Rand Journal of Economics* 28:S17–44.

Breyer, Stephen. 1982. *Regulation and Its Reform.* Cambridge, MA: Harvard University Press.

Brickley, James A. 1999. "Incentive Conflicts and Contractual Restraints: Evidence from Franchising." *Journal of Law and Economics* 42:745–74.

Brickley, James A. 2002. "Royalty Rates and Upfront Fees in Share Contracts: Evidence from Franchising." *Journal of Law, Economics and Organization* 18:511–35.

Brickley, James A., and Frederick H. Dark. 1987. "The Choice of Organizational Form: The Case of Franchising." *Journal of Financial Economics* 18:401–20.

Brickley, James A., Frederick H. Dark, and Michael S. Weisbach. 1991. "The Economic Effects of Franchise Termination Laws." *Journal of Law and Economics* 34:101–32.

Brickley, James A., Sanjog Misra, and Lawrence Van Horn. 2002. "Contract Duration: Evidence from Franchise Contracts." Working paper.

Brock, William A., and Jose A. Scheinkman. 1983. "Free Entry and the Sustainability of Natural Monopoly: Bertrand Revisited by Cournot," in David S. Evans, ed., *Breaking Up Bell.* New York: Elsevier Science Publishing Co., Inc.

Brodley, Joseph F. 1990. "Antitrust Law and Innovation Cooperation." *Journal of Economic Perspectives* 4:97–112.

Brown, Deborah J., and Lee F. Schrader. 1990. "Cholesterol Information and Shell Egg Consumption." *American Journal of Agricultural Economics* 72:548–55.

Brozen, Yale. 1971. "Bain's Concentration and Rates of Return Revisited." *Journal of Law and Economics* 14:351–69.

Brueckner, Jan K., Nicholas J. Dyer, and Pablo T. Spiller. 1992. "Fare Determination in Airline Hub-and-Spoke Networks." *Rand Journal of Economics* 23:309–33.

Brueckner, Jan K., and Pablo T. Spiller. 1991. "Competition and Mergers in Airline Networks." *International Journal of Industrial Organization* 9:323–42.

Brynjolfsson, Eric, and Michael Smith. 2000. "Frictionless Commerce? A Comparison of Internet and Conventional Retailers." *Management Science* 46:563–85.

Buchanan, James. 1965. "An Economic Theory of Clubs." *Economica* 32:1–14.

Bulow, Jeremy I. 1982. "Durable-Goods Monopolists." *Journal of Political Economy* 90:314–32.

Bulow, Jeremy I. 1986. "An Economic Theory of Planned Obsolescence." *Quarterly Journal of Economics* 101:729–49.

Bulow, Jeremy I., John D. Geanakoplos, and Paul D. Klemperer. 1985a. "Multimarket Oligopoly: Strategic Substitutes and Complements." *Journal of Political Economy* 95:488–511.

Bulow, Jeremy I., John D. Geanakoplos, and Paul D. Klemperer. 1985b. "Holding Idle Capacity to Deter Entry." *Economic Journal* 95:178–82.

Bulow, Jeremy I., and Paul Pfleiderer. 1983. "A Note on the Effect of Cost Changes on Prices." *Journal of Political Economy* 91:182–85.

Bulow, Jeremy I., and John Roberts. 1989. "The Simple Economics of Optimal Auctions." *Journal of Political Economy* 97:1060–90.

Burns, Malcolm R. 1986. "Predatory Pricing and the Acquisition Cost of Competitors." *Journal of Political Economy* 94:266–96.

Buschena, David E., and Jeffrey M. Perloff. 1991. "The Creation of Dominant Firm Market Power in the Coconut Oil Export Market." *American Journal of Agricultural Economics* 73:1000–8.

Butters, Gerard R. 1977. "Equilibrium Distributions of Sales and Advertising Prices." *Review of Economic Studies* 44:465–91.

Butz, David. 1990. "Durable-Good Monopoly and Best-Price Provisions." *American Economic Review* 80:1062–76.

Cady, John F. 1976. "An Estimate of the Price Effects of Restrictions on Drug Price Advertising." *Economic Inquiry* 14:493–510.

Calkins, Stephen. 1993. "Supreme Court Antitrust 1991–92: The Revenge of the Amici." *Antitrust Law Journal* 61:269–311.

Call, Gregory D., and Theodore E. Keeler. 1985. "Airline Deregulation, Fares, and Market Behavior: Some Empirical Evidence," in Andrew F. Daughety, ed., *Analytical Studies in Transport Economics.* New York: Cambridge University Press.

Calvo, Guillermo A., and Stanislaw Wellisz. 1979. "Supervision, Loss of Control, and the Optimum Size of the Firm." *Journal of Political Economy* 86:943–52.

Card, David. 1998. "Deregulation and Labor Earnings in the Airline Industry," in James Peoples, ed., *Regulatory Reform and Labor Markets, Recent Economic Thought Series,* Vol. 61. Boston: Dordrecht.

Carliner, Geoffrey. 1986. "Industrial Policies for Emerging Industries," in Paul R. Krugman, ed., *Strategic Trade Policy and the New International Economics.* Cambridge, MA: MIT Press.

Carlton, Dennis W. 1977. "Uncertainty, Production Lags, and Pricing." *American Economic Review* 67:244–49.

Carlton, Dennis W. 1978. "Market Behavior with Demand Uncertainty and Price Inflexibility." *American Economic Review* 68:571–87.

Carlton, Dennis W. 1979a. "Contracts, Price Rigidity, and Market Equilibrium." *Journal of Political Economy* 87:1034–62.

Carlton, Dennis W. 1979b. "Vertical Integration in Competitive Markets Under Uncertainty." *Journal of Industrial Economics* 27:189–209.

Carlton, Dennis W. 1982. "Planning and Market Structure," in John J. McCall, ed., *The Economics of Information and Uncertainty.* Chicago: University of Chicago Press, 47–72.

Carlton, Dennis W. 1983a. "The Disruptive Effect of Inflation on the Organization of Markets," in Robert Hall, ed., *Inflation.* Chicago: University of Chicago Press, 139–52.

Carlton, Dennis W. 1983b. "Equilibrium Fluctuations When Price and Delivery Lag Clear the Market." *Bell Journal of Economics* 14:562–72.

Carlton, Dennis W. 1983c. "A Reexamination of Delivered Pricing Systems." *Journal of Law and Economics* 26:51–70.

Carlton, Dennis W. 1984a. "Futures Markets: Their Purpose, Their History, Their Growth, Their Successes and Failures." *Journal of Futures Markets* 4:237–71.

Carlton, Dennis W. 1984b. *Market Behavior Under Uncertainty.* New York: Garland Press.

Carlton, Dennis W. 1985. "Delivery Lags as a Determinant of Demand." Unpublished.

Carlton, Dennis W. 1986. "The Rigidity of Prices." *American Economic Review* 76:637–58.

Carlton, Dennis W. 1989. "The Theory and Facts of How Markets Clear: Is Industrial Organization Useful for Understanding Macroeconomics?" in Richard Schmalensee and Robert D. Willig, eds., *The Handbook of Industrial Organization.* Amsterdam: North-Holland.

Carlton, Dennis W. 1990. "Comments on Vertical Integration and Market Foreclosure." *Brookings Papers on Economic Activity: Microeconomics* 277–83.

Carlton, Dennis W. 1991. "The Theory of Allocation and Its Implications for Marketing and Industrial Structure." *Journal of Law and Economics* 34:231–62.

Carlton, Dennis W. 2001. "A General Analysis of Exclusionary Conduct and Refusal to Deal—Why Aspen and Kodak Are Misguided." *Antitrust Law Journal* 68:659–83.

Carlton, Dennis W. 2003. "The Relevance for Antitrust Policy of Theoretical and Empirical Advances in Industrial Organization. *George Mason Law Review.*

Carlton, Dennis W. 2004a. "Using Economics to Improve Antitrust Policy." *Columbia Business Law Review.*

Carlton, Dennis W. 2004b. "The Proper Role for Antitrust in an International Setting." Keynote address: Second Annual Conference of the International Competition Network (ICN), Merida City, Mexico. *Columbia Business Law Review.*

Carlton, Dennis W., Gustavo Bamberger, and Roy Epstein. 1995. "Antitrust and Higher Education: Was There a Conspiracy to Restrict Financial Aid?" *Rand Journal of Economics* 26:131–47.

Carlton, Dennis W., and Judy Chevalier. 2001. "Free Riding and Sales Strategies for the Internet." *Journal of Industrial Economics* 49:441–61.

Carlton, Dennis W., and Robert Gertner. 1989. "Market Power and Mergers in Durable Good Industries." *Journal of Law and Economics* 32:S203–26.

Carlton, Dennis W., Robert Gertner, and Andrew Rosenfield. 1997. "Communication Among Competitors: Game Theory and Antitrust." *George Mason Law Review* 5:423–40.

Carlton, Dennis W., and Mark J. Klamer. 1983. "The Need for Coordination Among Firms, With Special Reference to Network Industries." *University of Chicago Law Review* 50:446–65.

Carlton, Dennis W., and Jeffrey M. Perloff. 1981. "Price Discrimination, Vertical Integration, and Divestiture in Natural Resources Markets." *Resources and Energy* 3:1–10.

Carlton, Dennis W., and Hal Sider. 1999. "Market Power and Vertical Restraints in Retailing: An Analysis of FTC v. Toys 'R' Us" in Daniel Slottje, ed., *The Role of the Academic Economist in Litigation Support.* Amsterdam: North-Holland.

Carlton, Dennis W., and Michael Waldman. 2002. "The Strategic Use of Tying to Preserve and Create Market Power in Evolving Industries." *Rand Journal of Economics* 33:194–220.

Carman, Hoy F., Richard D. Green, and Gay J. Mandour. 1992. "Commodity Advertising Pays . . . Or Does It?" *California Agriculture* 46:8–12.

Carmichael, C. M. 1987. "The Control of Export Credit Subsidies and Its Welfare Consequences." *Journal of International Economics* 23:1–19.

Carr, Jack L., and G. Frank Mathewson. 1988. "Unlimited Liability as a Barrier to Entry." *Journal of Political Economy* 96:766–84.

Castle, Emery N., and Kent A. Price. 1983. *U.S. Interests and Global Natural Resources.* Washington, D.C.: Johns Hopkins University Press.

Caswell, Julie A. 1992. "Current Information Levels on Food Labels." *American Journal of Agricultural Economics* 74:1196–1201.

Cave, Jonathan, and Stephen W. Salant. 1987. "Cartels That Vote: Agricultural Marketing Boards and Induced Voting Behavior," in Elizabeth Bailey, ed., *Regulation at the Crossroads.* Cambridge, MA: MIT Press.

Cave, Martin, and Robert Crandall. 2001. *Telecommunications Liberalization on Two Sides of the Atlantic.* Washington, D.C.: AEI-Brookings Joint Center for Regulatory Studies.

Caves, Douglas W., Laurits R. Christensen, Michael W. Tretheway, and Robert J. Windle. 1987. "An Assessment of the Efficiency Effects of U.S. Airline Deregulation via an International Comparison," in Elizabeth E. Bailey, ed., *Public Regulation: New Perspectives on Institutions and Policies.* Cambridge, MA: MIT Press.

Caves, Richard E. 1989. "International Differences in Industrial Organization," in Richard Schmalensee and Robert D. Willig, eds., *The Handbook of Industrial Organization.* Amsterdam: North-Holland.

Caves, Richard E. 1998. "Industrial Organization and New Findings on the Turnover and Mobility of Firms." *Journal of Economic Literature* 36:1947–82.

Caves, Richard E., Jeffrey A. Frankel, and Ronald W. Jones. 1999. *World Trade and Payments.* Reading, MA: Addison Wesley Longman.

Caves, Richard E., and William F. Murphy. 1976. "Franchising: Firms, Markets, and Intangible Assets." *Southern Economic Journal* 42:572–86.

Caves, Richard E., and Michael E. Porter. 1977. "From Entry Barriers to Mobility Barriers: Conjectural Decisions and Contrived Deterrence to New Competition." *Quarterly Journal of Economics* 91:241–61.

Caves, Richard E., and Marc J. Roberts. 1974. *Regulating the Product: Quality and Variety.* Cambridge, MA: Ballinger Publishing Company.

Caves, Richard E., and Masu Uekasa. 1976. *Industrial Organization in Japan.* Washington, D.C.: Brookings Institution

Caves, Richard E., Michael D. Whinston, and Mark A. Hurwitz. 1991. "Patent Expiration, Entry and Competition in the U.S. Pharmaceutical Industry." *Brookings Papers on Economic Activity* 1–48.

Cecchetti, Stephen G. 1985. "Staggered Contracts and the Frequency of Price Adjustment." *Quarterly Journal of Economics* 100:935–59.

Chadwick, E. 1859. "Results of Different Principles of Legislation and Administration in Europe; of Competition for the Field, as Compared with Competition within the Field, of Service." *Journal of the Royal Statistical Society* Series A, 22:381–420.

Chamberlin, Edward H. 1933. *The Theory of Monopolistic Competition.* Cambridge, MA: Harvard University Press.

Chan, Yuk-Shee, and Hayne E. Leland. 1982. "Prices and Qualities in Markets with Costly Information." *Review of Economic Studies* 49:499–516.

Chandler, Alfred D., Jr. 1977. *The Visible Hand: The Managerial Revolution in American Business.* Cambridge, MA: Harvard University Press.

Chaudhuri, Shubham, Pinelopi K. Goldberg, and Panle Jia. 2003. "The Effects of Extending Intellectual Property Rights Protection to Developing Countries: A Case Study of the Indian Pharmaceutical Market." National Bureau of Economic Research Working Paper 10159.

Chen, Yongmun. 2001. "On Vertical Mergers and Their Competitive Effects." *Rand Journal of Economics* 32:667–85.

Cheng, Leonard. 1988. "Assisting Domestic Industries under International Oligopoly: The Relevance of the Nature of Competition to Optimal Policies." *American Economic Review* 78:746–58.

Cheung, Steven N. S. 1982. "Property Rights in Trade Secrets." *Economic Inquiry* 20:40–52.

Chevalier, Judith. 1995. "Capital Structure and Product Market Competition: Empirical Evidence from the Supermarket Industry." *American Economic Review* 85:415–35.

Chevalier, Judith, Anil Kashyap, and Peter Rossi. 2000. "Why Don't Prices Rise During Periods of Peak Demand? Evidence from Scanner Data." Working paper.

Chevalier, Judith, and David Scharfstein. 1995. "Liquidity Constraints and the Cyclical Behavior of Markups." *American Economic Review* 85:390–96.

Chiang, Raymond, and Chester Spatt. 1982. "Imperfect Price Discrimination and Welfare." *Review of Economic Studies* 49:155–81.

Choi, Jay, and Christodoulos Stefandis. 2001. "Tying, Investment, and the Dynamic Leverage Theory." *Rand Journal of Economics* 32:52–71.

Clark, James M. 1923. *Studies in the Economics of Overhead Costs.* Chicago: University of Chicago Press.

Coase, Ronald H. 1937. "The Nature of the Firm." *Economica* 4:386–405.

Coase, Ronald H. 1946. "The Marginal Cost Controversy." *Economica* 14:150–54.

Coase, Ronald H. 1960. "The Problem of Social Cost." *Journal of Law and Economics* 3:1–44.

Coase, Ronald H. 1972. "Durability and Monopoly." *Journal of Law and Economics* 15:143–49.

Cohen, Wesley M., Richard C. Levin, and David C. Mowery. 1987. "Firm Size and R&D Intensity: A Re-Examination." *The Journal of Industrial Economics* 35:543–65.

Colantoni, C. S., O. A. Davis, and M. Swaminuthan. 1976. "Imperfect Consumers and Welfare Comparisons of Policies Concerning Information and Regulation." *Bell Journal of Economics* 7:602–15.

Cole, Barry F. 1991. *After the Breakup: Assessing the New Post-AT&T Divestiture Era.* New York: Columbia University Press.

Collins, Norman R., and Lee E. Preston. 1969. "Price-Cost Margins and Industry Structure." *Review of Economics and Statistics* 51:271–86.

Comanor, William S., and Robert H. Smiley. 1975. "Monopoly and the Distribution of Wealth." *Quarterly Journal of Economics* 89:177–94.

Comanor, William S., and Thomas A. Wilson. 1967. "Advertising, Market Structure, and Performance." *Review of Economics and Statistics* 49:423–40.

Comanor, William S., and Thomas A. Wilson. 1974. *Advertising and Market Power.* Cambridge, MA: Harvard University Press.

Comanor, William S., and Thomas A. Wilson. 1979. "Advertising and Competition: A Survey." *Journal of Economic Literature* 17:453–76.

Condon, Daniel. 2002. "Monopsony Power and the Market for Clergy: Some Evidence from the Census." *Quarterly Review of Economics and Finance* 42:889–900.

Connolly, Robert A., and Stephen Schwartz. 1985. "The Intertemporal Behavior of Economic Profits." *International Journal of Industrial Organization* 3:379–400.

Connor, John M. 2001. *Global Price Fixing: Our Customers Are the Enemy.* Boston: Kluwer Academic Publishers.

Connor, John M. 2003. "Private International Cartels: Effectiveness, Welfare, and Anticartel Enforcement." Purdue University working paper. **http://agecon.lib.umn.edu/cgibin/pdf_view.pl?paperid=11506&ftype=.pdf.**

Cooper, Russell, and Thomas W. Ross. 1984. "Prices, Product Qualities, and Asymmetric Information: The Competitive Case." *Review of Economic Studies* 51:197–207.

Corts, Kenneth. 1997. *Conduct Parameters and Market Power.* Cambridge, MA: Harvard Business School Press.

Corts, Kenneth. 1999. "Conduct Parameters and the Measurement of Market Power." *Journal of Econometrics* 88:227–50.

Cotterill, Ronald. 1986. "Market Power in the Retail Food Industry: Evidence from Vermont." *Review of Economics and Statistics* 68:379–86.

Cournot, Augustin A. 1963. *Researches into the Mathematical Principles of the Theory of Wealth.* Trans. Nathaniel T. Bacon. Homewood, IL: Richard D. Irwin.

Courville, Leon. 1974. "Regulation and Efficiency in the Electric Utility Industry." *Bell Journal of Economics* 5:53–74.

Cowling, Keith, and Dennis C. Mueller. 1978. "The Social Costs of Monopoly." *Economic Journal* 88:727–48.

Cowling, Keith, and Michael Waterson. 1976. "Price-Cost Margins and Market Structure." *Economica* 43:267–74.

Crandall, Robert W. 1987. "The Effects of U.S. Trade Protection for Autos and Steel." *Brookings Papers on Economic Activity* 271–88.

Crandall, Robert W. 1991. *After the Breakup: U.S. Telecommunications in a More Competitive Era.* Washington, D.C.: Brookings Institution.

Crawford, Gregory S. 2001. "The Discriminatory Incentives to Bundle: The Case of Cable Television." Duke University working paper.

Crew, Michael A., and Paul R. Kleindorfer. 1978. "Reliability and Public Utility Pricing." *American Economic Review* 68:31–40.

Crews, Clyde, Jr. 2003. *Ten Thousand Commandments.* Washington, D.C.: Cato Institute.

Crocker, Keith J. 1986. "A Reexamination of the 'Lemons' Market When Warranties Are Not Pre-Purchase Quality Signals." *Information Economics and Policy* 2:147–62.

Crocker, Keith J., and Kenneth J. Reynolds. 1993. "The Efficiency of Incomplete Contracts: An Empirical Analysis of Air Force Engine Procurement." *Rand Journal of Economics* 24:126–46.

Cubbin, John, and Paul A. Geroski. 1987. "The Convergence of Profits in the Long Run: Inter-Firm and Inter-Industry Comparisons." *Journal of Industrial Economics* 35:427–42.

Cummins, J. David, ed. 2002. *Deregulating Property Liability Insurance: Restoring Competition and Increasing Market*

Efficiency. Washington, D.C.: AEI-Brookings Center for Regulatory Studies.

Curry, D., and P. Reisz. 1988. "Prices and Price/Quality Relationships: A Longitudinal Analysis." *Journal of Marketing* 52:36–51.

Cyert, Richard M., and James G. March, eds. 1963. *Behavioral Theory of the Firm.* Englewood Cliffs, NJ: Prentice-Hall.

Dana, James, Jr. 1998. "Advance Purchase Discounts and Price Discrimination in Competitive Markets." *Journal of Political Economy* 106:395–422.

Dana, James, Jr. 1999. "Equilibrium Price Dispersion Under Demand Uncertainty: The Roles of Costly Capacity and Market Structure." *Rand Journal of Economics* 632–60.

Dana, James, Jr. 2001. "Competition in Price and Availability When Availability Is Unobservable." *Rand Journal of Economics* 32:497–513.

Darby, Michael R., and Edi Karni. 1973. "Free Competition and the Optimal Amount of Fraud." *Journal of Law and Economics* 16:67–88.

Darpa, Arup, and Sandeep Kapur. 2001. "Pricing on the Internet." *Oxford Review of Economic Policy* 17:202–16.

Dasgupta, Partha, and Eric Maskin. 1986. "The Existence of Equilibrium in Discontinuous Economic Games, I: Theory, and II: Applications." *Review of Economic Studies* 53:1–26 and 27–42.

Dasgupta, Partha, and Joseph E. Stiglitz. 1980. "Uncertainty, Industrial Structure, and the Speed of R&D." *Bell Journal of Economics* 11:1–28.

D'Aspremont, C., J. Jaskold Gabszewicz, and J.F. Thisse. 1979. "On Hotelling's 'Stability in Competition.'" *Econometrica* 47:1145–50.

Daughety, Andrew F. 1985. "Reconsidering Cournot: The Cournot Equilibrium Is Consistent." *Rand Journal of Economics* 16:368–79.

Davidson, Carl, and Raymond Deneckere. 1986. "Long-Run Competition in Capacity, Short-Run Competition in Prices, and the Cournot Model." *Rand Journal of Economics* 17:404–15.

Davidson, Carl, and Lawrence W. Martin. 1985. "General Equilibrium Tax Incidence Under Imperfect Competition: A Quantity-Setting Supergame Analysis." *Journal of Political Economy* 93:1212–23.

Davies, Stephen W., and Anthony J. McGuinness. 1982. "Dumping at Less Than Marginal Cost." *Journal of International Economics* 12:169–82.

Davis, Steven, John Haltwanger, and Scott Schuk. 1996. "Small Business and Job Creation: Dissecting the Myth and Reassessing the Facts." *Small Business Economics* 8:297–315.

DeAlessi, Louis. 1974. "An Economic Analysis of Government Ownership and Regulation: Theory and Evidence from the Electric Power Industry." *Public Choice* 19:1–42.

DeBoer, Larry. 1992. "Economies of Scale and Input Substitution in Public Libraries." *Journal of Urban Economics* 2:257–68.

DeBondt, Raymond R. 1976. "Limit Pricing, Uncertain Entry, and the Entry Lag." *Econometrica* 44:939–46.

Debreu, Gerard. 1959. *Theory of Value: An Axiomatic Analysis of Economic Equilibrium.* New York: John Wiley and Sons.

DeBrock, Lawrence M. 1985. "Market Structure, Innovation and Optimal Patent Life." *Journal of Law and Economics* 4:223–44.

Dechert, W. Davis. 1984. "Has the Averch-Johnson Effect Been Theoretically Justified?" *Journal of Economic Dynamics and Control* 8:1–17.

Demsetz, Harold. 1968. "Why Regulate Utilities?" *Journal of Law and Economics* 11:55–65.

Demsetz, Harold. 1973. "Industry Structure, Market Rivalry, and Public Policy." *Journal of Law and Economics* 16:1–9.

Deneckere, Raymond, and Carl Davidson. 1985. "Incentives to Form Coalitions with Bertrand Competition." *Rand Journal of Economics* 16:473–86.

Deneckere, Raymond, and James Peck. 1995. "Competition over Price and Service Rate When Demand is Stochastic: A Strategic Analysis." *Rand Journal of Economics* 26:148–62.

Deneckere, Raymond, and Michael Rothschild. 1986. "Monopolistic Competition and Preference Diversity." *Review of Economic Studies* 59:361–73.

Deodhar, Satish Y., and Ian M. Sheldon. 1995. "Is Foreign Trade (Im)perfectly Competitive?: An Analysis of the German Market for Banana Imports." *Journal of Agricultural Economics* 46(3 [September]):336–48.

Depken, Craig A., II, David R. Kamerschen, and Arthur Snow. 2002. "Generic Advertising of Intermediate Goods: Theory and Evidence on Free Riding." *Review of Industrial Organization* 20:205–20.

de Roos, Nicholas. 1999. "Examining Models of Collusion: The Market for Lysine." Working paper.

DeVany, Arthur S., and Thomas R. Saving. 1977. "Product Quality, Uncertainty, and Regulation: The Trucking Industry." *American Economic Review* 67:583–94.

Devine, D. Grant. 1978. "A Review of the Experimental Effects of Increased Price Information on the Performance of Canadian Retail Food Stores in the 1970s." *Canadian Journal of Agricultural Economics* 26:24–29.

Devine, D. Grant, and Bruce W. Marion. 1979. "The Influence of Consumer Price Information on Retail Pricing and Consumer Behavior." *American Journal of Agricultural Economics* 61:228–37.

Devine, D. Grant, and Bruce W. Marion. 1980. "The Influence of Consumer Price Information on Retail Pricing and Consumer Behavior: Reply." *American Journal of Agricultural Economics* 62:267–69.

Diamond, Peter. 1971. "A Model of Price Adjustment." *Journal of Economic Theory* 3:156–68.

Diamond, Peter. 1982. "Aggregate Demand Management in Search Equilibrium." *Journal of Political Economy* 90:881–94.

Diamond, Peter, and Michael Rothschild. 1978. *Uncertainty in Economics.* New York: Academic Press.

Dick, Andrew R. 1991. "Learning by Doing and Dumping in the Semiconductor Industry." *Journal of Law and Economics* 34:133–59.

Dijkgraaf, E., and R. H. J. M. Gradus. 2003. "Cost Savings of Contracting Out Refuse Collection." *Empirica* 30:149–61.

Dixit, Avinash K. 1979. "A Model of Duopoly Suggesting a Theory of Entry Barriers." *Bell Journal of Economics* 10:20–32.

Dixit, Avinash K. 1980. "The Role of Investment in Entry Deterrence." *Economic Journal* 90:95–106.

Dixit, Avinash K. 1984. "International Trade Policies for Oligopolistic Industries." *Economic Journal* 94:1–16.

Dixit, Avinash K. 1988a. "Antidumping and Countervailing Duties under Oligopoly." *European Economic Review* 32:55–68.

Dixit, Avinash K. 1988b. "Optimal Trade and Industrial Policy for the U.S. Automobile Industry," in Robert Feenstra, ed., *Empirical Methods for International Trade.* Cambridge, MA: MIT Press.

Dixit, Avinash K. 1989. "Entry and Exit Decisions Under Uncertainty." *Journal of Political Economy* 97:620–38.

Dixit, Avinash K., and Barry Nalebuff. 1991. *Thinking Strategically.* New York: W. W. Norton and Co.

Dixit, Avinash K., and Victor Norman. 1978. "Advertising and Welfare." *Bell Journal of Economics* 9:1–17.

Dixit, Avinash K., and Victor Norman. 1979. "Advertising and Welfare: Reply." *Bell Journal of Economics* 10:728–29.

Dixit, Avinash K., and Victor Norman. 1980. "Advertising and Welfare: Another Reply." *Bell Journal of Economics* 11:753–54.

Dixit, Avinash K., and Joseph E. Stiglitz. 1977. "Monopolistic Competition and Optimum Product Diversity." *American Economic Review* 67:297–308.

Djankov, Simeon, Rafael LaPorta, Florencio Lopez-De-Silanes, and Andrei Shleifer. 2002. "The Regulation of Entry." *Quarterly Journal of Economics* 117:1–37.

Dodson, Joe A., Jr., and Eitan Muller. 1978. "Models of New Product Diffusion Through Advertising and Word-of-Mouth." *Management Science* 24:1568–78.

Domberger, Simon. 1979. "Price Adjustment and Market Structure." *Economic Journal* 89:96–108.

Domowitz, Ian, Glenn R. Hubbard, and Bruce C. Petersen. 1986a. "The Intertemporal Stability of the Concentration-Margins Relationship." *Journal of Industrial Economics* 35:13–34.

Domowitz, Ian, Glenn R. Hubbard, and Bruce C. Petersen. 1986b. "Business Cycles and the Relationship Between Concentration and Price-Cost Margins." *Rand Journal of Economics* 17:1–17.

Domowitz, Ian, Glenn R. Hubbard, and Bruce C. Petersen. 1987. "Oligopoly Supergames: Some Empirical Evidence on Prices and Margins." *Journal of Industrial Economics* 35:379–98.

Domowitz, Ian, Glenn R. Hubbard, and Bruce C. Petersen. 1988. "Market Structure and Cyclical Fluctuations in U.S. Manufacturing." *Review of Economics and Statistics* 70:55–66.

Dorfman, Robert, and Peter O. Steiner. 1954. "Optimal Advertising and Optimal Quality." *American Economic Review* 44:826–36.

Douglas, George W., and James C. Miller III. 1974. *Economic Regulation of Domestic Air Transport: Theory and Policy.* Washington, D.C.: Brookings Institution.

Dranove, David, and Neil Gandal. 2003. "The DVD vs. DIVX Standard War: Empirical Evidence of Network Effects and Preannoncement." *Journal of Economics and Management Strategy* 12:363–86.

Dreze, Jacques H. 1975. "Existence of an Exchange Equilibrium Under Price Rigidities." *International Economic Review* 16:301–20.

Dudley, Susan, and Melinda Warren. 2003. "Regulatory Spending Soars." Report, Mercatus Center, George Mason University and Weidenbaum Center, Washington University.

Dunne, Timothy, Mark Roberts, and Larry Samuelson. 1988. "Patterns of Firm Entry and Exit in U.S. Manufacturing Industries." *Rand Journal of Economics* 19:495–515.

Easterbrook, Frank H. 1981. "Predatory Strategies and Counterstrategies." *University of Chicago Law Review* 48:263–337.

Easterbrook, Frank H. 2003. "When Is It Worthwhile to Use Courts to Search for Exclusionary Conduct?" *Columbia Business Law Review* 345–58.

Easterbrook, Frank H., William M. Landes, and Richard A. Posner. 1980. "Contribution Among Antitrust Defendants: A Legal and Economic Analysis." *Journal of Law and Economics* 23:331–70.

Eastman, Harry C., and Stefan Stykolt. 1960. "A Model for the Study of Protected Oligopolies." *Economic Journal* 70:336–47.

Eaton, B. Curtis. 1976. "Free Entry in One-Dimensional Models: Pure Profits and Multiple Equilibria." *Journal of Regional Science* 16:21–33.

Eaton, B. Curtis, and Richard G. Lipsey. 1980. "Exit Barriers Are Entry Barriers." *Bell Journal of Economics and Management Science* 11:721–29.

Eaton, B. Curtis, and Richard G. Lipsey. 1989. "Product Differentiation," in Richard Schmalensee and Robert D. Willig, eds., *The Handbook of Industrial Organization.* Amsterdam: North-Holland.

Eaton, B. Curtis, and Roger Ware. 1987. "A Theory of Market Structure with Sequential Entry." *Rand Journal of Economics* 18:1–16.

Eaton, Jonathan, and Gene M. Grossman. 1986a. "Optimal Trade and Industrial Policy Under Oligopoly." *Quarterly Journal of Economics* 101:383–406.

Eaton, Jonathan, and Gene M. Grossman. 1986b. "The Provision of Information as Marketing Strategy." *Oxford Economic Papers* 38:166–83.

Eckard, E. Woodrow, Jr. 1994. "An Empirical Test of the Free Rider and Market Power Hypotheses: A Comment." *Review of Economics and Statistics* 76:586–89.

Eckbo, Espen B. 1983. "Horizontal Mergers, Collusion, and Stockholder Wealth." *Journal of Financial Economics* 11:241–73.

Eckbo, Paul L. 1976. *The Future of World Oil.* Cambridge, MA: Ballinger.

Eckert, Ross D. 1973. "On the Incentives of Regulators: The Case of Taxicabs." *Public Choice* 14:83–100.

Eckert, Ross D. 1981. "The Life Cycle of Regulatory Commissioners." *Journal of Law and Economics* 24:113–20.

Economic Report of the President. 1987. Washington, D.C.: U.S. Government Printing Office, Ch. 5.

Economides, Nicholas. 1986. "Nash Equilibrium in Duopoly with Products Defined by Two Characteristics." *Rand Journal of Economics* 17:431–39.

Economides, Nicholas. 1988a. "Desirability of Compatibility in the Absence of Network Externalities." *American Economic Review* 79:1165–81.

Economides, Nicholas. 1988b. "The Economics of Trademarks." *Trademark Reporter* 78:523–39.

Economides, Nicholas. 1989. "Symmetric Equilibrium Existence and Optimality in Differentiated Products Markets." *Journal of Economic Theory* 47:178–94.

Economides, Nicholas. 1996. "The Economics of Networks." *International Journal of Industrial Organization* 14:673–700.

Economides, Nicholas. 1999. "The Telecommunications Act of 1996 and Its Impact." *Japan and the World Economy* 11:435–83.

Eden, Benjamin. 1990. "Marginal Cost Pricing When Spot Markets Are Complete." *Journal of Political Economy* 98:1293–1306.

Edlin, Aaron S. 1997. "Do Guaranteed-Low-Price Policies Guarantee High Prices, and Can Antitrust Rise to the Challenge?" *Harvard Law Review* 111:528–75.

Edlin, Aaron S., Mario Epelbaum, and Walter P. Heller. 1998. "Is Perfect Price Discrimination Really Efficient?: Welfare and Existence in General Equilibrium." *Econometrica* 66:897–922.

Edwards, Franklin R. 1973. "Advertising and Competition in Banking." *Antitrust Bulletin* 18:23–32.

Ekelund, Robert B., Jr., and William P. Gramm. 1970. "Advertising and Concentration: Some New Evidence." *Antitrust Bulletin* 5:243–49.

Ekelund, Robert B., Jr., John D. Jackson, David S. Saurman, William F. Shugart III, and Robert D. Tollison. 1987. "Exclusive Territories and Advertising Restrictions in the Malt Beverage Industry." Manuscript.

Ekelund, Robert B., Jr., and Charles Maurice. 1969. "An Empirical Investigation of Advertising and Concentration: Comment." *Journal of Industrial Economics* 18:76–80.

Ekelund, Robert B., Jr., and David S. Saurman. 1988. *Advertising and the Market Process.* San Francisco: Pacific Research Institute for Public Policy.

Ellickson, Paul B. 2000. "Vertical Product Differentiation and Concentration in the Supermarket Industry." Working paper, Simon School of Business Administration.

Ellingsen, Tore. 1991. "Strategic Buyers and the Social Cost of Monopoly." *American Economic Review* 81:648–57.

Ellison, Glenn. 1994. "Theories of Cartel Stability and the Joint Executive Committee." *Rand Journal of Economics* 25:37–57.

Elzinga, Kenneth G. 1986. "The Beer Industry," in Walter Adams, ed., *The Structure of American Industry.* New York: Macmillan, 203–38.

Elzinga, Kenneth G., and Thomas F. Hogarty. 1978. "*Utah Pie* and the Consequences of Robinson-Patman." *Journal of Law and Economics* 21:427–34.

Emons, Winand, and George Sheldon. 2002. "The Market for Used Cars: A New Test of the Lemons Model." University of Bern, **http://www.hwwa.de/Publikationen/Discussion_Paper/2002/187.pdf.**

Encoau, David, and Paul A. Geroski. 1984. "Price Dynamics and Competition in Five Countries." No. 8414, University of Southhampton.

Encoau, David, and Paul A. Geroski. 1986. "Price Dynamics and Competition in Five Countries." *OECD Economic Studies* 6:47–74.

Epple, Dennis. 1987. "Rent Control with Reputation: Theory and Evidence." Working Paper, Graduate School of Industrial Administration, Pittsburgh: Carnegie Mellon University.

Epple, Dennis, and Artur Raviv. 1979. "Product Reliability and Market Structure." *Southern Economic Journal* 46:280–87.

Ericson, Richard, and Ariel Pakes. 1995. "Markov-Perfect Industry Dynamics—A Framework for Empirical Work." *Review of Economic Studies* 62:53–82.

Ericson, Richard, and Ariel Pakes. 1998. "Empirical Implications of Alternative Models of Firm Dynamics." *Journal of Economic Theory* 79:1–45.

Ethier, Wilfred. 1982. "Dumping." *Journal of Political Economy* 90:487–506.

Ethier, Wilfred J. 2003. "Intellectual Property Rights and Dispute Settlement in the World Trade Organization." University of Pennsylvania working paper.

Evans, David S. 1987a. "The Relationship Between Firm Growth, Size, and Age: Estimates for 100 Manufacturing Industries." *Journal of Industrial Economics* 35:569–81.

Evans, David S. 1987b. "Tests of Alternative Theories of Firm Growth." *Journal of Political Economy* 95:657–74.

Evans, David S., Franklin Fisher, Daniel Rubinfeld, and Richard Schmalensee. 2002. "Did Microsoft Harm Consumers? Two Opposing Views." *American Enterprise Institute*, Washington, D.C.

Evans, David S., and James J. Heckman. 1982a. "Natural Monopoly," in David S. Evans, ed., *Breaking Up Bell.* New York: Elsevier Science Publishing Co., Inc.

Evans, David S., and James J. Heckman. 1982b. "Multiproduct Cost-Function Estimates and Natural Monopoly Tests for the Bell System," in David S. Evans, ed., *Breaking Up Bell.* New York: Elsevier Science Publishing Co., Inc.

Evans, R., and Eric Maskin. 1989. "Efficient Renegotiation-Proof Equilibria in Repeated Games." *Games and Economic Behavior* 1:361–69.

Evans, William N., and Ioanmis N. Kessides. 1993. "Localized Market Power in the U.S. Airline Industry." *Review of Economics and Statistics* 75:66–75.

Fargeix, André, and Jeffrey M. Perloff. 1989. "The Effects of Tariffs in Markets with Vertical Restraints." *Journal of International Economics* 26:99–117.

Farrell, Joseph. 1987. "Cheap Talk, Coordination, and Entry." *Rand Journal of Economics* 18:34–39.

Farrell, Joseph, and Paul Klemperer. Forthcoming. "Coordination and Lock-In: Competition with Switching Costs and Networks Effects," in Michael Armstrong and Robert Porter, eds., *Handbook of Industrial Organization,* Vol. 3. Amsterdam: North-Holland.

Farrell, Joseph, and Eric Maskin. 1989. "Renegotiation in Repeated Games." *Games and Economic Behavior* 1:327–60.

Farrell, Joseph, and Garth Saloner. 1985. "Standardization, Compatibility, and Innovation." *Rand Journal of Economics* 16:70–83.

Farrell, Joseph, and Garth Saloner. 1986a. "Installed Base and Compatibility: Innovation, Product Preannouncements, and Predation." *American Economic Review* 76:940–55.

Farrell, Joseph, and Garth Saloner. 1986b. "Standardization and Variety." *Economics Letters* 20:71–74.

Farrell, Joseph, and Carl Shapiro. 1990. "Horizontal Mergers: An Equilibrium Analysis." *American Economic Review* 80:107–26.

Faulhaber, Gerald R. 1975. "Cross-Subsidization: Pricing in Public Enterprises." *American Economic Review* 65:966–77.

Federal Trade Commission, Bureau of Consumer Protection. 1978. *Standards and Certification, Proposed Rule and Staff Report.* Washington, D.C.: U.S. Government Printing Office.

Federal Trade Commission. 1979. *Consumer Information Remedies, Policy Review Session.* Washington, D.C.: U.S. Government Printing Office.

Feenstra, Robert C., ed. 1988. *Empirical Methods for International Trade.* Cambridge, MA: MIT Press.

Feldstein, Martin. 1972a. "Distributional Equity and the Optimal Structure of Public Prices." *American Economic Review* 62:32–36.

Feldstein, Martin. 1972b. "Equity and Efficiency in Public Pricing." *Quarterly Journal of Economics* 86:175–87.

Fershtman, Chaim, and Ariel Pakes. 2000. "A Dynamic Oligopoly with Collusion and Price Wars." *Rand Journal of Economics* 31:207–236.

Finger, J. Michael, and Andrei Flate. 2003. "WTO Rules That Allow New Trade Restrictions: The Public Interest Is a Bastard Child." U.N. Millennium Project Task Force on Trade.

Fischer, Stanley. 1977. "Long-Term Contracts, Rational Expectations, and the Optimal Money Supply Rule." *Journal of Political Economy* 85:191–205.

Fisher, Anthony C. 1981. *Resource and Environmental Economics.* Cambridge: Cambridge University Press.

Fisher, Franklin M. 1974. "Alcoa Revisited: Comment." *Journal of Economic Theory* 9:357–59.

Fisher, Franklin M. 1985. "The Social Costs of Monopoly and Regulation: Posner Reconsidered." *Journal of Political Economy* 93:410–16.

Fisher, Franklin M. 1987. "On the Misuse of the Profit-Sales Ratio to Infer Monopoly Power." *Rand Journal of Economics* 18:384–96.

Fisher, Franklin M., P. H. Cootner, and Martin N. Bailey. 1972. "An Econometric Model of the World Copper Industry." *Bell Journal of Economics* 3:568–609.

Fisher, Franklin M., and John J. McGowan. 1979. "Advertising and Welfare: Comment." *Bell Journal of Economics* 10:726–27.

Fisher, Franklin M., and John J. McGowan. 1983. "On the Misuse of Accounting Rates of Return to Infer Monopoly Profits." *American Economic Review* 73:82–97.

Fisher, Franklin M., John J. McGowan, and Joen E. Greenwood. 1983. *Folded, Spindled, and Mutilated: Economic Analysis and U.S. v. IBM.* Cambridge, MA: MIT Press.

Fishman, Arthur, and Rafael Rob. 2000. "Product Innovation by a Durable-Good Monopoly." *Rand Journal of Economics* 31:237–52.

Fitzpatrick, Mary E. 1987. "A Test of Passive Regulation Using an Endogenous Switching Regression." Economic Analysis Group Discussion Paper 87–5. Washington, D.C.: Antitrust Division, U.S. Department of Justice.

Flaherty, M. Therese. 1980. "Dynamic Limit Pricing, Barriers to Entry, and Rational Firms." *Journal of Economic Theory* 23:160–82.

Fluet, Claude, and Paolo G. Garella. 2002. "Advertising and Prices as Signals of Quality in a Regime of Price Rivalry." *International Journal of Industrial Organization* 20:907–30.

Fouraker, Lawrence, and Sidney Siegel. 1963. *Bargaining Behavior.* New York: McGraw-Hill.

Fraas, Arthur G., and Douglas F. Greer. 1977. "Market Structure and Price Collusion: An Empirical Analysis." *Journal of Industrial Economics* 26:21–44.

Francois, Joseph, and Laura Baughman. 2003. "The Unintended Consequences of U.S. Steel Import Tariffs: A Quantification of the Impact During 2002." CITAC Foundation, Washington, D.C.

Fraumeni, Barbara M., and Dale W. Jorgenson. 1980. "Rates of Return by Industrial Sector in the United States, 1948–1976." *American Economic Review* 70(May):326–30.

Freeman, Richard B. 1983. "Unionism, Price-Cost Margins and the Return on Capital." National Bureau of Economic Research Working Paper no. 1164.

Friedlaender, Ann F. 1992. "Coal Rates and Revenue Adequacy in a Quasi-Regulated Rail Industry." *Rand Journal of Economics* 23:376–94.

Friedlaender, Ann F., Ernst R. Berndt, and Gerard McCullough. 1992. "Governance Structure, Managerial Characteristics, and Firm Performance in the Deregulated Rail Industry." *Brookings Papers on Economic Activity* 95–169.

Friedlaender, Ann F., and Richard H. Spady. 1980. "A Derived Demand Function for Freight Transportation." *Review of Economics and Statistics* 62:432–41.

Friedlaender, Ann F., Clifford Winston, and Kung Wang. 1983. "Costs, Technology, and Productivity in the U.S. Automobile Industry." *Bell Journal of Economics* 14:1–20.

Friedman, James W. 1967. "An Experimental Study of Cooperative Duopoly." *Econometrica* 35:1979–97.

Friedman, James W. 1971. "A Noncooperative Equilibrium for Supergames." *Review of Economic Studies* 28:1–12.

Friedman, James W. 1977. *Oligopoly and the Theory of Games.* Amsterdam: North-Holland.

Friedman, James W. 1983. *Oligopoly Theory.* Cambridge: Cambridge University Press.

Friedman, James W. 1986. *Game Theory with Applications to Economics.* Oxford: Oxford University Press.

Froeb, Luke M., Robert A. Koyak, and Gregory J. Werden. 1993. "What Is the Effect of Bid-Rigging on Prices?" *Economics Letters* 42:419–23.

Fromm, Gary. 1981. *Studies in Public Regulation.* Cambridge, MA: MIT Press.

Fudenberg, Drew, Richard Gilbert, Joseph E. Stiglitz, and Jean Tirole. 1983. "Preemption, Leap-frogging, and Competition in Patent Races." *European Economic Review* 22:3–31.

Fudenberg, Drew, and Eric Maskin. 1986. "The Folk Theorem in Repeated Games with Discounting and with Incomplete Information." *Econometrica* 54:533–54.

Fudenberg, Drew, and Jean Tirole. 1983. "Capital as a Commitment: Strategic Investment to Deter Mobility." *Journal of Economic Theory* 31:227–50.

Fudenberg, Drew, and Jean Tirole. 1984. "The Fat Cat Effect, the Puppy-Dog Play, and the Lean and Hungry Look." *American Economic Review* 74(May):361–66.

Fudenberg, Drew, and Jean Tirole. 1986a. "A 'Signal-Jamming' Theory of Predation." *Rand Journal of Economics* 17:366–76.

Fudenberg, Drew, and Jean Tirole. 1986b. *Dynamic Models of Oligopoly.* London: Harwood Academic Publishers.

Fudenberg, Drew, and Jean Tirole. 1989. "Noncooperative Game Theory for Industrial Organization: An Introduction and Overview," in Richard Schmalensee and Robert D. Willig, eds., *The Handbook of Industrial Organization.* Amsterdam: North-Holland.

Fudenberg, Drew, and Jean Tirole. 1991. *Game Theory.* Cambridge, MA: MIT Press.

Fudenberg, Drew, and Jean Tirole. 1998. "Upgrades, Tradeins, and Buybacks." *Rand Journal of Economics* 29:235–58.

Fuller, John G. 1962. *The Gentlemen Conspirators: The Story of the Price-Fixers in the Electrical Industry.* New York: Grove Press.

Fuss, Melvyn A., and Leonard Waverman. 1981. "Regulation and the Multiproduct Firm: The Case of Telecommunications in Canada," in Gary Fromm, ed., *Studies in Public Regulation.* Cambridge, MA: MIT Press.

Gabor, André. 1980. "Price and Consumer Protection," in David Morris, ed., *Economics of Consumer Protection.* London: Heinemann Educational Books.

Gabor, André, and C. W. J. Granger. 1961. "On the Price Consciousness of Consumers." *Applied Statistics* 10:170–88.

Galbraith, John K. 1952. *American Capitalism.* Boston: Houghton Mifflin.

Gale, Ian L., and Thomas J. Holmes. 1992. "The Efficiency of Advance-Purchase Discounts in the Presence of Aggregate Demand Uncertainty." *International Journal of Industrial Organization* 10:413–37.

Gale, Ian L., and Thomas J. Holmes. 1993. "Advance-Purchase Discounts and Monopoly Allocation of Capacity." *American Economic Review* 83:135–46.

Gallick, Edward C., and David E. Sisk. 1984. "Specialized Assets and Taxi Regulation: An Inquiry into the Possible Efficiency Motivation of Regulation." Bureau of Economics Working Paper no. 119. Washington, D.C.: Federal Trade Commission.

Gallini, Nancy T. 1984. "Deterrence Through Market Sharing: A Strategic Incentive for Licensing." *American Economic Review* 74:931–41.

Gallini, Nancy T. 2002. "The Economics of Patents: Lessons from Recent U.S. Patent Reform." *Journal of Economic Perspectives* 16:131–54.

Gallini, Nancy T., and Nancy Lutz. 1992. "Dual Distribution and Royalty Fees in Franchising." *Journal of Law, Economics and Organization* 8:471–501.

Gallini, Nancy T., and Suzanne Scotchmer. 2001. "Intellectual Property: When Is It the Best Incentive System?" in Adam Jaffe, Josh Lerner, and Scott Stern, eds., *Innovation Policy and the Economy,* Vol. 2. Cambridge, MA: MIT Press.

Gallini, Nancy T., and Ralph A. Winter. 1985. "Licensing in the Theory of Innovation." *Rand Journal of Economics* 16:237–52.

Gallo, Joseph C., Kenneth G. Dau-Schmidt, Joseph L. Craycraft, and Charles J. Parker. 1994. "Criminal Penalties Under the Sherman Act: A Study of Law and Economics." *Research in Law and Economics* 16:25–71.

Gandal, Neil, Sarit Markovich, and Michael Riordan. 2003. "Ain't It 'Suite'—Strategic Bundling in the PC Office Software Market." Unpublished. Tel Aviv University.

Gardner, Bruce L. 1984. "Price Discrimination or Price Stabilization: Debating with Models of U.S. Dairy Policy." *American Journal of Agricultural Economics* 66:763–68.

Garman, David, and Daniel Richards. 1992. "Wage-Price Flexibility, Market Power, and the Cyclical Behavior of Real Wages, 1959–80." *Quarterly Journal of Economics* 107:1437–50.

Garoyan, Leon, and James G. Youde. 1975. *Marketing Orders in California: A Description.* University of California Cooperative Extension Leaflet 2719.

Gaskins, Darius W., Jr. 1971. "Dynamic Limit Pricing: Optimal Pricing Under Threat of Entry." *Journal of Economic Theory* 3:306–22.

Gaskins, Darius W., Jr. 1974. "Alcoa Revisited: The Welfare Implications of a Secondhand Market." *Journal of Economic Theory* 7:254–71.

Gatsios, Konstantine, and Larry Karp. 1992. "How Anti-Merger Laws Can Reduce Investment, Help Producers, and Hurt Consumers." *Journal of Industrial Economics* 40:339–48.

Gaudet, Gérard, and Stephen W. Salant. 1991. "Increasing the Profits of a Subset of Firms in Oligopoly Models with Strategic Substitutes." *American Economic Review* 81:658–65.

Gelfand, Matthew D., and Pablo T. Spiller. 1987. "Entry Barriers and Multiproduct Oligopolies: Do They Forebear or Spoil?" *International Journal of Industrial Organization* 5:101–13.

Genesove, David, and Wallace Mullin. 1997. "Predation and Its Rate of Return: The Sugar Industry, 1887–1914." National Bureau of Economic Research Working Paper 6032.

Genesove, David, and Wallace Mullin. 1998. "Testing Static Oligopoly Models: Conduct and Cost in the Sugar Industry, 1890–1914." *Rand Journal of Economics* 29:355–77.

Geroski, Paul A. 1981. "Specification and Testing the Profits-Concentration Relationship: Some Experiments for the United Kingdom." *Economica* 48:279–88.

Geroski, Paul A. 1991. "The Empirical Analysis of Entry, Strategic Entry Deterrence and Market Selection." London Business School Working Paper.

Geroski, Paul A. 1991. "Entry and the Rate of Innnovation." *Economic Innovation of New Technology* 1:203–14.

Geroski, Paul A. 1991. *Market Dynamics and Entry.* Oxford: Basil Blackwell.

Geroski, Paul A. 1995. "What Do We Know About Entry." *International Journal of Industrial Organization* 13:421–40.

Gerstner, E. 1985. "Do Higher Prices Signal Higher Qualities?" *Journal of Marketing Research* 22:209–15.

Gerwig, Robert W. 1962. "Natural Gas Production: A Study of Costs of Regulation." *Journal of Law and Economics* 5:69–92.

Ghemawat, Pankaj, and Barry Nalebuff. 1985. "Exit." *Rand Journal of Economics* 16:184–94.

Gibbons, Robert. 1992. *Game Theory for Applied Economists.* Princeton, NJ: Princeton University Press.

Gilbert, Richard J. 1981. "Patents, Sleeping Patents, and Entry Deterrence," in Steven C. Salop, ed., *Strategy, Predation, and Antitrust Analysis.* Washington, D.C.: Federal Trade Commission, 205–69.

Gilbert, Richard J. 1989. "Mobility Barriers and the Value of Incumbency," in Richard Schmalensee and Robert D. Willig, eds., *The Handbook of Industrial Organization.* Amsterdam: North-Holland.

Gilbert, Richard J. 2002. "Antitrust for Patent Pools: A Century of Policy Evolution." University of California, Berkeley, working paper.

Gilbert, Richard J., and Marvin Lieberman. 1987. "Investment and Coordination in Oligopolistic Industries." *Rand Journal of Economics* 18:17–33.

Gilbert, Richard J., and David M. G. Newbery. 1982. "Preemptive Patenting and the Persistence of Monopoly." *American Economic Review* 72:514–26.

Gilbert, Richard J., and David M. G. Newbery. 1988. "Regulation Games." Department of Economics Working Paper no. 8879. University of California, Berkeley.

Gilbert, Richard J., and Carl Shapiro. 1990. "Optimal Patent Length and Breadth." *Rand Journal of Economics* 21:106–112.

Gilligan, Thomas. 1992. "Imperfect Competition and Basing Point Pricing: Evidence from the Softwood Plywood Industry." *American Economic Review* 82:1106–19.

Ginarte, Juan C., and Walter G. Park. 1997. "Determinants of Patent Rights: A Cross-National Study." *Research Policy* 26:283–301.

Ginter, James L., Murray A. Young, and Peter R. Dickson. 1987. "A Market Efficiency Study of Used Car Reliability and Prices." *Journal of Consumer Affairs* 21:258–76.

Godek, Paul E. 1985. "Industry Structure and Redistribution Through Trade Restrictions." *Journal of Law and Economics* 28:687–703.

Golan, Amos, Larry S. Karp, and Jeffrey M. Perloff. 2000. "Estimating Coke and Pepsi's Price and Advertising Strategies." *Journal of Business and Economic Statistics* 18:398–409.

Golbe, Devra L., and Lawrence J. White. 1988. "A Time Series Analysis of Mergers and Acquisitions in the U.S. Economy," in Alan J. Auerbach, ed., *Corporate Takeovers: Causes and Consequences.* Chicago: University of Chicago Press.

Gollop, Frank M., and Mark J. Roberts. 1979. "Firm Interdependence in Oligopolistic Markets." *Journal of Econometrics* 3:313–31.

Gomez-Lobo, André S., and Stefan Szymanski. 2001. "A Law of Large Numbers: Bidding and Compulsory Competitive Tendering for Refuse Collection Contracts." *Review of Industrial Organization* 18:105–13.

Gonenc, Rauf, and Giuseppe Nicoletti. 2000. *Regulation, Market Structure and Performance in Air Passenger Transportation.* Organization for Economic Cooperation and Development.

Gordon, Robert. 1983. "A Century of Evidence on Wage and Price Stickiness in the United States, the United Kingdom, and Japan," in James Tobin, ed., *Macroeconomics, Prices, and Quantities: Essays in Memory of Arthur M. Okun.* Washington, D.C.: The Brookings Institution, 85–134.

Gould, John P. 1974. "Risk, Stochastic Preference, and the Value of Information." *Journal of Economic Theory* 8:64–85.

Gould, John P. 1978. "Inventories and Stochastic Demand: Equilibrium Models of the Firm and Industry." *Journal of Business* 51:1–42.

Gow, R. Hamish, and Johan F. M. Swinnen. 1998. "Up- and Downstream Restructuring, Foreign Direct Investment, and Hold-Up Problems in Agricultural Transition." *European Review of Agricultural Economics* 25:331–50.

Grabowski, Henry, and John Vernon. 1979. "Substitution Laws and Innovation in the Pharmaceutical Industry (Regulation and Innovation)." *Law and Contemporary Problems* 43:43–66.

Grabowski, Henry, and John Vernon. 1986. "Longer Patents for Lower Imitation Barriers: The 1984 Drug Act." *American Economic Review* 76:195–98.

Grabowski, Henry, and John Vernon. 1992. "Brand Loyalty, Entry and Price Competition in Pharmaceuticals after the 1984 Drug Act." *Journal of Law and Economics* 35: 331–50.

Graham, David R., Daniel P. Kaplan, and David S. Sibley. 1983. "Efficiency and Competition in the Airline Industry." *Bell Journal of Economics* 14:118–38.

Green, Edward J., and Robert H. Porter. 1984. "Noncooperative Collusion Under Imperfect Price Information." *Econometrica* 52:87–100.

Griliches, Zvi, ed. 1984. *R&D, Patents, and Productivity.* Chicago: University of Chicago Press.

Griliches, Zvi. 1990. "Patent Statistics as Economic Indicators: A Survey." *Journal of Economic Literature* 28:1661–707.

Grossman, Gene M., and Carl Shapiro. 1984. "Informative Advertising with Differentiated Products." *Review of Economic Studies* 51:63–81.

Grossman, Gene M., and Carl Shapiro. 1986. "Research Joint Ventures: An Antitrust Analysis." *Journal of Law, Economics, and Organization* 2:315–37.

Grossman, Sanford J. 1981a. "Nash Equilibrium and the Industrial Organization of Markets with Large Fixed Costs." *Econometrica* 49:1149–72.

Grossman, Sanford J. 1981b. "The Informational Role of Warranties and Private Disclosure About Product Quality." *Journal of Law and Economics* 24:461–83.

Grossman, Sanford J., and Oliver Hart. 1980. "Disclosure Laws and Takeover Bids." *Journal of Finance* 35:323–34.

Grossman, Sanford J., and Joseph E. Stiglitz. 1980. "On the Impossibility of Informationally Efficient Markets." *American Economic Review* 70:393–408.

Gruenspecht, Howard K. 1988a. "Dumping and Dynamic Competition." *Journal of International Economics* 25:225–48.

Gruenspecht, Howard K. 1988b. "Export Subsidies for Differentiated Products." *Journal of International Economics* 24:331–44.

Guerin-Calvert, Margaret E. 1994. "Vertical Integration as a Threat to Competition: Airline Computer Reservation Systems (1992)," in John E. Kwoka, Jr. and Lawrence J. White, eds., *The Antitrust Revolution: The Role of Economics.* New York: HarperCollins Publishers.

Gul, Faruk. 1987. "Foundations of Dynamic Oligopoly." *Rand Journal of Economics* 18:248–54.

Gul, Faruk, Hugo Sonnenschein, and Robert Wilson. 1986. "Foundations of Dynamic Monopoly and the Coase Conjecture." *Journal of Economic Theory* 39:155–90.

Hadfield, Gillian K. 1990. "Problematic Relations: Franchising and the Law of Incomplete Contracts." *Stanford Law Review* 42:927–92.

Hadfield, Gillian K. 1991. "Credible Spatial Preemption Through Franchising." *Rand Journal of Economics* 22:531–43.

Hajivassiliou, Vassilis A. 1989. "Measurement Errors in Switching Regressions Models: With Applications to Price-Fixing Behavior." Cowles Foundation for Research in Economics Working Paper.

Hall, Bronwyn H. 1987. "The Relationship Between Firm Size and Firm Growth in the U.S. Manufacturing Sector." *Journal of Industrial Economics* 35:583–605.

Hall, Bronwyn H. 1988. "The Effect of Takeover Activity on Corporate Research and Development," in Alan J. Auerbach, ed., *Corporate Takeovers: Causes and Consequences.* Chicago: University of Chicago Press.

Hall, Bronwyn H. Forthcoming. "Innovation and Diffusion," in J. Fagerberg, D. Mowery, and R. R. Nelson, eds., *Handbook of Innovation.* Oxford University Press.

Hall, R. L., and C. J. Hitch. 1939. "Price Theory and Business Behavior." *Oxford Economic Papers* 2:12–45.

Hall, Robert E. 1978. "The Macroeconomic Impact of Changes in Income Taxes in the Short and Medium Runs." *Journal of Political Economy* 86:571–85.

Hall, Robert E. 1988a. "A Non-Competitive Equilibrium Model of Fluctuations." National Bureau of Economic Research, Working Paper no. 2576.

Hall, Robert E. 1988b. "The Relationship Between Price and Marginal Cost in U.S. Industry." *Journal of Political Economy* 96:921–47.

Haltiwanger, John, and Louis J. Maccini. 1988. "A Model of Inventory and Layoff Behavior Under Uncertainty." *Economic Journal* 98:731–45.

Halverson, James T. 1988. "The Future of Horizontal Restraints Analysis." *Antitrust Law Journal* 57:33–48.

Harberger, Arnold. 1954. "Monopoly and Resource Allocation." *American Economic Review* 44:77–79.

Harberger, Arnold C. 1971. "Three Basic Postulates for Applied Welfare Economics: An Interpretive Essay." *Journal of Economic Literature* 9:109–38.

Harris, Christopher, and John Vickers. 1985. "Patent Races and the Persistence of Monopoly," in Paul A. Geroski, Louis Phlips, and Alistair Ulph, eds., *Oligopoly, Competition, and Welfare.* New York: Basil Blackwell.

Harris, Maury N. 1976. "Entry and Barriers to Entry." *Industrial Organization Review* 4:165–74.

Harris, Milton, and Artur Raviv. 1981. "Monopoly Pricing Schemes with Demand Uncertainty." *American Economic Review* 71:347–65.

Harris, Richard. 1984. "Applied General Equilibrium Analysis of Small Open Economies with Scale Economies and Imperfect Competition." *American Economic Review* 74:1016–32.

Harris, Richard with David Cox. 1984. *Trade, Industry Policy, and Canadian Manufacturing.* Toronto: Ontario Economic Council, University of Toronto Press.

Harsanyi, John C. 1967–1968. "Games with Incomplete Information Played by Bayesian Players." *Management Science* 14:159–82, 320–34, and 486–502.

Hart, Oliver D. 1979. "Monopolistic Competition in a Large Economy with Differentiated Commodities." *The Review of Economic Studies* 46:1–30.

Hart, Oliver D. 1982. "A Model of Imperfect Competition with Keynesian Features." *Quarterly Journal of Economics* 97:109–38.

Hart, Oliver D. 1985. "Monopolistic Competition in the Spirit of Chamberlin: A General Model." *Review of Economic Studies* 52:529–46.

Hart, Oliver, and Jean Tirole. 1990. "Vertical Integration and Market Foreclosure." *Brookings Papers on Economic Activity. Microeconomics* 205–76.

Hart, P. E., and Eleanor Morgan. 1977. "Market Structure and Economic Performance in the United Kingdom." *Journal of Industrial Economics* 25:177–93.

Hausman, Jerry. 1997a. "Valuation of New Goods Under Perfect and Imperfect Competition," in Timothy Bresnahan and Robert Gordon, eds., *Economics of New Goods,* University of Chicago Press.

Hausman, Jerry. 1997b. "Valuing the Effect of Regulation on New Services in Telecommunications." *Brookings Papers on Economic Activity: Microeconomics* 1–38.

Hausman, Jerry, and Gregory Leonard. 1997. "Economic Analyses of Differentiated Products Mergers Using Real World Data." *George Mason Law Review* 5:321–46.

Hausman, Jerry A., Gregory Leonard, and J. Douglas Zona. 1994. "Competitive Analysis with Differentiated Products." *Annals D'Economique et de Statistique* 34:159–80.

Hausman, Jerry A., and Jeffrey K. MacKie-Mason. 1988. "Price Discrimination and Patent Policy." *Rand Journal of Economics* 19:253–65.

Hausman, William J., and John L. Neufeld. 1984. "Time-of-Day Pricing in the U.S. Electric Power Industry at the Turn of the Century." *Rand Journal of Economics* 15:116–26.

Hay, George A. 1998. "Facilitating Practices: The *Ethyl* Case (1984)," in John E. Kwoka, Jr. and Lawrence J. White, eds., *The Antitrust Revolution: Economics, Competition, and Policy.* New York: Oxford University Press.

Hay, George A., and Daniel Kelley. 1974. "An Empirical Survey of Price-Fixing Conspiracies." *Journal of Law and Economics* 17:13–38.

Heien, Dale. 1977. "The Cost of U.S. Dairy Price Support Programs: 1949–1974." *Review of Economics and Statistics* 59:1–8.

Helpman, Elhanan. 1988. "Imperfect Competition and International Trade: Evidence from Fourteen Countries," in A. Michael Spence and Heather A. Hazard, eds., *International Competitiveness.* Cambridge, MA: Ballinger Publishing Co.

Helpman, Elhanan, and Paul R. Krugman. 1985. *Market Structure and Foreign Trade: Increasing Returns, Imperfect Competition, and the International Economy.* Cambridge, MA: MIT Press.

Helpman, Elhanan, and Paul R. Krugman. 1989. *Trade Policy and Market Structure.* Cambridge, MA: MIT Press.

Hendel, Igal. 1999. "Estimating Multiple-Discrete Choice Models: An Application to Computerization Returns." *Review of Economic Studies* 25(2):423–46.

Hendel, Igal, and Alessandro Lizzeri. 1999a. "Adverse Selection in Durable Goods Markets." *American Economic Review* 89:1097–1115.

Hendel, Igal, and Alessandro Lizzeri. 1999b. "Interfering with Secondary Markets." *Rand Journal of Economics* 30:1–21.

Hendel, Igal, and Alessandro Lizzeri. 2002. "The Role of Leasing Under Adverse Selection." *Journal of Political Economy* 110:113–43.

Henderson, James J., and Richard E. Quandt. 1980. *Microeconomic Theory.* New York: McGraw-Hill.

Heston, Alan, Robert Summers, and Bettina Aten. 2002. Penn World Table Version 6.1, Center for International Comparisons at the University of Pennsylvania (CICUP), October.

Hilke, John C. 1984. "Early Mandatory Disclosure Regulations." Bureau of Economics, Federal Trade Commission Working Paper no. 111. Washington, D.C.: U.S. Government Printing Office.

Hill, D. J., R. R. Piggott, and Garry R. Griffith. 2001. "Profitability of Incremental Generic Promotion of Australian Dairy Products." *Agricultural Economics* 26:253–66.

Hillman, Arye L., and Eliakim Katz. 1986. "Domestic Uncertainty and Foreign Dumping." *Canadian Journal of Economics* 19:403–16.

Hirshleifer, Jack. 1971. "The Private and Social Value of Information and the Reward to Inventive Activity." *American Economic Review* 61:561–74.

Hoekman, Bernard. 2003. "Cancun: Crisis or Catharsis." Unpublished remarks, Brookings-George Washington Trade Roundtable.

Holmes, James M., Patricia A. Hutton, and Edward Weber. 1991. "A Functional-Form-Free Test of the Research and Development/Firm Size Relationship." *Journal of Business and Economic Statistics* 9:85–90.

Holmes, Thomas J. 1989. "The Effects of Third-Degree Price Discrimination in Oligopoly." *American Economic Review* 79:244–50.

Holmstrom, Bengt. 1979. "Moral Hazard and Observability." *Bell Journal of Economics* 10:74–91.

Holt, Charles A., Jr. 1985. "An Experimental Test of the Consistent-Conjectures Hypothesis." *American Economic Review* 75:314–25.

Holt, Charles A., Jr. 1995. "Industrial Organization: A Survey of Laboratory Research" in John Kagal and Alvin Roth, eds., *The Handbook of Experimental Economics.* Princeton, NJ: Princeton University Press.

Hopenhayn, Hugo A. 1992. "Entry, Exit, and Firm Dynamics in Long Run Equilibrium." *Econometrica* 60:1127–50.

Horlick, Gary N. 1989. "The United States Antidumping System," in John H. Jackson and Edwin A. Vermulst, eds., *Antidumping Law and Practice.* Ann Arbor: University of Michigan Press.

Horstmann, Ignatius J., and James R. Markusen. 1986. "Up Your Average Cost Curve: Inefficient Entry and the New Protectionism." *Journal of International Economics* 20:225–49.

Horvath, Michael, Fabiano Schivardi, and Michael Woywode. 2001. "On Industry Life-Cycles: Delay, Entry, and Shakeout in Beer Brewing." *International Journal of Industrial Organization* 19:1023–52.

Hotelling, Harold. 1929. "Stability in Competition." *Economic Journal* 39:41–57.

Houck, James P. 1986. *Elements of Agricultural Trade Policies.* Prospect Heights, IL: Waveland Press, Inc.

Houthakker, Hendrik. 1985. "Book Review" of Fisher et al. (1983). *Journal of Political Economy* 93:618–21.

Hoxby, Carolyn. 2000. "Benevolent Colluders? The Effects of Antitrust Action on College Financial Aid and Tuition." National Bureau of Economic Research Working Paper 754.

Hubbard, Glenn, and Robert Weiner. 1989. "Contracting and Price Flexibility in Product Markets." *Review of Economics and Statistics* 71:80–89.

Hufbauer, Gary Clyde, and Joanna Shelton Erb. 1984. *Subsidies in International Trade.* Washington, D.C.: Institute for International Economics.

Hughes, James W., Michael J. Moore, and Edward A. Snyder. 2002. "'Napsterizing' Pharmaceuticals: Access, Innovation, and Consumer Welfare." National Bureau of Economic Research Working Paper 9229.

Hui, Kai-Lung, and Ivan Png. 2003. "Piracy and the Legitimate Demand for Recorded Music." *Contributions to Economic Analysis & Policy,* 2. **http://www.bepress.com/ bejeap.**

Hurdle, Gloria J., Richard L. Johnson, Andrew S. Joskow, Gregory J. Werden, and Michael A. Williams. 1989. "Concentration, Potential Entry, and Performance in the Airline Industry." *Journal of Industrial Economics* 38:119–39.

Hurwitz, James D., William E. Kovacic, Thomas A. Sheehan, III, and Robert H. Lande. 1981. "Current Legal Standards of Predation," in Steven C. Salop, ed., *Strategy, Predation, and Antitrust Analyses.* Washington, D.C.: Federal Trade Commission.

Hyde, Charles E., and Jeffrey M. Perloff. 1998. "Multimarket Market Power Estimation: The Australian Retail Meat Sector." *Applied Economics* 30:1169–76.

International Journal of Industrial Organization. 1996. Special Issue on Network Economies. Vol. 14.

Ippolito, Pauline M. 1986. "Consumer Protection Economics: A Selective Survey," in Pauline M. Ippolito and David T. Scheffman, eds., *Empirical Approaches to Consumer Protection Economics.* Federal Trade Commission. Washington, D.C.: U.S. Government Printing Office.

Ippolito, Pauline M. 1991. "Resale Price Maintenance: Empirical Evidence from Litigation." *Journal of Law and Economics* 34(2):263–94.

Ippolito, Richard A., and Robert T. Masson. 1978. "The Social Cost of Government Regulation of Milk." *Journal of Law and Economics* 21:33–66.

Ireland, Norman J. 1992. "On the Welfare Effects of Regulating Price Discrimination." *Journal of Industrial Economics* 40:237–48.

Irwin, Douglas A., and Nina Pavcnik. 2001. "Airbus Versus Boeing Revisited: International Competition in the Aircraft Market." National Bureau of Economic Research Working Paper 8648. **http://papers.nber.org/papers/ w8648.pdf.**

Irwin, Marley R. 1971. "The Communication Industry," in Walter Adams, ed., *The Structure of American Industry.* New York: Macmillan.

Isaac, Mark R., and Vernon L. Smith. 1985. "In Search of Predatory Pricing." *Journal of Political Economy* 93:320–45.

Isé, Sabrina J., and Jeffrey M. Perloff. 1997. "Effects of FCC Regulations on Television Profits." *Information Economics and Policy* 9:37–49.

Iwata, Gyoichi. 1974. "Measurement of Conjectural Variations in Oligopoly." *Econometrica* 42:947–66.

Jacquemin, Alexis. 1990. "Horizontal Concentration and European Merger Policy." *European Economic Review* 34:539–50.

Jacquemin, Alexis, and Margaret E. Slade. 1989. "Cartels, Collusion, and Horizontal Merger," in Richard

Schmalensee and Robert D. Willig, eds., *The Handbook of Industrial Organization.* Amsterdam: North-Holland.

Jaffe, Adam B. 2000. "The U.S. Patent System in Transition: Policy Innovation and the Innovation Process." *Research Policy* 29:531–57.

Jarrell, Gregg A. 1981. "The Economic Effects of Federal Regulation of the Market for New Security Issues." *Journal of Law and Economics* 24:613–75.

Jarrell, Gregg A., James A. Brickley, and Jeffrey N. Netter. 1988. "The Market for Corporate Control: The Empirical Evidence Since 1980." *Journal of Economic Perspectives* 2:49–68.

Jarrell, Gregg A., and Annette B. Poulsen. 1987. "Shark Repellents and Stock Prices: The Effects of Antitakeover Amendments Since 1980." *Journal of Financial Economics* 19:127–68.

Jenny, Frédéric, and André-Paul Weber. 1983. "Aggregate Welfare Loss Due to Monopoly Power in the French Economy: Some Tentative Estimates." *The Journal of Industrial Economics* 32:113–30.

Jensen, Elizabeth J. 1987. "Research Expenditures and the Discovery of New Drugs." *Journal of Industrial Economics* 36:83–95.

Jensen, Michael C. 1988. "Takeovers: Their Causes and Consequences." *Journal of Economic Perspectives* 2:21–48.

Jensen, Michael C., and Richard S. Ruback. 1983. "The Market for Corporate Control: The Scientific Evidence." *Journal of Financial Economics* 11:5–50.

Jesse, Edward V., and Aaron C. Johnson, Jr. 1981. *Effectiveness of Federal Marketing Orders for Fruits and Vegetables.* U.S. Department of Agriculture, Economics and Statistics Service, Agricultural Economic Report no. 471.

Jin, Ginger Zhe, and Phillip Leslie. 2003. "The Effects of Disclosure Regulation: Evidence from Restaurants." *Quarterly Journal of Economics* 118:409–51.

Johnson, D. Gale. 1973. *Farm Commodity Programs.* Washington, D.C.: American Enterprise Institute.

Jones, Charles I., and John C. Williams. 1998. "Measuring the Social Return to R&D." *Quarterly Journal of Economics* 113:1119–35.

Jordan, N. John, and Bruce L. Jaffee. 1987. "The Use of Exclusive Territories in the Distribution of Beer: Theoretical and Empirical Observations." *Antitrust Bulletin* 9:275–89.

Jorde, Thomas M., and David J. Teece. 1988. *Innovation, Cooperation, and Antitrust.* Berkeley: University of California, Berkeley, School of Business Administration.

Jorde, Thomas M., and David J. Teece. 1990. "Innovation and Cooperation: Implications for Competition and Antitrust." *Journal of Economic Perspectives* 4:75–96.

Joskow, Paul L. 1973. "Pricing Decisions of Regulated Firms: A Behavioral Approach." *Bell Journal of Economics* 4:118–40.

Joskow, Paul L. 1974. "Inflation and Environmental Concern: Structural Change in the Process of Public Utility Price Regulation." *Journal of Law and Economics* 17:291–328.

Joskow, Paul L. 2000a. "Deregulation and Regulatory Reform in the U.S. Electric Power Sector," in Sam Peltzman and Clifford Winston, eds., *Deregulation of Network Industries: What's Next?* AEI-Brookings Center for Regulatory Studies. Washington, D.C.: Brookings Institute, 113–54.

Joskow, Paul L. 2000b. *Economic Regulation.* Cheltenham, UK: Edward Elgar Publishing.

Joskow, Paul L., and Roger C. Noll. 1981. "Regulation in Theory and Practice: An Overview," in Gary Fromm, ed., *Studies in Public Regulation.* Cambridge, MA: MIT Press.

Joskow, Paul L., and Nancy L. Rose. 1989. "The Effects of Economic Regulation," in Richard Schmalensee and Robert D. Willig, eds., *The Handbook of Industrial Organization.* Amsterdam: North-Holland.

Jovanovic, Boyan. 1982. "Selection and Evolution of Industry." *Econometrica* 50:649–70.

Jovanovic, Boyan. 1983. "Truthful Disclosure of Information." *Bell Journal of Economics* 13:36–44.

Jovanovic, Boyan, and Glenn MacDonald. 1994. "The Life Cycle of a Competitive Industry." *Journal of Political Economy* 104:322–47.

Jovanovic, Boyan, and Peter Rousseau. "Mergers and Technological Change: 1885-1998." Unpublished paper, University of Chicago. May 15, 2001.

Judd, Kenneth L., and Bruce C. Petersen. 1986. "Dynamic Limit Pricing and Internal Finance." *Journal of Economic Theory* 39:368–99.

Just, Richard E., and Wen S. Chern. 1980. "Tomatoes, Technology, and Oligopsony." *Bell Journal of Economics* 11:584–602.

Kahn, Alfred E. 1970. *The Economics of Regulation.* Vol. 1. New York: John Wiley and Sons, Inc.

Kahn, Alfred E. 1975. *The Economics of Regulation.* Vol. 2. New York: John Wiley and Sons, Inc.

Kahn, Alfred E. 1988. "Surprises of Airline Deregulation." *American Economic Review* 78:316–21.

Kahn, Charles. 1986. "The Durable-Goods Monopolist and Consistency with Increasing Costs." *Econometrica* 54:275–94.

Kahnemann, Daniel, Paul Slovic, and Amos Tversky, eds. 1982. *Judgement Under Uncertainty: Heuristics and Biases.* Cambridge: Cambridge University Press.

Kaldor, Nicholas. 1935. "Market Imperfection and Excess Capacity." *Economica* 2:33–50.

Kaldor, Nicholas. 1949–50. "The Economic Aspects of Advertising." *Review of Economic Studies* 18:1–27.

Kalt, Joseph. 1988. "The Political Economy of Protectionism: Tariffs and Retaliation in the Timber Industry," in Robert E. Baldwin, ed., *Trade Policy Issues and Empirical Analysis.* Chicago: University of Chicago Press.

Kamerschen, David R. 1966. "An Estimation of the Welfare Losses for Monopoly in the American Economy." *Western Economic Journal* 4:221–36.

Kamien, Morton I., and Nancy L. Schwartz. 1971. "Limit Pricing and Uncertain Entry." *Econometrica* 39 (May):441–54.

Kamien, Morton I., and Nancy L. Schwartz. 1974. "Product Durability Under Monopoly and Competition." *Econometrica* 42:289–301.

Kamien, Morton I., and Nancy L. Schwartz. 1982. *Market Structure and Innovation.* Cambridge: Cambridge University Press.

Kanafani, Adib, and Theodore E. Keeler. 1989. "New Entrants and Safety," in Leon N. Moses and Ian Savage, eds., *Transportation Safety in an Age of Deregulation.* Oxford: Oxford University Press.

Kandel, Eugene. 1996. "The Right to Return." *Journal of Law and Economics* 39:329–56.

Kaplan, Steven N., ed. 2000. "Mergers and Productivity." National Bureau of Economic Research Conference, University of Chicago.

Kaplan, Steven N., and Jeremy C. Stein. 1993. "The Evolution of Buyout Pricing and Financial Structure in the 1980s." *Quarterly Journal of Economics* (May):313–57.

Kaplan, Steven N., and Michael S. Weisbach. 1992. "The Success of Acquisitions: Evidence from Divestitures." *Journal of Finance* 47:107–38.

Karp, Larry S. 1996. "Depreciation Erodes the Coase Conjecture." *European Economic Review* 40:473–90.

Karp, Larry S., and Jeffrey M. Perloff. 1989a. "Oligopoly in the Rice Export Market." *Review of Economics and Statistics* 71:462–70.

Karp, Larry S., and Jeffrey M. Perloff. 1989b. "Estimating Market Structure and Tax Incidence: The Japanese Television Market." *Journal of Industrial Economics* 37:225–39.

Karp, Larry S., and Jeffrey M. Perloff. 1992. "The Long-Run Value of Inflexibility," in L. Alan Winters, ed., *Trade Flows and Trade Policy After '1992.'* Cambridge: Cambridge University Press.

Karp, Larry S., and Jeffrey M. Perloff. 1993a. "A Dynamic Model of Oligopoly in the Coffee Export Market." *American Journal of Agricultural Economics* 75:448–57.

Karp, Larry S., and Jeffrey M. Perloff. 1993b. "Industrial Policy as an Alternative to Trade Policy: Helping by Hurting." *Review of International Economics* 1:253–62.

Karp, Larry S., and Jeffrey M. Perloff. 1995a. "The Failure of Strategic Industrial Policies Due to the Manipulation by Firms." *International Review of Economics and Finance* 4:1–16.

Karp, Larry S., and Jeffrey M. Perloff. 1995b. "Why Industrial Policies Fail: Limited Commitment." *International Economic Review* 36:887–905.

Karp, Larry S., and Jeffrey M. Perloff. 1996. "The Optimal Suppression of a Low-Cost Technology by a Durable-Good Monopoly." *Rand Journal of Economics* 27:346–64.

Kashyap, Anil. 1995. "Sticky Prices: New Evidence from Retail Catalogues." *Quarterly Journal of Economics* 110:245–74.

Katz, Barbara G., and Joel Owen. 1992. "On the Existence of Franchise Contracts and Some of Their Implications." *International Journal of Industrial Organization* 10:567–93.

Katz, Michael L. 1983. "Nonuniform Pricing, Output, and Welfare under Monopoly." *Review of Economic Studies* 50:37–56.

Katz, Michael L. 1984. "Price Discrimination and Monopolistic Competition." *Econometrica* 52:1453–72.

Katz, Michael L. 1987. "The Welfare Effects of Third-Degree Price Discrimination in Intermediate Goods Markets." *American Economic Review* 77:154–67.

Katz, Michael L. 1989. "Vertical Contractual Relations," in Richard Schmalensee and Robert D. Willig, eds., *The Handbook of Industrial Organization.* Amsterdam: North-Holland.

Katz, Michael L., and Carl Shapiro. 1985a. "On the Licensing of Innovations." *Rand Journal of Economics* 16:504–20.

Katz, Michael L., and Carl Shapiro. 1985b. "Network Externalities, Competition and Compatibility." *American Economic Review* 75:424–40.

Katz, Michael L., and Carl Shapiro. 1986. "How to License Intangible Property." *Quarterly Journal of Economics* 101:567–90.

Katz, Michael L., and Carl Shapiro. 1987. "R&D Rivalry with Licensing or Imitation." *American Economic Review* 77:402–20.

Katz, Michael L., and Carl Shapiro. 1994. "Systems Competition and Network Effects." *Journal of Economic Perspectives* 8:93–115.

Kawai, M., K. Watanabe, and A. Mori. 1992. "Pre-cultural Behaviors Observed in Free-ranging Japanese Monkeys on Koshima Islet over the Past 25 Years." *Primate Report* 32:143–53.

Keeler, Theodore E. 1983. *Railroads, Freight, and Public Policy.* Washington, D.C.: The Brookings Institution.

Keeler, Theodore E. 1989. "Deregulation and Scale Economies in the U.S. Trucking Industry: An Econometric Extension of the Survivor Principle." *Journal of Law and Economics* 32:229–55.

Keeton, William R. 1980. *Equilibrium Credit Rationing.* New York: Garland Press.

Kenney, Roy W., and Benjamin Klein. 1983. "The Economics of Block Booking." *Journal of Law and Economics* 26:491–540.

Kessel, Reuben. 1958. "Price Discrimination in Medicine." *Journal of Law and Economics* 1:20–54.

Kihlstrom, Richard, and Michael Riordan. 1984. "Advertising as a Signal." *Journal of Political Economy* 92:427–50.

Kim, Jae-Cheol. 1985. "The Market for 'Lemons' Reconsidered: A Model of the Used Car Market with Asymmetric Information." *American Economic Review* 75:836–43.

Kindleberger, Charles P. 1986. *The World in Depression, 1929–1939.* Berkeley: University of California Press.

Kitch, Edmund W. 1975. "The Nature and Function of the Patent System." *Journal of Law and Economics* 13:1–37.

Kitch, Edmund W., Marc Isaacson, and Daniel Kaspar. 1971. "The Regulation of Taxicabs in Chicago." *Journal of Law and Economics* 14:285–350.

Klein, Benjamin, Robert G. Crawford, and Armen A. Alchian. 1978. "Vertical Integration, Appropriable Rents, and the Competitive Contracting Process." *Journal of Law and Economics* 21:297–326.

Klein, Benjamin, and Keith Leffler. 1981. "The Role of Market Forces in Assuring Contractual Performance." *Journal of Political Economy* 89:615–41.

Klein, Benjamin, and Kevin M. Murphy. 1988. "Vertical Restraints as Contract Enforcement Mechanisms." *Journal of Law and Economics* 31:265–98.

Klemperer, Paul. 1987. "The Competitiveness of Markets with Switching Costs." *Rand Journal of Economics* 18:138–50.

Klemperer, Paul. 1990. "Competition When Consumers Have Switching Costs: An Overview." The 1990 *Review of Economic Studies* Lecture to the Royal Economic Society Conference (Nottingham, UK), St. Catherine's College and Institute of Economics & Statistics, Oxford University.

Klemperer, Paul. 1999. "Auction Theory: A Guide to the Literature." *Journal of Economic Surveys* 13:227–86.

Klemperer, Paul. 2001. "Why Every Economist Should Learn Some Auction Theory" in *Advances in Economics and Econometrics: Invited Lecture to Eighth World Congress of the Econometric Society.*

Klepper, Steven, and Elizabeth Grady. 1990. "The Evolution of New Industries and the Determants of Market Structure." *Rand Journal of Economics* 21:27–44.

Klepper, Steven, and Kenneth Simons. 2000. "The Making of an Oligopoly: Firm Survival and Technological Change in the Evolution of the U.S. Tire Industry." *Journal of Political Economy* 108:728–60.

Klevorick, Alvin K. 1971. "The 'Optimal' Fair Rate of Return." *Bell Journal of Economics* 2:122–53.

Koenker, Roger W., and Martin K. Perry. 1981. "Product Differentiation, Monopolistic Competition, and Public Policy." *Bell Journal of Economics* 12:217–31.

Koller, Roland L. 1971. "The Myth of Predatory Pricing." *Antitrust Law and Economics Review* 3:105–23.

Kolstad, Charles D., and Frank A. Wolak, Jr. 1983. "Competition in Interregional Taxation: The Case of Western Coal." *Journal of Political Economy* 91:443–60.

Kolstad, Charles D., and Frank A. Wolak, Jr. 1985. "Strategy and Market Structure in Western Coal Taxation." *Review of Economics and Statistics* 67:239–49.

Kolstad, Charles D., and Frank A. Wolak, Jr. 1986. "Conjectural Variation and the Indeterminacy of Duopolistic Equilibria." *Canadian Journal of Economics* 19:656–77.

Koopmans, Tjalling, and Martin Beckmann. 1957. "Assignment Problems and the Location of Economic Activities." *Econometrica* 25:53–76.

Kotowitz, Yehuda, and G. Frank Mathewson. 1986. "Advertising and Consumer Learning," in Pauline M. Ippolito and David T. Scheffman, eds., *Empirical Approaches to Consumer Protection Economics.* Federal Trade Commission. Washington, D.C.: U.S. Government Printing Office, 109–34.

Krattenmaker, Thomas G., and Steven C. Salop. 1986. "Anticompetitive Exclusion: Raising Rivals' Costs to Achieve Power Over Price." *Yale Law Journal* 96:209–93.

Kreps, David M., Paul Milgrom, John Roberts, and Robert Wilson. 1982. "Rational Cooperation in the Finitely Repeated Prisoners' Dilemma." *Journal of Economic Theory* 27:245–52.

Kreps, David M., and José Scheinkman. 1983. "Quality Precommitment and Bertrand Competition Yield Cournot Outcomes." *Bell Journal of Economics* 14:326–37.

Kreps, David M., and A. Michael Spence. 1984. "Modelling the Role of History in Industrial Organization," in George Feiwel, ed., *Contemporary Issues in Modern Microeconomics.* London: Macmillan.

Kreps, David M., and Robert Wilson. 1982a. "Reputation and Imperfect Information." *Journal of Economic Theory* 27:253–79.

Kreps, David M., and Robert Wilson. 1982b. "Sequential Equilibrium." *Econometrica* 50:863–94.

Krugman, Paul R. 1984. "The U.S. Response to Industrial Targeting." *Brookings Papers on Economic Activity* 77–121.

Krugman, Paul R. 1989. "Industrial Organization and International Trade," in Richard Schmalensee and Robert D. Willig, eds., *The Handbook of Industrial Organization.* Amsterdam: North-Holland.

Krugman, Paul R., and Maurice Obstfeld. 1997. *International Economics: Theory and Policy.* Reading, MA: Addison Wesley Longman.

Kumar, Praveen. 2002. "Price and Quality Discrimination in Durable Goods Monopoly with Resale Trading." *International Journal of Industrial Organization* 20:1313–39.

Kwerel, Evan R. 1980. "Economic Welfare and the Production of Information by a Monopolist: The Case of Drug Testing." *Bell Journal of Economics* 11:505–18.

Kwoka, John E., Jr. 1977. "Pricing Under Federal Milk Market Regulation." *Economic Inquiry* 15:367–84.

Kwoka, John E., Jr. 1979. "The Effect of Market Share Distribution on Industry Performance." *Review of Economics and Statistics* 61:101–9.

Kwoka, John E., Jr. 1984. "Advertising and the Price and Quality of Optometric Services." *American Economic Review* 74:211–16.

Kwoka, John E., Jr., and David Ravenscraft. 1985. "Cooperation vs. Rivalry: Price-Cost Margins by Line of Business." Working Paper no. 127, U.S. Federal Trade Commission.

Kwoka, John E., Jr., and Lawrence J. White, eds. 2004. *The Antitrust Revolution: Economics, Competition, and Policy,* fourth edition. New York: Oxford University Press.

Lach, Saul, and Daniel Tsiddon. 1996. "Staggering and Synchronization in Price Setting: Evidence from Multi-Product Firms." *American Economic Review* 86:1175–96.

Lacko, James M. 1986. *Product Quality and Information in the Used Car Market.* Federal Trade Commission, Bureau of Economics Staff Report. Washington, D.C.: U.S. Government Printing Office.

Laffer, Arthur B. 1969. "Vertical Integration by Corporations, 1929–1965." *Review of Economics and Statistics* 51:91–93.

Lafferty, Ronald N., Robert H. Lande, and John B. Kirkwood, eds. 1984. *Impact Evaluations of Federal Trade Commission Vertical Restraint Cases.* Washington, D.C.: Bureau of Competition, Bureau of Economics, Federal Trade Commission (August).

Laffont, Jean-Jacques, and Jean Tirole. 1993. *A Theory of Incentives in Procurement and Regulation.* Cambridge, MA: MIT Press.

Laffont, Jean-Jacques, Patrick Rey, and Jean Tirole. 1998a. "Network Competition: I. Overview and Non-Discriminatory Pricing." *Rand Journal of Economics* 29:1–37.

Laffont, Jean-Jacques, Patrick Rey, and Jean Tirole. 1998b. "Network Competition: II. Price Discrimination." *Rand Journal of Economics.* 29:38–56.

Lafontaine, Francine. 1992. "Agency Theory and Franchising: Some Empirical Results." *Rand Journal of Economics* 23:263–83.

Lafontaine, Francine. 1995. "Pricing Decisions in Franchised Chains: A Look at the Restaurant and Fast Food Industry." National Bureau of Economic Research Working Paper 5247.

LaFrance, Jeffrey T., and Harry de Gorter. 1985. "Regulation in a Dynamic Market: The U.S. Dairy Industry." *American Journal of Agricultural Economics* 67:821–32.

Lambin, Jean Jacques. 1976. *Advertising, Competition and Market Conduct in Oligopoly over Time.* Amsterdam: North-Holland.

Lamm, R. McFall. 1981. "Prices and Concentration in the Food Retailing Industry." *Journal of Industrial Economics* 30:67–78.

Lancaster, Kelvin J. 1966. "A New Approach to Consumer Theory." *Journal of Political Economy* 74:132–57.

Lancaster, Kelvin J. 1971. *Variety, Equity and Efficiency.* New York: Columbia University Press.

Lancaster, Kelvin J. 1979. *Consumer Demand: A New Approach.* New York: Columbia University Press.

Landes, William M. 1983. "Optimal Sanctions for Antitrust Violations." *University of Chicago Law Review* 50:652–78.

Landes, William M., and Richard A. Posner. 1979. "Should Indirect Purchasers Have Standing to Sue Under the Antitrust Laws? An Economic Analysis of the Rule of *Illinois Brick.*" *University of Chicago Law Review* 46:602–35.

Landes, William M., and Richard A. Posner. 1981. "Market Power in Antitrust Cases." *Harvard Law Review* 95:937–96.

Landes, William M., and Richard A. Posner. 1987. "Trademark Law: An Economic Perspective." *Journal of Law and Economics* 30:265–309.

Landes, William M., and Richard A. Posner. 2003. *The Economic Structure of Intellectual Property Law.* Cambridge, MA: Harvard University Press.

Lanjouw, Jean O. 1998. "Patent Protection in the Shadow of Infringement: Simulation Estimations of Patent Value." *Review of Economic Studies* 65:671–710.

Lanjouw, Jean O., and Iain M. Cockburn. 2001. "New Pills for Poor People? Empirical Evidence After GATT." *World Development* 29:265–89.

Lapham, Lewis H., Michael Pollan, and Eric Etheridge. 1987. *Harper's Index Book.* New York: Henry Holt and Company.

Lau, Lawrence J. 1982. "On Identifying the Degree of Competitiveness from Industry Price and Output Data." *Economics Letters* 10:93–99.

Lave, Lester B. 1962. "An Empirical Approach to the Prisoners' Dilemma Game." *Quarterly Journal of Economics* 75:424–36.

Lave, Lester B. 1963. "The Value of Better Weather Information to the Raisin Industry." *Econometrica* 31:151–64.

Lavey, Warren, and Dennis W. Carlton. 1983. "Economic Goals and Remedies of the AT&T Modified Judgment." *Georgetown Law Review* 17:1497–1518.

Law, Stephen M., and James F. Nolan. 2002. "Measuring the Impact of Regulation: A Study of Canadian Basic Cable Television." *Review of Industrial Organization* 21:231–49.

Leahy, Arthur. 1997. "Advertising and Concentration: A Survey of the Empirical Evidence." *Quarterly Journal of Business and Economics* 26:35–50.

Lean, David F., Jonathan D. Ogur, and Robert P. Rogers. 1982. *Competition and Collusion in Electrical Equipment Markets: An Economic Assessment.* Washington, D.C.: Federal Trade Commission.

LeBlanc, Greg. 1992. "Signalling Strength: Limit Pricing and Predatory Pricing." *Rand Journal of Economics* 23:493–506.

Lederer, Phillip J., and Arthur P. Hurter, Jr. 1986. "Competition of Firms: Discriminatory Pricing and Location." *Econometrica* 54:623–40.

Lee, Lung-Fei, and Robert H. Porter. 1984. "Switching Regression Models with Imperfect Sample Separation Information with an Application on Cartel Stability." *Econometrica* 52:391–418.

Lee, Tenpao, C. Phillip Baumel, and Patricia Harris. 1987. "Market Structure, Conduct, and Performance of the Class I Railroad Industry, 1971–1984." *Transportation Journal* 26:54–66.

Lee, Tom, and Louis Wilde. 1980. "Market Structure and Innovation: A Reformulation." *Quarterly Journal of Economics* 94:429–36.

Leibenstein, Harvey. 1966. "Allocative Inefficiency vs. X-Inefficiency." *American Economic Review* 56:392–415.

Leidy, Michael P., and Bernard M. Hoekman. 1990. "Production Effects of Price and Cost-Based Antidumping Law Under Flexible Exchange Rates." *Canadian Journal of Economics* 24:873–95.

Leland, Hayne E. 1979a. "Quacks, Lemons, and Licensing: A Theory of Minimum Quality Standards." *Journal of Political Economy* 87:1328–46.

Leland, Hayne E. 1979b. "Minimum Quality Standards in Markets with Asymmetric Information," in Simon Rottenberg, ed., *Occupational Licensure.* Washington, D.C.: American Enterprise Institute.

Leontief, Wassily. 1946. "The Price Theory of the Guaranteed Annual Wage Contract." *Journal of Political Economy* 54:76–80.

Lerner, Abba P. 1934. "The Concept of Monopoly and the Measurement of Monopoly Power." *Review of Economic Studies* 1:157–75.

Lerner, Abba P. 1936. "The Symmetry Between Import and Export Taxes." *Economica* 3:306–13.

Lerner, Joshua, and Jean Tirole. 2002a. "Some Simple Economics of Open Source." *Journal of Industrial Economics* 52:197–234.

Lerner, Joshua, and Jean Tirole. 2002b. "Efficient Patent Pools." National Bureau of Economic Research Working Paper 9175.

Lesser, William H., and W. Keith Bryant. 1980. "The Influence of Consumer Price Information on Retail Pricing and Consumer Behavior: Comment." *American Journal of Agricultural Economics* 62:265–66.

Levenstein, Margaret. 1993. "Vertical Restraints in the Bromine Cartel: The Role of Distributors in Facilitating Collusion." National Bureau of Economic Research Working Paper Series on Historical Factors in Long Run Growth: 49.

Levin, Richard C., Alvin K. Klevorick, Richard R. Nelson, and Sidney G. Winter. 1987. "Appropriating the Returns from Industrial Research and Development." *Brookings Papers on Economic Activity* 3: 783–820.

Levin, Sharon G., Stanford L. Levin, and John B. Meisel. 1987. "A Dynamic Analysis of the Adoption of a New

Technology: The Case of Optical Scanners." *Review of Economics and Statistics* 69:12–17.

Levy, Daniel, Mark Bergen, Shantanu Dutta, and Robert Venable. 1997. "The Magnitude of Menu Costs: Direct Evidence from Large Supermarket Chains." *Quarterly Journal of Economics* 112:791–826.

Levy, Daniel, and Andrew Young. 2002. "The Real Thing: Nominal Rigidity of the Nickel Coke, 1886-1959." Working paper.

Li, Wei, and Lixim Xu. 2002. "The Impact of Privatization and Competition in the Telecommunications Sector Around the World." Working Paper 02-13, University of Virginia, Warden Graduate School of Business.

Lichtenberg, Frank R. 1987. "The Effect of Government Funding on Private Industrial Research and Development: A Re-Assessment." *The Journal of Industrial Economics* 36:97–104.

Lichtenberg, Frank R. 1992. "Industrial De-Diversification and Its Consequences for Productivity." *Journal of Economic Behavior and Organization* 18:427–38.

Lichtenberg, Frank R., and Donald Siegel. 1987. "Productivity and Changes in Ownership of Manufacturing Plants." *Brookings Papers on Economic Activity* 3:643–83.

Lieberman, Marvin B. 1987. "Patents, Learning by Doing, and Market Structure in the Chemical Processing Industries." *International Journal of Industrial Organization* 5:257–76.

Lieberman, Marvin B. 1990. "Exit from Declining Industries: 'Shakeout' or 'Stakeout'?" *Rand Journal of Economics* 21:538–54.

Lieberman, Marvin B. 1991. "Determinants of Vertical Integration: An Empirical Test," *Journal of Industrial Economics* 39:451–66.

Liebowitz, Stanley J. 1982a. "Durability, Market Structure, and New-Used Goods Models." *American Economic Review* 72:816–24.

Liebowitz, Stanley J. 1982b. "What Do Census Price-Cost Margins Measure?" *Journal of Law and Economics* 25:231–46.

Liebowitz, Stanley J., and Stephen E. Margolis. 1990. "The Fable of the Keys." *Journal of Law and Economics* 33:1–26.

Liebowitz, Stanley J., and Stephen E. Margolis. 1994. "Network Externality: An Uncommon Tragedy." *Journal of Economic Perspectives* 8:133–50.

Linnemer, Laurent. 2002. "Price and Advertising as Signals of Quality When Some Consumers Are Informed." *International Journal of Industrial Organization* 20:931–47.

Lipsey, Richard G., and Peter O. Steiner. 1981. *Economics*, 6th ed. New York: Harper & Row.

Liu, Donald J., and Olan D. Forker. 1988. "Generic Fluid Milk Advertising, Demand Expansion, and Supply Response: The Case of New York City." *American Journal of Agricultural Economics* 70:229–36.

Livesay, Harold C., and Patrick C. Porter. 1969. "Vertical Integration in American Manufacturing, 1899–1948." *Journal of Economic History* 29:494–500.

Lopatka, John, and Paul Godek. 1992. "Another Look at *Alcoa:* Raising Rivals' Costs Does Not Improve the View." *Journal of Law and Economics* 21:538–54.

Lopez, R. E. 1984. "Measuring Oligopoly Power and Production Responses of the Canadian Food Processing Industry." *Journal of Agricultural Economics* 35:219–30.

Lott, John R., Jr. 1999. *Are Predatory Commitments Credible: What Should the Courts Believe?* Chicago: University of Chicago Press.

Lott, John R., Jr., and Russell Roberts. 1991. "A Guide to the Pitfalls of Identifying Price Discrimination." *Economic Inquiry* 29:14–23.

Loury, Glenn C. 1979. "Market Structure and Innovation." *Quarterly Journal of Economics* 93:395–410.

Lown, Cara, Carol Osler, Philip Strahan, and Amir Sufi. 2000. "The Changing Landscape of the Financial Services Industry: What Lies Ahead." *Federal Reserve Bank of New York Economic Policy Review* 6:36–59.

Lucas, Robert E., Jr. 1981. *Studies in Business-Cycle Theory.* Cambridge, MA: MIT Press.

Luce, R. Duncan, and Howard Raiffa. 1957. *Games and Decisions.* New York: John Wiley and Sons.

Luksetich, William, and Harold Lofgren. 1976. "Price, Advertising, and Liquor Prices." *Industrial Organization Review* 4:13–25.

Lustgarten, Steven H. 1975a. "Administered Inflation: A Reappraisal." *Economic Inquiry* 13:191–206.

Lustgarten, Steven H. 1975b. "The Impact of Buyer Concentration in Manufacturing Industries." *Review of Economics and Statistics* 57:125–32.

Lustgarten, Steven H., and Stavros B. Thomadakis. 1980. "Valuation Response to New Information: A Test of Resource Mobility and Market Structure." *Journal of Political Economy* 88:977–93.

Lynch, Michael, Ross Miller, Charles R. Plott, and Russell Porter. 1986. *Experimental Studies of Markets with Buyers Ignorant of Quality Before Purchase: When Do 'Lemons' Drive Out High-Quality Products?* Bureau of Economics, Federal Trade Commission. Washington, D.C.: U.S. Government Printing Office.

Lynk, William J. 1999. "Tying and Exclusive Dealing: *Jefferson Parish Hospital v. Hyde* (1984)," in John E. Kwoka, Jr. and Lawrence J. White, eds., *The Antitrust Revolution: Economics, Competition, and Policy.* New York: Oxford University Press.

Lyons, Bruce. 2002. "Could Politicians Be More Right Than Economists? A Theory of Merger Standards." Working Paper CCR 02-1, University of East Anglia, Norwich, UK.

MacAvoy, Paul W. 1965. *The Economic Effects of Regulation.* Cambridge, MA: MIT Press.

MacAvoy, Paul W. 1979. *The Regulated Industries and the Economy.* New York: W.W. Norton.

MacAvoy, Paul W. 1992. "Deregulation by Means of Antitrust Divestiture: How Well Has It Worked in the Telephone Industry?" *Regulation* 15:88–92.

MacAvoy, Paul W. 2000. *The Natural Gas Market: Sixty Years of Regulation and Deregulation.* New Haven, CT: Yale University Press.

Maccini, Louis J. 1973. "On Optimal Delivery Lags." *Journal of Economic Theory* 6:107–25.

MacDonald, James M. 1987. "Competition and Rail Rates for the Shipment of Corn, Soybeans, and Wheat." *Rand Journal of Economics* 18:151–63.

MacDonald, James M. 2000. "Demand, Information, and Competition: Why Do Food Prices Fall at Seasonal Demand Peaks?" *Journal of Industrial Economics* 48:27–45.

MacKie-Mason, Jeffrey K., and Robert S. Pindyck. 1986. "Cartel Theory and Cartel Experience in International Minerals Markets," in Richard L. Gordon, Henry D. Jacoby, and Martin B. Zimmerman, eds., *Energy: Markets & Regulation: Essays in Honor of M. A. Adelman.* Cambridge, MA: MIT Press.

Maddigan, Ruth J. 1981. "The Measurement of Vertical Integration." *Review of Economics and Statistics* 93:328–35.

Madhavan, Ananth N., Robert T. Masson, and William H. Lesser. 1994. "Cooperation for Monopolization? An Empirical Analysis of Cartelization." *Review of Economics and Statistics* 76:161–75.

Maggi, Giovanni. 1996. "Strategic Trade Policies with Endogenous Mode of Competition." *American Economic Review* 86:237–58.

Mairesse, Jacques. 1991. "R&D and Productivity: A Survey of Econometric Studies at the Firm Level." *STI Review* 8:9–43.

Malinvaud, Edmund. 1979. *The Theory of Unemployment Reconsidered.* New York: Halsted Press.

Mallela, Parthasaradhi, and Babu Nahata. 1980. "Theory of Vertical Control with Variable Proportions." *Journal of Political Economy* 88:1009–25.

Maloney, Michael T., Robert E. McCormick, and Robert D. Tollison. 1979. "Achieving Cartel Profits Through Unionization." *Southern Economic Journal* 46:628–34.

Mankiw, N. Gregory. 1985. "Small Menu Costs and Large Business Cycles: A Macroeconomic Model." *Quarterly Journal of Economics* 100:529–38.

Mankiw, N. Gregory, and David Roemer, eds. 1991. *New Keynesian Economics,* vols. 1 and 2. Cambridge, MA: MIT Press.

Mann, H. Michael. 1966. "Seller Concentration, Barriers to Entry, and the Rates of Return in Thirty Industries, 1950–1960." *Review of Economics and Statistics* 48:290–307.

Mann, H. Michael, John A. Henning, and James W. Meehan, Jr. 1967. "Advertising and Concentration: An Empirical Investigation." *Journal of Industrial Economics* 16:34–45.

Mansfield, Edwin. 1968. *Industrial Research and Technological Innovation: An Econometric Analysis.* New York: W. W. Norton & Co.

Mansfield, Edwin. 1984. "R&D and Innovation: Some Empirical Findings," in Zvi Griliches, ed., *R&D, Patents and Productivity.* Chicago: University of Chicago Press.

Mansfield, Edwin. 1985. "How Rapidly Does New Industrial Technology Leak Out?" *Journal of Industrial Economics* 34:217–23.

Mansfield, Edwin. 1998. "Academic Research and Industrial Innovation: An Update of Empirical Findings." *Research Policy* 26:773–76.

Mansfield, Edwin, John Rapoport, Anthony Romeo, Samuel Wagner, and George Beardsley. 1977. "Social and Private Rates of Return from Industrial Innovations." *Quarterly Journal of Economics* 91:221–40.

Mansfield, Edwin, Anthony Romeo, Mark Schwartz, David Teece, Samuel Wagner, and Peter Brach. 1982. *Technology Transfer, Productivity, and Economic Policy.* New York: W. W. Norton & Co.

Mansfield, Edwin, Mark Schwartz, and Samuel Wagner. 1981. "Imitation Costs and Patents: An Empirical Study." *Economic Journal* 91:907–18.

March, James G., and Herbert A. Simon. 1958. *Organizations.* New York: John Wiley and Sons.

Markusen, James R., and Anthony J. Venables. 1988. "Trade Policy with Increasing Returns and Imperfect Competition: Contradictory Results from Competing Assumptions." *The Journal of International Economics* 24:299–316.

Marris, Robin. 1964. *The Economic Theory of Managerial Capitalism.* Glencoe, IL: Free Press of Glencoe.

Marshall, Alfred. 1920. *Principles of Economics.* Philadelphia: Porcupine Press.

Martin, Robert E. 1982. "Monopoly Power and the Recycling of Raw Materials." *Journal of Industrial Economics* 30:405–19.

Martin, Robert E. 1988. "Franchising and Risk Management." *American Economic Review* 78:954–68.

Martin, Steven. "Oligopoly Limit Pricing: Strategic Substitutes, Strategic Complements." *International Journal of Industrial Organization* 13:14–65.

Marvel, Howard P. 1978. "Competition and Price Levels in the Retail Gasoline Market." *Review of Economics and Statistics* 60:252–58.

Marvel, Howard P. 1982. "Exclusive Dealing." *Journal of Law and Economics* 25:1–25.

Marvel, Howard P., and Stephen McCafferty. 1984. "Resale Price Maintenance and Quality Certification." *Rand Journal of Economics* 15:346–59.

Mas-Collel, Andreu, Michael Dennis Whinston, and Jerry Green. 1995. *Microeconomic Theory*. New York: Oxford University Press.

Maskin, Eric, and John Riley. 1984. "Monopoly with Incomplete Information." *Rand Journal of Economics* 14:171–96.

Maskin, Eric, and Jean Tirole. 1988a. "A Theory of Dynamic Oligopoly, I: Overview and Quantity Competition with Large Fixed Costs." *Econometrica* 56:549–69.

Maskin, Eric, and Jean Tirole. 1988b. "A Theory of Dynamic Oligopoly, II: Price Competition, Kinked Demand Curves, and Edgeworth Cycles. *Econometrica* 56:571–99.

Mason, Edward S. 1939. "Price and Production Policies of Large-Scale Enterprise." *American Economic Review,* supp. 29:61–74.

Mason, Edward S. 1949. "The Current State of the Monopoly Problem in the United States." *Harvard Law Review* 62:1265–85.

Masson, Robert T., and Joseph Shaanan. 1984. "Social Costs of Oligopoly and the Value of Competition." *Economic Journal* 94:520–35.

Masten, Scott E. 1984. "The Organization of Production: Evidence from the Aerospace Industry." *Journal of Law and Economics* 27:403–17.

Masten, Scott E., and Edward Snyder. 1993. "United States v. United Shoe Machinery Corporation: On the Merits," *Journal of Law and Economics* 36:33–70.

Mathewson, G. Frank, and Ralph A. Winter. 1984. "An Economic Theory of Vertical Restraints." *Rand Journal of Economics* 15:27–38.

Mathewson, G. Frank, and Ralph A. Winter. 1997. "Tying as a Response to Demand Uncertainty." *Rand Journal of Economics* 28:566–83.

Matthews, Steven, and Andrew Postlewaite. 1985. "Quality Testing and Disclosure." *Rand Journal of Economics* 16:328–40.

Matutes, Carmen. 1985. "Studies in the Theory of Cartels and Product Innovation." Unpublished University of California, Berkeley, Ph. D. dissertation.

Matutes, Carmen, and Pierre Regibeau. 1988. "Mix and Match: Product Compatibility Without Externalities." *Rand Journal of Economics* 19:221–34.

Matutes, Carmen, and Pierre Regibeau. 1992. "Compatibility and Bundling of Complementary Goods in a Duopoly." *Journal of Industrial Economics* 40:37–54.

Maurizi, Alex R. 1972. "The Effect of Laws Against Price Advertising: The Case of Retail Gasoline." *Western Economic Journal* 10:321–29.

Maynes, Scott E., and Terje Assum. 1982. "Informationally Imperfect Consumer Markets: Empirical Findings and Policy Implications." *The Journal of Consumer Affairs* 16:62–87.

Mazzeo, Michael. 2002. "Product Choice and Oligopoly Market Structure." *Rand Journal of Economics* 33:221–42.

McAfee, R. Preston, and John McMillan. 1987. "Auctions and Bidding." *Journal of Economic Literature* 25:699–738.

McAfee, R. Preston, John McMillan, and Michael Whinston. 1989. "Multi-Product Monopoly, Commodity Bundling, and Correlation of Values." *Quarterly Journal of Economics* 103:371–83.

McAfee, R. Preston, and Michael Williams. 1992. "Horizontal Mergers and Antitrust Policy." *Journal of Industrial Economics* 40:181–87.

McAllister, Henry. 1961. "Government Price Statistics." Hearings before the Subcommittee on Economic Statistics of the Joint Economic Committee, 87th Cong., 1st Session. Washington, D.C.: U.S. Government Printing Office.

McConnell, J. D. 1968. "The Development of Brand Loyalty: An Experimental Study." *Journal of Marketing Research* 5:13–19.

McCorriston, Steve. 1993. "The Welfare Implications of Oligopoly." *European Review of Agricultural Economics* 20:1–17.

McCracken, Vicki A., Robert D. Boynton, and Brian F. Blake. 1982. "The Impact of Comparative Food Price Information on Consumers and Grocery Retailers: Some Preliminary Findings of a Field Experiment." *The Journal of Consumer Affairs* 16:224–39.

McFarland, Henry. 1987. "Did Railroad Deregulation Lead to Monopoly Pricing? An Application of Q." *Journal of Business* 60:385–400.

McFarland, Henry. 1989. "The Effect of U.S. Railroad Deregulation on Shipper, Labor, and Capital." Economic

Analysis Group Discussion Paper EAG 89–4. Washington, D.C.: Antitrust Division, U.S. Department of Justice.

McGee, John S. 1958. "Predatory Price Cutting: The Standard Oil (N.J.) Case." *Journal of Law and Economics* 1:37–69.

McGee, John S. 1966. "Patent Exploitation: Some Economic and Legal Problems." *Journal of Law and Economics* 9:135–62.

McGuire, Paul, and Ariel Pakes. 1994. "Computing Markov-Perfect Nash Equilibria—Numerical Implications of a Dynamic Differentiated Product Model." *Rand Journal of Economics* 25:555–89.

McKay, D. J. 1977. "Two Essays on the Economics of Electricity Supply." Ph.D. dissertation, California Institute of Technology.

McKenzie, Richard B., and Norman Keith Womer. 1991. "The Impact of the Airline Deregulation Process on Air-Travel Safety." Washington University Center for the Study of American Business Working Paper 143.

McNeil, Kenneth, John R. Nevin, David M. Trubek, Richard E. Miller, and Lauren Edelman. 1978. "Market Discrimination Against the Poor and the Impact of Consumer Disclosure Laws: The Used Car Industry." Institute for Research on Poverty Discussion Paper no. 486-78, University of Wisconsin-Madison.

Mead, Walter J. 1979. "The Performance of Government Energy Regulation." *American Economic Review* 69:352–56.

Means, Gardiner C. 1935. "Industrial Prices and Their Relative Inflexibility." Senate Document 13, 74th Congress, 1st session. Washington, D.C.: U.S. Government Printing Office.

Means, Gardiner C.. 1972. "The Administered Price Thesis Reconfirmed." *American Economic Review* 63:292–306.

Megginson, William, and Jeffrey Netter. 2001. "From State to Market: A Survey of Empirical Studies on Privatization." *Journal of Economic Literature* 39:321–89.

Meyer, John R., Clinton J. Oster, Jr., and John S. Strong. 1987a. "Airline Financial Performance Since Deregulation," in John R. Meyer and Clinton V. Oster, Jr., eds., *Deregulation and the Future of Intercity Passenger Travel.* Cambridge, MA: MIT Press.

Meyer, John R., Clinton J. Oster, Jr., and John S. Strong. 1987b. "The Effect on Travelers: Fares and Service," in John R. Meyer and Clinton V. Oster, Jr., eds., *Deregulation and the Future of Intercity Passenger Travel.* Cambridge, MA: MIT Press.

Milgrom, Paul. 1981. "Good News and Bad News: Representation Theorems and Applications." *Bell Journal of Economics* 12:380–91.

Milgrom, Paul, and John Roberts. 1982a. "Limit Pricing and Entry Under Incomplete Information: An Equilibrium Analysis." *Econometrica* 50:443–59.

Milgrom, Paul, and John Roberts. 1982b. "Predation, Reputation and Entry Deterrence." *Journal of Economic Theory* 27:280–312.

Milgrom, Paul, and John Roberts. 1986. "Price and Advertising Signals of Product Quality." *Journal of Political Economy* 94:796–821.

Miller, Richard A. 1969. "Market Structure and Industrial Performance: Relation of Profit Rate to Concentration, Advertising Intensity, and Diversity." *Journal of Industrial Economics* 17:104–18.

Mills, David E., and Laurence Schumann. 1985. "Industry Structure with Fluctuating Demand." *American Economic Review* 75:758–67.

Mills, Edwin. 1962. *Prices, Output and Inventory Policy.* New York: John Wiley and Sons.

Mills, Frederick C. 1927. *The Behavior of Prices.* New York: National Bureau of Economic Research.

Mills, Frederick C. 1936. *Prices in Recession and Recovery.* New York: National Bureau of Economic Research.

Milyo, Jeffrey, and Joel Waldfogel. 1999. "The Effect of Price Advertising on Prices: Evidence in the Wake of 44 *Liquormart.*" *American Economic Review* 89:1081–96.

Minkler, Alanson P., and Timothy A. Park. 1994. "Asset Specificity and Vertical Integration in Franchising." *Review of Industrial Organization* 9:409–23.

Mirrlees, James. 1971. "An Exploration in the Theory of Optimum Income Taxation." *Review of Economic Studies* 38:175–208.

Miwa, Yoshiro. 1996. *Firms and Industrial Organization in Japan.* New York: New York University Press.

Modigliani, Franco. 1958. "New Developments on the Oligopoly Front." *Journal of Political Economy* 66:215–32.

Monroe, Kent B. 1976. "The Influence of Price Differences and Brand Familiarity on Brand Preferences." *Journal of Consumer Research* 3:42–49.

Monteverde, Kirk, and David J. Teece. 1982. "Appropriable Rents and Quasi-Vertical Integration." *Journal of Law and Economics* 25:403–18.

Moore, Thomas Gale. 1986. "U.S. Airline Deregulation: Its Effect on Passengers, Capital, and Labor." *Journal of Law and Economics* 29:1–28.

Morris, Scot. 1991. *The Emperor Who Ate the Bible and More Strange Facts and Useless Information.* New York: Doubleday.

Morrison, Steven A., and Clifford Winston. 1986. *The Economic Effects of Airline Deregulation.* Washington, D.C.: Brookings Institution.

Morrison, Steven A., and Clifford Winston. 1990. "The Dynamics of Airline Pricing and Competition." *American Economic Review* 80:389–93.

Mortimer, Julie. 2002. "The Effects of Revenue Sharing Contracts on Welfare in Vertically Separated Markets: Evidence from the Video Rental Industry." Unpublished.

Morton, Fiona. 1997. "Entry and Predation: British Shipping Cartels 1879-1929." *Journal of Economics and Management Strategy* 6:679–724.

Moser, Petra. 2003. "How Do Patent Laws Influence Innovation? Evidence from Nineteenth-Century World Fairs." National Bureau of Economic Research Working Paper 9909.

Mueller, Dennis C. 1985. *Profits in the Long Run.* Cambridge: Cambridge University Press.

Mueller, Dennis C. 1997. "Merger Policy in the United States: A Reconsideration." *Review of Industrial Organization* 12:655–85.

Mueller, Willard F., and Frederick E. Geithman. 1991. "An Empirical Test of the Free Rider and Market Power Hypotheses." *Review of Economics and Statistics,* 73:301–8.

Muris, Timothy J., and Fred S. McChesney. 1979. "Advertising and the Price and Quality of Legal Services: The Case for Legal Clinics." *American Bar Foundation Research Journal* 1:179–207.

Mussa, Michael, and Sherwin Rosen. 1978. "Monopoly and Product Quality." *Journal of Economic Theory* 18:301–17.

Myerson, Roger B. 1991. *Game Theory: Analysis of Conflict.* Cambridge, MA: Harvard University Press.

Nadiri, M. Ishaq, and Sherwin Rosen. 1973. *A Disequilibrium Model of the Demand for Factors of Production.* New York: National Bureau of Economic Research and Columbia University Press.

Nalebuff, Barry. 2004. "GE—Honeywell (2001)," in John E. Kwoka and Lawrence J. White, eds., *The Antitrust Revolution,* 4th ed. Oxford: Oxford University Press.

Narasimhan, Chakravarthi. 1984. "A Price Discrimination Theory of Coupons." *Marketing Science* 3:128–47.

Nash, John F. 1951. "Non-Cooperative Games." *Annals of Mathematics* 54:286–95.

Neary, J. Peter. 1991. "Export Subsidies and Price Competition," in Elhanan Helpman and Assaf Razin, eds., *International Trade and Industrial Policy.* Cambridge, MA: MIT Press.

Nelson, Jon P. 2003. "Advertising Bans, Monopoly, and Alcohol Demand: Testing for Substitution Effects Using State Panel Data." *Review of Industrial Organization* 22:1–25.

Nelson, Phillip. 1970. "Information and Consumer Behavior." *Journal of Political Economy* 78:311–29.

Nelson, Phillip. 1974. "Advertising as Information." *Journal of Political Economy* 81:729–54.

Nelson, Ralph. 1959. *Merger Movement in American Industry, 1895-1956.* Princeton, NJ: Princeton University Press.

Nelson, Richard. 1959. "The Simple Economics of Basic Research." *Journal of Political Economy* 67:297–306.

Nelson, Richard R., and Sidney G. Winter. 1982. "The Schumpeterian Tradeoff Revisited." *American Economic Review* 73:114–32.

Nevo, Aviv. 2000. "A Practitioner's Guide to Estimation of Random-Coefficients Logit Models of Demand." *Journal of Economics and Management Strategy* 98:513–48.

Nevo, Aviv. 2001. "Measuring Market Power in the Ready-to-Eat Cereal Industry." *Econometrica* 69:307–42.

Nichols, Len M. 1985. "Advertising and Economic Welfare." *American Economic Review* 75:213–18.

Noel, Michael. 2001. "Edgeworth Price Cycles, Cost-based Pricing and Sticky Pricing in Retail Gasoline Markets." Unpublished, working paper, University of California, San Diego.

Noether, Monica. 1986. "The Effect of Government Policy Changes on the Supply of Physicians: Expansion of a Competitive Fringe." *Journal of Law and Economics* 29:231–62.

Noll, Roger G. 1989. "Economic Perspectives on the Politics of Regulation," in Richard Schmalensee and Robert D. Willig, eds., *The Handbook of Industrial Organization.* Amsterdam: North-Holland.

Noll, Roger G., and Bruce M. Owen. 1994. "The Anticompetitive Uses of Regulation: *U.S. v. AT&T* (1982)," in John E. Kwoka, Jr. and Lawrence J. White, eds., *The Antitrust Revolution: The Role of Economics.* New York: HarperCollins Publishers.

Nordhaus, William D. 1969. *Inventions, Growth, and Welfare: A Theoretical Treatment of Technological Change.* Cambridge, MA: MIT Press.

Noussair, Charles, Stephane Robin, and Bernard Ruffieux. 2002. "Do Consumers Not Care about Biotech Foods or Do They Just Not Read the Labels?" *Economics Letters* 75:47–53.

Novakovic, Andrew M., and Robert D. Boynton. 1984. "Do Changes in Farmer-First Handler Exchange Eliminate the Need for Government Intervention?" *American Journal of Agricultural Economics* 66:769–75.

Novos, Ian E., and Michael Waldman. 1984. "The Effects of Increased Copyright Protection: An Analytical Approach." *Journal of Political Economy* 92:236–46.

Novshek, William. 1980. "Equilibrium in Simple Spatial (or Differentiated Product) Models." *Journal of Economic Theory* 22:313–26.

Nuckton, Carole F. 1978. *Demand Relationships for California Tree Fruits, Grapes, and Nuts: A Review of Past Studies.* Giannini Foundation of Agricultural Economics, Special Report 3247. University of California at Berkeley.

Nuckton, Carole F. 1980. *Demand Relationships for Vegetables: A Review of Past Studies.* Giannini Foundation of Agricultural Economics, Special Report 80-1. University of California at Berkeley.

O'Huallacháin, Breandán. 1996. "Vertical Integration in American Manufacturing: Evidence of the 1980s." *Professional Geographer* 48:343–356.

Oi, Walter Y. 1971. "A Disneyland Dilemma: Two-Part Tariffs for a Mickey Mouse Monopoly." *Quarterly Journal of Economics* 85:77–96.

Okun, Arthur. 1981. *Prices and Quantities: A Macroeconomic Analysis.* Washington, D.C.: The Brookings Institution.

Okuno, Masahiro, Andrew Postlewaite, and John Roberts. 1980. "Oligopoly and Competition in Large Markets." *American Economic Review* 70:22–31.

Oliver, Daniel. 1988. *Competition Deserves More Than Lip Service.* St. Louis: Center for the Study of American Business, Washington University.

Olsen, Edgar O. 1972. "An Econometric Analysis of Rent Control." *Journal of Political Economy* 80:1081–1100.

Ontario Economic Council. 1978. *Government Regulation: Issues and Alternatives.* Toronto: Ontario Economic Council.

Ordover, Janusz A., and Garth Saloner. 1989. "Predation, Monopolization, and Antitrust," in Richard Schmalensee and Robert D. Willig, eds., *The Handbook of Industrial Organization.* Amsterdam: North-Holland.

Ordover, Janusz A., Garth Saloner, and Steven C. Salop. 1990. "Equilibrium Vertical Foreclosure." *American Economic Review* 80:127–42.

Ordover, Janusz A., and Robert D. Willig. 1981. "An Economic Definition of Predation: Pricing and Product Innovation." *Yale Law Journal* 91:8–53.

Ordover, Janusz A., and Robert D. Willig. 1985. "Antitrust for High-Technology Industries: Assessing Research Joint Ventures and Mergers." *Journal of Law and Economics* 28:311–33.

Organization for Economic Cooperation and Development. 1985. *Competition Policy and the Professions.* Paris: OECD.

Ornstein, Stanley I. 1977. *Industrial Concentration and Advertising Intensity.* Washington, D.C.: American Enterprise Institute for Public Policy Research.

Ornstein, Stanley I., and Dominique M. Hanssens. 1987. "Resale Price Maintenance: Output Increasing or Restricting? The Case of Distilled Spirits in the United States." *Journal of Industrial Economics* 36:1–18.

Ornstein, Stanley I., J. Fred Westen, Michael Intriligator, and Ronald Shrieves. 1973. "Determinants of Market Structure." *Southern Economic Journal* 39:612–25.

Osborne, D. K. 1976. "Cartel Problems." *American Economic Review* 66:835–44.

Oster, Sharon M., and John M. Quigley. 1977. "Regulatory Barriers to the Diffusion of Innovation: Some Evidence from Building Codes." *Bell Journal of Economics* 8:361–77.

Otsuka, Yasuji, and Bradley M. Braun, 2002. "Taxation by Regulation and Regulation by Taxation: The Case of Local TV Regulation." *Review of Industrial Organization* 21:21–40.

Overstreet, Thomas R., Jr. 1983. *Resale Price Maintenance: Economic Theories and Empirical Evidence.* Washington, D.C.: Federal Trade Commission, Bureau of Economics Staff Report (November).

Pakes, Ariel. 1986. "Patents as Options: Some Estimates of the Value of Holding European Patent Stocks." *Econometrica* 54:775–84.

Pakes, Ariel, and Richard Ericson. 1998. "Empirical Applications of Alternative Models of Firm Dynamics." *Journal of Economic Theory* 79:1–45.

Panzar, John C. 1979. "Equilibrium and Welfare in Unregulated Airline Markets." *American Economic Review* 69:92–95.

Panzar, John C. 1981. "Comments," in Gary Fromm, ed., *Studies in Public Regulation.* Cambridge, MA: MIT Press, 365–69.

Panzar, John C. 1989. "Determinants of Firm and Industry Structure," in Richard Schmalensee and Robert D, Willig, eds., *The Handbook of Industrial Organization.* Amsterdam: North-Holland.

Panzar, John C., and James N. Rosse. 1987. "Testing for 'Monopoly' Equilibrium." *Journal of Industrial Economics* 35:443–56.

Panzar, John C., and Robert D. Willig. 1977a. "Economies of Scale in Multi-Output Production." *Quarterly Journal of Economics* 91:481–93.

Panzar, John C., and Robert D. Willig. 1977b. "Free Entry and the Sustainability of Natural Monopoly." *Bell Journal of Economics* 8:1–22.

Pascale, Richard T. 1984. "Perspectives on Strategy: The Real Story Behind Honda's Success." *California Management Review* 26:47–72.

Pashigian, B. Peter. 1976. "Consequences and Causes of Public Ownership of Urban Transit Facilities." *Journal of Political Economy* 84:1239–60.

Pashigian, B. Peter. 1984. "The Effect of Environmental Regulation on Optimal Plant Size and Factor Shares." *Journal of Law and Economics* 27:1–28.

Patinkin, Don. 1947. "Multiple-Plant Firms, Cartels, and Imperfect Competition." *Quarterly Journal of Economics* 61:173–205.

Paulter, Paul A. 2001. "Evidence on Mergers and Acquisitions." Bureau of Economics, Federal Trade Commission, Working Paper 243.

Pauly, Mark V., and Mark A. Satterthwaite. 1981. "The Pricing of Primary Care Physicians' Services: A Test of the Role of Consumer Information." *Bell Journal of Economics* 12:488–506.

Pearce, David G. 1984. "Rationalizable Strategic Behavior and the Problem of Perfection." *Econometrica* 52: 1029–50.

Peltzman, Sam. 1971. "Pricing in Public Enterprises: Electric Utilities in the United States." *Journal of Law and Economics* 14:109–48.

Peltzman, Sam. 1973. "An Evaluation of Consumer Protection Legislation: The 1962 Drug Amendments." *Journal of Political Economy* 81:1049–91.

Peltzman, Sam. 1976. "Toward a More General Theory of Regulation." *Journal of Law and Economics* 19:211–40.

Peltzman, Sam. 1977. "The Gains and Losses from Industrial Concentration." *Journal of Law and Economics* 20:229–63.

Peltzman, Sam. 1989. "The Economic Theory of Regulations After a Decade of Deregulation." *Brookings Papers on Economic Activity* 1–41.

Peltzman, Sam. 1993. "George Stigler's Contribution to the Economic Analysis of Regulation." *Journal of Political Economy* 101:818–32.

Peltzman, Sam, and Clifford Winston, eds. 2000. *Deregulation of Network Industries: What's Next?* Washington, D.C.: AEI-Brookings Joint Center for Regulatory Studies.

Peoples, James. 1998. "Deregulation and the Labor Market." *Journal of Economic Perspectives* 12:111–30.

Perloff, Jeffrey M. 1998. "Droit de Suite." Peter Newman, ed., *New Palgrave Dictionary of Economics and the Law,* Vol. 1. New York: Stockton Press, 645–48.

Perloff, Jeffrey M., and Steven C. Salop. 1985. "Equilibrium with Product Differentiation." *Review of Economic Studies* 52:107–20.

Perloff, Jeffrey M., and Steven C. Salop. 1986. "Firm-Specific Information, Product Differentiation, and Industry Equilibrium." *Oxford Economic Papers* 38:184–202.

Perloff, Jeffrey M., and Edward Z. Shen, 2001. "Collinearity in Linear Structural Models of Market Power." **http://are.berkeley.edu/~perloff/PDF/linear.pdf.**

Perry, Martin K. 1980. "Forward Integration by Alcoa: 1888–1930." *Journal of Industrial Economics* 29:37–53.

Perry, Martin K. 1989. "Vertical Integration: Determinants and Effects," in Richard Schmalensee and Robert D. Willig, eds., *The Handbook of Industrial Organization.* Amsterdam: North-Holland.

Perry, Martin K., and Robert H. Porter. 1986. "Resale Price Maintenance and Exclusive Territories in the Presence of Retail Service Externalities." Bell Communications Research, Inc., Economics Discussion Paper 20 (May).

Pesendorfer, Martin. 2000. "A Study of Collusion in First Price Auctions." *Review of Economic Studies* 67:381–411.

Peterman, John. 1975. *"The Federal Trade Commission* v. *The Brown Shoe Company."* *Journal of Law and Economics* 18:361–421.

Peterman, John. 1979. "The *International Salt* Case." *Journal of Law and Economics* 22:351–64.

Peters, Craig. 2003. "Evaluating the Performance of Merger Simulation: Evidence from the U.S. Airline Industry." Economic Analysis Group 03-1, Dept. of Justice.

Petersen, H. Craig. 1975. "An Empirical Test of Regulatory Effects." *Bell Journal of Economics* 6:111–26.

Petrin, Amil. 2002. "Quantifying the Benefits of New Products: The Case of the Minivan." *Journal of Political Economy* 110(4):705–29.

Pettingill, John S. 1979. "Monopolistic Competition and Optimum Product Diversity: Comment." *American Economic Review* 69:957–60.

Phelps, Edmund S., and John B. Taylor. 1977. "Stabilizing Powers of Monetary Policy Under Rational Expectations." *Journal of Political Economy* 85:163–90.

Phillips, Almarin. 1972. "An Econometric Study of Price-Fixing, Market Structure, and Performance in British Industry in the Early 1950s," in Keith Cowling, ed., *Market Structure and Corporate Behaviour: Theory and Empirical Analysis of the Firm.* London: Gray-Mills Publishing, 177–92.

Phillips, Almarin, ed. 1975. *Promoting Competition in Regulated Markets.* Washington, D.C.: The Brookings Institution.

Phlips, Louis. 1983. *The Economics of Price Discrimination: Four Essays in Applied Price Theory.* New York: Cambridge University Press.

Pindyck, Robert S. 1977. "Cartel Pricing and the Structure of the World Bauxite Market." *Bell Journal of Economics* 8:343–60.

Pindyck, Robert S. 1978. "Gains to Producers from the Cartelization of Exhaustible Resources." *Review of Economics and Statistics* 60:238–51.

Pindyck, Robert S. 1979. "The Cartelization of World Commodity Markets." *American Economic Review* 69:154–8.

Pindyck, Robert S. 1985. "The Measurement of Monopoly Power in Dynamic Markets." *Journal of Law and Economics* 28:193–222.

Pirrong, Stephen C. 1987. "An Application of Core Theory to the Study of Ocean Shipping Markets." Ph.D. dissertation, University of Chicago.

Pirrong, Stephen C. 1992. "An Application of Core Theory to the Analysis of Ocean Shipping Markets." *Journal of Law and Economics* 35:89–131.

Pittman, Russell W. 1984. "Predatory Investment: U.S. vs. IBM." *International Journal of Industrial Organization* 2:341–65.

Pittman, Russell W. 1988. "Rent-Seeking and Market Structure: Comment." *Public Choice* 58:173–85.

Pittman, Russell W. 1992. "Merger Law in Central and Eastern Europe." U.S. Department of Justice, Antitrust Division Discussion Paper EAG92-2.

Plott, Charles R. 1982. "Industrial Organization Theory and Experimental Economics." *Journal of Economic Literature* 20:1485–1527.

Polinsky, A. Mitchell. 1979. "Controlling Externalities and Protecting Entitlements: Property Right, Liability Rule, and Tax-Subsidy Approaches." *Journal of Legal Studies* 8:1–48.

Polinsky, A. Mitchell. 1987. "Fixed-Price versus Spot-Price Contracts: A Study in Risk Allocation." *Journal of Law, Economics and Organization* 31:27–46.

Porter, Michael E. 1980. *Competitive Strategy: Techniques for Analyzing Industries and Competitors.* New York: The Free Press.

Porter, Michael E. 1985. *Competitive Advantage: Creating and Sustaining Superior Performance.* New York: The Free Press.

Porter, Robert H. 1983a. "A Study of Cartel Stability: The Joint Executive Committee, 1880–1886." *Bell Journal of Economics* 14:301–14.

Porter, Robert H. 1983b. "Optimal Cartel Trigger-Price Strategies." *Journal of Economic Theory* 29:313–38.

Porter, Robert H., and J. Douglas Zona. 1999. "Ohio School Milk Markets: An Analysis of Bidding." *Rand Journal of Economics* 30:263–88.

Posner, Richard A. 1970. "A Statistical Study of Antitrust Enforcement." *Journal of Law and Economics* 13:365–419.

Posner, Richard A. 1971. "Taxation by Regulation." *Bell Journal of Economics* 2:22–50.

Posner, Richard A. 1972. "The Appropriate Scope of Regulation in the Cable Television Industry." *Bell Journal of Economics* 3:98–129.

Posner, Richard A. 1974. "Theories of Economic Regulation." *Bell Journal of Economics* 5:335–58.

Posner, Richard A. 1975. "The Social Costs of Monopoly and Regulation." *Journal of Political Economy* 83:807–27.

Posner, Richard A. 1976. *The Robinson-Patman Act: Federal Regulation of Price Differences.* Washington, D.C.: American Enterprise Institute.

Posner, Richard A. 1981. "The Next Step in the Antitrust Treatment of Restricted Distribution: Per Se Legality." *University of Chicago Law Review* 48: 6–26.

Posner, Richard A. 2003. *Antitrust Law: An Economic Perspective.* Chicago: University of Chicago Press.

Posner, Richard A., and Frank H. Easterbrook. 1980. *Antitrust Cases, Economic Notes, and Other Materials.* St. Paul, MN: West Publishing Co.

Prager, Robin A. 1990. "Firm Behavior in Franchise Monopoly Markets." *Rand Journal of Economics* 21:211–25.

Pratt, John W., David A. Wise, and Richard Zeckhauser. 1979. "Price Differences in Almost Competitive Markets." *Quarterly Journal of Economics* 93:189–211.

Pratten, C. F. 1971. "Economies of Scale in Manufacturing Industry." Occasional Paper no. 28. Cambridge: Cambridge University Press (Department of Applied Economics).

Prescott, Edward. 1975. "Efficiency of the Natural Rate." *Journal of Political Economy* 83: 1229–36.

Preston, Lee E. 1994. "Territorial Restraints: *GTE Sylvania* (1977)," in John E. Kwoka, Jr., and Lawrence J. White, eds., *The Antitrust Revolution: The Role of Economics.* New York: HarperCollins Publishers.

Pryor, Frederic L. 1972. "An International Comparison of Concentration Ratios." *Review of Economics and Statistics* 54:130–40.

Pulliam, H. Ronald, Graham H. Pyke, and Thomas Caraco. 1982. "The Scanning Behavior of Juncos: A Game-Theoretical Approach." *Journal of Theoretical Biology* 95:89–103.

Qualls, P. David. 1979. "Market Structure and the Cyclical Flexibility of Price-Cost Margins." *Journal of Business* 52:305–25.

Ramsey, Frank P. 1927. "A Contribution to the Theory of Taxation." *Economic Journal* 37:47–61.

Rasmussen, Eric. 1988. "Mutual Banks and Stock Banks." *Journal of Law and Economics* 31:395–421.

Rasmussen, Eric, J. Mark Ramseyer, and John Wiley. 2000. "Naked Exclusion: Reply." *American Economic Review* 90:310–11.

Rausser, Gordon C. 1992. "Predatory Versus Productive Government: The Case of U.S. Agricultural Policies." *Journal of Economic Perspectives* 6:133–57.

Ravenscraft, David J., and Frederic M. Scherer. 1987. *Mergers, Sell-offs and Economic Efficiency.* Washington, D.C.: Brookings Institution.

Reagan, Patricia B. 1982. "Inventory and Price Behavior." *Review of Economic Studies* 49:137–42.

Reeves, Eoin, and Michael Barrow. 2000. "The Impact of Contracting Out on the Costs of Refuse Collection Services: The Case of Ireland." *Economic and Social Review* 31:129–150.

Reiffen, David, and Andrew N. Kleit. 1990. "Terminal Railroad Revisited: Foreclosure of an Essential Facility or Simple Horizontal Monopoly?" *Journal of Law and Economics* 33:419–37.

Reiffen, David, and Michael Vita. 1995. "Comment: Is There New Thinking on Vertical Mergers?" *Antitrust Law Journal* 63:917–41.

Reinganum, Jennifer F. 1979. "A Simple Model of Equilibrium Price Dispersion." *Journal of Political Economy* 87:851–58.

Reinganum, Jennifer F. 1982. "Dynamic Games of R&D: Patent Protection and Competitive Behavior." *Econometrica* 50:671–88.

Reinganum, Jennifer F. 1984. "Practical Implications of Game Theoretic Models of R&D." *American Economic Review* 74:61–66.

Reinganum, Jennifer F. 1989. "The Timing of Innovation: Research, Development, and Diffusion," in Richard Schmalensee and Robert D, Willig, eds., *The Handbook of Industrial Organization.* Amsterdam: North-Holland.

Reppy, Judith. 1994. "Defense Companies' Strategies in a Declining Market: Implications for Government Policy." *Peace Economics, Peace Science and Public Policy* 1:1–8.

Rey, Patrick, and Joseph E. Stiglitz. 1988. "Vertical Restraints and Producers' Competition." *European Economic Review* 32:561–66.

Rey, Patrick, and Joseph Stiglitz. 1995. "The Role of Exclusive Territories in Producers' Competition." *Rand Journal of Economics* 26:431–51.

Rey, Patrick, and Jean Tirole. 1986. "The Logic of Vertical Restraints." *American Economic Review* 76:921–39.

Rey, Patrick, and Jean Tirole. Forthcoming. "A Primer on Foreclosure," in Mark Armstrong and Robert Porter, eds., *Handbook in Industrial Organization*, Vol. 3. Amsterdam: North-Holland.

Riordan, Michael H. 1984. "On Delegating Price Authority to a Regulated Firm." *Rand Journal of Economics* 15:108–15.

Riordan, Michael H. 1992. "Regulation and Preemptive Technology Adoption." *Rand Journal of Economics* 23:334–49.

Riordan, Michael H. 1998. "Anticompetitive Vertical Integration by a Dominant Firm." *American Economic Review* 88:1232–48.

Riordan, Michael, and Steven Salop. 1995. "Evaluating Vertical Mergers: A Post-Chicago Approach." *Antitrust Law Journal* 63:513–68.

Riordan, Michael H., and David E. M. Sappington. 1987. "Awarding Monopoly Franchises." *American Economic Review* 77:375–87.

Roberts, Mark J. 1984. "Testing Oligopolistic Behavior." *International Journal of Industrial Organization* 2:367–83.

Roberts, Mark J., and Larry Samuelson. 1988. "An Empirical Analysis of Dynamic, Nonprice Competition in an Oligopolistic Industry." *Rand Journal of Economics* 19:200–20.

Robinson, Joan. 1934. "What Is Perfect Competition?" *Quarterly Journal of Economics* 49:104–20.

Roeger, Werner. 1995. "Can Imperfect Competition Explain the Difference Between Primal and Dual Productivity Measures? Estimates for U.S. Manufacturing." *Journal of Political Economy* 103:316–330.

Rogers, Robert P. 1992. "The Minimum Optimal Steel Plant and the Survivor Technique of Cost Estimation." *Atlantic Economic Journal* 21:30–37.

Rogerson, William P. 1986. "Advertising as a Signal When Price Guarantees Quality." Center for Mathematical Studies in Economics and Management Science Discussion Paper No. 704, Northwestern University.

Rogerson, William P. 1988. "Price Advertising and the Deterioration of Product Quality." *Review of Economic Studies* 55:215–29.

Rohlfs, Jeffrey. 1974. "Econometric Analysis of Supply in Concentrated Markets." *International Economic Review* 15:69–74.

Roll, Richard. 1986. "The Hubris Hypothesis of Corporate Takeovers." *Journal of Business* 59:197–216.

Romano, Richard E. 1991. "When Excessive Consumption is Rational." *American Economic Review* 81:553–64.

Romano, Roberta. 1985. "Law as a Product: Some Pieces of the Incorporation Puzzle." *Journal of Law Economics and Organization* 1:225–83.

Rose, Nancy L. 1987. "Labor Rent Sharing and Regulation: Evidence from the Trucking Industry." *Journal of Political Economy* 95:1146–78.

Rose, Nancy L. 1989. "The Financial Influences on Airline Safety," in Leon N. Moses and Ian Savage, eds., *Safety Performance under Deregulation.* Oxford: Oxford University Press.

Rosen, Sherwin. 1974. "Hedonic Prices and Implicit Markets: Product Differentiation in Pure Competition." *Journal of Political Economy* 82:34–55.

Rosenstein-Rodan, P. N. 1961. "International Aid for Underdeveloped Countries." *Review of Economics and Statistics* 43:107–38.

Ross, Thomas W. 1984. "Winners and Losers Under the Robinson-Patman Act." *Journal of Law and Economics* 27:243–71.

Ross, Thomas W. 1988. "Brand Information and Price." *The Journal of Industrial Economics* 36:301–14.

Ross, Thomas W. 1990. "On the Vertical Integration of Successive Monopolies." Manuscript.

Rosse, James N. 1970. "Estimating Cost Function Parameters without Using Cost Data: Illustrated Methodology." *Econometrica* 38:256–75.

Rosse, James N., and John C. Panzar. 1977. "Chamberlin versus Robinson: An Empirical Test for Monopoly Rents." Studies in Industry Economics, Research Paper no. 77, Stanford University.

Rotemberg, Julio J. 1982. "Sticky Prices in the United States." *Journal of Political Economy* 90:1187–1211.

Rotemberg, Julio J., and Garth Saloner. 1986. "A Supergame-Theoretic Model of Price Wars During Booms." *American Economic Review* 76:390–407.

Rotemberg, Julio J., and Garth Saloner. 1987. "The Relative Rigidity of Monopoly Pricing." *American Economic Review* 77:917–26.

Rotemberg, Julio J., and Garth Saloner. 1989. "The Cyclical Behavior of Strategic Inventories." *Quarterly Journal of Economics* 104:73–97.

Rotemberg, Julio J., and Michael Woodford. 1991. "Markups and the Business Cycle," in Oliver Blanchard and Stanley Fischer, eds., *NBER Macroeconomic Annual 1996.* Cambridge, MA: MIT Press.

Rothschild, Michael. 1974. "Models of Market Organization with Imperfect Information: A Survey." *Journal of Political Economy* 82:1283–1308.

Rothschild, R., John S. Heywood, and Kristen Monaco. 2000. "Spatial Price Discrimination and the Merger Paradox." *Regional Science and Urban Economics* 30:491–506.

Ruback, Richard S., and Martin B. Zimmerman. 1984. "Unionization and Profitability: Evidence from the Capital Market." *Journal of Political Economy* 92:1134–57.

Rubin, Paul H. 1978. "The Theory of the Firm and the Structure of the Franchise Contract." *Journal of Law and Economics* 21:223–33.

Ruffin, R. J. 1971. "Cournot Oligopoly and Competitive Behavior." *Review of Economic Studies* 38:493–502.

Rust, John. 1986. "When Is It Optimal to Kill Off the Market for Used Durable Goods?" *Econometrica* 54:65–86.

Saffer, Henry, and Dhaval Dave. 2002. "Alcohol Consumption and Alcohol Advertising Bans." *Applied Economics* 34:1325–34.

Salant, Stephen W. 1987. "Treble Damage Awards in Private Lawsuits for Price Fixing." *Journal of Political Economy* 95:1326–36.

Salant, Stephen W., Sheldon Switzer, and Robert Reynolds. 1983. "Losses from Horizontal Merger: The Effects of an Exogenous Change in Industry Structure on Cournot-Nash Equilibrium." *Quarterly Journal of Economics* 98:185–99.

Salinger, Michael A. 1984. "Tobin's *q*, Unionization, and the Concentration-Profits Relationship." *Rand Journal of Economics* 15:159–70.

Salinger, Michael A. 1988. "Vertical Mergers and Market Foreclosure." *Quarterly Journal of Economics* 103:345–56.

Saloner, Garth, and Andrea Shepard. 1995. "Adoption of Technologies with Network Effects: An Empirical Examination of Automated Teller Machines." *Rand Journal of Economics* 26:479–501.

Salop, Steven C. 1976. "Information and Monopolistic Competition." *American Economic Review* 66:240–45.

Salop, Steven C. 1978. "Parables of Information Transmission in Markets," in Andrew A. Mitchell, ed., *The Effect of Information on Consumer and Market Behavior.* Chicago: American Marketing Association, 3–12.

Salop, Steven C. 1979a. "Monopolistic Competition with Outside Goods." *Bell Journal of Economics* 10:141–56.

Salop, Steven C. 1979b. "Strategic Entry Deterrence." *American Economic Review* 69:335–38.

Salop, Steven C., ed. 1981. *Strategy, Predation, and Antitrust Analysis.* Washington, D.C.: Federal Trade Commission.

Salop, Steven C. 1986. "Practices that (Credibly) Facilitate Oligopoly Coordination," in Joseph E. Stiglitz and G. Frank Mathewson, eds., *New Developments in the Analysis of Market Structure.* Cambridge, MA: MIT Press, Chap. 9, 265–90.

Salop, Steven C. 1998. "Vertical Mergers and Monopoly Leverage," in Peter Newman, ed., *New Palgrave Dictionary of Economics and the Law.* New York: Stockton Press.

Salop, Steven C., and David T. Scheffman. 1987. "Cost-Raising Strategies." *Journal of Industrial Economics* 36:19–34.

Salop, Steven C., David T. Scheffman, and Warren Schwartz. 1984. "A Bidding Analysis of Special Interest Regulation: Raising Rivals' Costs in a Rent-Seeking Society," in *Political Economy of Regulation: Private Interests in the Regulatory Process.* Washington, D.C.: Federal Trade Commission.

Salop, Steven C., and Joseph Stiglitz. 1977. "Bargains and Ripoffs: A Model of Monopolistically Competitive Price Dispersion." *Review of Economic Studies* 44:493–510.

Salop, Steven C., and Lawrence J. White. 1986. "Economic Analysis of Private Antitrust Litigation." *Georgetown Law Journal* 74:1001–64.

Sattinger, Michael. 1984. "Value of an Additional Firm in Monopolistic Competition." *Review of Economic Studies* 51:321–22.

Schankerman, Mark. 1998. "How Valuable Is Patent Protection? Estimates by Technology Field." *Rand Journal of Economics* 29:77–107.

Schary, Martha. 1991. "The Probability of Exit." *Rand Journal of Economics* 22:339–53.

Scheffman, David, and Pablo Spiller. 1987. "Geographic Market Definition Under the U.S. Department of Justice Merger Guidelines." *Journal of Law and Economics* 30:123–48.

Scherer, Frederic. M. 1979. "The Welfare Economics of Product Variety: An Application to the Ready-to-Eat Cereals Industry." *Journal of Industrial Economics* 28:113–34.

Scherer, Frederic M. 1980. *Industrial Market Structure and Economic Performance.* Boston: Houghton Mifflin.

Scherer, Frederic M. 1981. "Comments on 'Patents, Sleeping Patents, and Entry Deterrence,'" in Steven C. Salop, ed., *Strategy, Predation, and Antitrust Analysis.* Washington, D.C.: Federal Trade Commission.

Scherer, Frederic M. 1984. *Innovation and Growth: Schumpeterian Perspectives.* Cambridge, MA: MIT Press.

Scherer, Frederic M. 1988. "Corporate Takeovers: The Efficiency Arguments." *Journal of Economic Perspectives* 2:69–82.

Scherer, Frederic M., Alan Beckenstein, Erich Kaufer, and R. Dennis Murphy. 1975. *The Economics of Multi-Plant Operation: An International Comparison Study.* Cambridge, MA: Harvard University Press.

Scherer, Frederic M., and David Ross. 1990. *Industrial Market Structure and Economic Performance.* Boston: Houghton Mifflin.

Schmalensee, Richard. 1973. *The Economics of Advertising.* New York: Humanities Press.

Schmalensee, Richard. 1974. "Brand Loyalty and Barriers to Entry." *Southern Economic Journal* 40:579–88.

Schmalensee, Richard. 1976. "Advertising and Profitability: Further Implications of the Null Hypothesis." *Journal of Industrial Economics* 25:45–54.

Schmalensee, Richard. 1977. "Comparative Static Properties of Regulated Airline Oligopolies." *Bell Journal of Economics* 8:565–76.

Schmalensee, Richard. 1978a. "A Model of Advertising and Product Quality." *Journal of Political Economy* 86:485–503.

Schmalensee, Richard. 1978b. "Entry Deterrence in the Ready-to-Eat Breakfast Cereal Industry." *Bell Journal of Economics* 9:305–27.

Schmalensee, Richard. 1979a. "Market Structure, Durability, and Quality: A Selective Survey." *Economic Inquiry* 17:177–96.

Schmalensee, Richard. 1979b. *The Control of Natural Monopolies.* Lexington, MA: Lexington Books.

Schmalensee, Richard. 1981a. "Monopolistic Two-Part Pricing Arrangements." *Bell Journal of Economics* 12:445–66.

Schmalensee, Richard. 1981b. "Output and Welfare Effects of Monopolistic Third Degree Price Discrimination." *American Economic Review* 71:242–47.

Schmalensee, Richard. 1982. "Product Differentiation Advantages of Pioneering Brands." *American Economic Review* 72:346–65.

Schmalensee, Richard. 1985. "Do Markets Differ Much?" *American Economic Review* 75:341–51.

Schmalensee, Richard. 1987. "Collusion versus Differential Efficiency: Testing Alternative Hypotheses." *Journal of Industrial Economics* 35:399–425.

Schmalensee, Richard. 1989. "Inter-Industry Studies of Structure and Performance," in Richard Schmalensee and Robert D. Willig, eds., *The Handbook of Industrial Organization.* Amsterdam: North-Holland.

Schmittmann, Michael, and Wolfgang Vonnemann. 1992. "Mergers and Acquisitions in Europe 1993: The New EC Merger Control Regulation and Its Effect on National Merger Control in Germany." *Antitrust Bulletin* 37:1025–1046.

Schroeter, John R., and Azzeddine Azzam. 1991. "Marketing Margins, Market Power, and Price Uncertainty." *American Journal of Agricultural Economics* 73:990–99.

Schroeter, John R., Scott L. Smith, and Steven R. Cox. 1987. "Advertising and Competition in Routine Legal Service Markets: An Empirical Investigation." *Journal of Industrial Economics* 36:49–60.

Schumpeter, Joseph. 1950. *Capitalism, Socialism, and Democracy.* 3rd ed. New York: Harper & Row.

Schwert, G. William. 1981. "Using Financial Data to Measure Effects of Regulation." *Journal of Law and Economics* 24:121–58.

Scitovsky, Tibor. 1950. "Ignorance as a Source of Oligopoly Power." *American Economic Review* 40:48–53.

Scotchmer, Suzanne, and Jerry Green. 1990. "Novelty and Disclosure in Patent Law." *Rand Journal of Economics* 21:131–46.

Scott, John T. 1984. "Firm versus Industry Variability in R&D Intensity," in Zvi Griliches, ed., *R&D, Patents, and Productivity.* Chicago: University of Chicago Press.

Scott, John T. 1991a. "Multimarket Contact among Diversified Oligopolists." *International Journal of Industrial Organization* 9:225–38.

Scott, John T. 1991b. "Research Diversity Induced by Rivalry," in Zoltan J. Acs and David B. Audretsch, eds., *Innovation and Technological Change: An International Comparison.* New York: Harvester Wheatsheaf.

Seade, Jesus. 1980. "On the Effects of Entry." *Econometrica* 48:479–89.

Segal, Ilya R., and Michael D. Whinston. 1996. "Naked Exclusion and Buyer Coordination." Harvard Institute of Economic Research Discussion Paper 1780.

Segal, Ilya R., and Michael D. Whinston. 2000a. "Exclusive Contracts and the Protection of Investments." *Rand Journal of Economics* 31:603–33.

Segal, Ilya R., and Michael D. Whinston. 2000b. "Naked Exclusion: Comment." *American Economic Review* 90:296–309.

Seldon, Barry J., and Khosrow Doroodian. 1989. "A Simultaneous Model of Cigarette Advertising." *Review of Economics and Statistics* 71:673–77.

Selten, Reinhard. 1975. "Reexamination of the Perfectness Concept for Equilibrium Points in Extensive Games." *International Journal of Game Theory* 4:25–55.

Selten, Reinhard. 1978. "The Chain Store Paradox." *Theory and Decisions* 9:127–59.

Sexton, Richard J. 1981. "Welfare Loss from Inaccurate Information: An Economic Model with Application to Food Labels." *Journal of Consumer Affairs* 15:214–31.

Sexton, Richard J., James A. Chalfant, Humei Wang, and Mingxia Zhang. 2002. "Grocery Retailer Pricing and Its Effects on Producers." *ARE Update,* University of California Giannini Foundation 5:10–11.

Shaffer, S. 1982. "A Nonstructural Test for Competition in Financial Markets." *Proceedings of a Conference on Bank Structure and Competition.* Chicago: Federal Reserve Bank of Chicago.

Shapiro, Carl. 1980. "Advertising and Welfare: Comment." *Bell Journal of Economics* 11:749–52.

Shapiro, Carl. 1982. "Consumer Information, Product Quality, and Seller Reputation." *Bell Journal of Economics* 13:20–35.

Shapiro, Carl. 1983. "Premiums for High-Quality Products as Returns to Reputation." *Quarterly Journal of Economics* 98:659–79.

Shapiro, Carl. 1989. "Theories of Oligopoly Behavior," in Richard Schmalensee and Robert D. Willig, eds., *The Handbook of Industrial Organization.* Amsterdam: North-Holland.

Shapiro, Carl, and Robert D. Willig. 1990. "On the Antitrust Treatment of Production Joint Ventures." *Journal of Economic Perspectives* 4:113–30.

Shapiro, Matthew. 1987. "Measuring Market Power in U.S. Industry." National Bureau of Economic Research Working Paper no. 2212.

Sharkey, William W. 1982. *The Theory of Natural Monopoly.* New York: Cambridge University Press.

Shepard, Andrea. 1993. "Contractual Form, Retail Price, and Asset Characteristics in Gasoline Retailing." *Rand Journal of Economics* 24:58–77.

Shepard, Lawrence. 1978. "The Economic Effects of Repealing Fair-Trade Laws." *Journal of Consumer Affairs* 12:220–36.

Sheshinski, Eytan. 1971. "Welfare Aspects of a Regulatory Constraint: Note." *American Economic Review* 61:175–78.

Shin, Richard T., and John S. Ying. 1992. "Unnatural Monopolies in Local Telephone." *Rand Journal of Economics* 23:171–83.

Shishido-Topel, Lynn M. 1984. "An Economic Analysis of Exclusive Dealing." Ph.D. dissertation, University of California, Los Angeles.

Shleifer, Andrei. 1986. "Implementation Cycles." *Journal of Political Economy* 94:1163–90.

Shleifer, Andrei, and Lawrence Summers. 1988. "Hostile Takeovers as Breaches of Trust," in Alan J. Auerbach, ed., *Corporate Takeovers: Causes and Consequences.* Chicago: University of Chicago Press.

Shleifer, Andrei, and Robert W. Vishny. 1988. "Value Maximization and the Acquisition Process." *Journal of Economic Perspectives* 2:7–20.

Shleifer, Andrei, and Robert W. Vishny. 1999. *The Grabbing Hand: Government Pathologies and Their Cures.* Cambridge, MA: Harvard University Press.

Shubik, Martin. 1959. *Strategy and Market Structure.* New York: John Wiley and Sons.

Shubik, Martin. 1982 (vol. 1), and 1984 (vol. 2). *Game Theory in the Social Sciences.* Cambridge, MA: MIT Press.

Shubik, Martin, with Richard Levitan. 1980. *Market Structure and Behavior.* Cambridge, MA: Harvard University Press.

Shy, Oz, and Jacques F. Thisse. 1999. "A Strategic Approach to Software Protection." *Journal of Economics and Management Strategy* 8:164–90.

Siberston, Aubrey. 1972. "Economies of Scale in Theory and Practice." *Economic Journal* 82:369–91.

Sickles, Robin C., David Good, and Richard L. Johnson. 1986. "Allocative Distortions and the Regulatory Transition of the U.S. Airline Industry." *Journal of Econometrics* 33:143–63.

Siegfried, John J., and Christopher Latta. 1998. "Competition in the Retail College Textbook Market." *Economics of Education Review* 17:105–15.

Sieper, E., and Peter L. Swan. 1973. "Monopoly and Competition in the Market for Durable Goods." *Review of Economic Studies* 40:333–51.

Simon, Herbert A. 1957. *Models of Man.* New York: John Wiley and Sons.

Simon, Herbert A. 1959. "Theories of Decision-Making in Economics and Behavioral Science." *American Economic Review* 49:253–83.

Slade, Margaret E. 1986. "Conjectures, Firm Characteristics, and Market Structure." *International Journal of Industrial Organization* 4:347–69.

Slade, Margaret E. 1987a. "Interfirm Rivalry in a Repeated Game: An Empirical Test of Tacit Collusion." *Journal of Industrial Economics* 35:499–516.

Slade, Margaret E. 1987b. "Conjectures, Firm Characteristics and Market Structure: An Analysis of Vancouver's Gasoline-Price Wars." Mimeo.

Slade, Margaret E. 1992. "Vancouver's Gasoline Price Wars: An Empirical Exercise in Uncovering Supergame Strategies." *Review of Economic Studies* 59:257–76.

Smallwood, Dennis E., and John Conlisk. 1979. "Product Quality in Markets Where Consumers Are Imperfectly Informed." *Quarterly Journal of Economics* 93:1–23.

Smith, Adam. (n.d.) *An Inquiry into the Nature and Causes of the Wealth of Nations.* New York: Random House. Also, Smith, Adam. 1937. *The Wealth of Nations.* New York: The Modern Library.

Smith, Richard. 1982. "Franchise Regulation: An Economic Analysis of State Restrictions on Automobile Distribution." *Journal of Law and Economics* 25:125–57.

Smithson, Charles W. 1978. "The Degree of Regulation and the Monopoly Firm: Further Empirical Evidence." *Southern Economic Journal* 44:568–80.

Smithson, Charles W., and Christopher R. Thomas. 1988. "Measuring the Cost to Consumers of Product Defects: The Value of 'Lemon Insurance.'" *Journal of Law and Economics* 31(2):485–502.

Snyder, Edward A. 1990. "The Effect of Higher Criminal Penalties on Antitrust Enforcement." *Journal of Law and Economics* 33:439–62.

Solow, John L. 1998. "An Economic Analysis of the Droit de Suite." *Journal of Cultural Economics* 22:209–26.

Spann, Robert M. 1974. "Rate-of-Return Regulation and Efficiency in Production: An Empirical Test of the Averch-Johnson Thesis." *Bell Journal of Economics* 5:38–52.

Spence, A. Michael. 1975. "Monopoly, Quality, and Regulation." *Bell Journal of Economics* 6:407–14.

Spence, A. Michael. 1976. "Product Selection, Fixed Costs, and Monopolistic Competition." *Review of Economic Studies* 43:217–36.

Spence, A. Michael. 1977a. "Entry, Capacity, Investment and Oligopolistic Pricing." *Bell Journal of Economics* 8:534–44.

Spence, A. Michael. 1977b. "Nonlinear Prices and Welfare." *Journal of Public Economics* 8:12–18.

Spence, A. Michael. 1978a. "Tacit Coordination and Imperfect Information." *Canadian Journal of Economics* 11:490–505.

Spence, A. Michael. 1978b. "Efficient Collusion and Reaction Functions." *Canadian Journal of Economics* 11:527–33.

Spence, A. Michael. 1979. "Investment Strategy and Growth in a New Market." *Bell Journal of Economics* 10:1–19.

Spence, A. Michael. 1981a. "The Learning Curve and Competition." *Bell Journal of Economics* 12:49–70.

Spence, A. Michael. 1981b. "Competition, Entry and Antitrust Policy," in Steven C. Salop, ed., *Strategy, Predation, and Antitrust Analysis.* Washington, D.C.: Federal Trade Commission.

Spencer, Barbara J., and James A. Brander. 1983. "International R&D Rivalry and Industrial Strategy." *Review of Economic Studies* 50:707–22.

Spiller, Pablo T. 1983. "The Differential Impact of Airline Regulation on Individual Firms and Markets: An Empirical Analysis." *Journal of Law and Economics* 26:655–89.

Spiller, Pablo T. 1985. "On Vertical Merger." *Journal of Law, Economics, and Organization* 1:285–312.

Spiller, Pablo T. 1990. "Politicians, Interest Groups, and Regulators: A Multiple-Principals Agency Theory of Regulation, or 'Let Them Be Bribed.'" *Journal of Law and Economics* 33:65–101.

Spiller, Pablo T., and Edwardo Favaro. 1984. "The Effects of Entry Regulation on Oligopolistic Interaction: The Uruguayan Banking Sector." *Rand Journal of Economics* 15:244–54.

Sproul, Michael F. 1993. "Antitrust and Prices." *Journal of Political Economy* 101:741–45.

Spulber, Daniel F. 1989. *Regulation and Markets.* Cambridge, MA: MIT Press.

Stackelberg, Heinrich von. 1934. *Marktform und gleichgewicht.* Vienna: Julius Springer. Reprinted in *The Theory of the Market Economy.* Trans. A. T. Peacock. London: William Hodge, 1952.

Stahl, Dale O. II. 1989. "Oligopolistic Pricing with Sequential Consumer Search." *American Economic Review* 79:700–12.

Staiger, Robert W., and Frank A. Wolak. 1991a. "Strategic Use of Antidumping Law to Enforce Tacit International Collusion." National Bureau of Economic Research, Working Paper no. 3016.

Staiger, Robert W., and Frank A. Wolak. 1991b. "The Effect of Domestic Antidumping Law in the Presence of Foreign Monopoly." National Bureau of Economic Research, Working Paper no. 3254.

Staiger, Robert W., and Frank A. Wolak. 1992. "Collusive Pricing with Capacity Constraints in the Presence of Demand Uncertainty." *Rand Journal of Economics* 23:203–20.

Stansell, Stanley R., and Daniel R. Hollas. 1988. "An Examination of the Economic Efficiency of Class I Railroads: A Profit Function Analysis." *Review of Industrial Organization* 3:93–117.

Stanworth, John, David Purdy, Stuart Price, and Nicos Zafivis. 1998. "Franchise Versus Conventional Small Business Failure Rates in the US and UK: More Similarities Than Differences." *International Small Business Journal* 16:56–69.

Stegeman, Mark. 1991. "Advertising in Competitive Markets." *American Economic Review* 81:210–23.

Steiner, Robert L. 1973. "Does Advertising Lower Consumer Prices?" *Journal of Marketing* 37:19–26.

Stevens, Barbara J. 1978. "Scale, Market Structure, and the Cost of Refuse Collection." *Review of Economics and Statistics* 60:438–48.

Stigler, George. 1939. "Production and Distribution in the Short Run." *Journal of Political Economy* 47:305–27.

Stigler, George. 1950. "Monopoly and Oligopoly by Merger." *American Economic Review* 40:23–34.

Stigler, George. 1951. "The Division of Labor Is Limited by the Extent of the Market." *Journal of Political Economy* 59:185–93.

Stigler, George. 1956. "The Statistics of Monopoly and Merger." *Journal of Political Economy* 64:33–40.

Stigler, George. 1961. "The Economics of Information." *Journal of Political Economy* 69:213–25.

Stigler, George. 1963. *Capital and Rates of Return in Manufacturing Industries.* Princeton, NJ: Princeton University Press.

Stigler, George. 1964a. "A Theory of Oligopoly." *Journal of Political Economy* 72. Reprinted as Chapter 5 in George Stigler, *The Organization of Industry.* Homewood, IL: Richard D. Irwin, 1968, 39–63.

Stigler, George. 1964b. "Public Regulation of the Securities Markets." *Journal of Business* 37:117–42.

Stigler, George. 1965. "The Dominant Firm and the Inverted Umbrella." *Journal of Law and Economics* 8. Reprinted as Chapter 9 in George Stigler, *The Organization of Industry.* Homewood, IL: Richard D. Irwin, 108–22.

Stigler, George. 1968. *The Organization of Industry.* Homewood, IL: Richard D. Irwin.

Stigler, George. 1968a. "Barriers to Entry, Economies of Scale, and Firm Size," in George Stigler, *The Organization of Industry.* Homewood, IL: Richard D. Irwin.

Stigler, George. 1968b. "Economics of Scale." *Journal of Law and Economics* 1: 5–71. Reprinted as Chapter 7 in George Stigler, *The Organization of Industry.* Homewood, IL: Richard D. Irwin.

Stigler, George. 1968c. "A Note on Block Booking," in George Stigler, *The Organization of Industry.* Homewood, IL: Richard D. Irwin.

Stigler, George. 1968d. "Price and Non-Price Competition." *Journal of Political Economy* 76:149–54.

Stigler, George. 1971. "The Theory of Economic Regulation." *Bell Journal of Economics* 2:3–21.

Stigler, George, and Gary S. Becker. 1977. "De Gusibus Non Et Disputandum." *American Economic Review* 67:76–90.

Stigler, George, and Claire Friedland. 1962. "What Can Regulators Regulate? The Case of Electricity." *Journal of Law and Economics* 5:1–16.

Stigler, George, and James K. Kindahl. 1970. *Behavior of Industrial Prices.* New York: National Bureau of Economic Research.

Stigler, George, and James K. Kindahl. 1973. "Industrial Prices, as Administered by Dr. Means." *American Economic Review* 63:717–21.

Stigler, George, and Robert A. Sherwin. 1985. "The Extent of the Market." *Journal of Law and Economics* 29:555–85.

Stigler, Stephen M. 1986. *The History of Statistics.* Cambridge, MA: Harvard University Press.

Stiglitz, Joseph E. 1976. "Prices and Queues as Screening Devices in Competitive Markets." IMSS Technical Report no. 212, Stanford University.

Stiglitz, Joseph E. 1979. "Equilibrium in Product Markets with Imperfect Information." *American Economic Review* 69:339–45.

Stiglitz, Joseph E. 1984. "Price Rigidities and Market Structure." *American Economic Review* 74:350–55.

Stiglitz, Joseph E. 1989. "Imperfect Information in the Product Market," in Richard Schmalensee and Robert D. Willig, eds., *The Handbook of Industrial Organization.* Amsterdam: North-Holland.

Stiglitz, Joseph E., and Andrew Weiss. 1981. "Credit Rationing in Markets with Imperfect Information." *American Economic Review* 71:393–410.

Stillman, Robert S. 1983. "Examining Antitrust Policy Toward Horizontal Mergers." *Journal of Financial Economics* 11:225–40.

Stokey, Nancy L. 1979. "Intertemporal Price Discrimination." *Quarterly Journal of Economics* 94:355–71.

Stokey, Nancy L. 1981. "Rational Expectations and Durable-Goods Pricing." *Bell Journal of Economics* 12:112–28.

Stole, Lars. Forthcoming. "Price Discrimination in Competitive Environments," in Mark Armstrong and Robert Porter, eds., *Handbook of Industrial Organization,* Vol. 3.

Strickland, Allyn D., and Leonard W. Weiss. 1976. "Advertising, Concentration, and Price-Cost Margins." *Journal of Political Economy* 84:1109–21.

Sullivan, Daniel. 1985. "Testing Hypotheses About Firm Behavior in the Cigarette Industry." *Journal of Political Economy* 93:586–98.

Sultan, Ralph G. M. 1974, 1975. *Pricing in the Electrical Oligopoly.* Boston: Harvard Business School, vols. I and II.

Sumner, Daniel A. 1981. "Measurement of Monopoly Behavior: An Application to the Cigarette Industry." *Journal of Political Economy* 89:1010–19.

Sun, Xiaolun. 1993. "The Effects of Antidumping Law Enforcement." University of California, Department of Agricultural & Resource Economics Working Paper.

Suslow, Valerie Y. 1986a. "Commitment and Monopoly Pricing in Durable-Goods Models." *International Journal of Industrial Organization* 4:451–60.

Suslow, Valerie Y. 1986b. "Estimating Monopoly Behavior with Competitive Recycling: An Application to Alcoa." *Rand Journal of Economics* 17:389–403.

Suslow, Valerie Y. 1992. "Cartel Contract Duration: Empirical Evidence from International Cartels." Working Paper.

Sutton, John. 1989. "Endogenous Sunk Costs and the Structure of Advertising Intensive Industries." *European Economic Review* 33:335–344.

Sutton, John. 1991. *Sunk Costs and Market Structure.* Cambridge, MA: MIT Press.

Sutton, John. 1997. "Gibrat's Legacy." *Journal of Economic Literature* 34:40–59.

Sutton, John. 1998. *Technology and Market Structure.* Cambridge, MA: MIT Press.

Suzuki, Nobuhiro, Harry M. Kaiser, John E. Lenz, Kohei Kobayasi, and Olan D. Forker. 1994. "Evaluating Generic Milk Promotion Effectiveness with an Imperfect Competition Model." *American Journal of Agricultural Economics* 76:296–302.

Swan, Peter L. 1970. "Durability of Consumption Goods." *American Economic Review* 60:88–94.

Swan, Peter L. 1977. "Product Durability Under Monopoly and Competition: Comment." *Econometrica* 45:229–35.

Swan, Peter L. 1980. "Alcoa: The Influence of Recycling on Monopoly Power." *Journal of Political Economy* 88:76–99.

Swann, Dennis D., Dennis O'Brien, W. Peter Maunder, and W. Stewart Howe. 1974. *Competition in British Industry; Restrictive Practices Legislation in Theory and Practice.* London: Allen & Unwin.

Sweezy, Paul M. 1939. "Demand under Conditions of Oligopoly." *Journal of Political Economy* 47:568–73.

Sykes, Alan. 1999. "Regulatory Protectionism and the Law of International Trade." *University of Chicago Law Review* 66:1–46.

Sylos-Labini, Paolo. 1962. *Oligopoly and Technical Progress.* Cambridge, MA: Harvard University Press.

Symposium on Price Cap Regulation. 1989. *Rand Journal of Economics* 20:369–472.

Syverson, Chad. 2003. "Market Structure and Productivity: A Concrete Example." University of Chicago, Department of Economics.

Takayama, Akira. 1969. "Behavior of the Firm Under Regulatory Constraint." *American Economic Review* 59:255–60.

Tang, Alex, and Yulong Ma. 2002. "The Intrastate Deregulation and the Operating Performance of Trucking Firms." *American Business Review* 20:33–42.

Taylor, Charles T., and Z. Aubrey Silberston. 1973. *The Economic Impact of the Patent System.* Cambridge: Cambridge University Press.

Tellis, Gerard J., and Birger Wernerfelt. 1987. "Competitive Price and Quality Under Asymmetric Information." *Marketing Science* 6:240–53.

Telser, Lester G. 1960. "Why Should Manufacturers Want Fair Trade?" *Journal of Law and Economics* 3:86–105.

Telser, Lester G. 1964. "Advertising and Competition." *Journal of Political Economy* 73:537–62.

Telser, Lester G. 1966. "Supply and Demand for Advertising Messages." *American Economic Review* 56:457–66.

Telser, Lester G. 1969. "Another Look at Advertising and Concentration." *Journal of Industrial Economics* 18:85–94.

Telser, Lester G. 1969. "On the Regulation of Industry: A Note." *Journal of Political Economy* 77:937–52.

Telser, Lester G. 1972. *Competition, Collusion and Game Theory.* Chicago: Aldine-Atherton.

Telser, Lester G. 1978. *Economic Theory and the Core.* Chicago: University of Chicago Press.

Telser, Lester G., and Harlow N. Higgenbotham. 1977. "Organized Futures Markets: Costs and Benefits." *Journal of Political Economy* 85: 969–1000.

Telson, Michael L. 1975. "The Economics of Alternative Levels of Reliability for Electric Power Generation Systems." *Bell Journal of Economics* 6:679–94.

Tenant, Richard B. 1950. *The American Cigarette Industry: A Study in Economic Analysis and Public Policy.* New Haven, CT: Yale University Press.

Thisse, Jacques-François, and Xavier Vives. 1992. "Basing Point Pricing: Competition Versus Collusion." *The Journal of Industrial Economics* 40:249–60.

Thomadakis, Stavros B. 1977. "A Value-Based Test of Profitability and Market Structure." *Review of Economics and Statistics* 59:179–85.

Thomas, Lacey Glenn. 1990. "Regulation and Firm Size: FDA Impacts on Innovation." *Rand Journal of Economics* 21:497–517.

Tirole, Jean. 1988. *The Theory of Industrial Organization.* Cambridge, MA: MIT Press.

Tirole, Jean. forthcoming. "Vertical Foreclosure," in Mark Armstrong and Robert Porter, eds., *Handbook in Industrial Organization,* Vol. 3. Amsterdam: North-Holland.

Tisdell, Clem. 1974. "Patenting and Licensing of Government Inventions—General Issues Raised by Australian Policy." *Australian Economic Papers* 13:188–208.

Topel, Robert H. 1982. "Inventories, Layoffs, and the Short-Run Demand for Labor." *American Economic Review* 72:769–87.

Town, Robert J. 1991. "Price Wars and Demand Fluctuations: A Reexamination of the Joint Executive Committee." U.S. Department of Justice Antitrust Division Discussion Paper EAG91-5.

Trajtenberg, Manuel. 1989. "The Welfare Analysis of Product Innovations, with an Application to Computerized Tomography Scanners." *Journal of Political Economy* 97:444–79.

Tremblay, Victor J., and Kumiko Okuyama. 2001. "Advertising Restrictions, Competition, and Alcohol Consumption." *Contemporary Economic Policy* 19:313–21.

Tucker, Irvin B., and Ronald P. Wilder. 1977. "Trends in Vertical Integration in the U.S. Manufacturing Sector." *Journal of Industrial Economics* 26:81–94.

Tucker, Rufus. 1938. "The Reasons for Price Rigidity." *American Economic Review* 28:41–54.

Ulen, Thomas S. 1980. "The Market for Regulation: The ICC from 1887 to 1920." *American Economic Review* 70:306–10.

Ulph, Alistair. 1987. "Recent Advances in Oligopoly Theory from a Game Theory Perspective." *Journal of Economic Surveys* 1:149–72.

Ulrich, Alvin, Hartley Furtan, and Andrew Schmitz. 1986. "Public and Private Returns from Joint Venture Research: An Example from Agriculture." *Quarterly Journal of Economics* 101:103–29.

U.S. Department of Labor, Bureau of Labor Statistics. 1975. *Characteristics of Major Collective Bargaining Agreements, July 1, 1974.* Bulletin 1888. Washington, D.C.: Government Printing Office.

Usher, Dan. 1964. "The Welfare Economics of Invention." *Economica* 31:279–87.

Varian, Hal R. 1980. "A Model of Sales." *American Economic Review* 70:651–59.

Varian, Hal R. 1984. *Microeconomic Analysis.* New York: W. W. Norton.

Varian, Hal R. 1985. "Price Discrimination and Social Welfare." *American Economic Review* 75:870–75.

Varian, Hal R. 1989. "Price Discrimination," in Richard Schmalensee and Robert D. Willig, eds., *The Handbook of Industrial Organization.* Amsterdam: North-Holland.

Vercammen, James, and Andrew Schmitz. 1992. "Supply Management and Import Concessions." *Canadian Journal of Economics* 25:957–71.

Vernon, John M. 1971. "Concentration, Promotion, and Market Share Stability in the Pharmaceutical Industry." *Journal of Industrial Economics* 19:246–66.

Vernon, John M., and Daniel A. Graham. 1971. "Profitability of Monopolization by Vertical Integration." *Journal of Political Economy* 79:924–25.

Vickery, Graham. 1986. "International Flows of Technology—Recent Trends and Developments." *STI Review* (Autumn):47–84.

Villas-Boas, Sofia Berto. 2002. "Vertical Contracts Between Manufacturers and Retailers: An Empirical Analysis."

Unpublished Ph.D. Thesis, University of California, Berkeley.

Viner, Jacob. 1923. *Dumping: A Problem in International Trade.* Chicago: University of Chicago Press.

Vining, Daniel R., Jr., and Thomas C. Elwertowski. 1976. "The Relationship Between Relative Prices and the General Price Level." *American Economic Review* 66:699–708.

Viscusi, W. Kip. 1996. "Economic Foundation of the Current Regulatory Reform Efforts." *Journal of Economic Perspectives* 10:119–34.

Viscusi, W. Kip, John M. Vernon, and Joseph E. Harrington, Jr. 2000. *Economics of Regulation and Antitrust.* Lexington, MA: D.C. Heath and Company.

von Neumann, John, and Oskar Morgenstern. 1944. *Theory of Games and Economic Behavior.* Princeton, NJ: Princeton University Press.

von Stackelberg: see Stackelberg, von.

von Weizsäcker, C. C. 1980. "A Welfare Analysis of Barriers to Entry." *Bell Journal of Economics* 11:399–420.

Voos, Paula B., and Lawrence R. Mishel. 1986. "The Union Impact on Profits: Evidence from Industry Price-Cost Margin Data." *Journal of Labor Economics* 4:105–33.

Wachter, Michael L., and Oliver E. Williamson. 1978. "Obligational Markets and the Mechanics of Inflation." *Bell Journal of Economics* 9:549–71.

Waldman, Michael. 1987. "Noncooperative Entry Deterrence, Uncertainty, and the Free-Rider Problem." *Review of Economic Studies* 54:301–10.

Waldman, Michael. 1993. "A New Perspective on Planned Obsolescence." *Quarterly Journal of Economics* 58:273–83.

Waldman, Michael. 1997. "Eliminating the Market for Secondhand Goods: An Alternative Explanation for Leasing." *Journal of Law and Economics* 40:61–92.

Waldman, Michael. 2003. "Durable Goods Theory for Real World Markets." *Journal of Economic Perspectives* 17:131–54.

Wallace, Donald H. 1937. *Market Control in the Aluminum Industry.* Cambridge, MA: Harvard University Press.

Walton, Clarence C., and Frederick W. Cleveland. 1964. *Corporations on Trial: The Electric Cases.* Belmont, CA: Wadsworth.

Wann, Joyce J., and Richard J. Sexton. 1992. "Imperfect Competition in Multiproduct Food Industries with Application to Pear Processing." *American Journal of Agricultural Economics,* 74(4 [Nov.]): 980–90.

Ward, Michael B., Jay P. Shimshack, Jeffrey M. Perloff, and J. Michael Harris. 2002. "Effects of the Private-Label Invasion in Food Industries." *American Journal of Agricultural Economics* 84:961–73.

Warren, Melinda, and William F. Lauber. 1998. "Regulatory Changes and Trends: An Analysis of the 1999 Federal Budget." Center for the Study of American Business Regulatory Budget Report 21.

Warren-Boulton, Frederick R. 1974. "Vertical Control with Variable Proportions." *Journal of Political Economy* 82:783–802.

Warren-Boulton, Frederick R. 1994. "Resale Price Maintenance Re-examined: *Monsanto v. Spray-Rite* (1984)," in John E. Kwoka, Jr. and Lawrence J. White, eds., *The Antitrust Revolution: The Role of Economics.* New York: HarperCollins Publishers.

Waterson, Michael. 1987. "Recent Developments in the Theory of Natural Monopoly." *Journal of Economic Surveys* 1:59–80.

Webb, Michael A. 1987. "Antidumping Laws, Production Location and Prices." *Journal of International Economics* 22:363–68.

Weidenbaum, Murray. 1987. "The Benefits of Deregulation." Contemporary Issues Series 25, Center for the Study of American Business, St. Louis: Washington University.

Weiher, Jesse C., Robin C. Sickles, and Jeffrey M. Perloff. 2002. "Market Power in the U.S. Airline Industry," in D. J. Slottje, ed., *Economic Issues in Measuring Market Power. Contributions to Economic Analysis,* Vol. 255. Amsterdam: Elsevier.

Weiman, David, and Richard Levin. 1994. "Preying for Monopoly—The Case of Southern Bell Telephone Company, 1894-1912." *Journal of Political Economy* 102:103–26.

Weiss, Avi. 1992. "The Role of Firm-Specific Capital in Vertical Mergers." *Journal of Law and Economics* 35:71–88.

Weiss, Leonard W. 1964. "The Survival Technique and the Extent of Suboptimal Capacity." *Journal of Political Economy* 72:246–61.

Weiss, Leonard W. 1969. "Advertising, Profits and Corporate Taxes." *Review of Economics and Statistics* 51:421–30.

Weiss, Leonard W. 1974. "The Concentration-Profits Relationship and Antitrust," in Harvey J. Goldschmid, H. Michael Mann, and J. Fred Weston, eds., *Industrial Concentration: The New Learning.* Boston: Little, Brown.

Weiss, Leonard W. 1976. "Optimal Plant Size and the Extent of Suboptimal Capacity," in R. T. Masson and P. D. Qualls, eds., *Essays on Industrial Organization in Honor of Joe S. Bain.* Cambridge, MA: Ballinger.

Weiss, Leonard W. 1977. "Stigler, Kindahl, and Means on Administered Prices." *American Economic Review* 67:610–19.

Weiss, Leonard W. 1981. "State Regulation of Public Utilities and Marginal-Cost Pricing," in Leonard W. Weiss and Michael W. Klass, eds., *Case Studies in Regulation: Revolution and Reform.* Boston: Little, Brown and Company.

Weiss, Leonard W., and Michael W. Klass, eds. 1981. *Case Studies in Regulation: Revolution and Reform.* Boston: Little, Brown and Company.

Weiss, Leonard W., George Pascoe, and Stephen Martin. 1983. "The Size of Selling Costs." *Review of Economics and Statistics* 65:668–72.

Weiss, Leonard W., and Allyn D. Strickland. 1982. *Regulation: A Case Approach.* New York: McGraw-Hill.

Weitzman, Martin L. 1983. "Contestable Markets: An Uprising in the Theory of Industrial Structure: Comment." *American Economic Review* 73:486–87.

Wendel, Jeanne. 1976. "Firm-Regulator Interaction with Respect to Firm Cost Reduction Activities." *Bell Journal of Economics* 7:631–40.

West, Douglas S., and Balder von Hohenbalken. 1984. "Spatial Predation in a Canadian Retail Oligopoly." *Journal of Regional Science* 24:415–29.

Weston, J. Fred, and Stephen Lustgarten. 1974. "Concentration and Wage-Price Changes," in Harvey J. Goldschmidt et al., eds., *Industrial Concentration: The New Learning.* Boston: Little, Brown, 307–38.

Whinston, Michael. 1990. "Tying, Foreclosure, and Exclusion." *American Economic Review* 80:837–59.

Whinston, Michael. 2001. "Exclusivity and Tying in U.S. v. Microsoft: What We Know, and Don't Know." *Journal of Economic Perspectives* 15:63–80.

White, Lawrence J. 1972. "Quality Variation When Prices Are Regulated." *Bell Journal of Economics* 3:425–36.

White, Lawrence J. 1976. "Searching for the Critical Industrial Concentration Ratio," in Stephen Goldfeld and Richard E. Quandt, eds., *Studies in Non-Linear Estimation.* Cambridge, MA: Ballinger.

White, Lawrence J. 1985. "Resale Price Maintenance and the Problem of Marginal and Inframarginal Customers." *Contemporary Policy Issues* 3:17–22.

White, Lawrence J. 1988. "Litan's *What Should Banks Do?*: A Review Essay." *Rand Journal of Economics* 19:305–15.

White, Lawrence J., ed. 1989. *Private Antitrust Litigation: New Evidence, New Learning.* Cambridge, MA: MIT Press.

White, Lawrence J. 1991. *The S&L Debacle—Public Policy Lessons for Bank and Thrift Regulation.* Oxford: Oxford University Press.

White, Lawrence J. 2002. "Trends in Aggregate Concentration in the United States." *Journal of Economic Perspectives* 16:137–60.

White, Michelle J. 2002. "The 'Arms Race' on American Roads." National Bureau of Economic Research Working Paper 9302.

Whitman, Douglas Glen. 2003. *Strange Brew: Alcohol and Government Monopoly.* Oakland, CA: The Independent Institute.

Whyte, Glen. 1994. "The Role of Asset Specificity in the Vertical Integration Decision." *Journal of Economic Behavior and Organization* 23:287–302.

Wilde, Louis L., and Alan Schwartz. 1979. "Equilibrium Comparison Shopping." *Review of Economic Studies* 46:543–53.

Williams, George. 2002. *Airline Competition: Deregulation's Mixed Legacy.* Burlington, VT: Ashgate.

Williams, John D. 1966. *The Compleat Strategyst.* New York: McGraw-Hill.

Williamson, Oliver E. 1964. *The Economics of Discretionary Behavior: Managerial Objectives in a Theory of the Firm.* Englewood Cliffs, NJ: Prentice-Hall.

Williamson, Oliver E. 1967. "The Economics of Defense Contracting: Incentives and Performance," in R. N. McKean, ed., *Issues in Defense Economics.* New York: Columbia University Press.

Williamson, Oliver E. 1968. "Wage Rates as a Barrier to Entry: The Pennington Case." *Quarterly Journal of Economics* 82:85–116.

Williamson, Oliver E. 1968–69. "Economies as an Antitrust Defense: The Welfare Trade-offs." *American Economic Review* 58:18–36; 58:372–76; and 59:954–69.

Williamson, Oliver E. 1971. "Administrative Controls and Regulatory Behavior," in H. M. Trebling, ed., *Essays on Public Utility Pricing and Regulation.* Institute of Public Utilities, East Lansing, MI: Michigan State University.

Williamson, Oliver, E. 1975. *Markets and Hierarchies—Analysis and Antitrust Implications: A Study in the Economics of Internal Organization.* New York: The Free Press.

Williamson, Oliver E. 1976. "Franchise Bidding for Natural Monopolies—In General and with Respect to CATV." *Bell Journal of Economics* 7:73–104.

Williamson, Oliver E. 1977. "Predatory Pricing: A Strategic and Welfare Analysis." *Yale Law Journal* 87:284–339.

Williamson, Oliver E. 1985. *The Economic Institutions of Capitalism: Firms, Markets, Relational Contracting.* New York: The Free Press.

Williamson, Oliver E. 1987. *Antitrust Economics.* Cambridge, MA: Basil Blackwell, Inc.

Williamson, Oliver E. n.d. "Entry Deterrence in the RTE Cereal Industry: A Comment." Working paper.

Willig, Robert D. 1976. "Consumer's Surplus without Apology." *American Economic Review* 66:589–97.

Willig, Robert D., and William J. Baumol. 1987. "Railroad Deregulation: Using Competition as a Guide." *Regulation* 11:28–35.

Wilson, Robert. 1992. "Strategic Models of Entry Deterrence," in R. Aumann and S. Hart, eds., *Handbook of Game Theory.* Amsterdam: North-Holland.

Wilson, Robert. 1993. *Nonlinear Pricing.* Oxford: Oxford University Press.

Wimmer, Bradley S., and Brian Chezum. 2003. "An Empirical Examination of Quality Certification in a 'Lemons Market'," *Economic Inquiry* 41:279–91.

Wimmer, Bradley S., and John E. Garen. 1997. "Moral Hazard, Asset Specificity, Implicit Bonding, and Compensation: The Case of Franchising." *Economic Inquiry* 35:544–54.

Winston, Clifford. 1993. "Economic Deregulation: Days of Reckoning for Microeconomists." *Journal of Economic Literature* 31:1263–89.

Winter, Ralph A. 1993. "Vertical Control and Price versus Non-Price Competition." *Quarterly Journal of Economics* 108:61–76.

Wolak, Frank A., and Charles D. Kolstad. 1988. "Measuring Relative Market Power in the Western U.S. Coal Market Using Shapley Values." *Resources and Energy* 10:293–314.

Wolinsky, Asher. 1983. "Prices as Signals of Product Quality." *Review of Economic Studies* 50:647–58.

Wolinsky, Asher. 1986. "True Monopolistic Competition as a Result of Imperfect Information." *Quarterly Journal of Economics* 101:493–511.

Worcester, Dean A., Jr. 1973. "New Estimates of the Welfare Loss to Monopoly, United States: 1956–1969." *Southern Economic Journal* 40:234–45.

Wright, Brian D. 1983. "The Economics of Invention Incentives: Patents, Prizes, and Research Contracts." *American Economic Review* 73:691–707.

Yamey, B. S., ed. 1966. *Resale Price Maintenance.* Chicago: Aldine.

Yatchew, A. 2000. "Scale Economies in Electricity Distribution: A Semiparametric Analysis." *Journal of Applied Econometrics* 15:187–210.

Ying, John S., and Theodore E. Keeler. 1991. "Pricing in a Deregulated Environment: The Motor Carrier Experience." *Rand Journal of Economics* 22:264–73.

You, Zhikang, James E. Epperson, and Chung L. Huang. 1998. *Consumer Demand for Fresh Fruits and Vegetables in the United States.* Georgia Agricultural Experiment Stations Research Bulletin 431.

Zajac, E. E. 1970. "A Geometric Treatment of Averch-Johnson's Behavior of the Firm Model." *American Economic Review* 60: 117–25.

Zarnowitz, Victor. 1962. "Unfilled Orders, Price Changes, and Business Fluctuations." *Review of Economics and Statistics* 44:367–94.

Zarnowitz, Victor. 1973. *Orders, Production, and Investment: A Cyclical and Structural Analysis.* New York: National Bureau of Economic Research.

Zarnowitz, Victor. 1985. "Recent Work on Business Cycles in Historical Perspective: A Review of Theories and Evidence." *Journal of Economic Literature* 23:523–80.

Zbaracki, Mark, Mark Ritson, Daniel Levy, Shantanu Dutta, and Mark Bergen. 2003. "Managerial and Customer Cost of Price Adjustment: Direct Evidence from Industrial Markets." Economics working paper, no. 2003, Bar-Ilen University.

Zupan, Mark A. 1989. "Cable Franchise Renewals: Do Incumbent Firms Behave Opportunistically?" *Rand Journal of Economics* 20:473–82.

Glossary

adjustment costs: the expenses associated with changing the combination of inputs used in production.

administered prices: prices are under the control of firms and not subject to the laws of supply and demand.

adverse selection: only consumers with the least desirable characteristics, which are unobservable to the firm, buy the firm's product. For example, only the worst risks buy an insurance policy.

amortized: costs are allocated over the useful life of a machine.

antitrust laws: statutes that limit the market power exercised by firms and control how firms compete with each other.

asymmetric information: one party to a transaction knows a material fact the other party does not know.

average cost (AC, average total cost, ATC): total cost divided by output: $ATC = C(q)/q$.

average fixed cost (AFC): fixed cost divided by output: $AFC = F/q$.

average variable cost (AVC): variable cost divided by output: $AVC = VC(q)/q$.

avoidable costs: expenses, including fixed costs, that are not incurred if operations cease.

barrier to entry: anything that prevents an entrepreneur from instantaneously creating a new firm in a market (see long-run barrier to entry).

best-response (reaction) function: the relationship between the best (highest profit) action by a firm and the action taken by its rival.

bond covenants: restrictions imposed by bond holders on a corporation's operations, such as choices of investment projects or further financing.

bounded rationality: people's limited ability to enumerate and understand all future possibilities.

break the equilibrium: firms benefit from deviating from a proposed equilibrium, so it is not an equilibrium.

bundling: two or more goods are sold only in fixed proportions.

capital asset: something (such as a machine, building, or reputation) that lasts for many periods and that provides a service in each period.

capital costs: the total rental fees if all the capital assets were rented.

capture theory: an industry "captures" (persuades, bribes, or threatens) the regulators, so that the regulators do what the industry wants (see *interest-group theory*).

cartel: an association of firms that explicitly agree to coordinate their activities, typically to maximize joint profits (*cooperative oligopoly*).

certification: an assurance that a particular product has been found to meet or exceed a given standard.

characteristic space: there is an axis showing the amount of each characteristic or attribute. Each brand and each consumer's preferred product can be located in this space according to its characteristics.

Coase Conjecture: a durable goods monopolist that sells its product has less market power—indeed, in the extreme case, no market power—when compared to a monopoly that rents the durable good.

competition: a market has many potential buyers and sellers and has no entry or exit barriers.

concentrated: an industry is said to be concentrated if a few firms make most of the sales.

conduct: behavior of firms (or other economic actors).

conglomerate merger: firms in unrelated businesses combine.

conscious parallelism (*tacit collusion*): the coordinated actions of firms in an oligopoly despite the lack of an explicit cartel agreement.

constant returns to scale: average costs do not vary with output.

consumer surplus: the amount above the price paid that a consumer would willingly spend, if necessary, to consume the units purchased.

contestable: a market is contestable if there is free entry and exit.

contribution: payments to a guilty defendant from other culpable parties.

cooperative oligopoly: a small group of firms (an oligopoly) that coordinate their actions to maximize joint profits (act like a *cartel*).

cooperative strategic behavior: actions that make it easier for firms in an industry to coordinate their actions and to limit their competitive responses.

copyright: an exclusive right granted a creator to produce, publish, or sell an artistic, dramatic, literary, or musical work.

corporations: companies whose capital is divided into shares that are held by individuals who have only limited responsibility for the debts of the company.

credible strategies: those sets of actions by a firm that are in the firm's best interest.

credible threat: a firm's strategy that its rivals believe is rational in the sense that it is in the firm's best interest to continue to employ it.

cross-elasticity of demand: the percentage change in quantity demanded in response to a 1 percent change in another product's price.

deadweight loss (*DWL*): the cost to society of a market that does not operate optimally.

decreasing returns to scale (*diseconomies of scale*): average cost rises with output.

delivered pricing: the total delivered price (inclusive of freight) that a buyer must pay is a function of the buyer's distance from a specific location (a basing point) but not from the seller's location.

depreciation: the decline in the value of an asset during the year.

discriminatory dumping: a firm charges a lower price in a foreign market than in the domestic market so as to *price discriminate.*

diseconomies of scale (*decreasing returns to scale*): average cost rises with output.

dominant firm: a price-setting firm that faces smaller, price-taking firms.

dominant strategy: a strategy that leads to as high or higher a payoff as any other regardless of the strategy chosen by a rival firm.

downstream firms: firms that produce the final good.

dumping: a firm sells its product abroad at a price below its domestic price or below its costs.

durable goods: goods that last for several time periods.

Dutch auction: an auction in which the price starts out very high and is slowly lowered until one person agrees to buy at that price.

dynamic limit pricing: a firm sets its prices (or quantities) over time so as to reduce or eliminate the incentives of rivals to enter a market.

economies of scale (*increasing returns to scale*): average cost falls as output increases.

economies of scope: it is less costly for one firm to perform two activities than for two specialized firms to perform them separately.

efficient production: given the inputs used, no more output could be produced with existing technology.

elastic: a demand (supply) curve is elastic if a 1 percent increase in price reduces (increases) the quantity demanded (supplied) by more than 1 percent (the absolute value of the elasticity of demand is greater than 1).

elasticity of demand: the percentage change in quantity demanded in response to a 1 percent change in price.

elasticity of supply: the percentage change in quantity supplied in response to a 1 percent change in price.

English auction: an auction in which bids start low and rise until there is no one willing to bid any higher.

entry condition: firms enter the market when profits are positive and exit when profits are negative.

essential facilities: scarce resources that a competitor needs to use to survive.

exchange rate: the price of one currency in terms of another currency.

exclusionary actions: what a firm does to eliminate rivals from a market or harm them, thereby either helping to maintain or create a monopoly.

exclusive dealing: a manufacturer forbids its distributors to sell the products of competing manufacturers.

exclusive territory: a single distributor is the only one that can sell a product within a particular region.

expensed: costs that are counted as they are incurred.

experience qualities: a product has these qualities if a customer must consume the product to determine its quality.

extensive-form representation of a game: a decision tree of the order in which firms make their moves, each firm's strategy at the time of its move, and the payoffs.

externality: the direct effect on the well-being of a consumer or the production capability of a firm from the actions of other consumers or firms.

fighting brand: a product that a firm sells at a low price and whose availability is limited to those areas and products where a rival is successful.

firm: an organization that transforms inputs (resources it purchases) into outputs (valued products that it sells).

firm's supply curve: the quantity that a competitive firm is willing to supply at any given price (the *MC* curve above minimum *AVC*).

first-best optimum: the unconstrained maximum (typically a solution that maximizes welfare).

first-degree price discrimination (*perfect price discrimination*): a monopoly is able to charge the maximum each consumer is willing to pay for each unit of the product.

first-mover advantage: the first firm to enter incurs lower costs (such as marketing) because it faces no rivals.

fixed costs (*F*): expenses that do not vary with the level of output.

fixed-proportions production function: inputs are always used in a particular proportion.

FOB pricing: the buyer pays a free-on-board (FOB) price, where the seller loads the good onto the transport carrier at no cost to the buyer, plus the actual freight.

franchise: the right to sell a product or use a brand name.

franchise bidding: a government or other franchisor sells the right to a monopoly or other franchise to the highest bidder.

free riding: when one agent (firm) benefits from the actions of another without paying for it.

fringe: a group of small price-taking firms in a market with a dominant firm.

game: any competition in which strategies are used.

game of imperfect information: a firm must choose an action without observing the simultaneous (or earlier) move of its rivals.

game theory: formal models are used to analyze conflict and cooperation between players.

going private: the managers buy ownership of a corporation.

greenmail: management buys back the shares of someone engaged in a hostile takeover attempt at a premium.

Herfindahl-Hirschman Index (*HHI*): the sum of the squared market shares of each firm in the industry.

heterogeneous or **differentiated** goods: related products that are viewed by consumers as imperfect substitutes.

homogeneous or **undifferentiated** goods: products that are viewed as identical by consumers.

horizontal merger: firms that compete within the same industry combine.

hostile takeover: a change in the ownership of a corporation despite opposition by the original managers or owners.

increasing returns to scale (*economies of scale*): average cost falls as output increases.

industrial organization: the study of the structure of firms and markets and of their interactions.

inelastic: a demand (supply) curve is inelastic if a 1 percent increase in price reduces (increases) the quantity demanded (supplied) by less than 1 percent (the elasticity is less than 1 in absolute value).

informational advertising: promotional activity that describes a product's objective characteristics.

interest-group theory: firms, consumers, or other groups capture a regulatory body (see *capture theory*).

internalize the externality: force someone who is causing an externality to bear the full social costs (for example, force a firm to pay for the pollution it creates).

intertemporal substitution: delaying consumption or production to a later time.

joint venture: coordinated activities by more than one firm. A research joint venture is an R&D project financed and managed cooperatively by several firms.

junk bonds: high-yield bonds that are backed by a corporation's assets and that are considered riskier than typical corporate bonds.

learning by doing: costs fall with production because workers become more skilled at their jobs due to experience or because better ways of producing are discovered.

legal standing: the right to bring a suit.

Lerner Index of market power (*price-cost margin*): a measure of the markup of price over marginal cost: $(p - MC)/p$.

leveraged buyout (*LBO*): the funds to purchase a corporation are raised through bonds based on the corporation's assets.

license: a permit granted by a patent holder to another firm to produce the product or use the new process.

limited liability: if a corporation fails (is unable to pay its bills), the shareholders need not pay for the debt using their personal assets.

limit pricing: a firm sets its price and output so that there is not enough demand left for another firm to profitably enter the market.

location (*spatial*) **models:** monopolistic competition models in which consumers view each firm's product as having a particular location in geographic or product (characteristic) space.

long run: a sufficiently lengthy period of time such that all factors of production can be costlessly varied.

long-run barriers to entry: a cost that must be incurred by a new entrant that incumbents do not (or have not had to) bear.

marginal cost (*MC*): the increment, or addition, to cost that results from producing one more unit of output.

marginal outlay schedule: the marginal cost to a monopsony of buying additional units.

marginal revenue (*MR*): the extra revenues that a firm receives when it produces one more unit of the product.

market clearing: the equilibration of the quantities supplied and demanded.

market definition: the competing products and geographic area in which competition occurs that determines the price for a given product.

market environment: all factors that influence the market outcome (prices, quantities, profits, welfare), including the beliefs of customers and of rivals, the number of actual and potential rivals, the production technology of each firm, and the costs or speed with which a rival can enter the industry.

market failures: distortions or inefficient production due to improper pricing.

market power: the ability of a firm to set price profitably above competitive levels (marginal cost).

market supply curve: the horizontal sum of the supply curves of each firm.

meeting-competition clause: a provision in a supply contract that guarantees the buyer that if another firm offers a lower price, the seller will match it or release the buyer from the contract.

merger: a transaction in which the assets of one or more firms are combined in a new firm.

minimum efficient scale (*MES*): the size plant that can produce the smallest amount of output such that long-run average costs are minimized.

monopolistic competition: a market structure in which firms have *market power,* the ability to raise price profitably above marginal cost, yet they make zero economic profits.

monopoly: a single seller in a market.

monopsony: a single buyer in a market.

moral hazard: an individual has an incentive to take an action that is unobservable to a firm and is socially inefficient in response to the firm's offer. For example, an individual with fire insurance may be tempted to burn the insured building.

most-favored-nation clause: a sales contract provision that guarantees the buyer that the seller is not selling at a lower price to another buyer.

Nash equilibrium: holding the strategies of all other firms constant, no firm can obtain a higher payoff (profit) by choosing a different strategy.

natural monopoly: a situation where total production costs would rise if two or more firms produced instead of just one firm.

negative externality: a bad that is not priced (such as pollution).

noncooperative oligopoly: a small number of firms acting independently but aware of one another's existence.

noncooperative strategic behavior: actions of a firm that is trying to maximize its profits by improving its position relative to its rivals.

nonlinear pricing: when a consumer's total expenditure on an item does not rise linearly (proportionately) with the amount purchased.

nonuniform pricing: charging different customers different prices for the same product or charging a single customer a price that varies depending on how many units the customer buys.

normal-form representation of a game: a matrix that shows all the strategies available to each player (who must choose actions simultaneously) and the payoffs to each player for each combination of strategies.

normal profit: best possible profit from an alternative use of the resource.

oligopoly: the only sellers in a market are a small number of firms and they face no threat of entry.

opportunistic behavior: taking advantage of another when allowed by circumstances.

opportunity cost: the value of the best foregone alternative use of the resources employed.

package tie-in sale: two or more goods are sold only in fixed proportions.

patent: an exclusive right granted an inventor to a new and useful product, process, substance, or design.

patent race: several firms compete to be the first to make the discovery and be granted a patent.

payoff: the reward (such as profits) received at the end of a game.

perfect competition: a market outcome in which all firms produce homogeneous, perfectly divisible output and face no barriers to entry or exit; producers and consumers have full information, incur no transaction costs, and are price takers; and there are no externalities.

perfect Nash equilibrium: a Nash equilibrium in which strategies (threats) are credible (see *subgame perfect Nash equilibrium*).

perfect price discrimination (*first-degree price discrimination*): a monopoly is able to charge the maximum each consumer is willing to pay for each unit of the product.

performance: the success of a market in producing benefits for society.

per se violation: an action that, by itself, is illegal.

persuasive advertising: promotional activities designed to shift consumers' tastes.

planned obsolescence: purposely making a durable good short-lived.

players: strategic decision makers in game theory, such as oligopolistic firms.

poison pill: if a successful hostile takeover occurs, the corporation must make available stock at bargain prices to original shareholders (but not to someone who takes over the firm).

positive externality: an uncompensated action that benefits others.

predatory dumping: a firm sets an extremely low price in a foreign country so as to predate against that country's firms (*predatory pricing*).

predatory pricing: a firm first lowers its price in order to drive rivals out of business and scare off potential entrants and then raises its price when its rivals exit the market (in most definitions, the firm lowers price below some measure of cost).

price controls: limits on how high firms may set prices.

price-cost margin: a measure of the markup of price over marginal cost: $(p - MC)/p$ (see *Lerner Index*).

price discrimination: nonuniform pricing in which a firm charges different categories of customers different unit prices for the identical good or charges each consumer a nonuniform price on different units of the good.

price dispersion: stores charge different prices for the identical good.

price rigidity: prices do not vary in response to fluctuations in cost and demand.

price setter: a firm with *market power* that can profitably set its price above the competitive price.

price supports: a price level that prices are kept at or above by government purchases.

price taker: a firm that does not have the ability (*market power*) to set its price profitably above the competitive price.

principal-agent relationship: the principal (firm or individual) hires the agent (another firm or individual) to perform an action in a manner that the principal cannot fully control.

prisoners' dilemma game: firms have dominant strategies that lead to a payoff that is inferior to what they could achieve if they cooperated.

producer surplus: the largest amount that could be subtracted from a supplier's revenues and yet leave the supplier willing to produce the product.

produce-to-order: firms wait for orders and then produce.

produce-to-stock: firms produce first, hold inventories, and then sell the inventoried products.

product differentiation: related products that do not have identical characteristics so that consumers do not view them as perfect substitutes.

production possibility frontier (*PPF*): the feasible combinations of number of brands and quantity per brand that can be produced with society's total inputs (generally, the feasible outputs that can be produced efficiently).

production technology: the relationship between inputs and output reflecting the maximum possible output that can be produced from a given set of inputs.

property rights: exclusive rights to use some asset (goods or services).

public good: something useful which, if supplied to one person, can be made available to others at no extra cost.

quality discrimination: a firm offers consumers a choice of different quality products in order to effectively price discriminate.

quantity discounts: a firm's price varies with the number of units of the good that a customer buys so that the average price paid declines as the number of units purchased increases.

quantity forcing: a sales quota that a manufacturer places on the distributor; the distributor must sell a minimum number of units.

quasi-rents: payments above the minimum amount necessary to keep a firm operating in the short run.

quasi-vertical integration (or quasi-integration or partial vertical integration): where one firm owns a specific physical asset that one of its suppliers uses.

Ramsey pricing: regulated prices that maximize consumer welfare subject to the requirement that revenues cover costs.

rate of return: a measure of how much is earned per dollar of investment.

reciprocal dumping: firms in two (or more) countries dump in the other's country.

refinements: restrictions on the possible equilibria.

rent: a payment to the owner of an input beyond the minimum necessary to cause it to be used.

rent seeking: the expenditure of resources to attain a monopoly with its associated rent or profit.

replacement cost: the long-run cost of buying a comparable quality asset.

representative consumer model: a monopolistic competition model in which the typical consumer views all brands as equally good substitutes for each other; hence brands are treated symmetrically.

requirements tie-in sale: customers who purchase one product from a firm are required to make all their purchases of another product from that firm.

resale price maintenance: the manufacturer sets a minimum price that may be charged by retailers. (Some people also use this term to refer to the setting of a maximum price.)

residual demand: the demand curve facing a particular firm, which is market demand less the quantity supplied by rival firms at any given price.

risk-adjusted rate of return: the rate of return earned by competitive firms engaged in projects with the same level of risk as that of the firm under analysis.

royalty: a payment for the right (*license*) to produce the product or use the process of a patent holder.

rule of reason: the balancing of the pro- and anticompetitive effects of an action to determine its legality; that is, the action involved is not *per se* illegal (always illegal).

search qualities: a product has these qualities if a consumer can establish the product's quality prior to purchase by inspection.

second-best optimum: the best possible outcome subject to a constraint that violates one of the conditions for a first-best outcome.

self-selection constraint: a restriction on a firm's pricing structure such that consumers in any group do not prefer another group's two-part tariff schedule.

short run: a time period so brief that some factors of production cannot be costlessly varied.

shutdown point: the price at which a firm ceases operating.

spatial (*location*) **models:** monopolistic competition models in which consumers view each firm's product as having a particular location in geographic or product (characteristic) space.

specialized asset: a piece of capital that is tailor-made for one or a few specific buyers.

spurious product differentiation: consumers mistakenly believe that physically identical brands differ.

standard: a metric or scale for evaluating the quality of a particular product.

static analysis: models of markets that last for only one period.

strategic behavior: a set of actions a firm takes to influence the market environment so as to increase its profits.

strategy: a battle plan of the actions of a player.

structure: those factors that determine the competitiveness of a market.

subgame: a new game that starts in any period t and lasts to the end of the game.

subgame perfect Nash equilibrium (*perfect Nash equilibrium*): a *Nash equilibrium* in which the original strategies are Nash equilibria (best responses) in any *subgame*.

sunk cost: the portion of fixed costs that is not recoverable.

supergames: repeated games where players know their rivals' previous actions and condition their actions in each period on these previous actions.

sustainable: an equilibrium where a natural monopoly prices such that it covers its costs yet does not induce entry.

tacit collusion (*conscious parallelism*): the coordinated actions of firms in an oligopoly despite the lack of an explicit cartel agreement.

third-degree price discrimination: a firm charges consumers in different groups different unit prices.

tie-in sale: a customer may purchase one product only if another product is also purchased.

Tobin's q: the ratio of the market value of a firm (as measured by the market value of its outstanding stock and debt) to the replacement cost of the firm's assets.

total costs (C): the sum of all fixed and variable costs: $C = F + VC$.

trademark: words, symbols, or other marks used to distinguish a good or service provided by one firm from those provided by other firms.

transaction costs: the expenses of trading with others besides the price.

transfer prices: prices that are set not by the market but by a firm for internal use to allocate goods among its divisions.

treble damages: three times actual damages (awarded in antitrust cases).

trigger price: cartel members agree that if the market price drops below this price, each firm will expand its output.

two-part tariff: a firm charges a consumer a fee (the first tariff) for the right to buy as many units of the product as the consumer wants at a specified price (the second tariff).

unitary elasticity: a demand curve has unitary price elasticity if a 1 percent increase in price reduces the quantity demanded by 1 percent (the absolute value of its elasticity of demand is 1).

upstream firms: firms that supply the inputs in the production process.

variable costs (VC): expenses that change with the level of output.

variable-proportions production function: one input can be substituted for another to some degree.

vertical merger: a firm buys its supplier or vice versa.

vertical restrictions: binding contractual limitations on price, other terms, or behavior that one nonintegrated firm imposes upon another firm from which it buys or to which it sells.

vertically integrated: a firm that participates in more than one successive stage of the production or distribution of goods or services.

white knight: in order to prevent a hostile takeover, an individual or firm is invited to obtain control of a corporation by its managers with the understanding that the new owner will leave current management in place.

Answers to Odd-Numbered Problems

I was gratified to be able to answer promptly. I said I don't know. —*Mark Twain*

Chapter 2

1. Although some monitoring problems increase with size, large firms exist because some benefits also increase with size, and other monitoring problems decrease as size increases. For example, the average cost of monitoring quality may fall with size if the firm can obtain reliable results by checking a small percentage of a large output.
3. Transaction costs are likely to be relatively high in (a), (b), and (c). In these three cases, there is likely to be only one firm.
5. No. Even if all costs are fixed, marginal cost need not be zero. For example, if a firm is operating at full capacity and is unable to produce more output, its marginal costs are effectively infinitely large (at no finite cost can an extra unit of output be produced).
7. The marginal cost of an extra car is 70. Producing 100 cars and 200 trucks in the same plant costs \$33,000 (10,000 + (70 × 100) + (80 × 200)). Producing them in two separate plants costs \$17,000 for cars and \$26,000 for trucks. Thus, the savings from jointly producing them is \$10,000 (the extra fixed cost). The measure of scope economies is 10,000/33,000 or about 0.3.
9. If all plants are in the same area, they face similar costs. If the industry is in equilibrium, then a wide range of plant sizes indicates that the *AC* curve has a flat section over a wide range of output. If plants are located in different countries, they are likely to face different costs, so that all one can conclude is that the efficient-scale plant may vary considerably depending on cost conditions.

Chapter 3

1. No, a tax of \$1 per unit of output raises the *AC* and *MC* curves of the firm by \$1. As a result, the output at which the *AC* curve reaches its minimum is unchanged by the tax. If all competitive firms are identical and there are an unlimited number of firms ready to produce, then each firm operates at the minimum of its *AC* curve in the long run.
3. a. The supply curve is horizontal at $p = \$10$. The supply and demand curves intersect at $p = \$10$, $Q = 990$.
   b. If the one firm with a fixed capacity of 10 enters, that firm's entry leaves unchanged the supply curve beyond 10 units. Supply and demand intersect at the same p and Q as in (a).
   c. Positive economic profits for some firms are not inconsistent with long-run competitive equilibrium. The new firm in (b) earns a profit of \$10.
   d. The marginal cost of the last unit supplied is \$10. If demand expands or contracts, the firms with \$10 marginal costs vary their output.
   e. The less efficient firms earn 0.
   f. Yes. Otherwise additional entry or exit would occur.
5. When there are no shutdown costs, the *AC* curve coincides with the *AVC* curve, and the shutdown point becomes the minimum point of the *AC* curve.

Chapter 4

1. The monopoly's profit is $(p - 4)(10 - p)$. A p of \$7 maximizes its profit. If $p = \$7$, $Q = 3$. Because $dQ/dp = -1$, the elasticity, $(dQ/dp)(p/Q)$, is $-7/3$.
3. Because $Q = 5/p$, $dQ/dp = -5/p^2$, and the elasticity, $(dQ/dp)(p/Q)$, is $(-5/p^2)[p/(5/p)] = -1$. Total revenue equals pQ, which always equals 5. Because revenue always equals \$5, the monopoly maximizes its profit where its total costs are as low as possible. That is, the monopoly should produce as little as possible, one unit, to maximize its profit at \$4.
5. Under competition, all 5 units are always sold, so that the supply curve is vertical at $Q = 5$. Supply equals demand at $Q = 5$, $p = 5$. The monopoly maximizes its profit. If it sells fewer than 5 units, its profit falls because its marginal revenue is positive if output is less than 5 (and hence above its marginal cost). If the monopoly sells 5 units, price equals 5. Hence, monopoly and competition produce identical results.

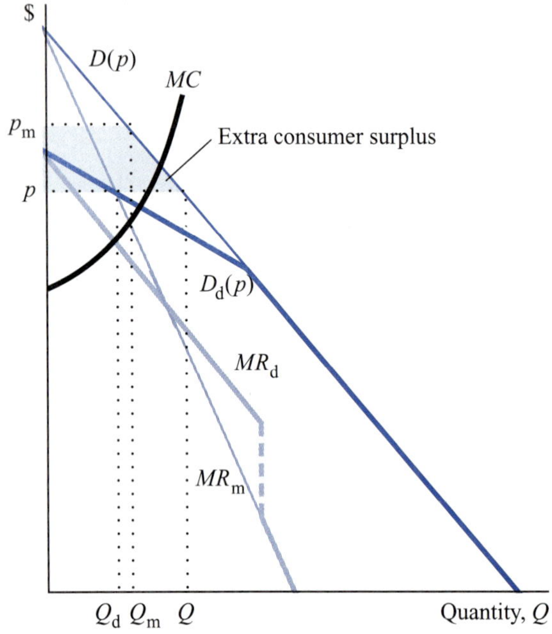

7. In the figure, the dominant firm sells Q_d, whereas the monopoly sells Q_m. Because the monopoly could have sold Q_d and chose not to, it must make higher profits at Q_m. The monopoly's costs to produce the extra output are the area under the *MC* curve between Q_d and Q_m. Its extra revenues are the area under the marginal revenue curve, MR_m, between Q_d and Q_m. Thus, by producing Q_m instead of Q_d, its profit increases by the area between the MR_m and the *MC* curve between Q_d and Q_m. On the first Q_d units, the monopoly's costs are the same as the dominant firm's (by assumption), and it receives a higher price, p_m instead of p. Thus, the monopoly makes more on the first Q_d units as well, and hence must make higher profits overall. The figure shows the consumers' gain.
9. In the figure in the answer to Problem 4.7 above, if the *MC* curve crosses the MR_d and the MR_m curves below the point where the marginal revenue curves cross, a dominant firm produces more than does a monopoly.

Chapter 5

1. Your drawing should look like Figure 4.6b if you assume no entry, where the cartel acts as though it is a dominant firm. If you assume free entry, your drawing should look like Figure 4.7b. If the cartel's marginal costs are low enough so that it maximizes its profits at a price below the noncartel member's shut-down price, the cartel drives the fringe out of business.
3. Your graph should show that as the demand curve becomes flatter at a given point (that is, its elasticity increases), the cartel's residual demand curve also becomes flatter. As a result, the intersection of *MC* and residual *MR* occurs at a lower quantity and a lower price.
5. Because noncartel members produce more than cartel members, shifting one of the n firms from the cartel to the noncartel group increases output, all else the same. Increasing the number of noncartel firms, j, causes the cartel's quantity to fall, as we show by differentiating Equation 5A.11:

$$\frac{dQ_m}{dj} = -\frac{(a - bd)(be + n)}{(be + 2n - j)^2} < 0.$$

This derivative is negative because $(a - bd)$ is positive (were it not, Q_m would be negative). Total output, Q, is the sum of the fringe supply, $j(p - d)/e$, and Q_m (Equation 5A.11). After substituting for p from Equation 5A.1 and rearranging terms:

$$Q = (nbe + 2nj - j^2)(a - bd)/D,$$

where $D = (be + 2n - j)(be + j)$. Differentiating this expression for Q with respect to j, we obtain

$$\frac{dQ}{dj} = \frac{2(n - j)(b^2e^2 + nbe)(a - bd)}{D^2} > 0.$$

Because total output increases, price must fall.

Chapter 6

1. A sufficient condition for the Cournot and Bertrand equilibria to be identical is for the market demand curve to be horizontal (perfectly elastic). Another sufficient condition is for there to be an infinite number of firms, so that the elasticity facing any one firm is infinite.
3. It pays for both firms to cooperate and charge the high price. Neither firm has an incentive to deviate from this strategy.
5. The modified table appears at the top of the next page.

Answer to Chapter 6, Problem 5:

Number of Firms	Market Elasticity, ϵ	Lerner's Measure	Consumer Surplus	Social Welfare	Deadweight Loss
2	−1.0833	.4615	115.2	230.4	28.8
5	−.6666	.3	180	252	7.2
10	−.5271	.1884	214.4	257.2	2.0
50	−.4166	.048	249.1	259.1	.1
1,000	−.3903	.0026	258.7	259.2	.0

Chapter 7

1. A franchise or lump-sum tax shifts up a firm's average cost, but not its marginal cost curve. As a result, a franchise tax has no effect on a monopoly unless it causes it to shut down. The quantity that maximizes the before-tax profits maximizes the after-tax profits as well.

   The tax does affect individual competitive firms. If all competitive firms are identical and there is free entry, then, after the tax, firms still in the industry are producing at a higher minimum average cost (reflecting the tax) and a higher quantity. Because the price is higher, less total quantity is consumed; thus, because each firm produces more than without the tax, there are fewer competitive firms.

   The tax also affects monopolistically competitive firms, but the effects are complex and depend on the shapes of the demand and cost curves. Table 7.2 shows what happens with a linear demand curve and a cost function $= mq + F$. For example, if $F = \$1.60$ and a franchise tax of \$4.80 is applied, the equilibrium number of firms drops from 17 to 8, output per firm doubles from 40 to 80, and the price rises from 32¢ to 36¢. See the answer to Problem 7.5 below for a more formal approach.

3. Table 7.2 shows three monopolistic competition equilibria (for F of \$6.40, \$1.60, and \$0). In the third of these equilibria ($F = \$0$), there is an infinite number of firms; the competitive price, 28¢, is charged; and output equals 720 (using the demand curve, $Q = 1{,}000 - 1000p$). Where $F = \$1.60$, there are 17 firms in equilibrium; the price, 32¢, is above the competitive level; and total output is only 680. However, suppose that one more firm were to produce at the same level (40 units) as the existing firms. Output would equal 720, and price would equal MC, 28¢. Similarly, at the equilibrium with $F = \$6.40$, industry output is 640, and price is 36¢. Yet, if one more firm were to produce at the same level as these firms, industry output would equal 720, where price equals MC. Indeed, it is positive fixed costs that keep the Cournot, monopolistic competition equilibrium from being efficient. Where fixed costs are positive, there is only room for one fewer firm than would make market output equal the competitive output at $F = 0$. There is only room in the sense that if one more firm were to enter, all firms would lose money.

5. A technological innovation that lowers fixed costs has the opposite effect of a franchise tax, discussed in the answer to Problem 7.1 above. A technological change that lowers marginal cost tends to increase output, but the exact effect depends on the shapes of the demand and cost curves.

   Formally, suppose the market demand curve is linear, $p = a - bnq$, where there are n identical firms, each of which produces q units of output with total costs $mq + F$. Each firm's profits are

$$\pi_i = (a - bnq)q - mq - F.$$

If the firms play Cournot, each firm's profit-maximizing, first-order condition is $MR = MC$:

$$a - b(n + 1)q = m.$$

Free entry implies that firms enter until price equals average cost $a - bnq = m + F/q$. Combining the first-order condition and the entry condition to eliminate m and rearranging terms yields $q = \sqrt{F/b}$. Thus,

$$\frac{dq}{dF} = \frac{1}{2\sqrt{bF}} > 0.$$

That is, as F falls, $q = \sqrt{F/b}$ falls in equilibrium, as shown in Table 7.2 and discussed in the answer to

Problem 7.1 above. Using $q = \sqrt{F/b}$ and the free-entry equation,

$$n = \frac{a - m}{\sqrt{bF}} - 1.$$

Differentiating this expression with respect to F, we obtain

$$\frac{dn}{dF} = -\frac{(a - m)}{2F\sqrt{bF}} < 0.$$

Thus, technological progress that lowers F increases the number of firms. The change in total output is

$$\frac{dnq}{dF} = n\frac{dq}{dF} + q\frac{dn}{dF}$$

$$= \frac{2\sqrt{bF} - a + m}{2bF} < 0,$$

using the first-order condition and manipulating. The change in price is $dp/dF = -b(dnq/dF) > 0$. Similarly, $dn/dm < 0$, $dq/dm = 0$, $dnq/dm < 0$, and $dp/dm = 1$.

Chapter 8

1. As commonly measured, the price-cost margin excludes capital and advertising costs. Moreover, even when costs include advertising, the cost measure typically expenses advertising rather than depreciating it (as is proper if advertising effects are long-lasting). It is possible that these sources of bias can be partially offset by including advertising/output and capital/output ratios on the right-hand side of the regression.

   However, it is very likely that this adjustment will not solve the problem. Both ratios are endogenous variables and are chosen simultaneously with price. Therefore, appropriate simultaneous equation econometric techniques should be used. Moreover, it is not always true that including these ratios linearly is appropriate. For example, if advertising depreciation is nonlinear, including advertising-output ratios on the right-hand side of the equation will not remove the bias. Moreover, if rental rates on capital are not constant over time, including capital/output ratios with a single time-independent coefficient is wrong.

3. The domestic concentration ratio based on data from only domestic firms is an upper bound on the relevant concentration ratio if the good is also imported. If imports in an industry increase over time, domestic concentration ratios may become less correlated with price-cost margins, because those industries are increasingly competitive.
5. In a perfectly competitive world, each firm's price equals marginal cost even in the short run. With entry, the profit of the last entrant equals zero. Firms that are relatively efficient earn profits. In a noncompetitive world (for example, one with monopolistic competition), price can exceed marginal cost. With entry, price can remain above marginal cost, but the profit of the last firm to enter typically is driven to zero in the long run.

Chapter 9

1. No producers of aluminum wire can survive. The price of aluminum ingot is so high that there is not enough profit left between the price of aluminum wire and the price of aluminum ingot.
3. Senior citizens may be less costly to serve than others. They may litter the theater less, and their preferences for movies may be easier to predict than those of teenagers, so that there are fewer unsold seats.
5. The first consumer's demand curve forms a rectangle. It is horizontal from zero to 1 unit at \$10 and then drops to zero at 1 unit. The maximum consumer surplus that can be captured is the entire area under the demand curve. The monopoly captures this consumer surplus if it sets its price equal to \$10. Similarly, the monopoly captures all the consumer surplus of the second consumer by charging \$9. There is no consumption inefficiency because there are no further transactions between the consumers that would increase at least one consumer's welfare.

Chapter 10

1. Suppose the coupon entitles the consumer to a 10¢ price reduction, and the consumer has 20 coupons. The firm may want to lower the price to the consumer on 20 units by 10¢ rather than lowering the price on 1 unit by \$2.
3. The consumer's budget constraint is $Y + X^2 = 100$, so that $Y = 100 - X^2$. Utility equals $100 - X^2 + 10X$. The X that maximizes utility is 5.

5. Monopoly 1 maximizes $p_1(10 - 2p_1 + p_2)$ and Monopoly 2 maximizes $p_2(10 + p_1 - 2p_2)$. The two first-order conditions are $10 - 4p_1 + p_2 = 0$ and $10 + p_1 - 4p_2 = 0$. Solving yields $p_1 = p_2 = 10/3$. A monopoly of both products chooses p_1 and p_2 to maximize $p_1(10 - 2p_1 + p_2) + p_2(10 + p_1 - 2p_2)$. The two first-order conditions are $10 - 4p_1 + p_2 + p_2 = 0$ and $p_1 + 10 + p_1 - 4p_2 = 0$. Solving yields $p_1 = p_2 = 5$.
7. If you price each dish separately, you maximize your profit by charging \$11 for the halibut and \$8 for pie. At these prices, Customers *a* and *b* buy only pie and Customer *c* buys only halibut. You earn \$7 = \$8 (price of pie) − \$1 (cost of pie) on each of the two dishes of pie you sell and \$10 on the halibut, for a total profit of \$24. If you only sell a pure bundle, you charge \$12 and earn a profit of \$30 = (\$12 − \$2) × 3, where \$2 is the cost of producing both dishes. Unlike in the example in the text, you cannot do better using mixed bundling (because each customer places a value on each good that is equal to or greater than its marginal cost). Suppose you set the bundle price at \$12, the price of halibut at \$10.99, and the price of pie at \$9.99. Customer *a* buys only the pie (the bundle costs \$2.01 more and that customer only values halibut at \$2), Customer *b* buys the bundle, and Customer *c* buys only the halibut (you sell 2 pies and 2 halibuts). You make \$8.99 from Customer *a*, \$9.99 from Customer *c*, and \$10 from Customer *b* for a total of \$28.98.

Chapter 11

1. Swaps can save transportation costs. If the paper firm in New York had to ship to its California customer and the paper firm in California had to ship to its New York customer, freight costs would be higher than if the firms shipped to the customers located in their own states. Swaps can also facilitate collusion. Suppose two firms collude by assigning customers to each other. This division of the market makes collusion easier because it lowers the cost of detecting a rival's sales to another firm's assigned customers. In the absence of swaps, the assignment of customers to firms may be too costly because of transportation costs.
3. If all firms have a high debt/equity ratio, and if going bankrupt is a blot on a manager's record, then the incentive to cut price is reduced. If firms differ widely in their debt/equity ratios, if new firms can enter, or if the interest rates on debt vary widely across firms, the price level is not likely to be affected by whether a few firms have high debt/equity ratios.
5. The discounted present value of the annual loss of \$1 million is \$8.51 million, using the formula given in the question. The discounted present value of the annual gain of π_m from Year 21 onward is \$1.49π_m. In order for the gain to exceed the loss, π_m must exceed \$5.7 million.

Chapter 12

1. The profit of a franchisee is $\pi = R(q)(1 - \alpha) - C(q)$, where $R(q)$ is revenues (sales), $C(q)$ is cost, and royalties are a times revenues. The franchisee bears all costs but receives only part of the revenues. Therefore, the franchisee sells less than is optimal. Its first-order condition for profit maximization is $(1 - \alpha)R'(q) = C'(q)$, instead of $R'(q) = C'(q)$. If royalties are β share of (before royalty) profits, $\pi = [R(q) - C(q)](1 - \beta)$. The same q that maximizes preroyalty profits maximizes postroyalty profits. Thus, the franchisee sells the optimal amount. Presumably, franchisers collect royalties as a percent of sales, in spite of this reasoning, because observing profits is more difficult than observing revenues. That is, franchisees may be better able to lie about costs than revenues (see also the answer to Problem 12.5).
3. If a pure profits tax is only collected at the retail level, there is a greater incentive to vertically integrate, even with fixed-proportions production. For example, an integrated firm could charge its own retailer a very high price for the factor it supplies. As a result, profits at the downstream level are relatively low (and hence relatively untaxed), and profits at the upstream level are relatively high. If the tax is collected both upstream and downstream, this incentive is removed. A sales tax at the retail level does not provide a similar incentive to integrate.
5. The franchiser (Kentucky Fried Chicken) uses the number of barrels to check the veracity of its retailers so as to guarantee they pay all the royalties they owe. The only obvious way to avoid this monitoring device is to sell chicken in other containers. Spot checks by the franchiser may discourage this avoidance technique. The argument for allowing this approach is that it facilitates vertical relations.

Chapter 13

1. If owners of a car quickly learn whether the car is a lemon, we would expect that a disproportionate number of owners who try to sell a new car quickly have lemons.
3. Many authors (including us) agree to royalties that are a percentage of revenues rather than profits. Such a royalty

system gives the publisher the incentive to produce too few books because the publisher incurs the full marginal cost of printing the last book but only gets a fraction of the revenues, $1 - \alpha$. As a result, joint profits are lower than they would be under the other two systems, where the publisher has the incentive to produce the optimal number of books. One possible reason that authors do not want royalties that are a percentage of profits is that they are afraid that the publisher may lie about its costs. Even without lying, authors and publishers could differ about appropriate costs because many costs of publishing are joint costs, and it is hard to allocate costs between various books. You may have read in newspapers that movie actors entitled to a percentage of profits are constantly suing producers who tell them that their hit movie produced no profits because of large costs. Publishers may be hesitant to pay authors lump-sum royalties because authors would then have little incentive to produce products that will sell well. See also the answer to Problem 12.1.

5. A consumer might reasonably infer that the brand name conveys quality. If the banana is of low quality, consumers will avoid this brand in the future. Thus, any firm that plans to remain in the market will only brand its banana if it believes consumers will view it as being better than unbranded bananas.

Chapter 14

1. Shapiro (1980) illustrates his point using an example with two consumers in which each consumer's demand is $q(p)$, and the monopoly produces with constant marginal cost, m. By assumption, before advertising, only one consumer knows about the product, and after advertising, both know it exists. Advertising does not change tastes; it merely informs the unaware consumer that the product exists. The preadvertising demand curve, $q(p)$, is half of the postadvertising demand curve, $2q(p)$, which is the horizontal sum of the demand of the two consumers. The monopoly charges p^* in either case, where p^* maximizes $(p - m)q(p)$ and $(p - m)2q(p)$, because m is constant. In the preadvertising equilibrium, point E in the figure, output is $q^* = q(p^*)$. In the postadvertising equilibrium, E', output is $2q^*$.

   In the preadvertising equilibrium, E, only one potential consumer purchases the good, so welfare is the area under the $q(p)$ demand curve between 0 and q^* above m. Advertising has a distributive gain, shown in the accompanying figure by the shaded triangle, which reflects the gain in consumer surplus from informing the other consumer. That is, consumer surplus is the area under the $2q(p)$ demand curve if the two consumers each consume half of the output, instead of having one consumer consume it all and the other, none. Because the monopoly does not capture this gain, it has *too little* incentive to advertise.

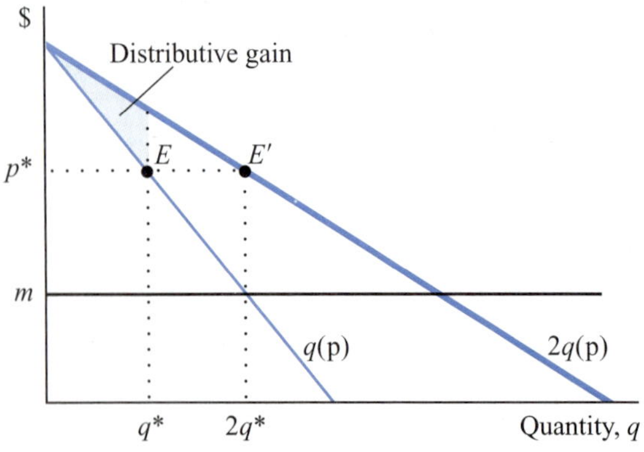

3. See Butters (1977) for an analysis of this problem. If firms are advertising that they have low prices, then the analysis is similar to that of the tourist-native model in Chapter 13. It is possible that, in equilibrium, some stores charge high prices and other stores charge low prices.

5. The monopoly's problem is

$$\max_{Q,\alpha} \pi = pQ - mQ - \alpha$$

$$= (a + \alpha - bQ)Q - mQ - \alpha.$$

   The first-order conditions are

$$\frac{\partial \pi}{\partial Q} = a + \alpha - 2bQ - m = 0$$

$$\frac{\partial \pi}{\partial \alpha} = Q - 1 = 0.$$

   That is, $Q = 1$ and $\alpha = 2b + m - a$.

Chapter 15

1. Let the demand for tractor services be $D(R)$, where R is the rental rate of tractors, and let the elasticity of demand for tractor services be ϵ. The demand for tractors facing the monopoly, $D^*(R)$, is $D(R) - 20$. The elasticity of demand for new tractors, ϵ^*, is then,

$$\frac{dD^*}{dR}\frac{R}{D^*} = \frac{dD}{dR}\frac{R}{D(R) - 20}$$

$$= \frac{dD}{dR}\frac{R}{D(R)}\frac{D(R)}{D(R) - 20}$$

$$= \epsilon\frac{D(R)}{D(R) - 20},$$

because $dD^*/dR = d(D(R) - 20)/dR = dD/dR$. That is, $\epsilon^* = \epsilon(N + O)/N$, where N is the number of new tractors, $D(R) - 20$, and O is the number of old tractors, 20. Holding the elasticity for tractor services, ϵ, constant, then as the ratio of old to new machines, O/N, rises, so does the elasticity for new tractors, ϵ^*.

3. Given high transaction costs, the demand for new tractors is not affected by the stock of old tractors if the farmers who currently need tractors are not the same ones who already own old tractors. However, if the same farmers that need tractors today already own old tractors from before, the analysis is the same as in Problem 15.1.
5. If many other firms make tractors that are close substitutes for the four-wheel-drive tractor produced by a monopoly, then the elasticity for tractor services, ϵ (defined in the answer to Problem 15.1), is high and thus the monopoly has little market power: ϵ^* is high.
7. By so doing, the artist credibly commits not to produce more prints in the future. As a result, the artist can sell the existing prints for more than if the future supply were not so limited.

Chapter 16

1. A sales tax reduces the profits from a monopoly without affecting the costs of research. Because the benefits fall and the costs do not, research effort falls.
3. In Figure 16.1, a longer patent life does not affect the cost curve, but shifts up the expected benefit curve, reflecting the longer time that the patent winner receives monopoly rents. As a result, the expected benefit and cost curves intersect further to the right (larger number of firms). Typically, the number of firms competing increases with patent life.
5. Suppose that each firm that races to make a discovery must incur a fixed cost to enter the race (for example, the expense of setting up a research lab). If there is a constant marginal cost of additional research effort, then each research firm is operating in a region of falling average costs. These fixed costs give society an incentive to reduce the number of research firms if one research firm can conduct many independent projects.

Chapter 17

1. If the bakery produces 50 loaves, it always can sell them at \$5 each. Costs are \$50, so the bakery's profits are \$200. If the bakery produces 100, it incurs costs of \$100 and earns revenues of either \$500 or \$250, or \$375 on average. Hence, its average profits are \$275, and producing 100 is optimal. If the price is \$1.50, when the bakery produces 50 loaves, its profits are \$25. When the bakery produces 100, its revenues are either \$150 or \$75, or \$112.50 on average; its costs are \$100; and its average profit is \$12.50. Hence, producing 50 is optimal. (*Note:* You should be able to show that the optimal output must be 0, 50, or 100 for any given price.)
3. A competitive firm chooses quantity so that price equals marginal cost. As price rises above the shut-down point, the price-average cost margin increases.
5. If it is costly to use the price system, the variability of a customer's demand affects the supplier's cost, and so customers with different demand variabilities pay different prices. There is no price discrimination when prices vary according to costs.

Chapter 18

1. Yes. The authorized wholesale distributor in one country can find it profitable to ship to the other country. By so doing, the distributor avoids paying promotional expenses at home and free rides off the promotional expense of the distributor in the other country. There is no incentive for anyone to buy at retail and ship the product abroad.
3. With no tax, $p_1 = p_2 = 5$, $q_1 = q_2 = 10$, and each firm earns a profit of \$50. With the export tax, buyers pay a price of \$7, firms receive a price (after tax) of \$4, $q_1 = q_2 = 8$, and each firm earns a profit of \$32 (after paying the tax).
5. In the competitive equilibrium, $p = 9$, $Q = 9$. If $t = 2$, $Q = 8$, consumers pay \$10, and the seller receives \$8. The monopsony solution is $Q = 6$, $p = 12$. This same quantity is achieved with a tariff of \$6.

Chapter 19

1. If a customer has signed a contract of fixed duration, rival suppliers are precluded from obtaining (at least some of) the customer's business. If there is competition

initially to sign up the customer, the fact that the contracts last for 10 years does not necessarily prevent the customer from paying a competitive price. If the contracts prevent rivals from reaching a scale required for efficiency, competition could be reduced.

3. Unclear. In some industries, collusion could lead to efficiency gains that outweigh any harm caused by elevated collusive pricing. It may be a difficult task for an enforcement agency to identify such industries, however.
5. The formula says that the direct price elasticity of good i equals (in absolute value) the sum of all cross-elasticities of good i with respect to the price of good j. If a cross-elasticity is large and positive, the price elasticity tends to be large, and market power tends to be low. The relevant cross-elasticity, according to the formula, is the one relating the quantity of Product A to the price of Product B.

Chapter 20

1. In Figure 20.3, at $\underline{p}$, the profits are zero, so $(p_a - p^*)Q_a$ = fixed costs = Areas $A + B$. The consumer surplus, and hence welfare, is the area under the demand curve and above p_a between 0 and Q_a. At $(\underline{p} - p^*)Q_a$, total welfare equals Areas $A + C$ minus $(p_a - p^*)Q_a$. That is, at $\underline{p} = p_a$, total welfare is equal to two triangles, a triangle equal to the consumer surplus at $\underline{p} = p_a$ and a second triangle that lies under the demand curve and above p^* between Q_a and Q^*. Thus, welfare must be higher at $\underline{p} = p^*$ than at $\underline{p} = p_a$.
3. An acreage quota causes farmers to use more of other inputs, such as labor and fertilizer, so that output does not fall as much as acreage. This inefficiency in production leads to deadweight loss. It also causes the supply curve to shift to the left, but by a smaller percentage than acreage falls. Holding the support price constant, the government buys less excessive crops than without acreage controls.
5. One alternative is to give farmers cash. Such a program improves farmers' well-being at lower cost than existing programs. It does not cause the production and distribution inefficiencies described in the chapter.
7. Because of the asymmetry in returns, rate-of-return regulation provides limited incentives to invent. If a firm makes an important discovery that, say, lowers its costs of production, its profit rises less than in proportion to the social gain. If it is unsuccessful in making the discovery, the firm bears the expense and has a lower profit. This problem in an industry with rapid innovation can be reduced if regulators are slow to change the cost basis in calculating the rate of return.

Legal Case Index

Author Index

Subject Index